CLARKSON AND KEATING CRIMINAL LAW: TEXT AND MATERIALS

EIGHTH EDITION

By

H.M. KEATING LL. M.
*Professor of Criminal Law and Criminal Responsibility,
University of Sussex*

S.R. CUNNINGHAM LL. B., LL. M., Ph. D.
Professor of Law, University of Leicester

T. ELLIOTT LL. B., LL. M., Ph. D.
Lecturer in Law, University of Leicester

M.A. WALTERS LL. B., LL. M., MSc., DPhil.
Senior Lecturer in Law, University of Sussex

SWEET & MAXWELL

THOMSON REUTERS

Published in 2014 by
Thomson Reuters (Professional) UK Limited
trading as Sweet & Maxwell,
Friars House, 160 Blackfriars Road, London SE1 8EZ
(Registered in England & Wales, Company No 1679046.
Registered Office and address for service:
2nd Floor, 1 Mark Square, Leonard Street, London EC2A 4EG)

For further information on our products and services, visit www.sweetandmaxwell.co.uk

Typeset by Servis Filmsetting ltd, Stockport, Cheshire
Printed and bound in Great Britain by CPI Group (UK) Ltd, Croydon, CR0 4YY

No natural forests were destroyed to make this product;
Only farmed timber was used and re-planted

British Library Cataloguing in Publication Data
A CIP catalogue record for this book
Is available from the British Library

ISBN 978-0-414-03297-2

Thomson Reuters and the Thomson Reuters Logo are trademarks of Thomson Reuters.
Sweet & Maxwell ® is a registered trademark of Thomson Reuters (Legal) Limited.

First Edition	1984
Reprinted	1986
Reprinted	1988
Second Edition	1990
Reprinted	1991
Reprinted	1993
Third Edition	1994
Reprinted	1994
Reprinted	1995
Fourth Edition	1998
Reprinted	1999
Reprinted	2000
Reprinted	2001 (twice)
Reprinted	2002
Fifth Edition	2003
Sixth Edition	2007
Seventh Edition	2010
Eighth Edition	2014

CLARKSON AND KEATING
CRIMINAL LAW:
TEXT AND MATERIALS

PREFACE

The aim of this book is to examine the main principles and rules of the criminal law and to expose the theoretical bases upon which they are founded.

The criminal law is the backdrop to the operation of the whole criminal justice system. It informs the way in which victims, the public, the police and other law enforcement agencies, the CPS and judges and other court personnel react and operate. It is, therefore, inextricably linked to issues of criminal procedure, criminology, moral philosophy and penology. Fletcher has stated that "the criminal law should express the way we live". It is a reflection of community values aimed at isolating the blameworthy who are deserving of punishment. Equally, it is a means of social control; it attempts to uphold, as well as reflect, these community values; it sets a standard, albeit at times a minimal one, of necessary compliance. In short, it is a set of moral commandments that are backed up by the legal threat of punishment. It thus follows that whether sanctions are imposed on the basis of desert or on utilitarian grounds, the rules of the criminal law and the punishment of offenders are the two sides of the same coin. A whole range of substantive issues—such as, whether "recklessness" should include "inadvertence", whether one can justify the existence of offences of "strict liability", how the boundaries of the law of "attempt" and "accessorial" crime should be drawn, and so on—are, in reality, issues relating to the justification of punishment in such cases. A true appreciation of the substantive criminal law must thus involve some understanding of the rationale of punishment and why conduct is criminalised—and it is in this context that we have sought to present the main rules of the law.

Like many other works in this field, this is a book on the actual rules of the criminal law. We have attempted to provide a full analysis of these main rules on the topics covered. But, in doing this, we have attempted the more ambitious task of using the law to extract, and develop, some fundamental ideas underlying the law. We have explored, in the context of punishment, such issues as: the relationship between blame and harm, the criteria for identifying the blameworthy, the structure of offences in relation to each other and whether such structure fairly represents the differing wrongdoing involved, and the role of the general defences. In short, we have attempted to subject the criminal law to the beginnings of a philosophical analysis that can throw some light on the substantive rules.

The criminal law changes with great rapidity and, therefore, substantial updating has taken place for the 8th edition. In particular, the changes to the law on self-defence brought about by the Crime and Courts Act 2013, the impact of decisions such as *Hughes* on causation, *Gnango* on participation and transferred malice, *Sadique* and *Pace* on inchoate offences, *R. v B*, *McNally* and *Assange* on consent and *Clinton* on loss of control are considered. It has also been possible to add a new section on restorative justice to Ch.1 and hate crime to Ch.7. Coverage is also given to new reform proposals such as the Law Commission Papers on Fitness to Plead and Insanity and Automatism, and to scholarly commentary published since the 7th edition on the full range of substantive issues.

We have been anxious to ensure that this book is accessible to, and easily digestible by, undergraduate and other students concerned with criminal law. We have approached our task, and included appropriate materials, with this concern very much in mind. We have tried to cover the range of competing views and present them in a discursive manner allowing the reader to make choices—while not being afraid to state our own preferences.

By now the format of this book should be familiar. It is neither a straight "textbook", nor a "cases and materials" book. Instead, we have tried to combine what we regard as the best features of both such styles—a book with the flow and coherence of a textbook thus providing the reader with guidance and direction, but one that also enables a substantial amount of original material from a diversity of sources to be absorbed.

We are very grateful to our publishers for their help and patience during the preparation of this book.

This is the first edition of the book written without one of the two original authors, Chris Clarkson. It has been a novel experience but we very much hope that his trust in us to carry the book forward is proved justified with this edition. This is also the last edition of this book with which Heather Keating will be involved. She leaves the book in Sally's most capable hands and is delighted that two new authors have joined for this edition, each bringing new expertise to the book. As ever, Heather Keating would like to express her thanks to her children for the support they have shown during the writing of this book. She dedicates her share of the book to them and also to her co-author, Chris, without whom this book would not have been written.

Sally Kyd Cunningham would like to thank her son for tolerating her preoccupation with work, her parents for their support, her co-authors for their good-natured co-operation, and Dr Steven Cammiss for his helpful suggestions. It has been a privilege and a pleasure to work with Heather on three editions of the book, and Sally is very proud to take forward, with the assistance of Tracey and Mark, the established name of Clarkson and Keating. Her share of this edition is dedicated to her former colleague and mentor, and continuing leisure-time-rich friend, Chris Clarkson.

Tracey Elliott would like to thank Chris Clarkson, Heather Keating and Sally Kyd Cunningham for inviting her to join the Clarkson and Keating writing team, her co-authors for their helpful comments, and Professor Janet Ulph for her willingness to look at, and comment upon, drafts relating to some of the knottier aspects of property law. It has been a real pleasure to work on this edition of the book. On a personal note, she would like to thank her parents for their support, and her daughters for tolerating the general decline in household tidiness whilst she has been working on this edition. Her share of this edition is dedicated to her former colleague, Chris Clarkson, whose presence in the School of Law at Leicester is much missed.

Mark Austin Walters would also like to thank Heather and Sally for asking him to join the authorship of Clarkson and Keating; a book that he has fond memories of using over ten years ago when completing his LL.B. In particular, he would like to personally express gratitude to Heather for her generous support and advice during the drafting of parts of this new edition. Mark would also like to thank his husband for putting up with his late night writing habits and to his parents for their continuous encouragement and support.

This book has been written with reference to the law as it stood on April 1, 2014, although it has been possible to incorporate some subsequent changes to the law.

H.M. KEATING
S.R. KYD CUNNINGHAM
T. ELLIOTT
M.A. WALTERS
May, 2014

ACKNOWLEDGEMENTS

Grateful acknowledgment is made to the following authors and publishers for permission to quote from their works:

Adler, Z.: "Rape—the Intention of Parliament and the practice of the Courts" (1982) 45 M.L.R. 664, Blackwell Publishers

Almond, Paul: Corporate Manslaughter and Regulatory Reform, (2013), p.xiii. Reprinted with permissions from Palgrave Macmillan.

Amirthalingam, K.: "Caldwell Recklessness is Dead, Long Live Mens rea's Fecklessness" (2004) 67 M.L.R. 491 at 492. Blackwell Publishers

Andenaes, J.: "General Prevention" (1952) 43 J. Crim. L., C. & P.S. 176. Reprinted by special permission of Northwestern University School of Law, Journal of Criminal Law and Criminology

——: "The General Preventive Effects of Punishment" 114 U. Pa. L. Rev. 949 (1966). Reproduced with permission of The University of Pennsylvania Law Review

Ashworth, A.: "Belief, Intent and Criminal Liability" in Eekelaar, J. and Bell, J. (eds): Oxford Essays in Jurisprudence, Third Series (1987). Oxford University Press

——: "Change of Normative Position: Determining the Contorus of Culpability in Criminal Law" (2008) 11 New Criminal Law Review 232–256. Reproduced with the permission of Andrew Ashworth

——: "'Manslaughter': Generic or Nominate Offences?" in Clarkson C.M.V. and Cunningham S.R. (eds), Criminal Liabillity for Non-Aggressive Death (2008), pp.243; 246–247. Reproduced with the permission of Ashgate

——: Principles of Criminal Law (2006), pp.230–231, 438. Oxford University Press

——: and Mitchell, B.: Rethinking English Homicide Law (2000), pp.38–45, 154–155, 158–160. Oxford University Press

——: "Robbery Re-assessed" [2002] Crim. L.R. 851

——: "The Scope of Liability for Omissions" (1989) 105 L.Q.R. 424

——: "The Doctrine of Provocation" [1976] C.L.J. 292 at 300. Cambridge University Press and reproduced with the permission of Andrew Ashworth

——: Sentencing and Criminal Justice, 3rd edn (2000), p.188. Cambridge University Press

——: Sentencing and Penal Policy (1983). Reproduced with the permission of Orion Publishing Group

——: "Testing Fidelity to Legal Values: Official Involvement and Criminal Justice" (2000) 63 M.L.R. 633, Blackwell Publishers

——: and Temkin, J.: "The Sexual Offences Act 2003: (1) Rape, Sexual Assaults and the Problems of Consent" [2004] Crim. L.R. 328

——: "Transferred Malice and Punishment for Unforeseen Consequences" in P.R. Glazebrook (ed.) Reshaping the Criminal Law (1978). Reprinted by permission of Oxford University Press

Austin, J.: Lecturers on Jurisprudence, 5th edn (1911) XVIII-XIX Vol 1. Thoemmes Press

Bartle, R.: Administering Justice: Crime and the New Magistrate (1985), quoted from Nelken, D., "Criminal Law and Criminal Justice" in Dennis, I. (ed.), Criminal Law and Justice (1987), p.149

Beale, J.H.: "Retreat from a Murderous Assault" (1903) 16 Harv. L. Rev. 567

Beattie, J.: "Baroness Scotland refuses to Resign after E5K Fine for Hiring an Illegal Worker" The Mirror, September 23, 2009

Bentham, J.: "An Introduction to the Principles of Morals and Legislation" in Bentham and Mill, The Utilitarians (1961). Anchor Publishing

Bergman, D.: Deaths at Work: Accidents or Corporate Crime, 1991. Reprinted by permission of The Workers Educational Association

Blom-Cooper, L: with Morris, T.: With Malice Afterthought, (2004), pp.56–57. Reproduced with permission of Hart Publishing

Bottoms, A.E.: "An Introduction to The Coming Crisis'" in Bottoms, A.E. and Preston, R.H., The Coming Penal Crisis (1980). Scottish Academic Press Ltd

——: "Morality, Crime, Compliance and Public Policy" in Bottoms A. and Tonry M., Ideology, Crime and Criminal Justice (2002), p.25. Reproduced with the permission of Willan Publishing

Brady, J.: "Punishing Attempts" (1980) 63 The Monist 246, 247-250. Copyright of The Monist: An International Quarterly Journal of General Philosophical Inquiry, Open Court Publishing Company, Chicago, Illinois. Reprinted by permission

Brady, J.B.: "Recklessness, Negligence, Indifference and Awareness" (1980) 43 M.L.R. 381, Blackwell Publishers

——: "Strict Liability Offences: A Justification" (1972) 8 Crim. L. Bulletin 217

Braithwaite, J.: Crime, Shame and Reintegration (1989), pp.77–79. Cambridge University Press

—— and Pettit, P.: Not Just Deserts: A Republican Theory of Criminal Justice (1990), pp.158–159. By permission of Oxford University Press

Brownlee, I.D.: "Superior Orders—Time for a New Realism?" [1989] Crim. L.R. 396

Brett, P.: Inquiry into Criminal Guilt (1963). Reproduced with the expressed permission of the Lawbook Co, part of Thomson Reuters

Buchanan, A. and Virgo, G.: "Duress and Mental Abnormality" [1999] Crim. L.R. 517

Buxton, R.: "The Human Rights Act and the Substantive Criminal Law" [2000] Crim. L.R. 331

Card, R.: "Reform of the Law of Conspiracy" [1973] Crim. L.R. 674

Cardozo, B.N.: "What Medicine Can do For Law", from Law and Literature (1947), pp.99–100, 390. Harcourt Brace & Co, Australia

Chalmers, James and Fiona Leverick: "Tracking the Creation of Criminal Offences" [2013] Criminal Law Review 543, pp.549-550. Reproduced with permission of Sweet & Maxwell

Clarkson, C.M.V.: "Aggravated Endangerment Offences" (2007) 60 Current Legal Problems 278 at 282–283. Reprinted by permission of Oxford Journal of Legal Studies

——: "Context and Culpability in Involuntary Manslaughter: Principle or Instinct?" in Ashworth, A. and Mitchell, B. (eds): Rethinking English Homicide Law (2000). Oxford University Press

——: "Corporate Manslaughter: Need for a New Offence?" in Clarkson, C.M.V. and Cunningham, S.R. (eds), Criminal Liability for Non-Aggressive Deaths (2008), pp.84–86. Reprinted by permission of Ashgate

——: "Corporate Culpability" (1997) Web Journal of Current Legal Issues. Reproduced with Permission of the Web Journal of Current Legal Issues

——: "General Endangerment Offences: The Way Forward?" (2005) 32(2) University of Western Australia Law Review 131. Reproduced with permission

——: Understanding Criminal Law, 4th edn (2005), pp.171–172

——: and Keating, H.M.: "Codification: Offences against the Person under the Draft Criminal Code" (1986) 50 J. Crim. L. 405

Clough, J.: Principles of Cybercrime (2010), pp183-185. Cambridge University Press

Coffee, J.: "No Soul to Damn: No Body to Kick': An Unscandalised Inquiry into the Problem of Corporate Punishment" (1981) 79 Mich.L.Rev. 386. Reproduced with the kind permission of Professor J. Coffee

Cohen, M.R.: "Moral Aspects of the Criminal Law" (1940) 49 Yale Law Journal 987 at 1012–1014, 1025. Reprinted by permission of the Yale Law Journal Company, Inc.

Colvin, E.: "Corporate Personality and Criminal Liability" (1995) 6 Criminal Law Forum 1 at 8. Kluwer Academic Publishers B.V

Cook, D.: Rich Law, Poor Law: Different Responses To Tax and Supplementary Benefit Fraud (1989), p.160. Oxford University Press

Cooper, J.: "The Sentencing Guidelines Council–a Practical Perspective" [2008] Crim. L.R. 277

Cowley, D.: "The Retreat from Morgan" [1982] Crim. L.R. 198 at 206–208

Cross, R.: "Reflections on Bratty's Case" (1962) 78 L.Q.R. 236

——: and Ashworth, A.: The English Sentencing System, 3rd edn (1981). Reproduced with the permission of Butterworths a division of LexisNexis Butterworths Tolley

Cunningham, S.: "Recklessness: being reckless and acting recklessly" (2010) 21 K.J.J. 445 at 457–460

Dashwood, A.: "Logic and the Lords in Majewski" [1977] Crim. L.R. 532, 591

Davis, M.: "Why Attempts Deserve Less Punishment than Complete Crimes", Law & Philosophy 5 (1986), p.28–29. Reprinted by permission of Kluwer Academic Publishers B.V

"Death, Drugs and Duties" [2009] Archbold News 6

Denehy, K.: cited in Goldstein, Dershowitz and Schwartz, Criminal Law: Theory and Process (1974), pp.835–836. Reproduced with permission of Macmillan

Dennis, I.: "Duress, Murder and Criminal Responsibility" (1980) 96 L.Q.R. 208

——: "On Necessity as a Defence to Crime: Possibilities, Problems and the Limits of Justification and Excuse" (2009) Criminal Law and Philosophy 29. With permission of Springer

Devlin, P.: Morals and the Criminal Law (reprinted in The Enforcement of Morals) (1965), pp.7–8, 14–17. Oxford University Press with permission from the British Academy

Dingwall, G.: "Intoxicated Mistakes and the Need for Self-Defence" (2007) M.L.R. 127 at 128. Wiley Publishing

Dressler, J.: Understanding Criminal Law (1987). Reproduced with permission of M. Bender/Lexis Nexis

Duff, R.A.: Answering for Crime: Responsibility and Liability in the Criminal Law (2007), pp.113, 130–132. Reprinted by permission of Hart Publishing, Oxford

——: Criminal Attempts (1986), pp.351–352, 354, 395–396. Oxford University Press

——: Intention Agency and Criminal Liability: Philosophy of Action and the Criminal Law (1990), pp.47–48, 111–113, 120–121, 172. Wiley-Blackwell

——: "Intention, Mens Rea and the Law Commission Report" [1980] Crim. L.R. 147

——: "Intentions Legal and Philosophical" (1989) 9 Oxford Journal of Legal Studies 76. By permission of Oxford University Press

——: "Perversions and Subversions of Criminal Law", in R.A. Duff, L. Farmer, S.E. Marshall, M. Renzo and V. Tadros, The Boundaries of the Criminal Law (2010), pp.89-90, 107-10. Reproduced with permission of Oxford University Press

——: with Garland, D.: A Reader on Punishment (1994), p.239. Oxford University Press

——: von Hirsch, A.: "Responsibility, Retribution and the Voluntary': A Response to Williams" [1997] C.L.J. 103. Reproduced with the permission of A. Duff and A. von Hirsch

——: "Recklessness" [1980] Crim. L.R. 282 at 289–292

——: "Theories and Policies Underlying Guidelines Systems" (2005) 105 Columbia Law Review 1162. Reprinted with permission of Antony Duff

——: Trials and Punishments (1986), pp.27, 263–264. Cambridge University Press

——: "Whose Luck Is It Anyway?" in C.M.V. Clarkson and S.R. Cunningham (eds), Criminal Liability for Non-Aggressive Death (2008), pp.76–77. Reproduced with permission of Ashgate

——: von Hirsch, A.: "Responsibility, Retribution and the Voluntary': A Response to Williams" [1997] C.L.J. 103. Reproduced with the permission of A. Duff and A. von Hirsch

Editorial, "The Criminology of Attempts" [1986] Crim. L.R. 769

Elliot, C. and de Than, C.: "Restructuring the Homicide Offences to Tackle Violence, Discrimination and Drugs in a Modern Society" (2009) 20 K.L.J. 69-88. Reprinted by permission of Hart Publishing

Ewing, A.C.: "A Study of Punishment II: Punishment as viewed by the Philosopher" (1943) 21 Can. B. Rev. 102 at 116 (41). Canadian Bar Review

Executive Advisory Committee on Sentencing in New York, Crime and Punishment in New York (1979), p.220. Reprinted with the permission of the National Criminal Justice Referral Center

Feinberg, J.: "The Expressive Function of Punishment" (1965) The Monist, Vol.49, No.3, 397–423. Copyright of The Monist: An International Quarterly Journal of General Philosophical Inquiry, Open Court Publishing Company, Chicago, Illinois. Reprinted by permission

——: The Moral Limits of the Criminal Law: Harm to Others (1984), pp.1–2, 26, 33, 34, 36, 215–216. Oxford University Press

——: The Moral Limits Of The Criminal Law, Vol.2, Offense To Others, pp.1–2, 26. Oxford University Press

Feldman, D.: Civil Liberties and Human Rights in England and Wales, 2nd edn (2002), pp.715–716. By permission of Oxford University Press

Fine, R.P. and Cohen, G.M.: "Is Criminal Negligence a Defensible Basis for Penal Liability" (1967) 16 Buffalo L. Rev. 749. Reproduced with permission Buffalo Law Review

Finnis, J.: "Intention and Side-effects" in Frey, R.G., and Morris, C.W. (eds), Liability and Responsibility (1991), p.46. Cambridge University Press

——: "The Restoration of Retribution" (1971) 32 Analysis 131. Basil Blackwell

Fisse, B.: "Recent Developments in Corporate Criminal Law and Corporate Liability to Monetary Penalties" (1990) 13 UNSWLV 1. Reprinted by permission of the University of New South Wales Law Journal

—— and Braithwaite, J.: "The Allocation of Responsibility for Corporate Crime: Individualism, Collectivism and Accountability" (1988) 11 Sydney Law Review 468

Fletcher, G.P.: Rethinking Criminal Law (1978), pp.82–29, 138–139, 149–150, 152–154, 161–163, 165–166, 235–236, 246–247, 419, 474, 482, 601, 679, 696–697, 707, 709–710, 770–771, 801–802, 847–848, 857–858. Oxford University Press

——: "The Theory of Criminal Negligence: A Comparative Analysis", 119 U. Pa. L. Rev. 401, 415–18 (1971). Reprinted with the permission of the University of Pennsylvania Law Review

Floud, J.: "Dangerousness and Criminal Justice" (1982) 22 Brit. J. Criminol. 213 at 220. Reproduced by permission of Oxford University Press

Frankel, M.E.: Criminal Sentences: Law Without Order (1973), pp.21–22. Hill and Wang, a division of Farrar, Strauss and Giroux, LLC

Frase, R.S.: "Sentencing Policy Development under the Minnesota Sentencing Guidelines" in von Hirsch, A., Ashworth, A. and Roberts, J. (eds), Principled Sentencing, 3rd edn (2009), p.275. Oxford University Press

Freeman, S.: "Criminal Liability and the Duty to Aid the Distressed", 142 U. Pa. L. Rev. 1455, 1489 (1994). Reprinted by permission of University of Pennsylvania Law Review

Freud, S.: A General Introduction to Psychoanalysis (1958), p.48. Reproduced with the permission of Unwin Hyman Limited

Funk, T.M.: "Justifying Justifications" (1999) 19 Oxford Journal of Legal Studies 631. Reproduced With permission of Oxford University Press

Gardner, J: "Justifications and Reasons" in Simester, A.P. and Smith, A.T.H. (eds), Harm and Culpability (1996), pp.107–108. Oxford University Press

——: and Jung, H: "Making Sense of Mens Rea: Anthony Duff's Account" (1991) 11 OJLS 559. By permission of Oxford University Press

——: "The Gist of Excuses" (1998) 1 Buffalo Criminal Law Review 575

——: and Shute, S.: "The Wrongness of Rape" in Horder, J. (ed.), Oxford Essays in Jurisprudence (2000), p.205. Oxford University Press

Glazebrook, P.R.: "Thief or Swindler: Who Cares?" [1991] C.L.J. 389. Reproduced with the kind permission of P.R. Glazebrook

Gobert, J.:"Controlling Corporate Criminality: Penal Sanctions and Beyond" [1998] 2 Web J.C.L.I. Web Journal of Current Legal Issues

Goff, R.: "The Mental Element in the Crime of Murder" (1988) 104 L.Q.R. 30

Goldstein, A.: ——: and Katz, J.: "Abolish the Insanity Defense'—Why Not?" (1963) 72 Yale Law Journal 853–876. Reprinted by permission of The Yale Law Journal Company, Inc.

——: "Conspiracy to Defraud the United States" (1959) 68 Yale Law Journal 405 at 405–406, 414

——: The Insanity Defense (1967). Published by Yale University Press

Green, S.P.: 13 Ways to Steal a Bicycle: Theft Law in the Information Age (2012), pp.112–113. Reprinted with permission of Harvard University Press

——: Lying, Cheating, and Stealing (2006), pp.78–80. Oxford University Press

Griew, E.: "Dishonesty: The Objections to Feely and Ghosh" [1985] Crim. L.R. 341

Gross, H.: A Theory of Criminal Justice (1979), pp.125, 276, 400–401, 425. Oxford University Press

Gusfield, J.R.: "On Legislating Morals: The Symbolic Process of Designating Deviance" 56 Cal. L. Rev. 54 (1968). Reprinted by permission of the California Law Review, University of California, Berkeley

Hale, Matthew: History of the Pleas of the Crown (1736). Reprinted by permission of Clark: Lawbook Exchange, Ltd., 2003

Hart, H.L.A.: "Acts of Will and Responsbility", Stevens & Sons and of the Faculty of Law, University of Sheffield/Oxford University Press

——: Honoré, A.M.: Causation in the Law, 2nd edn (1985), pp.29, 33–34, 37, 42, 77–80,103–104, 326, 340–341, 388. Reprinted by permission of Oxford University Press

——: "Changing Conceptions of Responsibility" in Punishment and Responsibility: Essays in the Philosophy of Law (1968), pp.186–209. Reproduced with the permission of Magnes Press and Oxford University Press

——: "Immorality and Treason", 62 The Listener 162–163 (July 30, 1959)

——: "Intention and Punishment" is reprinted from the Oxford Review No.4, February 1967, by permission of the Editor/Oxford University Press

——: "Legal Responsibility and Excuses" from the proceedings of the first annual New York Institute of Philosophy, 9 and 10 February 1957, published in Determinism and Freedom (1958) edited by Sidney Hook, and is reprinted by permission of the publishers Oxford University Press and Ernest Hook

——: "Murder and the Principles of Punishment: England and the United States" *c 1858 by Northwestern University School of Law/Oxford University Press

——: "Negligence, Mens rea and the Elimination of Responsibility" in Punishment and Responsibility (Essays in the Philosophy of Law) (1968), pp.152–157. OUP USA

——: Punishment and Responsibility, Essays in the Philosophy of Law (1968), pp.119–122, 152, 183. Reprinted by permission of Oxford University Press

——: "Punishment and the Elimination of Responsibility". Continuum Press/Oxford University Press

——: Postscript: Responsibility and Retribution from Punishment and Responsibility: Essays in The Philosophy of Law (1968), pp.210–237. Reproduced with the permission of Oxford University Press and The New York Review of Books

——: "Prolegomenon to the Principles of Punishment" in Punishment and Responsibility, Essays In the Philosophy of Law (1968) published by Oxford University Press. Reprinted courtesy of the Editor of the Aristotelian Society, 2010

——: "Punishment and Elimination of Responsibility" in Punishment and Responsibility, Essays in the Philosophy of Law (1968), pp.152–157. Oxford University Press

Hepburn, J.: "Occasional Property Crime", Meier, R. (ed.), Major Forms of Crime (1984), pp.88–89, 1984 by Sage Publications

Her Majesty's Stationery Office: Various extracts

Herring, J.: "Victims as Defendants: When Victims Participate in Crimes Against Themselves" in Alan Reed and Michael Bohlander (ed.), Participation in Crime: Domestic and Comparative Perspectives, p.84, 90-91. Reprinted with permission from Ashgate

Herring, R.: "Mum's Not the Word: An Analysis of Section 5" in C.M.V. Clarkson and S.R. Cunningham (eds), Criminal Liability for Non-Aggressive Death (2008), pp.152–153. Reproduced with permission of Ashgate

——: Palser, E.: "The Duty of Care in Gross Negligence Manslaughter" [2007] Crim. L.R. 24 von Hirsch, A.: et al.: Criminal Deterrence and Sentence Severity (1999), pp.41, 48. Reproduced with permission of Hart Publishing

——: Doing Justice—The Choice of Punishments (Report of the Committee for the Study of Incarceration), pp.45–49, 86–87. Copyright 1976. Reprinted by permission of Hill and Wang, a division of Farrar, Strauss and Giroux, LLC

——: and Ashworth, A.: "Extending Sentences for Dangerousness: Reflections on the Bottoms-Brownsword Model" in von Hirsch, A., Ashworth, A., and Roberts, J. (eds), Principled Sentencing, 3rd edn (2009), pp.86–87. Reprinted with permission of Hart Publishing

——: and Jareborg, N.: "Gauging Criminal Harm: A Living-Standard Analysis" (1991) 11 Oxford Journal of Legal Studies 1. By permission of Oxford University Press

——: and Julian V. Roberts, "Legislating sentencing principles: the provisions of the Criminal Justice Act 2003 relating to sentencing purposes and the role of previous convictions" [2004] Crim. L.R. 639 at 642

——: "Ordinal and Cardinal Desert" in von Hirsch, A. and Ashworth, A. (eds.), Principled Sentencing (1992), pp.209–210. Reproduced with permission of Andrew von Hirsch

——: Past or Future Crimes: Deservedness and Dangerousness in the Sentencing of Criminals (1985), pp.35–36. Reprinted by permission of Rutgers University Press and Andrew von Hirsch

——: "Prediction of Criminal Conduct and Preventative Confinement of Convicted Persons" (1972) 21 Buffalo L. Rev. 717. Reprinted by permission of Buffalo Law Review

——: and Ashworth, A.: Proportionate Sentencing, pp.17–18, 94. Oxford University Press Hodge, J.: Alcohol and Violence (1993). Reproducedfrom:Taylor P.J. (ed.), Violence in Society. London: RCP, 1993. Reprinted by permission of Royal College of Physicians, London

Holmes, O.W.: The Common Law (1882). Reprinted by permission of Dover Publications Inc, New York

Holton, R. and Shute, S.: "Self-Control in the Modern Provocation Defence" (2007) Oxford Journal of Legal Studies 27(1) 49 at 50. Reproduced with permission of Oxford University Press

Honoré, A.M.: Responsibility and Fault (1999), pp.135–137. Reprinted with permission of Hart Publishing Ltd

——: "The Dependence of Morality on Law" (1993) 13 Oxford Journal of Legal Studies 1. By Permission of Oxford University Press

Horder, J.: Provocation and Responsibility (1992), p.190. Oxford University Press

——: Homicide and the Politics of Law Reform (2012), pp.75; 86-87. Reprinted with permission of Oxford University Press

——: "Sobering Up? The Law Commission on Criminal Intoxication" (1995) 58 M.L.R. 534, Blackwell Publishers

——: Oxford Essays in Jurisprudence (2000), p.205. Oxford University Press

——: and McGowan, L.: "Manslaughter by Causing Another's Suicide" [2006] Crim. L.R. 1035

——: "Sobering Up? The Law Commission on Criminal Intoxication" [1995] 58 M.L.R. 534. Reproduced with permission of Blackwell Publishing

Hughes, G.: "Criminal Omissions" (1958) 67 Yale Law Journal 590–637. Reprinted by permission Of The Yale Law Journal Company, Inc.

——: "Morals and the Criminal Law" (1962) 71 Yale Law Journal 662–682. Reprinted by Permission of The Yale Law Journal Company, Inc.

Husak, D.: "Does Criminal Liability Require An Act" in Duff, R.A. (ed) Philosophy and the Criminal Law (1998). Cambridge University Press

——: Philosophy of Criminal Law (1987), p.100. The Rowman & Littlefield Publishing Group

——: "The Criminal Law as Last Resort" (2004) 24 Oxford Journal of Legal Studies 207. Reproduced with permission of Oxford University Press

The Incorporated Council of Law Reporting for England and Wales: Weekly Law Reports, Queen's Bench Division, Appeal Cases and King's Bench Law Reports

The Independent: Extract from February 23, 1990. Copyright The Independent Newspaper

Jones, T.H.: "Causation, homicide and the supply of drugs" (2006) 26 LS 139 at 153–154. Reproduced with permission of Oxford University Press

Johnson, P.: The Unnecessary Crime of Conspiracy (1973) 61 California Law Review 1137. Reprinted by permission of the California Law Review, University of California, Berkeley

Kadish, S.H.: "Complicity, Cause and Blame: A Study in the Interpretation of Doctrine" (1985) 73 Cal. L. Rev. 324. Reprinted by permission of the California Law Review, University of California, Berkeley

——: "Excusing Crime" (1987) 75 California Law Review 257. 1987. Reprinted by permission of The California Law Review, University of California, Berkeley

Kaplan, J.: "The Role of Law in Drug Control" [1971] Duke Law Journal 1065. (1971). Published by Duke University School of Law

Katz, L.: Bad Acts and Guilty Minds (1987). Reprinted by permission of The University of Chicago Press

Keating, H. and Jo Bridgeman: "Compassionate Killings: The Case for a Partial Defence", (2012) 75 M.L.R. 697-721 at 720. Reprinted with permission of Modern Law Review

Kenny, A.: Freewill and Responsibility (1978), pp.85–92. Reprinted with permission of Routledge

Lacey, N.: "Partial Defences to Homicide" in Ashworth, A. And Mitchell, B. (eds): Rethinking English Homicide Law (2000). Oxford University Press

——: State Punishment: Political Principles and Community Values (1988), pp.24–26. Reproduced with permission of Routledge

——: The Hamlyn Lectures 2007, The Prisoners' Dilemma: Political Economy and Punishment in Contemporary Democracies (2008), p.76

La Fave, W.R. and Scott, A.W.: Criminal Law, 2nd edn (1986). Reprinted by permission of the West Group

Lanham, D.: "Accomplices and Transferred Malice" (1980) 96 L.Q.R. 110

——: "Accomplices, Principles and Causation" (1980) 12 Melbourne University Law Review 490, 510–11

——: "Larsonneur Revisited" [1976] Crim. L.R. 276

Lawson, F.H. and Rudden, B.: The Law of Property (1982), p.190. Oxford University Press

Leavens, A.: A Causation Approach to Criminal Omissions (1988) 76 California Law Review 547. 1988. Reprinted by permission of the California Law Review, University of California, Berkeley

Lewis, C.S.: "The Humanitarian Theory of Punishment" (1953) VI Res Judicatae 224. Reprinted by permission of the Melbourne University Law Review

Lichtenstein, F.: cited in Goldstein, Dershowitz and Schwartz, Criminal Law: Theory and Process (1974), p.835

Lloyd-Bostock, S.: "The Ordinary Man, and the Psychology of Attributing Causes and Responsibility" (1979) 45 M.L.R. 143. Blackwell Publishers

Luckenbill, D.F.: "Murder and Assault" in Meier, R.F., Major Forms of Crime (1984), p.32. Sage Publications

McGlynn, C. and Rackley, E.: "Criminalising Extreme Pornography: A Lost Opportunity" [2009] Crim. L.R. 245

McGregor, J.: Is it Rape? On Acquaintance Rape and Taking Women's Consent Seriously (2005). Reproduced by permission of Ashgate

——: "Why When She Says No She Doesn't Mean Maybe and She Doesn't Mean Yes: A Critical Reconstruction of Consent, Sex and the Law (1996) 2 Legal Theory 175, Cambridge University Press

MacKenna, Sir B.: "Causing Death by Reckless or Dangerous Driving: A Suggestion" [1970] Crim. L.R. 67

Mabbott, J.D.: "Freewill and Punishment" in Lewis, H.D. (ed.), Contemporary British Philosophy, (1956), pp.289, 303. Reproduced with the permission of Unwin Hyman Limited

Mackay, R.D.: Mental Condition Defences in the Criminal Law (1995), p.104. Oxford University Press

Mead, G.: "Contracting into Crime: A Theory of Criminal Omissions" (1991) 11 Oxford Journal of Legal Studies 147. By permission of Oxford University Press

Model Penal Code: Extracts from Tentative Drafts No. 4 (1955), 8 (1958) and Model Penal Code Proposed Official Draft (1962). American Law Institute. All rights reserved

Moore, M.: Act and Crime (1993), p.59. Oxford University Press

Morris, A.: Women, Crime and Criminal Justice (1987) Reprinted by permission of Wiley-Blackwell

Morris, N.: Madness and the Criminal Law 1982 by The University of Chicago Press, pp.31–32, 61–64. All rights reserved

—— and Howard, C.: Studies in Criminal Law (1964), pp.175–176, 199. Reprinted with permission by Oxford University Press

Morris, T. and Blom-Cooper, L.: A Calendar of Murder: Criminal Homicide in England since 1957 (1964) Michael Joseph Publishers Ltd. Dr Terence Morris and Louis Blom-Cooper 1964.

——: With Malice Afterthought (2004), pp.56–57. Reprinted by permission of Hart Publishing

Mueller, G.: "The Mens Rea of Accomplice Liability" (1988) 61 South. Calif. L.R. 2169 at 2172. With the permission of the University of Southern California

Murphy, D.J.I.: Customers and Thieves—An Ethnography of Shoplifting (1986), p.240. (Ashgate Publishing Ltd) D.J.I. Murphy

Newell, P.: Children are People Too (1989), p.12. Bedford Square Press

Norrie, A.: "A Critique of Criminal Causation" (1991) 54 M.L.R. 685, Blackwell/Wiley Publishers

——: "After Woollin" [1999] Crim. L R. 532

——: "Between Orthodox Subjectivism and Moral Contextualism: Intention and the Consultation Paper" [2006] Crim. L.R. 486–513

——: Crime, Reason and History: A Critical Introduction to Criminal Law, 2nd edn (2001), p.119. Cambridge University Press

——: "Oblique Intention and Legal Politics" [1989] Crim. L.R. 793

——: "Subjectivism, Objectivism and the Limits of Criminal Recklessness" (1992) 12 Oxford Journal of Legal Studies 45. By permission of Oxford University Press

Note, "The Conspiracy Dilemma: Prosecution of Group Crimes or Protection of Individual Defendants" (1948) 62 Harv. L. Rev. 276 at 283–284. Harvard University Press

O'Donovan, K.: "Defences for Battered Women Who Kill" (1991) 18 JL & S 219, Blackwell Publishers

Ormerod, D.: Fortson, R.;"Serious Crime Act 2007: the Part 2 Offences" [2009] Crim. L.R. 389

——: Smith and Hogan Criminal Law, 12th edn (2008), p.558. Oxford University Press

——: and Taylor, R.: "The Corporate Manslaughter and Corporate Homicide Act 2007" [2008] Crim. L.R. 589

——: "The Fraud Act 2006 – Criminalising Lying?" [2007] Crim. L.R. 193

Packer, H.L.: "Mens Reas and the Supreme Court" (1962) Sup. Ct. Rev. 107 at 109. Reprinted by permission of The University of Chicago Press

——: The Limits of The Criminal Sanction (1969), pp.262–264, 296. Used with the permission of Stanford University Press

Padfield, N.: "Clean Water and Muddy Causation: Is Causation a Question of Law or Fact, or Just a Way of Allocating Blame?" [1995] Crim. L.R. 683

Parry, D.L.: "Judicial Approaches to Due Diligence" [1995] Crim. L.R. 695

Pearce, F. and Tombs, S.: Toxic Capitalism: Corporate Crime and the Chemical Industry (1998), p.153. With kind permission of Professors Pearce and Tombs

Pedain, A.: "Intention and the Terrorist Example" [2003] Crim. L.R. 579

Pickard, T.: "Culpable Mistakes and Rape: Relating Mens Rea to the Crime", (1980) 30 University of Toronto Law Journal 75. Reprinted by permission of University of Toronto Press Incorporated. http://www.utpjournals.com

xvi   Acknowledgements

Quick, O.L. and Wells, C.: "Getting Tough with Defences" [2006] Crim L.R. 514–525

Richardson, G.: "Strict Liability for Regulatory Crime: The Empirical Research" [1987] Crim. L.R. 295

Roberts J. (eds): Principled Sentencing, 3rd edn (2009), pp.153–154, 157. Reproduced with permission of Hart Publishing

Roberts, J.V.: "Revisiting the Recidivist Sentencing Premium" in von Hirsch, A., Ashworth, A. and Robinson, P.: "Criminal Law Defences: A Systematic Analysis" (1982) 82 Columbia Law Review 199. Reprinted with permission of the Columbia Law Review

——: Criminal Law Defences, Vol.2, 1984. Reprinted by permission of the West Group

——: "Hybrid Principles for the Distribution of Criminal Sanctions" (1988) 82 Northwestern University Law Review 19. Reprinted by special permission of Northwestern University Law Review

Robinson, P.H.: Distrubutive Principles of Criminal Law: Who Should be Punished and How Much? (2008), pp.5–6, 18–19, 103–105. Reproduced with permission of Oxford University Press

——: and Darley J.M.: "Does Criminal Law Deter? A Behavioural Science Investigation" (2004) 24 O.J.L.S. 173–205 at pp.180–181. Reproduced with permission of Oxford University Press

Rosenhan, D.L.: "On Being Sane in Insane Place". Science (1973) Vol.199, pp.250–258. Reprinted (abstracted/excerpted) with permission of Springer

Rumney, P. and Morgan-Taylor, M.: "Recognizing the Male Victim: Gender Neutrality and the Law of Rape" (1997) 26 Anglo-American Law Review 198. Reproduced with the permission of Philip Rumney

Schulhofer, S.: "Harm and Punishment: A Critique of emphasis on the results conduct in the Criminal Law" 122 U. Pa. L. Rev. 1497 (1974). Reprinted by permission of University of Pennsylvania Law Review

——: Unwanted Sex: The Culture of Intimidation and the Failure of the Law (1998), pp.56–57. Harvard University Press

Shute, S. and Horder, J.: "Thieving and Deceiving: What is the Difference?" (1993) 56 M.L.R. 548, Blackwell Publishers

——: "The Second Law Commission Consultation Paper on Consent: Something Old, Something New, Something Borrowed: Three Aspects of the Project" [1996] Crim. L.R. 684

Simester, A.P.: Appraising Strict Liability (2005), p.26. Oxford University Press

——: and Sullivan, G.R. (eds): Criminal Law: Theory and Doctrine (2007), pp.228, 419. Reprinted by permission of Hart Publishing

——: and Sullivan, G.R. (eds): Harm and Culpability (1964), pp.103, 107–108. Oxford University Press

——: "Intoxication is Never a Defence" [2009] Crim. L.R. 3

Simpson, A.W.B.: "The Butler Committee's Report: The Legal Aspects" (1976) 16 British Journal of Criminology. By permission of Oxford University Press

Smith, A.T.H.: "Error and Mistake in Law in Anglo-American Criminal Law" (1985) 14 Anglo-American Law Review 3. With kind permission of Vathek Publishing

Smith, J.C.: "Commentary on Broome v Perkins" [1987] Crim. L.R. 272

——: "Commentary on DPP v Huskinson" [1988 Crim L.R. 621

——: "Commentary on R v Walker" [1984] Crim. L.R. 113

——: "The Element of Chance in Criminal Liability" [1971] Crim. L.R. 63

Smith, K.J.M.: A Modern Treatise on the Law of Complicity (1991), p.5. Oxford University Press

——: "Duress and Steadfastness: In Pursuit of the Unintelligible" [1999] Crim. L.R. 363

——: "Withdrawal in Complicity: A Restatement of Principles" [2001] Crim. L.R. 769

Smith, P.F.: Smith (ed.),"Omissions and the Duty Myth" in Law: Essays in Honour of J.C. Smith (1986), pp.85–86. With permission of Lexis Nexis

Spencer, J.R.: The Sexual Offences Act 2003: (2) Child and Family Offences [2004] Crim. L.R. 347

Stephen, J.F.: A History of the Criminal Law of England (1883), pp.81–82

——: Liberty, Equality, Fraternity (1874) at 138. Reproduced by permission of The Liberty Fund
Stevenson, K. and Harris, C.: "Inaccessible and Unknowable: Accretion and Uncertainty in Modern Criminal Law" (2008) 29 Liverpool Law Review 247. With permission of Springer Netherlands

Stuart, D.: "Mens Rea, Negligence and Attempts" [1968] Crim. L.R. 647

Sullivan, G.R.: "Participating in Crime: Law Com No.305–Joint Criminal Ventures" [2008] Crim. L.R. 19

Szasz, T.S.: "The Myth of Mental Illness" (1960) 15 American Psychologist 113. American Psychological Association

Tadros, V.: "Rape without Consent" [2006] 26 Oxford Journal of Legal Studies 515 at 515–516. Reproduced with permission of Oxford University Press

——: "The Characters of Excuse" (2001) 21 Oxford Journal of Legal Studies 495. By permission of Oxford University Press

"The Philosophical Foundations of Consent in the Criminal Law" (1997) 17 Oxford Journal of Legal Studies 389. Reproduced by permission of Oxford University Press

Taylor, R.: "The Model of Tolerance and Self-Restraint" in Reed and Bohlander (eds), Loss of Control and Diminished Responsibility (2011), p.57. Reprinted with permission of Ashgate

Tolmie, J.: "Alcoholism and Criminal Liability" (2001) 64 M.L.R. 688, Blackwell Publishers

Tonry, M.: "Prediction and Classification: Legal and Ethical Issues" in Gottfredson and Tonry (eds), Prediction and Classification: Criminal Justice Decision Making (1987), p.397. By permission of The University of Chicago Press

——: Sentencing Matters (1996), pp.13–24. Used by permission of Oxford University Press, Inc

Turner, J.W.C.: Kenny's Outlines of Criminal Law (19th edn, 1966), pp.20–21. Cambridge University Press

——: Russell on Crime, 12th edn (1964), p.128

Veltford, H. and Lee, G.: "The Coconut Grove Fire: A Study in Scapegoating" Journal of Abnormal and Social Psychology XXXVIII (No.2 Clinical Supp 1943) 138. Journal of Abnormal and Social Psychology

Walker, N.: Punishment, Danger and Stigma (1980), pp.98–99. Reproduced by permission of Basil Blackwell

——: "Punishing, Denouncing or Reducing Crime" in Glazebrook, P. (ed.), Reshaping the Criminal Law (1978), p.393

Wasik, M.: "Abandoning Criminal Intent" [1980] Crim. L.R. 785

——: "Partial Excuses in the Criminal Law" (1982) 45 M.L.R. 516, Blackwell Publishers

Weihofen, H.: "Retribution is Obsolete," National Probation and Parole Association News, XXXIX (1960) 1, 4

Wells, C.: "Swatting the Subjectivist Bug" [1982] Crim. L.R. 209

White, R.W.: The Abnormal Personality (1948), pp.203–205, 288. American Psychological Association.

Williams, G.:"Recklessness Redefined" [1982] C.L.J. 252.

——: "Temporary Appropriation should be Theft" [1981] Crim. L.R. 129

——: Textbook of Criminal Law, 1st edn (1978), p.461
——: Textbook of Criminal Law, 2nd edn (1983), p.503
——: The Mental Element in Crime (1965). Reproduced with permission of Magnes Press
Wilson, W: "A Rational Scheme of Liability for Participating in Crime" [2008] Crim. L.R. 3
——: "Dealing with Drug-induced Homicide" in C.M.V. Clarkson and S.R. Cunningham (eds) Criminal
        Liability for Non-Aggressive Death (2008), pp.194–195. Reproduced with permission of Ashgate
——: "Doctrinal Rationality after Woollin" (1999) 62 M.L.R. 448, Blackwell Publishers
——: "Is Hurting People Wrong" 1992 Journal of Social Welfare and Family Law 388. Routledge/
        Taylor & Francis Ltd, www.tandf.co.uk/journals
——: "Murder and the Structure of Homicide" in Ashworth, A. and Mitchell, B. (eds) Rethinking English
        Homicide Law (2000). Oxford University Press
Winkler, E.: "Is the Killing/Letting-Die Distinction Normatively Neutral?" Dialogue XXX (1991) 309
Wooton, Baroness: Crime and the Criminal Law, 2nd edn (1981), pp.90–91

Zedner, L.: "Reparation and Retribution: Are They Reconcilable?" (1994) 57 M.L.R. 228 at 248–249
        & 250
Zeitlin, L.R.: "A Little Larceny Can Do a Lot for Employee Morale", Psychology Today (June 1974),
        22–26, 64. Reprinted with Permission by Psychology Today, 2010. www.Psychologytoday.com

While every care has been taken to establish and acknowledge copyright, and contact the copyright
owners, the publishers tender their apologies for any accidental infringement. They would be pleased
to come to a suitable arrangement with the rightful owners in each case.

CONTENTS

TABLE OF CASES

TABLE OF STATUTES

TABLE OF STATUTORY INSTRUMENTS

1

CRIME AND PUNISHMENT

I. Introduction

An attempt to comprehend the rules of criminal law must involve some understanding of the function of those rules. It would of course be possible simply to list the rules relating to various offences, e.g. murder, rape, and attempt, but such a stark analysis would not be particularly helpful or illuminating. The student of criminal law must be in a position to evaluate such rules and answer important questions. Why do we regard murder as more serious than manslaughter, when in both cases the victim has been killed? In rape does, or should, it make any difference whether the "rapist" believed that his victim was consenting? Why do we hold someone liable for attempted murder if no harm has been caused to the victim, because, say, the gun was defective and could never have injured anyone? Should such a person be held liable? These and numerous other fundamental questions that will be posed in the course of this book cannot be answered, and the present rules and reform proposals cannot be evaluated, without understanding the objective of these rules.

The function of the criminal law is to lay down a set of standards of what is permissible or not. It is a method of social control, a framework specifying the parameters of acceptable behaviour. The same is, of course, true of all law and indeed of ethical systems such as morality and religion. Family law, for example, is a set of rules stating whom one may marry, when a divorce may be obtained and so on. If one breaches these rules, for example, by trying to marry a close relative, the law provides a sanction, namely, the marriage is void. Similarly, the law of contract details how and when a contract comes into existence and stipulates the sanction for failing to comply with these rules (the contract may be void) or for failing to perform one's obligations under the contract (one may be liable for damages). All these rules are designed to ensure compliance therewith and the sanctions are those deemed most appropriate to ensure such compliance.

Similarly, the criminal law is a series of rules, with its own set of sanctions, aimed at controlling behaviour. For example, the rules provide that if you drive a motor car, you must drive carefully; if you operate a business, you must ensure that the work environment is not dangerous; you must not steal, or kill or injure other people and so on. What distinguishes the criminal law from other mechanisms of social control, and from other branches of law, is the sanction that is employed to back up the rules, namely, stigmatic punishment. If you steal property, the law of property (concerned with regulating property rights) might say that the "transaction" is void and you do not become the owner of the property. The criminal law, on the other hand, provides its own special sanction: if you steal property you are liable to be sent to prison for a maximum of seven years. The convicted thief is subjected to the shame and censure of public punishment.

Of course, one must not assume from this that the criminal law (or any other mechanism of social control) will operate perfectly. At all stages of the process from criminalisation to punishment there is scope for the mechanism to falter. It may well be that there are groups in society powerful enough to prevent the criminalisation of behaviour that otherwise appears to be a prime candidate for such treatment. An enormous number of crimes are never reported to the police; many persons who offend go undetected, are not prosecuted or not punished. The entire criminal justice system is riddled with discretion which tends to give the system the appearance of incoherence, but it is our view that, as a backdrop against which all these decisions must be made, there is a system of criminal law that is capable of internal consistency and it is that system that will be explored in this book.

In order to make sense of the criminal law and of the substantive rules that make up the whole, it is important to establish a framework. First, what conduct should be prohibited by the criminal law? If one accepts that one of the objects of the criminal law is to prevent people unjustifiably being deprived of their property, why should it be theft (a criminal offence) if you take property away from someone, but only breach of contract (generally, not a criminal offence) if you take their property pursuant to a contract without performing your obligations under that contract? If one understands why theft is criminalised, but breach of contract is not, one can begin to understand how theft should be defined so as to distinguish it from breach of contract. The substantive rules can start making sense (or be seen to be in need of reform to the extent they do not make sense).

Secondly, why do we punish those who break the rules of the criminal law? In the above theft example, why is the property law sanction not sufficient? Who do we punish and how much punishment should be imposed? Do we punish people simply because they deserve punishment or because we wish to make an example of them in order to deter others and so on? Again, the answer to these questions will often provide the key to an understanding of the rules themselves. For example, should duress be a defence in the criminal law, and if so, to what crimes? If punishing largely for desert reasons, such a defence should be available as a person subjected to duress is blameless and does not deserve punishment. On the other hand, if deterrence is seen as the main rationale of punishment, perhaps there ought to be no defence of duress, or it should not be available for the most serious crimes. A person subjected to duress might need the threat of punishment as a deterrent against giving in to the threat. In short, the structure of the substantive rules of the criminal law will depend on the view taken as to the purposes of punishment; the issue is of more fundamental importance than whether an individual judge happens to stress deterrence or reform when sentencing. Understanding the rationale of punishment will enable us to understand, evaluate, criticise and suggest reforms of those substantive rules.

It is these two crucial questions that are the subject of this first chapter.

II. What Conduct Ought to be Criminal?

A. Introduction

What conduct should be criminalised? We seem content to leave some "wrongful" conduct to morality or religion: for example, telling lies as to why an essay has not been completed on time. Other such conduct is left to the law of tort, for example, telling lies about other people so as to damage their reputation, or to the law of contract, for example, deliberately not performing one's obligations under a contract. On the other hand, if we tell a lie as a result of which another person gives us property, we commit the crime of fraud, contrary to the Fraud Act 2006. Is there any *principle* explaining why the last form of conduct is criminalised but not the others? Why, in a competitive capitalist society, is insider dealing (using privileged information to buy and sell shares on the stock exchange) a criminal offence?[1] On what basis was the decision made to make possession of indecent

---

[1]   Criminal Justice Act 1993 s.52.

photographs of children a criminal offence as well as the taking of them?[2] Similar questions can be addressed to many areas of human conduct, but, in an attempt to sharpen the focus of this section, we shall lay particular emphasis on the laws relating to sado-masochism between consenting adults.

It must be conceded at the outset that many, if not most, decisions to criminalise conduct are simply a response either to pressure groups or to perceived public opinion. This is well illustrated by the campaign to criminalise the possession of most handguns—even those held in sports clubs—in the wake of the Dunblane massacre where one man, armed with a handgun, shot and killed 16 children. A combination of factors—an organised campaign by a pressure group comprising parents of the children, a well-orchestrated press crusade, and a Government and an opposition party preparing for a general election with both determined to demonstrate a toughness against crime—conspired to ensure the speedy passage of the Firearms (Amendment) Act 1997 through Parliament. The creation of numerous other offences over the past two decades can be accounted for in the same way. For example, the alleged rise in football hooliganism led to the Football (Offences) Act 1991 which creates the offences of throwing missiles, indecent or racialist chanting and going on to the playing area at designated football matches. As a result of several highly publicised cases of fighting dogs severely injuring people, the Dangerous Dogs Act 1991 creates various offences relating to breeding, selling or allowing such dogs to be in public places without a muzzle and lead. In short, there has been an alarming tendency on the part of the Government, in particular, to adopt the view that if there is a problem, an instant panacea is to be found by criminalising the conduct in question. In 2008 it was reported that the Labour Government had, since its election in 1997, created 3,605 new criminal offences, one for almost every day it had been in power.[3] Some of these had been well publicised, such as the offence of hunting wild mammals with dogs under the Hunting Act 2004. Others, however, are offences which pass into existence almost unnoticed, such as the offence of repairing vehicles on a road[4] or willfully pretending to be a barrister (undergraduate mooters beware!).[5] In 2010, the Coalition Government expressed a commitment to prevent the proliferation of unnecessary new criminal offences and established a "Criminal Offences Gateway", which requires that proposals to create new offences receive clearance from the Secretary of State for Justice, who will approve such proposals only where he is satisfied that the proposed offences are necessary.[6] In addition, the Ministry of Justice has pledged to publish figures relating to the numbers of offences created. Figures for the 12 months ending May 2013 indicate that, in that year, 327 new criminal offences were created,[7] and Chalmers and Leverick have suggested that, in the year 2010–2011, 1,760 criminal offences were created, which indicates that the Government has a long way to go before it meets its commitment.[8]

This "frenzied approach to law-making" has led some commentators to assert that it is not possible

---

[2]   Possession of indecent photos of children was made a criminal offence by s.160 of the Criminal Justice Act 1988; the taking of such photos was made a criminal offence under the Protection of Children Act 1978 s.1(1)(a). The Coroners and Justice Act 2009 s.62 prohibits the possession of prohibited images of children (pornographic images that are grossly offensive, disgusting or otherwise of an obscene character).

[3]   *The Independent*, September 4, 2008.

[4]   Clean Neighbourhoods and Environment Act 2005 s.4.

[5]   Legal Services Act 2007 s.181.

[6]   Ministry of Justice, *Criminal Offences Gateway Guidance* (2011), available at: *http://www.justice.gov.uk/downloads/legislation/criminal-offences-gateway-guidance.pdf* [Accessed March 2014].

[7]   Ministry of Justice, *Revision: New Criminal Offences, England and Wales 1st June 2009–31st May 2013: Statistics Bulletin* (2014).

[8]   J. Chalmers and F. Leverick, "Tracking the Creation of Criminal Offences" [2013] Crim. L.R. 543–560. They suggest that the Ministry of Justice figures for that year substantially underestimate the number of new offences created. Cf. J. Chalmers and F. Leverick, "Scotland: Twice as Much Criminal Law as England" [2013] 17 Edin. L.R. 376–381.

to find any unifying thread explaining the content of the criminal law.[9] However, occasionally a more principled debate emerges. For instance, in the 1950s, the Wolfenden Committee[10] which investigated offences of homosexuality and prostitution sought to provide a theoretical framework against which the decision to criminalise conduct should be made. More recently, the Law Commission undertook a similar task in examining the extent to which consent should be a defence to various activities such as sado-masochism and various types of fighting. The aim of this section is to explore whether there are any principles that *ought* to inform a debate on whether conduct should be criminalised or decriminalised.

B. Criteria for Criminalisation

It is common to assert that there are two conditions that need to be satisfied before criminalisation of conduct is justified:

(i)   The conduct must be *wrongful*.

(ii) It must be *necessary* to employ the *criminal law* to condemn or prevent such conduct.[11]

Since 2000, there has been a third condition:

(iii) It must be *permissible* to criminalise the activity. Criminalisation of the conduct must not contravene the European Convention on Human Rights brought into force in the United Kingdom by the Human Rights Act 1998.

1. Wrongful conduct

Conduct should not be prohibited unless it can be regarded as wrongful. There is, however, no agreement as to the criteria for establishing wrongfulness. Three main strands of thinking can be discerned. First, there is the view that conduct is wrongful if it is immoral (legal moralism). Secondly, many assert that conduct is only wrongful if it causes harm or serious offence to others (the harm principle or liberalism). Thirdly, there are those who assert that conduct is wrongful if it causes harm to others or to the actor (paternalism). Each of these competing views will be discussed in turn.

(i) Legal moralism

Few would deny that the criminal law has a moral content[12]; many actions prohibited by the criminal law, such as theft and violence to the person, are undoubted moral wrongs. Even in the absence of a prohibitory law, a large majority would still feel that the actions were deeply wrong. Immoral conduct is something that offends against the community spirit. In a secular age, it need have no special religious connotations at all; immorality is not necessarily the same thing as sin, which has a religious connotation.[13] It is, however, no simple matter to define what it means for something to be "morally wrong".

---

[9]   N. Lacey, "Contingency and Criminalisation" in Ian Loveland (ed.), *The Frontiers of Criminality. Modern Legal Studies* (London: Sweet & Maxwell, 1995).

[10] Report of the Committee on Homosexual Offences and Prostitution (1957).

[11] H. Packer, *The Limits of the Criminal Sanction* (California: Stanford University Press, 1968).

[12] Some theorists, adopting a conflict view of society, would argue that the criminal law represents nothing more than the vested interests of the powerful, e.g. R. Quinney, *The Social Reality of Crime* (Boston: Little, Brown and Co, 1970).

[13] G. Hughes, "Morals and the Criminal Law" (1962) 71 Yale L.J. 662 at 666–669.

Tony Honoré, "The Dependence of Morality on Law" (1993) 13 O.J.L.S. 1 at 2:

"How are we to understand morality, a term with rather uncertain limits? It is concerned with conduct that has a significant impact on other people, and perhaps also animals, individually or collectively, and with the restraints on behaviour that we should accept because of this. Moral criticism assesses behaviour in the light of its impact on others. It excludes purely self-regarding behaviour. Moreover, since we live in groups and communities, and belong to states and other political entities, the central core of morality is concerned with how to co-exist and co-operate with others. The core of morality is, in a broad sense, political."

Moreover, one needs to be alert to the difficulties inherent in ascertaining moral opinion. Not only does moral opinion change over time but

"[t]o assume a common culture or a normative consensus in American society (for example) as in most modern societies, is to ignore the deep and divisive role of class, ethnic, religious, status, and regional culture conflicts which often produce widely opposing definitions of goodness, truth, and moral virtue."[14]

Leaving aside the problem of defining morality, one must still question the nature of the relationship between immorality and the criminal law. Is it just historical coincidence that both should operate so often in the same fields of activity or is it possible to state some more definite relationship?

Hyman Gross, A Theory of Criminal Justice (1979), pp.13–15:

"It seems obvious that those crimes of violence, theft and destruction that stand as paradigms of crime and comprise the core of any penal code are also moral wrongs. Everyone has a right to be free of such harm inflicted by others, and when murder, rape, arson, assault or larceny is committed there is also a moral wrong since a moral duty to refrain from doing harm to others has been breached. The right to be free of such harm does not have its origin in law but in a general consensus on the rights enjoyed by any member of society, or even by any person, no matter how he lives. This consensus is a more fundamental element of society even than the law, and for that reason the violation of such a right is a moral wrong and not simply a legal wrong.

But beyond the most obvious crimes, legions of others are on the books for the reason that doing what is prohibited (or failing to do what is required) makes life hazardous or unpleasant. Members of the public are entitled to live and to work in safety and to enjoy life in public places without fear, disquiet or embarrassment . . . these rights are also moral rights and not simply legal rights, since entitlement to the security and freedom that they represent is a matter of fundamental social consensus and not a matter simply of legal enactment.

Other crimes that are not common crimes are morally wrong for a different reason. Income tax fraud or draft evasion seem to place an unfair burden on others or deprive others of what is due to them."[15]

Herbert L. Packer, The Limits of the Criminal Sanction (1969), pp.262–264:

"Leaving aside for the moment what we mean by immoral, we may discern an analogy between the requirement of culpability in the individual case and a limiting criterion for the legislative invocation of the criminal sanction: only conduct generally considered 'immoral' should be treated as criminal. Several reasons support this prudential limitation. To begin with, the principles of selection we use in determining what kinds of undesirable conduct to treat as criminal should surely include at least one that is responsible to the basic character of the criminal sanction, i.e. its quality of moral condemnation. To put it another way, we should use the strengths of the sanction rather than ignore or undermine them. If the conduct with which the original sanction deals is already regarded

---

14   J.R. Gusfield, "On Legislating Morals: The Symbolic Process of Designating Deviance" (1968) 56 Cal. L. Rev. 54 at 55–56.
15   Gross argues further that committing a crime is necessarily a moral wrong because it involves violating a "solemn promise to live according to the rules" of society. However, we are here concerned with the *content* of these rules and their relationship to morality.

as being morally wrong, the processes of the criminal law have, so to speak, a 'leg up' on the job. This is a matter partly of public attitude and partly of the morale maintained by those who operate the criminal process. The way to keep those processes running at peak efficiency is to ensure that those who operate them are convinced that what they are doing is right. The surest way to persuade them that what they are doing is right is to have them act only against what they think is wrong. If the criminal sanction is widely used to deal with morally neutral behaviour, law enforcement officials are likely to be at least subconsciously defensive about their work, and the public will find the criminal law a confusing guide to moral, or even acceptable, behaviour. [Packer then dismisses the argument that the criminal law can be used to shape people's views on immorality, and continues]: . . . The question remains: whose morality are we talking about? It is easy to slide into the assumption that somewhere in society there is an authoritative body of moral sentiment to which the law should look. That assumption becomes particularly dangerous . . . when it is used to buttress the assertion that the immorality of a given form of conduct is a *sufficient* condition for declaring the conduct to be criminal. But when one is talking about immorality as a *necessary* condition for invocation of the criminal sanction, the inquiry should simply be whether there exists any significant body of dissent from the proposition that the conduct in question is immoral. Is there a social group that will be alienated or offended by making (or keeping) the conduct in question criminal? If there is, then prudence dictates caution in employing the criminal sanction. We can sum up this prudential limitation as follows: the criminal sanction should ordinarily be limited to conduct that is viewed, without significant social dissent, as immoral. The calendar of crimes should not be enlarged beyond that point and, as views about morality shift, should be contracted."

Are sado-masochistic encounters between consenting adults immoral? In *Brown*[16] the House of Lords was called upon to decide whether consent to sado-masochistic acts could be a defence to charges of assault occasioning actual bodily harm contrary to s.47 of the Offences Against the Person Act 1861. By a majority of three to two it was decided that consent was no defence to such charges. Lord Templeman (in the majority) stated:

"Society is entitled and bound to protect itself against a cult of violence. Pleasure derived from the infliction of pain is an evil thing. Cruelty is uncivilised."[17]

Lord Lowry (also in the majority) argued that

"[w]hat the appellants are obliged to propose is that the deliberate and painful infliction of physical injury should be exempted from the operation of statutory provisions the object of which is to prevent or punish that very thing, the reason for the proposed exemption being that both those who will inflict and those who will suffer the injury wish to satisfy a perverted and depraved sexual desire. Sado-masochistic homosexual activity cannot be regarded as conducive to the enhancement or enjoyment of family life or conducive to the welfare of society."[18]

Finally, Lord Mustill (in the minority) was of the view

"that whatever the outsider might feel about the subject matter of the prosecutions—perhaps horror, amazement or incomprehension, perhaps sadness—very few could read even a summary of the other activities without disgust".[19]

Even if one accepts that the House of Lords is in tune with current morality, does this mean that one is *bound* to criminalise sado-masochistic conduct?

---

[16]   *R. v Brown (Anthony Joseph)* [1994] 1 A.C. 212. The facts and an extract from the case are given at pp.315–318.
[17]   *Brown* [1994] 1 A.C. 212 at 237.
[18]   *Brown* [1994] 1 A.C. 212 at 255.
[19]   *Brown* [1994] 1 A.C. 212 at 256–257.

Some commentators have argued that it is possible to pinpoint more precisely the relationship between the criminal law and morality: they believe that not only is immorality a necessary condition for invocation of the criminal sanction, but that it is a sufficient one. It is not necessary to search for further justification (harm, enforceability, etc.) before the criminal law can be brought into action; the fact that the conduct is morally wrong is enough. This view is epitomised by such statements by James Fitzjames Stephen as "How can the State or the public be competent to determine any question whatever if it is not competent to decide that gross vice is a bad thing? I do not think the State ought to stand bandying compliments with pimps."[20]

Graphic though this picture is, the view that immorality is a sufficient condition is now likely to be couched in more qualified terms.

Patrick Devlin, Morals and the Criminal Law (reprinted in The Enforcement of Morals) (1965), pp.7–8, 14–17:

"I think it is clear that the criminal law as we know it is based upon moral principle. In a number of crimes its function is simply to enforce a moral principle and nothing else. The law, both criminal and civil, claims to be able to speak about morality and immorality generally. Where does it get its authority to do this and how does it settle the moral principles which it enforces? Undoubtedly, as a matter of history, it derived from Christian teaching. But I think that the strict logician is right when he says that the law can no longer rely on doctrines in which citizens are entitled to disbelieve. It is necessary therefore to look for some other source . . . I have framed three interrogatories addressed to myself to answer.

(1) Has society the right to pass judgment at all on the matters of morals? Ought there, in other words, to be a public morality, or are morals always a matter for private judgment?

(2) If society has the right to pass judgment, has it also the right to use the weapon of the law to enforce it?

(3) If so, ought it to use that weapon in all cases or only in some: and if only in some on what principles should it distinguish? . . .

[Lord Devlin then explained that a public morality is one of the vital ingredients of a society, and that the State has the right to safeguard anything that is essential to its existence. In other words, he answered the first two questions affirmatively.]

In what circumstances the State should exercise its power is the third of the interrogatories I have framed. But before I get to it I must raise a point which might have been brought up in any one of the three. How are the moral judgments of society to be ascertained . . . It is surely not enough that they should be reached by the opinion of the majority; it would be too much to require the individual assent of every citizen. English law has evolved and regularly uses a standard which does not depend on the counting of heads. It is that of the reasonable man. He is not to be confused with the rational man. He is not expected to reason about anything and his judgment may be largely a matter of feeling . . . for my purpose I should like to call him the man in the jury box . . .

Immorality then, for the purpose of the law, is what every right-minded person is presumed to consider immoral. Any immorality is capable of affecting society injuriously and in effect to a greater or lesser extent it usually does: this is what gives the law *locus standi*. It cannot be shut out. But—and this brings me to the third question—the individual has a *locus standi* too; he cannot be expected to surrender to the judgment of society the whole conduct of his life. It is the old familiar question of striking a balance between the rights and interests of society and those of the individual . . . there must be toleration of the maximum individual freedom that is consistent with the integrity of society. Nothing should be punished by the law that does not lie beyond the limit of tolerance. It is not nearly enough to say that a majority dislike a practice: there must be a real feeling of reprobation . . . I do not think one can ignore disgust if it is deeply felt and not manufactured. Its presence is a good indication that the bounds of toleration are being reached . . .

[B]efore a society can put a practice beyond the limits of tolerance there must be a deliberate judgment

---

[20]   James Fitzjames Stephen, *Liberty, Equality, Fraternity* (New York: Holt & Williams, 1873) p.125.

that the practice is injurious to society . . . We should ask ourselves in the first instance whether, looking at it calmly and dispassionately, we regard it as a vice so abominable that its mere presence is an offence. If that is the genuine feeling of the society in which we live, I do not see how society can be denied the right to eradicate it."

Criminal sanctions, according to Devlin, should be determined by the deep disgust (dispassionately felt) of the right-minded person, or, more accurately, they should depend upon the law-maker's interpretation of the likelihood of the right-minded person being deeply disgusted.

Devlin's criteria are easily applied to many crimes, such as murder and rape. Other crimes such as theft would also undoubtedly be regarded as immoral and generally attract "the real feeling of reprobation", even if not "disgust".

This thesis becomes more difficult when applied to Devlin's own example of homosexuality. (He was responding to the Wolfenden Report, which had recommended decriminalising homosexual acts between consenting adult males in private.) According to Devlin, although "some people sincerely believe that homosexuality is neither immoral nor unnatural",[21] there is nevertheless a collective judgment against it, and a deep feeling of disgust towards it.[22] But Hughes questions this use of "depth of disgust" as an appropriate yardstick and suggests that:

"It is not beyond the bounds of possibility that proper inquiry might reveal that, while the ordinary man contemplates homosexual behaviour with aversion and distaste, the knowledge of this practice by others does not disgust him so deeply as Lord Devlin suspects."[23]

Was it just a coincidence that the activities in *Brown* took place during homosexual encounters? It has been pointed out that prostitutes regularly receive beatings as part of their sexual encounters, even if the degrees of sado-masochism described in *Brown* are probably rarer. The implication for some commentators is that, despite all the window-dressing that talk of "harm" provides, this is really a case about the immorality of certain types of homosexual encounters.[24]

Whether one accepts such an argument or not, the result of the wide ruling in *Brown* is that most such violent encounters must be regarded as illegal if actual bodily harm results. It is irrelevant whether sexual pleasure is involved as consent is no defence. Some have applauded this conclusion:

William Wilson, "Is Hurting People Wrong?" [1992] J. of Social Welfare and Fam. Law 388 at 393, 395:

"[*Brown*] should be treated, not as a test case for sexual freedom but for the idea that even a tolerant, pluralistic society must enforce one fundamental residual moral value. Quite simply, it may be argued, hurting people is wrong, and this is so whether the victim consents or not, and whether the purpose is to fulfil a sexual need, to induce a state of euphoric narcosis, punish an errant child. . .

---

[21]   Patrick Devlin, *Morals and the Criminal Law* (reprinted in *The Enforcement of Morals*) (1965), p.8.
[22]   In 1987 it was estimated that 74% of the population regarded homosexual relations as "always" or "mostly" wrong (S. Harding, "Trends in Permissiveness" in Jowell, Witherspoon and Brook (eds), *British Social Attitudes, the 5th Report* (Aldershot: Gower, 1988), p.36. However, by 2012 that figure had fallen to 28% (*British Social Attitudes*, 30th Report, 2013) available at: *http://bsa-30.natcen.ac.uk/* [Accessed March 2014], p.16.
[23]   G. Hughes, "Morals and the Criminal Law" (1962) 71 Yale L.J. 662 at 676–678.
[24]   L. Bibbings and P. Alldridge accuse their Lordships of being homophobic: "Sexual Expression, Body Alteration, and the Defence of Consent" (1993) J. Law & Soc. 356 at 358. cf. S. Cowan, "Criminalizing SM: Disavowing the Erotic, Instatiating Violence", in R.A. Duff et al., *The Structures of the Criminal Law* (Oxford: OUP, 2011), Ch.4.

How is the balance between freedom and coercion to be drawn? Is the public interest to be secured, in other words, by allowing citizens absolute licence to pursue their own conceptions of the good life, which we take to be the basic moral premise upon which coercion is to be ordered? Or is it to be restricted in order to achieve some more valuable public good, namely societal cohesion and public order? . . . [A] fundamental building block in our moral society is the social taboo against the infliction of injury on another. Remove this building block and not only do sensibilities stand to be damaged but, over time, perhaps our very commitment to the sanctity of life. To reduce this fundamental moral issue to an issue about the presence or absence of consent may be to miss what is really at stake, namely our humanity, as presently conceived. If sadism is allowable, if consented to, then it is consent rather than moral conviction which polices the barrier between a society of would-be sadists and the kind of society most of us would like to inhabit."[25]

A line has to be drawn between that which society will allow, or turn a blind eye to, or condemn informally and that which it will condemn by means of the criminal law. One yardstick offered by Devlin is the depth of disgust. Another, offered by Wilson, is that of autonomy being "trumped" where the activity is against the "public interest". In the case of *Brown*, Lord Mustill dissented on the issue of where this line should be drawn.

R. v Brown [1994] 1 A.C. 212 (House of Lords)

LORD MUSTILL:

"When proposing that the conduct is not rightly so charged I do not invite your Lordships' House to endorse it as morally acceptable. Nor do I pronounce in favour of a libertarian doctrine specifically related to sexual matters . . . What I do say is that these are questions of private morality; that the standards by which they fall to be judged are not those of the criminal law; and that if these standards are to be upheld the individual must enforce them upon himself according to his own moral standards, or have them enforced against him by moral pressures exerted by whatever religious or other community to whose ethical ideals he responds. The point from which I invite your Lordships to depart is simply this, that the state should interfere with the rights of an individual to live his or her life as he or she may choose no more than is necessary to ensure a proper balance between the special interests of the individual and the general interests of the individuals who together comprise the population at large. Thus, whilst acknowledging that very many people, if asked whether the appellants' conduct was wrong, would reply, 'Yes, repulsively wrong', I would at the same time assert that this does not in itself mean that the prosecution of the appellants . . . is well-founded."

However, according to the law as it now stands, boxing, for example, stands one side of the line, while sado-masochism falls on the other.[26]

What can be concluded at this stage is that Lord Devlin's yardstick is not a sound basis upon which to take decisions to criminalise, especially if cloaked behind a mask of public interest. Not only may it be a thin disguise for the criminalisation of immorality simpliciter[27] (as advocated by Stephen more than a century ago) but the criteria employed are too limited. One cannot, as Lord Devlin has done, throw rationality completely to the winds in order to replace it with the reasonable man's disgust—which, as Hart points out, may be based on "ignorance, superstition or misunderstanding".[28] Instead:

---

[25] cf. D.J. Baker, "The Moral Limits of Consent as a Defence in the Criminal Law" (2009) 12 New Crim. L. Rev. 93–121, who suggests that the consent of the participants in *Brown* was not sufficient to override the harm inflicted on the participants because it violated their dignity as human beings and that the criminalization of the defendants in that case was prima facie fair because their actions were "wrongfully harmful in the objective sense" (at p.101, see also pp.117–118).

[26] See below, pp.315–322.

[27] For a defence of Lord Devlin, see E.V. Rostow, "The Enforcement of Morals" [1960] C.L.J. 174 where he suggests that Lord Devlin so qualifies his central conditions with cries for tolerance, etc. that the gap between him and his critics is very small.

[28] H.L.A. Hart, "Immorality and Treason" 62 *The Listener* 163 (July 30, 1959).

"the examination of existing law and the debate about proposed laws should be conducted by making as explicit a statement as is possible of the values that the law is designed to protect, by a careful investigation of the harm done to those values by the conduct prohibited or which it is sought to prohibit, and by a careful consideration of the probable efficacy of legal prohibition. In this debate the prevalence of feelings of disgust or revulsion in the community is one factor to be considered and no more than that."[29]

In other words, whilst moral wrongdoing (with all its attendant difficulties of identification) may be a necessary condition for the imposition of the criminal law, it ought not to be a sufficient one. This has been recognised by Duff in his consideration of the limits of criminal responsibility and the criminal law.[30]

R.A. Duff, "Peversions and Subversions of Criminal Law", in R.A. Duff et al., The Boundaries of the Criminal Law (Oxford: OUP, 2010), pp.89–90, 107–108:

"To say that the criminal law is concerned with wrongs (with moral wrongs) is to espouse some form of Legal Moralism . . . For the negative Legal Moralist, wrongdoing is a necessary condition of criminal liability and punishment. We should not criminalize conduct that is not in some relevant way morally wrongful, nor impose criminal liability on those who are not morally culpable, but the wrongfulness of the conduct and the culpability of its agent do not give us positive reason to criminalize it: the practice's 'general justifying aim' does not include ensuring the conviction and punishment of the morally guilty. For the positive Legal Moralist, by contrast, the moral wrongfulness of the conduct and its agent's culpability give us positive reason to criminalize it: a central purpose of criminal law as a distinctive mode of legal regulation is to define, and provide for the formal condemnation and punishment of, various kinds of wrongdoing. . .

. . .

A positive Legal Moralist must hold that we have reason to criminalize any public wrong: any such wrong is our collective business; we have reason to call its perpetrator to answer for it and to censure him as a wrongdoer. That is not yet to say, however, that we have conclusive reason to do so: quite apart from the fact that the costs, both material and moral, of enforcing the criminalization of a public wrong might be so great, and the chances of doing it justly and effectively so small, that we should not on balance seek to criminalize it, we might have two other kinds of reason for not criminalizing a public wrong.

First, some public wrongs are too trivial to justify the attention of the criminal law: even if a better system of criminal justice than our own was able to provide appropriately modest, non-oppressive procedures and punishments for minor offences, some wrongs are too minor to warrant even that much formal attention. For just one example, there are kinds of incivility that we may display to each other in public places (barging rudely along a crowded street, for instance) that constitute civic wrongs, and that merit comment from others, but that it would be absurd to think of criminalizing; that is why any sane system of criminal law recognizes a *de minimis* principle.

Second, however, there might be kinds of public wrong that cause or threaten serious harm, but that we should not criminalize because it is more important to ensure that the harm is repaired or paid for, and to allocate the costs of such repair or compensation justly, than to call those who cause it to public, criminal account; and, perhaps, because criminalizing the conduct would hinder the attempt to allocate its costs fairly—if, for instance, those who caused the harm would then be less likely to admit their responsibility for it. In such cases we would see reason to prefer something more like a civil-law than a criminal-law response. . ."

---

[29]   Hughes, "Morals and the Criminal Law" (1962) 71 Yale L.J. 662 at 682. He points out that this approach will still contain elements of irrationality but that it is better than the "throwing the baby out with the bath water" (Hart, "Immorality and Treason", 62 *The Listener* 163) approach of Devlin.

[30]   See also: R.A. Duff, *Answering for Crime: Responsibility and Liability in the Criminal Law* (Oxford: Hart Publishing, 2007), Chs 4–6; M.S. Moore, *Placing Blame: A Theory of Criminal Law* (Oxford: OUP, 1997). Duff has described himself as a "positive Legal Moralist": R.A. Duff, "Peversions and Subversions of Criminal Law", in R.A. Duff et al., *The Boundaries of the Criminal Law* (Oxford: OUP, 2010), p.91. cf. M. Thorburn, "Constitutionalism and the Limits of the Criminal Law", in R.A. Duff et al., *The Structures of the Criminal Law* (Oxford: OUP, 2011), Ch.5, for a critique of Moore and Duff's approaches to legal moralism.

(ii) Liberalism: the harm and offence principle

A basic tenet of liberalism is that respect must be shown to the principle of individual autonomy—the notion that people possess free will and must be allowed, to the maximum extent possible, to make free choices. The state should only intervene to restrict autonomy when it is necessary to prevent harm or serious offence to others.

The Law Commission, Consent in the Criminal Law (Consultation Paper No.139, 1995) Appendix C, para.C.85:

"The liberal and the moralist disagree fundamentally about the value of autonomy. The liberal can agree with the moralist that the world would be a better place with less of this evil in it, and the liberal might even set about trying to reduce the evil by argument, persuasion, exhortation and/or education of the young. But she will not use the criminal law to this end because she accords primacy to the value of autonomy and the mutually reinforcing ideals of value pluralism and toleration. Given the diversity of human needs, tastes and talents there must be a diversity of eligible life-styles, careers and options to give everybody a fair chance of living a fulfilling, stimulating and enjoyable life. Some of these life-styles will be incompatible or even mutually contradictory, but the liberal will demand that each should extend to the others a degree of tolerance and respect, within the limits set by the harm and offence principles. The liberal asserts that her political theory is the most appropriate for a multicultural and pluralistic society."

H.L.A. Hart, "Immorality and Treason" 62 The Listener 162–163 (July 30, 1959):

"The Wolfenden Committee on Homosexual Offences and Prostitution recommended by a majority of 12 to 1 that homosexual behaviour between consenting adults in private should no longer be a criminal offence. One of the Committee's principal grounds for this recommendation was expressed in its report in this way: 'There must remain a realm of private morality and immorality which in brief and crude terms is not the law's business.' I shall call this the liberal point of view: for it is a special application of those wider principles of liberal thought which John Stuart Mill formulated in his essay on Liberty. Mill's most famous words, less cautious perhaps than the Wolfenden Committee's were:

> 'The only purpose for which power can be rightfully exercised over any member of a civilized community against his will is to prevent harm to others. His own good, either physical or moral, is not a sufficient warrant. He cannot rightfully be compelled to do or forbear . . . because in the opinion of others to do so would be wise or even right.'

The liberal point of view has often been attacked, both before and after Mill. I shall discuss here the repudiation of it made by Sir Patrick Devlin . . .

Mill's formulation of the liberal point of view may well be too simple. The grounds for interfering with human liberty are more various than the single criterion of 'harm to others' suggests: cruelty to animals or organizing prostitution for gain do not, as Mill himself saw, fall easily under the description of harm to others. Conversely, even where there is harm to others in the most literal sense, there may well be other principles limiting the extent to which harmful activities should be repressed by law. So there are multiple criteria, not a single criterion, determining when human liberty may be restricted. Perhaps this is what Sir Patrick means by a curious distinction which he often stresses between theoretical and practical limits. But with all its simplicities the liberal point of view is a better guide than Sir Patrick to clear thought in the proper relation of morality to the criminal law: for it stresses what he obscures—namely, the points at which thought is needed before we turn popular morality into criminal law.

No doubt we would all agree that consensus of moral opinion on certain matters is essential if society is to be worth living in. Laws against murder, theft, and much else would be of little use if they were not supported by a widely diffused conviction that what these laws forbid is also immoral. So much is obvious. But it does not follow that everything to which the moral vetoes of accepted morality attach is of equal importance to society; nor is there the slightest reason for thinking of morality as a seamless web: one which will fall to pieces carrying society with it, unless all its emphatic vetoes are enforced by law. Surely even in the face of the moral feeling that is up to concert pitch—the trio of intolerance, indignation, and disgust—we must pause to think. We must ask a question at two different levels which Sir Patrick never clearly enough identifies or separates. First, we must ask whether a practice which offends moral feeling is harmful, independently of its repercussion on the general moral code. Secondly, what about repercussion on the moral code? Is it really true that failure to translate this item of general morality into criminal law will jeopardize the whole fabric of morality and so society?

We cannot escape thinking about these two different questions merely by repeating to ourselves the vague nostrum: 'This is part of public morality and public morality must be preserved if society is to exist.' Sometimes Sir Patrick seems to admit this, for he says in words which both Mill and the Wolfenden Report might have used, that there must be the maximum respect for individual liberty consistent with the integrity of society. Yet this, as his contrasting examples of fornication and homosexuality show, turns out to mean only that the immorality which the law may punish must be generally felt to be intolerable. This plainly is no adequate substitute for a reasoned estimate of the damage to the fabric of society likely to ensue if it is not suppressed."

An immediate problem with the harm and offence principle is that one needs a careful definition of these terms. A trader who sets up a legitimate business in competition with another can severely harm that other person by taking away all their business but, in a capitalist society where business competition is encouraged, this can hardly constitute the sort of harm that ought to be criminalised. Similarly, picking one's nose in public might cause deep offence to observers but, again, it would be unthinkable to assert that such conduct should be criminal.

With regard to the concept of harm, a distinction is often drawn between primary and secondary harms.

J. Kaplan, "The Role of the Law in Drug Control" [1971] Duke L.J. 1065 at 1065–1068:

"Typically the use of the law to prevent conduct which harms only the actor himself is distinguished from the use of the law as a means of preventing the individual from harming others, including society at large. In practice, however, this is not an easy distinction to draw, for there are few actions in which one can engage that threaten harm only to himself.

The purest example of laws aimed at such conduct are the statutes which require the driver of a motorcycle to wear a protective helmet. It is true that one can argue that the helmet really protects others, since it shields the motorcyclist from thrown pebbles which might make him lose control and injure innocent pedestrians or automobile drivers. Though this approach makes the problem easier, it is disingenuous. As a result, many courts and commentators have refused to take it and have assumed that the helmet protects only the cyclist himself.

Though the helmetless cyclist does not expose others to any appreciable physical danger, he does drive in a society that is committed to preventing people from dying of their injuries. Thus, rather than allowing the cyclist to die unnecessarily, society is prepared to undertake the enormous expense of treating him until he either expires or recovers. In Professor Robert Bartel's apt phrase, the helmetless cyclist exposes others to 'public ward' harm—the danger of having to treat him should he not be killed outright. It is on this theory that society feels it has the right to demand that he do his share to protect himself.

The expense and inconvenience that the helmetless driver may cause does not, however, stop at public ward harm. Insofar as his failure to wear a helmet results in his own injury, he may force society to assume the cost of his neglected responsibilities to others. Here the issue cannot be avoided by saying that it is all society's fault for not letting him die in the street at minimal cost, because his responsibilities must still be fulfilled. As an emotional matter, moreover, non-support justifications for laws which attempt to prevent self-harming conduct often command considerably more power than do public ward justifications. Thus, despite the enormous public ward justifications for halting alcohol abuse, one of the most powerful Prohibitionist posters contained a drawing of a saloon with a father drinking at the bar while his clean, but poorly dressed little daughter stood in the doorway saying, 'Father, Father, please come home. Mother needs you.' The same public interest which underlies non-support laws, then, can also justify helmetless cyclist laws—at least in the case of those who owe someone a support obligation.

In addition to the public ward and non-support justifications for forbidding conduct which on first glance would appear to harm only the actor, a further justification exists which might be called the 'modelling' justification.

Modelling is the psychological term for the process by which one repeats a type of behaviour one sees in others. Modelling of behaviour may thus occur where the watcher first learns that the behaviour which he had thought impossible can indeed be performed; where the watcher, by observing, learns how to do it; where he simply gets the idea from watching; or where he, for any one of many reasons, imitates the action. It is true, of course, that the same values which underlie the freedom of communication may interfere with preventing the harm caused by modelling. The individual who models the helmetless cyclist does so without coercion, and, apart from the indirect harms discussed, he harms only himself. Nevertheless, where those persons society tries to protect from modelling are children, the fact that the helmetless cyclist in a causal sense may have caused the modelling, which in turn might lead to injury, may be very significant. Children are regarded as much more likely than adults to model dangerous conduct, and we certainly acknowledge a greater responsibility to protect them from harm.

The final justification by which some may find social harm in conduct which appears to harm only the actor might be called the 'categorical imperative' justification. This relies on the fact that although an act might harm only the actor if performed by relatively few people, it could cause harm to everyone if it were performed by almost all. This justification is not heard in the helmetless cyclist case, but it is heard with respect to some sexual and drug laws."

If one were to apply the distinction made by Kaplan between harms which may be referred to as primary (involving direct harm to others) and secondary (involving indirect harm to others) to the examples we have employed before, theft would clearly belong to the former category; it causes harm to others and can be criminalised on that basis. But what of sado-masochistic activities between consenting adults? Those involved in such activities would argue that no primary harm is caused, since participants not only consent to physical pain but positively desire it. However, it could be argued that secondary harm is caused; one might wish to employ Kaplan's "modelling" and "categorical imperative" justifications. Similar arguments were in fact raised in the case of *Brown*[31] where it was alleged that a young man had been corrupted by being introduced into the sado-masochistic ring. In other words, the potential, if not the reality, for harm to others existed.[32]

Kaplan's "modelling" justification can be seen in operation more recently in relation to the offence of "extreme pornography" under s.63 of the Criminal Justice and Immigration Act 2008. This provision criminalises the possession (not the production or supply) of pornography that is deemed to be "extreme" due to its portrayal of one of a number of acts listed in s.63(7)[33] and which "is grossly offensive, disgusting or otherwise of an obscene character".[34] At first glance this test seems to indicate that the Government, in choosing to create this new offence, did so on the basis of legal moralism.[35] However, McGlynn and Rackley suggest that an offence of possessing extreme pornography could be justified under the harm principle, and identify "cultural harm" as a type of harm that such criminalisation might seek to prevent.[36] "Cultural harm", they assert, is "a concept of harm which moves beyond arguments of immediate cause and effect".[37] Ultimately, the harm that allowing the possession of extreme pornography threatens to cause is that it might "contribute to a climate in which sexual vio-

---

[31]   *Brown* [1994] 1 A.C. 212.

[32]   cf. The "risk of harm" test relied on in relation to the regulation of pornography: V.E. Munro and J. Scoular, "Harm, Vulnerability, and Citizenship: Constitutional Concerns in the Criminalization of Contemporary Sex Work", in R.A. Duff et al., *The Constitution of the Criminal Law* (Oxford: OUP, 2013), Ch.3.

[33]   The acts are: an act which threatens a person's life; an act which results, or is likely to result, in serious injury to a person's anus, breasts or genitals; an act which involves sexual interference with a human corpse; and a person performing an act of intercourse or oral sex with an animal (whether dead or alive).

[34]   Criminal Justice and Immigration Act 2008 s.63(6). cf. the offence of possession of prohibited images of children created by the Coroners and Justice Act 2009 s.62, which uses the same terminology.

[35]   cf. the Sexual Offences Act 2003 ss.63 and 64, which criminalise consensual incest between adults. It has been argued that legal moralism lies behind these offences, rather than any clear harm related or public interest justification: T. Hömle, "Consensual Adult Incest: A Sex Offence?" [2014] 76 New Crim. L. Rev. 76; J.R. Spencer, "Incest and Article 8 of the European Convention on Human Rights" (2013) 72 C.L.J. 5. cf. *Stubing v Germany* [2013] 1 F.L.R. 107.

[36]   C. McGlynn and E. Rackley, "Criminalising Extreme Pornography: A Lost Opportunity" [2009] Crim. L.R. 245.

[37]   McGlynn and Rackley, "Criminalising Extreme Pornography: A Lost Opportunity" [2009] Crim. L.R. 245 at 257.

lence is not taken seriously".[38] McGlynn and Rackley are of the opinion that the Government's purpose in enacting the legislation "should have been about changing the cultural and social environment in which sexual violence is marginalised, in which rape conviction rates are at an all time low and in which pornography is becoming (if possible) even more ubiquitous". Whilst the Government's original consultation paper[39] justified its proposals on this ground, amongst others, following opposition from "arch liberals" the proposals were amended and the Government "[u]ltimately . . . fell back on the easy tradition of the conservative-moralistic and disgust-based arguments which consume the [Obscene Publications Act]".[40]

In *Brown* the majority stressed yet other relevant harms. Lord Jauncey stated that

"it would appear to be good luck rather than good judgment which has prevented serious injury from occurring. Wounds can easily become septic if not properly treated, the free flow of blood from a person who is HIV positive or who has AIDS can infect another and an inflicter who is carried away by sexual excitement or by drink or drugs could very easily inflict pain and injury beyond the level to which the receiver had consented . . . When considering the public interest potential for harm is just as relevant as actual harm."[41]

What this discussion suggests is that the distinction between primary and secondary harms does not provide us with a basis for making decisions as to whether to criminalise conduct. Not only may it be a front for the criminalisation of immorality *simpliciter* but also it does not enable us to answer which (if any) secondary harms should be prohibited by the criminal law. Just as no-one today argues that all immoral acts ought to be criminal, so no-one argues that all secondary harms ought to be criminal. "The obvious secondary harm resulting from such almost universally performed acts as over-eating or poor nutrition is the *reductio ad absurdum* of such arguments."[42]

One of the most sophisticated efforts at defining the harm and offence principle is that provided by Joel Feinberg in a series of books, spanning four volumes, entitled *The Moral Limits of the Criminal Law*.

Joel Feinberg, The Moral Limits of the Criminal Law: Harm to Others (1984), pp.33, 34, 36, 215–216:

"Harm . . . [means] the thwarting, setting back, or defeating of an interest . . . One's interests . . . consist of all those things in which one has a stake . . . Only setbacks of interests that are wrongs, and wrongs that are setbacks to interest, are to count as harms in the appropriate sense . . .

This interpretation thus excludes set-back interests produced by justified or excused conduct ('harms' that are not wrongs) . . . A harm in the appropriate sense then will be produced by morally indefensible conduct that not only sets back the victim's interest, but also violates his right . . .

Minor or trivial harms *are* harms despite their minor magnitude and triviality, but below a certain threshold

---

[38] McGlynn and Rackley, "Criminalising Extreme Pornography: A Lost Opportunity" [2009] Crim. L.R. 245 at 257.
[39] Home Office Consultation Paper: *On the Possession of Extreme Pornographic Material* (2005).
[40] McGlynn and Rackley, "Criminalising Extreme Pornography: A Lost Opportunity" [2009] Crim. L.R. 245 at 257 at 258. See also, E. Rackley and C. McGlynn, "Prosecuting the Possession of Extreme Pornography: A Misunderstood and Mis-Used Law" [2013] Crim. L.R. 400–405. cf. P. Johnson, "Law, Morality and Disgust: The Regulation of 'Extreme Pornography' in England and Wales" (2010) 19 Social & Legal Studies 147–163, who argues that: "The morality test in section 63, enables a 'measurement' of harm to be made that is more appropriate to the aims of the legislation. It provides a flexible way to continually pose the crucial question that underpins the justification for the legislation: 'is the private possession of these images harmful to the moral values of society'?" (at pp.154–155).
[41] *Brown* [1994] 1 A.C. 212, 245–246.
[42] J. Kaplan, "The Role of the Law in Drug Control" [1971] Duke Law Journal 1065, 1068.

they are not to count as harms for the purposes of the harm principle, for legal interference with trivia is likely to cause more harm than it prevents . . .

Where the kind of conduct in question . . . does create a danger to some degree, legislators employing the harm principle must use various rules of thumb as best they can:

a. the greater the *gravity* of a possible harm, the less probable its occurrence need be to justify prohibition of the conduct that threatens to produce it;

b. the greater the *probability* of harm, the less grave the harm need be to justify coercion;

c. the greater the *magnitude of the risk* of harm, itself compounded out of gravity and probability, the less reasonable it is to accept the risk;

d. the more *valuable* (useful) the dangerous conduct, both to the actor and others, the more reasonable it is to take the risk of harmful consequences . . .

e. the more reasonable the risk of harm (the danger), the weaker is the case for prohibiting the conduct that creates it."

Joel Feinberg, The Moral Limits of the Criminal Law: Offense to Others (1985), pp.1–2, 26:

"It is always a good reason in support of a proposed criminal prohibition that it would probably be an effective way of preventing serious offense (as opposed to injury or harm) to persons other than the actor, and that it is probably a necessary means to that end . . .

The offense principle requires that the disliked state of mind . . . be produced wrongfully by another party . . .

[It is necessary] to weigh, in each main category and context of offensiveness, the seriousness of the offense caused to unwilling witnesses against the reasonableness of the offender's conduct. The seriousness of the offensiveness would be determined by (1) the intensity and durability of the repugnance produced, and the extent to which repugnance could be anticipated to be the general reaction of strangers to the conduct displayed or represented (conduct offensive only to persons with an abnormal susceptibility to offense would not count as *very* offensive); (2) the ease with which unwilling witnesses can avoid the offensive displays; and (3) whether or not the witnesses have willingly assumed the risk of being offended either through curiosity or the anticipation of pleasure . . .

These factors would be weighed as a group against the reasonableness of the offending party's conduct as determined by (1) its personal importance to the actors themselves and its social utility generally, remembering always the enormous social utility of unhampered expression (in those cases where expression is involved); (2) the availability of alternative times and places where the conduct in question would cause less offense; (3) the extent, if any, to which the offense is caused with spiteful motives. In addition, the legislature would examine the prior established character of various neighbourhoods, and consider establishing licensed zones in areas where the conduct in question is known to be already prevalent, so that people inclined to be offended are not likely to stumble on it to their surprise . . .

[Feinberg argues that the law should not treat offence as if it was as serious as harm and, where possible, should use other modes of regulation such as injunctions or licensing procedures (p.3).]"

The Law Commission, Consent in the Criminal Law (Consultation Paper No.139, 1995), Appendix C, para.C.41:

"Liberals support the offence principle because some forms of offence can be so extreme and protracted that they unacceptably infringe the autonomy of unwilling observers and are therefore, on liberal principles, legitimate candidates for criminalisation. The liberal is, however, extremely cautious in using the criminal law to this end and will only endorse an offence principle that is properly qualified and carefully circumscribed. The reason is clear; since just about every conceivable activity might give offence to *somebody*, *everybody's* autonomy would be severely and unacceptably curtailed if the criminal law routinely targeted offensive conduct . . . The liberal, at any rate, will only countenance criminalising offence which is extreme and unavoidable, and this can never be said of activity which takes place in private."

It follows that while picking one's nose in public might be an offence to sensibility,[43] it could never, using Feinberg's criteria, amount to *serious* offence. On the other hand, if one were travelling on a bus and the passengers in the seat directly opposite perform mutual fellatio or cunnilingus to climax accompanied by sound effects,[44] it could be argued that the test of serious offence is made out.

The critical definition of harm and offence is that it involves a *wrongful* set-back to another's interests. Whether conduct is wrongful is ultimately to be based on moral judgments. Accordingly, if a victim consents to injury or the risk of injury, as is the case with sado-masochistic beatings, that person has not been wronged and so has not been harmed. Similarly, the legitimate businessperson has not wronged the competitor and so no harm has been caused.

(iii) Legal paternalism

Legal paternalism involves allowing the criminal law to be used to protect a person from harm to themselves. The law is entitled to interfere with a person's autonomy for their own good and to enhance their welfare. If it were established that consuming certain drugs was harmful to the person concerned, the paternalist would criminalise the sale and possession of such drugs. The legal paternalist is, however, only interested in enhancing the interests that a person actually has and not in protecting interests that they ought to have. As Roberts puts it:

> "So a paternalist in my sense may interfere with another person's self-regarding actions in order to protect those interests which the other would recognise as authentically his (e.g. his interests in continued life and bodily security) but not for the sake of interests the other disowns (e.g. his (moral) interest in not having gay sex)."[45]

There are, however, problems with a paternalistic approach.

The Law Commission, Consent in the Criminal Law (Consultation Paper No.139, 1995), Appendix C, para.C.63:

"[T]he paternalist argues from a philosophical slippery slope and is at constant risk of taking a tumble. The fact is that many of us make life-style choices which do not promote our immediate or long-term interests. Smoking certainly falls into this category of choices: for the paternalist it should be a clear target for criminalisation. But the point goes much further. If (as seems plausible) a balanced, healthy diet and regular exercise would be in every person's interests, the paternalist has a reason for criminalising fatty foods and sedentary life-styles. Risk-taking without good reason would also be ruled out. Sky-diving, mountaineering and most contact sports would have to be criminalised. In principle, the paternalist seems to be committed to using the criminal law to turn us all into super-fit, clean-living 'spartans' whether we like it or not."

Despite this,[46] the Law Commission has proposed, in relation to sado-masochistic activities, that the law be based on an approach "redolent of a paternalism that is softened at the edges".[47] Accordingly,

---

[43]   H. Gross, *A Theory of Criminal Justice* (New York: OUP, 1979), p.120.
[44]   J. Feinberg, *The Moral Limits of the Criminal Law: Offense to Others* (New York: OUP, 1985), p.12. cf. A.P. Simester and A. von Hirsch, *Crimes, Harms and Wrongs: On the Principles of Criminalization* (Oxford: Hart Publishing, 2011), pp.97–107.
[45]   P. Roberts, "The Philosophical Foundations of Consent in the Criminal Law" (1997) 17(3) O.J.L.S. 389 at 394.
[46]   "Appendix C: Consent and the Criminal Law: Philosophical Foundations" was specially commissioned by the Law Commission and written by Paul Roberts. While reproducing his advice, the Law Commission felt itself unable to adopt the approach he favours (para.2.1).
[47]   "Appendix C: Consent and the Criminal Law: Philosophical Foundations", para.2.15.

while people should be generally entitled to make choices for themselves and consent to injury, even fairly serious injury, they should not be permitted to consent to seriously disabling injury. Because people have interests in their physical health, the normal functioning of their bodies and in avoiding intense pain or grotesque disfigurement, the Law Commission takes the view that anybody who consents to seriously disabling injury "has made a mistake and that to be really disabled is against his or her interests".[48] An exception is, however, proposed in relation to activities that are "very widely regarded as beneficial"[49] such as surgery and risky sports. By allowing people to consent to a range of injuries in sado-masochism, the Law Commission clearly regards its paternalistic view as being softened in favour of liberalism. However, by not allowing people to consent to seriously disabling injuries in the course of sado-masochism while not criminalising the same injuries in the course of, say, boxing, it is possible to assert that in reality the Law Commission has adopted a stance of paternalism hardened at the edges by legal moralism.

It is also the case that paternalism is used inconsistently as a justification for the control of certain drugs. One might expect that drugs offences be classed in seriousness according to the harm that they might potentially cause the user and/or any secondary victims. Studies of the harmfulness of drugs have shown that this is not in fact how the criminal law operates. The Misuse of Drugs Act 1971 categorises prohibited drugs in three classes A, B and C. Possession and supply of such drugs are prohibited, with the maximum sentence for such offences depending upon the class of drug involved.[50] Examples of those drugs falling within Class A are heroin and cocaine, whilst amphetamines (speed) are Class B. Cannabis, having been temporarily downgraded to Class C, has again been reclassified as a Class B drug.[51]

House of Commons Science and Technology Committee, Drug Classification: Making a Hash of It?, Fifth Report of Session 2005–06 (2006), p.3:

"With respect to the ABC classification system, we have identified significant anomalies in the classification of individual drugs and a regrettable lack of consistency in the rationale used to make classification decisions. In addition, we have expressed concern at the Government's proclivity for using the classification system as a means of 'sending out signals' to potential users and society at large—it is at odds with the stated objective of classifying drugs on the basis of harm and the Government has not made any attempt to develop an evidence base on which to draw in determining the 'signal' being sent out."

Evidence provided to the committee suggests, for example, that magic mushrooms, currently classed as a Class A drug, are far less harmful than other drugs in the same category. Official statistics suggest that only one person died from taking such drugs between the years 1993 and 2000; the drugs are thought not to be addictive, and that it is estimated that one would need to consume one's own body weight in magic mushrooms for the dose to be lethal.[52] In comparison, some drugs which are not even prohibited under law are far more harmful.[53] Alcohol and tobacco

---

[48]   "Appendix C: Consent and the Criminal Law: Philosophical Foundations", para.2.18.
[49]   "Appendix C: Consent and the Criminal Law: Philosophical Foundations", para.2.18.
[50]   For offences of possession, Class A drugs attract a maximum sentence of seven-years' imprisonment, for Class B drugs the maximum sentence is five years and for Class C drugs it is two years.
[51]   Misuse of Drugs Act 1971 (Amendment) Order 2008 (SI 2008/3130) art.2(2)(a) (in force from January 26, 2009).
[52]   House of Commons Science and Technology Committee, Drug Classification: Making a Hash of It?, Fifth Report of Session 2005–06 (2006), p.27. For further discussion of the criminalisation of magic mushrooms, see C. Walsh, "Magic Mushrooms and the Law" [2005] Crim. L.R. 773–783.
[53]   See, for example, recent press discussion in relation to the dangers of "legal highs": H. Macdonell, "Three Scots die each month after taking legal highs", Daily Telegraph, March 26, 2014; Editorial, "Legal highs blow yet another hole in our drugs policy", The Independent, March 14, 2014; M. Daly, "Not regulating 'legal highs' condemns drug users to playing Russian roulette", The Guardian, March 3, 2014.

were ranked by some as being as harmful as the Class A drugs of LSD and ecstasy, and it has been estimated that together alcohol and tobacco cause "approximately 40 times the total number of deaths from all illegal drugs combined".[54] If drugs offences are to be justified in terms of paternalism surely they should bear some relation to the degree of harm they actually cause.

Whilst paternalism has been subjected to much criticism, the harm principle has also been criticised in recent years for failing to curb the expansion of the criminal law,[55] and it may be seen as being both underinclusive, "since it cannot—or cannot without serious distortion—capture kinds of conduct that clearly should be criminalized",[56] and over-inclusive, "in that it renders 'criminalizable' at least in principle, kinds of conduct that should not be criminalized".[57] There is potential for the principle to be used to justify highly intrusive state intervention into the private life of individuals, for example it might be seen as justifying the criminalisation of parents who cause harm or a risk of harm to their children's health by failing to have them immunised, or smoking at home, or feeding them excessive quantities of calorie-dense food.[58] Feinberg has suggested that, in the case of offensive conduct and speech, there is a particular danger of over-criminalisation because of the tendency of law-makers to overreact to it.[59] Stanton-Ife has also argued that the manner in which the harm principle accounts for crimes in general, in terms of interests, fails adequately to explain the gravity of some particularly horrific crimes, because it "has the effect of shoehorning all crimes into one box",[60] regarding the victims of crime as those whose interests have been violated, when the reality is that the victims of horrific crimes "have been violated themselves".[61]

2. Is it necessary to employ the criminal law?

Whichever of the above views is adopted as the correct basis upon which to justify the determination that conduct is wrongful, most commentators accept that this is merely a minimal or necessary, but not a sufficient, condition. Assuming the conduct in question is adjudged to be wrongful, there is a further condition to be established. It must be *necessary* to use the *criminal law*

---

[54]   House of Commons Science and Technology Committee, *Drug Classification: Making a Hash of It?*, Fifth Report of Session 2005–06 (2006), p.47. See P.R. Ferguson, "'Smoke gets in your eyes . . .' the criminalisation of smoking in enclosed public places, the harm principle and the limits of the criminal sanction" (2011) 3 *Legal Studies* 259–278, who argues that the risk of harm to non-smokers from passive smoking is preferable as a justification for this criminalisation to legal paternalism.

[55]   B.E. Harcourt, "The Collapse of the Harm Principle" (1999) 90 J. Crim. L. & Criminology 109. cf. Thorburn, "Constitutionalism and the Limits of the Criminal Law", in R.A. Duff et al., *The Structures of the Criminal Law* (Oxford: OUP, 2011).

[56]   R.A. Duff et al., "Introduction: The Boundaries of the Criminal Law", in R.A. Duff et al., *The Boundaries of the Criminal Law* (Oxford: OUP, 2010), p.20.

[57]   Duff et al., "Introduction: The Boundaries of the Criminal Law", in R.A. Duff et al., *The Boundaries of the Criminal Law* (Oxford: OUP, 2010), p.20.

[58]   Nuffield Council on Bioethics, *Public Health: Ethical Issues* (2007), para.5.39; T. Elliott, "Pursued by the 'fat police'? The obesity 'epidemic' and the criminal law", in A.M. Viens, J. Coggon and A. Kessel, *Criminal Law, Philosophy and Public Health Practice* (Cambridge: CUP, 2013), Ch.6.

[59]   J. Feinberg, *The Moral Limits of the Criminal Law: Offense to Others* (Oxford: OUP, 1985), p.5. See, for example, the use which has been made of the Malicious Communications Act 1988 s.1 and the Communications Act 2003 s.127, to prosecute "flame trolls", who send offensive or provocative messages via social media. Recent prosecutions include that of student Liam Stacey for posting a racist comment on Twitter about the footballer Fabrice Muamba and the "twitter joke" trial of Paul Chambers (whose appeal against conviction was subsequently allowed: *Chambers v DPP* [2012] EWHC 2157 (Admin); [2013] 1 W.L.R. 1833). The CPS, in its *Guidelines on Prosecuting Cases Involving Communications Sent via Social Media* (2013) has indicated that prosecutions under s.1 of the Malicious Communications Act 1988 and s.127 of the Communications Act 2003 should only be brought where the communication in question is grossly offensive: "Just because the content expressed in the communication is in bad taste, controversial or unpopular, and may cause offence to individuals or a specific community, this is not in itself sufficient reason to engage the criminal law" (para.39).

[60]   J. Stanton-Ife, "Horrific Crime", in R.A. Duff et al., *The Boundaries of the Criminal Law* (Oxford: OUP, 2010), Ch.6, p.162.

[61]   Stanton-Ife, "Horrific Crime", in R.A. Duff et al., *The Boundaries of the Criminal Law* (Oxford: OUP, 2010), Ch.6, p.162.

to condemn and try to prevent the wrongful conduct. In other words, the criminal law should be used as a "last resort".

Douglas Husak, "The Criminal Law as Last Resort" (2004) 24 O.J.L.S. 207 at 211–212:

"Why not require the state to have a compelling interest for *each* criminal law it enacts? The standards applicable to infringements of fundamental rights (like speech) should be invoked *whenever* persons become subject to punishment. This theory would require the law in question to be *necessary* to achieve a compelling government purpose. In other words, the government's objective must be essential, and the law must be the least restrictive means to attain it. To qualify as the least restrictive means, the law must be *narrowly tailored* to serve the compelling state interest. The requirement of narrow tailoring has two dimensions. First, criminal laws should not be *overinclusive*, proscribing instances of conduct beyond those that serve the compelling state interest. Next, criminal laws should not be *underinclusive*, and must apply equally to each instance of conduct the state has the same compelling interest to proscribe. The state must treat us as equals in protecting our interest not to be punished; it should not punish some while sparing others if it has the same compelling reason to punish both. Of course, this theory cannot be implemented without criteria to decide which state interests are compelling; attempts to identify these interests are bound to generate enormous dispute. Moreover, since the law must be necessary to achieve the compelling government purpose, the state objective must be more difficult to attain *without* resorting to punishment. This latter requirement, it would seem, expresses the last resort principle. A criminal statute cannot be necessary to accomplish a purpose if other means could do so more easily."[62]

Husak is building upon the work of others here, in particular that of Packer, who listed the following as conditions to be met before the criminal law can be applied:

Herbert L. Packer, The Limits of the Criminal Sanction (1969), pp.267–272:

"Goals of Punishment:
    To begin with, there is the obvious point that unless at least *one* utilitarian mode of prevention is likely to be served by employing the criminal sanction against a particular form of conduct, we had better forget about it. Sneezing in church is a relatively uncontroversial example . . . [A] utilitarian case for defining conduct as criminal can best be made in situations where both deterrence and incapacitation are effective: where people are relatively likely to be deflected by the possibility of being caught *and* where punishment is likely to prevent the commission of further crimes. There are many situations in which the two are not correlated and . . . very few in which they are . . .
    Remoteness and Triviality:
    The conduct proscribed by any criminal code can be ranked in a hierarchy of remoteness from the ultimate harm that the law seeks to prevent. We prohibit the sale of liquor to an intoxicated person to lessen the likelihood that he will drive while drunk (an offense), crash into another car (an offense), injure an occupant of the other car (an offense), or cause the death of someone in the other car (an offense). There we have a spectrum of remoteness ranging from the illegal sale of liquor to manslaughter. Similarly, we make it an offense to possess tools specially adapted for burglary so that we may reduce the incidence of burglary (an offense), and thereby reduce the incidence of further offences, such as larceny, robbery, rape, and even murder, that can ensue from burglary. Mayhem or murder might not be intended by most burglars, but they are nonetheless possible results of the confrontation between burglar and victim.
    One of the most delicate problems in framing criminal proscriptions is to locate the point farthest removed from the ultimate harm apprehended at which meaningful preventive intervention can take place. If dangerous conduct can be deterred and dangerous persons identified well short of the point at which the danger becomes

---

62   See also: D. Husak, *Overcriminalization: The Limits of the Criminal Law* (Oxford: OUP, 2008); D. Husak, "Reservations about *Overcriminalization*" (2011) 14 New Crim. L. Rev.97. cf. N. Jareborg, "Criminalisation as a Last Resort (Ultima Ratio)" (2004–2005) 2 Ohio State J. of Crim. Law 521.

acute, so much the better. Or so it seems. Actually, increasing the radius of the criminal law in the interest of early intervention is a very risky business. The first question in every case is, or should be: how high is the probability that the preparatory conduct, if not inhibited by the threat of criminal punishment, will result in an ultimate harm of the sort that the law should try to prevent? A related consideration is whether the preparatory conduct is itself socially useful, or at least neutral, so that its proscription or curtailment might unduly inhibit people from doing what they should otherwise be free to do. To put the issue in terms that are familiar in the law, is the risk substantial and is it justifiable? . . .

Still another consideration relates to the problem of enforcement. By and large, the further removed the conduct in question is from the ultimate harm apprehended, the more difficult it is going to be to detect the occurrence of the conduct and to apprehend people who engage in it. Considerations of maximizing personal freedom and of minimizing the strain on law enforcement combine, then, to suggest considerable caution in the progression towards the remote end of the spectrum.

An example that is amusing because it is so extreme is a recent action of the New York City Council. At the urgent request of the Fire Commissioner, the Council voted to make it a criminal offense, punishable by a hundred-dollar fine, a thirty-day jail term or both, to smoke in bed in a hotel, motel, or other place of public abode. A subsidiary provision required that a notice to that effect be displayed by the proprietor of every place covered by the ban. Now, nobody doubts that a great many serious and sometimes fatal accidents are caused by people's smoking in bed and that it would be a far better thing if people did not smoke in bed. But consider the impossibility of enforcing such a prohibition without the most detailed kind of surveillance. Consider the invasions of privacy that such surveillance would entail. And, enforcement problems aside, consider the effect of announcing that such commonly engaged in conduct has now become criminal. One wonders what was accomplished by the criminal prohibition that would not equally well be accomplished by requiring hotels to display in each room a notice warning about the danger. Alternatively, the solution might have been to make it criminal to cause a fire by smoking in bed, regardless of the amount of harm done. That kind of prohibition would at least have been enforceable, whether or not it was enforced. As it is, given the well-known relationship between intoxication and fires resulting from smoking in bed, I suppose travellers should be grateful that the City Council did not go one step further and make it a crime to go to bed drunk in a New York hotel.

The idea of a criminal conviction no longer inspires the awe that it once did, because of the tendency of legislative bodies (like the New York City Council in this example) to prescribe criminal penalties simply as a means of expressing their disapproval of conduct. This tendency results in two kinds of triviality: triviality of object and triviality of intention. By triviality of object I mean the selection of behaviour for which the regular imposition of criminal punishment is disproportionate. By triviality of intention I mean an attitude of indifference or cynicism on the part of legislators toward the actual enforcement of the proscriptions they vote for. Both forms of triviality should be carefully avoided. A rational legislator should not vote to subject previously legal conduct to criminal proscription unless he is prepared to say, first, that the conduct being proscribed is so threatening to important social interests that he is willing to see people who engage in it subjected to criminal punishment and, second, that he expects law enforcement to devote adequate resources to detecting, apprehending, and convicting violators. The two will tend in most cases to be complementary . . . [Such trivial offences should be decriminalised and made 'civil offences' or 'infractions.']."

Packer then identifies further conditions that need to be taken into account when making the "ultimate decision" about criminalisation. In addition to what has been said so far, we need to avoid the possibility of creating a "crime tariff"[63]; by this he means that the demand for the illegalised activity or product may be so inelastic that rather than reducing the incidence of the activity, it merely drives it underground and forces the price up. The provision of illegal abortions and the sale of narcotics are cases in point. The same may well be true of sado-masochistic activities.

We may finally consider dangers pointed to by both Packer[64] and Kadish (in the context of a discussion of sexual crimes) which are all too likely to materialise if conduct is criminalised (or not decriminalised) without careful investigation:

---

63   Packer, *The Limits of the Criminal Sanction* (California: Stanford University Press, 1968), pp.277–282.
64   Packer, *The Limits of the Criminal Sanction* (California: Stanford University Press, 1968), pp.282–295.

Sanford Kadish, "The Crisis of Overcriminalisation" (1967) 374 Annals 157 at 159–162:

"But law enforcement pays a price for using the criminal law . . . [to enforce morality]. First, the moral message communicated by the law is contradicted by the total absence of enforcement; for while the public sees the conduct condemned in words, it also sees in the dramatic absence of prosecutions that it is not condemned in deed. Moral adjurations vulnerable to a charge of hypocrisy are self-defeating no less in law than elsewhere. Second, the spectacle of nullification of the legislature's solemn commands is an unhealthy influence on law enforcement generally. It tends to breed a cynicism and an indifference to the criminal-law processes which augment tendencies towards disrespect for those who make and enforce the law, a disrespect which is already widely in evidence. In addition:

'Dead letter laws, far from promoting a sense of security, which is the main function of the penal law, actually impair that security by holding the threat of prosecution over the heads of people whom we have no intention to punish.'[65]

Finally, these laws invite discriminatory enforcement against persons selected for prosecution on grounds unrelated to the evil against which these laws are purportedly addressed, whether those grounds be

'the prodding of some reform group, a newspaper-generated hysteria over some local sex crime, a vice drive which is put on by the local authorities to distract attention from defects in their administration of the city government.' . . ."

In returning to the example of sado-masochism it may be useful at this point to summarise Packer's criteria:

Herbert L. Packer, The Limits of the Criminal Sanction (1969), p.296:

"(1) The conduct is prominent in most people's view of socially threatening behaviour, and is not condoned by any significant segment of society.

(2) Subjecting it to the criminal sanction is not inconsistent with the goals of punishment.

(3) Suppressing it will not inhibit socially desirable conduct.

(4) It may be dealt with through even-handed and nondiscriminatory enforcement.

(5) Controlling it through the criminal process will not expose that process to severe qualitative or quantitative strains.

(6) There are no reasonable alternatives to the criminal sanction for dealing with it.[66]

---

[65] Although female circumcision was prohibited by the Prohibition of Female Circumcision Act 1985 (later repealed and replaced by the Female Genital Mutilation Act 2003), until 2014 there had been no prosecution in England and the practice nevertheless continued (M. Atoki, "Should Female Circumcision Continue to be Banned?" (1995) 3 *Feminist Legal Studies* 223 at 235). Keir Starmer, a former DPP, has suggested that this failure of the law to achieve its goals was because investigating authorities took the wrong approach to gathering the necessary evidence to support a prosecution: "We sat back and waited for a girl to walk into a police station": L. Bannerman and F. Gibb, "Britain urged to take tougher line on female mutilation", *The Times*, January 23, 2014. The DPP finally announced the first prosecution (of a doctor) under the 2003 Act on the March 12, 2014: *First Prosecutions for Female Genital Mutilation*, available at: *http://www.cps.gov.uk/news/ latest_news/first_prosecutions_for_female_genital_mutilation/* [Accessed March 2014]. cf. the position in relation to those who assist terminally ill relatives to travel to the Dignitas Clinic in Switzerland to commit assisted suicide. Strictly speaking, their conduct amounts to the offence of assisting suicide under the Suicide Act 1961 s.2 (see below, pp.757–760), but no prosecution has yet been brought in such a case: *http://www.cps.gov.uk/publications/prosecution/assisted_suicide.html* [Accessed April 2014].

[66] Whilst Packer identified the need for criminal law to achieve utilitarian goals as a determinative factor in applying this

These criteria can be used in making up a kind of priority list of conduct for which the legislature might consider invoking the criminal sanction."

What conclusions are to be drawn about the example of sado-masochism used throughout this section? In *Brown* the activities all took place with the consent of the passive partners. Was it appropriate to invoke the criminal law? The majority felt that the public interest took over at the point of actual bodily harm. Consent can thus only operate as a defence to a narrow range of activities involving minimal harm. They largely dealt with the matter as one of violence. But, surely, "violence" presupposes something that is against the will of the recipient. The whole approach of the majority amounts to little more than pure moralism. The piercing of genitals for sexual purposes is apparently unlawful. Ear-piercing and cosmetic body piercing is lawful.[67] As has been commented: "Eroticism makes a difference."[68] The minority, on the other hand, dealt with the matter as one of private sexual morality and felt that it was only when grievous bodily harm had been caused that consent should be no defence.

Ultimately, it would seem it is impossible to answer questions such as whether sado-masochism ought to be criminalised without taking a moral stance on the subject, even if one starts out from the position that conduct ought only to be criminalised if it is "wrongful":

R.A. Duff, Answering for Crime: Responsibility and Liability in the Criminal Law (2007), pp.130–132:

"[A] standard liberal response [to the House of Lords decision in *Brown*] would be to argue that whether or not the physical injuries were inflicted constituted harm, the 'victims' were not wronged. '*Volenti non fit iniuria*': consent might not negate harm, but it negates the wrongfulness that criminalisation requires. A 'bold' liberal would stick to this principle, however serious the physical harm involved: if someone who is rationally competent truly gives informed consent to what another does to him, he is not wronged, and the conduct therefore cannot legitimately be criminalised. However, as one imagines cases involving progressively more serious physical (or psychological) harms, even quite bold liberals tend to become uneasy, and find it harder to insist that consent should always preclude criminalisation.

What grounds such unease is not, I suspect, just the degree of seriousness of the physical injuries caused, but a conception of the meaning of the actions that deliberately inflict them: if the point of the action is to inflict extreme pain or serious injury, or to degrade and humiliate others in a ritual of torture, consent surely cannot legitimate it. I might consent to be treated in ways that degrade or deny my humanity; but that does not render the treatment other than wrongful. That is why a more plausible argument for acquitting the *Brown* defendants would appeal not simply to consent (whilst implicitly admitting that the 'victims' were harmed), but to the meaning of the actions in their context: although to the ignorant outsider their activities look like exercises in degradation and humiliation, we should realise that this way of finding sexual gratification is, within that sub-culture, a way in which the participants express their love and respect for each other. But such an argument abandons the Harm Principle, and moves onto the Legal Moralist's ground. For the argument is that the *Brown* defendants' conduct is worthy at least of our moral respect: it is oriented towards morally legitimate ends (mutual sexual pleasure); it is informed by morally admirable values (love and respect); even if the means by which those ends are pursued and those values are expressed are unusual, and to others' eyes shocking, when understood in their particular context they lose their *morally* shocking character. The argument is thus also that their conduct is not harmful: for it fulfils, rather than setting back, the interests of those involved. We need not accept it for ourselves, or approve

---

criterion, Husak notes that there may often be alternatives to the criminal law in *preventing* a particular conduct or harm. However, Husak notes that punishment for crimes additionally has an *expressive* function in stigmatising conduct we wish to censure. It is this latter function which will often determine whether it is necessary to employ the criminal law: D. Husak, "The Criminal Law as Last Resort" (2004) 24 O.J.L.S. 207. See above, fn.62.

67   See below, p.316.
68   L. Bibbings and P. Alldridge, "Sexual Expression, Body Alteration, and the Defence of Consent" (1993) 20 J. Law & Soc. 356 at 362. cf. S. Cowan, "Criminalizing SM: Disavowing the Erotic, Instatiating Violence", in R.A. Duff et al., *The Structures of the Criminal Law* (Oxford: OUP, 2011).

of it; we may still think it wrong. But we should not see it as meriting public condemnation, since it does not violate the values of mutual respect and concern by which our collective life as a polity is supposedly structured.

A liberal might be tempted to argue that the morality or otherwise of such conduct should not be what is at issue: as consensual sexual activity, it is a matter of 'private' morality which is, 'in brief and crude terms, not the law's business'.[69] The argument just offered was meant to show that this quick liberal response is inadequate. To show that we have no good reason to criminalise such conduct, according to the Harm Principle, we must show either that it is not harmful or that, though harmful, it is not wrongful. To show that it was not harmful we must attend, I have suggested, to its moral significance as an aspect of mutually respectful sexual relationships—which brings to bear a moralised conception of harm. To show that it was not wrongful we cannot, I have suggested, simply appeal to consent, but must look at the substantive character of the conduct, and in particular at whether it must count as degrading or dehumanizing."

Arguably, Duff's position that conduct should be criminalised only if it is wrongful, and that wrongful conduct includes that which is "degrading or dehumanizing", brings us no closer to finding a workable test which would allow us to determine whether a particular activity ought to be criminalised or not, since it depends on the moral view taken on whether such activity is "dehumanizing" or not. However, his discussion brings us to the almost inevitable conclusion that no single theory can dictate the content of the criminal law:

"Instead of trying to find some single concept or value that will capture *the* essence of crime or *the* essential characteristic in virtue of which crimes are property punished we should opt for a pluralism that recognises a diversity of reasons for criminalisation".[70]

3. Is it permissible to criminalise the conduct?

Even assuming the above criteria have been met, namely that the conduct is regarded as "wrongful" and it is thought "necessary" to invoke the powers of the criminal law to condemn the activity, there is a final hurdle to be overcome before the conduct should be declared (or remain) criminal. Such criminalisation must not contravene the European Convention on Human Rights which was made directly applicable in English law by the Human Rights Act 1998.

These provisions operate in two ways. First, any new Bill proposing to criminalise conduct must be accompanied by a statement by the Minister responsible that the provisions of the Bill are compatible with the Convention.[71]

Secondly, it is possible that existing criminal offences are structured in such a way as to offend the provisions of the ECHR. For example, the European Commission has found that it was a contravention of art.8 (respect for private life) and art.14 (non-discrimination) to have different ages of consent for heterosexuals and homosexuals.[72] This led to a change of English law, rendering the age of consent the same for all persons.[73] Under the Human Rights Act 1998, courts are obliged to interpret all legislation "so far as it is possible to do so" in a manner that is compatible with Convention rights.[74] Courts are thus mandated to *interpret* legislation to achieve this result if possible, but they are not permitted to *legislate* (in the sense of rewriting statutory provisions)

---

[69]   The Committee on Homosexual Offences and Prostitution (Wolfenden Committee), The Report of the Departmental Committee on Homosexual Offences and Prostitution (London, HMSO, 1957) para.61.

[70]   R.A. Duff, *Answering for Crime: Responsibility and Liability in the Criminal Law* (Oxford: Hart, 2007), p.139.

[71]   Human Rights Act 1998 s.19: this applies to all Bills and not only those creating criminal offences.

[72]   *Sutherland v United Kingdom* [1998] E.H.R.L.R. 117.

[73]   Sexual Offences (Amendment) Act 2000 s.1.

[74]   Human Rights Act 1998 s.3(1).

"if it is necessary in order to obtain compliance to radically alter the effect of the legislation this will be an indication that more than interpretation is involved".[75]

While every effort must be made to interpret provisions to ensure compatibility, if this is not possible then, as "a measure of last resort",[76] the High Court and appellate courts may make a declaration of incompatibility. While this does not affect the actual validity of the incompatible legislation, there is an obligation to bring the law into conformity with the Convention since otherwise the United Kingdom will not meet its obligations under art.1 of the Convention "to secure to everyone within their jurisdiction the rights and freedoms" set out in the Convention.

Similarly, courts are obliged to ensure compatibility between the common law and the Convention even if this involves courts having to override previous authority. While English courts have displayed some reluctance to go down this route, increasingly challenges to established authorities are being mounted. For example, in *Misra*[77] the Court of Appeal was faced with the argument that certain aspects of a leading House of Lords' decision, *Adomako*,[78] were incompatible with the Convention. While rejecting this argument on its merits, the Court of Appeal clearly regarded itself as having such a power. A court in Jersey has actually exercised this power in holding that the common law defence of insanity is incompatible with the ECHR.[79]

While the importance of the ECHR cannot be over-estimated, it must be conceded that its impact on the substantive criminal law (as opposed to criminal procedure, evidence and sentencing) has, to date, been somewhat limited. For example, art.8 provides a right to respect for private life. Prima facie, one might think that the decision in *Brown* would be incompatible with this: all the sado-masochistic activities in this case were consensual and in private. If a right to private life is to mean anything, it ought to encompass persons expressing their sexuality in the privacy of their own homes. Indeed, the decision in *Brown* was challenged on this basis in the European Court of Human Rights in *Laskey*.[80] However, the European Court, while conceding that there was a violation of the right to respect for private life in art.8(1), nevertheless ruled that criminalisation in cases involving "violence" was justifiable under art.8(2) which permits invasions of privacy if it is "necessary in a democratic society . . . for the protection of health or morals".

To date, despite the fact that the Convention applies directly in English law, there is little evidence of English judges adopting a less moralistic/paternalistic stance.[81] The English courts have held, for example, that art.6 is "not concerned with the fairness of provisions of substantive law" and that Contracting States are free "to choose how to define the essential elements of an offence".[82] Further,

---

[75]   *Poplar Housing and Regeneration Community Association Ltd v Donoghue* [2002] Q.B. 48.
[76]   *R. v A (No.2)* [2002] 1 A.C. 45.
[77]   *R. v Misra (Amit)* [2005] 1 Cr. App. R. 21.
[78]   *R. v Adomako (John Asare)* [1995] 1 A.C. 171. In *R. v Nursing (Ligaya)* [2013] 1 W.L.R. 1031, the Court of Appeal held that the offence of willful neglect of an adult lacking capacity under the Mental Capacity Act 2005 was sufficiently certain (cf. *R. v Hopkins (Annette)* [2011] EWCA Crim 1513; (2012) 123 B.M.L.R. 1).
[79]   *Attorney-General v Jason Prior* [2001] *Jersey Law Reports* 146. See Mackay and Gearty [2001] Crim. L.R. 560. This position was doubted by the Court of Appeal in Jersey (*Attorney-General v Prior* [2002] Jersey Law Reports 11) and it has not been followed in Guernsey (*R. v Harvey* Unreported August 3, 2001). See Mackay [2002] Crim. L.R. 728 and Law Commission, *Insanity and Automatism: Supplementary Material to the Scoping Paper* (2012), paras 5.34–5.35, and C.70–73.
[80]   *Laskey v United Kingdom* (1997) 24 E.H.R.R. 39.
[81]   Recourse to the European Court of Human Rights is still retained if all domestic remedies have been exhausted (ECHR art.34).
[82]   *R. v G* [2003] 1 Cr. App. R. 23. See also *R. v G* [2009] 1 A.C. 92 (discussed in Ch.3 at p.240–241), followed in *Brown* [2013] UKSC 43; *Concannon* [2002] Crim. L.R. 211. J. Arkinstall and C. O'Brien, "Table of Cases under the Human Rights Act" [2002] E.H.R.L.R. 364 provides a comprehensive list of English cases under the Human Rights Act 1998: in only one of the cases cited was there a successful challenge under the Act (*Percy* [2001] EWHC Admin 1125 concerned with the Public Order Act 1985 s.5).

legislation passed since the coming into force of the Human Rights Act suggests that the Act has failed to produce a more liberal effect on law-making, and that a moralistic stance persists. When the ban on hunting was being debated in Parliament various bodies, such as the Countryside Alliance, argued that any such ban would breach human rights and be incompatible with the Convention. The Bill was passed, however, and the Court of Appeal has since confirmed that the Hunting Act 2004 does not breach art.8 (right to respect for private life), art.11 (right to freedom of assembly and association), or art.1 of Protocol 1 (right to property).[83] One of the difficulties of implementing the Human Rights Act is that often Parliament and the courts will have to weigh the rights of would-be perpetrators of crime against those of would-be victims. For example, the Racial and Religious Hatred Act 2006 creates, amongst others, an offence of publishing or distributing written material which is threatening with intent to stir up religious hatred. Such an offence must balance the risk of harm caused by religious hatred and freedom of religion against freedom of expression (art.10). It is yet to be confirmed by the courts that this balance has been struck.

It is more often the procedural law, rather than substantive criminal law, which is confirmed as falling foul of the Human Rights Act. The example of detention without trial for suspected terrorists is a salient example of the Government introducing laws to satisfy public demand without applying time-honoured principles of justice that existed long before the Human Rights Act was passed. Whilst procedural law is beyond the scope of this book this example does show, at least, that the courts now have a power that they are willing to exercise in making a declaration of incompatibility against laws passed by Parliament.[84]

The Human Rights Act clearly has a proscriptive effect on criminalisation, in that conduct should not be criminalised if this would breach one of the rights contained within the ECHR. It has been suggested, furthermore, that the Human Rights Act might also have a prescriptive effect on judicial decision-making. Rogers notes that there is a line of authority from the European Court of Human Rights supporting the claim that the substantive criminal law is subject to the doctrine of positive obligations, meaning that the law must be effective in deterring threats to fundamental rights.[85] Thus, not only must the law not breach rights by criminalising conduct, it must also avoid breaching those rights by failing to deter individuals who threaten the rights of third parties. For example, in ensuring the right to life (art.2), an effective law of self-defence must be clear on the degree of force permissible[86] and, in guaranteeing the right to be free from inhuman or degrading treatment (art.3), the parameters of any lawful defence of chastisement available to parents who assault their children must clearly be defined.[87] However, this interpretation of the duties under the ECHR arguably has a minimal contribution to make to the determination of whether criminalisation of particular conduct is justified, since if it is recognised that a right needs to be protected under the Convention, the question

---

[83]   *R. (on the application of) Countryside Alliance v Attorney General* [2006] EWCA Civ 817 upheld by the House of Lords: [2007] UKHL 52; [2007] 1 A.C. 719.

[84]   The House of Lords has, for example, made a declaration of incompatibility in relation to s.23 of the Anti-terrorism, Crime and Security Act 2001 (detention without trial for suspected terrorists) on the basis that it was found to be in breach of the right to liberty provided in art.5 of the ECHR: *A (FC) (Appellants) v Secretary of State for the Home Department (Respondent)* [2004] UKHL 56. cf. *Beghal v DPP* [2013] EWHC 2573: The power to stop, question and detain a person at a port or border under the Terrorism Act 2000 Sch.7, not incompatible with ECHR art.8 (an appeal is outstanding); *Gillan v United Kingdom* (2010) E.H.R.R. 45: Police powers under the Terrorism Act 2000 s.44 to stop and search, which provided a wide discretion to stop and search in public without reasonable suspicion of wrongdoing, were held to be in breach of art.8). See further, A. Ashworth, "A Decade of Human Rights in Criminal Justice" [2014] Crim. L.R. 325–337.

[85]   J. Rogers, "Applying the Doctrine of Positive Obligations in the European Convention on Human Rights to Domestic Substantive Criminal law in Domestic Proceedings" [2003] Crim. L.R. 690.

[86]   *McCann v United Kingdom* (1996) 21 E.H.R.R. 97.

[87]   *A v United Kingdom* (1999) 27 E.H.R.R. 611.

which remains to be answered is whether it is *necessary* to use the criminal law (rather than some other mechanism) to realise such protection.[88]

The precise effect of the Convention and the nature of the various challenges to the substantive criminal law will be explored in the relevant sections of this book, particularly in relation to the structure of the defences to criminal liability which is the area that seems most likely to be affected. For present purposes, it is sufficient to conclude that while the test of permissibility of criminalisation under the ECHR could provide some check on unbridled moralism, the ultimate decision as to whether any particular criminalisation is justifiable will remain to be determined by the other criteria considered above. Stevenson and Harris argue that J.S. Mill's harm principle is, as a benchmark for criminalising conduct, implicit in the ECHR. Whilst this may not be beyond doubt, they identify a fundamental, overarching problem resulting from the legislature's tendency to create new offences with little regard for a set of criteria such as that laid-out by Packer: that of "accretion".

Kim Stevenson and Candida Harris, "Inaccessible and Unknowable: Accretion and Uncertainty in Modern Criminal Law" (2008) 29 Liverpool L. Rev. 247 at 258:

"This inexorable spread of criminal liability has the practical consequence of reducing the effectiveness of the law. In the computing world this type of accretion is known as 'bloatware'. As development progresses, the project, which may start as a simple and even elegant program, acquires more bells and whistles, more complexity, and more quantitative functionality ('It can do this! It can do that!'). But all this is achieved at the expense of stability and qualitative functionality in terms of ease of use. The process of legislative accretion has resulted in criminal law and the criminal justice system becoming similarly bloated. One of the most serious consequences is the injection of extreme uncertainty into the domain. In software terms, such uncertainty could be the bug which causes the system to fail, equally in criminal justice terms it has already infected its integrity."

The tendency for legislation to be enacted in a piecemeal fashion, with many offences being created, amended and repealed by Statutory Instrument, also means that it can be difficult to ascertain what the current law is, because the law cannot be found in a single document or place.

James Chalmers and Fiona Leverick, "Tracking the Creation of Criminal Offences" [2013] Criminal L. Rev. 543 at 549–550:

"Some criminal offences are created by remarkably inaccessible and tortuous forms of legislative drafting. Consider, for example, the Parliamentary Voting System and Constituencies Act 2011, which made provision for the Alternative Vote referendum. Schedule 4 of that Act provided that various provisions of the Representation of the People Act 1983, including many criminal offences, should apply in respect of the referendum. However, Sch.4 also listed a whole series of 'modifications'—amendments or substitutions of entire provisions—which should apply to the 1983 Act for this purpose. The consequence is that trying to work out exactly what electoral offences existed as a result of the 2011 Act is an extremely cumbersome process. There is no amended text of the 1983 Act available, because the 2011 Act did not actually amend the 1983 Act—it merely created a modified zombie version of the 1983 Act for a limited time. Anyone seeking to understand the offences created must read the two statutes side by side, substituting words and provisions where appropriate . . . this particular drafting

---

[88]   Minkkinen has argued that there are not two questions to answer here (i.e. whether the criminalisation is necessary under the last resort principle and whether it is permissible under the ECHR). Instead he argues that the last resort principle should be recognised as a legal principle, which requires that laws must be drafted in accordance with constitutional rights (including the ECHR) and in doing so all alternatives to criminalisation as the solution to a social harm must first be properly examined and verifiably ruled out before criminalisation is allowed: "'If Taken in Earnest': Criminal Law Doctrine and the Last Resort" (2006) 45 Howard J. 521.

technique seems to contribute little to the requirements of accessibility or fair notice. Similar difficulties arise with complex provisions which cross-refer to European Union provisions, and which give no indication on their own face of exactly what conduct is prohibited."

On occasions, the labyrinthine and complex nature of modern legislation may mean that lawyers and even eminent judges find it difficult to ascertain what the law is.[89] In *Chambers*[90] the defendant appealed against a confiscation order of £61,120 imposed when he was convicted of being knowingly concerned in the smuggling of cigarettes into the United Kingdom without paying excise duty. The Court of Appeal only discovered at the eleventh hour that the Excise Goods Regulations 1992, which had been relied upon by the prosecution as establishing the legal requirement to pay duty, had in fact been superseded by the Tobacco Products Regulations 2001, and had not applied to tobacco products for over five years. Allowing the appeal, Toulson LJ observed that:

> "To a worryingly large extent, statutory law is not practically accessible today, even to the courts whose constitutional duty it is to interpret and enforce it."[91]

If the criminal law is to avoid its own version of "bloatware" the legislature's current run of "binge law-making"[92] needs to be curbed. It is difficult, however, to apply any of the criteria set out earlier in this chapter without some consideration for what the criminal justice system is trying to achieve in punishing those who breach the law.

III. PUNISHMENT

There are two main schools of thought that underpin justifications for punishing those who commit criminal offences: (i) retributivist; and (ii) consequentialist.[93] Both retributivist and consequentialist theories of punishment have long histories. Retributivist theories became popular in the 18th century and, although falling out of fashion during the mid-1990s, made a resurgence in the latter part of the 20th century; remaining a cornerstone of the criminal justice system today. "Retribution", as a basis for punishment, is strongly associated with the work of Kant and Hegel, both of whom asserted that criminal offenders are moral agents who are deserving of punishment. "The annulment of the crime is retribution"[94] and is the symbolic restoration of the wrong committed. Retribution is therefore

---

[89]   In addition, certain criminal statutes create offences which are extremely vague and broad and/or which may be regarded as pre-inchoate in that they criminalise conduct which falls short of the "more than merely preparatory" conduct required for an attempt (see below, Ch.5). For example, the Terrorism Act 2006 s.5, makes it an offence for a person, "with intent to commit an act of terrorism or to assist another to do so, to engage in 'any conduct in preparation for giving effect to' that intention". As Ashworth and Zedner observe: "The conduct may therefore be perfectly normal and non-dangerous of itself—buying a map, a railway timetable or a computer manual may fulfil the actus reus": A. Ashworth and L. Zedner, "Just Prevention: Preventive Rationales and the Limits of the Criminal Law", in R.A. Duff and S. Green, *Philosophical Foundations of the Criminal Law* (Oxford: OUP, 2011), Ch.13, p.285. Where offences are drafted in such a fashion, considerable reliance must be placed upon prosecutorial discretion in relation to the decision to charge, and this may add further uncertainty to the law. See J. Rogers, "The Role of the Public Prosecutor in Applying and Developing the Substantive Criminal Law", in R.A. Duff et al., *The Constitution of the Criminal Law* (Oxford: OUP, 2013), Ch.4 and J. Hodgson and V. Tadros, "The Impossibility of Defining Terrorism" (2013) 16 New. Crim. L.R. 526.

[90]   *R. v Chambers (William)* [2008] EWCA Crim 2467. cf. A. Ashworth, "Ignorance of the Criminal Law and Duties to Avoid it" [2011] 74 M.L.R. 1–26.

[91]   *Chambers* [2008] EWCA Crim 2467 at [64].

[92]   J.R. Spencer, "The Drafting of Criminal Legislation: Need it be so Impenetrable?" (2008) 67(3) C.L.J. 585–605.

[93]   Also referred to as utilitarian theories of punishment. A consequentialist seeks to achieve a consequence at any price; a utilitarian sets a price on the achievement of that goal: in this context, only the minimum amount of punishment thought necessary to achieve the consequence can be justified.

[94]   G.W.F. Hegel, *Hegel's Philosophy of Right*, T M. Knox (trans.) (Oxford: OUP, 1967), para.101.

backward looking in that it seeks to punish the wrong doer in order to restore the balance or moral equilibrium that is disturbed by an offence.[95]

Consequentialist theories, on the other hand, are forward looking to the *consequences* of punishment. The theories of "deterrence", "incapacitation", and "rehabilitation" (described more fully below) have been associated with philosophers such as Cesare Beccaria and Jeremy Bentham who have argued that any form of punishment should achieve a "greater good"—namely crime reduction.

In addition to these theories of punishment is a relatively new purpose of sentencing which although not in itself a justification for punishing someone is nonetheless now an important means through which the state can respond to criminal wrongdoing—that of *reparation*. We therefore turn to a discussion of reparation later in this chapter.

A. Retribution

The word "retribution" is used in several senses. Sometimes it is employed to indicate either vengeance or expiation, but more commonly today it refers to giving offenders their "just deserts" and/or using punishment as a system of censure.

1. Vengeance

J.F. Stephen, A History of the Criminal Law of England Vol.II (1883), pp.81–82:

"[T]he infliction of punishment by law gives definite expression and a solemn ratification and justification to the hatred which is excited by the commission of the offence . . . The criminal law thus proceeds upon the principle that it is morally right to hate criminals, and it confirms and justifies that sentiment by inflicting upon criminals, punishments which express it . . . I am also of opinion that this close alliance between criminal law and moral sentiment is in all ways healthy and advantageous to the community. I think it highly desirable that criminals should be hated, that the punishments inflicted upon them should be so contrived as to give expression to that hatred."

This desire for vengeance supposedly operates at two levels. First, it is asserted that punishment satisfies the victim's (or relatives' and friends') desire for vengeance and the state is merely exacting vengeance on their behalf to prevent private retaliation.

Secondly, it is asserted that there is a public need for vengeance. It is argued that there is an instinctive demand which is active in every human being to retaliate. This reaction is not only understandable but desirable as a socially acceptable outlet for our aggressions. If there were no punishment our aggressions would become repressed to the point when they might break out in an anti-social manner.[96] Such views find little serious support today and have been alleged to "represent the breakdown of human intelligence, as well as good will. It shows perhaps the ugliest phase of our human nature".[97]

2. Expiation

According to this view, the offender must be made to work off his guilt; they must be purified through suffering. This is regarded as a species of retribution in that the offender is "paying his debt" owed to society and, in so doing, becomes reconciled with that society. The focus is on the past crime; the attempt is to wipe the slate clean.

---

[95] For an overview of retributivist rationales, see S. Easton and C. Piper, *Sentencing and Punishment: The Quest for Justice* (Oxford: OUP, 2012), pp 51–56.

[96] E.W. Puttkammer, *Administration of Criminal Justice* (Chicago: University of Chicago Press, 1953).

[97] M.R. Cohen, "Moral Aspects of the Criminal Law" (1940) 49 Yale L.J. 987 at 1025.

These ideas stem largely from the religious influences on our culture, but some would argue that there is a deeper psychological explanation underlying an offender's need for expiation. From the time we are children we are conditioned to expect punishment when we have done wrong. Guilt is a state of tension which gives rise to a need for the removal of this tension. We are conditioned to expect this relief through punishment. The most famous illustration of this form of punishment comes from Dostoyevsky's *Crime and Punishment* in which Raskolnikov, after committing a brutal murder, becomes obsessed with feelings of guilt and eventually gives himself up as the only means of coming to terms with himself and achieving peace of mind.

While society might offer an offender the opportunity of expiation, it cannot insist or demand it as the will or desire for *true* expiation must proceed from the defendant himself. One is not necessarily dealing with true expiation of sin. Society simply deems the offender to have purged his guilt by punishment. A modern advocate of this penance theory is Duff.[98]

R.A. Duff, "Theories and Policies Underlying Guidelines Systems" (2005) 105 Columbia L. Rev. 1162 at 1182–1183:

"The aim . . . is that the offender should come to understand, and so to repent, that wrong as a wrong both against the individual victim (where there was one) and against the wider political community to which they both belong . . .

Central to this richer purpose is an attempt to turn the offender's punishment from a purely one-way process of communication from polity to offender into a two-way process in which there is then a communication back from the offender to the victim and the community: What is to be communicated is a kind of symbolic apology, which is given material and thus more forceful expression by the penal 'hard treatment' that the offender undergoes."

Duff's views have, however, attracted criticism.

Andrew von Hirsch and Andrew Ashworth, Proportionate Sentencing (2005), p.94:

"[T]he offender has no choice but to undergo such deprivations; treating the expiatory pains of punishment as a kind of enforced apology thus raises the problem of compulsory attitudinizing—which may be viewed as a form of demeaning treatment . . . [T]here remains the key question of whether this is a proper function of the state. Perhaps an abbot may be entitled to impose penances designed to make erring novices expiate their sins. But why may the *state* do the same to its citizens in a free society?"

3. Just deserts

Over the last two decades "theories" of punishment such as deterrence and rehabilitation have come under increasing attack both by academics and law-makers.[99] The view that has fast gained ascendancy is that people who have broken the law deserve to be punished.[100] The idea is simple: he who harms must be harmed in return. In other words, the harmer gets his "just deserts". In this way we are according such persons respect as autonomous and responsible human beings who have chosen to commit a crime and must therefore face the consequences of their decisions.

---

[98]   R.A. Duff, *Punishment, Communication and Community* (New York: OUP, 2001).

[99]   For a good bibliography, see A. von Hirsch, A. Ashworth and J. Roberts, *Principled Sentencing*, 3rd edn (Oxford: Hart, 2009).

[100]   The Criminal Justice Act 1991 was largely based on this philosophy. Over the past 30 years a significant number of states in the United States have undertaken major sentencing reforms based primarily on just deserts thinking. The public tends to view this as the rationale of punishment: J. M. Walker and N. Hough, *Public Attitudes to Sentencing* (Aldershot: Gower, 1988), pp.185–186.

Andrew von Hirsch, Doing Justice—The Choice of Punishments (Report of the Committee for the Study of Incarceration) (1976), pp.45–49:

"In everyday thinking about punishment, the idea of desert figures prominently. Ask the person on the street why a wrongdoer should be punished, and he is likely to say that he 'deserves' it . . .

To say someone 'deserves' to be rewarded or punished is to refer to his *past* conduct, and assert that its merit or demerit is reason for according him pleasant or unpleasant treatment. The focus on the past is critical. That a student has written an outstanding paper is grounds for asserting that he deserves an award; but that the award will yield him or others future benefits (however desirable those might be) cannot be grounds for claiming he deserves it. The same holds for punishment: to assert that someone deserves to be punished is to look at his past wrongdoing as reason for having him penalized. This orientation to the past distinguishes desert from the other purported aims of punishment—deterrence, incapacitation, rehabilitation—which seek to justify the criminal sanction by its prospective usefulness in preventing crime."

C.S. Lewis, "The Humanitarian Theory of Punishment" (1953) VI Res Judicatae 224:

"[T]he concept of Desert is the only connecting link between punishment and justice. It is only as deserved or undeserved that a sentence can be just or unjust . . . There is no sense in talking about a 'just deterrent' or a 'just cure.' We demand of a deterrent not whether it is just but whether it will deter. We demand of a cure not whether it is just but whether it succeeds. Thus when we cease to consider what the criminal deserves and consider only what will cure him or deter others, we have tacitly removed him from the sphere of justice altogether: instead of a person, a subject of rights, we now have a mere object, a patient, a 'case.'

The distinction will become clearer if we ask who will be qualified to determine sentences . . . [if] sentences are no longer held to derive their propriety from the criminal's deservings . . . [S]o long as we are thinking in terms of Desert, the propriety of the penal code, being a moral question, is a question on which every man has the right to an opinion, not because he follows this or that profession, but because he is simply a man, a rational animal enjoying the Natural Light. But all this is changed when we drop the concept of Desert . . .

The Humanitarian theory, then, removes sentences from the hands of jurists whom the public conscience is entitled to criticize and places them in the hands of technical experts whose special sciences do not even employ such categories as rights or justice . . .

[T]he Humanitarian theory wants simply to abolish Justice and substitute Mercy for it. This means that you start being 'kind' to people before you have considered their rights, and then force upon them supposed kindnesses which they in fact had a right to refuse, and finally kindnesses which no one but you will recognise as kindnesses and which the recipient will feel as abominable cruelties. You have overshot the mark. Mercy detached from Justice, grows unmerciful."

There are two main strands to this just-deserts thinking.

(i) Just deserts as eliminating an unfair advantage

Andrew von Hirsch, Doing Justice—The Choice of Punishments (Report of the Committee for the Study of Incarceration) (1976), pp.45–49:

"A useful place to begin is with Kant's explanation of deserved punishment, which he based on the idea of fair dealing among free individuals. To realise their own freedom, he contended, members of society have the reciprocal obligation to limit their behaviour so as not to interfere with the freedom of others. When someone infringes another's rights, he gains an unfair advantage over all others in the society—since he has failed to constrain his own behaviour while benefitting from other persons' forbearance from interfering with his rights. The punishment—by imposing a counterbalancing disadvantage on the violator—restores the equilibrium: after having undergone the punishment, the violator ceases to be at advantage over his non-violating fellows As Herbert Morris puts it in a recent restatement of the Kantian argument:

'A person who violates the rules has something others have—the benefits of the system [of mutual non-interference with others' rights]—but by renouncing what others have assumed, the burdens of self-restraint, he has acquired an unfair advantage. Matters are not even until this advantage is in some way erased Justice—that is punishing such individuals—restores the equilibrium of benefits and burdens' ('Persons and Punishment', 52 *The Monist* 475, 478 (1968))."

According to this view, by committing a crime, offenders have gained an unfair advantage over all others who have "toed the line" and restrained themselves from committing crime. They are "free riders" who have failed to observe the moral constraints that others have accepted.[101] Punishment is necessary to take away the benefits gained. Social equilibrium must be restored. Offenders deserve punishment in order to destroy their unfair advantage. Finnis describes the advantage as one of "indulging a (wrongful) self-preference, of permitting himself an excessive freedom in choosing" which, in turn, is punished so that "the criminal has the disadvantage of having his wayward will restricted in its freedom by being subjected to the representative 'will of society' (the 'will' which he disregarded in disregarding the law)".[102]

Jean Hampton, in a variation on this theme, argues that crime involves the infliction of a moral injury; the victim is diminished in value. Punishment is necessary "to vindicate the value of the victim".[103] The defendant by committing the crime is asserting an unjustified superiority over the victim which must be nullified through punishment.

The concept of just deserts has, however, attracted criticism.

John Braithwaite and Philip Pettit, Not Just Deserts: A Republican Theory of Criminal Justice (1990), pp.158–159:

"A first objection to this justification for punishment is that law-abiding conduct is not always burdensome and crime is not always advantageous. The rapist might contract syphilis or the burglar break a leg. The conspiracy or the attempted murder might fail. Is the crime to be punished even though no benefits accrued?

The benefits and burdens theorist has a reply to this. He can say that it is self-restraint which is the burden, and unrestricted liberty the benefit that criminals gain by eschewing self-restraint. But is the self-restraint of not committing murder really a burden to our law-abiding readers? Even under conditions of unrestricted liberty most of us have no interest in or attraction to committing murder, and so the burden is no actual inconvenience. On the contrary, one influential view is that educating ourselves to adopt a moral character which abhors evil makes us 'better off'. . .

[It has been argued that] the burden of self-restraint still does limit options . . . and to have choice is better than not having it . . . Is it a burden in this sense that you are unable to fly to Mars tomorrow? The point we would stress is that some burdens have practical significance for people and some do not. It seems a weak basis for locking people up that they renounced burdens which are not felt to be burdens by most law-abiding citizens."

Nicola Lacey, State Punishment: Political Principles and Community Values (1988), pp.24–26:

"[Desert theories do not give] very clear practical guidance about the fair measure of punishment in particular cases. What actual punishment would forfeit a set of rights equivalent to those violated by a rapist, a petty thief, a reckless driver? As in the case of the law of the talion and the culpability principle, resort to arguments from conventionally agreed, customary or consequence-based penalty scales seem hard to avoid. Secondly, real difficulties have been raised about the social contract tradition itself; in what sense can a *fictitious* agree-

---

[101]   H. Morris, "Persons and Punishment" (1968) 52 *The Monist* 475.
[102]   J. Finnis, "The Restoration of Retribution" (1971) 32 *Analysis* 131.
[103]   J. Hampton, "Correcting Harms versus Righting Wrongs: The Goal of Retribution" (1992) 39 U.C.L.A. Law Rev. 1659 at 1686.

ment generate obligations for real people? Furthermore, these views are dependent for their force on the existence of a fair set of rules. This is not fatal in itself, but the criteria which dictate that there is indeed a just equilibrium which can be restored are not generated by the forfeiture of rights or unfair advantage principles alone. The views do pre-suppose an independent account of what counts as an unfair advantage and a just equilibrium.

Finally, it seems legitimate to ask whether the metaphorical ideas of restoring relationships of justice or moral equilibria outweigh the obvious disvalues attached to the suffering and other costs of punishment. Do these theories really ignore such costs completely? If not, what weight do they accord to them? In what real sense does punishment 'restore the right'? Do these theories really remove the mystery attaching to the original, simple desert principle, or are they, too, a form of moral alchemy? Or, in trying to avoid the mystery, do they not collapse into versions of utilitarian or other consequentialist justification? Even the more sophisticated versions barely rise above the level of metaphor, and leave us with the suspicion that the idea of desert cannot be distinguished from a principle of vengeance or the unappealing assertion that two wrongs somehow make a right."

According to these criticisms, it appears that "just deserts" theory struggles to stand up to critical and theoretical scrutiny. Of particular concern to critics is that the harming of wrong doers in order to rebalance the social equilibrium, rather than putting right the wrongs committed, simply doubles the amount of harm that is now inflicted. Perhaps, then, a more cogently formed justification for retribution can be found in the need for public censure and denunciation.

(ii) Just deserts as censure or denunciation

While some just deserts theorists claim that desert is in itself the only purpose of punishment in that "punishing the guilty achieves something good—namely, justice",[104] others argue that punishment based on desert is necessary to express disapproval and censure of the conduct and the offender.[105]

Andrew von Hirsch, Doing Justice—The Choice of Punishments (Report of the Committee for the Study of Incarceration) (1976), pp.45–49:

"[The theory relating to eliminating an unfair advantage] does not explain why that deprivation should take the peculiar form of punishment. Punishment differs from other purposefully inflicted deprivations in the moral disapproval it expresses: punishing someone conveys in dramatic fashion that his conduct was wrong and that he is blameworthy for having committed it. Why, then, does the violator deserve to be *punished*, instead of being made to suffer another kind of deprivation that connotes no special moral stigma?

To answer this question it becomes necessary, we think, to focus specifically on the reprobation implicit in punishment and argue that *it* is deserved. Someone who infringes the rights of others, the argument runs, does wrong and deserves blame for his conduct. It is because he deserves blame that the sanctioning authority is entitled to choose a response that expresses moral disapproval; namely, punishment. In other words, the sanction ought not only to deprive the offender of the 'advantage' obtained by his disregard of the rules (the Kantian explanation); but do so in a manner that ascribes blame (the reprobative explanation)."

Joel Feinberg, "The Expressive Function of Punishment" (1965) 49(3) The Monist 397–423:

"[P]unishment is a conventional device for the expression of attitudes of resentment and indignation, and of judgments of disapproval and reprobation, on the part either of the punishing authority himself or of those 'in

---

[104]   M.S. Moore, "The Moral Worth of Retribution", in E. Schoeman (ed.), *Responsibility, Character, and the Emotions: New Essays in Moral Philosophy* (Cambridge: CUP, 1987).

[105]   A. von Hirsch, *Past or Future Crimes: Deservedness and Dangerousness in the Sentencing of Criminals* (Boston: Rutgers University Press, 1985), p.52.

whose name' the punishment is inflicted. Punishment, in short, has a *symbolic significance* largely missing from other kinds of penalties.

Consider the standard international practice of demanding that a nation whose agent has unlawfully violated the complaining nation's rights should punish the offending agent. For example, suppose that an airplane of nation A fires on an airplane of nation B while the latter is flying over international waters. Very likely high authorities in nation B will send a note of protest to their counterparts in nation A demanding, among other things, that the transgressive pilot be punished. Punishing the pilot is an emphatic, dramatic, and well-understood way of *condemning* and thereby *disavowing* his act. It tells the world that the pilot had no right to do what he did, that he was on his own in doing it, that his government does not condone that sort of thing. It testifies thereby to government A's recognition of the violated rights of government B in the affected area and, therefore, to the wrongfulness of the pilot's act. Failure to punish the pilot tells the world that government A does not consider him to have been personally at fault. That in turn is to claim responsibility for the act, which in effect labels that act as an 'instrument of deliberate national policy' and hence an act of war. In that case either formal hostilities or humiliating loss of face by one side or the other almost certainly will follow. None of this scenario makes any sense without the clearly understood reprobative symbolism of punishment. In quite parallel ways punishment enables employers to disavow the acts of their employees (though not civil liability for those acts), and fathers the destructive acts of their sons."

Royal Commission on Capital Punishment, Minutes of Evidence, Ninth Day, December 1, 1949, Memorandum Submitted by the Rt. Hon. Lord Justice Denning, 207:

"Punishment is the way in which society expresses its denunciation of wrongdoing: and, in order to maintain respect for law, it is essential that the punishment inflicted for grave crimes should adequately reflect the revulsion felt by the great majority of citizens for them. It is a mistake to consider the objects of punishment as being deterrent or reformative or preventive and nothing else. If that were so, we should not send to prison a man who was guilty of motor manslaughter, but only disqualify him from driving; but would public opinion be content with this? The truth is that some crimes are so outrageous that society insists on adequate punishment, because the wrong-doer deserves it, irrespective of whether it is a deterrent or not . . . In my view the ultimate justification of any punishment is, not that it is a deterrent, but that it is the emphatic denunciation by the community of a crime."

Andrew von Hirsch and Andrew Ashworth, Proportionate Sentencing (2005), pp.17–18:

"A central reason for such a blaming response concerns penal censure's role as moral communication to the act's perpetrator. The punishment conveys to the actor a certain critical normative message concerning his conduct: for example, that he has culpably harmed or risked harming someone, and is disapproved of for having done so. This message treats him as a moral agent—that is, an agent capable of moral deliberation. He is being confronted with disapproval in virtues of the wrongfulness of his conduct, and not solely in order to produce preventive or other societal benefits that such censure might achieve . . .

Penal censure also has the role of addressing third parties—namely, members of the public. Unlike blame in everyday contexts, the criminal sanction announces in advance that specified categories of conduct are punishable. Because the prescribed sanctions are of a kind that express disapprobation, this conveys the message that the conduct is deemed reprehensible."

The role of censure is thus to ensure that the offender recognises the immorality of his actions. Simultaneously, his punishment provides a message to the victim and to society more broadly that his conduct has caused harm and that he is at fault for this. Denunciation theory can also serve to educate the public by reaffirming social values and reinforcing inhibitions against crime. Von Hirsch and Ashworth argue that any preventive effects of public censure must only be seen as complementing retribution and not as a primary justification for punishment. The utilitarian benefits of this theory, termed educative deterrence, will be discussed in the next section. There are two main advantages to punishment based on just deserts. First, it means that limits are placed on state power in that excessive exemplary or incapacitative sentences become unacceptable. Secondly, it helps reduce unjustifiable sentencing disparity in that two offenders committing the same crime will receive similar punishments, irrespective of race, culture or background. These are matters to which we shall return towards the end of this chapter.

B. Deterrence

Unlike retributive theories, deterrent theories are forward looking in that they are concerned with the consequences of punishment; their aim is to reduce further crime by the threat or example of punishment. Deterrence is commonly thought to operate at three levels.[106]

1. Individual deterrence

Deterrent theories seek to discourage crime. In the case of individual deterrence[107] it is hoped that the experience of punishment will be so unpleasant that the offender will not reoffend. The task of the sentencer is to look to the future and select the sentence which is likely to have most impact on the individual. In the case of some offenders, no punishment at all may be necessary as the risk of the convicted person reoffending may be minimal. In other cases the required sentence may be very severe.

It is often said that every time a crime is committed the theory of deterrence is weakened; it is an argument that has some force when applied to the reoffender. One can argue that a reconviction reveals the failure of the previous sentence. However, it is notoriously difficult to measure and assess this.[108] The one-year proven reconviction rate between 2010 and 2011 was 26.9 per cent.[109] In terms of the deterrent effect of punishment the figures do not read well:

> "The proven re-offending rates range from 11.2 per cent for offenders with no previous offences to 48.2 per cent for offenders with 11 or more previous offences."[110]

This data could be read as suggesting that each time an offender is convicted and punished he or she is more likely to go on to reoffend. Punishment may, therefore, have the opposite effect to that which is intended.

Nevertheless, the figures could also be construed as suggesting that what is needed is a more severe penalty than that merited by the present offence at an early stage in the defendant's criminal career to have a strong deterrent effect. Indeed, this kind of approach was encapsulated in the much discussed "short, sharp shock" that imposed detention centre orders on young offenders under the Criminal Justice Act 1982.[111] Alternatively, the sentence should be increased higher for persistent offenders after each offence is committed until a point is reached at which the penalty will deter the

---

[106]   Absolute deterrence may be considered a fourth level but as it applies to the criminal justice system in its entirety, as against an individual theory of punishment, it is not discussed in detail in this chapter. We simply note here that absolute deterrence is the theory that by having a body of criminal laws and a justice system which enforces those laws people will be deterred from committing crimes. It is almost impossible to test the plausibility of this theory as it would require the abolition of the criminal justice system of England and Wales in order to test whether an increase in crime occurs. As we will see, there are similarities between absolute deterrence and that which is viewed as educative.

[107]   Sometimes referred to as "specific deterrence".

[108]   N. Walker and N. Padfield, *Sentencing: Theory, Practice and Law*, 2nd edn (Oxford: OUP, 1996), pp.79–95.

[109]   Ministry of Justice, *Proven Re-offending Statistics Quarterly Bulletin July 2010 to June 2011, England and Wales* (2013).

[110]   Ministry of Justice, *Proven Re-offending Statistics Quarterly Bulletin July 2010 to June 2011, England and Wales* (2013), p. 11.

[111]   Abolished by the Criminal Justice Act 1988 s.123.

offender. Even if research established (and all indications are to the contrary[112]) that such measures were more effective in preventing recidivism, there is the problem of whether it is just to impose a more severe punishment than that merited by the offence.

2. General deterrence

Under this theory it is the threat of punishment that deters people from committing crimes. At the legislative level, Parliament lays down penalties to threaten those who might contemplate crime. At the sentencing level, offenders are punished in order that others will be discouraged from committing crimes; this punishment is held up as an example of what will happen if others engage in similar activities. Jeremy Bentham was a key proponent of general deterrence.[113] Bentham started from the position that all punishment is pain and as such should be avoided. However, punishment should be used where it can produce a greater benefit to society than the pain that such punishment will inflict on the individual offender. This costs benefits analysis is based on the idea of "utility". Utility means the minimisation of pain and suffering and the maximisation of pleasure. Bentham argued that in calculating the costs and benefits of our actions we assess a number of factors including the intensity of pain and pleasure but also the certainty or uncertainty of the benefit/pain occurring. Based upon this, Bentham argued that we can devise social policies which maximise pleasure and minimise pain in society. When this theory is applied to punishment we see punishment is only justified by the good consequences that will be returned to society. Yet to a large extent, the theory of general deterrence assumes that people will be deterred from committing crime by the threat of a certain level of punishment. Is this assumption justifiable?

J. Andenaes, "The General Preventive Effects of Punishment" (1966) 114 U. Pa. L. Rev. 949 at 960–970:

"Reports on conditions of disorganisation following wars, revolution or mutinies provide ample documentation as to how lawlessness may flourish when the probability of detection, apprehension and conviction is low. In these situations, however, many factors work together. The most clear cut examples of the importance of the risk of detection itself are provided by cases in which society functions normally but all policing activity is paralyzed by a police strike or a similar condition. For example, the following official report was made on lawlessness during a 1919 police strike, starting at midnight on July 31st, during which nearly half of the Liverpool policemen were out of service: 'In this district the strike was accompanied by threats, violence and intimidation on the part of lawless persons. Many assaults on the constables who remained on duty were committed. Owing to the sudden nature of the strike the authorities were afforded no opportunity to make adequate provision to cope with the position. Looting of shops commenced about 10pm on August 1st, and continued for some days. In all about 400 shops were looted. Military were requisitioned, special constables sworn in, and police brought from other centers.' (Mannheim, *Social Aspects of Crime in England Between the Wars*, 156–157 (1940).)

A somewhat similar situation occurred in Denmark when the German occupation forces arrested the entire police force in September, 1944. During the remainder of the occupation period all policing was performed by an improvised unarmed watch corps, who were ineffective except in those instances when they were able to capture the criminal red handed. The general crime rate rose immediately, but there was a great discrepancy between the various types of crime. The number of cases of robbery increased generally in Copenhagen during the war, rising from ten per year in 1939 to ten per month in 1943. But after the Germans arrested the police in 1944, the figure rose to over a hundred per month and continued to rise. Larcenies reported to the insurance companies quickly increased tenfold or more. The fact that penalties were greatly increased for criminals who were caught

---

112   This was the main reason for the abolition of detention centre orders (C. Emmins and G. Scanlan, *The Criminal Justice Act 1988* (New York: Hyperion Books, 1988), p.101).

113   J. Bentham, *An Introduction to the Principles of Morals and Legislation* (London: Pickering, 1823).

and brought before the courts did not offset the fact that most crimes were going undetected. On the other hand, crimes like embezzlement and fraud, where the criminal is usually known if the crime itself is discovered, do not seem to have increased notably.

The involuntary experiments in Liverpool and Copenhagen showed a reduction in law obedience following a reduction of risks. Examples of the opposite are also reported—the number of crimes decreases as the hazards rise. Tarde mentions that the number of cases of poisoning decreased when research in chemistry and toxicology made it possible to discover with greater certainty the causes as well as the perpetrator of this type of crime. (Tarde, *Penal Philosophy* 476 (1912)). A decline in bank robberies and kidnappings in the United States is reported to have followed the enactment of federal legislation which increased the likelihood of punishment (Taft, *Criminology* 322, 361 (rev. ed. 1950))."

This belief that punishment can deter crime assumes that actors are rational beings who calculate the risks involved in their actions. They can calculate the chances of being apprehended and punished (taking into account the amount of punishment) and can weigh this against the benefits to them in committing the crime. What is important to note here is that punishment in and of itself may not always be enough to deter the rational offender, but rather it is the degree of risk that is attached to being caught, combined with the penalty which is then attached to the crime, which will ultimately determine whether someone chooses to offend. However, as various criminologists have pointed out, many offenders will not think "rationally" before taking such risks.

Paul Robinson and John M. Darley, "Does Criminal Law Deter? A Behavioural Science Investigation" (2004) 24 Oxford J. of Legal Studies 173 at 179, 184, 185, 192–3:

"Available evidence suggests that potential offenders as a group are people who are less inclined to think at all about the consequences of their conduct or to guide their conduct accordingly. They often are risk-seekers, rather than risk-avoiders, and as a group are more impulsive than the average. Further, conduct decisions commonly are altered by alcohol and drug intake. In Anderson's sample, an astounding 66 per cent of those interviewed reported that 'recent drug use' contributed to the commission of the crime.

There are a number of other temporary states of mind that are likely to drive out rational considerations of punishment, such as desires for revenge or retaliation, and suddenly-induced rages or angers, the duration of which can extend from minutes to days. Other states of mind can be in place for longer durations and also can induce flawed reasoning. For instance, paranoia—feelings that others are immediate and overwhelming threats—is known to cycle over the course of months. When it is acute, it is likely that the degree of threat felt will override considerations of the deterrent weight of possible punishments. The grandiose component of manic-depression, which occurs when the manic-depressive cycles into the manic phase, can give the person experiencing it a feeling of incredible brilliance that is likely to cause him to underestimate the likelihood of the not-so-brilliant forces of law ever catching and convicting him.

Consider this picture of the effect of reduced probability of punishment in light of the known rates of arrest and conviction for various crimes. The overall average of conviction for criminal offences committed is 1.3 per cent . . .

We suspect that most citizens would be shocked at how low the punishment rates are, which suggests that the perception of detection rates tends to be higher than the rates actually are. Luckily for deterrence, people tend to overestimate the occurrence of rare events. This error is useful because it is the perceived rate of punishment rather than the actual rate that counts for deterrent effect. Probably the best summary is that the average person's perception of punishment rates is low, but at least higher than the reality.

But, and again, the group of persons who are the most likely offenders—those who have already committed an offence will account for the majority of future crimes—have a greater incentive than other people to learn the actual punishment rates. Thus, the career criminals—just the persons at whom we would wish to aim our deterrent threat of punishment—are the persons most likely to realize how low the punishment rates really are and, therefore, to perceive a lower chance of punishment than non-crime prone people.

There is also some evidence that many offenders tend to overestimate their own ability to avoid the mistakes that have led to others like them being caught . . .

The net effect is that most criminals do not think they will be caught and punished. In [one] study when asked about the risk of being caught, it was found that

'76 percent of active criminals and 89 percent of the most violent criminals either perceive no risk of apprehension or have no thought about the likely punishments for their crimes'.

[With regard to the amount of punishment affecting deterrence]: Potential offenders may come from social groups in which the threat of stigma for being convicted as a felon may not be as high as it is for other persons. In fact, for many offenders, conviction and imprisonment may lead to very little if any loss of status and respect in the communities within which they function. Similarly, it is likely that potential offenders as a group live a more deprived existence than the average person, and thus the threat of prison, with its provision for meals and shelter, is not so worse an alternative to their current existence as it would be for the more well-to-do person.

Our ultimate conclusion, which we think the evidence strongly supports, is that the threat of punishment amount under current practices is at best unpredictable and at worst unreliable in modulating the threatened amount of punishment."

Research into the behaviour of criminals supports many of the points made in the preceding extract. For example, Gill's research, based on interviews with commercial robbers, concluded that few of them thought there was a high chance of being caught. The less organised and amateurish robbers did not plan their crimes, acted impulsively and gave no thought to being caught or to the consequences of their actions. On the other hand, the more organised and professional robbers planned to minimise the risks and concluded there was a low chance of apprehension.[114] Wright and Decker's American research into burglary found that most burglars in their sample perceived themselves, when committing the offence, to be "in a situation of immediate need" and "consciously refused to dwell on the possibility of getting caught".[115] Similar English research confirms that most burglars are not rational calculators but act on the spur-of-the-moment.[116]

Research into the effectiveness of punishment as a deterrent also provides little support to advocates of deterrence theory. For instance, an international review of empirical evidence into marginal deterrence[117] by Doob and Webster found that "sentence severity has no effect on the level of crime in society".[118] Even research into the use of most severe of punishments—that of the death penalty—has found no reliable evidence that is reduces homicide rates.[119] Moreover, a major Cambridge-based analysis of research asserted that increasing sentence severity could actually have "possible counterproductive effects relating to reduced differential disincentives against the most serious crimes of violence" and could cause "destigmatisation of punishment if severe sanctions are very widely employed".[120]

In addition to the empirical objections to the effectiveness of punishment as a deterrent, there is the fundamental moral objection that deterrent sentencing involves using a person as a means to an end. Punishing people to deter others—rather than punishing them for what they have done—is not showing respect for their autonomy. If sentencing for deterrent reasons only, one becomes free to impose any sentence as long as it is felt to be an effective deterrent. In the past, this has led to the

---

[114]   M. Gill, *Commercial Robbery* (London: Blackstone Press, 2000), p.106.
[115]   P.T. Wright and S.H. Decker, *Burglars on the Job: Streetlife and Residential Break-ins* (Northeastern, 1994), pp.61, 137.
[116]   T. Bennett and R. Wright, *Burglars on Burglary* (Aldershot: Gower, 1984).
[117]   Whether increasing the severity of a punishment affects the prevalence of an offence.
[118]   A. Doob and C. Webster, "Sentence Severity and Crime: Accepting the Null Hypothesis" (2003) 30 *Crime and Jusctie: A Review of Research* 143. See also, Home Office, *Making Punishments Work: Report of a Review of the Sentencing Framework for England and Wales* (Halliday Report), (2001).
[119]   R. Hood and C. Hoyle, *The Death Penalty: A World Wide Perspective* (Oxford: OUP, 2008).
[120]   A. von Hirsch et al, Criminal Deterrence and Sentence Severity, (Oxford: Hart Publishing, 1999), pp.41, 48.

imposition of exemplary sentences. For example, exemplary sentences were imposed in the early 1970s to prevent the sudden increase of muggings of elderly people[121] and to contain football hooliganism in the late 1970s.[122] More recently, enhanced sentences were used for many of those convicted of offences during the 2011 London Riots in an attempt to deter future incidents of social unrest. In supporting the use of such sentences Lord Judge CJ in *Blackshaw* stated:

> "Those who deliberately participate in disturbances of this magnitude, causing injury and damage and fear to even the most stout-hearted of citizens, and who individually commit further crimes during the course of the riots are committing aggravated crimes. They must be punished accordingly, and sentences should be designed to deter others from similar activity."[123]

However, over the past few decades there has been an increasing acceptance that such sentences are unjust:

> "When you punish a man *in terrorem*, make of him an 'example' to others, you are admittedly using him as a means to an end: someone else's end. This, in itself, would be a very wicked thing to do . . . Why, in Heaven's name, am I to be sacrificed to the good of society in this way?—unless, of course, I deserve it?"[124]

As a consequence of research findings suggesting the ineffectiveness of deterrence and because of these principled objections, in the late 1980s deterrence, as a purpose of punishment, began to fall out of favour. The White Paper preceding the Criminal Justice Act 1991 concluded that

> "it is unrealistic to construct sentencing arrangements on the assumption that most offenders will weigh up the possibilities in advance and base their conduct on rational calculation".[125]

The 1991 Act followed this by outlawing exemplary sentences and, subject to exceptions, endorsing the concept of desert. However, since then much legislation,[126] debate and rhetoric[127] about sentencing has been based on deterrence. This culminated in s.142 of the Criminal Justice Act 2003 which expressly endorses deterrence as a one of the five purposes of punishment. During the 2000s, the proliferation of knife crime and the theft of lead both led the courts to impose longer sentences for the purposes of deterrence.[128] The Court of Appeal has, however, warned that sentencing judges should refer to statistics to support their view that a particular crime is prevalent, justifying the imposition of a longer sentence in the hope that the trend can be reversed.[129]

Whatever the "evidence", successive governments have believed (or think the electorate believe) in

---

[121]   For example, *R. v Storey (Paul Edwin)* (1973) 57 Cr. App. R. 840.

[122]   For example, *R. Motley (Gary)* (1978) 66 Cr. App. R. 274.

[123]   *R v. Blackshaw* [2011] EWCA Crim 2312; [2012] Cr. App. R. (S) 114 at 677.

[124]   C.S. Lewis, "The Humanitarian Theory of Punishment" (1953) *VI Res Judicatae* 224.

[125]   *Crime, Justice and Protecting the Public* (1990) Cmnd 965, para.2.8.

[126]   For example, the Crime (Sentences) Act 1997 containing minimum sentences for burglars and drug-dealers upon a third conviction (since repealed by the Powers of Criminal Courts (Sentencing) Act 2000).

[127]   D. M. Kahan, "The Secret Ambition of Deterrence" (1999) 113 Harv. L. Rev. 413 argues that in general "the real value of deterrence—its secret ambition—is to quiet illiberal conflict between contending cultural styles and moral outlooks"; the rhetoric of deterrence is a liberal ploy to defuse or suppress contentious moral issues; it is a cover-up: "the real significance of liberal theory [relating to deterrence] lies not in what it says but in what it stops us from saying".

[128]   *R. v Lanham (Stephen)* [2009] 1 Cr. App. R. (S.) 105; *R. v Povey* [2009] 1 Cr. App. R. (S.) 42.

[129]   *Povey* [2009] 1 Cr. App. R. (S.) 42.

the effectiveness of punishment as a deterrent. It is unfortunate that such thinking is not informed by the distinction, referred to above, between absolute deterrence (few doubt that punishment in general does have a broad deterrent effect for at least some crimes) and marginal deterrence where evidence that increasing the severity of punishments has an increased deterrent effect is noticeably lacking.

3. Educative deterrence

Under the theory of general deterrence, a person who is contemplating committing a crime is deterred by the positive threat that he will suffer the same punishment as others have suffered. However, punishment can have a more profound subconscious effect on society. Punishment of criminals builds up in the community over a period of time the habit of not breaking the law. It creates unconscious inhibitions against committing crimes and thus serves to educate the public as to the proper distinction between good and bad conduct. Every time someone is punished for theft the public morality that theft is wrong is strengthened and our habit of not stealing is reinforced. If suddenly nobody were to be punished for theft and this state of affairs were to endure for a considerable period of time, our inhibitions against stealing and our moral view that theft was wrong would start breaking down. The criminal law and the punishment that flows from breaking it, play an important role in supporting and shaping positive social mores. Take, for example, the introduction of hate crime offences (examined later in Ch.7) in the latter part of the 20th century. These new aggravated offences carry enhanced penalties where an offender is motivated, or where he demonstrates, racial or religious hostility during the commission of an offence. Over a period of time, the acceptability of public displays of such hostilities reduces as the unacceptability of such behaviours begins to penetrate the public conscience. Changes to the way in which society behaves towards certain minority groups can at least in part be attributable to the criminalisation of hate and the punishment of those who commit "hate crimes". As such, the role of deterrence may in fact prove to be a powerful means of social control.

A.E. Bottoms, "Morality, Crime, Compliance and Public Policy", in A.E. Bottoms and M. Tonry, Ideology, Crime and Criminal Justice (2002), p.25:

"[I]n a more differentiated society rather than prohibitions arising out of positive morality, they may on occasion not reflect positive morality at all, but rather may be imposed by those in power in the hope of securing obedience through deterrent calculation. Even in such a case, however, sometimes (though not always) the fact of the prohibition, and citizens' evolving response to it, can influence the development of a new strand of positive morality. Something very like this seems to have occurred in relation to drinking and driving: in Britain there is now substantially greater moral disapproval of such behaviour than was the case thirty or so years ago when it was first made a criminal offence."[130]

J. Andenaes, "General Prevention" (1952) 43 J. Crim. L., C. & P.S. 176 at 179–181:

"Later theory puts much stress on the ability of penal law to arouse or strengthen inhibitions of another sort. In Swedish discussion the *moralising*—in other words the *educational*—function has been greatly stressed. The idea is that punishment as a concrete expression of society's disapproval of an act helps to form and to strengthen

---

[130] See, however, the research cited in P. Robinson and J. Darley, "Does Criminal Law Deter? A Behavioural Science Investigation" (2004) 24 O.J.L.S. 177 indicating that the deterrent effect of many drink/driving laws has been temporary (at 199).

the public's moral code and thereby creates conscious and unconscious inhibitions against committing crime. Unconscious inhibitions against committing forbidden acts can also be aroused without appealing to the individual's concepts of morality. Purely as a matter of habit, with fear, respect for authority or social imitation as connecting links, it is possible to induce favourable attitudes toward this or that action and unfavourable attitudes toward another action. We find the clearest example of this in the military, where extended inculcation of discipline and stern reaction against breach thereof can induce a purely automatic, habitual response—not only where obeying specific orders is concerned, but also with regard to general orders and regulations . . .

. . . To the lawmaker, the achievement of inhibition and habit is of greater value than mere deterrence. For these apply in cases where a person need not fear detection and punishment, and they can apply without the person even having knowledge of the legal prohibition."

John Braithwaite, Crime, Shame and Reintegration (1989), pp.77–79:

"Community-wide shaming is necessary because most crimes are not experienced within the average household. Children need to learn about the evil of murder, rape, car theft, and environmental pollution offenses through condemnation of the local butcher or the far away image on the television screen . . .

Essentially, societal processes of shaming do three things:

1. They give content to a day-to-day socialization of children which occurs mainly through induction. As we have just seen, shaming supplies the morals which build consciences. The evil of acts beyond the immediate experience of children is more effectively communicated by shaming than by pure reasoning.

2. Societal incidents of shaming remind parents of the wide range of evils about which they must moralize with their children. Parents do not have to keep a checklist of crimes, a curriculum of sins, to discuss with their offspring. In a society where shaming is important, societal incidents of shaming will trigger vicarious shaming within the family so that the criminal code is eventually more or less automatically covered Of course societies which shame only half-heartedly run a risk that the full curriculum of crimes will not be covered. Both this point and the last one could be summarized in another way by saying that public shaming puts pressure on parents, teachers and neighbours to ensure that they engage in private shaming which is sufficiently systematic.

3. Societal shaming in considerable measure takes over from parental socialization once children move away from the influence of the family and the school. Put another way, shaming generalizes beyond childhood principles learnt during the early years of life.

This third principle is about the 'criminal law as a moral eye-opener' as Andenaes calls it. As a child, I may have learnt the principle that killing is wrong, but when I leave the familiar surroundings of the family to work in the unfamilar environment of a nuclear power plant, I am taught by a nuclear safety regulatory system that to breach certain safety laws can cost lives, and so persons who breach them are treated with a comparable level of shame. The principle that illegal killing is shameful is generalized. To the extent that genuine shame is not directed against those who defy the safety rules, however, I am liable to take them much less seriously. Unfortunately, societal shaming processes often do fail to generalize to organizational crime.

Recent years in some Western societies have seen more effective shaming directed at certain kinds of offenses—drunk driving, occupational health and safety and environmental offenses, and political corruption, for example. This shaming has for many adults integrated new categories of wrongdoing (for which they had not been socialized as children) into the moral frameworks pre-existing from their childhood.

While most citizens are aware of the content of most criminal laws, knowledge of what the law requires of citizens in detail can be enhanced by cases of public shaming. Through shaming directed at new legal frontiers, feminists in many countries have clarified for citizens just what sexual harassment, rape within marriage, and employment discrimination mean. Social change is increasingly rapid, particularly in the face of burgeoning technologies which require new moralities of nuclear, environmental and consumer safety, responsible use of new technologies of information exchange and electronic funds transfer, ethical exploitation of new institutions such as futures exchanges, and so on. Shaming is thus particularly vital in sustaining a contemporarily relevant legal and moral order."

In the United States these ideas have been pushed to the limit by the introduction of "shaming penalties". For example, persons convicted of drunken driving have been required to put special bumper stickers on their cars,[131] or wear a pink fluorescent bracelet,[132] publicising their conviction. One woman was made to place an advertisement in her local paper stating that she bought drugs in front of her children.[133]

This theory should be contrasted with the retributive theory of denunciation. The theories are similar in that punishment, under both theories, is performing a symbolic, expressive function—but there is an important difference between them. The idea of denunciation, as with all retributive theories, is not concerned with the effects of punishment. It is not a forward-looking theory aimed at preventing crime. Rather, it is concerned with the relation of the punishment to the past event, the crime. It is concerned that there be a relationship between the gravity of the offence and the degree of censure or denunciation. The educative theory, on the other hand, is exclusively forward looking, as are all deterrent theories. Punishment is used as a means of preventing crime and maintaining obedience to the law.

The educative theory rests upon an important premise, namely, that public morality and inhibitions against committing crimes are created and/or preserved by the regular punishment of others. This is a difficult premise to test although some research suggests a clear link between criminality and moral assessments of behaviour. For instance, Kaufmann asked a group of subjects to evaluate the morality of certain behaviour (failing to rescue a drowning man). Some subjects were told that this behaviour was criminal; others were told that there was no duty to rescue. The former group judged the inaction more harshly than the latter group.[134] Similarly, Walker and Marsh discovered that subjects stated that their disapproval of not wearing a seat-belt would increase when this became an offence.[135] Clearly most laws are designed to have some symbolic or expressive function. The point asserted here (and so difficult to validate—although one's intuitions do indicate some plausibility to the claim) is that *punishment* (or at least the real possibility thereof) pursuant to criminal liability is what gives the law its sting.[136]

C. Incapacitation

There are two types of incapacitation: collective and selective. Collective incapacitation refers to a strategy of incapacitating large numbers of "would be" offenders in order to decrease crime levels overall. Selective incapacitation aims to identify and incapacitate certain types of offenders who are most likely to re-offend. This approach entails determining which offenders are the most dangerous. This is normally done by looking at a person's past behaviours and predicting whether he is likely to re-offend. In the case of *Sargent*,[137] Lawton LJ acknowledged

"that there are some offenders for whom neither deterrence nor rehabilitation works. They will go on committing crimes as long as they are able to do so. In those cases the only protection which the public has is that such persons should be locked up for a long period."

---

[131]   *Goldschmitt v State*, 490 So. 2d 123 (Fla. 1986).
[132]   *Ballenger v State*, 210 Ga. App. 627, 436 S.E. 2d 793 (1993).
[133]   *The Guardian*, February 4, 1997.
[134]   H. Kaufmann, "Legality and Harmfulness of a Bystander's Failure to Intervene as Determinants of Moral Judgment", in J.R. Macaulay and L. Berkowitz (eds), *Altruism and Helping Behaviour: Social Psychological Studies of Some Antecedents and Consequences* (New York: New York Academic Press, 1970).
[135]   N. Walker and C. Marsh, "Do Sentences Affect Public Disapproval?" (1984) 24 Brit. J. Criminol. 27.
[136]   Contra Walker and Marsh (above) who concluded that public disapproval of conduct was not influenced by *severity* of punishment.
[137]   *R. v Sargeant* (1975) 60 Cr. App. R. 74.

Such protective sentencing aims to render the criminal incapable of committing more crimes; it thus "incapacitates" the offender. The particular punishment chosen at one stage in our penal history might have been the death penalty, severance of limbs or deportation to a colony. Today it is likely to be imprisonment, although other community measures such as a curfew order or disqualification from driving can also be viewed as incapacitative sentences. In countries such as France, Sweden, Denmark and Poland, and in some states in the United States, chemical castration can be used to incapacitate sex offenders, although some of these jurisdictions require the offender to consent to the procedure.[138] The real hallmark of an incapacitative sentence, however, is that it is likely to be longer or more severe than that which would normally be imposed for the offence.

There is much public support for the view that there are cases where society needs protection[139] and that it is permissible to incarcerate dangerous offenders who pose a threat to society for longer than non-dangerous offenders committing the same offence. Further, research has revealed that a significant amount of crime is being committed by relatively few persons, for example those on bail, and so "a policy of selective incapacitation aimed at such 'career criminals' promises a high yield of crime prevention for a low investment of resources".[140]

There are, however, significant objections to incapacitative sentencing. First, such a practice can only be justified (if at all) if predictions of dangerousness are accurate.

Andrew von Hirsch, "Prediction of Criminal Conduct and Preventive Confinement of Convicted Persons" (1972) 21 Buffalo L. Rev. 717 at 735–736:

"What makes violence so particularly difficult to predict is not merely its rarity, but its situational quality. Deterministic models to the contrary notwithstanding, violence generally is not a quality which inheres in certain 'dangerous' individuals: it is an occurrence which may erupt—or may not—in certain crisis situations. Whether it does erupt, whether it is reported, whether the perpetrator is apprehended and punished depends upon a wide variety of fortuitous circumstances, largely beyond the actor's control. Not only the actor's proclivities, but the decisions of other individuals—the victim, the bystanders, the police, the magistrate—may determine whether an act of violence occurs and whether it comes to be included in the criminal statistics."

The substantial literature that has developed on the subject of prediction is in broad agreement that for every three persons predicted to commit violent offences, only one will do so. It has become common to refer to those who do not reoffend as "false positives" and for most commentators this is taken to mean that a false prediction of dangerousness was made. However, that view has been challenged by Norval Morris. He argues that if an unexploded bomb were found in the early post-war days in London and then safely defused no-one would talk about it subsequently as if it had not been dangerous simply because it had not caused any damage. He thinks there is no difference in principle between the analogy of the bomb and dangerous people: "In sum, that the person predicted as dangerous does no future injury does not mean that the classification was erroneous."[141]

Nigel Walker, Punishment, Danger and Stigma (1980), pp.98–99:

"[In challenging the anti-protectionist's view] . . . let us accept that in our present state of partial ignorance any labelling of the individual as a future perpetrator of violence is going to be mistaken in the majority of cases. Does

[138] A. Chrisafis, "Killing puts 'castration' on French agenda", *The Guardian*, September 3, 2009.
[139] J.M. Walker and N. Hough, *Public Attitudes to Sentencing: Surveys From Five Countries* (Aldershot: Gower, 1988), pp.178–179.
[140] R.A. Duff and D. Garland, *A Reader on Punishment* (Oxford: OUP, 1994), p.239.
[141] N. Morris, "On 'Dangerousness' in the Judicial Process" (1982) Record of Assn of the Bar of the City of New York 102 at 115.

it follow that it is wrong to apply this label? Only if we swallow two assumptions. One is that it is *morally wrong* to make mistakes of this kind. Everyone would agree that it is *regrettable*; but if the decision is taken with good intentions, and one has done one's best, with the available information, to minimise the percentage of mistaken detentions, is it *morally wrong*? Only if we swallow the second assumption—namely the anti-protectionist's insistence that our overriding objective must be to minimise the total number of mistaken decisions, treating a mistaken decision to detain as exactly equal to a mistaken decision to release. The anti-protectionist is using two neat rhetorical tricks at once. By referring to mistaken detentions and mistaken releases simply as 'mistakes,' he is implying that they all count the same; and by glossing over the difference between 'regrettable' and 'morally wrong,' he is implying that it is our moral duty to go for the smallest number of mistakes irrespective of their nature.

    To put this point in concrete terms, suppose that you have in custody three men who have done serious violence to more or less innocent victims. Suppose too that the best actuarial information you can get tells you that one of them—but not *which* one—will do more violence if released. The anti-protectionist is saying that it is your moral duty to release all three instead of continuing to detain all three because release will involve only one mistaken decision instead of two mistaken decisions. Yet the one mistaken release would mean injury or death to someone, while the two mistaken detentions would mean something quite different: the continued deprivation of freedom for three men of whom an unidentifiable two would not do anybody injury if released."[142]

Most other commentators, however, have greater difficulty justifying the continued incarceration of offenders when predictions are so inaccurate and when many of the most useful predictors are controversial. Beyond the obvious factors of number and type of previous convictions, other considerations might be indicative of future offending. However, to include predictors such as sex, race, age, intelligence, educational attainments, etc. would be unacceptable as "factors which are beyond the offender's control and not logically related to culpability".[143]

    The second central objection to incapacitative sentences is that, even if predictions were accurate, it is wrong in principle to punish someone for what they might do in the future. Such a practice amounts to a radical departure from the constraints of just deserts under which punishment should be proportionate to the seriousness of the current offence committed.

Andrew von Hirsch, Past or Future Crimes (1985), p.11:

"Advocates of the desert model opposed the use of individual prediction in sentencing as a matter of principle, not merely because of such forecasts' tendency to error. Their objection to predictive sentencing was simply that it led to undeserved punishments and would do so even if the false-positive rate could be reduced. The use of predictions, accurate or not, meant that those identified as future recidivists would be treated more severely than those not so identified, not because of differences in the blameworthiness of their past conduct, but because of crimes they supposedly would commit in future. It was felt that punishment, as a blaming institution, was warranted only for past culpable choices and could not justly be levied for future conduct. Unless the person actually made the wrongful choice he was predicted to make, he ought not to be condemned for that choice—and hence should not suffer punishment for it."

Most commonly, predictions of dangerousness are based on previous convictions (along, often, with psychiatric reports). The objection to this is that the offender has already been punished for the past crimes and so this amounts to punishing them again for these offences.

    For some, the need to protect the public outweighs such objections. The Floud Report on Dangerous

---

[142] For a critique of Walker's views, see D. Wood, "Dangerous Offenders and the Morality of Protective Sentencing" [1988] Crim. L.R. 424 at 425–429.

[143] M. Tonry, "Prediction and Classification: Legal and Ethical Issues", in D.M. Gottfredson and M. Tonry (eds), *Prediction and Classification: Criminal Justice Decision Making* (Chicago: University of Chicago Press Journals, 1987), p.397.

Offenders[144] took it "as axiomatic that the public is entitled to the protection of a special sentence"[145] against grave harm and recommended a special sentencing framework of sentencing for dangerous offenders. This was done by a utilitarian balancing of risks argument: the harm done to the convicted offender in being punished longer than is deserved is outweighed by the prospect of harm done to the public should the offender be released at an earlier time. In short, where there is a risk of grave harm to potential victims, the rights of such victims should prevail over the rights of a convicted offender. To make such arguments, however, is to enter onto a slippery slope in terms of due process and the criminal law.

Andrew von Hirsch and Andrew Ashworth, "Extending Sentences for Dangerousness: Reflections on the Bottoms-Brownsword Model", in A. von Hirsch, A. Ashworth and J. Roberts (eds) Principled Sentencing, 3rd edn (2009), pp.86–87:

"To view the state's law-enforcement duties as 'rights' which victims hold against the state—which may then be 'balanced' against the offender's moral entitlement not to be treated unfairly—would reduce the entire analysis into a form of cost-benefit reckoning. An offender's entitlement to fair treatment then could readily be 'trumped' by crime-prevention concerns, because these now could be redenominated as purported 'rights' of potential victims. It could be argued, for example, that the proof-beyond-reasonable-doubt standard in criminal trials be diluted—because this might promote a victim's 'right' not to be victimised by actually guilty individuals who could be acquitted under the higher standard and might go out to commit further crimes. It ought not be permissible to dilute important requirements of fairness so easily."

It is, however, possible to justify attaching weight to previous convictions within a retributive framework. There are two views here that are employed by just deserts theorists. First, under the principle of "cumulative sentencing", persistent offenders can be regarded as more blameworthy because they have failed to learn lessons from previous convictions and ensuing punishments. They have persisted in criminal behaviour after being specifically warned and punished. Under this view, there should be no ceiling to the possible punishment. With each repeated defiance of the law, the offender is more blameworthy and deserving of greater punishment. Roberts compares recidivist offending with premeditated offending.

Julian V. Roberts, "Revisiting the Recidivist Sentencing Premium", in A. von Hirsch, A. Ashworth and J. Roberts (eds), Principled Sentencing, 3rd edn (2009), pp.153–154, 157:

"The existence of a number of prior convictions changes our evaluation of the mental state of the offender at the time of the commission of the crime. He or she approaches the fresh offence having been charged, convicted and sentenced, possibly on many occasions. Awareness of this previous legal censure should recall the individual to respect the law; the offender who reoffends is therefore similar to the offender who plans the offence. Both are worthy of a greater degree of moral reprobation to reflect their enhanced level of culpability. The conduct of the premeditated offender and the repeat offender both represent a more marked departure from acceptable conduct.

. . .

   To conclude, although previous convictions are excluded from a consideration of the seriousness of the offence, they should enter the sentencing equation through the determination of the offender's level of culpability. It is patently unreasonable to ignore a characteristic such as previous offending that practitioners, victims, offenders and the community regard as highly relevant to the determination of sentence. The best solution to this stand-off

---

[144]   J. Floud and W. Young, *Dangerousness and Criminal Justice* (London: Heineman, 1981).
[145]   J. Floud, "Dangerousness and Criminal Justice" (1982) 22 Brit. J. Criminol. 213 at 220.

between theory and practice involves recognising the relevance of previous convictions to offender blameworthiness (and consequently sentence severity), and then constraining their influence on the determination of sentence."

An alternative way of justifying, in terms of desert, extra weight attaching to previous convictions is the theory of "progressive loss of mitigation".

Andrew Ashworth, Sentencing and Criminal Justice, 5th edn (2010), pp. 201–202:

"The argument . . . is based on the idea of a lapse and tolerance . . . [and] the idea of giving someone a 'second chance'. So the justification for the discount for first offenders rests partly on recognition of human fallibility, and partly on respect for people's ability to respond to the censure expressed in the sentence. The justification for the gradual losing of that mitigation on second and third convictions is that the 'second chance' has been given and not taken: the offender has forfeited the tolerance, and its associated sentence discount, because the subsequent criminal choices show insufficient response to the public censure. In principle, therefore, the second offence deserves greater censure than the first . . . and the third offence may be censured fully."

While this latter theory has its attractions, it is unlikely to be politically acceptable as it would involve treating an offender with 30 previous convictions the same as one with three or four convictions. Indeed, the Criminal Justice Act 2003 prefers the "cumulative sentencing" approach to the "progressive loss of mitigation" model. Section 143(2) provides that all related, recent previous convictions must be treated as aggravating factors in assessing the seriousness of the current offence.[146]

The danger of this whole approach is that these theories can be seized upon as providing an intellectual justification for increasing sentencing severity within a desert framework when in reality the previous convictions are simply being used as predictors of future reoffending or dangerousness. For example, the Halliday Report endorsed the notion that persons with previous convictions deserve, in retributive terms, greater punishment but then added that this "coincidentally" enabled the risk of reoffending to be taken into account. The Report then suggested that levels of punishment could be adjusted up or down by "plus or minus 100 per cent".[147] Such an approach is not compatible with any desert-based theory permitting weight to be attached to previous convictions.

The Criminal Justice Act 2003 states that one of the purposes of sentencing is "the protection of the public".[148] Sections 224–236 set out the key provisions for sentencing "dangerous offenders". Prior to 2012, the courts could impose a sentence of imprisonment based on the grounds of public protection (commonly referred to as IPPs).[149] These indeterminate sentences included a set minimum term after which release depended on the Parole Board's judgment that it was safe to release the offender. The indefinite nature of IPPs meant that they were highly controversial instruments of the law and after much resistance from human rights advocates they were subsequently repealed by the Legal Aid, Sentencing and Punishment of Offenders Act 2012.[150] However the Act is not retrospective, meaning that the 6,000 prisoners[151] already serving IPPs will continue to be imprisoned for an indefinite period of time.

---

[146] See A. von Hirsch and J. Roberts, "Legislating Sentencing Principles: the Provisions of the Criminal Justice Act 2003 Relating to Sentencing Purposes and the Role of Previous Convictions" [2004] Crim. L.R. 639.

[147] Halliday Report (2001).

[148] Criminal Justice Act 2003 s.142(1)(d).

[149] Previously prescribed under s.225(3) of the Criminal Justice Act 2003.

[150] Legal Aid, Sentencing and Punishment of Offenders Act 2012 c.10 Pt 3 c.5 s.123(a).

[151] Data taken from the Sentencing Council at: *http://sentencingcouncil.judiciary.gov.uk/sentencing/indeterminate-prison-sentences.htm* [Accessed April 30, 2014].

While the repeal of indeterminate sentences is to be welcomed there remains essentially two "tough" determinate sentences for offenders classified as "dangerous". First, a sentence of life imprisonment must be imposed if the offender has committed a "serious offence"[152] carrying a maximum of life imprisonment and "the court considers that the seriousness of the offence [or offences] . . . justify the imposition of a sentence of imprisonment for life".[153] Secondly, an extended sentence may be imposed where a "specified offence"[154] has been committed. This involves the offender serving the deserved sentence plus an "extension period" during which the offender is subject to licence.[155]

These provisions depend on a risk assessment that the offender is dangerous. The court must be of the opinion that there is a "significant risk to members of the public of serious harm occasioned by the commission by him of further specified offences".[156] The Criminal Justice Act 2003 introduced a presumption of dangerousness if the offender had one previous conviction for a specified offence (a provision akin to the "three strikes and you're out" legislation found in many states in the United States). However, recent changes to the Act[157] have moved away from a presumption of dangerousness, with the courts endorsing the view that imprisonment for public protection should be seen as a last resort.[158] Although this change in approach is to be welcomed it is still the case that these provisions relating to dangerous offenders, taken as a whole, are deeply disturbing. As suggested earlier in this section, they breach a fundamental principle of justice in that offenders are receiving sentences longer than they deserve. If this were justifiable (which we doubt), it could only be on the basis that there is a reliable prediction that the offender presents a "vivid danger"[159] to others. As seen, there is no empirical evidence suggesting that such reliable predictions can be made. Previous convictions, pre-sentence and psychiatric reports provide no firm basis for concluding that a person is so dangerous as to justify an incapacitative sentence.

D. Rehabilitation

Punishment with the aim of reforming or rehabilitating the offender has constituted one of the most ambitious developments in penal theory. The aim is to secure conformity, not through fear (which is the more limited object of deterrence) but through some inner positive motivation on the part of the individual. The process has been described as "improving [the offender's] . . . character so that he is less often inclined to commit offences again even when he can do so without fear of the penalty".[160] The source of the change in motivation or improvement in behaviour has been variously described but remains one of the ambiguities of the concept of reform.

The origins of the rehabilitative ideal are inextricably linked with the humanitarian movement for prison reform and many who defend the ideal stress the importance of offender welfare. Advocates of rehabilitation asserted that a more humane response to criminality would help to soften strict "law

---

[152] A "serious offence" is a specified offence that is punishable by life imprisonment or by a determinate sentence of ten years or more (Criminal Justice Act 2003 s.224(2)).

[153] Criminal Justice Act 2003 s.225(2)(b).

[154] As listed under Sch.15A to the Criminal Justice Act 2003.

[155] Criminal Justice Act 2003 s.226A.

[156] Criminal Justice Act 2003 s.225(1)(b), Guidelines on the assessment of dangerous can be found in s.229. Guidance on how to approach this issue was also given in *R. v Lang (Stephen Howard)* [2006] 2 Cr. App. R. (S.) 3.

[157] Criminal Justice and Immigration Act 2008 s.17, amending s.229 of the Criminal Justice Act 2003.

[158] D.A. Thomas, "Commentary on Attorney General's Reference (No.55 of 2008)" [2009] Crim. L.R. 221.

[159] A.E. Bottoms and R. Brownsword, "The Dangerousness Debate after the Floud Report" (1982) 22 Brit. J. Criminol. 229.

[160] N. Walker "Punishing, Denouncing or Reducing Crime", in P.R. Glazebrook (ed.), *Reshaping the Criminal Law* (London: Stevens, 1978), p.393.

and order" attitudes.[161] The great penal reformers of the 18th century, Beccaria, Bentham, Eden and Romilly, all supported a system of punishment which combined deterrent with rehabilitative features. It was their belief, however, that rehabilitation could come from punishment itself—by, for example, a period of solitude which would induce remorse, repentance and reform. Indeed, the first penitentiary in the United States was created by the Quakers in Philadelphia in 1793 in order that prisoners could pay "penance" for their sins and thereby become "cleansed".[162] The object was to make offenders "better persons" capable of being reintegrated into society (rather than simply purging their sins and thereby repaying their debt to society, which is the more limited object of expiation). When, towards the end of the 19th century the aim of rehabilitation became (with deterrence) part of official penal policy in this country, there was more than an element of this thinking present in the measures taken.

Whilst it soon became clear that, far from making "better individuals", solitude had a severely damaging impact upon offenders, the belief that reform should be a concomitant of punishment continued to hold sway for the first half of the 20th century at least. The moral or religious exhortations to improve were gradually replaced by the behavioural sciences and medicine. In the post-war period, criminality came to be viewed as an illness that was caused by psychiatric, psychological and social conditions. As more was learned about the antecedents of human conduct it was hoped that therapeutic measures could be designed which would reform the offender's behaviour.

H. Weihofen, "Retribution is Obsolete," National Probation and Parole Association News, XXXIX (1960) 1, 4:

"Crime and criminal responsibility are not mere interesting abstractions for the amusement of philosophers dreaming up metaphysical constructs. Crime is a reality, an ever present danger which in some cases is literally a matter of life and death.

The voices of ignorance and hate are loud enough now to shout down almost every effort to improve criminal administration by substituting rational for irrational solutions, a rehabilitative for a punitive approach. The rationale of these programs calls for understanding the sociological, economic and cultural sources of criminality, the psychology of criminals and our reactions to criminality. This is too sophisticated for the single-minded devotees of punishment . . .

I resent the apostles of punishment-for-its-own-sake arrogating to themselves words like 'moral' and 'justice' and implying in consequence that those who scorn their metaphysics are amoral or at least unconcerned with moral values. Surely the feeling of concern for the offender as a human being; the desire to save him from a criminal career and to help him redeem himself as a member of the human family; the even wider concern to prevent others from falling into criminality by searching out the influences and conditions that produce those frustrating and embittering defeats, degradations and humiliations of the human spirit that turn a man against his fellow men; the effort, therefore, to give men those advantages that will help them to keep their feet on the right path—better education, more healthful dwellings, readier aid for casualties of sickness, accident and failures of employment—surely all of this is not a less moral ideal than that which knows only one measure of morality, an eye for an eye and a tooth for a tooth.

Half a century ago, Winston Churchill said, in the House of Commons:

'The mood and temper of the public with regard to the treatment of crime and criminals is one of the most unfailing tests of the civilisation of any country. A calm, dispassionate recognition of the rights of the accused, and even of the convicted criminal against the State—a constant heart searching by all charged with the duty of punishment—a desire and eagerness to rehabilitate in the world of industry those who have paid their due in the hard coinage of punishment: tireless efforts towards the discovery of curative and regenerative processes:

---

[161]   See e.g. F.T. Cullen and K.E. Gilbert, *Reaffirming Rehabilitation* (Cincinnati: Anderson Publishing Co, 1982).
[162]   See C. Walker, *Crime and Punishment in Great Britain* (Edinburgh: Edinburgh University Press, 1968), pp.134–138, and N. Morris, *The Future of Imprisonment* (Chicago: University of Chicago Press, 1974).

unfailing faith that there is a treasure, if you can only find it, in the heart of every man. These are the symbols which, in the treatment of crime and criminals mark and measure the stored-up strength of a nation.'

Yes; and I would add, these are the sign and proof of its morality."

Rehabilitative sentencing involves a focus on the individual offender's needs ensuring that the sentence, or programme within a sentence, will help change the offender's behaviour, attitude and responses. A number of non-custodial measures were introduced in the 1960s and 1970s, such as community service orders, about which rehabilitative claims were made—although the introduction of such measures was perhaps more influenced by a desire to reduce the prison population.

However, despite the attractiveness of the idea of rehabilitating offenders so that they would not wish to reoffend, the 1970s saw a major decline in the rehabilitative ideal. As can be seen from the following extracts, criticism has taken many forms. The gist of the case against the rehabilitative ideal is as follows. First, it is highly interventionist and paternalistic, ultimately giving the state the power to try to alter the character and personality of the offender. Apart from raising images of a "Clockwork Orange" society and presenting grave human rights concerns, it also means that judges, who are trained in law and not psychiatry, are not the most appropriate persons to carry out the task of sentencing. This would be best left to "experts" (psychiatrists, etc.). Such ideas were condemned as removing the requirement of justice from sentencing.

The second casualty of the rehabilitative ideal is proportionality. Instead of looking to the past—to the offence committed—the sentencer is only concerned with the future needs of the offender. The sentence should be chosen which has the best chance of bringing about the desired change; thus the principle of treating like cases in a like manner has little part to play. Proportionality links punishment to the seriousness of the offence whereas under the rehabilitative ideal there are few like cases. There ought, in theory at least, to be complete individualisation of sentences—the sentences should depend, not on the offence, but on the offender. This, of course, inevitably leads to widespread sentencing disparity which breaches a fundamental principle of justice that people be accorded equal treatment before the law. It also leads in some cases to excessively long sentences being passed to allow time for rehabilitation.[163]

Finally, research began to question whether rehabilitative programmes actually work. In an influential article in 1974, Martinson concluded that "with few and isolated exceptions, the rehabilitative efforts that have been reported so far have had no appreciable effect on recidivism".[164] Initially such attacks were deflected by the argument that the criminal justice system was not truly committed to rehabilitation; often it was sacrificed completely to other competing ideals (such as deterrence), or that appropriate means had yet to be found to have the desired impact upon the defendant.

Whether rehabilitation has been successful is normally measured by studies of recidivism, few of which lent much support to the idea that rehabilitation works for the majority of offenders. However, there were some studies concentrating on treatment strategies for specific categories of offenders which revealed some success and, indeed, Martinson wrote an article in 1979 in which he partially recanted on his earlier views.[165] Nevertheless, the notion that "nothing works" had entered the psyche of penologists and that, coupled with ethical concerns about the treatment model, led to a demand that punishment be more firmly linked to just deserts.

---

[163]   R. Cross, *Punishment, Prison and the Public* (London: Stevens, 1971).
[164]   R. Martinson, "What Works?" (1974) *Public Interest* 35. Martinson's article has been misquoted as stating that "nothing works". See also, D. Lipton, R. Martinson and J. Wilks, *The Effectiveness of Correctional Treatment* (New York: Praeger, 1975).
[165]   R. Martinson, "New Findings, New Views: A Note of Caution Regarding Sentencing Reform" (1979) 7 Hofstra L. Rev. 243.

A.E. Bottoms, "An Introduction to 'The Coming Crisis'", in A.E. Bottoms and R.H. Preston, The Coming Penal Crisis (1980), pp.1–3:

"First, and the dominant factor in much current penal consideration, comes *the collapse of the rehabilitative ideal*. . . . A succession of negative research reports has—with a few exceptions which do not seriously disturb the conclusion—suggested that different types of treatment make little or no difference to the subsequent reconviction rates of offenders. . . . As the Serota Report (ACPS 1977) succinctly put it:

'A steadily accumulating volume of research has shown that, if reconviction rates are used to measure the success or failure of sentencing policy, there is virtually nothing to choose between different lengths of custodial sentence, different types of institutional regime, and even between custodial and non-custodial treatment; (para.8).'

But the objections to the treatment (or rehabilitation) ethic have not been solely based on empirical demonstrations of lack of efficacy. Strong theoretical objections have also been raised, perhaps most influentially in the American Friends Service Committee's (1971) *Struggle for Justice*, which argued that there was:

'compelling evidence that the individualised-treatment model, the ideal towards which reformers have been urging us for at least a century, is theoretically faulty, systematically discriminatory in application, and inconsistent with some of our most basic concepts of justice (p.12).'

What lies behind these claims?

(i) *'Theoretically faulty'*—because, it can be claimed, the treatment model implies that criminal behaviour has its roots in the deficiencies of the individual and his upbringing, and that if these are remedied, the crime rate will be cut; but this medical analogy is inappropriate, and crime is far more a result of the overall organization of society than of the deficiencies of the individual.

(ii) *'Systematically discriminatory'*—because the treatment model typically takes more severe coercive action in cases of 'unsatisfactory' home circumstances or 'dubious' moral background; but these judgments are made by middle-class workers who unwittingly but systematically discriminate against the poor and the disadvantaged, and in favour of the 'good' homes of the privileged.

(iii) *'Inconsistent with justice'*—because judgments involving the liberty of the individual are made (in the name of 'casework' or whatever) on the basis of extremely impressionistic evidence which is usually not revealed to the offender, and which he cannot therefore challenge; and the result may be, for example, that some will serve long sentences for trivial crimes because their 'attitudes have not improved,' while others convicted of serious crime but who have allegedly 'responded' are let out.

Underneath criticisms like these, it will be noted, lies a fundamental conviction by the critics as to the essentially *coercive* nature of the rehabilitative ideal . . . Many adherents of the ideal blinded themselves as to this coerciveness, in the false belief that benevolent intentions preclude a coercive result."

M. Cohen, "Moral Aspects of the Criminal Law" (1940) 49 Yale L.J. 987 at 1012–1014:

"The growing belief in education and in the healing powers of medicine encourages people to suppose that the delinquent may be re-educated to become a useful member of society. Even from the strictest economic point of view, individual men and women are the most valuable assets of any society. Is it not better to save them for a life of usefulness rather than punish them by imprisonment which generally makes them worse after they leave than before they entered?

There are, however, a number of highly questionable assumptions back of this theory which need to be critically examined.

We have already had occasion to question the assumption that crime is a physical or mental disease. We may now raise the question whether it is curable and if so at what cost to society? Benevolent social reformers are apt to ignore the amount of cold calculating business shrewdness among criminals. Some hot-blooded ones may respond to emotional appeal; but they are also likely to back-slide when opportunity or temptation comes along. Human beings are not putty that can be remolded at will by benevolent intentions . . . The analogy of the criminal law to medicine breaks down. The surgeon can determine with a fair degree of accuracy when there is an inflamed appendix or cancerous growth, so that by cutting it out he can remove a definite cause of distress. Is there in the complex of our social system any one cause of crime which any social physician can as readily remove on the basis of similarly verifiable knowledge?

Let us abandon the light-hearted pretension that any of us know how all cases of criminality can be readily cured, and ask the more modest and serious question: to what can criminals be re-educated or re-conditioned so that they can live useful lives? It would indeed be illiberal dogmatism to deny all possibility and desirability of effort along this line. Yet we must keep in mind our human limitations.

If the causes of crime are determined by the life of certain groups, it is foolish to deal with the individual as if he were a self-sufficient and self-determining system. We must deal with the whole group to which he naturally belongs or gravitates and which determines his morale. Otherwise we have to adapt him completely to some other group or social condition, which is indeed a very difficult problem in social engineering.

And here we must not neglect the question of cost. When we refer to any measure as impracticable, we generally mean that the cost is too great. There is doubtless a tremendous expense in maintaining our present system of punishment. But this expense is not unlimited. Suppose that fiendish perpetrators of horrible crimes on children could be reformed by being sent first for several years to a special hospital. Will people vote large funds for such purposes when honest law-abiding citizens so often cannot get adequate hospital facilities?"

C.S. Lewis, "The Humanitarian Theory of Punishment" (1953) VI Res Judicatae 224:

"[O]nly the psychotherapist can tell us what is likely to cure. It will be in vain for the rest of us, speaking simply as men, to say, 'but this punishment is hideously unjust, hideously disproportionate to the criminal's deserts.' The experts with perfect logic will reply 'but nobody was talking about deserts. No one was talking about *punishment* in your archaic vindictive sense of the word . . . Here are the statistics proving that this other treatment cures. What is your trouble?' . . .

To be 'cured' against one's will and cured of states which we may not regard as a disease is to be put on a level with those who have not yet reached the age of reason or those who never will: to be classed with infants, imbeciles, and domestic animals. But to be punished however severely, because we have deserved it, because we 'ought to have known better,' is to be treated as a human person."

Von Hirsch has suggested that much of the true appeal of rehabilitative ideology lies in the fact that its advocates were able both to have their cake and eat it:

"[I]t offered both therapy and restraint. One did not have to assume that all criminals were redeemable but could merely hope that some might be. Therapy could be tried on apparently amenable defendants, but always with a fail-safe: the offender who seemed unsuitable for, or unresponsive to, treatment could be separated from the community."[166]

Despite these concerns, the rehabilitative ideal has undergone something of a revival over the last two decades with the catch-phrase "what works" replacing the gloom of "nothing works" that had dominated the previous decade.[167] Various programmes have been introduced for offenders who have received both custodial and non-custodial sentences. Apart from drug and alcohol programmes, there has been a growing implementation of cognitive-behavioural programmes: these focus on training offenders in decision-making and problem-solving, management of emotions (such as anger-management), negotiation skills and critical reasoning with offenders being encouraged to

---

[166]   A. von Hirsch, *Past or Future Crimes* (Manchester: Manchester University Press, 1987), p.5.
[167]   See, generally, M. Tonry, "Obsolescence and Immanence in Penal Theory and Policy" (2005) 105 Col. L.R. 1233.

reflect on the consequences of their actions. Programmes also include various educational and life-skills courses, such as ones aimed at improving literacy and numeracy, designed to improve offenders' chances of employment. New statistical techniques of meta-analysis (aggregating findings from a number of smaller studies) have been employed and are revealing some success for these programmes particularly in relation to certain types of offenders.[168] For example, in the United States, a number of different programmes of varying effectiveness are used in dealing with drug offenders.

Paul H. Robinson, Distrubutive Principles of Criminal Law: Who Should be Punished and How Much? (Oxford, 2008), pp.103–105:

"Prisoners incarcerated for drug offenses represent a large proportion of all inmates. . . . Drug use is also linked to the commission of violent crimes, property crimes, and public disorder offenses. . . . Given the implications of drug use and dependency, successful drug rehabilitation programs could offer the hope of significantly reducing recidivism (and, if extended to potential offenders, might avoid the original offending).

Programs for persons coping with addiction include among others: drug courts, pharmacological treatment, outpatient drug treatment, residential drug treatment, and prison-based therapeutic community treatment.

. . .

Perhaps the most promising response to ending drug use and related criminality is the therapeutic community approach. This model functions by establishing a 'community' to help individuals overcome substance abuse. Treatment generally occurs in stages at a drug-free residential facility, with an emphasis on both the use of group therapy and individual self-help. The principle is to use the peer-reinforcement power of the community of individuals in recovery as well as that of staff to facilitate the learning and assimilation of substance-free social norms. In the prison setting, the therapeutic community approach begins with removing participants from the general prison population to undergo intensive addiction therapy. Ideally, the in-prison treatment is followed by therapy coupled with work release in the transitional, pre-release phase, and then monitoring and therapy in the post-release after-release phase. A best-practice model established in Delaware found significant improvements in both the likelihood of being drug free and re-arrest free after five years for those who completed a therapeutic community program. . . . Even with the positive outcomes, however, nearly 50 percent of the aftercare group would be expected to be rearrested within five years, but this is compared with nearly 75 percent of those receiving no treatment. Thus, while reductions in recidivism can be achieved, the recidivism rates for such offenders remain high."

In the UK, there has been a greater commitment to evidence-based initiatives and research during the 2000s. In 2001, The Halliday Report strongly endorsed the "What Works" strategies and programmes and estimated that they could lead to a reduction in the overall reconviction rate of 5 to 15 per cent on the basis that "some things can work for some people, provided the right programmes are selected and implemented properly".[169]

The Criminal Justice Act 2003 expressly states that one of the purposes of sentencing is "the reform and rehabilitation of offenders".[170] When a community sentence is passed, a range of "requirements" may be made as a community order: for example an unpaid work requirement, a drug rehabilitation requirement or a supervision requirement.[171] Such requirements must be tailored to ensure they are the "most suitable for the offender".[172] However, such rehabilitative sentences may only be imposed within the confines of the just deserts principle of proportionality on the basis

---

[168] J. McGuire (ed.), *What Works: Reducing Reoffending* (Chichester: John Wiley, 1995); P. Raynor, "Community Penalties, Probation, and Offender Management", in M. Maguire, R. Morgan and R. Reiner (eds), *The Oxford Handbook of Criminology*, 5th edn (Oxford: OUP, 2012); Parliamentary All-Party Penal Affairs Group, *Changing Offending Behaviour—Some Things Work* (1999).

[169] Halliday Report (2001), paras 1.49, 1.50.

[170] Criminal Justice Act 2003 s.142(1)(c).

[171] Criminal Justice Act 2003 s.177(1).

[172] Criminal Justice Act 2003 s.148(2)(a). Some of the requirements that can be imposed are not rehabilitative in their aim: for example, a prohibited activity requirement or a curfew requirement.

that the offence is "serious enough to warrant such a sentence".[173] More recently the legislation has been amended so as to "include in the order at least one requirement imposed for the purpose of punishment" or "a fine".[174] Such provisions indicate that retribution must remain the central purpose of sentencing.

Norval Morris and Collin Howard, Studies in Criminal Law (1964), pp.175–176:

"[P]ower over a criminal's life should not be taken in excess of that which would be taken were his reform not considered as one of our purposes. Let the maximum of his punishment be never greater than that which would be justified by the other aims of our system of criminal justice. Within the term of that sentence, let us utilise our reformative skills to assist him towards social readjustment, but never put forward the possibility of reforming him to justify an extension of power over him. The jailer in a white coat with a degree in a behavioural science remains a jailer."

E. Reparation

Though not strictly a theory of punishment, reparation is now of significant importance to any discussion about crime and punishment. This is because the use of reparation as a sentencing purpose, and more generally as a means of responding to offending, has proliferated within England and Wales over the past 10–15 years. Its growth is a reflection of a movement towards including victims more centrally within the criminal justice process. Critics of conventional methods of criminal justice have argued that the system fails to respond adequately to the needs of victims, offenders and local communities. Traditionally, the commission of an offence has been viewed as a violation against the state which, as representative of society, must punish the offender. Victims and other community members are often involved in the criminal process merely as sources of evidence, such as prosecution witnesses. Nils Christie has argued that the state has, in effect, appropriated conflict from those which are most affected by it.[175] Rather than those directly impacted by an offence helping to resolve the harms it causes, legal professionals are tasked with prosecuting offenders and administering what they consider to be "deserved" punishment.

Reparation, on the other hand, is concerned with the restoration of harms caused by crime. It is intrinsically linked to what is now commonly referred to as "restorative justice" (RJ), a contemporary theory and practice of justice which developed within Western jurisdictions from the late 1970s.[176] There is no single definition of RJ, but many advocates assert that it is based on the premise that crime is a wound to human relations which requires convalescence. This is best achieved by those most affected by the offence, including the victim, the offender and other community members. Howard Zehr explains that:

"Crime is a violation of people and relationships. It creates obligations to make things right. Justice involves the victim, the offence, and the community in a search for solutions which promote repair, reconciliation, and reassurance."[177]

---

173   Criminal Justice Act 2003 s.148(1).
174   Criminal Justice Act 2003 s.177(1)(2A).
175   N. Christie, "Conflicts as Property" (1977) 17 Brit. J. Criminol. 1.
176   Christie, "Conflicts as Property" (1977) 17 Brit. J. Criminol. 1. Though it is often claimed that the RJ is rooted to ancient and/or indigenous practices of justice, see G. Maxwell and A. Morris, *Families, Victims and Culture: Youth Justice in New Zealand* (Wellington, Institute of Criminology, Victoria University of Wellington and Social Policy Agency, 1993).
177   H. Zehr, *Changing Lenses: A New Focus for Crime and Justice* (Scottdale, Pennsylvania: Herald Press, 1990), p. 181.

In order to restore harm the offender must first take responsibility for his actions. Part of the restorative process is the facilitation of inclusive dialogue which involves the shaming of the offender. Braithwaite asserts:

"Because shaming is a participatory form of social control, compared with formal sanctioning which is more professionalized than participatory, shaming builds consciences through citizens being instruments as well as targets of social control. Participation in expressions of abhorrence toward the criminal acts of others is part of what makes crime an abhorrent choice for us ourselves to make."[178]

Social condemnation is expressed both via the offender's active participation in a restorative intervention and through the disapproval which is conveyed by the community participants in restorative meetings. The "stakeholders" of an offence (i.e. the victim, offender and their community supporters) help the offender to understand the hurt and suffering that he has caused. Maxwell and Morris explain that such a process is likely to induce feelings of remorse which are the result of "empathy or understanding the effects on victims".[179] In turn it is argued that the offender is less likely to reoffend because he will have seen first-hand the direct impacts of his actions.

One of the first formal introductions of RJ *within* the criminal justice system was implemented by the Thames Valley Police during the mid-1990s. Using the Australian Wagga Wagga model of RJ, the police implemented a new restorative cautioning scheme as a means of disposing of minor offences.[180] This involved a script being used by police officers who facilitated victim-offender mediations (VOM). Meetings involved direct dialogue between victims and offenders who came together to discuss the impacts of the offence and how best the offender can make good the harm he has done. The use of restorative justice practices by other police services has quickly proliferated, with 33 out of the 43 police services across England and Wales now using some form of restorative justice.[181]

Restorative justice is also used within the Youth Justice System[182] as well as for adults by probation services and within some prisons.[183] A popular measure used by practitioners within these parts of the justice system is the family group conference (conferencing). Conferencing involves the participation of victims, offenders and their community supporters in a direct meeting that aims to find restoration for all involved. Conferences, like VOM, are facilitated by restorative practitioners who create safe spaces for participants to talk about their experiences of victimisation. The stakeholders decide together how the offender should repair any harms caused. Meetings often end with the parties signing a "reparation agreement" which outlines the undertakings which have been agreed.

The growing body of empirical evidence for RJ has provided positive findings on its effectiveness, particularly in relation to victim satisfaction with conferencing. Studies conducted in Australia, England and the United States, many of which have used control groups comparing restorative conferencing with the court process, have found higher satisfaction levels amongst victims when compared to court.[184] Furthermore, the emotional traumas caused by crime, such as fear, anger and anxiety, have also been shown to reduce more significantly post RJ. Yet while these findings

---

[178]   John Braithwaite, *Crime, Shame and Reintegration* (Cambridge: Cambridge University Press, 1989), p. 80.

[179]   G. Maxwell and A. Morris, "The Role of Shame, Guilt, and Remorse in Restorative Justice Processes for Young People", in E. Weitekamp and H. Kerner (eds), *Restorative Justice: Theoretical Foundations* (Cullompton, Devon: Willan Publishing, 2002) pp. 280–281.

[180]   C. Hoyle, R. Young and R. Hill, *Proceed with Caution: An Evaluation of the Thames Valley Police Initiative in Restorative Cautioning* (York: Joseph Rowntree Foundation, 2002).

[181]   Criminal Justice Joint Inspection (CJJI), *Facing Up to Offending: Use of Restorative Justice in the Criminal Justice System* (London: HMIC, HMI Probation, HMI Prisons and the HMCPSI, 2012), p.15.

[182]   For example, Referral Orders, see the Powers of the Criminal Courts (Sentencing) Act 2000 ss.16–32 and Sch.1.

[183]   Referral Orders, see the Powers of the Criminal Courts (Sentencing) Act 2000 ss.16–32 and Sch.1.

[184]   L. Sherman and H. Strang, *Restorative Justice: The Evidence* (London: The Smith Institute, 2007).

are encouraging, studies that have examined the effect of RJ on reoffending rates have produced findings that are far from unequivocal. For example, although some studies have shown reductions in reoffending rates for certain violent offences, other studies have found little to no difference in reoffending levels between court processes and RJ; with some research suggesting that RJ may even increase recidivism.[185]

The increased emphasis that is now placed on restoring harm (as against punishing offenders) has resulted in "reparation" becoming one of the five prescribed sentencing purposes as set out in the Criminal Justice Act 2003. This means that sentencers can consider the purpose of restoring harm when determining an appropriate penalty for every defendant that comes before them. More recently, the Government has outlined a vision that RJ should become accessible for victims at "all stages of the criminal justice system".[186] Indeed, the Practice Code for Victims now states that victims are entitled to receive information on Restorative Justice from the police, including how they can take part.[187] Judges will also soon be provided with the powers to defer sentence for a restorative meeting to take place between the victim and offender.[188]

It is yet unknown to what extent the use of RJ between conviction and sentencing will affect the sentencer's use of other theories of punishment. Indeed many criminologists have questioned whether RJ can ever be used in conjunction with theories of punishment which focus on harming offenders as a means of resolving crime—it being considered antithetical to the restorative ideal. Others have, however, suggested that RJ can be reconciled with the current system of retribution. In particular, the act of repairing can in itself be conceived as a form of punishment due to the fact that it requires the offender to make amends while restricting his freedom to do as he pleases.

L. Zedner, "Reparation and Retribution: Are They Reconcilable?" (1994) 57 M.L.R. 228 at 248–249 and 250.

"[I]t might be argued that both reparation and retribution derive their 'authority' from the offence itself and impose penalties according to the seriousness of the particular crime. Unlike the utilitarian aims of general deterrence or rehabilitation which import wider notions of societal good, both retribution and reparation exclude (or nearly exclude) consideration of factors beyond the particular offence. The offender's personal history, the social or economic causes of crime or the need to prevent future offending (all of which extend the limits of intrusion by the state under deterrent or rehabilitative theories) are here deemed irrelevant. As such, both retributive and reparative justice, it is said, impose strict constraints on the intrusion of the state into the lives of offenders. This apparent congruity is not, however, as close as it first seems. The seriousness of the offence is set according to two different sets of criteria. Retribution demands punishment proportional primarily to the intent of the offender, whereas reparative justice derives its 'proportionality' from the harm inflicted on the victim. Whilst intent is generally focused on outcomes, and intent and harm may thus coincide, the two may point to very different levels of gravity. If reparation and retribution were to be wholly reconciled, then it would be necessary to devise a measure which integrated intent and harm in setting offence seriousness. A greater difficulty still is that, if reparative justice is to be more than a criminal analogue to civil damages, then it should go beyond the offence itself to enquire about its wider social costs and the means to making them good. . . .

The danger, however, is that the attempt to accommodate reparative justice to the rationale of punishment so perverts its underlying rationale as to strip it of much of its original appeal, not least its commitment to repairing ruptured social bonds. We are accustomed to seeing criminal justice as the repressive arm of the state, but might it not better be conceived as one end of a continuum of practices by which social order is maintained?

---

[185]   Sherman and H. Strang, *Restorative Justice: The Evidence* (2007).

[186]   Ministry of Justice, *Restorative Justice Action Plan for the Criminal Justice System* (2012), p.5.

[187]   Ministry of Justice, *Code of Practice for Victims of Crime* (2013). Pursuant to s.33 of the Domestic Violence, Crime and Victims Act 2004.

[188]   Crime and Courts Act 2013, Sch.16, Pt 2.

Punishment has a very limited ability to control crime and, to the extent that it is disintegrative, it inflicts further damage on society. Given that the high profile 'law and order policies' . . . have done little to stem spiralling crime figures, perhaps it is time to explore the integrative potential of reparative justice on its own terms."

Whether RJ will become a main focus within criminal justice or simply a practice which operates at the periphery of the system may well depend on whether society accepts the use of reparation on its own merits. However, there are a number of difficulties that the theory and practice of RJ is yet to get to grips with which may yet limit its application. One concern is that many restorative practices pivot around the concept of "community". The notion of community has been ill-defined leaving its exact meaning elusive. Many questions arise such as, how do we locate any given community? When should community members be invited to participate in restorative processes? How should they participate? Can a broad concept such as "community" ever be consistently applied to criminal offences?[189] Linked to these issues are concerns relating to the legitimacy of victims and community members determining how an offender will repair the harms of crime. For instance, Ashworth questions whether the expansion of RJ practices will encroach upon the right of the offender to be sentenced by an independent and impartial tribunal.[190] These issues are yet to be resolved and it is therefore far from clear to what extent RJ will shape the future of criminal justice in England and Wales.

F. Combining the Theories

It is difficult to make any sense of the above competing "theories" until one knows precisely what question they are trying to answer. Building on the work of Hart[191] one can distinguish four separate questions:

1. What is the purpose of punishment?
2. Who may be punished?
3. How much punishment should be imposed?
4. What type of punishment should be imposed?

Many commentators have attempted to combine both retributive and utilitarian considerations in answering these questions. One approach, exemplified by Hart, is that a distinction needs to be drawn between two issues. First, one needs to ascertain what the purpose of the whole institution of punishment is; Hart called this "the general justifying aim" and the justification for this was to be found in utilitarian considerations. In short, the reason why we have an institution of punishment is because we want to reduce crime. However, there is a second separate issue of "distribution": this relates to the second two questions above, namely, who to punish and how much punishment? According to Hart the question of distribution should be answered in retributive terms. Only persons who have committed criminal offences deserve punishment and the amount of punishment should be proportionate to the seriousness of the crime. According to this approach, one could say that the aim of the institution of punishment was, for example, deterrence but one would not be justified in

---

[189]   A. Crawford, "The State, Community and Restorative Justice: Heresy, Nostalgia and Butterfly Collecting", in L. Walgrave (ed.), *Restorative Justice and the Law* (Cullompton, Devon: Willan Publishing, 2002).

[190]   A. Ashworth, "Responsibilities, Rights and Restorative Justice" (2002) 42 Brit. J. Criminol. 578.

[191]   "Prolegomenon to the Principles of Punishment", in H.L.A. Hart, *Punishment and Responsibility* (Oxford: Clarendon Press, 1969), p.1.

punishing innocent people (say, the children of the offender) purely because this might be an effective deterrent. Punishment can only be justified in a particular case on the retributive basis that it is deserved.

George P. Fletcher, Rethinking Criminal Law (1978), p.419:

"The analogy that comes to mind is the distinction between justifying the income tax as a whole and justifying the imposition of burdens on particular taxpayers. The justification of the system as a whole is raising revenue for the government; the justification of burdens on particular taxpayers is (roughly) the taxpayer's relative ability to pay. It would obviously be improper to interweave these two levels of justification and justify the denial of claim for a charitable deduction on the ground of the claimant's relative ability to pay. Similarly, if the justification for the criminal law as a whole is the isolation of dangerous offenders, it is improper to decide particular cases by appealing to the alleged offender's relative dangerousness."

One could advocate such a "dualist"[192] approach but, instead of accepting Hart's views, one could argue, for instance, that the aim of the institution of punishment is desert but that one needs utilitarian justifications to punish in individual cases.[193] Much of this chapter has been devoted to answering the first question: what is the purpose of punishment? Nothing further need be added here. The focus of the remainder of this section is on whether a dualist approach is justifiable and, if so, how matters of distribution of punishment should be determined. In assessing this it is helpful to examine the above three distributive questions separately.

1. Who may be punished?

H.L.A. Hart, "Prolegomenon to the Principles of Punishment", in Punishment and Responsibility (1968), pp.11–13, 21–24:

"The root question to be considered is, however, why we attach the moral importance which we do to retribution in Distribution. . . .

The standard example used by philosophers to bring out the importance of retribution in Distribution is that of a wholly innocent person who has not even unintentionally done anything which the law punishes if done intentionally. It is supposed that in order to avert some social catastrophe officials of the system fabricate evidence on which he is charged, tried, convicted and sent to prison or death. Or it is supposed that without resort to any fraud more persons may be deterred from crime if wives and children of offenders were punished vicariously for their crimes. In some forms, this kind of thing may be ruled out by a consistent sufficiently comprehensive utilitarianism. Certainly expedients involving fraud or faked charges might be very difficult to justify on utilitarian grounds . . . [Such an approach] would awaken such apprehension and insecurity that any gain from the exercise of these powers would by any utilitarian calculation be offset by the misery caused by their existence. But official resort to this kind of fraud on a particular occasion in breach of the rules and the subsequent indemnification of the officials responsible might save many lives and so be thought to yield a clear surplus of value. Certainly vicarious punishment of an offender's family might do so and legal systems have occasionally resorted to this . . . In extreme cases many might still think it right to resort to these expedients but we should do so with the sense of sacrificing an important principle. We should be conscious of choosing the lesser of two evils, and this would be inexplicable if the principle sacrificed to utility were itself only a requirement of utility. . . .

It is clear that like all principles of Justice it (punishment) is concerned with the adjustment of claims between a multiplicity of persons. It incorporates the idea that each individual person is to be protected against the claim of the rest for the highest possible measure of security, happiness or welfare which could be got at his expense

---

192   D. Wood, "Retribution, Crime Reduction and the Justification of Punishment" (2002) 22 O.J.L.S. 301.
193   A.H. Goldman, "The Paradox of Punishment" (1979) 9 *Philosophy and Public Affairs* 42.

by condemning him for a breach of the rules and punishing him. For this a moral licence is required in the form of proof that the person punished broke the law by an action which was the outcome of his free choice, and the recognition of excuses is the most we can do to ensure that the terms of the licence are observed. Here perhaps, the elucidation of this restrictive principle should stop. Perhaps we (or I) ought simply to say that it is a requirement of Justice, and Justice simply consists of principles to be observed in adjusting the competing claims of human beings which (i) treat all alike as persons by attaching special significance to human voluntary action and (ii) forbid the use of one human being for the benefit of others except in return for his voluntary actions against them. . . .

We may look upon the principle that punishment must be reserved for voluntary offences from two different points of view. The first is that of the rest of society considered as *harmed* by the offence (either because one of its members has been injured or because the authority of the law essential to its existence has been challenged or both). The principle then appears as one securing that the suffering involved in punishment falls upon those who have voluntarily harmed others: this is valued, not as the Aim of punishment, but as the only fair terms on which the General Aim (protection of society, maintenance of respect for law, etc.) may be pursued.

The second point of view is that of society concerned not as harmed by the crime but as *offering* individuals including the criminal the protection of the laws on terms which are fair, because they not only consist of a framework of reciprocal rights and duties, but because within this framework each individual is given a *fair* opportunity to choose between keeping the law required for society's protection or paying the penalty. From the first point of view the actual punishment of a criminal appears not merely as something useful to society (General Aim) but as justly extracted from the criminal who has voluntarily done harm; from the second it appears as a price justly extracted because the criminal had a fair opportunity beforehand to avoid liability to pay."

This dualist approach has been criticised on the basis that confining retribution to the issue of distribution of punishment amounts to a down-grading of its importance.[194] It has been further suggested that the whole dualist enterprise is flawed.

Nicola Lacey, State Punishment: Political Principles and Community Values (1988), pp.51–52:

"All these hybrid theories proceed on the assumption that there are genuinely separate questions to be answered: . . . It seems to be true . . . that rules themselves contain their own conditions of application. No sensible system has rules and then fails to apply them: prima facie, the reasons for having the rules generate the reasons for applying them in individual cases. This seems to indicate that the principle of distribution, if one is (as it seems to be) needed, must come in at the first stage: *a* principle of distribution is inevitably contained within or at least envisaged by the general justifying aim of the rules. And if the general justifying aim is straightforwardly utilitarian, the project of grafting on a separate distributive principle, begins to look deeply problematic, for utilitarianism does *not*, as its critics sometimes claim, lack such a principle. It rather embodies criteria of distribution which are vulnerable to serious objection. It is necessary, then, to identify an alternative general justifying aim which incorporates or is consistent with an acceptable distributive principle, rather than to separate different questions and give different answers to them. Conversely, I think it can be argued that a justification for institutions of punishment must include a justification for their actual use in individual cases, and that the individual question is in some ways primary: can any single infliction of punishment ever be justified? The mere fact that such an infliction is according to rules does not seem to generate any additional justification in itself. In justifying a system of rules, we generally assume that those rules will be applied: therefore the justification which we seek must also justify the application of the rules. For these reasons it is my belief that the . . . Hartian distinction does not really withstand close analysis."[195]

Lacey's approach is, however, dependent on the "general justifying aim" itself embodying *effective* criteria of "distribution". To assess this let us briefly consider the utilitarian response to the problem of punishing the innocent. Why not punish an innocent person if, say, it would be an effective deterrent?

---

[194]   Wood, "Retribution, Crime Reduction and the Justification of Punishment" (2002) 22 O.J.L.S. 301 at 307.
[195]   For a similar argument, see J. Braithwaite and P. Pettit, *Not Just Deserts. A Republican Theory of Criminal Justice* (New York: OUP, 1992), p.167.

The answer here is that such punishment could never in fact be an effective deterrent as punishment would become a lottery and there would be no special disincentive to would-be offenders. Punishing the innocent would cause suffering to the victim, general insecurity, disrespect for the law and could encourage the guilty person to reoffend. In short, such punishment would cause more evil than it prevented and thus could not be justifiable.

Further, even if the "general justifying aim" did embody criteria of distribution, *why would they be any better* than those yielded by the concept of just deserts, which, as demonstrated in the Hart extract above, provides fair, consistent and just results?

2. How severely do we punish?

The amount of punishment imposed again depends on the rationale for the imposition of that punishment. Let us start with the utilitarian view of punishment. How would a utilitarian determine the amount of punishment to be imposed for a particular offence? If it were thought necessary, for example, for reasons of deterrence, could extreme sentences be imposed that bore no relationship to the seriousness of the crime? Could one give life sentences for parking on double yellow lines if this were thought to be an effective deterrent? Could one give life sentences to persons who repeatedly stole milk bottles from doorsteps if this would prevent the recurrence of the crime?

The classic answer to this question is still that provided by Jeremy Bentham, that all punishment is evil and ought only to be imposed to achieve some greater good—and, accordingly, one should only impose the minimum punishment necessary to achieve that objective.

Jeremy Bentham, "An Introduction to the Principles of Morals and Legislation", Ch.13, in Bentham and Mill, The Utilitarians (1961), pp.162, 166:

"The general object which all laws have, or ought to have, in common, is to augment the total happiness of the community; and therefore, in the first place, to exclude, as far as may be, every thing that tends to subtract from that happiness: in other words, to exclude mischief.

But all punishment is mischief: all punishment in itself is evil. Upon the principle of utility, if it ought at all to be admitted, it ought only to be admitted in as far as it promises to exclude some greater evil.

It is plain, therefore, that in the following cases punishment ought not to be inflicted.

1. Where it is *groundless*: where there is no mischief for it to prevent, the act not being mischievous upon the whole.

2. Where it must be *inefficacious*: where it cannot act so as to prevent the mischief.

3. Where it is *unprofitable*; or too *expensive*: where the mischief it would produce would be greater than what it prevented.

4. Where it is *needless*: where the mischief may be prevented, or cease of itself, without it: that is, at a cheaper rate . . .

Now the evil of the punishment divides itself into four branches, by which so many different sets of persons are affected. 1. The evil of *coercion* or *restraint*: or the pain which it gives a man not to be able to do the act, whatever it be, which by the apprehension of the punishment he is deterred from doing. This is felt by those by whom the law is *observed*. 2. The evil of *apprehension*: or the pain which a man, who has exposed himself to punishment, feels at the thought of undergoing it. This is felt by those by whom the law has been *broken*, and so feel themselves in *danger* of its being executed upon them. 3. The evil of *sufferance*: or the pain which a man feels, in virtue of the punishment itself, from the time when he begins to undergo it. This is felt by those by whom the law is broken, and upon whom it comes actually to be executed. 4. The pain of sympathy, and the other *derivative* evils resulting to the persons who are in *connection* with the several classes of original sufferers just mentioned."

Accordingly, the utilitarian reason why we do not punish parking on a double yellow line with life imprisonment is that it is thought that the aim of deterrence can be effectively achieved at a lower cost—and crime must be prevented as economically in terms of the suffering of the offender as possible. Further, such an extreme sentence would undoubtedly attract public sympathy for the offender and thus

> "instead of reaffirming the law and intensifying men's consciousness that the kind of act punished is wrong, will have the opposite effect of casting discredit on the law and making the action of the law-breaker appear excusable or even almost heroic".[196]

The problem with this approach is that while it might explain why preposterous sentences cannot be imposed for minor crimes, it does not necessarily prohibit exemplary sentences whereby one person is given *a longer sentence than is deserved*. Desert theory is emphatic here: the crime itself provides the necessary guidance as to the amount of punishment necessary. The punishment must be proportionate to the crime; it must "fit" the crime. Desert theorists, such as von Hirsch, argue that punishment must be proportionate to the seriousness of the crime in order to reflect an *appropriate degree of censure*.

Andrew von Hirsch, Past or Future Crimes (1985), pp.35–36:

"The requirement of proportionate punishment is derived directly from the censuring implications of the criminal sanction. Once one has created an institution with the condemnatory connotations that punishment has, then it is a requirement of justice, not merely of efficient law enforcement, to punish offenders according to the degree of reprehensibleness of their conduct. Disproportionate punishments are unjust not because they are ineffectual or possibly counterproductive, but because the state purports to condemn the actor for his conduct and yet visits more or less censure on him than the gravity of that conduct warrants.

. . . As long as the state continues to respond to violence, theft, or fraud, or similarly noxious conduct through the institution of the criminal sanction, it is necessarily treating those whom it punishes as wrongdoers and condemning them for their conduct. If it thus condemns, then the severity of the state's response ought to reflect the degree of blameworthiness, that is, the gravity, of actors' conduct.

This argument uses a commonly understood concept, employed in everyday life: the notion of censure. The idea is that once one has established a condemnatory institution to respond to criminal acts, one ought then to allocate its sanctions in a manner that comports with the reprehensibleness of those acts."

How does one determine what level of punishment is proportionate to the seriousness of the crime?

Andrew von Hirsch, "Ordinal and Cardinal Desert", in A. von Hirsch and A. Ashworth (eds), Principled Sentencing (1992), pp.209–210:

"One must distinguish between *ordinal* and *cardinal* magnitudes of punishment: That is, between (1) the question of how defendants should be punished relative to each other, and (2) the question of what absolute severity levels should be chosen to anchor the penalty scale . . .

For modern desert theory, this distinction is critical. Advocates of desert-oriented sentencing such as myself do not assert that desert is determinative for all purposes. Rather, our claim is a more restricted one, to wit: desert is a determinative principle in deciding ordinal magnitudes, but only a limiting principle in deciding cardinal magnitudes. To see what this means in practice, consider the crime of burglary. The issues of ordinal magnitude deal with how a particular burglary should be penalized compared to other burglaries and to other more or less serious crimes. When desert theorists assert that desert is a determining principle here, they mean

---

196   A.C. Ewing, "A Study of Punishment II: Punishment as Viewed by the Philosopher" (1943) 21 Can. B. Rev. 102 at 116.

that the ordering of penalties must meet the following two requirements. The first is the requirement of *parity*: criminal conduct of equal seriousness should be punished equally, with deviations from such equality permitted only where special circumstances alter the harm or culpability—that is, the degree of blameworthiness—of the defendant's conduct. The other is that of *rank ordering*: penalties should be ranked and spaced to reflect the ranking and spacing in degree of seriousness among crimes. What desert theorists object to is deciding these questions of *comparative* punishments on grounds other than the blameworthiness of the defendant's conduct: for example, to punish a particular burglar more severely than other burglars not because his particular crime is any worse but because he is a worse risk or because giving him a higher-than-usual punishment would make him an example to others.

To espouse this view does not, however, require one to hold that desert is determinative in deciding cardinal magnitudes. Here, rather, most modern desert theorists—certainly I—would admit that desert is a limiting principle only. I do not claim to know precisely how tough or lenient a sentencing scale should be, but only that punishments beyond certain levels of harshness or leniency are *undeserved*."

A final, but critical, issue remains. *Must* one punish to the exact extent dictated by the seriousness of the crime, or does the concept of just deserts merely provide a ceiling beyond which punishment is undeserved?

The strict Kantian response is that the offender must be punished to that extent, *no more and no less*, which is necessary to destroy the unfair advantage gained from committing the crime. A failure to punish the offender, either at all, or to the extent necessary to eliminate the advantage gained, would not restore social equilibrium and would amount to society endorsing the criminal's acts and thus becoming participants in it. It would further involve failing to treat the criminal as a responsible human being who deserves the consequences of their actions.

On the other hand, drawing on the approach advocated by Hart earlier in this section, it could be that the concept of just deserts should only specify the maximum possible penalty beyond which punishment is undeserved.[197] Within a permissible range, punishment is deserved—one is justified in punishing—but one has a choice as to the severity of the punishment, that choice being informed by all the circumstances of the offence and perhaps even by utilitarian considerations. In short, within a range set by desert principles, the precise allocation of punishment could be determined on a utilitarian basis. This approach, sometimes called limited or *negative retributivism*, was endorsed by the Halliday Report[198] which proposed that desert should provide a "punitive envelope"[199] indicating a permissible range of sentence. No sentence outside that range would be permissible. However, once the "envelope was opened", the actual sentence imposed, within the defined limits, would depend on utilitarian considerations. Within the range the sentencer would select the punishment that would most closely serve the purpose of crime reduction (and reparation) in the individual case. This would involve an assessment of the likelihood of reoffending and the measures most likely to reduce that risk.[200]

Nicola Lacey, State Punishment: Political Principles and Community Values (1988), pp.54–55:

"The idea that desert furnishes the state with a non-conclusive reason to punish raises the question of what types of extra reasons must be adduced in order to produce a justification of particular acts of punishment. On some accounts, apparently non-utilitarian factors are appealed to—factors such as fairness and justice. But it is clear

---

[197]   N. Morris, *Punishment, Desert and Rehabilitation* (Washington, D.C.: US Government Printing Office, 1976).
[198]   Halliday Report (2001).
[199]   Halliday Report (2001), para.2.39.
[200]   Halliday Report (2001), para.2.31. See E. Baker and C.M.V. Clarkson, "Making Punishments Work? An Evaluation of the Halliday Report on Sentencing in England and Wales" [2002] Crim. L.R. 81.

that the most obvious candidates are utilitarian reasons such as prevention, deterrence, avoidance of private vengeance and so on. It is important to note that on most weak retributivist views desert operates not only as the central justification but also as a limit on the amount of punishment: the only function of the consequentialist considerations is to add an element which provides the sufficient reason for some punitive action. On this view, consequentialism cannot tell us whom to punish or how much to punish; it merely defeats the argument from the pointlessness of purely retributive punishment. The difficulty here is that these utilitarian arguments do purport to provide not just an explanation of when we may exercise our right or power of punishment, but actually to make it right for us to punish. According to utilitarianism, it is right to punish wherever such an action maximises the aggregate of pleasure over pain. It is thus hard to see how it is that the weak retributive principle fails to become redundant. In addition, it is not clear whether the desert argument is intended to apply to the design of institutions and the utilitarian one to individual acts of punishment . . . If this were so, we would be invited to endorse the unattractive vision of a legal system based on a principle of desert, in which individual acts of punishment were left to judicial discretion which should be exercised on the basis of consequentialist reasoning, or else of a system in which the legislator made utilitarian generalisations in framing the rules which were nevertheless primarily based on considerations of desert."

As Lacey makes clear, sentencing cannot be left to unfettered judicial discretion. Justice demands that like cases be treated alike. There needs to be an organising principle to structure and control such discretion. The Halliday Report made some effort in this direction—but was ultimately flawed for two reasons. First, the limits of permissible punishment based on desert were overly influenced by the existence of previous convictions.[201] This leaves too broad a band within which punishment is "deserved". Secondly, once the envelope has been opened, utilitarianism takes complete control and there is insufficient guidance as to the relationship between the various utilitarian considerations. Halliday's recommendations were not adopted in their entirety, but instead a potential problem with the ensuing Criminal Justice Act 2003 is that s.142(1) lists multiple purposes of sentencing.

Criminal Justice Act 2003 s.142(1)

"Purposes of sentencing
  Any court dealing with an offender in respect of his offence must have regard to the following purposes of sentencing—

  (a) the punishment of offenders,

  (b) the reduction of crime (including its reduction by deterrence),

  (c) the reform and rehabilitation of offenders,

  (d) the protection of the public,

  (e) the making of reparation by offenders to persons affected by their offences."

No relative weighting or ranking of these purposes is provided, creating the danger that different sentencers might pick and choose and prioritise different sentencing purposes, in turn creating the potential for sentencing disparity. Von Hirsch and Roberts have criticised what they see as a return to the "'smorgasbord' approach to sentencing aims".[202]

---

[201] Halliday Report (2001), pp.39–40.

[202] A. von Hirsch and J.V. Roberts, "Legislating Sentencing Principles: The Provisions of the Criminal Justice Act 2003 Relating to Sentencing Purposes and the Role of Previous Convictions" [2004] Crim. L.R. 639 at 642.

Andrew von Hirsch and Julian V. Roberts, "Legislating Sentencing Principles: The Provisions of the Criminal Justice Act 2003 Relating to Sentencing Purposes and the Role of Previous Convictions" [2004] Crim. L.R. 639 at 642.

"Section 142 lists [deserved] punishment, deterrence, incapacitation, rehabilitation, and reparation to victims as aims which the judge must consider in each sentencing case. It does not indicate what priority should be observed among these various aims.

The recent penological literature does not support this new emphasis on crime-preventive aims in sentencing; indeed, the leading English authorities on sentencing continue to endorse an emphasis on proportionality in imposing criminal sentences. The initiative has come, instead, from the Home Office. Developing measures to prevent crime and reduce re-offending has for years been part of the Government's criminal justice policy strategy. It is not surprising therefore that these ideas have permeated the area of sentencing and finally reached the statute book. Starting with claims made by Mr Jack Straw while shadow Home Secretary, senior Home Office officials have asserted their increasing impatience with a proportionality standard for sentencing, and recommended that greater weight be given in sentencing to crime prevention concerns. In part, such officials' stated reasons reflect concern with assuaging public opinion."

This listing approach to sentencing purposes has also received more direct criticism from within the House of Commons.

House of Commons Justice Committee, Sentencing Guidelines and Parliament: Building a Bridge, HC 715, July 2009, para.66:

"The five aims of sentencing set out in the Criminal Justice Act 2003 are neither internally coherent nor consistently applied. It is not clear whether the aims are intended to be a hierarchical list or a menu to be combined differently in different cases. It is not clear how the purposes of sentencing relate to, or should be reflected in, sentencing guidelines. As a result, the public, criminal justice organisations, victims, sentencers and the Government all have different expectations as to what sentencing is trying to achieve—suggesting that someone, inevitably, will be disappointed."

The Government's rather weak response to this was that:

"It would be, in the Government's view, inadvisable and counterproductive to attempt to prioritise the purposes of sentencing in a manner which would be incompatible with the flexible nature set out in the statute. The balancing of the criteria is a case-specific decision for the sentencer to make."[203]

Despite the breadth of conflicting sentencing purposes provided in s.142 of the Act, there are various other provisions which can be read as preserving an emphasis on proportionality in sentencing. The first of these is s.143(1) which states that:

"In considering the seriousness of any offence, the court must consider the offender's culpability in committing the offence and any harm which the offence caused, was intended to cause or might forseeably have caused."

Section 152(2) also states that:

"The court must not pass a custodial sentence unless it is of the opinion that the offence . . . was so serious that neither a fine alone nor a community sentence can be justified for the offence."

---

[203] Ministry of Justice, *Government Response to the Justice Select Committee's Report: "Sentencing Guidelines and Parliament: Building a Bridge"*, Cmnd 7716 (2009), p.7.

Following this is s.153(2), which reads, in part, as follows:

> "[T]he custodial sentence must be for the shortest term (not exceeding the permitted maximum) that in the opinion of the court is commensurate with the seriousness of the offence . . ."

Together these sections suggest that retribution, and with it the principle of proportionality, is the dominant purpose of sentencing in England and Wales. In fact, the Sentencing Guidelines Council has since confirmed that the principle of proportionality is to remain the touchstone of sentencing in England and Wales.[204]

3. What type of punishment?

Once a determination is made about how much punishment is warranted, the courts must then decide what method of punishment ought to be employed. This is yet another complex decision that sentencers must make.

Paul H. Robinson, "Hybrid Principles for the Distribution of Criminal Sanctions" (1988) 82 Northwestern University L. Rev. 19 at 34–36:

"The [next] issue, concerning the method of sanction, is distinguishable from the distribution of amount. Two offenders may merit the same *amount* of sanction yet different *methods* of sanctioning may be suitable for imposing that amount. These two issues—how much for whom and what method—are not only functionally distinguishable but also may properly be subject to different distributive principles.

Each of the distributive purposes may treat the different issues differently. Effective crime control can be furthered through a variety of mechanisms—by setting the amount or the method of sanction, as well as by setting enforcement and prosecution patterns and expenditures. Satisfaction of desert concerns, by contrast, depends almost exclusively on the amount issue—who receives how much; the method issue (as well as the resource allocation issues) is generally not relevant.

The desert requirement of a proper ordinal ranking of offenders by overall blameworthiness, for example, concerns the ranking of *amounts* of sanction. As long as the ordinal ranking is correct, the *method* by which each amount is imposed is not relevant to desert. If one month in the state prison is the punitive equivalent to five months of weekends in the local jail, then desert is satisfied even if the more blameworthy offender gets probation, with a condition of seven months of weekends in jail, while the less blameworthy offender goes to prison for one month. It is critical, of course, that the sanction equivalencies be properly set. Some empirical research has been done on perceptions of relative seriousness of sanctions, but the work is still in its infancy.

With an estimate of equivalencies, one can construct a sentencing system that allows independent determination of the amount and method issues. The principles governing the 'amount' issue can generate total 'sanction units' for each offender, which can then be allocated to a particular sanctioning method or combination of methods according to a different set of 'method' principles. As long as the issues can be effectively segregated in practice, one can develop a hybrid distributive principle for governing the amount of sanction that is different from the principle used to determine the method of sanction. One could, for example, emphasize desert in determining the amount of sanction, but ignore it in determining the method. The selection of method could be made to maximize pure utilitarian concerns without infringing desert interests—a precious no-loss, all-win opportunity.

The separation of amount and method issues has other important collateral advantages. For example, unwarranted disparity in sentencing primarily concerns disparity in amount, rather than disparity in method. Thus, one might significantly reduce judicial sentencing discretion on the amount issue, in order to reduce disparity among judges, yet maintain broad judicial discretion on the method issue. As long as the total 'sanction units' for an offender are satisfied and the sanction equivalencies are properly set, it does not matter what method or methods an individual judge selects; the punitive 'bite' will be the same."

---

[204] Sentencing Guidelines Council, *Overarching Principles: Seriousness* (2004). See further discussion below on the role of the sentencing guidelines.

According to this analysis, within a desert framework, decisions as to the type of punishment can be based on utilitarian considerations. For instance, when imposing a (deserved) community sentence involving a community order the court should normally obtain a pre-sentence report and then decide which requirements to impose and should indicate the purposes to be achieved thereby. For example, a court could impose a supervision requirement or an alcohol treatment requirement aimed at the rehabilitation of the offender. Alternatively, a curfew requirement, an exclusion requirement or a prohibited activity request could be imposed aimed at protecting the public.

G. Sentencing Guidelines

Until the rise of the just deserts movement, sentencers were generally free to impose whatever sentence they deemed appropriate—up to the maximum permitted. In England there were, however, constraints: a "tariff" was developed by the judges which broadly indicated a range of sentences for "normal cases" and defendants had a right of appeal where an excessive penalty beyond the tariff was imposed. It is interesting to contrast this with the position in the United States where the just deserts movement began its revival. Judicial sentencing discretion there was virtually unlimited and in a majority of states no appeal against sentence was permitted.

Such broad discretionary powers meant several things in both jurisdictions. Different judges could impose different sentences for different reasons without having to give any explanation in open court. For example, some judges could impose a sentence for deterrent reasons but other judges in similar cases could sentence offenders in order to rehabilitate them. Even the same judge was not always consistent in sentencing. There was no agreement among judges as to what criteria ought to be taken into account in the sentencing decision and what weight ought to be given to factors such as previous convictions, age, good family, perceived future dangerousness, whether the accused pleaded guilty and other such matters. Criticism of this lack of consistency was speedily met with the response that sentences were individualised; they were tailored to meet the needs of the defendant and therefore consistency in punishments for similar crimes was not to be expected. The result was widespread sentencing disparity with similar cases being treated differently.

In England a 1979 study on sentencing practice in the magistrates' court revealed sometimes wide disparities in the use of fines and imprisonment:

> "Almost all clerks and chairmen emphasised the necessity for the establishment and maintenance of a consistent policy in their own individual courts but this concern did not extend to maintaining consistency with their neighbours. It was more important, they believed, that the decision taken by the courts should be determined by the particular characteristics of the offenders coming before it and of the district it served than that wider consistency be achieved at the expense of sensitivity."[205]

Even more startling evidence of sentencing disparity began to emerge from the United States.

Marvin E. Frankel, Criminal Sentences—Law Without Order (1973), pp.21–22:

"Take, for instance, the case of two men we received last spring. The first man had been convicted of cashing a cheque for $58.40. He was out of work at the time of his offence, and when his wife became ill and he needed

---

[205]   R. Tarling and M. Weatheritt, *Sentencing Practice in Magistrates' Courts* (H.O.R.S. No.56, 1979), p.45. See also N.A.C.R.O., *The Real Alternative* (1989), pp.10–17; J. Corbett, "Magistrates' Courts Clerks' Sentencing Behaviour: An Experimental Study", in S. Lloyd-Bostock and D. Pennington (eds), *The Psychology of Sentencing* (Oxford: Centre for Socio-Legal Studies, 1987), p.205; and Liberty, *Unequal before the Law; Sentencing in Magistrates' Courts in England and Wales 1981–1990* (1992).

money for rent, food and doctor's bills, he became the victim of temptation. He had no prior criminal record. The other man cashed a cheque for $35.20. He was also out of work and his wife had left him for another man. His prior record consisted of a drunk charge and a non-support charge. Our examination of these two cases indicated no significant differences for sentencing purposes but they appeared before different judges and the first man received 15 years in prison and the second man 30 days . . .

In one of our institutions a middle-aged credit union treasurer is serving 117 days for embezzling $24,000 in order to cover his gambling debts. On the other hand, another middle-aged embezzler with a fine past record and a fine family is serving 20 years, with 5 years probation to follow."

Another consequence of judges sentencing for a mixture of reasons, many of them utilitarian, was that excessively long sentences were being imposed in some cases. In particular, the rationale of exemplary sentencing resulted in some persons receiving sentences in excess of those imposed on others committing similar crimes.

One final point about the pre-just deserts era ought to be borne in mind. Offenders sent to prison were entitled to remission of their sentence (for good behaviour in prison) and to release on parole after a specified period. The decision as to whether to release someone on parole was highly discretionary and effectively amounted to a prisoner being sentenced a second time—but this time behind closed doors. This meant that when two offenders received the same sentence for the same crime, one could be released far sooner than the other. This, of course, could lead to even greater disparity.

It was a combination of all these factors that provided fertile soil for the growth of the just deserts movement. The agenda was set: judicial discretion had to be controlled; sentencing disparity had to be eliminated: this would necessarily involve eliminating disproportionately long sentences; there needed to be "truth in sentencing": equal sentences imposed in open court had to mean the same thing for different offenders. The concept of just deserts with its liberal emphasis on justice involving like cases being treated alike was the obvious facilitator. However, it was clearly not enough simply to embrace the concept of just deserts and reduce the importance of utilitarian considerations. Different judges could have different conceptions of what sentence was deserved in any particular case. What was needed was a mechanism for ensuring that judicial discretion was controlled by forcing judges to sentence in accordance with agreed and objective standards of desert. The response in many states in the United States was sharp and dramatic. In England it has been slower and somewhat different. Let us consider the developments in each country in turn.

1. United States

In the United States a significant number of states[206] have developed numerical sentencing guidelines under which judicial discretion is retained, but specific criteria or guidelines are developed to structure and control the exercise of that discretion. The legislature continues to set maximum terms. A specialised body, usually referred to as a Sentencing Commission, is created to establish sentencing guidelines within these broad statutory boundaries. These guidelines are generally based on two factors: the severity of the offence and the offender's prior criminal history. Offences are ranked in order of their seriousness and the Commission specifies a limited number of aggravating and mitigating circumstances which increase or decrease the severity of the offence. Factors relating to the offender's prior criminal history include previous convictions, prior incarcerations and whether the person was on parole or probation at the time the offence was committed. For each combination

---

[206] For a full list of these states, see R.S. Frase, "State Sentencing Guidelines: Diversity, Consensus and Unresolved Policy Issues" (2005) 105 Col. L.R. 1190.

of offence and offender, including a consideration of aggravating or mitigating circumstances, the guidelines provide a narrow sentencing range. The sentencing judge is expected to impose a sentence within this range, but if there are special circumstances not adequately taken into account by the guidelines, there may be a departure from the guidelines; reasons for the departure must be given and the sentence then becomes automatically subject to appellate review.

Under such schemes the sentence imposed on an offender is the sentence that will actually be served (except for "good time" reductions). Accordingly, there is no necessity for a Parole Board.

The role of the Sentencing Commission is viewed as crucial. Unlike the legislature, such a body would have the time and expertise to establish guidelines on the basis of careful study of existing sentencing practices; it could periodically alter these guidelines on the basis of on-going experience; theoretically, it would be removed from partisan politics; it would be a publicly accountable body; its rule-making would be on the record and open to public scrutiny.

The best known example of such guidelines is to be found in Minnesota (Figure 1). The italicised numbers within each grid denote the presumptive sentencing range in months within which a sentence may be imposed without it being deemed a departure.[207] All felony offences are assigned an appropriate level of severity. The offences listed on the grid are examples of frequently occurring offences within each severity level. The offender's criminal history score is computed by assigning points to previous convictions (one-half point for each previous conviction at levels 1–2; one point for each previous conviction at levels 3–5; one-and-a-half points for convictions at levels 6–8; and two points for convictions at levels 9–11), custody status at the time of the offence (e.g. if the offender was on probation), prior misdemeanour record and prior juvenile record. Cumulative points may accrue on a single occasion when offenders are sentenced concurrently for more than one offence.[208]

The presumptive sentence for cases contained in the shaded cells should be "stayed" (delayed until some future date; if the offender complies with imposed conditions until that date, the case is discharged[209]). The presumptive sentence for cases contained in cells above and to the right of the solid line should be "executed" (served immediately).

The presumptive penalty may be departed from in cases involving "substantial and compelling circumstances". The Sentencing Guidelines provide a non-exclusive list of mitigating factors (e.g. that the victim was the aggressor in the incident) and aggravating factors (e.g. that the victim was particularly vulnerable due to age or infirmity) that may be used as reasons for departure. They are also explicit that race, sex, employment and social factors may *not* be used as reasons for departure. Parole is abolished and replaced by a specified reduction (up to one-third off) for good behaviour in prison.

These guidelines appear to have been tolerably successful in reducing disparity. In 2012 the durational departure rate[210] was 15.1 per cent.[211] This can, of course, be justified. Justice not only demands that like cases be treated alike, but that different cases be treated differently. It is inevitable that in reducing all serious crimes to only 11 categories over-generalised solutions are imposed and fine-tuning has to be achieved on a case-by-case basis which involves departing from the presumptive penalty.

---

[207] Originally, this range was much narrower; it was expanded in 2004: R.H. Wandall, "Equality by Numbers or Words: A Comparative Study of Sentencing Structures in Minnesota and in Denmark" (2006) 17 *Criminal Law Forum* 1 at 13, 35.

[208] *State v Hernandez*, 311 N.W. 2d 478 (Minn. 1981).

[209] Almost 80% of prison sentences are in fact stayed: Frase, "State Sentencing Guidelines: Diversity, Consensus and Unresolved Policy Issues" (2005) 105 Col. L.R. 1190 at 1214.

[210] This is where the court orders a sentence with a duration that is other than the presumptive fixed duration or range in the appropriate cell on the applicable Grid.

[211] Minnesota Sentencing Guidelines Commission, *Sentencing Practices: Annual Summary Statistics for Felony Offenders* (2013), p.58, available at *http://www.msgc.state.mn.us/msgc5/sentencing_practices.htm* [Accessed April 30, 2014].

Figure 1 Minnesota Sentencing Guidelines Grid, Effective August 1, 2013

Sentencing Guidelines Grid

Presumptive sentence lengths are in months.

Italicised numbers within the grid denote the discretionary range within which a court may sentence without the sentence being deemed a departure. Offenders with stayed felony sentences may be subject to local confinement.

SEVERITY LEVEL OF CONVICTION OFFENSE (Example offenses listed in italics)		CRIMINAL HISTORY SCORE						
		0	1	2	3	4	5	6 or more
Murder, 2nd Degree (intentional murder; drive-by shootings)	11	306 *261–367*	326 *278–391*	346 *295–415*	366 *312–439*	386 *329–463*	406 *346–480²*	426 *363–480²*
Murder, 3rd Degree Murder, 2nd Degree (unintentional murder)	10	150 *128–180*	165 *141–198*	180 *153–216*	195 *166–234*	210 *179–252*	225 *192–270*	240 *204–288*
Assault, 1st Degree Controlled Substance Crime, 1st Degree	9	86 *74–103*	98 *84–117*	110 *94–132*	122 *104–146*	134 *114–160*	146 *125–175*	158 *135–189*
Aggravated Robbery, 1st Degree Controlled Substance Crime, 2nd Degree	8	48 *41–57*	58 *50–69*	68 *58–81*	78 *67–93*	88 *75–105*	98 *84–117*	108 *92–129*
Felony DWI	7	36	42	48	54 *46–64*	60 *51–72*	66 *57–79*	72 *62–84²*
Controlled Substance Crime, 3rd Degree	6	21	27	33	39 *34–46*	45 *39–54*	51 *44–61*	57 *49–68*
Residential Burglary Simple Robbery	5	18	23	28	33 *29–39*	38 *33–45*	43 *37–51*	48 *41–57*
Nonresidential Burglary	4	12¹	15	18	21	24 *21–28*	27 *23–32*	30 *26–36*
Theft Crimes (Over $5,000)	3	12¹	13	15	17	19 *17–22*	21 *18–25*	23 *20–27*
Theft Crimes ($5,000 or less) Check Forgery ($251–$2,500)	2	12¹	12¹	13	15	17	19	21 *18–25*
Sale of Simulated Controlled Substance	1	12¹	12¹	12¹	13	15	17	19 *17–22*

☐ Presumptive commitment to state imprisonment. First-degree murder has a mandatory life sentence and is excluded from the Guidelines under Minn. Stat. § 609.185. See Guidelines section 2.E. Mandatory Sentences, for policies regarding those sentences controlled by law.

▓ Presumptive stayed sentence; at the discretion of the court, up to one year of confinement and other non-jail sanctions can be imposed as conditions of probation. However, certain offenses in the shaded area of the Grid always carry a presumptive commitment to state prison. Guidelines sections 2.C. Presumptive Sentence and 2.E. Mandatory Sentences.

¹ 12¹ = One year and one day.
² Minn. Stat. § 244.09 requires that the Guidelines provide a range for sentences that are presumptive commitment to state imprisonment of 15% lower and 20% higher than the fixed duration displayed, provided that the minimum sentence is not less than one year and one day and the maximum sentence is not more than the statutory maximum. Guidelines section 2.C.1–2. Presumptive Sentence.

CRIMINAL HISTORY SCORE

However, it should be noted that these guidelines are only applicable for more serious crimes for which a prison sentence of at least one year's imprisonment may be imposed. They do not apply to non-custodial sentences or to lesser crimes. This is a common approach in the United States although a few states, such as Tennessee, have developed guidelines for all sentences.[212] It is, of course, immensely difficult to subject non-custodial sentences—and the choices to be made between them—to numerical guidelines. Nevertheless, it is a major criticism of the Minnesota Guidelines that for all lesser crimes the potential for sentencing disparity continues.

Further, it must be recalled that the guidelines only deal with the control of discretion at the sentencing stage of the criminal justice process. Inevitably, since the introduction of the guidelines much discretion has been shifted to the prosecutor who, through the use of plea bargaining, can agree to a reduced charge. Such practices are effectively determining the sentence in most cases. This means that offenders are not being sentenced for the crime they committed, but rather for the crime to which they have pleaded guilty.[213] This, coupled with an apparent tendency on the part of prosecutors to insist that offenders plead guilty to a number of charges so that their offender score is raised,[214] can lead to disparity and injustice being removed to an earlier and less visible stage of the process.

Another problem with numerical guidelines in the United States is that they often co-exist alongside "three strikes and you're out" laws and other mandatory sentences which effectively trump the guidelines. The result can be significant sentencing disparity.

Finally, a very real danger of implementing such a guideline system must be emphasised. In Minnesota the original guidelines were introduced in 1980 with the avowed and laudable aim of reducing prison populations. Such guidelines are, however, amenable to hijack by the law-and-order brigade intent on increasing penalties. This has occurred in Minnesota where the presumptive penalties have been increased twice since their inception. In 1989, after several highly-publicised homicides and considerable legislative pressure, the Sentencing Commission *doubled* several initial penalties: for example, the presumptive penalty for aggravated robbery was increased from 24 to 48 months. At the same time it doubled the number of points accorded to prior convictions thereby again increasing the potential for, and duration of, imprisonment. The result was an increase in the incarceration rate.[215]

R.A. Duff, "Theories and Policies Underlying Guidelines Systems" (2005) 105 Columbia L. Rev. 1162 at 1173–1174:

"Numerical sentencing guideline schemes . . . will be unable to capture relevant differences between individual cases, and will fail to do substantive justice to or between individual offenders. Such schemes will lump together under the same offence category individual offences that vary significantly in their character and seriousness; they will assign the same criminal history score to offenders whose relevant characteristics, culpability and prospects vary significantly; in addition, what they define as 'the same sentence' (a specified number of months or years in prison) will encompass what are in their substantive character and impact vastly different punishments. They will thus appear to do justice, by treating 'like' cases 'alike'. But they will achieve that appearance only by imposing artificial definitions of likeness on offences, offenders and sentences."[216]

---

[212]   Frase, "State Sentencing Guidelines: Diversity, Consensus and Unresolved Policy Issues" (2005) 105 Col. L.R. 1190.

[213]   The United States Sentencing Commission initially sought to introduce guidelines allowing offenders to be sentenced according to the real crime they committed rather than the one for which they admitted guilt. The Commission was, however, ultimately forced to abandon such a scheme because of difficulties of establishing the "real" crime (United States Sentencing Commission, *2001 Federal Sentencing Guidline Manual*, A.4(a)).

[214]   M. Tonry, "Sentencing Guidlines and Sentencing Commissions—the Second Generation", in K. Pease and M. Wasik (eds), *Sentencing Reform: Guidance or Guidelines* (Manchester: Manchester University Press, 1987), p.39.

[215]   Frase, "State Sentencing Guidelines: Diversity, Consensus and Unresolved Policy Issues" (2005) 105 Col. L.R. 1190.

[216]   See also R.H. Wandall, "Equality by Numbers or Words: A Comparative Study of Sentencing Structures in Minnesota and in Denmark" (2006) 17 *Criminal Law Forum* 1.

Michael Tonry, Sentencing Matters (1996), pp.13–24:

"The irony of 'just deserts' is that it backfired. The overriding aim was to make sentencing principled and fair . . . If indeterminate sentencing sometimes produced racial and class disparities, other unwanted disparities, and sentences grossly out of proportion to the crimes of which offenders were convicted, there was much to be said for proposals to scale the severity of punishments to the seriousness of crimes and thereby to satisfy the first tenet of equal treatment to: 'treat like cases alike.' In practice the effect was to focus attention solely on offenders' crimes and criminal records, to the exclusion of ethically important differences in their circumstances, and thereby to fail the second tenet of equal treatment to 'treat different cases differently.'

Reduced to their core elements, just desert theories are based on the intuitively powerful idea that punishment should be *deserved*, the empirical premise that most people agree about the comparative seriousness of crimes, and the proposal that crimes be ranked in order of their seriousness and punishments proportioned to those rankings . . . In practice, however, while most academic proponents of desert theories favor overall *reduction* in the severity of punishments, the result has been both to make punishment more severe and to create disparities as extreme as any that existed under indeterminate sentencing.

. . . [B]ecause desert theories place primary emphasis on linking deserved punishments to the severity of crimes, in the interest of treating like cases alike, they lead to disregard of other ethically relevant differences between offenders—like their personal backgrounds and the effects of punishment on them and their families— and thereby often treat unlike cases alike . . .

Just deserts, sometimes characterized as expressing a 'principle of proportionality', is sound in theory but defective in practice. In an ideal world in which all citizens have equal opportunities for self-realization and material advancement, the idea that deserved punishments can be calibrated precisely to the offender's culpability, and that punishments should be apportioned accordingly, has much to commend it. Somewhat awkwardly for desert theories, however, ours is a world that in a number of respects falls short of the ideal.

. . . In just deserts principle, two offenders who commit the same offense and have similar criminal records deserve the same penalty. If applicable guidelines specify a two-year prison sentence, both should receive it. If one, however, is unemployed and has no permanent residence, and the other works and supports a family, many people will want to treat them differently. Partly, this is because the second seems more stable, more integrated into society, and somehow more worthy. Partly also, and equally important, it is because the second offender's spouse and children—who have committed no crime—will also suffer . . .

Judges, prosecutors, and other officials make decisions about whole people, and not about generic offenders who have committed offence X and have criminal history Y. Not surprisingly, they often feel moved to take the individual offender's circumstances into account in deciding what to do.

Another defect . . . [is that in] objective terms, punishments that technically are the same may be very different. A 'generic' two-year prison sentence . . . may range from time spent in a crowded, fear-ridden maximum security prison under lockup twenty-three hours per day to confinement under electronic monitoring in the offender's home, with medium and minimum security prisons, forestry camps, and halfway houses in between. All count as two years' deprivation of liberty, but all offenders and most observers see them as vastly different.

In subjective terms as well, two years' imprisonment in a single setting will have very different meanings to different offenders who have committed the same crime. Two years' imprisonment in a maximum security prison may be a rite of passage for a Los Angeles gang member. For an attractive, effeminate twenty-year-old, it may mean the terror of repeated sexual victimization. For a forty-year-old head of household, it may mean the loss of a job and a home and a family. For the unhealthy seventy-year-old, it may be a death sentence.

. . . By offering policy makers a rationale for sentencing that reduced relevant considerations to two that can be scaled on the axes of grids, [just desert theories] reified three-dimensional defendants into two-dimensional abstractions. When policy makers think of abstractions rather than people, it is easy to respond to an electoral opponent's possible 'soft on crime' accusations by voting to increase sentences or to establish mandatory penalties . . . If a two-dimensional grid is chalked on to a legislative committee's blackboard, it takes little effort to erase numbers and replace them with higher ones."

2. England and Wales

There have been significant responses in England and Wales to sentencing disparity. First, since 1989 the Attorney-General has been able to refer an unduly lenient sentence, imposed by the Crown Court, to the Court of Appeal which has the power to increase that sentence.[217] A disparate sentence can be an unduly light one as well as an unduly heavy one and so this right of appeal does go some way towards the elimination of unwarranted disparity. However, it is only Crown Court sentences (and not ones from magistrates' courts), and only sentences imposed for "indictable only" offences, that are referable. These account for fewer than 20 per cent of sentences imposed in the Crown Court.[218] Nevertheless, between 60 and 80 sentences are reviewed by the Court of Appeal for undue lenience each year and 88 per cent of these are found to be unduly lenient.[219]

Secondly, in an attempt to structure sentencing discretion in the Crown Court, the Court of Appeal in the 1970s started handing down *guideline judgments*. These have usually occurred when a number of appeals have been heard at the same time and the Court of Appeal has taken the opportunity to make generalised statements about sentencing for that type of offence.

There are now guideline judgments dealing with a wide range of offences. There is evidence that some of these decisions have resulted in sharp increases in sentencing levels.[220] Further, it is uncertain to what extent these guideline judgments have helped control sentencing disparity. The problem was that guideline judgments, while helpful in indicating starting points for the severity of sentences, and in listing aggravating and mitigating circumstances, were insufficiently precise, in mathematical terms, as to how much sentences could be increased or decreased.[221] Further, such judgments tended to concentrate on the more serious crimes with the result that there was insufficient guidance for cases dealing with less serious crimes where non-custodial sentences were likely.[222]

In response to such criticisms a Sentencing Advisory Panel was established in 1999.[223] Its function was to give advice to the Court of Appeal which was obliged to have regard to these views and, if practicable or at the next appropriate opportunity, include guidelines in its judgment.

The Criminal Justice Act 2003 set up a new body, the Sentencing Guidelines Council, which was empowered to issue "definitive guidelines" based on advice provided by the Sentencing Advisory Panel. In 2009 the Sentencing Guidelines Council and the Sentencing Advisory Panel were subsumed into a single body called the Sentencing Council.[224] The Council is made up of eight "judicial" and six "non-judicial" members, selected by the Lord Chief Justice and Lord Chancellor, respectively.[225] The Council is entrusted with preparing draft guidelines with the requirement to consult with the Lord Chief Justice and House of Commons Justice Select Committee before producing definitive guidelines. The Council's guidelines may be general in nature or limited to a particular category of offence or offender.[226] In passing any sentence the courts "must . . . follow any sentencing guideline . . . unless the court is satisfied that it would be contrary to the interests of justice to do so".[227] The Council has issued definitive guidelines, amongst others, on the following matters: fundamental principles for measuring the seriousness of offences; the new sentences in the Criminal Justice Act 2003; discounts

---

[217]   Criminal Justice Act 1988 s.36.
[218]   S. Shute, "Who Passes Unduly Lenient Sentences? How Were They Listed?: A Survey of Attorney-General's Reference Cases, 1989–1997" [1999] Crim. L.R. 603.
[219]   Shute, "Who Passes Unduly Lenient Sentences? How Were They Listed?: A Survey of Attorney-General's Reference Cases, 1989–1997" [1999] Crim. L.R. 603.
[220]   R. Ranyard, B. Hebenton and K. Pease, "An Analysis of a Guideline Case as Applied to the Offence of Rape" (1994) 33 Howard J.C.J. 203 at 215.
[221]   Ranyard, Hebenton and Pease, "An Analysis of a Guideline Case as Applied to the Offence of Rape" (1994) 33 Howard J.C.J. 203 at 208–209.
[222]   A. Ashworth, *Sentencing and Criminal Justice*, 3rd edn (Cambridge: CUP, 2000), p.32.
[223]   Crime and Disorder Act 1998 ss.80–81.
[224]   Established under s.118 of the Coroners and Justice Act 2009.
[225]   Coroners and Justice Act 2009 Sch.15.
[226]   Coroners and Justice Act 2009 s.120(2)
[227]   Coroners and Justice Act 2009 s.125(1).

for guilty pleas; manslaughter by reason of provocation; robbery; sexual offences; assaults on children and child cruelty; failure to surrender to bail; assaults; breach of anti-social behaviour orders; causing death by driving; theft and burglary from a non-dwelling; attempted murder; fraud; corporate manslaughter and health and safety offences causing death; and youth sentencing.

The importance of courts having regard to these guidelines was stressed in *Oosthuizen*[228]: the guidelines must be brought to the sentencer's attention; the sentencer must have regard to them but it did "not necessarily follow that in every case a guideline will be followed".

The Sentencing Council has also published a definitive guideline for sentencing in magistrates' courts,[229] having taken over responsibility for such guidelines from the Magistrates' Association. This 200-page document covers most of the offences regularly coming before a magistrates' court, and contains explanatory material that sets out a common approach to more general issues. The duty on judges to have regard to sentencing guidelines now applies equally to magistrates for the first time. It should be noted that magistrates deal with around 97 per cent of all criminal cases, and although one often thinks of imprisonment as the "normal" punishment for criminal offences, in magistrates' courts the penalty applied in around 75 per cent of cases is a fine.[230] A major question for sentencers has been whether fines should try to be allocated to ensure equality of financial impact on offenders of different means. A £100 fine for someone of considerable means will not have the same impact as it would do on someone surviving on income support, for example. Raine and Dunstan note that in trying to achieve this goal of equality of financial impact, or "equity", sentencers may find that they come into conflict with the additional, and perhaps more important, goals of proportionality (the just deserts requirement that the penalty fit the crime) and consistency in sentencing (minimising disparity in sentencing in two similar cases).[231] The unit fine scheme under the Criminal Justice Act 1991 was one initiative that tried to ensure equality of impact but was extremely complex and was abandoned after the media reported apparent disparities and disproportionate sentences.[232] However, s.164 of the Criminal Justice Act 2003 has tried to continue the spirit of the unit fines system, in that it requires sentencers to take account of both offenders' financial means and offence seriousness in setting fine levels. The Sentencing Council's 2008 version of the Magistrates' Court Sentencing Guidelines take a "fresh approach and methodology for fines setting"[233] in the hope that equity, proportionality and consistency can all be achieved, although research carried out prior to the final version of the guidelines being published raises doubts about the ability of such guidelines to succeed in their goals, given that case studies produced a large variation in sentencing due to sentencers interpreting the guidance in line with their personal experience and "sense of justice". [234]

There will always be tension between the need to ensure that sentencers can do justice without their discretion becoming unduly fettered and the desire to discourage disparity in sentencing. These reforms constitute a major step towards ensuring consistency in sentencing. The Sentencing Council has taken a "narrative" approach in producing its guidelines for indictable offences, tending to consist

---

[228] *R. v Oosthuizen (Lee)* [2006] 1 Cr. App. R. (S.) 73.

[229] Sentencing Guidelines Council, *Magistrates' Court Sentencing Guidleines: Definitive Guideline* (2008).

[230] J. Raine and E. Dunstan, "How Well do Sentencing Guidelines Work?: Equity, Proportionality and Consistency in the Determination of Fine Levels in the Magistrates' Courts of England and Wales" (2009) 48 *The Howard Journal* 13 at 15.

[231] Raine and Dunstan, "How Well do Sentencing Guidelines Work?: Equity, Proportionality and Consistency in the Determination of Fine Levels in the Magistrates' Courts of England and Wales" (2009) 48 *The Howard Journal* 13 at 15.

[232] Raine and Dunstan, "How Well do Sentencing Guidelines Work?: Equity, Proportionality and Consistency in the Determination of Fine Levels in the Magistrates' Courts of England and Wales" (2009) 48 *The Howard Journal* 13 at 15.

[233] Raine and Dunstan, "How Well do Sentencing Guidelines Work?: Equity, Proportionality and Consistency in the Determination of Fine Levels in the Magistrates' Courts of England and Wales" (2009) 48 *The Howard Journal* 13 at 22.

[234] Raine and Dunstan, "How Well do Sentencing Guidelines Work?: Equity, Proportionality and Consistency in the Determination of Fine Levels in the Magistrates' Courts of England and Wales" (2009) 48 *The Howard Journal* 13 at 29.

of a first part discussing the features of the offence and factors that might increase or decrease its seriousness, and a second part which is set out in the form of a table, assigning a sentencing range to different levels of offence seriousness.[235] The approach to be taken by sentencers has been carefully set out in the magistrates' guidelines, explaining the factors to be taken into account in a step-by-step methodology. Sentencers should start with looking at offence seriousness, the starting point for sentencing under the Criminal Justice Act 2003, by assessing culpability of the offender and harm caused or threatened by the offence. This should lead the sentencer to identify a "starting point" for the sentence. Consideration should then be given to any mitigating or aggravating factors, to either move up or down the sentencing "range" from the starting point. Although the range is set to try to encourage consistency in sentencing, it is possible for a sentence to be passed outside the range laid down in the guidelines. Once a provisional sentence has been arrived at, sentencers should then look at whether that sentence should be reduced due to offender mitigation (e.g. whether the offender has shown remorse) or a guilty plea. Unlike sentencing grids from the United States, such as the Minnesota Guidelines, definitive guidelines produced by the Sentencing Council do not provide an automatic increase in sentence for previous convictions. However, the Sentencing Council notes that previous convictions may take a sentence beyond the sentencing range provided.[236] Apart from the question, discussed above, of whether offenders with previous convictions deserve longer sentences than first-time offenders, this ability to increase a prison sentence based on past behaviour may contribute to a practical problem that has recently reached crisis point: that of overcrowding in prisons. The size of the problem, examined in a report by Lord Carter,[237] can be summarised by reference to the fact that since the mid-1990s the prison population in England and Wales has increased by 60 per cent, resulting in England and Wales having the second highest prison population per capita in prison capacity in Western Europe.[238] To help remedy the situation, Carter recommended that in addition to the building of more prisons, including three "Titan" prisons,[239] the Government should look to create a new, more structured, sentencing framework with a Sentencing Commission akin to those found in the United States. The advantage of such frameworks is that they allow for the efficient management of prison places.

R.S. Frase, "Sentencing Policy Development under the Minnesota Sentencing Guidelines", in A. von Hirsch, A. Ashworth and J. Roberts (eds) Principled Sentencing, 3rd edn (2009), p.275:

"Guidelines sentencing remains sufficiently predictable to permit accurate forecasts of resource impacts, and the Commission and the Legislature take these forecasts seriously and tailor their proposals to limit State and local resource impacts. As a result, the State's prison population, although growing rapidly, has grown more slowly than in many other States over the past 26 years and has almost always remained within rated capacity."

Following on from the Carter Report, a Sentencing Commission Working Group, chaired by Lord Justice Gage, was established to explore the viability of a structured framework overseen by a

---

[235]   A. Ashworth, "Techniques for Reducing Sentencing Disparity", in A. von Hirsch, A. Ashworth and J. Roberts (eds) Principled Sentencing, 3rd edn (Oxford: OUP, 2009).

[236]   Research has found that in a significant number of cases (46% of 222 offences of assault, sexual assault and robbery), sentencers imposed a sentence outside the guideline ranges for the levels of offence seriousness described: Sentencing Commission Working Group, Crown Court Sentencing Survey, July 2008.

[237]   Lord Carter, Securing the Future: Proposals for the Efficient and Sustainable Use of Custody in England and Wales (2007).

[238]   Only Spain has a higher rate of imprisonment. G. Berman and A. Dar, Prison Population Statistics (2013).

[239]   Large prisons to house approximately 2,500 prisoners per prison (Carter, Securing the Future: Proposals for the Efficient and Sustainable Use of Custody in England and Wales (2007), p.38).

Sentencing Commission, and issued a consultation paper,[240] followed by a report,[241] in 2008. Having visited Minnesota and North Carolina, the Working Group expressed the view that it was

"conscious that the specific design of the USA sentencing grids, particularly the way that account is taken of previous criminal history, is overly formulaic and mechanistic to an extent that is inimical to our tradition of judicial discretion. However, the greater predictability and consistency that may be achieved by a structured sentencing framework makes it worthy of consideration".[242]

Such a move would certainly not be welcomed by all, however. Wasik notes that the advantages of the English approach are that sentencing guidelines are able to focus on generic sentencing issues rather than just offence-specific guidelines and that the Sentencing Council is able to resist political pressure and media hype.[243] Wasik concedes that although sentencing grids such as those in Minnesota allow for a more effective management of the prison population, this is at the expense of judges' discretion, allowing little leeway either side of the presumptive numerical sentence, and argues that the objective of the Sentencing Council is preferable; that is: "uniformity of approach, not uniformity of outcome".[244]

Not all are convinced that the Sentencing Council's guidelines provide the right balance between sentencing discretion and a structured approach, however. Cooper has argued that much of the guidance has become rhetoric:

"Aware, as any conscientious and realistic tribunal is, of the desirability of rendering their judgments less vulnerable to appeal, judges and advocates use the guidelines, not as helpful signposts to a proper disposal, but rather as fireproofing for any subsequent appeal. Box-ticking has tended to replace a careful consideration of the individual and pertinent facts of the case."[245]

A more fundamental objection to Carter's suggestion to import the idea of a Sentencing Commission from America is noted by Wasik:

"There is a deep irony in importing lessons on prison policy from a country where the sentenced custodial population is running at a rate of about 750 per 100,000, five times as high as in England and Wales (148) and 10 times the rate of imprisonment in much of the rest of Europe."[246]

He points out that better models for reducing prison population can be found in Scandinavia. Work by Lacey similarly highlights the stark reality that the United States is the last country one ought to take as a model for society's use of the prison system. She takes a rather different view of the increasing prison population, in essence attributing the higher rates of incarceration in the United Kingdom and the United States compared to countries within Scandinavia, northern Europe and Japan, to the electoral systems and market economies of those countries.

---

[240] Sentencing Commission Working Group, *A Structured Sentencing Framework and Sentencing Commission: Consultation Paper* (2008).

[241] Sentencing Commission Working Group, *Sentencing Guidelines in England and Wales: An Evolutionary Approach* (2008).

[242] Sentencing Commission Working Group, *Sentencing Guidelines in England and Wales: An Evolutionary Approach* (2008), para.1.7.

[243] M. Wasik, "Sentencing Guidelines in England and Wales—State of the Art" [2008] Crim. L.R. 253 at 254.

[244] Wasik, "Sentencing Guidelines in England and Wales—State of the Art" [2008] Crim. L.R. 253 at 259.

[245] J. Cooper, "The Sentencing Guidelines Council—a Practical Perspective" [2008] Crim. L.R. 277 at 280.

[246] Wasik, "Sentencing Guidelines in England and Wales—State of the Art" [2008] Crim. L.R. 253 at 263.

Nicola Lacey, The Hamlyn Lectures 2007, The Prisoners' Dilemma: Political Economy and Punishment in Contemporary Democracies (2008), p.76:

"To sum up, in liberal market economies with majoritarian electoral systems, particularly under conditions of relatively low trust in politicians, relatively low deference to the expertise of criminal justice professionals, and a weakening of the ideological divide between political parties as they become increasingly focused on the median voter and correspondingly less able to make commitments to a stable party base, the unmediated responsiveness of politics to popular opinion in the adversarial context of the two-party system makes it harder for governments to resist a ratcheting up of penal severity."

Lacey's proposal for reducing the prison population and the tendency towards social exclusion which punishment produces is that criminal justice policy ought to be removed from party politics altogether and placed in the hands of an independent body. She recognises that this suggestion may seem "impossibly utopian"[247] but arguably such a move would not be inconsistent with the introduction of an American-style Sentencing Commission, depending on how such a body would operate. An alternative way to minimise the effects of party politics might be to require sentencing guidelines to be placed before Parliament in their entirety for parliamentary approval. This approach has been advocated by the New Zealand Law Commission,[248] and was considered by the Sentencing Commission Working Group, the members of which were in disagreement as to its merits. Although controversial, Lacey's proposal to remove sentencing from politics altogether, as opposed to increasing the input of politicians by involving Parliament as a whole, would surely be a more effective way of controlling the prison population and could be the solution to the problem Carter was entrusted with addressing.

Despite the lack of a Sentencing Commission within England and Wales, the Sentencing Council does have several duties which may have the effect of controlling imprisonment rates. First, the Council must produce a resource assessment when issuing any draft or definitive guidelines.[249] This will assess the likely impact of the guidelines on prison places and the provision of probation services. In addition to this, the Council's annual report must include an assessment of the effect which any changes in the sentencing practice of courts are having or are likely to have on prison places and the provision of probation services.[250] This is not quite the Sentencing Commission envisaged by Carter, since the Council continues to work on an ad hoc, or "penny numbers"[251] basis, with the Lord Chancellor and Court of Appeal given the option of proposing that sentencing guidelines be prepared in relation to specific offences or sentencing matters.[252] It will not involve the systematic ranking of all existing offences in order of seriousness, something which Ormerod notes would be a massive task.[253] It was the prospect of such a lengthy exercise that prompted the Sentencing Commission Working Group to abandon the idea of a grid-like framework and American-style Sentencing Commission.[254]

---

[247] Lacey, *The Hamlyn Lectures 2007*, p.195.
[248] W. Young and C. Browning, "New Zealand's Sentencing Council" [2008] 4 Crim L.R. 287. However, in New Zealand sentencing guidelines do not require positive approval by Parliament. Rather, the guidelines will automatically come into force unless they are disallowed by negative resolution within a specified period.
[249] Coroners and Justice Act 2009 s.127.
[250] Coroners and Justice Act 2009 s.130.
[251] A. Ashworth, Oral Evidence taken before the Justice Committee on the Sentencing Commission, October 14, 2008, HC (2007–08) 1095-I, Q 37, quoted in House of Commons Justice Committee, *Sentencing Guidelines and Parliament: building a bridge*, HC 715, (2009), para.350.
[252] Coroners and Justice Act 2009 s.124
[253] D. Ormerod, *Editorial* [2008] Crim. L.R. 413.
[254] Sentencing Commission Working Group, *Sentencing Guidelines in England and Wales: An Evolutionary Approach* (2008), para.3.11.

It is a major theme of this book that all offences should be structured and labelled to reflect a hierarchy of seriousness. The extent to which seriousness should be reflected in the substantive law or left to the sentencing stage (being regulated by sentencing guidelines) is a crucial matter. It is to these issues of substantive law—and the relationship between that law and sentencing—that the remainder of this book is devoted.

2

THE GENERAL PRINCIPLES OF CRIMINAL LIABILITY

I. INTRODUCTION

The criminal law is an institution of blame and punishment. Blame is attached to the defendant's conduct and if that conduct violates the law they are punished for it (whether for retributive or deterrent, etc. reasons). However, in what circumstances are we to blame someone for their conduct, and blame them to a degree sufficient to justify the imposition of punishment? And in what circumstances can someone's actions be said to have violated the law?

Generally, the law is concerned with punishing harmful actions that are committed in circumstances or in conditions in which we can fairly blame the perpetrator of the actions. This is, of course, only a general proposition. Not all acts that are criminal cause an obvious harm. With the crime of attempt, for instance, no actual harm has been caused. Similarly, criminal liability is often imposed in circumstances where many feel that no blame can be attached to the actor. Thus, in crimes of strict liability a person who has acted to the best of their ability can be punished if, albeit inadvertently, they violate a statute making certain conduct criminal. The question of whether such conduct, which either involves no obvious harm or is generally perceived to involve no blameworthiness, should be punishable will be considered later in this book.

Let us return to the general proposition which can be broken down into two limbs.

1. Harmful conduct: Sometimes "conduct" can in itself be forbidden on the basis that it constitutes or threatens a harm. Alternatively, it is conduct that causes a harmful result that is forbidden by the criminal law. The word "conduct" is here used in its broadest sense to encompass an omission to act or even a state of affairs. The law has developed a short-hand term, actus reus, to describe this.

2. Committed in conditions in which we can fairly blame the actor: The problem here is to determine the indicators of blame. It is widely accepted that two such indicators exist:

(a) *Mens rea.* Some would only blame those who acted with a subjective mental element (for example, intending to kill). Others would blame those whose actions objectively failed to conform to a set standard. Either way, the law has developed a short-hand term, mens rea, to describe this.[1]

---

[1] Whether an objective failure to conform to a set standard of behaviour (negligence) is accurately described as a species of mens rea is a controversial matter. See pp.145–146 where a distinction is drawn between cognitive mens rea (involving a subjective mental element) and normative mens rea (involving an assessment of culpability taking account of all the circumstances including a failure to conform to set standards).

(b) *Absence of defence.* A defendant might have committed an actus reus and have mens rea but, because of the circumstances, we might not wish to hold them liable and punish them. They might have a valid defence in that they acted, say, in self-defence or under duress.

One way of interpreting this is that the constituent ingredients of a crime are three-fold, actus reus, mens rea and the absence of a valid defence.[2]

There are, however, other modes of analysing the constituent elements of a crime. Glanville Williams, for instance, argued that all elements of a crime are divisible into either actus reus or mens rea and that the actus reus requirement includes absence of defence.[3] Others argue that mens rea means blameworthiness in the sense of mental element (or, possibly, negligence) plus absence of defence.[4]

This divergence of views can be illustrated simply. The crime of murder is defined as the "unlawful killing of a human being with malice aforethought". The constituent elements of this crime can be analysed in three ways:

(1) There are three elements—the actus reus of killing a human being, the mens rea of malice aforethought, and the requirement of unlawfulness indicating the absence of any defence.

(2) The actus reus is unlawfully killing a human being; the requirement of unlawfulness (absence of defence) is part of the actus reus.[5] The mens rea requirement is malice aforethought.

(3) The actus reus is killing a human being. The mens rea is the element of blameworthiness which encompasses both the malice aforethought and the unlawfulness (absence of defence) requirement.

The possible importance of these different modes of analysis will be discussed later but, for the moment, the fact that there are these very different modes of analysis serves to emphasise an important point. The terms actus reus and mens rea are no more than tools that are useful in the exposition of the criminal law. Dividing crime into its constituent elements in this way should be no more than a matter of analytical convenience.[6] Whether defendants are to be convicted should depend on important principles aimed at deciding whether their conduct deserves condemnation as criminal; such questions should not be answered by reference only to definitions of actus reus and mens rea. Questions of policy should not be determined by reference to definition and terminology.[7]

In *Miller*, Lord Diplock disapproved of such terminology:

"My Lords, it would I think be conducive to clarity of analysis of the ingredients of a crime that is created by statute, as are the greater majority of criminal offences today, if we were to avoid bad

---

[2]   D. Lanham, "Larsonneur Revisited" [1976] Crim. L.R. 276.

[3]   *Criminal Law: The General Part* (1961), p.20; G. Williams, "Statutory Exceptions to Liability and the Burden of Proof" (1976) 126 New L.J. 1032 at 1034; see also *Williams (Gladstone)* (1984) 78 Cr. App. R. 276.

[4]   S.H. Kadish, "The Decline of Innocence" (1968) 26 C.L.J. 273 at 273–275.

[5]   This claim is only plausible with regard to justificatory defences. The distinction between justificatory and excusatory defences is discussed at pp294–306.

[6]   See, however, pp.218–219 where judicial decisions have lost sight of this simple point and made criminal liability dependent upon a particular mode of analysing the constituent elements of a crime.

[7]   A.T.H. Smith, "On *Actus reus* and *Mens rea*", in P.R. Glazebrook (ed.), *Reshaping the Criminal Law: Essays in Honour of Glanville Williams* (London: Stevens, 1978), pp.95, 96, 102.

Latin and instead to think and speak about the conduct of the accused and his state of mind at the time of that conduct, instead of speaking of actus reus and mens rea."[8]

In this book we have chosen to disregard Lord Diplock's command. We shall analyse crimes in terms of actus reus, mens rea and absence of defence. We do this for the simple reason that as long as one appreciates that these terms are no more than tools, they are tools that *can* usefully aid the clear exposition of the rules of criminal law. Further, they have been so much part of the criminal law vocabulary for hundreds of years, and still are, that many of the cases to be discussed in this book would be highly confusing, if not totally meaningless, without some understanding of the orthodox meaning of these terms.

In this chapter we shall consider the primary basis of criminal liability in terms of actus reus and mens rea. For the sake of clarity the discussion of the general defences has been reserved for a separate chapter.

II. Actus Reus

A. Introduction

To many people, evil thoughts, desires and intentions are as reprehensible as evil deeds and, if we had the means to detect such criminal propensities, we would be justified in punishing such persons. The law, however, is not concerned with punishing people for thinking evil thoughts or having evil intentions.[9] The law will not interfere unless there has been some conduct, some physical manifestation of the evil intention.[10] Some crimes only require the slightest manifestation: in conspiracy, for example, all that is needed is an agreement to commit a crime. However, minimal as it might be, this agreement is nevertheless a physical manifestation of the evil intention; it is conduct and can form the basis of an actus reus.

Why does the law insist upon an actus reus as a prerequisite of criminal liability?

Powell v State of Texas 392 US 514 (1968) (Supreme Court of the United States)

BLACK J:

"The reasons for this refusal to permit conviction without proof of an act are difficult to spell out, but they are nonetheless perceived and universally expressed in our criminal law. Evidence of propensity can be considered relatively unreliable and more difficult for a defendant to rebut: the requirement of a specific act thus provides some protection against false charges. Perhaps more fundamental is the difficulty of distinguishing, in the absence of any conduct, between desires of the day-dream variety and fixed intentions that may pose a real threat to society; extending the criminal law to cover both types of desire would be unthinkable, since

'[t]here can hardly be anyone who has never thought evil. When a desire is inhibited it may find expression in fantasy; but it would be absurd to condemn this natural psychological mechanism as illegal.' (Glanville Williams (1961), p.2.)"

---

8   *R. v Miller (James)* [1983] 2 A.C. 161, 175. See also P.H. Robinson, "Should the Criminal Law Abandon the *Actus Reus* and *Mens Rea* Distinction?", in S. Shute, J. Gardner and J. Horder (eds), *Action and Value in Criminal Law* (Oxford: OUP, 1993) who argues that these phrases are misleading and obscure understanding.

9   For a view that it could be justifiable to punish evil intentions alone, see D. Husak, "Does Criminal Liability Require an Act?", in A. Duff (ed.), *Philosophy and the Criminal Law* (Cambridge: CUP, 1998). See, generally, R.A. Duff, *Answering for Crime* (Oxford: Hart, 2007), pp.102–105.

10   Duff, *Answering for Crime* (2007), pp.95–101.

Further, in addition to it being morally inappropriate to punish mere intentions, there is doubt as to whether people have sufficient control over their thoughts to be held responsible for them.[11]

A. Goldstein, "Conspiracy to Defraud the United States" (1959) 68 Yale L.J. 405 at 405–406:

"[The notion of not punishing evil intentions alone] expresses today, as it did three centuries ago, the feeling that the individual thinking evil thoughts must be protected from a state which may class him as a threat to its security. Rooted in scepticism about the ability either to know what passes through the minds of men or to predict whether antisocial behaviour will follow from antisocial thoughts, the act requirement serves a number of closely-related objectives: it seeks to assure that the evil intent of the man branded a criminal has been *expressed in a manner signifying harm to society*; that there is no longer any substantial likelihood that he will be deterred by the threat of sanction; and that there has been an identifiable occurrence so that multiple prosecution and punishment may be minimized."

As seen above, a mere agreement to commit a crime is regarded as a sufficient manifestation of evil intentions to constitute the actus reus of conspiracy; similarly, mere words of instruction or encouragement are sufficient to render one liable for aiding and abetting a crime. Whether these ought to be regarded as a sufficient manifestation of evil intentions to justify the imposition of criminal liability is a question to be considered later.

B. Constituent Elements of Actus Reus

The actus reus of every crime is different. The actus reus of theft is the appropriation of property belonging to another[12] and the actus reus of rape is the penetration of the vagina, anus or mouth of another person who does not consent to the penetration.[13] With all crimes the actus reus is the external element of the crime—the objective requirement necessary to constitute the offence. Crimes can be divided into two categories and the essential elements of an actus reus depend on which of these two species of crime one is dealing with. First, there are crimes, known as conduct crimes, where the only external element required is the prohibited conduct itself. Thus the actus reus of the offence of dangerous driving is simply driving a mechanically propelled vehicle on a road or other public place.[14] No consequence of that dangerous driving need be established.[15] Secondly, there are other crimes, known as result crimes, where the external elements of the offence require proof that the conduct caused a prohibited result or consequence. Thus the actus reus of the offence of causing death by dangerous driving is causing the "death of another person by driving a mechanically propelled vehicle dangerously on a road or other public place".[16] Here it is necessary to establish that the dangerous driving caused the forbidden consequence specified in the actus reus, namely, the death of another person.

Conduct crimes provide a good illustration of the criminal law punishing offenders who have caused no obvious harm. However, it can be argued that in the above example there is a harm, namely causing danger to other road users. If this is indeed a harm, it is clearly a lesser harm than actually killing another road-user. Should this difference be reflected by differing penalties for the

---

[11]   Robinson, see fn.8 above at 191.
[12]   Theft Act 1968 s.1.
[13]   Sexual Offences Act 2003 s.1(1).
[14]   Road Traffic Act 1988 s.2.
[15]   Beyond the creation of a *danger* of injury to others or serious damage to property: Road Traffic Act 1988, s.2A(3).
[16]   Road Traffic Act 1988 s.1.

two offences? Or should one proceed on the basis that as the forbidden conduct is the same in both offences, the result (death) could be entirely fortuitous, thus not reflecting upon the driver's responsibility and consequently the two offences should carry the same penalty? This is an issue to which we shall return later in the book.

From the above it can be seen that both conduct crimes and result crimes have two elements in common: (1) both require an "act" or conduct, i.e. driving; and (2) both require that the act be carried out in defined *legally relevant circumstances*, i.e. on a road or other public place. If the same act of driving the car occurred in a private field, the actus reus of the offence would not be made out. It is only dangerous driving *on a road or other public place* that is prohibited. Similarly, the actus reus of theft requires that the property "belong to another". In the absence of this circumstance, for example, if the property is owned by the would-be thief, the actus reus of the crime is not made out. Just as mens rea may or may not be required for the act and for the consequences in result crimes, liability may similarly depend upon whether the accused has the required mental state in relation to the legally defined relevant circumstances. So, in theft, if the defendant honestly believes that they are the owner of the property, there would be no mens rea in relation to a vital element of the actus reus.[17]

With result crimes it is necessary to establish an additional third element, namely, that the act *caused* the prohibited consequence, for example, *caused* the death of another person. If poison is put into the drink of another person with intent to kill that person who subsequently dies with the drink found beside them, liability for murder cannot exist unless it was the poison that caused the death. If the deceased had died of a heart attack, the only possible charge would be attempted murder.[18]

Putting these elements together, it is common to find an actus reus described as:

(1) an "act";

(2) committed in legally relevant circumstances; and

(3) (for result crimes) causing the prohibited result.

One final point needs to be made by way of introduction. Whilst many crimes are so defined that the defendant may be convicted on the basis of the actus reus alone without need for proof of *mens rea* (crimes of so-called strict liability), the converse is not true. There must always be an actus reus for liability to be at issue at all. If, for example, in an alleged case of theft, the property already belongs to the person taking it, then despite any intention to steal, the actions cannot amount to the crime of theft. Similarly, where a defendant persuades another to purchase his car by representing that it is free from encumbrances, believing he is lying, he cannot be found guilty of fraud if it turns out that it was in fact free from encumbrances.[19] The defendant has unwittingly told the truth; the car was his to sell and his dishonest state of mind counts for nothing. The fact that a defendant believes he has committed an actus reus is not enough. The actus reus must be proved objectively to exist.

We are now in a position to examine in greater detail the requirements of an actus reus.

---

[17]   Theft Act 1968 s.2(1)(a).
[18]   *R. v White (John)* [1910] 2 K.B. 124; See also *Re Hensler* (1870) 11 Cox C.C. 570.
[19]   *R. v Deller (Charles Avon)* (1952) 36 Cr. App. R. 184. This case is commonly discussed in relation to *The Queen v George Dadson* (1850) 2 Den. 35.

1. An "act"

(i) The act must be voluntary

The distinction between an act and any accompanying mental element required by the law for the imposition of liability has already been drawn. Thus, if we define murder as killing when there is an intention to kill or cause serious harm we can readily accept the acquittal of someone whose claim that it was all a dreadful accident is accepted by the courts. But the circumstances of the accident might lead us to very different conclusions about the basis of the acquittal. If the defendant claims that the accident lay in thinking the weapon was an imitation one rather than a real one, then this translates into a denial of mens rea; the defendant did not have the necessary intention to kill or cause serious harm. However, if the defendant claims to have shot the victim as a result of stumbling down some icy steps, the "accident" here appears to be of a more fundamental kind. The act itself seems defective. Punishment seems inappropriate—even if we were dealing with a crime where no mental element was required (crimes of strict liability). The difficulty lies in trying to pin-point the defect. The law has generally shied away from identifying why it is inappropriate to punish in such circumstances beyond affirming that acts must be "voluntary". Instead, it has been left to academic lawyers and philosophers to explore what this means.

John Austin, Lectures on Jurisprudence (5th edn) (XVIII–XIX) Vol.I, 411–415:

"Certain movements of our bodies follow invariably and immediately our wishes and desires for those same movements. Provided, that is, that the bodily organ be sane, and the desired movement be not prevented by any outward obstacle . . . These antecedent wishes and these consequent movements, are human volitions and acts (strictly and properly so-called) . . . And as these are the only volitions, so are the bodily movements by which they are immediately followed the only acts or actions (properly so-called). It will be admitted on the mere statement, that the only objects which can be called acts are consequences of volitions. A voluntary movement of my body, or a movement which follows a volition, is an act. The *in*voluntary movements which (for example) are the consequences of certain diseases, are *not* acts."

We are asked, therefore, to divide the human act into two elements: the desire for the muscular movement and the movement itself. In the case of the defendant who kills another as a result of falling down some steps, there would be no accountability for the harm done because of the absence of a willed or desired muscular movement. However, this breakdown of human behaviour has been fiercely criticised. Hart points out that, described in these terms, it cannot apply to omissions (where to speak of the necessity for a willed failure to move one's muscles is not only clumsy but an inaccurate reflection of the law).[20] Furthermore, such an analysis does not reflect the reality of our movements.

H.L.A. Hart, Punishment and Responsibility (1968), pp.101–102:

"[A] desire to contract our muscles is a very rare occurrence: there are no doubt *some* special occasions when it would be quite right to say that what we are doing is contracting our muscles, and that we have a desire to do this. An example of this is what we may do under instruction in a gymnasium. The instructor says 'lift your right hand and contract the muscles of the upper arm.' If we succeed in doing this (and it is not so easy) it would be quite appropriate

---

[20]   H.L.A. Hart, *Punishment and Responsibility* (Oxford: OUP, 1968), p.100: "It is surely absurd even to attempt to fit omissions into such a picture of voluntary or involuntary conduct . . . [because] in the case of omissions no muscular movement or contraction need occur . . . [Such a theory] would have very unwelcome consequences for legal responsibility: for the only omissions which would then be culpable would be deliberate omissions. We could then only punish those who failed to stop at traffic lights if they deliberately shot the lights."

to say we desired to and did contract our muscles . . . [But] when we shut a door, or when we hit someone, or when we fire a gun at a bird, these things are done without any previous thought of the muscular movements involved and without any desire to contract the muscles . . . The simple but important truth is that when we deliberate and think about actions, we do so not in terms of muscular movements but in the ordinary terminology of actions."

Glanville Williams, The Mental Element in Crime (1965), pp.17–18:

"[O]ne cannot by introspection, identify a conscious exercise of will previous to movement. Indeed, one cannot always find an exercise of will at all. Many acts are performed unthinkingly; not only a reflex like dropping a hot poker but much of the routine of life, such as shaving, eating, walking. We seem to switch on an 'automatic pilot' for many of the familiar tasks we perform; yet we are undoubtedly acting. Even when we make a conscious decision and act to carry it out, the act is something different from the preceding deliberation."

In this statement Williams, in accordance with many commentators, tacitly upholds the distinction drawn in English law between mens rea and actus reus. But other critics of the willed movement principle do not. Welzel,[21] a German philosopher, argued that the causal theory upon which this principle, and much of the criminal law rests, is misconceived. He does not accept that there are a set of desires which *cause* the movements to occur. Instead, he favours a view of acting that looks to the actor's goal. The distinction between a bodily movement and an "act" lies not in any preceding will but in the purpose of the actor—what they were seeking to achieve. According to this philosophical stance, not only is it wrong to divide up the act, as Austin and his supporters do, but to divide any mental state from its act would be equally invalid. The two, he would claim, are inextricably linked and are incapable of separate analysis.

More representative of the standard approach is the view of Williams that:

"Notwithstanding these difficulties of definition everyone understands the proposition that an act is something more than bodily movement—for bodily movement might occur in tripping and falling, which would not be described as an act."[22]

Broad consensus does seem to exist that it would be unjust to punish in these situations, despite the harm done. Those who feel that the willed movement analysis is unhelpful argue that what is missing is an ability to control one's actions. In no real sense are the actions "his"[23] and, therefore, criminal liability is inappropriate. At this point, however, the consensus breaks down. Some commentators argue that involuntariness

"is best analysed as representing a spectrum or continuum of potentially excusing conditions running from total incapacitation or involuntariness, as in sleep-walking or muscular spasm, to cases say of (concussion-induced) confusion. These conditions are all reducible to an absence of fault and therefore, . . . share the same underlying rationale of other excusing conditions such as duress, provocation and diminished responsibility."[24]

---

[21] For a discussion of Welzel's view, see G.P. Fletcher, *Rethinking Criminal Law* (Boston: Little Brown, 1978), pp.434–439.

[22] G. Williams, *The Mental Element in Crime* (Jerusalem: Magnes Press, 1965), p.18.

[23] This is not, as Packer says, to "be read as plunging into the deep waters of free will vs determinism . . . The law is not affirming that some conduct is the product of the free exercise of conscious volition; it is excluding, in a crude kind of way, conduct that in any view is not" (*The Limits of the Criminal Sanction* (California: Stanford University Press, 1969), p.76).

[24] K.J.M. Smith and W. Wilson, "Impaired Voluntariness and Criminal Responsibility: Reworking Hart's Theory of Excuses—The English Judicial Response" (1993) 13 O.J.L.S. 69 at 74.

In short, a person whose actions are classified as involuntary can be afforded a type of defence called an *excuse* and can be exempted from criminal liability. The essence of an excuse is that the actor is blameless. If it were the actor's own fault that the involuntary conduct occurred, the law will not excuse that conduct. If the reason that the person fell down the stairs was that they were extremely drunk, we are entitled to say that carrying a loaded gun in that state of intoxication is culpable conduct and, accordingly, the resultant death or injury ought not to be excused.

Other commentators, however, argue that in cases of involuntary conduct the absence of "the ordinary link between mind and behaviour",[25] is more fundamental than that involved when, for example, duress is pleaded. The defendant who shoots another because there is a gun pointed at their partner's head accepts that they have done it, but pleads that they lacked any real opportunity to do otherwise. The defendant who shoots another as a result of falling down steps denies authorship. There is a complete denial of basic responsibility and the defendant is afforded an *exemption*.[26] The defendant has done no wrong; there is nothing to excuse.[27]

Whatever the theoretical basis of the exemption from liability, the law has tended to describe these cases of involuntariness as involving a defence of *automatism*. The precise nature and effect of this defence depends on a variety of circumstances surrounding the involuntary conduct. Accordingly, detailed consideration of this exemption from liability based on involuntariness is best left to Ch.4 where defences are considered.

(ii) Status offences

The requirement that there must be an act and that this involves voluntary human conduct has caused particular problems in the context of what are known as "status offences" or "situational liability".

A crime can be defined in such a manner that no conduct is required, but the crime is committed when a certain state of affairs exists or the defendant is in a certain condition or is of a particular status. The following notorious case is a classic example of this.

R. v Larsonneur (1933) 24 Cr. App. R. 74 (Court of Criminal Appeal)

A French subject was permitted to land in the United Kingdom subject to certain conditions endorsed on her passport. These conditions were subsequently varied by a condition requiring her to depart from the United Kingdom not later than a certain date. On that date she went to the Irish Free State. An order for her deportation from the Irish Free State was made by the executive authorities of that country, and she was subsequently brought back to Holyhead in the custody of the Irish Free State police, who there handed her over to the police of the United Kingdom, by whom she was detained. She was convicted on a charge that she "being an alien to whom leave to land in the United Kingdom has been refused was found in the United Kingdom", contrary to arts 1(3)(g) and 18(1)(b) of the Aliens Order 1920. She appealed against her conviction.

MARSTON GARSIA, FOR THE APPELLANT:

"For an alien to whom leave to land has been refused to commit an offence under Art. 18(1) (b) of the Order three elements are necessary:

---

[25]   A. Ashworth and J. Horder, *Principles of Criminal Law*, 7th edn (Oxford: OUP, 2013), p.86.

[26]   J. Gardner, "The Gist of Excuses" [1998] 1 Buff. Crim. L.R. 575.

[27]   For a discussion of the importance of the distinction between exemptions and excuses, see C.M.V. Clarkson, *Understanding Criminal Law*, 4th edn (London: Sweet & Maxwell, 2005), pp.81–82 where it is suggested that it might be helpful to regard the former as "status excuses" and the latter as "non-status excuses".

i. the alien must land in the United Kingdom;

ii. such landing must be contrary to Art. 1 of the Order;

iii. the alien, having so landed in the United Kingdom, must be found therein.

Therefore the mere fact of being found in the United Kingdom after the time limited for her departure therefrom had expired was not in itself an offence, unless it could be proved in addition that she landed in the United Kingdom in contravention of Art. 1. Here the evidence showed that she had not landed at all, but that she had been landed by a superior force over which she had no control. Having thus come to be found in the United Kingdom, she was not guilty of any offence under Art. 18(1) (b)."

J. F. EASTWOOD, FOR THE CROWN:

"The whole point is whether the appellant was found within the United Kingdom; how she got here makes no difference at all. The word 'found' was used deliberately in the section so that if any alien who had no right to be here is here an offence is committed. By reason of Art. 1(4) of the Order she falls within the same category as one who had originally been prohibited from landing."

HEWART, LCJ:

"[T]he appellant is an alien. She has a French passport, which bears [a] statement . . . [requiring] 'departure from the United Kingdom not later than March 22, 1933.' . . . In fact, the appellant went to the Irish Free State and afterwards, in circumstances which are perfectly immaterial, so far as this appeal is concerned, came back to Holyhead. She was at Holyhead on April 21, 1933, a date after the day limited by the condition on her passport.
    In these circumstances, it seems to be quite clear that Art. 1(4) of the Aliens Order, 1920 . . . applies. The article is in the following terms:

'. . . An alien who fails to comply with any conditions so attached or varied, and an alien who is found in the United Kingdom at any time after the expiration of the period limited by any such conditions, shall for the purposes of this Order be deemed to be an alien to whom leave to land has been refused.'

The appellant was, therefore, on April 21, 1933, in the position in which she would have been if she had been prohibited from landing by the Secretary of State and, that being so, there is no reason to interfere with the finding of the jury. She was found here and was, therefore, deemed to be in the class of persons whose landing had been prohibited by the Secretary of State, by reason of the fact that she had violated the condition on her passport. The appeal, therefore, is dismissed and the recommendation for deportation remains."

Appeal dismissed

What is objectionable about convictions for status offences such as that in *Larsonneur* is that the defendant's actions are involuntary. There is nothing objectionable about the offence per se in *Larsonneur* and had Larsonneur brought herself voluntarily into the United Kingdom her conviction would have aroused no comment. It was the involuntary nature of her forced entry that provoked the controversy. In short, status offences are not objectionable if the defendant has control over the status. It would be wrong to have an offence of having a common cold but, as Husak argues, it could be justifiable to have an offence of having a beard, as this is a process over which one has control.[28] Under s.11(1) of the Terrorism Act 2000 it is a criminal offence to belong to a proscribed organisation such as Al-Qa'ida. This provision is not aimed merely at prohibiting the "act" of joining Al-Qa'ida; it applies equally to those who joined before the date of commencement of the Act. This looks as though it is punishing persons for the mere status of being members of Al-Qa'ida. However, s.11(2) provides

---

[28] D. Husak, *Philosophy of Criminal Law* (Oxford: OUP, 1987), p.102. Similarly, while it would be contrary to principle to make it an offence to be H.I.V. positive, it could be permissible to make it an offence to have sexual intercourse while H.I.V. positive.

a defence if one became a member before the organisation was proscribed and if one has not taken part in any of its activities while the organisation is proscribed. Thus, what is being punished in reality is a status over which there is control—evidenced by action (i.e. either joining Al-Qa'ida after the date of commencement of the Act or, if one joined before then, taking part in its activities).

Douglas Husak, "Does Criminal Liability Require An Act" in Antony Duff (ed.), Philosophy and the Criminal Law (1998), pp.75, 77–79:

"[P]ersons typically have *control* over their choices, and persons are responsible and deserve punishment only for those states of affairs over which they exercise control. I submit that the absence of control, and not the absence of action, establishes the outer boundary of deserved punishment and responsibility. I claim, in other words, that what I will call the *control requirement* should be substituted for the act requirement as a necessary condition of criminal liability and deserved punishment . . . The core idea behind the control requirement is that a person lacks responsibility for those states of affairs he or she is unable to prevent from taking place or obtaining. If the state of affairs for which he is responsible is an action, he must have been able not to perform that action. If the state of affairs is a status, he must have been able not to have that status . . . I propose to explicate control in terms of what it is reasonable to expect of persons. A person lacks control over a state of affairs and neither is nor ought to be criminally liable for it if it is unreasonable to expect him or her to have prevented that state of affairs from obtaining . . .

[T]he issue of whether an agent has control over a state of affairs admits of degrees . . . and one person may have more control over the same kind of state of affairs than another person . . . [L]ess control is needed before responsibility is imposed for an especially bad state of affairs than for a not-so-bad state of affairs."

Following this reasoning, status offences are only unjustifiable if the person had no control over their status. However, as seen earlier when examining involuntary conduct, the general requirement of voluntariness can be dispensed with if it was the defendant's own fault that their actions were involuntary, for example, if they chose to get very drunk. So, too, liability for a status offence becomes justifiable if it was the defendant's own fault they got into that status or were in that situation. It has even been argued that the decision in *Larsonneur* was justifiable because it was her own fault that she was in the situation of being an illegal immigrant.

David Lanham, "Larsonneur Revisited" [1976] Crim. L.R. 276 at 278–280:

"[The defence of physical compulsion is] not an absolute defence. It may, at least with regard to certain types of crime, be defeated if the defendant has been at fault in bringing about the situation which has exposed him to compulsion . . . It is the thesis of this paper that Miss Larsonneur was probably the author of her own misfortune and that the fact that at the last moment she was acting under compulsion was properly regarded as affording her no defence . . . Miss Larsonneur's recorded confession is worth quoting: . . .

'A short time ago my sister Mrs McCorry came to see me in France and invited me to visit her in London. On my arrival my sister introduced me to a Frenchman named René, who was living with her, and also introduced me to an Englishman named Harold Brown. René and Brown said they would arrange a marriage for me with an Englishman and they later introduced me to a man named George Drayton. We tried to get married at Guildford but the police stopped the marriage. They took my French passport from me but returned it the same day, telling me that the Home Office had ordered me to leave the country at once. Brown and René told me not to worry as they were going to get legal advice.

Next day I went to Ireland with Brown. We travelled as Mr & Mrs Wiggins. Brown said he had seen a solicitor, and that if I went to Ireland I would be in order. I naturally believed him. René and Drayton also travelled to Ireland, but not with us. There were difficulties in Ireland about marrying and eventually the police told me to leave Ireland by April 17. I wanted to leave Ireland at once, but René and Brown told me that everything would be alright (*sic*.), and that they were trying to find an Irish priest willing to marry us. I think it terrible that I should be the only one to suffer.'"

It is difficult to see that this justifies the decision in *Larsonneur*. What is meant by the defendant being "at fault"? Surely the fault must be related in some way to the offence charged. In our earlier example of the drunken person carrying a gun and falling down the stairs, it is legitimate to assert that the ensuing results were the fault of the defendant. The fault of getting drunk while in possession of a gun and any offence committed with that gun are clearly connected. Trying to go through a marriage of convenience (not an unlawful act) is not connected in the same way to the offence committed by Larsonneur.

Winzar v Chief Constable of Kent, The Times, March 28, 1983, Co/1111/82 (Lexis) (Queen's Bench Divisional Court)

The defendant was brought on a stretcher to hospital. The doctor discovered that he was merely drunk and asked him to leave. He was later seen slumped on a seat in the corridor and so the police were called. They removed him to the roadway, "formed the opinion he was drunk", and placed him in their car parked nearby. He was charged with being found drunk in a highway and convicted.

ROBERT GOFF LJ:

"Does the fact that the Appellant was only momentarily on the highway and not there of his own volition, prevent his conviction of the offence of being found drunk in a highway?. . .

In my judgment, looking at the purpose of this particular offence, it is designed . . . to deal with the nuisance which can be caused by persons who are drunk in a public place. This kind of offence is caused quite simply when a person is found drunk in a public place or in a highway . . . [A]n example . . . illustrates how sensible that conclusion is. Suppose a person was found as being drunk in a restaurant or a place of that kind and was asked to leave. If he was asked to leave, he would walk out of the door of the restaurant and would be in a public place or in a highway of his own volition. He would be there of his own volition because he had responded to a request. However, if a man in a restaurant made a thorough nuisance of himself, was asked to leave, objected and was ejected, in those circumstances, he would not be in a public place of his own volition because he would have been put there either by a gentleman on the door of the restaurant, or by a police officer, who might have been called to deal with the man in question. It would be nonsense if one were to say that the man who responded to the plea to leave could be said to be found drunk in a public place or in a highway, whereas the man who had been compelled to leave could not.

This leads me to the conclusion that a person is 'found to be drunk in a public place or in a highway,' within the meaning of those words as used in the section, when he is perceived to be drunk in a public place. It is enough for the commission of the offence if (1) a person is in a public place or a highway, (2) he is drunk, and (3) in those circumstances he is perceived to be there and to be drunk. Once those criteria have been fulfilled, he is liable to be convicted of the offence of being found drunk in a highway. Finally, I turn to the question: Does it matter if the Appellant was only momentarily in the highway? In my judgment, it makes no difference. A man may be perceived to be drunk in the highway for five minutes, for one minute or for ten seconds. However short the period of time, if a man is perceived to be drunk in a highway, he is guilty of the offence under the section. Of course, if the period of time is very short, the penalty imposed may be minimal; indeed in such circumstances a police officer, using his discretion, may think it unnecessary to charge the man. The point is simply that the offence is committed if a person is perceived to be drunk in a public place or in the highway. Once that criterion is fulfilled, then the offence is committed."

Conviction affirmed

Again it could be argued that it was Winzar's "fault" he was in that situation. The report does not make it clear how he got to be taken to the hospital. Presumably he must have been found drunk in some other public place, or have summoned medical assistance when he was only drunk and not in need of medical attention.

A different approach to a similar problem was adopted by the Supreme Court of Alabama.

Martin v State, 31 Ala. App. 334, 17 So. 2d 427 (1944) (Alabama Court of Appeals)

SIMPSON J:

"Appellant was convicted of being drunk on a public highway, and appeals. Officers of the law arrested him at his home and took him onto the highway where he allegedly committed the proscribed acts, viz. manifested a drunken condition by using loud and profane language. The pertinent provisions of our statute are:

'Any person who, while intoxicated or drunk, appears in any public place where one or more persons are present, . . . and manifests a drunken condition by boisterous or indecent conduct, or loud and profane discourse, shall, on conviction be fined' (Code 1940, Title 14, Section 120).

Under the plain terms of this statute a voluntary appearance is presupposed. The rule has been declared, and we think it sound, that an accusation of drunkenness in a designated public place cannot be established by proof that the accused, while in an intoxicated condition, was involuntarily and forcibly carried to that place by the arresting officer.

Conviction of appellant was contrary to this announced principle and in our view, erroneous. It appears that no legal conviction can be sustained under the evidence, so, consonant with the prevailing rule, the judgment of the trial court is reversed and one here rendered discharging appellant."[29]

Can this case be reconciled with *Larsonneur* and *Winzar* on the basis that Martin was arrested in his own home and therefore could not in any way be blamed for his resultant situation?

Herbert L. Packer, The Limits of the Criminal Sanction (1969), pp.78–79:

"There is a strong tradition in Anglo-American law of treating certain kinds of status, such as vagrancy, as criminal. To be a person 'without visible means of living who has the physical ability to work, and who does not seek employment, nor labor when employment is offered him' (in the words of a now-repealed California statute) may perhaps be characterized as engaging in a kind of omissive conduct: but common sense rebels at the use of the word 'conduct' to describe a condition that does not 'take place' but rather exists without reference to discrete points of time. It must be acknowledged that when the law makes the status of vagrancy or the status of 'being a common drunkard' (that phrase redolent of Elizabethan England) a criminal offense, it is departing from the restriction to conduct. Laws of this sort are in fact very much on the way out. Courts are giving them a helpful push on the road to oblivion . . .

Offenses of status can best be understood as embodiments of the preventive ideal at a time when the criminal law offered no alternatives. Their demise is the result, whatever the rubric under which it is accomplished, of the development of alternatives that have permitted us the previously unavailable luxury of recognizing that such offenses are anomalies in the criminal law. There has always been pressure to rid the community of people who are perceived as dangerous, threatening, or merely odd. That pressure, until fairly recently, has had to find its outlet almost entirely in the criminal law. But the extraordinary expansion of the concept of illness, and especially of mental illness, that has taken place during the last century has furnished us another set of outlets. Now we can afford to insist on the doctrinal purity from which crimes of status represent so marked a lapse."

It has been argued that status offences could be regarded as contrary to art.6(1) of the ECHR.[30] The best approach would be to focus on the voluntariness of the defendant's actions. On this basis the question is simply whether Larsonneur, Winzar and Martin had control over their status or, even if they did not, whether it was their own fault that they allowed themselves to get into that status. It is only this approach that is likely to be regarded as compatible with the ECHR.

---

[29]   See also *O'Sullivan v Fisher* [1954] S.A.S.R. 33 (S. Aust.); *Achterdam* (1911) E.D.L. 336 (S.A.).

[30]   G.R. Sullivan, "Strict Liability for Criminal Offences in England and Wales Following Incorporation into English Law of the European Convention on Human Rights", in A.P. Simester (ed.), *Appraising Strict Liability* (New York: OUP, 2005), p.208.

R. v Robinson-Pierre [2013] EWCA Crim 2396 (Court of Appeal, Criminal Division)

Police arrived at the defendant's house with a search warrant and without prior warning broke open the front door of the house, after which the defendant's dog attacked the officers, both inside and later outside the house. The defendant was convicted of being the owner of a dog which caused injury while dangerously out of control in a public place, contrary to s.3(1) and (4) Dangerous Dogs Act 1991. He appealed against his conviction on the basis that the offence does not allow conviction of an owner who did not by his act or omission cause the dog to be in a public place or cause the dog to become dangerously out of control.

PITCHFORD LJ:

"38. Professor Ormerod recognises . . . a category of offences in which the *actus reus* is represented by a state of affairs. In such a case there is no act or omission by, or state of mind of, the defendant that must be established, merely the existence of the prohibited state of affairs . . . Professor Ormerod concludes that:

'As a matter of principle, even "state of affairs" offences ought to require proof that D either caused the state of affairs or failed to terminate it or to act in order to do so when it was within his control and possible to do so.'

This is a view that will have many supporters. However, we have no doubt that the supremacy of Parliament embraces the power to create 'state of affairs' offences in which no causative link between the prohibited state of affairs and the defendant need be established. The legal issue is not, in our view, whether in principle such offences can be created but whether in any particular enactment Parliament intended to create one.

. . .

42. On analysis of section 3, we do not consider that it was Parliament's intention to create an offence without regard to the ability of the owner (or someone to whom he had entrusted responsibility) to take and keep control of the dog. There must, in our view, be some causal connection between having charge of the dog and the prohibited state of affairs that has arisen. In our view, section 3 (1) requires proof by the prosecution of an act or omission of the defendant (with or without fault) that to some (more than minimal) degree caused or permitted the prohibited state of affairs to come about.

. . .

46. It seems to us that had the jury been directed to consider whether any act or omission of the appellant had made a more than minimal contribution to the presence of the dog in a public place, dangerously out of control, it is likely they would have concluded that he did by his failure to make any attempt after its escape to take the dog under his control before it entered a public place. However, the learned judge . . . did not direct the jury to consider the issue. . . In these circumstances the appellant . . . was not given the opportunity to meet an assertion that by his act or omission after the escape from the house he caused or contributed to the prohibited state of affairs. We cannot in these circumstances be sure that the verdicts of the jury were safe."

Appeal allowed

In this case the Court of Appeal, whilst finding that the offence of being the owner of a dangerous dog did in fact require an act or omission on the part of the dog owner in contributing to the state of affairs of the dog being out of control in public place, came to that conclusion not on the grounds of principle, but through an analysis of the statute. The implication is that if Parliament chooses to word an offence in such a way as to make a defendant liable irrespective of his control, or lack thereof, over the situation, it is free to do so. On principled grounds, that cannot be right.

(iii) Omissions

Most crimes are committed by positive action and thus the requirement of an "act" will usually be met by a positive act. However, in certain circumstances a failure to act may be deemed to constitute the requisite "act". A failure to act may result in the imposition of criminal liability in two situations.

1. In conduct crimes the failure to act may itself, without more, constitute the crime. This usually occurs in statutory crimes which are specifically defined in terms of an omission to act, for example, failing to provide for a child in one's care[31] or failing to provide a specimen of breath under the breathalyser legislation.[32]

2. In result crimes the failure to act may contribute towards the harm specified in the offence and may thus, in certain circumstances, be deemed the requisite "act" for the purposes of the offence. This will only be so if the actor is under a duty to act. For example, a father would be under a duty to rescue his child drowning in a shallow pool; his failure to act would constitute the requisite "act" of the crime of homicide. However, a stranger could with impunity watch the same child drowning. There is no general duty to act in English law. As Lord Diplock stated in *Miller*: "The conduct of the parabolical priest and Levite on the road to Jericho may have been indeed deplorable, but English law has not so far developed to the stage of treating it as criminal."[33]

Thus criminal liability in these cases is completely dependent upon the existence of a duty to act. It is to this, and other related problems, that we now turn.

(a) *Duty to act*

Whether there is a duty to act is a question of law. The judge must direct the jury that if they find certain facts established, there will or will not be a duty to act. For example, in *Evans* (below) the victim was supplied with heroin (by her half-sister) which she self-injected and died of heroin poisoning. It was a matter of fact for the jury whether it was the defendant who supplied the drugs. If the jury were satisfied that she did supply the drugs, then, as a matter of law, she was under a duty to act.

R. v Evans [2009] 2 Cr. App. R. 10 (Court of Appeal, Criminal Division)

Lord Judge CJ:

"45. In some cases, such as those arising from a doctor/patient relationship where the existence of the duty is not in dispute, the judge may well direct the jury that a duty of care exists. Such a direction would be proper. But if, for example, the doctor were on holiday at the material time, and the deceased asked a casual question over a drink, it may well be that the question whether a doctor/patient relationship existed, and accordingly whether a duty of care arose, would be in dispute. In any cases where the issue is in dispute, and therefore in more complex cases, and assuming that the judge has found that it would be open to the jury to find that there was a duty of care, or a duty to act, the jury should be directed that if facts a + b and/or c or d are established, then in law a duty will arise, but if facts x or y or z were present, the duty would be negatived."

---

[31]   Children and Young Persons Act 1933 s.1(2)(a).
[32]   Road Traffic Act 1988 s.6(4).
[33]   *R. v Miller (James)* [1983] 2 A.C. 161 at 175.

It is not entirely certain when a duty to act will arise.[34] However, it is generally thought that the following situations, while their parameters are not clearly defined, will give rise to a duty to act.

1. Special relationship

This special relationship may be professional or familial. A doctor owes a duty to their patients. There may also be a duty to act where there is a close family relationship. Parents are under a duty to aid their small children; husbands and wives are under a duty to aid each other.[35]

In *Downes*[36] a parent, being a member of a religious sect called the Peculiar People, who believed in prayer rather than in medicine, failed to call a doctor for his sick child who died. Downes was convicted of manslaughter.[37] It is not entirely certain what relationships possess the "features of familial duty or responsibility".[38] In *Evans* it was held that while a mother owed such a duty to her nearly 17-year-old daughter, no such duty was owed by the daughter's half-sister.[39]

It used to be asserted that the reason for the imposition of a duty of care in such cases was that the blood or marriage relationship was so strong as to generate a legal duty to preserve life. In the United States decision of *People v Beardsley*,[40] for instance, it was held that a man owes no duty to act to aid his "week-end mistress", as distinguished from his wife. However, such a rationale can no longer be accepted. The true reason for the existence of a duty in such cases must be the interdependence that springs from shared family life or close communal living.[41] In such a situation one comes to rely on the other members of the family and it is this reliance and expectation of assistance, if necessary, that generates the duty to act, rather than any blood or marriage tie. In *Shepherd*[42] it was held that no duty to act is owed by a parent to her 18-year-old "entirely emancipated" daughter. In such a case there would not be the same expectation of assistance as with a dependent child. Accordingly, it is suggested that separated spouses owe no duty to each other, and with other relatives it is not a question of blood or marriage relationship but the assumption of responsibility that generates the reliance and expectation of assistance and hence the legal duty to act. In *Stone*, Lane LJ did allude to the fact that the victim "was a blood relation of the appellant" but it is clear from his ensuing comments that the true basis of the duty to act was the fact that the appellant had taken the victim into his home and assumed responsibility for her.[43]

2. Assumption of responsibility

If the defendant assumes responsibility towards another or voluntarily assumes a duty towards another, then they become under a legal duty to act.

---

34   The first draft of the Criminal Code Bill specified the circumstances in which one would be under a duty to act (cl.20(2)). These detailed proposals were dropped from the revised Draft Criminal Code; they were regarded as matters that should remain for the development of the common law (Law Com. No.77, Vol.2, para.7.12). The Draft Criminal Law Bill 1993 cl.19, follows this latter approach (Law Com. No.218, *Legislating the Criminal Code: Offences against the Person and General Principles*, Cmnd.2370 (1993)).

35   *R. v Smith* [1979] Crim. L.R. 251; *R. v Hood (Kenneth)* [2004] 1 Cr. App. R.(S.) 73.

36   *Downes* (1875) 13 Cox C.C. 111.

37   In this case and in *Shepherd* (fn.42 below) it was indicated that the duty was imposed by statute (Poor Law Amendment Act 1868 s.37). In *Downes*, Coleridge CJ deliberately left open the question of whether there would be a duty to act in the absence of such a statutory duty. While many of the earlier cases were decided on this basis, it is now generally accepted that there is a *common law* duty to act in such cases but there is little express authority on this point.

38   *R. v Evans (Gemma)* [2009] 2 Cr. App. R. 10 at [20].

39   *Evans* [2009] 2 Cr. App. R. 10 at [20], [34].

40   *People v Beardsley* 150 Mich. 206; 113 N.W. 1128; 13 L.R.A.(N.S.) 1020; 121 Am. St. Rep. 617; 13 Ann. Cas. 39 (1907). This case was cited with approval in England in *Sinclair* [1998] EWCA Crim 2590.

41   G.P. Fletcher, *Rethinking Criminal Law* (Boston: Little Brown, 1978), p.613.

42   *Shepherd* (1862) 9 Cox C.C. 123.

43   *R. v Stone (John Edward)* [1977] Q.B. 354.

R. v Instan [1893] 1 Q.B. 450 (Court for Crown Cases Reserved)

The defendant lived with her 73-year-old aunt. The aunt, who had been healthy until shortly before her death, developed gangrene in her leg. During the last 12 days of her life she could not fend for herself, move about or summon help. Only the defendant knew of her state and gave her aunt no food and did not seek medical assistance. The defendant was charged with manslaughter and was convicted.

LORD COLERIDGE CJ:

"We are all of the opinion that this conviction must be affirmed. It would not be correct to say that every moral obligation involves a legal duty; but every legal duty is founded on a moral obligation. A legal common law duty is nothing else than the enforcing by law of that which is a moral obligation without legal enforcement. There can be no question in this case that it was the clear duty of the prisoner to impart to the deceased so much as was necessary to sustain life of the food which she from time to time took in, and which was paid for by the deceased's own money for the purpose of the maintenance of herself and the prisoner; it was only through the instrumentality of the prisoner that the deceased could get the food. There was, therefore, a common law duty imposed upon the prisoner which she did not discharge.

Nor can there be any question that the failure of the prisoner to discharge her legal duty at least accelerated the death of the deceased, if it did not actually cause it. There is no case directly in point; but it would be a slur upon and a discredit to the administration of justice in this country if there were any doubt as to the legal principle, or as to the present case being within it. The prisoner was under a moral obligation to the deceased from which arose a legal duty towards her; that legal duty the prisoner has wilfully and deliberately left unperformed, with the consequence that there has been an acceleration of the death of the deceased owing to the non-performance of that legal duty."

Conviction affirmed

In *Stone*[44] the defendants took the anorexic and infirm sister of one of them into their home. She failed to look after herself or feed herself properly and eventually died. The defendants were held to have assumed a responsibility by taking her into their home and so were under a legal duty either to summon help or to care for her.

R. v Sinclair [1998] EWCA Crim 2590 (Court of Appeal, Criminal Division)

Sinclair and his friend, the deceased, visited a flat owned by Johnson in order to buy methadone from another man there. Needles and syringes were available in the flat. Sinclair and the deceased each injected themselves with the methadone at 14.30. The deceased became unconscious. Sinclair remained with him for much the afternoon and night. Both he and Johnson took limited and ineffectual remedial action such as pouring water over the deceased (and Johnson administered a saline solution) but an ambulance was only called at 06.30 the following morning. The deceased was certified dead on arrival at hospital. Sinclair and Johnson were convicted of manslaughter and appealed.

ROSE LJ:

"[Counsel for the defendant] referred to a decision of the New South Wales Supreme Court in *Tak Tak* 1988 NSWLR 226 which emphasised, as a pre-condition for a legal duty of care to arise, the need for the disabled person to be secluded by the defendant to prevent others from affording aid . . .

So far as Johnson is concerned, there is no English authority in which a duty of care has been held to arise, over a period of hours, on the part of a medically unqualified stranger. *Beardsley* and *Tak Tak* are both persuasive authorities pointing away from the existence of any such duty, although we do not accept in the light of *Stone*

---

44   *R. v Stone (John Edward)* [1977] Q.B. 354. An extract from this case can be found at pp.105–106.

and *Dobinson*, that the concept of seclusion is, in English law, a necessary prerequisite to the existence of a legal duty of care. But Johnson did not know the deceased. His only connection with him was that he had come to his house and there taken methadone and remained until he died. Others were coming and going in the meantime. The fact that Johnson had prepared and administered to the deceased saline solutions does not, as it seems to us, demonstrate on his part a voluntary assumption of a legal duty of care rather than a desultory attempt to be of assistance. In our judgment, the facts in relation to Johnson were not capable of giving rise to a legal duty of care . . .

Sinclair was in a different position. The evidence was that he was a close friend of the deceased for many years and the two had lived together almost as brothers. It was Sinclair who paid for and supplied the deceased with the first dose of methadone and helped him to obtain the second dose. He knew that the deceased was not an addict. He remained with the deceased throughout the period of his unconsciousness and, for a substantial period, was the only person with him. In the light of this evidence, there was in our judgment material on which the jury properly directed, could have found that Sinclair owed the deceased a legal duty of care.

[The appeal was, however, allowed on the ground that a fuller direction on causation should have been given: as to whether acceleration of the moment of death was other than minimal.]"

Appeal allowed

This case was cited with approval in *Ruffell*.[45] The appellant and the deceased took drugs together which led to the death of the latter. The Court of Appeal approved the trial judge's reasoning that there was a sufficient nexus between the parties to give rise to a duty of care because

"the deceased was a guest of the appellant in the appellant's family home and he was a friend . . . that had taken upon himself the duty of trying to revive him."

In *Evans* (where the deceased died of heroin poisoning) it was held that merely placing her in a recovery position, putting her to bed and taking turns to check if she was alright would not be sufficient to amount to an assumption of responsibility.[46] However, it was added that in certain circumstances there could be a voluntary assumption of responsibility where the defendant does acts which "led the victim, or others, to become dependent on him to act".[47]

Geoffrey Mead, "Contracting into Crime: A Theory of Criminal Omissions" (1991) 11 O.J.L.S. 147 at 168:

"The presence of an undertaking often gives rise to other reasons for the presence of a duty . . . If D has given an undertaking he may be in the best position to avert the harm. I shall refer to this as the 'Best Position' argument. This may be for one or more of the following reasons. First, he is more likely to be aware that a person may be in a position of peril and in need of assistance. He will know of the vulnerability of the victim in a way that others may not. Second, he may be more capable of carrying out the required task than will a third party. We might assume that, in most cases where D undertakes to do a particular thing, he feels he has the ability to do it, whereas a third party, who has not given such an undertaking will not necessarily possess the required skills to do what is needed in order to avert danger to V. The third point is that if other people are aware of the undertaking they might feel it unproductive for them to get involved as well. They might reasonably think that they would simply get in the way and hinder the proper completion of the task in question."

The real problem in these cases is one of determining the circumstances in which a person can be said to have undertaken a duty towards another. A ship captain would be liable for failing to pick up a seaman,

---

45   *R. v Ruffell (Stephen David)* [2003] 2 Cr. App. R. (S.) 53.
46   *Evans* [2009] 2 Cr. App. R. 10 at [34], [35].
47   *Evans* [2009] 2 Cr. App. R. 10 at [36].

or a passenger, who had fallen overboard.[48] Depending on the circumstances of employment, an employer could be liable for failing to aid their endangered employee. And as LaFave and Scott assert:

> "If two mountain climbers, climbing together, are off by themselves on a mountainside, and one falls into a crevass, it would seem that the nature of their joint enterprise, involving a relationship of mutual reliance, ought to impose a duty upon the one mountaineer to extricate his imperilled colleague. So also if two people, though not closely related, live together under one roof, one may have a duty to act to aid the other who becomes helpless."[49]

Following this, in *Beardsley* if the parties had lived together or embarked on a dangerous joint enterprise together, as opposed to an adulterous weekend, the defendant would probably have been held to have assumed a duty to act. Again, as suggested before, it ought to be a question of whether, because of the relationship or the circumstances or both together, the parties rely on assistance from each other. *Sinclair* is explicable on this basis. While Johnson was effectively in as good a position as Sinclair to render aid (following Mead's Best Position argument), it was the closeness of the relationship between Sinclair and the deceased and their embarking on the enterprise of procuring drugs together that would have led the deceased to rely on assistance from Sinclair. Although at his house, Johnson was a stranger. There would not have been the same reliance on, and expectation of, assistance from him.

3. Contractual duty

A duty to assist others may arise out of a contract. A lifeguard employed at a swimming pool to ensure the safety of swimmers cannot sit idly by while a swimmer is drowning.

In *Pittwood*[50] a railway gate-keeper, who was employed to keep a gate shut whenever a train was passing, was held liable for manslaughter when he forgot to shut the gate with the result that a train hit a hay-cart crossing the railway line and killed a man.

Again, the basis of the duty in these cases is not so much the contract itself, but rather the fact that the contract is evidence of an assumption of responsibility creating an expectation in the mind of others that the defendant will act. The public expect railway gate-keepers to act and close the gates of railway crossings when trains are approaching. It is their reliance on this fact that creates the duty to act. The fact that the railway gate-keeper has been contracted to perform these duties is merely strong evidence that they have assumed these responsibilities. It is submitted that the position would be no different if, during a strike, a volunteer offered (without any contract) to perform these duties. The fact that they had undertaken this responsibility would cause the public to rely upon them performing these tasks. On this basis, this whole category (along with the first category above) simply becomes a species of the second category, namely the assumption of responsibility.

4. Statutory duty

A failure to act may in itself, without more, constitute a criminal offence. Failing to provide for a child in one's care is a criminal offence contrary to s.1(1) of the Children and Young Persons Act 1933, even if this failure to act causes no further harm. Similarly, ss.2–7 of the Health and Safety at Work, etc. Act 1974 impose duties on employers to operate a safe working environment. A specific penalty is provided for breach of this duty irrespective of whether any other harm results.

---

[48]   *US v Knowles*, 26 Fed. Cas. 800 (N.D. Cal. 1864).
[49]   W.R. Lafare and A.W. Scott, *Criminal Law*, 2nd edn (Eagan: West Group, 1986), p.204.
[50]   *R. v Pittwood (Philip)* (1902) 19 T.L.R. 37.

However, unlike breaches of common law duties, a breach of a statutory duty will not always constitute the necessary "act" for the purpose of an ulterior offence if further harm results from the breach of duty. In *Lowe*,[51] a man neglected his nine-week-old daughter by failing to call for a doctor when she became ill. He was charged with neglecting the child contrary to s.1(1) of the Children and Young Persons Act 1933 and with manslaughter. One way in which manslaughter can be committed is by committing an unlawful act that is dangerous and causes death (constructive manslaughter). It was held that the requirement of an unlawful act was not satisfied by an omission. Phillimore LJ stated:

"We think there is a clear distinction between an act of omission and an act of commission likely to cause harm. Whatever may be the position in regard to the latter it does not follow that the same is true of the former. In other words if I strike a child in a manner likely to cause harm it is right that if the child dies I may be charged with manslaughter. If, however, I omit to do something with the result that it suffers injury to health which results in its death, we think that a charge of manslaughter should not be an inevitable consequence, even if the omission is deliberate."

This case provides an interesting illustration of the reluctance of the English courts to impose criminal liability for omissions to act. Phillimore LJ is suggesting that there needs to be a higher degree of blameworthiness for crimes committed through omission than for crimes where there has been a positive act of commission and so an omission will not suffice for constructive manslaughter because this species of manslaughter[52] only requires a relatively low degree of culpability. Similarly, if a worker were to die as a result of an employer's breach of statutory duty the employer would not be liable for constructive manslaughter because, as the Law Commission has noted, Parliament, in creating this duty, has provided a specific and limited punishment for its breach.[53] This approach is only justifiable if positive acts are regarded as "worse" than omissions.[54]

5. Creation of a dangerous situation

R. v Miller [1983] 2 A.C. 161 (House of Lords)

One night while squatting in someone else's house, the appellant lit a cigarette and then lay down on a mattress in one of the rooms. He fell asleep before he had finished smoking the cigarette and it dropped onto the mattress. Later he woke up and saw that the mattress was smoldering. He did nothing about it; he merely moved to another room and went to sleep again. The house caught fire. The appellant was rescued and subsequently charged with arson, contrary to s.1(1) and (3) of the Criminal Damage Act 1971. At this trial he submitted that there was no case to go to the jury because his omission to put out the fire, which he had started accidentally, could not in the circumstances amount to a sufficient actus reus. The judge ruled that once he had discovered the mattress was smouldering the appellant had been under a duty to act. The appellant was convicted. The Court of Appeal upheld his conviction on the ground that his whole course of conduct constituted a continuous actus reus. On appeal, to the House of Lords:

---

[51] *Lowe* [1973] 1 Q.B. 702. An extract from this case can be found at p.710.
[52] The species of gross negligence manslaughter might be the more appropriate charge in such cases, however.
[53] Law Commission Consultation Paper No.122, *Legislating the Criminal Code: Offences against the Person and General Principles* (1992), para.6.19.
[54] See pp.103–104.

LORD DIPLOCK:

"I see no rational ground for excluding from conduct capable of giving rise to criminal liability, conduct which consists of failing to take measures that lie within one's power to counteract a danger that one has oneself created, if at the time of such conduct one's state of mind is such as constitutes a necessary ingredient of the offence . . .

I cannot see any good reason why, so far as liability under criminal law is concerned, it should matter at what point of time before the resultant damage is complete a person becomes aware that he has done a physical act which, whether or not he appreciated that it would at the time when he did it, does in fact create a risk that property of another will be damaged; provided that, at the moment of awareness, it lies within his power to take steps, either himself or by calling for the assistance of the fire brigade if this be necessary, to prevent or minimise the damage to the property at risk.

Let me take first the case of the person who has thrown away a lighted cigarette expecting it to go out harmlessly, but later becomes aware that, although he did not intend it to do so, it has, in the event, caused some inflammable material to smolder and that unless the smoldering is extinguished promptly, an act that the person who dropped the cigarette could perform without danger to himself or difficulty, the inflammable material will be likely to burst into flames and damage some other person's property. The person who dropped the cigarette deliberately refrains from doing anything to extinguish the smoldering. His reason for so refraining is that he intends that the risk which his own act had originally created, though it was only subsequently that he became aware of this, should fructify in actual damage to that other person's property; and what he so intends, in fact occurs. There can be no sensible reason why he should not be guilty of arson. If he would be guilty of arson, having appreciated the risk of damage at the very moment of dropping the lighted cigarette, it would be quite irrational that he should *not* be guilty if he first appreciated the risk at some later point in time but when it was still possible for him to take steps to prevent or minimise the damage . . .

The recorder, in his lucid summing up to the jury . . . told them that the accused having by his own act started a fire in the mattress which, when he became aware of its existence, presented an obvious risk of damaging the house, became under a duty to take some action to put it out. The Court of Appeal upheld the conviction, but its ratio decidendi appears to be somewhat different from that of the recorder. As I understand the judgment, in effect it treats the whole course of conduct of the accused, from the moment at which he fell asleep and dropped the cigarette on to the mattress until the time the damage to the house by fire was complete, as a continuous act of the accused, and holds that it is sufficient to constitute the statutory offence of arson if at any stage in that course of conduct the state of mind of the accused, when he fails to try to prevent or minimise the damage which will result from his initial act, although it lies within his power to do so, is that of being reckless whether property belonging to another would be damaged.

My Lords, these alternative ways of analysing the legal theory that justifies [the] decision . . . provoked academic controversy. Each theory has distinguished support. Professor J.C. Smith espouses the 'duty theory' (see [1982] Crim.L.R.526 at 528); Professor Glanville Williams . . . now prefers that of the continuous act (see [1982] Crim.L.R.773). When applied to cases where a person has unknowingly done an act which sets in train events that, when he becomes aware of them, present an obvious risk that property belonging to another will be damaged, both theories lead to an identical result; and since what your Lordships are concerned with is to give guidance to trial judges in their task of summing up to juries, I would for this purpose adopt the duty theory as being the easier to explain to a jury; though I would commend the use of the word 'responsibility,' rather than 'duty' which is more appropriate to civil than to criminal law, since it suggests an obligation owed to another person, i.e. the person to whom the endangered property belongs, whereas a criminal statute defines combinations of conduct and state of mind which render a person liable to punishment by the state itself . . .

[A] suitable direction to the jury would be: that the accused is guilty of the offence under s.1 (1) of the Criminal Damage Act 1971 if, when he does become aware that the events in question have happened as a result of his own act, he does not try to prevent or reduce the risk of damage by his own efforts or if necessary by sending for help from the fire brigade, and [if he has the appropriate *mens rea* at the time of failing to act]."

Appeal dismissed

Lord Diplock's reasoning is to be welcomed. We all bear a responsibility for our actions, even if those actions are unintentional. They are *our* actions. Where others are placed in danger from these actions, they expect us to "do something". They would rely on us to provide reasonable assistance, even if that only amounts to summoning help. Further, "the person who creates a danger may be more aware than others of the existence of the danger, and ought not feel a reluctance to intervene that may be felt by others".[55] Accordingly, we should be under a duty to act when we become aware of the danger. On this basis it is irrelevant whether the defendant's initial actions involved any fault. Thus if, as in *Fagan v MPC*,[56] the defendant accidentally parks his car with a wheel resting on a policeman's foot, we would surely be justified in saying that the defendant had assumed a responsibility (to get off the foot); his initial action would raise an expectation on the part of the police officer that he would act. He is under a duty to act.

It is, however, difficult to determine the precise circumstances in which a duty can be said to arise because of the creation of a "dangerous situation". In *DPP v Santana-Bermudez*[57] the defendant stated that he had no needles on him and was then searched by a police officer. The police officer put her fingers in the defendant's pocket and was pierced by a hypodermic needle. On a charge of assault occasioning actual bodily harm it was stated by the Court of Appeal that the defendant had created a dangerous situation by having the needles in his pocket and not telling the police officer they were there. This provided an evidential basis that he was under a duty and had breached that duty.

R. v Evans [2009] 2 Cr. App. R. 10 (Court of Appeal, Criminal Division)

The appellant, Gemma Evans, supplied her half-sister, Carly, with drugs. Carly became very ill. The appellant, knowing this, took ineffectual steps to care for her. Carly died from heroin poisoning. The appellant was convicted of manslaughter by gross negligence and appealed.

LORD JUDGE:

"20 The question in this appeal is not whether the appellant may be guilty of manslaughter for having been concerned in the supply of the heroin which caused the deceased's death. It is whether, notwithstanding that their relationship lacked the features of familial duty or responsibility which marked her mother's relationship with the deceased, she was under a duty to take reasonable steps for the safety of the deceased once she appreciated that the heroin she procured for her was having a potentially fatal impact on her health.

21 When omission or failure to act are in issue two aspects of manslaughter are engaged . . . The second arises when the defendant has created a dangerous situation and when, notwithstanding his appreciation of the consequent risks, he fails to take any reasonable preventative steps . . . [His Lordship then discussed *Miller* and other authorities, including the drug supply cases of *Khan* and *Sinclair*.]

31 . . . The duty necessary to found gross negligence manslaughter is plainly not confined to cases of a familial or professional relationship between the defendant and the deceased. In our judgment, . . . for the purposes of gross negligence manslaughter, when a person has created or contributed to the creation of a state of affairs which he knows, or ought reasonably to know, has become life threatening, a consequent duty on him to act by taking reasonable steps to save the other's life will normally arise . . .

34 The judge . . . directed the jury that they had heard that the appellant

'did perform some acts to assist Carly during the evening of 2nd May, in particular she and her mother placed Carly in the recovery position and they took turns to look to see if she was alright. However, I direct you that as a matter of law there is nothing in that course of conduct which is capable of amounting to an acceptance or an assumption by Gemma Evans of responsibility for Carly so as to give rise to a duty of care. In the present case, the only matter which in law is capable of giving rise to a duty of care owed by Gemma Evans to Carly Townsend would be if Gemma Evans did, on this occasion, as the prosecution allege, act as an intermediary, giving the drugs to Carly . . .'

35 In relation to the circumstances in which a duty of care might arise in this case, these observations must be seen in their context, which is that the only issue of fact which the jury had to decide was the supply issue. Unless

---

55   G. Meade, "Contracting into Crime: A Theory of Criminal Omissions" (1991) 11 O.J.L.S. 147 at 171.
56   [1969] 1 Q.B. 439. The actual reasoning adopted in this case was somewhat different to the proposal here: see pp.203–204.
57   *DPP v Santa-Bermudez* [2004] Crim. L.R. 471.

the jury was sure of this fact, the remaining undisputed areas of appellant's involvement . . . would, on the judge's directions, have been insufficient for the purposes of gross negligence manslaughter. Without her involvement in the supply of heroin, the jury was directed that there was no duty on the appellant to act even after she became aware of the serious adverse effect of the drug taking on Carly. If on the other hand she was so involved, that fact, taken with the other undisputed facts would, and on our analysis of the relevant principles did give rise to a duty on the appellant to act. In law the judge's directions about the ingredients of gross negligence manslaughter, as applied to this case, were correct.

36 We would merely record that the judge's direction that a duty to act did not arise from a voluntary assumption of risk by the appellant may have been appropriate in this case, but it would not be of universal application where, for example, a voluntary assumption of risk by the defendant had led the victim, or others, to become dependent on him to act."

Appeal dismissed

When precisely does the duty to act arise in these cases where a dangerous situation has been created? One view is that it arises on the initial creation of the dangerous situation. This would mean that the duty arose in *Miller* when the fire was accidentally started[58] and in *Evans* when the drugs were supplied. However, this view is no longer tenable because, as will be seen later in this chapter when causation is discussed, the victim's self-injection of the drugs breaks the causal chain.[59] Accordingly, as is clear from the dicta above in both *Miller* and *Evans*, the duty only arises when the defendant realises that her acts have created a dangerous situation. In *Miller* Lord Diplock refers to the duty arising when the defendant "becomes aware that the events in question have happened as a result of his own act". This is echoed in *Evans* when it is stated that the duty arises "once she appreciated that the heroin she procured for her was having a potentially fatal impact on her health".[60] On this basis, if a drug-supplier sells drugs to a client and then leaves the scene before the client self-injects, the supplier will not be under any duty to act. As Rogers points out:

"Professional drug suppliers . . . now have every incentive not even to associate with their clients after supplying the drug . . . So the burden of the duty of care in *Evans* will fall more typically upon those close friends or family members who supply the drug and then stay with the victim. . . Any policy based reasoning which accepts that the dealer, who knowingly supplies potentially lethal drugs for profit, should not be guilty of any form of manslaughter when a client dies—but which tolerates the punishment of any one else who was involved with the victim—is seriously flawed."[61]

In *Evans*, it was added that the duty arises when the defendant "knows, *or ought reasonably to know*" that the state of affairs has become life-threatening. The italicised words are obiter as the defendant in *Evans* was well aware that her sister's life was in danger. For many crimes, such as arson in *Miller*, a defendant who did not himself appreciate the danger would lack mens rea and so not be liable in any event. But for crimes that can be committed negligently or through gross negligence as was the case in *Evans*, the italicised words become important. It can be argued that it would be inappropriate to impose a duty to act on a person who was completely unaware of the fact that they had created a dangerous situation. The opposing view is that if the dangers are obvious, the defendant should not escape liability simply because she did not appreciate that fact. If negligence (or gross negligence) suffices for the crime, then negligence should also suffice in determining whether a duty to act has arisen.

---

[58]   A.P. Simester, J.R. Spencer, G.R. Sullivan and G.J. Virgo, Criminal Law: Theory and Doctrine, 5th edn (Oxford: Hart 2013), p.72.
[59]   *R. v Kennedy (Simon)* [2008] 1 A.C. 269; G. Williams, "Gross Negligence Manslaughter and Duty of Care in 'Drugs' Cases: R v Evans" [2009] Crim. L.R. 631 at 638.
[60]   *Evans* [2009] 2 Cr. App. R. 10 at [20].
[61]   "Death, Drugs and Duties" [2009] *Archbold News* 6, 6–9.

(b) *Performance of duty*

Assuming that the defendant is under a duty to act, how much danger, inconvenience or expense must they undergo in order to fulfil that duty and avoid criminal liability?

United States v Knowles, 26 Fed. Cas. 801 (No.15, 540) (N.D. Cal. 1864) (District Court, Northern District California)

The defendant was captain of the American ship *Charger* when a seaman, Swainson, accidentally fell into the sea and drowned. The defendant was charged with manslaughter on the ground that death had been caused by his wilful omission to rescue Swainson when it was his duty to do so.

FIELD, CIRCUIT JUSTICE (charging jury):

"Now, in the case of a person falling overboard from a ship at sea, whether a passenger or seaman, when he is not killed by the fall, there is no question as to the duty of the commander. He is bound, both by law and by contract, to do everything consistent with the safety of the ship and of the passengers and crew, necessary to rescue the person overboard, and for that purpose to stop the vessel, lower the boats, and throw to him such buoys or other articles which can be readily obtained, that may serve to support him in the water until he is reached by the boats and saved. No matter what delay in the voyage may be occasioned, or what expense to the owners may be incurred, nothing will excuse the commander for any omission to take these steps to save the person overboard, provided they can be taken with a due regard to the safety of the ship and others remaining on board. Subject to this condition, every person at sea, whether passenger or seaman, has a right to all reasonable efforts of the commander of the vessel for his rescue, in case he should by accident fall or be thrown overboard. Any neglect to make such efforts would be criminal, and if followed by the loss of the person overboard, when by them he might have been saved, the commander would be guilty of manslaughter . . .

If you are satisfied that the fall was not immediately fatal, the next inquiry will be whether Swainson could have been saved by any reasonable efforts of the captain, in the then condition of the sea and weather. That the wind was high there can be no doubt. The vessel was going at the time, at the rate of twelve knots an hour; it had averaged, for several hours, ten knots an hour. A wind capable of propelling a vessel at that speed would, in a few hours, create a strong sea. To stop the ship, change its course, go back to the position where the seaman fell overboard, and lower the boats, would have required a good deal of time, according to the testimony of several witnesses. In the meanwhile, the man overboard must have drifted a good way from the spot where he fell. To these considerations, you will add the probable shock and consequent exhaustion which Swainson must have experienced from the fall, even supposing that he was not immediately killed.

It is not sufficient for you to believe that possibly he might have been saved. To find the defendant guilty, you must come to the conclusion that he would, beyond a reasonable doubt, have been saved if proper efforts to save him had been reasonably made, and that his death was the consequence of the defendant's negligence in this respect. Beside the condition of the weather and sea, you must also take into consideration the character of the boats attached to the ship. According to testimony of the mate, they were small and unfit for a rough sea."

The jury returned a verdict of acquittal

Vehicle Inspectorate v Nuttall [1999] 1 W.L.R. 629 (House of Lords)

The defendant, an owner of a coach business, did not examine charts produced by tachographs installed in his vehicles and was convicted of permitting his drivers to contravene various requirements of s.96(11A) of the Transport Act 1968.

LORD HOBHOUSE OF WOODBOROUGH:

"This offence of permitting is a crime of omission which arises from the duty to act and involves the failure to perform that duty. What actual conduct will amount to the offence of permitting will be a question of fact depending on the circumstances of the particular case. For example, an employer whose employees are always, to his knowledge, back in the yard within the required time need not carry out the same checks as one whose employees are sent out on longer journeys which will necessitate the taking of breaks if the Regulations are not to be infringed. Such an employer must certainly carry out some checks . . . The test of reasonableness must be applied objectively having regard to the relevant circumstances which will vary from case to case. But it is not a question of the employer doing what he thinks is reasonable. He must do whatever is involved in taking the reasonable steps to prevent breaches. It is an objective not a subjective criterion. If he does not perform his duty, he has committed the *actus reus* of the offence . . .

The employer is under a positive duty to take the steps which an employer can reasonably take to detect and prevent breaches. He is not required to do the impossible; but he is not at liberty to omit to take those reasonable steps."

In *Hood*[62] the defendant delayed three weeks in summoning medical assistance for his wife who had accidentally fallen and broken several bones which ultimately led to her death. The fact that the wife did not want to go to hospital and could herself have called for assistance did not affect the fact that the husband had breached his duty—although these factors were relevant to sentencing.

(c) *Distinguishing positive acts from omissions*

The distinction between positive acts and omissions is crucial as criminal liability will only be imposed for the latter if a duty to act can be established. However, it is not always clear whether one is dealing with a positive act or an omission. For example, if a road worker digs a deep hole in the road and then forgets to place a cover over it with the result that a child falls in the hole and is killed, has the death been caused by the positive act of digging the hole or the omission to cover the hole?

Katz has suggested that the test for distinguishing an act from an omission should be as follows: "if the defendant did not exist, would the harmful outcome in question still have occurred in the way it did?".[63] On this test the road worker is clearly acting as their existence is critical to the causing of death. On the other hand, there is an omission where the stranger fails to rescue the drowning child because the child would still have died even if the stranger had not existed. In *Environmental Agency v Empress Car Co. (Abertillery) Ltd*[64] a company maintained a diesel oil tank on its premises. An outlet from the tank, governed by a tap, had no lock. A vandal opened the tap causing pollution to a river. The House of Lords held that "maintaining a tank of diesel is doing something" and therefore amounted to a positive act. This is consistent with Katz's theory. If the company had not existed, the pollution would never have occurred.

(d) *Omissions and causation*

When a mother fails to rescue her drowning child, how can her inactivity be said to cause the death of the child? Hogan has written:

"[T]here is no way you can cause an event by doing nothing . . . to prevent it. If grandma's skirts are ignited by her careless proximity to the gas oven, the delinquent grandson cannot be said to have killed her by his failure to dowse her . . . To say to the child, 'You have killed your grandmother' would simply be untrue."[65]

---

62   *Hood* [2004] 1 Cr. App. R. (S.) 73.
63   L. Katz, *Bad Acts and Guilty Minds: Conundrums of the Criminal Law* (Chicago: University of Chicago Press, 1987), p.143. For further discussion of the distinction between acts and omissions, see A.P. Simester, "Why Omissions are Special" (1995) 1 *Legal Theory* 311.
64   *Environmental Agency v Empress Car Co. (Abertillery) Ltd* [1999] 2 A.C. 22.
65   B. Hogan, "Omissions and the Duty Myth", in P. Smith (ed.), *Criminal Law: Essays in Honour of J. C. Smith* (London: Butterworths, 1986), pp.85–86.

This view cannot be tenable. When we examine causation we shall see that many actions could potentially be classed as "causes" of consequences. When the child drowns in the pool with the mother watching and doing nothing, we could say that the causes of the child's death were the following: that the child was in the park and was taken near the pool, that the child fell in the pool, that there was sufficient water in the pool for him to drown, that he could not swim, that his lungs filled with water, or that his mother did not rescue him when she could easily have done so. Hart and Honoré, in the leading work on causation, argue that in selecting a cause from a list such as this, one will count as causes those things or events that are a deviation from normal or required behaviour: "when such man-made normal conditions are established, deviation from them will be regarded as exceptional and so rank as the cause of harm".[66] In our list there are two exceptional occurrences: the child fell in the pool and the mother failed to rescue him. Both are deviations from what might be expected and can thus be held to be causes of the death of the child.

Arthur Leavens, "A Causation Approach to Criminal Omissions" (1988) 76 Cal. L. Rev. 547, 572–575:

"[I]t seems at first inappropriate to apply commonsense causation analysis to an individual's failure to engage in particular conduct. If one focuses solely on the circumstances of an omission at the time directly preceding the harm, the omission often appears not to have affected the at rest state of affairs. For example, a person sitting in the park while a nearby flower dies from lack of water is usually not considered to have caused the plant's demise, even if a full watercan sits nearby . . .

The difficulty in conceptualizing an omission as a causal force is that omissions do not seem to fit within the parameters of the physical cause and effect model. In the physical paradigm, there is a direct and identifiable chain of events through which the actor can readily be seen as intervening and changing what existed before. In cases of omission, however, the actor does not physically alter the status quo, but rather appears simply to permit the preexisting state of affairs to continue. Without direct physical involvement in the causal process leading to a particular result, an omitter seems no more causally responsible for the result than anyone else . . .

Such a view of causation is flawed because its inquiry is too limited. It depends on a definition of the status quo as the existing physical state of affairs at the precise time of the omission, much as if we took a picture of the scene at the moment before the omission and then compared it to a similar picture taken immediately thereafter, searching for a change in circumstances physically attributable to the omissive conduct. Our everyday notions of causation, however, are not so limited because we understand that the status quo encompasses more than the physical state of affairs at a given time. Indeed, in everyday usage the status quo is taken to include expected patterns of conduct, including actions designed to avert certain unwanted results. When, for example, a driver parks a car on a steep hill, it is normal to set the parking brake and put the car in gear. If the driver forgets to do so and the car subsequently rolls down the hill, smashing into another car, we would say that the failure to park properly was a departure from the status quo. This failure, not the visibly steep hill or the predicate act of pulling the car to the curb, was the cause of the collision.

Once we realize that a particular undesirable state of affairs can be avoided by taking certain precautions, we usually incorporate these precautions into what we see as the normal or at rest state of affairs. A failure to engage in the preventive conduct in these cases can thus be seen as an intervention that disturbs the status quo. When such a failure to act is a necessary condition (a 'but for' cause) of a particular harm, then that failure fairly can be said to cause that harm. In the above example, the driver's failure to park the car in a proper manner caused the accident as surely as if he had actually driven his car into the other . . .

[W]e do expect certain persons to engage in particular types of preventive conduct as a matter of routine. Because of this expectation, we perceive any failure of those persons to take prescribed actions as a departure from normality. While we do not see the bystander's failure to water the flower as the cause of its withering away, we take a different view of such a failure by the park's gardener. We expect that the gardener will take reasonable steps to prevent the flower's demise, that is, his preventive conduct represents normality. A departure from that status quo—his failure to water—is thus more than a necessary condition of the flower's death: it causes that result every bit as much as the act of an intruder pulling the plant from its soil.

---

[66]   H.L.A. Hart and T. Honoré, *Causation in the Law*, 2nd edn (Oxford: OUP, 1985), p.37.

Of course, society's expectation of particular preventive conduct could be described as merely another formulation of 'duty.'

A 'duty' sufficient to support criminal sanctions must be founded on both an empirically valid expectation that persons in similar circumstances will act to prevent a harm—the probability aspect of normality—and also a deeply ingrained common understanding that society relies on that individual to prevent the harm—the normative aspect of normality. Thus parents have a 'duty' to prevent harm to their children because empirically, almost all parents act this way, and normatively, our society would consider it reprehensible if they did not. It is this combination of deviance—departing from a pattern of regular performance—and reprehensibility—being blameworthy—that makes us conclude that failure to act caused the harm."

Following this reasoning, it is only those who are under a duty to act, according to the rules examined above, who can be said to cause a result through their failure to act. This conclusion has important implications in the next section where we consider whether there should be a general duty to act.

(e) A general duty to act?

It is often asserted that liability for omissions ought not to be restricted to those cases where there is a legal duty to act, as currently defined. The person who sees a strange child drowning in a shallow pool of water and neglects to rescue him when she could have easily done so with no danger to herself, has killed that child as surely as if she had held the child's head under the water and ought to be punished to the same extent. If one of the objects of the criminal law and punishment is to stimulate socially approved conduct then the imposition of criminal liability in such cases would encourage people to act in situations such as these.

Andrew Ashworth, "The Scope of Liability for Omissions" (1989) 105 L.Q.R. 424 at 430–432:

"Individuals tend to place a high value on interpersonal contacts, relationships, mutual support and the fulfilment of obligations, and a society which values collective goals and collective goods may therefore provide a wider range of worthwhile opportunities for individual development . . . The counter-argument to the conventional view is thus that a duty to co-operate with or to assist others should not be ruled out *ab initio* by an asocial and falsely restricted view of individual autonomy . . .

Individuals need others, or the actions of others, for a wide variety of tasks which assist each one of us to maximise the pursuit of our personal goals. A community or society may be regarded as a network of relationships which support one another by direct and indirect means . . .

. . . It follows that there is a good case for encouraging co-operation at the minimal level of the duty to assist persons in peril, so long as the assistance does not endanger the person rendering it . . .

. . . The foundation of the argument is that a level of social co-operation and social responsibility is both good and necessary for the realisation of individual autonomy . . . Each member of society is valued intrinsically, and the value of one citizen's life is generally greater than the value of another citizen's temporary freedom. Thus it is the element of emergency which heightens the social responsibility in 'rescue' cases, and which focusses other people's vital interests into a 'deliberative priority,' and it is immediacy to *me* that generates *my* obligation. The concepts of immediacy and the opportunity of help (usually because of physical nearness) can thus be used to generate, and to limit the scope of, the duty of assistance to those in peril."

Samuel Freeman, "Criminal Liability and the Duty to Aid the Distressed" (1994) 142 University of Pennsylvania L. Rev. 1455 at 1489:

"Given . . . the significant fact that each of us is about as likely to benefit from this duty as to be inconvenienced by it, the political argument for the legalization of a duty to aid the distressed is that it promotes a common good, namely the safety and security of all persons in society. Since each person is sufficiently likely to benefit from this legal duty at some crucial point in their lifetime, it is a collectively rational legal constraint."

Feinberg argues that any person in peril becomes one's neighbour for the purposes of the moral exhortation "love thy neighbour" and is therefore owed a duty: "When it comes to *aiding the imperiled*, all people who happen to find themselves in a position to help—all who have by chance wandered into the vicinity, or 'portable neighborhood,' of the imperiled party—are his 'neighbours,' with reciprocal dependencies, expectations, duties, and claims."[67]

Graham Hughes, "Criminal Omissions" (1958) 67 Yale L.J. 590 at 626, 634:

"But a view of moral responsibility is surely outmoded which imposes liability on the father who does not warn his child of the precipice before him, but not on a stranger who neglects to warn the child . . . The law often lags a half century or so behind public mores, but the spectacle cannot be lightly entertained in a field of this importance. The duty to take active steps to save others, and a liability for homicide in the absence of such action, could well be based on the defendant's clear recognition of the victim's peril plus his failure to take steps which might reasonably be taken without risk to himself to warn or protect the victim . . .

Conventional criticisms of the imposition of a duty to rescue are usually based on objections to compelling one man to serve another, to creating a fear of prosecution which might cause citizens to interfere officiously in the affairs of others, and to the feasibility of imposing liability on a crowd of spectators all of whom had knowledge of the peril but were too selfish to intervene. These objections, however, do not seem to have much merit. To the first, the reply may be made that the evil of interfering with individual liberty by compelling assistance is much outweighed by the good of preserving human life. The second is a speculation which would be difficult to support. The third point appears to pose a real difficulty, but it is no different from a situation which commonly occurs in offenses of commission. In a riot, for example, it is difficult if not impossible to bring all the participants to book, but this has never been considered an obstacle to trial and punishment of those who can be reached. If a crowd of spectators stands by and watches a child drown in shallow water, nothing seems objectionable in trying and punishing all who can be tracked down and cannot show a reasonable excuse. To think that such an example of selfish group inertia could exist in our society is distressing, but, if it did, there would be every reason for invoking the criminal law against it.

The time is ripe for Anglo-American systems to translate into legislative fact the modern consciousness of interdependence. Surely, it is not in socialist countries alone that the duty of a citizen to help his fellows in these situations of extreme peril can be recognized."

There are many arguments as to why English law should not introduce a general duty to act. The central argument relates to individual liberty and autonomy.[68] Our freedom should only be restricted insofar as it is necessary to prevent persons causing harm to others. Further,

"the criminal law should recognise an individual's choices rather than allowing liability to be governed by chance, and the obligation to assist someone in peril may be thrust upon a chance passerby, who may well prefer not to become involved at all".[69]

It is further argued that the imperilled stranger has no *right* to be rescued and therefore the defendant is under no *duty* to rescue.[70]

These arguments are fortified by the claim that it is basic to our morality that it is worse to, say, shoot or drown a victim than merely to look the other way when they are drowning. As Fletcher puts it:

---

[67]   J. Feinberg, *Harm to Others* (New York: OUP, 1984), p.133.

[68]   A.P. Simester, "Why Omissions are Special" (1995) 1 *Legal Theory* 311.

[69]   A. Ashworth, "The Scope of Criminal Liability for Omissions" (1989) 105 L.Q.R. 424 at 425–426.

[70]   J. Murphy, "Blackmail: A Preliminary Inquiry", *The Monist* 63, No.2 (1980) n.6; L.K. Stell, "Dueling and the Right to Life" 90 (1979) *Ethics* 7 at 12 cites John Stuart Mill's distinction between perfect and imperfect obligations: "Duties of perfect obligation are those duties in virtue of which a correlative right resides in some person or persons; duties of imperfect obligation are those moral obligations which do not give birth to any right." (*Utilitarianism* (1957), p.61).

"The difference between killing and letting die, between creating a risk, and tolerating a risk, is one of the principles that sets the framework for assessing moral responsibility."[71]

This point is underlined by Moore: "Drowning [a child] makes the world a worse place, whereas not preventing its drowning only fails to improve the world."[72]

Leo Katz, Bad Acts and Guilty Minds (1987), p.145:

"[T]he consequences of an omission are generally less certain than those of an act. Holding somebody's head under water is more likely to kill him than not throwing him a life vest.

But there is a deeper, moral, reason why killing-by-omission offends us less than killing-by-commission. Compare these two situations. (1) Bert will die unless Berta gives him one of her kidneys. Berta is ailing and doesn't want to risk an operation. So she lets Bert die. (2) Berta will die unless Bert gives her his only kidney. She kills Bert and takes his kidney. In both 1 and 2 Berta brings about Bert's death to assure her own survival; in 1 she does it by an omission, in 2 by an act. Why are we less offended by her conduct in 1 than 2? Because in 1 she simply holds on to her own kidney, whereas in 2 she appropriates somebody else's kidney. We value personal autonomy and Berta's conduct in 2 offends against that value, while her conduct in 1 doesn't. Our sentiments about every other case of omission can be understood by analogizing it to these two cases. The person who fails to prevent harm that would occur even if he didn't exist simply fails to give away something he owns. The person who brings about harm that wouldn't occur if he didn't exist takes away something owned by someone else. Both persons may be callous, but only the latter offends our sense of personal autonomy."

Husak suggests the reason why it is worse to kill than to let die is because the defendant has more control in the former than in the latter situation

"persons generally exercise far less control over what happens as a result of their omission than as a result of their positive actions. Control over a consequence is typically exercised by positive action."[73]

English law has endorsed this view that it is worse to kill than to "let die". In *Airedale NHS Trust v Bland* the House of Lords ruled that in certain circumstances it was lawful for doctors to let a patient die but it was illegal actively to bring a patient's life to an end:

"So to act is to cross the Rubicon which runs between on the one hand the care of the living patient and on the other hand euthanasia—actively causing his death to avoid or to end his suffering. Euthanasia is not lawful at common law."[74]

Additionally, there are many objections of a more practical nature to any idea of introducing a general duty to act. If a large crowd watches someone drown, would they all be liable? How much help need be given? After dragging a drowning person from the sea, would one be under a duty to provide mouth-to-mouth resuscitation (irrespective of risk of disease) and then drive the rescued person to the nearest hospital if necessary? How much danger would the rescuer be expected to risk? What if the rescuer's efforts exacerbated the situation and worsened the plight of the imperilled person? Might

---

[71]   Fletcher, *Rethinking Criminal Law* (1978), p.601.
[72]   M. Moore, *Act and Crime: The Philosophy of Action and Its Implications for Criminal Law* (Oxford: Clarendon Press, 1993), p.59.
[73]   Husak, *Philosophy of Criminal Law* (1987), p.100. Husak advocates replacing the actus reus requirement in criminal law generally with a "control principle".
[74]   *Airedale NHS Trust v Bland* [1993] A.C. 789 at 865.

not such a law be counterproductive in that fear of being forced to intervene might keep people away from places where they might be called upon to help?

A final objection to any attempt to introduce a general duty to act is that it will not usually be possible to establish causation in situations other than those where at present there is a duty to act.

R. v Stone and Dobinson [1977] 1 Q.B. 354 (Court of Appeal, Criminal Division)

The facts appear from the judgment of Geoffrey Lane LJ.

GEOFFREY LANE LJ:

"[The two appellants were convicted of manslaughter and now appeal against conviction. Stone and his housekeeper/mistress, Dobinson, admitted Stone's younger sister, Fanny, aged 61, to their household].

[Fanny] was eccentric in many ways. She was morbidly and unnecessarily anxious about putting on weight and so denied herself proper meals. She would take to her room for days . . .

[T]here can be no doubt that Fanny's condition over the succeeding weeks and months must have deteriorated rapidly. By July 1975 she was, it seems, unable or unwilling to leave her bed and, on July 19, the next-door neighbour, Mrs Wilson, gallantly volunteered to help the female appellant to wash Fanny. She states:

'On July 19 Mrs Dobinson and I went to Fanny's room in order to clean her up. When I went into the room there was not a strong smell until I moved her. Her nightdress was wet and messed with her own excreta and the dress had to be cut off. I saw her back was sore; I hadn't seen anything like that before. I took the bedclothes off the bed. They were all wet through and messed. And so was the mattress. I was there for about two hours and Mrs Dobinson helped. She was raw, her back, shoulders, bottom and down below between her legs. Mrs Dobinson appeared to me to be upset because Fanny had never let her attend to her before. I advised Mrs Dobinson to go to the social services.'

Emily West, the licensee of the local public house, the Crossed Daggers, gave evidence to the effect that during the whole of the period, from July 19 onwards, the appellants came to the public house every night at about 7 p.m. The appellant Dobinson was worried and told Emily West that Fanny would not wash, go to the toilet or eat or drink. As a result Emily West immediately advised Dobinson to get a doctor and when told that Fanny's doctor lived at Doncaster, Emily West suggested getting a local one. It seems that some efforts were made to get a local doctor, but the neighbour who volunteered to do the telephoning (the appellants being incapable of managing the instrument themselves) was unsuccessful.

On August 2, 1975 Fanny was found by Dobinson to be dead in her bed. The police were called. On arrival they found there was no ventilation in the bedroom . . . Under the bed was an empty polythene bucket. Otherwise there was no food, washing or toilet facilities in the room. There was excrement on the bed and floor. It was a scene of dreadful degradation.

The pathologist, Dr Usher, gave evidence that the deceased was naked, emaciated, weighing five stone and five pounds, her body ingrained with dirt, lying in a pool of excrement . . . There was a tidemark of excreta corresponding with the position in which her body was lying. At the mortuary, Dr Usher found the deceased's body to be ulcerated over the right hip joint and on the underside of the left knee; in each case the ulceration went down to the bone. There were maggots in the ulcers . . . Such ulcers could not have been produced in less than two or three weeks . . . Her stomach contained no food products but a lot of bile stained fluid. She had not eaten recently. He found no natural disease. The disinclination to eat was a condition of anorexia nervosa which was not a physical condition but a condition of the brain or mind. She had been requiring urgent medical attention for some days or even weeks. He said:

'If two weeks prior to my seeing the body she had gone into hospital there is a distinct possibility that they may have saved her; and three weeks earlier the chances would have been good. If her condition on July 19 was no worse than that described by Mrs Wilson, then her survival would have been probable.'. . .

The prosecution alleged that in the circumstances the appellants had undertaken the duty of caring for Fanny who was incapable of looking after herself, that they had, with gross negligence, failed in that duty, that such failure caused her death and they were guilty of manslaughter . . .

[Counsel for the appellant] suggests that the situation here is unlike any reported case. Fanny came to this house as a lodger. Largely, if not entirely due to her own eccentricity and failure to look after herself or feed herself properly, she became increasingly infirm and immobile and eventually unable to look after herself. Is it to be said, asks [counsel for the appellant] rhetorically, that by the mere fact of becoming infirm and helpless in these circumstances she casts a duty on her brother and the appellant Dobinson to take steps to have her looked after or taken into hospital? The suggestion is that, heartless though it may seem, this is one of those situations where the appellants were entitled to do nothing; where no duty was cast upon them to help, any more than it is cast upon a man to rescue a stranger from drowning, however easy such a rescue might be.

This court rejects that proposition. Whether Fanny was a lodger or not she was a blood relation of the appellant Stone; she was occupying a room in his house; the appellant Dobinson had undertaken the duty of trying to wash her, of taking such food to her as she required. There was ample evidence that each appellant was aware of the poor condition she was in by mid-July. It was not disputed that no effort was made to summon an ambulance or the social services or the police despite the entreaties of Mrs Wilson and Mrs West. A social worker used to visit Cyril. No word was spoken to him. All these were matters which the jury were entitled to take into account when considering whether the necessary assumption of a duty to care for Fanny had been proved.

This was not a situation analogous to the drowning stranger. They did make efforts to care. They tried to get a doctor; they tried to discover the previous doctor. The appellant Dobinson helped with the washing and the provision of food. All these matters were put before the jury in terms which we find it impossible to fault. The jury were entitled to find that the duty had been assumed. They were entitled to conclude that once Fanny became helplessly infirm, as she had by July 19, the appellants were, in the circumstances, obliged either to summon help or else to care for Fanny themselves."

Appeal dismissed

If there were a general duty to act in English law, would Mrs Wilson (whose daughter was a nurse) and even Emily West be charged with manslaughter? If either of them had summoned medical assistance then Fanny's life might have been saved.

The answer here must be in the negative. It is possible to hold that Stone and Dobinson caused Fanny's death because it was their deviation from an expected norm that stands out as exceptional among the candidates for causation. The inactions of Mrs Wilson and Emily West do not stand out as wholly exceptional. Fanny was dependent and reasonably relied upon Stone and Dobinson. It is this reliance that generates a duty on their part to take care of her. It is the breach of this duty that stands out as a "deviation" and thus a cause. On the other hand, Fanny did not rely on Mrs Wilson or Emily West any more than she would have relied on a passing milkman who happened to become aware of her situation. This lack of reliance means that Mrs Wilson and Emily West will not be held to have assumed a responsibility towards Fanny under the present law. Their failure to act will not stand out as exceptional or a deviation from the norm. They did not cause her death.

Does this thesis, which would be fatal to any argument in favour of a general duty to act, apply in all cases? It will be recalled that Leavens, in an earlier extract,[75] used the example of a person sitting on a park bench watching a flower die from lack of water even though a full water can was nearby. We would not say that that person caused the death of the flower. As she was under no duty to water the flower, her failure to act was unexceptional. But we would say that the park's gardener caused the death of the flower if he failed to water it. Because of his duty (by contract), his failure becomes significant; it represents a marked alteration of the status quo and can count as a cause.

What of the mother and the stranger who fail to rescue the child from the shallow pool of water? It has been argued that there is no difficulty in establishing a causal link in both these cases.[76] In one sense, the actions of both did cause the death of the child: but for their failures to act, the child would

---

[75]   See pp.101–102.
[76]   G. Hughes, "Criminal Omissions" (1958) 67 Yale L.J. 590 at 627; J. Hall, *General Principles of Criminal Law* (Indianapolis: The Bobs-Merrill Co., 1947), pp.256–266.

have survived. But, again, it is the mother's failure that stands out as the more significant cause of death. Like the appellants in *Stone and Dobinson* the mother has a special responsibility to the child. It is the failure to exercise this responsibility that is "exceptional" or a significant "deviation" from the expected and thus the substantial cause of the death. It is the existence of this duty that converts a mere cause into a legally sufficient cause. The stranger has no special responsibility towards the child and, therefore, while his omission might be morally deplorable, it is not "exceptional" in the same sense as when the mother fails to save her own child.

Another way of expressing this is that a cause alters the status quo. The status quo is something that exists, "including expected patterns of conduct",[77] whether we are there or not. A mother has a special relationship towards her drowning child. *That relationship becomes part of the status quo.* Her failure to act alters the status quo and is thus a cause of the result. The stranger's failure to act has no impact on the status quo. Events simply take their normal (but tragic) course; the stranger's acts do not count as a legal cause of the consequence.

Thus, to summarise, it would be pointless to impose a general duty to act as the only people who could be held responsible in terms of causation would be those who owed duties to their victims under one of the recognised heads. It is only *because of* the special relationship, the assumption of duty, etc. that causation is established. Without this pre-existing duty the causative link between the inactivity and the ensuing consequence would be too remote.[78]

In discussing whether there ought to be a general duty to act we have, until now, assumed that the purpose of such a general duty is that a breach thereof constitutes the requisite "act" for the purposes of some ulterior offence—for example, a failure to rescue becomes the requisite act for the purposes of a homicide offence. It is, however, not necessary to go as far as this. The law could still issue its moral directive that people must render assistance to others, but avoid all problems of causation and mens rea, by the creation of separate offences imposing limited and complete liability for a failure to act. A failure to act would render one liable for this separate offence. In the United States the state of Vermont has such a provision.

12 Vt. Stat. Ann. s.519. (Emergency Medical Care)

"(a) A person who knows that another is exposed to grave physical harm shall, to the extent that the same can be rendered without danger or peril to himself or without interference with important duties owed to others, give reasonable assistance to the exposed person unless that assistance or care is being provided by others.

(b) A person who provides reasonable assistance in compliance with subsection (a) of this section shall not be liable in civil damages unless his acts constitute gross negligence or unless he will receive or expects to receive remuneration. Nothing contained in this subsection shall alter existing law with respect to tort liability of a practitioner of the healing arts for acts committed in the ordinary course of his practice.

(c) A person who wilfully violates subsection (a) of this section shall be fined not more than $100.00."[79]

If such a provision were part of English law then defendants such as Stone and Dobinson could have been charged with this offence instead of manslaughter. Some might argue that this would have been preferable: in moral terms one can condemn Stone and Dobinson for neglecting Fanny; but can we really condemn them morally for *killing* Fanny? Of course, if such a provision were introduced in

---

77   A. Leavens, see p.101.
78   This point was recognised in *Miller* [1983] 2 A.C. 161, when Lord Diplock indicated that a "passive bystander" could not be said to have caused a fire, or presumably any injuries sustained in the fire.
79   Many continental Criminal Codes contain similar and even broader provisions. See A. Ashworth and E. Steiner, "Criminal Omissions and Public Duties: The French Experience" (1990) 10 L.S. 153; Hughes, (1958) 67 Yale L.J. 590 at 627 at 631–634.

England, without more, Stone and Dobinson would have been guilty of both this offence *and* man-slaughter, their duty to act being now statutory in addition to the other grounds giving rise to their duty. It would need to be made clear whether such a new provision was *replacing* the possibility of any criminal liability for an ulterior offence or not. Where there is a duty under one of the already estab-lished heads, there is a strong case for continuing to impose criminal liability for the ulterior offence. The mother who watches her young child drown in the shallow pool *ought* arguably to be liable for manslaughter (at least) and not merely liable for a lesser offence of failing to act. This would, of course, leave unresolved the problem of whether defendants like Stone and Dobinson should simply be charged with the new statutory offence or whether they should be charged with manslaughter on the basis that they have breached one of the existing categories of duty. Similar questions are raised in relation to recent proposals to create an offence of failing to report suspected child abuse, applicable to professionals.[80] If a teacher suspected that one of her pupils was being abused at home, and failed to report her suspicions to the authorities, would she then be liable for manslaughter if that child subsequently died as a result of such abuse?

R. A. Duff, Answering for Crime: Responsibility and Liability in the Criminal Law (2007), p.113:

"When the law does criminalise failures to prevent harm, it should normally distinguish them from active harm-doings, as distinct and lesser offences: it can do this either by criminalising only the failure to act, without assign-ing criminal responsibility for the actual harm, or by distinguishing omissive from active responsibility for the harm."

One offence which ignores Duff's suggestion is that of causing or allowing the death of a child or vul-nerable adult in one's household.[81] This offence, discussed in Ch.8, can be committed either through a positive act, or through an omission, but in either case the penalty is a maximum of 14 years' impris-onment. Ashworth suggests that many people may be unaware of the existence of this offence and of the duty that arises, leading to rule-of-law concerns.[82] If the law is to be effective in enforcing moral duties that arise, the existence of such offences needs to be effectively communicated to members of the public. That becomes a particular issue where the legislature chooses to create a large number of offences criminalising omissions. Ashworth reports that 42 (26 per cent) of the offences created by primary legislation in 2005 are offences of omission.[83]

(f) Punishment of omissions

Under English law, once liability for an offence has been established, one is liable to any punishment up to the maximum, regardless of whether one's "act" consisted of positive action or an omission to act. This approach can be defended: the harm is the same in both cases and sometimes it is difficult to distinguish between acts of commission and omissions to act.

On the other hand, it can be argued that omissions ought on principle to be punished less severely than positive acts and that this lesser level of punishment should be clearly articulated. One of the views considered earlier was that it was worse to "kill" than to "let die". If this were accepted, it should be reflected at the punishment level. In *Hood* a sentence for gross negligence manslaughter was

---

80   A. Ashworth, "The Boundaries of Criminal Law: Offences of Failure to Report" [2014] Crim. L.R. 1.
81   Domestic Violence, Crime and Victims Act 2004 s.5.
82   A. Ashworth, "Ignorance of the Criminal Law, and Duties to Avoid it" (2011) 74(1) M.L.R. 1 at 18.
83   Ashworth, "Ignorance of the Criminal Law, and Duties to Avoid it" (2011) 74(1) M.L.R. 1 at 13.

reduced on the ground, inter alia, that the offence was one of "pure omission".[84] Adopting such an approach could have the advantage of encouraging the courts to be less inflexible in their attitude towards the imposition of criminal liability based on omissions.

2. Legally relevant circumstances

It was seen earlier in this chapter that the traditional definition of an actus reus involves: (1) an act (2) committed in legally relevant circumstances, (3) that (for result crimes) causes the prohibited consequence. An example is the crime of causing death by dangerous driving which requires that the defendant caused the death by dangerously driving a mechanically propelled vehicle on a road or other public place. The act of dangerous driving must be committed in the legally relevant circumstance that it was on a road or other public place and it must have caused death.

For most crimes it is not important whether an element of an offence is classified as being part of the act or as a legally relevant circumstance or as a consequence. For example, in the above offence it makes no difference whether the requisite act is "driving a mechanically propelled vehicle" or whether the act is driving a vehicle in the legally relevant circumstance of it being mechanically propelled. However, for some crimes a different mens rea is required for different elements of the actus reus and for these crimes it is important to be able to distinguish between acts, circumstances and consequences. For example, the crime of attempting to commit s.1(2) of the Criminal Damage Act 1971 requires the defendant to attempt to commit criminal damage being reckless as to whether life would be endangered. As will be seen in Ch.5, for attempted crime the defendant must intend the consequence but can be reckless as to surrounding circumstances. Whether the offence element of "whether the life of another would be thereby endangered" is a legally relevant circumstance or a consequence becomes a critical issue.[85]

3. Causation

(i) Introduction

Commonwealth v Welansky, 316 Mass. 383, 55 N.E. 2d 902 (1944) (Supreme Judicial Court of Massachusetts)

On the evening of November 28, 1942 a fire broke out at the New Cocoanut Grove, a nightclub in Boston. The fire quickly spread throughout the crowded premises. Panic resulted and nearly 500 people died of burns, smoke inhalation, or injuries suffered in the attempt to escape. Who caused the death of these people?[86] There were several candidates for blame:

1. The waiter, Stanley Tomaszewski

A prankster had turned off a light bulb set in a decorative palm tree. A bartender ordered Stanley, a sixteen year old boy, to light the bulb. He got a stool, lit a match in order to see the bulb and turned the bulb in its socket. The flame of his match ignited the artificial palm tree which in turn speedily ignited a low cloth ceiling near it. Did Stanley cause the death of the 500 victims? Initially he was

---

[84] *Hood* [2004] 1 Cr. App. R.(S.) 73.
[85] See p.488 where this point and the case in which it arose (*Attorney-General's Reference (No.3 of 1992)* (1994) 98 Cr. App. R. 383) are discussed.
[86] The ensuing discussion of *Welansky* is drawn from the report of the case itself, from H.R. Veltford and G.E. Lee, "The Cocoanut Grove Fire: A Study in Scapegoating", *Journal of Abnormal and Social Psychology*, XXXVIII (No.2 clinical supp.; 1943) 138 at 141–154, and from J. Goldstein, A. M. Dershowitz and R.D. Schwartz, *Criminal Law: Theory and Process* (Macmillan, 1974), pp.833–837.

blamed by the local press, but as other "scapegoats" were found, he was exonerated from blame and treated with 'near adulation' and started receiving 'fan letters.' But for the next 28 years Stanley received abusive telephone calls in the middle of the night and his life was threatened "hundreds of times by people who blame me for the fire".[87]

2. The prankster

The prankster who turned off the light bulb was also blamed initially in the press, but as his identity was never discovered, his condemnation was shortlived. Can he be said to have caused the death of the victims?

3. Public officials

The week before, the Fire Department had inspected the Cocoanut Grove and approved it as safe, despite the fact that there was a lack of adequate fire-exits and that highly inflammable materials were used throughout the nightclub and, in particular, in the decorative palm tree and in the low cloth ceiling. Did the particular fire inspector cause the deaths?

The local press also blamed other public officials. They condemned the Fire Commissioner on the basis that he was responsible for his subordinate's performance of duty. They castigated a Captain in the Police Department who was inside the club at the time of the fire on inspection duties for not enforcing the law against over-crowding. Even the mayor was blamed for appointing such "negligent" and "lax" heads of departments and because he had taken no action to adopt a new building code that had been in the hands of the City Council for the previous four years. Did any of these public officials cause the deaths?

4. The owners

The nightclub was owned and run by Barnett Welansky. In decorating and equipping the club he had used defective wiring and installed the inflammable decorations. There were insufficient exit doors and some of these doors were kept locked. At the time of the fire Barnett Welansky was confined in hospital with a serious illness—his brother James Welansky and an employee, Jacob Goldfine, 'assumed some of [his] duties at the night club, but made no change in methods.'[88] To what extent can it be said that the death of the victims was caused by Barnett Welansky or by his two delegates?

The result

Barnett Welansky and his two delegates were charged with manslaughter. The two delegates were acquitted by the jury, but Barnett Welansky was convicted of manslaughter and sentenced to a term of imprisonment of not less than twelve years and not more than fifteen years. Welansky's appeal was dismissed. Thus both the trial court and the Supreme Judicial Court of Massachusetts clearly found that Barnett Welansky caused the death of the victims of the fire. After serving three years of his sentence, Welansky, who was suffering from terminal cancer and was not expected to live for more than another year, was granted a full and complete pardon by the Governor of Massachusetts.

---

[87]   *The Boston Globe*, December 28, 1970, p.10, col.3. See Goldstein, Dershowitz and Schwartz, *Criminal Law: Theory and Process* (1974), p.836.
[88]   *Welansky* 55 N.E. 2d 902 at 905.

It is interesting to contrast the views expressed in two of the many letters addressed to the Governor prior to his granting a pardon.

(i) "If Welansky was guilty of manslaughter in connection with the terrible deaths resulting from the Cocoanut Grove fire, then it was a technical guilt and nothing more. Certainly, in those circumstances, the sentence that was imposed upon him by the court was much too severe . . . It may well be true that in appropriate cases, such as criminals whom the public would have a right to fear if they were released, that the criminal's health should not be taken into consideration, but in this particular case where there was no intention to do harm in the first place, but through a succession of misfortunes a man has been found guilty of manslaughter only from a technical point of view and not otherwise, [he is deserving of a pardon.]"[89]

(ii) "I vehemently oppose any pardon for Barnett Welansky whose criminal re-construction of the Cocoanut Grove building sacrificed 492 human beings. I am a close relative of one of the victims. This horrible holocaust was a civic disgrace. It would become even more unspeakable were this man to be freed. In his petition for premature freedom, Welansky claims illness—says he wants to spend the rest of his days with his family. I recall 492 persons (one in particular) who wanted to live out their lives with their families. *They are dead*. He also disclaims guilt because he was at home the night of the fire.

Guiltless? He *accepted guilt* when he criminally flouted the building laws in callously renovating his nightclub and did *not* have the work done according to the plans which he had had okayed.

He evaded the law when he employed a young fellow to do some electrical wiring and *knew* that his worker did not have the proper license to do this work. Has it been *absolutely proven* that faulty wiring *did not* cause this fire? Although he was not present he *knew* that his illegally reconstructed club was open for public attendance the night of the fire.

Governor Tobin, consider the fact of locked exits in a place of public patronage. Hundreds died because a locked exit barred their way to the street's safety. These facts are on public record. They also are hideous facts burning deeply into the hearts of hundreds of heartbroken families."[90]

H. Veltford and G. Lee, "The Cocoanut Grove Fire: A Study in Scapegoating" Journal of Abnormal and Social Psychology, XXXVIII (No.2 clinical supp; 1943), 138:

"The people [of Boston] felt some person or persons must be held responsible; attaching responsibility to mere laws or to the *panic* provided neither sufficient outlet for their emotions nor opportunity for punishment . . .

Significantly, newspapers and public alike overlooked the fact that the panic created by the fire must have been largely responsible for the great loss of life. In spite of statements by officials immediately after the fire, the people were not ready to accept the fact that 'the Boston tragedy was due in part to a psychological collapse.' To the extent that they ignored this fact, the blame that the newspapers and public placed on various persons involved in the fire was disproportionate to their responsibility."

Sally Lloyd-Bostock, "The Ordinary Man, and the Psychology of Attributing Causes and Responsibility" (1979) 42 M.L.R. 143 at 155–156:

"Walster ('Assignment of Responsibility for an Accident' (1963) 3, 1 Journal of Personality and Social Psychology, 73–79) . . . found that people attributed more responsibility for an accident (in which a car parked unbraked ran down a hill) as the severity of the consequence increased. She formulated a version of what has become known as 'the defensive attribution hypothesis'. Chance happenings over which the individual has no control (and,

---

89   Letter by F. Lichtenstein, cited in See Goldstein, Dershowitz and Schwartz, *Criminal Law: Theory and Process* (1974), p.835.
90   Letter by K. Denehy, cited in See Goldstein, Dershowitz and Schwartz, *Criminal Law: Theory and Process* (1974), pp.835–836.

hence, no responsibility) are threatening. Therefore, when faced with an accident with serious consequences, an individual will seek to attribute responsibility to somebody in order to protect himself from acknowledging that the accident could happen to anyone, including himself. The need to protect himself in this way will increase with increasing severity of outcome . . .

Often more than one kind of responsibility may be attributed in relation to the same event. For example, a *Sunday Times* article (April 13, 1977) after describing at some length the circumstances surrounding the collision between two jumbo jets at Santa Cruz airport in Tenerife, concluded by attributing responsibility—'Blame for the world's worst aviation tragedy will no doubt be apportioned in time. One name will certainly not feature in any official inquest however: Antonio Cubillo. It is he who, no matter how indirectly, must shoulder responsibility for what happened at Santa Cruz.' (Cubillo was leader of the movement which claimed responsibility for a bomb at Las Palmas airport. As a result of the bomb, aircraft, including those in the accident, were diverted to Santa Cruz, overloading the airport.) This illustrates a number of interesting things about reactions to disasters and attributing responsibility for them in newspapers. The writers recognise that it will differ from other attributions, and that Antonio Cubillo's causal contribution will in other contexts be insufficient grounds. It is a non-legal attribution of responsibility, but even if nobody quarrelled with it in this context, it is clearly not *the* everyday answer to the question 'who is responsible for the crash?', nor does it exemplify *the* common-sense principles on which questions about remoteness of causes, etc. are decided.

The fact that everyday judgments are related to everyday purposes and consequences must be a major limitation on the usefulness of comparisons between legal and ordinary common-sense notions of cause and fault."

(ii) Approaches to causation

In such cases how does the law determine which of several candidates actually caused the result? How far does the chain of causation extend? Welansky did not start the fire. Why was he liable for the resultant deaths? If the waiter had deliberately started the fire, would Welansky still have been liable or would the chain of causation have then been broken? While attempts have been made to discover a metaphysical rationale for the law's rules on causation,[91] the more usual approach is that legal doctrines are shaped by other considerations and do not map metaphysical causal reality.[92] What are these other considerations?

There are three approaches that can be adopted in relation to the problem of causation.

(a) *"Policy" approach*

There are no underlying general *principles* of causation. Judges simply resort to considerations of "policy" to determine whether a particular defendant caused the specified harm.

H.L.A. Hart and Tony Honoré, Causation in the Law, 2nd edn (1985), pp.103–104:

"For writers of the first school 'policy' is just a name for an immense variety of considerations which do weigh and should weigh with courts considering the question of the existence or extent of responsibility. No exhaustive enumeration can be given of such factors and no general principles can be laid down as to how a balance should be struck between them. Policy, on this interpretation, is atomized: the courts must focus attention on the precise way in which harm has eventuated in a particular case, and then ask and answer, in a more or less intuitive fashion, whether or not on these particular facts a defendant should be held responsible. The court's function is to pass judgments acceptable to society for their time and place on these matters, and general policies can never take the place of judgment. Edgerton says,

'It neither is nor should be possible to extract rules which cover the subject (of legal cause) and are definite enough to solve cases . . . The solution . . . depends upon a balancing of considerations which tend to show

---

[91]   M. Moore, "The Metaphysics of Causal Intervention" (2000) 88 Cal. L.R. 827.
[92]   S.J. Morse, "The Moral Metaphysics of Causation and Results" (2000) 88 Cal. L.R. 879.

that it is or is not reasonable or just to treat the act as the cause of the harm . . . these considerations are indefinite in number and in value and incommensurable' (Legal Cause, (1924) U.Pa.L.R. 211)."

Norrie argues that any "principles" that might exist require "constant supplementation by policy considerations to reach decisions in individual cases" because causation can only be explained by taking into account the social context within which people act.[93]

In holding that Welansky caused the death of the victims of the Cocoanut Grove fire, were the judges (and jury) simply giving effect to their conceptions of justice, expediency or "policy"? In deciding who to prosecute, are prosecutors to be guided by the same considerations of "policy"? Is such an ad hoc approach acceptable? It must be remembered that, apart from crimes of strict liability, criminal liability does not necessarily follow from a finding that causation is established. Some mens rea or culpability must also be found to exist. If policy considerations are to affect legal decisions, should they not be reserved for the mens rea assessment, or is it unrealistic to divorce policy considerations from any one aspect of a crime?

(b) *Mens rea approach*

TIhere are two strands to the argument here. The first is that causation will generally be established if the defendant has mens rea. It is often stated (for example, in the Hart and Honoré extract below) that an intended consequence can never be too remote. Because recklessness (or gross negligence) could be attributed to Welansky, causation could be established. The alternative analysis (theoretically quite different, but similar in effect) is that because of the doctrine of mens rea and the test of responsibility, principles of causation are unnecessary in the criminal law. Any factual cause can be held to be the legal cause because actual liability will be limited to those who have mens rea.

"Under the modern conception of mens rea no hardship can result from any finely drawn investigation of causes, since the more remote the cause the greater the difficulty of proving that the accused person intended or realised what the effect of it would be."[94]

In *Welansky* the prankster's action of switching off the light bulb was *a* cause of the fire and subsequent deaths, but as mens rea could never be attributed to him, there was no point in prosecuting him. On the other hand, because Welansky was blameworthy he was prosecuted and convicted. Under these views all the "real work" is done by the doctrine of mens rea. Either the rules on causation are shaped by the existence of mens rea, or, alternatively, no rules on causation are necessary. All that is needed, in either case, is a simple proposition that the defendant's act must have been *a* cause in the sense that without it the ultimate harm would not have occurred (known as the *sine qua non* rule or "but for" causation: *but for* the prankster turning off the bulb, the fire would never have started and the patrons would not have died).

There are problems with these approaches. How can they be adopted when dealing with crimes of strict liability? Clearly, the first view that causation is only established if there is a "blameable" cause[95] is problematic. Particularly when dealing with strict liability offences, the courts have tended

---

93   A. Norrie, "A Critique of Criminal Causation" (1991) 54 M.L.R. 685 at 701.

94   C.S. Kenny and J.W.C. Turner, *Kenny's Outlines of Criminal Law*, 19th edn (Cambridge, CUP, 1966), pp.20–21. See *Royall v The Queen* (1991) 65 A.L.J.R. 451, per McHugh J., discussed in S. Shute, "Causation: Foreseeability v Natural Consequences" (1992) 55 M.L.R. 584.

95   G. Williams, *Textbook of Criminal Law*, 2nd edn (London: Stevens, 1983), p.381.

to emphasise that whether causation is established is a question of fact and not law.[96] It has been argued that this amounts to an invitation to juries and magistrates only to find causation established if the defendant was blameworthy:

"By delegating the question of causation to the finders of fact, the courts are able to avoid the rigours of strict liability. The device allows both courts and Parliament to bury their heads in the sand, and to avoid any reassessment of the role of strict liability in criminal law. The courts undermine the rigidity of the strict liability rules by allowing juries to introduce a judgmental or culpability element into their decision-making on causation."[97]

However, in *Environment Agency v Empress Car Co (Abertillery) Ltd*[98] it was expressly stated that causation may be established even though the defendant did not intend the harm and was not even negligent; any other approach would defeat the object of strict liability legislation. Under the second view, causation would be established on a simple "but for" basis in all cases regardless of how far removed the act was from the result. Such an approach would be unacceptable and does not represent the law. While it is arguable that causation is more easily established in cases of strict liability, it is nevertheless clear that legal rules of causation do exist. As stated in *Environment Agency v Empress Car Co (Abertillery) Ltd*: "while liability is strict . . . it is not an absolute liability in the sense that all that has to be shown is that the polluting matter escaped from the defendant's land".[99] In *Alphacell v Woodward*[100] it was indicated that causation depended on a "proper attribution of responsibility". While "responsibility" in this context should not be confused with culpability, it is clear that more than "but for" causation needs to be established. This was most recently confirmed by the Supreme Court in the case of *Hughes*,[101] extracted below.

Even in cases where mens rea is established, there are problems with these approaches to causation.[102] The result would be that Welansky, because he had mens rea (as defined in that case), would still have been liable even if the waiter, Stanley, had deliberately started the fire with the intention of killing everyone in the nightclub. Would such a result be acceptable? If these views are correct, is it right that *all* liability should turn on such a nebulous and elusive concept as mens rea? It might well be thought better to clarify and strengthen the rules on causation which could lead to a diminution of the importance of the doctrine of mens rea.

(c) *Quest for general principles*

Not satisfied with the above approaches, attempts have been made to formulate general principles of causation that could be applicable in all cases. Two of these attempted formulations will be presented:

(1) Hart and Honoré's principles derived from our commonsense notions of causation; and

(2) proposals by the Criminal Law Team of the Law Commission.

---

[96] *National Rivers Authority v Yorkshire Water Services Ltd* [1994] 4 All E.R. 274; *Alphacell v Woodward* [1972] A.C. 824.
[97] N. Padfield, "Clean Water and Muddy Causation: Is Causation a Question of Law or Fact, or Just a Way of Allocating Blame?" [1995] Crim. L.R. 683 at 692–693.
[98] *Empress Car Co (Abertillery) Ltd* [1999] 2 A.C. 22. See also *Southern Water Authority v Pegrum and Pegrum* [1989] Crim. L.R. 442.
[99] *Empress Car Co (Abertillery) Ltd* [1999] 2 A.C. 22 at 33.
[100] *Alphacell v Woodward* [1972] A.C. 854.
[101] [2014] 1 Cr. App. R. 6 at [29].
[102] V. Tadros, *Criminal Responsibility* (Oxford: OUP, 2005), pp.175–181.

(i) Hart and Honoré's principles of causation

Events do not have single "causes", but only occur when there is a combination of a complex set of conditions. We might identify the dropping of a lighted cigarette in a waste-paper basket as the cause of a fire but in reality this leads to a fire only if certain other conditions are satisfied: there must be oxygen in the air, there must be combustible material in the waste-paper basket, and so on. Each of these conditions is equally necessary if a fire is to be started. How are we to select one of this complex set of conditions as the cause?

H.L.A. Hart and Tony Honoré, Causation in the Law, 2nd edn (1985), pp.29, 33–34, 42, 77–80, 326, 340–341:

"Human action in the simple cases, where we produce some desired effect by the manipulation of an object in our environment, is an interference in the natural course of events which *makes a difference* in the way these develop . . . Common experience teaches us that, left to themselves, the things we manipulate, since they have a 'nature' or characteristic way of behaving, would persist in states or exhibit changes different from those which we have learnt to bring about in them by our manipulation. The notion that a cause is essentially something which interferes with or intervenes in the course of events which would normally take place, is central to our commonsense concept of cause . . .

[I]n distinguishing between causes and conditions two contrasts are of prime importance. These are the contrasts between what is abnormal and what is normal in relation to any given thing or subject-matter, and between a free deliberate human action and all other conditions . . .

(a) Abnormal and normal conditions

. . . In the case of a building destroyed by fire 'mere conditions' will be factors such as the oxygen in the air, the presence of combustible material or the dryness of the building . . . These factors are, of course, just those which are present alike both in the case where such accidents occur and in the normal cases where they do not; and it is this consideration that leads us to reject them as the cause of the accident, even though it is true that without them the accident would not have occurred . . . such factors do not 'make the difference' between disaster and normal functioning, as . . . the dropping of a lighted cigarette [does] . . .

(b) Voluntary action

. . . [A] voluntary human action intended to bring about what in fact happens, and in the manner in which it happens, has a special place in causal inquiries; not so much because this, if present among a set of conditions required for the production of the effect, is often treated as the cause (though this is true), but because, when the question is how far back a cause shall be traced through a number of intervening causes, such a voluntary action very often is regarded both as a limit and also as still the cause even though other later abnormal occurrences are recognized as causes . . .

[However in certain cases even when an actor intends to achieve a result (and that result occurs), the chain of causation between the actor's conduct and the result might be broken.]

Tracing consequences

. . . A hits B who falls to the ground stunned and bruised by the blow; at that moment a tree crashes to the ground and kills B. A has certainly caused B's bruises but not his death . . .

The connexion between A's action and B's death . . . would naturally be described in the language of *coincidence*. 'It was a coincidence: it just happened that, at the very moment when A knocked B down, a tree crashed at the very place where he fell and killed him.' . . . We speak of a coincidence whenever the conjunction of two or more events in certain spatial or temporal relations (1) is very unlikely by ordinary standards and (2) is for some reason significant or important, provided (3) that they occur without human contrivance and (4) are independent of each other . . .

In the present case the fall of the tree just as B was struck down within its range satisfies the four criteria for a coincidence which we have enumerated. First, though neither event was of a very rare or exceptional kind, their conjunction would be rated very unlikely judged by the standards of ordinary experience. Secondly, this conjunction was causally significant for it was a necessary part of the process terminating in B's death. Thirdly, this conjunction was not consciously designed by A; had he known of the impending fall of the tree and hit B with the intention that he should fall within its range B's death would not have been the result of any coincidence. A would certainly have caused it. The common-sense principle that a contrived conjunction cannot be a coincidence is the element of truth in the legal maxim (too broadly stated even for legal purposes) that an intended consequence cannot be too 'remote'. Fourthly, each member of the conjunction in this case was independent of the other; whereas if B had fallen against the tree with an impact sufficient to bring it down on him, this sequence of physical events, though freakish in its way, would not be a coincidence and in most contexts of ordinary life, as in the law, the course of events would be summarized by saying that in this case, unlike that of the coincidence, A's act was the cause of B's death, since each stage is the effect of the preceding stage. Thus, the blow forced the victim against the tree, the effect of this was to make the tree fall and the fall of the tree killed the victim.

One further criterion in addition to these four must be satisfied if a conjunction of events is to rank as a coincidence and as a limit when the consequences of the action are traced . . . An abnormal *condition* existing at the time of a human intervention is distinguished both by ordinary thought and, with a striking consistency, by most legal systems from an abnormal event or conjunction of events subsequent to that intervention; the former, unlike the latter, are not ranked as coincidences or 'extraneous' causes when the consequences of the intervention come to be traced. Thus A innocently gives B a tap over the head of a normally quite harmless character, but because B is then suffering from some rare disease the tap has, as we say, 'fatal results'. In this case A has caused B's death though unintentionally. The scope of the principle which thus distinguishes contemporaneous abnormal conditions from subsequent events is unclear; but at least where a human being initiates some physical change in a thing, animal, or person, abnormal physical states of the object affected, existing at the time, are ranked as part of the circumstances in which the cause 'operates'. In the familiar controlling imagery these are part of 'the stage already set' before the 'intervention'.

. . . Just how unlikely must a conjunction be to rank as a coincidence, and in the light of what knowledge is likelihood to be assessed? The only answer is: 'very unlikely in the light of the knowledge available to ordinary men.'

. . . [S]o in criminal law courts have often limited responsibility by appealing to the causal distinctions embedded in ordinary thought, with their emphasis on voluntary interventions and abnormal or coincidental events as factors negativing responsibility.

Voluntary conduct

The free, deliberate, and informed intervention of a second person, not acting in concert with the first, and intending to bring about the harm which in fact occurs or recklessly courting it, is normally held to relieve the first actor of criminal responsibility. One must distinguish, however, the situation where the first actor's conduct was sufficient in the existing circumstances to bring about the harm (. . . the case for holding the first actor responsible despite the voluntary intervention of the second is naturally much stronger) . . . from that where it was not sufficient without the intervention of the second actor (. . . here most decisions relieve the first actor of responsibility) . . .

Abnormality

The basic principle here is that a physical state or event, even if subsequent to the act of the defendant, does not negative causal connection if it is normal or usual in the context. In criminal as in civil law a conjunction of events amounting to a coincidence is held to negative causal connection." A central problem with this analysis is that everything depends on one's definition of "normal", "abnormal" and "voluntary". As Norrie says:

> "Thus, individuals are held to be causes until something abnormal intervenes, but what is abnormal depends upon social perception, and therefore upon a socio-political label being stuck upon it. Similarly, causation stretches as far as the new voluntary act of a third party, but what is meant by voluntary can be as narrow or as broad as one likes, depending upon how much one is prepared to recognise the social character of the lives of individuals."[103]

(ii) Proposals by the Criminal Law Team of the Law Commission

In 1989 the Law Commission's Draft Criminal Code Bill contained a "restatement" of the then current law.[104] The central provision was that an intervening act would not break the causal chain if it was not foreseen and was not reasonably foreseeable. Responding to important developments in the law (to be explored in this section), the following proposals were suggested in 2002.[105] These proposals have never been carried forward into a Law Commission Consultation Paper or Report.

Criminal Law Team of the Law Commission, Draft Criminal Code: External Elements: Draft Report (2002):

"(1) Subject to subsections (2) to (5), a defendant causes a result which is an element of an offence when—

(a) he does an act which makes a substantial and operative contribution to its occurrence; or

(b) he omits to do an act, which he is under a duty to do according to the law relating to the offence, and the failure to do the act makes a substantial and operative contribution to its occurrence.

(2) The finders of fact may conclude that a defendant's act or omission did not make a substantial and operative contribution to the occurrence of a result if compared with

(a) the voluntary intervention of another person; as

(b) an unforseeable natural event; unless

(i)   the defendant is subject to a legal duty to guard against the very harm that the intervention or event causes; and

(ii) the intervention was not so extraordinary as to be unforeseeable to a reasonable person in the defendant's position; and

(iii) it would have been practicable for the defendant to have taken steps to prevent the intervention.

---

[103] Norrie, "A Critique of Criminal Causation" (1991) 54 M.L.R. 685 at 692.
[104] Law Commission Paper No.177 cl.17. See the 6th edition of this book, p.451.
[105] D. Ormerod, *Smith and Hogan, Criminal Law*, 12th edn (Oxford: OUP, 2008), pp.92–93.

(3) The intervention of another person is not voluntary unless it is:

(a) free, deliberate and informed; and

(b) performed or undertaken without any physical participation from the defendant.

(4) A natural event is not unforeseeable unless:

(a) the defendant did not foresee it; and

(b) it could not have been foreseen by any reasonable person in the defendant's position.

[(5) states that subject to exceptions 'a person who procures, assists or encourages another to cause a result that is an element of an offence does not himself cause that result so as to be guilty of the offence as a principal'.]"

(iii) The law's response

In order to establish causation for the purposes of criminal liability it is necessary that there be both factual and legal causation. Most of the cases have concerned homicide and offences against the person and so discussion here will be primarily (but not exclusively) limited to these areas. The problems of causation in relation to omissions and participation in crime are discussed when dealing with those topics.

(a) *Factual causation*

The defendant's actions must be a *sine qua non* (or "but for" cause) of the result. "But for" the defendant striking the victim, she would not have died. In *White*[106] the defendant put cyanide in his mother's drink with intent to kill her. She had a heart attack and died before she had drunk any of the poisoned mixture. The defendant had not caused her death. His actions were not even a "but for" cause of her death.

(b) *Legal causation*

We have seen, however, that there may be a wide range of "but for" causers. For example, in *Welansky*, the waiter, the prankster and Welansky all satisfied this test. The law, in selecting those who are causally responsible, insists that the defendant's actions be the "operative",[107] "substantial",[108] "beyond the de minimus range",[109] or "proximate",[110] cause of the prohibited consequence; they must "contribute significantly" to the result.[111] As seen above, the Criminal Law Team of the Law Commission proposed that the act or omission must make a "substantial and operative contribution" to the result. The problem with these terms is their elasticity. They can be made as broad or narrow as one likes and essentially take one no further in the quest for principles of causation.

The creation of a new statutory homicide offence of causing death by driving whilst unlicensed, disqualified or uninsured[112] has recently highlighted the need for legal causation to be established, and confirmed that factual "but for" causation is insufficient on its own to establish liability. The offence is a constructive crime, and "a rare example of double strict liability"[113] in that to be liable no mens rea is

---

106   *White* [1910] 2 K.B. 124.
107   *R. v Malcherek (Richard Tadeusz)* (1981) 73 Cr. App. R. 173.
108   *R. v Smith (Thomas Joseph)* [1959] 2 Q.B. 35; *R. v Mitchell (Ronald James)* [1983] 2 W.L.R. 938.
109   *R. v Cato (Ronald Philip)* [1976] 1 W.L.R. 110; *R. v Notman* [1994] Crim. L.R. 518.
110   Hart and Honoré, *Causation in the Law*, 2nd edn (1985), p.4.
111   *R. v Pagett (David Keith)* (1983) 75 Cr. App. R. 279.
112   Road Traffic Act 1988 s.3ZB.
113   *Hughes* [2014] 1 Cr. App. R. 6 at [17].

needed to be proved either in relation to the underlying offence of driving without a licence, insurance or whilst disqualified, nor in relation to the causing of death. In the case of *Williams*[114] the Court of Appeal held that no blameworthy driving was required to be proved; it was enough that the defendant was driving without insurance etc. and had been involved in a fatal collision. The result of this decision was that the Court of Appeal interpreted Parliament's intention to be that any *sine qua non* connection between the defendant's illicit driving and the deceased's death would suffice as a legally sufficient cause of the death,[115] and that criminal liability could arise in situations where the defendant would not be found liable for the death under civil law. It was not long before this interpretation of the law was put to the test in front of the Supreme Court.

R. v Hughes [2014] 1 Cr. App. R. 6 (Supreme Court)

The defendant, who did not have a full driving licence and was uninsured, was driving his camper van in a faultless manner when he collided with a car coming in the opposite direction which had veered onto the wrong side of the road. The driver of the car, who had taken a significant quantity of heroin, was over-tired, and had been driving erratically for some time, died from his injuries. The defendant was charged with two counts of causing the death of another person by driving a motor vehicle on a road while uninsured and otherwise than in accordance with a licence, contrary to s.3ZB of the Road Traffic Act 1988. At trial, the Crown accepted that there was nothing that the defendant could have done to avoid the collision. On a preliminary point, the judge ruled that the defendant had not committed either offence because he had not caused the death of the car driver. However, the Court of Appeal allowed the Crown's appeal, holding that it was not an element of the offence that the defendant's driving had to exhibit any fault contributing to the accident and that it was enough that the defendant was uninsured, or without a full licence, and that his vehicle had been involved in the fatal collision and that, therefore, the trial should resume. The defendant appealed.

LORD HUGHES and LORD TOULSON:

"23 The law has frequently to confront the distinction between 'cause' in the sense of a sine qua non without which the consequence would not have occurred, and 'cause' in the sense of something which was a legally effective cause of that consequence. The former, which is often conveniently referred to as a 'but for' event, is not necessarily enough to be a legally effective cause. If it were, the woman who asked her neighbour to go to the station in his car to collect her husband would be held to have caused her husband's death if he perished in a fatal road accident on the way home. In the case law there is a well recognised distinction between conduct which sets the stage for an occurrence and conduct which on a common sense view is regarded as instrumental in bringing about the occurrence. There is a helpful review of this topic in the judgment of Glidewell LJ in *Galoo Ltd v Bright Grahame Murray* [1994] 1 W.L.R. 1360 . Amongst a number of English and Commonwealth cases of high authority, he cited, at 1373–1374, the judgment of the High Court of Australia in *March v E & MH Stramare Pty Ltd* (1991) 171 C.L.R. 506 at 515, in which Mason CJ emphasised that it is wrong to place too much weight on the 'but for' test to the exclusion of the 'common sense' approach which the common law has always favoured, and that ultimately the common law approach is not susceptible to a formula.

24 In the earlier s.3ZB case of Williams the principal focus of the argument was the defendant's submission that the new offence under s.3ZB depended on proof of some fault in the driving of the defendant. That submission failed in large part because of the simultaneous creation by the 2006 Act of the second new offence of causing death by careless driving by inserting s.2B into the 1988 Act . . . In the present case, as in that of Williams, there is no suggestion that there was anything which the defendant either did or omitted to do in the

---

[114]   *R. v Williams (Jason John)* [2010] EWCA Crim 2552.
[115]   G.R. Sullivan and A.P. Simester, "Causation Without Limits: Causing Death While Driving Without a Licence, While Disqualified or Without Insurance" [2012] Crim. L.R. 753–766.

driving of the car which contributed to the least extent to the fatality. The driving of the two defendants was, no doubt, a 'but for' cause of the death. It set the scene or provided the background to, or occasion for, the fatal collision. But that does not resolve the question whether it was a legally effective cause.

25 By the test of common sense, whilst the driving by Mr Hughes created the opportunity for his car to be run into by Mr Dickinson, what brought about the latter's death was his own dangerous driving under the influence of drugs. It was a matter of the merest chance that what he hit when he veered onto the wrong side of the road for the last of several times was the oncoming vehicle which Mr Hughes was driving. He might just as easily have gone off the road and hit a tree, in which case nobody would suggest that his death was caused by the planting of the tree, although that too would have been a sine qua non.

26 This is a statute creating a penal provision, and one of very considerable severity. The offence created is a form of homicide. To label a person a criminal killer of another is of the greatest gravity. The defendant is at risk of imprisonment for a substantial term . . . It is undoubtedly open to Parliament to legislate to create a harsh offence or penalty, just as it is open to it to take away fundamental rights, but it is not to be assumed to have done so unless that interpretation of its statute is compelled, and compelled by the language of the statute itself. The rule of construction which applies to penal legislation, and, a fortiori, to legislation which carries the penalty of imprisonment, is not identical to, but is somewhat analogous to, the principle of statutory interpretation known as the principle of legality.

27 . . . [T]he gravity of a conviction for homicide, for which the sentence may be a term of imprisonment, is such that if Parliament wishes to displace the normal approach to causation recognised by the common law, and substitute a different rule, it must do so unambiguously. Where, as here, Parliament has plainly chosen not to adopt unequivocal language which was readily available, it follows that an intention to create the meaning contended for by the Crown cannot be attributed to it.

. . .

35 The certified question in this case asks:

'Is an offence contrary to section 3ZB of the Road Traffic Act 1988, as amended by section 21(1) of the Road Safety Act 2006, committed by an unlicensed, disqualified or uninsured driver when the circumstances are that the manner of his or her driving is faultless and the deceased was (in terms of civil law) 100% responsible for causing the fatal accident or collision?'

36 For the reasons set out, enquiry into apportionment of liability in civil terms is not appropriate to a criminal trial. But it must follow from the use of the expression "causes . . . death . . . by driving" that s.3ZB requires at least some act or omission in the control of the car, which involves some element of fault, whether amounting to careless/inconsiderate driving or not, and which contributes in some more than minimal way to the death. It is not necessary that such act or omission be the principal cause of the death. In which circumstances the offence under s.3ZB will then add to the other offences of causing death by driving must remain to be worked out as factual scenarios are presented to the courts. In the present case, the agreed facts are that there was nothing which Mr Hughes did in the manner of his driving which contributed in any way to the death. It follows that the Recorder of Newcastle was correct to rule that he had not in law caused the death by his driving. The appeal should be allowed and that ruling restored."

Appeal allowed

Before examining the cases further, it might be helpful to set out some preliminary propositions.

1. General propositions

1. The defendant's actions need not be the scientific or medical cause of the result. In *McKechnie*[116] the defendant hit the victim over the head with a television set. These injuries prevented doctors operating on the victim's duodenal ulcer. The medical cause of death was a burst duodenal ulcer. The defendant was nevertheless held to have legally caused that death.

---

[116]   *R. v McKechnie (Roy Maurer)* (1992) 94 Cr. App. R. 51.

2. One can cause death or other injury by fright or shock without touching one's victim. For example, in *Watson*[117] a burglar entered a house and verbally abused the elderly householder who died of a heart attack shortly afterwards. The burglar was held to have caused the death of the householder.

3. The defendant must "take his victim as he finds him". In *Hayward*[118] the defendant chased his wife into the street. She fell down and he kicked her arm. She died. Medical evidence established that she had a persistent thyrus gland and such persons could die from a combination of fright or strong emotion and physical exertion. The defendant was convicted of manslaughter. This proposition will be explored further in due course.

4. The defendant's actions need not be the sole cause of the consequence. In *Hughes* the principal cause of the deceased's death was his own dangerous driving:

"*if* the driving of Mr Hughes was a cause of the death at all, this is the familiar case of concurrent causes. There are many examples of two or more concurrent causes of an event, all effective causes in law. A road traffic accident is one of the commoner cases, for such events are only too often the result of a combination of acts or omissions on the part of two or more persons. Where there are multiple legally effective causes, whether of a road traffic accident or of any other event, it suffices if the act or omission under consideration is a significant (or substantial) cause, in the sense that it is not de minimis or minimal. It need not be the only or the principal cause."[119]

In several of the medical cases, shortly to be discussed, the defendant attacked a victim who then received negligent treatment. As stated in *Cheshire*: 'the accused's acts need not be the sole cause or even the main cause of death, it being sufficient that his acts contributed significantly to that result'.[120] In such cases it is possible for both the original attacker and the doctors to be found to have caused the death. The civil law concept of contributory negligence plays no role in the criminal law rules on causation.

5. A *novus actus interveniens* will break the chain of causation. A *novus actus interveniens* is an intervening act or event that takes over as the new "operative" cause, relegating the defendant's actions to the realms of the history of the case. This point needs more detailed explanation.

2. Novus actus interveniens

After the defendant has acted, some other act or event or omission could occur which might have the potential to break the chain of causation. This can be a natural event, the act of a third party, or an act of the victim. In these cases the problem is whether this intervening act or event is so significant as to become the new *sole* cause of the result.

Two general principles can be stated at the outset. First, as seen above in the Hart and Honoré extract, a voluntary ("free, deliberate and informed") act by a third party will normally break the chain of causation. Secondly, with regard to acts of the victim or natural events, only those acts or events

---

[117]   *R. v Watson (Clarence Archibald)* [1989] 1 W.L.R. 684. See also *Towers* (1874) 12 Cox C.C. 530 and *Hayward* (1908) 21 Cox C.C. 692. For a medical explanation of how one can frighten someone to death, see A. Busuttil and A. McCall Smith, "Fright, Stress and Homicide" (1990) 54 Jo.C.L. 257.
[118]   *Hayward* (1908) 21 Cox C.C. 692.
[119]   *Hughes* [2014] 1 Cr. App. R. 6 at [22].
[120]   *R. v Cheshire (David William)* (1991) 93 Cr. App. R. 251.

that are "daft or unexpected" and not reasonably foreseeable will break the chain of causation. These principles, and whether they are reconcilable, can now be examined in more depth.

(a) *Natural events*

What is the position if the defendant attacks a victim and leaves them unconscious in a field where they are struck by lightning and killed? The rule here is that if the supervening natural event (being struck by lightning) is not reasonably foreseeable, it will break the chain of causation. As Hart and Honoré state, in the extract above, such an event is a "coincidence".

On the other hand, if the supervening natural event is reasonably foreseeable, the causal chain will not be broken. In *Hart*[121] the defendant attacked a victim and left her unconscious on a beach below the high-water mark where she was drowned by the incoming tide. Such an event was reasonably foreseeable and the defendant was held to have caused the death of the victim.

(b) *Human intervention*

It is useful here to distinguish between the actions of a third party and actions by the victim.

(i) Acts of third party

It will be recalled that, according to Hart and Honoré, causation cannot be traced through the voluntary action of a third party. The free, deliberate and informed intervention of a third party breaks the chain of causation. For example, if I stab my victim who is lying in the street dying and you come along and shoot the victim killing them instantly, your action will break the chain of causation. However, if you merely kick the victim, accelerating death by a matter of seconds, your "voluntary action" will not break the causal chain. The issue is one of determining the circumstances in which the voluntary action of a third party will be so significant as to break the causal chain.

R. v Latif [1996] 2 Cr. App. R. 92 (House of Lords)

The defendant was charged with importing controlled drugs into the country. In fact, the drugs were knowingly brought in by a customs officer acting with a paid informant, Homi.

LORD STEYN:

"The general principle is that the free, deliberate and informed intervention of a second person, who intends to exploit the situation created by the first, but is not acting in concert with him, is held to relieve the first actor of criminal responsibility. For example, if a thief had stolen the heroin after Shahzad delivered it to Honi, and imported it into the United Kingdom, the chain of causation would plainly have been broken. The general principle must also be applicable to the role of the customs officers in this case. They acted in full knowledge of the content of the packages. They did not act in concert with Shahzad. They acted deliberately for their own purposes whatever those might have been. In my view consistency and legal principle do not permit us to create an exception to the general principle of causation to take care of the particular problem thrown up by this case."

Appeal dismissed (as defendants were guilty of an attempt to commit the offence)

---

121 *Hart* [1986] NZLR 48, cited by A.P. Simester, J.R. Spencer, G.R. Sullivan and G.J. Virgo, *Criminal Law: Theory and Doctrine*, 5th edn (Oxford: Hart 2013), p.84.

Rafferty v R. [2007] EWCA Crim 1846

The appellant and two others seriously assaulted and the robbed the victim on a beach. The appellant took the victim's debit card and went to try to draw money from a cashpoint machine. While he was away, the others dragged the victim into the sea where he drowned. The appellant was convicted of manslaughter and appealed.

HOOPER LJ:

"[40] . . . Hart and Honore . . . [wrote]

'The free deliberate and informed intervention of a second person, who intends to exploit the situation created by the first, but is not acting in concert with him, is normally held to relieve the first actor of criminal responsibility.' . . .

[43] . . . [T]he judge gave the following direction on *novus actus interveniens* [that the jury had to be sure]:

'that the drowning of [the victim] by [the others] was not such a new and intervening act in the chain of events, which was so completely different from the injuries for which Rafferty was responsible, that it overwhelmed those injuries and destroyed any causal connection between them and the death of [the victim].'

[44] We have reached the conclusion that no jury could properly conclude that the drowning of [the victim] by [the others] was other than a new and intervening act in the chain of events."

Appeal allowed

This principle that the free, deliberate and informed intervention of a third party breaks the causal chain was not applied in the following much-criticised House of Lords' decision.

Environment Agency v Empress Car Co (Abertillery) Ltd [1999] 2 A.C. 22 (House of Lords)

The appellant company maintained a diesel oil tank on its premises. An outlet from the tank was governed by a tap which had no lock. An unknown person (probably a vandal) opened the tap causing the oil to run into a river. The company was convicted of causing polluting matter to enter controlled waters contrary to s.85(1) of the Water Resources Act 1991.

LORD HOFFMANN:

"[O]ne cannot give a commonsense answer to a question of causation for the purpose of attributing responsibility under some rule without knowing the purpose and scope of the rule . . .

What, therefore, is the nature of the duty imposed by s.85(1)? . . . It is immediately clear that the liability imposed is strict: it does not require mens rea in the sense of intention or negligence. Strict liability is imposed in the interests of protecting controlled waters from pollution . . .

. . . [T]o frame the question as 'who or what caused the result under consideration' is wrong and distracting, because it may have more than one right answer. The question is whether the defendant caused the pollution. How is foreseeability a relevant factor to consider in answering this question? . . . [T]he question is not whether the consequences ought to have been foreseen; it is whether the defendant caused the pollution. And foreseeability is not the criterion for deciding whether a person caused something or not. People often cause things which they could not have foreseen.

The true commonsense distinction is, in my view, between acts and events which, although not necessarily foreseeable in the particular case, are in the generality a normal and familiar fact of life, and facts or events which are abnormal and extraordinary . . . There is nothing unusual about people putting unlawful substances into the sewage system and the same, regrettably, is true about ordinary vandalism. So when these things happen, one does not say: that was an extraordinary coincidence, which negatived the causal connection between the original act of accumulating the polluting substance and its escape . . . On the other hand, the example I gave of the terrorist attack would be something so unusual that one would not regard the defendant's conduct as having caused the escape at all . . .

I shall try to summarise the effect of this discussion . . .

(2) The prosecution need not prove that the defendant did something which was the *immediate* cause of the pollution: maintaining tanks, lagoons or sewage systems full of noxious liquid is doing something, even if the immediate cause of the pollution was lack of maintenance, a natural event or the act of a third party.

(3) When the prosecution has identified something which the defendant did, the justices must decide whether it caused the pollution. They should not be diverted by questions like 'What was the cause of the pollution?' or 'Did something else cause the pollution?' Because to say that something else caused the pollution (like brambles clogging the pumps or vandalism by third parties) is not inconsistent with the defendant having caused it as well.

(4) If the defendant did something which produced a situation in which the polluting matter could escape but a necessary condition of the actual escape which happened was also the act of a third party or a natural event, the justices should consider whether the act or event should be regarded as a normal fact of life or something extraordinary. If it was in the general run of things a matter of ordinary occurrence, it will not negative the causal effect of the defendant's acts, even if it was not foreseeable that it would happen to that particular defendant or take that particular form. If it can be regarded as something extraordinary, it will be open to the justices to hold that the defendant did not cause the pollution.

(5) The distinction between ordinary and extraordinary is one of fact."

Appeal dismissed

This decision has received a hostile reception on the basis that while the test laid down in this case (ordinary v extraordinary events) is the correct test for natural events (such as brambles clogging the pumps), it is not the appropriate test for the voluntary actions of third parties: the acts of the vandal should have been held to have caused the pollution to the river.

However, the decision is perhaps understandable in policy terms. The offence here was one of strict liability. Many offences are deliberately made ones of strict liability to ensure that persons and companies take every precaution to prevent the harm occurring. Such persons are under a legal duty to guard against the harm that is caused, albeit by another; this includes taking steps to prevent deliberate interventions by third parties. This decision has been followed in other strict liability cases. In *Environment Agency v Brook Plc*[122] it was held that leakage of pollution caused by a latent fault in a seal was a rare but ordinary fact of life. Although the bursting of the seal was unforeseeable, it was not an extraordinary event breaking the causal chain. In *Express Ltd (t/a Express Dairies Distribution) v Environment Agency*[123] it was held that a vehicle tyre blow out, while rare, was an event in the "ordinary run of things". Lord Hoffmann's use of the term "extraordinary" in the context of third party acts or natural events was approved.

However, it is doubtful whether this reasoning should apply to non-strict liability offences. Lord Hoffmann has stated, extra-judicially, that the voluntary intervention rule should be applied to crimes where fault is required; it is only where liability is strict that the wider rule endorsed in *Empress* is appropriate.[124] Such a limitation has now been introduced by the House of Lords' decision of *Kennedy (No.2)* which strongly reaffirms the free, deliberate and informed intervention principle and arguably restricts *Empress* to offences of strict liability or, even more narrowly, to "cases of pollution and envi-

---

[122]   *Environment Agency v Brook Plc, The Times*, March 26, 1998.
[123]   *Express Ltd (t/a Express Dairies Distribution) v Environment Agency* [2003] 2 All E.R. 778.
[124]   Hoffmann, "Causation" (2005) 30 L.Q.R. 121.

ronmental crimes".[125] *Kennedy (No.2)* is extracted and discussed below.

The voluntary intervention test involves a determination of whether the act of the third party is "free, deliberate and informed".

R. v Pagett (1983) 76 Cr. App. R. 279 (Court of Appeal, Criminal Division)

The appellant shot at police officers who were attempting to arrest him for various serious offences. He had a girl with him and against her will used her body to shield himself from any retaliation by the officers. The officers returned the appellant's fire; three of their bullets hit the girl; she died from these wounds. The appellant was convicted of manslaughter and appealed to the Court of Appeal.

GOFF LJ:

"[One of the] specific points raised on behalf of the appellant . . . [was that] the learned judge . . . ought to have held that the appellant had not in the circumstances of this case caused the death of the deceased. The learned judge, in directing himself upon the law, ought to have held that where the act which immediately resulted in a fatal injury was the act of another party, albeit in legitimate self-defence, then the ensuing death was too remote or indirect to be imputed to the original aggressor . . .

[I]t was pressed upon us by [counsel for the appellant] that there either was, or should be, a . . . rule of English law, whereby, as a matter of policy, no man should be convicted of homicide (or, we imagine, any crime of violence to another person) unless he himself, or another person acting in concert with him, fired the shot (or, we imagine, struck the blow) which was the immediate cause of the victim's death (or injury).

No English authority was cited to us in support of any such proposition, and we know of none. So far as we are aware, there is no such rule in English law; and . . . we can see no basis in principle for any such rule in English law . . .

In our judgment, the question whether an accused person can be held guilty of homicide, either murder or manslaughter, of a victim the immediate cause of whose death is the act of another person must be determined on the ordinary principles of causation . . .

In cases of homicide, it is rarely necessary to give the jury any direction on causation as such . . . Even where it is necessary to direct the jury's minds to the question of causation, it is usually enough to direct them simply that in law the accused's act need not be the sole cause, or even the main cause, of the victim's death, it being enough that his act contributed significantly to that result. Occasionally, however, a specific issue of causation may arise. One such case is where although an act of the accused constitutes a *causa sine qua non* of (or necessary condition for) the death of the victim, nevertheless the intervention of a third person may be regarded as the sole cause of the victim's death, thereby relieving the accused of criminal responsibility. Such intervention, if it has such an effect, has often been described by lawyers as a *novus actus interveniens* . . .

Professors Hart and Honoré, *Causation in the Law* . . . consider the circumstances in which the intervention of a third person, not acting in concert with the accused, may have the effect of relieving the accused of criminal responsibility. The criterion which they suggest should be applied in such circumstances is whether the intervention is voluntary, *i.e.* whether it is 'free, deliberate and informed'. We resist the temptation of expressing the judicial opinion whether we find ourselves in complete agreement with that definition; though we certainly consider it to be broadly correct and supported by authority. Among the examples which the authors give of non-voluntary conduct, which is not effective to relieve the accused of responsibility, are two which are germane to the present case, *viz.* a reasonable act performed for the purpose of self-preservation, and an act done in performance of a legal duty.

There can, we consider, be no doubt that a reasonable act performed for the purpose of self-preservation, being of course itself an act caused by the accused's own act, does not operate as a *novus actus interveniens* . . . Now one form of self-preservation is self-defence; for present purposes, we can see no distinction in principle between an attempt to escape the consequences of the accused's act, and a response which takes the form of self-defence. Furthermore, in our judgment, if a reasonable act of self-defence, against the act of the accused causes the death of a third party we can see no reason in principle why the act of self-defence, being an involuntary act caused by the act of the accused, should relieve the accused from criminal responsibility for the death of the third party . . .

The principles which we have stated are principles of law . . . It follows that where, in any particular case, there

---

[125]   Ormerod, Commentary to *Kennedy (No.2)* [2008] Crim. L.R. 224.

is an issue concerned with what we have for convenience called *novus actus interveniens*, it will be appropriate for the judge to direct the jury in accordance with these principles.

    . . . [I]t is for the judge to direct the jury with reference to the relevant principles of law relating to causation, and then to leave it to the jury to decide, in the light of those principles, whether or not the relevant causal link has been established."

Appeal dismissed

In this case the self-defensive actions of the police were regarded as "involuntary" and so did not constitute a "free, deliberate and informed" intervention and, accordingly, did not break the causal chain. The fact that they were acting negligently[126] was not relevant. What, though, of a case in which two gunmen engaged in a shoot-out causes the death of an innocent member of the public who happens to be passing by? Could it be said that not only the first gunman, from whose weapon the fatal shot was fired, but also his adversary at whom he was shooting, caused the death? According to the dissenting judgment of Lord Kerr in *Gnango*, the answer is no: by returning fire the second gunman does not "cause" the first gunman to fire again; the first gunman's act of firing another shot is a free, deliberate and informed act breaking the chain of causation between the second gunman's engagement in the shoot-out, and the passer-by's death. [127] Unlike the police officers in *Pagett*, the gunman in *Gnango* was not acting involuntarily as it was his choice to fire the first shot in an act of aggression. As will be seen later, the second gunman was, however, found liable for murder in this case.[128]

    In several of the leading cases it has been action on the part of doctors, often acting negligently, that has been alleged to be a novus actus interveniens.

R. v Smith [1959] 2 Q.B. 35 (Courts Martial Appeal Court)

During a fight in a barracks the appellant twice stabbed the victim, Private Creed, with a bayonet. He appealed against his conviction for murder on the ground, inter alia, that the summing up by the judge-advocate on the question of causation was defective.

LORD PARKER CJ:

"The second ground concerns a question of causation. The deceased man in fact received two bayonet wounds, one in the arm and one in the back. The one in the back, unknown to anybody, had pierced the lung and caused haemorrhage. There followed a series of unfortunate occurrences. A fellow-member of his company tried to carry him to the medical reception station. On the way he tripped over a wire and dropped the deceased man. He picked him up again, went a little further, and fell apparently a second time, causing the deceased man to be dropped on to the ground. Thereafter he did not try a third time but went for help, and ultimately the deceased man was brought into the reception station. There, the medical officer, Captain Millward, and his orderly were trying to cope with a number of other cases . . . and it is clear that they did not appreciate the seriousness of the deceased man's condition or exactly what had happened. A transfusion of saline solution was attempted and failed. When his breathing seemed impaired, he was given oxygen and artificial respiration was applied, and, in fact, he died after he had been in the station about an hour, which was about two hours after the original stabbing. It is now known that, having regard to the injuries which the man had in fact suffered, his lung being pierced, the treatment that he was given was thoroughly bad and might well have affected his chances of recovery. There was evidence that there is a tendency for a wound of this sort to heal and for the haemorrhage to stop. No doubt his being dropped on the ground and having artificial respiration applied would halt or at any rate impede the

---

126   Some 10 years later the deceased girl's mother was awarded damages against the police for their negligent handling of the siege (*The Guardian*, December 4 and 5, 1990).
127   *R. v Gnango (Armel)* [2011] UKSC 59 at [131]–[132].
128   See p.208 below and Ch.6 at p.560 where this case is extracted.

chances of healing. Further, there were no facilities whatsoever for blood transfusion, which would have been the best possible treatment. There was evidence that, if he had received immediate and different treatment, he might not have died. Indeed, had facilities for blood transfusion been available and been administered, Dr Camps, who gave evidence for the defence, said that his chances of recovery were as high as 75 per cent.

In these circumstances Mr Bowen [counsel for the appellant] urges that not only was a careful summing-up required but that a correct direction to the court would have been that they must be satisfied that the death of Private Creed was a natural consequence and the sole consequence of the wound sustained by him and flowed directly from it. If there was, says Mr Bowen, any other cause, whether resulting from negligence or not, if, as he contends here, something happened which impeded the chance of the deceased recovering, then the death did not result from the wound. The court is quite unable to accept that contention. It seems to the court that if at the time of death the original wound is still an operating cause and a substantial cause, then the death can properly be said to be the result of the wound, albeit that some other cause of death is also operating. Only if it can be said that the original wounding is merely the setting in which another cause operates can it be said that the death does not result from the wound. Putting it in another way, only if the second cause is so overwhelming as to make the original wound merely part of the history can it be said that the death does not flow from the wound . . .

Mr Bowen placed great reliance on . . . *Jordan* . . . The court is satisfied that *Jordan's* case was a very particular case depending on its exact facts . . .

In the present case . . . a man is stabbed in the back, his lung is pierced and haemorrhage results; two hours later he dies of haemorrhage from that wound; in the interval there is no time for a careful examination, and the treatment given turns out in the light of subsequent knowledge to have been inappropriate and, indeed, harmful. In those circumstances no reasonable jury or court could, properly directed, in our view possibly come to any other conclusion than that the death resulted from the original wound."

Appeal dismissed

R. v Jordan (1956) 40 Cr. App. R. 152 (Court of Appeal, Criminal Division)

The appellant stabbed the deceased who died some days later in hospital. Jordan, who had been convicted of murder, sought to adduce further medical evidence on appeal to the effect that the wound was not the cause of death.

HALLET J:

"There were two things other than the wound which were stated by these two medical witnesses to have brought about death. The stab wound had penetrated the intestine in two places, but it was mainly healed at the time of death. With a view to preventing infection it was thought right to administer an antibiotic, terramycin.

It was agreed by the two additional witnesses that that was the proper course to take, and a proper dose was administered. Some people, however, are intolerant to terramycin, and Beaumont was one of those people. After the initial doses he developed diarrhoea, which was only properly attributable, in the opinion of those doctors, to the fact that the patient was intolerant to terramycin. Thereupon the administration of terramycin was stopped, but unfortunately the very next day the resumption of such administration was ordered by another doctor and it was recommenced the following day. The two doctors both take the same view about it. Dr Simpson said that to introduce a poisonous substance after the intolerance of the patient was shown was palpably wrong. Mr Blackburn agreed.

Other steps were taken which were also regarded by the doctors as wrong—namely, the intravenous introduction of wholly abnormal quantities of liquid far exceeding the output. As a result the lungs became waterlogged and pulmonary oedema was discovered. Mr Blackburn said that he was not surprised to see that condition after the introduction of so much liquid, and that pulmonary oedema leads to broncho-pneumonia as an inevitable sequel, and it was from broncho-pneumonia that Beaumont died.

We are disposed to accept it as the law that death resulting from any normal treatment employed to deal with a felonious injury may be regarded as caused by the felonious injury . . . It is sufficient to point out here that this was not normal treatment. Not only one feature, but two separate and independent features, of treatment were, in the opinion of the doctors, palpably wrong and these produced the symptoms discovered at the post-mortem examination which were the direct and immediate cause of death, namely, the pneumonia resulting from the condition of oedema which was found . . .

We feel no uncertainty at all that, whatever direction had been given to the jury and however correct it had been, the jury would have felt precluded from saying that they were satisfied that death was caused by the stab wound."

Conviction quashed

R. v Cheshire (1991) 93 Cr. App. R. 251 (Court of Appeal, Criminal Division)

The appellant shot the deceased in the leg and stomach. As part of his treatment in hospital a tracheotomy tube was placed in his windpipe. Some two months later, at a time when his wounds were no longer threatening his life, his windpipe became obstructed and he died. This was due to a narrowing of the windpipe where the tracheotomy had been performed—a rare but not unknown complication. At the appellant's trial for murder evidence was given that the medical treatment had been negligent. The trial judge directed the jury that only recklessness, and not negligence, could break the causal chain. He was convicted of murder and appealed.

BELDAM LJ:

"[Causation] is a question of fact for the jury, but it is a question of fact to be decided in accordance with legal principles explained to the jury by the judge . . .
    In the criminal law the jury . . . will we think derive little assistance from figures of speech more appropriate for conveying degrees of fault or blame in questions of apportionment . . . [W]e think such figures of speech are to be avoided in giving guidance to a jury on the question of causation . . .
    [W]hen the victim of a criminal attack is treated for wounds or injuries by doctors or other medical staff attempting to repair the harm done, it will only be in the most extraordinary and unusual case that such treatment can be said to be so independent of the acts of the accused that it could be regarded in law as the cause of the victim's death to the exclusion of the accused's acts . . .
    [T]he accused's acts need not be the sole cause or even the main cause of death it being sufficient that his acts contributed significantly to that result. Even though negligence in the treatment of the victim was the immediate cause of his death, the jury should not regard it as excluding the responsibility of the accused unless the negligent treatment was so independent of his acts, and in itself so potent in causing death, that they regard the contribution made by his acts as insignificant.
    It is not the function of the jury to evaluate competing causes or to choose which is dominant provided they are satisfied that the accused's acts can fairly be said to have made a significant contribution to the victim's death. We think the word 'significant' conveys the necessary substance of a contribution made to the death which is more than negligible . . .
    [W]e think that the judge erred when he invited the jury to consider the degree of fault in the medical treatment rather than its consequences, [but] we consider that no miscarriage of justice has actually occurred. Even if more experienced doctors than those who attended the deceased would have recognised the rare complication in time to have prevented the deceased's death, that complication was a direct consequence of the appellant's acts, which remained a significant cause of his death."

Appeal dismissed

R. v Mellor [1996] 2 Cr. App. R. 245 (Court of Appeal, Criminal Division)

The appellant was charged with the murder of an elderly man who, after being attacked, died in hospital two days later. It was alleged that negligence by the hospital staff broke the chain of causation. The appellant was convicted and appealed.

SCHIEMANN LJ:

"The immediate cause of death was broncho-pneumonia which, upon the evidence, was brought on directly by the injuries inflicted by the appellant. Those injuries were certainly the cause of death. Probably if the appellant had been administered sufficient oxygen in time, the broncho-pneumonia would not have been fatal, and therefore the failure to administer sufficient oxygen could be regarded as a cause of death. It was asserted on behalf of the appellant, and supported by expert evidence, that the failure to administer sufficient oxygen in time amounted to negligence or incompetence . . .

In homicide cases, where the victim of the alleged crime does not die immediately, supervening events will occur which are likely to have some causative effect leading to the victim's death; for example, a delay in the arrival of the ambulance, a delay in resuscitation, the victim's individual response to medical or surgical treatment, and the quality of medical, surgical and nursing care. Sometimes such an event may be the result of negligence or mistake or bad luck. It is a question of fact and degree in each case for the jury to decide, having regard to the gravity of the supervening event, however caused, whether the injuries inflicted by the defendant were a significant cause of death.

The onus on the Crown is to make the jury sure that the injuries inflicted by the defendant were a significant cause of death. However, the Crown have no onus of establishing that any supervening event was not a significant cause of death or that there was no medical negligence in the deceased's treatment.

. . . In appropriate cases the jury can be told that there may be a number of significant causes leading to a victim's death. So as long as the Crown proves that the injuries inflicted by the defendant were at least a significant, if not the only, cause of death that will be sufficient to prove the nexus between injury and death . . .

In our judgment, it is undesirable in most cases for juries to be asked to embark upon the question of whether medical negligence as a significant contributory cause of death has been negatived because it diverts the jury from the relevant question, namely, has the accused's act contributed significantly to the victim's death?"

Appeal dismissed

The effect of these decisions is that the actions of medical practitioners will (almost) never break the causal chain. It is irrelevant that the doctors were negligent or even reckless. It will require a "most extraordinary and unusual case" (*Cheshire*) for this to occur. Perhaps *Jordan* was such a case. The original wound had almost healed and had become part of the background. The victim was effectively killed by the administration of a drug to which he was known to be allergic. However, even on these facts subsequent cases have been careful to confine *Jordan* as being a "very exceptional"[129] case. Indeed, it is difficult to see that *Jordan* is really different from some of the other cases. In *Smith* the victim's treatment was "thoroughly bad". In *Jordan* it was "palpably wrong". In *Smith* the victim had a 75 per cent chance of recovery had he received proper medical treatment. In *Jordan* the victim's wounds had almost healed. Hart and Honoré argue that abnormal contingencies constitute a "coincidence" and break the chain of causation. It is difficult to see that the treatment in *Jordan* was an abnormal contingency, but that this was not the case in *Smith*. Of course, it could be argued that the victim in *Jordan* died from the drugs prescribed by the doctors whereas in *Smith* he died from loss of blood caused by the stab wound inflicted by the defendant. This cannot be the explanation. The victim in *Cheshire* did not die from his wounds. He died because the doctors inserted a tracheotomy tube in his windpipe and were negligent in their subsequent treatment. Why was this not an abnormal contingency?

The picture that starts to emerge is that Hart and Honoré's "abnormal contingency" and "coincidence" are hollow concepts that can be interpreted as the courts see fit. In short, all these "principled tests" provide no more than a veil under which decisions are ultimately based on policy considerations. With a National Health Service hard pressed for funds the courts are not going to exempt violent assailants from liability because their victims did not receive the best treatment—except in what can be regarded as very exceptional cases such as *Jordan*.

Are these cases consistent with the now dominant principle that a "free, deliberate and informed" intervention by a third party (the doctors) will break the causal chain? Ashworth has argued that "doctors work under pressure, occasionally having to make rapid decisions, but they are trained

---

[129]   *Malcherek* (1981) 73 Cr. App. R. 173.

and trusted to exercise clinical judgment in these circumstances. Doctors are under a duty to treat patients, but they surely do so voluntarily".[130]

However, the better view is that the doctors, in most of these cases, were simply performing their duty to their patients and so their actions cannot count as sufficiently free or voluntary to break the causal chain (although it is hard to see why this did not apply to the doctors in *Jordan*). "Voluntariness" here does not mean literal voluntariness. In *Pagett* the court accepted the examples given by Hart and Honoré of non-voluntary conduct which included "a reasonable act . . . done in performance of a legal duty". The actions of the doctors can be brought within this: doctors owe a legal duty to their patients. Whether their actions constitute a "reasonable act" in the discharge of that duty is obviously a context-sensitive issue in which the pressures of hard-worked doctors operating in an under-funded National Health Service must be taken into account.

(ii) Acts of victim

a. Victim escaping

R. v Roberts (1972) 56 Cr. App. R. 95 (Court of Appeal, Criminal Division)

A girl who was a passenger in the appellant's car injured herself by jumping out of the car while it was in motion. Her explanation was that the appellant had made sexual advances to her and was trying to pull her coat off. The appellant was convicted of an assault occasioning actual bodily harm. He appealed on the ground, inter alia, that causation had not been established.

STEPHENSON LJ:

"The test is: Was it the natural result of what the alleged assailant said and did, in the sense that it was something that could reasonably have been foreseen as the consequence of what he was saying or doing? As it was put in one of the old cases, it had got to be shown to be his act, and if of course the victim does something so 'daft', in the words of the appellant in this case, or so unexpected, not that this particular assailant did not actually foresee it but that no reasonable man could be expected to foresee it, then it is only in a very remote and unreal sense a consequence of his assault, it is really occasioned by a voluntary act on the part of the victim which could not reasonably be foreseen and which breaks the chain of causation between the assault and the harm or injury."

Appeal dismissed

R. v Mackie (1973) 57 Cr. App. R. 453 (Court of Appeal, Criminal Division)

A three-year-old boy whom the appellant was looking after fell downstairs while running away in fear of being ill-treated by the appellant. The boy died. The appellant appealed against conviction for manslaughter.

STEPHENSON LJ:

"The victim was a child of three and regard must be had to his age in considering whether his reaction was well-founded or well-grounded on an apprehension of immediate violence (in the language of the old cases appropriate to adults) and therefore reasonably to be expected . . . [T]he issue is whether the boy 'over-reacted' in a way which the appellant could not reasonably be expected to have foreseen . . . At the end of the summing-up the judge came back to these questions in suggesting what the vital points might be: First, was the boy in fear of Mackie? Secondly, did that cause him to try to escape? Thirdly, if he was in fear, was that fear well-founded?"

Appeal dismissed

---

[130]   Ashworth and Horder, *Principles of Criminal Law*, 7th edn (2013), p.111.

R. v Williams and Davis (1992) 95 Cr. App. R. 1 (Court of Appeal, Criminal Division)

The appellants gave a lift to a hitch-hiker and allegedly tried to rob him. The hitch-hiker jumped from the moving car (travelling about 30 mph) and died from head injuries caused by falling into the road. The appellants were convicted of manslaughter and appealed.

STUART-SMITH LJ:

"There must be some proportionality between the gravity of the threat and the action of the deceased in seeking to escape from it . . . [T]he deceased's conduct . . . [must] be something that a reasonable and responsible man in the assailant's shoes would have foreseen . . . [T]he nature of the threat is of importance in considering both the foreseeability of harm to the victim from the threat and the question whether the deceased's conduct was proportionate to the threat, that is to say that it was within the ambit of reasonableness and not so daft as to make it his own voluntary act which amounted to a *novus actus interveniens* and consequently broke the chain of causation. It should of course be borne in mind that a victim may in the agony of the moment do the wrong thing . . .

The jury should consider two questions: first, whether it was reasonably foreseeable that some harm, albeit not serious harm, was likely to result from the threat itself; and, secondly, whether the deceased's reaction in jumping from the moving car was within the range of responses which might be expected from a victim placed in the situation which he was. The jury should bear in mind any particular characteristic of the victim and the fact that in the agony of the moment he may act without thought and deliberation . . .

In our judgment the failure of the judge to give any direction on causation was a misdirection and the conviction on this count must be quashed."

Appeals allowed

In *Corbett*[131] the defendant assaulted a drunk, mentally-handicapped man who, in the course of running away, fell into a gutter where he was struck by a passing car and killed. The Court of Appeal approved the trial judge's direction that the issue was whether the victim's reaction was within the foreseeable range and, in assessing this, they had to decide whether this was something that might be expected as a reaction of somebody in that state. While the test of foreseeability allows account to be taken of the victim's situation and characteristics, this is not true of defendants. In *Marjoram*[132] it was stated that the test of reasonable foresight is purely objective and so no account could be taken of the age or sex or any other characteristics of the defendant—otherwise, where two defendants with different characteristics acted together, one might be held to have caused the result but not the other.

Are these cases consistent with the rule that the "free, deliberate and informed" intervention of a third party will break the chain of causation? One view is that this rule does not apply to the actions of victims as they are not "third parties". Such an argument seems implausible and would be inconsistent with the now leading House of Lords' decision of *Kennedy (No.2)*, which is discussed below. The better view is that these cases are consistent with the "free, deliberate and informed" intervention rule. The fear of the victims in these cases was such that they had no real choice but to do as they did. It will be recalled that one of Hart and Honoré's examples of non-voluntary conduct, approved in *Pagett*, was a "reasonable act performed for the purpose of self-preservation" such as an act by the victim in attempting to escape from the violence of the defendant.

---

[131]   *R. v Corbett (Christopher)* [1996] Crim. L.R. 594.
[132]   *R. v M (Richard) (A Juvenile)* [2000] Crim. L.R. 372.

b. Drugs supplied to victim

What is the position if the defendant supplies drugs to another who injects herself and dies? Will the act of self-injection constitute a voluntary intervening act, breaking the chain of causation? In *Kennedy (No.1)*[133] this view was rejected and it was held that the supplier could be regarded as having caused the death of the person self-injecting the drugs. However, in *Dias*[134] it was held that the injector has a choice whether to inject and so this can break the causal chain. In *Finlay*[135] it was held that causation can be established on such facts as the defendant was a "joint principal in V's act". In this case the *Empress* principles were applied: only if the acts of the injector were "extraordinary" would the causal chain be broken. *Kennedy (No.1)* and *Finlay* have now been overruled by the following decision.

R. v Kennedy (No.2) [2008] 1 A.C. 269 (House of Lords)

The appellant prepared a "hit" of heroin for the deceased and gave him the syringe ready for injection. The deceased injected himself and returned the syringe to the appellant who left the room. The injection resulted in the death of the deceased. The appellant was convicted of manslaughter and appealed.

LORD BINGHAM OF CORNHILL:

"2 The question certified by the Court of Appeal (Criminal Division) for the opinion of the House neatly encapsulates the question raised by this appeal:

'When is it appropriate to find someone guilty of manslaughter where that person has been involved in the supply of a class A controlled drug, which is then freely and voluntarily self-administered by the person to whom it was supplied, and the administration of the drug then causes his death?' . . .

14 The criminal law generally assumes the existence of free will. The law recognises certain exceptions, in the case of the young, those who for any reason are not fully responsible for their actions, and the vulnerable, and it acknowledges situations of duress and necessity, as also of deception and mistake. But, generally speaking, informed adults of sound mind are treated as autonomous beings able to make their own decisions how they will act, and none of the exceptions is relied on as possibly applicable in this case. Thus D is not to be treated as causing V to act in a certain way if V makes a voluntary and informed decision to act in that way rather than another. There are many classic statements to this effect. In his article "Finis for Novus Actus?" [1989] CLJ 391, 392, Professor Glanville Williams wrote:

'I may suggest reasons to you for doing something; I may urge you to do it, tell you it will pay you to do it, tell you it is your duty to do it. My efforts may perhaps make it very much more likely that you will do it. But they do not cause you to do it, in the sense in which one causes a kettle of water to boil by putting it on the stove. Your volitional act is regarded (within the doctrine of responsibility) as setting a new "chain of causation" going, irrespective of what has happened before.'

In chapter XII of *Causation in the Law*, 2nd ed (1985), p 326, Hart & Honoré wrote:

'The free, deliberate, and informed intervention of a second person, who intends to exploit the situation created by the first, but is not acting in concert with him, is normally held to relieve the first actor of criminal responsibility.'

---

[133]   *Kennedy (No.1)* [1999] Crim. L.R. 65.
[134]   *Dias* [2001] 2 Cr. App. R. 96.
[135]   *R. v Finlay (Paul Anthony)* [2003] EWCA Crim 3868.

This statement was cited by the House with approval in *R v Latif* [1996] 1 WLR 104, 115. The principle is fundamental and not controversial.

15 Questions of causation frequently arise in many areas of the law, but causation is not a single, unvarying concept to be mechanically applied without regard to the context in which the question arises. That was the point which Lord Hoffmann, with the express concurrence of three other members of the House, was at pains to make in *Environment Agency (formerly National Rivers Authority) v Empress Car Co (Abertillery) Ltd* [1999] 2 AC 22. The House was not in that decision purporting to lay down general rules governing causation in criminal law. It was construing, with reference to the facts of the case before it, a statutory provision imposing strict criminal liability on those who cause pollution of controlled waters. Lord Hoffmann made clear that common sense answers to questions of causation will differ according to the purpose for which the question is asked; that one cannot give a common sense answer to a question of causation for the purpose of attributing responsibility under some rule without knowing the purpose and scope of the rule; that strict liability was imposed in the interests of protecting controlled waters; and that in the situation under consideration the act of the defendant could properly be held to have caused the pollution even though an ordinary act of a third party was the immediate cause of the diesel oil flowing into the river. It is worth underlining that the relevant question was the cause of the pollution, not the cause of the third party's act.

16 The committee would not wish to throw any doubt on the correctness of the *Empress Car* case. But the reasoning in that case cannot be applied to the wholly different context of causing a noxious thing to be administered to or taken by another person contrary to section 23 of the 1861 Act . . .

18 . . . If the conduct of the deceased was not criminal he was not a principal offender, and it of course follows that the appellant cannot be liable as a secondary party. It also follows that there is no meaningful legal sense in which the appellant can be said to have been a principal jointly with the deceased, or to have been acting in concert. The finding that the deceased freely and voluntarily administered the injection to himself, knowing what it was, is fatal to any contention that the appellant caused the heroin to be administered to the deceased or taken by him . . .

20 [Counsel for the appellant] relied on *R v Rogers* [2003] 1 WLR 1374 . . . The relevant finding was that the defendant physically assisted the deceased by holding his belt round the deceased's arm as a tourniquet, so as to raise a vein in which the deceased could insert a syringe, while the deceased injected himself. It was argued in support of his appeal to the Court of Appeal that the defendant had committed no unlawful act for purposes of either count. This contention was rejected. The court held that it was unreal and artificial to separate the tourniquet from the injection. By applying and holding the tourniquet the defendant played a part in the mechanics of the injection which had caused the death. There is, clearly, a difficult borderline between contributory acts which may properly be regarded as administering a noxious thing and acts which may not. But the crucial question is not whether the defendant facilitated or contributed to administration of the noxious thing but whether he went further and administered it. What matters, in a case such as *R v Rogers* and the present, is whether the injection itself was the result of a voluntary and informed decision by the person injecting himself. In *R v Rogers*, as in the present case, it was. That case was, therefore, wrongly decided . . .

24 It is possible to imagine factual scenarios in which two people could properly be regarded as acting together to administer an injection. But nothing of the kind was the case here. As in *R v Dalby* [1982] 1 WLR 425 and *R v Dias* [2002] 2 Cr App R 96 the appellant supplied the drug to the deceased, who then had a choice, knowing the facts, whether to inject himself or not. The heroin was, as the certified question correctly recognises, self-administered, not jointly administered. The appellant did not administer the drug. Nor, for reasons already given, did the appellant cause the drug to be administered to or taken by the deceased.

25 The answer to the certified question is: 'In the case of a fully-informed and responsible adult, never.'"

Appeal allowed

The restriction of *Empress* to its particular context (strict liability offences of pollution) is to be welcomed. Further, it is clear that the general rule, confirmed in *Latif*, that a voluntary intervention will break the causal chain is accepted.[136] Cases where the defendant and the deceased are acting in concert are regarded as exceptions to the general principle.[137] The following is an example of such an exceptional case.

---

[136]   The approach adopted in *Kennedy (No.2)* has since been rejected in Scotland: *MacAngus and Kane v H.M. Advocate* [2009] H.C.J.A.C. 8.

[137]   T.H. Jones, "Causation, Homicide and the Supply of Drugs" (2006) 26 L.S. 139 at 149.

R. v Burgess; Byram [2008] EWCA Crim 516 (Court of Appeal, Criminal Division)

SIR IGOR JUDGE:

"12 If a defendant may be convicted on the basis that the fatal dose was jointly administered, then it follows that he is not automatically entitled to be acquitted if the deceased rather than the defendant physically operated the plunger on the syringe and caused the drug to enter his body. In the present case there was evidence which might reasonably have lead a jury to conclude that this appellant had indeed jointly participated in the administration of the fatal dose of heroin. From the interviews as they developed, it emerged that he supplied the deceased with the heroin, which he, the appellant, drew into the syringe . . . He did not hand the syringe to the deceased but he took it and the needle to the deceased's arm, where he found an appropriate vein. He laid the tip of the needle against the skin of the deceased above that vein. It is not clear from the interview that he ever in fact let go of the syringe, but on his account the deceased depressed the plunger. Having done so, the appellant assisted in the physical withdrawal of the plunger from the deceased's arm . . .

13 . . . [O]n his own account, it would have been open to the jury to convict the appellant on the basis identified by Lord Bingham of Cornhill in *Kennedy*."

It has been suggested that *Kennedy (No.2)* is inconsistent with the victim escape cases where, if the victim's actions are reasonably foreseeable, they will not break the causal chain. In most drug-supply cases it is reasonably foreseeable that the drugs will be taken. That is why they are supplied.[138]

It was argued earlier that the "free, deliberate and informed" intervention rule, endorsed in *Kennedy (No.2)*, is reconcilable with the "reasonable foresight" test employed in the escape cases. In escaping from an assailant, the reasonably foreseeable actions of a victim can be regarded as involuntary (a point accepted in *Pagett*). In cases such as *Kennedy (No.2)*, however, while it was reasonably foreseeable that the victim would inject the drugs, that injection was a voluntary act and, where there is a conflict between the two rules (the reasonable foresight rule and the voluntary intervention rule), the latter should trump the former. However, there are difficulties applying this reasoning in all drug-supply cases. If a drug addict, deprived of drugs, injects the drugs supplied, it seems implausible to argue that this is the product of a free, informed and voluntary choice. Possibly, the only sensible solution is that the drug-taker's actions should normally be regarded as voluntary unless it was not free and informed because of age, mental condition or improper pressure or influence.[139] In *Khan*[140] a 15-year-old prostitute victim took heroin for probably the first time

> "there must be some doubt . . . [whether her actions] should have been regarded as truly capable of consenting to the risks inherent in heroin use; her assumption of risk . . . 'seems at the borderline of voluntariness.'"[141]

Such an approach would be consistent with the policy and fair-labelling arguments that drug-suppliers ought generally to be labelled and punished as drug-suppliers and not as manslaughterers. In cases with facts such as *Kennedy (No.2)* the general rule should be that the recipient "has a choice". This is not an instance of non-voluntary conduct coming within the examples given by Hart and Honoré and approved in *Pagett*. Ultimately, it should be for the jury, applying the voluntary intervention test, to determine whether this was a voluntary choice breaking the chain of causation.

---

[138]   L. Cherkassky, "Kennedy and Unlawful Act Manslaughter: An Unorthodox Application of the Doctrine of Causation" (2008) 72 Jo.C.L. 387.

[139]   R. Heaton, "Principals? No Principles" [2004] Crim. L.R. 463 at 464.

[140]   *R. v Khan (Rungzabe)* [1998] Crim. L.R. 830.

[141]   *MacAngus and Kane v H.M. Advocate* [2009] H.C.J.A.C. 8, citing T. H. Jones, "Causation, Homicide and the Supply of Drugs" (2006) 26 L.S. 139.

Beyond cases of drug supply, the courts seem to have demonstrated some inconsistency in the way in which voluntariness might be interpreted. It was held in *Hughes* that the deceased's own dangerous driving did not break the chain of causation as he "did not voluntarily and deliberately kill himself; he drove dangerously and without thought and as a result caused the collision in which he died".[142] It is not clear that the Supreme Court interpreted the test correctly in applying *Kennedy (No.2)* in a context other than drug supply here. Given that the deceased in *Kennedy* itself did not take a conscious decision to commit suicide, only to take the risk involved in self-injecting heroin without necessarily giving any thought to the outcome, it is not clear why the decision of the deceased in *Hughes* to take the risk of driving after taking heroin should not act in an equivalent way to break the causal chain.[143]

c. Other victim action/inaction/condition

There have been cases where the victim has refused medical treatment and consequently died. Such cases have been treated as manifestations of the principle that one must "take one's victim as one finds him". In *Hayward*[144] and *McKechnie*[145] it was held that if a victim had a physical weakness (a thyrus gland and a duodenal ulcer respectively) which hastened death following an assault, the defendant could not claim a break in causation merely because a healthy victim might not have died. In the following cases this principle was applied to the psychological condition of the victim. The defendant must "take his victim as he finds him in mind as well as in body".

R. v Blaue (1975) 61 Cr. App. R. 271 (Court of Appeal, Criminal Division)

The appellant stabbed a woman piercing her lung. She refused to have a blood transfusion as it was contrary to her religious beliefs as1 a Jehovah's Witness. The surgeon advised her that without the transfusion she would die. Medical evidence established that with the transfusion she would have survived. She died and the appellant was convicted of manslaughter (on grounds of diminished responsibility). He appealed on the ground that causation was not established.

LAWTON LJ:

"Maule J's direction to the jury reflected the common law's answer to the problem. He who inflicted an injury which resulted in death could not excuse himself by pleading that his victim could have avoided death by taking greater care of himself. See Hale, *Pleas of the Crown* (1800 ed.) pp. 426–428. The common law in Sir Matthew Hale's time probably was in line with contemporary concepts of ethics. A man who did a wrongful act was deemed *morally* responsible for the natural and probable consequences of that act. [Counsel for the appellant] . . . asked us to remember that since Sir Matthew Hale's day the rigour of the law relating to homicide has been eased in favour of the accused. It has been—but this has come about through the development of the concept of intent, not by reason of a different view of causation . . .

The physical cause of death in this case was the bleeding into the pleural cavity arising from the penetration of the lung. This had not been brought about by any decision made by the deceased girl but by the stab wound.

[Counsel for the appellant] . . . tried to overcome this line of reasoning by submitting that the jury should have been directed that, if they thought the girl's decision not to have a blood transfusion was an unreasonable one, then the chain of causation would have been broken. At once the question arises—reasonable by whose standards? Those of Jehovah's Witnesses? Humanists? Roman Catholics? Protestants of Anglo-Saxon descent? The man on the Clapham omnibus? But he might well be an admirer of Eleazar who suffered death rather than eat

---

[142] *Hughes* [2014] 1 Cr. App. R. 6 at [22].
[143] Simester and Sullivan explain this apparent anomaly on the basis that "[t]he difference lies in a peculiarity of constitutive manslaughter: V's taking of the drug was freely chosen in Kennedy, and it was not caused by Kennedy's unlawful act of supplying the heroin": A.P. Simester and G.R Sullivan, "Causation as Fault" (2014) 73(1) C.L.J. 14–17 at 16.
[144] *Hayward* (1908) 21 Cox C.C. 692.
[145] *R. v McKechnie (Roy Maurer)* (1992) 94 Cr. App. R. 51.

the flesh of swine . . . or of Sir Thomas More who, unlike nearly all his contemporaries, was unwilling to accept Henry VIII as Head of the Church in England. Those brought up in the Hebraic and Christian traditions would probably be reluctant to accept that these martyrs caused their own deaths.

As was pointed out to . . . [counsel for the appellant] in the course of argument, two cases, each raising the same issue of reasonableness because of religious beliefs, could produce different verdicts depending on where the cases were tried . . . It has long been the policy of the law that those who use violence on other people must take their victims as they find them. This in our judgment means the whole man, not just the physical man. It does not lie in the mouth of the assailant to say that his victim's religious beliefs which inhibited him from accepting certain kinds of treatment were unreasonable. The question for decision is what caused her death. The answer is the stab wound. The fact that the victim refused to stop this end coming about did not break the causal connection between the act and death."[146]

Appeal dismissed

Other cases have concerned victims who, in a state of anguish or fear as a result of the defendant's attack, have committed suicide. In the American case of *Lewis*[147] the defendant shot the deceased in the abdomen—a wound that would have caused death in an hour. The deceased, however, cut his own throat and died within five minutes. The court conceded that the defendant would nevertheless be liable if the self-inflicted knife wound could be causally connected to the defendant's gunshot wound, i.e. if it was self-inflicted because of grief or pain or through a desire to shield the defendant. Temple J stated:

"But, if the deceased did die from the effect of the knife wound alone, no doubt the defendant would be responsible, if it was made to appear . . . that the knife wound was caused by the wound inflicted by the defendant, in the natural course of events. If the relation was causal, and the wounded condition of the deceased was not merely the occasion upon which another cause intervened, not produced by the first wound, or related to it in other than in a causal way, then the defendant is guilty of a homicide. But, if the wounded condition only afforded an opportunity for another unconnected person to kill, the defendant would not be guilty."

Lewis is a decision from the United States. Would it be followed here?

R. v Dear [1996] Crim. L.R. 595 (Court of Appeal, Criminal Division) (Lexis Transcript, March 14, 1996)

The appellant slashed the victim repeatedly with a Stanley knife. The victim died two days later. The defence was that the deceased committed suicide either by reopening his wounds or, the wounds having reopened themselves, by failing to take steps to stop the bleeding. The trial judge directed the jury that causation was established if the victim did what he did because of the wounds and would not have done so unless he had been wounded. The chain of causation would only be broken if the victim acted only for some reason unconnected to the attack on him, for example, shame at his own prior conduct (it was alleged that the victim had sexually interfered with the appellant's daughter). The appellant was convicted of murder and appealed.

ROSE LJ:

"[Counsel for the appellant argues that] 'voluntary' suicide . . . is a *novus actus interveniens*. A suicide where the deceased can be taken to know and understand the nature of his act, and thus exercise a choice, is a *novus actus*, even if it follows upon an attack upon the victim . . .

---

[146] See also *Holland* (1841) 2 Mood. & R. 351 where a victim, who could have recovered, ignored medical advice and died two weeks later; the original assailant was held to have caused the death.
[147] *Lewis* 124 Cal. 551, 57 Pac. 470 (1889).

[E]ven assuming that there was evidence of suicide, through shame or some other reason unrelated to the defendant's conduct . . . this did not . . . render inaccurate . . . the direction which the judge gave on causation . . .

The correct approach in the criminal law is . . .: were the injuries inflicted by the defendant an operating and significant cause of death? That question, in our judgment, is necessarily answered, not by philosophical analysis, but by common sense according to all the circumstances of the particular case.

In the present case the cause of the deceased's death was bleeding from the artery which the defendant had severed. Whether or not the resumption or continuation of that bleeding was deliberately caused by the deceased, the jury were entitled to find that the defendant's conduct made an operative and significant contribution to the death."

Appeal dismissed

Smith commented on this case that if

"the wounds were effectively healed when D took the Stanley knife to himself, it is not so clear that the wounds were an operating and substantial cause of death. Arguably, it was then the same as if he had cut his throat or blown his brains out."[148]

In *R. v Dhaliwal*[149] a woman who had been subjected to various forms of abuse committed suicide. In the Court of Appeal it was stated obiter that "at least arguably" the defendant's violence could be regarded as the cause of her death.

Jeremy Horder and Laura McGowan, "Manslaughter by Causing Another's Suicide" [2006] Crim. L.R. 1035 at 1042–3:

"When a relationship is characterised by persistent domestic abuse (especially in the kind of cultural and religious context to be found in *Dhaliwal*), the experience of living with the abuse is liable to affect the victim's decision-making processes, and to influence the range and character of actions she regards as legitimate, inevitable or natural . . .

There has been strong support for an approach to causation in which the destructive effect domestic abuse has on the victim's autonomy can be regarded as rendering the defendant criminally responsible for the victim's suicide . . .

It might be that a decision on the part of a victim of abuse to commit suicide is best explained, in straightforward causal terms, by a depressive condition induced by the abuse . . . [H]is abuse triggered the operation of a special vulnerability of the victim. On our account, however, the causal link between the abuse and the suicide can be (lack of) freedom-based, and need not be based on a victim's special vulnerability. An abuse-based controlling influence can, in this context, make a decision to commit suicide something that the victim was not truly free to avoid, because other avoiding actions were in practical terms ruled out by the effect of that influence."

"Victim condition" cases such as *Blaue* are straightforward applications of Hart and Honoré's "abnormal condition" exception. The "abnormality" of the victim does not break the chain of causation. However, there is a problem in these cases where the defendant is held to take his victim as he finds him. In *Blaue* the victim's physical or mental condition is counted as an "abnormal condition" and thus unable to rank as a coincidence. But in the cases of victims escaping from attackers, such as *Roberts* and *Mackie*, the victim's psychological make-up that might have induced flight from the defendant is disregarded and insistence is placed on such actions being reasonable, likely or foreseeable. Perhaps this was simply because there was no evidence of the victims suffering from any particular psychological condition. However, what if the victim, because of an established pre-existing neurotic

---

[148] *R. v Dear* [1996] Crim. L.R. 596.
[149] *R. v Dhaliwal* [2006] EWCA Crim 1139.

condition, grossly over-reacts to a minor assault: for example, jumps from the 10th floor of a building because the defendant placed his arm around her shoulder? Under the *Blaue* principle the defendant must take his victim as he finds them and causation is established. Under the *Roberts* principle such a victim's action could probably be viewed as "daft" and so break the causal chain. How can this divergence of approach be explained?

Perhaps the best way of resolving this issue is by recognising the centrality of the "free, deliberate and informed" intervention test endorsed in *Kennedy (No.2)*. If the victim's suicide or leaping from a moving car was voluntary it breaks the chain of causation. This was the solution adopted in *Pagett, Latif* and *Kennedy (No.2)* for determining whether the actions of a third person (or the victim) constituted a *novus actus interveniens*. Horder and McGowan offer this same solution in cases where an abused woman commits suicide. In relation to cases where the victim is escaping from the violence of the defendant, the courts, in assessing whether the response is reasonable have taken account of any particular idiosyncrasies of the victim. In *Blaue* the issue is whether it is reasonably foreseeable that a Jehovah's Witness would refuse a blood transfusion. This was the approach approved in *Williams and Davis* where it was held that, in assessing whether the victim's response in jumping out of the car was reasonably foreseeable one had to bear in mind "any particular characteristic of the victim". In *Corbett* the issue was whether the reaction of a victim "in that state" was foreseeable. This test enables the victim's condition or characteristics to be taken into account and provides some indication of whether the victim's actions were voluntary or not. If it were reasonably foreseeable that the person with the neurotic condition would jump from the building, that victim's actions can be regarded as involuntary. (The defendant, in this example, would not be liable for the resultant death as there would be no relevant culpability.)

On the other hand, in cases where there is no evidence of any particular characteristics or mental condition, such as *Roberts*, the test is simply whether the response is reasonable. The fact that a victim with particular characteristics does an act that is reasonably foreseeable is, in such cases, indicative that that act was "involuntary". In *Blaue* it was reasonably foreseeable that a Jehovah's Witness would refuse a blood transfusion. Because of her religion she had no choice. Most Jehovah Witnesses would do the same; that is why such a reaction is reasonably foreseeable and can be regarded as involuntary. On the other hand, if a person, not being a Jehovah's Witness refused a blood transfusion in similar circumstances, in the absence of any medical explanation this could not be regarded as reasonably foreseeable which indicates that the decision was a voluntary one breaking the chain of causation. Again, ultimately, it is for the jury, having been properly directed as to the application of the voluntary intervention test, to determine whether such a decision amounted to a voluntary choice breaking the chain of causation.

(iv) Conclusion

It is interesting that, leaving aside the medical and strict liability judgments, many of the problem cases discussed above involved constructive manslaughter,[150] which is a species of crime where no mens rea is required as to the final result. *Hughes* similarly involved a constructive homicide offence. The other leading case, *Roberts*, involved s.47 of the Offences Against the Person Act 1861 which, as another constructive crime, also does not require mens rea as to the result. This tends to lend some credence to the view that principles of causation are subservient to those of mens rea. Where there is clear mens rea as to the result, problems of causation will not be allowed to intrude. (*Dear* is an exception here.) But, where one is dealing with constructive crime, the job cannot be left to mens rea and it

---

[150]   The defendant was convicted of murder in *Dear*. In *Blaue* the conviction was for manslaughter by diminished responsibility.

is in this area that "principles", such as they are, have started emerging. However, even in these, and certainly in the other cases, it would be a mistake to ignore the role of policy: for example, the policy of not allowing medical treatment to break the chain of causation or the policy of respecting a victim's religious beliefs in *Blaue*.

It must be remembered that most of the defendants in the above cases could have been charged with, or found guilty of, lesser offences. Pagett was convicted of possession of a firearm, kidnapping and attempted murder. Kennedy was convicted of supplying a Class A drug to another. McKechnie was charged, in the alternative, with causing grievous bodily harm with intent. Blaue could have been convicted of attempted murder, Hayward of assault, Hughes of driving whilst uninsured and unlicensed driving, and so on. Welansky could have been found guilty of a violation of safety regulations. Policy considerations dictated that they all be blamed and punished for something, but the question is: what were the policy considerations that dictated they be found liable for homicide offences, as opposed to these lesser offences? It is interesting how much importance has been attached to the resulting harm as opposed to the more immediate "wrongdoing" of the defendant. Whether this approach is justifiable is one of the main themes of the next chapter.

III. Mens Rea

A. Blame and Responsibility

The normal consequence of a criminal conviction is punishment. The offender is subjected to censure and blame. Blame and censure are only appropriate if the offender was morally responsible for his behaviour. We do not blame animals, small children and the insane that have caused a harm because we do not hold them responsible. In a liberal society where political freedom is valued, people must be free from criminal liability and punishment unless they "voluntarily" break the law[151] in the sense of doing something that they can properly acknowledge as wrongdoing.[152] A morally responsible agent is one who understands the social norms to which he is subject[153] and can understand and accept responsibility for wrongdoing (whether or not this is associated with feelings of guilt). Such an agent can understand the "communicative enterprise of punishment"[154] in a way that young children and the insane cannot. The state may use its coercive powers against citizens who lack responsibility (for example, imposing tax on the purchase of goods[155]), but the use of its censuring powers of punishment in such cases would not be consistent with the demands of political freedom. There would be no freedom in a state that chose to punish persons with green eyes. In short, the link between responsibility and criminal liability is one of the hallmarks of a free society.

How is responsibility assessed? There are two main theories: the capacity theory and the character theory.[156]

Under the capacity theory, the necessary attributes are knowledge, reason and control (which include the capacity to make choices).[157]

---

151 B. Williams, "Moral Responsibility and Political Freedom" [1997] C.L.J. 96.
152 R.A. Duff and A. von Hirsch, "Responsibility, Retribution and the 'Voluntary': A Response to Williams" [1997] C.L.J. 103 at 109.
153 F.G. Jacobs, *Criminal Responsibility* (London: Orion Publishing Group, 1971), p.13.
154 Duff and von Hirsch "Responsibility, Retribution and the 'Voluntary': A Response to Williams" [1997] C.L.J. 103 at 109.
155 Duff and von Hirsch "Responsibility, Retribution and the 'Voluntary': A Response to Williams" [1997] C.L.J. 103 at 104.
156 See generally, N. Lacey, *State Punishment: Political Principles and Community Values* (London: Routledge, 1988), pp.62–68; J. Horder, "Criminal Culpability: The Possibility of a General Theory" (1993) 12 *Law and Philosophy* 193; N. Lacey, "In Search of the Responsible Subject: History, Philosophy and Social Sciences in Criminal Law Theory" (2001) 64 M.L.R. 350. V. Tadros, *Criminal Responsibility* (Oxford: OUP, 2005), Ch.2.
157 Arenella would insist that an actor also be capable of some form of moral evaluation and be able to incorporate these

H.L.A. Hart, Punishment and Responsibility: Essays in the Philosophy of Law (1968), p.152:

"What is crucial is that those whom we punish should have had, when they acted, the normal capacities, physical and mental, for doing what the law requires and abstaining from what it forbids, and a fair opportunity to exercise these capacities. Where these capacities and opportunities are absent, as they are in different ways in the varied cases of accident, mistake, paralysis, reflex action, coercion, insanity etc., the moral protest is that it is morally wrong to punish because 'he could not have helped it' or 'he could not have done otherwise' or 'he had no real choice'."

According to this traditional view, because the defendant could choose to do otherwise we are entitled to hold them morally blameworthy and to punish them. Because it is difficult to say that the mentally disordered defendant could have done otherwise they are exonerated from blame and punishment.[158]

This capacity theory can be applied to crimes of recklessness and negligence.

Antony Duff and Andrew von Hirsch, "Responsibility, Retribution and the 'Voluntary': A Response to Williams" [1997] C.L.J. 103 at 109–110:

"We might do better to focus on the notion of rational agency. By this, we mean not action that is in fact guided by good reasons; but action which is in principle susceptible to being guided by reasons, done by an agent who would be capable of recognising whether such reasons are good ones . . . [I]t seems to us to be the best way to try to capture the idea of moral responsibility which is appropriate to ascriptions of criminal liability: what we condemn the agent for is a failure to recognise, to accept, or to be adequately motivated by, reasons for action (those offered by the law) which were within his grasp."

There have been many challenges to this notion that people are free or autonomous agents capable of rational action and free choice. The argument here is that this conception of individuals as autonomous, self-determined beings ignores the social context within which people operate. As Norrie puts it: "while we feel in control of what we say or do, we sometimes appear only to speak the parts bequeathed to us by history and context".[159] An extension of this argument is known as determinism. According to this view, all human action is the result of preceding events and conditions (environmental, biological or even chemical). All actions are "determined" and freedom of will is a myth. Under this view, a person cannot be held responsible for something that they were inevitably going to do. In the following decision the court was faced with just such a determinist argument.

State v Sikora 44 N.J. 453, 210 A. 2d. 193 (1965) (Supreme Court of New Jersey)

The defendant, Sikora, was charged with murder and produced psychodynamic evidence that as a result of his genetic makeup and upbringing he was incapable of exercising free will.

FRANCIS J:

"In appearing as a witness, Dr Galen indicated his function was to help the court understand 'the dynamics of what happened to this man with his particular history at this particular time in his life.' . . . Basically Dr Galen's thesis is that man is a helpless victim of his genes and his lifelong environment; that unconscious forces from within dictate the individual's behaviour without his being able to alter it . . .

---

moral beliefs and values into practical judgments about how to act. ("Convicting the Morally Blameless: Reassessing the Relationship between Legal and Moral Accountability" (1992) 39 U.C.L.A. Law Rev. 1511.) This approach is not accepted by present English law. See below, pp.396–397.

[158]   Because of the danger of repetition of harm in such circumstances, it might be necessary to retain control over the defendant.

[159]   A. Norrie, "The Limits of Justice: Finding Fault in the Criminal Law" (1996) 59 M.L.R. 540 at 552.

In short the doctor opined that the circumstances to which Sikora had been subjected imposed on his personality disorder a stress that impaired or removed his ability consciously to premeditate or weigh a design to kill. The tension was so great that he could handle it only by an automatic reaction motivated by the predetermined influence of his unconscious. Plainly the doctor meant that Sikora's response was not a voluntary exercise of his free will . . .

For protection of society the law accepts the thesis that all men are invested with free will and capable of choosing between right and wrong. In the present state of scientific knowledge that thesis cannot be put aside in the administration of the criminal law. Criminal blameworthiness cannot be judged on a basis that negates free will and excuses the offence, wholly or partially, on opinion evidence that the offender's psychological processes or mechanisms were such that even though he knew right from wrong he was predetermined to act the way he did at that time because of unconscious influences set in motion by the emotional stresses then confronting him. In a world of reality such persons must be held responsible for their behaviour . . .

Criminal responsibility must be judged at the level of the conscious. If a person thinks, plans and executes the plan at that level, the criminality of his act cannot be denied, wholly or partially, because although he did not realise it, his conscious was influenced to think, to plan and to execute the plan by unconscious influences which were the product of his genes and his lifelong environment . . . If the law were to accept such a medical doctrine . . . the legal doctrine of *mens rea* would all but disappear from the law . . . Criminal responsibility, as society now knows it, would vanish from the scene, and some other basis for dealing with the offender would have to be found."

George P. Fletcher, Rethinking Criminal Law (1978), pp.801–802:

"It is difficult to resolve [the issue of determinism and responsibility] except by noting that we all blame and criticise others, and in turn subject ourselves to blame and criticism, on the assumption of responsibility for our conduct. In order to defend the criminal law against the determinist critique, we need not introduce freighted terms like 'freedom of the will.' Nor need we 'posit' freedom as though we were developing a geometric system on the basis of axioms. The point is simply that the criminal law should express the way we live. Our culture is built on the assumption that, absent valid claims of excuse, we are accountable for what we do. If that cultural presupposition should someday prove to be empirically false, there will be far more radical changes in our way of life than those expressed in the criminal law."

Tony Honoré, Responsibility and Fault (1999), pp.135–137:

"It is sometimes said that determinism, if true, is irrelevant to the moral and legal responsibility of human agents. But can this be the case, given that intelligent people have been and are concerned to show that the things that go wrong in our society are better tackled by eliminating the causes of wrongdoing than by punishing, censuring or isolating the wrongdoers?

To avoid a superficial discussion of a complex issue, I assume that it makes sense to treat people as the authors of and hence responsible for their actions . . .

The worry remains that, though it may make sense to treat people as responsible for their conduct, if human actions are caused by circumstances, people are not really responsible for what they do. However beneficial it may be to treat them as if they were, to do so is to resort to a salutary lie. And salutary lies stop being salutary when the deception is revealed. Are people's actions in fact caused by their hereditary make-up and external circumstances? No one can be sure. Though valuable work has been done by psychologists, neurologists and sociologists the precise regularities involved, if they exist, await discovery . . . Even so, we tend to assume that something determines people's decisions. That nothing determined them would imply that they were not merely unpredictable but inexplicable: a belief that would be truly alarming.

Should this disturb us? It seems that even 'strong psychophysical explanations' bordering on psychological laws are compatible with the notions of choice, decision, action and intention to which we are committed when we treat people as responsible. To suppose, as a working hypothesis, that our decisions are determined does not make it implausible or illogical to treat ourselves as the authors of our actions when we judge ourselves and others as social beings. How far back is it rational to go in tracing causes must depend on the purpose for which we want to get at the cause of something that has gone wrong. This must also apply to the causes of human conduct. It is rational to treat people as the authors of their actions in the context of a system of responsibility that we regard as valuable both for individuals and for society as a whole. To treat human action as a stopping point beyond which causal inquiries are not ordinarily pursued is sensible and indeed indispensable."

The alternative conception of responsibility is one based upon the character of the defendant.

> "Actions for which we hold a person fully responsible are those in which her usual character is centrally expressed. The finding of a mental element such as intention or recklessness on the character model provides an important piece of evidence from which the existence of character responsibility may be inferred, given that single acts do not always indicate settled dispositions."[160]

Thus we would hold responsible a person who makes unreasonable mistakes because such behaviour manifests an undesirable character trait of practical indifference to others. On the other hand, a person who acts under duress is not expressing their usual character. As they have been forced to act in a particular way, we are unable to draw an inference to a flawed character. This approach does have certain attractions; not least it accords with our tendency to regard as significant the fact that someone acts "out of character" and may be more in keeping with the function of the criminal law as a form of social control. However, it is this intuitive appeal that reveals a central weakness of this character theory. The infliction of a serious harm could be regarded as non-culpable if the agent acted "out of character".[161] But how would we know if any action were uncharacteristic of the agent? This theory is unlikely to replace the capacity conception of responsibility because it looks too much like punishing people for what they are rather than for what they do. Such a person

> "remains a moral cripple, a flawed person in his own eyes, a person who understands that he committed a crime because of 'the kind of person he is' . . . [This amounts to an] enormous and sadistic cruelty."[162]

B. Blame and Mens Rea

The fact that one is a responsible agent does not necessarily mean that criminal liability is justifiable when a harm is caused or a wrong committed. Duff puts it that

> "responsibility is a necessary but not a sufficient condition of liability. I am liable to conviction or blame for X only if I am responsible for X; but I can be responsible for X without being thus liable."[163]

The question is thus: in what circumstances should the actions of a responsible actor be held criminal? The answer is: when they are sufficiently blameworthy in causing the harm or committing the wrong. The mechanisms for establishing this appropriate degree of blame are the subject of the ensuing sections. But it should be emphasised at the outset that the indicators of blame are largely fashioned according to which of the above competing conceptions of responsibility we adopt. For example, if we

---

[160] N. Lacey, *State Punishment: Political Principles and Community Values* (London: Routledge, 1988), p.66.

[161] M.S. Moore, "Choice, Character and Excuse" (1990) 7 *Social Philosophy and Policy* 29; J. Horder, "Criminal Culpability: The Possibility of a General Theory" (1993) *Law and Philosophy* 193 at 207.

[162] J.R. Lindgren, "Criminal Responsibility Reconsidered" (1987) 6 *Law and Philosophy* 89 at 94. This criticism of the character theory is rejected by V. Tadros, *Criminal Responsibility* (Oxford: OUP, 2005), pp.49–51.

[163] R.A. Duff, *Answering for Crime: Responsibility and Liability in the Criminal Law* (Oxford: Hart, 2007), p.20.

adopted the "character conception" of responsibility, we might need to evaluate an actor's motivations because a laudable motive would not reveal a flawed character. The law, however, has been fearful of adopting such a course as it might necessitate exempting from blame those who rob the rich to give to the poor or those who, as in *Chandler v DPP*,[164] commit offences to express their opposition to nuclear weapons. Accordingly, the law adopts the stance that motive is generally irrelevant to the assessment and has instead preferred the "capacity conception" of responsibility. We blame those who have control over their actions and have chosen to commit a crime. The process of choosing to commit a crime is a mental process involving *cognition* (knowing or realising that a consequence could occur or that a circumstance could exist). This mental state became known as mens rea. (We shall see, however, that more recently the term mens rea has been expanded to encompass more than pure mental states.)

Some commentators have rejected the need for mens rea before criminal liability is justified and have argued that liability should be based on harm done.

Baroness Wootton, Crime and the Criminal Law, 2nd edn (1981), pp.43, 46–48:

"If the law says that certain things are not to be done, it is illogical to confine this prohibition to occasions on which they are done from malice aforethought; for at least the material consequences of an action, and the reasons for prohibiting it, are the same whether it is the result of sinister malicious plotting, of negligence or of sheer accident. A man is equally dead and his relatives equally bereaved whether he was stabbed or run over by a drunken motorist or by an incompetent one; and the inconvenience caused by the loss of your bicycle is unaffected by the question whether or not the youth who removed it had the intention of putting it back, if in fact he had not done so at the time of his arrest. It is true, of course, as Professor Hart has argued, that the material consequences of an action by no means exhaust its effects.

'If one person hits another, the person struck does not think of the other as just a cause of pain to him. If the blow was light but deliberate, it has a significance for the person struck quite different from an accidental much heavier blow.'

To ignore this difference, he argues, is to outrage 'distinctions which not only underlie morality but pervade the whole of our social life.' That these distinctions are widely appreciated and keenly felt no one would deny. Often perhaps they derive their force from a purely punitive or retributive attitude; but alternatively they may be held to be relevant to an assessment of the social damage that results from a criminal act. Just as a heavy blow does more damage than a light one, so also perhaps does a blow which involves psychological injury do more damage than one in which the hurt is purely physical.

The conclusion to which this argument leads is, I think, not that the presence or absence of the guilty mind is unimportant, but that *mens rea* has, so to speak—and this is the crux of the matter—*got into the wrong place*. Traditionally, the requirement of the guilty mind is written into the actual definition of a crime. No guilty intention, no crime, is the rule. Obviously this makes sense if the law's concern is with wickedness: where there is no guilty intention, there can be no wickedness. But it is equally obvious, on the other hand, that an action does not become innocuous merely because whoever performed it meant no harm. If the object of the criminal law is to prevent the occurrence of socially damaging actions, it would be absurd to turn a blind eye to those which were due to carelessness, negligence or even accident. The question of motivation is *in the first instance* irrelevant.

But only in the first instance. At a later stage, that is to say, after what is now known as a conviction, the presence or absence of guilty intention is all-important for its effect on the appropriate measures to be taken to prevent a recurrence of the forbidden act. The prevention of accidental deaths presents different problems from those involved in the prevention of wilful murders. The result of the actions of the careless, the mistaken, the wicked and the merely unfortunate may be indistinguishable from one another, but each case calls for a different

---

[164]   *Chandler* [1964] A.C. 763.

treatment. Tradition, however, is very strong, and the notion that these differences are relevant only after the fact has been established that the accused committed the forbidden act seems still to be deeply abhorrent to the legal mind."

Hart has taken issue with these claims by putting forward what has become the classic justification of the doctrine of mens rea.[165] He clearly believed in people's ability to determine their own actions and rested his defence of mens rea upon that belief. Even if one accepts people as "responsible", it does not mean that the notion of "wickedness" need automatically be accepted as well, nor that one, therefore, punishes retributively on the basis of it. Instead, as we have seen, the value of punishment rests on the "simple idea that unless a man has the capacity and a fair opportunity or chance to adjust his behaviour to the law its penalties ought not to be applied to him".[166] By punishing when there is some mental element, one acknowledges a person's capacity and has given them the chance not to overstep the legal boundaries of action. It gives people the maximum power to determine their own future. The person who has exercised self-restraint and who has made the right choices is not made to suffer for mistakes or accidents.

H.L.A. Hart, Punishment and Responsibility (1968), p.183:

"If you strike me, the judgment that the blow was deliberate will elicit fear, indignation, anger, resentment: these are not voluntary responses; but the same judgment will enter into deliberations about my future voluntary conduct towards you and will colour all my social relations with you. Shall I be your friend or enemy? Offer soothing words? Or return the blow? All this will be different if the blow is not voluntary. This is how human nature in society actually is and as yet we have no power to alter it. The bearing of this fundamental fact on the law is this. If as our legal moralists maintain it is important for the law to reflect common judgments of morality, it is surely even more important that it should in general reflect in its judgments on human conduct distinctions which not only underlie morality, but pervade the whole of our social life. This it would fail to do if it treated men merely as alterable, predictable, curable or manipulative things."

These views have been widely accepted by the criminal law. But what does "mens rea" mean?

J.F. Stephen, History of the Criminal Law of England, Vol.II (1883), pp.94–95:

"The maxim, *'Actus non facit reum nisi mens sit rea'*, is sometimes said to be the fundamental maxim of the whole criminal law . . .

It is frequently though ignorantly supposed to mean that there cannot be such a thing as legal guilt where there is no moral guilt, which is obviously untrue, as there is always a possibility of a conflict between law and morals.

It also suggests the notion that there is some state of mind called a '*mens rea*,' the absence of which, on any particular occasion, deprives what would otherwise be a crime of its criminal character. This also is untrue. There is no one such state of mind, as any one may convince himself by considering the definitions of dissimilar crimes. A pointsman falls asleep, and thereby causes a railway accident and the death of a passenger; he is guilty of manslaughter. He deliberately and by elaborate devices produces the same result: he is guilty of murder. If in each case there is a *mens rea*, as the maxim seems to imply, *mens rea* must be a name for two states of mind, not merely differing from but opposed to each other, for what two states of mind can resemble each other less than indolence and an active desire to kill?

The truth is that the maxim about *mens rea* means no more than that the definition of all or nearly all crimes contains not only an outward and visible element, but a mental element, varying according to the different

---

[165]   H.L.A. Hart, *Punishment and Responsibility* (Oxford: OUP, 1968), Ch.3.
[166]   Hart, *Punishment and Responsibility* (Oxford: OUP, 1968), p.181.

nature of different crimes. Thus, in reference to murder, the *mens rea* is any state of mind which comes within the description of malice aforethought. In reference to theft the *mens rea* is an intention to deprive the owner of his property permanently, . . . Hence the only means of arriving at a full comprehension of the expression *mens rea* is by a detailed examination of the definitions of particular crimes, and therefore the expression itself is unmeaning."

Mens rea is the term generally used to indicate the mental element required by the definition of the crime. Older law and statutes used evaluative terms such as "malice aforethought" and "maliciously". For the past century, and particularly the last half-century, more cognitive terms such as knowledge and belief in relation to circumstances, and intention and recklessness in relation to consequences, have become prevalent. The courts have embraced these new concepts and have reinterpreted the older terms in the light of them. For example, "maliciously" in s.20 of the Offences Against the Person Act 1861 has been construed as meaning "recklessly". Other forms of affective (as opposed to cognitive) mens rea also exist. For example, theft requires "dishonesty": this is a state of mind relating to the wrongfulness of actions.

However, the term mens rea has also been used to describe other forms of culpability that do not necessarily involve a "state of mind" in its cognitive sense of intending or being subjectively aware that a consequence could occur. For example, in the 1980s the law adopted an "objective" test of recklessness that involved a failure to foresee an obvious risk (an interpretation abandoned in 2003). Also, it has long been established that the mens rea for one species of manslaughter is satisfied by proof of gross negligence. In *Misra* it was stated that:

"the term '*mens rea*' is also used to describe the ingredient of fault or culpability before criminal liability for the defendant's actions may be established . . . The requirement for gross negligence provides the necessary element of culpability."[167]

The Sentencing Advisory Panel has stated that there are four levels of culpability: intention, recklessness, knowledge and negligence.[168] Indeed, there is an increasing number of crimes for which only negligence is required. A prime example of this is the crime of rape. It would be churlish to describe rape as a crime not involving mens rea.

One approach to this issue would be to conclude that there are two species of mens rea. First, there is "cognitive mens rea" which involves intention or foresight on the part of the defendant. Secondly, there is "normative mens rea" under which an assessment of culpability involves an evaluation of the defendant's actions, taking into account all the circumstances including the defendant's state of mind.[169]

Kumaralingham Amirthalingam, "Caldwell Recklessness is Dead, Long Live Mens rea's Fecklessness" (2004) 67 M.L.R. 491 at 492:

"The doctrine of mens rea itself needs to be restored to its normative roots of attributing blameworthiness . . . Briefly, blameworthiness goes beyond mere conduct responsibility; it is a normative enquiry as to whether the person deserves to be labelled and punished as a criminal. The blameworthiness of an accused is not determined merely by enquiring whether there existed a 'subjective' mens rea; it requires an additional crucial step of asking

---

[167] *R. v Misra (Amit)* [2005] 1 Cr. App. R. 21 at 57.
[168] *Overarching Principles: Seriousness* (2004), p.4. In its most recent report, negligence is no longer regarded as demonstrating culpability (*Advice to Sentencing Guidelines Council: Overarching Principles of Sentencing* (2010), para.83).
[169] C.M.V. Clarkson, *Understanding Criminal Law* (London: Sweet & Maxwell, 2005), pp.19–20, 56.

whether the 'mens was rea'. This inquiry involves an 'objective' element and includes inadvertence within mens rea."[170]

This approach, which is more consistent with the "character conception" of responsibility, has the advantage that it focuses attention on the central issue whether the defendant is blameworthy.[171] In many cases cognitive mens rea is a prime indicator of blameworthiness but an assessment of blame can be based on other non-cognitive factors. For example, a defendant can be blamed for causing a harm when, even though there was no awareness of the possibility of the harm occurring at the time of acting, it was the defendant's own fault for getting themselves into a situation or condition (for example, intoxicated) whereby they were deprived of the capacity for awareness. Also, the fact that a defendant has cognitive mens rea does not conclusively establish that they are blameworthy. They might intentionally bring about a prohibited harm but be exempt from blame because of a recognised excuse or justification (for example, duress or self-defence).

Accordingly, it must be borne in mind throughout this book that the term "mens rea" is no more than a tool in the identification of culpability. The construction of the various mens rea terms, such as recklessness, should be governed by the central quest of identifying blameworthiness. For example, in assessing whether "recklessness" should be interpreted as including a failure to consider obvious risks, the central issue is whether such a failure can be regarded as sufficiently culpable to justify the imposition of criminal liability.

C. Proof of Cognitive Mens Rea

Most of the mens rea concepts mentioned above require proof of a person's state of mind. Did the actual defendant intend the consequence or foresee the risk of it occurring? This is commonly described as being a "subjective" test. Such a subjective test assumes that a person's state of mind is ascertainable. However, is it possible to inquire into a person's mind to ascertain what their intentions were when they committed the crime (maybe many months or even years previously)? As Ackner J said in his summing-up to the jury in *Hyam*:

"There is no scientific measurement or yardstick for gauging a person's intention. Unfortunately, there is no form of meter which one can fix to an accused person, like an amp meter or something of that kind, in order to ascertain what the intention is, no X-ray machine which will produce a useful picture."[172]

Despite the scientific impossibility of ascertaining what a person's state of mind was at the time of the alleged crime, cognitive mens rea requires courts to try to establish these subjective states of mind. How is this done?

Without direct evidence of a person's state of mind, such as a confession (although even this might not be reliable), mens rea has to be established by drawing inferences from facts; the jury must consider all the circumstantial evidence—the conduct of the defendant before, during and after the crime, motive, statements by the defendant, type of weapon used, etc.—and from that infer what the defendant must have intended. The jury can only perform this task by trying to ascertain what any normal or

---

[170]   Amirthalingam suggests that mens rea could be construed as follows: the "mens" should refer to the state of mind of the defendant and the "rea" should involve a normative evaluation of that mental state in all the circumstances. The better view is that this evaluation should include—but not be limited to—the defendant's mental state.

[171]   This approach was rejected in *R. v Kingston (Barry)* [1995] 2 A.C. 355.

[172]   No.6530, C.72, Warwick Crown Court; tried November 22–24, 1972.

reasonable person would have intended or foreseen in those circumstances. From this developed the important maxim that a person must be taken to intend the natural and probable consequences of their actions. This maxim, which of course went a long way towards destroying any subjective notion of mens rea, was interpreted rigidly by the House of Lords in the following decision.

Director of Public Prosecutions v Smith [1961] A.C. 290 (House of Lords)

The respondent was driving a car in which there was stolen property. He was stopped by a police officer who told him to draw into the near side. The respondent began to do so and the constable walked beside the car. Then the respondent suddenly accelerated down an adjoining road. The constable succeeded in hanging on to the car which pursued an erratic course until he was thrown off in the path of a vehicle which ran over him, killing him.

At his trial for murder, the respondent maintained that he had no intention of killing or causing serious injury to the constable. Donovan J directed the jury

"if you are satisfied that he must, as a reasonable man, have contemplated that grievous bodily harm was likely to result to that officer and that such harm did happen and the officer died in consequence, then the accused is guilty of capital murder."

The jury returned a verdict of guilty. The Court of Criminal Appeal quashed his conviction on the ground of misdirection. The Crown appealed to the House of Lords.

VISCOUNT KILMUIR:

"The unlawful and voluntary act must clearly be aimed at someone in order to eliminate cases of negligence or of careless or dangerous driving. Once, however, the jury are satisfied as to that, it matters not what the accused in fact contemplated as the probable result or whether he ever contemplated at all, provided he was in law responsible and accountable for his actions, that is, was a man capable of forming an intent, not insane within the M'Naghten Rules and not suffering from diminished responsibility. On the assumption that he is so accountable for his actions, the sole question is whether the unlawful and voluntary act was of such a kind that grievous bodily harm was the natural and probable result. The only test available for this is what the ordinary responsible man would, in all the circumstances of the case, have contemplated as the natural and probable result. That, indeed, has always been the law . . .

Another criticism of the summing-up and one which found favour in the Court of Criminal Appeal concerned the manner in which the trial judge dealt with the presumption that a man intends the natural and probable consequences of his acts. The real question is whether the jury should have been told that it was rebuttable. In truth, however, as I see it, this is merely another way of applying the test of the reasonable man. Provided that the presumption is applied, once the accused's knowledge of the circumstances and the nature of his acts have been ascertained, the only thing that could rebut the presumption would be proof of incapacity to form an intent, insanity or diminished responsibility. In the present case, therefore, there was no need to explain to the jury that the presumption was rebuttable."

Appeal allowed

This decision was greeted with howls of derision by most English commentators.[173] The exact effect of the decision was never settled: did it lay down an irrebuttable evidential presumption that intention was to be ascertained objectively for all crimes? Or did it lay down a new mens rea for murder—a completely objective test where it was only necessary to establish that death or grievous bodily harm

---

[173]   Fletcher regards the reaction to this case as "even more unfortunate" than the decision itself in that English judges and commentators have "gone to the opposite extreme" in eschewing "any reliance on the projected behaviour of a reasonable person" (*Rethinking Criminal Law* (Oxford: OUP, 1978), p.704).

was objectively foreseeable? Either way, its effect was profound. Murder (and possibly all crimes) had been transformed into a crime of negligence: if the reasonable man would have foreseen the harm, the defendant was liable.

Intense criticism of this decision[174] led to the passing of the Criminal Justice Act 1967 s.8:

"A court or jury, in determining whether a person has committed an offence—

(a) shall not be bound in law to infer that he intended or foresaw a result of his actions by reason only of its being a natural and probable consequence of these actions; but

(b) shall decide whether he did intend or foresee that result by reference to all the evidence, drawing such inferences from the evidence as appear proper in the circumstances."

The legislature has thus clearly endorsed the idea that intention is to be subjectively ascertained—as must foresight.[175] Of course, one way to establish a person's state of mind is by obtaining a confession. There is evidence that this has led to the police exerting more pressure to get confessions from defendants to strengthen the case for the prosecution.[176] The results have been seen in a number of successful appeals against convictions.

Section 8 does not actually solve the practical problem of proving mens rea at all; it merely states what ought to be done in theory. It is true that if there is clear evidence that the defendant did not intend a result, the jury can so find. But in what circumstances would a jury conclude that while a reasonable man would have foreseen a result, the defendant did not? Surely this would generally only occur where there was clear evidence that the defendant's state of mind was in some material way different from that of the reasonable man—say, because they were a schizophrenic. But Viscount Kilmuir in *DPP v Smith* was careful to exclude those persons not capable of conforming to the standards of the reasonable man.

In other cases, however, it is doubtful if juries can do otherwise than draw inferences from conduct and apply their own standards, the standards of ordinary people: "If I had been in that situation, what would I have foreseen?" Perhaps this is what was meant by the startling extract from a training manual for magistrates which stated:

"It is sometimes said on the defendant's behalf that he did not intend to inflict the particular injury which the victim suffered. This is always a weak point because any sane person who commits an act of violence must expect injury to result. The fact that it happens to be greater than anticipated provides no excuse whatsoever."[177]

The Court of Appeal can sometimes pay lip-service to s.8 and quash convictions because the jury was not clearly directed that the test of intention is subjective.[178] Nevertheless, in reality, it seems likely that in many (if not most) cases s.8 is impracticable and juries in fact have to apply objective tests. As we shall see, this is one of the reasons why subjectivism has come under attack and there have been increasing calls for a more objectivist approach towards the ascertainment of mens rea—particularly recklessness.

---

[174] e.g. Law Commission, *Imputed Criminal Intent (Director of Public Prosecutions v Smith)*, 1965.
[175] See also *Frankland (Graham Ralph) v The Queen* [1987] A.C. 576 where the Privy Council reiterated the point that the test is a subjective one.
[176] A. Sanders, "Some Dangers of Policy Oriented Research—The Case of Prosecutions" in I. Dennis (ed.), *Criminal Law and Justice* (London: Sweet & Maxwell, 1987), p.208.
[177] R. Bartle, *Crime and the New Magistrate* (London: B. Rose, 1985), quoted from D. Nelken, "Criminal Law and Criminal Justice" in I. Dennis (ed.), *Criminal Law and Justice* (London: Sweet & Maxwell, 1987), p.149.
[178] *R. v Ingram* [1975] Crim. L.R. 457.

We are now in a position to examine some of the core mens rea concepts, in particular, intention, recklessness and negligence. Other mens rea concepts, such as dishonesty and knowledge, are discussed later in the book in relation to the offences to which they apply. Which of these mens rea concepts is applicable depends on the definition of the offence on question. For some offences, this is specified by statute. For example, s.1 of the Theft Act 1968 defines theft as requiring proof of dishonesty. For other offences, case-law has established the type of mens rea required. For example, for an assault proof of recklessness suffices.[179]

D. Intention

1. Introduction

For many crimes it is unnecessary to dist1inguish intention from recklessness because proof of either will suffice. For example, s.1(1) of the Criminal Damage Act 1971 provides that it is an offence to destroy or damage any property belonging to another "intending to destroy or damage any such property or being reckless as to whether any such property would be destroyed or damaged". However, there are some crimes that can only be committed intentionally: for example, s.18 of the Offences Against the Person Act 1861 makes it an offence to wound or cause grievous bodily harm "with intent to cause grievous bodily harm". For these crimes it is essential to define intention with some precision in order to distinguish it from recklessness.

2. The law

As seen above, s.8 of the Criminal Justice Act 1967 lays down an evidential rule as to *how* intention is to be proved and makes it clear that intention is a subjective state of mind. What matters is whether the defendant intended the result, not whether the reasonable man would have intended it. In trying to ascertain what the defendant did intend, the court or jury must draw inferences from all the relevant evidence.

However, while this is clear as to the process for ascertaining intention, there is no statutory definition of intention in English law. Indeed, over the past few decades there has been much controversy over the actual meaning of the concept "intention". Two views have dominated this debate.

(1) A consequence is intended when it is the aim or the objective of the actor. This is called "direct" intention.

(2) A consequence is intended when it is the aim or objective of the actor, or is foreseen as a virtual, practical or moral certainty. If this second state of mind is classed as intention, it is usually called "oblique" intention.

The courts used to adopt an even broader view in holding that a consequence was intended when it was foreseen as a probable or likely result of the defendant's actions.[180] In *Hyam*,[181] for instance, Mrs

---

179   *R. v Venna (Henson George)* [1976] Q.B. 421.
180   This was the view (obiter) of the House of Lords in *R. v Lemon (Denis)* [1979] A.C. 617, and was arguably the view adopted in *Hyam v DPP* [1975] A.C. 55. The alternative interpretation of *Hyam* is that the House of Lords was there defining "malice aforethought", the mens rea of murder—and not defining "intention". See generally, J. Buzzard, "Intent" [1978] Crim. L.R. 5 and J.C. Smith, "'Intent': A Reply" [1978] Crim. L.R. 14.
181   *Hyam* [1975] A.C. 55.

Hyam poured petrol through the letterbox of the house of her lover's new mistress and then ignited it knowing people were asleep in the house. She claimed that she had not meant to kill but had foreseen death or grievous bodily harm as a highly probable result of her actions. Her conviction for murder was upheld with the House of Lords arguably ruling that her state of mind amounted to an *intention* to kill or cause grievous bodily harm.

However, since then there has been a retreat from this position and it is now clear that foresight of a consequence as probable, likely or even highly probable does not amount to intention. However, the precise status and meaning of oblique intention has greatly troubled the courts.

R. v Moloney [1985] A.C. 905 (House of Lords)

The appellant and his stepfather, both of whom had been drinking heavily, engaged in a contest to ascertain who was quicker on the draw with a shotgun. The appellant shot and killed his stepfather but claimed he had not realised the gun was pointing at him. He was convicted of murder and his appeal was dismissed by the Court of Appeal. He appealed to the House of Lords.

LORD BRIDGE OF HARWICH:

"[L] ooking on their facts at the decided cases where a crime of specific intent was under consideration, they suggest to me that the probability of the consequence taken to have been foreseen must be little short of overwhelming before it will suffice to establish the necessary intent. The golden rule should be that, when directing a jury on the mental element necessary in a crime of specific intent, the judge should avoid any elaboration or paraphrase of what is meant by intent, and leave it to the jury's good sense to decide whether the accused acted with the necessary intent, unless the judge is convinced that, on the facts and having regard to the way the case has been presented to the jury in evidence and argument, some further explanation or elaboration is strictly necessary to avoid misunderstanding. In trials for murder or wounding with intent, I find it very difficult to visualise a case where any such explanation or elaboration could be required, if the offence consisted of a direct attack on the victim with a weapon . . . Even where the death results indirectly from the act of the accused, I believe the cases that will call for a direction by reference to foresight of consequences will be of extremely rare occurrence . . .

I do not, of course, by what I have said in the foregoing paragraph, mean to question the necessity, which frequently arises, to explain to a jury that intention is something quite distinct from motive or desire. But this can normally be quite simply explained by reference to the case before the court or, if necessary, by some homely example. A man who, at London Airport, boards a plane which he knows to be bound for Manchester, clearly intends to travel to Manchester, even though Manchester is the last place he wants to be and his motive for boarding the plane is simply to escape pursuit. The possibility that the plane may have engine trouble and be diverted to Luton does not affect the matter. By boarding the Manchester plane, the man conclusively demonstrates his intention to go there, because it is a moral certainty that that is where he will arrive . . .

Starting from the proposition . . . that the mental element in murder requires proof of an intention to kill or cause really serious injury, the first fundamental question to be answered is whether there is any rule of substantive law that foresight by the accused of one of those eventualities as a probable consequence of his voluntary act, where the probability can be defined as exceeding a certain degree, is equivalent or alternative to the necessary intention. I would answer this question in the negative . . .

The irrationality of any such rule of substantive law stems from the fact that it is impossible to define degrees of probability, in any of the infinite variety of situations arising in human affairs, in precise or scientific terms . . .

I am firmly of opinion that foresight of consequences, as an element bearing on the issue of intention in murder, or indeed any other crime of specific intent, belongs, not to the substantive law, but to the law of evidence . . .

In the rare cases in which it is necessary to direct a jury by reference to foresight of consequences, I do not believe it is necessary for the judge to do more than invite the jury to consider two questions. First, was death or really serious injury in a murder case (or whatever relevant consequence must be proved to have been intended in any other case) a natural consequence of the defendant's voluntary act? Secondly, did the defendant foresee that consequence as being a natural consequence of his act? The jury should then be told that if they answer yes to both questions it is a proper inference for them to draw that he intended that consequence."

Appeal allowed

R. v Hancock and Shankland [1986] A.C. 455 (House of Lords)

The defendants, two striking miners, pushed a large lump of concrete from a bridge on to a convoy of cars below carrying a miner to work. The concrete struck a taxi's windscreen and killed the driver. The defendants claimed they had not meant to kill or cause serious injury. Their plan was to drop the concrete in the middle lane of the carriageway while the convoy was in the nearside lane. Their aim was to frighten the miner or block the road in order to prevent him from getting to work. The defendants were convicted of murder. The Court of Appeal allowed their appeals and substituted verdicts of manslaughter. The Crown appealed to the House of Lords.

LORD SCARMAN:

"[T]he cases to which the guidance was expressly limited by the House in *Moloney*, i.e. the 'rare cases' in which it is necessary to direct a jury by reference to foresight of consequences, are unlikely to be so rare or so exceptional as the House believed. As the House then recognised, the guidelines as formulated are applicable to cases of any crime of specific intent, and not merely murder. But further and disturbingly crimes of violence where the purpose is by open violence to protest, demonstrate, obstruct, or frighten are on the increase. Violence is used by some as a means of public communication. Inevitably there will be casualties: and inevitably death will on occasions result. If death results, is the perpetrator of the violent act guilty of murder? It will depend on his intent . . .

The question for the House is, therefore, whether the *Moloney* guidelines are sound . . .

[Lord Bridge of Harwich in *Moloney*] omitted any reference in his guidelines to probability. I agree with the Court of Appeal that the probability of a consequence is a factor of sufficient importance to be drawn specifically to the attention of the jury and to be explained. In a murder case where it is necessary to direct a jury on the issue of intent by reference to foresight of consequences the probability of death or serious injury resulting from the act done may be critically important. Its importance will depend on the degree of probability: if the likelihood that death or serious injury will result is high, the probability of that result may be seen as overwhelming evidence of the existence of the intent to kill or injure. Failure to explain the relevance of probability may, therefore, mislead a jury into thinking that it is of little or no importance . . . In my judgment, therefore, the *Moloney* guidelines as they stand are unsafe and misleading. They require a reference to probability. They also require an explanation that the greater the probability of a consequence the more likely it is that the consequence was foreseen and that if that consequence was foreseen the greater the probability is that that consequence was also intended. But juries also require to be reminded that the decision is theirs to be reached upon a consideration of all the evidence . . .

In a case where foresight of a consequence is part of the evidence supporting a prosecution submission that the accused intended the consequence, the judge, if he thinks some general observations would help the jury, could well, having in mind section 8 of the Criminal Justice Act 1967, emphasise that the probability, however high, of a consequence is only a factor, though it may in some cases be a very significant factor, to be considered with all the other evidence in determining whether the accused intended to bring it about. The distinction between the offence and the evidence relied on to prove it is vital . . .

For these reasons I would hold that the *Moloney* guidelines are defective and should not be used as they stand without further explanation."

Appeal dismissed

R. v Nedrick [1986] 1 W.L.R. 1025 (Court of Appeal, Criminal Division)

The appellant poured paraffin through the letterbox of a house and set light to it. The house caught fire and a child died. The appellant claimed that he did not want anyone to die. He was convicted of murder and appealed.

LORD LANE CJ:

"What then does a jury have to decide so far as the mental element in murder is concerned? It simply has to decide whether the defendant intended to kill or do serious bodily harm. In order to reach that decision the jury must pay regard to all the relevant circumstances, including what the defendant himself said and did.

In the great majority of cases a direction to that effect will be enough, particularly where the defendant's actions amounted to a direct attack upon his victim, because in such cases the evidence relating to the defendant's desire or motive will be clear and his intent will have been the same as his desire or motive. But in some cases, of which this is one, the defendant does an act which is manifestly dangerous and as a result someone dies. The primary desire or motive of the defendant may not have been to harm that person, or indeed anyone. In that situation what further directions should a jury be given as to the mental state which they must find to exist in the defendant if murder is to be proved?

We have endeavoured to crystallise the effect of their Lordships' speeches in *R. v Moloney* and *R. v Hancock* in a way which we hope may be helpful to judges who have to handle this type of case.

It may be advisable first of all to explain to the jury that a man may intend to achieve a certain result whilst at the same time not desiring it to come about . . .

When determining whether the defendant had the necessary intent, it may therefore be helpful for a jury to ask themselves two questions. (1) How probable was the consequence which resulted from the defendant's voluntary act? (2) Did he foresee that consequence?

If he did not appreciate that death or serious harm was likely to result from his act, he cannot have intended to bring it about. If he did, but thought that the risk to which he was exposing the person killed was only slight, then it may be easy for the jury to conclude that he did not intend to bring about that result. On the other hand, if the jury are satisfied that at the material time the defendant recognised that death or serious harm would be virtually certain (barring some unforeseen intervention) to result from his voluntary act, then that is a fact from which they may find it easy to infer that he intended to kill or do serious bodily harm, even though he may not have had any desire to achieve that result.

. . .

Where the charge is murder and in the rare cases where the simple direction is not enough, the jury should be directed that they are not entitled to infer the necessary intention, unless they feel sure that death or serious bodily harm was a virtual certainty (barring some unforeseen intervention) as a result of the defendant's actions and that the defendant appreciated that such was the case.[182]

Where a man realises that it is for all practical purposes inevitable that his actions will result in death or serious harm, the inference may be irresistible that he intended that result, however little he may have desired or wished it to happen. The decision is one for the jury to be reached upon a consideration of all the evidence."

Appeal allowed
Conviction of manslaughter substituted

R. v Woollin [1999] 1 A.C. 82 (House of Lords)

The appellant lost his temper with his three-month-old son and threw him with great force causing the child to hit his head on something hard and die. In an interview the appellant admitted that he had realised there was a risk of serious injury. The trial judge directed the jury that they might infer intention if they were satisfied that the appellant appreciated that there was a substantial risk that he would cause serious harm. The appellant was convicted of murder and appealed on the ground that the judge should not have used the phrase "substantial risk", which is a test of recklessness, but should have used the phrase "virtual certainty".

LORD STEYN:

"The Crown did not contend that the appellant desired to kill his son or to cause him serious injury. The issue was whether the appellant nevertheless had the intention to cause serious harm . . .

I approach the issues arising on this appeal on the basis that it does not follow that 'intent' necessarily has precisely the same meaning in every context in the criminal law. The focus of the present appeal is the crime of murder. Lord Bridge observed in *Moloney* [that] . . .

---

[182]   This section was italicised by Lord Steyn in *Woollin* when he cited this passage with approval.

'But looking on their facts at the decided cases where a crime of specific intent was under consideration, including *Reg v Hyam* itself, they suggest to me that the probability of the consequence taken to have been foreseen must be little short of overwhelming before it will suffice to *establish* the necessary intent.' (My emphasis added.)

Lord Bridge paraphrased this idea in terms of 'moral certainty.' In the result the House adopted a narrower test of what may constitute intention which is similar to the 'virtual certainty' test in *Nedrick* . . .

In *Hancock*, Lord Scarman did not express disagreement with the test of foresight of a probability which is 'little short of overwhelming' as enunciated in *Moloney* . . . Moreover, Lord Scarman thought that where explanation is required the jury should be directed as to the relevance of probability without expressly stating the matter in terms of any particular level of probability. The manner in which trial judges were to direct juries was left unclear . . .

[His Lordship then cited from *Nedrick*, including the italicised passage on p.152]

While I have thought it right to give the full text of Lord Lane's observations, it is obvious that the italicised passage contains the critical direction. The effect of the critical direction is that a result foreseen as virtually certain is an intended result.

It is now possible to consider the Crown's direct challenge to the correctness of *Nedrick*. First, the Crown argued that *Nedrick* prevents the jury from considering all the evidence in the case relevant to intention. The argument is that this is contrary to the provisions of section 8 of the Act of 1967 . . . [Section 8] is no more than a legislative instruction that in considering their findings on intention or foresight the jury must take into account all relevant evidence: *Nedrick* is undoubtedly concerned with the mental element which is sufficient for murder . . . But, as Lord Lane CJ emphasised in the last sentence of *Nedrick*: 'The decision is one for the jury to be reached upon a consideration of all the evidence.' *Nedrick* does not prevent a jury from considering all the evidence: it merely stated what state of mind (in the absence of a purpose to kill or to cause serious harm) is sufficient for murder. I would therefore reject the Crown's first argument.

In the second place the Crown submitted that *Nedrick* is in conflict with the decision of the House in *Hancock*. Counsel argued that in order to bring some coherence to the process of determining intention Lord Lane CJ specified a minimum level of foresight, namely virtual certainty. But that is not in conflict with the decision in *Hancock* which, apart from disapproving Lord Bridge's 'natural consequence' model direction, approved *Moloney* in all other respects. And in *Moloney* Lord Bridge said, that if a person foresees the probability of a consequence as little short of overwhelming, this 'will suffice to *establish* the necessary intent' (my emphasis) . . .

The Crown did not argue that as a matter of policy foresight of a virtual certainty is too narrow a test in murder . . . Moreover, over a period of 12 years since *Nedrick* the test of foresight of virtual certainty has apparently caused no practical difficulties. It is simple and clear. It is true that it may exclude a conviction of murder in the often cited terrorist example where a member of the bomb disposal team is killed. In such a case it may realistically be said that the terrorist did not foresee the killing of a member of the bomb disposal team as a virtual certainty. That may be a consequence of not framing the principle in terms of risk-taking. Such cases ought to cause no substantial difficulty since immediately below murder there is available a verdict of manslaughter which may attract in the discretion of the court a life sentence . . . I am satisfied that the *Nedrick* test, which was squarely based on the decision of the House in *Moloney*, is pitched at the right level of foresight . . .

It may be appropriate to give a direction in accordance with *Nedrick* in any case in which the defendant may not have desired the result of his act. But I accept the trial judge is best placed to decide what direction is required by the circumstances of the case . . .

It follows that the judge should not have departed from the *Nedrick* direction. By using the phrase 'substantial risk' the judge blurred the line between intention and recklessness, and hence between murder and manslaughter. The misdirection enlarged the scope of the mental element required for murder. It was a material misdirection . . . The conviction of murder must be quashed.

The status of Nedrick

In my view Lord Lane CJ's judgment in *Nedrick* provided valuable assistance to trial judges . . . [His Lordship then repeated part of Lord Lane's judgment]:

'. . . (B) Where the charge is murder and in the rare cases where the simple direction is not enough, the jury should be directed that they are not entitled to infer the necessary intention, unless they feel sure that death or serious bodily harm was a virtual certainty (barring some unforeseen intervention) as a result of the defendant's actions and that the defendant appreciated that such was the case. (C) Where a man realises that it is for all practical purposes inevitable that his actions will result in death or serious harm, the inference may be irresistible that he intended that result, however little he may have desired or wished it to happen. The decision is one for the jury to be reached upon a consideration of all the evidence.' (Lettering added.)

. . . [It has been observed] that the use of the words 'to infer' in (B) may detract from the clarity of the model direction. I agree. I would substitute the words 'to find'. Thirdly, the first sentence of (C) does not form part of the model direction. But it would always be right for the judge to say, as Lord Lane CJ put it, that the decision is for the jury upon a consideration of all the evidence in the case."

Appeal allowed

The following conclusions can be drawn from these cases:

(i) Wanting result

A defendant who wants a result to happen or is prepared to do acts to achieve a consequence even if not (emotionally) desired[183]—when it is the aim or objective (direct intention)—clearly intends that result.

R.A. Duff, Intention, Agency and Criminal Liability: Philosophy of Action and the Criminal Law (1990), pp.47–48:

"To say that she intended to bring about a particular result is to say that that result formed at least part of her reason for acting as she did . . . What Mrs Hyam did fitted both the description 'setting fire to the house' and the description 'making work for the fire brigade': what makes the former description, but not the latter, appropriate as a description of her intended action is its relation to her reasons for action."

Duff goes on to suggest that direct intention can be measured by employing a "test of failure": would the defendant count their actions as a failure if the result did not ensue?[184] Employing this test, Mrs Hyam did not directly intend to kill or cause injury because she would not have regarded her actions as a failure had no one been killed or injured.

Such wanted results are intended even if the chances of the result occurring are slim: if the defendant shoots at their victim half a mile away knowing that they could easily miss, they still intend to kill because that is what they are trying to do. Lord Reid has expressed this point in terms of a golfing analogy:

"If I say I intend to reach the green, people will believe me although we all know that the odds are ten to one against my succeeding."[185]

---

183   In *R. v Hales (Ricky)* [2005] EWCA Crim 1118 it was held that it was enough that the defendant was "prepared to kill" in order to escape police custody (at [28]).
184   At p.61. See also R.A. Duff, "Intention, Mens Rea and the Law Commission Report" [1980] Crim. L.R. 147 at 150–151.
185   *Gollins v Gollins* [1964] A.C. 644 at 664.

However, no matter how much one may want to achieve a result, one can only be said to intend it if one recognises that there is a chance of achieving it. If one does not believe that the consequence is a possible result of one's actions one can hardly be said to be trying to achieve it.[186]

(ii) Question of fact for jury

In the normal case the term "intention" should not be given a legal definition. Judges should refrain from giving juries guidance as to what it means. This is particularly true in common cases where there has been a direct attack upon the victim.[187] Whether a defendant intended a result is a question of fact which only the jury, applying their common sense to an ordinary English word, can answer. It is thus impossible to define intention or to know precisely what it means. It could well mean different things to different juries. Presumably, although one is only guessing, most juries will opt for the ordinary, common-sense meaning, namely, "as 'a decision to bring about a certain consequence' or as the aim".[188]

(iii) "Exceptional" cases: oblique intention

However, there may be other cases where a defendant has a purpose other than causing the prohibited harm—but where that result is an inevitable or likely consequence. For example, the defendant's main aim in *Nedrick* was to burn down the house in order to frighten its occupant but, in so doing, causing death was a likely result. In *Woollin*, it was again emphasised that a direction was only necessary in cases where the defendant does not desire the consequence that has occurred. In *Moloney*, Lord Bridge thought such guidance would only be necessary in "rare" and "exceptional" cases.[189] However, Lord Scarman in *Hancock* stated that such cases would not be at all rare or exceptional—and, accordingly, guidance to the jury will be necessary in most cases where the defendant has a primary aim in acting other than causing the prohibited harm.[190] Despite this, more recent cases have stressed that a *Woollin* direction will only be required in "rare circumstances".[191] Further, giving a *Woollin* direction when it is not appropriate can amount to a misdirection providing grounds for quashing a conviction because it can lead to the trial judge analysing the evidence differently from how it should be analysed in the normal cases of direct intention.[192]

So, in rare cases it is permissible to give juries some guidance. However, it is far from clear precisely what intention does mean in such cases. The central problem is that there are two possible interpretations of *Woollin*:

(i) *Definitional interpretation*: a new extended *definition* of intention has been laid down. If a consequence is foreseen as virtually certain the jury may be told that this amounts to intention. This view is supported by two passages in *Woollin*. First, Lord Steyn cited with approval from *Moloney*

---

[186]   R.A. Duff, "The Obscure Intentions of the House of Lords" [1986] Crim. L.R. 771 at 779; R.A. Duff, *Intention, Agency and Criminal Liability: Philosophy of Action and the Criminal Law* (London: Blackwell, 1990), p.58.
[187]   *Gregory and Mott* [1995] Crim. L.R. 507; *R. v Fallon* [1994] Crim. L.R. 519.
[188]   *Mohan* [1976] 1 Q.B. 1.
[189]   See also *Gilmour* [2000] Cr. App. R. 407.
[190]   In *R. v Walker (John Charles)* (1990) 90 Cr. App. R. 226, it was held that a mere request from a jury for a further direction did not make the case a rare and exceptional one requiring a direction on foresight.
[191]   *R. v MD* [2004] EWCA Crim 1391 at [29]. See also *R. v Allen (Tony John)* [2005] EWCA Crim 1344 at [63] and *Hales* [2005] EWCA Crim 1118 at [27].
[192]   *MD* [2004] EWCA Crim 1391 at [36].

that "if a person foresees the probability of a consequence as little short of overwhelming, this will suffice *to establish* the necessary intent" (Lord Steyn's emphasis). Secondly, after citing the italicised passage from *Nedrick* (p.152), Lord Steyn added: "The effect of the critical direction is that a result foreseen as virtually certain *is* an intended result" (our emphasis). This interpretation is strengthened by the fact that in *Woollin* the Crown did not contend that the appellant desired to kill or seriously injure his son. The case proceeded on the basis that there could be another species of intention apart from direct intention.

(ii) *Evidential interpretation*: there is still no definition of intention. Where a consequence is foreseen as virtually certain this is evidence entitling a court or jury to find intention. Lord Steyn emphasised his approval of the critical direction in *Nedrick* (the italicised passage on p.152). While he substituted "find" in place of "infer",[193] he endorsed the *Nedrick* view that the jury was "not entitled to [find] the necessary intention unless they feel sure that death or serious bodily harm was a virtual certainty . . . and the defendant appreciated that such was the case". While endorsing the virtual certainty test as evidence from which the jury is entitled to find intention, Lord Steyn immediately went on to rule that the *Nedrick* proposition (first sentence of (C) cited in *Woollin*) that the inference may be irresistible, does not form part of the model direction. This seems to confirm that there is no test of intention. While foresight of a virtual certainty is a prerequisite to a finding of intention, the jury may (is "entitled to") find intention in such cases, but equally they may not. This evidential interpretation was adopted in the following case.

R. v Matthews and Alleyne [2003] 2 Cr. App. R. 30 (Court of Appeal, Criminal Division)

The defendants deliberately threw a non-swimmer into a deep, wide river where he drowned. They were convicted of murder and appealed on the ground that the trial judge had misdirected the jury that if they were satisfied the defendants foresaw death as virtually certain they had to convict (i.e. that the trial judge adopted the definitional interpretation).

RIX LJ:

"Mr Coker for the Crown on this appeal submits that in *Woollin* the House of Lords has finally moved away from a rule of evidence to a rule of substantive law. In this connection he drew attention to a sentence in Lord Steyn's speech where he says . . . that—

'The effect of the critical direction is that a result foreseen as virtually certain is an intended result.' . . .

In our judgment, however, the law has not yet reached a *definition* of intent in murder in terms of appreciation of a virtual certainty . . . [W]e do not regard *Woollin* as yet reaching or laying down a substantive rule of law. On the contrary, it is clear from the discussion in *Woollin* as a whole that *Nedrick* was derived from the existing law, at that time ending in *Moloney* and *Hancock*, and that the critical direction in *Nedrick* was approved, subject to the change of one word.

   In these circumstances we think that the judge did go further than the law as it stands at present permitted him to go . . .

---

[193] Some commentators have suggested that the substitution of "find" for "infer" "seems a clear indication that the connection between virtual certainty and intention is not merely evidential" (A. Simester, 'Murder, Mens Rea and the House of Lords-Again' (1999) 115 L.Q.R. 17). However, the jury is only *entitled* to find intention suggesting that this is still an evidential proposition.

Having said that, however, we think that, once what is required is an appreciation of virtual certainty of death, and not some lesser foresight of merely probable consequences, there is very little to choose between a rule of evidence and one of substantive law. It is probably this thought that led Lord Steyn to say that a result foreseen as virtually certain is an intended result. . . .

We also think that on the particular facts of this case, reflected in the judge's directions, the question of the appellants' intentions to save Jonathan from drowning highlight the irresistible nature of the inference or finding of intent to kill, once the jury were sure both that the defendants appreciated the virtual certainty of death '(barring some attempt to save him)' and that at the time of throwing Jonathan from the bridge they then 'had no intentions of saving him'. If the jury were sure that the appellants appreciated the virtual certainty of Jonathan's death when they threw him from the bridge and also that they then had no intention of saving him from such death, it is impossible to see how the jury could not have found that the appellants intended Jonathan to die."

Appeal dismissed

In an ambiguous judgment in *Stringer*[194] Toulson LJ seemed to accept that if a consequence was foreseen as virtually certain, a finding of intention "was bound to follow". Despite this, the evidential interpretation endorsed in *Matthews and Alleyne* appears to represent the current law. Nevertheless, the question still remains: which of these interpretations is preferable? The definitional interpretation has the advantage of being simpler and more workable. There are two separate species of intent: direct intent (aim/purpose) and oblique intent (foresight of virtual certainty). Each is clearly defined and proof of either will suffice (for murder, at any rate: see below). It avoids the absurdity of having to infer one state of mind (intention) from another state of mind (foresight of virtual certainty).

William Wilson, "Doctrinal Rationality after Woollin" (1999) 62 Modern L. Rev. 448 at 451–452:

"What a person foresees is not necessarily even probative of what he means to achieve. Direct intention and foresight are different states of mind, in the same way that love is different from acquisitiveness. Proving that a person foresees a consequence as probable/ highly probable is no more conclusive of an intention to produce that consequence than counting an art dealer's acquisitions can establish his love of art."

The problem with the evidential interpretation is that if one is inferring (or finding) intention from foresight of a virtual certainty, one must know what intention means. If intention (A) may be found from foresight of a virtual certainty (B), (A) and (B) must logically mean different things. But what does intention (A) mean? It is not foresight of a virtual certainty (B) because that is merely an evidential pre-condition.[195] It should not mean direct intention[196] because juries should only be given a *Nedrick/ Woollin* direction in cases where the defendant does not aim at achieving the consequence. It is a logical nonsense to tell the jury that because the defendant does not want the result they are going to be given the special direction but that if they are satisfied that the defendant foresaw the consequence as a virtual certainty, they may conclude that he did want it after all.

The result is that intention can only mean something mysterious: "some ineffable, indefinable

---

194   *R. v Stringer (Matthew)* [2008] EWCA Crim 1222.
195   W. Wilson, "Doctrinal Rationality after *Woollin*" (1999) 62 M.L.R. 448 at 155.
196   Norrie has argued that one can only infer intention from foresight where intention connotes direct intention plus foresight of a moral certainty (oblique intention) because one cannot infer a mental state (A) from the facts (b) where A and b are qualitatively different (A. Norrie, "Oblique Intention and Legal Politics" [1989] Crim. L.R. 793 at 803). However, as Duff has effectively responded: "intention is inferable from foresight only if they are distinct"; if they are the same thing, no further inference is needed ("The Politics of Intention: A Response to Norrie" [1990] Crim. L.R. 637 at 639).

notion of intent, locked in the breasts of the jurors".[197] Where there is such a "logical gap"[198] between foresight of a virtual certainty and this mysterious, undefined concept of intention, it becomes difficult to predict when and in what circumstances the finding of intent will or will not be made. Such anapproach allows the jury maximum flexibility to make moral assessments of the defendant's actions and to do justice as they perceive it.[199]

On the other hand, the definitional interpretation places the jury in a moral straight-jacket. If the defendant foresees a consequence as virtually certain the jury is bound (in theory) to conclude that the test of oblique intention is satisfied.

Alan Norrie, "After Woollin" [1999] Criminal L. Rev. 532 at 538:

"[There] are cases where there is a 'moral threshold' such that even though the accused could foresee a result as virtually certain, it is so at odds with his moral conception of what he was doing that it could not be conceived as a result that he intended . . . [T]here is a good argument for saying that a person does not intend indirectly those results which may be foreseen as virtually certain where they are at serious moral odds with what he intended to do . . . [Judges] and juries would be 'entitled' to find, in terms of *principle* and without strain, that the moral threshold between what the accused intended and what she foresaw as virtually certain was sufficiently large to avoid attribution of fault."

In most cases (certainly murder cases) what the defendant foresees is not going to be "at serious moral odds with what he intended to do". Such defendants are usually engaged in reprehensible conduct such as that in *Matthews and Alleyne* where it was stated that *on the facts* the inference was "irresistible" and that if the defendants appreciated the virtual certainty of death, it would be "impossible" for the jury not to find the requisite intention to kill.

However, as argued by Norrie, the advantage of the evidential interpretation is that in other cases where their sympathy is aroused the jury is given a "get out clause"[200] in that while they are entitled to find intention, equally they are entitled not to find intention. This approach gives juries "moral elbow-room"[201] to acquit in such cases without having to resort to perverse verdicts. As Wilson puts it: by not having a strict definition of intention the judge or jury have a "flexible friend, which, in appropriate circumstances can allow good intentions to take doctrinal precedence over knowledge".[202]

R. v Steane [1947] K.B. 997 (Court of Criminal Appeal)

The appellant, a British film actor, was resident and working in Germany before World War II. When war broke out he was arrested. As a result of threats to place his wife and children in a concentration camp and physical threats to himself, the appellant reluctantly agreed to broadcast on the radio for the Germans. For four months he read the news three times a day. After the war he was convicted of doing acts likely to assist the enemy, with intent to assist the enemy, contrary to reg.2A of the Defence

---

[197] J. Smith "Commentary to *Woollin*" [1998] Crim. L.R. 891.
[198] Duff, "The Obscure Intentions of the House of Lords" [1986] Crim. L.R. 771.
[199] This approach is criticised in C.M.V. Clarkson, *Understanding Criminal Law*, 4th edn (London: Sweet & Maxwell, 2005), p.213. Norrie says it "permits the law to have its principled cake of subjectivism, and to eat it" ("Oblique Intention and Legal Politics" [1989] Crim. L.R. 793 at 806).
[200] W. Wilson, "Doctrinal Rationality after *Woollin*" (1999) 62 M.L.R. 448 at 456.
[201] J. Horder, "Intention in the Criminal Law—A Rejoinder" (1995) 58 M.L.R. 678 at 687.
[202] "Murder and the Structure of Homicide", in A. Ashworth and B. Mitchell (eds), *Rethinking English Homicide Law* (Oxford: OUP, 2000), p.48.

(General) Regulations 1939 and was sentenced to three years' imprisonment. He appealed against the conviction.

GODDARD LCJ:

"The appellant also asserted . . . that he never had the slightest idea or intention of assisting the enemy and what he did was done to save his wife and children . . .

The . . . difficult question that arises, however, is in connection with the direction to the jury with regard to whether these acts were done with the intention of assisting the enemy . . . While no doubt the motive of a man's act and his intention of doing the act are in law different things, it is nonetheless true that in many offences a specific intention is a necessary ingredient, and the jury have to be satisfied that a particular act was done with that specific intent . . .

An illustration . . . would be if a person deliberately took down his blackout curtains or shutters with the result that light appeared on the outside of his house, perhaps during an air raid; it might well be that no evidence or explanation were given and if all that was proved was that during that raid the prisoner exposed lights by a deliberate act, a jury could infer that he intended to signal or assist the enemy. But if the evidence in the case showed, for instance, that he or someone was overcome by heat and that he tore down the blackout to ventilate the room, the jury would certainly have to consider whether his act was done with the intent to assist the enemy or with some other intent, so that while he would be guilty of an offence against the Blackout Regulations, he would not be guilty of the offence of attempting to assist the enemy . . .

British soldiers who were set to work on the Burma Road, or if invasion had unhappily taken place, British subjects who might have been set to work by the enemy digging trenches would undoubtedly be doing acts likely to assist the enemy. It would be unnecessary surely in their cases to consider any of the niceties of the law relating to duress because no jury would find that merely doing this work they were intending to assist the enemy . . . The proper direction to the jury in this case would have been that it was for the prosecution to prove the criminal intent, and that while the jury would be entitled to presume that intent if they thought that the act was done as the result of the free uncontrolled action of the accused, they would not be entitled to presume it if the circumstances showed that the act was done in subjection to the power of the enemy or was as equally consistent with an innocent intent as with a criminal intent, for example, a desire to save his wife and children from a concentration camp. They should only convict if satisfied by the evidence that the act complained of was in fact done to assist the enemy and if there was doubt about the matter the prisoner was entitled to be acquitted."

Conviction quashed

If this case were decided today under the definitional interpretation of *Woollin*, the jury would be forced (short of a perverse verdict) to conclude that Steane intended to assist the enemy: he would certainly have foreseen that consequence as a virtual certainty. However, under the evidential interpretation the jury would have the moral elbow-room to conclude that, despite such foresight, the result was not intended.

This approach also provides flexibility in medical cases where doctors administer drugs or other treatment with lawful motives (for example, to relieve pain) but knowing the treatment will kill the patient.

Re A (conjoined twins: surgical separation) [2000] 4 All E.R. 961 (Court of Appeal, Civil Division)

The issue in this case was whether a declaration should be made that it would be lawful for doctors to separate conjoined twins even though such a procedure would certainly result in the death of the weaker twin. One of the matters canvassed was whether the doctors would have the mens rea of murder, namely, an intention to kill or cause grievous bodily harm.

WARD LJ:

"I have to ask myself whether I am satisfied that the doctors recognise that death or serious harm will be virtu-ally certain (barring some unforeseen intervention) to result from carrying out this operation. If so, the doctors intend to kill or do that serious harm even though they may not have any desire to achieve that result. It is common ground that they appreciate that death to Mary would result from the severance of the common aorta. Unpalatable though it may be . . . to stigmatise the doctors with 'murderous intent', that is what in law they will have if they perform the operation and Mary dies as a result.

The doctrine of double effect . . . teaches that an act which produces a bad effect is nevertheless morally permissible if the action is good in itself, the intention is solely to produce the good effect, the good effect is not produced through the bad effect and there is sufficient reason to permit the bad effect. It may be difficult to reconcile with *R. v Woollin* . . . I can readily see how the doctrine works when doctors are treating one patient administering pain-killing drugs for the sole good purpose of relieving pain, yet appreciating the bad side-effect that it will hasten the patient's death. I simply fail to see how it can apply here where the side-effect to the good cure for Jodie is another patient's, Mary's, death, and when the treatment cannot have been undertaken to effect any benefit for Mary."

BROOKE LJ:

"[A]n English court would inevitably find that the surgeons intended to kill Mary, however little they desired that end, because her death would be the virtual certain consequence of their acts, and they would realize that for all practical purposes her death would inevitably follow . . ."

ROBERT WALKER LJ:

"However the stark facts of *R. v Woollin* and the speeches in the House of Lords in that case say nothing at all about the situation in which an individual acts for a good purpose which cannot be achieved without also having bad consequences (which may be merely possible, or very probable, or virtually certain). This is the doctrine (or dilemma) of double effect. In one class of case the good purpose and the foreseen but undesired consequence (what Bentham called 'oblique intention') are both directed at the same individual. This can be illustrated by a doctor's duty to his patient . . . [H]e may in order to palliate severe pain, administer large doses of analgesics even though he knows that the likely consequence will be to shorten the patient's life . . . In these cases the doctrine of double effect prevents the doctor's foresight of accelerated death from counting as a guilty intention. This type of double effect cannot be relevant to conduct directed towards Mary . . .

There is another class of case in which a person may be faced with the dilemma of whether to save himself or others at the cost of harm or even death to a third person. The dilemma generally arises as the result of an emer-gency . . . [such as] disasters at sea. If a person, faced with such a dilemma, acts with the intention of saving his own life (or the lives of others) it may be said that that leaves no room for a guilty intention to harm or even kill the third person. Equally, it may be said that although he must (on *R. v Woollin* principles) be taken to have intended the death which he foresaw as virtually certain, he has a defence of necessity. That is the way the submission was put by Miss Davies . . .

In *Gillick v West Norfolk and Wisbech Area Health Authority* [1986] 1 A.C. 112 at 190, Lord Scarman . . . said . . .

'The bona fide exercise by a doctor of his clinical judgment must be a complete negation of the guilty mind which is an essential ingredient of the criminal offence . . .'.

Here the court is concerned with the possibility of the commission of a much more serious criminal offence, that is murder. But in the wholly exceptional case of these conjoined twins I consider that the same principles apply . . . Mary's death would be foreseen as an inevitable consequence of an operation which is intended, and is necessary, to save Jodie's life. But Mary's death would not be the purpose or intention of the surgery."

This case is significant in two respects. First, it demonstrates the difference between the two inter-pretations of intention. Ward LJ and Brooke LJ, in effect, followed the definitional interpretation. The doctors would foresee death as a virtual certainty and therefore they *would* intend death.[203] However, Robert Walker LJ (implicitly) allowed himself moral elbow-room in holding that the doctors would not intend to kill the weaker twin because that was not "the purpose or intention of the surgery."

Secondly, this divergence of approach brings to the fore a central dilemma here. Is intention a psychological state of mind or a moral conclusion?[204] While Robert Walker LJ clearly adopted the latter view that there was no intention because the doctors would not be morally responsible for the death, the other two members of the Court of Appeal proceeded on the basis that intention is a psychological state. The issue was quite simply whether the doctors would, as a matter of fact, foresee death as a virtual certainty.

A conclusion that a defendant is criminally liable must, of course, involve a judgment of moral responsibility but the issue is ascertaining where such moral assessments should be located: ought they to be part of the question whether the defendant intended a result or should they affect the issue of whether a defence is available? For example, Ward LJ and Brooke LJ were clear that the doctors would not be guilty of murder but they achieved this result by holding that, while they would intend death, they would be afforded a defence of medical necessity. Similarly, *Steane* could have been decided on the basis that he did intend to assist the enemy but had a defence of duress because he was forced to broadcast.

The argument in favour of the view that intention should be a moral conclusion is that actions must pass a "threshold of responsibility" before there can be intention. For example, the teacher who gives a student a (deserved) bad mark knowing it will upset the pupil does not intend such upset because of a moral assessment that the teacher is only performing her duty to grade properly.[205] On this basis Norrie argues that

> "there is a *moral* objection in common sense to saying [that Steane obliquely intended to assist the enemy], which stems from the duress under which Steane operated. The threats to his family represented the basis of a moral excuse for saying that he did not possess the oblique intention to assist the enemy, but only intended to save his family."[206]

Another way of making such moral assessments is to examine the defendant's *attitudes* towards the risks they are creating.

Antje Pedain, "Intention and the Terrorist Example" [2003] Crim. L.R. 579 at 589, 586, 587:

"If intending something means to endorse it as the consequence of one's voluntary actions, then the issue is not about whether you endorse it as the certain, the likely or the unlikely consequence of your behaviour. It is about endorsement as such. The point is about whether you give that consequence your blessing . . .
[The author applies this 'endorsement test' to the facts of *Woollin*] The *reason* why we allow Woollin to distance himself from the foreseeable consequences of his actions is that he did not endorse injury or death even as a possibility . . . [and to the facts of *Hyam*] [T]he sense of 'not wanting something to happen' is the sense of not caring about an outcome, of having no interest in it or being indifferent to its occurrence. This is the sense in which Hyam did 'not want' Mrs Booth's daughters to die in the fire. That in itself is insufficient for her to disassociate herself from this consequence of her intentional conduct."

---

203 A similar approach was approved (obiter) in *Burke v General Medical Council* [2005] EWCA Civ 1003.
204 A.P. Simester and S. Shute, *Letter to the Editor* [2000] Crim. L.R. 204.
205 R.A. Duff, "Intention, Mens Rea and the Law Commission Report" [1980] Crim. L.R. 147 at 152–154.
206 Norrie, "Oblique Intention and Legal Politics" [1989] Crim. L.R. 793 at 797.

Under the evidential interpretation such an approach would be helpful to a jury in deciding whether to draw the inference of intention or not.[207]

These approaches are, however, highly problematic in less straightforward cases particularly where the defendant's actions do not unambiguously reveal their attitude or where there is uncertainty as to whether the defendant does have a moral excuse or not.

Chandler v DPP [1964] A.C. 763 (House of Lords)

The appellants were deeply opposed to nuclear weapons. In order to demonstrate their opposition they planned non-violent action to immobilise an aircraft at an RAF station for a period of six hours. They were convicted of conspiracy to commit a breach of s.1 of the Official Secrets Act 1911, namely entering a prohibited place for "a purpose prejudicial to the safety or interests of the state". The trial judge ruled that they were not entitled to call evidence to show that it would be for the benefit of the country to give up nuclear armaments. He directed the jury to convict if they were satisfied that the immediate purpose of the appellants was the obstruction of an aircraft. Their appeal was dismissed by the Court of Criminal Appeals. They appealed to the House of Lords.

RADCLIFFE LJ:

"The trial judge . . . directed the jury that they should not be influenced by what, he said, was the undisputed fact that the views as to the wrongness and, indeed, unwisdom of nuclear weapons held by the appellants were deeply and passionately held and that they were honest and sincere views. In effect he put it to the jury that they should look on the appellants as having made their entry for two separate purposes, an immediate purpose of obstructing the airfield, and a further or long-term purpose of inducing or compelling the Government to abandon nuclear weapons in the true interests of the state. His ruling was that, if they found the immediate purpose proved, that of obstruction, they ought to find the appellants guilty of offences under section 1 of the Act, regardless of whether they might think the long-term purpose in itself beneficial or, at any rate, non-prejudicial to the interests and safety of the state. In my opinion there was nothing defective in law in this ruling."

Appeal dismissed

Following the definitional interpretation of *Woollin* the defendants in *Chandler* would clearly be liable—a view consistent with the notion that intention is a psychological state of mind. The moral judgment as to liability would be left to the determination of whether they should be afforded a defence—which they would not.[208] On the other hand, under the evidential interpretation of *Woollin*, the jury would be able to evaluate the motives of the defendants in deciding whether to find intention or not. There are, however, problems with this latter approach. First, whether intention would be "found" or not in a case such as *Chandler* would depend largely on the "political" persuasions of the jury, thus generating uncertainty and inconsistency. Secondly, it results in a blurring of the distinction between the elements of an offence and exculpatory defences.[209] Would it mean that Steane could have done *anything* (for example, blow up an aeroplane killing hundreds of people) to save his family?[210]

---

[207]   Assuming the consequence was foreseen as virtually certain. Note that Pedain's argument is that this should not be a prerequisite: all that she requires is an intention to expose someone to a risk coupled with endorsement of the possible consequences. Such an approach would significantly broaden the current English concept of intention.

[208]   See pp.383–384.

[209]   W. Wilson, "A Plea for Rationality in the Law of Murder" (1990) 10 L.S. 307 at 310.

[210]   Duff, "The Politics of Intention: A Response to Norrie" [1990] Crim. L.R. 637 at 638.

Such an important question as whether duress should be a defence to murder should not be left to the vagaries of a jury decision. It raises fundamental moral questions, which should be determined as a matter of law within the parameters of the defence of duress.

(iv) A variable meaning?

In *Moloney* and *Hancock* it was stressed that the court was not only dealing with murder, but with all crimes of "intention". In short, according to these cases intention bears the same meaning throughout the criminal law.

However, Lord Steyn in *Woollin* was careful to limit the scope of his judgment:

"I approach the issues arising on this appeal on the basis that it does not follow that 'intent' necessarily has the same meaning in every context in the criminal law."

The impact of this limitation is, of course, dependent on which of the two interpretations of *Woollin*, discussed above, is adopted. If, as generally accepted, *Woollin* is interpreted as not defining intention, but simply confirming *Nedrick* that the jury is "entitled to find" intention where there is foresight of a virtual certainty, then this limitation is unimportant as the *Nedrick* test was broadly accepted as applying to all crimes that required intention.[211] However, if *Woollin* is interpreted as laying down a definition of intention, this would mean that there is a definition of intention for the crime of murder, but for all other crimes resort would still have to be had to *Nedrick*.

It is, of course, possible to argue that the concept "intention" should have a chameleon-like character and change its meaning according to its context. For example, Glanville Williams has argued that "intent" should generally include foresight of a virtual certainty, but that there are three exceptions where it should bear its narrowest, purposive meaning of "direct" intent: namely, offences of causing mental stress or annoyance; certain instances of complicity; and treason.[212] Duff, on the other hand, also argues for a concept of "oblique" intention but with three different exceptions where only "direct" intention should suffice. His exceptions are attempted crimes, other "with intent" crimes where there has to be an intention to cause a result not specified in the actus reus of the crime and, finally, the doctrine of implied malice.[213]

Such an approach is unacceptable. As can be seen from the divergent views of the above writers, agreement as to which crimes should require which type of intention would be impossible to secure and would only increase the uncertainty in this area of law. Further, it is difficult to see that there is any justifiable legal policy underpinning a variable meaning for "intention". Also, such an approach would simply lead to complication and complexity. If the *Woollin* limitation were accepted it would mean that intention to cause grievous bodily harm for murder would be governed by *Woollin* but for s.18 of the Offences Against the Person Act 1861 it would be governed by *Nedrick*.

Both in terms of principle and pragmatism, the concept "intention" should bear the same meaning throughout the criminal law. If it were felt that for certain crimes this fixed meaning was inappropriate, then an additional or alternative species of mens rea should be stipulated—without the concept of "intention" having to shrink or expand to meet the exigencies of all situations.

---

[211]   This view was adopted *in R. v Purcell (Frank)* (1986) 83 Cr. App. R. 45; *R. v AMK (Property Management)* [1985] Crim. L.R. 600; *Bryson* [1985] Crim. L.R. 669; *R. v Burke (Alisdair David)* [1988] Crim. L.R. 839.

[212]   Glanville Williams, "Oblique Intention" [1987] C.L.J. 417 at 435–437.

[213]   Duff, "Intention, Mens Rea and the Law Commission Report" [1980] Crim. L.R. 147; R.A. Duff, "Intentions Legal and Philosophical" (1989) 9 O.J.L.S. 76. A similar argument for a variable meaning has been put forward by Judge Buzzard ("Intent" [1978] Crim. L.R. 5).

3. Evaluation

From the above discussion, it should be clear that in the wake of *Woollin* foresight of a virtual certainty is an alternative species of intention or, at least, an evidential precondition to a finding of intention. The implications of these two interpretations have been assessed. However, a final question remains. *Should* foresight of a virtual certainty suffice for intention? Is such an approach too narrow in that intention should perhaps be found to exist in a wider range of cases such as where a consequence is foreseen as probable or likely? Or, is the foresight of a virtual certainty approach too broad in that intention should be restricted to its core meaning of direct intention (aim/purpose)? It is suggested that an appropriate meaning can only be ascribed to "intention" after the following four matters have been considered.

(a) *Semantic precision*

There ought to be some semantic precision about the law's use of the word "intention" so that it correlates with the layman's perceptions of the word. Intention is an ordinary word in everyday usage. The criminal law ought to reflect the values of society and, thus, if the word "intention" is to have any useful function, it ought to bear this ordinary meaning. As Duff states:

> "[T]he 'appeal to ordinary language' should not be despised: not just because it may cause confusion if the law uses terms whose legal and extra-legal meanings differ radically; but because the term's ordinary usage reflects our moral understanding of its relevance to ascriptions of responsibility, and of those distinctions which we regard as morally significant. Thus if it is any part of the law's purpose to assign legal liability in accordance with moral responsibility, there must be a presumption in favour of preserving the ordinary meanings of the concepts through which responsibility is assigned."[214]

Further, the task of the jury is made easier when legal terms are given their ordinary meanings. It was this desire to avoid confusing juries that led the Court of Appeal in the earlier case of *Belfon* to reject broader interpretations of intention:

> "There has never been any need to explain what 'intent' means . . . Juries do not seem to have experienced any difficulty in understanding the word 'intent' without further explanation."[215]

It was this reasoning that led Lord Bridge in *Moloney* to his view that generally juries needed no guidance as to the meaning of "intention". It was a matter of fact to be decided by them according to the ordinary usage of the word.

On the other hand, as Lacey has suggested

> "if ordinary usage is as consistent and reliable as [the House of Lords] presumably think it is given the importance they accord to it, guidelines would be irrelevant".[216]

In short, it is not always easy to ascertain the "ordinary, everyday" meaning of words. This difficulty in assigning an "ordinary" meaning to intention is illustrated by the fact that while most commentators agree with the Oxford English Dictionary definition of "intend" as aim or design, Lord Cross in the now discredited House of Lords' decision of *Hyam* considered that the "ordinary man" would equate

---

214   Duff, "Intention, Mens Rea and the Law Commission Report" [1980] Crim. L.R. 147 at 148.
215   *R. v Belfon (Horace Adrian)* (1976) 63 Cr. App. R. 59 at 60.
216   N. Lacey, "A Clear Concept of Intention: Elusive or Illusory?" (1993) M.L.R. 621 at 634.

foresight of injury with intentionally causing injury. It may well be that Lord Cross was falling into the common trap of confusing the issue of how ordinary people would describe the concept of intention with the issue of whom ordinary people would want to hold responsible for their actions. However, despite this potential problem, it seems tolerably clear that to most people the term "intend" means "aiming at" or "meaning to achieve". The consequence must be one's purpose, objective or goal. Even the Law Commission in an earlier draft Bill accepts that it is attributing an artificial meaning to the word intention when it defined its "standard test of intention" as being "either [to] intend or have no substantial doubt"[217] that a result will occur. Having no substantial doubt is clearly accepted as being something different from intention. As has been stated:

> "Oblique intention is not really any kind of intention at all. It is a label for a different sort of mental state altogether, namely foresight or, in Model Penal Code terminology, knowledge. Calling it a species of intention is pure obfuscation."[218]

Should intention be defined or simply left to the jury? It is becoming increasingly common in criminal law to leave crucial issues such as this to the jury. For instance, one of the critical concepts in theft, "dishonesty", is largely left to jury determination. However, a concept such as "dishonesty" involves the application of standards; ethical stances have to be taken. In short, a judgment has to be made as to the morality of the defendant's actions. The jury, as the mouthpiece of community values, is probably the most appropriate body to express such judgments. It has been argued that this is no less true of the concept "intention" and that judicial reliance on "the haven of 'ordinary language'"[219] allows judges to let in through the back door ethical questions concerning the appropriateness of criminal liability "under the guise of supplementing conceptual analysis in a value-neutral way".[220] As already seen, however, many commentators argue that the meaning to be attributed to "intention" should involve moral judgments but these are less various, and perhaps more capable of reduction to a single formula, than the never-ending range of factors affecting ethical judgments as to the meaning of a concept such as dishonesty.[221] Accordingly, it would be preferable for "intention" to be given a legal definition, and that definition should largely reflect the ordinary meaning of the word.

(b) *Capable of proof*

Proponents of both the definitional and the evidential interpretation of intention often assume that foresight is easier to prove than a person's purposes in acting (direct intention).

M. Cathleen Kaveny, "Inferring Intention from Foresight" [2004] 120 L.Q.R. 81 at 87, 83, 82, 89, 91, 93:

"Both [approaches to intention] assume that a defendant's foresight is simpler and easier to discern than his intent. Both assert a reliable relationship of evidential inference between foresight and intent. Finally, both maintain that the best way to pin down a defendant's intention is to move *through* foresight . . . [T]here is a

---

[217] Law Commission Paper No.89, *Report on the Mental Element of Crime* (1978), p.56.
[218] C. Finkelstein, "No Harm No Foul? Objectivism and the Law of Attempts" (1999) 18 *Law and Philosophy* 69 at 75.
[219] Lacey, "A Clear Concept of Intention: Elusive or Illusory?" (1993) M.L.R. 621 at 633. Lacey has argued that the appeal to "ordinary usage" implies that the criminal law "operates on the basis of widely shared meanings and widely endorsed judgments. It hence suppresses the idea that criminal law is hierarchical, an exercise of power, based on meanings which are imposed" (p.636).
[220] Horder, "Intention in the Criminal Law—a Rejoinder" (1995) 58 M.L.R. 678 at 679, summarising Lacey's views.
[221] C.M.V. Clarkson and H.M. Keating, "Codification: Offences against the Person under the Draft Criminal Code" (1986) 50 J. Crim. L. 405 at 410.

conceptual distinction between intention and all degrees of foresight . . . *no degree of foresight can, by itself, be the basis of a reliable inference of intention* . . . An agent may foresee a given result of his action as virtually certain, but nonetheless not intend it (*e.g.* a chemotherapy patient with respect to hair loss); on the other hand, he may intend to achieve a result he predicts is highly unlikely to come about (*e.g.* a diplomat with respect to a peace treaty) . . .

[W]e are concerned not with probability in the abstract, but rather with the assessment of probability by human beings . . . Unfortunately, there appears to be no uniformity in the way people assess probability or even in the way they use terms pertaining to probability . . .

Additional complications and possibilities for error arise because the jury's evaluation of the defendant's assessment of probability is both retrospective and second-hand. To what degree is their judgment about his foresight of bad consequences likely to be affected by their belief that the defendant was a bad person doing a bad thing? . . . Foresight, unlike intention (which bridges the thinking, acting agent and the world), is a purely mental state. In itself, it leaves no immediate traces in the world, and is propelled by no momentum. Short of eliciting a true confession, how do we determine another person's foresight of the consequences of his action?"

(c) *Distinction from recklessness*

The law ought to define intention in such a manner that it can be clearly distinguished from recklessness. One of the main problems with the old *Hyam* formulation that foresight of a probable or highly probable consequence amounted to intention was that no principle could be discerned to establish the cut-off point between recklessness and intention. Foreseeing a consequence as probable or likely was intention but foreseeing it as less than probable was recklessness. Such a test involved having to define "probable" and "likely".[222] While these problems are perhaps reduced after *Woollin*, they have not been eradicated. The boundary between intention and recklessness has simply shifted. If a consequence is foreseen as extremely likely this will presumably still amount to recklessness whereas if it is foreseen as virtually certain it can count as intention (or intention can be found). No principled basis for distinguishing between these two states of mind exists because, in both situations, the consequence is not the objective of the action. In both, it is simply a by-product of the actor's actions that is foreseen as having varying chances of occurring. The only clear basis for drawing the distinction would be to limit intention to direct intention.

(d) *Moral content*

The final factor to be taken into account in ascribing a meaning to the concept of intention is the most important, but also the most elusive. Is there a moral difference between foreseeing a consequence as likely, foreseeing it as virtually certain and aiming at it? If so, where should this "moral line" be drawn?

First, should intention be given a broad meaning so as to include foresight of a consequence as merely probable or likely? If there is no significant moral difference between the person who aims to achieve a consequence and the person who merely foresees that a consequence is probable, then one *might* be justified in describing both as intention; but if there is a moral distinction between the two, this distinction should be reflected by the law in order that different levels of liability and punishment can be imposed.

H.L.A. Hart, "Intention and Punishment" in Punishment and Responsibility (1968), pp.119–122:

"[Hart cites the case of *R. v Desmond, Barrett and Others* (*The Times*, April 28, 1868) where the defendant, Barrett, dynamited a prison wall in order to effect the escape of two Irish Fenians imprisoned therein. Though the plot failed, the explosion killed some persons living nearby].

---

[222] For a discussion of these issues, see the 4th edn of this book at p.147.

[F]or the law, a foreseen outcome is enough, even if it was unwanted by the agent, even if he thought of it as an undesirable by-product of his activities, and in Desmond's case this is what the death of those killed by the explosion was. It was no part of Barrett's purpose or aim to kill or injure anyone; the victims' deaths were not a means to his end; to bring them about was not his reason or part of his reason for igniting the fuse, but he was convicted on the ground that he foresaw their death or serious injury . . .

The reason [that the law should neglect the difference between direct intention and foreseeing the consequence] is, I suggest, that both the case of direct intention and that of oblique intention share one feature which any system of assigning responsibility for conduct must always regard as of crucial importance. This can be seen if we compare the actual facts of the Desmond case with a case of direct intention. Suppose Barrett shot the prison guard in order to obtain from them the keys to release the prisoners. Both in the actual Desmond case and in this imaginary variant, so far as Barrett had control over the alternative between the victims' dying or living, his choice tipped the balance; in both these cases he had control over and may be considered to have chosen the outcome, since he consciously opted for the course leading to the victims' deaths. Whether he sought to achieve this as an end or a means to his end, or merely foresaw it as an unwelcome consequence of his intervention, is irrelevant at the stage of conviction where the question of control is crucial. However, when it comes to the question of sentence and the determination of the severity of punishment it may be (though I am not at all sure that this is in fact the case) that on both a retributive and a utilitarian theory of punishment the distinction between direct and oblique intention is relevant."

This "control" test of intention is similar to the views of Lord Diplock in *Hyam* when he equated desiring a consequence with foreseeing that consequence as likely because "what is common to both these states of mind is willingness to produce the particular evil consequence".

Even if one accepts Hart's premise that the actor has "control" in both situations, does this necessarily mean that both states of mind must be defined as "intention", and that both deserve the same level of criminal liability? The actor who acts recklessly in merely foreseeing a remote possibility of a consequence occurring, is also "in control", but if one were to designate such actions as being intentional, one would have eliminated much of the concept of recklessness.

This view that intention should include foresight of probable consequences has been firmly rejected by English law (in *Moloney* and *Hancock*) and no longer commands serious support from commentators.

The prevailing view, both judicial and extra-judicial, is that intention should extend beyond its core meaning to include foresight of a consequence as a virtual, practical or moral certainty ("oblique intent").

Glanville Williams, Textbook of Criminal Law, 2nd edn (1983), pp.84–85:

"Clearly, a person can be taken to intend a consequence that follows under his nose from what he continues to do, and the law should be the same where he is aware that a consequence in the future is the certain or practically certain result of what he does. As Lord Hailsham said in *Hyam*, 'intention' includes 'the means as well as the end and the inseparable consequences of the end as well as the means.' (What he evidently meant was the consequences known to the defendant to be inseparable.) . . .

To take a hypothetical case: suppose that a villain of the deepest dye sends an insured parcel on an aircraft, and includes in it a time-bomb by which he intends to bring down the plane and consequently to destroy the parcel. His immediate intention is merely to collect on the insurance. He does not care whether the people on board live or die, but he knows that success in his scheme will inevitably involve their deaths as a side-effect. On the theoretical point, common sense suggests that the notion of intention should be extended to this situation; it should not merely be regarded as a case of recklessness. A consequence should normally be taken as intended although it was not desired, if it was foreseen by the actor as the *virtually certain* accompaniment of what he intended. This is not the same as saying that any consequence foreseen as *probable* is intended . . .

Clearly, one cannot confine the notion of foresight of certainty to certainty in the most absolute sense. It is a question of human certainty, or virtual certainty, or practical certainty. This is still not the same as speaking in terms of probability."

The Law Commission (Law Com. No.177), A Criminal Code for England and Wales, Commentary on Draft Criminal Code Bill (1989), paras 8.14–8.16:

"Acting in order to bring about a result is, as it were, the standard case of 'intending' to cause a result. But we are satisfied that a definition of 'intention' for criminal law purposes must refer, as Lord Hailsham of St Marylebone L.C. expressed it in *Hyam* to 'the means as well as the end and the inseparable consequences of the end as well as the means.' Where a person acts in order to achieve a particular purpose, knowing that this cannot be done without causing another result, he must be held to intend to cause that other result. The other result may be a pre-condition—as where D, in order to injure P, throws a brick through the window behind which he knows P to be standing; or it may be a necessary concomitant of the first result—as (to use a much quoted example) where D blows up an aeroplane in flight in order to recover on the insurance covering its cargo, knowing that the crew will inevitably be killed. D intends to break the window and he intends to kill the crew. But there is no absolute certainty in human affairs. P *might* fling up the window while the brick is in flight. The crew *might* make a miraculous escape by parachute. D's purpose might be achieved without causing the second result—but these are only remote possibilities and D, if he contemplates them at all (which may be unlikely), must know that they are only remote possibilities. The result will occur, and D knows that it will occur, 'in the ordinary course of events . . . unless something supervenes to prevent it.' It is, and he knows it is, 'a virtual certainty.' . . .

A person's awareness of any degree of probability (short of virtual certainty) that a particular result will follow from his acts ought not, we believe, to be classed as an 'intention' to cause that result for criminal law purposes."

The view that foresight of a virtual certainty amounts to intention has long been embraced by law reform bodies.[223]

In 2005, the Law Commission published a Consultation Paper on homicide seeking views as to whether the law should adopt a definition of intention as a matter of law (the definitional approach) or whether it should set preconditions which must be satisfied before the jury may find that a person acted intentionally (the evidential approach).[224] After consultation, the Law Commission concluded that the latter approach should be adopted.

Law Commission, No.304, Murder, Manslaughter and Infanticide (2006), para.3.27:

"We recommend that the existing law governing the meaning of intention is codified as follows:

(1) A person should be taken to intend a result if he or she acts in order to bring it about.

(2) In cases where the judge believes that justice may not be done unless an expanded understanding of intention is given, the jury should be directed as follows: an intention to bring about a result may be found if it is shown that the defendant thought that the result was a virtually certain consequence of his or her action."

There are, however, contrary views that intention should not be expanded so as to include oblique intention. The argument here is that there are strong moral justifications for distinguishing between an actor who foresees a result as virtually certain and one who tries to achieve that result. A person's

---

[223] Criminal Law Revision Committee (14th Report, *Offences against the Person*, Cmnd.7844 (1980), para.10; Law Commission, *Draft Criminal Code* (1989); Law Commission, *Draft Criminal Law Bill* (1993). These proposals did not use the terminology of "virtual certainty" but rather "knows that it would occur in the ordinary course of events if he were to succeed in his purpose of causing some other result". This approach also represents the common law position in the United States where Burger CJ in *United States v United States Gypsum* (438 US 422) held that a person intended a result "when he knows that the result is practically certain to follow from his conduct, whatever his desire may be as to that result". The Canadian Law Reform Commission produced an even stricter definition that the defendant must act "in order to effect: (a) that consequence; or (b) another consequence which he knows involves that consequence" (Report 31, *Recodifying Criminal Law* (1987); see J.C. Smith, "A Note on 'Intention'" [1990] Crim. L.R. 85).

[224] Law Commission Consultation Paper No.177, *A New Homicide Act for England and Wales?* (2005), paras 4.3, 4.4.

objectives or aims influence our perceptions of their character as a moral agent. Actions become more reprehensible if they are deliberate and purposeful. A boy, throwing a ball dangerously near a window and realising that it is virtually certain that in the course of his game he could break the window, will instinctively cry out: "I didn't mean to break it", when the window is duly shattered. Our characterisation of the boy as a moral agent would be different if he had deliberately taken aim and thrown the ball, trying to break the window. As Duff says:

"To do what I believe will help the enemy, or cause injury, may be counted criminal even when I do it for reasons which have nothing to do with helping the enemy or causing injury: but to act with the intention of helping the enemy, or causing injury, gives a quite different moral character to the action, which we may wish to mark by making only that an offence, or by making it a more serious offence."[225]

John Finnis, "Intention and Side-effects" in R.G. Frey and Christopher W. Morris, Liability and Responsibility (1991), p.46:

"[I]t is well to recall how foreign to the commonsense concept of intention is the academics' notion that what is foreseen as certain is intended.

One who hangs curtains knowing that the sunlight will make them fade does not thereby intend that they shall fade. Those who wear shoes don't intend them to wear out. Those who fly the Atlantic foreseeing certain jetlag don't do so with the intention to get jetlag; those who drink too heavily rarely intend the hangover they know is certain . . . Indeed, we might call the academics' extended notion of intent the Pseudo-Masochist Theory of Intention—for it holds that those who foresee that their actions will have painful effects upon themselves *intend* those effects."

R. A. Duff, Intention, Agency and Criminal Liability: Philosophy of Action and the Criminal Law (1990), pp.111–113:

"[A] non-consequentialist view . . . finds an intrinsic moral difference in intended action; a significance which depends not on its expected consequences, but on the intentions which structure it . . . One who tries to kill me . . . *attacks* my life and my most basic rights; and the harm which I suffer in being murdered (or in being the victim of an attempted murder) essentially involves this wrongful attack on me. The point is not that a murder victim suffers the same (consequential) harm of death as a victim of natural causes, and also suffers the *separate* harm of being attacked: it is that she suffers the distinctive harm of being killed by one who attacks her life. The 'harm' at which the law of murder is aimed is thus not just the consequential harm of death, but the harm which is *intrinsic* to an attack on another's life . . . [A]n attack is an action which is *intended* to do harm . . . It is through the intentions with which I act that I engage in the world as an agent, and relate myself most closely to the actual and potential effects of my actions; and the central or fundamental kind of wrong-doing is to *direct* my actions towards evil—to *intend* and to *try* to do what is evil."[226]

This is the approach recommended in the United States by the American Law Institute's Model Penal Code and which has been widely adopted in state code revisions throughout the United States. The Code does not adopt the view of intention favoured by the Law Commission and leading commentators in England. It adopts the narrower view that a person acts intentionally "when it is his conscious

---

[225] Duff, "Intention, Mens Rea and The Law Commission Report" [1980] Crim. L.R. 147 at 159.
[226] Duff does, however, go on to argue that such direct intention should only be required in exceptional cases (see p.161 above).

object to engage in conduct of that nature or to cause such a result".[227] What of foresight of a virtual certainty? The Model Penal Code does not assimilate this with intention, nor does it relegate it to the realms of recklessness. Instead, it has created a special category of mens rea between intention and recklessness, namely, knowledge. Section 202(2)(b) defines "knowingly" in the following terms:

"A person acts knowingly with respect to a material element of an offense when: . . . (ii) if the element involves a result of his conduct, he is aware that it is practically certain that his conduct will cause such a result."

The commentary to this sub-section recognises that the distinction drawn is a narrow one and is "no doubt inconsequential for most purposes of liability". But apart from being conceptually necessary and helping to promote clarity of definition, the distinction does have some practical utility as

"there are areas where the discrimination is required . . . This is true in treason, for example, in so far as a purpose to aid the enemy is an ingredient of the offense . . . and in attempts and conspiracy, where a true purpose to effect the criminal result is requisite for liability . . . The distinction also has utility in differentiating among grades of an offense for purposes of sentence, e.g. in the case of homicide."[228]

Thus, according to this view, there is a moral, as well as a linguistic, justification for drawing this fine distinction. Indeed, there are some states in the United States that have employed this Model Penal Code terminology and have felt the distinction to be sufficiently material to warrant using it as the basis for a grading of homicide offences. Alaska provides that it is murder in the first degree to kill "with intent to cause the death of another person", but only murder in the second degree to kill "knowing that the conduct is substantially certain to cause death".[229] New Hampshire provides that it is first degree murder to kill "purposely" and second degree murder to kill "knowingly".[230]

One final question remains. How should one classify cases where a consequence is foreseen as *certain*, as opposed to virtually certain? In these situations the consequence is foreseen as something that *must* happen; it is a condition precedent to the occurrence of the actor's primary aim.[231] To take the classic example where I intend to shoot you; you are standing behind a glass window that cannot open. Do I intend to break the window? In this case I foresee it as certain that I will break the glass; I cannot shoot you without doing so. This means that breaking the glass is my aim or objective, albeit only a secondary aim or objective to my main one of killing you. It is a necessary and "wanted" means to my end. I intend to break the window. Lord Hailsham in *Hyam* endorsed this when he spoke of

"intention, which embraces, in addition to the end, all the necessary consequences of an action including the means to the end and any consequences intended along with the end".[232]

---

227   American Law Institute, Model Penal Code s.2.02(2)(a) prefers the term "purposely". However, most code revisions have used this same definition for the term "intention".
228   American Law Institute, Model Penal Code, Tent. Draft No.4 (1955) art.2, pp.124, 125.
229   Alaska Stat. tit. 11 ss.11.41.100, 110.
230   N.H. Rev. Stat. Ann. ss.630: 1-a, b.
231   This need not be scientific certainty, but the consequence must be inseparable in terms of the agent's conception of the world as he understands it (A.P. Simester, "Moral Certainty and the Boundaries of Intention" (1996) 16 O.J.L.S. 445 at 459).
232   *Hyam* [1975] A.C. 55 at 73.

However, where an undesired consequence is only foreseen as "virtually certain" or "morally certain" it ceases to be an inescapable consequence or a necessary means to an end. It thus ceases to be a secondary aim and should no longer be described as intention. In the celebrated example where I blow up an aircraft in flight in order to obtain the insurance money and the passengers are killed, I would foresee the death of these passengers as virtually certain. But, if it is not my object to kill them, the fact that there is a chance (albeit one in a million) that they could parachute to safety, means that their death is not a necessary means to an end and cannot be described as intention. Using Duff's "test of failure",[233] blowing up the aeroplane without killing the occupants would not mark the failure of the enterprise, but would represent the ultimate in success. Similarly, flying across the Atlantic and not suffering jetlag would be a cause for celebration. On the other hand, failing to break the window represents a failure of the agent's action because this necessarily involves not killing the person behind it. The line of demarcation is a thin one and would only apply in the most exceptional cases.[234] Nevertheless, it is a conceptually clear distinction and provides a principled basis for distinguishing intention from recklessness. There is no intention to kill the passengers on the aeroplane, but there is an intention to break the glass.

If there are indeed linguistic, practical and moral justifications for distinguishing between intention (including the condition precedent cases) and foresight of the virtually certain, English law would surely not be justified in following the Law Commission's proposal (whether finally accepted as a definition of intention or as an evidential proposition from which intention can be inferred) to treat both as "intention".

E. Recklessness

1. Background

Some crimes, such as attempt, can only be committed intentionally and so it is crucial to be able to distinguish intention from recklessness. This line of demarcation depends, as we have just seen, on how broadly one chooses to define "intention". Any degree of foresight less than that specified in the definition of intention will constitute recklessness. But a large number of crimes can be committed "intentionally or recklessly". Indeed, the Draft Criminal Code 1989 proposes that recklessness should be the basic fault element for *all* offences (unless otherwise stated).[235] For all these crimes the distinction between intention and recklessness is unimportant; what matters, instead, is the distinction between recklessness and negligence or other forms of conduct not regarded as equally blameworthy. This demarcation is vital as it has been the general policy of English law to punish reckless wrongdoing, but, with notable exceptions, to exempt negligent wrongdoing from criminal liability.

---

[233] See p.154.
[234] Norrie, above, fn.196 and the Law Commission, above, p.154, both deny the possibility of drawing such a distinction on the basis that virtual certainty "denote[s] the only kind of certainty that it is ever possible to have in any practical intervention in the natural or social world" (Norrie). This ignores the fact that one is dealing with a subjective concept. It is the defendant's aims and foresight that matter. To most defendants firing at the person standing behind the window, it is only possible to shoot the victim by breaking the glass. The fact that it might actually be possible to achieve the result without breaking the window (an earthquake might break the glass at the critical moment) does not alter the fact that the defendant is trying to break the window.
[235] Law Commission Paper No.177 (1989) cl.20(1).

2. Law prior to G: two species of recklessness

The concept of "recklessness" has had a chequered and uncertain history with judges vacillating as to whether it meant "gross negligence"[236] (an objective major deviation from the standards of the reasonable person) or whether it meant simply failing to foresee an obvious risk or whether it should be limited to cases where the defendant subjectively realised that there was a possibility of the consequence occurring (or the circumstance existing) but carried on regardless. By the beginning of the present century and until the landmark decision of G,[237] however, it had become established that there were two distinct species of recklessness.

(i) Cunningham recklessness

By the late 1970s, following the leading decision of *Cunningham*,[238] a subjective meaning of recklessness had been approved. Recklessness entailed the conscious running of an unjustifiable risk. The following case illustrates this approach.

R. v Stephenson [1979] Q.B. 695 (Court of Appeal, Criminal Division)

The appellant, who had crept into a hollow in the side of a large straw stack to sleep, felt cold and lit a fire of twigs and straw inside the hollow. The stack caught fire and was damaged. He was charged with arson contrary to s.1(1) of the Criminal Damage Act 1971. Evidence on his behalf was given by a consultant psychiatrist that the appellant suffered from schizophrenia that could have the effect of depriving him of the ability of a normal person to foresee or appreciate the risk of damage from the act of lighting the fire. The judge directed the jury that a person was "reckless as to whether any such property would be destroyed or damaged", within s.1(1) of the 1971 Act, if he closed his mind to the obvious fact of risk from his act, and that schizophrenia might be a reason which made a person close his mind to the obvious fact of risk. The jury returned a verdict of guilty and the appellant was convicted. He appealed against the conviction on the ground, inter alia, of a misdirection by the judge on what constituted recklessness.

GEOFFREY LANE LJ:

"Does the word 'reckless' require that the defendant must be proved actually to have foreseen the risk of some damage resulting from his actions and nevertheless to have run the risk (the subjective test), or is it sufficient to prove that the risk of damage resulting would have been obvious to any reasonable person in the defendant's position (the objective test)? In our view it is the subjective test which is correct.

. . . A man is reckless when he carries out the deliberate act appreciating that there is a risk that damage to property may result from his act. It is however not the taking of every risk which could properly be classed as reckless. The risk must be one which it is in all the circumstances unreasonable for him to take.

Proof of the requisite knowledge in the mind of the defendant will in most cases present little difficulty. The fact that the risk of some damage would have been obvious to anyone in his right mind in the position of the defendant is not conclusive proof of the defendant's knowledge, but it may well be and in many cases doubtless will be a matter which will drive the jury to the conclusion that the defendant himself must have appreciated the risk. The fact that he may have been in a temper at the time would not normally deprive him of knowledge or

---

[236] *Andrews v DPP* [1937] A.C. 576.
[237] *R. v G* [2004] 1 A.C. 1034.
[238] *R. v Cunningham (Roy)* [1957] 2 Q.B. 396. See also *R. v Briggs (Basil Ian)* [1977] 1 W.L.R. 605; *R. v Parker (Daryl Clive)* [1977] 1 W.L.R. 600; Law Commission Paper No.89, *Report on the Mental Element in Crime*, 1978, paras 20–21.

foresight of the risk. If he had the necessary knowledge or foresight and his bad temper merely caused him to disregard it or put it to the back of his mind not caring whether the risk materialised, or if it merely deprived him of the self-control necessary to prevent him from taking the risk of which he was aware, then his bad temper will not avail him. This was the concept which the court in *R. v Parker (Daryl)* [1977] 1 W.L.R. 600, 604 was trying to express when it used the words 'or closing his mind to the obvious fact that there is some risk of damage resulting from that act.' . . . We wish to make it clear that the test remains subjective, that the knowledge or appreciation of risk of some damage must have entered the defendant's mind even though he may have suppressed it or driven it out . . .

How do these pronouncements affect the present appeal? The appellant, through no fault of his own, was in a mental condition which might have prevented him from appreciating the risk which would have been obvious to any normal person. When the judge said to the jury 'there may be . . . all kinds of reasons which make a man close his mind to the obvious fact—among them may be schizophrenia'—we think he was guilty of a misapprehension, albeit possibly an understandable misapprehension. The schizophrenia was on the evidence something which might have prevented the idea of danger entering the appellant's mind at all. If that was the truth of the matter, then the appellant was entitled to be acquitted. That was something which was never left clearly to the jury to decide."

Appeal allowed

Under this "subjective" approach, the definition of recklessness, both as to consequences and circumstances,[239] imposes a double test:

(1) whether the defendant foresaw the possibility of the consequence occurring; and

(2) whether it was unjustifiable or unreasonable to take the risk.

Whether a risk is justifiable or not depends on the social importance of the acts and on the chances of the forbidden consequence occurring. As the Law Commission has stated:

"The operation of public transport, for example, is inevitably accompanied by risks of accident beyond the control of the operator, yet it is socially necessary that these risks be taken. Dangerous surgical operations must be carried out in the interests of the life and health of the patient, yet the taking of these risks is socially justifiable."[240]

Thus if there is perceived to be a one in a thousand chance of high-speed trains being involved in an accident, the social value of high-speed public transport is such as to render the taking of such a remote risk justifiable, but if it is realised that there is a one in 20 chance of these trains being involved in an accident, then the chances of an accident occurring outweighs the social importance of the activity and it becomes unjustifiable to take such a risk. On the other hand, if there is the same (subjectively perceived) one in a thousand chance of killing a friend while playing Russian roulette, the complete absence of any social value attached to the activity renders the taking of the risk unjustifiable. Thus the test involves a subtle balancing operation between the following questions: how socially useful is the activity? What are the perceived chances of the harm occurring? How serious is the harm that could occur? For example, in *Vehicle Inspectorate v Nuttall*[241] it was stated that if one was dealing with conduct that could imperil the safety of the public, foresight of the slightest possibility (of a breach of contraventions) would suffice.

---

[239] For the sake of simplicity, the remainder of this section will refer only to consequences, but this should be taken to include circumstances.

[240] Law Commission Paper No.31, *Working Paper on the Mental Element in Crime*, p.53.

[241] *Vehicle Inspectorate v Nuttall* [1999] 1 W.L.R. 629.

Whether a risk is justifiable or unreasonable is an objective issue and does not depend on the defendant's view of the matter. For example, in *Dodman*[242] it was stated that it was irrelevant that the defendant did not know his conduct was wrongful. Of course, the question whether there is any social utility in an activity is a highly evaluative one which has led some writers to argue that the concept of recklessness is an inherently political one.[243] This is true inasmuch as a value judgment is involved, a point that can always be made when employing a value-ridden concept such as "reasonableness".[244] The advantage, however, of employing such a concept and leaving it to members of the jury is that they can reflect the ever-shifting notions of social utility.

The Law Commission in the Draft Criminal Law Bill 1993[245] has endorsed this "subjective" approach, as has the Draft Offences Against the Person Bill 1998, cl.14(2) of which provides:

"A person acts recklessly with respect to a result if he is aware of a risk that it will occur and it is unrea-sonable to take that risk having regard to the circumstances as he knows or believes them to be."

(ii) Caldwell/Lawrence recklessness

In 1981 there was a radical change of direction when the House of Lords handed down two judg-ments on the same day, both concerned with the meaning of recklessness. It should be stressed that this change only affected the first limb of the test cited above, namely, whether the defendant must foresee the possibility of harm occurring. It did not affect the second requirement that it must be unjustifiable to take the risk.

R. v Caldwell [1982] A.C. 341 (House of Lords)

1The respondent had done some work for the owner of a hotel as the result of which he had a quarrel with the owner, got drunk and set fire to the hotel in revenge. The fire was discovered and put out before any serious damage was caused and none of the 10 guests in the hotel at the time was injured. The respondent was indicted on two counts of arson under s.1(1) and (2) of the Criminal Damage Act 1971. At his trial he pleaded not guilty to the more serious charge under s.1(2) of damaging property with intent to endanger life or being reckless whether life would be endangered. He claimed that he was so drunk at the time that the thought that he might be endangering the lives of the people in the hotel had never crossed his mind. The trial judge directed the jury that drunkenness was not a defence to a charge under s.1(2) and he was convicted.

The Court of Appeal allowed his appeal. The Crown appealed to the House of Lords, where in order to decide whether drunkenness was a defence to a charge under s.1(2), the House ruled that it was necessary to decide upon the precise meaning of the term recklessness as employed in s.1(2).

LORD DIPLOCK (with whom Lord Keith and Lord Roskill concurred):

"[T]he popular or dictionary meaning is careless, regardless, or heedless, of the possible harmful consequences of one's acts. It presupposes that if thought were given to the matter by the doer before the act was done, it would have been apparent to him that there was a real risk of its having the relevant harmful consequences; but, granted this, recklessness covers a whole range of states of mind from failing to give any thought at all to whether

---

242   *R. v Dodman (Darryl Philip)* [1998] 2 Cr. App. R. 338.
243   A. Norrie, "Subjectivism, Objectivism and the Limits of Criminal Recklessness" (1992) 12 O.J.L.S. 45.
244   J.A.G. Griffiths, *The Politics of the Judiciary*, 4th edn (London: Fontana Press, 1991).
245   Law Commission Paper No.218, *Legislating the Criminal Code: Offences against the Person and General Principles* (1993).

or not there is any risk of those harmful consequences, to recognising the existence of the risk and nevertheless deciding to ignore it . . .

My Lords, the restricted meaning [adopted by] the Court of Appeal in *R. v Cunningham* . . . called for a meticulous analysis by the jury of the thoughts that passed through the mind of the accused at or before the time he did the act that caused the damage, in order to see on which side of a narrow dividing line they fell. If it had crossed his mind that there was a risk that someone's property might be damaged but, because his mind was affected by rage or excitement or confused by drink, he did not appreciate the seriousness of the risk or trusted that good luck would prevent its happening, this state of mind would amount to malice [a term used in the Malicious Damage Act 1861] in the restricted meaning placed upon that term by the Court of Appeal; whereas if, for any of these reasons, he did not even trouble to give his mind to the question whether there was any risk of damaging the property, this state of mind would not suffice to make him guilty of an offence under the Malicious Damage Act 1861.

Neither state of mind seems to me to be less blameworthy than the other; but if the difference between the two constituted the distinction between what does and what does not in legal theory amount to a guilty state of mind for the purposes of a statutory offence of damage to property, it would not be a practicable distinction for use in a trial by jury. The only person who knows what the accused's mental processes were is the accused himself—and probably not even he can recall them accurately when the rage or excitement under which he acted has passed, or he has sobered up if he were under the influence of drink at the relevant time. If the accused gives evidence that because of his rage, excitement or drunkenness the risk of particular harmful consequences of his acts simply did not occur to him, a jury would find it hard to be satisfied beyond reasonable doubt that his true mental process was not that, but was the slightly different mental process required if one applies the restricted meaning of 'being reckless as to whether' something would happen, adopted by the Court of Appeal in *R. v Cunningham*.

My Lords, I can see no reason why Parliament when it decided to revise the law as to offences of damage to property should go out of its way to perpetuate fine and impracticable distinctions such as these, between one mental state and another. One would think that the sooner they were got rid of, the better . . .

'Reckless' as used in the new statutory definition of the *mens rea* of these offences is an ordinary English word. It had not by 1971 become a term of legal art with some more limited esoteric meaning than that which it bore in ordinary speech—a meaning which surely includes not only deciding to ignore a risk of harmful consequences resulting from one's acts that one has recognised as existing, but also failing to give any thought to whether or not there is any such risk in circumstances where, if any thought were given to the matter it would be obvious that there was.

If one is attaching labels, the latter state of mind is neither more nor less 'subjective' than the first. But the label solves nothing. It is a statement of the obvious; *mens rea* is by definition, a state of mind of the accused himself at the time he did the physical act that constitutes the *actus reus* of the offence; it cannot be the mental state of some non-existent, hypothetical person.

Nevertheless, to decide whether someone has been 'reckless' as to whether harmful consequences of a particular kind will result from his act, as distinguished from his actually intending such harmful consequences to follow, does call for some consideration of how the mind of the ordinary prudent individual would have reacted to a similar situation. If there were nothing in the circumstances that ought to have drawn the attention of an ordinary prudent individual to the possibility of that kind of harmful consequence, the accused would not be described as 'reckless' in the natural meaning of that word for failing to address his mind to the possibility; nor, if the risk of the harmful consequences was so slight that the ordinary prudent individual upon due consideration of the risk would not be deterred from treating it as negligible, could the accused be described as 'reckless' in its ordinary sense if, having considered the risk, he decided to ignore it. (In this connection the gravity of the possible harmful consequences would be an important factor. To endanger life must be one of the most grave.) So to this extent, even if one ascribes to 'reckless' only the restricted meaning, adopted by the Court of Appeal in *R. v Stephenson* of foreseeing that a particular kind of harm might happen and yet going on to take the risk of it, it involves a test that would be described in part as 'objective' in current legal jargon. Questions of criminal liability are seldom solved by simply asking whether the test is subjective or objective.

In my opinion, a person charged with an offence under section 1(1) of the Criminal Damage Act 1971 is 'reckless as to whether any such property would be destroyed or damaged' if (1) he does an act which in fact creates an obvious risk that property will be destroyed or damaged and (2) when he does the act he either has not given any thought to the possibility of there being any such risk or has recognised that there was some risk involved and has nonetheless gone on to do it. That would be a proper direction to the jury; cases in the Court of Appeal which held otherwise should be regarded as overruled. [His Lordship then went on to consider the defence of drunkenness.]"

LORD EDMUND-DAVIES (with whom Lord Wilberforce concurred) dissenting:

"[I]t is well known that the Criminal Damage Act 1971 was in the main the work of the Law Commission, who, in their Working Paper No. 31, Codification of the Criminal Law, General Principles, The Mental Element in Crime (issued in June, 1970) defined recklessness by saying, at p.52:

'A person is reckless if, (a) knowing that there is a risk that an event may result from his conduct or that a circumstance may exist, he takes that risk, and (b) it is unreasonable for him to take it, having regard to the degree and nature of the risk which he knows to be present.'

It was surely with this contemporaneous definition and the much respected decision of R. v Cunningham in mind that the draftsman proceeded to his task of drafting the Criminal Damage Act 1971.

It has therefore to be said that, unlike negligence, which has to be judged objectively, recklessness involves foresight of consequences, combined with an objective judgment of the reasonableness of the risk taken. And recklessness in vacuo is an incomprehensible notion. It must relate to foresight of risk of the particular kind relevant to the charge preferred, which, for the purpose of section 1(2), is the risk of endangering life and nothing other than that.

So if a defendant says of a particular risk, 'it never crossed my mind,' a jury could not on those words alone properly convict him of recklessness simply because they considered that the risk ought to have crossed his mind, though his words might well lead to a finding of negligence. But a defendant's admission that he 'closed his mind' to a particular risk could prove fatal, for:

'A person cannot, in any intelligible meaning of the words, close his mind to a risk unless he first realises that there is a risk; and if he realises that there is a risk, that is the end of the matter.' See Glanville Williams, Textbook of Criminal Law (1978), p.79.

In the absence of exculpatory factors, the defendant's state of mind is therefore all-important where recklessness is an element in the offence charged and section 8 of the Criminal Justice Act 1967 has laid down that:

'A court or jury, in determining whether a person has committed an offence—(a) shall not be bound by law to infer that he intended or foresaw a result of his actions by reason only of its being a natural and probable consequence of those actions; but (b) shall decide whether he did intend or foresee that result by reference to all the evidence, drawing such inferences from the evidence as appear proper in the circumstances.'

My Lords, it is unnecessary to examine at length the proposition that ascertainment of the state of mind known as 'recklessness' is a subjective exercise . . . [His Lordship then went on to consider the defence of drunkenness]."

Appeal dismissed

R. v Lawrence [1982] A.C. 510 (House of Lords)

The appellant was riding his motorcycle at an excessive speed along an urban road and ran into and killed a pedestrian who was crossing the road. The appellant was convicted of causing death by reckless driving, contrary to s.1 of the Road Traffic Act 1972 and appealed against his conviction.

Lord Diplock (with whom Lord Fraser, Lord Roskill and Lord Bridge agreed):

"[His Lordship cited sections 1 and 2 of the Road Traffic Act 1972, as amended by section 50(1) of the Criminal Law Act 1977:

'1. A person who causes the death of another person by driving a motor vehicle on a road recklessly shall be guilty of an offence.

2. A person who drives a motor vehicle on a road recklessly shall be guilty of an offence.'[246]

He then contrasted these with the 'lesser offence' of section 3 of the Road Traffic Act 1972:

'If a person drives a motor vehicle on a road without due care and attention, or without reasonable consideration for other persons using the road, he shall be guilty of an offence.']

So section 3 takes care of the kind of inattention or misjudgment to which the ordinarily careful motorist is occasionally subject without its necessarily involving any moral turpitude, although it causes inconvenience and annoyance to other users of the road . . .

The context in which the word 'reckless' appears in section 1 of the Criminal Damage Act 1971 differs in two respects from the context in which the word 'recklessly' appears in sections 1 and 2 of the Road Traffic Act 1972, as now amended. In the Criminal Damage Act 1971 the *actus reus*, the physical act of destroying or damaging property belonging to another, is in itself a tort. It is not something that one does regularly as part of the ordinary routine of daily life, such as driving a car or a motor cycle. So there is something out of the ordinary to call the doer's attention to what he is doing and its possible consequences, which is absent in road traffic offences. The other difference in context is that in section 1 of the Criminal Damage Act 1971 the *mens rea* of the offences is defined as being reckless as to whether particular harmful consequences would occur, whereas in sections 1 and 2 of the Road Traffic Act 1972, as now amended, the possible harmful consequences of which the driver must be shown to have been heedless are left to be implied from the use of the word 'recklessly' itself. In ordinary usage 'recklessly' as descriptive of a physical act such as driving a motor vehicle which can be performed in a variety of different ways, some of them entailing danger and some of them not, refers not only to the state of mind of the doer of the act when he decides to do it but also qualifies the manner in which the act itself is performed. One does not speak of a person acting 'recklessly,' even though he has given no thought at all to the consequences of his act, unless the act is one that presents a real risk of harmful consequences which anyone acting with reasonable prudence would recognise and give heed to. So the *actus reus* of the offence under sections 1 and 2 is not simply driving a motor vehicle on a road, but driving it in a manner which in fact creates a real risk of harmful consequences resulting from it. Since driving in such a manner as to do no worse than create a risk of causing inconvenience or annoyance to other road users constitutes the lesser offence under section 3, the manner of driving that constitutes the *actus reus* of an offence under sections 1 and 2 must be worse than that; it must be such as to create a real risk of causing physical injury to someone else who happens to be using the road or damage to property more substantial than the kind of minor damage that may be caused by an error of judgment in the course of parking one's car.

I turn now to the *mens rea* . . . Recklessness on the part of the doer of an act does pre-suppose that there is something in the circumstances that would have drawn the attention of an ordinary prudent individual to the possibility that his act was capable of causing the kind of serious harmful consequences that the section which creates the offence was intended to prevent, and that the risk of those harmful consequences occurring was not so slight that an ordinary prudent individual would feel justified in treating them as negligible. It is only when this is so that the doer of the act is acting 'recklessly' if before doing the act, he either fails to give any thought to the possibility of there being any such risk or, having recognised that there was such risk, he nevertheless goes on to do it.

In my view, an appropriate instruction to the jury on what is meant by driving recklessly would be that they must be satisfied of two things:

First, that the defendant was in fact driving the vehicle in such a manner as to create an obvious and serious risk of causing physical injury to some other person who might happen to be using the road or of doing substantial damage to property; and

Second, that in driving in that manner the defendant did so without having given any thought to the possibility of there being any such risk or, having recognised that there was some risk involved, had nonetheless gone on to take it . . .

If satisfied that an obvious and serious risk was created by the manner of the defendant's driving, the jury are entitled to infer that he was in one or other of the states of mind required to constitute the offence and will prob-

---

[246] The Road Traffic Act 1988, as amended by the Road Traffic Act 1991, has replaced these offences with those of causing death by dangerous driving (s.1) and dangerous driving (s.2).

ably do so; but regard must be given to any explanation he gives as to his state of mind which may displace the inference."

Appeal dismissed

R. v Reid (1992) 95 Cr. App. R. 391 (House of Lords)

LORD KEITH OF KINKEL:

"The precise state of mind of a person who drives in the manner indicated must in the vast majority of cases be quite incapable of ascertainment. Absence of something from a person's mind is as much part of his state of mind as its presence. Inadvertence to risk is no less a subjective state of mind than is disregard of a recognised risk."

LORD GOFF OF CHIEVELEY:

"I think it is wise to bear in mind the possibility that words such as reckless or recklessly, which can be used in a number of different contexts, may not necessarily be expected to bear the same meaning in all statutory provisions in which they are found . . . Indeed, it can be argued with force that, in many cases of failing to think, the degree of blameworthiness to be attached to the driver can be greater than that to be attached in some cases to the driver who recognised the risk and decided to disregard it. This is because the unspoken premise which seems to me to underlie Lord Diplock's statement of the law in *Lawrence* (and perhaps also in *Caldwell*) is that the defendant is engaged in an activity which he knows to be potentially dangerous."

(a) *Implications of Caldwell/Lawrence recklessness*

These decisions had a profound effect on English criminal law. What was the precise meaning of recklessness under this test?

1. Ruling out the risk

This *Caldwell/Lawrence* test of recklessness excludes from its ambit the defendant who stops to think whether there is a risk, concludes there is no risk and consequently acts. Such a person does not come within the test which requires that the actor must have either "not given any thought to the possibility of there being any such risk" (because thought has been given to such a possibility) or must have "recognised that there was some risk involved" (because the possibility of there being a risk has been dismissed). Accordingly, there can be no recklessness. This has been described as a "lacuna" (a gap) in the law of recklessness.[247] Thus if Stephenson could have established that he had contemplated the possibility of the straw stack catching fire but had dismissed the possibility (say, because of his schizophrenia) then he could not be held reckless under Lord Diplock's test. Such an actor would of course be negligent. The existence of the lacuna, as supported in the case of *Shimmen*,[248] is an important feature distinguishing negligence from *Caldwell/Lawrence* recklessness. The defendant in that case was showing off his martial-arts skills to some friends. He aimed a kick at a plate-glass window contending that he believed he had the necessary muscular control and skill to avoid breaking the window. He did however break it and was charged with criminal damage contrary to s.1(1) of the Criminal Damage Act 1971. Taylor J interpreted the defendant's state of mind as being that he was aware of the risk and took precautions which he intended to eliminate the risk, but which were plainly inadequate for this purpose. As such, the defendant's state of mind did not fall into the so-called lacuna, since he had not completely ruled out the risk. However, in deciding this, Taylor J was

---

[247]   G. Williams, "Recklessness Redefined" [1981] C.L.J. 252 at 278–281; G. Williams, "Divergent Interpretations of Recklessness" (1982) 132 N.L.J. 289, 313, 336 at 313–314, 336; J. Smith [1981] Crim. L.R. 393, 394.
[248]   *Chief Constable of Avon v Shimmen* (1987) 84 Cr. App. R. 7.

acknowledging that such a lacuna might exist in a case where the defendant considers the possibility of a result occurring and then comes to the conclusion that there is no risk.

However, the whole approach towards a lacuna is highly questionable. In *Shimmen* the court was drawing an impossibly fine distinction. A defendant who rules out a risk by mistakenly concluding that there is no risk is not reckless. On the other hand, the defendant who thinks there is no risk because they are taking all steps to eliminate the risk, is reckless. Such hair-splitting distinctions, apart from lacking any solid moral foundation, can only give rise to numerous interpretive problems.

2. Creating an obvious risk

Lord Diplock stated that recklessness involved the doing of an act "which in fact creates an obvious risk" of the relevant harm occurring. What was meant by the phrase "creates an obvious risk"? Obvious to whom? To the reasonable person? Or, to the defendant? There was a strong argument that the risk must have been obvious to the defendant himself had he bothered to think about the matter.[249] Indeed, there are dicta in *Caldwell* that recklessness "presupposes that, if thought were given to the matter by the doer before the act was done, it would have been apparent to *him*"[250] that there were risks involved. However, there are numerous other passages in both *Caldwell* and *Lawrence*, fortified by the model direction in *Caldwell*, that the risk must have been obvious to the "ordinary prudent individual". This was the view endorsed by later decisions.

Elliott v C. (A Minor) (1983) 77 Cr. App. R. 103 (Queen's Bench Divisional Court)

The defendant was a 14-year-old schoolgirl, with learning difficulties. After staying out all night without sleep she poured white spirit on the carpet of a garden shed and then threw two lighted matches on the spirit. The shed was destroyed by fire. She was charged with criminal damage contrary to s.1(1) of the Criminal Damage Act 1971, it being alleged that she had been reckless as to whether the shed be destroyed. The justices concluded that because of her age, lack of understanding, lack of experience and exhaustion, the risk of destroying the shed would not have been obvious to her if she had given any thought to the matter. Accordingly they found she was not reckless and dismissed the information. The prosecutor appealed by way of case stated.

GLIDEWELL J:

"Mr Moses [counsel for the prosecution] submits that the phrase 'creates an obvious risk' means that the risk is one which must have been obvious to a reasonably prudent man, not necessarily to the particular defendant if he or she had given thought to it. It follows, says Mr Moses, that if the risk is one which would have been obvious to a reasonably prudent person, once it has also been proved that the particular defendant gave no thought to the possibility of there being such a risk, it is not a defence that because of limited intelligence or exhaustion she would not have appreciated the risk even if she had thought about it . . .

In the light of [the authorities, viz. *Caldwell*, *Lawrence* and *Miller*], we are in my judgment bound to hold that the word 'reckless' in section 1 of the Criminal Damage Act 1971 has the meaning ascribed to it by Mr Moses."

Appeal allowed

---

[249] Williams, "Recklessness Redefined" [1981] C.L.J. 252; Williams, "Divergent Interpretations of Recklessness" (1982) 132 N.L.J. 289, 313, 336 at 289–290; G. Syrota, "A Radical Change in the Law of Recklessness" [1982] Crim. L.R. 97.
[250] Above, p.174 (emphasis added).

This approach was followed in *R (Stephen Malcolm)*,[251] where it was held that the risk had to be obvious to an ordinary prudent person and it was not appropriate to endow such an ordinary prudent person with the characteristics of the defendant—say, age and sex.[252] In *Bell*,[253] the defendant, who had a history of mental illness, suffered a schizophrenic attack and feeling he was being driven on by an outside force which he thought was God, used his car as a "weapon to attack various targets which he regarded as evil", namely, a Butlins holiday camp. He was held to be acting recklessly in that he had failed to foresee obvious risks. The fact that he might have been unable to foresee those risks was irrelevant; they were obvious to ordinary prudent people. Under this purely objective test the schizophrenic Stephenson would clearly have been regarded as having acted recklessly.

Such an approach was unfortunate. It is only possible to defend the *Caldwell/Lawrence* test of recklessness if one is dealing with an actor who is *capable* of improving their behaviour. We have seen that the notion of responsibility, upon which the doctrine of mens rea is premised, is based on choice. We can blame a defendant for making the wrong choice. How can we realistically blame the schizophrenics in *Stephenson* or *Bell* or the young girl in *Elliott v C*? They were not able to assume the responsibility we expect most people to shoulder. They "chose" to act as they did only in the most meaningless sense of the word "choice". And, crucially, their actions did not demonstrate lack of concern; they were simply the inevitable product of their inadequacy. No civilised society should blame people for inadequacies or immaturity over which they have no control (as opposed to self-induced inadequacies such as the drunkenness in *Caldwell*).

3. Distinguishing Caldwell/Lawrence recklessness from negligence

Negligence is a failure to exercise such care, skill or foresight as a reasonable person would exercise in the circumstances. The test is a purely objective one. The conduct of the defendant is measured against that of an ordinary, reasonably careful person.

The *Caldwell/Lawrence* recklessness test was widely regarded as laying down an objective standard in that the defendant need not subjectively realise that there are risks involved. Following *Elliott v C*, it was only necessary that those risks be obvious to the ordinary prudent individual. This looks at first glance like a definition of negligence. However, closer inspection reveals that there was still a distinction between such recklessness and negligence for the following reasons.

First, it was tolerably clear that a defendant who considered a risk, but ruled it out, was not acting recklessly. Such a defendant may, however, be acting negligently if the reasonable person in that situation would not have so dismissed the risk.

Secondly, Lord Diplock's judgment in *Lawrence* indicates that something more than negligence simpliciter is required for a finding of recklessness. He insisted that an "obvious and serious risk" be established. "Serious" risk here seems to refer to the degree of likelihood of the risk materialising.[254] There is a distinction between a risk being merely "obvious" (negligence) and being "obvious and serious" (recklessness).

Lord Diplock encapsulated this distinction in *Lawrence* by indicating that there must be "moral turpitude" for a finding of recklessness, while no such "moral turpitude" was necessary for the "lesser offence" of careless driving which is a crime of negligence.[255] Crimes of recklessness are "worse" than

---

[251] *R. v R (Stephen Malcolm)* (1984) 79 Cr. App. R. 334.
[252] This approach of endowing the reasonable person with such characteristics was employed in the former partial defence of provocation (and in its replacement, loss of control) and in the defence of duress.
[253] *R. v Bell (David)* [1984] 3 All E.R. 842.
[254] Williams, "Recklessness Redefined" [1981] C.L.J. 252 at 276. In *Lamb* [1990] Crim. L.R. 522 it was held that juries must be directed that the risk must be serious in reckless driving cases.
[255] *Simpson v Peat* [1952] 2 Q.B. 24.

crimes of negligence. In the former, the defendant, by failing to consider the consequences of actions (or considering them and acting regardless), manifests an attitude of indifference which is culpable. A negligent actor simply makes an "error of judgment". This distinction is intolerably difficult to draw.

4. A variable meaning

The concept of recklessness is employed in both statutory and common law offences. During the period that the law employed two tests of recklessness, a critical issue was whether recklessness bore its *Cunningham* or its *Caldwell/Lawrence* meaning.

In *Seymour*[256] the House of Lords indicated that recklessness should bear its *Caldwell/Lawrence* meaning throughout the criminal law, whether the offence was a statutory or a common law one. However, in *Reid* it was made clear that recklessness could be interpreted differently for different offences. Lord Goff said of recklessness that "as used in our law, it has more than one meaning". Lord Browne-Wilkinson said that he did "not accept that the constituent elements of recklessness must be the same in all statutes. In particular [various] factors may lead to the word being given different meanings in different statutes."[257]

The unfortunate result was that for some offences recklessness bore its *Caldwell/Lawrence* meaning but for other offences it bore its *Cunningham* meaning. For example, the *Caldwell/Lawrence* test of recklessness applied to criminal damage and was held to be applicable to several lesser-known offences.[258] On the other hand, it had become established that the subjective *Cunningham* test applies to aiding and abetting offences,[259] to conspiracy to damage property being reckless as to whether life is endangered[260] and to false imprisonment.[261] It had also become widely accepted as being applicable to the central offences against the person such as common assault and assault occasioning actual bodily harm,[262] and as being applicable to other lesser-known offences.[263]

The result was confusion and unpredictability. The stage was thus set for the courts and/or Parliament to make a choice between the two tests.

3. Present law

As will be seen later, both tests had supporters but one thing was agreed upon: with the exception of some of the (now repealed) driving offences requiring recklessness, the two tests of recklessness should not be allowed to co-exist. The matter was brought to a head and largely resolved by the following leading House of Lords' decision. While the ratio of this decision is limited to criminal damage, it has been interpreted, as we shall see, as applying to other offences as well, resulting in the effective demise of *Caldwell/Lawrence* recklessness.

---

[256] *R. v Seymour (Edward John)* [1983] 2 A.C. 493.
[257] At 412. Lord Ackner endorsed this view (at 402).
[258] Air Navigation Order 1980 art.45, made under ss.60 and 61 of the Civil Aviation Act 1982 prohibiting reckless acts likely to endanger aircraft or persons therein (*Warburton-Pitt* (1991) 92 Cr. App. R. 135); Data Protection Act 1984 s.5 (subsequently repealed by the Data Protection Act 1998) (*Data Protection Registrar v Amnesty International* [1995] Crim. L.R. 633). For further examples, see D. Ormerod, *Smith and Hogan: Criminal Law*, 12th edn (Oxford: OUP, 2008), p.114.
[259] *Blakely v DPP* [1991] Crim. L.R. 763.
[260] *Mir, The Independent*, May 23, 1994.
[261] *James, The Times*, October 2, 1997.
[262] This point was, however, not beyond doubt: see the 5th edn of this book, pp.164–165.
[263] For example, the Sea Fishing (Enforcement of Community Control Measures) Regulations 1985 reg.3(2) (*Large v Mainprize* [1990] 1 All E.R. 331).

R. v G [2004] 1 A.C. 1034 (House of Lords)

Two boys, aged 11 and 12 respectively, set fire to newspapers and threw them under a wheelie-bin. The bin was set alight and adjoining buildings caught fire causing some £1 million damage. They claimed they thought the lit newspapers would burn themselves out on the concrete floor and that it never crossed their minds that there was a risk of the fire spreading. They were convicted of arson with the trial judge ruling that whether there was an obvious risk of the property being damaged was to be assessed by reference to the reasonable man and not a person endowed with the characteristics of the defendants: "the ordinary reasonable bystander is an adult". The defendants were convicted. Their appeal to the Court of Appeal was dismissed and they appealed to the House of Lords.

LORD BINGHAM OF CORNHILL:

"The task confronting the House in this appeal is, first of all, one of statutory construction: what did Parliament mean when it used the word 'reckless' in section 1(1) and (2) of the 1971 Act? In so expressing the question I mean to make it as plain as I can that I am not addressing the meaning of 'reckless' in any other statutory or common law context. In particular, but perhaps needlessly since 'recklessly' has now been banished from the lexicon of driving offences, I would wish to throw no doubt on the decisions of the House in *R v Lawrence* and *R v Reid* . . .

[Lord Bingham, along with the other two Law Lords extracted below, engaged in a detailed historical analysis and concluded that Parliament, in enacting the Criminal Damage Act 1971, intended to give effect to the Law Commission's proposals that 'reckless' bear its subjective *Cunningham* meaning. *Caldwell* was based on a 'mis-interpretation' of that Act. Additionally, he put forward three other reasons to justify departing from *Caldwell*.]

First, it is a salutary principle that conviction of serious crime should depend on proof not simply that the defendant caused (by act or omission) an injurious result to another but that his state of mind when so acting was culpable . . . The most obviously culpable state of mind is no doubt an intention to cause the injurious result, but knowing disregard of an appreciated and unacceptable risk of causing an injurious result or a deliberate closing of the mind to such risk would be readily accepted as culpable also. It is clearly blameworthy to take an obvious and significant risk of causing injury to another. But it is not clearly blameworthy to do something involving a risk of injury to another if (for reasons other than self-induced intoxication: *R v Majewski* [1977] AC 443) one genuinely does not perceive the risk. Such a person may fairly be accused of stupidity or lack of imagination, but neither of those failings should expose him to conviction of serious crime or the risk of punishment.

Secondly, the present case shows, more clearly than any other reported case since *R v Caldwell*, that the model direction formulated by Lord Diplock is capable of leading to obvious unfairness . . . [T]he trial judge regretted the direction he (quite rightly) felt compelled to give, and it is evident that this direction offended the jury's sense of fairness. The sense of fairness of 12 representative citizens sitting as a jury (or of a smaller group of lay justices sitting as a bench of magistrates) is the bedrock on which the administration of criminal justice in this country is built. A law which runs counter to that sense must cause concern . . . It is neither moral nor just to convict a defendant (least of all a child) on the strength of what someone else would have apprehended if the defendant himself had no such apprehension . . .

Thirdly, I do not think the criticism of *R v Caldwell* expressed by academics, judges and practitioners should be ignored . . .

It is perhaps unfortunate that the question at issue in [*Caldwell*] fell to be answered in a case of self-induced intoxication. For one instinctively recoils from the notion that a defendant can escape the criminal consequences of his injurious conduct by drinking himself into a state where he is blind to the risk he is causing to others. In *R v Caldwell* it seems to have been assumed that the risk would have been obvious to the defendant had he been sober. Further, the context did not require the House to give close consideration to the liability of those (such as the very young and the mentally handicapped) who were not normal reasonable adults. The overruling by the majority of *R v Stephenson* does however make it questionable whether such consideration would have led to a different result.

In the course of argument before the House it was suggested that the rule in *R v Caldwell* might be modified, in cases involving children, by requiring comparison not with normal reasonable adults but with normal reasonable children of the same age. This is a suggestion with some attractions but it is open to four compelling objections. First, even this modification would offend the principle that conviction should depend on proving the state of mind of the individual defendant to be culpable. Second, if the rule were modified in relation to children on grounds of their immaturity it would be anomalous if it were not also modified in relation to the mentally handicapped on grounds of their limited understanding. Third, any modification along these lines would open the door to difficult and contentious argument concerning the qualities and characteristics to be taken into account for purposes of the comparison. Fourth, to adopt this modification would be to substitute one misinterpretation of section 1 for another. There is no warrant in the Act or in the travaux préparatoires which preceded it for such an interpretation.

A further refinement, advanced by Professor Glanville Williams in his article 'Recklessness Redefined' [1981] CLJ 252, 270–271 . . . is that a defendant should only be regarded as having acted recklessly by virtue of his failure to give any thought to an obvious risk that property would be destroyed or damaged, where such risk would have been obvious to him if he had given any thought to the matter. This refinement also has attractions, although it does not meet the objection of principle and does not represent a correct interpretation of the section. It is, in my opinion, open to the further objection of over-complicating the task of the jury (or bench of justices). It is one thing to decide whether a defendant can be believed when he says that the thought of a given risk never crossed his mind. It is another, and much more speculative, task to decide whether the risk would have been obvious to him if the thought had crossed his mind. The simpler the jury's task, the more likely is its verdict to be reliable."

LORD STEYN:

"The accepted meaning of recklessness [before *Caldwell*] involved foresight of consequences. This subjective state of mind is to be inferred 'by reference to all the evidence, drawing such inferences from the evidence as appear proper in the circumstances' [citing section 8 of the Criminal Justice Act 1967] . . . That is what Parliament intended by implementing the Law Commission proposals.

This interpretation of section 1 of the 1971 Act would fit in with the general tendency in modern times of our criminal law. The shift is towards adopting a subjective approach. It is generally necessary to look at the matter in the light of how it would have appeared to the defendant . . . I regard section 8 of the Criminal Justice Act 1967, as of central importance.

[His Lordship then cited the leading decisions on mistake which have mostly adopted a subjective approach: see pp.210–214.]

That brings me to the question whether the subjective interpretation of recklessness might allow wrongdoers who ought to be convicted of serious crime to escape conviction. Experience before *R v Caldwell* did not warrant such a conclusion. In any event, as Lord Edmund-Davies explained, if a defendant closes his mind to a risk he must realise that there is a risk and, on the evidence, that will usually be decisive . . .

In my view the case for departing from *R v Caldwell* has been shown to be irresistible . . . I agree with the reasons given by Lord Bingham of Cornhill. I have nothing to add to his observations on self-induced intoxication."

LORD ROGER OF EARLSFERRY:

"Cases of self-induced intoxication are an exception to the general rule. In our judgment the decision of the House of Lords in *R v Majewski* makes it clear that they are such an exception . . .

It does not follow, however, that Lord Diplock's broader concept of recklessness was undesirable in terms of legal policy. On the contrary, there is much to be said for the view that, if the law is to operate with the concept of recklessness, then it may properly treat as reckless the man who acts without even troubling to give his mind to a risk that would have been obvious to him if he had thought about it. This approach may be better suited to some offences than to others. For example, in the context of reckless driving . . .

[However] I have come to share your Lordships' view that we should indeed overrule *R v Caldwell* and set the law back on the track that Parliament originally intended it to follow. If Parliament now thinks it preferable for the 1971 Act to cover culpably inadvertent as well as advertent wrongdoers, it can so enact."

Appeal allowed

This unanimous decision by the House of Lords adopts the *Cunningham* view that recklessness involves foresight of the possibility of an unjustified risk.

Three further points emerge from the judgments. First, Lord Steyn, added that "if a defendant closes his mind to a risk he must realise that there is a risk" and so will be reckless. In *Booth v CPS*[264]

---

[264] *Booth v CPS* [2006] EWHC 192 (Admin).

the defendant ran across a road without checking whether it was safe to cross; he collided with a car, denting it. It was held that "aware of those risks (risk of collision and damage to property), he then deliberately put them out of his mind . . . The magistrates have found that the appellant was aware of the risk and closed his mind to it . . . [Accordingly], they had applied the correct test [of recklessness as laid down in *G*]".

Secondly, the law on self-induced intoxication (which was the context in which *Caldwell* was decided) is unaffected. Lord Bingham exempted self-induced intoxication stating that "one instinctively recoils from the notion that a defendant can escape the criminal consequences of his injurious conduct by drinking himself into a state where he is blind to the risk he is causing to others". The law on self-induced intoxication is discussed in Ch.4.

Thirdly, and very importantly, Lord Bingham (with whom all their Lordships agreed) restricted his judgment to the meaning of recklessness in the Criminal Damage Act 1971:

"I mean to make it as plain as I can that I am not addressing the meaning of 'recklessness' in any other statute or common law context."

In particular, he approved the *Lawrence* meaning of recklessness adopted for offences involving reckless driving. Lord Rodger also stated that that *Caldwell* "may be better suited to some offences than to others. For example, in the context of reckless driving".

However, all offences involving reckless driving have been abolished and replaced by offences requiring dangerous driving. Prior to *G*, *Caldwell* had become largely restricted to the offence of criminal damage and, as regards that offence at least, it has been overruled. However, as seen earlier, there were a few other offences, apart from criminal damage, that had employed the *Caldwell* test of recklessness. Technically, these decisions have not been overruled by *G* and *Caldwell* recklessness is still applicable to them. However, these are mostly obscure, little-used offences and it can be confidently predicted that for them and other such offences that fall for consideration, the new test laid down so firmly in *G* will be applicable. As was stated in *Brady*,[265] "many of their Lordships observations [in *G*] have much wider application" and apply to crimes other than criminal damage. In *Attorney-General's Reference (No.3 of 2003)* the Court of Appeal stated that in *G* "general principles were laid down".[266]

4. Evaluation

English law has progressed to the point where there is, for almost all offences, now only one test of recklessness. *Cunningham* recklessness has prevailed over *Caldwell/Lawrence* recklessness. However, while certainty and simplicity in this area of the law is to be welcomed, it is less clear that the House of Lords in *G* did in fact adopt the better test in terms of policy and principle. Most of the decision is devoted to a technical, historical examination as to the meaning intended by Parliament when it enacted the Criminal Damage Act 1971 and to judicial decisions relating to the interpretation of that Act. The only discussion of matters of policy and principle are extracted above. It is to these issues that we now turn.

---

[265] *Brady* [2006] EWCA Crim 2413.
[266] *Attorney-General's Reference (No.3 of 2003)* [2004] Cr. App. R. 367 at 371. See also *R. v C* [2007] EWCA Crim 1068. It is, of course, possible for Parliament expressly to provide an objective definition of recklessness in a specific statute: see, for example, Uranium Enrichment Technology (Prohibition of Disclosure) Regulations 2004, SI 2004/1818 (made under the Anti-terrorism Crime and Security Act 2001 s.80(7)), reg.2(2) of which defines recklessness as including being "indifferent" as to whether a risk is created and "fail[ing] to give any thought to the possibility" of creating a risk.

The argument over the merits or otherwise of *Caldwell/Lawrence* is a dispute as to whether blame-worthiness is dependent on cognition. Are we justified in blaming only those who realise that their actions could cause the prohibited harm? This was described earlier as "cognitive mens rea". Or, should the law adopt what was earlier described as "normative mens rea" under which an assessment of culpability involves an evaluation of the defendant's actions, taking into account all the circum-stances including, but not limited to, the defendant's state of mind?

Many of the arguments over which of these two approaches should be adopted have focused on whether negligence is an appropriate basis for the imposition of criminal liability and reference should be made to the next section where this issue is addressed. However, as discussed earlier, *Caldwell/Lawrence* recklessness was not synonymous with pure negligence. In particular, as the House of Lords in *Reid* emphasised, *Caldwell/Lawrence* recklessness still involved looking at the defendant's attitude, motive, emotional state and capacities.[267] Not all cases of inadvertence are regarded as involving blameworthiness. Where the inadvertence arose from drink, rage, an attitude of indifference or wilful blindness the defendant could be adjudged blameworthy and therefore reckless. But where the lack of foresight arose from some other factor over which the defendant had no control such as "some condition not involving fault on his part" (Lord Keith in *Reid*) there is no blame and no recklessness. Accordingly, the remainder of this section focuses on whether the House of Lords in *G* was right to jettison the *Caldwell/Lawrence* test of recklessness.

Lord Diplock's reasoning in *Caldwell* and *Lawrence* has been described as "pathetically inadequate",[268] "slap-happy", and "profoundly regrettable".[269] The case for cognitive mens rea is that recklessness is a species of mens rea and mens rea should be based on the notion of responsibility which involves ideas of choice. The defendant has chosen to act in a certain way and that choice only becomes blameworthy if there was knowledge that the actions could cause the prohibited harm. For example, in the infamous case of *Lamb*[270] the defendant pointed a revolver at his best friend in jest and pulled the trigger. His friend was similarly treating the incident as a joke. The revolver had a five-chambered cylinder which, unknown to the defendant, rotated clockwise each time the trigger was pulled. There were two bullets in the chambers but, before firing, neither was in the chamber opposite the barrel. The pulling of the trigger caused the cylinder to rotate, placing a bullet opposite the barrel so that it was struck by the striking pin. The bullet was discharged killing his friend. Lamb's defence was that he was unaware that the pulling of the trigger would bring one bullet into the firing position opposite the barrel and thus the killing was an accident. Lamb was convicted of manslaughter and sentenced to three years' imprisonment. On appeal this conviction was quashed because of a misdi-rection on the law of manslaughter. However, the Court of Appeal stated that with a proper direction, Lamb would have been convicted and no criticism was made of the sentence originally imposed. Glanville Williams has written of this:

"I do not hesitate to say that I regard the sentence as outrageous, a wholly mistaken exercise of judicial discretion. Lamb was a fool, but there is no need to punish fools to that degree. There is no need to punish Lamb at all. He had killed his friend, and that was punishment enough."[271]

---

[267] J. Stannard, "Subjectivism, Objectivism, and the Draft Criminal Code" (1985) 101 L.Q.R. 540 at 543.
[268] J. Smith [1981] Crim. L.R. 393 at 394.
[269] Williams, "Recklessness Redefined" [1981] C.L.J. 252.
[270] *Lamb* [1967] 2 Q.B. 981.
[271] Above, fn.268 at 281–282.

According to this view, because there was no advertence to the possibility of the consequence occurring, blame becomes inappropriate.

However, there are opposing views supporting a broader normative approach to mens rea under which the decisions in *Caldwell/Lawrence* could be supported. There are two central arguments here. The first relates to the immense difficulty in proving a person's state of mind. As seen earlier, in most cases where there is no confession, juries, in drawing inferences from conduct, can do little other than apply their own standards as being the standards of ordinary people. If, in the circumstances, they think they would have foreseen a result, then, unless there is an explanation that the defendant is in some way materially different from them, for example suffering from a mental illness, they will conclude that the defendant did foresee the result.

R.A. Duff, Intention, Agency and Criminal Liability (1990), pp.120–121:

"Our inferences from another's behaviour to his mental states cannot be based on correlations which we have observed between the behaviour of others and their mental states: for we can never directly observe the mental states of others. The only case in which we can observe correlations between external behaviour and inner mental states is our own. I am directly aware of my own mental states, and can observe correlations between them and my external behaviour and situation; these observed correlations must provide the basis of my inferences from the behaviour of others to their mental states.

This is the Argument from Analogy. I see bodies around me, which resemble mine and behave in ways similar to mine. I know that my body is connected to a mind. So I infer, by analogy with my own case, that these other bodies are also connected to minds [and have similar responses to mine to stimuli]."

The difficulties in proving a person's state of mind were an important reason behind Lord Diplock's conclusion in *Caldwell* that recklessness should be given a more objective meaning. He described the distinction between consciously running a risk and failing to appreciate a risk as "not being a practicable distinction for use in a trial by jury". He stated that

"[t]he only person who knows what the accused's mental processes were is the accused himself, and probably not even he can recall them accurately when the rage or excitement under which he acted has passed".

He was not prepared to perpetuate such "fine and impracticable distinctions".

This, taken to its logical conclusion, is the argument that, because it is unrealistic to believe that one can reliably determine the state of a person's mind, the criminal law should not attempt to make criminal liability turn on states of mind.

The second strand to the arguments supporting the objectively-based test in *Caldwell/Lawrence* relates to the central question of how culpability *should* be established.

John Gardner and Heike Jung, "Making Sense of Mens Rea: Anthony Duff's Account" (1991) 11 O.J.L.S. 559 at 574–575:

"Recklessness is a vice or personal fault, like dishonesty, cowardice and self-indulgence. Vices are identified in part by reference to the ends or motives of those whose actions exhibit them. A reckless person, in morality, is one who takes large risks for the sake of relatively unimportant ends. Recklessness, as a moral phenomenon cannot be identified except in terms of the agent's flimsy motives . . .

It is true that the presence or absence of advertence to a risk on the part of an agent can sometimes make a difference, like so many other factors, to the scale of that agent's moral culpability. 'Objectivists' are wrong if they deny this. But inadvertence only mitigates a reckless agent's moral culpability, as a rule, if she has attenuated cognitive capacities, and even then it does not normally entail that her fault is converted from recklessness to something else, like carelessness, but only that her recklessness is diminished in scale. The quality of the motive is an essential part of what distinguishes a reckless person from a careless person in moral evaluations, and that distinction cannot be replicated by relying on any other factor instead, such as advertence to the risk."

R.A. Duff, "Recklessness" [1980] Crim.L.R.282 at 289–292:

"[There is a] view that inadvertence, however negligent, cannot constitute *mens rea* since we cannot blame a man for what he does not know. That view has been convincingly demolished: whether I notice some aspect of my action or its context may depend on the attention I pay to what I am doing, and be thus within my control; failures of attention may be as 'voluntary' and culpable as other omissions . . .

Some failures of attention or realisation may manifest, not mere stupidity or 'thoughtlessness,' but the same indifference or disregard which characterises the conscious risk-taker as reckless. If I intend to injure someone seriously, I may not realise that this might kill them: not because I am mistaken about the likely effect of my assault, but because it 'just doesn't occur to me'—I am blind to that aspect of my action. But such blindness to such an essential and integral aspect of a serious assault, though possible, itself manifests a 'reckless disregard' for my victim's life no different from that of an assailant who knows he is endangering life . . .

[M]y failure to realise this aspect of my action expresses a certain attitude to it. I do not realise it because I regard it as unimportant; my failure expresses my complete lack of concern about it. In general, the extent to which I notice or realise the various aspects of my action, its context, and its results, is a function as much of my attitudes and values as of my powers of observation and attention: to say that I forgot or did not realise something is to admit that I thought it unimportant, and thus to convict myself of a serious lack of concern for it (which is why a bridegroom would hardly mitigate his offence of missing his wedding by the plea that he forgot it). If, as I have suggested, an agent is reckless to the extent that his actions manifest a serious kind of 'practical indifference,' a 'willingness' to bring about some harm, then such recklessness, indifference, and willingness can be exhibited as much in his failure to notice obvious and important aspects of his action as in his conscious risk-taking. A man may be reckless even though, and even partly because, he does not realise the risk which is in fact an essential and significant aspect of his action."

R.A. Duff, Intention, Agency and Criminal Liability: Philosophy of Action and the Criminal Law (1990), p.172:

"[A]n appropriate general test of recklessness would be—did the agent's conduct (including any conscious risk-taking, any failure to notice an obvious risk created by her action, and any unreasonable belief on which she acted) display a seriously culpable practical indifference to the interests which her action in fact threatened?"

Duff stresses that this is still a subjective test. What matters is the defendant's "practical indifference"; it is subjective to them. Recklessness is not just failing to conform to an objective standard:

"for what matters is not just that, but why, the agent fails to notice an obvious risk; she is reckless only if she fails to notice it because she does not care about it."[272]

On this basis he rejects the conclusion in *Caldwell*: it cannot be established that because Caldwell failed to notice the risk to life from his actions that he was displaying reckless indifference thereto. On the other hand, the defendant in *Lawrence* was driving recklessly: no-one could drive in the manner in which he did unless they were utterly indifferent to the safety of others.

This approach, endorsed to some extent in *Reid*, presents an immediate problem. On what basis are we to decide that Lawrence displayed this practical indifference but that Caldwell did not?

---

[272]   R.A. Duff, *Intention, Agency and Criminal Liability* (London: Blackwell, 1990), pp.165–166. Similarly, Horder argues that rather than basing culpability on cognition, we should adopt "a moral theory whose focus is the evaluation of actions stemming from the desires associated with emotions". ("Cognition, Emotion, and Criminal Culpability" (1990) 106 L.Q.R. 469 at 476.)

Alan Norrie, "Subjectivism, Objectivism and the Limits of Criminal Recklessness" (1992) 12 O.J.L.S. 45 at 50–52:

"This then raises the broader question of how one could tell the callous from the stupid, the negligent or the thoughtless. Is it not likely that one person's callousness will be another person's stupidity, negligence or thoughtlessness? [What matters] on Duff's analysis is the attitude of the interpretive audience to the conduct on display. It is the inference which 'we,' the observers of the events, or the jury, draw from the facts of the case which is relevant . . . [Norrie then gives the rape example of a man who makes an unreasonable mistake as to the woman's consent to sexual intercourse. While Duff would describe this as utter practical indifference to the woman's interests and therefore recklessness, there might be others in our 'society characterised by male chauvinism' who might have different views 'about how willing women are to be forcibly seduced.']

This is not a matter of social consensus in a sexist society. The world ought to be as Duff wants it to be but it is not. So the 'we' who judge callous indifference to consent to be unreasonable cannot claim that our judgment is apolitical because universal. And the attribution of responsibility on the basis of a conception of practical indifference therefore relies here upon an interpretation of behaviour and attitude that may have nothing to do with the way in which the defendant himself would explain them. It requires the reading onto, the imposition of an interpretation of, an attitude on behaviour from 'outside.' It is practical indifference as interpreted objectively by an audience, and having no necessary subjective link with the accused. The accused does not necessarily share Duff's worldview, and hence interpretation of attitudes, yet may be adjudged subjectively guilty on Duff's account. It may be right to argue politically that the law ought to promote Duff's enlightened values through the requirement of a particular moral attitude, but it should not be presented as a form of subjectivism."

There is much to be said for Norrie's criticisms. Why is Duff so confident that Lawrence did not care about the risks of his driving? Presumably, driving as he did posed severe risks to his own life and safety as well. Was he indifferent to that as well? Lord Diplock in *Lawrence* was clearly imposing (his own) objective standard

"to ensure that young tearaways and others who drive cars or motor cycles disgracefully will not get off of a charge of reckless driving by saying that they were perfectly convinced that their manner of driving presented no danger, because they were so clever that they could always avoid a mishap. The object of the offence of reckless driving is to catch the driver who flagrantly disregards rules of prudence, whatever he may think about the safety of his behaviour."[273]

Nevertheless, Duff's test of "practical indifference" does offer the distinct advantage that it enables one to escape from some of the rigours of the more formally objective test as laid down in *Caldwell* and then subsequently applied in *Elliott v C (a Minor)* without having to return to a full-blooded test based on cognition. Indeed, one might not really ascertain what the defendant's true attitude was, but equally under the cognitive tests one never really establishes what the defendant foresaw. One simply draws inferences from facts and then tries to deduce what that state of mind must have been. The *Caldwell/Lawrence* test of recklessness (assuming the dicta in *Reid*, qualifying it, had been built upon) is at least asking the right questions: who can we adjudge to be reckless in the sense that they are blameworthy and deserving of punishment? Those who advert to the risks involved in their actions might[274] well be blameworthy but there is no reason why the inquiry should stop there.

The case being made here is that the *Caldwell/Lawrence* concept of recklessness was right to have freed itself from the shackles of cognition and that provided that the dicta in *Reid* (which are not dissimilar to the ideas of Duff) had been accepted, this recklessness test should not have been

---

[273]   Williams, "Recklessness Redefined" [1981] C.L.J. 252 at 272.
[274]   It is interesting that Duff concludes that advertent risk-taking necessarily exhibits practical indifference whereas inadvertent risk-taking has to pass the "lack of concern" test thereby demonstrating indifference. This is criticised by Gardner and Jung, above, p.186.

abandoned by the House of Lords in *G*. Whether we might ever want to distinguish advertence from inadvertence in assessing appropriate *levels* of criminal liability or punishment is a matter to which we shall return shortly.

F. Negligence

1. Introduction

When people cause harm accidentally, in circumstances where they are acting impeccably, they will not be blamed; indeed, they will probably get our sympathy. However, the "accident" may have been one which, with some simple care and precautions, could have been avoided. In this latter situation our tendency is now to blame the actor: "You should have been more careful." The question is whether this moral blame should be translated into criminal liability.

The legal concept of negligence has developed to reflect this responsibility that is attributed in everyday life. The following is a classic definition of negligence:

> "A person is negligent if he fails to exercise such care, skill or foresight as a reasonable man in his situation would exercise."[275]

2. Negligence as a basis of liability

For much of the last century the law was strongly committed to subjectivism in the form of cognitive mens rea. Negligence was regarded as imposing an objective test which could not be accommodated within such an approach and, accordingly, particularly at common law, negligence was not widely utilised in the criminal law.

There were, however, notable exceptions at common law. First, there has long been a crime of careless driving (now driving without due care and attention or without reasonable consideration for other persons contrary to s.3 of the Road Traffic Act 1988). Secondly, in extreme cases where death results, the law has been prepared to depart from its traditional insistence on advertence and allow liability for negligence, provided the defendant had shown such lack of care that the conduct could be regarded as extremely negligent. The law thus developed the idea that there can be degrees of negligence and that a person can be liable for manslaughter if there is gross negligence. Thirdly, for much of the last century there was a trend that mistakes in relation to certain defences had to be reasonable. For example, if a person claimed that they were acting in self-defence but in reality they were mistaken in their belief that they were under attack, the defence would only be available if the mistake were reasonable. As we shall see shortly, the courts over the past 25 years have largely abandoned this approach to mistaken beliefs in defences.

However, over the past few decades the law has tended to expand these exceptions and has started to adopt a normative theory of mens rea under which the defendant's actions in the circumstances are subjected to a broader moral assessment. From this perspective it is legitimate to regard negligence as a species of mens rea. As seen earlier, the Sentencing Advisory Panel regards negligence as one means (along with intention, recklessness and knowledge) of establishing culpability.[276] With the proliferation of statutory offences regulating commercial and other aspects of daily life these views have been gaining ground and have led to the creation of many new offences based on negligence: for example,

---

[275] Law Commission, Working Paper No.31, p.57.
[276] *Overarching Principles: Seriousness* (2004), p.4. See above, fn.168.

insider dealing,[277] supplying intoxicating substances to under-age persons,[278] harassment[279] and selling firearms or ammunition to "another person whom he knows or has reasonable cause for believing to be drunk or of unsound mind".[280] Further, as we shall see, many prima facie strict liability offences allow "due diligence" defences. If the defendant can establish that she was not negligent she will escape liability. For example, s.21 of the Food Safety Act 1990 provides a defence to any person who "took all reasonable precautions and exercised all due diligence to avoid the commission of the offence".

More recently, negligence as to an aspect of the actus reus has been employed for some serious criminal offences. Prior to the Sexual Offences Act 2003, rape and other sexual offences required subjective mens rea. For example, if a man honestly believed the other was consenting to intercourse he would not be guilty of rape, no matter how unreasonable that belief.[281] The Sexual Offences Act 2003 abandoned this subjectivist stance and substituted negligence as a new basis of liability; under the Act the defendant is liable unless he *reasonably* believed that the other was consenting. The Domestic Violence, Crime and Victims Act 2004 s.5 introduced the new crime of causing or allowing the death of a child or vulnerable adult. This offence can be committed negligently, the test being whether the defendant was, *or ought to have been*, aware of a significant risk of serious physical harm being caused to the deceased.

3. Negligence and capacity

Negligence was earlier defined as failing to exercise such care, skill or foresight as a reasonable person *in that situation* would exercise. Rape requires that the defendant have no reasonable belief in the other's consent and s.1(2) of the Sexual Offences Act 2003 provides that "whether a belief is reasonable is to be determined *having regard to all the circumstances*". What is meant by "in that situation" and "having regard to all the circumstances"? Does this mean that the defendant's characteristics or capacities must be taken into account?[282]

In the following classic exposition of negligence, Hart suggested that the characteristics and capacities of the defendant should be taken into account.

H.L.A. Hart, "Negligence, Mens Rea and the Elimination of Responsibility" in Punishment and Responsibility (Essays in the Philosophy of Law) (1968), pp.152–157:

"What is crucial is that those whom we punish should have had, when they acted, the normal capacities, physical and mental, for doing what the law requires and abstaining from what it forbids, and a fair opportunity to exercise these capacities. Where these capacities and opportunities are absent, as they are in different ways in the varied cases of accident, mistake, paralysis, reflex action, coercion, insanity, etc., the moral protest is that it is morally

---

277   Criminal Justice Act 1993 s.52.
278   Intoxicating Substance (Supply) Act 1985 s.1(1)
279   Protection from Harassment Act 1997 ss.1(1), 2(1).
280   Firearms Act 1968 s.25.
281   *DPP v Morgan* [1976] A.C. 182.
282   This question will be addressed in more detail below in Ch.7. The Court of Appeal recently considered the question of whether account can or cannot be taken of the defendant's mental condition in deciding whether he held a reasonable belief in consent. It was held that a defendant's delusional belief in consent owing to his schizophrenia cannot in law render reasonable a belief that his partner was consenting when she was not. Beliefs in consent arising from conditions such as delusional psychotic illness or personality disorders must be judged by objective standards of reasonableness and not by taking into account a mental disorder which induced a belief which could not reasonably arise without it: *R. v B* [2013] 1 Cr. App. R. 36.

wrong to punish because 'he could not have helped it' or 'he could not have done otherwise' or 'he had no real choice'. But . . . there is no reason (unless we are to reject the whole business of responsibility and punishment) *always* to make this protest when someone who 'just didn't think' is punished for carelessness. For in some cases at least we may say 'he could have thought about what he was doing' with just as much rational confidence as one can say of any intentional wrong-doing 'he could have done otherwise'.

Of course, the law compromises with competing values over this matter of the subjective element in responsibility . . .

The most important compromise which legal systems make over the subjective element consists in its adoption of what has been unhappily termed the 'objective standard'. This may lead to an individual being treated for the purposes of conviction and punishment as if he possessed capacities for control of his conduct which he did not possess, but which an ordinary or reasonable man possesses and would have exercised. The expression 'objective' and its partner 'subjective' are unhappy because, as far as negligence is concerned, they obscure the real issue. We may be tempted to say with Dr Turner that just because the negligent man does not have 'the thought of harm in his mind,' to hold him responsible for negligence is *necessarily* to adopt an objective standard and to abandon the 'subjective' element in responsibility. It then becomes vital to distinguish this (mistaken) thesis from the position brought about by the use of objective standards in the application of laws which make negligence criminally punishable. For, when negligence is made criminally punishable, this itself leaves open the question: whether, before we punish, both or only the first of the following two questions must be answered affirmatively.

(i)   Did the accused fail to take those precautions which any reasonable man with normal capacities would in the circumstances have taken?

(ii)   Could the accused, given his mental and physical capacities, have taken those precautions? . . . If our conditions of liability are invariant and not flexible, *i.e.* if they are not adjusted to the capacities of the accused, then some individuals will be held liable for negligence though they could not have helped their failure to comply with the standard. In *such* cases, indeed, criminal responsibility will be made independent of any 'subjective element', since the accused could not have conformed to the required standard. But this result is nothing to do with negligence being taken as a basis for criminal liability; precisely the same result will be reached if, in considering whether a person acted intentionally, we were to attribute to him foresight of consequences which a reasonable man would have foreseen but which he did not. 'Absolute liability' results, not from the admission of the principle that one who has been grossly negligent is criminally responsible for the consequent harm even if 'he had no idea in his mind of harm to anyone,' but from the refusal in the application of this principle to consider the capacities of an individual who has fallen below the standard of care.

It is of course quite arguable that no legal system could afford to individualise the conditions of liability so far as to discover and excuse all those who could not attain the average or reasonable man's standard. It may, in practice, be impossible to do more than excuse those who suffer from gross forms of incapacity, *viz.* infants, or the insane, or those afflicted with recognisably inadequate powers of control over their movements, or who are clearly unable to detect, or extricate themselves, from situations in which their disability may work harm. Some confusion is, however, engendered by certain inappropriate ways of describing these excusable cases, which we are tempted to use in a system which, like our own, defines negligence in terms of what the reasonable man would do. We may find ourselves asking whether the infant, the insane, or those suffering from paralysis did all that a reasonable man would *in the circumstances* do, taking 'circumstances' (most queerly) to include personal qualities like being an infant, insane or paralysed. This paradoxical approach leads to many difficulties. To avoid them we need to hold apart the primary question (1) What *would* the reasonable man with ordinary capacities have done in these circumstances? from the second question (2), *Could* the accused with his capacities have done that? Reference to such factors as lunacy or disease should be made in answering only the second of these questions. This simple, and surely realistic, approach avoids difficulties which the notion of individualising the standard of care has presented for certain writers; for these difficulties are usually created by the mistaken assumption that the only way of allowing for individual incapacities is to treat them as part of the 'circumstances' in which the reasonable man is supposed to be acting. Thus Dr Glanville Williams said that if 'regard must be had to the make-up and circumstances of the particular offender, one would seem on a determinist view of conduct to be pushed to the conclusion that there is no standard of conduct at all. For if every characteristic of the individual is taken into account, including his heredity the conclusion is that he could not help doing as he did.' (The General Part (1st Ed.) p.82.)

But 'determinism' presents no special difficulty here. The question is whether that individual had the capacity (inherited or not) to act otherwise than he did, and 'determinism' has no relevance to the case of one who is accused of negligence which it does not have to one accused of intentionally killing."

Judicial support for this approach can be found in the case of *RSPA v C*.[283] A 15-year-old girl was charged with causing unnecessary suffering to a domestic cat contrary to s.1(a) of the Protection of Animals Act 1911. In determining whether she was negligent the issue was whether her age and position in the household (her father had decided that the cat should not receive veterinary care) should be taken into account. It was held that the fact the defendant was a youth and part of her father's household was relevant in determining whether her actions were reasonable.[284]

This approach is to be welcomed. If such an approach had been adopted in the recklessness case of *Elliott v C*, it could well have lessened the criticism levelled at the *Caldwell/Lawrence* test. The Law Commission has similarly endorsed this approach in relation to gross negligence for the purposes of manslaughter stressing that it is important that

"the grossness of negligence be made relative to someone's individual capacity to appreciate the nature and degree of risks, which may be affected by youth or disability."[285]

However, the degree to which individual characteristics or qualities should be taken into account is brought into question in relation to regulatory offences, where an individual is expected to live up to a particular standard of care as a condition of engaging in a particular, risky activity. The obvious example of offences of negligence forming part of a regulatory regime is that of driving offences such as careless and dangerous driving. Both are offences of negligence, but of different degrees: careless driving requires that the defendant drove below the standard of driving expected of a competent and careful driver;[286] dangerous driving that the defendant's driving fell far below that standard and that it would have been obvious to a competent and careful driver that such driving was dangerous.[287] All those who take control of a potentially lethal weapon such as a car are expected to live up to the standard of a competent and careful driver, whether they are on their first driving lesson or have thirty years of experience of driving. That this is an entirely objective test was in question following the case of *Milton*, in which a police officer, trained to drive at an advanced standard, argued that whilst it might be dangerous for other drivers to drive at speeds of up to twice the permitted speed limit, the fact that he was particularly skilled was a characteristic which meant that it was not dangerous for *him* to do so. This argument was upheld on appeal to the Divisional Court and the officer's conviction quashed, with Smith LJ arguing that to allow such circumstances to be taken into account "does not offend against the requirement that the test for dangerous driving is objective. It simply refines the objective test by reference to existing circumstances".[288] The Court of Appeal, however, did not agree, later overruling *Milton* in the case of *Bannister*.[289] That case had very similar facts to *Milton*; a police advanced driver drove at speeds of up to 113mph on a motorway in the dark and wet, and spun

---

[283]   *RSPA v C* [2006] EWHC 1069 (Admin).
[284]   It should be noted that the offence under the Protection of Animals Act 1911 has now been replaced by s.4 of the Animal Welfare Act 2006. It was recently held in relation to that offence, that the requirement that the defendant "knew, or ought reasonably to have known, that the act, or failure to act" would cause an animal to suffer was an entirely objective test of negligence: *R. (Gray) v Aylesbury Crown Court* [2013] EWHC Admin 500.
[285]   Law Commission Consultation Paper No.177, *A New Homicide Act for England and Wales?* (2005), para.3.185.
[286]   Road Traffic Act 1988 s.3ZA.
[287]   Road Traffic Act 1988 s.2A.
[288]   *Milton v DPP* [2007] R.T.R. 43 at [27].
[289]   *R. v Bannister (Craig)* [2010] R.T.R. 4.

out of control and crashed. The defendant argued that, on the basis of *Milton*, he was not guilty of dangerous driving as it was relevant that he had completed an advanced training course which had enabled him to drive safely at high speed in the conditions concerned, even if it would not be safe for the ordinary competent and careful driver. The Court of Appeal overruled *Milton*, and held that taking into account the driving skills of a particular driver was inconsistent with the objective test set out in the Road Traffic Act. The special skill, or lack of skill, of a driver was an irrelevant circumstance when considering whether the driving was dangerous. This decision is to be welcomed; to continue with the position in *Milton* would allow arguments to be made by a defendant that although their driving did not meet the standard of a competent and careful driver, they should not be assessed according to that standard because of a lack of skill or experience in driving and could not be expected to do more than their incompetent best. That would undermine the regulatory regime of driving offences put in place for the safety of all road users.

4. Should negligence be a basis for the attribution of criminal responsibility?

Robert P. Fine and Gary M. Cohen, "Is Criminal Negligence a Defensible Basis for Penal Liability" (1967) 16 Buffalo L.Rev. 749 at 750–752:

"[T]he question is raised as to the advisability of punishing negligent conduct with criminal sanctions. Professor Edwin Keedy responded to this question as follows:

'If the defendant, being mistaken as to the material facts, is to be punished because his mistake is one an average man would not make, punishment will sometimes be inflicted when *the criminal mind does not exist*. Such a result is contrary to fundamental principles, and is plainly unjust, for a man should not be held criminal because of lack of intelligence.' (Keedy, "Ignorance and Mistake in the Criminal Law" 22 Harv.L.Rev. 75, 84 (1908) (Emphasis added)).

This argument is persuasive, especially when considered in conjunction with the traditional concepts and goals of criminal punishment.

The concept of criminal punishment is based on one, or a combination, of four theories: deterrence, retribution, rehabilitation and incapacitation.

The deterrence theory of criminal law is based on the hypothesis that the prospective offender knows that he will be punished for any criminal activity, and, therefore, will adjust his behaviour to avoid committing a criminal act. This theory rests on the idea of 'rational utility,' *i.e.* prospective offenders will weigh the evil of the sanction against the gain of the contemplated crime. However, punishment of a negligent offender in no way implements this theory, since the negligent harm-doer is, by definition, unaware of the risk he imposes on society. It is questionable whether holding an individual criminally liable for acts the risks of which he has failed to perceive will deter him from failing to perceive in the future.

The often-criticised retributive theory of criminal law presupposes a 'moral guilt,' which justifies society in seeking its revenge against the offender. This 'moral guilt' is ascribed to those forms of conduct which society deems threatening to its very existence, such as murder and larceny. However, the negligent harm-doer has not actually committed this type of morally reprehensible act, but has merely made an error in judgment. This type of error is an everyday occurrence, although it may deviate from a normal standard of care. Nevertheless, such conduct does not approach the moral turpitude against which the criminal law should seek revenge. It is difficult to comprehend how retribution requires such mistakes to be criminally punished.

It is also doubtful whether the negligent offender can be rehabilitated in any way by criminal punishment. Rehabilitation presupposes a 'warped sense of values' which can be corrected. Since inadvertence, and not a deficient sense of values, has caused the 'crime', there appears to be nothing to rehabilitate.

The underlying goal of the incapacitation theory is to protect society by isolating an individual so as to prevent him from perpetrating a similar crime in the future. However, this approach is only justifiable if less stringent methods will not further the same goal of protecting society. For example, an insane individual would not be criminally incarcerated, if the less stringent means of medical treatment would afford the same societal protection. Likewise, with a criminally negligent individual, the appropriate remedy is not incarceration, but 'to exclude him from the activity in which he is a danger'.

The conclusion drawn from this analysis is that there appears to be no reasonable justification for punishing negligence as a criminal act under any of these four theories. It does not further the purposes of deterrence, retribution, rehabilitation or incapacitation; hence, there is no rational basis for the imposition of criminal liability on negligent conduct . . .

In addition, Hall ("Negligent Behaviour Should be Excluded from Penal Liability" 36 Colum.L.Rev. (1963)), suggests scientific arguments for the exclusion of negligence from penal liability. One contention is that the incorporation of negligence into the penal law imposes an impossible function on judges, namely, to determine whether a person, about whom very little is known, had the competence and sensitivity to appreciate certain dangers in a particular situation when the facts plainly indicate that he did not exhibit that competence."

The opposing view is that "punishment supplies men with an additional motive to take care before acting, to use their faculties and to draw upon their experience".[290] As Brett puts it:

"It is common knowledge that as soon as traffic police appear on the roads drivers begin to pay greater attention to what they are doing, and the standard of driving rises sharply."[291]

Further, perhaps those who fail to consider the obvious consequences of their actions reveal their dangerousness and need incapacitation (say, having their driving licence removed) and rehabilitation.

However, many of the arguments in favour of negligence as a basis for the imposition of criminal liability have not concentrated on such utilitarian considerations, but have stressed that judgments of blameworthiness should not be limited to cases where the defendant realises that harm could occur. Even accepting the premise of responsibility involving the notion of choice, we can blame those who make choices of which we disapprove. We can blame Lamb[292] for acting as he did in total disregard of an obvious and serious risk. In the context of recklessness, Lord Diplock in *Caldwell* regarded non-advertence as no less blameworthy than advertence. Lord Goff in *Reid* went further and said that

"it can be argued with force that, in many cases of failing to think, the degree of blameworthiness to be attached to the driver can be greater than that to be attached in some cases to the driver who recognized the risk and decided to disregard it."[293]

George P. Fletcher, "The Theory of Criminal Negligence: A Comparative Analysis" (1971) 119 U. Pa. L. Rev. 401 at 415–418:

"At first blush it seems odd that anyone would argue that negligence is not an appropriate ground for censuring the conduct of another . . . In daily conduct, we all confidently blame others who fail to advert to significant risks. If we confront a motorist driving without his lights on and thereby endangering the lives of many others, we would hardly condition our condemnation of his conduct on whether he knew his lights were off. His failure to find out

---

[290]   Model Penal Code, *Tentative Draft No.4*, pp.126–127.
[291]   P. Brett, *An Inquiry into Criminal Guilt* (Sydney: Law Book Company of Australasia, 1963), p.98.
[292]   Above, p.185.
[293]   *Reid* (1992) 95 Cr. App. R. 393 at 406.

whether his lights were on or off would itself be a basis for condemning him.[294] Yet theorists have repeatedly argued that this judicial practice is primitive and that, as a matter of principle, an actor must *choose* to do harm in order to be culpable and fairly subject to penal sanctions. Jerome Hall has vigorously advanced this view . . . [T] he proponents of punishing negligence have relied upon the same reply: the culpability of negligence is not the culpability of choice, but rather of failing to bring to bear one's faculties to perceive the risks that one is taking . . . The battleground of one segment of the literature is the role of culpability in justifying criminal sanctions. Jerome Hall argues, for example, that 'in the long history of ethics voluntary harm-doing is the essence of (culpability).' From this premise he reasons that negligence is involuntary, and that therefore it is unjust to punish negligent risk-taking. The question Hall raises is the right one. We do wish to know whether it is just to punish the negligent actor. It is not enough to show that punishing negligence has a deterrent impact on other potential risk-creators, for the goal of deterrence, however sound, does not speak to the fairness of forcing the specific defendant to be the object of exemplary sanctioning. Yet the issue of fairness to the defendant is not resolved by positing that negligence is not voluntary and therefore not culpable. Surely, the negligent actor, like the intentional actor, has the capacity of doing otherwise; he could have brought to bear his faculties to perceive and to avoid the risk he created. That is all we typically require to label conduct as voluntary . . .
With the idea of forfeiture in the foreground, culpability functions as the touchstone of the question whether by virtue of his illegal conduct, the violator has lost his moral standing to complain of being subjected to sanctions. If his illegal conduct is unexcused, if he had a fair chance of avoiding the violation and did not, we are inclined to regard the state's imposing a sanction as justified. The defendant's failure to exercise a responsibility shared by all, be it a responsibility to avoid intentional violations or to avoid creating substantial and unjustified risks, provides a warrant for the state's intrusion upon his autonomy as an individual. From the viewpoint of culpability as a standard of moral forfeiture, it seems fair and consistent to regard negligence as culpable and to subject the negligent offender to criminal sanctions."

5. Conclusion

There are deep tensions within English criminal law. On the one hand, much of the judiciary is deeply committed to subjectivism. For them, mens rea means cognitive mens rea. These views were strongly expressed in *G* and in a series of House of Lords' decisions dealing with mistake.[295] The Law Commission has also traditionally adopted this subjectivist stance. The Draft Criminal Code Bill 1989, for example, makes no mention of negligence, stating that recklessness should be the core fault element for every offence unless specifically otherwise provided.[296]

On the other hand, there is no denying that, at least for statutory offences, there is growing reliance on the concept of negligence. With the notable exception of gross negligence manslaughter, much of this increase has related to lesser offences. However, with rape and the other sexual offences and the offence of causing or allowing the death of a child or vulnerable adult now added to the list of crimes that can be committed negligently, the door to further utilisation of the concept has been thrown open.

G. Levels of Culpability

An important final point needs consideration. Assuming defendants who act with non-advertent recklessness (the now overruled *Caldwell/Lawrence* recklessness) or negligence are to be blamed and punished for the harms they cause, are they *as* blameworthy as those who might have caused the same harms intentionally or with subjective foresight of the risks they were running? If not, should the

---

294 Compare Williams, "Recklessness Redefined" [1981] C.L.J. 252 at 261: "can it possibly be said, with justice, that a driver who opens his door being momentarily forgetful of risk is 'no less blameworthy' than the driver who realises the possibility of causing injury to a cyclist whom he sees approaching but flings open his door regardless?".
295 See pp.210–214.
296 Law Commission Paper No.177 cl.20(1).

law reflect the differences in culpability by imposing different levels of liability and/or punishment? Should the law reflect the view that

> "to break your Ming china, deliberately or intentionally, is worse than to knock it over while waltzing wildly round the room and not thinking of what might get knocked over?"[297]

Further, is it worse to break your Ming china while waltzing round the room realising that you might knock it over than when you have no such realisation?

A. Kenny, Freewill and Responsibility (1978), pp.85–92:

"In the same way as the justification of the general requirement of *mens rea* flows from the nature of punishment and the nature of practical reasoning, so the justification of distinguishing between different degrees of *mens rea* arises from the different degrees of proximity to the actuality or possibility of practical reasoning in particular criminal behaviour. The same act, when performed negligently, may be punished less severely than when performed knowingly, and the same act when performed recklessly may be punished less severely than when performed intentionally. We must ask why this is so, and whether it should be so . . .

No doubt almost everyone would regard a reckless killer as more wicked than an inadvertent killer; but the law's principal concern is the prevention of harm, and the harm done by either killer is identical. Should not the penalty too be identical? No: for the point at which the threat of punishment is intended to be brought to bear upon practical reasoning is different in the two cases. The threat of punishment for negligence is meant to enforce at all times a standard of care to ensure that one's actions do not endanger life: the threat of punishment for recklessness is meant to operate at the specific points at which one is contemplating a course of action known to be life-endangering. The actions, therefore, on which the threat of punishment for negligence is brought to bear are less dangerous than those on which the threat of punishment for recklessness is brought to bear: for in general actions which, for all one knows, may be dangerous are less dangerous than actions which one positively knows to be a risk to life. Hence the more severe threat of punishment is held out to the citizen contemplating the more dangerous action.

Just as actions known to be likely to cause death are in general more dangerous than those not known to be so likely, so actions done with the intention of causing death are in general more dangerous than those merely foreseen as likely to cause death. (The latter, for instance, unlike the former, are compatible with the taking of precautions against the causing of death.) This perhaps offers a reason for punishing intentional homicide more severely than reckless homicide, just as reckless homicide is punished more severely than negligent homicide . . .

Thus we have seen the rationale, on the deterrent theory of punishment, for the discriminations made in law between the different forms of *mens rea* from negligence, recklessness and basic intent up to specific intent. It may well be thought that the theory behind such discriminations presupposes a coolness in calculation and a competence in the theory of games which it is unrealistic to impute to the average citizen tempted to commit a crime. On the other hand, it is surely not a mere accident that the gradations of severity in punishment which a comparatively recondite application of the theory of deterrence suggests should correspond in such large measure with the intuitions of moral common sense about the comparative wickedness of frames of mind.

In practice, of course, the deterrent effect of the law operates unevenly and erratically. The elaborate efforts of lawyers and academics to sort offences into precise categories and to fit crimes to punishment on impeccable theoretical grounds may well strike a layman as resembling an attempt to make a town clock accurate to a millisecond in a community most of whom are too short-sighted to see the clock-face, too deaf to hear the hours ring, and many of whom set no great store on punctuality in any case."

Do such utilitarian arguments adequately explain why we distinguish between different levels of culpability and reflect this by different punishments for each?

---

[297] Hart, above, p.190 at p.136.

James B. Brady, "Recklessness, Negligence, Indifference and Awareness" (1980) 43 M.L.R. 381 at 396–399:

What is the justification for the decreasing culpability attaching to intentional, reckless and negligent conduct? . . . First of all, I do not believe that an utilitarian rationale concerning the purpose of punishment will suffice. For example, it has been argued that the culpability distinction between intentional action and recklessness may be justified since there is a greater likelihood that an intentional action will result in harm. If the purpose of punishment is the prevention of harm, the argument goes, the degree of seriousness of the offence should be proportionate to the degree of dangerousness. On this theory we punish the intentional offender more because (a) a more severe penalty may be necessary to deter a person from accomplishing a result that is his aim or purpose than to deter one who acts knowing that there is a risk but whose purpose is not to bring about that result, and (b) the intentional offender may require a longer sentence, for purpose of reform or special deterrence, than the reckless or negligent offender . . . [T]hese arguments from an utilitarian rationale are not persuasive in general. For example, considering the class of negligent or reckless offenders as contrasted with the class of intentional offenders there seems to be no reason to believe that the former pose less of a continuing threat of harm than the latter. If the degree of seriousness of the offence were only dictated by utilitarian reasons, negligence might well be viewed as more serious, in light of the greater number of negligent harms in comparison to intentional harms, and might in special cases require more punishment for purposes of general or special deterrence than intentional offences require.

These distinctions between different modes are to be viewed as distinctions of culpability in the strict sense. If they are justified at all, they are justified because they mark moral distinctions. The strongest argument is that unless the law is to treat morally disparate cases alike the law should reflect these distinctions . . .

There does not seem to be any single criterion which fully captures our intuitions concerning degrees of culpability. One might argue, for example, that the distinctions could be maintained on the basis of the degree of voluntariness of the action. The reason that negligence, where the agent is unaware of the risk, is less blameworthy than recklessness is that negligent conduct is less voluntary than reckless conduct. But this will not explain the distinction between intentional and reckless conduct. Since in reckless conduct the agent is aware of the risk, it would seem that in both reckless and intentional action the agent has the choice of forbearing from his action. From a consideration of control of conduct, therefore, reckless conduct seems to be as voluntary as intentional conduct.

Suppose that we consider another theory, that it is the factor of likeliness to cause harm which is the criterion of blame. This is a different theory than the one discussed earlier which attempts to explain these distinctions on utilitarian grounds relating to a greater degree of likelihood of harm. The argument here is that the greater likelihood of harm marks a moral distinction and that one who engages in conduct which is more likely to cause harm is more culpable than one who engages in conduct with a lesser chance of harm. Under this theory the reason that intentional conduct is more culpable than recklessness causing the same harm is that harm is judged more likely to occur if that is the purpose of one's action than if it is the merely foreseen consequence of one's action.

To a certain extent this factor might explain some of the distinctions in culpability. It seems to be part of the reason, for example, for one who hopes that the harm will not occur, is more blameworthy than one who 'doesn't care one way or the other' in regard to a less likely risk. In this case 'hoping not' is not a mitigating factor because of the greater likelihood of the harm occurring.

But while the likelihood of harm is an important factor, it cannot explain other distinctions. For example, a person who causes harm with the desire of bringing about that harm is thought more culpable, even where the chance of his succeeding was slight, than a person who causes harm by recklessly taking a substantial risk. This cannot, of course, be explained on the grounds of likelihood of harm since the likelihood where the person intentionally takes a 'long shot' is less than where the person acts recklessly in regard to a likely risk. And in cases regarding the same risk, the person's hopes that the harm will not occur does reduce culpability in comparison with one who does not care at all. Again, the difference in degree cannot be explained on the basis of greater likelihood of harm since the risk is the same. Similarly, this theory evidently cannot explain the distinctions between negligent and reckless conduct involving the same risk of harm since, of course, the likelihood of harm is the same. Why then do we blame the reckless agent more? Here the answer seems to be that recklessness manifests a trait of the person that is not present to the same degree in negligence. The person who realises the risk would not have acted unless he was indifferent, in the broad sense, to the interests of others. We properly blame him more, since he is more indifferent. And the person who hopes that harm will not occur is less indifferent, in regard to the same risk, than one who does not care at all. Though again in some cases involving different degrees of risk 'hoping not' does not show a lesser degree of indifference."

Alternatively, there might be a different way of assessing whether an objective or subjective test of blameworthiness is appropriate, depending on the context in which the offence is committed.

Sally Cunningham, "Recklessness: Being Reckless and Acting Recklessly" (2010) 21 K.J.J. 445 at 457–460

"The key to the mistakes made by the courts is that they tried to find a definition of recklessness to apply to both conduct crimes and result crimes. Reckless driving is a conduct crime. It does not require any concrete harm to have been caused by the blameworthy conduct of the offender, since it exists to punish those who take risks and to regulate the dangerous activity of driving. Non-aggravated criminal damage [under s.1(1) Criminal Damage Act 1971] (and offences against the person such as assault are result crimes which require a specific harm to have been caused as part of the *actus reus* of the offence. These two different types of crimes should have been dealt with in entirely different ways by the courts, given their different natures.

This distinction was recognised by some of . . . the [relevant] cases . . . In *Murphy* [1980] Q.B. 434 the distinction was made between 'reckless' as an adjective describing an attitude towards certain possible consequences (result crime), and 'recklessly' as an adverb governing the accused's conduct (conduct crime). In each case the word 'reckless' or 'recklessly' is doing a different job, and so it makes sense that it should carry a different meaning. In one, 'recklessness' is describing a state of mind, whilst in the other it relates to the quality of D's act.

A similar argument was made in *Lawrence*. Counsel for the Crown contended that there are three basic categories of recklessness:

(a)   Recklessness as to circumstance ('conduct crimes')

(b)   Recklessness as to consequences ('result crimes') and

(c)   Recklessness as defined by statute in relation to a particular situation. (At p.514)

Reckless driving falls within the first category (a), whilst non-aggravated criminal damage is an example of the second category (b). It would therefore be consistent to have two different tests such as those given in *Murphy* and *Stephenson* for different offences. In giving his judgment in *Lawrence* Lord Diplock did admit that there was a difference between the context in which the word 'reckless' was used in relation to driving and in relation to criminal damage as the Crown had suggested, . . .

The distinction between the adjective 'reckless' and the adverb 'recklessly' can be seen in the drafting of relevant legislation. Section 2 of the Road Traffic Act 1988, prior to amendment by the Road Traffic Act 1991, stated that: 'a person who drives a motor vehicle on a road recklessly is guilty of an offence.' This uses recklessly as an adverb in describing how a particular type of conduct which is normally lawful, can be proscribed if a person goes about the activity in a particular way. Section 1(1) of the Criminal Damage Act 1971 requires that D destroy or damage property belonging to another intending to do so or 'being reckless' as to doing so. 'Reckless' describes D's state of mind when causing a proscribed harm, as an alternative to the state of mind of intention.

. . .

Examples of conduct crimes (reckless driving, child neglect, rape, aggravated criminal damage) all involve the creation of risks. But all of these activities are in themselves hazardous occupations if not carried out with care. The underlying risk is always present, in that: driving is inherently dangerous; caring for a child can easily end in tragedy if sufficient attention is not paid to the child's needs; there is the possibility of interfering with another individual's autonomy; damage to property can easily create danger of at least injury to others. Psychologists suggest that there is a fundamental distinction between 'risk and hazard'.

'Risk' (in any sense) is a measure of a subjective process. 'Hazard' is a measure of what actually happens independently of any subjective considerations. Strictly speaking, no individual is in a position to compare, in advance of any enterprise, the risk he is taking with the hazard the undertaking involves. The individual can only compare his risk (i.e. his expected success or failure) with his impression or guess of the hazard, or with past hazards.' (Cohen and Christensen, *Information and Choice*, (Edinburgh: Oliver and Boyd), 1970), p.101.)

If someone is engaging in hazardous conduct where the potential for risk exists, the question of whether she has foreseen that a risk might materialise is not relevant. The salient point is that she must take care in engaging in the activity to try to minimise the possibility of the potential risk occurring. If she fails to take sufficient care, creating a risk from a hazardous situation, she becomes blameworthy, whether or not she adverts to the risk. She has carried out the hazardous activity in a reckless manner if she fails to take care, thereby creating a risk which should have been avoided.

An objective test of *mens rea* is appropriate in relation to conduct crimes, because D is partaking in a dangerous activity and so *should* pay attention to the risks and is blameworthy if she does not. D ought to make her knowledge of a risk 'explicit', to use another term employed by Duff, by making herself alert to the potential risks involved in the activity and calling her latent knowledge to mind. If she fails to do so she is blameworthy and should attract criminal condemnation. On the other hand, in relation to result crimes we start from the position that a particular proscribed harm has been caused and need to work our way back from there in order to determine whether D's state of mind is sufficiently blameworthy in relation to that harm in order to attract criminal liability. A different test is appropriate to that employed in relation to conduct crimes."

Under this analysis, some offence definitions would need redrafting to properly reflect the species of mens rea required, and to perhaps use terms such as "negligently" rather than "recklessly" where an objective test is appropriate. Indeed, it may be that we should start to use a more varied selection of mens rea terms, rather than trying to stretch the traditional terms to fit what is needed.

Findlay Stark, "It's Only Words: On Meaning and Mens Rea" (2013) 72(1) C.L.J. 155 at 170–172

"It has been argued that, if the criminal law is to live up to its communicative ideal, citizens must be able to understand (normatively and semantically) and use the language of wrongdoing and liability adopted by the courts and the legislature in planning their conduct. Similarly, if the discretion accorded to criminal justice actors is to be controlled adequately, the criminal law's mens rea terms should be defined clearly and consistently.

But what are the courts and the legislature to do if they accept the argument from communication made here, yet want to ensure that the law can react appropriately to the competing principles and policies which affect different areas of the criminal law? . . . Tadros suggests that the courts may, in interpreting terms such as intention, be conservative and not seek to make generalisations which might damage some parts of the law. This approach results, however, in the courts using a small number of mens rea terms in different ways and leads to the potential confusion pointed to above. A better solution, it is submitted, would be to expand the range of mens rea terms presently utilised in the criminal law, and ensure that, when they were used, these words are defined consistently across offences.

A. A Way Forward

Consider again the definition of intention. Sometimes there does not seem to be a significant moral difference between meaning to bring about a certain result (for instance, death) and failing to be motivated sufficiently by the realisation that it is virtually certain that, if the defendant proceeds with his plan, that result will be brought about. It might be argued that the law would be missing something morally significant if it defined murder as only desired and purposeful killings. Therefore, foresight of a virtual certainty might be treated, for the law of murder, as being sufficient mens rea to secure culpability. This is the position at present in English law (with the added complication that nobody is sure if foresight of a virtual certainty *is* intention, or just something *morally equivalent* to it).

Rather than doing what the English courts have up until now done, however, and simply expanding the concept of intention *in this area* to include foresight of a virtual certainty, it would be more conducive to clarity if the mens rea of murder were expressed in terms of an intention to kill (or cause grievous bodily harm) *or* foresight of virtual certainty that death (or grievous bodily harm) would result from the defendant's action. 'Foresight of virtual certainty' could be conceived of as a separate category of mens rea from intention . . . It is *unacceptable*, because it makes inaccessible the message (and undermines the communicative enterprise) of the criminal law, to be conservative in the way that the English courts have been and, as a result, use the same words in different ways in different contexts. The courts should thus refuse to do so, and should define mens rea terms in a uniform fashion wherever they are encountered.

The benefit of using different *terms*, rather than different *definitions*, is obvious. It would avoid the need for the courts to *decide* when intention ought to include foresight and when it ought not to. This decision would be left to Parliament in drafting an offence . . . Intention would mean, if foresight of virtual certainty were separated from it, meaning to bring about a certain result—a definition that coheres sufficiently with the 'everyday' understanding of that term that it could be utilised effectively by citizens in planning or arguing about their conduct. It would also be clear to citizens what 'foresight of virtual certainty' means, and it would not be difficult to explain to them that, where foresight of virtual certainty *is* viewed as being sufficiently culpable to constitute mens rea then the definition of the crime is satisfied. Plans could be made fairly, on this basis, to avoid liability."

Stark goes on to note that similar problems have been faced by the courts in interpreting recklessness, and that they have put forward different interpretations of the word in order to "do justice" in a particular case. However, he submits that it would have been preferable for the courts to stick to a uniform definition of mens rea terms and require Parliamentary intervention to ameliorate the position. This is eventually what occurred in relation to the mens rea of rape, with the Sexual Offences Act 2003 being passed to ensure that an appropriately objective test is used in relation to belief in consent. Beyond rape, however, that leaves the legislature with a huge amount of work to do in redrafting offences to ensure that appropriate mens rea terms are used, a process which Stark recognises is extremely unlikely to happen. Despite this practical hurdle, the argument that the courts should make the difficulties faced by using current mens rea terms a more immediate problem for Parliament by refusing to stretch them to fit the requirements of a case "so that a more sensible debate over criminal fault can commence" has much to merit it.

IV. Relationship of Mens Rea to Actus Reus

A. Introduction

A general rule of the criminal law is that mens rea must exist in relation to the actus reus. Bearing in mind that an actus reus can consist of:

(1) an act;

(2) committed in certain specified circumstances; and

(3) leading to the prohibited consequence,

mens rea should exist in relation to each of these separate elements. However, it does not necessarily follow that the same degree of mens rea is required in relation to each. Thus the crime of attempt, for example, could require (1) an intentional act; (2) recklessness as to surrounding circumstances; and (3) an intention to bring about the forbidden consequences. But whatever the level of mens rea, it must exist "in relation to" the actus reus, or, to put it another way, the actus reus must be attributable to the mens rea. In order to understand this rule it is necessary to investigate two "principles" that are well established in criminal law, and to consider the problem of mistake.

B. Coincidence of Actus Reus and Mens Rea

In the Rhodesian case of *Shorty*[298] the defendant violently assaulted the deceased with intent to kill him. The defendant, genuinely believing the victim to be dead, attempted to dispose of the "body" by putting it down a sewer. The deceased was in fact still alive at the time but died of drowning in the sewer. The court ruled that these actions must be divided into:

(1) the assault which did not cause death—this was accompanied by an intent to kill; and

(2) the actus reus of murder (placing the "body" in a sewer with resultant drowning)—but this was not accompanied by mens rea at this stage.

Because the actus reus of murder did not coincide with the mens rea thereof, the defendant could not be convicted of murder. He was convicted only of attempted murder (stage 1), the actus reus of which did coincide with the requisite mens rea.

Is such a result realistic? The defendant intended to kill his victim; he did kill him. Should his mistake as to the method and time of death affect his liability?

Thabo Meli v R. [1954] 1 All E.R. 373 (Privy Council)

The appellants, in accordance with a pre-arranged plan, took a man to a hut, gave him beer so that he was partially intoxicated and then struck him over the head. Believing him to be dead, they took his body and rolled it over a low cliff, making the scene look like an accident. In fact the man was not dead, but died of exposure when unconscious at the foot of the cliff.

LORD REID:

"The point of law which was raised in this case can be simply stated. It is said that two acts were done:—first, the attack in the hut; and, secondly, the placing of the body outside afterwards—and that they were separate acts. It is said that, while the first act was accompanied by *mens rea*, it was not the cause of death; but that the second act, while it was the cause of death, was not accompanied by *mens rea*; and on that ground, it is said that the accused are not guilty of murder, though they may have been guilty of culpable homicide. It is said that the *mens rea* necessary to establish murder is an intention to kill, and that there could be no intention to kill when the accused thought that the man was already dead, so their original intention to kill had ceased before they did the act which caused the man's death. It appears to their Lordships impossible to divide up what was really one series of acts in this way. There is no doubt that the accused set out to do all these acts in order to achieve their plan, and as parts of their plan; and it is much too refined a ground of judgment to say that, because they were under a misapprehension at one stage and thought that their guilty purpose had been achieved before, in fact, it was achieved, therefore they are to escape the penalties of the law . . . Their crime is not reduced from murder to a lesser crime merely because the accused were under some misapprehension for a time during the completion of their criminal plot."

Appeal dismissed

Dealing with a similar situation (except there was no preconceived plan) in *Church*,[299] it was stated that the jury should have been told they could convict of murder

---

[298] *Shorty* (1950) S.R. 280.
[299] *R. v Church (Cyril David)* (1965) 49 Cr. App. R. 206.

"if they regarded the appellant's behaviour from the moment he first struck her to the moment when he threw her into the river as a series of acts designed to cause death or grievous bodily harm".[300]

R. v Le Brun (1992) 94 Cr. App. R. 101 (Court of Appeal, Criminal Division)

The defendant hit his wife on the chin knocking her unconscious. While trying to drag her body away (probably to avoid detection) he dropped her causing her to fracture her skull and die. He was convicted of manslaughter and appealed.

LORD LANE CJ:

"[After citing *Church* with approval his Lordship continued]

It seems to us that where the unlawful application of force and the eventual act causing death are parts of the same sequence of events, the same transaction, the fact that there is an appreciable interval of time between the two does not serve to exonerate the defendant from liability. That is certainly so where the appellant's subsequent actions which caused death, after the initial unlawful blow, are designed to conceal his commission of the original unlawful assault.

It would be possible to express the problem as one of causation. The original unlawful blow to the chin was a *causa sine qua* of the later *actus reus*. It was the opening event in a series which was to culminate in death: the first link in the chain of causation, to use another metaphor. It cannot be said that the actions of the appellant in dragging the victim away with the intention of evading liability broke the chain which linked the initial blow with the death.

In short, in circumstances such as the present . . . the act which causes death and the necessary mental state to constitute manslaughter need not coincide in point of time . . .

[The trial judge had drawn a correct distinction] between actions by the appellant which were designed to help his wife and actions which were not so designed: on the one hand that would be a way in which the prosecution could establish the connection if he was not trying to assist his wife; on the other hand if he was trying to assist his wife, the chain of causation would have been broken and the *nexus* between the two halves of the prosecution case would not exist."

Appeal dismissed

Ashworth argues that these decisions "take a rather elastic view of the contemporaneity principle, and seem to be motivated by considerations akin to constructive liability".[301] However, in all the above cases the so-called problem of a "coincidence of actus reus and mens rea" is illusory. In each case the defendant's actions caused the ultimate death (that is, the chain of causation was not broken); the defendant was held liable for either murder or manslaughter[302] depending on the mens rea present at the time of the original assault.

This approach was confirmed by the House of Lords in *Attorney-General's Reference (No.3 of 1994)* where Lord Mustill stated:

"The existence of an interval of time between the doing of an act by the defendant with the necessary wrongful intent and its impact on the victim in a manner which leads to death does not in itself prevent the intent, the act and the death from together amounting to murder, so long as there is an unbroken causal connection between the act and the death."[303]

---

[300]   See also *R. v Moore and Dorn* [1975] Crim. L.R. 229. In *Att-Gen's Reference (No.4 of 1980)* [1981] 1 W.L.R. 705 the Court of Appeal left open the question whether this "series of acts" test was a correct extension of the *Thabo Meli* principle.

[301]   Ashworth and Horder, *Principles of Criminal Law*, 7th edn (Oxford: OUP, 2013), p.159.

[302]   This solution was not adopted in *Shorty* (above, fn.298). It is submitted that under English causation principles, *Shorty* would be regarded as wrong.

[303]   *Attorney-General's Reference (No.3 of 1994)* [1997] 3 All E.R. 936 at 942.

Lord Hope added that

"the act which caused the death and the mental state which is needed to constitute manslaughter need not coincide in point of time . . . [as long as] the original unlawful and dangerous act, to which the required mental state is related, and the eventual death of the victim are both part of the same sequence of events."[304]

It has been suggested that this causation analysis will not apply and that the "continuing actus reus" doctrine will still be necessary in cases where the second event is the overwhelming cause of death and breaks the chain of causation[305]—for example, if the wife in *Le Brun* had been dropped by a Good Samaritan trying to take her to hospital.[306] The short answer to this is that if the second event is so overwhelming as to break the causal chain, it would not be regarded as part of the same "series of acts" (*Church*) or "same sequence of events" (*Le Brun*). The continuing actus reus principle would not apply.

In such cases where there are two separate incidents which cannot be conflated into a continuous act or the "same sequence of events", the jury must be unanimous as to which of the acts forms the basis of the defendant's liability.[307] In *Boreman*[308] the defendant seriously assaulted the victim (with the mens rea of murder) and later (perhaps accidentally) started a fire at the victim's flat. The victim died but the medical evidence was divided as to the cause of death. It was held that

"where the two possible means by which the killing is effected comprise completely different acts, happening at different times, it can properly be said that the jury ought to be unanimous on which act leads them to the decision to convict."

However, the appeal was dismissed on the ground that the jury must have been satisfied that the injuries were an operating cause of death.

There are other "coincidence cases" where the initial act is not accompanied by mens rea but the defendant forms mens rea at a later stage in the sequence of events.

Fagan v Metropolitan Police Commissioner [1969] 1 Q.B. 439 (Queen's Bench Divisional Court)

The appellant was told by a police officer to park his car in an exact position against the kerb. He drove the vehicle forward and stopped with its front off-side wheel on the constable's left foot. When told to reverse off, the appellant replied, "Fuck you, you can wait", and turned off the ignition. After several further requests, the appellant reversed the vehicle off the constable's foot. He was convicted of assaulting a police officer in the execution of his duty. On appeal he claimed that the initial driving on to the foot was unintentional and therefore not an assault, and that his refusal to drive off was not an "act" capable of amounting to an assault.

JAMES J:

"We think that the crucial question is whether, in this case, the act of the appellant can be said to be complete and spent at the moment of time when the car wheel came to rest on the foot, or whether his act is to be regarded as

[304] *Attorney-General's Reference (No.3 of 1994)* [1997] 3 All E.R. 936 at 956–957.
[305] A.P. Simester et al., *Criminal Law: Theory and Doctrine*, 5th edn (Oxford: Hart, 2013), p.171.
[306] D. Ormerod, *Smith and Hogan, Criminal Law*, 13th edn (Oxford: OUP, 2011), p.140.
[307] *Brown* (1983) 79 Cr. App. R. 115.
[308] *R. v Boreman (Victor)* [2000] 1 All E.R. 307.

a continuing act operating until the wheel was removed. In our judgment, a distinction is to be drawn between acts which are complete—though results may continue to flow—and those acts which are continuing . . . For an assault to be committed, both the elements of *actus reus* and *mens rea* must be present at the same time . . . It is not necessary that *mens rea* should be present at the inception of the *actus reus*, it can be superimposed on an existing act. On the other hand, the subsequent inception of *mens rea* cannot convert an act which has been completed without *mens rea* into an assault . . .

There was an act constituting a battery which at its inception was not criminal because there was no element of intention, but which became criminal from the moment the intention was formed to produce the apprehension which was flowing from the continuing act. The fallacy of the appellant's argument is that it seeks to equate the facts of this case with such a case as where a motorist has accidentally run over a person and, that action having been completed, fails to assist the victim with the intent that the victim should suffer."

Appeal dismissed

In *Miller*[309] the defendant fell asleep holding a lit cigarette which started a fire. When he awoke he failed to do anything about the fire but simply moved to another room. The House of Lords adopted the "duty theory" that by creating the dangerous situation (starting the fire) the defendant became under a duty to act and so could be held responsible for the omission to act. Lord Diplock, however, conceded that the "continuous act" theory would provide an alternative route to liability.

R. v Miller [1983] A.C. 161 (House of Lords)

LORD DIPLOCK:

"[T]he conduct of the accused, throughout the period from immediately before the moment of ignition to the completion of the damage to the property by the fire, is relevant; so is his state of mind throughout that period . . .

[The *ratio decidendi* of the Court of Appeal] treats the whole course of conduct of the accused, from the moment at which he fell asleep and dropped the cigarette on to the mattress until the time the damage to the house by fire was complete, as a continuous act of the accused, and holds that it is sufficient to constitute the statutory offence of arson if at any stage in that course of conduct the state of mind of the accused, when he fails to try to prevent or minimise the damage which will result from his initial act, although it lies within his power to do so, is that of being reckless as to whether property belonging to another would be damaged."

The Government has published a Consultation Document containing a Draft Bill which would deal with the problem in *Miller* in the following manner.

Home Office, Violence: Reforming the Offences Against the Person Act 1861, Draft Offences Against the Person Bill 1998 cl.16:

"(1) Where it is an offence under this Act to be at fault in causing a result by an act and a person lacks the fault required when he does an act that may cause or does cause the result, he nevertheless commits the offence if—

   (a) being aware that he has done the act and that the result may occur or (as the case may be) has occurred and may continue, and

   (b) with the fault required, he fails to take reasonable steps to prevent the result occurring or continuing and it does occur or continue."

This is, as indicated in *Miller*, a better way of resolving the problem. Rather than resorting to fictions concerning a "continuing *actus reus*", the defendant is effectively treated as having created a danger-

---

[309] *Miller* [1983] A.C. 161. A fuller extract from this case is provided at pp.95–96.

ous situation. This generates a duty to take reasonable steps to prevent harm resulting from that danger.

C. Transferred Malice

There are two well-established and accepted rules of criminal law:

(a) If a defendant causes the actus reus by a different method than she intended she is nevertheless liable. Thus if the defendant intended to kill her victim by stabbing him but after the first stab the victim fell and struck his head on a kerb, the blow killing him, the defendant is clearly guilty of murder and cannot claim that the death is accidental. She intended to kill her victim; by her actions she has killed the victim; she has mens rea in relation to the actus reus; she is liable.

(b) If the defendant is mistaken as to the identity of her victim, she is nevertheless liable. Thus if the defendant shoots at a victim thinking he is Smith but in fact he is Jones and Jones dies, the defendant is clearly guilty of murder. Again she is committed the actus reus of murder; she had the requisite mens rea; she is liable.

However, what of the following scenarios?

(a) What if the defendant fires her gun at Smith, but misses and hits a passing stranger, Jones, and kills him? If the defendant was unaware of the existence of Jones, can she nevertheless be liable for murder?

(b) What if the defendant throws a brick at Smith, but misses and breaks a window near Smith? If the defendant was unaware of the existence of the window, can she be liable for criminal damage?

The response of English law to these two situations is clear:

(a) The defendant will be liable for murder. She intended to cause the actus reus of murder; she did cause the actus reus of murder. Her malice against Smith is transferred to Jones. The actus reus of murder is killing a human being. This she has done, intentionally; the identity of the victim is irrelevant. The leading illustration of this principle is *Latimer*[310] where the defendant swung his belt at a man with whom he was quarrelling but the belt hit the face of a woman to whom he was talking. Lord Coleridge CJ held

"if a person has a malicious intent towards one person, and in carrying into effect that malicious intent he injures another man, he is guilty of what the law considers malice against the person so injured."

(b) The defendant will *not* be liable for criminal damage because the doctrine of transferred malice does not apply where the actus reus (criminal damage) is different from the mens rea (of an

---

[310] *Latimer* (1886) 17 Q.B.D. 369. For a more recent illustration of transferred malice (and where the doctrine was expressly approved), see *Mitchell* (1983) 75 Cr. App. R. 293. In *Jones (Peter)* [1987] Crim. L.R. 701 the doctrine was applied in a provocation case.

offence against the person). Only if the actus reus intended and the actus reus caused are the same can the malice be transferred from the one to the other. In *Pembliton*,[311] where the facts were similar to the hypothetical example, the defendant was acquitted (on appeal) of malicious damage to a window.

The rationale of, and limits to, the doctrine of transferred malice were explored in the following case. In order to understand the decision it is necessary to appreciate two rules to be explored in Ch.8. First, a foetus cannot be the victim of a crime of violence. If the foetus dies in utero, it cannot be murder or manslaughter. If, however, the child is born alive but later dies from violence aimed at it while in utero, the assailant may be liable for manslaughter. Secondly, the mens rea of murder is satisfied by either an intention to kill or an intention to cause grievous bodily harm.

Attorney-General's Reference (No. 3 of 1994) [1998] A.C. 245 (House of Lords)

The appellant stabbed a pregnant woman intending to cause her grievous bodily harm. As a result her child was born prematurely and 121 days later died because of the prematurity of the birth. The trial judge directed the jury to acquit the appellant of both murder and manslaughter because the foetus, at the time of the attack, was not a live person. The doctrine of transferred malice was not applicable because "the intent to stab the mother (a live person) could not be transferred to the foetus (not a live person)". On a reference by the Attorney-General, the Court of Appeal allowed the appeal on the ground that the foetus is part of the mother so that an intention to cause grievous bodily harm to the mother is equivalent to the same intent directed towards the foetus. The appellant appealed to the House of Lords.

LORD MUSTILL:

"[His Lordship rejected the Court of Appeal's views on the ground that] the mother and the foetus were two distinct organisms living symbiotically, not a single organism with two aspects. The mother's leg was part of the mother; the foetus was not. . . .

I turn to . . . 'transferred malice' . . . One explanation [of this rule is that it is] founded on the notion of risk. The person who committed a crime took the chance that the outcome would be worse than he expected . . . but as a foundation of a modern doctrine of transferred malice broad enough to encompass the present case it seems to me quite unsupportable . . .

[T]here was [also] the idea of 'general malice', of an evil disposition existing in the general and manifesting itself in the particular, uniting the aim of the offender and the result which his deeds actually produced. According to this theory, there was no need to 'transfer' the wrongful intent from the intended to the actual victim; for since the offender was . . . 'an enemy to all mankind in general', the actual victim was the direct object of the offender's enmity. Plainly, this will no longer do, for the last vestiges of the idea disappeared with the abolition of the murder/felony doctrine.

What explanation is left: for explanation there must be, since the 'transferred malice' concept is agreed on both sides to be sound law today? . . . [His Lordship then discussed *Pembliton* and *Latimer*.] I find it hard to base a modern law of murder on these two cases . . . [although the answers they gave] would be the same today. But the harking back to a concept of general malice, which amounts to no more than this, that a wrongful act displays a malevolence which can be attached to any adverse consequence, has long been out of date. And to speak of a particular malice which is 'transferred' simply disguises the problem by idiomatic language. The defendant's malice is directed at one objective, and when after the event the court treats it as directed at another object it is not recognising a 'transfer' but creating a new malice which never existed before. As Dr Glanville Williams pointed out . . . the doctrine is 'rather an arbitrary exception to general principles'. Like many of its kind this is useful enough to yield rough justice . . .

---

[311]   *Pembliton* (1874) 12 Cox 607.

My Lords, the purpose of this enquiry has been to see whether the existing rules are based on principles sound enough to justify their extension to a case where the defendant acts without an intent to injure either the foetus or the child which it will become. In my opinion they are not. To give an affirmative answer requires a double 'transfer' of intent: first from the mother to the foetus and then from the foetus to the child as yet unborn . . . For me, this is too much . . . I am willing to follow old laws until they are overturned, but not to make a new law on a basis for which there is no principle.

Moreover, even on a narrower approach the argument breaks down. The effect of transferred malice, as I understand it, is that the intended victim and the actual victim are treated as if they were one, so that what was intended to happen to the first person (but did not happen) is added to what actually did happen to the second person (but was not intended to happen), with the result that what was intended and what happened are married to make a notionally intended and actually consummated crime. The cases are treated as if the actual victim had been the intended victim from the start. To make any sense of this process there must, as it seems to me, be some compatibility between the original intention and the actual occurrence, and this is, indeed, what one finds in the cases. There is no such compatibility here. The defendant intended to commit and did commit an immediate crime of violence to the mother. He committed no relevant violence to the foetus, which was not a person, either at the time or in the future, and intended no harm to the foetus or to the human person which it would become . . . I would not overstrain the idea of transferred malice by trying to make it fit the present case.

Accordingly, . . . the judge was right to direct an acquittal on the count of murder.

[His Lordship then went on to hold that the appellant could have been guilty of manslaughter for which recourse to transferred malice was not necessary.]"

Appeal allowed

This decision can be supported because what was intended (grievous bodily harm to the mother) was qualitatively different to what occurred (death of the child who, at the time of the attack, was not legally a person). As Lord Mustill put it: for the doctrine of transferred malice to apply, there must be "some compatibility between the original intention and the actual occurrence".

Jeremy Horder, Transferred Malice and the Remoteness of Unexpected Outcomes from Intentions" [2006] Crim. L.R. 383 at 388, 385, 386, 388–389:

"In my terms, 'compatibility' can be maintained by asking the jury to consider whether the way in which the death of an unanticipated victim resulted was too remote from the death that the defendant intended or anticipated, for a conviction for murder . . . to constitute a representative label . . .

Example 1: D fires a gun at V1 intending to kill V1. D misses, but the noise of the gun being fired startles a bystander, V2, who consequently dies of a heart attack.

. . . What should matter in these examples is not only that the actual victims were unintended victims, but also that they died in an unanticipated way. This double element of deviation from D's plan is what, in principle, may make the deaths too 'remote' from what D intended for murder to be a representative label . . .

[T]he remoteness principle comes into play only when (a) the victim was not the intended victim; and (b) the victim was not killed in the way intended. These two conditions were met in *Attorney-General's Reference (No.3 of 1994)*. Although they are necessary conditions, they should not, however, be treated as sufficient conditions for the purposes of the remoteness principle. Crucial in this regard is the evidence that *B deliberately stabbed M in the abdomen, knowing that she was pregnant*. If D is aware that something might go awry, and *a fortiori* of how it may go awry, when they try to put their intention into effect, that awareness is highly relevant to the question of how far, morally speaking, D can distance himself from the unintended outcome. Morally speaking, it makes the outcome less 'remote' from what B intended, and more compatible with it."

It has been suggested that the solution to the example given by Horder is that there should be no liability because D was not causally responsible for the bystander's death.[312] This response is not

---

[312]   A.P. Simester, J.R. Spencer, G.R. Sullivan and G.J. Virgo, *Criminal Law: Theory and Doctrine*, 5th edn (Oxford: Hart 2013), p.166, n233.

tenable. As seen earlier in this chapter, where one person assaults another and a third person dies of fright, the chain of causation can be established.[313]

Horder's suggested approach is somewhat impractical. It involves leaving too much to the jury who have to decide whether the death is too remote from what was intended or anticipated for murder to constitute a representative label. This is effectively telling the jury that "if it looks like murder, if it feels like murder, then it is murder".

Real life has provided a complex scenario in which to consider the boundaries of the doctrine of transferred malice, albeit not quite as complex as Horder's fictional one. In the case of *Gnango*[314] two gunmen were engaged in a shoot-out in a car-park when a passer-by got caught in the crossfire and was killed. The gunman who fired the fatal shot was, for unknown reasons, not prosecuted, and the question for the court was whether the doctrine of transferred malice could be used, in conjunction with the doctrine of joint enterprise liability,[315] to convict the second gunman of the murder of the passer-by. The Supreme Court held that the defendant was indeed guilty of murder on the basis that he had aided and abetted the other gunman in the attempted murder of himself, and his malice towards himself could therefore be transferred to the passer-by. This is surely stretching the doctrine too far.[316]

Is the doctrine of transferred malice justifiable? Lord Mustill's clear dislike of the doctrine of transferred malice in *Attorney-General's Reference (No.3 of 1994)* echoes the earlier views of Ashworth.

Andrew Ashworth, "Transferred Malice and Punishment for Unforeseen Consequences" in P.R. Glazebrook (ed.), Reshaping the Criminal Law (1978), pp.77, 84–89:

"The principle that a person should not be convicted of an offence unless he brought about the proscribed harm either intentionally or recklessly is frequently urged . . . The doctrine known as transferred malice seems to stand out as an exception to this principle, for it results in criminal liability for consequences which would in ordinary language be described as accidental. The doctrine applies 'when an injury intended for one falls on another by accident.' . . .

But if the indictment charges D with wounding P with intent to do grievous bodily harm to P, contrary to section 18 of the Offences Against the Person Act 1861, is it not an affront to common sense to convict him in the knowledge that his intent was to harm O and not P?[317] . . . The apparent illogicality can of course be ignored in the belief that transferred malice represents a higher principle of criminal liability which must be applied even where the particular words of a statute do not sit happily with it . . .

What, if anything, would be lost if the doctrine were abolished here? Does our criminal law offer any acceptable alternative methods of dealing with these cases? There are two obvious possibilities—liability for the crime attempted (thus ignoring the accidental result), and liability for the actual result based on recklessness—and these will be examined in turn . . .

A conviction for attempt is possible in virtually all cases which fall within the doctrine of transferred liability . . . In *Latimer*, for example, D could quite simply have been convicted of the attempted unlawful wounding of O; and likewise in *Pembliton* there were strong grounds for convicting D of attempted unlawful wounding of persons in the crowd . . .

In many of the cases to which transferred malice applies, the harm to P was quite unforeseen. But in some of them D could be held liable for harm to P without invoking transferred malice—on the basis that, in attempting to harm O, he was reckless as to harming P . . . It is often said that in *Pembliton* the jury should have found D reckless as to damaging the window, and that this would have spared counsel and the courts much fruitless argument . . .

---

[313]   *Towers* (1874) 12 Cox C.C. 530.
[314]   *Gnango* [2012] [2011] UKSC 59.
[315]   See Ch.6 below.
[316]   See R. Buxton, "Being an accessory to one's own murder" [2012] Crim. L.R. 275–281.
[317]   This point was accepted in *Slimmings* [1999] Crim. L.R. 69. The indictment would need to specify that D caused grievous bodily harm to P with intent to cause grievous bodily harm to O.

The doctrine could, then, be abolished without material loss to criminal justice; and it is desirable that it should be. For, quite apart from any problems over the consistency of the doctrine with general principles of criminal liability, it attributes significance to matters of chance and results in a mischaracterisation of D's criminality which could simply and effectively be avoided by charging an attempt. What, then, are the objections to using the law of attempts?

The first is that it would be wrong for a person who intended to cause harm of a certain kind and did cause such a harm to escape with a lighter sentence merely because he was charged with an attempt . . .

A second objection . . . is that even if the punishment were the same, it is more appropriate to convict of the completed crime in the 'transferred malice' situation. Where D set out to cause harm of a certain kind and did cause harm of that kind, it seems empty and insufficient to convict him of a mere attempt. He has actually caused a loss to the community of the kind he intended to cause, and that fact should be recorded. Once again, however, this reasoning leans too heavily on results which may be entirely a matter of chance. In a system based on subjective liability, the legal label attached to D's offence should generally reflect his intentional act and not the chance result."

This hostility to the doctrine of transferred malice seems misplaced. Where the defendant intends to kill another human being and does kill another human being, albeit a different one from the one intended, is it fair to describe that result as a "matter of chance", exempting the defendant from liability for murder? Is this mistake as to the identity of the victim relevant in any *material* way?[318] Murder involves the intentional killing of a human being. If the defendant tries to kill Smith and instead kills Jones, the difference in result can hardly be sufficient to avoid the conclusion that the defendant intentionally killed a human being and deserves the label "murderer". Further, if the defendant detonates a bomb in a crowded pub, intentionally killing 20 strangers, he will be liable for their murder; the fact that their identity is unknown to him is irrelevant. Similarly, if he burns down a house intending to kill V1 but, unknown to him, V2 is also in the house and dies, he will be liable for the murder of both provided the indictment is drafted in a suitable manner. Where it is not only a different victim, but that victim is killed in a different way (as in the example given by Horder), the only relevant moral issue is whether the defendant can still be held to have caused death. The Law Commission and the Draft Offences Against the Person Bill 1998 have accepted the doctrine of transferred malice in its present form and have proposed a statutory provision to that effect.[319]

D. Mistake

A defendant may make many different types of mistake. Sometimes she will think she is committing no crime at all. At other times she will think that she is committing a different crime from the one that transpires. What is the law's response to such pleas?

In order for a mistake to be considered as a possible exculpatory factor, it must relate in a *relevant* way to the elements of the crime. If a driver makes a mistake and puts a foot on the accelerator thinking that he is putting it on the brake and so kills a pedestrian, this is not a relevant mistake as to an element of the crime of causing death by dangerous driving.[320] Indeed, instead of being an exculpatory factor, such a mistake is important evidence in establishing the critical element required for the crime, namely that the driving was "dangerous".

A mistake might have relevance to an exemption from liability in the following three situations:

[318] D. Stroud, *Mens Rea* (1914), p.184; G. Williams, "Convictions and Fair Labelling" [1983] C.L.J. 85 at 86–88.
[319] Draft Criminal Law Bill 1993 cl.32 (Law Com. No.218, 1993); Draft Offences against the Person Bill 1998 cl.17.
[320] *Attorney-General's Reference (No.4 of 2000)* [2001] Crim. L.R. 578.

(1) mistake as to one of the elements of the actus reus;

(2) mistake as to a defence element; or

(3) mistake as to law.

As we shall see, it is difficult to distinguish rigidly between these three, but such a classification is useful for purposes of exposition.

1. Mistake as to element of actus reus

For most crimes the defendant must have mens rea in relation to the actus reus. This means that she must have mens rea in relation to every element of the actus reus—often referred to as the "definitional elements". However, the mistake must not simply be one as to *some quality* of the definitional element. It must be as to the existence of the definitional element. For example, the actus reus of criminal damage is *destroying or damaging any property belonging to another*.[321] If the defendant thinks the property belongs to Smith when in fact it belongs to Jones, her mistake is irrelevant because she knows that the property belongs to another. On the other hand, if the defendant thinks the property belongs to herself this mistake now negates her mens rea. She does not have mens rea in relation to a definitional element and would thus escape liability.[322]

Section 170(2) of the Customs and Excise Management Act 1979 makes it an offence to be knowingly concerned in the fraudulent evasion of the prohibition on the importation of prohibited goods. In *Ellis*[323] the defendants believed they were importing prohibited pornographic goods but in fact it was prohibited drugs. Their convictions were upheld. They had mens rea in relation to the definitional element "prohibited goods". The precise nature and quality of such prohibited goods was of no more relevance than whether the property belonged to Smith or Jones in the earlier example.[324] In *Taaffe*[325] the defendant was charged with this offence when he imported cannabis resin into the country. He believed the substance was currency and that doing this was illegal, which it was not. The House of Lords held that there would be no liability in these circumstances. His mistake of fact meant he believed he was importing goods which were not prohibited.[326]

Where the mistake is as to the existence of a definitional element, the position used to be that the defendant would only escape liability if the mistake was a reasonable one. In *Tolson*[327] the defendant's husband deserted her and sailed for America. Inquiries revealed that the ship had been sunk and so, believing herself to be a widow, five years later she went through a marriage ceremony with another man. Later that year her husband returned from America and the defendant was charged with bigamy. Her conviction was quashed, on the basis that she had believed "in good faith and on reasonable grounds" that her husband was dead.

---

[321] Criminal Damage Act 1971 s.1(1).
[322] *Smith (David)* [1974] Q.B. 354.
[323] *R. v Ellis (Ian)* [1987] Crim. L.R. 44.
[324] J. Smith has pointed out that this decision might have been unexceptional when the importation of prohibited drugs and pornographic material were both punishable with two years' imprisonment—but it becomes questionable now that the penalties in relation to drugs have been increased ([1987] Crim. L.R. 46). In *Leeson* [2001] 1 Cr. App. R. 233 the defendant was in possession of cocaine (a Class A drug) but believed it was an amphetamine (a Class B drug). The court concluded that the relevance of the different classes of drugs related only to sentencing.
[325] *R. v Taaffe (Paul Desmond)* [1984] A.C. 539.
[326] See *R. v Forbes (Giles)* [2002] 2 A.C. 512 where the *"Taaffe* defence" was approved—but on the facts the jury had rejected the defence.
[327] *Tolson* (1889) 23 Q.B. 168.

However, the House of Lords in the following case effected a radical change of direction by holding that in certain circumstances an honest mistake would exempt a defendant from criminal liability. It was no longer necessary that the mistake be reasonable.

DPP v Morgan [1976] A.C. 182 (House of Lords)

A husband invited a number of companions to have sexual intercourse with his wife, apparently in order to be avenged for her real or imagined infidelity. He suggested that she might put up a struggle but that they were not to take it seriously; it was her way of increasing her sexual satisfaction. The men, so urged, had intercourse in turn without her consent. They were tried and convicted of rape; the husband was convicted of aiding and abetting rape. The judge directed the jury that the men were guilty of rape even if they in fact believed that Mrs Morgan consented if such belief was not based on reasonable grounds.

The question certified to the House of Lords was whether the defendants' belief in her consent had to be based on reasonable grounds.

LORD CROSS:

"In fact, however, I can see no objection to the inclusion of the element of reasonableness in what I may call a 'Tolson' case. If the words defining an offence provide either expressly or impliedly that a man is not to be guilty of it if he believes something to be true, then he cannot be found guilty if the jury think that he may have believed it to be true, however inadequate were his reasons for doing so. But, if the definition of the offence is on the face of it 'absolute' and the defendant is seeking to escape his prima facie liability by a defence of mistaken belief, I can see no hardship to him in requiring the mistake—if it is to afford him a defence—to be based on reasonable grounds. As Lord Diplock said in *Sweet v Parsley* [1970] A.C. 132, there is nothing unreasonable in the law requiring a citizen to take reasonable care to ascertain the facts relevant to his avoiding doing a prohibited act. To have intercourse with a woman who is not your wife is, even today, not generally considered to be a course of conduct which the law ought positively to encourage and it can be argued with force that it is only fair to the woman and not in the least unfair to the man that he should be under a duty to take reasonable care to ascertain that she is consenting to the intercourse and be at the risk of prosecution if he fails to take such care. So if the Sexual Offences Act 1956 had made it an offence to have intercourse with a woman who was not consenting to it, so that the defendant could only escape liability by the application of the 'Tolson' principle, I would not have thought the law unjust.

But, as I have said, section 1 of the Act of 1956, does not say that a man who has sexual intercourse with a woman who does not consent to it commits an offence; it says that a man who rapes a woman commits an offence. Rape is not a word in the use of which lawyers have a monopoly and the question to be answered in this case, as I see it, is whether according to the ordinary use of the English language a man can be said to have committed rape if he believed that the woman was consenting to the intercourse and would not have attempted to have it but for his belief, whatever his grounds for so believing. I do not think that he can. Rape, to my mind imports at least indifference as to the woman's consent. I think, moreover, that in this connection the ordinary man would distinguish between rape and bigamy. To the question whether a man who goes through a ceremony of marriage with a woman believing his wife to be dead, though she is not, commits bigamy, I think that he would reply 'Yes, —but I suppose that the law contains an escape clause for bigamists who are not really to blame.' On the other hand, to the question whether a man, who has intercourse with a woman believing on inadequate grounds that she is consenting to it, though she is not, commits rape, I think that he would reply 'No. If he was grossly careless then he may deserve to be punished but not for rape.' That being my view as to the meaning of the word 'rape' in ordinary parlance, I next ask myself whether the law gives it a different meaning. There is very little English authority on the point but what there is . . . accords with what I take to be the proper meaning of the word . . . For these reasons, I think that the summing up contained a misdirection.

The question which then arises as to the application of the proviso [to section 2(1) of the Criminal Appeal Act 1968] is far easier of solution . . . The jury obviously considered that the appellant's evidence as to the part played by Mrs Morgan was a pack of lies and one must assume that any other jury would take the same view as to the relative culpability of the parties . . . So I would apply the proviso and dismiss the appeal."

LORD HAILSHAM:

"No doubt it would be possible, by statute, to devise a law by which intercourse, voluntarily entered into, was an absolute offence subject to a 'defence' of belief whether honest or honest and reasonable, of which the 'evidential' burden is primarily on the defence and the 'probative' burden on the prosecution. But in my opinion such is not the crime of rape as it has hitherto been understood. The prohibited act in rape is to have intercourse without the victim's consent. The minimum *mens rea* or guilty mind in most common law offences, including rape, is the intention to do the prohibited act . . .

The only qualification I would make . . . is the refinement . . . that if the intention of the accused is to have intercourse nolens volens, that is recklessly and not caring whether the victim be a consenting party or not, that is equivalent on ordinary principles to an intent to do the prohibited act without the consent of the victim . . .

Once one has accepted, what seems to me abundantly clear, that the prohibited act in rape is non-consensual sexual intercourse, and that the guilty state of mind is an intention to commit it, it seems to me to follow as a matter of inexorable logic that there is no room either for a 'defence' of honest belief or mistake, or of a defence of honest and reasonable belief or mistake. Either the prosecution proves that the accused had the requisite intent, or it does not. In the former case it succeeds, and in the latter if fails. Since honest belief clearly negatives intent, the reasonableness or otherwise of that belief can only be evidence for or against the view that the belief and therefore the intent was actually held . . . Any other view, as for insertion of the word 'reasonable' can only have the effect of saying that a man intends something which he does not . . .

I am content to rest my view of the instant case on the crime of rape by saying that it is my opinion that the prohibited act is and always has been intercourse without consent of the victim and the mental element is and always has been the intention to commit that act, or the equivalent intention of having intercourse willy-nilly not caring whether the victim consents or no [*sic*]. A failure to prove this involves an acquittal because the intent, an essential ingredient, is lacking. It matters not why it is lacking if only it is not there, and in particular it matters not that the intention is lacking only because of a belief not based on reasonable grounds . . .

For the above reasons I would answer the question certified in the negative, but would apply the proviso to the Criminal Appeal Act on the ground that no miscarriage of justice has or conceivably could have occurred."

LORD SIMON:

"It remains to consider why the law requires, in such circumstances, that the belief in a state of affairs whereby the *actus* would not be *reus* must be held on reasonable grounds . . .

. . . The policy of the law in this regard could well derive from its concern to hold a fair balance between victim and accused. It would hardly seem just to fob off a victim of a savage assault with such comfort as he could derive from knowing that his injury was caused by a belief, however absurd, that he was about to attack the accused. A respectable woman who has been ravished would hardly feel that she was vindicated by being told that her assailant must go unpunished because he believed, quite unreasonably, that she was consenting to sexual intercourse with him . . .

I would therefore answer the question certified for your Lordships' consideration, Yes. But, even did I consider that it should be answered No, I would, for the reasons given by my noble and learned friends, think this a suitable case to apply the proviso."

[Lord Fraser held that the defendant's belief in the woman's consent did not have to be based on reasonable grounds; Lord Edmund-Davies, however, felt that only the legislature could effect such a reform in the law.]

Appeal dismissed

B (A Minor) v DPP [2000] A.C. 428 (House of Lords)

The defendant, a 15-year-old boy, invited a 13-year-old girl to perform oral sex with him on a bus. He was charged with the offence of inciting a girl under the age of 14 to commit an act of gross indecency, contrary to s.1(1) of the Indecency with Children Act 1960 (an offence now repealed by the Sexual Offences Act 2003). He honestly believed that she was over 14 years of age.

LORD NICHOLLS OF BIRKENHEAD:

"The 'reasonable belief' school of thought held unchallenged sway for many years. But over the last quarter of a century there have been several important cases where a defence of honest but mistaken belief was raised. In deciding these cases the courts have placed new, or renewed, emphasis on the subjective nature of the mental element in criminal offences. The courts have rejected the reasonable belief approach and preferred the honest belief approach. When mens rea is ousted by a mistaken belief, it is as well ousted by an unreasonable belief as by a reasonable belief . . . [I]t is the defendant's belief, not the grounds on which it is based, which goes to negative the intent . . .

Considered as a matter of principle, the honest belief approach must be preferable. By definition the mental element in a crime is concerned with a subjective state of mind, such as intent or belief. To the extent that an overriding objective limit ('on reasonable grounds') is introduced, the subjective element is displaced. To that extent a person who lacks the necessary intent or belief may nevertheless commit the offence. When that occurs the defendant's 'fault' lies exclusively in falling short of an objective standard. His crime lies in his negligence. A statute may so provide expressly or by necessary implication. But this can have no place in a common law principle, of general application, which is concerned with the need for a mental element as an essential ingredient of a criminal offence . . .

There has been a general shift from objectivism to subjectivism in this branch of the law. It is now settled as a matter of general principle that mistake, whether reasonable or not, is a defence where it prevents the defendant from having the *mens rea* which the law requires for the crime with which he is charged. It would be in disharmony with this development now to rule that in respect of a defence under subsection 1(1) of the Act of 1960 the belief must be based on reasonable grounds."

Appeal allowed

One year later the House of Lords reaffirmed this approach in *R. v K,*[328] an appeal involving indecent assault on a girl under the age of 16 contrary to s.14(1) of the Sexual Offences Act 1956. A 26-year-old man committed sexual acts with a consenting 14-year-old girl believing she was aged 16 or over. Under s.14(2), a girl under the age of 16 could not give valid consent for the purposes of this offence. It was held that the actus reus of this offence involved "an indecent act done . . . with or without the consent of the other person being a person under the age of 16 years" and that, as regards mens rea, the prosecution "must be prepared to prove that the defendant did not have an honest belief that the other person was in fact consenting and not under 16 years of age". Lord Bingham did, however, stress that while the defendant's belief need only be honest and genuine and need not be reasonable, "the more unreasonable the belief, the less likely it is to be accepted as genuine".

These decisions on mistake in relation to rape and the other sexual offences have now been overruled by the Sexual Offences Act 2003. Section 1(1) provides that the mens rea of rape is satisfied if the defendant does not reasonably believe that the other is consenting. Sections 9 to 12 of this Act create various "child sex offences". For those offences where the age of 16 is the material age there is provision that the belief that the child is 16 or over must be reasonable.

However, in relation to other offences where statute does not specifically insist on mistakes being reasonable in order to exculpate defendants, the principle established by *Morgan* and its progeny continues to apply. The appropriateness of this approach is considered later in this section but, for now, two points need to be noted.

First, it is incorrect to talk of a "defence of mistake". It is not a defence: the defendant does not have to prove anything. The prosecution has to prove mens rea. If there is a mistake as to an actus reus element, the prosecution will have failed to prove its case. The principle is clear. A mistake as to a definitional element can negate mens rea; it is irrelevant whether the mistake is reasonable or not; reasonableness is only relevant as a matter of evidence in determining whether a belief was in fact honestly held.

---

[328]   *R. v K* [2002] 1 A.C. 462.

Secondly, given this clear principle, what is the status today of *Tolson* which required a mistake, for the crime of bigamy, to be reasonable? This case was approved in *Morgan* with Lord Cross stating that *Tolson* was dealing with a prima facie strict liability offence and in such cases any "defence of mistaken belief" needed to be reasonable. One view is that the Tolson principle still operates for bigamy because bigamy is a crime of negligence.[329] If the defendant makes an unreasonable mistake, they are negligent. However, *Tolson* was disapproved in *B (A Minor) v DPP*. Lord Nicholls, in addition to the passages extracted above, cited *Sweet v Parsley* on this point and concluded that this view was "out of step with this recent line of authority" and that the dicta from those cases "must in future be read as though the reference to reasonable grounds were omitted". It thus appears that *Tolson* is no longer good authority.

2. Mistake as to a defence element

There is another type of mistake a defendant can make. He might have made a mistake in thinking he was entitled to a defence. For example, a defendant might admit that he intentionally killed another but claim that he thought that he was being attacked and was therefore defending himself, when, in reality, he had made a mistake and was not under attack.[330]

Originally, and even for a few years after *Morgan*, the courts insisted that only *reasonable* mistakes as to defence elements would suffice to exempt a person from liability.[331] However, in relation to mistakes affecting self-defence the courts soon abandoned the requirement that the mistake be reasonable. Whether this subjectivist approach is compatible with art.2 of the European Convention on Human Rights will be considered later.[332]

R. v Williams (Gladstone) (1984) 78 Cr. App. R. 276 (Court of Appeal, Criminal Division)

The appellant saw a man, Mason, dragging a youth along a street and striking him; the youth was calling for help. Mason claimed he was a police officer and was arresting the youth for mugging a lady. When he was unable to produce a warrant card, a struggle ensued during which the appellant punched Mason, who sustained injuries to his face. The appellant, who was charged with assault occasioning actual bodily harm, claimed that he honestly believed Mason was unlawfully assaulting the youth and that he was trying to rescue the youth. (One is entitled to use reasonable force to prevent an unlawful assault on another.) However, the appellant had made a mistake. While Mason was not a police officer, he had nevertheless seen the youth seize the woman's handbag and was acting lawfully in restraining the youth with a view to taking him to a police station. At his trial, the jury were directed that the appellant's mistake would only be relevant if it were a reasonable one. He was convicted and appealed on the ground of a misdirection.

LANE LCJ:

"'Assault'. . . is an act by which the defendant, intentionally or recklessly, applies unlawful force to the complainant. There are circumstances in which force may be applied to another lawfully. Taking a few examples: first, where the victim consents, as in lawful sports, the application of force to another will, generally speaking, not be

---

[329] Ormerod, *Smith and Hogan, Criminal Law*, 13th edn (2011), p.332.
[330] There is a further type of mistake that a defendant can make with regard to self-defence. He might mistakenly believe that it is necessary to use more force than is actually necessary. See pp.338–340
[331] *Albert v Lavin* [1982] A.C. 546.
[332] At pp.332–333, 336.

unlawful. Secondly, where the defendant is acting in self-defence: the exercise of any necessary and reasonable force to protect himself from unlawful violence is not unlawful. Thirdly, by virtue of section 3 of the Criminal Law Act 1967, a person may use such force as is reasonable in the circumstances in the prevention of crime or in effecting or assisting in the lawful arrest of an offender or suspected offender or persons unlawfully at large. In each of those cases the defendant will be guilty if the jury are sure that first of all he applied force to the person of another, and secondly that he had the necessary mental element to constitute guilt.

The mental element necessary to constitute guilt is the intent to apply unlawful force to the victim. We do not believe that the mental element can be substantiated by simply showing an intent to apply force and no more.

What then is the situation if the defendant is labouring under a mistake of fact as to the circumstances? What if he believes, but believes mistakenly, that the victim is consenting, or that it is necessary to defend himself, or that a crime is being committed which he intends to prevent? He must then be judged against the mistaken facts as he believes them to be. If judged against those facts or circumstances the prosecution fail to establish his guilt, then he is entitled to be acquitted.

The next question is, does it make any difference if the mistake of the defendant was one which, viewed objectively by a reasonable onlooker, was an unreasonable mistake? . . . The reasonableness or unreasonableness of the defendant's belief is material to the question of whether the belief was held by the defendant at all. If the belief was in fact held, its unreasonableness, so far as guilt or innocence is concerned, is neither here nor there. It is irrelevant. Were it otherwise, the defendant would be convicted because he was negligent in failing to recognise that the victim was not consenting or that a crime was not being committed and so on. In other words the jury should be directed first of all that the prosecution have the burden or duty of proving the unlawfulness of the defendant's actions; secondly, if the defendant may have been labouring under a mistake as to the facts, he must be judged according to his mistaken views of the facts; thirdly, that is so whether the mistake was, on an objective view, a reasonable mistake or not . . .

We have read the recommendations of the Criminal Law Revision Committee, Part IX, paragraph 72(a), in which the following passage appears:

'The common law defence of self-defence should be replaced by a statutory defence providing that a person may use such force as is reasonable in the circumstances as he believes them to be in the defence of himself or any other person.'

In the view of this Court that represents the law as expressed in *Morgan*."

Appeal allowed

Beckford v R. [1988] A.C. 130 (Privy Council)

The appellant was a police officer who was a member of an armed posse which chased, shot and killed a fleeing man. The appellant claimed he had killed in self-defence. The trial judge directed the jury that the belief that life was in danger had to be a reasonable belief. The Court of Appeal of Jamaica confirmed this. The appellant appealed to the Privy Council.

LORD GRIFFITHS:

"There can be no doubt that prior to the decision of the House of Lords in *R. v Morgan* the whole weight of authority supported the view that it was an essential element of self-defence not only that the accused believed that he was being attacked or in imminent danger of being attacked but also that such belief was based on reasonable grounds . . .

The question then is whether the present Lord Chief Justice, Lord Lane, in *R. v Williams (Gladstone)*, was right to depart from the law as declared by his predecessors in the light of the decision of the House of Lords in *R. v Morgan* . . .

It is because it is an essential element of all crimes of violence that the violence or the threat of violence should be unlawful that self-defence, if raised as an issue in a criminal trial, must be disproved by the prosecution. If the prosecution fail to do so the accused is entitled to be acquitted because the prosecution will have failed to prove an essential element of the crime namely that the violence used by the accused was unlawful.

If then a genuine belief, albeit without reasonable grounds, is a defence to rape because it negatives the necessary intention, so also must a genuine belief in facts which if true would justify self-defence be a defence to a crime of personal violence because the belief negatives the intent to act unlawfully . . .

There may be a fear that the abandonment of the objective standard demanded by the existence of reasonable grounds for belief will result in the success of too many spurious claims of self-defence. The English experience has not shown this to be the case. The Judicial Studies Board with the approval of the Lord Chief Justice has produced a model direction on self-defence which is now widely used by judges when summing up to juries. The direction contains the following guidance:

'Whether the plea is self-defence or defence of another, if the defendant may have been labouring under a mistake as to the facts, he must be judged according to his mistaken belief of the facts: that is so whether the mistake was, on an objective view, a reasonable mistake or not.'"

Appeal allowed

In *Faraj*[333] the defendant restrained a victim mistakenly thinking he was a burglar. On a charge of false imprisonment it was held that he was entitled to a defence of defence of property if he honestly believed the victim was a burglar, irrespective of the reasonableness of this belief.

These cases clearly establish that, in order to afford a defence, a mistake in relation to the need to resort to self-defence (or defence of property) need only be honest; it need not be a reasonable mistake. This has now been confirmed by s.76(3) of the Criminal Justice and Immigration Act 2008 which provides that whether force can be used is to be decided "by reference to the circumstances as D believed them to be".

This subjective approach, however, has not been adopted with other defences. In *Graham*[334] it was held that the defence of duress would only be available to one who reasonably believed that they were being subjected to the requisite threats for a defence of duress. This approach was approved by the House of Lords in *Howe*[335] and *Hasan*.[336] The same test was applied in *Martin*[337] to "duress of circumstances".[338] In *O'Grady*[339] it was held that a person who made a drunken mistake in thinking he was being attacked was not entitled to a defence. In *Fotheringham*[340] the defendant made a drunken mistake when having non-consensual intercourse with his 14-year-old babysitter: he thought it was his wife. It was held that such a drunken mistake was no defence. While it was held in both these cases that drunken mistakes were no defence, if, in fact, despite the defendant's drunkenness, the mistake made was a perfectly reasonable mistake that an ordinary sober person would have made, it should be a defence. Section 76(5) of the Criminal Justice and Immigration Act 2008 now provides that a defendant pleading self-defence cannot rely on "any mistaken belief attributable to intoxication". If the mistake was a reasonable one, it would presumably not be *attributable* to the intoxication; the intoxication would be coincidental; the same mistake would probably have been made if he had been sober. The Law Commission endorses this approach: where the defendant is voluntarily intoxicated, "D's actual belief is to be taken into account only if D would have held the same belief if not intoxicated".[341]

How can this divergence of approach, between mistakes as to consent and self-defence on the one hand, and duress, duress of circumstances and drunkenness on the other hand, be explained?

---

[333] *R. v Faraj (Shwan)* [2007] EWCA Crim 1033.
[334] *Graham* [1982] 1 W.L.R. 294.
[335] *R. v Howe (Michael Anthony)* [1987] A.C. 417.
[336] *R. v Hasan (Aytach)* [2005] 2 A.C. 467.
[337] *R. v Martin (Colin)* [1989] 1 All E.R. 652.
[338] However, in *R. v Martin (David Paul)* [2000] 2 Cr. App. R. 42 it was held that the *Williams (Gladstone)* principle did apply to duress. It will be argued (in Ch.4) that this decision is wrong and ought not to be followed.
[339] *O'Grady* [1987] Q.B. 995. See also *Hatton* [2006] Crim. L.R. 353.
[340] *R. v Fotheringham (William Bruce)* (1989) 88 Cr. App. R. 206 at 416.
[341] Law Commission Paper No.314, *Intoxication and Criminal Liability* (2009), Draft Criminal Law (Intoxication) Bill 2009 cl.5(3) (b).

In *Williams (Gladstone)* and *Beckford* the court drew a distinction between mistakes which affect definitional elements (where the mistake need only be genuine) and mistakes as to a defence element (where the mistake must be reasonable). According to these cases it is part of the definitional elements that the defendant be acting "unlawfully"; self-defensive action renders conduct lawful and so if a defendant has made a mistake as to the need for self-defensive action, there is no mens rea in relation to that definitional element of "unlawfulness".

Glanville Williams, Textbook of Criminal Law, 2nd edn (1983), p.138:

"No other rule of the substantive criminal law distinguishes between the definitional and defence elements of a crime, and it is a distinction that is impossible to draw satisfactorily. (Our notion of what issue is a 'defence,' in so far as we have any clear notion, seems to depend largely on whether we think that the defendant should be required to take the initiative in introducing it, *i.e.* on whether he should bear an evidential burden in respect of it. But there is no reason why the distribution of evidential burdens should affect the rules of liability.) A rule creating a *defence* merely supplies additional details of the scope of the *offence*. To regard the offence as subsisting independently of its limitations and qualifications is unrealistic. The defence is a negative condition of the offence, and is therefore an integral part of it. What we regard as part of the offence and what as part of a defence depends only on traditional habits of thought or accidents of legal drafting; it should have no bearing on the important question of criminal liability. For example, it is purely a matter of convenient drafting whether a statute says, on the one hand, that damaging the property of another without his consent is a crime, or, on the other hand, that damaging the property of another is a crime but that his consent is a defence. In fact we regard the non-consent of the owner as a definitional element, but there is no particular reason why this should be so, and the question of guilt or innocence should not depend on it."

It is difficult to determine on what basis an offence or a defence requirement should be classified as either a definitional or a defence element.[342] For example, if a defendant honestly believes that he is being subjected to duress, could one not say that he lacks mens rea in relation to the definitional element of "unlawfulness"? If so, why did *Graham* and *Martin* insist that such mistakes be reasonable?

Another possible explanation is that mistakes as to justificatory defences need only be honest but that mistakes as to excusatory defences must be reasonable. Consent and self-defence are both justificatory defences. Justificatory conduct is in effect "approved of"—or, at least, tolerated as acceptable conduct. Thus a person acting in self-defence is effectively doing "right"; they are doing what we expect them to do; they are restricting unprovoked aggression; in effect, they are acting lawfully. A person who honestly thinks that they are acting in a justified and thus lawful manner are not blameworthy and there is no point punishing them. Accordingly, an honest mistaken belief will suffice to exempt from criminal liability.

On the other hand, duress and intoxication raise excusatory defences. When conduct is excused, it remains wrong and unacceptable (i.e. unlawful) but because the defendant has an excuse, we punish them less or not at all. If, thinking he is being subjected to duress a defendant robs a bank, this is "wrong and disapproved of" conduct—but we might wish to exempt the defendant from liability if they had been subjected to terrible threats. But because the conduct remains wrong we will only excuse those who have a plausible excuse—and a plausible excuse is a reasonable one. The same analysis is true of drunken mistakes. The defendant has acted unlawfully and will only be afforded an excuse if the mistake was one that a sober, reasonable person would have made.

---

[342] See R.H.S. Tur, "Subjectivism and Objectivism: Towards Synthesis", in S. Shute, J. Gardner and J. Horder, *Action and Value in Criminal Law* (Oxford: OUP, 1993), p.213 at pp.217–222 for a view that this process of reclassifying defence elements as definitional elements has been largely a matter of "dry legal technique" flowing from a commitment to subjectivism with the consequence that pressing moral and public concerns have been overlooked.

This approach presupposes that there is a water-tight distinction between justification and excuse. As will be seen in Ch.4, where these defences are explored more fully, this is not always the case.[343] For example, it is uncertain how "duress of circumstances" should be classified. The approach in *Martin*[344] suggests it is an excuse while in *Martin (D.P.)*[345] it was held that the defence was analogous to self-defence, which is a justificatory defence.

Nevertheless, to summarise, the position at the moment would seem to be that with regard to mistakes as to definitional elements (which include mistakes as to justificatory defences) an honest mistake will exempt a defendant from criminal liability. However, with regard to mistakes as to excusatory defences, only a reasonable mistake will entitle a defendant to such exemption.

This whole approach had been condemned by the Law Commission who in the Draft Criminal Code Bill 1989 proposed that "a person who acts in the belief that a circumstance exists has any defence that he would have if the circumstance existed".[346]

3. Evaluation of the law

How are we to evaluate the law's response to the problem of mistake? Are we to approve of *Morgan* and its progeny? Are the present distinctions drawn by the law based upon sound policy considerations or should we adopt the Law Commission's proposal of allowing an honest mistake to exculpate in all cases?

D. Cowley, "The Retreat from Morgan" [1982] Crim. L.R. 198 at 206–208:

"One theory suggests that whether the objective test of mistake applies depends upon where in respect of the relevant issue the evidential burden lies, and that where an evidential burden lies on the accused to show that he believed in facts inconsistent with the offence,

'a bald assertion of belief for which the accused can indicate no reasonable ground is evidence of insufficient substance to raise any issue requiring the jury's consideration' (*per* Lord Simon in *Morgan*).

It is respectfully submitted that this theory is unsound and that there is no connection between the incidence of the evidential burden and the question whether the mistake must be reasonable, the main reason being that an evidential burden on the defendant merely requires him to give some *reasonable evidence of belief* as opposed to *evidence of reasonable belief*. It may well be the case that his assertion of belief is not 'bald' but is fully corroborated by independent evidence leading the jury to accept that the unreasonable belief was in fact held and, in such circumstances, the defendant will have discharged the burden cast upon him.

An alternative reason for requiring the belief to be reasonable put forward by Lord Simon is the fact that the victim must be 'vindicated' by punishing *e.g.* an assailant who has made an unreasonable mistake: 'the policy of the law in this regard could well derive from its concern to hold a fair balance between the victim and the accused. It would hardly seem just to fob off a victim of a savage assault with such comfort as he could derive from knowing that his inquiry was caused by a belief, however absurd, that he was about to attack the accused. One cannot but agree with Professor Williams' opinion ((1975) New L.J. p.968) that this is not only a somewhat old-fashioned view of the criminal law but also fails to explain who is vindicated when a bigamist is punished. The lawful spouse, in particular, may not care a jot about the bigamy.

Perhaps . . . [an] insistence on there being reasonable grounds for mistaken belief can, rather, be put down to a simple lack of confidence in the jury as the final arbiter of fact. If so, such judicial mistrust is very reminiscent of the somewhat misconceived and blinkered popular reaction to the decision in *Morgan*. What was apparently

---

[343]   For a criticism of our suggested approach, see A.P. Simester, J.R. Spencer, G.R. Sullivan and G.J. Virgo, *Criminal Law: Theory and Doctrine*, 5th edn (Oxford: Hart 2013), p.619.

[344]   Above, fn.337.

[345]   *Martin* [2000] 2 Cr. App. R. 42.

[346]   Law Commission Paper No.177 cl.41(1).

overlooked by those whose passions were aroused by *Morgan's* effect on the law of rape, and those whose railing against the case implied a serious lack of faith in the tribunal of fact in criminal cases, was not only the total lack of gullibility of that particular jury who decided that the defendants' tale as to Mrs Morgan's consent to their intercourse with her was a 'pack of lies', but also the ultimate result of the case—the dismissal of the defendants' appeals against conviction. There is little evidence there to support the often heard claim that a requirement of mere honest belief facilitates bogus defences, and before seeking to impose any kind of restriction upon the freedom of the jury to determine issues of fact the judiciary might reflect upon the oft-quoted words of Dixon J. that a 'lack of confidence in the ability of a tribunal correctly to estimate evidence of states of mind and the like can never be sufficient ground for excluding from inquiry the most fundamental element in a rational and humane criminal code' *Thomas v R*. (1937) 59 C.L.R. 278 at 309."

George P. Fletcher, Rethinking Criminal Law (1978), pp.696–697, 707, 709–710:

"[W]e would be naive to think we had a definitive, unassailable solution to the enduring problem of determining when mistakes must be reasonable in order to have an exculpatory effect. The thesis is tentative, and to aid those who might wish to carry the effort further, we should restate the critical premises for recognising that some mistakes have a categorical exculpatory effect.

1. The definition of an offence is the violation of a prohibitory norm.

2. The prohibitory norm identifies the minimal set of objective circumstances necessary, in the given cultural context, to state a coherent moral or social imperative.

3. There is no violation of a prohibitory norm unless the actor acts intentionally or knowingly with respect to the elements of the definition (the prohibitory norm) . . .

A mistake as to one of these elements . . . has the same effect in barring liability for an intentional offence as the absence of one of the objective elements . . . Of course, if the offense is one that can be committed negligently, then the mistake only bars conviction for the intentional offence. The premises supporting the alternative track requiring mistakes to be reasonable are the following:

4. Relevant mistakes about elements extrinsic to the definition are excuses.

5. Elements of justification are extrinsic to the definition.

6. Excuses are not valid unless they negate the actor's culpability.

7. A mistake does not negate culpability unless the making of the mistake was blameless . . .

[Fletcher admits that this distinction is as yet fragile. For example, he finds the issue of consent in *Morgan* to be justificatory, rather than definitional.]. . . [I]n the field of putative self-defense and other imagined circumstances of justified conduct, it is generally assumed that the mistake must be reasonable. We could interpret this requirement as a concern about whether the actor's mistake is free from fault. But the doctrine could also be read as a theory about the justifying effect of appearances. If the circumstances warrant a reasonable belief, the actor is entitled to rely upon appearances, whatever the facts may actually be . . . [C]ommon-law courts are reluctant to reveal to the jury the extent to which a conviction rests on a moral assessment of the actor's wrongful conduct . . . As a step toward overcoming these inhibitions about moral discourse, we should try to state precisely how individuals can be fairly blamed for making mistakes or for remaining inadvertent to the risks implicit in their conduct. The inquiry encompasses not only mistakes in the narrow sense, but the culpability of inadvertent negligence."

Andrew Ashworth and Jeremy Horder, Principles of Criminal law, 7th edn (2013), p. 217:

"[T]he law should adopt [a] more context-sensitive approach, taking some account of the circumstances of the act, of D's responsibilities, and of what may reasonably be expected in such situations. The consequence may be not to require knowledge of a certain circumstance in the definition of the offence, but to require reasonable grounds for a belief. In rape cases these considerations militate in favour of a requirement of reasonable grounds for any mistake, as the Sexual Offences Act 2003 now provides; reasonable grounds should also be required in respect of age requirements for consensual sexual conduct . . . In principle, it is also right to require reasonable grounds before allowing the acquittal of a police officer with firearms training, as in *Beckford v R*. Of course, any such infusion of objective principles must recognize the exigencies of the moment, and must not expect more of D than society ought to expect in that particular situation. That is a necessary safeguard of individual autonomy. The general point, however, is that there may be good reasons for society to require a certain standard of conduct if the conditions were not such as to preclude it, particularly where the potential harm involved is serious."

This "context-sensitive" approach can be welcomed. Owing to their training we can legitimately expect a higher standard of responsibility from police officers or members of the armed forces who inflict force on others believing they are acting in self-defence: we can insist that their mistakes be reasonable if they are to escape liability. So too with rape: because of the necessary proximity between the parties and thus the ease of ascertaining whether there is consent, only reasonable mistakes should exculpate. Similarly, the basis of the decision in *R. v K* is flawed. The effect of this case is that a middle-aged paedophile could (under the law prior to the Sexual Offences Act 2003) escape liability for an indecent assault on a girl under the age of 16 on the basis that he genuinely believed, albeit unreasonably, that she was 16. Surely, if older men want to have sex with "children" they should be under a duty to ensure that the person is at least 16 and ought only to be able to "rely on appearances" (Fletcher) if other reasonable people would also have thought the girl was over 16.

This context-sensitive approach has been accepted for rape and other sexual offences in the Sexual Offences Act 2003. However, this view was rejected by the self-defence provisions in the Criminal Justice and Immigration Act 2008 where no distinction is drawn between the mistaken beliefs of the police or military personnel and similar mistakes of ordinary people.[347]

However, as these examples show, looking at the problem another way, the question becomes: in what contexts will a mere honest, but unreasonable, mistake serve to exculpate? Given the sorts of interests the criminal law seeks to protect (bodily integrity, property rights etc.), can we not demand of all defendants that only reasonable mistakes will suffice for exemption of liability? Most people would accept that Williams (Gladstone) be allowed to "rely on appearances"—but, again, this means only relying on reasonable mistakes. Ashworth argues that we should not expect more of a defendant "than society ought to expect in that particular situation". Following the above argument, we ought always to expect ordinary persons to avoid making unreasonable mistakes. However, we can have no such expectations when dealing with defendants whose mental capacities are such that they are unable to achieve this standard, for example, mentally vulnerable defendants with severe learning difficulties. This argument then reduces itself to a proposition similar to that encountered earlier when we examined Hart's favoured test of negligence: we are entitled to blame persons for their unreasonable conduct (and unreasonable mistakes) provided they had the capacity to act according to that standard.

4. Mistake as to law

Traditionally, mistakes of law have been regarded as generally irrelevant. Citizens are presumed to know the law of the land—their ignorance or mistake cannot avail them. The reason often given is that the law sets an objective standard; citizens should not be able to make it subjective by their mistaken

---

347   A. Ashworth and J.Horder, *Principles of Criminal Law*, 7th edn (Oxford: OUP, 2013), p.218.

view of it,[348] or that it might encourage ignorance.[349]

However, this proposition that mistakes of law are irrelevant is somewhat misleading. Some mistakes of law can be highly relevant. In this context it is necessary to distinguish between:

(i)   mistake as to civil law; and

(ii) mistake as to criminal law.

(i) Mistake as to civil law

Some mistakes of civil law may negate the mens rea required for a crime. In *Smith (David)*[350] the defendant damaged property wrongly believing it was his own property. He was not liable. He had made a mistake of the civil law. As a result of this mistake he lacked the intention to damage property belonging to another.[351]

In essence, a mistake of civil law is (or results in) a mistake of *fact*, e.g. thinking one is damaging property belonging to oneself. Accordingly, such mistakes will be governed by the principles discussed above. So, where a defendant mistakenly believes that her first marriage has been dissolved by a foreign divorce entitled to recognition in England, she will, following the demise of *Tolson*, escape liability if her mistake as to the civil law on recognition of foreign divorces was honest and genuine.

(ii) Mistake as to criminal law

Here the maxim "ignorance of the law is no excuse" comes into operation. A mistake as to whether one's actions are criminal will generally be irrelevant. So if a defendant thinks it is legal to have more than one wife, the actus reus and mens rea of the crime of bigamy are present; he is merely alleging that he did not know bigamy was a crime and such a mistaken belief is irrelevant.[352]

This same principle extends to persons who know that a particular activity is criminal but mistakenly think they have not committed the crime. In *Lee*[353] the defendant honestly believed he had not failed a roadside breathalyser test and so, believing his arrest to be unlawful, punched the police officers. It was held that his belief in his innocence did not negate his liability for the offence of assault with intent to resist lawful arrest contrary to s.38 of the Offences Against the Person Act 1861. This decision is uncontroversial. Any other solution would have given carte blanche to all arrested persons to resist that arrest on the ground that they believed they were innocent and so the arrest was unlawful.[354]

In many cases, however, there are problems in distinguishing between mistakes of civil law and criminal law, and much turns on the wording of particular statutory provisions. Three cases demonstrate this. In *Grant v Borg*[355] the offence charged was under s.24(1)(b)(i) of the Immigration Act 1971,

---

[348]   J. Hall, *General Principles of Criminal Law*, 2nd edn (Clark: The Lawbook Exchange Ltd, 1960).

[349]   O.W. Holmes, *The Common Law* (Mineola: Dover Publications, 1881), p.45.

[350]   *Smith (David)* [1974] Q.B. 354.

[351]   Both the Criminal Damage Act 1971 s.2(5)(2)(a) and the Theft Act 1968 s.2(1) provide that defendants are not liable if they believe they have a legal right to damage or appropriate the property of another.

[352]   The Draft Criminal Code Bill 1989 (Law Com. No.177, 1989) endorses this approach: "Ignorance or mistake as to a matter of law does not affect liability to conviction of an offence except—(a) where it is so provided; or (b) where it negatives a fault element of the offence" (cl.21).

[353]   *Lee* [2001] 1 Cr. App. R. 293.

[354]   See also *Doring* [2002] Crim. L.R. 817 where a defendant claimed she did not believe what she was doing amounted to "management" of companies for the purpose of bankruptcy offences. This belief was dismissed as irrelevant.

[355]   *Grant v Borg* [1982] 1 W.L.R. 638.

which makes it an offence if a non-patrial "having only limited leave to . . . remain . . . knowingly . . . remains beyond the time limited by the leave".

The House of Lords held that a mistake as to whether "leave" had expired was a mistake of law and thus irrelevant. Lord Bridge went so far as to state that:

> "The principle that ignorance of the law is no defence in crime is so fundamental that to construe the word 'knowingly' in a criminal statute as requiring not merely knowledge of the facts material to the offender's guilt, but also knowledge of the relevant law, would be revolutionary and, to my mind, wholly unacceptable."[356]

But in this case there was no dispute that the defendant knew it was a crime to overstay his leave. The question was whether he might have been mistaken as to when his leave had expired—surely a question of civil law.

In *Secretary of State for Trade and Industry v Hart*[357] a somewhat different approach was adopted. In this case the defendant acted as the auditor of two companies while being disqualified from so acting because he was a director of the companies. He was charged with an offence under s.13(5) of the Companies Act 1976 which prohibited a person acting as auditor of a company "at a time when he knows that he is disqualified for appointment to that office". The defendant admitted he knew all the facts or circumstances disqualifying him, but did not know that he was disqualified in law—in other words, he was unaware of the disqualification and its criminal sanctions—surely a mistake as to whether he had committed a crime which, in principle, is not dissimilar to the mistake made in *Lee*. Yet the Divisional Court held the defendant must know he was disqualified; an awareness of the statutory restrictions was a prerequisite of liability. As Ormrod LJ said:

> "If that means that he is entitled to rely on ignorance of the law as a defence, in contrast to the usual rule, the answer is that the section gives him that right."[358]

In *Attorney-General's Reference (No.1 of 1995)*[359] the defendant was charged with an offence, contrary to s.3(1) of the Banking Act 1987, of accepting deposits in the course of acting as a deposit-taking business without being authorised to do so by the Bank of England. The defendants knew they were accepting deposits but had "no idea" they needed to be licensed by the Bank of England. It was held that as long as the defendants knew the facts which constituted the offence (which they did), they would be liable. The fact that they did not know it was an offence to act as they did without a licence was mere ignorance of the law and no defence. This decision seems correct. If they had mistakenly believed they had acquired a licence, this would be a mistake of fact or civil law (depending on the circumstances). Not knowing it was a crime to fail to acquire a licence was a mistake of criminal law.

A limited exception to the rule that ignorance of the law is no excuse is provided by s.3(2) of the Statutory Instruments Act 1946: it is a defence to a crime created by a Statutory Instrument if the instrument has not been published and reasonable steps have not been taken to bring its contents to the notice of the public or the defendant. Further, in *Rimmington*[360] Lord Bingham stated that under art.7 of the ECHR "the law must be adequately accessible—and an individual must have an indication

---

[356]   At 646. See to similar effect, *R. v Millward (Neil Frederick)* [1985] Q.B. 519.
[357]   *Secretary of State for Trade and Industry v Hart* [1982] 1 W.L.R. 481.
[358]   *Lee* [2001] 1 Cr. App. R. 293 at 487.
[359]   *Attorney-General's Reference (No.1 of 1995)* [1996] 4 All E.R. 21.
[360]   *R. v Rimmington (Anthony)* [2005] UKHL 63.

of the legal rules applicable in a given case". In *Christian*[361] Lord Woolf, in the Privy Council, stated that it was a "requirement of the rule of law" that persons must "be given actual or at least constructive notice of what the law requires". He added, however, that "the onus is firmly on a person . . . to take the action that is open to him to find out what are the provisions of that law".

A final question remains for consideration. Is it right that mistake or ignorance of the law should generally have no bearing on the imposition of criminal liability?

Paul Robinson, Criminal Law Defences (Vol.2) (1984), pp.375–376:

"Austin argues that to permit mistakes as to criminality as an excuse for criminal conduct would be to present insoluble problems of proof (Austin on Jurisprudence: 13th ed. 1920). Everyone could claim such ignorance and it could be disproved only with considerable difficulty.

An examination of the structure of a general mistake excuse gives this concern considerable support. It is the one excuse that has no disability, no observance and verifiable abnormality, to lend support to the actor's claim of an excusing condition. The mistaken actor, except for his mistake, is indistinguishable from all other 'normal' persons. Evidence of the defendant's excusing condition, of his ignorance of criminality, must come solely from circumstantial evidence of his state of mind.

The absence of a distinguishing abnormality not only makes it difficult to distinguish the defendant and to establish his excusing condition, but also makes it more difficult to maintain the integrity of the prohibition violated while excusing the actor for his violation. '[O]nce the conduct has been so defined [as criminal], one cannot usurp the lawmaking function by pleading that his ignorance must mean that the conduct is not criminal as to him.' (Packer, "The Model Penal Code and Beyond" 63 Colum. L. Rev. 594, 596–97, 1963). In light of the heightened need for clear proof and the simultaneous increased difficulty in reliably determining mistake of law claims, one may reasonably concur with Holmes that 'to admit [such an] excuse at all would be to encourage ignorance where the lawmaker has determined to make men know and obey . . .' (Holmes, The Common Law 48, 1881). It is on the basis of these arguments that 'ignorance of the law is no excuse' is a maxim of long standing."

A.T.H. Smith, "Error and Mistake of Law in Anglo-American Criminal Law" (1985) 14 Anglo-Am. L.R. 3 at 16–18:

"1. Problems of proof.
. . .[I]t may be argued that mistakes of fact and law and mistakes of law are not essentially different in kind, and since the inquiry is manifestly not impossible in the case of the former, it is equally not impossible in the latter. This response does not directly confront the brutal utilitarianism that lies behind the objection; it is not so much that proof is impossible but that the pursuit of absolute justice must be curtailed by considerations of social utility and the distribution of resources . . .
2. To admit the defence would be to encourage ignorance . . .
Even the utilitarian should allow that where a particular individual can show that he has taken all the steps that he conceivably can to conform his conduct to what he reasonably believes to be the dictates of the law, he has done all that can be asked of him.
3. The argument from legality. According to Jerome Hall, ((1976) 24 Am. Jo. Comp. Law 680) if the law were to assess a defendant's culpability on the footing of the law as he believed it to be, then for those purposes the law would be thus and so. This could undercut the rule of law, which relies on an objective law impartially administered by officials who declare what the law is. But this, as has been most persuasively argued, is to fail to distinguish between wrong-doing and attribution, justification and excuse. The mere fact that an individual is not held to be legally accountable for a wrong act does not mean that the act is not condemned; it means only that the actor is not to be blamed for what he did."

The present approach of English law is perhaps justifiable in relation to the major offences where there is a close correlation between law and morality, for instance, crimes of murder and rape and so

---

[361] *Christian* [2006] 2 A.C. 400.

on. In *Christian*[362] the defendants, from Pitcairn Island, argued that they did not know that the English law of rape and sexual abuse applied on their island. This argument was rejected on the ground that rape and sexual abuse are such obvious moral wrongs that they must have known that their conduct was criminal—even if they were unaware of the specific provisions of the law.

Similarly, the present law can be defended in relation to specialist activities in which the actor may be engaged.[363] However, when turning to the plethora of legislation surrounding modern life, one is forced to question whether this approach is either just or efficacious.

Ashworth[364] has argued that (at least) in cases where the defendant has relied upon incorrect official assurances there should be a defence of mistake of law or any prosecution should be stayed as an abuse of the process of court. He cites two cases. In the first, *Cambridgeshire and Isle of Ely County Council v Rust*[365] the defendant, having made enquiries of local and national authorities, set up a stall beside a highway. After operating and paying rates on the stall for three years, the defendant was prosecuted and convicted of an offence of pitching a stall on a highway with the Divisional Court holding that his mistake of law was irrelevant. However, in *Postermobile v Brent London Borough Council*[366] a prosecution was stayed for abuse of process in a case where the defendant had been told by officials from the Brent planning department that it would be lawful to erect advertising hoardings. It was held that persons should be able to rely on the statements of public officials: "it was not as though they had requested planning advice from one of the council's gardeners". More recently, though, Ashworth has argued in favour of a broader defence of ignorance of the criminal law in limited circumstances. He notes that this step has been taken in South Africa, where in *S v De Blom*[367] it was held that the defendant's ignorance of the law prohibiting her from taking jewellery out of the country negated the mens rea required for that offence.

Andrew Ashworth, "Ignorance of the Criminal Law, and Duties to Avoid it" (2011) 74 M.L.R. 1 at 24–26

"The aim of this article is to offer a critique of the common law doctrine on ignorance of the criminal law, with a view to moving discussions away from narrow (and unpersuasive) consequentialist arguments and opening up some wider issues of justice and political obligation. Three points have particular significance.

First, the common law doctrine that ignorance of the criminal law is no excuse has been shown to have insecure foundations. To exclude any defence based on ignorance of the criminal law is manifestly unfair, given the diverse, often technical, and changing content of the criminal law. To require actual knowledge of particular conduct's criminality would be to go too far in the other direction, since it is right to expect citizens to make reasonable efforts to find out the criminal law (so long as the State recognises its obligations too). It was argued that a defence of excusable or reasonable ignorance of the law would achieve the best alignment with fairness, bearing in mind the censure inherent in criminal conviction

Secondly, the State's duty of security requires not just the creation of laws to protect us from significant wrongs and harms, but also recognition of the State's obligations in relation to the accessibility of the criminal law and communication of its ambit to adults and to children. If the State takes proper steps to inform its citizens about the criminal law, the incidence of ignorance of the criminal law should decline, there would be fewer unfair convictions, and there might possibly be fewer crimes. The State's primary interest should be in ensuring maximum

---

[362] *Christian* [2006] 2 A.C. 400.
[363] Some countries provide a defence of mistake of law but exclude it in such situations, e.g. Norway (Penal Code of 1902–57, added 1939). See also A.L.I. Model Penal Code, Proposed Official Draft 1962 s.2.04(3). See G.P. Fletcher, *Rethinking Criminal Law* (London: Little, Brown, 1978), pp.713–736.
[364] Andrew Ashworth, "Testing Fidelity to Legal Values: Official Involvement and Criminal Justice" (2000) 63 M.L.R. 633.
[365] *Cambridgeshire and Isle of Ely County Council v Rust* [1972] 1 Q.B. 426.
[366] *Postermobile v Brent London Borough Council*, The Times, December 8, 1997.
[367] *S v De Blom* 1977 (3) S.A. 513.

law-abidance without having to bring prosecutions, and this is in the interests of potential victims too. This obligation also flows from the State's duty of justice, respecting the right of individuals not to be convicted of offences of which it was not reasonable to expect them to have knowledge.

Thirdly, the State's duties of security and justice are particularly engaged in relation to omissions. Offences of omission are unusual in English criminal law, and are known to be so, and therefore the State must make a particular effort to draw any such offence to people's attention . . .

These three points should lead the government, the Law Commission and the judiciary to re-appraise their approaches. The common law ignorance-of-law doctrine is theoretically and practically unsustainable. The criminal law, and particularly new crimes and extensions to existing crimes, must be properly communicated to the public. So much for the critical dimension of this article. Much more problematic is the task of devising a fair and workable response to excusable ignorance of the criminal law. Three particular difficulties may be mentioned in conclusion.

First, a defence of reasonable ignorance of the criminal law can only operate if there is a serviceable distinction between ignorance and mistakes of fact and ignorance and mistakes of law. . . .

Secondly, there are still people who find a nagging attraction in the *malum in se* concept. The argument above was that there are very few *mala in se*, because in a culturally diverse country there is a range of different views about right and wrong. That argument is strong in relation to sexual offences, where the boundaries may change in a generation or from one country to another nearby, but it may be much weaker for possession of some types of firearm. Moreover, when members of a household (indeed, a family) stand by and fail to intervene as another family member repeatedly beats his wife, are we not all drawn to the argument that they must have known that it was wrong not to intervene? The answer offered here is that there is a significant distinction between knowing something is wrong and knowing that it is a (serious) criminal offence; and that this distinction is supported by English law's general and known reluctance to recognise positive duties to intervene. Our sympathies may sometimes point in a different direction, but the *malum in se* argument is too uncertain and too unruly to be relied upon in circumstances where there is excusable or reasonable ignorance of the criminal law. More difficult to accommodate is the probability that many defendants may either suspect that their conduct is close to the borderline of crime or have a kind of partial ignorance, in the sense that they know there are prohibitions on firearms but do not know or are mistaken as to the details. Those cases have been treated here as falling within the ambit of reasonable ignorance, but some would prefer a narrower defence that does not extend to those who suspect that their conduct may be unlawful.

Thirdly, at two crucial stages—in developing the argument for a defence of reasonable or excusable ignorance of the criminal law, and in discussing the State's duty of justice—particular emphasis has been laid on the values of the rule of law and the principle of legality. The criminal law must be certain, prospective and accessible in order to guide people's behaviour. Yet liberal criminal lawyers must note the tension that this creates . . . The compromises are evident in the arguments . . . in favour of an individual's duty to take *reasonable* steps to discover the law; in favour of legal specification of duty-situations . . .; in favour of the State's duty to make the criminal law *reasonably* accessible, and to take *reasonable* steps to communicate it to adults and children, and so forth."

Ashworth points to the Sexual Offences Act 2003 as an example of a new piece of legislation which introduced a whole raft of offences, the details of which received little publicity. His argument that if citizens are to be able to expect to use the criminal law in order to guide their conduct and therefore the state has a duty to make the law certain and sufficiently publicised is a forceful one. With the vast array of regulatory offences, with constantly changing and varying standards of permissible conduct, for example, in relation to obscenity, with the law often being unclear and uncertain even to lawyers, do we necessarily blame all defendants who have made mistakes as to the criminal law? The paradigmatic blameworthy defendant is one who has culpably brought about the prohibited result or state of affairs and has acted in open defiance of the law. With mistake of law there is no such flouting of the rules. Bearing in mind that one is not justifying the wrong done, but merely excusing the actor—and, therefore, an excuse should only be available if the mistake was a reasonable one—there must surely be a strong case for exempting such an actor from criminal liability.

3

STRICT LIABILITY AND CORPORATE CULPABILITY

I. STRICT LIABILITY

A. Introduction

Under the general principles considered in Chapter 2, a finding of culpability or blameworthiness is necessary for the imposition of criminal liability. While this proposition is true for most serious criminal offences, there are nevertheless many offences for which no culpability need be established.[1] These are called crimes of strict liability. Liability is "strict" because the prosecution is relieved of the necessity of proving mens rea in relation to one or more of the elements of the actus reus.[2] In the first "modern" case of strict liability,[3] for example, the defendant was accused of selling adulterated milk. It was sufficient to prove that the milk was adulterated and that he was selling it; his mistake that he had thought the milk was pure was irrelevant. Similarly, in the much later case of *Alphacell v Woodward*[4] liability was established under s.2(1)(a) of the Rivers (Prevention of Pollution) Act 1951 by the defendants causing polluted water to enter a river. The fact that they had not known that the pollution was taking place and that they had mistakenly thought that their filtering system was operating efficiently did not exonerate them. A majority of strict liability crimes exist within schemes of regulation where the main emphasis is on the maintenance of standards such as safety. Regulatory schemes making extensive use of strict liability cover areas such as food, consumer protection, the environment, agriculture, the countryside, construction and fire. In these areas the main concern is to ensure compliance with the law and administrative remedies such as improvement notices are extensively used. However, as a last resort, a criminal prosecution can be brought. These offences are known as "regulatory offences". While much of the literature and debate in this area has revolved around these regulatory offences, it must be emphasised that there are countless other strict liability offences that do not exist within regulatory schemes.

---

[1] In 2000 it was estimated that more than half the (then) roughly 8,000 crimes in English law were ones involving strict liability (A. Ashworth, "Is the Criminal Law a Lost Cause?" (2000) 116 L.Q.R. 225).

[2] Most of these offences are statutory in origin.

[3] *Woodrow* (1846) 153 E.R. 907 (Exch.).

[4] *Alphacell v Woodward* [1972] A.C. 824.

B. The Law

How are the courts to determine whether an offence is one of strict liability? At first sight the issue resolves itself into a problem of statutory interpretation. When the legislature has done its job efficiently, there is no difficulty. It may indicate, by the inclusion of terms such as "knowingly" or "recklessly" that the offence being created is one requiring mens rea. It may, alternatively, make it clear that an offence of strict liability is being created.[5]

All too often, however, legislation is enacted with no indication as to whether the offence is one requiring proof of mens rea. In such cases it is for the courts to determine whether the offence is one of strict liability. The mere absence of mens rea terms is by no means indicative that no culpability is required. On the contrary, there is an "established common law presumption that a mental element, traditionally labelled mens rea, is an essential ingredient unless Parliament has indicated a contrary intention either expressly or by necessary implication".[6]

1. The presumption of mens rea

Sweet v Parsley [1970] A.C. 132 (House of Lords)

The defendant, a teacher, let rooms to students in a farmhouse in which she did not reside although she occasionally stayed overnight in the one room retained for her use. She exercised no control over the students beyond collecting rent from them and occasionally shouting at them to be quiet if on her visits there was excessive noise late at night.

She was convicted of being concerned in the management of premises which were used for the purpose of smoking cannabis contrary to s.5(b) of the Dangerous Drugs Act 1965, when such substances were found during a police search. The Divisional Court upheld her conviction on the basis that she was not only in a position of being able to choose her tenants but could have made it a term of the letting that the smoking of cannabis was prohibited.[7] She appealed to the House of Lords.

LORD REID:

"How has it come about that the Divisional Court has felt bound to reach such an obviously unjust result? It has in effect held that it was carrying out the will of Parliament because Parliament has chosen to make this an absolute offence. And, of course, if Parliament has so chosen the courts must carry out its will, and they cannot be blamed for any unjust consequences. But has Parliament so chosen? Our first duty is to consider the words of the Act: if they show a clear intention to create an absolute offence that is an end of the matter. But such cases are very rare. Sometimes the words of the section which creates a particular offence make it clear that *mens rea* is required in one form or another. Such cases are quite frequent. But in a very large number of cases there is no clear indication either way. In such cases there has for centuries been a presumption that Parliament did not intend to make criminals of persons who were in no way blameworthy in what they did. That means that whenever a section is silent as to *mens rea* there is a presumption that, in order to give effect to the will of Parliament, we must read in words appropriate to require *mens rea*.

In the absence of a clear indication in the Act that an offence is intended to be an absolute offence, it is necessary to go outside the Act and examine all relevant circumstances in order to establish that this must have been the intention of Parliament. I say 'must have been' because it is a universal principle that if a penal provision is reasonably capable of two interpretations, that interpretation which is most favourable to the accused must be adopted."

---

[5]   See, for example, the offence of causing the death of another person by driving a vehicle while uninsured (Road Traffic Act, s.322). The injustice of making this serious offence one of strict liability has been lessened by the Supreme Court in *Hughes* [2014] 1 Cr. App. R. (above p.119).

[6]   *B (A Minor) v DPP* [2000] 2 A.C. 428 at 460, per Lord Nicholls.

[7]   J.C. Smith [1968] Crim. L.R. 328 points out that such a term in the letting agreement would not have absolved the defendant from liability if the crime were one of strict liability.

LORD PEARCE:

"My Lords, the prosecution contend that any person who is concerned in the management of premises where cannabis is in fact smoked even once, is liable, though he had no knowledge and no guilty mind. This is, they argue, a practical act intended to prevent a practical evil. Only by convicting some innocents along with the guilty can sufficient pressure be put upon those who make their living by being concerned in the management of premises. Only thus can they be made alert to prevent cannabis being smoked there. And if the prosecution have to prove knowledge or *mens rea*, many prosecutions will fail and many of the guilty will escape. I find that argument wholly unacceptable.

The notion that some guilty mind is a constituent part of crime and punishment goes back far beyond our common law. And at common law *mens rea* is a necessary element in a crime. Since the Industrial Revolution the increasing complexity of life called into being new duties and crimes which took no account of intent. Those who undertake various industrial and other activities, especially where these affect the life and health of the citizen, may find themselves liable to statutory punishment regardless of knowledge or intent, both in respect of their own acts or neglect and those of their servants. But one must remember that normally *mens rea* is still an ingredient of any offence. Before the court will dispense with the necessity for *mens rea* it has to be satisfied that Parliament so intended. The mere absence of the word 'knowingly' is not enough. But the nature of the crime, the punishment, the absence of social obloquy, the particular mischief and the field of activity in which it occurs, and the wording of the particular section and its context, may show that Parliament intended that the act should be prevented by punishment regardless of intent or knowledge."

Appeal allowed

The strength of this presumption of mens rea has more recently been strongly affirmed.

B (A Minor) v DPP [2000] 2 A.C. 428 (House of Lords)

The defendant, a 15-year-old boy, invited a 13-year-old girl to perform oral sex on him on a bus. He was charged with the offence of inciting a girl under the age of 14 to commit an act of gross indecency, contrary to s.1(1) of the Indecency with Children Act 1960. He honestly believed she was over 14 years of age.

LORD NICHOLLS OF BIRKENHEAD:

"The starting point for a court is the established common law presumption that a mental element, traditionally labelled *mens rea*, is an essential ingredient unless Parliament has indicated a contrary intention either expressly or by necessary implication . . .

In section 1(1) of the Indecency with Children Act 1960 Parliament has not expressly negatived the need for a mental element in respect of the age element of the offence. The question, therefore, is whether, although not expressly negatived, the need for a mental element is negatived by necessary implication. 'Necessary implication' connotes an implication which is compellingly clear. Such an implication may be found in the language used, the nature of the offence, the mischief sought to be prevented and any other circumstances which may assist in determining what intention is properly to be attributed to Parliament when creating the offence.

I venture to think that, leaving aside the statutory context of section 1, there is no great difficulty in this case. The section created an entirely new criminal offence, in simple unadorned language. The offence so created is a serious offence. The more serious the offence, the greater is the weight to be attached to the presumption, because the more severe is the punishment and the graver the stigma which accompany a conviction. Under section 1 conviction originally attracted a punishment of up to two years' imprisonment. This has since been increased to a maximum of ten years' imprisonment. The notification requirements under Part I of the Sex Offenders Act 1997 now apply, no matter what the age of the offender: see Schedule 1, paragraph 1(1) (b). Further, in addition to being a serious offence, the offence is drawn broadly ('an act of gross indecency'). It can embrace conduct ranging from predatory approaches by a much older paedophile to consensual sexual experimentation between precocious teenagers of whom the offender may be the younger of the two. The conduct may be depraved by any acceptable standard, or it may be relatively innocuous behaviour in private between two young people. These factors reinforce, rather than negative, the application of the presumption in this case.

Similarly, it is far from clear that strict liability regarding the age ingredient of the offence would further the purpose of section 1 more effectively than would be the case if a mental element were read into this ingredient. There is no general agreement that strict liability is necessary to the enforcement of the law protecting children in sexual matters."

LORD HUTTON:

"It would be reasonable to infer that it was the intention of Parliament that liability under section 1(1) of the Act of 1960 should be strict so that an honest belief as to the age of the child would not be a defence. But the test is not whether it is a reasonable implication that the statute rules out *mens rea* as a constituent part of the crime—the test is whether it is a necessary implication. Applying this test, I am of the opinion that there are considerations which point to the conclusion that it is not a necessary implication."

Appeal allowed

This approach was reaffirmed by the House of Lords in *R. v K*[8] where it was held that the offence of indecent assault on a girl under the age of 16, contrary to s.14(1) of the Sexual Offences Act 1956 was an offence requiring mens rea and so the defendant, believing the girl to be aged 16 or over, could not be liable. Lord Steyn emphasised the point made by Lord Nicholls in *B (A Minor) v DPP* that the presumption of mens rea can only be displaced by "necessary implication which is compellingly clear".

The strength of the presumption of mens rea was again confirmed in *Kumar*[9] where it was held that the offence of buggery contrary to s.12 of the Sexual Offences Act 1956 required mens rea and so the defendant was entitled to a defence that he believed that the complainant had attained the age of 16. The House of Lords again applied the presumption in *DPP v Collins*[10] to the offence of sending a grossly offensive message by a public electronic communications network contrary to s.127(1)(a) of the Communications Act 2003.

In these cases where the presumption is applied, it is necessary for the courts to specify the precise form of mens rea that is being implied. This is generally taken to mean intention or subjective recklessness or knowledge or belief.[11] Negligence has not been regarded as sufficiently blameworthy for this purpose. Perhaps, despite the strength of the presumption emphasised in the above cases, it is this "all or nothing" approach (full subjective mens rea or strict liability) that has resulted in the presumption being displaced so often. If the courts had been prepared to utilise negligence as an appropriate fault requirement here, the presumption might have been applied in a wider range of situations.

2. Displacing the presumption

Gammon Ltd v Attorney-General of Hong Kong [1985] 1 A.C. 1 (Privy Council)

LORD SCARMAN:

"In their Lordships' opinion, the law may be stated in the following propositions: (1) there is a presumption of law that *mens rea* is required before a person can be held guilty of a criminal offence; (2) the presumption is particularly strong where the offence is 'truly criminal' in character; (3) the presumption applies to statutory offences, and can be displaced only if this is clearly or by necessary implication the effect of the statute; (4) the only situation in which the presumption can be displaced is where the statute is concerned with an issue of social concern, and public safety is such an issue; (5) even where a statute is concerned with such an issue, the presumption of *mens rea* stands unless it can also be shown that the creation of strict liability will be effective to promote the objects of the statute by encouraging greater vigilance to prevent the commission of the prohibited act."

The presumption in favour of mens rea can be overridden. Guiding criteria have gradually emerged as to when this is appropriate. These criteria, encapsulated in the *"Gammon* principles" above are now regularly applied as the appropriate test to determine whether an offence is one of strict liability.[12]

---

8   *R. v K* [2002] 1 A.C. 462.
9   *R. v Kumar (Aman)* [2005] Crim. L.R. 470.
10   *DPP v Collins* [2006] UKHL 40.
11   This was the approach adopted in the House of Lords' decisions of *B (A Minor) v DPP, R. v K* and *DPP v Collins*.
12   *R. v Bezzina (Anthony)* (1994) 99 Cr. App. R. 356; *R. v Brockley (Frank)* (1994) 99 Cr. App. R. 385; *R. v Blake (Albert Philip)*

(i) Type of offence

Strict liability is more likely to be imposed in relation to offences that:

- pertain to matters of social regulation and public welfare such as health and safety or road traffic;
- are regarded generally as only "quasi-criminal": that is, there is little or no stigma attached to their violation; and
- carry a light punishment, typically a fine.

Staples v United States 511 US 600 (1994) (Supreme Court of the United States)

STEVENS J:

"'Public welfare' offenses share certain characteristics: (1) they regulate 'dangerous or deleterious devices or products or obnoxious waste materials'; (2) they 'heighten the duties of those in control of particular industries, trades, properties or activities that affect public health, safety or welfare'; public welfare statutes render criminal 'a type of conduct that a reasonable person should know is subject to stringent public regulation and may seriously threaten the community's health or safety. The purposes of this legislation thus touch phases of the lives and health of people which, in the circumstances of modern industrialism, are largely beyond self-protection'. [A]n overriding public interest in health or safety may outweigh that risk [of injustice] when a person is dealing with products that are sufficiently dangerous or deleterious to make it reasonable to presume that he either knows, or should know, whether those products conform to special regulatory requirements[13] [citations omitted]".

Lim Chin Aik v The Queen [1963] A.C. 160 (Privy Council)

(For facts see below, p.235)

LORD EVERSHED:

"Where the subject matter of the statute is the regulation for the public welfare of a particular activity—statutes regulating the sale of food and drink are to be found among the earliest examples—it can be and frequently has been inferred that the legislature intended that such activities should be carried out under conditions of strict liability. The presumption is that the statute or statutory instrument can be effectively enforced only if those in charge of the relevant activities are made responsible for seeing that they are complied with. When such a presumption is to be inferred, it displaces the ordinary presumption of *mens rea*. Thus sellers of meat may be made responsible for seeing that meat is fit for human consumption and it is no answer for them to say that they were not aware that it was polluted. If that were a satisfactory answer, then the distribution of bad meat (and its far-reaching consequences) would not be effectively prevented."

It is, however, not always clear what a "public welfare" offence is. "The connection between 'public welfare'/'quasi' crime and strict liability is self-fulfilling at both a legislative and an interpretive level."[14] An offence can be held to be one of strict liability because it is only "quasi-criminal" and then because it is an offence of strict liability it can be labelled a "public welfare offence".

[1997] 1 All E.R. 963; *R. v Paine (Nicholas)* [1998] 1 Cr. App. R. 36; *R. v Ezeemo (Godwin Chukwnaenya)* [2012] EWCA Crim 2064.

[13] It has been stressed in the United States that, even with public welfare offences, mens rea is "generally" required (*PostersNThings Ltd v United States*, 511 U.S. 513 (1994)).

[14] C. Wells, *Corporations and Criminal Responsibility* (1993), p.8.

Muhamad v R. [2003] 2 W.L.R. 1050 (Court of Appeal, Criminal Division)

The appellant was convicted of materially contributing to the extent of his insolvency by gambling contrary to s.362(1)(a) of the Insolvency Act 1986 and appealed.

DYSON LJ:

"It is not clear to us whether an offence under section 362(1) (a) would have been classified by Lord Reid as 'quasi-criminal', or 'truly criminal'. A maximum penalty of two years' imprisonment is by no means insignificant, although it is towards the lower end of the scale of maximum custodial sentences. On the other hand, it is open to doubt whether, at any rate in 2002, such an offence would be regarded as 'truly criminal' . . .

The question whether the presumption of law that *mens rea* is required applies, and, if so, whether it has been displaced can be approached in two ways. One approach is to ask whether the act is truly criminal, on the basis that, if it is not, then the presumption does not apply at all. The other approach is to recognise that any offence in respect of which a person may be punished in a criminal court is, *prima facie*, sufficiently 'criminal' for the presumption to apply. But the more serious the offence, the greater the weight to be attached to the presumption, and conversely, the less serious the offence, the less weight to be attached. It is now clear that it is this latter approach which, according to our domestic law, must be applied.

The starting point, therefore, is to determine how serious an offence is created by section 362(1) (a), and accordingly how much weight, if any, should be attached to the presumption. Some weight must undoubtedly be given to the presumption, but in our judgment it can be readily displaced. As we have said, the maximum sentence indicates that Parliament considered this to be an offence of some significance, but not one of the utmost seriousness. This is not surprising. We do not believe that great stigma attaches to a conviction of this offence. In our view, this is not, and never has been, a particularly serious offence . . .

First, the 1986 Act created a clear and coherent regime. The majority of the offences include an express requirement of a mental element. This is achieved either in the section which creates the offence (for example, section 356(2)); or by reference to section 352 (which contains a reverse onus of proof provision). Only a few, of which section 362(1) (a) is one, do not specify a mental element. In our judgment, this is a clear pointer to Parliament's intention in relation to section 362(1) (a) . . .

Further support for the displacement of the presumption in relation to section 362(1) (a) emerges when a comparison is made of the maximum sentences provided for by the various offences created in Chapter VI of the 1986 Act. The offences where no mental element is specified, for the most part, attract considerably lower maximum sentences than those where a mental element is specified . . .

The next point relied on by [the prosecution] is the fact that gambling which harms a gambler's creditors is a matter of social concern. That is obviously right. It follows that this is a case where the fourth and fifth of Lord Scarman's propositions [in *Gammon*] are engaged. So too they were in *Harrow London Borough Council v Shah* [1999] 2.Cr.App.R.457. In that case, the Divisional Court had to decide whether the offence of selling National Lottery tickets to a person under the age of 16 was an offence of strict liability. The court decided that it was. In giving the leading judgment, Mitchell J said that the legislation dealt with an issue of social concern, and that it was an excellent example of the sort of legislation contemplated by Lord Scarman's fifth proposition. He said: 'That strict liability attaches to this offence will unquestionably encourage greater vigilance in preventing the commission of the prohibited act' . . .

It is self-evident that section 362(1) (a) is aimed at an issue of social concern. [A]n offence of strict liability may have a more chilling effect on gambling that may materially contribute to insolvency than an offence which requires a mental element. We are satisfied that strict liability will encourage greater vigilance to prevent gambling which will or may materially contribute to insolvency . . .

We conclude, therefore, that the offence created by section 362(1) (a) of the 1986 Act is one of strict liability."

Appeal dismissed

The approach towards offence seriousness expressed in the above cases is by no means universally applied. There are glaring examples of cases where strict liability has been imposed where the crime has the stamp of traditional criminality. For example, in *Warner*[15] it was held that the serious crime of

---

[15]   *Warner* [1969] A.C. 256.

possession of dangerous drugs contrary to s.1 of the Drugs (Prevention of Misuse) Act 1964 involved strict liability. Similarly, in *Land*[16] it was held that the offence of possessing an indecent photograph of a child contrary to s.1(1)(c) of the Protection of Children Act 1978 was one of strict liability.

R. v Blake [1997] 1 All E.R. 963 (Court of Appeal, Criminal Division)

The defendant, a disc jockey, was convicted of using a station for wireless telegraphy without a licence contrary to s.1(1) of the Wireless Telegraphy Act 1949. He claimed he had believed he was making a demonstration tape and was not aware he was in fact transmitting. He appealed on the ground that the offence was not one of strict liability.

HIRST LJ:

"[S]ince throughout the history of s.1(1), an offender has been potentially subject to a term of imprisonment, the offence is 'truly criminal' in character, and [thus] the presumption in favour of *mens rea* is particularly strong. However, it seems to us manifest that the purpose behind making unlicensed transmissions a serious criminal offence must have been one of social concern in the interests of public safety since undoubtedly the emergency services and air traffic controllers were using radio communications in 1949, albeit in a much more rudimentary form than nowadays. No doubt the much greater sophistication of these modes of communication, and the wider prevalence of pirate radio stations 40 years on, led to the substantial increase in the penalty in 1990.

Clearly, interference with transmissions by these vital public services poses a grave risk to wide sections of the public . . .

. . . [T]he imposition of an absolute offence must surely encourage greater vigilance on the part of those establishing or using a station, or installing or using the apparatus, to avoid committing the offence, *e.g.* in the case of users by carefully checking whether they are on air; it must also operate as a deterrent . . .

In these circumstances, we are satisfied that s.1(1) does create an absolute offence."

Appeal dismissed

In *Barnfather* it was held that the strict liability offence committed by a parent whose child failed regularly to attend at school involved

"a real stigma (being) attached . . . It suggests either an indifference to one's children, or incompetence at parenting, which in the case of the blameless parent will be unwarranted."[17]

As seen in *Muhamad*, it is often stated that the level of punishment attached to a crime is important in assessing whether the offence is one of strict liability. In the United States, the Model Penal Code proposes that the possibility of imprisonment should conclusively indicate that the offence is not one of strict liability.[18]

However, this is again only a guiding principle. In *Jackson*[19] it was held that strict liability was not precluded merely because the offence imposed the sanction of imprisonment. In many cases offences carrying reasonably severe penalties have been held to be crimes of strict liability. In *Hussain*,[20] the defendant was convicted of unlawful possession of a firearm contrary to s.1 of the Firearms Act 1968 even though he believed it was a toy used by his son. Despite the fact that this offence carried a maximum penalty of three years' imprisonment, it was held to be one of strict liability.

---

16   *R. v Land (Michael)* [1998] 1 All E.R. 403. See also *R. v Lemon (Denis)* [1979] A.C. 617.
17   *Barnfather v Islington Education Authority* [2003] 1 W.L.R. 2318 at [57]. See J. Horder, "Whose Values Should Determine When Liability is Strict?", in A.P. Simester (ed.), *Appraising Strict Liability* (Oxford: OUP, 2005).
18   Article 6.02(4).
19   *R. v Jackson (Robert Valentine)* [2007] 1 Cr. App. R. 28.
20   *Hussain* (1981) 47 Cr. App. R. 143.

Gammon Ltd v Attorney-General of Hong Kong [1985] 1 A.C. 1 (Privy Council)

The appellants were charged under Hong Kong Building Ordinances with deviating in a material way from work shown on an approved plan. It had to be determined whether they had to know that their deviation was material or whether liability was strict in relation to that element of the offence, the maximum penalty for which was a fine of $250,000 and imprisonment for three years.

LORD SCARMAN:

"The severity of the penalties is a more formidable point. But it has to be considered in the light of the Ordinance read as a whole . . . [T]here is nothing inconsistent with the purpose of the Ordinance in imposing severe penalties for offences of strict liability. The legislature could reasonably have intended severity to be a significant deterrent, bearing in mind the risks to public safety arising from some contraventions of the Ordinance. . . It must be crucially important that those who participate in or bear responsibility for the carrying out of works in a manner which complies with the requirements of the Ordinance should know that severe penalties await them in the event of any contravention or non-compliance with the Ordinance."

Appeal dismissed

One of the most serious offences created by the Sexual Offences Act 2003 is that of the crime of rape of a child under 13 (which carries a maximum penalty of life imprisonment). Yet this is an offence of strict liability: it is irrelevant that the defendant believes the child is over 13.[21] Whether strict liability for an offence as serious as this can be justified is a matter to which we shall return.

(ii) Statutory context

It has been repeatedly stated by the House of Lords that the presumption of mens rea can only be displaced if this is clearly or by necessary implication the effect of the statute. As the wording of the statute usually leaves the matter open, what is important is the statutory context of the provision in question.

Pharmaceutical Society of Great Britain v Storkwain Ltd (1986) 83 Cr. App. R. 359 (House of Lords)

The appellants, retail chemists, supplied prescription-only drugs in accordance with a forged prescription. They were charged with an offence contrary to s.58(2)(a) of the Medicines Act 1968 which provides that

"no person shall sell by retail, or supply in circumstances corresponding to retail sale, a medical product of a description, or falling within a class, specified in an order under this section except in accordance with a prescription by an appropriate practitioner."

It had to be determined whether this was an offence of strict liability.

LORD GOFF OF CHIEVELEY:

"It is, in my opinion, clear from the Act of 1968 that Parliament must have intended that the presumption of *mens rea* should be inapplicable to s.58(2) (a). First of all, it appears from the Act of 1968 that, where Parliament

---

[21]   *R. v G* [2009] 1 A.C. 92.

wished to recognize that *mens rea* should be an ingredient of an offence created by the Act, it has expressly so provided. Thus, taking first of all offences created under provisions of Part II of the Act of 1968, express requirements of *mens rea* are to be found in both s.45(2) and in s.46(1), (2) and (3) of the Act. More particularly, in relation to offences created in Part III and Parts V and VI of the Act of 1968, section 121 makes detailed provision for a requirement of *mens rea* in respect of certain specified sections of the Act, including ss.63 to 65 (which are contained in Part III), but significantly not s.58 . . . It is very difficult to avoid the conclusion that, by omitting s.58 from those sections to which s.121 is expressly made applicable, Parliament intended that there should be no implication of a requirement of *mens rea* in s.58(2) (a)."[22]

If several sections of a statute allow due diligence defences (see below) but the provision under consideration omits such a defence, it will be easier to infer strict liability.[23]

(iii) Effectiveness in promoting the objectives of the statute

Lim Chin Aik v The Queen [1963] A.C. 160 (Privy Council)

The defendant was convicted of contravening an immigration ordinance by remaining in Singapore after he had been declared a prohibited immigrant. There was no evidence that the prohibition order had been brought to his attention or that any effort had been made to do so. He appealed.

LORD EVERSHED:

"But it is not enough in their Lordships' opinion merely to label the statute as one dealing with a grave social evil and from that to infer that strict liability was intended. It is pertinent also to inquire whether putting the defendant under strict liability will assist in the enforcement of the regulations. That means there must be something he can do, directly or indirectly, by supervision or inspection, by improvement of his business methods or by exhorting those whom he may be expected to influence or control, which will promote the observance of the regulations. Unless this is so, there is no reason in penalising him, and it cannot be inferred that the legislature imposed strict liability merely in order to find a luckless victim. Their Lordships prefer [this] to the alternative view that strict liability follows simply from the nature of the subject matter and that persons whose conduct is beyond any sort of criticism can be dealt with by the imposition of a nominal penalty.[24]

Where it can be shown that the imposition of strict liability would result in the prosecution and conviction of a class of persons whose conduct could not in any way affect the observance of the law, their Lordships consider that, even where the statute is dealing with a grave social evil, strict liability is not likely to be intended. The subject-matter, the control of immigration, is not one in which the presumption of strict liability has generally been made. Nevertheless, if the courts of Singapore were of the view that unrestricted immigration is a social evil which it is the object of the Ordinance to control most rigorously, their Lordships would hesitate to disagree. That is a matter peculiarly within the cognisance of the local courts. But [counsel for the respondent] was unable to point to anything that the appellant could possibly have done so as to ensure that he complied with the regulations. It was not, for example, suggested that it would be practicable for him to make continuous inquiry to see whether an order had been made against him. Clearly one of the objects of the Ordinance is the expulsion of prohibited persons from Singapore, but there is nothing that a man can do about it if, before the commission of the offence, there is no practical or sensible way in which he can ascertain whether he is a prohibited person or not."

Appeal allowed

---

[22] See also *Sherras v De Rutzen* [1895] 1 Q.B. 918; *Neville v Mavroghenis* [1984] Crim. L.R. 42; and *R. v Bradish (Liam Christopher)* [1990] Crim. L.R. 723.
[23] K. Reid, "Strict Liability: Some Principles for Parliament" (2008) Statute L. Rev. 173 at 174; see also *R. v Deyemi (Danny)* [2007] EWCA Crim 2060 at [21].
[24] As happened in the case of *Hussain* (above, fn.20) where the defendant was only fined £100.

Matudi v The Crown [2003] EWCA Crim 697 (Court of Appeal, Criminal Division)

The defendant was convicted of importing animal products (meat from Africa) contrary to regs 21 and 37 of the Products of Animal Origin (Import and Export) Regulations 1996. The defendant received a consignment which he believed contained leaves and herbs; he had no idea that it contained any meat. He appealed on the ground that the offence ought to require mens rea.

SCOTT BAKER LJ:

"[Counsel for the defendant] argued that if Regulation 21 is interpreted as an absolute offence the importer is in an impossible position; he cannot control what the consignor puts into the consignment . . . In our judgment an importer will emphasise to his supplier that the contents of the consignment must correspond with the information on the accompanying documents. Also, it is up to importers to ensure that their consignments come from a reliable source. In our view it is too simplistic for the appellant to say there is nothing he could have done about it. Strict liability imposes a clear black and white obligation on importers. It is up to them to ensure that they contract with consignors that they can trust who do not take risks on lax procedures . . .

[The issue] is whether strict liability will be effective to promote the objects of the legislation. There will obviously be a temptation with some importers to by-pass the notice provisions and thus save the delay and expense involved in the consignment being diverted to a border inspection post. It seems to us that strict liability is inevitably going to make the regulation more effective . . .

[T]he mischief sought to be prevented . . . is likely to be better achieved if the offence is one of strict liability."

Appeal dismissed

3. Defences to strict liability

(i) General defences

A crime of strict liability is one where mens rea is not required in relation to one or more elements of the actus reus. Liability is thus strict and not absolute, although courts often misleadingly use this latter term. The importance of this point is only fully realised when one comes to consider what, if any, defences are available to a defendant charged with a strict liability offence. If the offence were "absolute" then no defences would save the defendant from the consequences of his actions. But, given that this is not the case, one has to consider whether the defendant may plead, for example, duress or self-defence or even automatism in answer to a charge. What would be the position if a dangerous dog was properly secured inside premises but let loose by a burglar? Prima facie the owner of the dog would be liable under s.3(1) of the Dangerous Dogs Act 1991 as this is a strict liability offence. However, in *Robinson-Pierre* it was held that the owner's conviction could not be upheld where the dog was released by a deliberate act of a third party (in this case police officers deliberately entering the property in execution of a search warrant) and the jury had not been given the opportunity to consider whether the owner had contributed to the events by his voluntary act or omission.[25]

One approach would be to make the availability of a defence depend upon the *nature* of the defence being raised. As we shall see, it is possible to distinguish between defences that are justificatory in nature (resulting in a determination that there was no wrongful act at all) and those that are excusatory (relieving the defendant from blame whilst acknowledging the wrongfulness

---

[25]   *R. v Robinson-Pierre (Symieon)* [2013] EWCA Crim 2396, see extract above p.89. The case drew upon the decision of *R. v Hughes (Michael)* [2013] UKSC 56. In this case, considered in more detail at p.119, the Supreme Court concluded that even though the offence of causing death whilst uninsured or without a full licence under the Road Traffic Act 1988 s.3ZB is an offence of strict liability, it still "requires some act or omission in the control of the car, which involves some element of fault . . . which contributes in some more than minimal way to the death" at [36].

of the conduct). In relation to strict liability offences, it would be logical to allow the defendant to plead defences that are justifications for conduct (such as self-defence) but to deny defences that are excuses (because the defendant is really claiming absence of blame, which is not in any event required). If this argument were adopted, the excusatory defences of insanity, infancy, intoxication, duress and automatism would be denied to the defendant. An approach consistent with this view was adopted in *DPP v Harper*[26] where it was held that insanity could only be a defence to crimes requiring mens rea and, accordingly, was not a defence to the strict liability offence of driving with excess alcohol.

The above argument, however, presupposes that the distinction between justificatory and excusatory defences is clear which, as will be seen, is not always the case. Further, if the underlying rationale of strict liability is the promotion of higher standards of care, this seems unlikely to be served by the punishment of, say, infants, the insane or others whose actions were involuntary. In *Hill v Baxter*[27] automatism was successfully pleaded to a charge of dangerous driving. If non-insane automatism can be a defence here, so too should insane automatism. After all, the essence of an automatism defence is a denial of the "voluntary act" requirement, which is an essential element of the actus reus, and not merely a denial of mens rea. Going even further, in *Martin*[28] it was held that duress of circumstances (classically regarded as an excuse) was a defence to the strict liability offence of driving while disqualified.[29] As we shall see, whether strict liability offences are ever justifiable is a controversial matter. Recognising that all established defences are available to such offences would go a long way towards "sweetening the bitter pill" of their (perhaps necessary) existence.

(ii) Due diligence defences

In addition to any general defences that may be available, there is the growing possibility that the offence may contain within it a specific defence. This will be based upon showing an absence of fault; these are often called "due diligence" defences. An example of such a defence is to be found in the Food Safety Act 1990. This Act creates a number of offences relating to the preparation and sale of food such as rendering food injurious to health and not complying with food safety requirements and selling food which is not of the nature or substance or quality demanded. Section 21(1) creates a due diligence defence:

> "[I]t shall be a defence for the person charged to prove that he took all reasonable precautions and exercised all due diligence to avoid the commission of the offence by himself or by a person under his control".

A research study into 41 Statutory Instruments concerning food found that 34 of them included due diligence defences.[30] This same research revealed extensive use of due diligence defences in the other main areas of regulatory crime: environmental health, trading and consumer laws and construction.

---

[26] *DPP v Harper* [1997] 1 W.L.R. 1406.
[27] *Hill v Baxter* [1958] 1 Q.B. 277.
[28] *R. v Martin (Colin)* [1989] 1 All E.R. 652.
[29] However, in *Hampshire CC v E* [2007] EWHC 2584 (Admin) some doubt was expressed about whether duress of circumstances could be pleaded in relation to the strict liability offence of failing to secure the attendance of a child at school under the Education Act 1996 s.444(1).
[30] A.P. Simester and P. Roberts, "Strict Liability in UK Regulation", in Macrory, *Regulatory Justice: Sanctioning in a Post-Hampton World* (2006), Annex E, E17.

Deborah L. Parry, "Judicial Approaches to Due Diligence" [1995] Crim. L.R. 695 at 701–702:

"[The author examined a series of cases dealing with the due diligence defence provided by section 39 of the Consumer Protection Act 1987 and concluded that while a flexible attitude was apparent in pricing cases, a very demanding standard was required for safety-related offences.]

[W]hilst at the trial a due diligence defence may succeed in a safety-related matter, in none of the appeal cases has it been established . . . [This causes] concern as strict liability offences may be appearing more like absolute offences . . .

If . . . it is felt by businesses that no one can ever 'win', there is a risk of the offences being viewed as unavoidable and of removing any stigma from convictions if it is known that even 'careful' defendants are convicted. It could certainly encourage many to opt for a plea of guilty plus mitigation, rather than expend time and money on establishing a defence."

Placing the burden on the defendant to establish due diligence does, however, present problems. In *Woolmington v DPP*[31] the House of Lords declared that it was for the prosecution to establish the guilt of the defendant. It was not the responsibility of the defendant to establish their innocence. Article 6(2) of the European Convention on Human Rights provides that "everyone charged with a criminal offence shall be presumed innocent until proven guilty according to law". This raises the issue of whether due diligence defences are compatible with art.6(2).

Broadly speaking, the courts have tackled this issue in the following manner. If a provision imposes a *legal burden* of proof on a defendant (where they are required to prove on a balance of probabilities that, in this context, they have exercised due diligence or reasonable care), it will be incompatible with the presumption of innocence unless the provision is serving a legitimate aim and is a proportionate and justifiable response. For example, in *Matthews*[32] the defendant was charged with possession of a knife contrary to s.139 of the Criminal Justice Act 1988 and claimed a due diligence defence under s.139(4) that he had good reason for having the article with him in a public place, namely, that it was to cut lino. It was held that this reverse burden of legal proof was not incompatible with art.6(2) because it was a justifiable and proportionate response: the reason for having a knife in a public place was something peculiarly within the knowledge of the accused; the reverse onus provision struck a fair balance between the interests of the community and the individual and went

> "no further than is necessary to accomplish Parliament's objective in protecting the public from the menace posed by persons having bladed articles in public places without good reason".[33]

However, if a reverse burden of proof is not regarded as a reasonable and proportionate response, the court can "read down" the provision as only placing an *evidential burden* on the defence. An evidential burden merely requires the defendant to raise sufficient evidence to show that the defence could apply but the burden remains on the prosecution to establish beyond reasonable doubt that the defence does not apply. For example, in *Lambert*[34] the defendant was charged with possession of a controlled drug with intent to supply, contrary to s.5(3) of the Misuse of Drugs Act 1971 but raised the due diligence defence available in s.28(2) and (3) that he did not know or suspect that he was possessing controlled drugs. The House of Lords declared, obiter, that placing a legal burden on the defendant would be incompatible with art.6(2) as being a disproportionate measure for such a serious offence. However, the majority stated that s.28(2) and (3) should be "read down" so that only an

---

[31]   *Woolmington v DPP* [1935] A.C. 462.
[32]   *R. v Matthews (Mark Anthony)* [2003] 2 Cr. App. R. 19.
[33]   A similar approach was adopted in *R. v Johnstone (Robert Alexander)* [2003] 2 Cr. App. R. 33.
[34]   *Lambert* [2001] 2 Cr. App. R. 511.

evidential burden was placed on the defendant and this would not be incompatible with the presumption of innocence established in art.6(2).[35] Such a "reading down" will almost always be possible[36] but, if the provision cannot be "read down", then as a last resort under s.4 of the Human Rights Act 1998 the court should declare the reverse burden incompatible with art.6(2).

The result of this approach is inevitable uncertainty. It is difficult to see why "a strong public interest in bladed articles not being carried in public" makes a due diligence defence a proportionate response while a similar defence to possession of drugs is a disproportionate response. We shall see in the next section that since the coming into force of the Human Rights Act 1998 the English courts have considered the status of some strict liability offences and have held that they are not, per se, incompatible with the European Convention. If such (admittedly lesser) offences without due diligence defences represent a proportionate response to a problem, it would be odd to hold that affording a due diligence defence with a reverse burden of legal proof (admittedly for more serious offences) could be incompatible with the ECHR. We shall shortly examine the many objections to offences of strict liability. As a response to these problems, courts in some Commonwealth countries, such as Canada, have declared that all strict liability offences should presumptively be construed as incorporating due diligence defences[37] and the Law Commission has also recently consulted on whether courts should be given a power to apply a due diligence defence to any statutory offence not requiring fault.[38] It would be a sad irony if human rights concerns, as expressed in *Lambert*, were to lead to a foreclosure of this option.

4. Strict liability and the European Convention on Human Rights

As seen above, in certain circumstances strict liability offences with reverse burdens of proof could be incompatible with art.6(2) of the European Convention. There is, however, a further argument that some strict liability offences could, in dispensing with any fault element, contravene other articles of the Convention. This approach has not been adopted by the English courts.[39]

Muhamad v R. [2003] 2 W.L.R. 1050 (Court of Appeal, Criminal Division)

The appellant was convicted of materially contributing to the extent of his insolvency by gambling, contrary to s.362(1)(a) of the Insolvency Act 1986.

DYSON LJ:

"[It is argued that Article 7] requires the criminal law to be sufficiently accessible and precise to enable an individual to know in advance whether his conduct is criminal. No gambler can necessarily know, when he places his bet, whether he runs a real risk of prosecution if he loses. The only way to avoid running this risk is not to gamble at all, or to gamble for low stakes. Without *mens rea* the offence is objectionably uncertain. Furthermore, a construction of strict liability is neither necessary in a democratic society, nor proportional to any legitimate aim . . .

---

[35]   A similar approach was approved in *R. v DPP Ex p. Kebeline* [2000] 1 Cr. App. R. 275 and applied in *Sheldrake v DPP* [2005] 1 A.C. 264.

[36]   I. Dennis, "Reverse Onuses and the Presumption of Innocence: In Search of Principle" [2005] Crim. L.R. 901.

[37]   *R. v City of Sault Ste Marie* (1978) 85 D.L.R. (3d) 161.

[38]   Law Commission Consultation Paper No.195, *Criminal Liability in Regulatory Contexts* (2010), para.1.68. The paper considers whether the test of due diligence should be less strict than is currently formulated (paras 1.78–1.79).

[39]   See generally, G.R. Sullivan, "Strict Liability for Criminal Offences in England and Wales Following Incorporation into English Law of the European Convention on Human Rights", in A.P. Simester (ed.), *Appraising Strict Liability* (Oxford: OUP, 2005).

[T]he narrow question that arises is whether the fact that the offence is one of strict liability is disproportionate so as to render it in breach of Article 7. We accept that a strict liability offence is easier to prove than one requiring a mental element, and that, if section 362(1)(a) is interpreted as creating an offence of strict liability, it may deter persons from gambling who, if the offence required a mental element, might not be so deterred. We do not consider that either of these consequences indicates that it is disproportionate to hold that the section creates an offence of strict liability. [I]f strict liability does have a chilling effect on gambling, we are not convinced that the imposition of strict liability is a disproportionate response to the need, in the public interest, to deter persons from gambling in such a way as to cause loss to their creditors.

We should add that, so far as concerns the ECHR, there is nothing objectionable in principle with strict liability offences. In *Salabiaku v France* 13 EHRR 379, at paragraph 27 the ECtHR said:

'27. As the Government and the Commission have pointed out, in principle the Contracting States remain free to apply the criminal law to an act where it is not carried out in the normal exercise of one of the rights protected under the Convention and, accordingly, to define the constituent elements of the resulting offence. In particular, and again in principle, the Contracting States may, *under certain conditions*, penalise a simple or objective fact as such, irrespective of whether it results from criminal intent or from negligence. Examples of such offences may be found in the laws of the Contracting States.'

In our judgment, therefore, there is nothing in the ECHR and in particular in Article 7 which requires us to reach a different conclusion from that which we expressed earlier on the basis of an application of domestic law principles. Upon its true construction, section 362(1)(a) creates an offence of strict liability" (italics added).

In *Barnfather* it was held that these "certain conditions" (italicised in above extract) related to procedural matters (such as reverse burdens of proof) and did not apply to the substantive elements of an offence. It was held that art.6(2) (presumption of innocence) does not impose any restrictions on the right of Parliament to create strict liability offences.[40] Lord Hope in *R. v G* stated that these "certain conditions" were simply referring to the fact that a strict liability offence could be incompatible with other articles of the Convention.[41] The ironic result (conceded in *Barnfather*) is that

"a state's laws are subject to fuller review when they include a defence which places a burden on the defence than they are when no defence at all is conferred."[42]

In *R. v G* it was held that the strict liability offence of rape of a child under 13 contrary to s.5 of the Sexual Offences Act 2003 was not incompatible with art.6.2 (presumption of innocence) or with art.8 (right to respect for privacy and family life) of the ECHR.

R. v G. [2009] 1 A.C. 92 (House of Lords)

The defendant, aged 15, had consensual sexual intercourse with a 12-year-old girl. He believed she was 15. He was convicted of rape of a child under 13 contrary to s.5 of the Sexual Offences Act 2003 and appealed.

LORD HOFFMANN:

"[3] . . . [T]he offence is one of strict liability and it is no defence that the accused believed the other person to be 13 or over.

---

40   *Barnfather* [2003] 1 W.L.R. 2318.
41   *R. v G* [2009] 1 A.C. 92 at [28]. Lord Hoffmann recommended that *Salabiaku v France* should in future be "ignored" (at [6]).
42   *Barnfather* [2003] 1 W.L.R. 2318 at [45].

[4] Article 6(1) guarantees fair procedure but not that either the civil or criminal law will have any particular substantive content . . . Likewise, article 6(2) requires him to be presumed innocent of the offence but does not say anything about what the mental or other elements of the offence should be. In *R v G* [2003] 1 Cr App R 343, para 33 Dyson LJ said:

'The position is quite clear. So far as article 6 is concerned, the fairness of the provisions of the substantive law of the contracting states is not a matter for investigation. The content and interpretation of domestic substantive law is not engaged by article 6.'

[7] The other ground of appeal is that the conviction violated the defendant's right of privacy under article 8 . . .
[10] Prosecutorial policy and sentencing do not fall under article 8. If the offence in question is a justifiable interference with private life, that is an end of the matter. If the prosecution has been unduly heavy handed, that may be unfair and unjust, but not an infringement of human rights."

BARONESS HALE:

"[54] In effect, therefore, the real complaint is that the defendant has been convicted of an offence bearing the label 'rape'. Parliament has very recently decided that this is the correct label to apply to this activity. In my view this does not engage the article 8 rights of the defendant at all, but if it does, it is entirely justified. The concept of private life 'covers the physical and moral integrity of the person, including his or her sexual life': *X and Y v The Netherlands* 8 EHRR 235, para 22. This does not mean that every sexual relationship, however brief or unsymmetrical, is worthy of respect, nor is every sexual act which a person wishes to perform. It does mean that the physical and moral integrity of the complainant, vulnerable by reason of her age if nothing else, was worthy of respect."

LORD MANCE:

"[70] In the final analysis, the core of the defendant's objection to what occurred lies in the stigma which he maintains he will sustain as a result of the heading attached to section 5. If he had any complaint on this score, it has to be, as I see it, on the basis that the use of the word 'rape' in that heading involves an unjustified stigma which will affect his 'right to establish and to develop relationships with other human beings, especially in the emotional field for the development and fulfilment of one's own personality'. However, the concept of 'statutory rape' has long been familiar as a description of the previous strict liability offence of unlawful sexual intercourse with a girl existing under section 5 of the Sexual Offences Act 1956. The actual ingredients of the offence are defined by the actual wording of the section. The ingredients are strict, but their strictness reflects the protective purpose of the section and the unreality or unreasonableness of speaking of any properly informed consent in relation to sexual intercourse with someone aged 12 or under . . .

[71] The criticism made is that the offence under section 5 should have been framed so as to contain an exception for a belief (at least if reasonably held) on the part of the defendant that the complainant was 13 or over, and/or possibly also for circumstances where the defendant was himself under a certain age. But the offence under section 5 is deliberately strict in its protective intention, and leaves such matters to be taken account of in sentencing."

Appeal dismissed[43]

The one area where the ECHR can have an impact is in relation to sentencing for strict liability offences. In *International Transport Roth GmbH*[44] it was stated that to be compatible with art.6(1) there needed to be an investigation into the culpability of defendants at the sentencing stage to ensure that a punitive response is proportionate to the offending. In *R. v G* the defendant had been sentenced to a 12-month detention and training order. The Court of Appeal reduced this to a conditional discharge for 12 months. (He had already spent five months in custody.) Baroness Hale and Lord Mance stated

---

[43]   An application by G to the ECtHR was declared inadmissible on similar reasoning to that of the House of Lords: *G v United Kingdom (Application No.37334/08)* (2011). See A. Ashworth, "Human Rights: Presumption of Innocence, Art. 6(2)" [2012] Crim L.R. 47. For a recent application of G see *R. v Brown (Richard)* [2013] UKSC 43.
[44]   *International Transport Roth GmbH v Secretary of State for the Home Department* [2002] 3 W.L.R. 344.

that this final sentence was rational and proportional, impliedly suggesting that the original sentence imposed might have been incompatible with the Convention.

5. Are strict liability offences justifiable?

The Law Commission has stated:

> "The criminal law should only be employed to deal with wrongdoers who deserve the stigma associated with criminal conviction because they have engaged in seriously reprehensible conduct. It should not be used as the primary means of promoting regulatory objectives."[45]

In the light of this strong statement of principle, possible justifications for the imposition of strict liability require close scrutiny, starting with the general purposes of punishment.

Herbert L. Packer, "Mens Rea and the Supreme Court" (1962) Sup. Ct. Rev. 107 at 109:

"To punish conduct without reference to the actor's state of mind is both inefficacious and unjust. It is inefficacious because conduct unaccompanied by an awareness of the factors making it criminal does not mark the actor as one who needs to be subjected to punishment in order to deter him or others from behaving similarly in the future, nor does it single him out as a socially dangerous individual who needs to be incapacitated or reformed. It is unjust because the actor is subjected to the stigma of a criminal conviction without being morally blameworthy."

From this, two major questions emerge:

(i)   Can strict liability be justified on utilitarian or instrumental grounds?

(ii) Is strict liability a morally justifiable doctrine?

(i) The utilitarian and instrumental arguments

In favour of strict liability, it is claimed that the interests of the public require that the highest possible standards of care be exercised by people engaged in certain forms of conduct and that "strict liability can reduce the risks of harm to private and public interests".[46] Expressed in utilitarian terms, the greater good to be achieved by occasionally convicting someone who may have taken all reasonable care to abide by the law could not be achieved to the same extent, if, for example, the defence of reasonable mistake were available.

R. Macrory, Regulatory Justice: Sanctioning in a Post-Hampton World (2006), paras D4–D8:

"D4 A core argument in favour of the use of strict liability offences is that it improves deterrence . . . This is likely to be especially important where the non-compliance involves technical and managerial complexities of which only the regulated body, rather than the regulator, has full knowledge.

D5 Prosecution of legitimate businesses should generally be a matter of last resort after other sanctioning

---

[45]   Law Commission Consultation Paper No.195, *Criminal Liability in Regulatory Contexts* (2010), para.1.28.
[46]   G. Lamond, "What is a Crime?" (2007) 27 O.J.L.S. 609 at 630.

tools have failed or where the offence is serious enough to warrant a prosecution in the first instance. However, without the existence of criminal offences which are reasonably easy to prove, the regulator's power to advise and warn regulated business would be seriously jeopardised: 'Routine enforcement is conducted against a background of the criminal law and the implied threat of invocation . . .'

D6 Strict liability offences are also an important tool in securing convictions of corporate entities . . .

D7 Strict liability for regulatory offences can also be justified on the grounds that business operating in regulatory areas can be said to implicitly accept the risk of criminal liability even where no intention or recklessness is involved . . . Strict liability encourages companies not just to do what they can reasonably be capable of, but to do everything possible to comply. Further, it may be consistent with a public view that regulatory breaches causing serious damage (such as a major pollution incident, or death or serious injury in the workplace or elsewhere) are truly criminal in their own right, whatever the state of mind of the perpetrator.

D8 Finally, in practice, any perceived injustices from strict criminal liability is tempered by the fact that 'fault creeps back in during the various stages of the enforcement process'. Prosecution bodies have discretion whether or not to prosecute in a particular case, and are more likely to prosecute where in their view there is some element of fault. Courts have discretion in the sentence they impose, and lack of intention or recklessness can be presented by the offender in mitigation."

United States v Dotterweich, 320 US (1943) 277 at 284–285 (Supreme Court of the United States)

FRANKFURTER J:

"The Food and Drugs Act of 1906 was an exertion by Congress of its power to keep impure and adulterated food and drugs out of the channels of commerce . . . The purposes of this legislation thus touch phases of the lives and health of people which, in the circumstances of modern industrialism, are largely beyond self-protection . . . In the interest of the larger good it puts the burden of acting at hazard upon a person otherwise innocent but standing in responsible relation to a public danger . . .

Hardship there doubtless may be under a statute which thus penalizes the transaction though consciousness of wrongdoing be totally wanting. Balancing relative hardships, Congress has preferred to place it upon those who have at least the opportunity of informing themselves of the existence of conditions imposed for the protection of consumers before sharing in illicit commerce, rather than to throw the hazard on the innocent public who are wholly helpless."

A. Kenny, Freewill and Responsibility (1978), p.93:

"The application of strict liability can be justified in special cases: particularly with regard to the conduct of a business. In such a case, even a strict liability statute makes an appeal to the practical reasoning of the citizens: in this case, when the decision is taken whether to enter the business the strictness of the liability is a cost to be weighed. Strict liability is most in place when it is brought to bear on corporations. In such cases there may not be, in advance, any individual on whom an obligation of care rests which would ground a charge of negligence for the causing of the harm which the statute wishes to prevent: the effect of the legislation may be to lead corporations to take the decision to appoint a person with the task of finding out how to prevent the harm in question."

Opponents of strict liability have argued that there is no evidence that a higher standard of care results from the imposition of strict liability. Those engaged in activities will only do what is reasonable to prevent harm. Indeed, some have argued that strict liability may operate as a disincentive to do even this. If operators know that prosecution could flow whatever precautions they take, they may be tempted to take none whatsoever. In other words, the defendant may as well be "hanged for a sheep as for a lamb".[47] Such an attitude scarcely increases respect for the law. There may be further harmful effects: the innocent may be made to feel insecure not only in general psychological terms but to the

---

[47]   P. Brett, *An Inquiry into Criminal Guilt* (Sydney: Law Book Co of Australia, 1963), p.8.

extent that they may be deterred from entering into socially beneficial enterprises governed by strict liability.[48]

James B. Brady, "Strict Liability Offences: A Justification" (1972) 8 Crim. L. Bulletin 217 at 224:

"There are two replies to this argument. First, there is little evidence to show that the effect of strict liability offences has been to make these socially beneficial enterprises less attractive. The second, and more important point is that a person who does not have the capacity to run (for example) a dairy in such a manner as to prevent the adulteration of milk is not to be protected on the sole ground that he is engaged in a 'socially beneficial' enterprise. An incompetent carrying on an enterprise in which there is the danger of widespread harm actually is not engaged in a 'socially beneficial' enterprise. There can be no objection, therefore, to his choosing not to enter the business."

In addition to the arguments above, a further instrumental argument may be adduced. Because of the sheer volume of criminal offences, particularly those of a regulatory nature, it is argued that it would be too time-consuming to require the prosecution to prove a mental element.

A.P. Simester, "Is Strict Liability Always Wrong?", in A.P. Simester (ed.), Appraising Strict Liability (2005), p.26:

"From an administrative perspective, the costs involved before and during trial are likely to be considerably decreased if [the activity] is made a criminal offence, since the number of elements required to be proved at trial, and the number of potential issues, is reduced. This consideration matters because criminal justice is very expensive. It is plausible that, if every one of a nation's offences required proof of *mens rea* with respect to all elements of the *actus reus*, administration of the criminal law would not be merely cumbersome but unaffordable . . . If it is impossible fully to protect victims from harm while maintaining a Rolls-Royce system of criminal justice, the conflicting interests of defendants and victims may be mediated, in part, by simplifying the *mens rea* elements of certain offences . . . The state should consider *which* offences to 'skimp' on. If the choice is either cutting corners or abandoning the prohibition altogether, a pared-down regulation (say, with reduced sanctions attached) may well be preferable."

Norval Morris and Colin Howard, Studies in Criminal Law (1964), p.199:

"[It is often alleged that there is] an administrative problem. Prosecutions are numerous: if P were required to prove a wrongful intention, in itself impossible in most regulatory offence cases, the speed at which these charges can at present be dealt with would be much diminished and overwhelming arrears of work would accumulate . . . There is no evidence of an administrative problem. Proof of absence of fault is admissible in mitigation of punishment. If such proof is admissible for one purpose, no loss of time is involved in admitting it for another. Prosecutions for regulatory offences may be numerous but so are prosecutions for many other offences, particularly the various forms of larceny. No one suggests that the pressure of work should be relieved by removing the requirement of *mens rea* from larceny. Indeed, it is arguable that, far from saving time, strict liability often wastes time by necessitating legal argument as to whether it applies to the case in hand."

Supporters of the expediency argument sometimes temper their support by claiming that prosecutorial discretion will prevent the obviously blameless being charged. There are, however, great difficulties with this approach. Prosecutorial discretion is notoriously unreliable; there is no guidance as to how extreme the case must be to justify a prosecution. Most importantly, it amounts to a negation of strict liability. To some extent at least, liability is being made to depend upon fault. We shall return to this point later.

---

[48]   R.B. Brandt, *Ethical Theory* (Englewood Cliffs: Prentice-Hall, 1959), p.493.

(ii) Is strict liability morally justifiable?

It has already been noted that the concept of mens rea is deeply embedded in the development of the criminal law. For many commentators its importance is so great that it cannot be trumped by utilitarian considerations. According to this view, the criminal law should only be invoked when the defendant has done something deserving of blame. Somebody who has taken all reasonable precautions is not blameworthy and does not deserve to be punished. Labelling a blameless person a criminal "amounts to systematic moral defamation by the state".[49]

The classic response to this argument is that while these views might be true of stigmatic crimes, most offences of strict liability are not "real" crimes, but, at most, are "quasi-criminal" offences.[50] Simester has argued that sometimes "strict liability may be legitimate in non-stigmatic offences".[51] In *Wings Ltd v Ellis* Lord Scarman referred to the Trade Descriptions Act 1968, which creates consumer protection offences, as being "not a truly criminal statute. Its purpose is not the enforcement of the criminal law but the maintenance of trading standards."[52]

Peter Brett, An Inquiry into Criminal Guilt (1963), pp.114–116:

"Let us now consider what ought to be the future of the doctrine of strict liability. There are those who believe that there is no great objection to it, and even that it serves a useful and proper social purpose. Sayre's general conclusion ('Public Welfare Offences', 33 Col. L. Rev. 55 (1933)) was that the doctrine was applicable only to the minor public welfare offences, despite his recognition of its applicability in some other fields, which he attempted to distinguish on special grounds. In his view there is no objection to applying strict liability so long as only a light penalty is involved; but it ought not to be applied to 'true crimes'. This seems rather like saying that it is all right to be unjust so long as you are not too unjust. My own position is that any doctrine which permits the infliction of punishment on a morally innocent man is reprehensible.

If my view is accepted, we are then faced with the question whether it can be implemented without imperilling the social fabric. There seems to be a strong belief that it cannot. The argument is that the regulation of public welfare has been successfully accomplished under a regime of strict liability, and that it is thus proved that 'strict liability regulation works'. This is doubtless true, but it does not take us one step further to the proposition that effective public welfare regulation will not work without strict liability. That proposition must for most countries remain empirically unverified, for the simple reason that it has never been tried out in practice.

A school of thought has sprung up in recent years which attempts to resolve the question by attaching new labels to strict liability offences. Thus it has been argued that the strict liability offences should be termed 'civil offences', and that to such offences mistake of fact should not be a defence. They would be punishable only by a fine, and not by any form of imprisonment.[53] The *Model Penal Code* appears to accept this basic position save that it proposes to treat the strict liability offences as still being criminal in nature, but classes them as violations: as such the punishment which may be imposed when they are committed without fault is strictly limited, and the determination whether to class an offence as a violation is left to the legislature.

The difficulty which I have with proposals of this kind is that their proponents seem to regard the injustice of punishing innocent conduct as a matter which may be disregarded if it takes place under a different label. My own view is that the injustice remains unaffected despite the semantic change. A fine continues to be a punishment whether it is labelled civil or criminal. I do not deny that the change of label may accomplish a removal of part, if not the whole, of the stigma which results from the mere fact of conviction for a crime; nor would I wish to diminish the importance of such a step. But when this step has been taken, there still remains the brute fact

---

[49]   A.P. Simester, "Is Strict Liability Always Wrong?", in A.P. Simester (ed.), *Appraising Strict Liability* (Oxford: OUP, 2005), p.34.

[50]   For a more nuanced argument that strict liability may be legitimate in the grading of offences, see, K.W. Simons, "Is Strict Liability in the Grading of Offences Consistent With Retributive Desert?" (2012) 32 O.J.L.S. 445.

[51]   Simester, "Is Strict Liability Always Wrong?", in A.P. Simester (ed.), *Appraising Strict Liability* (Oxford: OUP, 2005), p.21.

[52]   *Wings Ltd v Ellis* [1984] 3 All E.R. 577 at 587.

[53]   This view is, of course, relevant also to the deterrent argument. Some commentators have argued (e.g. Brady, above, p.244) that higher penalties might increase the deterrent effect.

that a man is being punished for innocent behaviour. I cannot reconcile this with any theory of justice with which I am acquainted."

The distinction drawn between "real" and "quasi-criminal" crimes or between stigmatic and non-stigmatic crimes (sometimes known as crimes *mala in se* and *mala prohibita*), is problematic. How is one to determine whether a crime is a stigmatic one or not? Is it based on whether the convicted person feels stigmatised (psychological stigma) or on whether such a person ought to feel stigmatised (normative stigma)?[54] Referring to the offence under the Insolvency Act 1986 in *Muhamad*, extracted above, Stanton-Ife asks:

> "How is it that stigma gets attached to criminal convictions on his Lordship's view? Does he mean the population at large or the business community or some other group does not *believe* this behaviour to be stigmatic or that it is not *deserving* of stigma, whatever any group of people may think about the matter?" (italics in original)[55]

Baroness Wootton argued that the distinction being drawn between crimes *mala in se* and *mala prohibita* does not rest on any inherent characteristics of the former category other than the antiquity of such crimes.[56] Particularly once one steps beyond offences that are part of a regulatory scheme, it becomes far from obvious that a clear line can be drawn between truly criminal and quasi-criminal offences. Even with regulatory offences there are problems with making them offences of strict liability because this "marginalises" such offences; nobody, least of all the perpetrator, has to take them seriously because, after all, they are not really criminal.

6. Enforcement

One of the classic arguments against strict liability is that it results in the prosecution and conviction of people who were not at fault and who might even have done everything they possibly could to avoid bringing about the harm. However, empirical studies of the enforcement of many strict liability offences do not always support this conclusion.

The case of *Storkwain*[57] provides an interesting case study. In this case the defendants were found guilty of the strict liability offence of supplying prescription-only drugs without a valid prescription; it had been forged. At first sight it seems that the defendants could not be blamed for what had happened. How, in a busy chemist, could checks be made as to the validity of every prescription? Yet closer examination of the case reveals that the Pharmaceutical Society (the regulatory body) which wanted to confirm the principle of strict liability, actually believed the pharmacist's conduct fell short of normal good practice. The prescription was a blatant forgery. Moreover, because the prescription was for controlled drugs it was expected that the pharmacist would telephone for confirmation. He did so, but, rather than checking in the directory, rang the number given on the prescription. Not surprisingly, the forgery was confirmed by an accomplice at the end of the phone. In conclusion then, the pharmacist was prosecuted because he was at fault; even a due diligence defence, had one existed, would not have saved him.[58]

---

54   J. Stanton-Ife, "Strict Liability: Stigma and Regret" (2007) 27 O.J.L.S 151.
55   Stanton-Ife, "Strict Liability: Stigma and Regret" (2007) 27 O.J.L.S 151 at 158.
56   B. Wootton, *Crime and the Criminal Law*, 2nd edn (London: Stevens and Son, 1981), pp.42–44.
57   *Pharmaceutical Society of Great Britain v Storkwain Ltd* (1986) 83 Cr. App. R. 359. See above, p.234.
58   B.S. Jackson, "Storkwein: A Case Study in Strict Liability and Self-Regulation" [1991] Crim. L.R. 892.

Empirical studies of many strict liability offences also point to highly selective enforcement practices amongst different enforcement agencies.[59] Fault appears to play an important role in the decision to prosecute (although the magnitude of the harm is also significant). However, compliance is more normally secured by means of co-operation rather than coercion and the self-image of the inspectors is that of educators and advisers rather than as police. Advice, repeat visits, warnings, improvement notices and the like are all much more likely to be used to secure compliance. For example, in 2005 the Health and Safety Executive commenced 712 prosecutions yet, in contrast, issued 8,445 enforcement notices (improvement notices, immediate prohibition notices and deferred prohibition notices).[60] The emphasis is on administrative procedures with the criminal law being a remedy of last resort.[61]

Other regulatory bodies may have a rather different self-image which will play a significant part in shaping prosecution policies. The Inland Revenue, Customs and Excise and the Department for Work and Pensions (as far as national insurance contributions are concerned) see their role as revenue collectors[62] and will try to secure a negotiated settlement in preference to prosecution. This does not mean, however, that such regulatory bodies would be happy to see mens rea incorporated into the substantive offences.

Genevra Richardson, "Strict Liability for Regulatory Crime: The Empirical Research" [1987] Crim. L.R. 295 at 303:

"The existing research also indicates that despite their effective rejection of strict liability in practice the majority of enforcement officers regard it with favour and urge its retention. Although prosecution and its direct threat are seldom used, routine enforcement is conducted against a background of the criminal law and the implicit threat of its invocation. The fewer the uncertainties which attach to the law, therefore, the stronger is the agencies' bargaining position."[63]

Not all agencies operate in the same way, however. As far as supplementary benefit payments are concerned, the Department for Work and Pensions appears to be much more willing to prosecute.[64] This policy, which appears to have been initiated by senior staff within the Department, has resulted in a number of initiatives against such fraudsters. It is rather more common, however, for enforcement policies to emerge from "the bottom up".

Such selective enforcement practices are disturbing in a number of respects. Most importantly, those policies which result in only flagrant breaches being prosecuted help to perpetuate in the mind of offenders and society the view that such activities are not really criminal despite the undoubted (and sometimes very substantial) harm caused.

The discrepancy in enforcement practices between the Inland Revenue and the Department for Work and Pensions has prompted the comment:

"At the heart of the contradictions in policy and practice is the ideological representation of the tax-payer as a 'giver' to the state and the supplementary benefit claimant as a 'taker' from the state."[65]

---

59   I. Paulus, *The Search for Pure Food: A Sociology of Legislation in Britain* (Littleton: Fred B. Rothman & Co, 1974); W.F. Carson, "White-Collar Crime and the Enforcement of Factory Legislation" (1970) 10 Brit. J. Criminol. 383.

60   R. Macrory, *Regulatory Justice: Sanctioning in a Post-Hampton World* (2006), para.4.19.

61   See generally, K. Hawkins, *Law as Last Resort* (New York: OUP, 2002).

62   Paulus, *The Search for Food: A Sociology of Legislation in Britain*, p.207-210.

63   See also Nelken's study of landlords and harassment: *The Limits of the Legal Process: A Study of Landlords, Law and Crime* (Milton Keynes: Open University Press, 1983).

64   D. Cook, *Rich Law, Poor Law: Differential Responses to Tax and Supplementary Benefit Fraud* (Oxford: Elsevier, 1989). There appears also to be some disparity in levels of punishment.

65   Cook, *Rich Law, Poor Law: Differential Responses to Tax and Supplementary Benefit Fraud* (1989), p.160.

One final point must be made here. There are a large number of strict liability offences that fall outside the regulatory schemes discussed above and where liability tends, indeed, to be strict. Many of the summary motoring offences, such as exceeding a speed limit, driving whilst disqualified, etc. would be cases in point. In this particular context, with prosecuting policies varying considerably from one area to another, it is much harder to ascertain what role, if any, is played by fault.

7. Sentencing

Sentences for strict liability offences (particularly white collar crimes) are generally light. This may be because a defendant is regarded as less blameworthy than for "real" crimes or may even be seen as blameless.

R. v Jackson [2007] Cr. App. R. 28 (Court of Appeal, Criminal Division)

HOOPER LJ:

"At the sentencing stage it is important for the court to determine the level of culpability to the criminal standard of proof. A pilot who knowingly or recklessly flies his plane at less than 100 ft may expect a higher sentence than one who flies lower than that height negligently (as did the appellant). Likewise if there is no knowledge or recklessness or negligence then it may well be that the appropriate penalty is one of an absolute discharge."

On the other hand, there may be a number of other factors having little to do with blame or the amount of harm caused that influence such sentencing practices. The fact that the defendant has lost her job or business may be seen as punishment enough. The level of fine may be affected by the sentencer's perception of the defendant's ability to pay.[66] The defendant's previous good character may be persuasive but likely to figure is, once again, the judgment that such offences are not really criminal. The result is that the fines imposed may be no more than "pin-pricks" to an organisation which may be able to write them off as a minor business expense.[67]

A further concern is the lack of uniformity in sentencing practice. Within an area of activity (for example, pollution) sentences can be erratic.[68] Some efforts have been made to address this in specific areas. For example, the Sentencing Advisory Panel has published advice to the Court of Appeal with sentencing guidelines on environmental offences.[69] However, the problem becomes exacerbated when sentences from different areas of activity are compared. Research has suggested, for example, that those engaged in supplementary benefits fraud are likely to be regarded less sympathetically than those engaged in tax evasion.[70]

---

[66] N. Padfield, "Clean Water and Muddy Causation: Is Causation a Question of Law or Fact, or Just a Way of Allocating Blame?" [1995] Crim. L.R. 683 at 693.

[67] H. Croall, *White Collar Crime* (1992), pp.112–125.

[68] Padfield, "Clean Water and Muddy Causation: Is Causation a Question of Law or Fact, or Just a Way of Allocating Blame?" [1995] Crim. L.R. 683 at 693.

[69] Sentencing Advisory Panel, *Environmental Offences: The Panel's Advice to the Court of Appeal* (2000).

[70] Cook, *Rich Law, Poor Law: Differential Responses to Tax and Supplementary Benefit Fraud* (1989), p.160.

8. Civil sanctions

Instead of employing strict criminal liability (or criminal punishments), more use could be made of civil/administrative law to ensure compliance with the law.

In 2009, Baroness Scotland, the Attorney-General, was "fined" (according to the press) £5,000 by the UK Border Agency for employing an illegal worker. Baroness Scotland is reported as saying:

> "It's a civil penalty just as if you drive into the city and don't pay a congestion charge. It's not a criminal offence. I made an administrative technical error."[71]

It is notoriously difficult to define a crime.[72] Perhaps the most widely-accepted definition is that of Glanville Williams that a crime is

> "an act that is capable of being followed by criminal proceedings, having one of the types of outcome (punishment, etc.) known to follow these proceedings".[73]

Applying this test to the Baroness Scotland case, this was indeed a civil penalty (and not a fine) that was imposed under s.15 of the Immigration, Asylum and Nationality Act 2006. Section 15 refers to a "penalty" and uses the civil language that "it is contrary to this section to employ". This can be contrasted with s.21 of the same Act which states that "a person commits an *offence* if he employs another *knowing* that the employee is subject to immigration control". Of course, the nomenclature chosen by Parliament is not determinative but what is important, in distinguishing this from a crime, is that this civil penalty "may be recovered by the Secretary of State as debt due to him".[74]

This does suggest a possible way forward. Instead of employing strict liability criminal offences, the civil law and civil sanctions could be utilised. If decriminalisation of existing strict liability offences were contemplated, there would need to be some assurance that the loss of procedural safeguards thereby occasioned would not be likely to lead to administrative malpractice and, of course, it would not satisfy critics such as Brett, who believe that relabeling offences using the language of civil law is mere semantics.[75]

An alternative approach is to retain (or create) strict liability offences as criminal offences but to utilise civil sanctions instead of traditional criminal punishments. In 2006, the Government commissioned the Macrory Report to examine regulatory sanctions.[76] This Report proposed that much regulatory non-compliance should be dealt with by administrative remedies outside the criminal justice system. These recommendations have been given effect to by the Regulatory Enforcement and Sanctions Act 2008 which allows Ministers to introduce statutory instruments providing civil sanctions to a wide range of strict liability offences contained in a long list of statutes: for example, the Control of Pollution Act 1974, the Dangerous Dogs Act 1991, the Fireworks Act 2003, the Food Safety Act 1990 and the Medicines Act 1968. In all, 142 statutes are listed.[77] These civil sanctions can also be

---

[71]   J. Beattie, "Baroness Scotland refuses to Resign after £5K Fine for Hiring an Illegal Worker", *The Mirror*, September 23, 2009.

[72]   D. Ormerod, *Smith and Hogan's: Criminal Law*, 13th edn (Oxford: OUP, 2011), pp.3–15.

[73]   "The Definition of Crime" (1955) 8 C.L.P. 107 at 128. See also Lamond, "What is a Crime?" (2007) 27 O.J.L.S. 609 at 630.

[74]   Section 18.

[75]   Above p.245.

[76]   *Regulatory Justice: Making Sanctions Effective* (Final Report, 2006) (Macrory Report). See also, Law Commission Consultation Paper No.195, *Criminal Liability in Regulatory Contexts* (2010), paras 3.21–3.51.

[77]   Schedule 6.

applied to a further 45 statutes under which Ministers have power by statutory instrument to create criminal offences.[78]

In these cases, where a Regulator (for example, the Environment Agency, the Food Standards Agency, the Health and Safety Executive, the Office of Fair Trading[79]) is satisfied beyond reasonable doubt that a person has committed one of the specified offences, instead of a criminal prosecution, the Regulator may impose one of the following civil sanctions:

(1) Fixed Monetary Penalty[80]: usually capped at £5,000.[81]

(2) Discretionary requirements.[82] The Regulator may impose one or more of the following:

- a Variable Monetary Penalty,
- a compliance notice, and
- a restoration notice.

(3) Stop notices[83] (preventing a person from carrying on an activity until specified steps have been taken).

(4) Enforcement undertakings[84] (an undertaking to take specified corrective action).

In all of these cases there is a right of appeal to a tribunal, but not to a court of law.[85] Provision may be made for the Regulator to recover monetary penalties either as a civil debt or, on the order of a court, as if payable under a court order.[86]

Under these provisions the criminal process and the criminal courts will be bypassed although a breach of any of the orders could ultimately result in judicial sanctions. These provisions do not involve any decriminalisation of existing offences. A criminal prosecution remains an option. As we have seen, those enforcement agencies already involved in such procedures rely upon the stick of the criminal sanction as their last resort.

9. Conclusion

Despite the weight of the arguments against strict liability offences, it would be naïve to imagine that they can all be transformed into offences requiring full mens rea or that they could all be decriminalised. It seems clear that there is a cogent argument in favour of strict liability for the most minor of offences. However, for the rest a number of possibilities exist.

First, it is open to the courts to extend the presumption in favour of mens rea.[87] One important enhancement, copied from Canada, would be to state that if the penalty for the offence involves imprisonment, then strict liability is precluded.[88]

---

[78]   Section 62, Sch.7.
[79]   Schedule 5 lists 27 designated regulators.
[80]   Section 39.
[81]   Ministry of Justice, *Guidance on Creating New Regulatory Penalties and Offences* (2009), para.11.
[82]   Section 42.
[83]   Section 46.
[84]   Section 50.
[85]   Section 54.
[86]   Section 52(2).
[87]   Under the Draft Criminal Code, cl.20, there is a presumption in favour of mens rea "unless otherwise provided" (Law Commission Paper No.177, *A Criminal Code for England and Wales* (1989)).
[88]   See A. Ashworth, "Editorial: Trumping Strict Liability" Crim. L. R. 721 at 721-723.

Secondly, again following the lead set elsewhere,[89] and as recommended in the Law Commission's consultation paper,[90] existing offences of strict liability could be converted into what would amount to offences of negligence by the general, rather than selective, use of due diligence defences. This would not have the effect of making the prosecutor's task too difficult because the onus would be on the defendant to show that he was not negligent. However, as seen, it is possible that such a general shifting of the burden of proof could be incompatible with the ECHR.

Thirdly, increased use of administrative procedures and civil sanctions (as under the Regulatory Enforcement and Sanctions Act 2008) could be made to secure compliance. This can have twin benefits. It can close the "compliance gap, where some regulators lack the appropriate enforcement tools to address regulatory non-compliance".[91] Also, through by-passing the criminal process, the civil sanctions will not carry the same stigma as a criminal conviction. This might lessen the objections to such strict liability offences. However, some caution is necessary here as this by-passing of the criminal process could result in a loss of the protection offered by the criminal justice system, for example, in relation to the burden of proof.

Many of the provisions in the Regulatory Enforcement and Sanctions Act 2008 are aimed at corporate non-compliance with regulatory laws (but are not limited to such cases). Perhaps this differentiation between individual and corporate responsibility should be extended. Many, if not most, strict liability offences govern the operations not of individuals but of businesses. Those who object to strict liability when applied to individuals might be prepared to support its use for corporations, especially if a wider range of sentencing options were introduced. It is to this, and related, matters that we now turn.

II. Corporate Criminal Liability

A. Introduction

The criminal law has developed as a mechanism for responding to individual wrongdoing. Individuals are regarded as autonomous. They are free to control their actions, to think and make decisions, including the choice to do wrong. Accordingly, such persons can be held responsible for those choices and can be praised or blamed and punished for them. This individualistic notion of responsibility does not naturally encompass artificial organisations such as companies.

Much of our lives today is affected by companies and other organisations: we work for them (in conditions that might be dangerous); we purchase their products (that might explode or poison us); we travel in their ferries and trains (that might be unsafe); we drink the water they provide (which might be unclean); and we breathe the air (into which they might have emitted their fumes). In short, companies can destroy our environment or kill or injure us but can they be held criminally responsible?

A company is a legal entity. It has a legal personality. It can sue and be sued in its own name and, as seen in the previous section on strict liability where many of the defendants were companies, it can be held criminally liable.[92] In principle, there is no reason why a company should not be capable of committing any criminal offence, subject to two exceptions. First, it is unlikely that a company could

---

[89] e.g. see the American Law Institute, Model Penal Code, Tent. Draft No.4, 1985, s.2.05 and comment at p.140.
[90] Above fn.38.
[91] Ministry of Justice, *Guidance on Creating New Regulatory Penalties and Offences* (2009), para.3.
[92] A partnership can be criminally liable as a separate entity from the partners if there are partnership assets available to meet any penalty imposed: *R. v W Stevenson & Sons (A Partnership)* [2008] EWCA Crim 273.

commit crimes that necessarily involve human action such as sexual offences and bigamy.[93] Secondly, as the only criminal penalty that can be imposed on a company in English law is a fine (apart from remedial orders and publicity orders), a company cannot be convicted of murder as this carries a mandatory sentence of life imprisonment.

While companies have long been held liable for a wide array of offences, such as pollution offences and offences involving financial irregularities, the whole issue of corporate criminal liability has become extremely high-profile and controversial in cases where the activities of companies have led to the death or injury of workers or members of the public. The interest in this subject was heightened by two sets of developments. First, there were a series of highly publicised "disasters" in which large numbers of persons were killed. In 1988, there was the Piper Alpha oil rig explosion in which 167 people were killed. The inquiry which followed identified "unsafe practices", "grave shortcomings" and "significant flaws" in the management's approach to safety as causes of the explosion and subsequent deaths.[94] In 1987, there was the King's Cross fire in which 31 people died and 60 people were injured, the cause being the failure of the various groups and individuals within the overall corporate structure to identify their respective areas of responsibility.[95] And, most infamously, in 1987 there was the Zeebrugge "disaster" in which the ferry, *Herald of Free Enterprise*, capsised killing 192 people. The official inquiry found that

> "from top to bottom the body corporate was infected with the disease of sloppiness . . . The failure on the part of the shore management to give proper and clear directions was a contributory cause of the disaster."[96]

Further, there have been a series of high-profile train crashes (Southall: seven killed and 151 injured; Paddington: 31 killed and over 400 injured; Hatfield: four killed and 102 injured) accompanied by mounting accusations of incompetence and complacency and poor safety management by the rail companies concerned.[97] More recently, there has been strong condemnation of deaths caused in hospitals. In 2006 it was revealed that 33 people had died from *C Difficile* bacterium over the previous two years at Stoke Mandeville Hospital. Over the same period this bacterium directly caused the deaths of 90 people and contributed to the deaths of a further 345 people at two Kent hospitals. In both cases a Healthcare Commission Report revealed "serious failings" by senior managers.[98]

---

[93] *R. v P&O European Ferries (Dover) Ltd* (1991) 93 Cr. App. R. 72 at 73. In *Richmond upon Thames LBC v Pinn & Wheeler Ltd, The Times*, February 14, 1989, it was held that a company could not be convicted of an offence of driving a lorry without a permit. The act of driving was a physical act which could only be performed by a natural person. In *R. v Robert Millar (Contractors) Ltd* [1970] 1 All E.R. 577 a company was convicted of causing death by dangerous driving. This was, however, on the basis that the company had counselled and procured the offence. In *Kosar v Bank of Scotland Plc t/a Halifax* [2011] EWHC 1050 (Admin) it was held that it would be possible for a corporation to commit the offence of harassment. In a private prosecution a bank was accused of committing the offence of harassment under s.2 of the Protection from Harassment Act 1997. The District Judge ordered the case to be dropped, on the basis that the offence could only be committed by a person who is an individual. Section 7(5) of the Act states: "references to a person, in the context of the harassment of a person, are references to a person who is an individual". The appellant argued this applied only to *victims* not to perpetrators. The High Court agreed, interpreting Parliament's intention as being that the body corporate could be a perpetrator but not a victim of this offence.

[94] Department of Energy, *The Public Inquiry into the Piper Alpha Disaster* (The Cullen Report) (1990) Cmnd.1310, paras 11.4, 11.14, 14.52.

[95] *Investigation into the Kings Cross Underground Fire* (1988) (Fennell Report).

[96] Department of Transport, *The Merchant Shipping Act 1894, M.V. Herald of Free Enterprise*, Report of Court No.8074 (Sheen Report), para.14.1. See further, pp.269–271.

[97] For example, the Cullen Report on the Paddington (Ladbroke Grove) train crash accused Railtrack of complacency and "underlying deficiencies in the management of safety" (*Ladbroke Grove Rail Enquiry* (Cullen Report), 2001). Other "disasters" that have contributed to the growing clamour for corporate accountability have included the Clapham Junction rail disaster in 1988 where faulty signalling caused the death of 35 people, the Purley train crash in 1989 where five people were killed and there were strong claims that British Rail management shortcomings had contributed to the crash.

[98] Healthcare Commission, *Investigation into Outbreaks of Clostridium Difficile at Stoke Mandeville Hospital, Buckinghamshire*

Secondly, there has been an increased awareness of the numbers of persons annually being killed and seriously injured in their places of work. In 2012/13, 148 people were killed at work. Over the same year, 78,222 workers were reported as having sustained injuries, of which 19,707 were classified as major injuries.[99] These figures do not reveal the full picture with the Health and Safety Executive (HSE) estimating that only half of reportable injuries at work were in fact reported to the authorities.[100] Other surveys have estimated that only about a quarter of reportable non-fatal injuries at work are actually reported.[101]

Many of these incidents will have been the result of corporate fault. The HSE itself has publicly stated in the past that 90 per cent of deaths could have been prevented and that "in 70 per cent of cases positive action by management could have saved lives".[102]

Frank Pearce and Steve Tombs, Toxic Capitalism: Corporate Crime and the Chemical Industry (1998), p.153–154:

"In report after report, the HSE and its Inspectorates have stated that managements bear primary responsibility for these 'accidents'. For example, . . . the HSE has stated that in 75 per cent of maintenance accidents in the chemical industry, site management were found to be 'wholly or partly responsible for failing to take all reason-ably practicable precautions to prevent an accident'; similarly, managements have been cited as responsible for approximately two out of three deaths in general manufacturing, three out of five farm deaths. 78 per cent of fatal maintenance accidents in manufacturing, 70 per cent of deaths in the construction industry, and so on . . . It seems clear that the predominance of the label 'accident' to such systematic failings . . . owes more to legal, social, political and economic modes of thought and balances of power—to a dominant ideological hegemony—than to any inherent features of the events themselves . . .

It is clear that for many instances of employee death, injury or ill-health arising out of work, the use of the term 'accident' is often inappropriate . . . [A] significant number of these incidents are the consequence of criminal acts of commission or omissions."

Increased publicity of these "disasters" and other work-related fatality cases has had a profound effect on "transmitting messages about risk to the wider population".[103] The result of these two developments has been mounting pressure for the introduction of laws making it easier to hold corporations accountable in such cases. This pressure led to the enactment of the Corporate Manslaughter and Corporate Homicide Act 2007 for cases where people have been killed through corporate gross negligence. This statute will be considered towards the end of this section but, first, more general issues concerning corporate criminal liability, and its application to other offences, must be considered.

Hospitals NHS Trust (2006); Healthcare Commission, *Investigation into Outbreak of Clostridium Difficile at Maidstone and Tunbridge Wells NHS Trust* (2007).

[99]   Health and Safety Executive, *Annual Statistics Report for Great Britain 2012/13*, available at *http://www.hse.gov.uk/statistics/overall/hssh1213.pdf* [Accessed June 6, 2014].

[100]   This is based on self-reported injury data. The legal reporting requirement changed in April 2012 from over three days' incapacitation to over seven days: HSE, *Annual Statistics Report for Great Britain 2012/13*.

[101]   Labour Force Surveys, cited by S. Tombs and D. Whyte, "A Crisis of Enforcement: The Decriminalization of Death and Injury at Work" (2008) 5 *Centre for Crime and Justice Studies*, p.2.

[102]   Health and Safety Executive, *Blackspot Construction* (1988), p.4. See also, Health and Safety Executive, *The Role of Managerial Leadership in Determining Workplace Safety Outcomes* (2003).

[103]   P. Almond, "Regulating Crisis: Evaluating the Potential Legitimizing Effects of 'Corporate Manslaughter' Cases" (2007) 29 *Law and Policy* 285 at 291–293.

B. Corporate or Personal Criminal Liability

A central question is whether the criminal law should hold *corporations* accountable or whether it should rather seek to punish the culpable individuals within the company. The argument in favour of only prosecuting individuals is that it is they who are blameworthy and deserve punishment. In some cases, an individual manager in order to secure promotion, for example, might implement a policy with short-term rewards but contrary to the long-term interests of the company. In such cases the company does not deserve blame and punishment. Further, it is argued that individuals within a company are the ones most amenable to deterrence. In order to deter the company itself fines would need to be huge. A company is only likely to be deterred if its expected costs exceed its expected gains. If a company anticipates making £10 million from a criminal act and the risk of apprehension is 20 per cent, it has been argued that the fine would need to be at least £50 million to have any hope of being an effective deterrent.[104] There is a further problem here with the "deterrence trap": this is where the risk of apprehension is so low that no penalty will operate as a deterrent.[105] In terms of incapacitation and rehabilitation, it could be said that it is the particular individuals who should be removed from office, disciplined or made to improve their work practices.

Finally, it is argued that punishment of a company by way of a fine amounts to punishment of innocent shareholders, creditors, employees who might be made redundant, or the public who will ultimately have to bear the burden of the fine. In short, the ones who will really suffer will be those whom the law is aiming to protect.

On the other hand, the case in favour of corporate criminal liability is formidable.

Brent Fisse and John Braithwaite, "The Allocation of Responsibility for Corporate Crime: Individualism, Collectivism and Accountability" (1988) 11 Sydney L. Rev. 468 at 479–508:

"In the case of organisations, individuals may be the most important parts, but there are other parts, as is evident from factories with manifest routines which operate to some extent independently of the biological agents who flick the switches. Organisations are systems . . . not just aggregations of individuals . . . Indeed, the entire personnel of an organisation may change without reshaping the corporate culture; this may be so even if the new incumbents have personalities quite different from those of the old . . . The fact is that organisations are blamed in their capacity as organisations for causing harm or taking risks in circumstances where they could have acted otherwise. We often react to corporate offenders not merely as impersonal harm-producing forces but as responsible, blameworthy entities. When people blame corporations they . . . [are not] pointing the finger at individuals behind the corporate mantle. They are condemning the fact that the organisation either implemented a policy of non-compliance or failed to exercise its collective capacity to avoid the offence for which blame attaches . . . We routinely hold organisations responsible for a decision when and because that decision instantiates an organisational policy and instantiates an organisational decision-making process which the organisation has chosen for itself . . .

Punishment directed at a corporate entity typically seeks to deter a wide range of individual associates from engaging in conduct directly or indirectly connected with the commission of an offence. Individual persons who are directly implicated in offences may be difficult or impossible to prosecute successfully, and those who influence the commission of offences indirectly may fall outside the scope of liability for complicity or other ancilliary heads of criminal liability . . . Companies value a good reputation for its own sake, just as do universities, sporting clubs and government agencies. Individuals who take on positions of power within such organisations, even if

---

[104]   J.C. Coffee, "'No Soul to Damn: No Body to Kick': An Unscandalised Inquiry into the Problem of Corporate Punishment" (1981) 79 Mich. L. Rev. 386 at 389 drawing on the work of R.A. Posner, *Economic Analysis of Law*, 2nd edn (Boston: Little, Brown, 1977), p.167.

[105]   Coffee, "'No Soul to Damn: No Body to Kick': An Unscandalised Inquiry into the Problem of Corporate Punishment" (1981) 79 Mich. L. Rev. 386 at 390.

they as individuals do not personally feel any deterrent effects of shaming directed at their organisation, may find that they confront role expectations to protect and enhance the repute of the organisation . . . Another factor which tends to limit the deterrent efficacy of individual criminal liability for corporate crime is the expendability of individuals within organizations . . . [T]he corporation 'marches on its elephantine way almost indifferent to its succession of riders.' The risk thus arises of rogue corporations exploiting their capacity to toss off a succession of individual riders and, if necessary, to indemnify them in some way . . . Consider also the extreme tactic adopted by some companies of setting up internal lines of accountability so as to have a 'vice-president responsible for going to jail.' By offering an attractive sacrifice the hope is that prosecutors will feel sufficiently satisfied with their efforts to refrain from pressing charges against the corporation or members of its managerial elite . . .

[I]n some respects corporations may be better endowed than individuals to be the subject of responsibil-ity. Corporations, it may be argued, have a number of advantages when it comes to rational decision-making, including access to a pool of intelligence and the resources to acquire a superior knowledge of legal and other obligations. The conclusion is thus invited that although corporations do not have a 'soul to be damned' they can deserve to be blamed . . .

[With regard to the argument that punishing companies amounts to punishment of innocent shareholders etc.] [f]irst, cost-bearing associates are not themselves subject to the stigma of conviction and criminal punish-ment—they are not convicts but corporate distributees. Secondly, employees and stockholders accede to a distributional scheme in which profits and losses from corporate activities are distributed on the basis of position in the company or type of investment rather than degree of deserved praise or blame . . . Thirdly, and above all, not to punish an enterprise at fault would be to allow corporations to accumulate and distribute to associates a pool of resources which does not reflect the social cost of production. Justice as fairness requires, as a minimum, that the cost of corporate offences be internalised by the enterprise."

Many large corporations have complex structures which make it difficult for outsiders to ascertain who is responsible for a particular decision. Punishing the company can trigger the most appropriate insti-tutional response in that the company is in the best position to identify and discipline its employees. In many cases, prosecution of individuals might be inappropriate as it ignores the corporate pressures that might have been placed upon them by the corporate structure; these pressures will often remain even after the individual has been sacrificed. It is only by punishment of the company itself that one can hope for a corporate response to the wrongdoing by the implementation of the appropriate safety procedures.

Modern companies now often promote themselves as distinct identifiable entities. Such advertising

"designed to 'humanise' the company in the interests of image-building, has reinforced the anthro-pomorphic perception of the company in the public mind, which in turn has led to a public demand to apportion blame and to criminalise and punish companies for serious transgressions".[106]

The concept of fair-labelling applies not just to offences themselves, but to whom we choose to blame for the offences committed. After the capsize of the *Herald of Free Enterprise* a manslaughter prosecution was brought against the company involved (P&O) and seven employees of the company. For reasons to be explored shortly, the judge directed acquittals against P&O and the five most senior employees. It is a telling fact that the relatives of the victims who died on the *Herald of Free Enterprise* were primarily interested in a prosecution of P&O and not of the individuals. Even the prosecution seemed of similar mind when it dropped the charges against the two most immediate "causers" of the sinking as soon as the judge had directed acquittals against P&O and its senior executives. Perhaps there was a realisation that junior employees should never have been left in a position where the entire safety of the ferry and its passengers depended on them without any adequate system of checks or controls. The true fault lay with the company.

---

[106]   L. Dunford and A. Ridley, "No Soul to be Damned, No Body to be Kicked: Responsibility, Blame and Corporate Punishment" (1996) 24 Int. J. Soc. L. 1 at 7.

However, a final and critical point must be stressed here. The above argument is that companies should be capable of being held criminally liable. This does *not* mean that individuals within the company should be exempt from liability. In appropriate cases, where an individual has committed the actus reus with the mens rea of the offence, they should also be liable. Indeed, in the case of small companies, particularly "one-person-companies", imposing criminal liability on the company, in addition to the individual, is somewhat pointless. Even in relation to larger companies, individual criminal liability should be imposed (in addition to corporate criminal liability). The central case for this is based on deterrence. People are more amenable to deterrence than corporations. The evidence suggests that employer groups are most vocal in their opposition to new laws when there is a risk that under those laws company directors or senior managers might go to prison.[107]

Indeed, for many statutory offences, there is specific provision for holding individuals liable when an offence is committed by a company. A standard form employed in many statutes, such as the Health and Safety at Work etc Act 1974 s.37(1), is as follows:

> "Where an offence under any of the relevant statutory provisions committed by a body corporate is proved to have been committed with the consent or connivance of, or to have been attributable to any neglect on the part of, any director, manager, secretary or other similar officer of the body corporate or a person who was purporting to act in any such capacity, he as well as the body corporate shall be guilty of that offence and shall be liable to be proceeded against and punished accordingly."

Liability under such a provision is broader and easier to establish than liability under the complex common law rules on accessorial liability. The extent to which this provision is utilised in the controversial cases of death at work is considered later in this section.

C. The Law

There are two ways in which a company can be criminally liable:

1. Vicarious liability

With many offences of strict liability and negligence a company can be vicariously liable for the acts of its employees in the course of their duties.

National Rivers Authority v Alfred McAlpine Homes East Ltd [1994] 4 All E.R. 286 (Queen's Bench Divisional Court)

The defendant company was charged with causing pollution, namely, wet cement, to enter controlled waters contrary to s.85(1) of the Water Resources Act 1991. Two employees of the company, the site agent and the site manager, accepted responsibility for the pollution. At their trial in the magistrates' court the company was acquitted on the ground that a company can only be criminally liable if the criminal acts are committed by senior persons within the company. The prosecution appealed by way of case stated.

---

[107]   C.M.V. Clarkson, "Corporate Manslaughter: Need for a Special Offence?" in C.M.V. Clarkson and S. Cunningham (eds), *Criminal Liability for Non-Aggressive Deaths* (Aldershot: Ashgate, 2008), p.88.

SIMON BROWN LJ:

"I for my part see *Alphacell* as an illustration of vicarious liability . . . [A]n employer is liable for pollution resulting from its own operations carried out under its essential control, save only where some third party acts in such a way as to interrupt the chain of causation . . . It is sufficient that those immediately responsible on site (those who in the event acknowledged what had occurred) were employees of the company and acting apparently within the course and scope of that employment."

MORLAND LJ:

"The object of the relevant words of s.85(1) and the crime created thereby is the keeping of streams free from pollution for the benefit of mankind generally and the world's flora and fauna. Most significantly deleterious acts of pollution will arise out of industrial, agricultural or commercial activities . . . In almost all cases the act or omission will be that of a person such as a workman, fitter or plant operative in a fairly low position in the hierarchy of the industrial, agricultural or commercial concern.

In my judgment, to make the offence an effective weapon in the defence of environmental protection, a company must by necessary implication be criminally liable for the acts or omissions of its servants or agents during activities being done for the company."

Appeal allowed
Case remitted for rehearing

The doctrine of vicarious liability is well established in English law in relation to strict liability offences dealing with matters such as pollution, food and drugs and trading standards.[108] It has also been applied to hybrid offences which are prima facie strict liability offences but allow a due diligence defence.[109] However, it is clear that vicarious liability will not necessarily apply to all offences of strict liability. In *Seaboard Offshore Ltd*[110] the House of Lords held that the doctrine of vicarious liability did not apply to the offence before it[111] irrespective of whether the offence was one of strict liability or not. Whether vicarious liability applies or not is a matter of statutory interpretation, taking into account the policy of the law and whether vicarious liability will assist enforcement.[112] For example, in *McAlpine* the law could only be made effective by holding the company vicariously liable. In *Seaboard* it was concluded that the statute was aimed at the safety policies of the company itself rather than the actions of menial employees. The result is that at present it is rather difficult to predict whether an offence will be held to be one to which the doctrine of vicarious liability will be applicable.

Is the doctrine of vicarious liability justifiable? The doctrine can be defended on pragmatic grounds. It is easy to apply. As long as someone (anyone) acting in the course of their employment has committed a crime the company can be held liable. It prevents companies shielding themselves from criminal liability by delegating potentially illegal operations to employees. Companies delegate powers to act, in their respective spheres, to all their employees and accordingly should be held responsible for their criminal acts. It is also argued that optimum deterrence is achieved through the imposition of vicarious liability in that companies will "know where they stand".[113] These arguments are, of course, particularly powerful when applied to strict liability offences. If no fault is required on the part of the individual committing the crime, there seems little point in requiring fault on the part of the company to be established. There are, however, strong arguments against the doctrine.

---

[108] *R. v British Steel Plc* [1995] I.C.R. 586.
[109] *Tesco Supermarkets Plc v Brent LBC* [1993] 2 All E.R. 718.
[110] *Seaboard Offshore Ltd v Secretary of State for Transport* [1994] 2 All E.R. 99.
[111] Merchant Shipping Act 1988 s.31: failing to take reasonable steps to ensure that a vessel is operated in a safe manner.
[112] See, for example, *R. v Gateway Foodmarkets Ltd* [1997] 2 Cr. App. R. 40.
[113] G.R. Sullivan, "The Attribution of Culpability to Limited Companies" [1996] C.L.J. 515 at 541.

Eric Colvin, "Corporate Personality and Criminal Liability" (1995) 6 Criminal Law Forum 1 at 8:

"Vicarious corporate liability has been criticized for being both underinclusive and overinclusive. It is underinclusive because it is activated only through the criminal liability of some individual. Where offenses require some form of fault, that fault must be present at the individual level. If it is not present at this level, there is no corporate liability regardless of the measure of corporate fault. Yet vicarious liability is also overinclusive because, if there is individual liability, corporate liability follows even in the absence of corporate fault. The general objection to vicarious liability in criminal law—that it divorces the determination of liability from an inquiry into culpability—applies to corporations as it does to other defendants. The special characteristics of corporations do not insulate them from the stigmatizing and penal consequences of a criminal conviction."

An example of the over-inclusiveness of the doctrine is that a company could be liable for an offence despite having adopted clear policies and having issued express instructions to avert the wrongdoing. It hardly seems justifiable to hold a company liable for the actions of a lowly employee who decides to breach company rules and commit a crime.

A possible compromise would be to make companies prima facie vicariously liable for all offences committed by employees in the course of their employment (whether a particular individual could be identified or not), but to afford a due diligence defence.

Council of Europe, Liability of Enterprises for Offences, Recommendation No. R (88) 18 (1990), 6–7:

"1(2) The enterprise should be [criminally] liable, whether a natural person who committed the acts or omissions constituting the offence can be identified or not.
    (4) The enterprise should be exonerated from liability where its management is not implicated in the offence and has taken all the necessary steps to prevent its commission."

A similar proposal would allow vicarious liability to apply to all offences, but only afford a due diligence defence to "non-regulatory offences that carry a stigma".[114]

2. Direct liability: the identification doctrine

When it comes to crimes involving blameworthiness the commitment to individualistic notions of responsibility meant that English criminal law was reluctant to hold companies criminally liable. However, as company law developed the fiction of corporate personality—the idea that a company was a legal "person" that could sue and be sued in its own name—the criminal law did not take long to lift this fiction and superimpose it on its individualist conception of criminal liability. The courts started "lifting the veil" of companies to see if there was an individual who had committed the actus reus of a crime with the appropriate mens rea. This individual had to be sufficiently important in the corporate structure for their acts to be identified with the company itself; in such circumstances the company could be criminally liable (as well as the individual). This is known as the identification doctrine.

Tesco Supermarkets Ltd v Nattrass [1972] A.C. 153 (House of Lords)

Tesco were prosecuted under s.11(2) of the Trade Descriptions Act 1968 for advertising outside their shop that they were selling goods for less than they were being offered for sale inside the shop. The

---

[114]   Sullivan, "The Attribution of Culpability to Limited Companies" [1996] C.L.J. 515 at 544.

fault for the incorrect advertisement lay with the local manager whose system of daily checks had broken down. Tesco claimed a defence under s.24 of the same Act that the "failure was due to the default of another person". The question then arose as to whether the local manager was "another person" or whether he was to be identified with the company.

LORD REID:

"I must start by considering the nature of the personality which by a fiction the law attributes to a corporation. A living person has a mind which can have knowledge or intention or be negligent and he has hands to carry out his intentions. A corporation has none of these: it must act through living persons, though not always one or the same person. Then the person who acts is not speaking or acting for the company. He is acting as the company and his mind which directs his acts is the mind of the company. There is no question of the company being vicariously liable. He is not acting as a servant, representative, agent or delegate. He is an embodiment of the company or, one could say, he hears and speaks through the persona of the company, within his appropriate sphere, and his mind is the mind of the company. If it is a guilty mind then that guilt is the guilt of the company. It must be a question of law whether . . . a person . . . is to be regarded as the company or merely as the company's servant or agent . . .

Reference is frequently made to the judgment of Denning LJ in *H.L. Bolton (Engineering) Co Ltd v T.J. Graham & Sons Ltd* [1957] 1 Q.B. 159. He said, at p.172:

'A company may in many ways be likened to a human body. It has a brain and nerve centre which controls what it does. It also has hands which hold the tools and act in accordance with directions from the centre. Some of the people in the company are mere servants and agents who are nothing more than hands to do the work and cannot be said to represent the mind or will. Others are directors and managers who represent the directing mind and will of the company, and control what it does. The state of mind of these managers is the state of mind of the company and is treated by the law as such.'

In that case the directors of the company only met once a year: they left the management of the business to others, and it was the intention of those managers which was imputed to the company. I think that was right. There have been attempts to apply Lord Denning's words to all servants of a company whose work is brain work, or who exercise some managerial discretion under the direction of superior officers of the company. I do not think that Lord Denning intended to refer to them. He only referred to those who 'represent the directing mind and will of the company, and control what it does.'

[The local manager was not to be identified with the company. He was, therefore, 'another person'.]"

Appeal allowed

There were significant objections to this strict interpretation of the identification doctrine particularly with larger companies where it is most unlikely that a senior manager will actually commit the actus reus of an offence with the accompanying mens rea. It is arguable that a more flexible approach was adopted by the Privy Council in the following case.

Meridian Global Funds Management Asia Ltd v Securities Commission [1995] 2 A.C. 500 (Privy Council)

The chief investment officer and senior portfolio manager of Meridian, unknown to the board of directors and managing director, invested in another company without making disclosures to the stock exchange as required by s.20(3) of the New Zealand Securities Amendment Act 1988. The company was convicted of failing to comply with s.20. The New Zealand Court of Appeal upheld the conviction on the basis that the investment manager was the directing mind and will of the company and so his knowledge was attributable to the company. The company appealed to the Judicial Committee of the Privy Council.

LORD HOFFMANN:

"Any proposition about a company necessarily involves a reference to a set of rules. A company exists because there is a rule (usually in a statute) which says that a *persona ficta* shall be deemed to exist and to have certain of the powers, rights and duties of a natural person . . . It is . . . a necessary part of corporate personality that there should be rules by which acts are attributed to the company. These may be called 'the rules of attribution'. . .

Judges sometimes say that a company 'as such' cannot do anything; it must act by servants or agents . . . [A] reference to a company 'as such' might suggest that there is something out there called the company of which one can meaningfully say that it can or cannot do something. There is in fact no such thing as the company as such, no ding an sich, only the applicable rules. To say that a company cannot do something means only that there is no one whose doing of that act would, under the applicable rules of attribution, count as the act of the company.

. . . [T]he criminal law . . . ordinarily impose[s] liability only for the *actus reus* and *mens rea* of the defendant himself. How is such a rule to be applied to a company?

. . . In such a case, the court must fashion a special rule of attribution for the particular substantive rule. This is always a matter of interpretation: given that it was intended to apply to a company, how was it intended to apply? Whose act (or knowledge, or state of mind) was *for this purpose* intended to count as the act etc. of the company? One finds the answer to this question by applying the usual canons of interpretation, taking into account the language of the rule (if it is a statute) and its content and policy.

. . . The policy of section 20 of the Securities Amendment Act 1988 is to compel, in fast-moving markets, the immediate disclosure of the identity of persons who become substantial security holders in public issuers. Notice must be given as soon as that person knows that he has become a substantial security holder. In the case of a corporate security holder, what rule should be implied as to the person whose knowledge for this purpose is to count as the knowledge of the company? Surely the person who, with the authority of the company, acquired the relevant interest. Otherwise the policy of the Act would be defeated. Companies would be able to allow employees to acquire interests on their behalf which made them substantial security holders but would not have to report them until the board or someone else in senior management got to know about it. This would put a premium on the board paying as little attention as possible to what its investment managers were doing. Their Lordships would therefore hold that upon the true construction of section 20(4) (e), the company knows that it has become a substantial security holder when that is known to the person who had authority to do the deal . . . It was therefore not necessary in this case to inquire whether [the investment officer] could have been described in some more general sense as the 'directing mind and will' of the company. But their Lordships would wish to guard themselves against being understood to mean that whenever a servant of a company has authority to do an act on its behalf, knowledge of that act will for all purposes be attributed to the company. It is a question of construction in each case as to whether the particular rule requires that the knowledge that an act has been done, or the state of mind with which it was done, should be attributed to the company . . . [T]he fact that a company's employee is authorised to drive a lorry does not in itself lead to the conclusion that if he kills someone by reckless driving, the company will be guilty of manslaughter. There is no inconsistency. Each is an example of an attribution rule for a particular purpose, tailored as it always must be to the terms and policies of the substantive rule."

Appeal dismissed

This decision is unfortunately ambiguous and could lead to uncertainty. Lord Hoffmann states that "the court must fashion a special rule of attribution for the particular substantive rule". On the facts of *Meridian* this was easy. The issue was whether the company knew it had invested in another company without making the required disclosures. The person who had "authority to do the deal" was the investment manager; his knowledge was attributed to the company. But what was the "special rule of attribution" that enabled this sensible result to be achieved? Is Lord Hoffmann saying that, depending on the statute, one has a choice between utilising the identification doctrine or imposing vicarious liability—and that the company here was vicariously liable for the acts of its investment manager? Or does it mean that, again depending on the statute, one can broaden the identification doctrine so that a company can be directly liable for the acts of someone not traditionally associated with the "controlling mind" of the company, which in this case was the investment manager? Perhaps the answer to these questions is not important. After all, the identification doctrine can be viewed as a very narrow form of vicarious liability:[115] companies can only be held "vicariously" liable for the acts of persons representing the controlling mind of the company. Whichever route is adopted, the effect of *Meridian* is the same. Companies can be liable for mens rea offences on the basis of acts by persons not traditionally regarded as senior enough under the *Tesco Supermarkets Ltd v Nattrass* formulation of the identification doctrine.

How is this approach to be applied to statutes dealing with non-regulatory areas and creating stigmatic offences, such as the Offences Against the Person Act 1861 or to cases where there is no statute to be construed? If the acts and knowledge of an investment manager can be attributed to a company for investment offences, logic would dictate that the acts and knowledge of a health and safety manager should be attributed to a company for all health and safety purposes which would include cases where a worker sustained serious injuries. In *Odyssey v OIC Run-Off Ltd*[116] it was stated that the *Meridian* principle was of general application and could be applied to "a substantive rule of judge made law" (whether the finality of a judgment could be displaced by the perjury of a party). In this case a company was identified through the acts of a former director because at the trial where the perjury took place, he was "part of a team which was helping to row [the company] to victory". However, Brooke LJ was careful to emphasise that this was a civil case where the approach to corporate liability was "fundamentally different". In a strong dissent, Buxton LJ stated that the same rules of attribution should be applied in both criminal and civil cases. His view was that *Meridian* is "at best an imperfect guide to the correct approach to the rule for attribution of a crime" and that he was "bound by *Tesco v Nattrass* to apply the 'directing mind and will' formulation, or something very near to it".[117]

Indeed, the following criminal decision confirmed that any flexibility introduced by *Meridian* in relation to statutory offences had no application to the common law offence of manslaughter.

Attorney-General's Reference (No.2 of 1999) [2000] 2 Cr. App. R. 207 (Court of Appeal, Criminal Division)

Following a train collision at Southall, seven passengers died and 151 were injured. Great Western Trains was prosecuted for manslaughter but was acquitted, as there was no human being with whom the company could be identified. On reference by the Attorney General:

ROSE LJ:

"There is, as it seems to us, no sound basis for suggesting that, by their recent decisions, the courts have started a process of moving from identification to personal liability as a basis for corporate liability for manslaughter . . . [T]he identification principle is in our judgment just as relevant to the *actus reus* as to *mens rea*. . .

In our judgment, unless an identified individual's conduct, characterisable as gross criminal negligence, can be attributed to the company the company is not, in the present state of the common law, liable for manslaughter. Civil negligence rules . . . are not apt to confer criminal liability on a company.

None of the authorities relied on by [counsel] as pointing to personal liability for manslaughter by a company supports that contention. In each, the decision was dependent on the purposive construction that the particular

---

[115] A.P. Simester, J.R. Spencer, G.R. Sullivan and G.J. Virgo, *Criminal Law: Theory and Doctrine*, 5th edn (Oxford: Hart, 2013), p.282.

[116] *Odyssey v OIC Run-Off Ltd, The Times*, March 17, 2000.

[117] In the Scottish case of *Transco plc v HM Advocate* (2004 S.L.T. 41) the English civil case of *El Ajou v Dollar Land Holdings* ([1994] 2 All E.R. 685) was discussed. In this latter case it was held that the directing mind and will of the company need not be the person with general management of the company; the directing mind of a company can be found in different persons for different activities. In *Transco*, Lord Hamilton described both *El Anjou* and *Meridian* as being of "no assistance" in a case dealing with corporate homicide (the Scottish equivalent of corporate manslaughter).

statute imposed . . . In each case there was an identified employee whose conduct was held to be that of the company. In each case it was held that the concept of directing mind and will had no application when construing the statute. But it was not suggested or implied that the concept of identification is dead or moribund in relation to common law offences . . . Indeed, Lord Hoffmann's speech in the *Meridian* case, in fashioning an additional special rule of attribution geared to the purpose of the statute, proceeded on the basis that the primary 'directing mind and will' rule still applies although it is not determinative in all cases. In other words, he was not departing from the identification theory but re-affirming its existence . . .

[T]he identification principle remains the only basis in common law for corporate liability for gross negligence manslaughter."

Opinion accordingly

The ratio of this decision only extends to the common law offence of corporate manslaughter (which, as we shall see, has now been abolished) and would probably apply to other common law offences. While the point has not been settled, it seems likely that it would also apply to statutes creating stigmatic offences, such as the Offences Against the Person Act 1861. So if a prosecution had been brought under the 1861 Act in relation to the 151 people seriously injured (probably under s.20), it would seem that the company would only have been liable if a person representing the controlling mind of the company had actually committed the offence. This is intolerably narrow. Managing Directors do not drive trains and it would be extraordinarily difficult, if not impossible, to establish that their gross negligence in the boardroom *caused* the death of workers or members of the public.

The extent of *Meridian* has even been brought into question in relation to regulatory offences. In *St Regis Paper Co Ltd.*[118] the trial judge relied on Lord Hoffmann's observations to conclude that the company defendant could be identified as having committed an offence of intentionally making a false entry in a record required to be kept under the condition of a permit (Pollution Prevention and Control Regulations 2000, reg.32) through the acts and state of mind of the technical manager of the smallest of five paper mills owned by company. The offence involved the manager making a false entry about the amount of solids the company was discharging into a river. The Court of Appeal quashed the conviction, holding that to attribute an employee's act to the company the individual must be seen as the directing mind and will of the company, and such persons would normally be on the board of directors, a managing director or some other superior officer of the company who carried out the functions of management and spoke and acted as the company. That was the case even though the offence fell within a regulatory regime, since if parliament had intended vicarious liability to be possible it would not have drafted the offence to require mens rea. The lesson to be learned from *Meridian*, noted Moses LJ, is the importance of construing the statute which creates the statutory offence in order to determine the rules of attribution applicable to the statutory offence in question.[119]

---

[118]   *R. v St Regis Paper Co Ltd* [2012] 1 Cr. App. R. 14.

[119]   This is in agreement with the Law Commission, which proposes that in the absence of specific legislative provisions setting out the basis upon which companies are to be found liable, the courts should treat the question of how corporate fault may be established as a matter of statutory interpretation. The Law Commission, however, would "encourage the courts not to presume that the identification doctrine applies when interpreting the scope of criminal offences applicable to companies": Law Commission Consultation Paper 195, *Criminal Liability in Regulatory Contexts* (2010), Proposal 13. Pinto and Evans argue that Moses LJ in *St Regis Paper Co* misinterpreted the statute, and that the particular provision of reg.32(1), rather than pointing away from liability for the company, invited the opposite conclusion. They suggest that for the purpose of the regulation it is the person who produced the daily environmental reports whose acts should be attributable to the company, and that would have been the technical manager. Despite the court acknowledging that the purpose of the statute was to protect the environment, the effect of the decision, they argue, is that a company can immunise itself against the risk of liability under the regulation by assigning the duty of keeping the record to a sufficiently lowly employee, which

That the question revolves around statutory interpretation in relation to offences specifically designed as part of a regulatory regime may not be particularly enlightening in determining the rules of attribution in relation to a statutory offence, such as one under the Offences Against the Person Act 1861, which was not drafted with the liability of corporations in mind. However, even if the more flexible *Meridian* approach were adopted, there would still be immense problems with the identification doctrine. It still requires an individual to be identified within the company whose acts and knowledge can be attributed to the company. In many cases the wrong might have occurred for the very reason that there was no person within the company responsible for, say, health and safety. Alternatively, the company's structures may be so complex and impenetrable, with decision-making buried at many different departmental levels, that it becomes impossible to pin-point any individual with responsibility for a particular area of activity. It is for these, and other, reasons, explored below, that there has been a call for the complete abandonment of the identification doctrine in English law.

D. Restructuring Corporate Criminal Liability

The identification doctrine is inadequate to deal with the reality of decision-making in many modern companies. Accordingly, several alternative methods for the establishment of corporate culpability have been suggested.

1. Aggregation doctrine

In *HM Coroner for East Kent, Ex p. Spooner*[120] the aggregation doctrine was considered and rejected.[121] Under this doctrine one aggregates all the acts and mental elements of the various relevant persons within the company to ascertain whether, aggregated together, they would amount to a crime if they had all been committed by one person. This doctrine has the advantage of recognising that in many cases it is not possible to isolate a single individual who has committed the crime with mens rea. This doctrine can deter companies from burying responsibility deep within the corporate structure.

However, this doctrine simply perpetuates the personification of companies myth. Instead of finding one person with whom the company can be identified (as required by the identification doctrine), one finds several people. The doctrine ignores the reality that the real essence of the wrongdoing might not be what each individual did but the fact that the company had no organisational structure or policy to prevent each individual doing what they did in a way that cumulatively amounts to a crime. Indeed, in the *Herald of Free Enterprise*[122] case it is doubtful whether the aggregation of the acts and omissions of the various personnel would have amounted to a corporate crime. The real fault in that case lay with the lack of policy and responsibility for safety within the company.

---

will not discourage environmental pollution: A. Pinto QC and M. Evans, *Corporate Criminal Liability*, 3rd edn, (London: Sweet & Maxwell, 2013), pp.60–61.

[120]   *R. v HM Coroner for East Kent, Ex p. Spooner* (1989) 88 Cr. App. R. 10.

[121]   This rejection was confirmed in *Attorney-General's Reference (No.2 of 1999)* [2000] 2 Cr. App. R. 207.

[122]   Below, pp.269–271.

2. Reactive corporate fault

A somewhat different approach to corporate criminal liability has been proposed by Fisse and Braithwaite. As many company structures are impenetrable to outsiders they propose that companies "activate and monitor [their own] private justice systems of corporate defendants".

Brent Fisse and John Braithwaite, "The Allocation of Responsibility for Corporate Crime: Individualism, Collectivism and Accountability" (1988) 11 Sydney L. Rev. 468 at 511–512:

"One possible approach would be to restructure the imposition of corporate liability so as to enforce internal accountability. Where the *actus reus* of an offence is proven to have been committed by or on behalf of a corporation, the court, if equipped with a suitable statutory injunctive power, could require the company (a) to conduct its own enquiry as to who was responsible within the organisation, (b) to take internal disciplinary measures against those responsible, and (c) to return a report detailing the action taken. If the corporate defendant returned a report demonstrating that due steps had been taken to discipline those responsible then corporate criminal liability would not be imposed. If the reaction of the company was inexcusably deficient then both the company and its top managers would be criminally liable for their failure to comply with the order of the court. The range of punishments for corporate defendants would include court-ordered adverse publicity, community service, and punitive injunctive sentences . . .

Where it can be proven that harm proscribed by the *actus reus* of an offence has been caused by conduct performed on behalf of a corporation, it is not unreasonable that the cost of investigating internal responsibility for that harm causing be borne by the corporate defendant rather than by taxpayers in general . . . Even though sanctions available to private justice systems—fines, dismissals, demotions, shame—may be less potent than some of those available in the public arena, it seems better to have weaker sanctions hitting the right targets than stronger weapons pounding the wrong targets."[123]

There are, however, many problems with this reactive fault doctrine. What corrective measures and disciplinary actions will suffice to avoid liability? Would a formal reprimand of an employee coupled with the circulation of an internal memorandum advising staff that certain actions need to be taken in future suffice?[124] If a company fails to take sufficient steps, what offence would be committed? If the company were to be liable for established offences such as theft or fraud, there would be a severe danger of "false labelling"[125] in that the established prerequisites of the crime, in terms of actus reus and mens rea, would not be made out. On the other hand, if new special offences relating to reactive fault were to be created, there is the danger that the crimes committed by such companies will continue to be perceived as "poor cousins" to the "real criminal offences". Convicting companies of a failure to comply with a court order conveys the same message as a conviction under the Health and Safety legislation. What is needed is a more direct public shaming of the company itself for the actual harm that the company's culpable acts have caused.

Nevertheless, such proposals could be useful for lesser regulatory offences and an approach along these lines is already adopted by English law to a certain extent. In these situations Statutory Notices can be imposed requiring a company to do or refrain from certain behaviour with failure to comply being a specific criminal offence. For example, it is common in environmental and health and safety law for such an approach to be adopted.[126] The Regulatory Enforcement and Sanctions Act 2008,

---

[123]   For a statutory model based on this proposal, see B. Fisse, "The Attribution of Criminal Liability to Corporations: A Statutory Model" (1991) 13 Sydney L. Rev. 277.
[124]   C.M.V. Clarkson, "Corporate Culpability" [1998] 2 Web J.C.L.I.
[125]   G.R. Sullivan, "The Attribution of Culpability to Limited Companies" [1996] C.L.J. 515 at 526.
[126]   See generally, Macrory Consultation Document, *Regulatory Justice: Sanctioning in a post-Hampton World* (2006), Annex F.

discussed earlier,[127] enables Regulators to serve Stop Notices on corporations prohibiting them from carrying on specified activities until certain steps have been taken.[128] Further, Regulators can accept Enforcement Undertakings from corporations that they will take specified action to secure that the offence does not continue or recur.[129] As will be seen at the end of this chapter, something similar has been introduced in relation to corporate liability for economic crime, in the form of Deferred Prosecution Agreements.

3. Corporate culture doctrine

What is needed is a recognition that corporate policies and behaviour often depend on the organisational structure and lines of authority within the corporation with responsibility for standard procedures, such as those relating to safety, being spread throughout the company. Corporate acts and policies are not simply an aggregation of individual choices but are often the acts and policies of the company itself. A company might have "no soul to be damned, and no body to be kicked",[130] but it can be likened to "an intelligent machine".[131] Much of the modern literature on corporate culpability has rejected the individualistic conceptions underlying the identification doctrine and favours an organisational model in which companies are seen as more than the sum of their total numbers: "they are discrete and unique moral entities which can be criminally culpable in their own right".[132] The focus should be on corporate structures and systems and on practices and policies and whether the corporation has allowed a "corporate culture" to develop which facilitated the commission of the crime. From such a corporate culture of non-compliance with the law, it becomes possible to infer corporate mens rea by the corporation itself.

Brent Fisse, "Recent Developments in Corporate Criminal Law and Corporate Liability to Monetary Penalties" (1990) 13 UNSWLJ 1 at 15–16:

"Corporate policy is the corporate equivalent of intention, and a company that conducts itself with an express or implied policy of non-compliance with a criminal prohibition exhibits corporate criminal intentionality . . . The concept of negligently failing to comply with the law is also applicable to a corporation as a collectivity. Corporations perform corporate roles in society and have collective capacities. Accordingly, they are subject to distinctly corporate standards of care.

Although it is possible to define corporate fault in terms of corporate policy and corporate negligence, the worry is that corporations will develop compliance systems that look immaculate on paper but which are not meant to be taken seriously by their personnel. One solution is to recognise that a corporation may have an implied policy of non-compliance . . . There would be merit in a rule that a company is deemed to have a policy of non-compliance where the company has failed to have in place a system whereby employees could report suspected or anticipated episodes of non-compliance directly to top management."

---

[127] At pp.249–250.
[128] Section 46.
[129] Section 50.
[130] J.C. Coffee, "'No Soul to Damn: No Body to Kick': an Unscandalised Inquiry into the Problem of Corporate Punishment" (1981) 79 Mich. L. Rev. 386.
[131] M. Dan-Cohen, *Rights, Persons, and Organisations: A Legal Theory for Bureaucratic Society* (Berkeley: University of California Press, 1986), p.49. For an argument that a company can be a culpability-bearing agent, see C.M.V. Clarkson, "Kicking Corporate Bodies and Damning Their Souls" (1996) 59 M.L.R. 557. See also, C. Wells, *Corporations and Criminal Responsibility*, 2nd edn (Oxford: OUP, 2001).
[132] T. Woolf, "The Criminal Code Act 1995 (Cth)—Towards a Realist Vision of Corporate Criminal Liability" (1997) 21 Crim. L.J. 257.

C.M.V. Clarkson, "Corporate Culpability" [1998] 2 Web Journal of Current Legal Issues:

"While it is perhaps easy to grasp the notion of a company being grossly negligent in that no subjective mental element is required, it is important to stress that both recklessness or intention can also be found in a company's policies, operational procedures and lack of precautions. If the corporate culture permitted or encouraged the wrongdoing, it may be easy to infer that the corporate body itself must have foreseen the possibility of the harm occurring (*Cunningham* recklessness) . . . or that the consequence was virtually certain to occur from which intention may be inferred (*Moloney/Hancock* intention). The important point about this approach is that it is not whether any individual within the company would have realised or foreseen the harm occurring but whether in a properly structured and organised careful company the risks would have been obvious . . . Possibly the only avenue of escape would be for a company to assert that while the risks looked objectively obvious, they had special expertise enabling them to rule out the risk (which would negate both . . . recklessness and intention). In the unlikely event of this claim being believed (bearing in mind that the risk clearly did materialise), the company would (rightly) escape liability.

The major objection to the corporate *mens rea* doctrine is the difficulty of determining whether the policies and practices of a company are sufficiently defective to be adjudged blameworthy to the requisite degree. In *Herald of Free Enterprise* this could easily have been done. The company had no proper safety procedures, no director responsible for safety and had received and ignored prior warnings of open-door sailings. In other cases, however, particularly where there is no pattern of wrongdoing, it could be more difficult to identify the policies and practices as amounting to *mens rea*. One method of addressing this problem in the United States would be to inquire whether a company had a Corporate Compliance Programme (a formal system or programme designed to ensure that all employees know the relevant laws affecting the company's operations and seeking to ensure corporate compliance with the law) which has been enforced in good faith."

In 2004, the Australian Capital Territory (ACT) introduced a new criminal offence (Industrial Manslaughter)[133] expressly endorsing this approach whereby mens rea can be inferred from a corporate culture. Recklessness is needed for the offence and is attributed to the company itself if it "expressly, tacitly or impliedly authorised or permitted the commission of the offence". Such authorisation or permission may be established by

"proving that a corporate culture existed within the corporation that directed, encouraged, tolerated or led to non-compliance with the contravened law; or proving that the corporation failed to create and maintain a corporate culture requiring compliance with the contravened law".[134]

Corporate culture is defined to mean

"an attitude, policy, rule, course of conduct or practice existing within the corporation generally or in that part of the corporation where the relevant conduct happens".[135]

In assessing whether a relevant corporate culture exists it is relevant to consider whether the employee etc. who committed the offence reasonably believed that senior managers of the corporation would have authorised or permitted the commission of the offence. (This would capture situations where, although corporate policy ostensibly prohibits conduct, it is in fact encouraged by management.)

Academic commentators[136] have suggested that the following factors could be relevant in establishing a corporate culture:

---

[133]   Crimes (Industrial Manslaughter) Amendment Act 2003, amending the Crimes Act 1900 (ACT).
[134]   Section 51(2)(c) and (d).
[135]   Section 51(6).
[136]   Cited in J. Clough and C. Mulhern, *The Prosecution of Companies* (Melbourne: OUP, 2002).

- Hierarchy of corporation: does the Board make efforts to comply with the law? Is the management structure organised in such a way as to encourage non-compliance (e.g. insulating certain officers from responsibility)?

- Corporate goals: are these realistic or so unrealistic as to encourage unlawful behaviour?

- Monitoring compliance: monitoring systems/internal audits/channels of communication for employees to report concerns.

- Circumstances of offence.

- Reactions to past violations.

- Incentives and indemnification.

We shall see later in this section that English law has endorsed a version of this approach in establishing liability for the new offence of corporate manslaughter.

4. Specific corporate offences

The discussion of the above approaches to establishing corporate criminal liability relates to mechanisms for holding corporations liable for established criminal offences that can be committed by individuals. These offences were all shaped around individualistic conceptions of liability making it difficult to fashion rules for corporate liability. Accordingly, an alternative approach could be the creation of special offences that can only be committed by corporations. These offences can then be specially designed to accommodate the reality of corporate decision-making. As we shall see, this has been done with the creation of a special offence of corporate manslaughter. The Bribery Act 2010 has created a special offence of failure of commercial organisations to prevent bribery.[137]

The Law Commission has conducted a general review of organisational liability. One of its proposals is that legislation should include specific provisions in criminal offences to indicate the basis on which companies may be found liable.[138]

E. Death and Injury at Work: A Case Study in Corporate Criminal Liability

The issues discussed above apply to all criminal offences that can be committed by corporations. However, it was the application of these rules in cases where workers or others had been killed or injured at work or through other corporate operations (such as transport) that proved most controversial. The result was a sustained and vigorous campaign for reform of the law which culminated in the Corporate Manslaughter and Corporate Homicide Act 2007. Before the provisions of this Act are examined, we need to explore why this area of the law has proved so controversial. This involves examining both how the law in this field has operated in practice and the particular shortcomings of the identification doctrine in such cases.

---

[137]   Section 7. See C. Wells, "Bribery: Corporate Liability under the Draft Bill 2009" [2009] Crim. L.R. 479.
[138]   Law Commission Consultation Paper No.195, *Criminal Liability in Regulatory Contexts* (2010), Proposal 13.

1. The law in action

Where someone has been killed or injured as a result of corporate activities, it is possible to have recourse to the main homicide and non-fatal offences against the person. However, the reality is that there have only ever been seven convictions of corporations for common law manslaughter in England and Wales[139] and prosecutions for other serious offences against the person are virtually unknown. Why is this?

An important explanation relates to enforcement procedures and public attitudes moulded by the media, the state and companies themselves. When persons are killed or seriously injured at work (even when they are members of the public) the typical response has in the past been to describe this as an "accident"—which in turn structures the official response.[140] While there is evidence that work-related fatalities are now regarded as very serious crimes,[141] crime in the streets is still generally regarded as worse than crime in the suites. In an attempt to increase safety at work and prevent such "accidents" the Health and Safety at Work etc. Act 1974 makes it an offence for an employer to breach a duty "to ensure, so far as is reasonably practicable, the health, safety and welfare at work of all his employees".[142] This and other similar offences under the Act are drafted without any reference to whether a worker is killed or injured or not. The crime is simply an endangerment offence involving the failure to maintain proper safety standards. This stands in strong contrast to the offences available when persons are killed or injured outside their workplaces which are structured in terms of the seriousness of the harm caused. This is true not only in cases of personal violence but also under the Road Traffic Act 1988. The different structure of the health and safety offences contributes to the overall sense that death and injury at work is not "real crime". The main body set up to enforce this legislation is the HSE which has the power to notify companies that certain safety matters require attention, to issue improvement or prohibition notices or to bring a criminal prosecution. It is only since 1998, as a result of a protocol agreed between the HSE, the CPS and the Association of Chief Police Officers (ACPO), that the police now attend the scene of every sudden workplace death.[143] When someone is seriously injured at work it is extremely rare for the police to conduct an investigation into the incident[144] and only about 10 per cent of non-fatal serious injuries are investigated by the HSE.[145]

Further, in those cases where an investigation is undertaken, the HSE does not regard its primary function as being one of initiating prosecutions, but rather as one of advising companies and of determining good practice.[146] The HSE's regulatory practice is underpinned by three concepts: self-regulation, co-operation and compliance seeking.[147] The HSE, under-manned and under-resourced,[148] with its policy

---

[139]   For details of these convictions, see C.M.V. Clarkson, "Corporate Manslaughter: Yet More Government Proposals" [2005] Crim. L.R. 677, n.9.

[140]   C. Wells, *Corporations and Criminal Responsibility*, 2nd edn (Oxford: OUP, 2001), p.11.

[141]   P. Almond, "Public Perceptions of Work-Related Fatality Cases: Reaching the Outer Limits of 'Popular Punitiveness'?" (2008) Brit. J. Criminol. 448.

[142]   Section 2(1).

[143]   Health and Safety Executive, *Work-Related Deaths: A Protocol for Liaison* (1998).

[144]   D. Bergman, *Deaths at Work: Accidents or Corporate Crime* (Workers Educational Association, London Hazards Centre, Inquest (London), 1991), p.17.

[145]   S. Tombs and D. Whyte, "A Crisis of Enforcement: The Decriminalization of Death and Injury at Work" (2008) 5 *Centre for Crime and Justice Studies* 5.

[146]   In 2012/13, 8,810 enforcement notices were issued while only 597 prosecutions were brought by the HSE: Health and Safety Executive, *Annual Statistics Report for Great Britain 201/13*, available at *http://www.hse.gov.uk/statistics/overall/hssh1213.pdf* [Accessed June 6, 2014].

[147]   P. Almond, "An Inspector's Eye View: The Prospective Enforcement of Work-Related Fatality Cases" (2006) 46 Brit. J. Criminol. 893 at 896.

[148]   Tombs and Whyte, "A Crisis of Enforcement: The Decriminalization of Death and Injury at Work" (2008) 5 *Centre for Crime and Justice Studies* 5–6.

of advising rather than prosecuting companies, will only press charges in cases that they believe represent a flagrant breach of the Health and Safety at Work etc. Act 1974. In cases where serious injuries have been sustained a prosecution (under the Health and Safety legislation) is only brought in 11 per cent of cases that were investigated (i.e. only in about 1 per cent of the total number of cases where a serious injury was sustained).[149] A majority of these prosecutions are brought in the magistrates' court (60 per cent[150]) as this is quicker and cheaper for the HSE.[151] Penalties there have traditionally been low.[152] This displacement of police powers by the primarily regulatory HSE simply marginalises corporate crime and contributes, even in those cases where there is a prosecution, to the general feeling that such deaths and injuries are not really "crime" or the products of corporate violence.

However, deaths in the work place began to be taken more seriously.

Paul Almond, Corporate Manslaughter and Regulatory Reform, (2013), p.xiii

"I was . . . undertaking fieldwork for my study of health and safety inspectors' attitudes in relation to work-related fatality cases, and I was speaking with a very experienced inspector about his 30-year career and the changes he had witnessed during that time. He identified what he saw as a paradox underpinning this area of regulation:

'When I joined HSE 27 years ago it wasn't a very important job to be honest, but it just seems to have grown and grown in importance . . . I remember investigating fatalities when nobody was interested in what was going on, it was just one of those things, people go to work and get killed, but it's a big event now. I wonder why, when actually we're safer, the importance of the subject seems to keep rising? In the time I've been an inspector, employee fatalities have fallen from about six or seven hundred a year down to about two hundred a year. You'd expect people to have said "right, we can pack in now", but they don't, the importance keeps growing. It's a conundrum.'

(2003:17)"

2. Failings of the identification doctrine

One reason for the lack of criminalisation in cases when people were killed as a result of corporate activities was that the identification doctrine made a conviction for homicide extremely difficult. This problem still persists when people are injured.

R. v HM Coroner for East Kent, Ex p. Spooner (1989) 88 Cr. App. R. 10 (Queen's Bench Divisional Court)

The applicants sought judicial review of the coroner's decision that a company could not be indicted for manslaughter and that the acts or omissions of the company personnel could not be aggregated so as to render the company liable.

---

[149]   Tombs and Whyte, "A Crisis of Enforcement: The Decriminalization of Death and Injury at Work" (2008) 5 *Centre for Crime and Justice Studies* 5–6.

[150]   Freedom of Information Request to HSE, 2009. In 2004/05, 80 per cent of prosecutions were brought in the magistrates' court (Sentencing Advisory Panel, *Advice to the Sentencing Guidelines Council: Sentencing for Corporate Manslaughter and Health and Safety Offences Involving Death* (2009)).

[151]   B. Hutter and S. Lloyd-Bostock, "The Power of Accidents" (1990) 30 Brit. J. Criminol. 409: "an inspector working on a prosecution or on a public inquiry is not out making visits to other premises" (p.421).

[152]   Until 1992 the maximum fine there was £2,000; this had since been increased to £20,000 for breaches of the general duties in ss.2–6 of Health and Safety at Work etc. Act 1974.

BINGHAM LJ:

"The inquest arises from the capsize of the vehicle ferry 'Herald of Free Enterprise' off Zeebrugge on March 6, 1987 and the huge loss of life, both of passengers and crew, to which that tragic disaster gave rise. Nearly 200 lives were lost, causing widespread grief, and the facts of the disaster are etched not only on the recollections of all who were involved, directly or indirectly, but on the consciousness of the nation as a whole.

Very shortly after the Secretary of State for Trade ordered a formal investigation under section 55 of the Merchant Shipping Act 1970, Sheen J. sitting with Assessors, was appointed to conduct it . . .

The investigation found that the immediate cause of the vessel's loss was that she sailed with her bow doors opened trimmed by the head, *i.e.* with her nose down. The manoeuvre in which she engaged led to the entry of water into the vehicle deck, the heavy listing of the vessel and her speedy capsize.

Sheen J. criticised a number of individuals who had failed to perform their duty, in particular those responsible for failing to close the bow doors, failing to see that the doors were closed and sailing without knowing that the doors were closed. He expressed his criticisms in strong terms. The vessel was owned and operated by Townsend Car Ferries Ltd, and that company also was the subject of severe criticism.

It is right that I should refer to the terms in which Sheen J. expressed those criticisms. In paragraph 14.1 of his report he said this:

'At first sight the faults which led to this disaster were the aforesaid errors of omission on the part of the Master, the Chief Officer and the assistant bosun, and also the failure by Captain Kirby to issue and enforce clear orders. But a full investigation into the circumstances of the disaster leads inexorably to the conclusion that the underlying or cardinal faults lay higher up in the Company. The Board of Directors did not appreciate their responsibility for the safe management of their ships. They did not apply their minds to the question: What orders should be given for the safety of our ships? The Directors did not have any proper comprehension of what their duties were. There appears to have been a lack of thought about the way in which the HERALD ought to have been organised for the Dover/Zeebrugge run. All concerned in management, from the members of the Board of Directors down to the junior superintendents, were guilty of fault in that all must be regarded as sharing responsibility for the failure of management. From top to bottom the body corporate was infected with the disease of sloppiness . . . The failure on the part of the shore management to give proper and clear directions was a contributory cause of the disaster. This is a serious finding which must be explained in some detail.'

The report then goes into very considerable detail and in the course of the present hearing three points are relied on as being particularly relevant. First, it is pointed out that the company and its representatives failed to give serious consideration to a proposal that lights should be fitted on the bridge of the vessel which would inform the Master whether the bow doors and, for that matter, the stern doors were closed or not. Such a warning system, if duly heeded by the Master, would have prevented this disaster. This was a suggestion which was made but seems unhappily to have been the subject of facetious comment.

Secondly, attention is drawn to the failure of the company and its representatives to report and collate information relating to previous incidents when vessels had sailed with their doors open. It appears that there were five or six such incidents between October 1983 and February 1987. Had knowledge of these repeated incidents been appreciated it should have alerted the officers of the company to the risk of disaster, but it appears that there was no person within the company who ever knew of all the incidents.

Thirdly, attention is drawn to the lack of any proper system within the company to ensure that the vessels were operated in accordance with the highest standards of safety. It is rightly urged upon us that where the result of an unsafe system is liable to be so grave, the onus on a company to ensure safe operation is correspondingly high.

At the very end of his report, Sheen J. answered the questions posed for the investigation by the Secretary of State. Question 3 was in these terms: 'Was the capsize of the "Herald of Free Enterprise" caused or contributed to by the fault of any person or persons and, if so, whom and in what respect?' The answer given to that question was: 'Yes, by the faults of the following,' and three individuals are listed. Then: '4. Townsend Car Ferries Limited at all levels from the Board of Directors through the managers of the Marine Department down to the Junior Superintendents . . .'

[The coroner] said this . . .

'although it is possible for several persons to be guilty individually of manslaughter, it is not permissible to aggregate several acts of neglect by different persons, so as to have gross negligence by a process of aggregation. That is a very important point of law . . .'

No criticism is I think made of what the coroner said about manslaughter as against a personal defendant, but criticism has been made before us as to what he said about aggregation. The point has been made that a company can be guilty of manslaughter as well as an individual . . . I am, however, tentatively of opinion that on appropriate facts the *mens rea* required for manslaughter can be established against a corporation. I see no reason in principle why such a charge should not be established. . . . [F]or a company to be criminally liable for manslaughter—on the assumption I am making that such a crime exists—it is required that the *mens rea* and the *actus reus* of manslaughter should be established not against those who acted for or in the name of the company but against those who were to be identified as the embodiment of the company itself. The coroner formed the view that there was no such case fit to be left to the jury against this company. I see no reason to disagree. I would add that I see no sustainable case in manslaughter against the directors who are named either.

I do not think the aggregation argument assists the applicants. Whether the defendant is a corporation or a personal defendant, the ingredients of manslaughter must be established by proving the necessary *mens rea* and *actus reus* of manslaughter against it or him by evidence properly to be relied on against it or him. A case against a personal defendant cannot be fortified by evidence against another defendant. The case against a corporation can only be made by evidence properly addressed to showing guilt on the part of the corporation as such. On the main substance of his ruling I am not persuaded that the coroner erred."

Applications refused

At the inquest, the jury ignored the coroner's instruction that there were no grounds for a verdict of corporate manslaughter and returned verdicts of unlawful death. Eventually, almost three years after the Zeebrugge deaths and after threats of a private prosecution, prosecutions for manslaughter were instituted against P&O (who had taken over Townsend) and seven employees of the company. At a preliminary hearing it was finally established that a company can be liable for manslaughter[153] but at the end of the prosecution case the trial judge, Turner J, directed acquittals against P&O and the five most senior employees.[154] This indicates that there was a case to be answered by the two most junior employees, Stanley, the assistant-bosun who had not closed the bow doors, and Sable, the loading officer/officer of the watch whose responsibility it was to check that the bow doors were closed. The prosecution immediately dropped all charges against these two on the ground that it was not in the public interest to proceed against them alone. The reason for directing an acquittal against P&O and the senior managers was that it could not be proved that the risks of open-door sailing were obvious to any of them.

The collapse of this prosecution is not surprising. There was no one individual, sufficiently high in the hierarchy of P&O, who could be said to have committed the actus reus and mens rea of manslaughter. For similar reasons, the failure to secure a manslaughter conviction in the *Great Western Trains* case, discussed above,[155] was predictable. In short, this whole approach of "humanising" companies will generally only be appropriate for small owner-managed companies where it will not be too difficult to pinpoint a senior individual with whom the company can be identified. For example, a corporate manslaughter conviction was obtained in *Kite*[156] where four teenagers had been drowned during a canoeing trip in Lyme Bay, because the company, OLL Ltd, was effectively a one-person company and as the trial judge put it: "Mr Kite and the company OLL, of which he is managing director, stand or fall together. One for all and all for one."[157] However, with larger companies, such as P&O, it will not

---

[153]   *DPP v P&O European Ferries (Dover) Ltd* (1991) 93 Cr. App. R. 73.
[154]   Unreported. Transcript: *R. v Alcindor* 1990 (Central Criminal Court, October 19, 1990). See D. Bergman, "Recklessness in the Boardroom" (1990) 140 N.L.J. 1496.
[155]   *Attorney-General's Reference (No.2 of 1999)* [2000] 2 Cr. App. R. 207.
[156]   *Kite, The Independent*, December 9, 1994.
[157]   Cited in Smith and Smith, "The Company Behind Bars", *Health and Safety at Work*, February 1995, p.10.

be easy to find a corporate officer who committed an offence that can be attributed to the company. The identification doctrine ignores the reality of modern corporate decision-making which is often the product of corporate policies and procedures rather than individual decisions.

3. Corporate manslaughter

The inadequacy of the law, particularly in relation to securing a manslaughter conviction against larger companies, led to a sustained campaign for reform of the law.

In 1996, the Law Commission responded to these calls for reform of the law and proposed the introduction of a new offence of "corporate killing".[158] It proposed abandonment of the identification doctrine and its replacement by a test of "management failure". When the Labour Government came to power in 1997, one of its pledges was to introduce an offence along these lines and in due course the Corporate Manslaughter and Corporate Homicide Act 2007 (hereafter termed the CMCH Act) was enacted and came into force in 2008.

This Act abolishes the "common law of manslaughter by gross negligence" in its application to corporations and other organisations. A new offence, corporate manslaughter,[159] is created. Individuals cannot be liable for aiding, abetting, counselling or procuring the new offence but can still be liable for the common law offence of manslaughter.

The offence of corporate manslaughter is defined as follows:

Corporate Manslaughter and Corporate Homicide Act 2007 s.1

"The offence
(1) An organisation to which this section applies is guilty of an offence if the way in which its activities are managed or organised—

(a) causes a person's death, and

(b) amounts to a gross breach of a relevant duty of care owed by the organisation to the deceased . . .

(3) An organisation is guilty of an offence under this section only if the way in which its activities are managed or organised by its senior management is a substantial element in the breach referred to in subsection (1)."

From this somewhat cumbersome offence definition, it can be seen that the following core ingredients need to be established:

- Organisation.

- Relevant duty of care.

- Senior management failure.

- Gross breach of duty.

- Causing death.

---

[158] Law Commission Paper No.237, *Legislating the Criminal Code: Involuntary Manslaughter* (1996).
[159] The offence is termed corporate homicide in Scotland.

Each of these ingredients will be examined in turn.

(i) Organisation

Despite the nomenclature of "corporate" manslaughter, the offence can be committed by any of the following specified "organisations".

Corporate Manslaughter and Corporate Homicide Act 2007 s.1(2)

"The organisations to which this section applies are—

(a) a corporation;

(b) a department or other body listed in Schedule 1;

(c) a police force;

(d) a partnership, or a trade union or employers' association, that is an employer."

Schedule 1 lists various government departments and other public bodies such as the Department of Transport, the Department of Health and Her Majesty's Revenue and Customs. This list may be amended by statutory instrument.[160] Crown immunity for all such bodies is removed by s.11. While this extension of the law to these other bodies is significant, we shall see in the next section that ss.3–7 provide that public authorities do not owe a relevant duty of care in a wide range of circumstances meaning that the lifting of crown immunity is largely a matter of "symbolism".[161]

(ii) Relevant duty of care

Corporate Manslaughter and Corporate Homicide Act 2007 s.2

"Meaning of 'relevant duty of care'

 (1) A 'relevant duty of care', in relation to an organisation, means any of the following duties owed by it under the law of negligence—

(a) a duty owed to its employees or to other persons working for the organisation or performing services for it;

(b) a duty owed as occupier of premises;

(c) a duty owed in connection with—

(i)   the supply by the organisation of goods or services (whether for consideration or not),
(ii)   the carrying on by the organisation of any construction or maintenance operations,
(iii)   the carrying on by the organisation of any other activity on a commercial basis, or
(iv)   the use or keeping by the organisation of any plant, vehicle or other thing;

(d) a duty owed to [a person held in custody] . . .

---

[160]   Section 22. Amendments have been made several times, in order to reflect restructuring of government departments, the most recent being in October 2013.

[161]   D. Ormerod and R.D. Taylor, "The Corporate Manslaughter and Corporate Homicide Act 2007" [2008] Crim. L.R. 589 at 597.

(5) For the purposes of this Act, whether a particular organisation owes a duty of care to a particular individual is a question of law.

The judge must make any findings of fact necessary to decide that question.
(6) For the purposes of this Act there is to be disregarded—

(a)   any rule of the common law that has the effect of preventing a duty of care from being owed by one person to another by reason of the fact that they are jointly engaged in unlawful conduct;

(b)   any such rule that has the effect of preventing a duty of care from being owed to a person by reason of his acceptance of a risk of harm."

As with the current law of manslaughter by gross negligence, the organisation must owe a relevant duty of care to the deceased. This is a duty owed under the civil law of negligence; whether a duty of care is owed is a question of law.

This requirement is drawn from the *Adomako*[162] test for gross negligence manslaughter under which the defendant must owe a duty of care to the deceased. However, under this common law test the civil law concept of duty of care has not been fully employed by the criminal law. In *Wacker*[163] it was stated that the law of tort and criminal law have different objectives and so concepts such as duty of care need to be adapted to the different areas of law in which they are being applied.[164] Accordingly, in this case it was held that the tortuous doctrine of *ex turpi causa non oritur actio* did not apply in a case where a lorry driver smuggled 58 illegal immigrants (who died) into the country. To preserve the effect of this decision and also to ensure that the civil law rules on *volenti non fit injuria* do not apply, s.2(6) specifically provides that neither doctrine applies for the purposes of corporate manslaughter. Thus a corporate defendant in a *Wacker*-type case will be regarded as being under a duty of care. Similarly, the fact that a worker has accepted a risk of harm will not prevent the employer company being under a duty of care.

The extent to which a duty of care is owed by public authorities, the military, police and law enforcement agencies, emergency services, child-protection and probation agencies are severely limited by ss.3–7 which provide various exemptions from liability. Some of these exemptions are "comprehensive".[165] Public authorities do not owe a relevant duty of care "in respect of a decision as to matters of public policy (including in particular the allocation of public resources or the weighing of competing public interests)".[166] Thus if the Department of Health makes a decision not to allocate public resources to, for example, the purchase of certain drugs, there will be no duty of care owed to any patients who might die because of the unavailability of the drug. The other comprehensive exemptions relate to military combat operations[167] and police operations dealing with terrorism and violent disorder.[168] Other exemptions are "partial". For example, with regard to other policing and law enforcement activities and the emergency response of fire authorities and other emergency response organisations, there is, in essence,[169] no duty of care in relation to their operational activities; there is only a duty of care where the death relates to the organisation's responsibility as employer or as occupier of premises.[170] So, for example, if a fire authority acts negligently while rescuing people from a fire, there will be no liability. However, if the fire authority negligently fails to maintain its fleet of fire engines with the result that a death is caused, the fire authority can be liable for the new offence.

It is to be hoped that the courts will not get bogged down with legal intricacies relating to whether a duty of care exists under the civil law or whether the case comes within the exclusions in ss.3–7. Indeed, it may be questioned whether it is appropriate to employ the civil law concept of duty of care here at all. The duty of care concept

---

[162]   *R. v Adomako (John Asare)* [1995] 1 A.C. 171.
[163]   *R. v Wacker (Perry)* [2003] 1 Cr. App. R. 22.
[164]   This point was endorsed in *R. v Willoughby (Keith Calverley)* [2004] EWCA Crim 3365.
[165]   Ministry of Justice, *Understanding the Corporate Manslaughter and Corporate Homicide Act 2007* (2007), p.9.
[166]   Section 3(1).
[167]   Section 4.
[168]   Section 5(1)(2).
[169]   Detail of these provisions is beyond the scope of this book. See Ormerod and Taylor, "The Corporate Manslaughter and Corporate Homicide Act 2007" [2008] Crim. L.R. 589 at 605–9.
[170]   For example, s.5(3).

has been developed and refined in the totally different context of claims for compensation. It is also a complex legal concept that is still evolving through judicial decisions. Given the special context of the new offence, it might have been better not to follow the contours of the law of gross negligence manslaughter and instead to have recognised that the focus of the new offence should be on breaches of health and safety that cause death. As shall be seen, such breaches form a critical component in the assessment of whether an organisation is liable. Such offences are specifically designed for regulating corporate conduct and are clear and well-established. The Law Commission's original proposal with no such requirement of a duty of care was superior.[171] However, the CMCH Act rejects this view.

(iii) Senior management failure

Corporate Manslaughter and Corporate Homicide Act 2007 s.1

"(3) An organisation is guilty of an offence under this section only if the way in which its activities are managed or organised by its senior management is a substantial element in the breach referred to in subsection (1) . . .
  (4)(c) 'senior management', in relation to an organisation, means the persons who play significant roles in—

(i)   the making of decisions about how the whole or a substantial part of its activities are to be managed or organised, or

(ii) the actual managing or organising of the whole or a substantial part of those activities."

Ministry of Justice, Understanding the Corporate Manslaughter and Corporate Homicide Act 2007 (2007), pp.12–14:

"The offence is concerned with the way in which activities were managed or organised. This represents a new approach to establishing corporate liability for manslaughter . . . and does not require the prosecution to establish failure on the part of particular individuals or managers. It is instead concerned with how an activity was being managed and the adequacy of those arrangements.

- This approach is not confined to a particular level of management within an organisation: the test considers how an activity was managed within the organisation as a whole. However, it will not be possible to convict an organisation unless a substantial part of the organisation's failure lay at a senior management level . . .

- Exactly who is a member of an organisation's senior management will depend on the nature and scale of an organisation's activities. Apart from directors and similar senior management positions, roles likely to be under consideration include regional managers in national organisations and the managers of different operational divisions . . .

Can the offence be avoided by senior management delegating responsibility for health and safety?

- No. The Act is concerned with the way an activity was being managed or organised and will consider how responsibility was being discharged at different levels of the organisation. Failures by senior managers to manage health and safety adequately, including through inappropriate delegation of health and safety matters, will therefore leave organisations vulnerable to corporate manslaughter . . . charges."

The above provisions focus on the way in which the organisation's activities are managed and organised by the *senior management*. This is to ensure "that the new offence is targeted at failings in the strategic management of an organisation's activities, rather than failings at relatively junior levels".[172]

---

[171]   Above, fn.158 at 4.
[172]   Home Office, *Corporate Manslaughter: The Government's Draft Bill for Reform* (2005), para.28.

The insistence in the Act on fault by senior management is a response to critics of earlier proposals who argued that because companies are purely creatures of law, crimes can only be committed by people and not companies and so the real issue is one of determining when the acts of these people should be attributed to a company.[173]

David Ormerod and Richard Taylor, "The Corporate Manslaughter and Corporate Homicide Act 2007" [2008] Crim. L.R. 589 at 593–594:

"This test returns the focus, at least to some extent, to the evaluation of the relative contribution of groups of individuals. It can thus be described as implementing a 'qualified aggregation principle' in two respects: (1) because it adds together the failings of a number of individuals or groups of individuals, not in creating an artificial level of fault of an appropriate degree than can be anthropomorphically attributed to the company but rather, in characterising the company's management failure as the aggregate of those (groups of) individuals' failures; and (2) because whilst the failures might be found in and aggregated from a variety of places within the company, there is a proviso or qualification that failures must include to an appropriate (substantial) extent, failure or failures by 'senior management'."

Once the decision had been made to abandon the identification doctrine (and not to adopt the aggregation doctrine)[174] and instead to focus "responsibility on the working practices of the organisation",[175] this insistence on identifying the "senior management" seems unduly restrictive and threatens to open the door to endless argument in court as to whether certain persons do or do not qualify as part of the "senior management". A further obvious problem with this approach is that it replicates one of the main problems with the previous law in that it could apply inequitably to small and large organisations. It will clearly be easier to identify senior management failings in small companies.[176] In essence, this senior management test is little more than a broadening of the identification doctrine. In effect, as suggested by Ormerod and Taylor, it is an endorsement of a version of the aggregation doctrine where, instead of identifying one senior directing mind, one aggregates the actions and culpability of several senior persons. It is unfortunate that the Law Commission approach was not adopted whereby the definition of a management failure removed the need to identify persons representing the senior management and placed the emphasis on the *activities* of the company: "the way in which its activities are managed or organised".[177] This placed the focus where it should be: on the activities and organisational practices of the company.

(iv) Gross breach of duty

Corporate Manslaughter and Corporate Homicide Act 2007 s.1(4)(b)

"[A] breach of a duty of care by an organisation is a 'gross' breach if the conduct alleged to amount to a breach of that duty falls far below what can reasonably be expected of the organisation in the circumstances."

---

[173]   G.R. Sullivan, "The Attribution of Culpability to Limited Companies" (1996) 55 C.L.J. 515; P.R. Glazebrook, "A Better Way of Convicting Businesses of Avoidable Deaths and Injuries" (2002) 61 L.Q.R. 405.

[174]   A point made explicitly in Home Office, *Corporate Manslaughter: The Government's Draft Bill for Reform* (2005), para.27.

[175]   Home Office, *Corporate Manslaughter: The Government's Draft Bill for Reform* (2005), para.26.

[176]   Of the first five companies to be successfully prosecuted under the Act, the largest is Lion Steel Equipment Ltd which had 142 employees: *R. v Lion Steel Equipment Ltd* Unreported July 2012; see: *http://www.judiciary.gov.uk/judgments/r-v-steel-equip-ltd-sentencing-remarks/*

[177]   Above fn.158.

This is following the contours of gross negligence manslaughter as laid down in *Adomako*.[178] There must be a *gross* breach of the relevant duty of care in the way the senior managers manage or organise the organisation's activities.

It is for the jury to determine whether a breach of duty is a "gross breach". One of the main criticisms of the *Adomako* test is that it is too vague. The jury has to assess, in an unstructured manner, the broad, open issue of whether the conduct was "so bad" that it deserves to be labelled manslaughter. In response to this, and to similar criticisms that the Law Commission's proposals were also too vague in this respect, the Act provides a range of statutory criteria for the jury in deciding whether there was a gross breach of duty.

Corporate Manslaughter and Corporate Homicide Act 2007 s.8

"Gross breach
Factors for jury

(1) This section applies where—

(a) it is established that an organisation owed a relevant duty of care to a person, and

(b) it falls to the jury to decide whether there was a gross breach of that duty.

(2) The jury must consider whether the evidence shows that the organisation failed to comply with any health and safety legislation that relates to the alleged breach, and if so—

(a) how serious that failure was;

(b) how much of a risk of death it posed.

(3) The jury may also—

(a) consider the extent to which the evidence shows that there were attitudes, policies, systems or accepted practices within the organisation that were likely to have encouraged any such failure as is mentioned in subsection (2), or to have produced tolerance of it;

(b) have regard to any health and safety guidance that relates to the alleged breach.

(4) This section does not prevent the jury from having regard to any other matters they consider relevant."

(a) *Failure to comply with health and safety legislation*

In deciding whether there has been a gross breach of duty, the jury must consider whether the organisation failed to comply with any health and safety legislation that relates to the alleged breach, and if so, (a) how serious that failure was; and (b) how much of a risk of death it posed.

Four points should be made with regard to this provision. First, the jury *must* consider the issues specified in s.8(2). This is to be welcomed. Companies are expected to comply with the health and safety legislation. Their failure to do so raises at least a prima facie case of a gross breach. Secondly, it is only compliance with health and safety *legislation* that must be considered. Whether there has been compliance with health and safety *guidance* is a matter to which the jury *may* have regard.[179] Thirdly, the jury must consider whether the *organisation* (as a whole) failed to comply with the health and safety legislation. While it has been stated that this "further supports the argument that the activities of non-senior managers are relevant in determining whether there has been a management

---

[178] *R. v Adomako (John Asare)* [1995] 1 A.C. 171. See below, pp.702–703.
[179] Section 8(3)(b).

failure",[180] the fact remains that the failure to comply with the health and safety legislation by the organisation must be substantially attributable to the way in which the organisation's activities are managed or organised by its *senior management*. Fourthly, it is right that not every (perhaps trivial) breach of health and safety laws should give rise to liability for the new offence. The jury must go on to assess *how serious* the failure was and how much of a *risk of death* it posed.

Of course, there is an inevitable circularity in asking whether conduct falls far below a standard and then measuring this by "how serious" is the failure to comply with the law. However, making these decisions in relation to something tangible (the breach of health and safety laws) is a helpful step compared to the position under *Adomako* where no guidance at all for the jury is specified. The approach is not without practical problems, though. As highlighted by Dobson,[181] proving breaches of health and safety legislation involves a reverse burden of proof, allowing a company to escape liability if it is able to show that it did what was practicable.[182] It is unclear whether such a reverse burden would apply when the jury is to assess whether a breach of health and safety legislation is occurred for the purposes of s.8.[183] Given that a company may well be facing charges of breach of health and safety legislation alongside a corporate manslaughter charge (see below), such procedural issues could become confusing for the jury.

(b) *Corporate culture*

As a result of the Parliamentary Subcommittees' Report on the 2005 Bill,[184] the Act has introduced a new, additional, test for the jury in determining whether the conduct "falls far below what can reasonably be expected of the organisation in the circumstances". The jury *may* also "consider the extent to which the evidence shows that there were attitudes, policies, systems or accepted practices within the organisation that were likely to have encouraged" the failure to comply with health and safety laws or to have produced tolerance of such a failure.

This is drawing upon the corporate culture test applied in the Australian Capital Territory (discussed earlier[185]). This approach has tried to escape from the notion that corporate acts must be linked to individual human beings' choices and acts. It has adopted an organisational model with the focus being on corporate structures and systems and on practices and policies and whether the corporation has allowed a "corporate culture" to develop which facilitated the commission of the crime. It should be noted that the Subcommittees' Report proposed this corporate culture test as a substitute for the senior management test. The Act has, however, utilised the corporate culture test as an additional mechanism to determine whether there has been the required senior management failure. While the Australian test has been criticised as too vague,[186] the provision in s.8(3) is less amenable to attack because it is an *additional* test to the breach of health and safety laws test. It is only when there has been a breach of health and safety laws that the jury *may* go on to consider the corporate culture within the corporation; the provision specifically relates to how the corporate culture encouraged

---

[180]   Ormerod and Taylor, "The Corporate Manslaughter and Corporate Homicide Act 2007" [2008] Crim. L.R. 589 at 603.
[181]   A. Dobson, "Shifting Sands: Multiple Counts in Prosecutions for Corporate Manslaughter" [2012] Crim. L.R. 200.
[182]   Health and Safety at Work etc. Act 1974 s.40.
[183]   Dobson notes that in *Cotswold Geotech Ltd* Field J held that s.40 of the Health and Safety at Work etc. Act 1974 did not apply when analysing s.8 of the Corporate Manslaughter and Corporate Homicide Act 2007. Dobson, "Shifting Sands: Multiple Counts in Prosecutions for Corporate Manslaughter" [2012] Crim. L.R. 200 at 207.
[184]   House of Commons, Home Affairs and Work and Pensions Committees, *Draft Corporate Manslaughter Bill*, First Joint Report of Session 2005–06 (2005).
[185]   Above, pp.266–267.
[186]   J. Clough and C. Mulhern, *The Prosecution of Corporations* (Melbourne: OUP, 2002), pp.140–147.

the failure to comply with the health and safety laws. This is a far more focused issue than the rather unstructured and broad test from Australia.

(c) *Any other relevant matters*

Neither of the above two provisions prevent the jury from having regard to "any other matters they consider relevant". It is difficult to see that this provision will be much utilised. It is unthinkable that a jury could conclude that there had been no breach of health and safety laws yet because of "other matters" there was a gross breach of duty. So the relevance of this provision must relate to the issue of "how serious" was the failure to comply with the health and safety laws. Such issues would normally fall to be determined by the corporate culture test.

(v) Causing death

In many cases when a death occurs at work, the most immediate cause of the death will be the act of a particular individual. To prevent arguments that this could constitute a free, deliberate and informed act breaking the chain of causation, the Law Commission Report recommended that liability could not be avoided on the ground that the most immediate cause of death was the act or omission of "an individual".[187] The Government rejected this approach.

Home Office, Corporate Manslaughter: The Government's Draft Bill for Reform, Cmnd.6497 (2005), para.51:

"The case law in this area has, however, developed since the Law Commission reported and we are satisfied that no separate provision is now needed. An intervening act will only break the chain of causation if it is extraordinary—and we do not consider that corporate liability should arise where an individual has intervened in the chain of events in an extraordinary fashion causing death, or the death was otherwise immediately caused by an extraordinary and unforeseeable event."

Accordingly, s.1(1)(a) simply specifies that the way in which the organisation managed or organised its activities must "cause a person's death". The normal rules on causation apply. This Home Office view was based on the then leading decision in *Empress Cars*.[188] However, since then the House of Lords has reaffirmed the supremacy of the rule that a chain of causation will be broken by the free, voluntary and informed action of a third party.[189] This has opened the door to arguments that the action of an individual employee, who is the most immediate cause of the death, will be regarded as voluntary and informed and will break the chain of causation. It is unfortunate that the Law Commission's proposal was not carried into the legislation.

Having outlined the main ingredients of the new offence, the following matters deserve consideration.

---

[187]   Law Commission Paper No.237, *Legislating the Criminal Code: Involuntary Manslaughter* (1996), para.8.39.
[188]   *Environmental Agency v Empress Car Co (Abertillery) Ltd* [1999] 2 A.C. 22. See pp.123–124.
[189]   *R. v Kennedy (Simon)* [2008] 1 A.C. 269. See pp.132–133.

(vi) Relationship to health and safety legislation

Corporate Manslaughter and Corporate Homicide Act 2007 s.19

"(1) Where in the same proceedings there is—

(a) a charge of corporate manslaughter . . . arising out of a particular set of circumstances, and

(b) a charge against the same defendant of a health and safety offence arising out of some or all of those circumstances,

the jury may, if the interests of justice so require, be invited to return a verdict on each charge.
(2) An organisation that has been convicted of corporate manslaughter . . . arising out of a particular set of circumstances may, if the interests of justice so require, be charged with a health and safety offence arising out of some or all of those circumstances."

An organisation may be charged with both corporate manslaughter and a health and safety offence and the jury may return a verdict on only the lesser charge. Under s.17 the consent of the Director of Public Prosecutions is required for a corporate manslaughter prosecution. The Act makes no change to the position that the CPS (and not the HSE) has responsibility for prosecuting the offence.[190]

Sentencing Guidelines Council, Corporate Manslaughter and Health and Safety Offences Causing Death: Definitive Guideline (2010), para.4:

"There are considerable differences between these two offences:

(a) because corporate manslaughter involves both a *gross* breach of duty of care and senior management failings as a substantial element in that breach, those cases will generally involve systemic failures; by contrast the HSWA offences are committed whenever the defendant cannot show that it was not reasonably practicable to avoid a risk of injury or lack of safety; that may mean that the failing is at an operational rather than systemic level and can mean in some cases that there has been only a very limited falling below the standard of reasonable practicability;

(b) in corporate manslaughter the burden of proof remains on the prosecution throughout; in particular this will ordinarily involve the prosecution identifying the acts or omissions which it relies upon as constituting the breach, and then proving them; by contrast, in a HSWA prosecution the prosecutor need only prove that there has been a failure to ensure safety or absence of risk, which it may often be able to do simply by pointing to the injury; once it has done so the burden of proof shifts to the defendant; the prosecution need not identify the precautions which it says ought to have been taken, nor need it prove how the accident happened (*R v Chargot* [2008] UKHL 73, *Electric Gate Services Ltd.* [2009] EWCA Crim 1942); usually however it will do so.

(c) in corporate manslaughter the prosecution must prove that the breach was *a* (but not necessarily *the only*) substantial cause of death; by contrast the HSWA offences can be proved without demonstrating that any injury was caused by the failure to ensure safety . . ."

---

[190] See generally, P. Almond, "An Inspector's Eye View: The Prospective Enforcement of Work-Related Fatality Cases" (2006) 46 Brit. J. Criminol. 893 at 896.

(vii) Abolition of liability of organisations for manslaughter at common law

Corporate Manslaughter and Corporate Homicide Act 2007 s.20

"The common law offence of manslaughter by gross negligence is abolished in its application to corporations, and in any application it has to other organisations to which section 1 applies."

While the common law offence of manslaughter by gross negligence is abolished in relation to organisations, it is not abolished, as shall be seen in the next section, in relation to individuals.

(viii) No individual liability

Corporate Manslaughter and Corporate Homicide Act 2007 s.18

"(1) An individual cannot be guilty of aiding, abetting, counselling or procuring the commission of an offence of corporate manslaughter."

One of the most controversial aspects of the new law is the exemption from liability for individuals, such as directors or managers. Section 18 provides that no individual can be liable for aiding, abetting, counselling or procuring an offence of corporate manslaughter committed by an organisation. Such persons can still be liable to prosecution under the Health and Safety legislation (Health and Safety at Work etc Act 1974 s.37) or for the common law offence of gross negligence manslaughter. However, the reality is that few company directors (mostly of small companies) are personally convicted under Health and Safety legislation and even fewer have been convicted of manslaughter.[191] With the introduction of the new corporate manslaughter offence, it was feared that even fewer prosecutions would be brought against individuals as prosecutors could view companies as easier targets.[192]

However, what appears to be emerging is a tendency to use prosecutions of both companies and their individual directors to open the door to plea bargains. In *Lion Steel*, for example, a guilty plea to corporate manslaughter was offered and accepted once the charges against the individual directors were dropped.[193] Woodley worries that this is cause for concern:

"Will plea bargains be offered as a matter of course in the hope that directors facing individual prosecution will instruct their company's solicitors to plead guilty? Or will the initiative come from those same directors to offer a corporate guilty plea in the hope or knowledge that any individual liability will be dropped with the added 'bonus' of a reduction in any subsequent fine on the company?"[194]

Antrobus concludes that in cases combining gross negligence manslaughter charges against individual directors and a corporate manslaughter charge against their company, where the prosecution seek to persuade the jury that the

---

[191]   For full statistics, see C.M.V. Clarkson, "Corporate Manslaughter: Yet More Government Proposals" [2005] Crim. L.R. 677 at 687.

[192]   J. Clough and C. Mulhern, *The Prosecution of Companies* (2002), p.9.

[193]   *R. v Lion Steel Equipment Ltd* Unreported July 2012; see: *http://www.judiciary.gov.uk/judgments/r-v-steel-equip-ltd-sentencing-remarks/*

[194]   M. Woodley, "Bargaining over Corporate Manslaughter—What Price a Life?" (2013) 77(1) J. of Crim. Law 33–40.

"corporate entity is little more than the vehicle of those directors, then the risk is run that the company's liability will stand or fall with the liability of those individuals. It is therefore tempting to conclude that in many respects the liability of corporations and their directors is little different from the situation prior to the CMCHA 2007 coming into force."[195]

(ix) Need for a special offence

The inadequacies of the old law were exposed earlier in this section. Reform of the law was essential. However, was it necessary to introduce a completely new offence? There are two views that can be adopted here.

The first view is that there was no need for the introduction of a new special offence. All unlawful killings should be prosecuted under the general law of homicide (in these situations, manslaughter). Whether someone is killed by an attack, by a car, by a negligent doctor or as a result of corporate activities should make no difference. As long as the identification doctrine were abolished or reformed, "corporate killings" could have been dealt with in the same way as other unlawful killings. Separate treatment through the introduction of a new offence could lead to a marginalisation of the seriousness of such killings. The offence will not be regarded as serious as "real" manslaughter and much of the law's censuring and symbolic role would be defeated.

Further, it is argued that there is the danger that this offence could be perceived by prosecutors as the "easy option" and so individual managers and directors would escape prosecution. As has been seen, the case for corporate liability is not a case for the exclusion of individual liability in appropriate cases. Finally, while the introduction of this new offence could greatly facilitate prosecutions in cases where death has been caused, the identification doctrine still continues to apply to all other cases, in particular, those where serious injury has been caused and with the high-profile problem of corporate killings being catered for, pressure for reform of the identification doctrine will be significantly reduced.

The alternative view is that the new offence can be supported.

C.M.V. Clarkson, "Corporate Manslaughter: Need for a New Offence?", in C.M.V. Clarkson and S.R. Cunningham (eds), Criminal Liability for Non-Aggressive Deaths (2008), pp.84–86:

"Special homicide offences are perhaps needed when there is something distinctive about the context in which the killing occurred that justifies labelling the offence as something different from manslaughter . . .

Where a death has been caused in the context of corporate activities, the killing is far removed from the paradigmatic manslaughter. Duff ('Criminalising Endangerment' in Duff, R.A. and Green, S. (eds), *Defining Crimes* (2005)) distinguishes attacks from endangerments and argues that there is a significant moral difference between them. Attacks manifest 'practical hostility' towards people and their interests. An attack involves being guided by the wrong reasons: I attack you because I want to harm you; this is not a reason by which I should be guided. Endangerment involves not being guided by the right reasons.

Corporate activities do not involve attacks on the interests of others. Harming people is not the object of corporate enterprises. Such activities are widely regarded as acceptable and beneficial . . . But if a company allows dangerous machinery or operations it is not being guided by all the reasons against allowing danger at work. These different actions reveal different wrongs (compared to attacks) and show the company's character in different lights . . . [D]eath is still the product of a lack of health and safety measures. It is very far-removed from manslaughter and so should be marked by the existence of a special offence. To underwrite this difference, it can be strongly argued that the label 'corporate killing' would have been more appropriate than 'corporate manslaughter'."

---

[195]   S. Antrobus, "The Criminal Liability of Directors for Health and Safety Breaches and Manslaughter" [2013] Crim. L.R. 309 at 322.

Further, this fear that such a new, separate offence could lead to its marginalisation could be misplaced. Having separate vehicular homicide offences has not resulted in trivialisation of their seriousness as can be seen by the sentences imposed in such cases.[196]

4. Corporate liability for non-fatal injuries

Early in the process that led to the CMCH Act it was suggested that the Act should be extended to cover cases where serious injuries had been caused by corporate gross negligence. As was seen earlier, the number of people seriously injured at work grossly exceeds the number killed (148 people killed; 19,707 seriously injured in 2012/13). It was argued that it was illogical that a company could be liable for the death of a worker but not for the serious injury to another worker when both might have been involved in the same incident and the second worker's life might only have been saved by the quick actions of the emergency services or by sheer luck.[197]

However, such a proposal was not pursued. The view that prevailed was that while it was acceptable to criminalise corporate manslaughter on the basis of gross negligence as such culpability has always sufficed for manslaughter, it would be anomalous and a major extension of the law to criminalise serious injury caused negligently as subjective mens rea has traditionally been required for non-fatal offences against the person. It was also felt that it could "lead to dilution of the corporate killing offence and could potentially over-stretch investigation and enforcement resources".[198] However, the most important reason for the limitation of the new offence to killings was because of political expedience:

> "it might lose its current clear focus on manslaughter, and the ensuing controversy and drafting difficulties might further delay the introduction of the actual Bill."[199]

Accordingly, for serious, stigmatic offences—such as non-fatal offences against the person (where vicarious liability cannot be applied)—the common law, with its notorious identification doctrine, continues to apply and will continue to hamper the prosecution of companies in cases where serious injury is caused at work. The most realistic charge will be for inflicting grievous bodily harm contrary to s.20 of this Act. However, for such a charge to succeed it will be necessary to prove that the senior person representing the directing mind and will of the company *inflicted* the grievous bodily harm and did so *foreseeing the risk of some harm*.[200] It will only be in the most extraordinary circumstances that this could be proved—which is why there have been no reported convictions to date for such a corporate offence. Such cases will continue to be prosecuted under the Health and Safety legislation. However, it can be anticipated that there will be calls for legislative intervention to extend the law to non-fatal offences. At the time the Act was passed, the Government was urged to consider the possibility of using the Corporate Manslaughter Act as a template for introducing further criminal offences, such as an offence of corporate grievous bodily harm, in due course.[201] This suggestion can be further

---

[196]   See Ch.8 below for further discussion.
[197]   House of Commons, Home Affairs and Work and Pensions Committee, *Draft Corporate Manslaughter Bill: First Report of Session 2005–06, Vol.I: Report*, para.77.
[198]   House of Commons, Home Affairs and Work and Pensions Committee, *Draft Corporate Manslaughter Bill: First Report of Session 2005–06, Vol.I: Report*, para.80.
[199]   House of Commons, Home Affairs and Work and Pensions Committee, *Draft Corporate Manslaughter Bill: First Report of Session 2005–06, Vol.I: Report*, para.81.
[200]   See pp.622–624.
[201]   House of Commons, Home Affairs and Work and Pensions Committees, *Draft Corporate Manslaughter Bill: First Report of Session 2005–06, Vol.I: Report*, para.81.

bolstered by the fact that such an offence would no longer be an anomaly, thanks to the introduction of a new offence of causing serious injury by dangerous driving in 2012.[202]

F. Punishment of Corporations[203]

It is useful to consider first sentencing in cases of corporate manslaughter and health and safety offences causing death and then to consider sentencing of other offences committed by organisations and other sentencing options.

1. Corporate manslaughter/health and safety offences causing death

(i) Fines

Traditionally, the main penalty imposed on corporations for these offences has been a fine. This continues to be the main penalty under the CMCH Act. As seen earlier, fines imposed on companies under the Health and Safety legislation have traditionally been low and could be described as little more than a "public morality tax".[204] This is one of the reasons contributing to the marginalisation of such offences. However, the last 15 years has seen a change of attitude. In *F Howe & Sons (Engineers) Ltd*[205] it was stated that:

> "Generally where death is the consequence of a criminal act it is regarded as an aggravating feature of the offence. The penalty should reflect public disquiet at the unnecessary loss of life . . . The objective of prosecutions for health and safety offences in the work place is to achieve a safe environment for those who work there and for other members of the public who may be affected. A fine needs to be large enough to bring that message home where the defendant is a company not only to those who manage it but also to its shareholders. [It was argued] that the fine should not be so large as to imperil the earnings of employees or create a risk of bankruptcy. Whilst in general we accept that submission . . . there may be cases where the offences are so serious that the defendant ought not to be in business."

The average fine following a death at work increased steadily between the twentieth and twenty-first centuries, and in a few high-profile cases the fines have been significant. In the *Great Western Trains* case a fine of £1.5 million was imposed following the Southall train crash. In 2005, the two biggest fines ever for breach of health and safety laws were imposed on Balfour Beatty (£10 million) and Network Rail (£3.5 million) following the Hatfield derailment where four people were killed and 70 injured.[206] However, while this new attitude to the level of fines is to be welcomed, it should be pointed out that the fine in the *Great Western Trains* case represented only 5.6 per cent of the company's profit for the preceding year.[207] Under the Criminal Justice Act 2003 s.164(3), the court must inquire into the financial circumstances of the offender before fixing the amount of a fine. Equality in sentencing

---

[202] Legal Aid, Sentencing and Punishment of Offenders Act 2012 s.143, inserting s.1A into the Road Traffic Act 1988.
[203] See generally, J. Gobert, "Controlling Corporate Criminality: Penal Sanctions and Beyond" [1998] Web J.C.L.I; M. Jefferson, "Corporate Criminal Liability: The Problem of Sanctions" (2001) 65 J. Crim. L. 235.
[204] Coffee, "'No Soul to Damn: No Body to Kick': an Unscandalised Inquiry into the Problem of Corporate Punishment" (1981) 79 Mich. L. Rev. 386 at 407.
[205] *R. v F Howe & Son (Engineers) Ltd* [1999] 2 Cr. App. R. (S.) 37.
[206] The fine on Balfour Beatty was reduced on appeal to £7.5 million (*R. v Balfour Beatty Rail Infrastructure Services Ltd* [2006] EWCA Crim 1586).
[207] S. Trotter, "Corporate Manslaughter" (2000) N.L.J. 454.

means equality of impact. If large corporations with vast profits were to be fined according to their means (say a percentage thereof) a new attitude to corporate violence and other crime might start emerging.

Since the CMCH Act, sentencing guidelines have been issued for both corporate manslaughter and for breaches of health and safety legislation causing death. The Sentencing Advisory Panel proposed that the starting point in cases where the gross breach of duty of care created a "very high" risk of death should be 5 per cent of the corporation's annual turnover, with a range of 2.5–10 per cent of annual turnover.[208] For health and safety causing death cases, a similar approach was recommended but with lesser starting points. For example, in cases where the breach of duty created a "very high" risk of death the starting point would be 2.5 per cent of annual turnover.

The Sentencing Guidelines Council has, however, rejected this proposal.

Sentencing Guidelines Council, Corporate Manslaughter and Health and Safety Offences Causing Death: Definitive Guideline (2010):

"B. Factors likely to affect seriousness

Seriousness should ordinarily be assessed first by asking:

(a) How foreseeable was serious injury? . . .

(b) How far short of the applicable standard did the defendant fall?

(c) How common is this kind of breach in this organisation? . . .

(d) How far up the organisation does the breach go? . . .

7. In addition, other factors are likely, if present, to aggravate the offence (the list is not exhaustive):

(a) more than one death, or very grave personal injury in addition to death;

(b) failure to heed warnings or advice, whether from officials such as the Inspectorate, or by employees (especially health and safety representatives) or other persons, or to respond appropriately to 'near misses' arising in similar circumstances;

(c) cost-cutting at the expense of safety;

(d) deliberate failure to obtain or comply with relevant licences, at least where the process of licensing involves some degree of control, assessment or observation by independent authorities with a health and safety responsibility;

(e) injury to vulnerable persons . . .

8. Conversely, the following factors, which are similarly non-exhaustive, are likely, if present, to afford mitigation:

(a) a prompt acceptance of responsibility;

(b) a high level of co-operation with the investigation, beyond that which will always be expected;

(c) genuine efforts to remedy the defect;

(d) a good health and safety record;

---

208 Sentencing Advisory Panel, *Advice to the Sentencing Guidelines Council: Sentencing for Corporate Manslaughter and Health and Safety Offences Involving Death* (2009). Where the risk of death was "high", the starting point would be 3.5 per cent; where there was "some" risk of death, it would be 2 per cent (p.23).

(e) a responsible attitude to health and safety, such as the commissioning of expert advice or the consultation of employees or others affected by the organisation's activities . . .

15. A fixed correlation between the fine and either turnover or profit is not appropriate. The circumstances of defendant organisations and the financial consequences of the fine will vary too much; . . .

16. The court should, however, look carefully at both turnover and profit, and also at assets, in order to gauge the resources of the defendant . . .

19. In assessing the financial consequences of a fine, the court should consider (inter alia) the following factors:

(i) the effect on the employment of the innocent may be relevant;

(ii) any effect upon shareholders will, however, not normally be relevant; those who invest in and finance a company take the risk that its management will result in financial loss;

(iii) the effect on directors will not, likewise, normally be relevant;

(iv) nor would it ordinarily be relevant that the prices charged by the defendant might in consequence be raised, at least unless the defendant is a monopoly supplier of public services;

(v) the effect upon the provision of services to the public will be relevant; although a public organisation such as a local authority, hospital trust or police force must be treated the same as a commercial company where the standards of behaviour to be expected are concerned, and must suffer a punitive fine for breach of them, a different approach to determining the level of fine may well be justified; . . .

(vi) the liability to pay civil compensation will ordinarily not be relevant; normally this will be provided by insurance . . . .

(vii) the cost of meeting any remedial order will not ordinarily be relevant, except to the overall financial position of the defendant; such an order requires no more than should already have been done;

(viii) whether the fine will have the effect of putting the defendant out of business will be relevant; in some bad cases this may be an acceptable consequence . . .

D. Level of fines

22 . . . Fines must be punitive and sufficient to have an impact on the defendant . . .

24. The offence of corporate manslaughter, because it requires gross breach at a senior level, will ordinarily involve a level of seriousness significantly greater than a health and safety offence. The appropriate fine will seldom be less than £500,000 and may be measured in millions of pounds.

25. The range of seriousness involved in health and safety offences is greater than for corporate manslaughter. However, where the offence is shown to have caused death, the appropriate fine will seldom be less than £100,000 and may be measured in hundreds of thousands of pounds or more."

Despite the appropriate fine being "seldom less than £500,000", none of the first five successful prosecutions for corporate manslaughter exceeded that amount. The largest company to be convicted, Lion Steel, was fined just shy of this supposed minimum at £480,000, the judge explaining this on the basis that a fine at the recommended level would "have a serious effect on the ability of the company to pay its way and sustain its business".[209] This is not to suggest, however, that judges will always balk at the idea of effectively applying the death penalty to companies. The first company convicted of corporate manslaughter, Cotswold Geotechnical Holdings, was fined £385,000, upheld on appeal, despite the fact that the company would probably have to go into liquidation to pay the fine.[210] The most recent conviction for corporate manslaughter, involving the first non-employee

---

[209] *R. v Lion Steel Equipment Ltd*, Unreported July 2012; see: *http://www.judiciary.gov.uk/judgments/r-v-steel-equip-ltd-sentencing-remarks/.pdf*. The amount of £480,000 did, however, take into account a reduction of 20 per cent due to the guilty plea.

[210] *R. v Cotswold Geotechnical Holdings Ltd* [2012] 1 Cr. App. R. (S.) 26.

death, was that of Princes Sporting Club, which pleaded guilty and was fined £135,000, amounting to all its assets.[211]

(ii) Penalties other than fines

The CMCH Act permits other penalties to be imposed.

Corporate Manslaughter and Corporate Homicide Act 2007

"Remedial orders and publicity orders

9 Power to order breach etc to be remedied
   (1) A court before which an organisation is convicted of corporate manslaughter or corporate homicide may make an order (a 'remedial order') requiring the organisation to take specified steps to remedy—

   (a) the breach mentioned in section 1(1) ('the relevant breach');

   (b) any matter that appears to the court to have resulted from the relevant breach and to have been a cause of the death;

   (c) any deficiency, as regards health and safety matters, in the organisation's policies, systems or practices of which the relevant breach appears to the court to be an indication . . .

   (5) An organisation that fails to comply with a remedial order is guilty of an offence, and liable on conviction on indictment to a fine.

10 Power to order conviction etc to be publicised
   (1) A court before which an organisation is convicted of corporate manslaughter or corporate homicide may make an order (a 'publicity order') requiring the organisation to publicise in a specified manner—

   (a) the fact that it has been convicted of the offence;

   (b) specified particulars of the offence;

   (c) the amount of any fine imposed;

   (d) the terms of any remedial order made."

These provisions are to be welcomed although it must be recognised that there is a risk that with the sanction for failing to comply with the order being a monetary penalty, a corporation could deliberately refuse to comply with the order, thus converting the remedial order into a fine.[212]
   Remedial orders are also available for HSWA offences.[213] Such orders are rarely imposed as, by the time an organisation is sentenced for an offence, the regulatory authorities are likely to have taken appropriate action.[214] Indeed, in *Lion Steel* the judge chose not to apply a remedial order following a guilty plea to corporate manslaughter on the basis that he was satisfied that the company's working protocols had been sufficiently improved since the fatality occurred.[215]
   The Sentencing Guidelines Council has stated that publicity orders "should ordinarily be imposed in cases of corporate manslaughter. The object is deterrence and punishment".[216] Again, in *Lion Steel* the judge failed to make full use of the sentencing options available to him, choosing not to make

---

[211]   H. Fidderman, "Fifth Corporate Manslaughter Case Claims First Non-Worker" (2014) 426 H.S.B. 15–22.
[212]   Gobert, "Controlling Corporate Criminality: Penal Sanctions and Beyond" [1998] Web J.C.L.I.
[213]   Health and Safety at Work etc. Act 1974 s.42.
[214]   Sentencing Advisory Panel, above, fn.208 at para.41.
[215]   Above fn.209.
[216]   At para.31.

a publicity order, instead commenting that such an order would "achieve nothing which will not be achieved by the reporting of these sentencing remarks".[217] The first publicity order for corporate manslaughter was issued in the Princes Sporting Club case.[218]

2. Other corporate offences; other sentencing options

With other offences committed by organisations the main penalty has again been a fine. However, increasingly, suggestions have been made that other sentencing options should be made available as there is doubt whether fines alone ensure that companies revise their internal operational procedures to guard against repetition of the offence.[219]

Because of these concerns and the fear that the public will ultimately have to bear the cost in terms of price rises, Coffee has advocated the imposition of "equity fines" whereby a company would be forced to issue shares to a public body (say, the Victim Compensation Fund) which would then dispose of them on the market.[220] As the company would have no need to raise immediate cash, there would be no need for consumers to bear the cost of price increases and no threat of redundancies.[221] And, as Coffee says:

> "Because the equity fine can vastly exceed the cash fine, the stock market will begin to discount the securities of those companies perceived to be vulnerable to future criminal prosecutions . . . [C]orporate managers will have an incentive to institute preventive monitoring controls to forestall this decline."[222]

Releasing such shares onto the market would increase the risk of a hostile takeover. As managers gain great psychological rewards in the form of power and prestige (as well as money) from their positions of authority in the corporation, the threat of losing these benefits is regarded by managers as a traumatic experience and they will defend their positions with great zeal.[223]

Other alternatives have been mooted and tried in other jurisdictions. For example, a community service order could be made against the company requiring it to engage in various projects. Thus a company convicted of a pollution offence could be required to clean up rivers or beaches. In imposing such orders a court could order senior management to be involved in the service:

> "Executive wrongdoers should not be able to delegate to employees responsibilities that are rightfully theirs . . . any more than a convicted defendant should be allowed to hire a substitute to serve his prison sentence."[224]

---

[217] *R. v Lion Steel Equipment Ltd* Unreported July 2012 at [48].
[218] Hidderman, above fn.211.
[219] Fisse, "The Attribution of Criminal Liability to Corporations: A Statutory Model" (1991) 13 Sydney L. Rev. 277 makes the point that fines are inappropriate in the context of offences committed by quasi-governmental authorities as they would simply result in "some budgetary shuffling with money deducted from one arm of government passing back into general revenue" (p.9).
[220] Coffee, "'No Soul to Damn: No Body to Kick': an Unscandalised Inquiry into the Problem of Corporate Punishment" (1981) 79 Mich. L. Rev. 386 at 413–424.
[221] J. Gobert, "Controlling Corporate Criminality: Penal Sanctions and Beyond" [1998] 2 Web J.C.L.I.
[222] Coffee, "'No Soul to Damn: No Body to Kick': an Unscandalised Inquiry into the Problem of Corporate Punishment" (1981) 79 Mich. L. Rev. 386 at 420.
[223] Coffee, "'No Soul to Damn: No Body to Kick': an Unscandalised Inquiry into the Problem of Corporate Punishment" (1981) 79 Mich. L. Rev. 386 at 412.
[224] Gobert, "Controlling Corporate Criminality: Penal Sanctions and Beyond" [1998] 2 Web J.C.L.I.

However, care must be taken here to ensure that the company does not profit, in terms of publicity and reputation, from involvement in such worthwhile projects. For example, in order to prevent this, the CMCH Act permits organisations to be ordered to place adverse publicity advertisements in newspapers.

An alternative sentence is corporate probation whereby companies could be forced to change those policies and procedures that allowed the offence to be committed. Courts could demand an internal restructuring of the company[225] or could appoint trustees or directors to examine the procedures of the company or to investigate who was responsible within the company. These measures, which would have to be financed by the company itself, would ensure that companies "rehabilitated themselves" and adopted whatever measures were necessary to prevent a reoccurrence of the wrongdoing.

In England and Wales the Macrory Report proposed a range of sanctioning regimes that would not involve a court prosecution. Some of these recommendations have been implemented by the Regulatory Enforcement and Sanctions Act 2008 and are discussed in the previous section on strict liability. Where a conviction has been obtained in the criminal courts, the following sanctions were recommended:

Macrory Report, Regulatory Justice: Making Sanctions Effective (Final Report, 2006):

"Profit Orders
4.49 . . . [I]it would be preferable if the criminal courts had the power to impose a profits order that is separate from any fine imposed. The Profit Order would be a non-judgmental sanction in that it reflected solely the profits made from non-compliance, while the fine imposed would reflect the court's assessment of the seriousness with which they regard the breach . . . Identifying and removing the financial benefit from a regulatory breach is something I believe would strengthen enforcement and send a clearer signal to industry that it is not acceptable to make financial gain from non-compliance . . .

Corporate Rehabilitation Orders
4.53 Corporate Rehabilitation Orders . . . contain provisions to enable a court to require a company to undertake specific actions or activities during a specified period . . . [with the] aim to rehabilitate the offender by ensuring tangible steps are taken that will address a company's poor practices and prevent future non-compliance. They involve a period of monitoring of the activities, policies and procedures of a business, with a view to organisational reform. . .

Community Projects
4.57 The range of requirements that could form the elements of Corporate Rehabilitation Orders should be flexible . . . It could, for example, include a requirement for the business to complete an appropriate community improvement project . . . Community projects would enable the business community to take responsibility for its actions within a local community and restore the harm it may have caused to the community or individuals . . .
4.58 Examples of community projects include funding and delivering an education campaign in a specific subject or funding and delivering a project in the built environment, such as a park or a garden, or making some donations to the local community of time or resource . . ."

While the Regulatory Enforcement and Sanctions Act 2008 accepted other recommendations by the Macrory Report,[226] it did not implement these particular proposals. Most recently, the Crime and Courts Act 2013 has introduced provisions which may have the same effect as such recommendations,

---

[225] B. Fisse, "Reconstructing Corporate Criminal Law: Deterrence, Retribution, Fault and Sanctions" (1983) 56 S. Cal. L. Rev. 1141, 1222. Probation is clearly more sensible in the context of offences committed by quasi-governmental bodies.
[226] See pp.249–250 above.

but not as sentences per se. Schedule 17 to the Act introduces Deferred Prosecution Agreements (DPA) as an alternative to trial and conviction of companies in relation to certain financial crimes. It should be noted that the wrongdoing this is proposed to tackle is quite different to that under discussion here, which has focused on injuries and fatalities caused by health and safety breaches. Instead, the target is economic crime, in the form of theft, fraud, forgery, money laundering, bribery etc.[227] Essentially, the DPA is a type of conditional caution for companies, which permits the prosecution to achieve the objectives of punishment without the cost of a trial. The prosecution commences proceedings against the company for one of the offences listed, after which such proceedings are automatically suspended once the prosecution and defendant company have negotiated the content of the DPA. So long as the terms of the DPA are met, the company will avoid the prosecution resuming. A DPA may impose the following requirements:

(a) to pay to the prosecutor a financial penalty;

(b) to compensate victims of the alleged offence;

(c) to donate money to a charity or other third party;

(d) to disgorge any profits made by P from the alleged offence;

(e) to implement a compliance programme or make changes to an existing compliance programme relating to P's policies or to the training of P's employees or both;

(f) to co-operate in any investigation related to the alleged offence;

(g) to pay any reasonable costs of the prosecutor in relation to the alleged offence or the DPA.[228]

The Ministry of Justice, in proposing the creation of DPAs, suggested that they were designed to overcome particular obstacles to successfully prosecuting a company for economic crime. Such obstacles stem from the law of corporate criminal liability, the increasingly sophisticated criminal behaviour in the area of economic crime, the size of commercial organisations and the difficulties of identifying criminal activity and of prosecution at national level for what can often be wrongdoing across a number of jurisdictions.[229] What is not clear is how DPAs circumvent the need for the Crown Prosecution Service to have collected sufficient evidence against a company for the relevant offences in order to be able to bring charges to begin with, before a DPA can be negotiated. Although the initiative has been imported from the United States, it is yet to be seen how they will operate in practice in this country.

   While DPAs are not relevant to corporate wrongdoing involving corporate violence, the point is that there is a range of sentencing options that could be employed to tackle corporate wrongdoing generally. As already stressed, nothing in this chapter should be taken as suggesting that corporate criminal liability should in all cases replace individual liability. In many cases where an individual has "gone out on a limb" it is that individual who should be prosecuted. In many cases both the company and individuals should be prosecuted. Indeed, culpable persons should never be allowed

---

[227] Part 2 of Schedule 17 sets out the offences to which DPAs can be applied. Some of these offences are also the subject of a recent sentencing guideline applying to corporate offenders: Sentencing Council, *Fraud, bribery and money laundering: corporate offenders: Definitive Guideline* (2014), available at *http://sentencingcouncil.judiciary.gov.uk/docs/Fraud_bribery_and_money_laundering_offences_-_Definitive_guideline.pdf.*

[228] Crime and Courts Act 2013 Sch.17 para.5.

[229] MoJ CP 9/2012 Consultation on a new enforcement tool to deal with economic crime committed by commercial organisations: Deferred Prosecution Agreements (May 2012).

to hide behind the corporate facade. Equally, however, in many cases the real fault will lie with the company and not with any individual. In such cases there should be a real possibility of a prosecution and conviction with appropriate, meaningful punishment being available to reflect the true guilt of the company.

4

GENERAL DEFENCES

I. JUSTIFICATION AND EXCUSE

A. Introduction

A defendant may commit the actus reus of an offence with the requisite mens rea and yet escape liability because he has a "general defence". For example, he may have intentionally killed his victim, but have been acting in self-defence because the victim had been trying to kill him. In such a case, assuming the requirements of self-defence are met, he escapes all liability.

It was seen in Ch.2 that there are different ways of analysing criminal liability. It could be, continuing the above example, that the defendant is regarded as having committed the actus reus with an appropriate mens rea but is afforded a defence which is a separate third element. This mode of analysis could be useful in describing the shifting burdens of proof in a criminal trial in those jurisdictions[1] where it is for the prosecution to prove beyond reasonable doubt that the defendant committed the actus reus with appropriate mens rea, but the burden then shifts to the defendant to establish on a balance of probabilities that he has a defence. This "procedural analysis" is employed in England and Wales with the defences of insanity[2] and diminished responsibility.[3] Such an approach is, however, not accurate in describing the burden of proof in other cases in England where, in relation to common law defences, the burden remains on the prosecution throughout.[4] Nor is this "procedural analysis" helpful in understanding the true bases of criminal liability: who, why and when persons should be adjudged blameworthy and held criminally responsible for their actions. Accordingly, a "substantive interpretation" tends to focus on the requirement of blameworthiness. Criminal liability is imposed on a blameworthy actor who causes a prohibited harm or prohibited act or omission. If a defendant has a "general defence" she is not blameworthy and, therefore, deserves to escape criminal liability. Accordingly, as Horder states, the way in which defences are defined and restricted "represents criminal law's contribution to society's commitment to the common good of upholding respect for the individual and general interests of persons" just as much as the definition and scope of offences.[5]

The term "general defences" is used to convey that such defences are available to all crimes. There are some defences that are not "general" but specific to particular offences: for example, loss of control (formerly provocation) and diminished responsibility are defences only to murder, reducing

---

[1]   e.g. Singapore and Malaysia: see K.L. Koh, C.M.V. Clarkson and N.A. Morgan, *Criminal Law in Singapore and Malaysia: Text and Materials* (Singapore: Malayan Law Journal 1989), p.103.
[2]   *Bratty v Attorney-General of Northern Ireland* [1963] A.C. 386.
[3]   Homicide Act 1957 s.2(2).
[4]   *Woolmington v Director of Public Prosecutions* [1935] A.C. 462; see D. Ormerod, *Smith and Hogan's Criminal Law*, 13th edn (Oxford: OUP, 2011), pp.29, 46.
[5]   J. Horder, *Excusing Crime* (Oxford: OUP, 2004), p.2.

liability to manslaughter. Such specific defences are dealt with later in relation to their particular offences. Further, it must be stressed that the title "general defences" is adopted purely for expository convenience. It is patently untrue that all these defences are available to all offences. For example, duress is not available for murder. Another problematic area is the extent to which the "general defences" are available to offences of strict liability.

These general defences used to be listed as isolated sets of identifiable conditions or circumstances which prevented a defendant being convicted. However, over the last 35 years a number of attempts have been made to bring defences within an overall theoretical framework. The chief advantage of this is that it enables more rational analysis of the ways in which the law has developed or been restricted.[6] Defences have been broadly classified into two groups: those that provide a *justification* for the defendant's conduct, and those that *excuse* his conduct.[7] However, commentators have reworked the category of excusatory defences and increasingly exclude from it those which amount to denials of responsibility. This latter group may be called *exemptions*. Most recently, as we will see, Duff has suggested a reworking of defences to introduce a fourth category.[8]

It must be stressed, however, that the classification of defences into groups is not watertight. This is true in a number of respects. First, at least some members of the judiciary appear to have less regard for the classifications than academic commentators.[9] Secondly, the categories themselves are still being refined. As we shall see, it has become commonplace to distinguish between the categories on the basis that excuses focus upon the actor and justifications upon actions. But it can be argued that in reality the focus has to be upon both actors and actions for both justifications and excuses. Thus, the distinction between the categories is blurred.[10] Finally, it may be difficult to locate a particular defence within just one category:

"In English law this is compounded by the law's cautious insistence on having a belt as well as braces: in general no excuse is accepted into the criminal law which is not also a partial justification, and no justification is accepted which is not also a partial excuse."[11]

Paul Robinson, "Criminal Law Defenses: A Systematic Analysis" (1982) 82 Col. L. R. 199 at 213, 221, 229:

"[J]ustification defences are not alterations of the statutory definition of the harm sought to be prevented or punished by an offense. The harm caused by the justified behaviour remains a legally recognised harm which is

---

6   But see W. Wilson, "The Structure of Defences" [2005] Crim. L.R. 108, where he argues that the best way of improving the doctrinal stability, coherence and consistency of defences is to focus upon a common template for the structure of defences rather than searching for an underlying unifying rationale for them.

7   The distinction was important before 1828 as, under the common law, a killer's goods were forfeited if the killing was excusable but not if it was justifiable. In 1828 forfeiture was abolished. See further, J.C. Smith, *Justification and Excuse in the Criminal Law* (Oxford: OUP, 1989), p.7. The revived interest in the distinction can largely be traced back to the publication in 1978 of G.P. Fletcher, *Rethinking Criminal Law* (Boston: Little, Brown, 1978).

8   R.A. Duff, *Answering for Crime: Responsibility and Liability in the Criminal Law* (Oxford: Hart Publishing, 2007).

9   See, for example, Robert Walker LJ in *Re A (Conjoined Twins: Surgical Operation)* [2000] 4 All E.R. 961 at 1064.

10 See further, C.M.V. Clarkson, "Necessary Action: A New Defence" [2004] Crim. L.R. 81 and contra W.M. Chan and A.P. Simester, "Duress, Necessity: How Many Defences?" (2005) 16 K.C.L.J. 121. Some commentators have found the classification so flawed that they have almost entirely abandoned it: see A.P. Simester, J.R. Spencer, G.R. Sullivan and G.J. Virgo, *Simester and Sullivan's Criminal Law: Theory and Doctrine*, 5th edn, (Oxford: Hart Publishing, 2013), pp.673–678.

11 J. Gardner, "Justifications and Reasons", in A.P. Simester and A.T.H. Smith (eds), *Harm and Culpability* (Oxford: Clarendon Press, 1996), p.122. See further, A. Simester, "On Justifications and Excuses", in L. Zedner and J. Roberts (eds), *Principles and Values in the Criminal Law and Criminal Justice: Essays in Honour of Andrew Ashworth* (Oxford: OUP, 2012).

to be avoided whenever possible. Under the special justifying circumstances, however, that harm is outweighed by the need to avoid an even greater harm or to further a great societal interest . . .

    Excuses admit that the deed may be wrong, but excuse the actor . . .

Justifications and excuses may seem similar in that both are general defenses which exculpate an actor because of his blamelessness . . . The conceptual distinction remains an important one, however. Justified conduct is correct behaviour which is encouraged or at least tolerated. In determining whether conduct is justified, the focus is on the *act*, not the actor. An excuse represents a legal conclusion that the conduct is wrong, undesirable, but that criminal liability is inappropriate because some characteristic of the actor vitiates society's desire to punish him. Excuses do not destroy blame . . . rather, they shift it from the actor to the excusing condition. The focus in excuses is on the *actor*. Acts are justified; actors are excused."

Robinson's analysis has been very influential, but, as we shall see, both his description of justifications and excuses has come under fire. At times it is far from clear-cut whether a particular defence is justificatory or excusatory in nature.

B. Justifications

Joshua Dressler, Understanding Criminal Law (1987), pp.180–183:

[V]arious theories of justification are espoused . . .

Moral Forfeiture

Some moral interests . . . may be forfeited as a result of morally wrong conduct. As a result of a person's improper conduct society may determine unilaterally that it will no longer recognize her interest in her life or property.

    The moral-forfeiture doctrine is frequently used to explain why taking human life in self-defence or in preventing the escape of a fleeing felon is justified. Pursuant to this principle, V, an aggressor or a felon, forfeits her legal interest in the protection of her life as a result of her morally wrong conduct . . . When D kills V in self-defence or in order to prevent her flight from a felony, no socially recognized harm has occurred. From the perspective of the homicide laws, the taking of V's life is viewed as no different than the killing of a fly or damage to an inanimate object.

    The forfeiture principle . . . is morally troubling because it involves the non-consensual loss of a valued right. When the principle is applied to the interest in human life it runs counter to the 'good and simple moral principle that human life is sacred'. A theory that treats human life as the equivalent of an inanimate object is troubling to those who believe in the sanctity of human life.

Securing Legal and Moral Rights

. . . The defendant's conduct is justified when it is determined that she had an affirmative right to protect a socially recognized interest that was threatened by the victim.

    For example, when D kills or seriously injures V, a lethal aggressor, her conduct may be justified because she was enforcing a natural right of personal autonomy that V's conduct threatened. As this theory views the situation, D is a citizen protecting her interest against the outlaw, V, who seeks to take away her rights. This principle of justification does not treat V's death as socially irrelevant (as does the forfeiture doctrine); rather, it views D's conduct as affirmatively proper.

    This concept is not without its critics . . . Once it is determined that V has intruded on a right belonging to D—e.g., the right to personal autonomy or the right to possess personal property—the theory suggests that D may use whatever force is necessary to enforce her rights, no matter how minor the intrusion on them. After all, she is in the right, and V is in the wrong, and Right should never give way to Wrong. In its unadulterated form, therefore, this justification theory may permit a disproportional response to the harm threatened.

Superior Interest

. . . Conduct may be justified by a straightforward balancing of competing interests. In this view, the victim's interests are not forfeited by her prior conduct nor does the defendant possess an unlimited right to act in enforcement of a particular interest. Pursuant to this principle the interests of D and V—and, more broadly, the interests of society in the values that they seek to enforce—are balanced. In each case there is a superior, or at least a non-inferior, interest. As long as such an interest is pursued, it is justified."

Some commentators have been of the view that "a defence is justificatory whenever it denies the objective wrongness of the act" and that "a justification is a defence, affirming that the act, state of affairs or consequences are on balance, to be socially approved, or are matters about which society is neutral".[12] However, other commentators decline to go this far.

John Gardner, "Justifications and Reasons", in A.P. Simester and A.T.H. Smith (eds), Harm and Culpability (1996), pp.107–108:

"In classifying some action as criminal, the law asserts that there are *prima facie* reasons against its performance—indeed reasons sufficient to make its performance *prima facie* wrongful. In providing a justificatory defence the law nevertheless concedes that one may sometimes have sufficient reason to perform the unlawful act, all things considered . . .

   The reasons against the action, which are the reasons for its criminalisation, may all have been defeated in the final analysis. It may have been alright for the defendant to act against them, all things considered. But it does not mean that they dropped out of the picture. That a reason is defeated does not mean that it is undermined or cancelled. It still continues to exert its rational appeal. It may indeed be a matter of bitter regret or disappointment that, thanks to the reasons which justified one's action, one nevertheless acted against the *prima facie* reasons for avoiding that action. It may even be a matter of regret or disappointment to the criminal law. The law certainly need not welcome it. But by granting a defence the law concedes that any regret or disappointment must be tolerated . . . By granting a *justificatory* defence the law concedes that this is true by virtue of the fact that the defendant had, at the time of her *prima facie* wrongful action, sufficient reason to perform it."

According to this view it is not enough that the action may be justified on a utilitarian, balancing of interests, basis (as favoured, for example, by Robinson). It is necessary to explore the reasons the defendant had for acting. In order to have a justificatory defence, the defendant's (explanatory) reasons for acting must correspond to the (guiding) reasons that exist for such actions.[13] In other words, her actual reasons for acting must be one of the accepted reasons for acting. As Tadros explains: justifications "operate where the defendant has acted for good reason".[14]

   Bringing the reasons for acting into the concept of a justification creates a dilemma for theorists. How should we respond to the person who acts for what she believes to be a good reason when in fact that reason does not exist? Duff gives the example of the person who deliberately breaks a window of a house in order to obtain entry so that she can provide assistance to a person she believes (wrongly) to be unconscious (the person in fact being simply asleep). Gardner would, at most, treat this as an excuse, if the mistake had been a reasonable one to make. Tadros would regard this still as a justifi-

---

12   G. Williams, "The Theory of Excuses" [1982] Crim. L.R. 732 at 735.
13   J. Gardner, "Justifications and Reasons", in A.P. Simester and A.T.H. Smith (eds), *Harm and Culpability* (Oxford: Clarendon Press, 1996), p.111.
14   V. Tadros, *Criminal Responsibility* (Oxford: OUP, 2005), p.265. Excuses, on the other hand, operate where the defendant has not acted for good reason. Tadros agrees with Gardner that the defendant must have not just been aware of the good reasons for acting but also must have been *motivated by them* in order for the reasons that the criminal prohibition should not be breached to be counterbalanced (pp.273–280).

cation.[15] Duff has suggested that this should be described as "warranted" and in so doing proposes a fourth category of defences:

> "[By] calling her action warranted we can do justice both to the way in which it unlike straightforwardly 'justified' actions (because it is not right) and to the ways in which it is unlike excused actions (because it is warranted)".[16]

Whether one confines one's analysis to a balancing of interests or looks for underlying guiding reasons for permitting action, the following defences can be classified as justificatory in nature:

(i) Self-defence

Under any of the above theories self-defence provides a justification. The interests of the person attacked are greater than those of the attacker. The aggressor's culpability in starting the fight tips the scales in favour of the defendant.[17] Further "a rule allowing defensive action tends to inhibit aggression, or at least to restrain its continuance, as a rule forbidding defensive action would tend to promote it".[18]

(ii) Necessity (where the harm threatened is greater than the harm caused)

Where a lesser evil is committed in order to prevent a greater evil (for example, criminal damage is caused to save the lives of 20 people), the interests of the latter outweigh the interests of the owner of the property. In the United States necessity is widely regarded as a paradigmatic example of justification.[19] This defence has only recently been admitted by English law, initially under the nomenclature of "duress of circumstances" and its parameters are as yet uncertain. As will be argued later, it is because of this classification of necessity as a justification that English judges, historically, showed reluctance to admit the defence at all. Perhaps if necessity had been viewed as an *excuse* only, there might have been a greater willingness to accept the defence into English law as it would have been seen as posing less threat to the established prohibitions of the criminal law. The closely related defence of duress is widely regarded as an excuse and in the leading case of *Howe*[20] the House of Lords seemed to think that the same principles applied to both. The recent "duress of circumstances" cases have a distinct excusatory flavour to them. Perhaps, then, if a fully-blown defence of necessity were to be admitted into English law it would be in an excusatory format. However, where the threatened harm is greater than the harm inflicted, the defence bears all the hallmarks, in principle, of a justification.

(iii) Public authority

The use of force by the police, for example, in effecting an arrest is justified, the superior interest being the enforcement of the law. The same applies to acts "to prevent or terminate crime" or "to prevent or terminate a breach of the peace".[21]

---

[15] Tadros, fn.14, above, pp.280–290.
[16] Duff, fn.8, above, p.276. Warrants are "close relatives" of justifications (p.266).
[17] Fletcher, fn.7 above, p.858.
[18] Williams, fn.12 above, p.739.
[19] The American Law Institute, Model Penal Code s.3.02; N.Y. Penal Law s.35.05.
[20] *R. v Howe (Michael Anthony)* [1987] A.C. 417.
[21] Draft Criminal Code Bill 1989 cl.44(1) (Law Com. No.177).

(iv) Discipline/chastisement

Parents are, controversially, regarded as justified in using force not amounting to actual bodily harm against their children, the superior interest being to "promote the welfare of the minor" and to prevent or punish misconduct.[22]

(v) Consent

Force against a person who has consented is justified, the superior interest being the value of human autonomy. Individuals are free and responsible agents and respect must be given to their right to consent to the infliction of force against them. However, in certain cases the interests of society prevail over any value attached to human autonomy and thus consent may not be given to certain types of force (mainly serious force such as death or grievous bodily harm, or disapproved-of-force such as sado-masochistic beatings inflicting injury).

C. Excuses

Duff suggests that, "to offer an excuse is to admit that I got it wrong: I acted as I should not have acted".[23] A defence is thus excusatory when a wrongful, unjustified act has been committed but, because of the excusing circumstances, the wrongdoer is not morally to blame for committing that act.

Sanford H. Kadish, "Excusing Crime" (1987) 75 Cal. L. Rev. 257 at 264:

"To blame a person is to express a moral criticism, and if the person's action does not deserve criticism, blaming him is a kind of falsehood and is, to the extent the person is injured by being blamed, unjust to him. It is this feature of our everyday moral practices that lies behind the law's excuses. Excuses, then, . . . represent no sentimental compromise with the demands of a moral code; they are, on the contrary, of the essence of a moral code."

According to this view, an excuse destroys blame. However, the theoretical basis upon which this is done is far from agreed:

"Two theories of excuses are currently popular in criminal law theory: the character theory and the capacity theory. In the former, the claim that the defendant makes is 'although I did it, I wasn't really myself'. In the latter, the claim is 'I did it but I couldn't have done otherwise. I had no real choice.'"[24]

While the capacity-based approach, which centred on notions of voluntariness,[25] was very influential during the latter part of the twentieth century, it has become subject to criticism.[26] More recently,

---

[22]   The American Law Institute, Model Penal Code, Proposed Official Draft (1962), s.308(1)(a). That this is a "superior interest" has become deeply contested. (*Tyrer v United Kingdom* (1978) Eur.Ct. Series A. Vol.26; *Campbell and Cosans v United Kingdom* (1980) 3 E.H.R.R. 531).

[23]   Duff, fn.8 above, p.287.

[24]   Tadros, fn.14 above, p.293.

[25]   See H.L.A. Hart, *Punishment and Responsibility* (Oxford: OUP, 1968).

[26]   See, for example, N. Lacey, "Partial Defences to Homicide" in A. Ashworth and B. Mitchell (eds), *Rethinking Homicide Law* (New York: OUP, 2000), pp.115–117; G. Mousourakis, *Criminal Responsibility and Partial Excuses* (Aldershot: Ashgate, 1998), pp.48–58.

debate has been divided as to whether a character-based analysis or a modified capacity-based analysis[27] offers the best way of understanding the role excuses play in the criminal law. Gardner, for example, prefers the character theory:

John Gardner, "The Gist of Excuses" (1998) 1 Buffalo Criminal Law Review 575 at 575–579:

"It is often said that the criminal law judges actions, not character. That is true, but misleading. It is true that, barring certain exceptional and troubling examples, crimes are actions . . . Nevertheless, the criminality of an action frequently falls to be determined, in part, according to standards of character—according to standards of courage, carefulness, honesty . . . Nobody can be a thief in English law, for instance, unless she acts dishonestly. There is, to be sure, a difference between asking whether the accused acted dishonestly, and asking whether she is dishonest. She is dishonest if and only if she tends to act dishonestly. In other words, judging a person dishonest has a diachronic aspect which judging an action dishonest lacks. But apart from this diachronic aspect, the standard by which we judge a person dishonest is exactly the same standard as that by which we judge an action dishonest. It is a standard of character, a standard which bears not only on what is done, but also on the spirit in which and reason for which it is done . . .

[S]ometimes, standards of character figure in the criminal law because they are built into the definition of particular criminal offenses . . . They also figure separately, however, in many of the criminal law's excusatory doctrines . . . On one familiar view, sometimes called the 'Humean' view, we should grant an excuse to somebody in respect of what he did if and only if what he did was no manifestation of his character. This view proceeds from the sound thought that excuses matter because a person's excused actions do not reflect badly on him—do not show him, personally, in a bad light. That being so, the thinking goes, an excuse must be something that blocks the path from an adverse judgment about an action to a correspondingly adverse judgment about the person whose action it is. The action is cowardly, say, but since this person does not otherwise tend towards cowardly actions, she herself is no coward. Her cowardly action is 'out of character'. And that, according to the Humean view, is the gist of excuses. But there is a good deal of confusion in this line of thought. For there is no such thing as a cowardly action which does not show its agent in a cowardly light. It is true that . . . one cowardly action does not make a coward. But . . . in my cowardly action, by definition, I manifest at least the *beginnings* of a cowardly tendency . . . Cowards are no more and no less than people who tend to perform cowardly actions. Their cowardly actions add up to *constitute*, not to evidence, their cowardice. Thus even if this cowardly action is my first, and is quite unprecedented, it necessarily counts constitutively and not merely evidentially against me whenever, thereafter, the question arises of whether I am a coward. And that is exactly what it means to say that my cowardly actions show me in a cowardly light. It follows that the Humean view unravels. If my excused actions do not show me in a cowardly light, they cannot, after all, be cowardly actions. That they are excused cannot therefore block the path from the judgment that I did something cowardly to the judgment that I am a coward. The excuse must intervene earlier to forestall the original judgment that this was a cowardly action . . .

So the gist of an excuse is not that the action was 'out of character', in the sense of being a departure from what we have come to expect from the person whose action it is. Quite the contrary, in fact. The gist of an excuse . . . is precisely that the person with the excuse lived up to our expectations . . . [T]he question, for excusatory purposes, is obviously not whether the person claiming the excuse lived up to expectations in the predictive sense of being true to form . . . The question is whether that person lived up to expectations in the *normative* sense. Did she manifest as much resilience, or loyalty, or thoroughness, or presence of mind as a person in her situation should have manifested? In the face of terrible threats, for example, did this person show as much fortitude as someone in his situation could properly be asked to show?. . . The character standards which are relevant to these and other excuses are not the standards of our own characters, not even the standards of most people's characters, but rather the standards to which our characters should, minimally, conform."[28]

---

[27]   Horder, fn.5 above, p.108 acknowledges that no theory is free from difficulty but defends capacity theory as the most important (pp.123–137). He comments that the courts have veered between two capacity theories—subjective and objective versions (p.131). His preference is for an objective version of the capacity theory.

[28]   Gardner further argues (fn.11 above, pp.580–587) that one cannot distinguish the capacity to act, say with the character trait of courage, from acting courageously. One either acts courageously or not; there is no underlying capacity

This assessment does not involve making broad or sweeping judgements about the individual's character as a person. Instead, the judgement, based in practice upon reasonableness, involves a specific assessment of whether the reasons upon which the action was taken correspond to the character standards to which we should conform.[29] Central to Gardner's argument is the point that those who claim excuses are not denying "responsibility" for their actions. This needs clarification because the word responsibility is ambiguous. Those who plead excusatory defences are obviously hoping to avoid responsibility in the sense of liability. However, they are not denying that they were their actions, for which there is an intelligible, rational explanation.[30] Indeed, Gardner argues it is part of being a self-respecting person

> "to be able to give an intelligible rational account of herself, to be able to show that her actions were the actions of someone who aspired to live up to the proper standards . . . She wants it to be the case that her actions were not truly wrongful, or if they were wrongful, that they were at any rate justified, or if they were not justified, that they were at any rate excused."[31]

It has been suggested that Gardner's explanation either leaves the category of excuses extremely limited or indeed that he is mistaken about the gist of excuses.[32] Other defences, such as involuntary intoxication, fall outside this analysis but some commentators have argued that they ought to provide an excuse.[33]

Victor Tadros, "The Characters of Excuse" (2001) 21 O.J.L.S. 495 at 498:

"In fact, I would suggest that there is no single gist of excuses. The criminal law is supervised by a multitude of principles. In arguing that one has an excuse, one attempts to show that whilst one's action was wrongful, the principles of the criminal law would not be served by imposing criminal liability. Excuses, then, mop up where exemptions, offence definitions and justifications would lead to convictions in inappropriate cases . . . [It] may be because the defendant underwent a fundamental, and reasonable, shift in character before committing the wrongful act. Or it may be because the defendant only exhibited a vice that is an inappropriate target for criminal liability. Or it may be for some other reason, say because the defendant was, beyond her control, placed in a situation in which she was deprived of a fair opportunity to make her behaviour conform to the criminal law. In my view, that is as much as can be said for the gist of excuses."

---

to act courageously that does or does not kick into operation. This view has been challenged by Tadros, fn.14 above, pp.294–297.

[29] See also Duff, fn.8 above (who favours a capacity based account of responsibility), where he argues that a person "offering an excuse does not claim that her action was itself reasonable; she admits that it was unreasonable: but she claims this was a reasonable unreasonableness . . . even a reasonable person . . . might have acted in that unreasonable way in that situation" (p.289).

[30] See further, J. Gardner, "The Mark of Responsibility" (2003) 23 O.J.L.S. 157 at 161 where he argues that responsibility in "the basic sense is none other than an ability to offer justifications and excuses . . . It is exactly what it sounds like: response-ability, an ability to respond".

[31] See fn.30, p.590. This idea that there is a normative priority to defences has been criticised but has also been answered by J. Gardner in "Reply to Critics" in *Offences and Defences: Selected Essays in the Philosophy of the Criminal Law* (Oxford: OUP, 2007), pp.269–276. See also, J. Gardner, "The Logic of Excuses and the Rationaility of Emotions" (2009) 43 *Value and Inquiry* 313 and C. Bennett, "Excuses, Justifications and the Normativity of Expressive Behaviour" (2012) 32 O.J.L.S. 563.

[32] Tadros, fn.14 above, p.293. This is a revision of the views Tadros expressed in "The Characters of Excuse" (2001) 21 O.J.L.S. 495 due to the fact that (as noted, fn.14 above) Tadros now characterises the defendant who acts under a reasonable mistake as justified. This leaves very little scope for the category of excuses as developed by Gardner.

[33] G.R. Sullivan, "Making Excuses" in A.P. Simester and A.T.H. Smith (eds), *Harm and Culpability* (Oxford: Clarendon Press, 1996).

One further issue arises. Just as we might wish to blame the intentional killer more than the negligent killer, so too we might wish to blame the provoked killer less than the unprovoked killer. In other words, there are degrees of blame that mean that some defences will not necessarily operate in an all or nothing fashion.

Martin Wasik, "Partial Excuses in the Criminal Law" (1982) 45 M.L.R. 516 at 524–525:

"A more helpful model of the operation of excuses in the criminal law would involve the recognition of a 'scale of excuse', running downwards from excusing conditions, through partial excuses to mitigating excuses. Excuses towards the higher end of the scale are those where maximum moral pressure for exculpation outweighs reasons of policy and practicality for not permitting the excuse. Automatism is an example. Those towards the lower end of the scale, while they may be morally significant, are out-weighed by practical and policy considerations. A general excusing condition of good motive is an example. Partial excuses fall into the centre of this range, and exhibit a fine balance between rival considerations. The partial excuse of provocation, for example, has been said to be '. . . an extremely strong exculpatory claim . . .' (Gross, p.158) . . . On the other hand this excusatory power should surely be weighed against the law's requirement of self-control . . .

All 'middle range' excuses may be regarded as potential partial excuses, but it is clearly not inevitable that they will turn out to be so. At a given stage in the history of criminal law, policy claims against admitting a particular excuse as an excusing condition will be seen as more or less compelling."[34]

Despite the continued debate surrounding the underlying rationale of excuses, it is possible to identify those defences which, broadly speaking, can be classified as excuses:

(i) Mistake

Sanford H. Kadish, "Excusing Crime" (1987) 75 Cal. L. Rev. 257 at 261:

"Other mens rea requirements, on the other hand, are excuses in mens rea clothing. They are excusing conditions because they serve to deny blame for a harm done. That they are cast in the form of mens rea requirements does not change their character . . . This is why accident and mistake are excuses, despite their formal character as definitional *mens rea* requirements."

We saw in Ch.2 that there is fierce controversy over whether mistake negates a definitional element of the crime (and, therefore, is simply lack of mens rea), or whether it is a defence that previously had to be based on reasonable grounds. This problem could easily be solved within the existing framework by asserting that *no* blame attaches to a person who makes a reasonable mistake (i.e. complete excuse), but that *some* blame attaches to the person who makes an unreasonable mistake, and he should be liable to *that* extent (i.e. a partial excuse).

(ii) Duress

Duress is generally treated as an excuse rather than a justification. Some cases have identified the defence as hinging upon the morally involuntary response of the actor, in other words that the defendant lacked a fair opportunity to conform to the law. It may also be explained by reference to Gardner's

---

[34]   Horder has since argued in favour of "a greatly enhanced role" for partial excuses; fn.5 above, pp.102, 139–190.

gist of excuses. It is not currently open to a defendant charged with murder or attempted murder to plead duress—although there have been proposals to reform the law in this respect.[35]

(iii) Loss of control (formerly provocation)

Although provocation may have originated as a justification, its transformation into a partial excuse under the common law became more or less complete. However, the new statutory defence of loss of control has restored an element of justification to the test. One of the attractions of pleading loss of control, as opposed to diminished responsibility, is that it gives self-respecting defendants the opportunity to give an intelligible rational account of their actions rather than denying any responsibility.

(iv) Intoxication

Whether intoxication should be regarded as a defence at all is a problematic issue that will be considered later. The courts very frequently refer to it in such terms. Where defendants lack mens rea because of voluntary intoxication, they will be acquitted of crimes requiring specific intent but will be convicted of lesser crimes of basic intent. Looked at in this way, intoxication appears to constitute a partial excuse.[36]

(v) Necessity (where the harm threatened is equal to the harm caused)

As shall be seen, it is unlikely that English law affords a defence in such situations. Necessity or "duress of circumstances" as it has become known is only available as a defence when the defendant acts "proportionately in order to avoid a threat of death or serious injury"[37] and, as "duress of circumstances", is not a defence to a charge of murder. Accordingly, the only situations where the defence could conceivably be available in English law where the harm threatened is equal to the harm caused would be where a defendant causes serious injury to avoid a threat of serious harm or (perhaps) commits what could be manslaughter to avoid a threat of death. In such cases, the defence cannot be regarded as justificatory as the harm being caused is not less than the harm being threatened, but such a defence might be regarded as an excuse. We can understand the predicament of an actor who claims to have had no real choice. If the defence were to be allowed in the context of homicide, one possibility would be to regard it as only a partial excuse, i.e. reducing murder to manslaughter, which is the approach adopted to loss of control.[38] However, given that the general principles that govern duress and duress of circumstances are increasingly regarded as "substantially the same", there have been proposals for a complete defence to be introduced.[39]

---

[35]   Law Commission, *Murder, Manslaughter and Infanticide*, Law Com. No.304 (2006), para.6.21.
[36]   Some commentators have focused upon the particular problem of "involuntary" intoxication where the defendant still has mens rea, to construct a variety of arguments concerning the role of defences. While such defendants would currently be found guilty, Sullivan has argued that a defence of blamelessness ought to be available, conjoining a lapse from previous good character with circumstances of destabilisation: fn.33 above, p.131. See further, Tadros, fn.14 above, pp.297–302.
[37]   *R. v Martin (Colin)* (1989) 88 Cr. App. R. 343 at 346.
[38]   The American Law Institute, Model Penal Code, Tent. Draft No.8 (1958), Comments to art.3, pp.8–9.
[39]   Law Com. No.304 (2006), fn.35, paras 6.7–6.8.

(vi) Superior orders

A defence of superior orders does not exist in English law. To the extent that obeying the orders of superiors is a defence in the United States, the harm done is justified on the basis that the superior interest protected is military discipline and effectiveness. The superiority of this interest is only over-turned when the unlawfulness of the order is obvious. Although, following this reasoning, superior orders could be tentatively classified as a justification, a better view could be that like duress, it consti-tutes an *excuse*. Such an approach could make the defence more politically acceptable and lead to its acceptance into English law. Whether this would be desirable is discussed later.

D. Exemptions

While the gist of excuses may remain contested, there has been a growing acceptance of the view that excuses are not denials of responsibility. There must be a basic responsibility for one's actions for them to be amenable to excuse. However, there are other situations where the actor bears no basic responsibility for his actions. This occurs where the defendant lacks practical reasoning skills and where the actions are not amenable to intelligible rational explanation. Defences in such situations (previously categorised as excuses) are now increasingly being regarded as *exemptions*:

> "[T]he focus on making sense of people's actions in the light of their reasons rightly brings to the surface the important point that those whose reasoning can't be made sense of in this way, whether because of profound mental illness or infancy or sleepwalking . . . are not responsible for their actions and therefore need no excuses for what they do."[40]

A number of defences operate as exemptions:

(i) Insanity

A defendant who, because of a disease of the mind, cannot appreciate the nature and quality of her act, or cannot appreciate that it is wrong, lacks the practical reasoning skills to be found responsible for what she has done. On this basis insanity ought to act as an exemption. However, as we shall see, the wording of the *M'Naghten* Rules tends to suggest otherwise.[41]

(ii) Diminished responsibility

"Diminished responsibility occupies the peculiar position of a 'partial exemption'—a position which is closely related to the specific context of the mandatory life sentence for murder."[42] It is, however, based on the notion that the actions were unreasonable:

> "The whole point of the diminished responsibility defence is that it depends on the unreasonable-ness of the defendant's reactions, i.e. their unamenability to intelligible rational explanation."[43]

---

[40] J. Gardner, "The Gist of Excuses" (1998) 1 *Buffalo Criminal Law Review* 575 at 589. See also Duff, fn.8 above, pp.284–292.
[41] Below, p.408.
[42] Lacey, fn.26 above, pp.119–120.
[43] Gardner, fn.40 above, p.591. This view is challenged by Horder, fn.5 above, pp.153 et seq.

(iii) Automatism

There is some dispute as to whether automatism is a defence or whether the need for voluntariness is part of the actus reus requirement.[44] What is clear is that automatism shares the same rationale as other conditions which give rise to exemption from criminal liability.

(iv) Lack of age

Very young children are not regarded as sufficiently responsible to engage in practical reasoning and, accordingly, are exempt from criminal liability when they commit a wrong.[45]

E. Significance of Distinctions

What is the point of the theoretical distinctions discussed above?

The distinction between justification, excuse and exemption is regarded by many commentators as the key to defining the parameters of each of the general defences. Tadros has described it as "central to the moral architecture of the criminal law".[46] For example, approaching duress as an excuse, and not as a justification, informs one as to how its rules should be framed. Its importance as a theoretical guide, therefore, cannot be overestimated. However, there is a practical utility as well. The distinction between defences has the following important consequences:

(a) Whether one is entitled to resist conduct for which the aggressor has a defence, or entitled to assist the aggressor, depends upon whether the aggressor's defence is justificatory or excusatory in nature.[47]

Paul Robinson, "Criminal Law Defenses: A Systematic Analysis" (1982) 82 Col. L. R. 199 at 274–275:

"Where an aggressor has a justification defence, the proper rule is clear: justified aggression should never be lawfully subject to resistance or interference. When conduct is deemed justified, it creates, by definition, a net benefit to society. The owner of a field should not be allowed to resist one who would burn it to stop a spreading fire, and others should be encouraged to assist, and not permitted to interfere.

An excused [or exempted] aggressor, on the other hand, should be subject to lawful resistance. That is, the victim of the psychotic attacker should be able lawfully to defend himself and to have others lawfully assist him in such defense. While the aggressor may be ultimately blameless, the conduct is clearly harmful. All required elements of the offense are satisfied and no justification exists."

Similar principles apply to accessories to crime. Thus in *Quick and Paddison*[48] the principal offender had a defence of automatism—an "exemption" under the above analysis. Paddison assisted him in his aggression and was held liable as an accessory. Had Quick's defence been justificatory in nature, say, acting reasonably to defend himself, then Paddison would have been entitled to assist him.

---

[44] See also K.J.M. Smith and W. Wilson, "Impaired Voluntariness and Criminal Responsibility: Reworking Hart's Theory of Excuses—the English Judicial Response" (1993) 13 O.J.L.S. 69 at 70–74.

[45] See further, Tadros, fn.14 above, p.372.

[46] Tadros, fn.14 above, p.266.

[47] But see Tadros who argues "that there is no clear relationship between the fact that D has a justification defence and the rights of third parties to assist D. Where D reasonably believes that a jogger is a mugger, in order for D2 to be justified in assisting D, D2 must also reasonably believe that the jogger is a mugger." (See Tadros above, p.291).

[48] *R. v Quick (William George); R. v Paddison (William)* [1973] Q.B. 910.

(b) When conduct is justified, some commentators argue that it is in effect "approved" of or, at least tolerated and there is, arguably, no need to try to prevent such conduct re-occurring. Where conduct is merely excused or exempted, however, society might wish to protect itself from repetition of such conduct and might wish to resort to coercive remedies against the defendant despite his acquittal. Thus a successful defence of insanity can lead to commitment in a secure mental hospital. Lack of age is a defence to a criminal charge, but separate care proceedings may follow under the Children Act 1989. Diminished responsibility exempts the actor from liability for murder, but not for manslaughter, enabling the court to take appropriate steps in relation to the defendant. So, too, intoxication is only an excuse to certain crimes—generally where there is a lesser included offence available to which it is no defence. Automatism, on the other hand, enables a defendant to escape all coercive measures, but, even here, there are suggestions that some new form of special verdict should be returned in such cases enabling a court to exercise some supervision over such a person to prevent recurrence of the involuntary action. The remaining excuses such as duress present little threat of repetition of the conduct and therefore there is no need to resort to coercive measures, but, in general, a finding of an exemption (as opposed to a justification) does alert one to the possibility of considering some form of restriction, whether criminal or civil, over the defendant.

The next two consequences of the distinction are admittedly somewhat speculative.

(c) Whether a defence is justificatory or excusatory may affect the law's response to defendants who claim to have made a mistake. Thus the law's response at present seems to be that those who make a mistake in relation to a *justification*, for example, self-defence, need only have made a genuine mistake. On the other hand, those who make a mistake in relation to an *excuse*, for example, duress, must have made a reasonable mistake to escape liability.[49]

(d) It has been suggested that the justification/excuse/exemption distinction provides the key to determining which of the general defences are available to crimes of strict liability. Justificatory defences are, but excusatory defences are not, available in such cases.[50] According to this view one could successfully plead self-defence to a strict liability offence, but could not plead intoxication or mistake to such an offence.

There is a certain logic to this view. The effect of an excusatory defence is that it destroys *blame*: the whole point of strict liability is that it is not concerned with blame. It would, therefore, be contradictory to allow excusatory defences to strict liability offences.[51] A fortiori, this argument would apply to exemptions. However, it is submitted that this argument is unacceptable. Duress is generally regarded as an excuse. It would surely be absurd to deny the defence of duress when an actor, with a gun pointed at their head, commits a minor traffic offence. Indeed, as seen in Ch.2, duress of circumstances, insanity and automatism have been held to apply to strict liability offences. This matter is discussed more fully in that chapter.[52]

(e) Where conduct is justified, some commentators suggest that the law, for conduct in those circumstances, is effectively amended.[53] A precedent is generated that others, in similar circumstances, may

---

49   Above, p.214.
50   M. Sornarajah, "Defences to Strict Liability Offences in Singapore and Malaysia" (1985) 27 Mal.L.R. 1.
51   Koh et al., fn.1 above, p.96.
52   See pp.236–239.
53   As we have seen, other commentators, such as Gardner, would not subscribe to this view.

act in the same manner. Excuses and exemptions, on the other hand, do not constitute exceptions or modifications to the law. They simply involve an assessment that in the particular circumstances it would be unjust to hold a particular actor accountable for their actions. This distinction, perhaps, needs clearer expression.

Paul Robinson, "Criminal Law Defenses: A Systematic Analysis" (1982) 82 Col. L. R. 199 at 245–247:

"When conduct is justified there is again nothing to condemn or punish. The defendant's conduct did not, under the circumstances, violate the prohibition of the law, and indeed may be desired and encouraged. Yet a harm or evil was inflicted, and such conduct should remain generally prohibited and condemned. Arson, for example, remains a crime even though the law may permit the burning of a field if it creates a fire break that saves an entire town, but when an actor is acquitted under a justification defense, the message to the public may be unclear, especially since the verdict of 'not guilty' gives no hint that a justification defense is at work. Thus, the condemnation and general deterrence of arson may be undercut. It might be desirable to alter the jury verdict to 'justified,' thereby acquitting the actor because his conduct caused no net harm, yet noting the continuing prohibition of arson . . .

Excuses have a great potential for undercutting the condemnation and general deterrence of the harmful conduct. Even taking the objective circumstances into account, the conduct in an excuse case *does* constitute a net harm or evil that is condemned by the criminal law. Society will continue to condemn and seek to deter such conduct even in identical circumstances. It is the *actor*, not the act, which causes us to excuse. Furthermore, the explanation for acquittal of the offender is much less apparent than in cases of justification. Excuses, for the most part, rely on subjective criteria like mental illness, mistake, or subnormality. Often only a person who is aware of the evidence adduced at trial will understand that acquittal is based upon these special characteristics of the actor, not an approval or tolerance of the act.

The limited value of a simple 'not guilty' verdict to convey the proper message accounts for some of the difficulties which have arisen in cases of excuse [such as *Dudley and Stephens*: see below, p.387] . . .

It may be because of this potential for misapprehension that an acquittal based on insanity is reported as a verdict of 'not guilty by reason of insanity'. . . .

The only sound approach is to recognize excuse defenses, but to minimize the danger of misperception of the acquittal by relying upon special verdicts—not guilty by reason of excuse—and assuring that the public understands that special message. Civil commitment and similar procedures outside the criminal justice system are available to further the goals of special deterrence and rehabilitation in the absence of condemnable culpability."

It is important to note, of course, that Robinson draws a distinction between excuses and justifications only. What we now call "exemptions" are included within the excusatory classification. However, his central message is the same. The moral message sent by an excuse or an exemption is different from that sent by justifications. This difference may be made clearer by the development of "special" verdicts. The case for this is, obviously, at its strongest in relation to exemptions. If, however, one takes the view that excuses, such as duress, are borderline justifications, the argument for a "special" verdict is very weak. Somebody who, according to Gardner's analysis, has lived up to the character standards of her role has done all that could reasonably be expected in the circumstances and should be entitled to a full and unqualified acquittal.

We are now in a position to examine the various defences.

II. Consent

A. Introduction

Certain crimes are defined in such a manner that they can only be committed without the victim's consent. Rape, for instance, is penile penetration of the vagina, anus or mouth of a person who does not consent to it.[54] In such cases a defendant who claims that a person was consenting to penetration is not pleading consent as a defence, but is claiming that one of the definitional elements of the offence is missing—that the actus reus of the crime has not been committed.[55] A definition that provided that it was rape to engage in these actions (with a special defence to cover those cases where consent was present) would seem wrong:

> "The reason is that it reflects a morality that is foreign to us. We simply do not think that there is always a reason against sexual intercourse. We are much happier, therefore, with a definition of rape which includes consent in the definition of the offence rather than allowing it to operate as a separate defence that only comes into play as an after-thought once the initial prohibition has been breached."[56]

Most crimes are, however, not expressly defined in such a manner, but the consent of the "victim" may exempt the defendant from liability. The issue of whether consent should be regarded as a "defence" was integral to the House of Lords' decision of *Brown*.[57] The majority took the view that consent should be regarded as a defence rather than as a definitional element. They then went on to conclude that it should not be available to the appellants who had been convicted of assault occasioning actual bodily harm following consensual sado-masochistic encounters. However, Lord Mustill, in the minority, approached the appeal as raising a question about the ambit of the offence rather than one involving a defence.[58]

Normally this distinction is of little importance,[59] but in *Brown*, where the court was engaged in law-making,[60] there can be no doubt that the "defence approach" made the decision of the majority somewhat easier. While one may have doubts about the conclusion they reached, it is submitted that consent should be regarded as a defence. The defendant admits that they have committed the full actus reus of the offence, but claims that the consent of the "victim" justifies the wrong they would otherwise be committing. As we have seen, a justificatory defence can be explained in terms of a superior interest being upheld. In relation to consent, that superior interest is human autonomy. The foundation of the criminal law is the concept of responsibility and here it finds expression in the freedom of people to consent to what would otherwise be a criminal offence. The question is one of ascertaining what limits, if any, there are to this freedom to consent. As we shall see, consent is not a defence to all crimes. Whether it is available as a defence depends on the following matters: whether the court is sure that the recipient[61] truly consented (including whether the recipient was responsible enough to make such decisions), the nature and degree of harm involved, and the rationale of consent as a defence.

---

54   Sexual Offences Act 2003 s.1.
55   *DPP v Morgan* [1976] A.C. 182.
56   S. Shute, "The Second Law Commission Consultation Paper on Consent: Something Old, Something New, Something Borrowed: Three Aspects of the Project" [1996] Crim. L.R. 684 at 690.
57   *R. v Brown (Anthony Joseph)* [1994] 1 A.C. 212.
58   See also *R. v Kimber (David Michael)* (1983) 77 Cr. App. R. 225 where it was implicit in the decision of the court that consent is not truly a defence. Cf. S. Cowan, "Criminalizing SM: Disavowing the Erotic, Instantiating Violence", in R.A. Duff, L. Farmer, S.E. Marshall, M. Renzo and V. Tadros, *The Structures of the Criminal Law* (Oxford: OUP, 2011), Ch.4.
59   The main difference between these two modes of analysis relates to cases where the defendant mistakenly believes his victim has consented. See above, pp.209–214. As to whether there is a difference in the burden of proof, see above, p.293.
60   J.C. Smith, "Commentary to *Brown*" [1993] Crim. L.R. 585.
61   This is the term adopted by Lord Mustill in *R. v Brown (Anthony Joseph)* [1994] 1 A.C. 212 (below, pp.313–316), in preference to the term "victim" because of the presence of consent. Significantly, the majority (with the exception of Lord Jauncey) tend to refer to the consenting participant as a "victim".

B. The Reality of Consent

Joan McGregor, "Why When She Says No She Doesn't Mean Maybe and She Doesn't Mean Yes: A Critical Reconstruction of Consent, Sex and the Law" (1996) 2 Legal Theory 175 at 192:

"There are a number of different ways of construing the nature and effect of consent. Consent is always given to the actions and projects of others. One common understanding of consent is that it 'authorizes' another to act in an area that is part of one's domain, e.g., giving power of attorney to another. Another way of thinking about consent is that of giving 'permission' to another. Joel Feinberg said, in Harm to Self, 'Any act that crosses the boundaries of a sovereign person's zone of autonomy requires that person's "permission"; otherwise it is wrongful' [p.177]. Conceiving of consent in either of these ways has normative significance, since it brings into existence new moral and legal relationships . . . Consent must, then, be deliberate and voluntary, since its explicit purpose is to change the world by changing the structure of rights and obligations of the parties involved.

Within the sovereign zone of our domain, all others have a duty to refrain from crossing over without our permission. Consent cancels that duty, at least in regard to the specific acts consented to, and for a specified time."

To act as such a "moral transformative"[62] consent must be full and free.[63] Indeed, within the context of sexual offences, consent is expressly defined along these lines: "a person consents if he agrees by choice, and has the freedom and capacity to make that choice".[64] Saying that the decision must be voluntary does not mean that every nuance is critical. Thus, the person who submits to intercourse rather than be beaten or killed is not regarded as having given real consent[65] but the person who has intercourse because a boyfriend has declared undying love, or because she believes that he is rich, cannot later claim that the consent was invalid if it turns out that the boyfriend was lying.[66] This latter example introduces another dimension: what information is critical to determining whether consent is full (and free)? In the example above the person might well claim that she would never have agreed to sex had she known that the boyfriend was lying but this will not prevent her consent being regarded as real. However, what if the boyfriend does not disclose that he is HIV positive?

R. v Dica [2004] Q.B. 1257 (Court of Appeal, Criminal Division)

The defendant, who was HIV positive, had unprotected consensual sexual intercourse with two women on a number of occasions in the course of relationships with them. Both women subsequently contracted HIV. The defendant was charged with inflicting grievous bodily harm contrary to s.20 of the Offences Against the Person Act 1861. The prosecution alleged that he had been reckless as to whether the women might become infected and that they would never have agreed to sexual intercourse had they known of his condition. The defendant was convicted and appealed, inter alia, on the issue of consent which the trial judge had withdrawn from the jury.

---

[62] L. Alexander, "The Moral Magic of Consent" (1996) 2 Legal Theory 165.

[63] In R. v Brown (Anthony Joseph) [1994] 1 A.C. 212, Lord Templeman (at 235) sought to cast doubt on the consent of the participants, describing it as "dubious or worthless." In fact, there was some doubt as to consent in one incident only. For the rest, as Lord Slynn stated (at 281): "Astonishing though it may seem, the persons involved positively wanted, asked for, the acts to be done to them." As to the description "worthless", one is presumably to interpret this as irrelevant, rather than as casting doubt on the responsibility of the participants.

[64] Sexual Offences Act 2003 s.74.

[65] See, e.g. R. v Doyle (Danny) [2010] EWCA Crim 119; R. v C [2012] EWCA Crim 2034.

[66] R. v McNally (Justine) [2013] EWCA Crim 1051 at [24]. See J. Herring, "Mistaken Sex" [2005] Crim. L.R. 511 for a critique of the current law in relation to this issue.

JUDGE LJ:

"The present case is concerned with and confined to s.20 offences alone . . . The question for decision is whether the victims' consent to sexual intercourse, which as a result of his alleged concealment was given in ignorance of the facts of the appellant's condition, necessarily amounted to consent to the risk of being infected by him. If that question must be answered 'Yes', the concept of consent in relation to s.20 is devoid of real meaning . . .

In our view, on the assumed fact now being considered [that they had not known of his condition], the answer is entirely straightforward. These victims consented to sexual intercourse. Accordingly the appellant is not guilty of rape. Given the long-term nature of the relationships, if the appellant concealed the truth about his condition from them, and therefore kept them in ignorance of it, there was no reason for them to think that they were running any risk of infection, and they were not consenting to it. On this basis, there would be no consent sufficient in law to provide the appellant with a defence to the charge under s.20."

[The court concluded that the defendant would have had a defence had the women known of his condition and agreed to sexual intercourse because they were still prepared to run the risks involved. Accordingly, the trial judge had been wrong to withdraw the issue of consent from the jury.]

Appeal allowed. Retrial ordered[67]

In the subsequent decision of *Konzani*,[68] the Court of Appeal stressed the need for informed consent—which would almost invariably have to result from disclosure by the person with HIV.[69] The argument that by consenting to unprotected sex the person is also impliedly consenting to the risk of infection was rejected.[70] Convictions have also been obtained under s.20 where defendants have failed to disclose infection with hepatitis B, and genital herpes, to their sexual partners. [71]

In *R. v B*,[72] it was held that the fact that the defendant (who was charged with rape) had not disclosed his HIV status was not relevant to the issue of consent to the act of sexual intercourse: the act remained consensual. However, it appears that the position is different if the defendant either actively deceives the complainant, or deliberately overrides a condition that the complainant has expressly stated must be complied with before consenting to sexual activity. In *Assange v Sweden*,[73] the Administrative Court held that a deception as to the use of a condom, although not one as to the "nature and purpose" of the act for the purposes of s.76 of the Sexual Offences Act 2003, could vitiate the complainant's freedom and choice to consent. In *R. (on the application of F) v DPP*, it was held that, where F had made it clear that the only basis upon which she was prepared to have sex with her husband was if he withdrew and did not ejaculate inside her, her consent was negatived when

---

[67]   The defendant was convicted and sentenced to four-and-a-half years' imprisonment.

[68]   *R. v Konzani (Feston)* [2005] EWCA Crim 706. See also *R. v Barnes (Mark)* [2004] EWCA Crim 3246 and *Cort* [2004] Q.B. 388.

[69]   *R. v Konzani (Feston)*, above at [41]. Exceptionally, informed consent might result even where there had been non-disclosure by the defendant if, for example, the relationship had developed between the person and the defendant while in hospital receiving treatment for the condition: at [44].

[70]   *R. v Konzani (Feston)*, above at [41]. See further, M. Weait, "Knowledge, Autonomy and Consent: *R v Konzani*" [2005] Crim. L.R. 763 and A. Pedain, "HIV and Responsible Sexual Behaviour" [2005] 64 C.L.J. 540 for contrasting critiques of the decisions in *R. v Dica (Mohammed)* [2004] Q.B. 1257 and *Konzani*. Cf. G.R. Mawhinney, "To be ill or to kill: the criminality of contagion" (2013) 77 J. Crim. L. 202–214 and M. Brazier, "Do no harm–do patients have responsibilities too?" [2006] 43 C.L.J. 397–422 at 408–409, who suggest that legal responsibility for the reckless transmission of disease might be extended.

[71]   In 2008, Ercan Yasar was sentenced to two years' imprisonment for reckless transmission of hepatitis: "Man jailed for passing on hepatitis B", *The Times*, November 19, 2008. In 2011, David Golding was sentenced to custody for giving his girlfriend genital herpes: , reduced on appeal to 3 months' imprisonment: R v Golding (David) [2014] EWCA Crim 889.

[72]   *R. v B* [2006] EWCA Crim 2945, [2007] 1 W.L.R. 1567, considered below, pp.656–657. Cf. S. Cowan, "Offenses of Sex or Violence? Consent, Fraud and HIV Transmission" (2014) 17 New Crim. L.Rev. 135.

[73]   *Assange v Sweden* [2011] EWHC 2849 (Admin) at [88]–[90].

he deliberately ejaculated in her vagina because she was "deprived of choice relating to the crucial feature on which her original consent to sexual intercourse was based".[74] In *McNally*,[75] a deception as to the gender of the defendant was held to vitiate consent. If an active deception as to the use of a condom can negative freedom and choice to consent, then it is likely that a similar stance would be taken by the courts in relation to a deception as to HIV (or other STD) status. However, it is not clear what deceptions will be held to vitiate consent, since the most guidance that the Court of Appeal was proposed to give on this issue was that "some deceptions (for example, in relation to wealth) will obviously not be sufficient to vitiate consent",[76] and that the evidence in relation to choice and freedom to consent should be approached in a "broad common sense way".[77] Nor is it clear precisely at what stage non-disclosure becomes an "active deception".[78]

In addition, the person must have sufficient capacity to give consent. Capacity may be lacking because of the individual's physical or mental condition. As far as medical treatment is concerned, action taken during an emergency to aid the patient may not constitute an assault even if done without consent.[79] In theory, at least, the question is whether the patient has the capacity to consent.[80] If, for example, a pregnant woman who needs an emergency caesarean operation has capacity to consent then her refusal ought to be respected, even if this places her life and that of her unborn child at risk.[81] In practice, however, the patient may be found to lack capacity and the operation will go ahead.[82]

As far as adults with severe learning difficulties or mental disabilities are concerned, capacity to consent is a sensitive issue. In *Jenkins*,[83] a young woman with a verbal mental age of two or three who did not understand sexual relationships, pregnancy or sexually transmitted diseases became pregnant. DNA tests on the aborted foetus (the decision being taken for her to have an abortion since she was unable to understand what had happened to her, to care for a child or give consent to an abortion) revealed that the father was a member of her residential staff. He was charged with rape but acquitted, the trial judge ruling that she had properly consented, as she simply had to submit to her animal instincts to be deemed to have consented. The Law Commission has expressed the

---

74   *R. (on the application of F) v DPP* [2013] EWHC 945 (Admin) at [26]. In this case, F was challenging the CPS's decision not to prosecute her husband for rape. For a critique of the judgments in *Assange v Sweden* and *R. (on the application of F) v DPP*, see J. Rogers, "Further Developments Under the Sexual Offences Act" [2013] *Archbold Review* 7.

75   *R. v McNally (Justine)* [2013] EWCA Crim 1051. See A. Sharpe, "Criminalizing sexual intimacy: transgendered defendants and the legal construction of non-consent" [2014] Crim L.R. 207–223. For further discussion in relation to deception and consent to sexual activity, see below, p.653–657.

76   *R. v McNally (Justine)*, above at [26].

77   *R. v McNally (Justine)*, above; *R (on the application of F) v DPP* [2013] EWHC 945 (Admin) at [26].

78   See Simester, et al., above, fn.10, p.770.

79   *F v West Berkshire HA* [1990] 2 A.C. 1, per Lord Donaldson MR (CA), p.13. The House of Lords held that such action was justified by necessity: see Lord Goff at p.76, and below, pp.386. Mental Capacity Act 2005, s.5, provides a statutory defence in respect of treatment provided without consent to persons 16 and over, provided that the treating person before doing the act takes reasonable steps to establish whether the patient (P) lacks capacity, and reasonably believes that P lacks capacity and that the treatment is in P's best interests.

80   Mental Capacity Act 2005, s.2 provides a statutory test for incapacity: "a person lacks capacity in relation to a matter if at the material time he is unable to make a decision for himself in relation to the matter because of an impairment of, or a disturbance in the functioning of, the mind or brain".

81   *St George's Healthcare NHS Trust v S* [1998] 3 All E.R. 673. Persons are not treated as lacking capacity merely because they make an unwise decision: Mental Capacity Act 2005, s.1(4). See further, Hale LJ, "A Pretty Pass: When is There a Right to Die?" (2003) 32 C.L.W.R. 1 at 7.

82   *Re S (Adult: Refusal of Treatment)* [1992] 3 W.L.R. 806; *Bolton Hospitals NHS Trust v O* [2002] EWHC 2871 (Fam); *Great Western Hospitals NHS Foundation Trust v AA* [2014] EWHC 132 (Fam). Cf. M. Thorpe, "The Caesarean Section Debate" (1997) 27 *Family Law* 663 at 663–664.

83   *Jenkins*, unreported, Central Criminal Court, January 10–12, 2000. Cited in Law Commission, *Consent in Sex Offences, A Report to the Home Office Sex Offences Review* (2000), paras 4.66–4.67.

view that, whilst the law should protect the sexual autonomy of the mentally disabled and others, it should also protect the vulnerable. Rightly, it concluded that the law should be so framed that there is no capacity to consent in situations such as *Jenkins* and recommended that the need to understand the reasonably foreseeable consequences of sexual activity should be fundamental to any capacity to consent to such activity.[84] A similar, autonomy-based approach was adopted by Baroness Hale in *R. v C*,[85] when she concluded that, in relation to sexual activity, to have capacity a person must be able to understand the information relevant to make a decision and weigh that information to make a choice. Capacity in this context is both person and situation specific: "One does not consent to sex in general. One consents to this act of sex with this person at this time and in this place".[86] The issue of the capacity of the mentally disabled also frequently arises in relation to medical treatment and will be considered further in the context of the decisions of *Bland* and *Re B*.[87]

Incapacity may also arise because of the age of the individual. In *Howard*,[88] for example, the alleged consent of a six-year-old to attempted sexual intercourse with the defendant was deemed invalid. It was judged that she was incapable of giving real consent. Whilst transparently the right decision in that particular case, the principle that there must be informed consent by minors may not always operate so simply. A six-year-old may truthfully be said not to have attained the "age of discretion" but can the same thing be said of 12- and 13-year-olds? The reality is that the "age of discretion" rests not only upon the mental and physical age of the child but also depends on the type of harm to which she has allegedly given her consent.[89] For example, in *Sutton*, it was held that boys of 10, 11 and 12 could consent to their naked bodies being touched in order to indicate the pose the photographer wanted.[90] However, had the touching been held to be indecent the same consent would have been held to be invalid and the photographer would have been convicted of indecent assault.[91] In *Gillick v West Norfolk and Wisbech AHA*[92] the court was concerned with whether contraceptive advice could be given to girls under the age of 16 without parental consent. The House of Lords ruled that parental rights to determine whether or not such a child should have medical treatment end "when the child achieves a sufficient understanding and intelligence to enable him or her to understand fully what is proposed."[93] A similar approach was adopted in *R. v D* in assessing whether a child could consent to

---

[84]   See also Law Commission, *Mental Incapacity*, Law Com No.231 (1995) and Mental Capacity Act 2005, s.3. The Sexual Offences Act 2003 creates offences which extend the protection afforded to those suffering from mental disorder (ss.30–41). While the provisions are welcome in many respects there is concern that they may criminalise the consensual sexual activities of people with learning difficulties. See e.g. B.E. McGuire and A.A. Bayley, "Relationships, sexuality and decision-making capacity in people with an intellectual disability" (2011) 24 *Current Opinion in Psychiatry* 398–402.

[85]   *R. v C* [2009] UKHL 42, [2009] 1 W.L.R. 1786, considered below, p.650. In this case the defendant was charged with the offence under Sexual Offences Act 2003 s.30, of sexual activity with a person with a mental disorder.

[86]   *R. v C*, above at [27]. This approach has not been followed by the civil courts: *IM v LM (Capacity to Consent to Sexual Relations)* [2014] EWCA Civ 37.

[87]   Below, p.311–313.

[88]   *R. v Howard (Robert Lesarian)* [1966] 1 W.L.R. 13.

[89]   Sexual Offences Act 2003 ss.5–7 creates offences of rape, assault by penetration and assault (by touching) of a child under 13 years old where the issue of consent is irrelevant. There is concern that the irrelevance of consent means that (consensual) sexual exploration between two 12-year-olds is always criminalised and that whether prosecutions are brought will depend upon the approach taken by the CPS. See further, pp.669–673.

[90]   *R. v Sutton (Terence)* [1977] 1 W.L.R. 1086. But see now Protection of Children Act 1978 s.1(1)(a), which prohibits the taking of indecent photographs of children. See J. Hall, "Can Children Consent to Indecent Assault?" [1996] Crim. L.R. 184, where he argues that *Sutton* was wrongly decided.

[91]   The offence of indecent assault upon boys under Sexual Offences Act 1956 s.14 (where the consent of a boy under the age of 16 is regarded as irrelevant for the purposes of determining whether there has been an indecent assault) was repealed by the Sexual Offences Act 2003.

[92]   *Gillick v West Norfolk and Wisbech AHA* [1986] A.C. 112.

[93]   *Gillick*, above, fn.92, per Lord Scarman at p.189. This test is approved by the Law Commission in Consultation Paper No.139,

what would otherwise be a kidnapping by one parent.[94] However, recent cases have undermined this "*Gillick*-competence" test by restricting it to cases of a child giving positive consent:

"[T]he courts have held that they have power, as part of their inherent parental jurisdiction, to over-ride the child's objections even when he does have sufficient understanding and has reached 16. They will start with a preference for respecting his views, but will not allow him to die, or probably suffer serious harm, through lack of treatment, especially if his illness is distorting his judgment."[95]

Thus, in *Re W*, a 16-year-old child suffering from anorexia nervosa refused medical treatment that would save her life. It was held that the court had the power to override her wishes even though she was "*Gillick*-competent".[96] It is probably also the case that parents can override their child's refusal of treatment.[97] Such an approach has been criticised on the basis that it is "an unattractive prospect that parents might have power to oblige a capable child to accept forcible treatment against his will and without any of the safeguards attached to legal proceedings."[98]

C. The Nature and Degree of Harm

Harm can be defined as any violation of an interest and, as we have already begun to see, there are violations of some interests to which courts will not allow consent to be given.

Whether consent will constitute a defence is ultimately a question of public policy that involves balancing the seriousness of the harm against the social utility or acceptability of the defendant's conduct. The greater the injury inflicted, the more the defendant must have some justification (in terms of social utility). Stephen J in *Coney* held:

"The principle as to consent seems to me to be this: When one person is indicted for inflicting personal injury upon another, the consent of the person who sustains the injury is no defence to the person who inflicts the injury, if the injury is of such a nature, or is inflicted under such circum-stances, that its infliction is injurious to the public as well as to the person injured."[99]

Thus, if a defendant kills a person at that other's request, it will still be murder;[100] this will be so even though the actions could be described as "mercy-killing" and even though self-murder (suicide) is

---

Consent in the Criminal Law (1995), para.5.21. See also *R. (on the application of Axon) v Secretary of State for Health* [2006] Q.B. 539. See further, E. Jackson, *Medical Law: Text, Cases and Materials*, 3rd edn (Oxford: OUP, 2013), pp.264–267

[94] *R. v D (Ian Malcolm)* [1984] A.C. 778.

[95] B.M. Hoggett, *Parents and Children*, 4th edn (London: Sweet & Maxwell, 1993), p.16.

[96] *Re W (A Minor) (Medical Treatment: Court's Jurisdiction)* [1993] Fam. 64. See further, *Re R (A Minor) (Wardship: Consent to Treatment)* [1992] Fam. 11; *Re J* [1992] 3 W.L.R. 521. Once minors reach the age of 16, Family Law Reform Act 1969, s.8 provides that their consent to medical treatment "shall be as effective" as if they were an adult. However, s.8(3) provides that this does not render ineffective "any consent which would have been effective if this section had not been enacted". The section is also silent in relation to treatment *refusals*.

[97] *Re R (A Minor) (Wardship: Consent to Treatment)* [1992] Fam. 11; *Re K W and H (Minors) (Consent to Medical Treatment)* [1993] 1 F.L.R. 845. A proper examination of this complex issue is beyond the scope of this book. See further, S. Gilmore and J. Herring, "'No' is the hardest word: consent and children's autonomy" (2011) 23 C.F.L.Q. 3–25; E. Cave, "Goodbye *Gillick*? Identifying and resolving problems with the concept of child competence" (2014) 34 L.S. 103–122.

[98] Hoggett, fn.95 above, p.16.

[99] *R. v Coney* (1882) 8 Q.B.D. 549.

[100] Or, possibly, manslaughter if the defendant is able to plead diminished responsibility. See e.g. *R (on the application of Nicklinson) v Ministry of Justice* [2013] EWCA Civ 961 at [25] (at the time of writing, the judgment of Supreme Court is awaited); *R. v Gnango (Armel)* [2011] UKSC 59, [2012] 1 A.C. 827 at [53], [59] and [69]–[71]; *Airedale NHS Trust v Bland* [1993] A.C. 789, per Lord Mustill at 892–893. In *Nicklinson*, the Court of Appeal rejected an argument based on necessity: see below, pp.757–760. In Stark's view, *Nicklinson* should have been argued on the ground that the defence of consent would

no longer a crime.[101] The Criminal Law Revision Committee rejected the proposal that such a killing "should be a special offence removed from the law of murder and should carry a reduced sentence, the reason being that such a killing did not present a threat to public security as did murder in general".[102] More recently, the Law Commission has declined to make any recommendation as to whether there should be an offence or partial defence of "mercy killing" (beyond a reformed partial defence of diminished responsibility) on the basis that the issue needs to be properly addressed by a specific review of this aspect of the law of homicide.[103] However, while active euthanasia and assisting suicide are prohibited in the UK,[104] the existence of the latter offence is increasingly controversial.[105] Moreover, in instances where compassionate assistance is given by relatives to help someone travel to Switzerland (where assisted suicide is lawful), prosecutions are likely to be very rare indeed.[106]

Increasingly, the courts have been called upon to determine the issue of the continuance of medical treatment. In *Re B*,[107] the patient had suffered an illness that left her paralysed from the neck down and requiring the support of a ventilator to breathe. Ms. B asked for the ventilator to be switched off and when the hospital refused, sought a declaration from the court that she had the capacity to make such a decision and that the hospital had been acting unlawfully in treating her in defiance of her wishes. She was found to be capable, the declaration was granted, and Ms. B was moved to a hospital prepared to carry out her wishes where she died shortly afterwards.[108] In other situations, relatives or

---

be available to a doctor assisting him to die, conceding, however, that such an argument would have been "doomed to fail": F. Stark, "Case Comment: Necessity and *Nicklinson*" [2013] Crim LR 949–965 at 949, 964. Consent would appear to be the more appropriate defence, since the essential plank of the case made by *Nicklinson* (and *Pretty* and *Purdy*) was that their autonomous wish to end their lives should be respected. However, given the current state of the law, it is not at all clear that leave would have been given to argue that consent could be a defence to assisted suicide or euthanasia.

[101] Suicide Act 1961 s.1.

[102] Criminal Law Revision Committee, 14th Report, *Offences Against the Person* (Cmnd.7844, 1980), para.128. The German Penal Code St.G.B. art.216 creates a special lesser offence of "killing on request" on the basis that the victim's consent reduces the wrongfulness of the killing. See further, V. Bergelson, "The Right to be Hurt: Testing the Boundaries of Consent" (2007) 75 George Washington L.R. 165–236 at 166–167. See Fletcher, fn.7 above, pp.332–334, where he distinguishes between voluntary, involuntary, passive and active euthanasia.

[103] Law Commission, *Murder, Manslaughter and Infanticide* (HMSO 2006), Law Com. No.304, fn.35 above, para.7.33. See paras 7.1–7.37. cf. H. Keating and J. Bridgeman, "Compassionate Killings: The Case for a Partial Defence" (2012) 75 M.L.R. 697. Whilst murder carries a carries a mandatory sentence of life imprisonment, in setting the minimum term the offender must serve, Criminal Justice Act 2003 s.269 and Sch.21 para.11(f) identifies one of the mitigating factors the judge should consider as the offender's belief that the killing was an act of mercy. See e.g. *R. v Inglis (Frances)* [2010] EWCA Crim 2637, [2011] 1 W.L.R. 1110.

[104] *R (on the application of Pretty) v Director of Public Prosecutions (Secretary of State for the Home Department Intervening)* [2002] 1 A.C. 800; *R (on the application of Purdy) v Director of Public Prosecutions* [2009] UKHL 45; *R (on the application of Nicklinson) v Ministry of Justice* [2013] EWCA Civ 961, CPS, Policy for Prosecutors in Respect of Cases of Assisted Suicide (2010), available at *http://www.cps.gov.uk/publications/prosecution/assisted_suicide.html* (last accessed April 2014). Cf. A. Norrie, "Legal Form and Moral Judgement: Euthanasia and Assisted Suicide", in R.A. Duff, L. Farmer, S.E. Marshall, M. Renzo and V. Tadros, *The Structures of the Criminal Law* (Oxford: OUP, 2011), Ch.7.

[105] A 2010 YouGov survey found that 88 % of (3,874) people questioned supported assisted suicide in at least some circumstances: The Commission on Assisted Dying, *Final Report* (2012), available at *http://www.demos.co.uk/files/476_CoAD_FinalReport_158x240_I_web_single-NEW_.pdf?1328113363* (last accessed April 2014). The Assisted Dying Bill 2013–14, a Private Member's Bill to enable competent adults who are terminally ill to be provided at their request with specified assistance to end their life, is currently progressing through Parliament. See *http://services.parliament.uk/bills/2013–14/assisteddying.html* (last accessed April 2014).

[106] Of 115 cases of people being assisted to travel to Switzerland, only eight were referred to the DPP (per Lord Hope in *Purdy* at [30]). In six of these cases, the decision not to prosecute was based upon a lack of evidence. In two cases it was held to be not in the public interest to bring a prosecution: see, for example, CPS: *Decision on Prosecution—The Death by Suicide of Daniel James* (2008); *No charges following the deaths of Sir Edward and Lady Downes* (2010), and *No charges following the death of Raymond Cutkelvin* (2010), available at *http://www.cps.gov.uk/publications/prosecution/assisted_suicide.html* (last accessed April 2014).

[107] *Re B (Adult: Refusal of Medical Treatment)* [2002] 2 All E.R. 449.

[108] See further, Hale LJ, fn.81 above.

the hospital treating the patient may raise the issue of withdrawing treatment. Many of these cases have concerned babies born with severe disabilities[109] but in the following case of *Bland*, the House of Lords was asked to make a declaration enabling life-sustaining treatment to be withdrawn from a young male patient who had been severely injured at the Hillsborough football ground disaster in 1989. The patient had suffered catastrophic and irreversible damage to the brain, which had left him in a condition known as a persistent vegetative state. Medical opinion was agreed that there was no hope of recovery or improvement.

Airedale NHS Trust v Bland [1993] A.C. 789 (House of Lords)

LORD GOFF:

"I must however stress, at this point, that the law draws a crucial distinction between cases in which a doctor decides not to provide, or to continue to provide, for his patient treatment or care which could or might prolong his life, and those in which he decides, for example by administering a lethal drug, actively to bring his patient's life to an end . . . the former may be lawful, either because the doctor is giving effect to his patient's wishes by withholding the treatment or care, or even in certain circumstances in which . . . the patient is incapacitated from stating whether or not he gives his consent. But it is not lawful for a doctor to administer a drug to his patient to bring about his death, even though that course is prompted by a humanitarian desire to end his suffering, however great that suffering may be: see *R. v Cox* (unreported), September 18, 1992. So to act is to cross the Rubicon which runs between on the one hand the care of his living patient and on the other hand euthanasia . . .

At the heart of this distinction lies a theoretical question. Why is it that the doctor who gives his patient a lethal injection which kills him commits an unlawful act and indeed is guilty of murder, whereas a doctor who, by discontinuing life support, allows his patient to die, may not act unlawfully—and will not do so, if he commits no breach of duty to his patient?. . .

I agree that the doctor's conduct in discontinuing life support can properly be categorised as an omission . . . But in the end the reason for that difference is that, whereas the law considers that discontinuance of life support may be consistent with the doctor's duty to care for his patient, it does not, for reasons of policy, consider that it forms any part of his duty to give his patient a lethal injection to put him out of his agony."

The declaration was affirmed by the House of Lords (dismissing the appeal by the Official Solicitor) on the basis that further treatment was futile and that prolonging the patient's life by medical treatment could not be said to be in his best interests. The decision was not simply based on the principle of "substituted judgment" (as it would have been in the United States, for example[110]). This is an approach which requires the court to ascertain what the patient would have wanted. Instead, in this country the concept of "substituted judgment" may be subsumed into the broader analysis of the best interests of the patient.[111] While in the United States consent is regarded as critical even in such cases, the courts in this country rejected the idea that, at common law, they had the power to give consent on behalf of an incapable adult, viewing their role as being confined to declaring whether or not treatment, or the withdrawal of treatment, was lawful.[112] Decision-making in such cases is now governed by the Mental Capacity Act 2005,[113] but the approach of the courts is similar:

---

[109]   See e.g. *Re J (A Minor) (Wardship: Medical Treatment)* [1991] 2 W.L.R. 140; *Re B (A Minor) (Wardship: Medical Treatment)* [1981] 1 W.L.R. 1421; *Re Wyatt* [2006] EWHC 319 (Fam); *Re OT* [2009] EWHC 633 (Fam); *NHS Trust v Baby X* [2012] EWHC 2188 (Fam). See further, Jackson, fn.93 above, p.258.

[110]   See, e.g. *Re Quinlan* (1976) 355 A. 2d 647; *Superintendent of Belchertown State School v Saikewicz*, 370 N.E. 2d 417; *In re Schiavo* (2003) 851 So.2d 182.

[111]   See further, W. Wilson, "Is Life Sacred?" (1995) 17 J. of Soc. Wel. and Fam. Law 131; M. Donnelly, *Healthcare Decision-making and the Law: Autonomy, Capacity and the Limits of Liberalism* (Cambridge: CUP, 2010).

[112]   *F v West Berkshire HA* [1990] 2 A.C. 1; *Airedale NHS Trust v Bland* [1993] A.C. 789.

[113]   Mental Capacity Act 2005 Code of Practice, paras 8.18–8.19, provide that as a matter of practice all decisions about the

life-sustaining treatment may be withdrawn if it is no longer in the best interests of the incapacitated person.[114] The statutory test for best interests incorporates an important element of substituted judgment: the patient's wishes and feelings must be considered, and from the patient's subjective point of view insofar as that is possible.[115] In *Re A (children) (conjoined twins)*,[116] the trial judge decided that the separation of the twins would be lawful, following *Bland*, because it amounted to a withdrawal of treatment. The Court of Appeal rejected this analysis.[117] While the concerns expressed in *Bland* itself about the omission/commission distinction were echoed, the Court of Appeal was unanimous in holding that positive acts would have to be performed to save Jodie's life and thus the lawfulness of the operation had to be based on other grounds.[118] The distinction between acts and omissions continues to be of utmost importance in cases such as *Bland* where the court is effectively giving consent to the withdrawal of treatment.[119]

What about injuries short of death? In the absence of any social utility[120] it is clear that consent will be no defence to really serious injuries.[121] In *Leach*,[122] for example, the "victim" organised his own crucifixion on Hampstead Heath. The defendants nailed him to a wooden cross, his hands pierced by 6-inch nails. The defendants were liable for unlawful wounding; the consent of the victim was disregarded. With regard to lesser injuries, the following leading decision establishes that one may consent to common assault which involves only minimal or no injury. It was also thought to establish that consent is not a defence where actual bodily harm occurs or where a wound is inflicted[123] unless it falls within a recognised exception such as sporting injuries.

R. v Brown (and other appeals) [1994] 1 A.C. 212 (House of Lords)

The appellants belonged to a group of sado-masochistic gay men who over a 10-year period participated in the commission of acts of violence against each other, including genital torture, for the sexual pleasure engendered in the giving and receiving of pain. The partner in each case consented to the acts being committed and sustained no permanent injury. The participants had code words that enabled them to indicate when the pain became excessive. The appellants were charged with assault occasioning actual bodily harm contrary to s.47, and with unlawful wounding contrary to s.20 of the Offences Against the Person Act 1861. The appellants changed their pleas to guilty when the trial judge ruled that consent was no defence to such charges and subsequently appealed.

---

proposed withholding or withdrawal of artificial nutrition and hydration from patients in a persistent vegetative state should be brought before the Court of Protection for approval.

[114] *Aintree University Hospitals NHS Foundation Trust v James* [2013] UKSC 67. Mental Capacity Act 2005, Explanatory Notes, para.28. Where a court is making a decision in relation to life-sustaining treatment, it must not, "in considering whether the treatment is in the best interests of the person concerned, be motivated by a desire to bring about his death", Mental Capacity Act 2005, s.4(6).

[115] *Aintree*, fn.114, above at [38] and [45]; Mental Capacity Act 2005 s.4.

[116] *Re A (Children) (Conjoined Twins: Medical Treatment) (No.1)* (2001) 57 B.M.L.R. 1 at 13.

[117] [2000] 4 All E.R. 961, per Ward LJ at p.1027 (cf. Brooke LJ at p.1027, Robert Walker LJ, pp.1060–1062).

[118] Below, p.390–392.

[119] See further, D.P. Price, "What shape to euthanasia after Bland? Historical, contemporary and futuristic paradigms" (2009) 125 L.Q.R. 142 at 155–157. See also L. Oates, "Life, Death and the Law" (2007) 36 *Common Law World Review* 1 (Laurence Oates was the Official Solicitor at the time of *Re A*).

[120] Including matters of contested social utility, such as boxing.

[121] *Wright* (1603) Co.Lit.f. 127 a–b; *R. v Cato (Ronald Philip)* [1976] 1 All E.R. 260; *R. v Andrews (Christopher Kenneth)* [2003] Crim. L.R. 477 and *R. v Brown (Anthony Joseph)* [1994] 1 A.C. 212.

[122] *Leach, The Times*, January 15, 1969.

[123] Offences contrary to the Offences Against the Person Act 1861 ss.47 and 20. Whether this applies in all cases or only in cases where the harm is deliberately inflicted is discussed below, p.322–323

LORD TEMPLEMAN:

"My Lords, the appellants were convicted of assaults occasioning actual bodily harm contrary to section 47 of the Offences against the Person Act 1861. . . The incidents which led to each conviction occurred in the course of consensual sado-masochistic encounters. The Court of Appeal upheld the convictions and certified the following point of law of general public importance:

'Where A wounds or assaults B occasioning him actual bodily harm in the course of a sado-masochistic encounter, does the prosecution have to prove lack of consent on the part of B before they can establish A's guilt under section 20 or section 47 of the Offences against the Person Act 1861?'

. . . In the present case each of the appellants intentionally inflicted violence upon another (to whom I refer as 'the victim') with the consent of the victim and thereby occasioned actual bodily harm or in some cases wounding or grievous bodily harm. Each appellant was therefore guilty of an offence under section 47 or section 20 of the Act of 1861 unless the consent of the victim was effective to prevent the commission of the offence or effective to constitute a defence to the charge.

In some circumstances violence is not punishable under the criminal law. When no actual bodily harm is caused, the consent of the person affected precludes him from complaining. There can be no conviction for the summary offence of common assault if the victim has consented to the assault. Even when violence is intentionally inflicted and results in actual bodily harm, wounding or serious bodily harm the accused is entitled to be acquitted if the injury was a foreseeable incident of a lawful activity in which the person injured was participating. Surgery involves intentional violence resulting in actual or sometimes serious bodily harm but surgery is a lawful activity. Other activities carried on with consent by or on behalf of the injured person have been accepted as lawful notwithstanding that they involve actual bodily harm or may cause serious bodily harm. Ritual circumcision, tattooing, ear-piercing and violent sports including boxing are lawful activities . . .

My Lords, the authorities dealing with the intentional infliction of bodily harm do not establish that consent is a defence to a charge under the Act of 1861. They establish that the courts have accepted that consent is a defence to the infliction of bodily harm in the course of some lawful activities. The question is whether the defence should be extended to the infliction of bodily harm in the course of sado-masochistic encounters . . . [This question] can only be decided by consideration of policy and public interest . . .

Counsel for some of the appellants argued that the defence of consent should be extended to the offence of occasioning actual bodily harm under section 47 of the Act of 1861 but should not be available to charges of serious wounding and the infliction of serious bodily harm under s.20. I do not consider that this solution is practicable. Sado-masochistic participants have no way of foretelling the degree of bodily harm which will result from their encounters . . .

Counsel for the appellants argued that consent should provide a defence to charges under both section 20 and section 47 because, it was said, every person has a right to deal with his body as he pleases. I do not consider that this slogan provides a sufficient guide to the policy decision which must now be made. It is an offence for a person to abuse his own body and mind by taking drugs. Although the law is often broken, the criminal law restrains a practice which is regarded as dangerous and injurious to individuals and which if allowed and extended is harmful to society generally. In any event the appellants in this case did not mutilate their own bodies. They inflicted bodily harm on willing victims. Suicide is no longer an offence but a person who assists another to commit suicide is guilty of murder or manslaughter.[124]

The assertion was made on behalf of the appellants that the sexual appetites of sadists and masochists can only be satisfied by the infliction of bodily harm and that the law should not punish the consensual achievement of sexual satisfaction. There was no evidence to support the assertion that sado-masochist activities are essential to the happiness of the appellants or any other participants but the argument would be acceptable if sado-masochism were only concerned with sex, as the appellants contend. In my opinion sado-masochism is not only concerned with sex. Sado-masochism is also concerned with violence. The evidence discloses that the

---

[124] With due respect to his Lordship, it is only murder if the defendant intentionally *causes* the death of the "victim". It is manslaughter if both had intended to die and the defendant unexpectedly survives. In other circumstances the crime involved is aiding and abetting suicide, contrary to Suicide Act 1961 s.2.

practices of the appellants were unpredictably dangerous and degrading to body and mind and were developed with increasing barbarity and taught to persons whose consents were dubious or worthless . . .

In principle there is a difference between violence which is incidental and violence which is inflicted for the indulgence of cruelty. The violence of sado-masochistic encounters involves the indulgence of cruelty by sadists and the degradation of victims . . . I am not prepared to invent a defence of consent for sado-masochistic encounters which breed and glorify cruelty and result in offences under sections 47 and 20 of the Act of 1861."

LORD MUSTILL (DISSENTING):

"Throughout the argument of the appeal I was attracted by an analysis on the following lines. First, one would construct a continuous spectrum of the infliction of bodily harm, with killing at one end and a trifling touch at the other. Next, with the help of reported cases one would identify the point on this spectrum at which consent ordinarily ceases to be an answer to a prosecution for inflicting harm. This could be called 'the critical level.' It would soon become plain however that this analysis is too simple and that there are certain types of special situation to which the general rule does not apply. Thus, for example, surgical treatment which requires a degree of bodily invasion well on the upper side of the critical level will nevertheless be legitimate if performed in accordance with good medical practice and the consent of the patient. Conversely, there will be cases in which even a moderate degree of harm cannot be legitimated by consent . . .

For all the intellectual neatness of this method I must recognise that it will not do, for it imposes on the reported cases and on the diversities of human life an order which they do not possess. Thus, when one comes to map out the spectrum of ordinary consensual physical harm, to which the special situations form exceptions, it is found that the task is almost impossible, since people do not ordinarily consent to the infliction of harm. In effect, either all or almost all the instances of the consensual infliction of violence are special . . .

Furthermore, when one examines the situations which are said to found such a theory it is seen that the idea of consent as the foundation of a defence has in many cases been forced on to the theory, whereas in reality the reason why the perpetrator of the harm is not liable is not because of the recipient's consent, but because the perpetrator has acted in a situation where the consent of the recipient forms one, but only one, of the elements which make the act legitimate . . .

I thus see no alternative but to adopt a much narrower and more empirical approach, by looking at the situations in which the recipient consents or is deemed to consent to the infliction of violence upon him, to see whether the decided cases teach us how to react to this new challenge . . .

[Lord Mustill concluded that the case law left the way open for the House to determine the issue completely anew.]

As I have ventured to formulate the crucial question, it asks whether there is good reason to impress upon section 47 an interpretation which penalises the relevant level of harm irrespective of consent, i.e., to recognise sado-masochistic activities as falling into a special category of acts, such as duelling and prize-fighting, which 'the law says shall not be done.' This is very important, for if the question were differently stated it might well yield a different answer. In particular, if it were held that as a matter of law all infliction of bodily harm above the level of common assault is incapable of being legitimated by consent, except in special circumstances, then we would have to consider whether the public interest required the recognition of private sexual activities as being in a specially exempt category. This would be an altogether more difficult question and one which . . . [should be answered by Parliament] . . . I ask myself . . . whether the Act of 1861 (a statute which . . . was clearly intended to penalise conduct of a quite different nature) should in this new situation be interpreted so as to make it criminal?

[His Lordship concluded that there were insufficient grounds to do so and allowed the appeals.]"

LORD SLYNN (DISSENTING):

"[T]here exist areas where the law disregards the victim's consent even where that consent is freely and fully given. These areas may relate to the person (e.g. a child); they may relate to the place (e.g. in public); they may relate to the nature of the harm done. It is the latter which is in issue in the present case.

I accept that consent cannot be said simply to be a defence to any act which one person does to another. A line has to be drawn as to what can and as to what cannot be the subject of consent . . .

[T]o be workable, it cannot be allowed to fluctuate within particular charges and in the interests of legal certainty it has to be accepted that consent can be given to acts which are said to constitute actual bodily harm and wounding. Grievous bodily harm I accept to be different by analogy with and as an extension of the old cases on maiming. Accordingly, I accept that other than for cases of grievous bodily harm or death, consent can be a defence. This in no way means that the acts done are approved of or encouraged."

Appeal dismissed

While this decision can only be profoundly regretted as legal moralism prevailing over human autonomy and the right of persons to express their sexuality as they see fit,[125] it did, in some respects, help to clarify the law. The majority, in their answer to the certified question, decided that consent can be a defence to common assault, but is generally no defence to an assault occasioning actual bodily harm or to an unlawful wounding. There are exceptions to this general rule based on "policy and public interest" which allow persons to consent to the infliction of actual bodily harm, wounding—and even serious bodily harm. These exceptions include activities such as surgery, tattooing, ear-piercing,[126] rough sport and extends to sexual activity with a known risk of serious sexual disease. However, the decision in *Brown* and its progeny leave certain questions unanswered:

1. While the House of Lords endorsed the existence of "well established exceptions", the parameters of these exceptions are far from clear. This is true, even in the context of sexual encounters.

R. v Wilson [1996] 2 Cr. App. R. 241 (Court of Appeal, Criminal Division)

The defendant was convicted of assaulting his wife contrary to s.47 of the Offences Against the Person Act 1861. He admitted to the police (who had been informed by the wife's doctor) that he had used a hot knife to brand his initials on her buttocks. The judge ruled that he was bound by the decision in *Brown*. On appeal:

RUSSELL LJ:

"We are abundantly satisfied that there is no factual comparison to be made between the instant case and . . . and *Brown*: Mrs Wilson not only consented to that which the appellant did, she instigated it. There was no aggressive intent on the part of the appellant. On the contrary, far from wishing to cause injury to his wife, the appellant's desire was to assist her in what she regarded as the acquisition of a desirable piece of personal adornment, perhaps in this day and age no less understandable than the piercing of nostrils or even tongues for the purposes of inserting decorative jewellery.

---

[125] See L. Bibbings and P. Alldridge, "Sexual Expression, Body Alteration, and the Defence of Consent" (1993) 20 J. Law and Society 356. The appellants attempted to rely (unsuccessfully) upon the European Convention on Human Rights (most importantly, upon art.8 which guarantees respect for private and family life) during the course of their defence. Subsequently, the European Court of Human Rights unanimously held that there had been no violation of art.8 (*Laskey, Jaggard and Brown v The United Kingdom* (1997) 24 E.H.R.R. 39). Cf. D. Baker, "The Moral Limits of Consent as a Defence in the Criminal Law" (2009) 12 New Crim.L.Rev. 93; E. Craig, "Capacity to Consent to Sexual Risk" (2014) 17 New Crim. L.Rev. 103 and Cowan, fn.58 above.

[126] In the unreported case of *Oversby*, Judge Rant QC ruled that the piercing of other parts of the body for decorative or cosmetic purposes was lawful, but that body piercing for sexual gratification was unlawful (cited in Law Commission, Consultation Paper No.139, fn.93 above, para.9.7). Cosmetic piercing is regulated by Local Government (Miscellaneous Provisions) Act 1982 s.15 (as amended by Local Government Act 2003 s.120). The Government has produced guidance for local authorities regulating piercing businesses, and model bylaws, which have been adopted by over a hundred authorities: L. Smith, *Regulation of Tattooing and Body Piercing Businesses*, House of Commons Standard Note SN/SC/5079. The Guidance follows the approach in *Oversby*: Department of Health, *Local Government Act 2003: Regulation of Cosmetic Piercing and Skin Colouring Businesses: Guidance on Section 120 and Schedule 6* (2004), para. 20. Since cosmetic nipple and genital piercing (on those over the age of 16) appear to be lawful, it is suggested that the motive of the person obtaining the piercing ought to be irrelevant. The *Oversby* approach is unworkable in practice and based on an outmoded attitude towards body modification and unacceptable legal moralism.

In our judgment *Brown* is not authority for the proposition that consent is no defence to a charge under section 47 of the 1861 Act, in all circumstances where actual bodily harm is deliberately inflicted. It is to be observed that the question certified for their Lordships in *Brown* related only to a 'sadomasochistic encounter'. However, their Lordships recognised in the course of their speeches, that it was necessary that there be exceptions to what is no more than a general proposition. The speeches of [several of their Lordships] . . . all refer to tattooing as being an activity which, if carried out with the consent of an adult, does not involve an offence under section 47, albeit that actual bodily harm is deliberately inflicted.

For our part, we cannot detect any logical difference between what the appellant did and what he might have done in the way of tattooing. The latter activity apparently requires no state authorisation, and the appellant was as free to engage in it as anyone else.

We do not think that we are entitled to assume that the method adopted by the appellant and his wife was any more dangerous or painful than tattooing . . . [W]e are firmly of the opinion that it is not in the public interest that activities such as the appellant's in this appeal should amount to criminal behaviour. Consensual activity between husband and wife, in the privacy of the matrimonial home, is not, in our judgment, a proper matter for criminal investigation, let alone criminal prosecution . . . In this field, in our judgment, the law should develop upon a case by case basis rather than upon general propositions to which, in the changing times we live, exceptions may arise from time to time not expressly covered by authority."

Appeal allowed

R. v Emmett, Case No. 9901191 ZR, The Times, October 15, 1999 (Court of Appeal, Criminal Division)

The defendant and his partner engaged in consensual sexual activity that on one occasion involved partial asphyxiation and on another occasion setting light to lighter fuel on her breast. As a result she suffered subconjunctival haemorrhages in both eyes, some bruising around her neck and a burn that at first was thought to be so serious as to require a skin graft. The offence came to light because the doctor treating the woman reported it to the police. The defendant was convicted of assault occasioning actual bodily harm. The trial judge distinguished *Wilson* and followed *Brown* in ruling that consent was no defence where the parties foresaw the risk of injuries. On appeal:

WRIGHT J:

"[W]e have come to the clear conclusion that the evidence in the instant case, in striking contrast to that in *Wilson*, made it plain that the actual or potential damage to which the appellant's partner was exposed in this case, plainly went far beyond that which was established by the evidence in *Wilson*. The lady suffered a serious, and what must have been, an excruciating painful burn . . . As to the process of partial asphyxiation . . . while it may now be fairly well known that the restriction of oxygen to the brain is capable of heightening sexual sensation, it is also, or should be, equally well-known that such a practice contains within itself a grave danger of brain damage or even death . . . The appellant was plainly aware of that danger . . . Accordingly, whether the line beyond which consent becomes immaterial is drawn at the point . . . at which common assault becomes assault occasioning actual bodily harm, or at some higher level, where the evidence looked at objectively reveals a realistic risk of more than a transient or trivial injury, it is plain, in our judgment, that the activities involved in by this appellant and his partner went well beyond that line . . .

[The appellant argues that] the involvement of the processes of the criminal law, in the consensual activities that were carried on in this couple's bedroom, amount to a breach of Article 8 of the European Convention on Human Rights [right to respect for private and family life]. . . It seems clear to us that once the conduct of the accused person has gone beyond the permitted limit, however that is defined, in inflicting injury upon or exposing to potential risk his or her partner, in the course of sado-masochistic games whether homo- or heterosexual, so that he or she *prima facie* at least has committed an offence of a sufficient degree of seriousness, the institution of a criminal investigation and, if appropriate, criminal proceedings cannot amount to a breach of Article 8."

Appeal dismissed

While this decision can be welcomed, as applying the same test to different types of sexual relationships, the judgment is non-committal about the precise point at which the state may intervene in one's private sexual life. Branding one's wife with a knife is permitted (by analogy with the "exception" of tattooing[127]) but the activities in this case "went well beyond that line". The reliance in *Wilson* on the fact that the branding had been done as an act of affection rather than aggression is unhelpful. Subsequently, the decisions of *Dica* and *Konzani* have attempted to render more coherent the law surrounding consent and sexual activity. In *Dica*, the court decided that if the women had known of the defendant's condition and continued to engage in sexual activity with him, their consent would have been an answer to a charge of inflicting grievous bodily harm.

R. v Dica [2004] Q.B. 1257 (Court of Appeal, Criminal Division)

JUDGE LJ:

"[*Emmett* and the case of *Boyea*[128]] demonstrate that violent conduct involving the deliberate and intentional infliction of bodily harm is and remains unlawful notwithstanding that its purpose is the sexual gratification of one or both participants. Notwithstanding their sexual overtones, these cases were concerned with violent crime, and the sexual overtones did not alter the fact that both parties were consenting to the deliberate infliction of serious harm or bodily injury on one participant by the other. To date, as a matter of public policy, it has not been thought appropriate for such violent conduct to be excused merely because there is a private consensual sexual element to it. The same public policy reason would prohibit the deliberate spreading of disease, including sexual disease.

In our judgment the impact of the authorities dealing with sexual gratification can too readily be misunderstood. It does not follow from them, and they do not suggest, that consensual acts of sexual intercourse are unlawful merely because there may be a known risk to the health of one or other participant. These participants are not intent on spreading or becoming infected with disease through sexual gratification. They are not indulging in serious violence for the purpose of sexual gratification. They are simply prepared, knowingly, to run the risk—not the certainty—of infection, as well as all the other risks inherent in and possible consequences of sexual intercourse, such as, and despite the most careful precautions, an unintended pregnancy . . .

These, and similar risks, have always been taken by adults consenting to sexual intercourse . . . Modern society has not thought to criminalise those who have willingly accepted the risks . . .

The problems of criminalizing the consensual taking of risks like these include the sheer impracticability of enforcement and the haphazard nature of its impact. The process would undermine the general understanding of the community that sexual relationships are pre-eminently private and essentially personal to the individuals involved in them . . .

In our judgment, interference of this kind with personal autonomy, and its level and extent, may only be made by Parliament."

While autonomy is upheld here (unlike in *Brown*) in respect of the choice of individuals to engage in risk-laden sexual activity, the distinction being drawn between violence and sex is no more illuminating or coherent than the distinction in *Wilson* between affection and aggression.

In 2013, Steven Lock was tried at Ipswich Crown Court for an offence under s.47 of the Offences Against the Person Act 1861. Inspired by the bestselling erotic work of fiction, *Fifty Shades of Grey*,[129] he had restrained his partner, who had signed a letter stating that she gave him permission to treat her

---

[127]   As P. Roberts points out ("Consent to Injury: How Far Can You Go?" [1997] 113 L.Q.R. 27 at 31), there is no authority that *branding* is an exception to the general liability rule and, thus, "Russell LJ was obliged to look for a new exception to cover Mr. Wilson's handiwork."

[128]   *R. v Boyea* (1992) 156 J.P. 505.

[129]   E.L. James, *Fifty Shades of Grey* (London: Arrow Publications, 2012), a novel about a heterosexual relationship which involves sado-masochistic sexual activity.

as a slave, and lashed her with a rope, causing 14 centimetre bruises to her buttocks. His defence was that this was a 'master and slave' sex game to which the complainant had consented, and that he had not intended to inflict injury. He was acquitted by the jury.[130] In *Brown*, Lord Mustill recognised that societal attitudes and behaviour change over time, and that the line between acceptable and unlawful behaviour might need to be revisited in the future:

"It also seems plain that as the general social appreciation of what is tolerable and of the proper role of the state in regulating the lives of individuals changes with the passage of time, so we shall expect to find that the assumption of the criminal justice system about what types of conduct are properly excluded from its scope, and about what is meant by going 'too far' will not remain constant."[131]

What is the position with regard to other exceptions? Consent is a defence to sports participants who injure one another in the course of their sporting activities. Lawful sports (excluding activities such as prize-fighting) are to be encouraged: they are "manly diversions, they tend to give strength, skill and activity, and may fit people for defence, public as well as personal, in time of need".[132] In *Billinghurst*, the jury was directed that rugby players consent to such force as can reasonably be expected during the game.[133] In *Barnes*, the defendant made, in the words of the prosecution, "a crushing tackle, which was late, unnecessary, reckless and high up the legs" upon a player on the opposing side in an amateur game of football which resulted in serious injuries to the ankle and calf bone of the player.[134] The defendant was convicted of maliciously inflicting grievous bodily harm under s.20 of the Offences Against the Person Act 1861. At his appeal, Lord Woolf stated that there was now a steady flow of cases coming before them which required them to give guidance. He stressed that prosecutions should be reserved for those situations where the conduct was sufficiently grave to be categorised as criminal. Given that most organised sports had their own disciplinary procedures for enforcing the rules and standards of conduct, it was not only unnecessary but also undesirable that criminal proceedings should generally occur. "If what occurs goes beyond what a player can reasonably be regarded as having accepted by taking part in the sport, this indicates that the conduct will not be covered by the defence" of consent. However, the threshold for it being regarded as criminal will vary depending on the sport in question and allowance should be made for the heat of the moment.[135] In

---

[130] T. Farmery, "Fifty Shades of Grey 'Master' is cleared of assault", *The Times*, January 23, 2013, p.11.Cf. the case of *M(M)*, tried at Woolwich Crown Court, where the defendant was acquitted of charges of assault by penetration, sexual assault and assault occasioning actual bodily harm arising out of sado-masochistic behaviour on one occasion: P. Murphy, "Flogging live complainants and dead horses: we may no longer need to be in bondage to *Brown*" [2011] Crim. L.R. 758–765. Cf. *R. v Meachen (David Nigel)* [2006] EWCA Crim 2414 and *Slingsby* [1995] Crim. L.R. 570, discussed below, p.322.

[131] *R. v Brown (Anthony Joseph)* [1994] 1 A.C. 212 at 267.

[132] M. Foster, *Crown Cases*, 3rd edn (M. Dodson, 1792), p.260.

[133] *R. v Billinghurst* [1978] Crim. L.R. 553. See further, J. Anderson, "No Licence for Thuggery: Violence, Sport and the Criminal Law" [2008] Crim. L.R. 751.

[134] *R. v Barnes (Mark)* [2004] EWCA Crim 3246.

[135] *R. v Barnes (Mark)*, fn.134, above at [12], [15] and [16]. The defendant's appeal against conviction was allowed on the basis that the judge's direction to the jury (in terms of deciding whether the incident had not been done by way of legitimate sport) had been inadequate. See further, B. Livings, "A Different Ball Game" [2007] 71 J. Crim. L. 534 and M. James, *Sports Law*, 2nd edn (Basingstoke: Palgrave Macmillan, 2013), Ch.6. Since *Barnes* there have been a number of criminal prosecutions of amateur football and rugby players, and it has been suggested that some confusion remains as to what acts warrant criminal prosecution: A. Pendlebury, "The Regulation of on-the-ball Offences: Challenges in Court" (2012) 10 *Entertainment and Sports Law Journal* 279–294.

those cases where criminal liability does result, the courts will ordinarily respond to such offending by imposing a custodial sentence.[136] Where does this analysis leave professional boxing?:

"For money, not recreation or personal improvement, each boxer tries to hurt the opponent more than he is hurt himself, and aims to end the contest prematurely by inflicting a brain injury serious enough to make the defendant unconscious . . . It is in my judgment best to regard this as another special situation which for the time being stands outside the ordinary law of violence because society chooses to tolerate it."[137]

In *H v Crown Prosecution Service*[138] the Administrative Court refused to hold that a teacher at a school for children with special needs, by accepting employment at that school, had impliedly consented to the use of minor violence against him by his pupils because, in that type of school, pupils would frequently exhibit aggressive and challenging behaviour. An argument that this situation was analogous to the contact sports cases and that, by analogy, such cases should be dealt with by the schools' internal disciplinary proceedings, rather than by the criminal law, was similarly rejected. The Court was concerned about possibly opening the floodgates to arguments that those dealing with difficult individuals impliedly consented to minor assaults upon them:

"For example, if teachers impliedly consent to common assault, what of other people such as support staff, dinner ladies and other students? Are they to be regarded as having impliedly consented to assaults upon them? One can also conceive of other situations where, if the defendant's contention is correct, it must logically follow that consent must be deemed to be given, for example by a nurse or doctor on a ward with difficult patients."[139]

There are a number of other special situations in addition to boxing where the deliberate infliction of bodily harm may be legitimated by consent. An example is the ritual circumcision of males.[140] The cultural acceptance this form of invasive action enjoys is very different to the position of female circumcision. This latter practice is mainly performed on young girls of African origin in order to protect their virginity. "[I]ts purpose lies in the control and oppression of women and the suppression of female sexuality."[141] Such circumcisions can cause very severe injuries and have been made criminal.[142] People over the age of 16 may give consent to other forms of surgical interference. Whether it is

---

[136]   See, e.g. *R. v Birkin (Paul Abbey)* [1988] Crim. L.R. 854; *Bowyer* [2001] EWCA Crim 1835; *R. v Cotterill (James Michael)* [2007] EWCA Crim 526; *R. v Lawrence (Jerome)* [2011] EWCA Crim 3129; *R. v Brown (Paul Brian)* [2011] EWCA Crim 786.

[137]   Per Lord Mustill in *R. v Brown (Anthony Joseph)* [1994] 1 A.C. 212 at 265. See further, M. Gunn and D. Ormerod, "The Legality of Boxing" (1995) 15 *Legal Studies* 181; J. Anderson, *The Legality of Boxing: A Punch Drunk Love?* (Abingdon: Birkbeck Law Press, 2007) and J. Anderson, "The right to a fair fight: sporting lessons on consensual harm" (2014) 17 New Crim.L.Rev 103. There are a number of martial arts activities which expose the participants to just as much potential risk as boxing, often without the same strict regulatory control (Law Commission Consultation Paper No.139, fn.93 above, para.1.6).

[138]   *H v Crown Prosecution Service* [2010] EWHC 1374 (Admin), [2012] Q.B. 257.

[139]   *H v Crown Prosecution Service*, fn.138, above, per Cranston J at [21].

[140]   Law Com., fn.93, above, para.3.25. Cf. M. Fox and M. Thompson, 'A Covenant with the Status Quo? Male Circumcision and the New BMA Guidance to Doctors' (2005) 31 *Journal of Medical Ethics* 463. Feldman has argued that nontherapeutic circumcision conducted without the consent of the patient may violate art.3 of the European Convention on Human Rights: D. Feldman, *Civil Liberties and Human Rights in England and Wales*, 2nd edn (Oxford: OUP, 2002), p.272. Cf. H Gilbert, 'Time to Reconsider the Lawfulness of Ritual Male Circumcision' [2007] EHRLR 279.

[141]   Bibbings and Alldridge, fn.125 above.

[142]   Female Genital Mutilation Act 2003 s.1. The offence carries a maximum sentence of 14 years' imprisonment. However, cosmetic genital surgery (e.g. labiaplasty) is lawful and apparently increasingly popular: C. Smyth, "Porn fuels rise in girls

the consent of the patient that renders the actions lawful or whether surgery forms a special category of its own is an issue which has yet to be fully resolved in the courts.[143] We know that at least one surgeon has performed amputation operations on two patients suffering from the rare medical disorder of apotemnophilia which induces in its sufferers the desire to have a (healthy) limb amputated.[144] The legality of this (and its rationale) was not tested by a prosecution but a similar scenario would provide a "limit" case for the courts on the issue of consent to surgery.

Finally, there is a problem concerning "rough horseplay". In *Jones*[145] it was held that this activity which occurs "in the school playground, in the barrack-room and on the factory floor"[146] was something that persons consent to as long as there is no intention to cause injury. Because of this, a group of schoolboys in *Jones* who had thrown their victims "some 9 or 10 feet" into the air causing, in one case, a ruptured spleen which necessitated a surgical operation for its removal, had their convictions for causing grievous bodily harm quashed. In *Brown*, Lord Mustill stated that the criminal law could not concern itself with such activities "provided that they do not go too far".[147] This public policy approach was adopted in *P* where it was held that in the context of horseplay consent might be highly material in negating what would otherwise be an unlawful act.[148] In this case two teenage defendants, after a post-exam celebration, threw the victim over a bridge to his death. Their convictions for manslaughter were upheld—not on the basis that consent was irrelevant in such circumstances—but on the basis that no consent had been given and it was abundantly clear that the victim had been actively resisting the defendants.

These cases have the potential to be a bully's charter.[149] It is far-fetched to suggest that the boys in *Jones* who were being held by several others to *prevent them running away* were genuinely consenting to being thrown into the air. To suggest that boys can consent to grievous bodily harm or a risk of death, but that sado-masochists, who are genuinely consenting, cannot consent to actual bodily harm, provides an interesting insight into the way some of our judiciary view the world. Violence in the playground or barrack-room is what is expected and normal in the male world; it is a "manly diversion". Two men wishing to express their sexuality together and in private are not doing the sort of thing "real men" do. It is an "evil thing" and "uncivilised"[150] and cannot be the subject of valid consent.

---

having risky genital cosmetic surgery", *The Times*, November 15, 2013. See T. Elliott, "Body Dysmorphic Disorder, Radical Surgery and the Limits of Consent" (2009) 17 *Medical Law Review* 149 at 178–181.

[143] This latter view is taken by Lord Mustill in *R. v Brown (Anthony Joseph)* [1994] 1 A.C. 212 at 266.

[144] "News: Surgeon Amputated Healthy Legs" (2000) *British Medical Journal* 320. The surgeon, Robert Smith, effectively barred from performing any more such operations in the UK because no hospital will permit this surgery to take place on their premises, has argued that the condition (now usually known as Body Integrity Identity Disorder) is analogous to Gender Identity Disorder and, thus, may be appropriately treated by surgery: G.M. Furth and R. Smith, *Amputee Identity Disorder: Information, Questions, Answers and Recommendations about Self-Demand Amputation* (First Books Library, 2002); C. Fracassini, "Call for NHS Amputation of Healthy Limbs" *The Times*, November 23, 2003. The legality of gender reassignment surgery is well established, see e.g. *Corbett v Corbett* [1971] P. 83; *Bellinger v Bellinger* [2003] 2 A.C. 467; Law Consultation Paper No.139, above, fn.126, paras 8.28–8.29. See further, Elliott, above, fn.142.

[145] *R. v Jones (Terance)* (1986) 83 Cr. App. R. 375. See also *R. v Aitken (Thomas Adam)* [1992] 1 W.L.R. 1006 and Law Commission Consultation Paper No.139, fn.93 above, paras 14.1–14.21.

[146] Per Lord Mustill in *R. v Brown (Anthony Joseph)* [1994] 1 A.C. 212 at 267.

[147] *R. v Brown (Anthony Joseph)*, fn.146 above, p.267.

[148] *R. v P* [2005] EWCA Crim 1960.

[149] The defence *may* even operate where the defendants make a drunken mistake as to the consent of the victim: see *R. v Richardson (Nigel John) and Irwin (Sean Anthony)* [1999] 1 Cr. App. R. 392. Below, p.443.

[150] Per Lord Templeman in *R. v Brown (Anthony Joseph)* [1994] 1 A.C. 212 at 237.

2. An assault occasioning actual bodily harm contrary to s.47 can be inflicted intentionally or recklessly. Indeed, the defendant need not foresee any bodily harm at all as the mens rea is the same as that of a common assault.[151] It is unclear whether consent can never be a defence to s.47[152] (apart from the recognised exceptions) or whether this is limited to cases where the actual bodily harm is *deliberately* inflicted.[153] There are dicta supporting this latter view.[154] On the other hand, the majority in *Brown* all answered the certified question in the negative. This question was framed with reference to "section 20 and section 47", both of which offences can be committed recklessly. Lord Jauncey was clear that consent could never be a defence to anyone charged with either a s.47 or a s.20 offence (apart from the well-established exceptions). Further, the majority approved of the dictum of Lord Lane in *Attorney-General's Reference (No.6 of 1980)* that it was not in the public interest that people should try to or should cause each other bodily harm (for no good reason) and that it was an assault if actual bodily harm was intended and/or caused.[155] Thus, it is possible that if actual bodily harm results, even though it is neither intended nor foreseen, consent would be negated.[156]

However, the better view is that whether consent can ever be a defence, in cases where the injury is not intended, depends on the context in which these injuries are inflicted. In *Brown* the certified question was expressly posed in relation to woundings or actual bodily harm "in the course of a sadomasochistic encounter" and it is arguable that it is only in such cases that consent is never a defence to a s.47 charge. It is only on "public interest" grounds that consent is not a defence here and presumably the "public interest" varies with the type of case involved. For example, we are all deemed to consent to a certain degree of bodily contact in everyday life when on buses, trains and so on. It seems perfectly plausible in such a case to argue that consent can be a defence to a s.47 charge if the actual bodily harm was not deliberately caused. We all consent not only to everyday touching but also to the risk of being pushed and jostled and perhaps injured. We certainly do not consent, however, to persons pushing us over and deliberately causing us actual bodily harm.

Similarly, with sexual activity (not of a sadomasochistic variety) it was held in *Dica*, as we have seen, that there could be consent to the risk of HIV (which is grievous bodily harm). In *Meachen*,[157] the defence case was that the complainant had consented, for her gratification, to the defendant inserting his finger into her anus. She suffered serious anal injury. On appeal, the defendant's conviction for inflicting grievous bodily harm contrary to s.20 was quashed. As her injuries had not been intended, her consent could provide a defence.[158]

3. In *Attorney-General's Reference (No.6 of 1980)* it was held that one could not consent to injuries sustained in a fight because such fighting (unless properly conducted under the Queensberry Rules)

---

[151] *R. v Savage (Susan)* [1992] 1 A.C. 699.

[152] In *R. v Emmett*, Case No. 9901191 ZR, *The Times*, October 15, 1999, it was stated that the issue was whether the line should be drawn between assault and s.47 "or at some higher level".

[153] Smith, fn.60 above: "It is important to note that [the decision in *R. v Brown (Anthony Joseph)*] is limited to the intentional infliction of bodily harm."

[154] Lord Templeman: "in principle there is a difference between violence which is incidental and violence which is inflicted for the indulgence of cruelty" (at 236). Lord Lowry: "If in the course of buggery . . . one participant, either with the other participant's consent or not, *deliberately* causes actual bodily harm to that other, an offence against s.47 has been committed." (at 256, emphasis added).

[155] *Attorney-General's Reference (No.6 of 1980)* [1981] Q.B. 715 at 719.

[156] Support for this proposition comes from the case of *R. v Boyea* (1992) 156 J.P. 505. See further, M.J. Allen, "Consent and Assault" [1994] 58 J. Crim. L. 183.

[157] *R. v Meachen (David Nigel)* [2006] EWCA Crim 2414.

[158] See also *Slingsby* [1995] Crim. L.R. 570, where the court gave some indication that it would restrict the negation of consent to those injuries which were intentionally or recklessly inflicted. Further, it may have been material that the court in *R. v Emmett*, Case No. 9901191 ZR, *The Times*, October 15, 1999 stressed that the defendant was "plainly aware of the danger".

was contrary to the public interest. What if the injuries sustained in the fight were not sufficient to amount to actual bodily harm, or if the prosecution chose for other reasons to charge only with common assault? Would consent be a defence to such a charge? In *Attorney-General's Reference (No.6 of 1980)* it was held that there could be an assault in such circumstances if actual bodily harm was "intended and/or caused".[159] If actual bodily harm is intended but not actually caused, the only possible charge is common assault. This issue is not directly addressed in *Brown* but would appear to be answered by the following, fairly typical statement by Lord Lowry that "everyone agrees that consent remains a complete defence to a charge of common assault".[160] Until this point has been resolved prosecutors are likely to avoid charging common assault in any case where consent is involved.

4. Subject to the above point, consent is a defence to assault. How can a defendant be guilty of the offence of *assault* occasioning actual bodily harm when there can be no liability for one of the elements of the offence, namely, the assault?

D. Reform Proposals

The judgments of their Lordships in *Brown* prompted the Law Commission to examine the law relating to consent. It adopts an essentially pragmatic approach and follows what it perceives to be the prevailing attitude in Parliament to questions of criminalisation,[161] that is, "paternalism softened at the edges when Parliament is confident that there is an effective system of regulatory control".[162]

Law Commission, Consent in the Criminal Law (Consultation Paper No.139, 1995), paras 4.47–4.51:

"4.47   We provisionally propose that the intentional causing of seriously disabling injury to another person should continue to be criminal, even if the person injured consents to such injury or to the risk of such injury.

4.48   We provisionally propose that—

(1) the reckless causing of seriously disabling injury should continue to be criminal, even if the injured person consents to such injury or to the risk of such injury; but

(2) a person causing seriously disabling injury to another person should not be regarded as having caused it recklessly unless—

(a) he or she was, at the time of the act or omission causing it, aware of a risk that such injury would result, and

(b) it was at that time contrary to the best interests of the other person, having regard to the circumstances known to the person causing the injury (including, if known to him or her, the fact that the other person consented to such injury or to the risk of it), to take that risk.

4.49   We provisionally propose that the intentional [and reckless (4.50)] causing of any injury to another person other than seriously disabling injury . . . should not be criminal if, at the time of the act or omission causing the injury, the other person consented to injury of the type caused.

4.51   . . .'seriously disabling injury' should be taken to refer to an injury or injuries which

(1) cause serious distress, and

---

[159] *Attorney-General's Reference (No.6 of 1980)* [1981] Q.B. 715.
[160] *R. v Brown (Anthony Joseph)* [1994] 1 A.C. 212 at 248.
[161] Consultation Paper No.139, fn.93, para.2.17.
[162] Consultation Paper No.139, fn.93, para.2.15.

(2) involve the loss of a bodily member or organ or permanent bodily injury or permanent functional impair-
     ment, or serious or permanent disfigurement, or severe and prolonged pain, or serious impairment of
     mental health, or prolonged unconsciousness;

and in determining whether an effect is permanent, no account should be taken of the fact that it may be
remediable by surgery.[163]

[The Law Commission then goes on to identify a number of exceptions. Persons may give consent to a higher level
of harm for medical treatment and surgery. There are a number of activities (such as tattooing, sport and horseplay) where the level of harm is to stay at that permitted by the present law. Those under the age of 18 would not
be able to consent to injuries intentionally caused for sexual, religious or spiritual purposes.]"

If implemented, these proposals would produce a law which would give rather more scope for the
defence of consent. The Law Commission acknowledges that there are still difficulties to be resolved[164]
but, beyond this, there are underlying assumptions which are not beyond challenge and to which we
now turn.

E. The Rationale of Consent as a Defence

An attempt to understand the basis upon which, and the extent to which, consent operates as a
defence involves a consideration of liberalism, paternalism and moralism. Those issues were considered in Ch.1 and will not be explored again here. However, two final insights may be presented.

George P. Fletcher, Rethinking Criminal Law (1978), pp.770–771:

"The principle that individuals are free and responsible agents informs the analysis of consent . . . Once accepted,
the value of autonomy does not lend itself to being offset by competing social interests. So far as the rationale
of consent is that individuals should be free to waive their rights, this capacity of waiver is not a contingent value,
subject to repeated balancing against the opposing array of interests.

There is some evidence that at the fringes, however, the principle of autonomy gives way to competing
social values. The prevailing view in Western legal systems is that the individual has the right to take his own
life or to torture himself, but he does not have the right to authorise others to do the killing or to perform a
sado-masochistic beating. That there is a personal right to suffer in these cases indicates that the rationale for
limiting personal autonomy is not a paternalistic governmental posture toward the victim's injuring himself. If
the issue were paternalism, the government should employ sanctions as well against suicide and other forms of
self-destruction.

A more convincing account of the distinction between self-injury and consenting to injury by others derives
from the danger of implicating other persons in dangerous forms of conduct. The individual who kills or mutilates
himself might affect the well-being of family and friends, but this result depends upon the actor's relationships
with other people. In contrast, the self-destructive individual who induces another person to kill or to mutilate
him implicates the latter in the violation of a significant social taboo. The person carrying out the killing or the
mutilation crosses the threshold into a realm of conduct that, the second time, might be more easily carried
out. And the second time, it might not be particularly significant whether the victim consents or not. Similarly, if
someone is encouraged to inflict a sado-masochistic beating on a consenting victim, the experience of inflicting
the beating might loosen the actor's inhibitions against sadism in general."

---

[163] Thus the question of whether the injury is seriously disabling would have to be established in addition to grievous bodily
       harm in cases where consent is claimed. See, D. Ormerod and M. Gunn, "Consent—A Second Bash" [1996] Crim. L.R. 694
       at 701, where they argue that this is too complex, confusing and unnecessary.
[164] With, for example, the concept of "horseplay": Consultation Paper No.139, fn.93, paras 14.1–14.21.

David Feldman, Civil Liberties and Human Rights in England and Wales, 2nd edn (2002), pp.715–716:

"[T]o imply . . . that carefully controlled, planned, and consensual violence as part of a sexual encounter has no redeeming social value, but to accept that boxing or rough and undisciplined play have social value which justifies the infliction of bodily harm, turns reality on its head. The object of respecting consent to the rough and tumble of sport (like consent to medical treatment) is primarily to protect the individual interests of the participants as they perceive them, rather than to advance any public interest. It is a recognition of individual autonomy, the right of individuals of sufficient understanding to make their own decisions about what is good for them. In principle, this should apply equally to people's sexual preferences. Indeed, it is hard to see how the interest (whether public or private) in allowing people to express their sexuality, which forms a fundamental part of people's personality, could be less important than the interest in allowing people to pursue sports. Sport is fun, but sex, for many people, is more than fun: it is a form of self-expression."

Even if one concedes that, in certain cases, consent ought not to provide a complete defence, do we blame such defendants *as much* as those who commit similar harms against their victims who are *not* consenting? Even if consent does not provide a complete justification, ought it not to provide a partial defence so as to reduce the defendant's level of criminal liability and/or punishment?

III. Self-defence

A. Introduction

Almost as long as the criminal law has been in existence it has consistently restricted the right of the individual to self-help; it is the function of the law to preserve law and order and protect the weak. There are, however, inevitably occasions when to depend upon the arrival of official help would be to court disaster and it would be extremely unjust if the remedy of self-help were altogether denied. The law recognises this and in certain situations deems the use of force to be lawful. It has been argued that:

"The source of [this] right is a comparison of the competing interests of the aggressor and the defender, as modified by the important fact that the aggressor is the one party responsible for the fight . . . As the party morally at fault for threatening the defender's interests, the aggressor is entitled to lesser consideration in the balancing process."[165]

The underlying rationale of defensive force may also be understood in terms of Gardner's analysis: "By granting a *justificatory* defence the law concedes that . . . the defendant had, at the time of her *prima facie* wrongful action, sufficient reason to perform it."[166] While most of the rules here were developed largely to cater for situations where the defendant is acting against an aggressor, Gardner's analysis provides a more complete explanation that covers cases where self-defensive action is taken against a non-culpable person such as a small child who is inadvertently threatening the defendant's interests.

---

[165] Fletcher, fn.7 above, pp.857–858. See also, S. Uniacke, *Permissible Killings: The Self-Defence Justification for Homicide* (Cambridge: OUP, 1994), Chs 4 and 5 where she rejects the argument that killings in self-defence are morally permissible because they are unintended (but merely foreseen) and argues that they are permissible because of "the moral asymmetry between the parties" (p.229)—a development of the theory of forfeiture.

[166] Gardner, fn.11 above, p.108.

Again, as with consent, it is possible to assert that necessary defence is not truly a "defence". A defendant acting in self-defence is acting lawfully—an element of the actus reus is thus not established.[167] As we have seen, this method of characterisation has important implications in cases where the defendant has made a mistake, i.e. mistakenly thinking he needs to defend himself or others.[168] But apart from such cases, the parameters of necessary defence are constant—irrespective of whether it is regarded as a defence, or a denial of a definitional element.

As we shall see in the context of both homicide and non-fatal offences against the person, most reported violent crime is between young males, typically when they are out for the evening.[169] Violence may flare up in such situations, which leads one of the parties to use defensive force. The dynamics of the interaction may not, however, be straightforward; the eventual victim may have precipitated the final outcome or the defendant could actually have been the initial aggressor;[170] in short, the division of responsibility between the victim and the defendant may be difficult to determine. Thus the law has developed fairly rigorous conditions before a plea based on the need to defend oneself will be accepted.

It is also true to say that the context within which these rules have been framed has been predominantly that of inter-male violence.[171] What this ignores (and what is still underrepresented by official statistics) is domestic violence. As we will see, the rules in relation to defensive force may make it difficult for the "battered woman" who retaliates to raise a successful plea.[172]

In recent years, the law of self-defence has come under intense scrutiny from the popular press, the public and politicians in relation to the force a householder may use in response to intruders.[173] As a consequence, s.76 of the Criminal Justice and Immigration Act 2008 was enacted in order to "clarify the operation of the existing defences."[174] The 2008 Act codifies the existing common law defence of self-defence and the statutory defence under s.3 of the Criminal Law Act 1967 of acting in prevention of crime. Section 76 does not abolish the common law; nor does it cover all of the issues dealt with by the common law. As such, the section has been criticised as "pointless"[175] and for ignoring the fact that the common law "urgently needs to be reformed".[176] Reform has come more recently, but not in the form envisaged by most legal scholars. In 2013, s.43 of the Crime and Courts Act 2013 amended the 2008 Act in relation to so-called "householder cases". The new provisions, in effect, legitimise the use of disproportionate force in self-defence in home invasion cases.[177]

---

[167] *R. v Abraham (Alan)* [1973] 1 W.L.R. 1270; *R. v Williams (Gladstone)* (1984) 78 Cr. App. R. 276.

[168] Above, p.214.

[169] Below, pp.677–678.

[170] *R. v Rashford (Nicholas)* [2006] Crim. L.R. 547; *R. v Keane* [2010] EWCA Crim 2514.

[171] See K. O'Donovan, "Defences for Battered Women Who Kill" (1991) 18 J. L. and Soc. 219; C. Wells, "Domestic Violence and Self-Defence" (1990) 140 N.L.J. 127; L.J. Taylor, "Provoked Reason in Men and Women: Heat of Passion Manslaughter and Imperfect Self-Defense" (1986) 33 U.C.L.A. Law Rev. 1679.

[172] See N. Wake, "Battered women, startled householders and psychological self-defence: Anglo-Australian perspectives" (2013) 77 J. Crim. L. 433.

[173] See, for example, the discussion in I. Dennis, "Editorial: Defending Self-Defence" [2010] Crim. L.R. 167.

[174] Criminal Justice and Immigration Act 2008 s.76(9).

[175] I. Dennis, "Editorial: A Pointless Exercise" [2008] Crim. L.R. 507.

[176] J. Rogers, "Have-a-go heroes" [2008] 158 N.L.J. 318 at 318.

[177] These provisions are discussed below, p.340–342.

B. The Triggering Conditions

What circumstances must exist in order for an actor to be justified in acting in self-defence? It is common to state that in "defensive force justifications an aggressor must present a threat of unjustified harm to the protected interest".[178] Two points need consideration here:

1. Threat of unjustified harm

In the paradigmatic self-defence scenario an innocent person is attacked by an unjustified aggressor and this triggers the right to self-defensive action. From this, it is clear that self-defence is not a defence against justified action, for example, against a police officer using reasonable force to make a lawful arrest. On the other hand, as seen earlier when the significance of the distinction between justifications, excuses and exemptions was explored, self-defence is permitted against an exempted actor. One is entitled to defend oneself against a small child firing a gun or an insane person wielding an axe. Such a person, while non-culpable, is still threatening unjustified harm.

Re A (Conjoined Twins: Surgical Separation) [2001] Fam. 147 (Court of Appeal, Civil Division)

"Jodie" and "Mary" were conjoined twins. Leaving them joined would result in the death of both of them within six months. A separation operation would certainly result in the death of Mary who was not capable of separate survival but would give Jodie a good prospect of a normal life. The issue was whether such an operation would be lawful despite the fact that it would result in the death of Mary under circumstances making the surgeons *prima facie* liable for murder.

WARD LJ:

"The reality here—harsh as it is to state it, and unnatural as it is that it should be happening—is that Mary is killing Jodie. That is the effect of the incontrovertible medical evidence and it is common ground in the case. Mary uses Jodie's heart and lungs to receive and use Jodie's oxygenated blood. This will cause Jodie's heart to fail and cause Jodie's death as surely as a slow drip of poison. How can it be just that Jodie should be required to tolerate that state of affairs? One does not need to label Mary with the American terminology which would paint her to be 'an unjust aggressor', which I feel is wholly inappropriate language for the sad and helpless position in which Mary finds herself. I have no difficulty in agreeing that this unique happening cannot be said to be unlawful. But it does not have to be unlawful. The six-year-old boy indiscriminately shooting all and sundry in the school playground is not acting unlawfully for he is too young for his acts to be so classified. But is he 'innocent' within the moral meaning of that word? . . . I am not qualified to answer that moral question . . . If I had to hazard a guess, I would venture the tentative view that the child is not morally innocent. What I am, however, competent to say is that *in law* killing that six-year-old boy in self-defence of others would be fully justified and the killing would not be unlawful. I can see no difference in essence between that resort to legitimate self-defence and the doctors coming to Jodie's defence and removing the threat of fatal harm to her presented by Mary's draining her lifeblood. The availability of such a plea of quasi-self-defence, modified to meet the quite exceptional circumstances nature has inflicted on the twins, makes intervention by the doctors lawful."

This view, expressed by Ward LJ, raises complex issues that cannot be fully explored here. For example, in self-defence cases, even against exempted actors such as the small child firing a gun, the defender is acting to protect his *actual* bodily integrity. It has been argued that "this particular norm

---

[178] P.H. Robinson, "Criminal Law Defenses: A Systematic Analysis" (1982) 82 Col. L. R. 199. Alternatively, it may be characterised as when the reasons for acting (defensively) outweigh or defeat the normal reasons that exist against the wrongful conduct.

is inapplicable to the case of bodies that come into existence with a conjoined circulatory system".[179] How does Mary's right to life square with Jodie's "right" to have her killed? On what basis can Mary be said to have "forfeited" her right not to have force used against her?[180] Can it be argued that a "luck-less" person like Mary who has become an "unjustified threat" has "opened up a gap" in her rights?[181] How can Mary be brought within the rationale of self-defence that she has "created a situation in which [her] otherwise protected interests are subject to injury because [she] has stepped outside the area where [she] can legitimately expect to remain free from interference"?[182] Probably the only way of resolving these intractable problems is by turning attention away from the person posing the unjust threat and focusing instead on the defender's normative position and whether he had sufficient reasons for his actions.[183] An alternative, and certainly easier, approach is that these cases of defensive action against a non-culpable actor should be removed from the ambit of self-defence and dealt with as cases of necessity, as a majority of the judges in *Re A (Conjoined Twins: Surgical Separation)* actually did.[184]

The position appears to be different when the defendant is acting in defence of property. In *DPP v Bayer*, it was held that the defence is only available against an unlawful or criminal act. In this case the defendants entered on to private land which was being drilled with genetically modified maize; to prevent the drilling they attached themselves to the tractors being used. On appeal, it was held that the common law "defence of property" was not available to them because the drilling of the seed was not unlawful.[185] While at one level it might be thought appropriate to have a more rigorous requirement in the context of property, it does expose an anomaly: is the law really saying that if one's house were set on fire by, say, a sleepwalker (who is not, therefore, committing a crime), one could do nothing to defend one's property? That cannot be the correct answer.

(i) Innocent third parties

The force used in response to a threat will typically be directed towards the person who is posing the threat; whether innocent or not. Only in exceptional circumstances may a defendant use force against an innocent *third* party in order to either resist personal violence and/or prevent a crime being committed by another.

R. v Hichens [2011] 2 Cr. App. R. 26

The defendant was convicted of assaulting the complainant (his girlfriend) who he had slapped in order to stop her from allowing O (her ex-boyfriend) from entering their apartment; the defendant, with good reason, anticipating violence from O. The trial judge withdrew the common law defence of self-defence and the s. 3 offence of acting in prevention of crime from the jury on the basis that the defences did not extend to situations where force is used against an innocent third party.

---

[179] S. Uniacke, "Was Mary's Death Murder?" (2001) Med. L.R. 208 at 214.
[180] Uniacke, fn.165 above.
[181] J. Horder, "Self-Defence, Necessity and Duress: Understanding the Relationship" (1998) XI *Canadian Journal of Law and Jurisprudence* 143.
[182] T.M. Funk, "Justifying Justifications" (1999) 19 O.J.L.S. 631 at 63.
[183] Gardner, fn.11 above.
[184] Below, p.390.
[185] *DPP v Bayer* [2004] 1 Cr. App. R. 38.

GROSS LJ:

"[30] It is next convenient to focus on two separate strands. The first is whether self-defence at common law and the use of force in the prevention of crime under s.3 of the Criminal Law Act 1967 are capable of extending to the use of force, against an innocent third party, to prevent a crime being committed by someone else. If and in so far as the judge thought that these defences were not capable of extending to the use of force against an innocent third party, we respectfully disagree, and indeed Mr Wicks did not seek to contend otherwise. Although we suspect that the facts capable realistically of giving rise to such a defence will only rarely be encountered, examples can be adduced and two will suffice:

1. A police constable bundles a passerby out of the way to get at a man he believes about to shoot with a firearm or detonate an explosive device;

2. Y seeks to give Z car keys with Z about to drive X, believing Z to be unfit to drive through drink, knocks the keys out of Y's hands and retains them.

As ever the fact that the defence is capable of being advanced is of course a very different question from whether it would succeed."

Appeal dismissed

Reluctantly, the court found that the judge was wrong to withdraw the defence of prevention of crime from the jury, however the conviction was nevertheless safe; the court concluding that the remoteness of the threat posed by O meant that no reasonable jury, even if properly directed, would have acquitted the defendant.

Lord Gross provides two examples of circumstances of when proportionate force may be used against an innocent party in either self-defence or acting in prevention of a crime. Section 76 remains silent on this issue and thus it is upon the common law that we must rely when deciphering which situations (involving innocent third parties) will give rise to the availability of these defences. This leaves yet another aspect of the law on self-defence uncertain.

2. Protected interest

The "protected interests" currently recognised by the common law are protection of self, protection of others, and property.[186] Overlapping these interests to a considerable extent is the further protected interest of acting in the prevention of crime.[187]

It seems only just that innocent persons who are attacked ought to be able to defend themselves and should also be able to go to the aid of their immediate family. But what if friends or even strangers are in need of help; should someone be blamed or protected if they choose to step in? Some authorities, including *Devlin v Armstrong* suggest that there must be "some special nexus or relationship between the person relying on the doctrine to justify what he did in aid of another, and that other."[188] However, it is now clear that no such limitation exists and it makes no difference whether one is defending oneself or a complete stranger.[189] This has important implications for pub and street

---

[186] Criminal Justice and Immigration Act 2008 s.76(10)(b) makes it clear that references to self-defence also includes the defence of other people.

[187] The overlap is not complete, e.g. if one defends oneself against an infant's attack, one is not preventing a "crime". For discussion of acting in prevention of crime, see below, p.335.

[188] *Devlin v Armstrong* [1971] N.I. 13 at 35–36. Bernadette Devlin M.P.'s relationship with her Londonderry constituents was held not to be sufficient.

[189] *R. v Williams (Gladstone)* (1984) 78 Cr. App. R. 276; *Tooley* (1709) 11 Mod. at 250, 88 E.R. at 1020; *Prince* (1875) 2 C.C.R. at 178; *People v Keatley* [1954] I.R. 12.

brawls. A fight between two people can soon escalate with persons who join in claiming that they are acting in defence of others. One may also use physical force to protect one's property.[190] As we shall see, however, one of the real dilemmas here is in defining how much defensive physical force one may use to protect one's property.

C. The Permitted Response

The law recognises the right to protect both personal and proprietary interests.[191] One can use violence to repel an attack. It is clear, however, that there are severe restrictions as to the circumstances in which one is justified in using such force. One does not have *carte blanche* to defend oneself entirely as one chooses. The law will simply not accept that it is justifiable to kill a human being in order to protect a much-loved pet guinea-pig. In order for conduct to be justified, the defender must only use *such force as is necessary* to avert the attack.

In many of the leading self-defence cases the aggressor has been killed. The importance that is attached to the sanctity of life (and the corresponding need for any exception to it to be closely circumscribed) is enshrined in art.2 of the European Convention on Human Rights.

"(1) Everyone's right to life shall be protected by law. No-one shall be deprived of his life intentionally save in execution of a sentence of a court following his conviction of a crime for which this penalty is provided by law.

(2) Deprivation of life shall not be regarded as inflicted in contravention of this article when it results from the use of force which is no more than absolutely necessary:

(a) in defence of any person from unlawful violence;

(b) in order to effect a lawful arrest or prevent the escape of a person lawfully detained."[192]

There are a number of preliminary points that need to be discussed here. First, art.2 of the European Convention on Human Rights deals only with the use of *fatal* force. Thus, it is of no relevance when less defensive force is used. In the interests of clarity and consistency it could be argued that the legal test for self-defence ought to be the same regardless of the level of force used so as to avoid a dual standard being applied. The use of non-lethal force is covered by art.3 (freedom from inhuman treatment) and art.5 (right to liberty and security of the person). These Articles do not contain explicit exceptions (such as those contained with art.2(2)), but the European Court of Human Rights has held that they are subject to an implied exception for injuries inflicted in self-defence.[193] While the attractions of having a single set of rules applying to all situations of self-defence are obvious, there could, nevertheless, be a case for employing a different (more rigorous) test in relation to fatal force given the sanctity of life.

---

[190] *Hussey* (1924) 18 Cr. App. R. 160. See further, Smith, fn.7 above, pp.109–112.
[191] It is clear that if self-defence arises on the facts it should be put to the jury even though the defence has not been raised by the defendant (*DPP v Bailey* [1995] 1 Cr. App. R. 257). The judge should also explain that the prosecution has to prove beyond reasonable doubt that the defendant was not acting in self-defence (*Anderson* [1995] Crim. L.R. 430).
[192] The final exception is: (c) in action lawfully taken for the purpose of quelling a riot or insurrection. Clearly, all three exceptions may be relevant when considering the defence of prevention of crime; below, p.335.
[193] *Rivas v France* [2005] Crim. L.R. 305; *RL and M-J D v France* [2005] Crim. L.R. 307. See further, A. Ashworth and J. Horder, *Principles of Criminal Law*, 7th edn (Oxford: OUP, 2013), p.118.

Secondly, art.2 of the European Convention on Human Rights refers to the "intentional" taking of life only. It has been argued that this means that the action must be taken with the "purpose" of killing and "that a person acting in order to defend themselves or others is not acting for the purpose of killing".[194] However, this view was rejected in *R. (Bennett) v HM Coroner for Inner South London* where it was held that the protection of art.2 is available in respect of unintentional as well as intentional deaths.[195]

Thirdly, it has been argued that art.2 of the European Convention on Human Rights will be confined to cases involving agents of the state but *Bennett* rejects the idea that a different test should be applied in the case of state officials, such as police officers, to that applicable in general to the issue of self-defence.[196]

Richard Buxton, The Human Rights Act and the Substantive Criminal Law [2000] Crim. L.R. 331 at 337–338:

"[U]nder Article 2 the subject has a right to have his life protected *by the state*. That obligation on the state's part is most clearly broken if . . . the killing is by state agents; or possibly where state agents culpably fail to enforce protective measures. But where . . . one citizen simply and unpredictably attacks another, the state, the respondent under Article 2, is only engaged if the *system* created by the state is inadequate to provide the system with protection. [I]t seems almost inconceivable that . . . [the European] Court would hold that the English legal system, including the English law of self-defence, does not give adequate protection to Englishmen against the prospect of being killed by other Englishmen; and even more inconceivable that an English tribunal would feel confident enough to say that that would be the opinion of the Strasbourg Court were the issue to be considered by it."

However, the *system* of English law has been found wanting in relation to protecting children against excessive physical punishment[197] and one cannot confidently predict, therefore, that the law of self-defence between citizens will be safe from challenge.[198]

Finally, art.2 of the European Convention on Human Rights only permits a killing to protect oneself or others against "unlawful violence". English domestic law allows one to act in protection of property. *If* art.2 is extended to cases involving non-lethal force (killing in defence of property would not be protected under current English law), would art.2 cover cases where force is used in protection of property? If not, there is again the prospect of a dual standard emerging: one set of rules for cases falling within the scope of the Convention and another set of rules for the remaining cases.

Accordingly, there has been considerable uncertainty about the extent to which art.2 of the European Convention on Human Rights might impact upon the English law of self-defence. The emphasis placed upon the sanctity of life in art.2 and the need for force used in the exceptions to be "absolutely necessary" appeared to cast some doubt on the compatibility of English Law with art.2. However, as we shall see, that doubt has now receded.[199]

---

[194] J.C. Smith, "The Use of Force in Public or Private Defence and Article 2" [2002] Crim. L.R. 956 at 957 citing *Re A (Conjoined Twins: Surgical Separation)* [2001] Fam. 147 as the authority.

[195] *R. (on the application of Bennett) v HM Coroner for Inner South London* [2006] EWHC 196 (Admin). The court added, however, that it was "not obvious that the absolute necessity requirement is appropriate where the death was neither intended nor foreseeable as an inevitable consequence of the force used" at [22]. See also F. Leverick, "Is English Law Incompatible with Article 2 of the ECHR" [2002] Crim. L.R. 347 and F. Leverick, "The Use of Force in Public or Private Defence and Article 2: A Reply to Professor Sir John Smith" [2002] Crim. L.R. 961.

[196] *Bennett*, above at [27]. On appeal, the Court of Appeal upheld the decision without discussing these particular issues: [2007] EWCA Civ 617.

[197] *A v United Kingdom* (1999) 28 E.H.R.R. 603; below, p.353.

[198] See Leverick, "Is English Law Incompatible with Article 2 of the ECHR", fn.195 above, pp.358–359.

[199] Although with the new section on householder cases in s.76 stating that only grossly disproportionate force will take the defendant outside the defence, this may well again become a live issue.

What is meant by the current requirement of English law that the defender must only use *such force as is necessary to avert the attack*? This involves a consideration of the following issues:

(i)   the necessity for *any* defensive action;

(ii) the amount of responsive force that may be used;

(iii) the duty to retreat; and

(iv) the imminence of the threatened attack.[200]

It is important to emphasise that with each of these one is ultimately balancing the competing interests of the initial aggressor and the defender, but, as the aggressor was the culpable one responsible for starting the violence, the law has tended to tip the scales in favour of the defender.

1. The necessity for any defensive action

It is quite clear that the person seeking to rely upon the defence must believe his action to be necessary; if he is, in reality, the aggressor seeking to disguise his status behind a smoke-screen of self-defence, the defence will not apply to him.[201] However, this does not mean that an initial aggressor is unable to rely on the defence if during an altercation the "tables have been turned".

R. v Keane [2010] EWCA Crim 2514 (Court of Appeal, Criminal Division)

The appellant was convicted of inflicting grievous bodily harm contrary to s.20 of the Offences Against the Person Act 1861. After a night out in several pubs the defendant was offered a lift home by three others he had met in one of the pubs. While stopping at a petrol station an argument broke out between the defendant and one of the other passengers, during which the defendant pushed the other passenger to the ground outside the car. The driver, having been inside the petrol station during this altercation, then returned to the car. After several words were spoken between him and the defendant, the defendant punched the driver hard in the face causing him to fall to the floor, hitting the back of his head heavily on the ground.

HUGHES LJ:

"[17] . . . it is certainly true that it is not the law that the fact that a defendant either started the fight or entered it willingly is always and inevitably a bar to self-defence arising. The law is as stated by Lord Hope, then the Lord Justice General, in the Scottish case of *Burns* 1995 SLT 1090 at 1093H. The Lord Justice General said this:

'it is now clear that the propositions in Hume and Macdonald that the accused must not have started the trouble, or provoked the quarrel, are stated too broadly. It is not accurate to say that a person who kills someone in a quarrel which he himself started, by provoking it or entering into it willingly, cannot plead self defence if his victim then retaliates. The question whether the plea of self defence is available depends, in a case of that kind, on whether the retaliation is such that the accused is entitled then to defend himself. That

---

[200]   As *R. v Harvey (Nadia Anne)* [2009] EWCA Crim. 469 makes clear, not all the elements of the defence will be relevant in any one case and thus need not be mechanically recited to the jury.

[201]   See also, *R. v Rashford (Nicholas)* [2006] Crim. L.R. 547. It is clear, however, that the defence will not succeed where the defendant uses force which, *unknown to him*, is justified by the circumstances: *Dadson* (1850) 4 Cox C.C. 358. See B. Hogan, "The *Dadson* Principle" [1989] Crim. L.R. 679 and R. L. Christopher, "Unknowing Justification and the Logical Necessity of the *Dadson* Principle in Self-Defence" (1995) 15 O.J.L.S. 229.

depends upon whether the violence offered by the victim was so out of proportion to the accused's own actings as to give rise to the reasonable apprehension that he was in an immediate danger from which he had no other means of escape, and whether the violence which he then used was no more than was necessary to preserve his own life or protect himself from serious injury.' . . .

[18] As to its practical application, we would commend attention to the recent decision of this court in *Harvey* [2009] EWCA Crim 469, which judgment we shall append to the present judgment. We venture to suggest that practitioners will gain a good deal of help from Moses LJ's treatment in Harvey of the proper approach to cases when self-defence arises. In that case the court considered a direction given by the judge inviting the jury to consider whether 'the tables had been turned'. It seems to us that that kind of homely expression, like 'the roles being reversed', can quite well encapsulate the question which may arise if an original aggressor claims the ability to rely on self-defence. We would commend it as suitable for a great many cases, subject only to this reminder. Lord Hope's formulation of the rule makes it clear that it is not enough to bring self-defence into issue that a defendant who started the fight is at some point during the fight for the time being getting the worst of it, merely because the victim is defending himself reasonably. In that event there has been no disproportionate act by the victim of the kind that Lord Hope is contemplating. The victim has not been turned into the aggressor. The tables have not been turned in that particular sense. The roles have not been reversed.

[19] Thirdly, however, in the present case the central proposition advanced on behalf of this defendant contains a fundamental flaw. It may well be true that if D provokes V to hit him, and succeeds so that V gives way to the invitation, V is acting unlawfully when he does so. It does not however follow that D thereby becomes entitled to rely on self-defence. There are many situations where two people are fighting and both are acting unlawfully, by which we mean other than in self-defence. It is true of every voluntary fight, challenge laid down and accepted. It is true of most fights in which one person deliberately incites and the other cheerfully responds with an unlawful use of force. We need to say as clearly as we may that it is not the law that if a defendant sets out to provoke another to punch him and succeeds, the defendant is then entitled to punch the other person. What that would do would be to legalise the common coin of the bully who confronts his victim with taunts which are deliberately designed to provide an excuse to hit him. The reason why it is not the law is that underlying the law of self-defence is the commonsense morality that what is not unlawful is force which is reasonably necessary. The force used by the bully in the situation postulated is not reasonably necessary. On the contrary, it has been engineered entirely unreasonably by the defendant. Exactly the same point emerges clearly from Lord Hope's formulation in Burns. In the situation postulated there has been no disproportionate reaction from the victim which removes from the defendant the quality of the aggressor and reverses the roles. Of course it might be different if the defendant set out to provoke a punch and the victim unexpectedly and disproportionately attacked him with a knife. That is not the case that we are considering."

Appeal dismissed

(i) Honest belief that force is necessary

What is the position if the response is not in fact necessary, but the defendant *genuinely* believes it is (because, say, he mistakenly believes he is about to be attacked)? It used to be thought that such a defendant would only escape liability if his mistake was a reasonable one.[202] In *Williams (Gladstone)*,[203] however, it was held by the Court of Appeal that the defendant's mistake need not be reasonable. Instead, he had to be judged according to his view of the facts.[204] In *Oatridge*, the Court of Appeal concluded that the defendant, who had been abused by her partner on previous occasions, was entitled to have her mistaken view of the incident, which led to her fatally stabbing him, considered by the jury.

---

[202] e.g. *Rose* (1884) 15 Cox 540, where the defendant shot and killed his father whom he mistakenly thought was killing his mother by cutting her throat; *Albert v Lavin* [1982] A.C. 546.

[203] *R. v Williams (Gladstone)* (1984) 78 Cr. App. R. 276.

[204] This was confirmed in *Beckford v The Queen* [1988] A.C. 130 and applied, for example, in *R. v Drane (Paul)* [2008] EWCA Crim 1746 and *R. v Faraj (Shwan)* [2007] EWCA Crim 1033.

"[T]he possibility of the appellant honestly believing that on this occasion the victim really was going to do what he had previously threatened—even if this was not in fact what he was going to do—was not so fanciful as to require its exclusion."[205]

The Criminal Justice and Immigration Act 2008 confirms the common law in this regard.[206]

As has already been noted, self-defence is regarded as a *justificatory* defence. This, however, can only be the case where the defendant is actually acting in self-defence. Where he has made a mistake and is, therefore, attacking the interests of an *innocent* party, his actions cannot be *justified* as not involving any wrongdoing. But in these cases, the law has decided that such a mistake negates blameworthiness and *excuses* the defendant from blame.[207] This whole approach of excusing all honest mistakes, even if unreasonable, is highly questionable. Suppose two police officers see a man in a car. They think he is a dangerous, wanted criminal. They stop the car to arrest the man. Genuinely believing him to be a violent criminal who would shoot them to effect an escape, they beat him nearly to death with their guns. It transpires that the victim is a completely innocent man. According to *Williams (Gladstone)* and s.76(3), the actions of the police officers must be judged according to their view of the facts. On that basis, assuming their response was not excessive, they will escape all liability.[208] That is because the officers thought force was necessary. Now, if their mistake was a reasonable one—i.e. if the facts were such that all reasonable police officers would similarly have thought that the man in the car was the wanted criminal and that it was necessary to use force against him—we have sympathy with the police officers' actions and would wish to exempt them from blame and criminal liability (leaving aside, for the moment, the issue of whether their response might have been excessive). However, if their mistake was an unreasonable one—if there were no reasonable grounds for thinking that the man was the wanted criminal or that he would attack them—then, surely, our response is entirely different. We are now appalled at the enormity of their error. We blame the police officers for making such an unreasonable mistake—and blame them to an extent that we feel they should be made criminally accountable for their actions. In other words, the former requirement that the defendant's mistake had to be based on reasonable grounds not only mitigated the practical difficulty of proving whether the defendant actually held the belief or not, but also reflected a more fundamental attitude towards the determination of culpability.

It is in this context that art.2 of the European Convention on Human Rights may come into play. There have been a number of decisions in which the European Court of Human Rights has held that in determining whether the killing was "absolutely necessary" the honest beliefs of the defenders must be based on "good reason".[209] In *Bubbins v UK*,[210] it was stated that the defendant must have an "honest belief, for good reason". However, having said this, the court then devoted much of its judgment to emphasising the actual belief of the police at the time the victim was shot. While it is possible to argue that s.76(3) might be incompatible with art.2, in *Bennett*, it was stated that the English rules

---

[205] *R. v Oatridge (Ganor)* [1992] Crim. L.R. 205 at 206.

[206] Criminal Justice and Immigration Act 2008 s.76(3), (4) and (5). See below, pp.335–336. As Rogers comments, "neither in principle nor on policy grounds can one defend treating the drunkard more harshly" than, for example, the incorrigible racist who wrongly believes himself to be under attack for that reason: fn.176 above, p.319.

[207] See further, Uniacke, fn.165 above, Ch.2 where she offers a more complex analysis of justification and excuse, based in part on a distinction between objective and agent-perspectival viewpoints.

[208] This is broadly what occurred in *Finch and Jardine* (Unreported, Central Criminal Court, October 12–19, 1982). See also P.A.J. Waddington, "'Overkill' or 'Minimum Force'" [1990] Crim. L.R. 695.

[209] *McCann v United Kingdom* (1996) 21 E.H.R.R. 97; *Andronicou v Cyprus* (1998) 25 E.H.R.R. 491; *Gul v Turkey* (2002) 34 E.H.R.R. 28.

[210] *Bubbins v UK* (2005) 41 E.H.R.R. 24.

on self-defence where someone is killed are not incompatible with the European Court of Human Rights.[211]

However, arguing that the approach taken in *Williams (Gladstone)* is misconceived does not necessarily mean that the old reasonableness test should simply be resurrected. If the assessment of reasonableness is based upon typical male responses to violence, then change is necessary. What is needed is a test that is capable of taking into account the characteristics of the defender, including, for example, prior history. The question ought to be whether it was reasonable for *that* person to have used such force in *that* situation. This will be considered further in the context of the next issue. In the meantime, as a result of *Williams (Gladstone)* as codified, we are unable to distinguish between those who, when every consideration has been taken of the anguish of the situation, are still blameworthy and those whom we would wish to excuse. In other words, as long as the belief that force is needed is an honest one, it matters not that other reasonable people would not have considered force necessary.[212]

2. The amount of responsive force must be reasonable in the circumstances

It has long been accepted that the defender may only use such force as is reasonable in the circumstances. The general rule is that the response must be proportionate to the attack. A person acting to repel an unlawful attack is, at the same time as trying to protect himself or others, usually also acting to prevent a crime. This latter situation was put on a statutory basis by the following provision.

Criminal Law Act 1967 s.3

"3.—(1) A person may use such force as is reasonable in the circumstances in the prevention of crime,[213] or in effecting or assisting in the lawful arrest of offenders or suspected offenders or of persons unlawfully at large.

(2) Subsection (1) above shall replace the rules of the common law on the question when force used for a purpose mentioned in the subsection is justified by that purpose."

Both s.3 and the common law rules relating to defensive force now have to be read in the light of s.76.

Criminal Justice and Immigration Act 2008 s.76

"76 Reasonable force for purposes of self-defence etc.

(1) This section applies where in proceedings for an offence—

(a) an issue arises as to whether a person charged with the offence ("D") is entitled to rely on a defence within subsection (2), and

(b) the question arises whether the degree of force used by D against a person ("V") was reasonable in the circumstances.

(2) The defences are—

---

[211]   *R. (on the application of Bennett) v HM Coroner for Inner South London* [2006] EWHC 196 (Admin).

[212]   Although, of course, this may provide evidence that the defendant did not in fact honestly believe force was required.

[213]   See *R. v Morris (Daryl Howard)* [2013] 2 Cr. App. R. 9. where it was held that a taxi driver had acted to prevent the offence of making off without payment by driving onto a pavement whereby he injured a passenger. Note s.3 is not available where the relevant crime has been completed by the time force is applied, *R. v Attwater (Mark Victor)* [2011] R.T.R. 12; See also *R. v Jones (Margaret)* [2006] 2 All E.R. 741 which decided that a crime for the purposes of s.3 was restricted to crimes under domestic law and not international law.

(a) the common law defence of self-defence;

(aa) the common law defence of defence of property; and

(b) the defences provided by section 3(1) of the Criminal Law Act 1967 (c. 58) or section 3(1) of the Criminal Law Act (Northern Ireland) 1967 (c. 18 (N.I.)) (use of force in prevention of crime or making arrest).

(3) The question whether the degree of force used by D was reasonable in the circumstances is to be decided by reference to the circumstances as D believed them to be, and subsections (4) to (8) also apply in connection with deciding that question.

(4) If D claims to have held a particular belief as regards the existence of any circumstances—

(a) the reasonableness or otherwise of that belief is relevant to the question whether D genuinely held it; but

(b) if it is determined that D did genuinely hold it, D is entitled to rely on it for the purposes of subsection (3), whether or not—

(i) it was mistaken, or

(ii) (if it was mistaken) the mistake was a reasonable one to have made.

(5) But subsection (4)(b) does not enable D to rely on any mistaken belief attributable to intoxication that was voluntarily induced.

(5A) In a householder case, the degree of force used by D is not to be regarded as having been reasonable in the circumstances as D believed them to be if it was grossly disproportionate in those circumstances.

(6) In a case other than a householder case, the degree of force used by D is not to be regarded as having been reasonable in the circumstances as D believed them to be if it was disproportionate in those circumstances.

(6A) In deciding the question mentioned in subsection (3), a possibility that D could have retreated is to be considered (so far as relevant) as a factor to be taken into account, rather than as giving rise to a duty to retreat.

(7) In deciding the question mentioned in subsection (3) the following considerations are to be taken into account (so far as relevant in the circumstances of the case)—

(a) that a person acting for a legitimate purpose may not be able to weigh to a nicety the exact measure of any necessary action; and

(b) that evidence of a person's having only done what the person honestly and instinctively thought was necessary for a legitimate purpose constitutes strong evidence that only reasonable action was taken by that person for that purpose.

(8) Subsections (6A) and (7) are not to be read as preventing other matters from being taken into account where they are relevant to deciding the question mentioned in subsection (3).

(8A) For the purposes of this section "a householder case" is a case where—

(a) the defence concerned is the common law defence of self-defence,

(b) the force concerned is force used by D while in or partly in a building, or part of a building, that is a dwelling or is forces accommodation (or is both),

(c) D is not a trespasser at the time the force is used, and

(d) at that time D believed V to be in, or entering, the building or part as a trespasser.

(8B) Where—

(a) a part of a building is a dwelling where D dwells,

(b) another part of the building is a place of work for D or another person who dwells in the first part, and

(c) that other part is internally accessible from the first part, that other part, and any internal means of access between the two parts, are each treated for the purposes of subsection (8A) as a part of a building that is a dwelling.

(8C) Where—

(a)   a part of a building is forces accommodation that is living or sleeping accommodation for D,

(b)   another part of the building is a place of work for D or another person for whom the first part is living or sleeping accommodation, and

(c)   that other part is internally accessible from the first part, that other part, and any internal means of access between the two parts, are each treated for the purposes of subsection (8A) as a part of a building that is forces accommodation.

(8D) Subsections (4) and (5) apply for the purposes of subsection (8A)(d) as they apply for the purposes of subsection (3).

(8E) The fact that a person derives title from a trespasser, or has the permission of a trespasser, does not prevent the person from being a trespasser for the purposes of subsection (8A).

(8F) In subsections (8A) to (8C)—

"building" includes a vehicle or vessel, and

"forces accommodation" means service living accommodation for the purposes of Part 3 of the Armed Forces Act 2006 by virtue of section 96(1)(a) or (b) of that Act.

(9) This section, except so far as making different provision for householder cases, is intended to clarify the operation of the existing defences mentioned in subsection (2).

(10) In this section—

(a)   "legitimate purpose" means—

(i)   the purpose of self-defence under the common law,

(ia)   the purpose of defence of property under the common law, or

(ii)   the prevention of crime or effecting or assisting in the lawful arrest of persons mentioned in the provisions referred to in subsection (2)(b);

(b)   references to self-defence include acting in defence of another person; and

(c)   references to the degree of force used are to the type and amount of force used."[214]

(i) Non-householder cases

What is meant by the words "reasonable" and "disproportionate" force under s.76? English law *used* to insist on a fairly rigorous and objective test of reasonableness. Such an approach can be supported when one recalls that necessary defence amounts to a *justification*:

"[C]haracterizing self-defence as justification . . . involves finding that the attacker's life has become of less value *to society* than the life of the person attacked. To reach this difficult conclusion, the law must make the self-defence elements strict enough to ensure that the attacker was really the more culpable party and that there was really no reasonable alternative to killing him."[215]

However, over the past 30 years or so, English cases have increasingly favoured the interests of the defender.

---

[214]   As amended by Legal Aid, Sentencing and Punishment of Offenders Act 2012, s.148 and Crime and Courts Act 2013 s.43.
[215]   D.L. Creach, "Partially Determined Imperfect Self-Defense: The Battered Wife Kills and Tells Why" (1982) 34 Stan. L.R. 616 at 632.

Re Attorney-General of Northern Ireland's Reference (No.1 of 1975) [1977] A.C. 105 (House of Lords)

The reference arose from a case in which a soldier had been charged with murder for shooting and killing someone whom he had mistakenly thought to be a member of the I.R.A.

LORD DIPLOCK:

"What amount of force is 'reasonable in the circumstances' for the purpose of preventing crime is, in my view, always a question for the jury in a jury trial, never a 'point of law' for the judge . . .

The jury would also have to consider how the circumstances in which the accused had to make his decision whether or not to use force and the shortness of the time available to him for reflection, might affect the judgment of a reasonable man . . . [The jury] should remind themselves that the postulated balancing of risk against risk, harm against harm, by the reasonable man is not undertaken in the calm analytical atmosphere of the courtroom after counsel with the benefit of hindsight have expounded at length the reasons for and against the kind of degree of force that was used by the accused; but in the brief second or two which the accused had to decide whether to shoot or not and under all the stresses to which he was exposed . . .

On the facts that are to be assumed for the purposes of the reference the only options open to the accused were either to let the deceased escape or to shoot at him with a service rifle. A reasonable man would know that a bullet from a self-loading rifle if it hit a human being, at any rate at the range at which the accused fired, would be likely to kill him or injure him seriously. So in one scale of the balance the harm to which the deceased would be exposed if the accused aimed to hit him was predictable and grave and the risk of its occurrence high. In the other scale of the balance it would be open to the jury to take the view that it would not be unreasonable to assess the level of harm to be averted by preventing the accused's escape as even graver—the killing or wounding of members of the patrol by terrorists in ambush and the effect of this success by members of the Provisional I.R.A. in encouraging the continuance of the armed insurrection and all the misery and destruction of life and property that terrorist activity in Northern Ireland has entailed. The jury would have to consider too what was the highest degree at which a reasonable man could have assessed the likelihood that such consequences might follow the escape of the deceased if the facts had been as the accused knew or believed them reasonably to be."

Decision of the Court of Criminal Appeal of Northern Ireland varied

Palmer v The Queen [1971] A.C. 814 (Privy Council)

The appellant, who carried a gun, went with other men to buy ganja. During a dispute they left with the ganja without paying; during the following chase one of the pursuers was shot by the appellant, who was charged and convicted of murder, although he had claimed self-defence.

LORD MORRIS:

"In their Lordships' view the defence of self-defence is one which can be and will be readily understood by any jury. It is a straightforward conception. It involves no obstruse legal thought . . . only common sense is needed for its understanding. It is both good law and good sense that a man who is attacked may defend himself. It is both good law and good sense that he may do, but may only do what is reasonably necessary. But everything will depend upon the particular facts and circumstances. Of these a jury can decide. It may in some cases be only sensible and clearly possible to take some simple avoiding action. Some attacks may be serious and dangerous. Others may not be. If there is some relatively minor attack it would not be common sense to permit some action of retaliation which was wholly out of proportion to the necessities of the situation. If an attack is serious so that it puts someone in immediate peril then immediate defensive action may be necessary . . . If the attack is all over and no sort of peril remains then the employment of force may be by way of revenge or punishment or by way of paying off an old score or may be pure aggression. There may no longer be any link with a necessity of defence. Of all these matters the good sense of the jury will be the arbiter . . . If there has been an attack so that defence is reasonably necessary, it will be recognised that a person defending himself cannot weigh to a nicety the exact measure of his necessary defensive action. If a jury thought that in a moment of unexpected anguish a person attacked had only done what he honestly and instinctively thought was necessary that would be most potent evidence that only reasonable defensive action had been taken. A jury will be told that the defence of self-defence, where the evidence makes the raising possible, will only fail if the prosecution show beyond doubt that what the accused did was not by way of self-defence."

Appeal dismissed

Building on dicta in *Palmer*, subsequent cases such as *Shannon*,[216] *Whyte*[217] and *Scarlett*[218] appeared increasingly to be abandoning the objective requirement. As long as the defendants thought that they were using an appropriate amount of force, it seemed there could be no conviction. This dramatic change of approach was entirely too crude and could have led to the result that the more habituated the defendant was to violence, the more retaliatory force they were allowed to use. The Court of Appeal finally halted the trend towards a completely subjective test.

R. v Owino [1996] 2 Cr. App. R. 128 (Court of Appeal, Criminal Division)

The defendant was charged with assault occasioning actual bodily harm upon his wife. He claimed that the injuries had been caused when he had acted defensively to stop her assaulting him. He was convicted and appealed on the ground (inter alia) that the jury had not been properly directed on the issue of self-defence.

COLLINS J:

"The essential elements of self-defence are clear enough. The jury have to decide whether a defendant honestly believed that the circumstances were such as required him to use force to defend himself from an attack or threatened attack. In this respect a defendant must be judged in accordance with his honest belief, even though that belief may have been mistaken. But the jury must then decide whether the force used was reasonable in the circumstances as he believed them to be . . .

What . . . [Beldam LJ in *Scarlett*] was not saying, in our view (and indeed if he had said it, it would be contrary to authority) was that the belief, however ill-founded, of the defendant that the degree of force he was using was reasonable, will enable him to do what he did . . . [I]f that argument was correct, then it would justify, for example, the shooting of someone who was merely threatening to throw a punch, on the basis that the defendant honestly believed, although unreasonably and mistakenly, that it was justifiable for him to use that degree of force. That clearly is not, and cannot be, the law."

Appeal dismissed

This was an important clarification of the law which quite properly discarded any suggestion of an entirely subjective test.[219] The initial aggressor, in making the attack, is culpable and deserves to forfeit some of his rights but he does not sacrifice every right. Allowing unreasonable retaliatory force to constitute a justification would be, in effect, to endorse it.

The requirement that the degree of force used by the defendant must be proportionate (i.e. reasonable) is an important element of self-defence. It means that English law appears to have done enough to avoid problems with art.2 of the European Convention on Human Rights. Article 2 states that fatal force may be used only if "absolutely necessary". In practice the European Court of Human Rights has looked for a "strictly proportionate" response although there has been a degree of flexibility in

---

[216] *R. v Shannon (James Russell)* (1980) 71 Cr. App. R. 192.
[217] *R. v Whyte (Ese Etenyin)* [1987] 3 All E.R. 416.
[218] *R. v Scarlett (John)* (1994) 98 Cr. App. R. 290. See also *Attorney-General's Reference (No.2 of 1983)* [1984] 2 W.L.R. 465.
[219] See also *R. v Yaman (Tolga)* [2012] EWCA Crim 1075 where the court held that The Criminal Justice and Immigration Act 2008 s.76 makes it clear that the trigger for using force is assessed subjectively while the defendant's response to it must be assessed objectively.

interpreting this.[220] In *R. (Bennett) v HM Coroner for Inner South London*, it was held that the English reasonableness test is compatible with art.2.

> "If any police officer reasonably decides that he must use lethal force, it will inevitably be because it is absolutely necessary to do so. To kill when it is not absolutely necessary to do so is surely to act unreasonably."[221]

It was accepted in this case that allowances must be made for the fact that decisions to use defensive force may be made in the heat of the moment under extraordinary pressure. Section 76 provides several times that the defensive force must be "reasonable in the circumstances" (s.76(1)(b), (3), (6)). This is defined in s.76(6) as "not to be regarded as having been reasonable in the circumstances as D believed them to be if it was disproportionate in those circumstances". Drawing on the precise wording in *Palmer*, s.76(7) states that account should be taken of the fact that the defendant may not be able "to weigh to a nicety" the amount of defensive force to use and that "the evidence of a person's having only done what the person honestly and instinctively thought was necessary for a legitimate purpose constitutes strong evidence[222] that only reasonable action was taken by that person for that purpose."[223] This second formulation is problematic. As Dennis has commented:

> "What is the significance of 'strong evidence'? Does it create some kind of presumption of reasonableness? And suppose the defendant's action was not instinctive, but a considered response to a situation justifying the use of force, as it might be in some cases of military or police operations—is this no longer a case of being strong evidence of reasonableness?"[224]

Rather than clarifying the operation of the common law, therefore, s.76 creates potential problems. However, one thing seems clear. Despite the insistence in s.76 that the defensive action be "reasonable in the circumstances", that action need not *actually* be objectively reasonable. Whether it is "reasonable" will be influenced by the defendant's *perception* of the situation. The more one moves away from an objective standard of proportionality, the more self-defence ceases to have features of a justificatory defence and takes on attributes of an excusatory defence.[225]

(ii) Householder cases

In *Martin*[226] the defendant was convicted of murder having shot a teenage burglar who broke into his isolated Norfolk farmhouse. This case attracted considerable publicity, much of it sympathetic to the defendant.[227] The difficulty is that, for many persons, such a degree of force is the only method

---

[220]   *Andronicou v Cyprus* (1998) 25 E.H.R.R. 491. See commentary by A. Ashworth, [1998] Crim. L.R. 823.

[221]   *R. (on the application of Bennett) v HM Coroner for Inner South London* [2006] EWHC 196 (Admin) at [25], upheld on appeal at [2007] EWCA Civ 61. See also *Bubbins v United Kingdom* (2005) 41 E.H.R.R. 24.

[222]   In *Palmer* the phrase "most potent evidence" was used.

[223]   The courts have noted that the jury, in particular, should be directed as to this principle, *R. v Yaman (Tolga)* [2012] EWCA Crim 1075.

[224]   Dennis, fn.175 above, pp.507–508.

[225]   For a theoretical exploration of objective, subjective and "hybrid" tests for self-defence, see H. Frowe, "A Practical Account of Self-Defence" (2010) 29 Law & Phil. 245.

[226]   *R. v Martin (Anthony Edward)* [2002] 2 W.L.R. 1. See below, p.344.

[227]   S. Yeo, "Killing in Defence of Property" (2000) N.L.J. 730 cites a poll indicating that fewer than 4% of people were in favour of Martin's conviction and sentence. The Government responded to the publicity by issuing "reassurance" to the public about the law (HO Press Release No. 004/2005, January 12, 2005) and the CPS has issued new guidance (below, p.350).

by which they can protect their property. If they are not permitted to use such force, they are in effect condemned to forfeiting their property and having to rely on subsequent legal remedies for redress— remedies that will often be useless. However, one might consider that the alternative is even worse. Are we to allow persons to go round inflicting death or severe personal injuries on others merely in defence of property? This seems to be the view upheld by art.2 of the European Convention on Human Rights. Fatal force may be used if "absolutely necessary", but only in response to "unlawful violence". In *Faraj*, it was held that if the defendant believes that the only threat is to his property rather than the person, reasonable force may be used to detain the intruder but no aggressive force is permitted.[228]

However, this can no longer be said to be true for householder cases. Changes made to s.76 in 2013 mean that cases involving trespassers in the home should now be treated differently to other cases of self-defence. Section 76(5A) states, "In a householder case, the degree of force used by D is not to be regarded as having been reasonable in the circumstances as D believed them to be if it was grossly disproportionate in those circumstances." This is to be contrasted with s.76(6) which states "In a case other than a householder case, the degree of force used by D is not to be regarded as having been reasonable in the circumstances as D believed them to be if it was disproportionate in those circum- stances." This now means that there are two separate tests for what is "reasonable" and "proportion- ate" in cases involving self-defence and defence of property. Notwithstanding the potential confusion this will give rise to in law, it is difficult to justify such a stark divergence in approach to these discrete forms of self-defence. As the court noted in *Bennett* (already outlined above), "[t]o kill when it is not absolutely necessary to do so is surely to act unreasonably". How then can killing in protection of one's property, in circumstances when the force used is disproportionate, ever be justified on the basis of reasonableness? During the second reading speech for the Crime and Courts Bill, the Secretary of State for the Home Department explained the reasoning for new provisions:

> "The Bill . . . delivers on our coalition commitment to ensure that the law is on the side of people who defend themselves when confronted by an intruder in their home. Few situations can be more frightening than when someone's own home is violated. Faced with that scenario, a person will do what it takes to protect themselves and their loved ones. They cannot be expected dispassionately to weigh up the niceties of whether the level of force they are using is proportionate in the circum- stances. If the intruder is injured, perhaps seriously, in such an encounter, the householder should not automatically be treated as the perpetrator where, with hindsight, the force used is considered to have been disproportionate. Clause 30 will ensure that, in such a context, the use of dispro- portionate force can be regarded as reasonable, while continuing to rule out the use of grossly disproportionate force."[229]

The assertion that householder cases are more frightening and threatening than situations where in the heat of the moment an individual must react to a perceived dangerous physical threat (that occurs outside the home) is far from convincing. In fact, the new test for householder cases may prove to make matters worse. For example, Wake asserts that "[t]he new provision, rather than protecting homeown- ers, could instead operate to place homeowners at an increased risk of violent attack . . . [as] 'startled householders' might become more inclined to intervene".[230] In turn, burglars now knowing that they might be killed or at least badly injured during the course of their crime may be more likely to carry dangerous weapons. Whether s.76(5A) will give rise to a "vigilantes charter", as various opponents of

---

[228] *R. v Faraj (Shwan)* [2007] EWCA Crim 1033.
[229] *Hansard*, HC, Vol.449, col.641 (January 14, 2013).
[230] Wake, fn.172 above.

the new provisions have asserted, remains to be seen.[231] What is clear is that the popular media has had a greater impact on self-defence law reform than those who practise this area of law.[232]

(iii) Defendant characteristics and the perception of danger

Section 76 has nothing specific to say about the degree of force that may be used by a householder or non-householder—nor, as we shall see, about the issues of pre-emptive force nor imminence. Further, it has failed to offer a solution to an issue that has beset the common law: how should the law respond when a defendant's perception of the danger he faces is distorted by a mental characteristic that he possesses? We shall see later that in relation to both the defence of duress and the common law of provocation the law has struggled to find an appropriate response. The following case grappled with the question of which characteristics may be taken into account when assessing the reasonableness of the defendant's response when the plea is one of self-defence.

R. v Martin [2002] 2 W.L.R. 1 (Court of Appeal, Criminal Division)

The defendant shot and killed a burglar and was convicted of murder. On appeal, new medical evidence was accepted that he was suffering from a paranoid personality disorder that would have made him perceive a much greater danger to his physical safety than the average person.

LORD WOOLF CJ:

"[It has been accepted in the law of provocation that the jury is] entitled to take into account some characteristic, whether temporary or permanent, which affected the degree of control which society could reasonably expect of a defendant and which it would be unjust not to take into account.

Is the same approach appropriate in the case of self-defence? There are policy reasons for distinguishing provocation from self-defence. Provocation only applies to murder but self-defence applies to all assaults. In addition, provocation does not provide a complete defence; it only reduces the offence from murder to manslaughter. There is also the undoubted fact that self-defence is raised in a great many cases resulting from minor assaults and it would be wholly disproportionate to encourage medical disputes in cases of that sort . . . As a matter of principle we would reject the suggestion that the approach of the majority in *Smith* in relation to provocation should be applied directly to the different issue of self-defence.

We would accept that the jury are entitled to take into account in relation to self-defence the physical characteristics of the defendant. However, we would not agree that it is appropriate, except in exceptional circumstances which would make the evidence especially probative, in deciding whether excessive force has been used to take into account whether the defendant is suffering from some psychiatric condition."

Verdict of manslaughter by reason of diminished responsibility substituted

Leaving aside the obvious absurdity of the view that medical evidence would be inappropriate in a "great many cases resulting from minor assaults" (which is tantamount to asserting that injustice is acceptable if the crime is a minor one), this approach can be supported. Unlike duress, for example, which is an excuse, self-defence provides a justification and so there is good reason to insist that the defendant's response be reasonable without account being taken of individual characteristics.

---

[231] Wake, fn.172 above .

[232] See further, an Editorial in the *Criminal Law Review* back in 2010 which stated: "A great virtue of the reasonableness standard is that it can be applied flexibly and appropriately in different contexts. It is not at all apparent that a 'grossly disproportionate' standard would be appropriate for all these contexts, even assuming that a case could be made for its application to domestic burglary. Different laws of self-defence for different social settings would then present nightmares of definition, to say nothing of the acute policy issues that would be raised. The present law works and is fair. It should be left alone." Editor, "Defending Self-defence" [2010] Crim L.R. 167 at 168.

In the case of *R. v Oye*,[233] the defendant had punched police officers believing they were evil spirits rushing him. There was psychiatric evidence before the jury at the Crown Court that the defendant was insane at the applicable time. The defendant appealed his conviction on the basis that the judge had failed adequately to address the issue of self-defence based on the fact that an insanely held delusion on the defendant's part that he was being attacked, causing him to respond violently, had entitled him to be acquitted on the basis of reasonable self-defence. The court held that the defendant could not rely on his delusional belief to support a claim that he had used reasonable force in self-defence because "[a]n insane person cannot set the standards of reasonableness as to the degree of force used by reference to his own insanity."[234] If such a claim was to succeed it would have "most disconcerting" implications as "[i]t could mean that the more insanely deluded a person may be in using violence in purported self-defence the more likely that an entire acquittal may result".[235]

3. The duty to retreat

It can be argued that if it is possible to escape from the attack by retreating then it is unnecessary and unreasonable to use defensive force.

Joseph H. Beale, "Retreat from a Murderous Assault" (1903) 16 Harv.L.Rev. 567 at 580–582:

"The conclusion of the courts which deny the duty to retreat is, as we have seen, more commonly rested upon two arguments: that no one can be compelled by a wrongdoer to yield his rights, and that no one should be forced by a wrongdoer to the ignominy, dishonor, and disgrace of a cowardly retreat.
As to the argument of right, the . . . law does not ordinarily secure the enjoyment of rights; it grants redress for a violation of rights . . .
    The argument based upon the honor of the assailed is more elusive and more difficult to answer . . . The feeling at the bottom of the argument is one beyond all law; it is the feeling which is responsible for the duel, for war, for lynching; the feeling which leads a jury to acquit the slayer of his wife's paramour; the feeling which would compel a true man to kill the ravisher of his daughter. We have outlived dueling, and we deprecate war and lynching; but it is only because the advance of civilization and culture has led us to control our feelings by our will. And yet in all these cases sober reflection would lead us to realize that the remedy is really worse than the disease. So it is in the case of killing to avoid a stain on one's honor. A really honorable man, a man of truly refined and elevated feeling, would perhaps always regret the apparent cowardice of a retreat, but he would regret ten times more, after the excitement of the contest was past, the thought that he had the blood of a fellow-being on his hands. It is undoubtedly distasteful to retreat; but it is ten times more distasteful to kill."

Glanville Williams, Textbook of Criminal Law, 1st edn (1978), p.461:

"[I]t seems unreasonable to require a token retreat by one who has not been involved in any kind of aggression. There is no point in requiring a token yielding away from one who is wholly to blame. The only value of a token yielding is to show a disinclination to fight on the part of a person who has previously shown that inclination."
    English law used to adopt a strict approach that a "retreat to the wall" was required before extreme

---

[233] *R. v Oye* [2014] 1 Cr. App. R. 11.
[234] *R. v Oye*, above at [47].
[235] *R. v Oye*, above at [45]. The defendant could, however, rely on the defence of insanity. Note that the physical characteristics of the defendant can be considered. For example, if the defendant is physically handicapped or is a pregnant woman (to borrow examples from duress) and less able to escape or use lesser force, this can be taken into account in assessing whether the actions were reasonable. This approach opens up the possibility of (weaker) women being permitted a wider range of defensive action against (stronger) men.

force could be justified.[236] Since then, however, there has been considerable amelioration of the rule. In *Julien* the law was stated thus:

> "It is not, as we understand it, the law that a person threatened must take to his heels and run in the dramatic way suggested . . . but what is necessary is that he should demonstrate by his actions that he does not want to fight. He must demonstrate that he is prepared to temporise and disengage and perhaps to make some physical withdrawal; and to the extent that that is necessary as a feature of the justification of self-defence, it is true, in our opinion, whether the charge is a homicide charge or something less serious."[237]

In *McInnes*,[238] this was accepted as an accurate statement of the law but Edmund-Davies LJ added that a failure to retreat is only one of the factors to be taken into account in determining the reasonableness of the defendant's conduct. This approach was confirmed in the case of *Bird*[239] and has now been adopted within s.76(6A), which states "[i]n deciding the question mentioned in subsection (3), a possibility that D could have retreated is to be considered (so far as relevant) as a factor to be taken into account, rather than as giving rise to a duty to retreat." This may militate against a woman who fails to leave a repeatedly violent partner being able to plead self-defence.

Katherine O'Donovan, "Defences for Battered Women Who Kill" (1991) 18 J. Law and Society 219 at 222, 235:

"Despite the abolition of the duty to retreat, retreat might be considered an appropriate response. In the context of killing following prolonged domestic violence the questions look rather different. There may be a history of previous retreat which, as it were, has not worked. How relevant is the previous relationship of those involved, the lack of a safe place to go, the ideology of family privacy, the presence of children? . . . leaving without one's children may seem a frightening prospect. But women's own accounts reveal emotional ties to the abuser which increase the difficulty of leaving. If the legal process is to come to terms with this it will have to accept that for many women connection to others is important. In other words, women's ways of looking at relationships will have to be valued equally with those of men.'

4. The imminence of the threatened attack

In Western films, the two protagonists tend to stand at opposite ends of a dusty street, each with his fingers hovering near his holster ready to draw and fire. In such films (apart from the occasional good one) the "baddie" will draw first; the "goodie" will then follow suit; he will inevitably be the quicker on the draw and the "baddie" will be killed. The film will then end with the "goodie" looking brave and honourable. The "baddie" drew first. The "goodie" was thus fully justified in acting in self-defence.

In such an example the threat is clearly imminent. But what is the case where the time between the threat and defensive action is drawn out? Section 76 is silent on the meaning of "imminence". In *Hichens*, Lord Gross simply notes:

> "Plainly both the common law and statutory defences have greater scope for operation where it is certain or nearly certain that a crime will be committed immediately if action is not taken.

---

[236]   Subject to certain exceptions: a person was not under a duty to retreat if he was in his own home or if it would leave his family or friends in danger.

[237]   *R. v Julien (Thomas)* (1969) 53 Cr. App. R. 407 at 411.

[238]   *R. v McInnes (Walter)* (1971) 55 Cr. App. R. 551.

[239]   *R. v Bird (Debbie)* [1985] 1 W.L.R. 816.

Conversely, the lower the degree of likelihood of a crime being committed and the greater the time between awareness of the risk and the time when the crime might be committed, so the scope for any defence to have any realistic prospect of success will be correspondingly reduced, even recognising, as we of course do, the subjective element in these defences."[240]

Furthermore, what if the "goodie" in our example above is the person to draw first in *anticipation* that violence will ensue? A plea of anticipatory self-defence would be meaningless in a Hollywood Western. By reaching for his gun first he would have become the aggressor. Life, however, is not lived on a Hollywood film-set and the criminal law has to reflect life as it is and mirror everyday values. Restricting rights of self-defence to purely defensive retaliation could effectively condemn some innocent persons to death or other injury. The problem may be particularly acute where a substantial difference in size and strength exists, as may well be the case when a woman is attacked by a man. In certain limited circumstances the law must permit the right to strike first. As Lord Griffiths said in *Beckford*, "A man about to be attacked does not have to wait for his assailant to strike the first blow or fire the first shot; circumstances may justify a pre-emptive strike."[241]

The problem, however, is in defining the parameters of such a right. Allowing too much anticipatory defensive action could become a charter for vigilantism.

Devlin v Armstrong [1971] N.I. 13 (Court of Appeal for Northern Ireland)

The defendant, during a riot in Londonderry, urged others to build barricades and throw petrol bombs at the police. She was convicted of riotous behaviour and incitement to riotous behaviour. She appealed on the basis that she thought her action necessary to prevent people being assaulted and property damaged by the police.

MACDERMOTT LJ:

"The plea of self-defence may afford a defence where the party raising it uses force, not merely to counter an actual attack, but to ward off or prevent an attack which he has honestly and reasonably anticipated. In that case, however, the anticipated attack must be imminent: see *R. v Chisam* (1963) 47 Cr.App.R.130 . . . and the excerpt from Lord Normand's judgment in *Owens v H.M. Advocate* (1946) S.C.(J.) 119 which is there quoted and which runs:

'In our opinion self-defence is made out when it is established to the satisfaction of the jury that the panel believed that he was in imminent danger and that he held that belief on reasonable grounds. Grounds for such belief may exist though they are founded on a genuine mistake of fact'. . .

However reasonable and convinced the appellant's apprehensions may have been, I find it impossible to hold that the danger she anticipated was sufficiently specific or imminent to justify the actions she took as measures of self-defence."

Appeal dismissed

In *Georgiades*,[242] the defendant was charged with possession of a firearm with intent to endanger life contrary to s.16 of the Firearms Act 1968. Police visited his flat. He came on to the balcony with

---

[240] [2011] 2 Cr.App.R.26 at [31]. See also, *R. v Keane* [2010] EWCA Crim 2514, discussed above.
[241] *Beckford v The Queen* [1988] A.C. 130 at 144. In *R. v Murphy (Michael Anthony)* [2007] EWCA Crim 2810, the Court of Appeal held that the jury does not necessarily have to be explicitly informed that pre-emptive force may be used in self-defence.
[242] *R. v Georgiades (Michael)* [1989] 1 W.L.R. 759.

a loaded shotgun and raised it to waist level before being arrested. He believed he was in danger of being attacked and had not realised his visitors were police officers. On appeal, it was held that self-defence should have been put to the jury. Accordingly, his conviction was set aside and a conviction for possessing a shortened firearm without a licence contrary to ss.1 and 4 of the Firearms Act 1968 was substituted.[243]

Malnik v DPP [1989] Crim. L.R. 451 (Queens Bench Divisional Court)

The appellant, acting as an "adviser" to X went to "visit" one J who was thought to have taken two of X's valuable cars without authority. As J was known to have a tendency to violent and irresponsible behaviour, the appellant (who was accompanied by three others) armed himself with a rice flail (two pieces of wood joined by a chain which the appellant was capable of using in connection with the martial arts). He was arrested approaching J's house. He was charged with having an offensive weapon in a public place without lawful authority or reasonable excuse contrary to s.1 of the Prevention of Crime Act 1953. The appellant argued that he had a reasonable excuse for having the flail with him, namely, that he had reasonable cause to believe that he was in imminent danger of being subjected to a violent attack. The appellant was convicted and appealed.
It was held

"dismissing the appeal, the magistrate had correctly concluded that as a matter of law the defence of reasonable excuse was not available to the appellant. The case of *Evans v Hughes* [in which it was held that there could be a defence to a charge of carrying an offensive weapon if there was 'an imminent particular threat affecting the particular circumstances in which the weapon was carried' [1972] 3 All E.R. 412] and *R. v Field* [one cannot drive people off the streets and compel them not to go to places where they might lawfully be because they might be subjected to an attack there—[1972] Crim.L.R.435] were distinguishable. Ordinarily, individuals could not legitimately arm themselves with an offensive weapon in order to repel unlawful violence which such individual had knowingly and deliberately brought about by creating a situation in which violence was liable to be inflicted. It was quite different where those concerned with security and law enforcement were concerned. If private citizens set out on expeditions such as this, armed with offensive weapons, the risk of unlawful violence and serious injury was great, and obvious. The policy of the law must therefore be against such conduct, which conclusion was consistent with the very narrow limits which previous decisions had imposed on the freedom of the citizen to arm himself against attack. It had been rightly concluded that the risk of violence could have been avoided and thus the need to carry weapons, by inviting the appropriate agency to repossess the cars by the usual means."

Appeal dismissed

Subsequently, the courts have emphasised how limited the circumstances are in which the defendant will be able to avoid liability for offences such as possessing a firearm with intent to endanger life: the risk of harm must be imminent.[244] Thus under the common law the part played by the requirement of imminence was pivotal. Research into battered women who kill reveals that it is this element that causes most difficulty. In Ewing's study of 100 cases of battered women who killed, he found certain features to be common: years of violence, inadequate help from the community and the police, an

---

[243] See also *Attorney-General's Reference (No.2 of 1983)* [1984] 2 W.L.R. 465 where the court held "[t]he defence of lawful object is available to a defendant against whom a charge under section 4 of the [Explosive Substances] Act of 1883 has been preferred, if he can satisfy the jury on balance of probabilities that his object was to protect himself or his family or his property against imminent apprehended attack and to do so by means which he believed were no more than reasonably necessary to meet the force used by the attackers." See further, D. Lanham, "Offensive Weapons and Self-defence" [2005] Crim. L.R. 85.

[244] See also *R. v Salih (Guner)* [2007] EWCA Crim 2750. See also D. Ormerod, "Firearms: possessing a firearm with intent to endanger life" [2008] Crim. L.R. 386.

inability to leave the situation and a killing that anticipated further violence or followed it, but did not fit the requirement of imminence.[245] A number of cases have involved women who have waited until their husbands were asleep before killing them.[246] This removed all possibility of pleading self-defence even though it may have seemed the only way out to the defendants. Other cases have concerned women who have gone to the kitchen to fetch a knife with which to respond to the attack.[247] Again, this could remove the possibility of pleading self-defence. Until the recent reforms to the partial defence of provocation, it might also have been deemed to be such "cooling down" time as to remove the possibility of this plea. The new partial defence of loss of control (which replaces provocation) does not contain the requirement that the loss of control be "sudden and temporary" and this means that such defendants may be able to plead either loss of control or diminished responsibility.[248]

It seems that the time-scale within which pre-emptive defensive action might be taken would be stretched when, as in the above cases, no actual violence had been used. But as Glanville Williams has pointed out

"[T]here is a distinction between the immediacy of the necessity for acting and the immediacy of the threatened violence. The use of force may be immediately necessary to prevent an attack in the future."[249]

Moreover, as has been stated before, in determining the necessity for acting at all, one does not have to jettison the requirement of reasonableness (as *Williams (Gladstone)* has done) in order to do justice to the differing sizes and strengths of attacker and defender.

The Criminal Law Revision Committee recommended the retention of the imminence rule: "it is desirable to make it clear that a man is not allowed to take the law into his own hands by striking before self-defence becomes necessary."[250] This view was reflected in the Draft Criminal Code Bill 1989.[251] However, the Law Commission subsequently concluded that the jury would be able to decide whether the use of pre-emptive force was reasonable without any specific reference to a requirement of imminence.[252] Accordingly, no reference was made to it in the Draft Bill. This approach had much to commend it because it raises the possibility, at least, of self-defence being available to battered women who kill. However, this cannot lead to the conclusion that the government adopted the Law Commission's view. All that s.76 does is to codify the common law, which as we have seen, upholds the requirement of imminence. An opportunity to improve the law has, thus, been lost.

5. Excessive self-defence

A successful plea of self-defence justifies the defendant's conduct and he goes free. Accordingly, despite the potential for s.76 to broaden the defence, the courts (aside from householder cases) are likely to continue to regard it as a rigorous test to satisfy. Where defendants who act in self-defence in public use excessive force the defence fails. Other defendants, such as the battered woman in *Ahluwalia*, who kill their violent partner while he is asleep, being fearful of violence when he awakes

---

[245] C.P. Ewing, *Battered Woman Who Kill: Psychological Self-Defence as Legal Justification* (Lanham: Lexington Books, 1987).
[246] *R. v Ahluwalia (Kiranjit)* (1993) 96 Cr. App. R. 133.
[247] *R. v Thornton (Sara Elizabeth) (No.1)* (1993) 96 Cr. App. R. 112.
[248] Below, pp.725–757.
[249] *Glanville Williams, Textbook of Criminal Law*, 2nd edn (London: Stevens & Sons, 1983), p.503.
[250] Criminal Law Revision Committee, 14th Report, fn.102 above, para.286.
[251] Law Com. No.177 (1989), fn.21 above, cl.44.
[252] Draft Criminal Law Bill 1993, Law Com. No.218 (1993), paras 39.6–39.7.

and knowing from past experience that their strength is inadequate to match his, will similarly fail to come within the test.[253] As we have seen, this is, however, no longer the case where the defendant acts in defence of their property during a home invasion. This means that we now have two separate tests for self-defence: one which rejects excessive force for defensive force used in the public domain and one that permits disproportionate force within the home.

This leads to the question, should excessive or premature defensive actions outside the home be regarded as completely unjustified? In terms of assessing their moral culpability, such persons are clearly not on a par with those who cold-bloodedly kill or injure others. Their reasons for acting are understandable. It is only the execution of those actions that is unacceptable. In short, there is a strong case for excusing, or at least partially excusing, such actors. Where the injuries inflicted are short of death, the fact that they were acting in self-defence can be taken into account as a mitigating factor in sentencing. But where they kill, the only verdict is murder with a mandatory sentence of life imprisonment.

In an effort to circumvent such injustice, courts have increasingly allowed such persons to avail themselves of the partial defences to murder. For example, battered women who kill are being afforded defences of diminished responsibility and loss of control which result in manslaughter verdicts. Apart from the fact that these defences do not cover all cases, this whole approach misses the point in fair labelling terms. If a person's reasons for acting are self-defensive and he is not acting *because* of an abnormality of mind or loss of control, what is needed is a defence—or partial defence—that accurately explains why he is not guilty of murder. Such thinking has led to increasing calls for the introduction of a new partial defence to murder termed "excessive self-defence", which would result in a manslaughter verdict.[254]

Such a defence exists in many other jurisdictions, for example, the Australian courts used to adopt an approach that persons who killed using excessive force were not guilty of murder, but only of manslaughter.[255] They were partially excused:

"[T]he moral culpability of a person who kills another in defending himself but who fails in a plea of self-defence only because the force which he believed to be necessary exceeded that which was reasonably necessary falls short of moral culpability ordinarily associated with murder".[256]

This approach recognised excessive self-defence as a partial excuse. However, the Australian courts have since abandoned this "half-way house"[257] and the House of Lords has confirmed that such an approach is not part of English law.

R. v Clegg [1995] 1 A.C. 482 (House of Lords)

The defendant, a soldier on duty in Northern Ireland, was on patrol when he shot and killed the driver of a stolen car and his passenger. He was charged with murder of the passenger and attempted murder of the driver. The defendant claimed that he had fired four shots in self-defence. The judge

---

[253] See further, S.S.M. Edwards, "Abolishing Provocation and Reframing Self-Defence—the Law Commission's Options for Reform" [2004] Crim. L.R. 181 where the law is condemned as "exorbitantly gendered".

[254] See, for example, Lacey, fn.26 above, pp.124, 129.

[255] *McKay* [1957] V.R. 560; *Howe* [1958] 100 C.L.R. 448. The Report of the Select Committee on Murder and Life Imprisonment, H.L. Paper 78–1, 1989, para. 89 expressed support for this approach. For an comparative analysis of householder's right to kill in England and Wales and Australia, see I. Dobinson and E. Elliott, "A householder's right to kill or injure an intruder under the Crime and Courts Act 2013: an Australian comparison" (2014) 78 J. Crim. L. 80.

[256] *Viro* (1976–78) 141 C.L.R. 88 at 139, per Mason J.

[257] *Zecevic* (1987) 71 A.L.R. 641. See D. Lanham, "Death of a Qualified Defence?" (1988) 104 L.Q.R. 239.

accepted this defence in relation to the first three shots. However, since the fourth shot (which was a significant cause of the passenger's death) was fired after the car had passed and the soldier was thus in no further danger, the defence was rejected. The defendant was convicted of murder and appealed.

LORD LLOYD OF BERWICK:

"Strictly speaking, the [issue of self-defence] does not arise on the facts of the present case. Since the danger had already passed when Private Clegg fired his fourth shot, there could be no question of self-defence, and therefore no question of excessive force in self-defence. But it is convenient to deal with this issue all the same . . . [His Lordship then surveyed the authorities, including *Palmer*.] In other words, there is no half-way house. There is no rule that a defendant who has used a greater degree of force than was necessary in the circumstances should be found guilty of manslaughter rather than murder . . . [S]o far as self-defence is concerned, it is all or nothing. The defence either succeeds or fails. If it succeeds, the defendant is acquitted. If it fails, he is guilty of murder . . . [His Lordship acknowledged the weight to be given to the views of those who argued for reform and concluded] I am not averse to judges developing law, or indeed making new law, when they can see their way clearly, even when questions of social policy are involved . . . But in the present case I am in no doubt that your Lordships should abstain from law-making. The reduction of what would otherwise be murder to manslaughter in a particular class of case seems to me essentially a matter for decision by the legislature, and not by this House in its judicial capacity. For the point in issue is, in truth, part of the wider issue whether the mandatory life sentence for murder should still be retained."

Appeal dismissed

In the wake of Clegg's conviction, the Government announced a review of the law relating to the use of lethal force in self-defence.

Report of the Interdepartmental Review of the Law on the use of Lethal Force in Self-Defence or the Prevention of Crime (1996), para.83:

"The availability of [a manslaughter] verdict might assist in a comparatively small number of cases in which, previously, the outcome had proved contentious. It might help the jury or court to meet the demands of justice where a defendant had acted sufficiently culpably to deserve a criminal conviction, yet had lacked the evil motive usually associated with murder. The review was not convinced, however, that providing an additional option of manslaughter would enable the court or jury to achieve a result which would necessarily always be seen to be just. More options required finer distinctions and judgments to be made. With more borders between cases, there could be more cases that were seen to fall unfairly on the wrong side of the borderline, this time between acquittal and conviction for manslaughter, and between conviction for murder and manslaughter."

Whether or not these reasons are regarded as convincing, the Government rejected any alteration to the law of murder in this respect. However, the matter was subsequently considered by the Law Commission as part of the review of the law of homicide.

Law Commission, Murder, Manslaughter and Infanticide (Law Com No.304), (2006), paras 5.53–5.57:

"Under the present law, if D's killing of V is regarded as an overreaction in self-defence, he or she must be convicted of murder unless he or she can succeed in a plea of provocation . . . D will . . . have to show that the provocation caused him or her to lose self-control at the time of the killing. It is not enough that D was frightened, but still in control of himself or herself.

In some circumstances, cases [such as these] should end in a first degree murder verdict. In our view, however, a rational approach to reaching the right verdict is currently hampered by arbitrariness and unfairness in the way the provocation defence is structured. In particular, D should not be prejudiced because he or she over-reacted in fear or panic . . .

Consequently, we are recommending that the provocation defence should be available where D killed in response to a fear of serious violence. D will be allowed to say that the effect of the fear of the threat, or of the fear of the threat coupled with the impact of the gross violence received, was such that, in the circumstances, someone of D's age and of an ordinary temperament might have reacted in the same or in a similar way . . .

This reform would have the additional benefit of giving Ds . . . more flexibility in how they choose to run their defence. If they are prepared to accept nothing less than total vindication of what they did, then they can plead nothing other than self-defence. In such a case, the outcome sought is complete acquittal . . . If D is not so confident that the jury will find his or her actions to have been fully justified, he or she can plead provocation—in the form of a fear of serious violence—instead of or alongside a plea of self-defence.

Having the latter option reduces the chance that D will be harshly adjudged to have committed first degree murder because the jury finds he or she overreacted. The jury can opt for the middle course: guilty of second degree murder on the grounds of provocation, leaving the judge with discretion over sentence."[258]

This recommendation, whereby using fatal excessive force would have resulted in a conviction for second degree murder by virtue of a reformed defence of provocation, was not adopted in its entirety by the Government. Instead, it has chosen to reform the law of provocation within the existing framework of murder and manslaughter. Section 54 of the Coroners and Justice Act 2009 creates a new partial defence to murder of loss of control. In order to rely upon this defence the defendant must have killed as a result of having lost control (which had a qualifying trigger) and, a person of the defendant's sex and age, with a normal degree of tolerance and self-restraint and in the circumstances of the defendant, might have reacted in a similar way. The relevant qualifying trigger in this context is that the defendant's loss of control was attributable to his fear of serious violence from V against the defendant or another person.[259] If pleaded successfully, liability is reduced to manslaughter. While this is to be welcomed in that it allows for a finer assessment of degrees of blame than is possible under current law, it is not applicable to all current instances of excessive self-defence. A defendant who loses self-control and kills due to a fear of serious violence being used against him will be able to rely on the defence; a defendant who, without loss of control, mistakenly uses a disproportionate amount of defensive force will fall outside the provisions. How common this latter occurrence will be under the potentially wider s.76 is as yet uncertain but the existing guidance from the Crown Prosecution Service on when it is appropriate to bring a prosecution may be indicative of how practice will develop. It may not be in the public interest to prosecute, for example, when it is alleged that the degree of force used is excessive "if the degree of force used is not very far beyond the threshold of what is reasonable." However, when such force "results in death or serious injury, it will be only in very rare circumstances indeed that a prosecution will not be needed in the public interest".[260]

At the same time as the controversy surrounding Private Clegg's conviction, the Government dismissed proposals to abolish the mandatory life sentence for murder.[261] It claimed that release provisions were flexible enough to deal adequately with less heinous murders. Indeed, Private Clegg was released after two and a half years' imprisonment.[262] Now, the fact that the offender acted to any extent in self-defence is regarded as a mitigating factor in the sentencing guidelines for the mandatory life sentence under the Criminal Justice Act 2003.[263] However, with the new provisions on house-

---

[258]   See also, Law Commission, *Partial Defences to Murder*, Law Com. No.290 (2004), paras 4.1–4.31.

[259]   Coroners and Justice Act 2009 s.55(3).

[260]   CPS, *Self-Defence and the Prevention of Crime*, available at *http://www.cps.gov.uk/legal/s_to_u/self_defence/* (last accessed May 2014).

[261]   First report, *Murder: the Mandatory Life Sentence* (H.C. 111, 1995), paras 23–27, 55–58. The Government's Reply, *Murder: the Mandatory Life Sentence* (Cmnd.3346, 1996).

[262]   Subsequently, new evidence was produced which suggested that Clegg may not have fired when the car had passed and a re-trial was ordered.

[263]   Criminal Justice Act 2003 Sch.21, 11(e). See *R. v Roe (Thomas Patrick)* [2008] EWCA Crim 2946.

holder cases potentially leading to complete acquittals for those who use excessive force to protect their homes, the contrast between these outcomes and the mandatory life sentence for those who use disproportionate force in public arenas will become starker than ever.

IV. CHASTISEMENT

Parents are entitled to take reasonable disciplinary measures against their children, including the use of moderate physical punishment, although this defence of "reasonable chastisement" was never meant to protect parents from criminal prosecution if the force used was excessive.[264] Deciding what is "moderate" (and lawful) on the one hand and "excessive" (and unlawful) on the other hand has always been problematic. Indeed, the whole issue of the physical punishment of children is deeply controversial especially in the light of art.3 of the European Convention on Human Rights, which prohibits inhuman or degrading treatment or punishment. In *A v United Kingdom*,[265] a boy was beaten with a cane by his step-father-to-be. The man was subsequently acquitted of assault occasioning actual bodily harm contrary to s.47 of the Offences Against the Person Act 1861, having pleaded reasonable chastisement. The boy's case was taken to the European Court of Human Rights where it was held that the United Kingdom was in breach of art.3 for failing to protect the child from such treatment.[266]

The Government accepted that the ruling required a change in the law to ensure that children would be protected from inhuman or degrading treatment. In 2000, it published a consultation paper in which it proposed to set out the defence of reasonable chastisement on a statutory basis.[267] These modest proposals, which would have required courts to have regard to the nature and context of the treatment, its duration, and its physical and mental effects[268] were subsequently abandoned.[269] However, international and domestic pressure to, at the very least, reform the defence continued.[270] In 2004, the defence was abolished by s.58 of the Children Act 2004 in those instances when physical punishment results in actual bodily harm to the child. It is retained for "mild" smacks where only transient harm is caused. As we shall see, the distinction between assault occasioning actual bodily harm and common assault is far from clear[271] and yet this is now the basis of the distinction between punishment which is unlawful and that which is permitted.

The Government chose to restrict rather than abolish the defence of reasonable chastisement, believing "that it would be quite unacceptable to outlaw physical punishment of a child by a parent. Nor, we believe, would the majority of parents support such a measure. It would be intrusive and incompatible with our aim of helping and encouraging parents in their role."[272] The Government was

---

[264] By nature, duration, degree or inflicted for the gratification of rage: *R. v Hopley* (1860) 2 F.& F. 202.

[265] *A v United Kingdom* (1999) 27 E.H.R.R. 611. See also *Campbell and Cosans v United Kingdom* (1980) 3 E.H.R.R. 531 and *Costello-Roberts v United Kingdom* (1993) 19 E.H.R.R. 12.

[266] The Court did not go so far as to state that all physical punishment of children breached art.3 of the European Convention on Human Rights.

[267] *Protecting Children, Supporting Parents: A Consultation Document on the Physical Punishment of Children* (London: Department of Health 2000).

[268] In order to constitute a breach, the ill-treatment would have to reach a minimum level of severity depending on all the circumstances identified here: para.5.3.

[269] On the basis that with the implementation of the Human Rights Act 1998 courts would, in any event, have to apply *A v United Kingdom*: Department of Health Press release, November 8, 2001. See *R. v H (Assault of Child: Reasonable Chastisement)* [2002] 1 Cr. App. R. 59.

[270] See further, H. Keating, "Protecting or Punishing Children: Physical Punishment, Human Rights and English Law Reform" [2006] 26 *Legal Studies* 394.

[271] See below, p.614.

[272] Above, fn.267, para.2.14.

influenced, in part, by the results of a survey conducted for them in which 88 per cent of respondents believed that it was sometimes necessary to smack a naughty child.[273] Certainly, the practice of physical punishment is widespread: one long-term survey of child-rearing practices revealed that over 60 per cent of parents say that they hit their one-year-olds, that children aged four are very likely to be hit between one and six times a week and that by the age of seven 91 per cent of boys and 59 per cent of girls had been hit or threatened with an implement.[274] However, a survey conducted on behalf of the N.S.P.C.C. found that 58 per cent of people would support law reform if they were sure that parents would not be prosecuted for trivial smacks.[275] It is argued that an outright ban, combined with an educational campaign and a very light touch in relation to prosecutions would do much more to protect children than the present, far from satisfactory, law.

The defence of reasonable chastisement is based on an archaic attitude that regards children as less than people.

"There is an injustice and illogicality in suggesting that it is acceptable to hit children, but that it is quite unacceptable to hit others, or for adults to hit anyone else. Hitting people is wrong—and children are people too."[276] It has also been argued that it unleashes a dangerous power, that some child abuse at least is discipline that has gone too far, and that it perpetuates a cycle of violence: children who have been abused tend in turn to become abusers.[277] Many other European countries have acted to ban the physical punishment of children[278] and it is to be hoped that the UK can be persuaded to follow suit. The immediate prospects are not good: the Government honoured a promise made when the legislation was passed to review it in 2007. Despite evidence, for example, that there was confusion as to what the law is among parents and prosecutors and that it has not deterred parents from continuing to use excessive levels of punishment, the government concluded that smacking is becoming less common and that s.58 has improved legal protection for children. It stated that while it did not condone smacking, it would not be outlawed because "unless there are clear reasons to intervene, parents should be free to bring up children as they see fit."[279]

In the meantime, all corporal punishment in schools is banned by s.131 of the Schools Standards and Framework Act 1998.[280] This was confirmed in the decision of *R. (on the application of Williamson) v Secretary of State for Education and Employment*,[281] in which it was decided that the power of parents to delegate to teachers the right to administer physical punishment at school had been removed by the legislation. The House of Lords accepted the argument that the practice of corporal punishment of children was a manifestation of the religious beliefs of the applicants (teachers and parents of

---

[273] *Protecting Children, Supporting Parents: A Consultation Document on the Physical Punishment of Children* (London: Department of Health 2000), para.2.9. Fewer than 1% of respondents thought punishment reasonable if it left marks and bruises which lasted for more than a few days.

[274] P. Newell, *Children are People Too: Case Against Physical Punishment* (London: Bedford Square, 1989), pp.53–66. See also M. Smith, *A Community Study of Physical Violence to Children in the Home* (1995).

[275] N.S.P.C.C. Press release March 21, 2002, available at *http://www.nspcc.org.uk*.

[276] Newell, fn.274 above, p.12.

[277] Crawford, "The Defence of Discipline: the Case for Abolition" (1982) 1 Med. L.R. 113.

[278] Sweden abolished physical punishment over 30 years ago: see J.E. Durrant, *A Generation without Smacking: the Impact of Sweden's Ban on Physical Punishment* (London: Save the Children Fund, 2000). Scotland came close to introducing a complete ban on hitting children aged under three in 2002. In the event, hitting anyone under the age of 16 on the head, shaking them or using an implement was made illegal: Criminal Justice Act (Scotland) 2003 s.51. See R. Smith, "'You can't hit me now': reforming the law of Scotland on the physical punishment of children" (2002) 17 S.L.T. 145.

[279] *Review of Section 58 of the Children Act 2004 Report* (Cmnd.7232, 2007), para 55. See further, C. Barton, "Hitting your children: common assault or common sense?" [2008] Fam Law 65.

[280] Amending Education Act 1996 s.548. This legislation applies to nursery schools as well as to those providing education for children of compulsory school age and to independent schools as well as state schools.

[281] *R. (on the application of Williamson) v Secretary of State for Education and Employment* [2005] 2 A.C. 246.

certain Christian schools) and, therefore, the ban did interfere with their rights under art.9 of the of the European Convention on Human Rights, enshrined in the Human Rights Act 1998. However, because the ban on physical punishment was justified by the need to protect the rights and freedoms of children art.9 had not been breached. It is, of course, still lawful for the parents to administer mild physical punishment at home for misbehaviour at school as long as it does not result in actual bodily harm.

V. Duress and Necessity

A. Introduction

The defence of *duress* arises where a defendant is threatened by another with death or serious injury if he does not commit a crime. For example, in *Hudson and Taylor*,[282] two girls gave false evidence in an unlawful wounding case in which they were the principal witnesses. When charged with perjury they claimed they had been threatened that they would be "cut up" unless they committed perjury; they had been so frightened that they had duly told the lies in court. It was held that the defence of duress should have been put to the jury. The source of the threat must be another person. This species of duress is sometimes termed "duress by threats".

The defence of *necessity* potentially arises where a defendant claims that she "had" to commit the crime, not because someone was threatening them, but because something (in the shape of surrounding circumstances which may or may not have been caused by a human being) deprived her of any real alternative. In short, she is claiming that she committed a crime to prevent a greater evil. For example, 10 people are climbing a ladder to safety from a vessel that is sinking. One of them is so petrified that he "freezes" on the ladder and cannot be persuaded to move. Eventually, he is pushed from the ladder and dies.[283] If charged with murder the survivors would claim that their actions were necessary and that it was better for one to die so that nine could live.

The defence of duress by threats has long been recognised by English law. However, until fairly recently it was commonly thought that the defence of necessity did not exist in English law. For example, in *Buckoke v Greater London Council*, it was stated (obiter) that the driver of a fire engine was compelled to stop at red traffic lights even though "he sees 200 yards down the road a blazing house with a man at an upstairs window in extreme peril . . . [and if he] waits for that time, the man's life will be lost". [284]

However, since the 1980s, the courts have been actively extending the defence of duress to apply to a broader range of situations where the threat does not necessarily arise from other persons, but where the defendant is faced with a crisis or emergency. This extended defence has been referred to as *duress of circumstances*. For example, in *Martin* the defendant drove his son to work (otherwise he would have been late and at risk of losing his job) because he feared his wife would commit suicide if he did not. He was afforded a defence to a charge of driving while disqualified on grounds of "duress of circumstances":

"English law does, in extreme circumstances, recognise a defence of necessity. Most commonly this defence arises as duress, that is pressure upon the accused's will from the wrongful threats or violence of another. Equally, however, it can arise from other objective dangers threatening the accused or others. Arising thus it is conveniently called 'duress of circumstances'."[285]

---

[282] *R. v Hudson and Taylor* [1971] 2 Q.B. 202.
[283] This seems to have happened during the sinking of the *Herald of Free Enterprise, The Times*, June 13, 1988. See *Re A (Conjoined Twins: Surgical Operation)* [2000] 4 All E.R. 961 at 1041.
[284] *Buckoke v Greater London Council* [1971] Ch. 655 at 668.
[285] *R. v Martin (Colin)* (1989) 88 Cr. App. R. 343 at 344.

R. v Shayler [2001] 1 W.L.R. 2206 (Court of Appeal, Criminal Division)

LORD WOOLF CJ:

"There is no reason of principle or authority for distinguishing the two forms of duress in relation to the elements of the defence which we have identified . . . The decision in *Abdul-Hussain* provides useful clarification of the earlier three pronged definition of necessity . . . It also reflects other decisions which have treated the defence of duress and necessity as being part of the same defence and the extended form of the defence as being nothing more than different labels for essentially the same thing, see *e.g. R. v Conway* [1988] 3 All E.R. 1025 at 1029 where it was said: 'As the learned editors point out in Smith and Hogan, *Criminal Law* (6th ed., 1988) p. 225, to admit a defence of "duress of circumstances" is a logical consequence of the existence of the defence of duress as that term is ordinarily understood, *i.e.* "do this or else". This approach does no more than recognise that duress is an example of necessity. Whether "duress of circumstances" is called "duress" or "necessity" does not matter. What is important is that, whatever it is called, it is subject to the same limitations as the "do this or else" species of duress.'"

It would be tempting, following this, simply to regard duress, duress of circumstances and necessity as three prongs of a single broad defence. However, while such a development might be perceived to be desirable, it would be both misleading and premature to conclude that English law has fully embraced this approach. First, as we shall see, in developing the defence of duress of circumstances the courts have largely, but not universally, accepted that the conditions for its application are the same as for duress by threats. We shall see that the two defences are not completely identical. More significantly, however, the rationale for the application of each defence is still contested. Duress by threats is, classically, seen as an excusatory defence: we understand the plight of the hapless person whose "will is overborne" by terrible threats. Duress of circumstances, however, appears to have a more justificatory flavour. The defendant has committed a crime to prevent something terrible befalling himself or others: he is driven to commit the crime by force of circumstances. Despite the fact that English law has cast this defence in an excusatory mould, duress of circumstances looks more like a synonym for necessity. Indeed, it has been referred to as "necessity by circumstances".[286] Yet, for the courts, the operation of the defence as a justification is reserved for instances of "pure" necessity, such as, life-saving actions by doctors. Defendants pleading that their actions (which involved conspiring to cause criminal damage at an R.A.F. airbase) were necessary to prevent an illegal war in Iraq will be deemed to be pleading excusatory duress of circumstances, if anything, and not justificatory necessity.[287] From the discussion at the start of this chapter, it is clear that the concepts of excuse and justification are themselves problematic: this is compounded here by an as yet developing state of the law. It may well be that a unifying rationale will emerge over time that is cut loose from justification or excuse. An alternative basis might be the reasonableness and proportionality of the defendant's actions. "Of course, an assessment whether a response is reasonable and proportionate must incorporate society's moral and political judgements about what sort of emergencies or threats can be averted."[288] In the meantime, the approach taken by the Court of Appeal,[289] emphasising the context-specific nature of duress by threats, duress of circumstances and necessity, leads one to be cautious about the prospects of the emergence of a single defence.

---

[286] *Quayle* [2005] 2 Cr. App. R. 527 at [35].

[287] *R. v Jones (Margaret)* [2005] Q.B. 259. In fact, this defence was denied to the defendants; below, p.383. See further, J. Gardner, "Direct Action and the Defence of Necessity" [2005] Crim. L.R. 371.

[288] Clarkson, fn.10 above, p.89.

[289] *Quayle* [2005] 2 Cr. App. R. 527. See also Chan and Simester, fn.10 above, where support is expressed for maintaining the distinctions between both justification and excuse and different defences.

This brings us to the second reason for distinguishing the defences. A fully fledged defence of necessity would be far broader than the present defence of duress of circumstances. As will be discussed later, it would involve a pure balancing of evils (whereas under the present law on duress of circumstances there has to be a threat of death or serious injury) and it would be a defence to all crimes (whereas duress of circumstances at present is not a defence to murder). As we shall see, it would be premature to regard such a broad necessity defence as having been accepted into English law.

The extent to which these are separate defences or are simply different labels for three prongs of a single defence will be explored in the following sections. As the three do not all share the same theoretical underpinnings and as they have developed differently and, to some extent, have different rules governing their applicability, they will be dealt with separately.

One final initial point should be made. Frequently, claims that the actions were done out of necessity or because of duress are made late, once the trial has commenced, and not, say, at the point of arrest. The burden to disprove such a claim beyond reasonable doubt is then placed upon the prosecution and it has been argued that this can cause very considerable problems: a claim of duress, it is said, is easily made and far from easily refuted.[290] It is a further reason why, after a period of increasing relaxation of the law, the House of Lords has made an effort to restrain the continued development of the defence of duress.[291]

B. Duress by Threats

As seen, this is the well-established defence that is afforded to persons who are threatened with death or serious injury unless they commit a crime. It is subject to very stringent qualifying conditions.[292]

1. Rationale of duress by threats as a defence

J.F. Stephen, History of the Criminal Law of England, Vol.2 (1883), pp.107–108:

"Criminal law is itself a system of compulsion on the widest scale. It is a collection of threats of injury to life, liberty and property if people do commit crimes. Are such threats to be withdrawn as soon as they are encountered by opposing threats? The law says to a man intending to commit murder, if you do it I will hang you. Is the law to withdraw its threat if someone else says, If you do not do it I will shoot you? Surely it is the moment when temptation to crime is strongest that the law should speak most clearly and emphatically to the contrary. It is, of course, a misfortune for a man that he should be placed between two fires, but it would be a much greater misfortune for society at large if criminals could confer impunity upon their agents by threatening them with death or violence if they refused to execute their commands. If impunity could be so secured a wide door would be opened to collusion, and encouragement would be given to associations of malefactors, secret or otherwise. No doubt the moral guilt of a person who commits a crime under compulsion is less than that of a person who commits it freely, but any effect which is thought proper may be given to this circumstance by a proportional mitigation of the offender's punishment. These reasons lead me to think that compulsion by threats ought in no case whatever to be admitted as an excuse for crime, though it may and ought to operate in mitigation of punishment in most though not in all cases."

---

[290] It is partly because of this that the Law Commission has recommended that if duress becomes a defence to murder and attempted murder that the burden should be placed upon the defendant to show, on balance of probabilities, that they acted under duress: Law Com. No.304 (2006), fn.35 above, para.6.101.

[291] R. v Hasan (Aytach) [2005] 2 A.C. 467 at [20] and [22] per Lord Bingham. The Court of Appeal has followed this lead: see, for example, R. v van Dao (Vinh) [2012] EWCA Crim 1717 at [44]–[49] per Goss LJ.

[292] Law Com. No.304 (2006), fn.35 above, para.6.9.

Law Commission, Report on Defences of General Application (Law Com. No.83) (1977), para.2.14:

"Those who favour the conclusion that duress should not afford a defence which absolves criminal liability contend that it can never be justifiable for a person to do wrong, in particular to do serious harm to another merely to avoid some harm to himself; that it is not for the individual to balance the doing of wrong against the avoidance of harm to himself. They argue that duress does not destroy the will or negative intention in the legal sense, but that it merely deflects the will so that intention conflicts with the wish; in short that it provides a motive for the wrongful act and that motive is, on general principle, irrelevant to whether a crime has been committed."

Abbott v The Queen [1977] A.C. 755 (Privy Council)

LORD SALMON:

"It seems incredible to their Lordships that in any civilised society, acts such as the appellant's whatever threats may have been made to him, could be regarded as excusable or within the law. We are not living in a dream world in which the mounting wave of violence and terrorism can be contained by strict logic and intellectual niceties alone. Common sense surely reveals the added dangers to which in this modern world the public would be exposed, if the change in the law proposed on behalf of the appellant were affected. It might well . . . prove to be a character for terrorists, gang leaders and kidnappers . . . [If the accused were allowed to go free he would now have] gained some real experience and expertise, he might again be approached by the terrorist who would make the same threats . . . [the accused] would then give a repeat performance, killing even more men, women and children. Is there any limit to the number of people you may kill to save your own life and that of your family?"

Those who oppose a defence of duress generally concede that it is a relevant matter to take into consideration in mitigation of sentence. For all crimes other than murder, courts have wide discretionary powers when sentencing and in extreme cases of duress only a minimal sentence need be imposed.[293] In relation to murder, the existence of duress does not figure as one of the bases for mitigating the length of the minimum term to be served.[294]

Thus the arguments against a general defence of duress fall broadly into two groups:

  (i)   the law would lose some of its deterrent effect if duress were allowed as a defence; and

  (ii) the defendant is morally blameworthy and, accordingly, deserves punishment. Because of the duress her blameworthiness might be *less* and so she can receive a mitigated sentence—but she is still, to some extent, morally blameworthy.

(i) Deterrence[295]

Was Stephen correct in asserting that "it is the moment when temptation to crime is strongest that the law should speak most clearly and emphatically to the contrary"? Are the law's threats likely to serve any useful purpose to a person placed in such a perilous situation?

---

[293] M. Wasik, "Duress and Criminal Responsibility" [1977] Crim. L.R. 453; I. Dennis, "Duress, Murder and Criminal Responsibility" (1980) 96 L.Q.R. 208 at 235–237. In *R. v A* [2012] EWCA Crim 434, the Court of Appeal found that there had been no viable case of duress but that the pressure the defendant had experienced had provided powerful mitigation in relation to the sentence for the offence of perverting the course of justice (at [63]).

[294] Criminal Justice Act 2003 Sch.21.

[295] The other utilitarian arguments hardly seem applicable here. A person who has committed a crime because of duress does not need rehabilitation. He is also not a danger to society needing incapacitation (unless, as Lord Salmon suggested in

Ian Dennis, "Duress, Murder and Criminal Responsibility" (1980) 96 L.Q.R. 208 at 234, 236:

"The deterrent argument is clear. If we assume that the accused acted as a reasonable man in not resisting the threat, and that both he and the reasonable man would act in the same way again whatever the attitude of the law, then the imposition of punishment cannot act as either an individual or a general deterrent. It will amount only to the useless infliction of a penalty and, on a utilitarian hypothesis, will therefore be unjustifiable . . .

[A] man under pressure to kill or be killed may well reason correctly that he does, at least, gain time by ignoring the law's prohibition; the alternative of heeding the prohibition and resisting the threat simply leads more quickly to unpleasant consequences. Secondly, if duress is to be taken into account anyway when sentence is passed, then the law's sanction for ignoring its threat is uncertain and may well not be heavy . . . An appeal to the deterrent value of the law disallowing duress as a defence is thus an empty gesture; the deterrent is ineffective because it is not immediate and because it is subverted by admitting duress through the back door as evidence in mitigation."

On the other hand, "[w]e do not and we cannot know what choices may be different if the actor thinks he has a chance of exculpation on the ground of his peculiar disabilities than if he knows that he does not,"[296] and thus:

"[t]here is an argument for saying that we should nourish the hope, however faint, that the threat of punishment may be enough to tip the balance of decision by those who have only doubtfully sufficient fortitude to undergo martyrdom for the sake of a moral principle".[297]

Further, quite apart from general deterrence, there is the more realistic "educative" species of deterrence that "legal norms and sanctions operate not only at the moment of climactic choice but also in the fashioning of values and of character".[298] The denial of a defence of duress would strengthen values so that persons in situations of duress would be less likely to submit to the threats.

(ii) Moral blameworthiness

Is the actor who submits to duress morally blameworthy and responsible for her actions so that she deserves punishment for them?

We saw in Ch.2 that moral responsibility has been traditionally confined to those who choose to break the law and thus *choose* to become subject to criminal liability.

H.L.A. Hart, Punishment and Responsibility (1968), pp.22–23:

"The . . . view is that of society . . . *offering* individuals including the criminal the protection of the laws on terms which are fair . . . because . . . each individual is given a *fair* opportunity to choose between keeping the law required for society's protection or paying the penalty . . .

Criminal punishment . . . consists simply in announcing certain standards of behaviour and attaching penalties for deviation, making it less eligible, and then leaving individuals to choose. This is a method of social control which maximises individual freedom within the coercive framework of law in a number of different ways . . . First, the individual has an option between obeying or paying . . . Secondly, this system not only enables individuals to exercise this choice but increases the power of individuals to identify beforehand periods when the law's punishments will not interfere with them and to plan their lives accordingly."

Abbott v The Queen [1977] A.C. 755, he was to be continually subjected to threats to induce him to commit crimes; this is highly unlikely—a terrorist or gang leader would be extremely foolish to use the same "agent", to whom the police were now alerted, more than once).

[296]   The American Law Institute, Model Penal Code, Tent. Draft No.10 (1960), Comments.
[297]   D. Baker, *Glanville Williams, Textbook of Criminal Law*, 3rd edn (London: Sweet & Maxwell, 2012), p.873.
[298]   Above, fn.296.

The question in duress is whether the actor had this "fair opportunity" to choose between conforming to the law or breaking it. Where the circumstances have overwhelmed his capacity for choice, where his freedom of choice is too restricted, we do not account him blameworthy and responsible. This is what was meant by Lord Widgery CJ in *Kray*,[299] when he spoke of the accused being "so terrified that he ceased to be an independent actor" and what he meant in *Hudson and Taylor*,[300] when he required that the defendant's "will" must have been "overborne"; the threats had to "neutralise the will". This does not mean that the defendant lacked mens rea.[301] Hudson and Taylor both told their lies deliberately and intentionally. As was emphasised by Lord Hailsham in the leading case of *Howe*:

> "[An] unacceptable view is that . . . duress as a defence affects only the existence or absence of mens rea. The true view is stated by Lord Kilbrandon (of the minority) in *Lynch* [1975] A.C. 653 . . . at p.703:
>
> > 'the decision of the threatened man whose constancy is overborne so that he yields to the threat, is a calculated decision to do what he knows to be wrong, and is therefore that of a man with, perhaps to some exceptionally limited extent, a "guilty mind". But he is at the same time a man whose mind is less guilty than is his who acts as he does but under no such constraint.'"[302]

So the basis of the defence of duress is that the defendant did not have an effective opportunity to make a choice as to whether to commit the crime. Of course, in one sense, the defendant does make a choice, but it is only "Hobson's choice". His dilemma is to choose between two "morally unacceptable courses of action".[303] As the external pressure is so great, in a moral sense, it "coerces" the actor into committing the crime. Fletcher describes such conduct as "morally involuntary".[304] Morally involuntary conduct is not blameworthy; the defendant does not deserve punishment.

R. v Ruzic (2001) S.C.C. 24 (Supreme Court of Canada)

LEBEL J:

"Moral involuntariness is also related to the notion that the defence of duress is an excuse . . . In using the expression 'moral involuntariness', we mean that the accused had no 'real' choice but to commit the offence. This recognizes that there was indeed an alternative to breaking the law, although in the case of duress that choice may be even more unpalatable—to be killed or physically harmed . . .

Punishing a person whose actions are involuntary in the physical sense is unjust because it conflicts with the assumption in criminal law that individuals are autonomous and freely choosing agents. It is similarly unjust to penalize an individual who acted in a morally involuntary fashion. This is so because his acts cannot realistically be attributed to him, as his will was constrained by some external force . . . [T]he accused's agency is not implicated in her doing. In the case of morally involuntary conduct, criminal attribution points not to the accused but to the exigent circumstances facing him, or to the threats of someone else."

---

[299] *R. v Kray (Ronald)* [1970] 1 Q.B. 125.
[300] *R. v Hudson and Taylor* [1971] 2 Q.B. 202.
[301] As was suggested by Lord Goddard CJ in *R. v Bourne (Sidney Joseph)* (1952) 36 Cr. App. R. 125. *Fisher* [2004] Crim. L.R. 938 confirms that duress does not negate either the actus reus or the mens rea.
[302] *R. v Howe (Michael Anthony)* [1987] 1 A.C. 417; see also Lord Bridge's similar comments in *Howe* at 436.
[303] J. Horder, "Occupying the Moral High Ground? The Law Commission on Duress" [1994] Crim. L.R. 334 at 340–341.
[304] Fletcher, fn.7 above, p.803.

In England, judges have also made repeated reference to the notion of moral involuntariness in the acceptance of duress as a defence[305]—primarily on the ground that it would be unjust or unfair to punish in such circumstances.[306]

DPP v Lynch [1975] A.C. 653 (House of Lords)

LORD MORRIS:

"[I]t is proper that any rational system of law should take fully into account the standards of honest and reasonable men. By those standards it is fair that actions and reactions may be tested. If then someone is really threatened with death or serious injury unless he does what he is told to do is the law to pay no heed to the miserable, agonising plight of such a person? For the law to understand not only how the timid but also the stalwart may in a moment of crisis behave is not to make the law weak but to make it just. In the calm of the court-room measures of fortitude or of heroic behaviour are surely not to be demanded when they could not in moments for decision reasonably have been expected even of the resolute and the well disposed . . .

The law must, I think, take a common sense view. If someone is forced at gun-point either to be inactive or to do something positive—must the law not remember that the instinct and perhaps the duty of self-preservation is powerful and natural? I think it must. A man who is attacked is allowed within reason to take necessary steps to defend himself. The law would be censorious and inhumane which did not recognise the appalling plight of a person who perhaps suddenly finds his life in jeopardy unless he submits and obeys."

Does recognising "the appalling plight" of the defendant reduce itself to taking motive into account? Norrie points out, "If 'doing justice' to a Lynch means taking into account his motives, it is unclear why 'doing justice' to everyone else means ignoring theirs."[307] Motive is generally irrelevant under the criminal law—because the law seeks to set an objective standard of behaviour—yet there can be no doubt that motives other than the threat of death or serious harm may be compelling. Indeed, as we shall see, this was one of the factors involved in the resistance of English law to the defence of necessity. However, as far as duress is concerned it has to be recognised that it is a "concession to human frailty"[308] which is available only when the threats are extreme. If one adopts the terminology of excuse/justification it is thus best viewed as the former rather than the latter.[309] The defendant has done wrong; he has violated the interests of an innocent person, but because of his appalling predicament, he is excused from blame.[310]

2. Parameters of the defence

In what circumstances may a defendant break the law but escape liability because of duress? When will the circumstances be such that we will not account the defendant blameworthy for their actions or as Gross puts it:

---

[305]   However, it is clear that moral involuntariness is not actually a requirement for the operation of the defence. If it were "the well-established requirements for duress as a defence (e.g. reasonable steadfastness) could have no place in a completely subjectively orientated defence where the only concern was whether the defendant's actions were 'morally involuntary'." Clarkson, fn.10 above, p.83.

[306]   With the exception of murder, attempted murder and some forms of treason.

[307]   A. Norrie, *Crime, Reason and History: A Critical Introduction to Criminal Law* (Cambridge: CUP, 1993), p.166.

[308]   *R. v Howe (Michael Anthony)* [1987] 1 A.C. 417; *R. v Shepherd (Martin Brian)* (1988) 86 Cr. App. R.47.

[309]   There are elements of a justificatory defence, however, which further illustrates the difficulties inherent in classification in relation to this area of law. In Lord Hailsham's speech in *R. v Howe (Michael Anthony)* [1987] A.C. 417, for example, he spoke of the defendant possibly regarding their choice "as the lesser of two evils". In other words, the defendant claims to have done the *right* thing (or, at least, the only reasonable thing) in the circumstances; this is a justificatory claim. The Law Commission rejected the notion of a balancing of harms approach; below, p.361. But see further, J. Horder, "Autonomy, Provocation and Duress" [1992] Crim. L.R.706.

[310]   *R. v Hasan (Aytach)* [2005] 2 A.C. 467 at [19] per Lord Bingham. S. Kadish, "Excusing Crime" (1987) 75 Cal. L. Rev. 257; K.J.M. Smith, "Must Heroes Behave Heroically?" [1989] Crim. L.R. 622.

"[H]ow shall the line be drawn to separate cases in which the constraint is sufficiently powerful to make blame inappropriate from cases in which constraint is simply a challenge to avoid harm to oneself as best one can while doing no harm to others? A line too far in either direction means injustice, for it is not right to allow with impunity harming that should have been avoided, nor is it right to punish for harm whose avoidance cannot reasonably be expected."[311]

John Gardner, "The Gist of Excuses" (1998) 1 Buffalo Criminal Law Review 575 at 578–579:

"The gist of an excuse . . . is precisely that the person with the excuse lived up to our expectations . . . in the *normative* sense. Did she manifest such resilience, or loyalty, or thoroughness, or presence of mind as a person in her situation should have manifested? In the face of terrible threats, for example, did this person show as much fortitude as someone in his situation could properly be asked to show? . . . The character standards which are relevant to these and other excuses are not the standards of our own characters, nor even the standards of most people's characters, but rather the standards to which our characters should, minimally conform."

Essentially, the attribution of blame involves a moral judgment relating, inter alia, to our expectations of how people should act in certain situations. This inevitably involves a comparison between the defendant's response and how we imagine *we,* or other "ordinary people", would respond in that situation. If we perceive that ordinary people would have responded as the defendant did, then we do not blame the defendant for their actions. But if we perceive that ordinary people would have withstood the threats, then we legitimately blame the defendant for a failure to do so.

This test provides us with the key to answering the following questions concerning the parameters of the defence of duress.

(i) Threat of death or serious harm

In making our moral judgment as to whether to blame the defendant, we would surely wish to compare the crime committed with the nature of the threats to which the defendant was exposed. Suppose a defendant had been threatened that his house would be burnt to the ground if he did not steal a tin of beans from the local supermarket. We would not blame a defendant who committed such a crime. Suppose a defendant who had access to the water supply of London was threatened with death or serious bodily harm if she did not place a deadly poison in the water supply. If she poisoned the water and 10,000 people died (as they knew would be the case), we would blame her for her actions because the harm she caused was so much greater than the harm threatened. This "balancing of harms" approach ought not to operate in a rigid mechanistic manner, but it is a useful aid to our moral judgment as to whether to blame the defendant.[312] This is broadly the approach of the Model Penal Code which states that any "use of, or a threat to use, unlawful force against his person[313] or the person of another, which a person of reasonable firmness in his situation would have been unable to resist"[314] will afford a defence of duress. Lord Wilberforce flirted with this notion in *Lynch* when he said that "[n]obody would dispute that the greater the degree of heinousness of the crime, the greater and

---

[311]   H. Gross, *A Theory of Criminal Justice* (New York: OUP, 1979), p.276.
[312]   Fletcher, fn.7 above, p.804.
[313]   Threats to property are surprisingly not included. The Commentary (To Tent. Draft No.8 1958) points out that threats to property are covered by the necessity defence in s.3.02.
[314]   The American Law Institute, Model Penal Code, Proposed Official Draft (1962), s.2.09(1).

less resistible must be the degree of pressure, if pressure is to excuse".[315] In *Howe*, Lord Hailsham said he "believe[d] that some degree of proportionality between the threat and the offence must, at least to some extent, be a prerequisite of the defence under the existing law".[316] English law, however, is committed to the view that only threats of death or serious harm will suffice for a defence of duress.[317] If the threats are less terrible they should be matters of mitigation only.[318]

What is meant be serious harm here? Must this be serious physical harm or will serious psychological harm suffice? For the purposes of offences against the person, the term "grievous bodily harm" has been interpreted to include serious psychiatric harm.[319] Such an approach was rejected in *Baker and Wilkins*[320] but *Shayler*[321] seems to support the view that a threat of serious psychological harm can suffice as it is stated that "protection of the physical and mental well-being of a person from serious harm is still being required". Of course, where the threat is one of serious psychological harm, it will be difficult (but not impossible) to satisfy the test, to be explored shortly, that the threat must be one of imminent harm.[322]

The Court of Appeal has recently stated that it had no doubt that rape would fall within the ambit of serious injury,[323] while in *van Dao*, it commented obiter that its provisional view was that it was "strongly disinclined" to allow a threat of false imprisonment (without any additional threat of serious harm) to suffice for a plea of duress on the basis that any widening of the defence would be ill-advised.[324]

The threat must be extraneous to the offender. In *Rodger and Rose*,[325] it was held that the defence of duress of circumstances was not available to a charge of breaking prison where the defendants claimed that if they had not escaped, they would have committed suicide.[326]

Law Commission, Working Paper No.55, Defences of General Application (1974), paras 16, 17:

"16 . . . We have considered whether a defence of duress could be framed in terms of the balancing of one harm against another, permitting it to be raised only when the harm to be inflicted upon the defendant is greater than the harm which he is obliged to do. For various reasons, however, we regard this as impracticable. In the first place, if the defence was so framed it would follow that where the defendant, to save his own life, imperilled the lives of more than one other person, the defence would be unavailable . . .

Secondly, a test involving the concept of balance of harms cannot, it seems to us, operate satisfactorily where the offences involved are of an entirely different character. There is, for example, no sensible means of weighing a threat of severe injury to the person against an enforced disclosure of information contrary to the Official Secrets

---

[315] *DPP for Northern Ireland v Lynch* [1975] A.C. 653 at 681.
[316] *R. v Howe (Michael Anthony)* [1987] 1 A.C. 417 at 432–433.
[317] *R. v Hudson and Taylor* [1971] 2 Q.B. 202; *DPP for Northern Ireland v Lynch* [1975] A.C. 653; *R. v Conway (Francis Gerald)* [1988] 3 W.L.R. 1238; *R. v Martin (Colin)* (1989) 88 Cr. App. R. 343; *DPP v Davis; DPP v Pittaway* [1994] Crim. L.R. 600.
[318] *R. v Hasan (Aytach)* [2005] 2 A.C. 467 at [22] per Lord Bingham; Law Commission, *Report on Defences of General Application*, Law Com. No.83 (1977), para.2.18.
[319] *R. v Ireland (Robert Matthew); R. v Burstow (Anthony Cristopher)* [1998] A.C. 147.
[320] *R. v Baker (Janet); R. v Wilkins (Carl)* [1997] Crim. L.R. 497.
[321] *R. v Shayler (David Michael)* [2001] 1 W.L.R. 2206.
[322] See further, J. Loveless, "Domestic Violence, Coercion and Duress" [2010] Crim. L.R. 93 where it is argued that this reduces the possibility of female victims of domestic violence pleading duress . See also *R. v A* [2012] EWCA Crim 434 and *R. v GAC* [2013] EWCA Crim 1472.
[323] *R. v A* [2012] EWCA Crim 434 per Lord Judge CJ at [63].
[324] *R. v van Dao (Vinh)* [2012] EWCA Crim 1717 at [33].
[325] *R. v Rodger (Andrew); R. v Rose (Keith John)* [1998] 1 Cr. App. R.143.
[326] This requirement has been insisted upon in *Quayle* [2005] 2 Cr. App. R. 527 in which the "necessity" of using cannabis for pain relief was the basis of defences in a number of appeals heard together. The plea of necessity was rejected: below, p.383.

Act which might lead to a danger to national security. Our provisional conclusion is, therefore, that in defining the kind of threats which are the subject of duress, it must be borne in mind that the basic justification of the defence is that it is a concession to human infirmity in situations of extreme peril.

17. This conclusion leads us to take the provisional view that duress ought for the future to be available only in cases where the threat is a threat of death or of serious injury."

This conclusion was confirmed in cl.25(1) of the Draft Criminal Law Bill 1993. The Law Commission's proposals would restrict the defence to threats of death or *life-threatening* harm where the offence charged is murder or attempted murder.[327] As it is largely accepted that it is the task of the criminal law to set objective standards of behaviour, it is hardly surprising that the defence of duress should be so closely circumscribed. It is only when the threats are extreme that the law can allow individual motive to be an excuse. This does, however, lead to anomalies in the law.[328] The Criminal Damage Act 1971 states that the fact that the defendant acted in order to protect property belonging to himself or another may be a lawful excuse for damage caused.[329]

(ii) Multiple threats

In *Valderrama-Vega*,[330] the defendant was threatened with the disclosure of his homosexuality, was under financial pressure and received threats of death or serious harm. The first two are incapable of amounting to duress but the court held that the jury was entitled to look at the cumulative effect of all of the threats. It was wrong to direct the jury that the threat of death or serious injury had to be the sole reason for him committing the crime. In *Ortiz*,[331] however, a direction that the threat to life be the sole threat was upheld, although the court also thought the use of the word "solely" should normally not be included. The special feature of *Ortiz* appears to have been the possibility of the defendant's actions also being motivated by the large amount of money he was making from dealing in cocaine and on that basis the authority of *Valderrama-Vega* is to be preferred.[332]

(iii) Threats to others

Law Commission, Working Paper No.55, Defences of General Application (1974), para.18:

"[W]e consider that no limitation should be placed upon the persons against whom the threat may be made. Obviously, a threat of imminent death, for example, to the defendant's wife or children ought to suffice for the defence;[333] but it is not, in our view, possible to maintain with confidence that it should not apply also in the case of threats to a friend[334] of the defendant nor, indeed, to someone he does not know. No rational dividing line is discernible in this context."

---

[327]   Law Com. No.304 (2006), fn.35 above, paras 6.73–6.76.
[328]   N. Padfield, "Duress, Necessity and the Law Commission" [1992] Crim. L.R. 778 at 782. See also *Shortland* [1996] 1 Cr. App. R.1 16 where it was held that the defence of marital coercion under Criminal Justice Act s.47 is quite distinct from duress and not confined to threats of physical harm.
[329]   Criminal Damage Act 1971 s.5(2)(b). *R. v Jones (Margaret)* [2005] Q.B. 259; *R. v Baker (Janet); R. v Wilkins (Carl)* [1997] Crim. L.R. 497. See Draft Criminal Code Bill 1989 cl.28(2)(e), Law Com. No.122 (1992).
[330]   *R. v Valderrama-Vega* [1985] Crim. L.R. 220.
[331]   *R. v Ortiz (Fernando)* (1986) 83 Cr. App. R. 173.
[332]   See also *DPP v Bell (Derek)* [1992] Crim. L.R. 176.
[333]   *R. v Ortiz (Fernando)* (1986) 83 Cr. App. R. 173: threats to wife and child sufficed; *R. v K* (1984) 148 J.P. 410: implicit threat to mother sufficed.
[334]   *R. v Wright (Shani Ann)* [2000] Crim. L.R. 510: threat to boyfriend sufficed.

"Duress of circumstances" cases have indicated that the threat can be to the defendant or "some other person",[335] and the Draft Criminal Law Bill 1993 provides that the threat must be to the defendant "or another".[336]

R. v Shayler [2001] 1 W.L.R. 2206 (Court of Appeal, Criminal Division)

The defendant, a former member of M.I.5, was charged with breaching s.1(1) of the Official Secrets Act 1989 by disclosing deficiencies in M.I.5. He claimed that it was necessary to do so because if M.I.5 continued to operate in this manner it would inevitably create a danger to the public. He was convicted and appealed.

LORD WOOLF CJ:

"It is also necessary to consider in greater detail the nature of the responsibility and the category of persons to whom the defendant must owe the responsibility for the purposes of the defence. Mr Shayler contends that, as a member of the government secret services, he owed a responsibility to the general public at large. His acts were necessary to protect a yet to be identified group from among the public for whose protection MI5 had responsibilities who would inevitably suffer because of MI5's incompetence . . .

So in our judgment the way to reconcile the authorities to which we have referred is to regard the defence as being available when a defendant commits an otherwise criminal act to avoid an imminent peril of danger to life or serious injury to himself or towards somebody for whom he reasonably regards himself as being responsible. That person may not be ascertained and may not be identifiable. However, if it is not possible to name the individuals beforehand, it has at least to be possible to describe the individuals by reference to the action which is threatened would be taken which would make them victims absent avoiding action being taken by the defendant. The defendant has responsibility for them because he is placed in a position where he is required to make a choice whether to take or not to take the action which it is said will avoid them being injured. Thus if the threat is to explode a bomb in a building if the defendant does not accede to what is demanded the defendant owes responsibility to those who would be in the building if the bomb exploded."

Appeal dismissed[337]

As this bomb example demonstrates, most endangered strangers can be brought within the test as being persons for whom the defendant "reasonably regards himself as being responsible"[338] provided they can be identified in a general way: for example, persons in a building. On the facts of *Shayler* itself, it was stated that "if it is possible to identify the members of the public at risk this will only be by hindsight. This creates difficulty over the requirement of responsibility".

Where the threat is directed against the defendant, her family or others to whom a direct responsibility is owed, one can legitimately describe the defendant's conduct as being "morally involuntary" and excusable. However, where strangers are involved, it is questionable whether a defendant should be permitted to, say, cause grievous bodily harm to one stranger in order to save another stranger from grievous bodily harm (especially as there must always be a chance, however small, that the threat will not be carried out). This is in effect allowing such defendants to choose between the two strangers. How are they to assess their relative "worth"? Of course, in many cases the harm to be inflicted by the defendant will be much less than that threatened against the stranger and in such

---

[335] *R. v Conway (Francis Gerald)* [1988] 3 W.L.R. 1238; *R. v Martin (Colin)* (1989) 88 Cr. App. R. 343.

[336] Law Com. No.218 (1993), fn.252 above, cl.25(2)(a).

[337] On appeal, the House of Lords declined to discuss these issues on the basis that the facts were "not within measurable distance of affording him a defence of necessity or duress of circumstances" (*R. v Shayler (David Michael)* [2002] 2 All E.R. 477 at 491).

[338] In *R. v Hasan (Aytach)* [2005] 2 A.C. 467, the House of Lords also adopted this test: see Lord Bingham's speech below, p.372.

situations it ought certainly to be an excuse that the defendant committed the crime to save the third party from, at least, serious injury.

(iv) Stipulated crime

Duress by threats is a defence where the defendant is threatened with death or serious injury unless he commits a particular, stipulated crime. What is the position if there is no link between the threat and the offence committed? In *Cole*,[339] the defendant robbed two building societies and claimed that he had done so to pay off a debt to moneylenders who had hit him with a baseball bat and had threatened him and his family. The Court of Appeal held that the defence of duress is only available if the threats are directed at the offence committed. In this case, the moneylenders had not stipulated that he commit robbery in order to meet their demands and there was, therefore, an insufficient nexus between the threat and the offence.

As we shall see, for the defence of "duress of circumstances" there is no requirement that the defendant commit a stipulated crime. For example, in *Martin*,[340] the evil to be averted was his wife committing suicide; the crime committed was driving while disqualified. There was no link between them. There are two views that can be adopted in relation to this. First, while duress and duress of circumstances are largely identical in the conditions for their application, there are differences and this is one of them. Secondly, if they are in reality two "prongs" of the same defence, simply bearing different labels to describe the different situations involved, it could be that *Cole* should no longer be regarded as good law. If a person's will is so overborne by terrible threats that her actions become "morally involuntary", it hardly seems material that they commit a crime other than the one stipulated.

(v) Belief in threat; steadfastness: subjective or objective

There are two issues here. First, what is the position if the defendant thinks that he has been threatened with death or serious injury but a reasonable person in his situation would not have interpreted the threat thus? Secondly, what is the position if the defendant is terrified by the threats and duly commits a crime, but the reasonable person would have "stood his ground" and not committed the crime? As the following two extracts demonstrate, these two questions are often dealt with jointly. However, as each raises rather different issues they will be dealt with separately after the extracts.

Law Commission, Report on Defences of General Application (Law Com. No.83) (1977), paras 2.27, 2.28:

"2.27. The defence of duress is essentially a concession to human weakness in the face of an overwhelming threat of harm by another, and it is therefore right that so far as possible the criteria to be applied should be subjective. It should be sufficient, provided always that there is a threat of harm, that the defendant believes that the threat is of death or serious personal injury and believes that there is no way of avoiding or preventing the threatened harm other than by committing the offence. That a reasonable person would not have so believed may be relevant in testing the defendant's evidence as to his own belief but it should not of itself disentitle the defendant to the defence.
2.28. It may be said that the whole test as to whether the requirements of duress exist should be subjective, but we feel that this would create too wide a defence. Serious personal injury can cover a wide range of threatened harm, and if the defence is to be available even in respect of the most serious offences, it would be unsatisfactory in the final event to dispense with some objective assessment of whether the defendant could reasonably have been

---

[339] *R. v Cole* [1994] Crim. L.R. 582.
[340] *R. v Martin (Colin)* (1989) 88 Cr. App. R. 343.

expected to resist the threat . . . We think that there should be an objective element in the requirements of the defence so that in the final event it will be for the jury to determine whether the threat was one which the defendant in question could not reasonably have been expected to resist. This will allow the jury to take into account the nature of the offence committed, its relationship to the threats which the defendant believed to exist, the threats themselves and the circumstances in which they were made, and the personal characteristics of the defendant. The last consideration is, we feel, a most important one. Threats directed against a weak, immature or disabled person may well be much more compelling than the same threats directed against a normal healthy person."

R. v Graham (1982) 74 Cr. App. R. 235 (Court of Appeal, Criminal Division)

The appellant, who was gay, lived in a flat with his wife and another gay man, K, in a *ménage à trois*. The appellant was taking drugs for anxiety which made him more susceptible to bullying. K was a violent man and was jealous of the appellant's wife. One night after the appellant and K had been drinking heavily, K put a flex round the wife's neck, pulled it tight and then told the appellant to take hold of the other end of the flex and pull on it. The appellant did so for about a minute as a result of which the wife was killed. The appellant was charged with murder, as was K, who pleaded guilty. The appellant pleaded not guilty and in evidence said that he had complied with K's demand to pull on the flex because of his fear of K. The Crown conceded that it was open to the appellant to raise the defence of duress and did not seek to contend that the defence was not available to a principal to murder. In his directions, the judge posed two questions for the jury: (i) the subjective question of whether the appellant took part in the killing because he feared for his life or personal safety as a result of K's words or conduct; and (ii) if so, the objective question of whether, taking into account all the circumstances, including the appellant's age, sex, sexual propensities and other personal characteristics, and his state of mind and the drink and drugs he had taken, it was reasonable for the appellant, because of fear of K, to take part in killing his wife. The judge further stated that the test of reasonableness in that context was whether, having regard to those circumstances, the appellant's behaviour reflected the degree of self-control and firmness of purpose to be expected from a person in today's society. The appellant was convicted of murder and appealed.

LORD LANE CJ:

"[T]he direction appropriate . . . [to the first question] should have been in these words: 'Was this man at the time of the killing taking part because he held a well-grounded fear of death [or serious physical injury] as a result of the words or conduct on the part of King?' The bracketed words may be too favourable to the defendant. The point was not argued before us.

. . . [Counsel for the appellant] contends that no second question arises at all; the test is purely subjective. He argues that if the appellant's will was in fact overborne by threats of the requisite cogency, he is entitled to be acquitted and no question arises as to whether a reasonable man, with or without his characteristics, would have reacted similarly . . .

[Counsel for the Crown], on the other hand, submits that such dicta as can be found on the point are in favour of a second test; this time an objective test . . .

As a matter of public policy, it seems to us essential to limit the defence of duress by means of an objective criterion formulated in terms of reasonableness. Consistency of approach in defences to criminal liability is obviously desirable. Provocation and duress are analogous. In provocation the words or actions of one person break the self-control of another. In duress the words or actions of one person break the will of another. The law requires a defendant to have the self-control reasonably to be expected to the ordinary citizen in his situation. It should likewise require him to have the steadfastness reasonably to be expected of the ordinary citizen in his situation. So too with self-defence, in which the law permits the use of no more force than is reasonable in the circumstances. And, in general, if a mistake is to excuse what would otherwise be criminal, the mistake must be a reasonable one.

It follows that we accept [counsel for the Crown's] submission that the direction in this case was too favourable to the appellant. The Crown having conceded that the issue of duress was open to the appellant and was raised on the evidence, the correct approach on the facts of this case would have been as follows: (1) Was the defendant, or may he have been, impelled to act as he did because, as a result of what he reasonably believed King had said or done, he had good cause to fear that if he did not so act King would kill him or (if this is to be added) cause him serious physical injury? (2) If so, have the prosecution made the jury sure that a sober person of reasonable firmness, sharing the characteristics of the defendant, would not have responded to whatever he reasonably believed King said or did by taking part in the killing? The fact that a defendant's will to resist has been eroded by the voluntary consumption of drink or drugs or both is not relevant to this test.

We doubt whether the Crown were right to concede that the question of duress ever arose on the facts of this case. The words and deeds of King relied on by the defence were far short of those needed to raise a threat of the requisite gravity. However, the Crown having made the concession, the judge was right to pose the second objective question to the jury. His only error lay in putting it too favourably to the appellant."

Appeal dismissed

(a) *Belief in threat*

According to *Graham*, the defendant must *reasonably* believe that he has been threatened with death or serious injury ("the first question").[341] It is interesting that Lord Lane asserts that "consistency of approach in defences to criminal liability is obviously desirable" yet in the self-defence case of *Williams (Gladstone)*,[342] he ruled that the defendant had to be judged according to the facts as he believed them to be. *Graham* has been approved by the House of Lords in *Howe*[343] and has been followed in a number of subsequent cases.[344] Suggestions from the Court of Appeal that an entirely subjective approach should be taken in duress cases[345] have fallen on stony ground: in *Hasan*, Lord Bingham stated that "there is no warrant for relaxing the requirement that the belief must be reasonable as well as genuine."[346]

This is the appropriate approach and the one recommended by the Law Commission.[347] As argued earlier, while mistakes as to justifications (such as self-defence) need only be honest, mistakes as to excuses (such as duress) should have to be reasonable as well. While this argument could potentially be problematic when applied to duress of circumstances which contains elements of a justificatory nature, the fact remains that the English courts have treated duress of circumstances as being an excuse. If excuses are to exempt defendants from liability, they should be plausible—i.e. reasonable—excuses.[348]

(b) *Steadfastness*

It is clear from *Graham* ("the second question") that the defendant must display reasonable steadfastness or bravery. This was also confirmed in *Howe*. The test is that the threats must be such that a person of reasonable firmness *sharing the characteristics of the defendant* would have given way to the threats. There have been a number of cases in which the courts have struggled to distinguish relevant characteristics from those which should be ignored.[349] In *Emery*, for example, the Court of Appeal held

---

341   The threat will usually be express but an implied threat can suffice: see *R. v N* [2007] EWCA Crim 3479.

342   *R. v Williams (Gladstone)* (1984) 78 Cr. App. R. 276.

343   *R. v Howe (Michael Anthony)* [1987] 1 A.C. 417.

344   For example, in *DPP v Davis; DPP v Pittaway* [1994] Crim. L.R. 600.

345   *R. v Martin (David Paul)* [2000] 2 Cr. App. R. 42 and *R. v Safi (Ali Ahmed)* [2004] 1 Cr. App. R. 14.

346   *R. v Hasan (Aytach)* [2005] 2 A.C. 467 at [23].

347   In relation to duress as a defence to murder and attempted murder, Law Com. No.304 (2006), fn.35 above, paras 6.77–6.82. The Law Commission takes the view that this would not prevent the particular circumstances of the defendant being taken into account in determining whether the belief was reasonably held.

348   In *R. v Cairns (John)* [1999] 2 Cr. App. R. 137, a duress of circumstances case, it was emphasised that the defendant must reasonably believe that there was a threat of death or serious injury.

349   *R. v Hegarty* [1994] Crim. L.R. 353 (evidence of emotional instability and a grossly elevated neurotic state inadmissible); *R. v Horne* [1994] Crim. L.R. 584 (evidence that unusually pliable and vulnerable to pressure inadmissible); *R. v Hurst (Marnie Michelle)* [1995] 1 Cr. App. R. 82 (evidence of possible effects upon defendant of child abuse as a child inadmissible);

that medical evidence about "learned or dependent helplessness" was rightly admitted in determining whether the defendant, charged with cruelty to a child, could have withstood threats from the child's father.[350] The following case attempted to synthesise the principles which have emerged.

R. v Bowen [1996] 2 Cr. App. R. 157 (Court of Appeal, Criminal Division)

The defendant was charged with obtaining services by deception. He claimed that he had been forced to do so, having been accosted by two men who threatened him and his family with petrol-bombing if he did not obtain the goods. He was convicted and appealed on the ground that his abnormal suggestibility and vulnerability (low I.Q. was added at the appeal stage) were relevant characteristics not put to the jury as affecting his ability to withstand the threats.

STUART-SMITH LJ:

"[T]he question remains, what are the relevant characteristics of the accused to which the jury should have regard in considering the second objective test? This question has given rise to considerable difficulty in recent cases. It seems clear that age and sex are, and physical health or disability may be, relevant characteristics. But beyond that it is not altogether easy to determine from the authorities what others may be relevant . . .
   [His Lordship then surveyed the case-law.]
   What principles are to be derived from these authorities? We think they are as follows:

(1) The mere fact that the accused is more pliable, vulnerable, timid or susceptible to threats than a normal person are not characteristics with which it is legitimate to invest the reasonable/ordinary person for the purpose of considering the objective test.

(2) The defendant may be in a category of persons who the jury may think less able to resist pressure than people not within that category. Obvious examples are age, where a young person may well not be so robust as a mature one;[351] possibly sex, though many women would doubtless consider they had as much moral courage to resist pressure as men; pregnancy, where there is added fear for the unborn child; serious physical disability, which may inhibit self protection; recognised mental illness or psychiatric condition, such as post traumatic stress disorder leading to learned helplessness.

(3) Characteristics which may be relevant in considering provocation, because they relate to the nature of the provocation, itself will not necessarily be relevant in cases of duress. Thus homosexuality may be relevant to provocation if the provocative words or conduct are related to this characteristic; it cannot be relevant in duress, since there is no reason to think that homosexuals are less robust in resisting threats of the kind that are relevant in duress cases.

(4) Characteristics due to self-induced abuse, such as alcohol, drugs or glue-sniffing, cannot be relevant.

(5) Psychiatric evidence may be admissible to show that the accused is suffering from some mental illness, mental impairment or recognised psychiatric condition provided persons generally suffering from such condition may be more susceptible to pressure and threats and thus to assist the jury in deciding whether a reasonable person suffering from such a condition might have been impelled to act as the defendant did. It is not admissible simply to show that in the doctor's opinion an accused, who is not suffering from such illness or condition, is especially timid, suggestible or vulnerable to pressure and threats. Nor is medical opinion admissible to bolster or support the credibility of the accused.

---

and R. v Flatt (David Sean) [1996] Crim. L.R. 576 (evidence of drug addiction excluded as a self-induced condition not a characteristic).
[350] R. v Emery (Sally Lorraine) (1993) 14 Cr. App. R. (S.) 394. The condition is also known as post-traumatic stress disorder. The defendant was convicted but her sentence was reduced on appeal from four years to 30 months. See also Antar [2004] All E.R. (D) 412.
[351] This relaxation of the standard could not, however, assist the 13-year-old defendant in R. v W [2007] EWCA Crim 1251 because he was charged with murder. See further A. Ashworth, "Murder: defence—young defendant—intention to kill—defendant's father instructing him to assist—murder" [2008] Crim. L.R. 138.

(6) Where counsel wishes to submit that the accused has some characteristic which falls within (2) above, this must be made plain to the judge. The question may arise in relation to the admissibility of medical evidence of the nature set out in (5). If so, the judge will have to rule at that stage. There may, however, be no medical evidence, or, as in this case, medical evidence may have been introduced for some other purpose, *e.g.* to challenge the admissibility or weight of a confession. In such a case counsel must raise the question before speeches in the absence of the jury, so that the judge can rule whether the alleged characteristic is capable of being relevant. If he rules that it is, then he must leave it to the jury.

(7) In the absence of some direction from the judge as to what characteristics are capable of being regarded as relevant, we think that the direction approved in *Graham* without more will not be as helpful as it might be, since the jury may be tempted, especially if there is evidence, as there was in this case, relating to suggestibility and vulnerability, to think that these are relevant. In most cases it is probably only the age and sex of the accused that is capable of being relevant. If so, the judge should, as he did in this case, confine the characteristics in question to these.

How are these principles to be applied in this case? [Counsel for the Crown] accepts, rightly in our opinion, that the evidence that the appellant was abnormally suggestible and a vulnerable individual is irrelevant. But she submits that the fact that he had, or may have had, a low I.Q. of 68 is relevant since it might inhibit his ability to seek the protection of the police. We do not agree. We do not see how low I.Q., short of mental impairment or mental defectiveness, can be said to be a characteristic that makes those who have it less courageous and less able to withstand threats and pressure."

Appeal dismissed

A. Buchanan and G. Virgo, "Duress and Mental Abnormality" [1999] Crim. L.R. 517 at 529–530:

"Diagnosis in psychiatry . . . [has moved] to an 'atheoretical' approach. Less emphasis is placed on causative factors, pathological changes or abnormalities of process underlying each disorder and more emphasis is placed on symptoms and signs. This change presents two related problems for the law as it relates to duress. The first is that, as a result, psychiatric conditions are now 'recognised' according to different criteria than was previously the case and these criteria cannot be relied upon to identify a group of people whose ability to withstand threats is reduced. The second is that if an atheoretical approach is adopted, psychiatric conditions cannot be said to 'cause' any aspect of behaviour because they themselves comprise no more or less than various aspects of behaviour.

It follows that the test . . . in *Bowen* . . . is unworkable and needs to be reformulated. There are two options . . . Second . . . [t]he crucial question would then be whether the defendant could reasonably be expected to have resisted the threat given his or her mental condition. It would not matter that the condition could not be described as recognized."

The Law Commission takes the view that, in so far as duress as a proposed defence to murder and attempted murder is concerned, the jury should be able to take into account all the circumstances of the defendant, including his or her age but not those which bear upon the defendant's capacity to withstand duress. This is controversial. It would mean that two different tests would exist. *Bowen* would continue to apply in non-homicide cases, but a more stringent test would be applied in instances where the crime charged was murder or attempted murder. The Law Commission justifies this in two ways. First, given the seriousness of the offence charged, a strict objective test should be maintained to limit the scope of the defence. Secondly, the defence of diminished responsibility is available for those defendants suffering from mental disorder who might be less able to withstand threats.[352]

However, one must ask whether this steadfastness rule—as under *Bowen* or as reformulated by the Law Commission for murder and attempted murder—serves any useful purpose? Bearing in mind

---

[352] Law Com No.304 (2006), fn.35 above, paras 6.83–6.86.

that duress can only be pleaded if there has been a threat of death or serious injury and that it is not currently a defence to murder, when would it ever be unreasonable to give in to such grave threats?

K.J.M. Smith, "Duress and Steadfastness: In Pursuit of the Unintelligible" [1999] Crim. L.R. 363 at 370, 375:

"Is it being maintained that, when faced with a belief in the threat of death or serious harm, the question is, *should* that defendant have capitulated bearing in mind their personal characteristics? In other words, does the reasonable steadfastness test envisage some defendants of strong emotional or physical disposition who will be denied a defence of duress and who must not choose self-preservation? . . . [N]o coherent function can be assigned to the steadfastness requirement . . .

[T]he presence of a steadfastness test deflects attention away from legitimate defence conditions relating to the neutralization or avoidance of threats . . . [T]he steadfastness requirement cannot coherently relate to anything other than the distinct conditions that defendants take all reasonable opportunities to escape from or neutralize an aggressor's threat."

(vi) Imminence of threat

It is generally stated that the defence of duress is only available if there is a threat of *immediate* harm. Thus in *Gill*,[353] the defendant was threatened with personal violence if he did not steal his employer's lorry. It was held obiter that he probably could not have pleaded duress because there had been a period of time during which he could have raised the alarm and wrecked the whole enterprise. As Lord Morris said in *Lynch*:

"[The question is whether] a person the subject of duress could reasonably have extricated himself or could have sought protection or had what has been called a 'safe avenue of escape'."[354]

This approach can be supported. We would blame someone who had a reasonable opportunity to raise the alarm and wreck the criminal enterprise,[355] but we would not blame someone who had no such opportunity. What is the position if the defendant has an opportunity to seek help but fears that police protection will be ineffective?

R. v Hudson and Taylor [1971] 2 Q.B. 202 (Court of Appeal, Criminal Division)

[The facts are set out, above, p.355.]

WIDGERY LJ:

"In the present case the threats . . . were likely to be no less compelling, because their execution could not be effected in the court room, if they could be carried out in the streets of Salford the same night . . .

[Counsel for the Crown] . . . submits on grounds of public policy that an accused should not be able to plead duress if he had the opportunity to ask for protection from the police before committing the offence and failed to do so. The argument does not distinguish cases in which the police would be able to provide effective protection, from those when they would not, and it would, in effect, restrict the defence of duress to cases where the person threatened had been kept in custody by the maker of the threats, or where the time interval between the making of the threats and the commission of the offence had made recourse to the police impossible . . .

---

[353]   *R. v Gill (Samuel James)* (1963) 47 Cr. App. R. 166. See also *R. v Cole* [1994] Crim. L.R. 582.
[354]   *DPP for Northern Ireland v Lynch* [1975] A.C. 653 at 668.
[355]   A. Ashworth, "Reason, Logic and Criminal Liability" (1975) 91 L.Q.R. 102 at 104.

In the opinion of this court it is always open to the Crown to prove that the accused failed to avail himself of some opportunity which was reasonably open to him to render the threat ineffective, and that upon this being established the threat in question can no longer be relied on by the defence. In deciding whether such an opportunity was reasonably open to the accused the jury should have regard to his age and circumstances, and to any risks to him which may be involved in the course of action relied upon."

Law Commission, Working Paper No.55, Defences of General Application (1974), para.20:

"We recognise that effective protection may not be continuously available; yet it seems to us that a defendant subject to this kind of threat must always be under a duty at least to seek that protection in order to reduce the possibility of its execution and failure to do so through fear of the consequences ought properly to be a factor in mitigation rather than a complete defence."[356]

In *Hudson and Taylor*, the threats could have been reported to the police, but the two young girls, aged 17 and 19, were convinced that the police protection would be ineffective. Are we to blame them for their failure to seek official protection? It would appear that their response was typical of the response of most ordinary girls of that age faced with such a predicament. It would be absurd to assert that the defence of duress would only be available to them if there had been a sniper sitting in court ready to execute his threats immediately. These views were echoed by Lord Griffiths in *Howe*:

"[I]f duress is introduced as a merciful concession to human frailty it seems hard to deny it to a man who knows full well that any official protection he may seek will not be effective to save him from the threat of death under which he has acted."[357]

However, *Hudson and Taylor* has always caused disquiet among some members of the judiciary and commentators: Glanville Williams, for example, described it as "an indulgent decision".[358]

R. v Hasan [2005] 2 A.C. 467 (House of Lords)

[The facts are set out below, p.372]

LORD BINGHAM:

"27. . . . [*Hudson*] had the unfortunate effect of weakening the requirement that execution of a threat must be reasonably believed to be imminent and immediate if it is to support a plea of duress . . . I can understand that the Court of Appeal in *R v Hudson* had sympathy with the predicament of the young appellants but I cannot, consistently with principle, accept that a witness testifying in the Crown Court of Manchester has no opportunity to avoid complying with a threat incapable of execution then or there . . .
28. . . . It should . . . be made clear to juries that if the retribution threatened against the defendant or his family or a person for whom he reasonably feels responsible is not such as he reasonably expects to follow on almost immediately on his failure to comply with the threat, there may be little if any room for doubt that he could take evasive action, whether by going to the police or in some other way, to avoid committing the offence with which he is charged."

---

[356] See also Law Com. No.83 (1977), fn.318 above, paras 2.29–2.3 1.
[357] *R. v Howe (Michael Anthony)* [1987] A.C. 417 at 433.
[358] Baker, fn.297 above, p.884. In *R. v Heath (Patrick Nicholas)* [2000] Crim. L.R. 109 the defence was denied to a defendant who had "more than one avenue of escape open to him" on the basis that he could have gone to the police or his parents. See also *R. v Baker and Ward* [1999] 2 Cr. App. R. 335.

This more robust stance[359] means that the approach taken by the Court of Appeal in *Abdul-Hussain*[360] in the context of duress of circumstances does not apply where the plea is one of duress by threats.[361] This latter case concerned an appeal by a group of Iraqis who had hijacked a Sudanese aeroplane. Their plea was they would be killed if returned to Iraq. Rose VP held that

"the execution of the threat need not be immediately in prospect . . . [and that] the period of time which elapses between the inception of the peril and the defendant's act, and between that act and execution of the threat, are relevant but not determinative factors for a judge and jury in deciding whether duress operates . . . In our judgment, although the judge was right to look for a close nexus between the threat and the criminal act, he interpreted the law too strictly in seeking a virtually spontaneous reaction." [362]

This difference in approach adopted with regard to duress by threats (*Hasan*) and duress of circumstances (*Abdul-Hussain*) to the issue of imminence reinforces the point that these defences are context-sensitive: the more one slides along the continuum from duress to duress of circumstances and through to necessity, the less rigorous this requirement becomes. This is because in cases of duress by threats the rationale for the excuse is that the defendant's "will has been overborne" whereas at the other extreme (necessity) the defendant is making a more rational choice. It was stressed in *Re A (Conjoined Twins)*,[363] a classic case of necessity, that the principle is "one of necessity, not emergency". In this case the death of both twins was not an immediate or even imminent prospect; they could both well have lived for many months. However, as their deaths within that period were a certainty, a severance operation that would kill the weaker twin was a necessity.

(vii) Defendants placing themselves in a position where they might be open to threats

Defendants who join a criminal association (whether terrorist, gangster or otherwise) which could force them to commit crimes can be blamed for their actions. In joining such an organisation fault can be laid at their door and their subsequent actions described as blameworthy. This is the approach adopted by English law which denies the defence of duress to such persons.

R. v Sharp [1987] 1 Q.B. 853 (Court of Appeal, Criminal Division)

The appellant joined a gang of robbers, knowing they used firearms. He participated in a robbery upon a sub-post office but claimed he had been forced to as one of the other robbers had threatened to kill him if he did not carry through the plan. He was convicted of manslaughter and appealed.

LORD LANE CJ:

"No one could question that if a person can avoid the effects of duress by escaping from the threats, without damage to himself, he must do so. In other words if there is a moment at which he is able to escape, so to speak, from the gun being held at his head by Hussey, or the equivalent of Hussey, he must do so. It seems to us to be part of the same argument, or at least to be so close to the same argument as to be practically indistinguishable from it, to say that a man must not voluntarily put himself in a position where he is likely to be subjected to such compulsion . . .

---

359   See also *R. v Aldridge (Jonathan)* [2006] EWCA Crim 1970 and *R. v N* [2007] EWCA Crim 3479.
360   *R. v Abdul-Hussain (Mustafa Shakir)* [1999] Crim. L.R. 570.
361   Alternatively, it is possible that *R. v Abdul-Hussain (Mustafa Shakir)*, above, has been impliedly overruled by *R. v Hasan (Aytach)* [2005] 2 A.C. 467.
362   This passage was approved in *R. v Shayler (David Michael)* [2001] 1 W.L.R. 2206.
363   *Re A (Conjoined Twins: Surgical Separation)* [2001] Fam. 147.

[I]n our judgment, where a person has voluntarily, and with knowledge of its nature, joined a criminal organisation or gang which he knew might bring pressure on him to commit an offence and was an active member when he was put under such pressure, he cannot avail himself of the defence of duress."

Appeal dismissed

R. v Baker and Ward [1999] 2 Cr. App. R. 335 (Court of Appeal, Criminal Division)

The defendants were drug dealers. They got into debt with their suppliers who threatened them with violence and instructed them to rob a store. Their defence to a charge of robbery was that they were acting under duress. They were convicted and appealed.

ROCH LJ:

"In some situations, the evidence may be so clear that the judge will be entitled to rule that the defence is not open to the accused, for example, where the accused has joined a terrorist organisation or a gang of armed robbers . . .

In another type of case, the accused, although not joining a gang or organisation, may have involved himself in criminal activities which bring him into contact with other criminals in circumstances where the accused knew or was aware that if he defaulted in fulfilling his role or in discharging obligations he assumed in relation to the other criminals he would be subjected to such compulsion. Drug dealing on a scale which is significant could be such a case. The present case was a case in which it was appropriate to leave to the jury the question whether the accused had voluntarily put themselves in a position where they were likely to be subjected to duress. The defence of duress will not be available to an accused in this situation if he is aware that there is a risk of pressure by way of violence or threats of death or violence to him or a member of his immediate family being brought to bear upon him. The purpose of the pressure has to be to coerce the accused into committing a criminal offence of the type for which he is being tried. If the accused had no reason to anticipate such pressure, then they would be entitled to rely upon duress."

Appeal allowed[364]

R. v Hasan [2005] 2 A.C. 467 (House of Lords)

The defendant worked as a driver and minder for a woman who ran an escort agency and was involved in prostitution. The woman's boyfriend, Sullivan, had a reputation for violence and was involved in drug dealing. The defendant was charged with aggravated burglary and claimed that he had been forced to commit the offence by Sullivan. He was convicted and appealed. The Court of Appeal allowed the appeal.

LORD BINGHAM:

"22. For many years it was possible to regard the defence of duress as something of an antiquarian curiosity, with little practical application . . . This has changed . . . This is borne out by the steady flow of cases reaching the appellate courts over the last 30 years or so . . . I must acknowledge that the features of duress . . . incline me, where policy choices are to be made, towards tightening rather than relaxing the conditions to be met before duress may be successfully relied upon . . .

29. . . . The Court of Appeal ruled that [the trial judge had misdirected the jury] . . . because the judge had not directed the jury to consider whether the defendant knew that he was likely to be subjected to threats to commit a crime of the type with which he was charged. It is this ruling which gave rise to the certified question on this part of the case, which is:

---

[364] On the basis that the jury was entitled to assistance from the trial judge in identifying the issues of fact which arose for their decision and the judge, by not answering the questions they had asked him, had failed to give them this assistance.

'Whether the defence of duress is excluded when as a result of the accused's voluntary association with others; (i) he foresaw (or possibly should have foreseen) the risk of being subjected to any compulsion by threats of violence, or (ii) only when he foresaw (or should have foreseen) the risk of being subjected to compulsion to commit criminal offences, and if the latter, (iii) only if the offences foreseen (or which should have been fore-seen) were of the same type (or possibly of the same type and gravity) as that ultimately committed.'

The Crown contend for answer (i) in its objective form. The defendant commends the third answer, omitting the first parenthesis . . .

37. The principal issue . . . is whether *R v Baker* correctly stated the law . . . The defendant is seeking to be wholly exonerated from the consequences of a crime deliberately committed. The prosecution must negative his defence of duress, if raised by the evidence, beyond reasonable doubt. The defendant is, ex hypothesi, a person who has voluntarily surrendered his will to the dominion of another. Nothing should turn on foresight of the manner in which, in the event, the dominant party chooses to exploit the defendant's subservience. There need not be foresight of coercion to commit crimes, although it is not easy to envisage circumstances in which a party might be coerced to act lawfully. In holding that there must be foresight of coercion to commit crimes of the kind with which the defendant is charged, *R v Baker* mis-stated the law.

38. There remains the question, which the Court of Appeal left open . . . whether the defendant's foresight must be judged by a subjective or an objective test: i.e. does the defendant lose the benefit of the defence of duress only if he actually foresaw the risk of coercion or does he lose it if he ought reasonably to have foreseen the risk of coercion, whether he actually foresaw the risk or not? I do not think any decided case has addressed this question, and I am conscious that application of an objective reasonableness test to the other ingredients of duress has attracted criticism . . . The practical importance of the distinction in this context may not be very great, since if a jury concluded that a person voluntarily associating with known criminals ought reasonably to have foreseen the risk of future coercion they would not, I think, be very likely to accept that he did not in fact do so. But since there is a choice to be made, policy in my view points towards an objective test of what the defendant, placed as he was and knowing what he did, ought reasonably to have foreseen. I am not persuaded otherwise by analogies based on self-defence or provocation . . . The policy of the law must be to discourage association with known criminals, and it should be slow to excuse the criminal conduct of those who do so. If a person voluntarily becomes or remains associated with others engaged in criminal activity in a situation where he knows or ought reasonably to know that he may be the subject of compulsion by them or their associates, he cannot rely on the defence of duress to excuse any act which he is thereafter compelled to do by them . . .

39. I would answer this certified question by saying that the defence of duress is excluded when as a result of the accused's voluntary association with others engaged in criminal activity he foresaw or ought reasonably to have foreseen the risk of being subjected to any compulsion by threats of violence."

Appeal allowed

Duress is an excuse and, on principle, there ought to be a plausible—or reasonable—excuse for the actions. The basis of the rule here is that a defendant has no plausible excuse and is blameworthy if he associates with such criminal enterprises or organisations. If the risks of compulsion were obvious, even though he gave no thought to them, the case for denying the defence is compelling.[365] However, it is true that Lord Bingham's approach is very robust: all that is required is that there is a foreseeable risk of being subjected to any compulsion by threats of violence. It is not necessary that the defendant foresaw or ought reasonably to have foreseen that he might be the subject of compulsion to commit a particular type of crime or any criminal offence at all.[366] It has been argued that this is unacceptably

---

[365] Under the Draft Criminal Law Bill 1993 cl.25(4), the defence is not available to a person who has knowingly and without reasonable excuse exposed themselves to the risk of a threat (Law Com. No.218 (1993), above). In its report on homicide, the Law Commission commented that the narrower approach adopted in *R. v Hasan (Aytach)* [2005] 2 A.C. 467 "will serve to exclude the most unmeritorious cases where the defence should simply not be available", Law Com. No.304 (2006), fn.35 above, para.6.52.

[366] Judicial Studies Board, *Specimen Directions: 49: Duress by Threats or Circumstances* (2008).

wide and that the defence should only be removed if there are foreseeable threats of serious violence to commit a crime[367] but *Hasan* is clearly the leading authority.[368]

(viii) Length of time after threats

The defendant can only rely upon the defence as long as the threat is operative. In *DPP v Davis; DPP v Pittaway*,[369] both defendants were charged separately with driving with excess alcohol, contrary to s.5(1)(a) of the Road Traffic Act 1988. Both pleaded duress. However, on appeal by way of case stated, the Divisional Court held (on a number of grounds) that there was no evidence of duress. In particular, the fact that one of the defendants had driven for two miles without any suggestion that he was being pursued and that the other had decided to drive off after a five minute pause in which no threat had materialised meant that duress could not apply.[370]

(ix) Crimes to which duress is a defence

If the defendant's conduct can be described as being "morally involuntary", and if we are satisfied that we do not blame the defendant for her actions, because ordinary people would have responded in the same way, it follows that she ought to have a defence to any crime. However, English law adopts the view that duress is a defence to all crimes *except* murder, attempted murder[371] and treason.[372] In *Lynch*, the House of Lords decided that duress was a defence to an accessory to murder but in *Abbott*, the Privy Council ruled that it was not a defence to the principal offender (the one who actually does the killing) of murder. In *Howe*,[373] the House of Lords held that duress was not a defence to murder, irrespective of the degree of participation.

DPP v Lynch [1975] A.C. 653 (House of Lords)

The appellant was ordered to drive members of the I.R.A. in Northern Ireland to a place where they intended to kill, and did kill, a policeman. The appellant claimed that he was convinced that he would be shot if he did not obey. He was convicted of murder, the trial judge holding that the defence of duress was not available to an accessory to murder. The Court of Criminal Appeal in Northern Ireland dismissed his appeal.

LORD MORRIS:

"It may be that the law must deny such a defence to an actual killer, and that the law will not be irrational if it does so.

---

[367] D. Ibbetson, "Duress Revisited" [2004] 64 C.L.J. 530 at 531. See also the speech of Baroness Hale in *R. v Hasan (Aytach)* [2005] 2 A.C. 467 at [77].

[368] It has been applied, for example, in *R. v Ali (Israr)* [2008] EWCA Crim 716 and *R. v Hussain (Mohammed)* [2008] EWCA Crim 1117.

[369] *DPP v Davis; DPP v Pittaway* [1994] Crim. L.R. 600.

[370] See *R. v Pommell* [1995] 2 Cr. App. R. 607; *DPP v Bell (Derek)* [1992] Crim. L.R. 176; *DPP v Jones* [1990] R.T.R. 33; *DPP v Tomkinson* [2001] R.T.R. 38; *DPP v Mullally* [2006] EWHC 3448 (Admin); and *CPS v Brown* [2007] EWHC 3274 (Admin) where similar reasoning was applied in duress of circumstances cases.

[371] *R. v Gotts* [1992] 2 A.C. 412.

[372] "Prosecutions for treason are virtually confined to the circumstances of war. Perhaps in war even the private citizen is expected to cast himself in a heroic mould." (Baker, fn.297 above, p.871). There are, however, dicta in *DPP for Northern Ireland v Lynch* [1975] A.C. 653 to the effect that duress could in some circumstances be a defence to treason. See, for example, Lord Morris at 672.

[373] *R. v Howe (Michael Anthony)* [1987] 1 A.C. 417.

Though it is not possible for the law always to be worked out on coldly logical lines there may be manifest factual differences and contrasts between the situation of an aider and abettor to a killing and that of the actual killer. Let two situations be supposed. In each let it be supposed that there is a real and effective threat of death. In one a person is required under such duress to drive a car to a place or to carry a gun to a place with knowledge that at such place it is planned that X is to be killed by those who are imposing their will. In the other situation let it be supposed that a person under such duress is told that he himself must there and then kill X. In either situation there is a terrible agonising choice of evils. In the former, to save his life, the person drives the car or carries the gun. He may cling to the hope that perhaps X will not be found at the place or that there will be a change of intention before the purpose is carried out or that in some unforeseen way the dire event of a killing will be averted. The final and fatal moment of decision has not arrived. He saves his own life at a time when the loss of another life is not a certainty. In the second (if indeed it is a situation likely to arise) the person is told that to save his life he himself must personally there and then take an innocent life. It is for him to pull the trigger or otherwise personally to do the act of killing. There, I think, before allowing duress as a defence it may be that the law will have to call a halt. May there still be force in what long ago was said by Hale?

'Again, if a man be desperately assaulted, and in peril of death, and cannot otherwise escape, unless to satisfy his assailant's fury he will kill an innocent person then present, the fear and actual force will not acquit him of the crime and punishment of murder, if he commit the fact; for he ought rather to die himself, than kill an innocent.'
(*Hale's Pleas of the Crown*, Vol. 1, p. 51.)"

Appeal allowed: new trial ordered

Abbott v The Queen [1977] A.C. 755 (Privy Council)

The appellant was ordered to kill a girl. He claimed he was afraid that if he did not obey he and his mother would be killed. He dug a hole for the body and held the girl while she was stabbed by another man. She was left dying in the hole while the appellant and others filled in the hole. Both the trial judge and the Court of Appeal of Trinidad and Tobago held that duress was not available as a defence.

LORD SALMON (delivering the majority judgment of their lordships):

"Counsel for the appellant has argued that the law now presupposes a degree of heroism of which the ordinary man is incapable and which therefore should not be expected of him and that modern conditions and concepts of humanity have rendered obsolete the rule that the actual killer cannot rely on duress as a defence. Their Lordships do not agree. In the trials of those responsible for wartime atrocities such as mass killings of men, women or children, inhuman experiments on human beings, often resulting in death, and like crimes, it was invariably argued for the defence that these atrocities should be excused on the ground that they resulted from superior orders and duress: if the accused had refused to do these dreadful things, they would have been shot and therefore they should be acquitted and allowed to go free. This argument has always been universally rejected. Their Lordships would be sorry indeed to see it accepted by the common law of England."

LORD WILBERFORCE AND LORD EDMUND-DAVIES dissenting:

"If the Crown is right, there is no let-out for any principal in the first degree, even if the duress be so dreadful as would be likely to wreck the morale of most men of reasonable courage, and even were the duress directed not against the person threatened but against other innocent people (in the present case, the appellant's mother) so that considerations of mere self-preservation are not operative. That is indeed 'a blueprint for heroism': *S. v Goliath*, 1972 (3) S.A. 1 . . .

The question that immediately arises is whether any acceptable distinction can invariably be drawn between a principal in the first degree to murder and one in the second degree, with the result that the latter *may* in certain circumstances be absolved by his plea of duress, while the former may never even advance such a plea.

The simple fact is that *no* acceptable basis of distinction has even now been advanced . . .

Lynch having been decided as it was, the most striking feature of the present appeal is the lack of any indication, in the judgment of the majority, *why* a flat declaration that in no circumstances whatsoever may the actual killer be absolved by a plea of duress makes for sounder law and better ethics. In truth, the contrary is the case. For example . . . no one can doubt that our law would today allow duress to be pleaded in answer to a charge, under section 18 of the Offences against the Person Act 1861, of wounding with intent. Yet, here again, should the victim die after the conclusion of the first trial, the accused when faced with a murder charge would be bereft of any such defence. It is not the mere lack of logic that troubles one. It is when one stops to consider why duress is *ever* permitted as a defence even to charges of great gravity that the lack of any moral reason justifying its *automatic* exclusion in such cases as the present becomes so baffling—and so important . . .

To hold that a principal in the first degree in murder is never in any circumstances to be entitled to plead duress, whereas a principal in the second degree may, is to import the possibility of grave injustice into the common law."

Appeal dismissed

R. v Howe [1987] 1 A.C. 417 (House of Lords)

Two appellants, Howe and Bannister, participated with others in torturing, kicking, punching and sexually abusing a man. The man was then strangled to death by one of the others. These events were repeated on a second occasion but this time it was Howe and Bannister who themselves killed the victim by strangling him with a shoelace. The appellants claimed that they had acted under duress at the orders of and through fear of one Murray. At their trial the judge, following *Lynch* and *Abbott*, directed the jury that duress could be a defence to the first killing where the appellants were only accessories, but not to the second killing where the appellants were the principal offenders. The Court of Appeal held this was correct. The appellants appealed to the House of Lords.

LORD HAILSHAM LC:

"In general, I must say that I do not at all accept in relation to the defence of murder it is either good morals, good policy or good law to suggest, as did the majority in *Lynch* and the minority in *Abbott* that the ordinary man of reasonable fortitude is not to be supposed to be capable of heroism if he is asked to take an innocent life rather than sacrifice his own. Doubtless in actual practice many will succumb to temptation, as they did in *Dudley and Stephens*. But many will not, and I do not believe that as a 'concession to human frailty' the former should be exempt from liability to criminal sanctions if they do. I have known in my own lifetime of too many acts of heroism by ordinary human beings of no more than ordinary fortitude to regard a law as either 'just or humane' which withdraws the protection of the criminal law from the innocent victim and casts the cloak of its protection upon the coward and the poltroon in the name of a 'concession to human frailty'.

I must not, however, underestimate the force of the arguments on the other side . . .
A long line of cases . . . establish duress as an available defence in a wide range of crimes, some at least, like wounding with intent to commit grievous bodily harm, carrying the heaviest penalties commensurate with their gravity. To cap this, it is pointed out that at least in theory, a defendant accused of this crime under section 18 of the Offences against the Person Act 1861, but acquitted on the grounds of duress, will still be liable to a charge of murder if the victim dies . . . I am not, perhaps, persuaded of this last point as much as I should. It is not simply an anomaly based on the defence of duress. It is a product of the peculiar *mens rea* allowed on a charge of murder which is not confined to an intent to kill . . .

I . . . believe that some degree of proportionality between the threat and the offence must, at least to some extent, be a prerequisite of the defence under existing law. Few would resist threats to the life of a loved one if the alternative were driving across the red lights or in excess of 70 m.p.h. on the motorway. But . . . it would take rather more than the threat of a slap on the wrist or even moderate pain or injury to discharge the evidential burden even in the case of a fairly serious assault. In such a case the 'concession to human frailty' is no more than to say that in such circumstances a reasonable man of average courage is entitled to embrace as a matter of choice the alternative which a reasonable man could regard as the lesser of two evils. Other considerations necessarily arise where the choice is between the threat of death or *a fortiori* of serious injury and deliberately taking an innocent life. In such a case a reasonable man might reflect that one innocent human life is at least as valuable as his own or that of his loved one. In such case a man cannot claim that he is choosing the lesser of two evils. Instead he is embracing the cognate but morally disreputable principle that the end justifies the means . . .

During the course of argument it was suggested that there was available to the House some sort of half way house between allowing these appeals and dismissing them. The argument ran that we might treat duress in murder as analogous to provocation, or perhaps diminished responsibility, and say that, in indictments for murder, duress might reduce the crime to one of manslaughter. I find myself quite unable to accept this. The cases show that duress, if available and made out, entitles the accused to a clean acquittal, without, it has been said, the 'stigma' of a conviction . . . [The suggestion] is also contrary to principle. Unlike the doctrine of provocation, which is based on emotional loss of control, the defence of duress, as I have already shown, is put forward as a 'concession to human frailty' whereby a conscious decision, it may be coolly undertaken, to sacrifice an innocent human life is made as an evil lesser than a wrong which might otherwise be suffered by the accused or his loved ones at the hands of a wrong doer."

LORD GRIFFITHS:

"It is therefore neither rational nor fair to make the defence dependent upon whether the accused is the actual killer or took some other part in the murder . . .

I am not troubled by some of the extreme examples cited in favour of allowing the defence to those who are not the killer such as a woman motorist being *hijacked* and forced to act as getaway driver or a pedestrian being forced to give misleading information to the police to protect robbery and murder in a shop. The short, practical answer is that it is inconceivable that such persons would be prosecuted; they would be called as the principal witnesses for the prosecution.

As I can find no fair and certain basis upon which to differentiate between participants to a murder and as I am firmly convinced that the law should not be extended to the killer, I would depart from the decision of this House in . . . *Lynch* and declare the law to be that duress is not available as a defence to a charge of murder, or to attempted murder. I add attempted murder because it is to be remembered that the prosecution have to prove an even more evil intent to convict of attempted murder than in actual murder.

. . . This leaves, of course, the anomaly that duress is available for the offence of wounding with intent but not to murder if the victim dies subsequently. But this flows from the special regard that the law has for human life, it may not be logical but it is real and has to be accepted.

[Lords Bridge, Brandon and Mackay agreed that duress should never be a defence to murder irrespective of the defendant's degree of participation. In addition to the above concerns over the special value accorded human life and the difficulty in drawing moral and legal distinctions between perpetrators and accomplices, the House felt there were three further reasons justifying their approach:

(1) if duress were to be made a defence to the perpetrator of murder, that should be done by Parliament, not the courts; the Law Commission (Law Com. No. 83) recommended ten years previously that duress should be a defence to the principal offender of murder; Parliament's failure to enact this recommendation is an indication that they have rejected the proposal.

(2) The defence of duress is imprecisely defined and extending it to murder would cause too much uncertainty;

(3) administrative remedies such as not prosecuting, use of parole and the royal prerogative would ensure that no injustice was perpetrated.]"

Appeals dismissed

R. v Gotts [1992] 2 A.C. 412 (House of Lords)

The defendant, aged 16, seriously injured his mother with a knife. In his defence to a charge of attempted murder he claimed that his father had threatened to shoot him unless he killed his mother. The judge ruled that such evidence was inadmissible since duress was not a defence to such a charge. The defendant pleaded guilty but then appealed.

LORD JAUNCEY:

"It is agreed that there is no English authority which deals directly with the availability of the defence of duress to a charge of attempted murder, but [Counsel for the appellant] . . . submitted that this is so because it has long been recognised that the defence of duress is available in respect of all crime except murder and treason . . .

My Lords, I share the view of Lord Griffiths [in *Howe*] that 'it would have been better had [the development of the defence of duress] not taken place and that duress had been regarded as a factor to be taken into account in mitigation' . . . At the time of the earlier writings on duress as a defence, offences against the person were much more likely to have involved only one or two victims. Weapons and substances capable of inflicting mass injury were not readily available to terrorists and other criminals as they are in the reputedly more civilised times in which we now live. While it is not now possible for this House to restrict the availability of the defence of duress in those cases where it has been recognised to exist, I feel constrained to express the personal view that given the climate of violence and terrorism which ordinary law-abiding citizens now have to face Parliament might do well to consider whether the defence should continue to be available in the case of all very serious crimes . . . The reason why duress has for so long been stated not to be available as a defence to a murder charge is that the law regards the sanctity of human life and the protection thereof as of paramount importance. Does that reason apply to attempted murder as well as to murder? As Lord Griffiths pointed out [in *Howe*] . . . an intent to kill must be proved in the case of attempted murder but not necessarily in the case of murder. Is there logic in affording the defence to one who intends to kill but fails and denying it to one who mistakenly kills intending only to injure? . . .

It is of course true that withholding the defence in any circumstances will create some anomalies but I would agree with Lord Griffiths . . . that nothing should be done to undermine in any way the highest duty of the law to protect the freedom and lives of those who live under it. I can therefore see no justification in logic, morality or law in affording to an attempted murderer the defence which is withheld from a murderer. The intent required of an attempted murderer is more evil than that required of the murderer and the line which divides the two is seldom, if ever, of the deliberate making of the criminal. A man shooting to kill but missing a vital organ by a hair's breadth can justify his action no more than can the man who hits the organ. It is pure chance that the attempted murderer is not a murderer . . .

I have no doubt that the Court of Appeal reached the correct decision and that the appeal should be dismissed."

Appeal dismissed

The fact that the defendant in *Gotts* was 16 years old made no difference to the outcome of the trial.[374] More starkly, in *W*, the fact that the defendant was 13 years old was irrelevant: the Court of Appeal accepted that there might be grounds for criticising a principle of law that did not afford such a boy any defence but the law was that a 13-year-old boy was responsible for his actions and duress no defence to a charge of murder.[375] As Ashworth has commented, the "decision was inevitable, but reflects badly on English criminal law".[376]

Is duress a defence to conspiracy and encouraging or assisting to murder? Authority on the point is very limited. In the Court of Appeal in *Gotts*, it was commented that there was "a legitimate distinction to be drawn" between these crimes and attempted murder because they are a "stage further away from the completed offence than is the attempt"[377] and this was the basis given for allowing duress to be pleaded in the unreported Crown Court decision of *Ness*.[378] Thus, while the defence is not available to murder or attempted murder (or treason), it is available to these other serious crimes as well as manslaughter, causing grievous bodily harm with intent contrary to s.18 of the Offences Against the Person Act 1861 and arson intending to endanger life or being reckless as to whether life is endangered contrary to s.1(2) of the Criminal Damage Act 1971.[379] As Lord Lowry stressed in his dissenting speech in *Gotts*, such anomalies are bound to result unless the defence is extended or denied to all crimes.[380] The view espoused by Lord Jauncey in *Gotts* that duress ought to be only a matter of

[374] The defendant was sentenced to three years' probation, so clearly some recognition was taken of his plight.
[375] *R. v W* [2007] EWCA Crim 1251.
[376] Ashworth, fn.351 above, p.139. The Law Commission considered whether there should be a special provision for duress affecting juveniles and young persons (although this received little support) (Law Com. No.304 (2006), fn.35 above, para.6.142). If duress were to become a defence to murder, the Law Commission's recommendation is that youth should continue to be a relevant characteristic.
[377] *R. v Gotts (Benjamin)* (1991) 92 Cr. App. R. 269 at 276.
[378] D. Ormerod, "Duress: conspiracy to murder" [2011] Crim. L.R. 645.
[379] *R. v Gotts (Benjamin)* (1991) 92 Cr. App. R. 269 at 273.
[380] *R. v Gotts* [1992] 2 A.C. 412 at 441.

mitigation in sentencing rather than a defence to serious crimes is one that needs to be resisted for the reasons explored at the beginning of this section.

What is disappointing about these decisions is the lack of attention paid to the theoretical basis of the defence. In *Gotts*, the House concentrated upon whether early writings established duress as a defence to attempted murder and then on its relationship to the crime of murder. At no time did they address fully why duress is a defence.[381] Prior to *Gotts*, *Howe* had already been roundly condemned as requiring unrealistic heroism.[382] Heroism might be a desirable quality but it is unduly harsh to sentence someone to life imprisonment for failing to achieve such heights. The criminal law should rest content if its exhortations induce persons to act reasonably. It seems an odd and an unjust law that can proclaim that the defendant has acted perfectly reasonably but is guilty of murder. And it is simply no answer to assert that injustice will be avoided either by the use of prosecutorial discretion or by more lenient sentencing.[383] Further, these platitudes have been heard before in other areas of criminal law—and been blatantly ignored.[384] In an otherwise policy-driven attempt to restrict the defence of duress, Lord Bingham in *Hasan* acknowledged that the logic of the argument for extending the defence to murder is irresistible.[385] This call for reform was endorsed by the Law Commission.

Law Commission, *Murder, Manslaughter and Infanticide* (Law Com No.304), (2006), paras 6.36–6.53:

"A full defence to first degree murder

In the CP, we provisionally proposed a different approach in relation to first degree murder [and duress] . . . There were two main reasons:

(1) We thought it important that there should be consistency with the partial defences of provocation and diminished responsibility, both of which we were proposing should reduce first degree murder to second degree murder;

(2) It would not be right for a person who had intentionally killed to be completely exonerated . . .

We now believe that, in this context, we exaggerated the importance of treating duress in a manner that was consistent with the way provocation and diminished responsibility fitted into our proposed structure . . .

We also acknowledge that we exaggerated the strength of the case for duress being a partial defence to first degree murder merely because, under our proposals, there would be more categories of murder. We now accept that . . . the mere fact that there are more categories of murder does not assist in deciding whether or not as a matter of principle duress should be a full defence to first degree murder . . .

The argument that duress should be a full defence to first degree murder has a moral basis. It is that the law should not stigmatise a person who, on the basis of a genuine and reasonably held belief, intentionally killed in fear of death or life-threatening injury in circumstances where a jury is satisfied that an ordinary person of reasonable fortitude might have acted in the same way . . .

[W]e believe that there is . . . force in the views expressed by consultees who believe that duress should be a complete defence to first degree murder. For example, [one consultee] said that withholding duress as a complete defence implies that the criminal law should support the view that 'people ought to act in an exceptionally

381   See J. Gardner, "Duress in Attempted Murder" (1991) 107 L.Q.R. 389 at 391; J. Gardner, "Duress in the House of Lords" (1992) 108 L.Q.R. 349.

382   Ormerod, fn.4 above, p.361; P. Alldridge, "Duress, Murder and the House of Lords" (1988) 52 Jo.C.L. 186; H.P. Milgate, "Duress and the Criminal Law: Another About Turn by the House of Lords" [1988] C.L.J. 61; L. Walters, "Murder under Duress and Judicial Decision-making in the House of Lords" (1988) 8 *Legal Studies* 61.

383   The sentencing guidelines for murder under Criminal Justice Act 2003 s.269 and Sch.21 remove much of the discretion formerly permitted judges and do not even include duress as a mitigating factor.

384   See the prosecution that was brought in *Anderton v Ryan* [1985] A.C. 560—exactly the sort of case in which the Law Commission (Law Com. Working Paper No.102) had predicted that a prosecution would never be brought.

385   *R. v Hasan (Aytach)* [2005] 2 A.C. 467.

moral and courageous way. They are being punished for giving way to what will often be enormous fear and wholly understandable human frailty.'

We also think it important to bear in mind the stringent qualifying conditions that attach to the defence. In particular, the majority in *Hasan* were firmly of the view that the defence ought not to be available to D if he or she saw or ought to have foreseen the risk of being subjected to any compulsion by threats of violence. We believe that this will serve to exclude the most unmeritorious cases where the defence should simply not be available. It is true that it will not itself exclude all undeserving cases but we believe that juries should be trusted not to accept the defence in undeserving cases.

Above all, we believe that it is essential to recognize and accord proper weight to the fact that for the defence to succeed, a jury must form a judgement that a reasonable person in D's position might have committed first degree murder. If a jury forms that judgment, we believe that D should be completely exonerated despite having intentionally killed."

The Law Commission's proposals in this respect are to be supported: duress should be a defence to all crimes.[386] What the defendant has done remains wrong but we can understand his predicament and excuse him. Given the severe threats, his actions are in effect morally involuntary. Perhaps if the majority in *Abbott* had realised this they might have produced a different result. Instead they seemed to think they were dealing with a justificatory defence when they spoke of duress bringing the defendant's act "within the law".[387] Lord Mackay in *Howe* spoke of a defendant subject to duress having a "right" to commit a crime.[388] This is simply not so. With excusatory defences one has no "right" to commit crimes. One is simply excused from blame: "To acquit him on grounds of duress is merely to sympathise, understand, commiserate with what he did."[389]

C. Duress of Circumstances

As seen earlier, until fairly recently it was clear that no general defence of necessity existed in English law. However, starting in the 1980s, the judiciary has been actively developing this area of law in a way that "can be likened to the overnight growth of a mushroom".[390] Rather than simply introducing or developing a new full-blown defence of necessity, the courts have chosen to expand the defence of duress by threats to cover what is termed "duress of circumstances". While often describing the defence as "necessity or duress of circumstances" or even as "duress of necessity"[391] the courts have been careful to ensure that the new defence of "duress of circumstances" has largely followed the contours of the existing defence of duress by threats. By emphasising the similarities between the two defences and, importantly, imposing similar rigorous restraints upon the defence, judges have been able to overcome their reluctance to admit a defence of necessity into English law.

The emergence of this defence occurred "more or less by accident".[392] In *Willer*,[393] the defendant was charged with reckless driving when he drove on a pavement to escape from a gang of youths. It was held that regardless of whether necessity had been established or was available, the defence of "duress

---

[386]   However, the Law Commission proposes that the burden of proof would lie with the defendant. This is controversial: see A. Ashworth, "Principles, Pragmatism and the Law Commission's Recommendations on Homicide Law Reform" [2007] Crim. L.R. 333 at 340–342.

[387]   *Abbott v The Queen* [1977] A.C. 755 at 766; see Fletcher, fn.7 above, p.832.

[388]   *R. v Howe (Michael Anthony)* [1987] A.C. 417 at 456; see Walters, fn.382, p.72 above.

[389]   L. Katz, *Bad Acts and Guilty Minds* (Chicago: University of Chicago Press, 1987), p.65.

[390]   D.W. Elliott, "Necessity, Duress and Self-Defence" [1989] Crim. L.R. 611 at 612.

[391]   *R. v Abdul-Hussain (Mustafa Shakir)* [1999] Crim. L.R. 570 and *R. v Cairns (John)* [1999] Cr. App. R. 137, respectively.

[392]   Ormerod, fn.4 above, p.362.

[393]   *R. v Willer (Mark Edward)* (1986) 83 Cr. App. R. 225.

of circumstances" was applicable.[394] "Duress of circumstances" was also considered in the case of *Conway*, another case of reckless driving.[395] The defendant pleaded that he had to make off in his car when approached by two men (who were in fact police officers) because his passenger was fearful of an attack. In saying that the defence of duress of circumstances should have been put to the jury, the Court of Appeal indicated that it was immaterial whether the defence was called necessity or duress. In *Bell*,[396] the Queen's Bench Divisional Court referred to the defence that was available to the defendant who had driven with excess alcohol in his blood in order to escape attackers as "duress/necessity".

R. v Martin (1989) 88 Cr. App. R. 343 (Court of Appeal, Criminal Division)

The defendant was charged with driving whilst disqualified under s.99(b) of the Road Traffic Act 1972. The facts appear from the judgment.

SIMON BROWN J:

"The circumstances which the appellant desired to advance by way of defence of necessity were essentially these. His wife has suicidal tendencies. On a number of occasions before the day in question she had attempted to take her own life. On the day in question her son, the appellant's stepson, had overslept. He had done so to the extent that he was bound to be late for work and at risk of losing his job unless, so it was asserted, the appellant drove him to work. The appellant's wife was distraught. She was shouting, screaming, banging her head against a wall. More particularly, it is said she was threatening suicide unless the appellant drove the boy to work.

The defence had a statement from a doctor which expressed the opinion that 'in view of her mental condition it is likely that Mrs Martin would have attempted suicide if her husband did not drive her son to work.'

The appellant's case . . . was that he genuinely, and he would suggest reasonably, believed that his wife would carry out that threat unless he did as she demanded. Despite his disqualification he therefore drove the boy. He was in fact apprehended by the police within about a quarter of a mile of the house.

Sceptically though one may regard that defence on the facts . . . the sole question before this court is whether those facts, had the jury accepted they were or might be true, amounted in law to a defence . . . As it was, such a defence was pre-empted by the ruling. Should it have been?

In our judgment the answer is plainly not. The authorities are now clear. Their effect is perhaps most conveniently to be found in the judgment of this court in *R. v Conway*. The decision reviews earlier relevant authorities.

The principles may be summarised thus. First, English law does, in extreme circumstances, recognise a defence of necessity. Most commonly this defence arises as duress, that is pressure on the accused's will from the wrongful threats or violence of another. Equally however it can arise from other objective dangers threatening the accused or others. Arising thus it is conveniently called 'duress of circumstances'.

Secondly, the defence is available only if, from an objective standpoint, the accused can be said to be acting reasonably and proportionately in order to avoid a threat of death or serious injury.

Thirdly, assuming the defence to be open to the accused on his account of the facts, the issue should be left to the jury, who should be directed to determine these two questions: first, was the accused, or may he have been, impelled to act as he did because as a result of what he reasonably believed to be the situation he had good cause to fear that otherwise death or serious physical injury would result? Second, if so, would a sober person of reasonable firmness, sharing the characteristics of the accused, have responded to that situation by acting as the accused acted? If the answer to both those questions was Yes, then the jury would acquit; the defence of necessity would have been established . . .

We see no material distinction between offences of reckless driving and driving whilst disqualified so far as the application and scope of this defence is concerned. Equally we can see no distinction in principle between various threats of death; it matters not whether the risk of death is by murder or by suicide or indeed by accident. One can illustrate the latter by considering a disqualified driver being driven by his wife, she suffering a heart attack in remote countryside and he needing instantly to get her to hospital.

---

[394] See also *R. v Denton (Stanley Arthur)* (1987) 131 S.J. 476.
[395] *R. v Conway (Francis Gerald)* [1988] 3 W.L.R. 1238. See P. Alldridge, "Duress, Duress of Circumstances and Necessity" (1989) 139 N.L.J. 911.
[396] *DPP v Bell (Derek)* [1992] Crim. L.R. 176. See also *DPP v Jones* [1990] R.T.R. 33 at 39.

It follows from this that the judge quite clearly did come to a wrong decision on the question of law, and the appellant should have been permitted to raise this defence for what it was worth before the jury."

Appeal allowed. Conviction quashed

R. v Pommell [1995] 2 Cr. App. R. 607 (Court of Appeal, Criminal Division)

The defendant was found by police at 8 a.m. at home in bed with a loaded sub-machine gun. He was charged with possession of a firearm, contrary to s.5(1)(a) of the Firearms Act 1968. In his defence he pleaded that he had taken the gun from someone the night before to prevent that person shooting some people who had killed a friend. He claimed that he had intended to take the gun to the police in the morning. He was convicted, the judge ruling that his failure to go to the police immediately robbed him of the defence of necessity.

KENNEDY LJ:

"There is an obvious attraction in the argument that if A finds B in possession of a gun which he is about to use to commit a crime, and if A is then able to persuade B to hand over the gun so that A may hand it to the police, A should not immediately upon taking possession of the gun become guilty of a criminal offence . . .

The strength of the argument that a person ought to be permitted to breach the letter of the criminal law in order to prevent a greater evil befalling himself or others has long been recognised . . . but it has, in English law, not given rise to a recognised general defence of necessity, and in relation to the charge of murder, the defence has been specifically held not to exist (see *Dudley and Stephens*). Even in relation to other offences, there are powerful arguments against recognising the general defence . . . [His Lordship then cited the Canadian decision of *Perka et al. v R.* (1985) 13 D.L.R. 1, where the court thought that a general defence would make the law too subjective, would enable illegal acts to be validated on the basis of expediency and would invite courts to second guess the Legislature.]

However, that does not really deal with the situation where someone commendably infringes a regulation in order to prevent another person from committing what everyone would accept as being a greater evil with a gun. In that situation it cannot be satisfactory to leave it to the prosecuting authority not to prosecute . . .

It was, as it seems to us, to meet this difficulty that the limited defence of duress of circumstances has been developed in English law in relation to road traffic offences . . . Professor Sir John Smith has written:

'All the cases so far have concerned road traffic offences but there are no grounds for supposing that the defence is limited to that kind of case. On the contrary, the defence, being closely related to the defence of duress by threats, appears to be general, applying to all crimes except murder, attempted murder and some forms of treason.' See [1992] Crim. L.R. 176.

We agree . . .

That leads us to the conclusion that in the present case the defence was open to the appellant . . . That leaves the question as to his continued possession of the gun thereafter . . . In our judgment, a person who has taken possession of a gun in circumstances where he has the defence of duress by circumstances must 'desist from committing the crime as soon as he reasonably can' (Smith and Hogan (7th ed.) p.239) . . . However, the situation does not seem to us to have been sufficiently clear cut [to remove the defence]. . . in the present case."

Appeal allowed. Retrial ordered

This approach has been followed in numerous other decisions[397] where it has been emphasised that both species of duress are governed by the same principles, which were canvassed above. Importantly, this means that the defence is not available to murder, attempted murder and certain forms of

---

[397] For example, *R. v Cairns (John)* [1999] 2 Cr. App. R. 137, and *R. v Abdul-Hussain (Mustafa Shakir)* [1999] Crim. L.R. 570, above. In *Hampshire County Council v E* [2007] EWHC 2584 (Admin) the court expressed some doubt about whether duress of circumstances could be pleaded in relation to an offence of strict liability (the crime in question being that of failing to secure the attendance of a child at school under Education Act 1996 s.444(1)), however, the better view is that it can be. In

treason. However, the rather different nature of the defences has involved some inevitable divergence in the application of the two defences. For example, as already seen, for duress by threats there must be a link between the threat and the crime whereas for duress of circumstances there is no such requirement. Further, the courts have taken a more flexible approach to the requirement of imminence with duress of circumstances than that pertaining to duress by threats.

In reality, duress of circumstances covers situations that are termed "necessity" in other jurisdictions. However, necessity is widely regarded as a *justificatory* defence. On that basis, duress of circumstances could logically be regarded similarly as a justification. However, by building on the blocks of duress by threats, the courts have been able to develop duress of circumstances as an excusatory defence.[398] It is recognised that defendants have done wrong but we do not think it appropriate, because of their plight, to blame them. This means that defendants can only be excused if they are able to satisfy stringent requirements: their will must be overborne by threats of death or serious bodily harm.

Such an approach leaves no scope for a claim that actions were justified and that the defendant's will was not overborne. In *Jones (Margaret)*,[399] the defendants argued that their actions in conspiring to cause criminal damage to an air-force base (where preparations were being made for war) were necessary in order to prevent an illegal war.[400] Just as in *Shayler*,[401] the court regarded this as, if anything,[402] an excusatory plea of duress of circumstances. Yet this does not satisfactorily reflect the reality of the defendants' claim. A further illustration is the case of *Quayle* in which a number of appeals were heard together.[403] All involved the possession or supply of cannabis for relief from chronic and acute pain. The Court of Appeal described the defendants' pleas as "necessity by extraneous circumstances" and took the view that, following *Hasan*, a restrictive approach to the defence was applicable. It was not possible to plead it in circumstances where it would legitimise conduct that was contrary to the clear legislative policy and scheme relating to controlled drugs.[404] In dismissing the appeals the Court of Appeal concluded:

"Where there is no imminent or immediate threat or peril, but only a general assertion of an internal motivation to engage in prohibited activities in order to prevent or alleviate pain, it is also difficult to identify any extraneous or objective factors by reference to which a jury could be expected to measure whether the motivation was such as to override the defendant's will or to force him to act as he did. If the response is that the defendant was not forced, but chose to act as he did, then [a continuous and deliberate course of otherwise unlawful self-help is unlikely to give rise to the defence]."[405]

R. v Gregory (Thomas Dennis) [2011] EWCA Crim 1712, for example, the court accepted that there might be circumstances when the defence might arise in answer to a charge of possession of a firearm without a certificate (Firearms Act 1968 s. 1)

[398] Padfield, fn.328 above .

[399] R. v Jones (Margaret) [2005] Q.B. 259.

[400] The case subsequently went to the House of Lords but did not deal with the issue of necessity of circumstances: [2006] UKHL 16.

[401] R. v Shayler (David Michael) [2001] 1 W.L.R. 2206.

[402] In both *Shayler* and *Jones* the defence failed. In *Jones*, the Court of Appeal held that the defence was limited to situations where the defendant was faced with a crime under domestic law. This has rightly been criticised. Ormerod, fn.4 above points out that the defence "was available to *Martin* when his wife was threatening suicide (not a crime)" (p.365). See further, Gardner, fn.287 above.

[403] Quayle [2005] 2 Cr. App. R. 527.

[404] This approach was followed in CS [2012] EWCA Crim 389 where it was held that it was not possible to plead necessity/duress of circumstances (the court left open the question of whether there was a difference between them) in answer to a charge of child abduction under Child Abduction Act 1984, s.1 as the purpose of the legislation was to prevent removal of a child from the jurisdiction so that he or she could remain under the protection of the court (at [13]). See further, D. Ormerod, "R v S: removing a child from the jurisdiction" [2012] Crim. L.R. 624.

[405] R. v Hasan (Aytach) [2005] 2 A.C. 467 at [81].

In *Quayle*, the court rejected the argument that denying a defence in these circumstances amounted to a breach of art.8 of the European Convention on Human Rights. Similarly, in *Altham*,[406] it was held that the denial of the defence did not breach art.3.

Recognition of the defence of excusatory necessity may, it seems, leave the development of justificatory necessity perpetually in the shadows. In the Draft Criminal Code Bill the Law Commission proposed statutory endorsement of the defence of duress of circumstances.[407] Since then, the Law Commission has considered the whole defence of duress as part of its review of the law of homicide. Prefacing its recommendations with the statement that there are two forms of duress: duress by threats and duress of circumstances, the Report acknowledges that the issue of whether duress should be a defence to murder has been discussed primarily in relation to duress by threats.[408] However, it takes the view that the general principles that govern duress of circumstances are substantially the same,[409] and thus, if the stringent requirements for the defence were met, a defendant would, if the recommendations became law, be able to plead duress of circumstances to a charge of murder.

D. Necessity

The defence of necessity is well-established in other jurisdictions and applies to situations where a defendant chooses to commit a crime in order to avert a greater evil. For example, in the Missouri decision of *State v Green*,[410] the defendant committed the crime of escaping from prison in order to avoid being raped.

1. Distinction between necessity and duress of circumstances

All the cases on duress of circumstances, considered above, concern situations of necessity and we have seen that many recent cases use the terms "duress of circumstances" and "necessity" interchangeably as simply being "different labels for essentially the same thing".[411]

There are, however, important differences between the two defences. Necessity is widely regarded in other jurisdictions as a justificatory defence whereas, as seen, the defence of duress of circumstances has been viewed as an excuse by English law. This difference in theoretical approach has important consequences for the rules that govern the developing defences,[412] although it has to be accepted that the courts are not always clear or consistent in their application of these rules.[413]

First, duress of circumstances is a defence only when there has been a threat of death or serious injury. With an excusatory defence, the essence of which involves the defendant's will being overborne and the actions being morally involuntary, one can perhaps understand the view that this will only be so if the threat is truly awesome as in the case of a threat of death or serious injury. With a justificatory defence, however, the emphasis is on the actor making a choice between two evils and pursuing the

---

[406] *R. v Altham (Lee)* [2006] EWCA Crim 7.

[407] Law Com. No.218 (1993), fn.252, cl.26. The defence would be available to all crimes—even murder—as with duress by threats (Law Com. Consultation Paper No.122, *Legislating the Criminal Code: Offences Against the Person and General Principles* (1992), para.19.9, confirmed in Law Com. No.218 (1993), fn.252 above, para.35.10).

[408] Law Com. No.304 (2006), fn.35 above, para.6.6.

[409] Above, para.6.8.

[410] *State v Green* 470 S.W.2d 565 (1971).

[411] *R. v Shayler (David Michael)* [2001] 1 W.L.R. 2206, above, p.363.

[412] See Clarkson, fn.10 above, where it is argued that the defences of self-defence, duress, duress of circumstances and necessity should be combined as one defence of "necessary action". This would have the advantage of simplicity and allow the focus to be upon the issue that unites all the defences: whether the defendant's response was reasonable and proportionate. See the critique of this proposal by Chan and Simester, fn.10 above .

[413] See, for example, *R. v S Ltd; R. v L Ltd* [2009] EWCA Crim 85 and comment thereto by D. Ormerod at [2009] Crim. L.R. 723.

lesser of them. So, with necessity the threat need not be of death or serious injury. The essence of the defence is that it involves a balancing of evils. The threat can take any form but the crime committed by the defendant must involve a lesser evil.

Secondly, with duress of circumstances the threat must be "imminent" in the sense of being operative on the mind of the defendant and overbearing his or her will. With necessity, the principle is one of "necessity, not emergency".[414] A rational choice is made to avert a greater evil that will necessarily occur even if it would be some time before it occurs.

Thirdly, the cases on duress of circumstances have allowed certain aspects of the vulnerability of the defendant to be taken into account; the test is whether the reasonable person, sharing the same characteristics as the defendant, would have given in to the threats. This is an appropriate test for determining whether a person should be excused because his will was overborne. With necessity, the focus is on the balancing of evils and not on the particular defendant's condition. There should be no scope for making allowance for the defendant's condition or vulnerability.

Finally, duress of circumstances is not a defence to murder, attempted murder or certain forms of treason. With necessity the focus is on the balancing of evils and judging the choices of the defendant. In principle, necessity ought to be a defence when the defendant kills one person in order to save the lives of more than one person.

2. The traditional approach of English law

Until the development of duress of circumstances in the 1980s, it was commonly thought that a defence of necessity did not exist in English law.[415] In O'Toole[416] and Wood v Richards,[417] an ambulance driver and a police officer, respectively, were involved in car accidents while rushing to answer emergency calls. Both were convicted of road traffic offences, necessity being no defence.[418] In Kitson,[419] a passenger woke up drunk in a car to find it running downhill; he steered the car on to a grass verge to avoid a possible accident; he was convicted of driving while under the influence of drink; the defence of necessity was not even raised. And in Southwark LBC v Williams where defendants in dire need of housing accommodation entered empty houses owned by the local authority, it was held that the defence of necessity did not apply. Lord Denning MR stated:

"If homelessness were once admitted as a defence to trespass, no one's house could be safe. Necessity would open a door which no man could shut. It would not only be those in extreme need who would enter. There would be others who would imagine that they were in need, or would invent a need, so as to gain entry."[420]

and Edmund Davis LJ held:

"[T]he law regards with the deepest suspicion any remedies of self-help, and permits those remedies

---

[414] Re A (Conjoined Twins: Surgical Separation) [2001] Fam. 147.

[415] R. v Dudley and Stephens (1884) 14 Q.B.D. 273 is usually cited to support this proposition. It has been argued that the facts of that case did not disclose a true case of necessity: Ormerod, fn.4 above, p.369, but it is submitted that the overall tenor of the judgment indicates that Lord Coleridge was simply not prepared to accept necessity as a defence to murder. The House of Lords in R. v Howe (Michael Anthony) (below, p.389) interpreted the case in this way.

[416] R. v O'Toole (Robert John) (1971) 55 Cr. App. R. 206.

[417] Wood v Richards [1977] Crim. L.R. 295.

[418] cf. Johnson v Phillips [1976] 1 W.L.R. 65 where necessity was accepted as a basis for convicting a defendant.

[419] R. v Kitson (Herbert) (1955) 39 Cr. App. R. 66.

[420] Southwark LBC v Williams [1971] Ch. 734 at 744.

to be resorted to only in very special circumstances. The reason for such circumspection is clear—necessity can very easily become simply a mask for anarchy."[421]

However, later in the same case Edmund-Davis LJ stated:

"[I]t appears that all the cases where a plea of necessity has succeeded are cases which deal with an urgent situation of imminent peril; for example, the forcible feeding of an obdurate suffragette . . . or performing an abortion to avert a grave threat to the life, or . . . health of a pregnant young girl who had been ravished in circumstances of great brutality."[422]

This apparent recognition of the defence of necessity in extreme cases demonstrates that there has never been a blanket condemnation of it in all guises and in all situations. The following two situations require separate consideration.

(i) Medical treatment

Edmund-Davies LJ spoke of the forced feeding of suffragettes and emergency abortions being defended on the basis of necessity. More recently, one interpretation of the case of *Gillick*[423] is that it involved a "hidden" defence of necessity. The doctor who prescribes contraceptive advice or treatment to a girl under the age of 16 does not commit the offence of aiding and abetting underage sexual inter-course if he does so (inter alia) in the belief that unless she receives it her physical or mental health would be likely to suffer.[424]

In *F v West Berkshire HA*,[425] it was held that doctors were justified in carrying out a sterilisation opera-tion upon a woman who was incapable of giving informed consent because of her mental handicap. Lord Goff's argument was based upon necessity; there was a grave risk of her becoming pregnant if she was not sterilised and it was agreed that such a condition would have a very disturbing impact upon her.[426]

What is significant about this development is that necessity is not used to excuse wrongful conduct but to justify conduct as the *right* thing to do. "[T]here is no question of the defence depending on the actor's resistance being overcome."[427] An example given by Lord Goff during his speech makes this clear: "a man who seizes another and forcibly drags him from the path of an oncoming vehicle, thereby saving him from injury or even death, commits no wrong".[428]

The Draft Criminal Law Bill 1993 recognises this underdeveloped justificatory defence in cl.36(2) by explicitly retaining "any distinct defence of necessity" at the same time as it codified duress by threats and duress of circumstances.[429]

(ii) Statutory defences that are in substance necessity

Some statutes expressly provide defences that are in substance defences of necessity. For example, fire-engines, police and ambulances are exempted from observing the speed limit in certain

---

[421]   *Southwark LBC v Williams*, at 745–746.
[422]   *Southwark LBC v Williams*, at 746.
[423]   *Gillick v West Norfolk and Wisbech AHA* [1986] A.C. 112.
[424]   Smith, fn.7 above, pp.64–68. Smith argues that there are many other "concealed defences" in the criminal law (pp.61–72).
[425]   *F v West Berkshire HA* [1990] 2 A.C. 1.
[426]   To similar effect, see *R. v Bournewood Community and Mental Health NHS Trust, ex parte L (Secretary of State for Health intervening)* [1999] A.C. 458.
[427]   Law Commission Consultation Paper No.122, (1992), fn.407 above, para.19.5.
[428]   *F v West Berkshire HA* [1990] 2 A.C. 1 at 74.
[429]   Law Com. No.218 (1993), fn.252 above.

circumstances,[430] and in specified circumstances they may treat a red traffic light as a warning to give way.[431] In such cases it is not possible to plead a general defence of necessity. The only possible defence is under the regulation itself.[432] Another important statutory example is that in order to protect property that is in immediate need of protection, it is permissible to destroy the property of another person.[433] This provision is meant, of course, to provide a defence to, say, a fireman who breaks down a door in order to rescue the occupants of a burning building. Remarkably, however, in 2008 a jury acquitted six climate change protesters charged with criminal damage to a coal fired power station, having heard defence arguments that the damage caused was lawfully excused by the need to prevent the even greater damage caused by climate change.[434]

Further, many statutes contain phrases such as "unlawful", "without lawful excuse" or "without reasonable excuse", which may be construed to cover situations in which a defence of necessity might be appropriate: for example, ss.8–10 of the old Forgery Act 1913 prohibited the possession of forged bank notes "without lawful authority or excuse".[435] In *Wuyts*,[436] it was held that if the defendant's sole purpose in retaining possession of the notes was to hand them to the police, it would have been a "lawful excuse".[437]

(iii) Necessity in relation to homicide

One of the greatest handicaps to the development of a general defence of necessity has been that the issue has usually arisen in homicide cases where "there is always a corpse, casting a shadow across the proceedings".[438]

R. v Dudley and Stephens (1884) 14 Q.B.D. 273 (Queens Bench Division)

The two defendants, with a third man and a 17-year-old boy, were cast away on the high seas in an open boat, 1,600 miles from land. They drifted in the boat for 20 days. When they had been eight days without food and six days without water, and fearing they would all die soon without some sustenance, the defendants killed the boy, who was likely to die first. The men ate his flesh and drank his blood for four days. They were then rescued by a passing vessel and were subsequently charged with murder. The jury found the facts of the case in a special verdict and the case was referred to the Queen's Bench Division for its decision.

LORD COLERIDGE CJ:

"[T]he prisoners put to death a weak and unoffending boy upon the chance of preserving their own lives by feeding upon his flesh and blood after he was killed, and with a certainty of depriving *him* of any possible chance of survival. The verdict finds in terms that: 'if the men had not fed upon the body of the boy, they would *probably*

---

[430] Road Traffic Regulation Act 1984 s.87.
[431] Traffic Signs Regulations and General Directions (SI 1981/859) reg.34(1)(b).
[432] *DPP v Harris (Nigel)* [1995] 1 Cr. App. R. 170. In such cases, if there is a threat of death or serious injury, duress of circumstances can be pleaded (*R. v Backshall (David Anthony)* [1999] Cr. App. R. 35).
[433] Criminal Damage Act 1971 s.5(2)(b).
[434] M. McCarthy, "Cleared: Jury decides that threat of global warming justifies breaking the law", *The Independent*, September 11, 2008.
[435] See now Forgery and Counterfeiting Act 1981 s.16(2).
[436] *R. v Wuyts (Nicholas Charles)* [1969] 2 Q.B. 474. See also *R. v Jones (Margaret)* [2005] Q.B. 259.
[437] For a full discussion of the circumstances when a statute can be construed to cover situations of necessity, see P.R. Glazebrook, "The Necessity Plea in English Criminal Law" [1972] C.L.J. 87.
[438] Alldridge, fn.395 above .

have not survived . . .' and that 'the boy, being in a much weaker condition, was *likely* to have died before them'. They might possibly have been picked up next day by a passing ship; they might not have been picked up at all; in either case it is obvious that the killing of the boy would have been an unnecessary and profitless act. It is found by the verdict that the boy was incapable of resistance, and, in fact, made none . . .

[I]t is admitted that the deliberate killing of this unoffending and unresisting boy was clearly murder, unless the killing can be justified by some well-recognised excuse admitted by the law. It is further admitted that there was in this case no such excuse, unless the killing was justified by what has been called 'necessity.' But the temptation to the act which existed here was not what the law has ever called necessity. Nor is this to be regretted. Though law and morality are not the same, and though many things may be immoral which are not necessarily illegal, yet the absolute divorce of law from morality would be of fatal consequence, and such divorce would follow if the temptation to murder in this case were to be held by law an absolute defence of it. It is not so. To preserve one's life is generally speaking, a duty, but it may be the plainest and the highest duty to sacrifice it. War is full of instances in which it is a man's duty not to live, but to die . . .

It is not needful to point out the awful danger of admitting the principle which has been contended for. Who is to be the judge of this sort of necessity? By what measure is the comparative value of lives to be measured? Is it to be strength, or intellect, or what? It is plain that the principle leaves to him who is to profit by it to determine the necessity which will justify him in deliberately taking another's life to save his own. In this case the weakest, the youngest, the most unresisting was chosen. Was it more necessary to kill *him* than one of the grown men? The answer be, No . . .

It must not be supposed that, in refusing to admit temptation to be an excuse for crime, it is forgotten how terrible the temptation was; how awful the suffering; how hard in such trials to keep the judgment straight and the conduct pure. We are often compelled to set up standards we cannot reach ourselves, and to lay down rules which we could not ourselves satisfy. But a man has no right to declare temptation to be an excuse, though he might himself have yielded to it, nor allow compassion for the criminal to change or weaken in any manner the legal definition of the crime. It is therefore our duty to declare that the prisoners' act in this case was wilful murder."

Judgment for the Crown. Sentence of death, later commuted to six months' imprisonment

B.N. Cardozo, "Law and Literature" from Selected Writings (1947), p.390:

"Where two or more are overtaken by a common disaster, there is no right on the part of one to save the lives of some by the killing of another. There is no rule of human jettison. Men there will often be who, when told that their going will be the salvation of the remnant, will choose the nobler part and make the plunge into the waters. In that supreme moment the darkness for them will be illuminated by the thought that those behind will ride to safety. If none of such mould are found aboard the boat, or too few to save the others, the human freight must be left to meet the chances of the waters. Who shall choose in such an hour between the victims and the saved? Who shall know when masts and sails of rescue may emerge out of the fog?"

United States v Holmes 26 Fed. Cas. 360 (1842) (Circuit Court, Eastern District, Pennsylvania)

The defendant along with eight other seamen and 32 passengers were in an overcrowded lifeboat. Fearing that the boat would sink he threw 16 passengers overboard. The crew were directed "'not to part man and wife, and not to throw over any women.' There was no other principle of selection." The next morning the survivors in the boat were all rescued.

BALDWIN CJ (directing jury):

"[M]an, in taking away the life of a fellow being, assumes an awful responsibility to God, and to society; and that the administrators of public justice do themselves assume that responsibility if, when called on to pass judicially upon the act, they yield to the indulgence of misapplied humanity. It is one thing to give a favourable interpretation to evidence in order to mitigate an offence. It is a different thing, when we are asked, not to extenuate, but to justify, the act . . . [T]he case does not become 'a case of necessity', unless all ordinary means of self-preservation have been exhausted. The peril must be instant, over-whelming, leaving no alternative but to lose our own life, or to take the life of another person . . .

[He then held that the seamen should have been sacrificed first as they were not in an equal position with the passengers as 'the sailor is bound . . . to undergo whatever hazard is necessary to preserve the boat and the passengers'. As between equals the decision as to who should be sacrificed should be made by drawing lots.]

When the solution has been made by lots, the victim yields of course to his fate, or, if he resists, force may be employed to coerce submission. Whether or not 'a case of necessity' has arisen, or whether the law under which death has been inflicted have been so exercised as to hold the executioner harmless, cannot depend on his own opinion; for no man may pass upon his own conduct when it concerns the rights and especially, when it affects the lives, of others . . . [H]omicide is sometimes justifiable; and the law defines the occasions in which it is so. The transaction must, therefore, be justified to the law . . .

[The jury returned a verdict of guilty. The defendant who had already been confined in jail for several months was sentenced to six months' imprisonment with hard labour and fined $20. The penalty was subsequently remitted.]"

American Law Institute, Model Penal Code, Tent. Draft No.8 (1958), Comments to art.3, pp.8–9:

"It would be particularly unfortunate to exclude homicidal conduct from the scope of the defense . . . For recognising that the sanctity of life has a supreme place in the hierarchy of values, it is nonetheless true that conduct which results in taking life may promote the very value sought to be protected by the law of homicide. Suppose, for example, that the actor has made a breach in a dike, knowing that this will inundate a farm, but taking the only course available to save a whole town. If he is charged with homicide of the inhabitants of the farm house, he can rightly point out that the object of the law of homicide is to save life, and that by his conduct he has effected a net saving of innocent lives. The life of every individual must be assumed in such a case to be of equal value and the numerical preponderance in the lives saved compared to those sacrificed surely establishes an ethical and legal justification for the act. So too a mountaineer, roped to a companion who has fallen over a precipice who holds on as long as possible but eventually cuts the rope, must certainly be granted the defense that he accelerated one death slightly but avoided the only alternative, the certain death of both.

. . . [T]he evil sought to be avoided [must] be a greater evil than that sought to be protected by the law defining the offense. For the result is that the defense would not be available to a defendant who killed A to save B, in circumstances where had he done nothing B would have been killed and A saved, assuming, of course, that there was not . . . aggression on either's part . . . Nor would the defense be available to one who acted to save himself at the expense of another, as by seizing a raft when men are shipwrecked . . . In all ordinary circumstances lives in being must be assumed, as we have said, to be of equal value, equally deserving the protection of the law."

Dudley and Stephens has, subsequently, received judicial confirmation.

R. v Howe [1987] 1 A.C. 417 (House of Lords)

[For facts see p.378]

LORD HAILSHAM L.C.:

"[I]f we were to allow this appeal [against a conviction for murder on the basis of duress], we should, I think, also have to say that *Dudley and Stephens* was bad law. There is, of course, an obvious distinction between duress and necessity as potential defences; duress arises from the wrongful threats of violence of another human being and necessity arises from any other objective dangers threatening the accused. This, however, is in my view a distinction without a relevant difference, since on this view duress is only that species of the genus of necessity which is caused by wrongful threats. I cannot see that there is any way in which a person of ordinary fortitude can be excused from the one type of pressure on his will rather than the other."

Lord Hailsham's view is that because the defences of duress and necessity are so similar, neither is available to the person who kills. This could be regarded as implicit acknowledgment of the existence of a defence of necessity to crimes other than murder, attempted murder and certain forms of treason. Perhaps it was dicta such as these that permitted the rapid development of the defence of duress of circumstances.

All the above extracts rightly treat necessity as a justificatory defence. In *Dudley and Stephens*, Lord Coleridge expressed the view that a defence of necessity would alter "the legal definition of the crime" which would only be the case if it acted as justificatory defence. This approach raises the intractable problem discussed in *Dudley and Stephens* and in *Holmes* of having to decide whose lives should be sacrificed. Perhaps the law might have developed in a different direction if the defendants in *Dudley and Stephens* had been viewed as pleading an excuse. It was not a case of the lives of the three men being superior to that of the cabin-boy. However, given that their lives were of equal value, due consideration should have been given to the awfulness of the situation they were in. The fact that their sentences were so rapidly commuted gives further strength to this argument. Indeed, it has been said that the pardon had been arranged well in advance of the sentences being passed.[439]

The shadow of *Dudley and Stephens* has long hung over English law. In 1974, the Law Commission proposed that a general defence of necessity be introduced into English law.[440] However, three years later it rejected the idea, going so far as to say that if a defence of necessity already existed at common law, it should be abolished. It felt that allowing such a defence to a charge of murder could effectively legalise euthanasia in England. For "human rights" reasons it would not be prepared to see necessity covering a situation where "an immediate blood transfusion must be made in order to save an injured person: the only one who has the same blood type as the injured refuses to give blood. Can he be overpowered and the blood taken from him?[441] Instead, the Draft Criminal Code Bill 1993 proposed a statutory formulation of duress of circumstances, cast as an excuse, but applying to all offences.

3. Emergence of a new defence?

By the turn of the century, English law thus appeared fairly settled. Whatever the nomenclature, necessity had been let in the back door under the guise of duress of circumstances and was viewed as an excuse with the implications discussed earlier, including the fact that it was not a defence to murder, attempted murder and certain forms of treason. This tranquillity was shattered by the following decision.

Re A (Conjoined Twins: Surgical Separation) [2001] Fam.147 (Court of Appeal, Civil Division)

"Jodie" and "Mary" were conjoined twins. Leaving them joined would result in the death of both of them within six months. A separation operation would certainly result in the death of Mary who was not capable of separate survival but would give Jodie a good prospect of a normal life. The parents objected to the operation and an application was made to the High Court and then to the Court of Appeal for a declaration, inter alia, that the operation would be lawful despite the fact that it would result in the death of Mary under circumstances making the surgeons prima facie liable for murder.

WARD LJ:

"The first important feature is that the doctors cannot be denied a right of choice if they are under a duty to choose. They are under a duty to Mary not to operate because it will kill Mary, but they are under a duty to Jodie to operate because not to do so will kill her . . . What then is the position where there is a conflict of duty? . . . Wilson J . . . in *Perka v The Queen* (1984) 13 DLR (4th) 1, 36 [stated]:

---

[439] Katz, fn.389 above, p.27.
[440] Law Commission Working Paper No.55, Defences of General Application (1974), para.57.
[441] Law Com. No.83 (1977), fn.318 above, para.4.27.

'the ethical considerations of the "charitable and the good" must be kept analytically distinct from duties imposed by law. Accordingly, where necessity is invoked as a justification for violation of the law, the justification must, in my view, be restricted to situations where the accused's act constitutes the discharge of a duty recognised by law. The justification is not, however, established simply by showing a conflict of legal duties. The rule of proportionality is central to the evaluation of a justification premised on two conflicting duties since the defence rests on the rightfulness of the accused's choice of one over the other.'

So far I agree . . . In [these] circumstances it seems to me that the law must allow an escape through choosing the lesser of the two evils. The law cannot say, 'Heads I win, tails you lose.' Faced as they are with an apparently irreconcilable conflict, the doctors should be in no different position from that in which the court itself was placed in the performance of its duty to give paramount consideration to the welfare of each child. The doctors must be given the same freedom of choice as the court has given itself and the doctors must make that choice along the same lines as the court has done, giving the sanctity of life principle its place in the balancing exercise that has to be undertaken. The respect the law must have for the right to life of each must go in the scales and weigh equally but other factors have to go in the scales as well. For the same reasons that led to my concluding that consent should be given to operate, so the conclusion has to be that the carrying out of the operation will be justified as the lesser evil and no unlawful act would be committed."

BROOKE LJ:

"I have described how in modern times Parliament has sometimes provided 'necessity' defences in statutes and how the courts in developing the defence of duress of circumstances have sometimes equated it with the defence of necessity. They do not, however, cover exactly the same ground. In cases of pure necessity the actor's mind is not irresistibly overborne by external pressures. The claim is that his or her conduct was not harmful because on a choice of two evils the choice of avoiding the greater harm was justified . . .

I have considered very carefully the policy reasons for the decision in *R. v Dudley and Stephens* supported as it was by the House of Lords in *R. v Howe*. These are, in short, that there were two insuperable objections to the proposition that necessity might be available as a defence for the *Mignonette* sailors. The first objection was evident in the court's questions: who is to be the judge of this sort of necessity? By what measure is the comparative value of lives to be measured? The second objection was that to permit such a defence would mark an absolute divorce of law from morality. In my judgment, neither of these objections are dispositive of the present case. Mary is, sadly, self-designated for a very early death. Nobody can extend her life beyond a very short span . . . [With regard to the second objection] all that a court can say is that it is not at all obvious that this is the sort of clear-cut case, marking an absolute divorce from law and morality, which was of such concern to Lord Coleridge CJ and his fellow judges.

There are sound reasons for holding that the existence of an emergency in the normal sense of the word is not an essential prerequisite for the application of the doctrine of necessity. The principle is one of necessity, not emergency . . .

If a sacrificial separation operation on conjoined twins were to be permitted in circumstances like these, there need be no room for the concern felt by Sir James Stephen that people would be too ready to avail themselves of exceptions to the law which they might suppose to apply to their cases, at the risk of other people's lives. Such an operation is, and is always likely to be, an exceptionally rare event . . .

According to Sir James Stephen there are three necessary requirements for the application of the doctrine of necessity: (i) the act is needed to avoid inevitable and irreparable evil; (ii) no more should be done than is reasonably necessary for the purpose to be achieved; (iii) the evil inflicted must not be disproportionate to the evil avoided. Given that the principles of modern family law point irresistibly to the conclusion that the interests of Jodie must be preferred to the conflicting interests of Mary, I consider that all three of these requirements are satisfied in this case."

ROBERT WALKER LJ:

"Duress of circumstances can therefore be seen as a third or residual category of necessity, along with self-defence and duress by threats. I do not think it matters whether these defences are regarded as justifications or excuses. Whatever label is used, the moral merits of the defence will vary with the circumstances . . .
In the absence of parliamentary intervention the law as to the defence of necessity is going to have to develop on a case by case basis . . . I would extend it, if it needs to be extended, to cover this case. It is a case of doctors owing conflicting legal, and not merely social or moral, duties. It is a case where the test of proportionality is met,

since it is a matter of life and death, and on the evidence Mary is bound to die soon in any event. It is not a case of evaluating the relative worth of two human lives, but of undertaking surgery without which neither life will have the bodily integrity, or wholeness, which is its due. It should not be regarded as a further step down a slippery slope because the case of conjoined twins presents an unique problem."

The full implications of this decision are still unfolding. A narrower interpretation is that this is an extension of the "medical necessity" principle discussed above. Ward LJ limited his judgment to cases where there was a conflict between a doctor's duties. A doctor is under a legal duty to do what is best for a patient. Here there were conflicting duties owed to the twins and, in exercising their duty, the doctors had to make a choice of the lesser of two evils. Although this narrower interpretation involves a significant extension of the law in that it allows doctors to kill their patients in these tightly-defined circumstances it does provide one of the many reasons why arguments in the courts that doctors should be able to plead necessity to a charge of assisting suicide (or even euthanasia) have been unsuccessful: in *Re A*, the conflict was resolved in favour of taking action to *preserve* at least one life. As Stark comments, this is what makes *Re A* distinguishable from cases such as *Nicklinson*.[442] In the words of the Court of Appeal in *Nicklinson*:

"[T]here is a world of difference between taking a life to save a life and taking a life because the deceased wishes it to end . . . [*Re A*] is too slender a thread on which to hang such a far-reaching development of the common law."[443]

A bolder interpretation of *Re A* is one which has the potential to lead to the development of a true defence of necessity, cut free from its theoretical links to duress. Many of the examples of necessity Brooke LJ cites and discusses extend beyond medical necessity and suggest a wider role for the defence.

Ian Dennis, "On Necessity as a Defence to Crime: Possibilities, Problems and the Limits of Justification and Excuse" (2009) Crim Law and Philos 29 at 44–45:

"It would seem, although this is not completely clear, that he [Brooke LJ] regarded this form of necessity defence as an act-utilitarian principle. It is not a statement of the classic 'lesser evils' form of necessity because it allows for harm to be done equal to that which is threatened, as long as the harm done is not disproportionate . . .

However, there are problems with an unqualified act-utilitarian principle. One of them is the potential devaluing of personal autonomy. Suppose P, a hospital patient, urgently needs a blood transfusion to survive, but she has a very rare blood group. As it happens, Q, the patient in the next bed, has the same rare blood group, but refuses to make a donation of blood even though she could do so without risk to herself. May, D, the doctor treating P, take the blood from Q without her consent? The blood is needed to avoid 'inevitable and irreparable evil', and the physical harm done in the form of assault on Q to obtain the blood is not disproportionate to the harm threatened of P's death. Is the assault on Q 'no more than reasonably necessary to achieve the purpose of preventing P's death?' Everything then turns on the one word 'reasonably'. A test of reasonableness is a flexible standard that inevitably requires an accommodation of competing values. But in states that subscribe to liberal democratic values personal autonomy is not something that can be traded against other values. Persons have

---

[442] Stark, fn.100 above, p.960. See also, S. Ost, "Euthanasia and the Defence of Necessity: Advocating a More Appropriate Legal Response" [2005] Crim. L.R. 355.

[443] *R (on the application of Nicklinson) v A Primary Care Trust* [2013] EWCA Civ 961 at [63]. The court further states that "it is simply not appropriate for the court to fashion a defence of necessity in such a complex and controversial field; this is a matter for Parliament" (at [56]). See below, p.759. (At the time of writing the decision of the Supreme Court is awaited.)

rights to be treated as ends in themselves and not as means to the achievement of other social goals. Accordingly, if Q chose to assert her autonomy by refusing her consent to give blood that would normally be the end of the matter, but the principle adopted by Brooke LJ, applied without qualification, would leave the matter in doubt."

Brooke LJ, when dealing with necessity as a defence to murder, was careful to limit his judgment to the killing of those already "designated for death". This means that a defendant cannot choose (by whatever criterion) to throw four people off a boat to their death in order to save 10 others: those four people have not been designated for death. Similarly, on the facts of *Dudley and Stephens* there would still not be a defence of necessity. While the cabin-boy was the weakest and most likely to die first, they could all have been rescued. He was not designated for death.

However, that still leaves situations, as the example from Dennis illustrates, where a defence of necessity could be pleaded to avoid "an inevitable and irreparable evil". Brooke L.J's interpretation could allow necessity as a defence to murder. For example, if after a car crash a driver and passenger were seriously injured but it was clear that the driver was dying with no prospect of recovery but the passenger's life could be saved, it could be open to paramedics or other emergency services personnel to kill the driver in cutting them loose if that was the only means by which they could get to the passenger in time to save his or her life. Professor Sir John Smith used an even more telling example:

"Following the destruction of the World Trade Centre in New York by hijacked aircraft it now appears to be recognised that it would be lawful to shoot down the plane, killing all the innocent passengers and crew if this were the only way to prevent a much greater impending disaster . . . Even if duress cannot be a defence to murder,[444] it seems quite clear that necessity can."[445]

What has yet to be determined is how far this will extend.

VI. Superior Orders

We have seen that the defence of duress can be rationalised on the basis that the defendant lacked effective and real choice in committing the crime; they were forced by someone else to do something that they were loath to do. In the same way, a subordinate may assert that they were forced by duty and loyalty to a superior to obey an order which lead them into conflict with the criminal law. Following this analogy it would seem that superior orders should constitute an *excuse*. The inferior has done wrong but is excused from blame. It is, however, clear that there is no such defence as superior orders in English law. Lord Salmon in the duress case of *Abbott*[446] said that the idea of such a defence "has always been universally rejected" and Lord Hailsham took a similar position in *Howe*.[447]

---

[444] Of course, if the recommendations of the Law Commission become law, duress (including duress of circumstances) would be a defence to murder. In fact, one of the illustrations given by the Law Commission is a classic illustration of necessity: Law Com. No.304 (2006), fn.35 above, para.6.61.

[445] See Ormerod, fn.4 above, p.372. See further, M. Bohlander, "In extremis—Hijacked Airplanes, 'Collateral Damage' and the Limits of the Criminal Law" [2006] Crim. L.R. 579 and D. Ormerod, "Letter to the Editor" [2006] Crim. L.R. 786 (responding to Bohlander's article). In Germany, the Act that allowed the Minister of Defence to order the shooting down of a plane in such circumstances (Aviation Security Act s.14(3)) has been held to be unconstitutional: K. Moler, "On Treating People as Means: The German Aviation Security Act, Human Dignity, and the German Federal Constitutional Court" [2006] P. L. 457. See further, P. Gaeta, "May Necessity be Available as a Defence for Torture in the Interrogation of Suspected Terrorists?" [2004] 2 J. Int'l Crim. Just. 785.

[446] *Abbott v The Queen* [1976] 3 W.L.R. 462 at 469.

[447] *R. v Howe (Michael Anthony)* [1987] A.C. 417 at 427.

In *Chiu-Cheung*[448] it was held that a person, who acted as an undercover agent to break a drug ring in Hong Kong, could be guilty of conspiring to traffic in dangerous drugs. The Privy Council confirmed that there was no general defence of superior orders as "neither the police, nor customs, nor any other members of the executive"[449] had any power to alter the terms of the Hong Kong Ordinance that made the export of heroin unlawful even though the court acknowledged that what the defendant had done was courageous and from the best of motives. In *Clegg*, the House of Lords held that the soldier would not be entitled to be acquitted by virtue of superior orders as "no such general defence [is] known to English law".[450] While such an approach might be uncontroversial in civil situations, the matter is not free from dispute in relation to military situations where it may be argued that the claims of duty, especially in war-time, are so strong as to warrant some kind of defence of superior orders.

McCall v McDowell, 1 Abb 212 Fed Cas. No.8673 (1867) (Circuit Court of California)

DEATY J:

"I cannot but think that the law should excuse the military subordinate when acting in obedience to the orders of his commander. Otherwise he is placed in the dangerous dilemma of being liable in damages to a third party[451] for obedience of an order or to the loss of his commission and disgrace for disobedience thereto[452] . . . The first duty of a soldier is obedience, and without this there can be neither discipline nor efficiency in an army. If every subordinate officer and soldier were at liberty to question the legality of the orders of the commander . . . the camp would be turned into a debating school, where the precious moment for action would be wasted in wordy conflicts between the advocates of conflicting opinions."

There have been numerous cases[453] in the United States which have attempted to recognise the "practical dilemma"[454] of the soldier by striking a balance between total immunity and total liability.

United States v Calley 22 U.S.M.C.A. 534 (1973) (US Court of Military Appeals)

Lieutenant Calley was a platoon leader engaged in sweeping out the enemy in part of Vietnam. He was charged with the premeditated murder of 22 infants, children, women and old men. His defence was that he was acting under the direct orders of his commanding officer; he had been told that under no circumstances were they to leave Vietnamese alive as they passed through the villages. He was to "waste them".

QUINN J:

[There is] ample evidence from which to find that Lieutenant Calley directed and personally participated in the intentional killing of men, women and children who were unarmed and in the custody of soldiers . . . [T]he uncontradicted evidence is that . . . they were offering no resistance. In his testimony, Calley admitted he was aware of the requirement that prisoners be treated with respect . . . he knew that the normal practice was to interrogate

---

[448] *Chiu-Cheung v The Queen* [1995] 1 A.C. 111.
[449] *Chiu-Cheung v The Queen*, above at 118.
[450] *R. v Clegg* [1995] 1 A.C. 482 at 498.
[451] Or subject to a criminal charge.
[452] The soldier may claim further that he would have been shot for disobedience (Nazi war criminals included this in their defences), thereby pleading duress.
[453] *United States v Kinder* (1953) A.C.M. 7321, 14 C.M.R. 742; *United States v Quarles* 350 U.S. II (1955). Both cases arose from incidents in the Korean War.
[454] I.D. Brownlie, "Superior Orders—Time for a New Realism?" [1989] Crim. L.R. 396 at 396.

villagers, release those who could satisfactorily account for themselves and evacuate the suspect among them for further examination . . .

We turn to the contention that the [trial] judge erred in his submission of the defense of superior orders to the court [by framing the instructions thus]: '[I] f you find that Lieutenant Calley received an order directing him to kill unresisting Vietnamese within his control . . . that order (as a matter of law) would be an illegal order. A determination that an order is illegal does not, of itself, assign criminal responsibility to the person following the order for acts done in compliance with it . . . [such] acts of a subordinate . . . are excused and impose no criminal liability upon him unless the superior's order is one which a man of ordinary sense and understanding would, under the circumstances, know to be unlawful, or if the order in question is actually known to the accused to be unlawful.'. . .

[Defence counsel urged that this was too high a standard for soldiers who may not be persons of ordinary sense and understanding; they argued for a lower test of 'commonest understanding'] . . . [W]hether Lieutenant Calley was the most ignorant person in the United States Army in Vietnam or the most intelligent, he must be presumed to know that he could not kill the people involved here . . . [the order was] so palpably illegal that whatever conceptual difference there may be between a person of 'commonest understanding' and a person of 'common understanding,' that difference could not have had any impact on a court."

Decision of the Court of Military Review affirmed[455]

This test of "palpable illegality" has been followed elsewhere. In the South African case of *Banda*, it was held that the defence was not available where the orders were "manifestly and palpably illegal and that a reasonable man in the circumstances of the soldier would know them to be".[456] This is also the test adopted by some international criminal law instruments. For example, art.33(1)(c) of the Rome Statute establishing the International Criminal Court provides that a defence of superior orders can never be available to orders that are "manifestly unlawful".[457]

The English approach of denying the existence of a defence of superior orders has been condemned as inappropriate and unrealistic.

Ian D. Brownlie, "Superior Orders—Time For a New Realism?" [1989] Crim. L.R. 396 at 411:

"It is inappropriate because the harm it is aimed at remedying, namely the abuse of executive fiat, is being perpetrated, if at all, by the superiors at various levels who have committed him to that situation. It is unrealistic because it requires the individual soldier to be able to make decisions on legal niceties in situations where sometimes his or her military competence and perhaps even instinct for physical survival will compel instant obedience. The strict 'no-defence' position is predicated upon assumptions about constitutional law and the possible consequences of allowing such a defence which cannot be demonstrated in practice . . . On the contrary, therefore, it is submitted that courts should be allowed to decide the bona fides of such a defence on the basis that military orders which are not manifestly illegal may give rise to a mistake of law . . . [which should be relevant]. It is in this way that the interests of justice both for the individual soldier and for the wider civil society in which, increasingly, the soldier is becoming involved, will best be served."

The problem with this analysis is that mistakes of law do not give rise to a defence in English law. Of course, the other general defence could be available to policemen or soldiers following orders. For example, a policeman could be ordered to shoot a suspected terrorist wrongly believed to be about

---

[455] In the *New York Times*, April 10, 1971, Marshall Burke argued that to hold Calley personally accountable was unjust; it was the whole nation that was accountable and ought to push for the end of the war. Goldstein argued against this view: "if future wars must be fought, there [must] be some expectation that each participant will abide by minimum standards of conduct which a law of crimes is designed to maintain." ("The Meaning of Calley", 194 (19) *The New Republic* 13–14.)

[456] *Banda* (1990) (3) S.A. 466 at 494.

[457] See further, S. Wallerstein, "Why English Law Should Not Recognise a Defence of Superior Orders" [2010] Crim. L.R. 109 at 110–114.

to detonate a bomb. Such a policeman could claim putative self-defence if they satisfied the requirements for this defence (honest belief in the necessity to shoot to save the lives of others).[458]

Given judicial pronouncements against superior orders (and both duress and duress of circumstances as defences to murder) it seems most unlikely that any change will take place. Moreover, there must remain grave doubts as to the wisdom of introducing a defence that would allow soldiers to kill innocent persons deliberately and claim that their actions were excused.

VII. Involuntary Conduct

A. Introduction

The need for voluntary conduct, and some of the philosophical problems associated with the meaning of terms such as "voluntary" and "involuntary", were discussed in Ch.2. A claim of involuntariness is a "denial of authorship"[459] and "it is only where defendants are agents and not mere causers of harm that they are to be regarded as responsible for causing that harm".[460] The object of this section is to examine the implications and consequences of a finding that conduct is involuntary. It is worth noting at the outset that the relationship between automatism, insanity and the law relating to defendants who commit offences whilst intoxicated is complex and that this area of law is currently under review by the Law Commission.[461]

If conduct is involuntary there is no actus reus (and certainly no mens rea). This indicates that the defendant should be exempted completely from criminal liability. For example, in the Australian case of *Cogden*,[462] a woman, in a somnambulistic state, dreaming that her daughter was being attacked by ghosts, spiders and North Korean soldiers, axed her to death. She was acquitted on the ground that her actions were not voluntary. Because a finding of involuntariness can potentially lead to a complete acquittal (with the danger that the conduct could be repeated), English courts have approached the problem of involuntariness with great circumspection and have adopted a restrictive approach as to when there should be a complete exemption from liability. This caution has manifested itself in three ways.

1. Narrow definition of involuntariness

The criminal law has adopted a narrow interpretation of "involuntary conduct". Not only is this because of the possibility of a complete acquittal, but also because of the difficulty of distinguishing a genuine claim from a fraudulent one. In *Bratty v Attorney-General for Northern Ireland*,[463] it was acknowledged that pleading a blackout is one of the first refuges of a guilty conscience and is a popular excuse.[464] Accordingly, the law has tended to the view that there is a continuum of involuntariness ranging from complete absence of consciousness, through persons acting in a confused or semi-conscious manner, to those who actually know what they are doing but claim that their actions were morally involuntary because their will was overborne and they were forced to act as they did. The courts, in determining

---

[458] See fn.446, pp.116–124.
[459] Ashworth and Horder, fn.193 above, p.86.
[460] J. Horder, "Pleading Involuntary Lack of Capacity" (1993) 52 C.L.J. 298 at 300.
[461] Law Commission, *Criminal Liability: Insanity and Automatism, A Discussion Paper* (2013), p.416.
[462] *Cogden* (1950) unreported. See N. Morris, "Somnambulistic Homicide: Ghosts, Spiders and North Koreans" V *Res Judicatae* 29.
[463] *Bratty v Attorney-General of Northern Ireland* [1963] A.C. 386.
[464] Citing Stable J in *Cooper v McKenna* [1960] Q.L.R. 406 at 419.

where to draw the line on this continuum, have been strongly influenced by the context, nature and dangerousness of the behaviour. In cases where the defendant is engaged in a particularly dangerous activity, such as driving a car, the law has adopted a strict stance that only a complete absence of consciousness will exempt from liability. In *Broome v Perkins*,[465] the defendant, when charged with driving without due care and attention, claimed to be in a hypoglycaemic condition. He was acquitted at first instance on the basis that his conduct was involuntary. However, an appeal by case stated resulted in a direction to the magistrates to convict. It was held that his actions were only automatic at intervals; at times "the respondent's mind must have been controlling his limbs (from the evidence) and thus he was driving".

J.C. Smith, Commentary to Broome v Perkins [1987] Crim. L.R. 272:

"The defendant was held not to be in a state of automatism throughout his journey because, from time to time, he apparently exercised conscious control over his car veering away from other vehicles so as to avoid a collision, braking violently when approaching the back of another vehicle and so on. This is a very harsh decision, resulting in the conviction of a person who appears to have suffered a misfortune, not to have been at fault in any real sense and to have behaved most responsibly by going to the police and saying that he believed he must have been involved in a road accident."

Despite this view, the same approach was adopted in *Attorney-General's Reference (No.2 of 1992)* where it was held that conduct was only involuntary if there was a total loss of voluntary control. In this case, the defendant, a lorry driver, crashed into a broken-down vehicle parked on the hard shoulder of a motorway and killed two people. Experts described the defendant's condition as "driving without awareness".[466] Whilst not asleep, "the driver's capacity to avoid a collision ceased to exist because of repetitive stimuli experienced on straight flat featureless motorways could induce a trance-like state". However, the expert acknowledged that this amounted to reduced or imperfect awareness and, accordingly, the Court of Appeal ruled that this could not amount to involuntary conduct.

This very robust approach, requiring that there be a complete loss of voluntary control, was confirmed recently in *Coley* in which Hughes LJ stated that:

"The essence of . . . [the defence] is that the movements or actions of the defendant at the material time were wholly involuntary. The better expression is complete destruction of voluntary control."[467]

As *Coley* concerned a defendant charged with attempted murder, the Law Commission is right to conclude that "the overwhelming weight of authority supports" the view that the requirement of total loss of control is not restricted to widely practiced dangerous activities, such as driving, only.[468]

---

[465] *Broome v Perkins* [1987] Crim. L.R. 271.

[466] *Attorney-General's Reference (No.2 of 1992)* (1993) 97 Cr. App. R. 429 at 431.

[467] *Coley (Scott) v The Queen* [2013] EWCA Crim 223 at [22]. Hughes LJ drew a distinction between the involuntary conduct required for a plea of automatism and the irrational conduct of the defendant (brought on by self-induced intoxication) at [22]–[23]. In *McGhee (Colin) v The Queen* (an appeal heard at the same time as *Coley*, Hughes LJ also distinguished automatism from disinhibited behaviour brought on by intoxication: at [46]. See further, R. Mackay, "R v Coley; R v McGhee; R v Harris: insanity–distinction between voluntary intoxication and disease of the mind caused by voluntary intoxication" [2013] Crim. L.R. 923.

[468] Law Commission Discussion Paper (2013), fn.461 above, para.5.29.

2. Preceding fault

The rationale for requiring voluntary conduct is that there can be no authorship or responsibility for involuntary conduct and, accordingly, blame is inappropriate. It is not a person's fault if she is attacked and, in a state of concussion, causes harm to another. Punishment is not deserved and no deterrent goals can be achieved by holding such a person criminally liable. In some situations, however, it might be the defendant's own fault that the state of involuntariness was brought about. In such cases, the courts, conscious of the fact that the defendant is not only blameworthy in precipitating the involuntariness but could do it again, have been careful to ensure that criminal liability is not evaded.

In *Quick and Paddison*, the defendant, a diabetic, was charged with an assault that occurred during a hypoglycaemic episode. This arose from eating too little and drinking too much alcohol after having taken insulin. It led to an aggressive outburst and an impairment of consciousness. Lawton LJ stated that

> "a self-induced incapacity will not excuse . . . nor will one which could have been reasonably fore-seen as a result of either doing, or omitting to do something, as, for example, taking alcohol against medical advice after using certain prescribed drugs, or failing to have regular meals while taking insulin."[469]

So, while "accidental" hypoglycaemia could have secured an acquittal, Quick's abuse of his body meant that he could be blamed for the ensuing hypoglycaemic episode. Although the conviction was actually reversed on appeal (on the basis that the issue of involuntariness should have been left to the jury), it was made clear that self-induced involuntariness will not provide a defence to crimes of basic intent.[470]

What, however, is meant by "preceding fault" in this context? Must the defendant know that his conduct will cause the involuntary conduct or is it sufficient that the reasonable person would know this? In *Quick and Paddison*, the question was whether the incapacity could reasonably have been foreseen. In *Bailey*,[471] the defendant was a diabetic who had not taken sufficient food after a dose of insulin to combat its effects. It was held (somewhat controversially) that it was not common knowledge amongst diabetics that such failure could lead to aggressive, dangerous or unpredictable behaviour. Accordingly, it could not be inferred that the defendant knew of the risks and he should not be penalised for his lack of knowledge.[472] One way of reconciling these cases would be to restrict the operation of the rule in *Quick and Paddison* to cases involving alcohol and drugs because it is so widely known that intoxicants can have such an effect[473] and, because of the statistical correlation between intoxication and crime, policy demands that no relief from criminal liability be afforded to intoxicated persons. Such an approach is arguably supported by *Hardie*,[474] where it was held that a defendant who took Valium could escape liability for subsequent involuntary conduct because it was not known to the defendant, nor generally known, that Valium could cause unpredictability and aggressiveness. The essence of the *Quick and Paddison* principle is that one can legitimately blame persons who, through their own fault, cause their own involuntary conduct. When such fault is established, the requirement of voluntariness is dispensed with—largely because that requirement is only there to

---

[469]   *R. v Quick (William George); R. v Paddison (William)* [1973] 1 Q.B. 910 at 922.
[470]   For the meaning of this term, see below, pp.431–441.
[471]   *R. v Bailey (John Graham)* [1983] 1 W.L.R. 760.
[472]   The appeal was in fact dismissed because of insufficient evidence that the defendant's actions had been involuntary.
[473]   *R. v Allen (Kevin)* [1988] Crim. L.R. 698.
[474]   *R. v Hardie* (1985) 80 Cr. App. R. 157.

protect the faultless.[475] The question of whether one can only blame those who knew of the risks they were running or whether blame is appropriate because the risks were obvious and they ought to have appreciated them raises broadly the same issues as were canvassed in relation to the concepts of recklessness and negligence in Ch.2.

It is important that there be precision in locating the act alleged to be involuntary. The rule that preceding fault negates automatism could be employed in driving cases where the driver falls asleep or suffers some form of attack that could have been predicted.[476] However, where the driver has previously had similar attacks, the act of driving can in itself amount to dangerous driving. In *Marison*,[477] the defendant suffered a hypoglycaemic episode while driving; he lost control of the car and caused the death of another driver.[478] It was held that even though the defendant had become an automaton at the moment of the accident, this was not a case of automatism. Being aware that he might have a hypoglycaemic attack while driving meant that the driver was "in a dangerously defective state due to diabetes". The offence of dangerous driving had already been committed before the attack occurred.

3. Cause of involuntariness

Bearing in mind the central point that a finding of involuntariness can lead to a complete acquittal, the courts have been anxious to investigate the cause of the involuntary conduct. If the cause of the involuntary conduct is something internal to the defendant—a disease of the mind—then clearly there is the potential danger that the involuntary conduct could be repeated. Society could need protection from such persons. Accordingly, where the defendant is suffering from a disease of the mind the involuntary conduct is described as insane automatism. Such an insane defendant, while escaping formal criminal liability, nevertheless receives a special verdict of "not guilty by reason of insanity" whereupon the courts have power to restrain the person. On the other hand, if the cause of the involuntary conduct is something external to the defendant—such as a blow on the head—there is little chance of repetition; the defendant is not dangerous. Such cases are described as non-insane automatism—or simply automatism—and the defendant is afforded a complete acquittal. Given this critical distinction between insanity and automatism, one way in which the courts can reduce the number of defendants escaping all liability is to expand the category of insanity thereby reducing the scope of the defence of automatism. Reclassifying the sleep-walking Mrs Cogden, for example, as suffering from an internal rather than an external condition would have a profound impact upon her treatment by the law.

The distinction between insanity and automatism is thus one of fundamental importance and each will be considered in turn.

B. Insanity

1. Introduction

The defence of insanity brings into sharp focus many of the issues discussed in previous chapters and has been the source of much debate.[479] Requiring a jury to decide whether a person accused of a crime

---

[475] See further, Smith and Wilson, fn.44 above.
[476] See *Kay v Butterworth* (1947) 173 L.T. 191; *Hill v Baxter* [1958] 1 Q.B. 277.
[477] *R. v Marison (Lee John)* [1996] Crim. L.R. 909.
[478] See further, J. Rumbold and M. Wasik, "Diabetic drivers, hypoglycaemic unawareness, and automatism" [2011] Crim. L.R. 863.
[479] This is despite the fact that there are only 20 or so findings of insanity per year (R. Mackay, "Ten more years of the Insanity Defence" [2012] Crim. L.R. 946).

is to be punished as criminal or "treated" as insane forces two major questions to the surface. The first addresses itself to the premise upon which the sane individual is punished. We have seen in Ch.2 that inherent in the criminal justice system is a view of people as responsible agents. Individuals possess freedom of will and can choose one course of action rather than another. If they step outside the limits of legal action we are, therefore, justified in imposing blame and punishment. By the same argument we cannot blame people who do not have this ability to choose or control their actions.[480] The insanity defence thus seeks to distinguish the responsible from those lacking responsibility. The difficulty lies in determining where the line between sanity and responsibility on the one hand, and insanity and irresponsibility on the other hand, is to be drawn. It has been increasingly argued that absolute states of sanity and insanity rarely (if ever) exist; instead there are shades of sanity. This attitude towards sanity and responsibility has expressed itself in a number of forms. For some commentators it has necessitated a more rigorous approach to the search for the crucial dividing line. For them the question of ascertaining who is responsible has been made more important, not less. The same doubt has, however, led others to demand that the insanity defence (or the concept of responsibility itself) be abolished. As we shall see, however, where the insanity defence has been abolished or amended, as in some of the states in the United States, it has often been in response to criticisms other than those concerning the principle of responsibility.

Secondly, how are the traditional objectives of punishment, which largely assume responsibility, affected when it comes to the punishment of the insane?

A.S. Goldstein, The Insanity Defense (1967), pp.11–15:

"At the present time, the objectives of the criminal law are ordinarily said to be retribution, deterrence and reha-bilitation . . . The *retributive* function building on the widely held feeling that the criminal owes the community a measure of suffering comparable to that which he has inflicted . . . channelled the anger of victims (and of their friends) lest they . . . [sought] revenge. But to do so, it was necessary to make a criminal conviction sufficiently con-sequential to satisfy those who were inclined to feel retributive . . . A corollary of this, however, was the feeling that so serious a sanction ought not to be imposed in situations in which the initial impulse to anger was likely to give way, even among victims, to feelings of compassion. These were situations in which the offender seemed so obvi-ously different from most men that he could not be blamed for what he had done. Even under a retributive theory, therefore, an insanity defense was needed to trace in outline those who could not be regarded as blameworthy . . .

Under the *deterrent* theory . . . the primary function of criminal law is to move men to conform to social norms, particularly those which cannot be left entirely to informal processes of social control or to those of the civil law. This is accomplished by announcing in a criminal code what conduct is prohibited and how much of a sanction of imprisonment or fine will be visited upon those who ignore the prohibition. Such a system can be effective only with men who can understand the signals directed at them by the code, who can respond to the warnings, and who feel the significance of the sanctions imposed upon violators . . . If a man cannot make the calculations or muster the feelings demanded of him by the theory, he is classed as insane. He lacks the requisite degree of intelligence, reasoning power and foresight of consequence. If he were held criminally responsible he would be made to suffer harsh sanctions without serving the purpose of individual deterrence.

It would still be possible, however, to conceive that such a man might serve the ends of general deterrence . . . [but] the examples are likely to deter only if the person who is not involved in the criminal process regards the lessons as applicable to him. He is likely to do so only if he identifies with the offender and with the offending situation. This feat of identification is difficult enough to achieve under ordinary circumstances . . . it is prob-ably hopeless if the deterrent example is so different from most men that the crime can be attributed to the difference . . .

---

[480]   Gross, fn.311 above, pp.361–362, points out that three contentions may be involved. It may, first, be thought that it is wrong in these situations to punish the accused *for being sick*, or, secondly, that it is wrong to punish someone for what they do *as a result of being sick*, or, lastly, that it is cruel to add to the suffering of someone who is sick: in other words, that it is wrong to punish someone *when* they are *sick*.

The third view of the insanity defense . . . tends to view deviant behaviour as psychological maladjustment, the product of forces beyond the individual's control; he is less to be blamed than to be helped to restore the balance between him and his background or his environment. The tacit assumption is that a paternal state can put him right by psychotherapy or by judicious social planning, if only the 'helping' professions are provided with the resources to do the job . . . This 'mental health' image has unquestionably captured the imagination of the reformers and has been propagated almost as a faith . . .

Because it is widely assumed that 'blame' plays a critical role in maintaining individual responsibility and social order, the insanity defense continues to be regarded as exceptional. It becomes the occasional device through which an offender is found to be inappropriate for the social purposes served by the criminal law. He is too much unlike the man in the street to permit his example to be useful for the purposes of deterrence. He is too far removed from normality to make us angry with him. But because he is sick rather than evil, society is cast as specially responsible for him and obligated to make him better."

A final preliminary point needs to be considered. Is the insanity defence really a "defence" at all? The issue of insanity is invariably included in discussions of defences to crime, yet this classification is not without its difficulties. To assert that a defendant has a defence to crime has connotations that may or may not prove to be applicable to the case of insanity. Three matters, in particular, require consideration.

(a) Is insanity regarded as a general exempting condition or as a specific excuse to a particular wrongful act? According to the analysis of defences at the start of this chapter, insanity should be perceived as akin to the general defence of infancy and act as an exemption. As the Law Commission has stated,[481] the defendant lacks *capacity-responsibility* for his "wrongful" actions— and thus requires no excuse. This incapacity may well be demonstrated in many ways other than the particular act. However, this analogy does not sit well with the current wording of the legal test for insanity. As we shall see, the *M'Naghten* Rules link the mental condition of the accused causally to the prohibited *act*. In other words, it appears to focus upon *attribution-responsibility*. Our inclusion of insanity as an exemption, therefore, is, in part, based upon the way it ought to operate and serves to highlight in advance one of the many flaws of the current test.[482]

(b) Is insanity a true defence or does it negate a definitional element? Support for the view that it performs this latter function comes from the argument that prior to the statutory creation of the special verdict, a finding of insanity would lead to a complete acquittal at common law.[483] Indeed, it has been argued further that this would still be true today of defendants pleading insanity in the magistrates' courts.[484] However, it may be that conclusions about whether insanity negates mens rea are best drawn once the *M'Naghten* Rules have been explored.

(c) In view of the consequences of a finding of insanity, can it really be said that it is a "defence"? The result of a successful plea of insanity is the special verdict of not guilty by reason of insanity.[485] As Goldstein has stated:

---

[481] Law Commission Discussion Paper (2013), fn.461 above, para.1.52, taking the view that this is the true rationale of the defence rather than simply a denial of mens rea.

[482] See V. Tadros, "Insanity and the Capacity for Criminal Responsibility" (2000) 5 *Edinburgh Law Review* 325 for an analysis of the significance of the difference between capacity and attribution responsibility.

[483] Criminal Lunatics Act 1800. S. White, "Insanity Defences and the Magistrates' Courts" [1991] Crim. L.R. 501 at 502.

[484] White, above, *R. v Horseferry Road Magistrates Court, ex parte K* [1996] 2 Cr. App. R. 574 confirms that it is still possible to raise the insanity defence at summary trial. See further, comment by J.C. Smith, [1997] Crim. L.R. 132; S. White and P. Bowen, "Insanity Defences in Summary Trials" [1997] 61 J. Crim. L. 198. See, for example, *R (on the application of Surat Singh) v (1) Stratford Magistrates' Court (2) Crown Prosecution Service (Interested Party)* [2007] EWCA 1582 (Admin).

[485] Criminal Procedure (Insanity) Act 1964 s.1. On the origins of the special verdict, see A. Loughnan, "'Manifest madness': towards a new understanding of the insanity defence" (2007) 70 M.L.R. 379.

"In virtually every state a successful insanity defense does not bring freedom with it. Instead it has become the occasion for either mandatory commitment to a mental hospital or for an exercise of discretion by the court regarding the advisability of such commitment."[486]

In this country, as a result of the Criminal Procedure (Insanity and Unfitness to Plead) Act 1991 (as amended by the Domestic Violence, Crimes and Victims Act 2004), we have moved from the first position Goldstein describes to the second. It can be argued, therefore, that the "defence" is merely a way of substituting one method of state control for another. The state may not hold the defendant responsible for her actions but still retains the right to dispose of her as it thinks fit.

2. The law

(i) Fitness to plead

There is little point in going through the ritual of a criminal trial if the defendant is unable to comprehend what is happening.

R.A. Duff, Trials and Punishments (1986), pp.27, 263–264:

"[W]hat is crucial here (apart from considerations of past deserts or of future consequences) is the offender's capacity to understand and respond to her imprisonment as a *punishment*: if she is now so disordered that she lacks this capacity she is not fit to be punished, whether or not she committed an offence which merited punishment, and whether or not imprisonment would be the most efficient way of protecting others against her. For punishment aims and must aim, if it is to be properly justified, to *address* the offender as a rational and responsible agent: if she cannot understand what is being done to her, or why it is being done, or how it is related as a punishment to her past offence, her punishment becomes a travesty . . .

This means that an offender who is fit to be punished . . . must be capable not only of grasping the fact that what is being done to her is done because she has broken the law, but also of grasping and responding to its moral meaning and purpose as a punishment. She must have the capacity and the potential for the kind of penitential redemption which punishment aims to induce: which means she must already have some concern which punishment may reawaken and strengthen, for the values which she has flouted, or at least that she has some moral concerns which would enable her to come, through her punishment, to understand and care for the values which the law embodies."[487]

Accordingly, before there can be a trial, a defendant must be found "fit to plead".[488] The earliest criteria employed by the courts to determine this were that the defendant had to be able to understand the charge, challenge jurors, and follow evidence.[489] These criteria were developed in relation to defendants who were deaf and dumb rather than defendants who were mentally ill and thus the test concentrated upon ability to communicate and intelligence (because at the time deaf mutes were widely regarded as suffering from mental disabilities):

"Because the focus was on mental deficiency . . . delusions, disorders of mood and other features common to mental illness which were clearly relevant to the notion of unfitness to plead . . . had no

---

[486] A.S. Goldstein, *The Insanity Defense* (London: Yale University Press, 1967), p.19.
[487] See further, R.D. Mackay, *Mental Condition Defences in the Criminal Law* (Oxford: Clarendon Press, 1995), pp.216–219.
[488] The issue of fitness may be raised by the prosecution or the defence or by the judge. On the origins of the concept of fitness to plead, see D. Grubin, "What Constitutes Fitness to Plead?" [1993] Crim. L.R. 748.
[489] *Dyson* (1831) 7 C. & P. 305; *Pritchard* (1836) 7 C. & P. 303. *R. v Podola (Guenther Fritz Erwin)* [1960] 1 Q.B. 325 decided that the burden of proof rests upon the defence if they raise the issue of fitness.

role in the concept . . . regardless of how they might impinge on a defendant's chances of having a fair trial."[490]

Subsequently, the requirement that the defendant be able to instruct counsel was added.[491] What is significant about this development was that it arose from a case dealing with a mentally ill defendant and emphasis was not placed upon ability to communicate or intelligence but upon the capacity of the defendant properly to instruct counsel. Since then, however, this distinction has been lost and for more than 150 years the test has concentrated upon cognitive ability. In *M*, the judge broke the issues down thus: the defendant has to be capable of: (i) understanding the charges they face; (ii) deciding whether to plead guilty; (iii) challenging jurors; (iv) instructing solicitors and counsel; (v) following the proceedings; and (vi) giving evidence.[492] It is clear that defendants may be found fit to plead and yet have substantial learning difficulties. In *SC v United Kingdom*,[493] the defendant was an 11-year-old boy with an intellectual ability of between a six- to eight-year-old child. He did not appear to grasp the role of the jury nor to understand the fact that he risked a custodial sentence if found guilty. Yet the medical expert who examined the boy concluded that he was, on balance, fit to plead. The boy was found guilty and in due course complained to the European Court of Human Rights that, because of his age and low intellectual ability, he was unable to participate effectively at his trial, contrary to art.6 of the European Convention on Human Rights. The European Court concluded by a majority that art.6 had been violated and explained:

"The court accepts the government's argument that art 6(1) does not require that a child on trial for a criminal offence should understand or be capable of understanding every point or evidential detail. Given the sophistication of modern legal systems, many adults of normal intelligence are unable to comprehend all the intricacies and exchanges which take place in the courtroom . . . However, 'effective participation' in this context presupposes that the accused has a broad understanding of the nature of the trial process and of what is at stake for him or her, including the significance of any penalty which may be imposed. It means that he or she, if necessary with the assistance of, for example, an interpreter, lawyer, social worker or friend, should be able to understand the general thrust of what is said in court. The defendant should be able to follow what is said by the prosecution witnesses and, if represented, to explain to his own lawyers his version of events, point out any statements with which he disagrees and make them aware of any facts which should be put forward in his defence."[494]

While this decision applies to child defendants only, there is a compelling argument that it should apply whether the defendant is a child or an adult. The point is not that defendants should conduct their defence wisely or well—simply that "effective participation" under art.6 of the European Convention on Human Rights should lead to a higher threshold of competency than the current test of fitness.[495] In the light of long-standing concerns over whether the test is finding fit those who should not be tried, the Law Commission has commenced a review of the law. In 2010, it provisionally recommended a test, based upon the Mental Capacity Act 2005, of "decision-making capacity" which

---

[490] Grubin, fn.488 above, p.753. In *R. v Moyle (Peter Geoffrey)* [2009] Crim. L.R. 586 the court confirmed that paranoid delusions will not necessarily prevent a defendant being found fit to plead: it will depend upon the nature of the delusions the defendant experiences.

[491] *Davies* (1853) C.L.C. 326.

[492] *M* [2003] All E.R. (D) 199.

[493] *SC v United Kingdom* [2005] 1 F.C.R. 347. See also *R. v Miller (Scott William)* [2006] EWCA Crim 2391 where the defendant was found fit to plead despite having an IQ of 66 which placed him in the bottom 2.5% of the population.

[494] *SC v United Kingdom*, above at [29]. See further, *T v United Kingdom* [2002] 2 All E.R. 1024.

[495] See further, Grubin, fn.488 above. A further problem relates to hysterical amnesiacs who can recall nothing of the crime they are alleged to have committed. According to *R. v Podola (Guenther Fritz Erwin)* [1960] 1 Q.B. 325, they will be found fit to plead.

would replace the *Pritchard* formula as re-stated in *M*.[496] However, given the responses to the consultation it has recently embarked upon a further period of discussion, including whether reform should supplement the current cognitive test with a decisional competence limb, as advocated by Mackay,[497] rather than jettisoning it completely. The outcome of this stage of the project will not be known until 2015, but because reform is regarded as pressing, it is being prioritised over the review of insanity and automatism. [498]

Some important reforms have taken place. The Criminal Procedure (Insanity and Unfitness to Plead) Act 1991 as amended by the Domestic Violence, Crimes and Victims Act 2004, has substantially altered the consequences of a finding of unfitness or "disability". Where the judge[499] finds that the defendant is under a disability the jury are empanelled to decide whether the defendant has done the act or omission charged. If they conclude that the defendant has not done so the jury "shall return a verdict of acquittal as if on the count in question the trial had proceeded to a conclusion".[500] The defendant goes free.

The alternative is for the jury to find that the defendant is under a disability but did the act or omission charged.[501] In *Antoine*, the House of Lords ruled that this requires a finding that the actus reus is established only.[502] It overruled the previous decision of *Egan*, in which the Court of Appeal had held that the mens rea of the offence need also be established.[503] While the interpretation favoured by the House of Lords accords with that of Parliament in debates during the passage of the 1991 Act, the level of protection for unfit defendants has been reduced.[504] Judges have also found it difficult sometimes to identify which elements of an offence constitute the actus reus for these purposes. In *R. v B*, the Court of Appeal ruled that the trial judge had been wrong not to instruct the jury to consider whether the defendant's observation of two boys had been "for the purpose of sexual gratification" when considering whether the defendant had done the "injurious act" of the offence of voyeurism under s.67 of the Sexual Offences Act 2003.[505] However, the general rule that only the actus reus need be proved is subject to qualification. Where, for example, the unfit person participated in the offence as a secondary party rather than as the principal, it will be necessary to refer to the basis of secondary liability. Thus, the jury will have to be satisfied that the unfit person participated with knowledge of the

---

[496] Law Commission Consultation Paper No.197, *Unfitness to Plead* (2010).

[497] R.D. Mackay, "On being Insane in Jersey Part Three" [2004] Crim. L.R. 291, discussing the decision of *O'Driscoll* in which Jersey adopted a test based upon "effective participation". See also, Mackay, "Unfitness to plead – some observations of the Law Commission's consultation paper" [2011] Crim. L.R. 433.

[498] Law Commission Discussion Paper (2013), fn.461 above, paras 1.10–1.15.

[499] Prior to Domestic Violence, Crimes and Victims Act 2004 s.22, a jury performed this function. Under Criminal Procedure (Insanity) Act 1964, s.4(5), as amended by Domestic Violence, Crimes and Victims Act 2004 s.22, the court may not make a determination of fitness except upon the evidence of two or more registered practitioners (one of whom is duly approved under the Mental Health Act 1983). Thus, as Ormerod notes, "if the accused simply asserts that he is unfit, without the medical evidence of two registered practitioners, the judge may continue with the trial, at his discretion. In doing so the judge is not determining whether D is 'fit' to be tried, but is simply not satisfied to the relevant standard and in accordance with the prescribed statutory procedure that the accused is 'unfit'", D. Ormerod, "Unfitness to plead: Criminal Procedure (Insanity) Act 1964 s.4, as amended–unfitness to plead" [2010] Crim. L.R. 796 at 798 (commenting on *R. v Ghulam (Habib)* [2009] EWCA Crim 2285).

[500] Criminal Procedure (Insanity and Unfitness to Plead) Act 1991 s.2, substituting a new s.4A(4) to the Criminal Procedure (Insanity) Act 1964.

[501] In *R. v Norman (Leslie)* [2008] EWCA Crim 1810, the court made recommendations as to the conduct of such cases. Because of concerns over public safety, it also urged the government to consider granting the courts a power to order retrial of the issue as to whether the defendant did the act where the original finding has to be quashed at [34].This lacuna was also highlighted in *R. v McKenzie (Michael Anthony)* [2011] EWCA Crim 1550.

[502] *R. v Antoine (Pierre Harrison)* [2001] 1 A.C. 340. See also *Attorney-General's Reference (No. 3 of 1998)* [1999] 2 Cr. App. R. 214.

[503] *R. v Egan (Michael)* [1998] 1 Cr. App. R. 121.

[504] See further, R.D. Mackay and G. Kearns, "The Trial of the Facts and Unfitness to Plead" [1997] Crim. L.R. 644.

[505] *R. v B* [2012] EWCA Crim 770.

activities of the principal offender and surrounding circumstances before he or she can be held to have "done the act or omission charged".[506] Where the jury comes to the conclusion that the person did the act or omission the judge may make a hospital order (with or without a restriction order), a supervision order or an order for absolute discharge.[507]

Research has shown that the judges have responded positively to this increased flexibility and there is also evidence that, after years of decline, the use of the plea has increased since the implementation of the 1991 Act.[508] At the same time as its use has been increasing, however, the 1991 Act has been subject to a fundamental challenge. In H,[509] it was argued that the procedure to establish whether the person has done the act or omission is to all intents and purposes a procedure to determine a criminal charge and thus ought to attract the protection provided in art.6 of the European Convention on Human Rights (the right to a fair trial) of the European Convention on Human Rights. This protection was absent because the defendant, being unfit to plead, could not give instructions and participate fully in his defence. The House of Lords rejected this claim, holding that the procedure lacked the essential features of the criminal process and that it would be highly anomalous if a procedure introduced to protect those unable to defend themselves at trial was to be found incompatible with the Convention. However, while s.4A may now be safe from a human rights challenge, the Law Commission is right to include the procedure as well as the test for fitness within its review.

(ii) Insanity as a "defence"

In many of the most extreme cases the defendant will not be found fit to stand trial. Accordingly, the insanity defence is usually reserved for problematic and borderline cases.

Before examining the test for insanity it should be noted that, exceptionally, the burden of proof rests with defendants to show on a balance of probabilities that they were insane at the time of the act[510] and that it is for the judge to determine whether a defence raised by defendants is, in fact, one of insanity. The question of reverse burden of proof has become deeply problematic with the implementation of the European Convention on Human Rights. The issue is whether placing the burden of proof upon the defendant contravenes the presumption of innocence protected by art.6(2) of the European Convention on Human Rights. While the point has yet to be tested in relation to insanity, one indication of the way in which courts may now approach reverse burdens of proof is given by the decision of Kebeline,[511] where

---

[506] *Martin* [2003] 2 Cr. App. R. 332.

[507] Criminal Procedure (Insanity) Act 1964 s.5 amended by Domestic Violence, Crimes and Victims Act 2004 s.24. The same forms of disposal are now also available where the charge is murder. However, under s.5(3) where the court has the power to make a hospital order (broadly, because of the nature of the defendant's condition) a hospital order with a restriction order must be made. The reforms made by s.24 mean that the law relating to disposal is now compatible with the right to liberty under art.5 of the European Convention on Human Rights.

[508] R.D. Mackay, "A continued upturn in unfitness to plead—more disability in relation to trial under the 1991 Act" [2007] Crim. L.R. 530. See also Appendix C of the Law Commission Consultation Paper, fn.496 above: Mackay's research reveals that there were 725 findings of unfitness to plead between 2002 and 2008.

[509] *H* [2003] All E.R. (D) 293.

[510] *Woolmington v Director of Public Prosecutions* [1935] A.C. 462 at 475–476. The same is true for diminished responsibility: Homicide Act 1957 s.2(2). There are difficulties with this exception. For example, if a defendant pleads (simple) lack of mens rea the burden of proof rests with the prosecution to prove beyond reasonable doubt that he did have mens rea; however, if the defendant adds that the absence of mens rea was due to a disease of the mind the burden then shifts to the defendant. If the defendant pleads automatism the burden will only shift in cases of insane automatism. See further, T. Jones, "Insanity, Automatism and the Burden of Proof on the Accused" [1995] 111 L.Q.R. 475.

[511] *R. v Director of Public Prosecutions, ex parte Kebeline* [1999] 3 W.L.R. 972. The case, decided prior to the Human Rights Act 1998, dealt with reverse burdens of proof under the Prevention of Terrorism Act 1989 which the Divisional Court found to be in flagrant breach of art.6(2) of the European Convention on Human Rights. The House of Lords took a much more

it was suggested by the House of Lords that these might be re-interpreted as imposing an evidential burden upon the defendant only.

(a) *The M'Naghten Rules*

M'Naghten's Case (1843) 10 C & F, 200, 8 Eng. Rep. 718

The defendant was indicted for the murder of Edward Drummond, Secretary to the Prime Minister, Sir Robert Peel. The defence introduced evidence of the defendant's insanity, particularly his obsession with certain morbid delusions. The presiding judge, Lord Tindal CJ, directed the jury in the following terms: "The question to be asked is whether . . . the prisoner had or had not the use of his understanding, so as to know that he was doing a wrong and wicked act." The jury returned a verdict of not guilty by reason of insanity. The furore occasioned by the verdict led to the whole issue of insanity being debated in the House of Lords. As a result, five questions were put to the judges of the day; the answers to questions two and three form the basis of the "*M'Naghten* Rules" by which lack of criminal responsibility is tested.

LORD TINDAL CJ:

"Your lordships are pleased to inquire of us, secondly, 'What are the proper questions to be submitted to the jury, where a person alleged to be afflicted with insane delusion respecting one or more particular subjects or persons, is charged with the commission of a crime (murder, for example), and insanity is set up as a defence?' And, thirdly, 'In what terms ought the question to be left to the jury as to the prisoner's state of mind at the time when the act was committed?' And as these two questions appear to us to be more conveniently answered together, we have to submit our opinion to be, that the jurors ought to be told in all cases that every man is to be presumed to be sane, and to possess a sufficient degree of reason to be responsible for his crimes, until the contrary be proved to their satisfaction; and that to establish a defence on the ground of insanity, *it must be clearly proved that, at the time of the committing of the act, the party accused was labouring under such a defect of reason, from disease of the mind, as not to know the nature and quality of the act he was doing; or, if he did know it, that he did not know he was doing what was wrong*. The mode of putting the latter part of the question to the jury on these occasions has generally been, whether the accused at the time of doing the act knew the difference between right and wrong: which mode, though rarely, if ever, leading to any mistake with the jury, is not, as we conceive, so accurate when put generally and in the abstract, as when put with reference to the party's knowledge of right and wrong in respect to the very act with which he is charged. If the question were to be put as to the knowledge of the accused solely and exclusively with reference to the law of the land, it might tend to confound the jury, by inducing them to believe that an actual knowledge of the law of the land was essential in order to lead to a conviction; whereas the law is administered upon the principle that every one must be taken conclusively to know it, without proof that he does know it. If the accused was conscious that the act was one which he ought not to do, and if the act was at the same time contrary to the law of the land, he is punishable; and the usual course therefore has been to leave the question to the jury, whether the party accused had a sufficient degree of reason to know that he was doing an act that was wrong: and this course we think is correct, accompanied with such observations and explanations as the circumstances of each particular case may require." (emphasis added)

Although the essence of the *M'Naghten* Rules may be simply stated—it asks whether the defendant knew what they was doing at the time the crime was committed—certain of the phrases used in the formulation of the rules have been subject to much judicial (and academic) interpretation.

One can envisage the *M'Naghten* Rules as a series of hurdles over which the defendant must jump in order to be excused liability.

---

qualified approach, arguing that each instance of the reverse burden would have to be considered on its own merits and that would include how the burden operated in practice.

(i) Disease of the mind

The defendant must, first, be suffering from a *"disease of the mind"*. This phrase

"initially seems to have attracted no judicial scrutiny . . . However, the development of the automatism defence changed this. For suddenly the courts were confronted by the fact that a successful defence based on 'unconscious involuntary action' could result in an unqualified acquittal. For obvious social defence reasons this fact began to worry the courts and in order to restrict the availability of such acquittals the judiciary began to develop a complex body of law built upon the phrase 'disease of the mind'."[512]

The case of *Kemp*[513] (where the defendant suffered from arteriosclerosis which induced a state of unconsciousness during which he attacked his wife with a hammer) makes it clear that the condition of the brain is irrelevant. The test is not necessarily whether there is some damage to that physical entity (although the mental disease may have a physical origin) but, more widely, whether the mental faculties of reason, understanding and memory are impaired or absent. This approach has been affirmed by the House of Lords.

R. v Sullivan [1984] A.C. 156 (House of Lords)

The defendant was charged with inflicting grievous bodily harm, contrary to s.20 of the Offences Against the Person Act 1861, after he had attacked Payne, his friend, during the post-ictal stage of an epileptic seizure. The trial judge ruled that this amounted to insanity rather than automatism; consequently, the defendant changed his plea to guilty to the lesser offence of assault occasioning actual bodily harm. He then appealed against conviction on the basis that he should have been allowed to raise the issue of automatism.[514]

LORD DIPLOCK:

"The M'Naghten Rules have been used as a comprehensive definition for this purpose by the courts for the last 140 years. Most importantly, they were so used by this House in *Bratty v Attorney-General for Northern Ireland* [1963] A.C. 386. That case was in some respects the converse of the instant case. Bratty was charged with murdering a girl by strangulation. He claimed to have been unconscious of what he was doing at the time he strangled the girl and he sought to run as alternative defences non-insane automatism and insanity. The only evidential foundation that he laid for either of these pleas was medical evidence that he might have been suffering from psychomotor epilepsy which, if he were, would account for his having been unconscious of what he was doing. No other pathological explanation of his actions having been carried out in a state of automatism was supported by evidence. The trial judge first put the defence of insanity to the jury. The jury rejected it; they declined to bring in the special verdict. Thereupon, the judge refused to put to the jury the alternative defence of automatism. His refusal was upheld by the Court of Criminal Appeal of Northern Ireland and subsequently by this House.

The question before this House was whether, the jury having rejected the plea of insanity, there was any evidence on non-insane automatism fit to be left to the jury. The ratio decidendi of its dismissal of the appeal was that the jury having negatived the explanation that Bratty might have been acting unconsciously in the course of an attack of psychomotor epilepsy, there was no evidential foundation for the suggestion that he was acting unconsciously from any other cause.

In the instant case, as in *Bratty*, the only evidential foundation that was laid for any finding by the jury that Mr

---

[512] Mackay, fn.487 above, p.97.
[513] *R. v Kemp (Albert)* [1957] 1 Q.B. 399.
[514] For an informative discussion of the medical background to this case, see N. Eastman, "Defending the Mentally Ill" in R.D. Mackay and K. Russell (eds), *Psychiatry and the Criminal Process* (Leicester: Milttak Limited, 1986).

Sullivan was acting unconsciously and involuntarily when he was kicking Mr Payne, was that when he did so he was in the post-ictal stage of a seizure of psychomotor epilepsy. The evidential foundation in the case of Bratty, that he was suffering from psychomotor epilepsy at the time he did the act with which he was charged, was very weak and was rejected by the jury; the evidence in Mr Sullivan's case, that he was so suffering when he was kicking Mr Payne, was very strong and would almost inevitably be accepted by a properly directed jury. It would be the duty of the judge to direct the jury that if they did accept that evidence the law required them to bring in a special verdict and none other. The governing statutory provision is to be found in section 2 of the Trial of Lunatics Act 1883. This says 'the jury *shall* return a special verdict . . .'

My Lords, I can deal briefly with the various grounds on which it has been submitted that the instant case can be distinguished from what constituted the *ratio decidendi* in *Bratty v Attorney-General for Northern Ireland*, and that it falls outside the ambit of the M'Naghten Rules.

First, it is submitted the medical evidence in the instant case shows that psychomotor epilepsy is not a disease of the mind, whereas in *Bratty* it was accepted by all the doctors that it was. The only evidential basis for this submission is that Dr Fenwick said that in medical terms to constitute a 'disease of the mind' or 'mental illness,' which he appeared to regard as interchangeable descriptions, a disorder of brain functions (which undoubtedly occurs during a seizure in psychomotor epilepsy) must be prolonged for a period of time usually more than a day; while Dr Taylor would have it that the disorder must continue for a minimum of a month to qualify for the description 'a disease of the mind.'

The nomenclature adopted by the medical profession may change from time to time; Bratty was tried in 1961. But the meaning of the expression 'disease of the mind' as the cause of 'a defect of reason' remains unchanged for the purposes of the application of the M'Naghten Rules. I agree with what was said by Devlin J in *R. v Kemp* that 'mind' in the M'Naghten Rules is used in the ordinary sense of the mental faculties of reason, memory and understanding. If the effect of a disease is to impair these faculties so severely as to have either of the consequences referred to in the latter part of the rules, it matters not whether the aetiology of the impairment is organic, as in epilepsy, or functional, or whether the impairment itself is permanent or is transient and intermittent, provided that it subsisted at the time of commission of the act. The purpose of the legislation relating to the defence of insanity, ever since its origin in 1800, has been to protect society against recurrence of the dangerous conduct. The duration of a temporary suspension of the mental faculties, of reason, memory and understanding, particularly if, as in Mr Sullivan's case, it is recurrent, cannot on any rational ground be relevant to the application by the courts of the M'Naghten Rules, though it may be relevant to the course adopted by the Secretary of State, to whom the responsibility for how the defendant is to be dealt with passes after the return of the special verdict 'not guilty by reason of insanity.'

To avoid misunderstanding I ought perhaps to add that in expressing my agreement with what was said by Devlin J in *Kemp*, where the disease that caused the temporary and intermittent impairment of the mental faculties was arteriosclerosis, I do not regard that learned judge as excluding the possibility of non-insane automatism (for which the proper verdict would be a verdict of 'not guilty') in cases where temporary impairment (not being self-induced by consuming drink or drugs) results from some external physical factor such as a blow on the head causing concussion or the administration of an anaesthetic for therapeutic purposes . . . The instant case, however, does not in my view afford an appropriate occasion for exploring possible causes of non-insane automatism . . .

My Lords, it is natural to feel reluctant to attach the label of insanity to a sufferer from psychomotor epilepsy of the kind to which Mr Sullivan was subject, even though the expression in the context of a special verdict of 'not guilty by reason of insanity' is a technical one which includes a purely temporary and intermittent suspension of the mental faculties of reason, memory and understanding resulting from the occurrence of an epileptic fit. But the label is contained in the current statute, it has appeared in this statute's predecessors ever since 1800. It does not lie within the power of the courts to alter it. Only Parliament can do that. It has done so twice; it could do so once again.

Sympathise though I do with Mr Sullivan, I see no other course open to your Lordships than to dismiss this appeal."

Appeal dismissed

R. v Burgess [1991] 2 W.L.R. 1206 (Court of Appeal, Criminal Division)

The defendant attacked his friend, Miss Curtis, with a bottle and then a video-recorder, finally putting a hand round her throat. The defendant claimed that he was acting unconsciously in that he had been sleep-walking and was thus entitled to be acquitted as a non-insane automaton. The trial judge ruled that the jury had to decide whether the defendant was acting consciously or whether he was not guilty by reason of insanity. The jury returned the latter verdict against which the defendant appealed.

LORD LANE CJ:

"Where the defence of automatism is raised by the defendant, two questions fall to be decided by the judge before the defence can be left to the jury. The first is whether a proper evidential foundation for the defence of automatism has been laid. The second is whether the evidence shows the case to be one of insane automatism, that is to say, a case which falls within the M'Naghten Rules, or one of non-insane automatism . . . There can be no doubt but that the appellant on the basis of the jury's verdict, was labouring under . . . such a defect of reason as not to know what he was doing when he wounded Miss Curtis. The question is whether that was from 'disease of the mind'. . .

The appellant plainly suffered from a defect of reason from some sort of failure (for lack of a better term) of the mind causing him to act as he did without conscious motivation. His mind was to some extent controlling his actions which were purposive rather than the result of muscular spasm, but without his being consciously aware of what he was doing. Can it be said that that 'failure' was a *disease* of the mind rather than a defect or failure of the mind not due to disease? That is the distinction, by no means easy to draw, upon which this case depends, as others have depended in the past.

One can perhaps narrow the field of enquiry still further by eliminating what are sometimes called the 'external factors' such as concussion caused by a blow on the head. There were no such factors here. Whatever the cause may have been, it was an internal cause.

[His Lordship then cited the case of *Sullivan*]

What help does one derive from the authorities as to the meaning of 'disease' in this context? Lord Denning in *Bratty v Attorney-General for Northern Ireland* [1963] A.C. 236, 412 said:

> . . . 'It seems to me that any mental disorder which has manifested itself in violence and is prone to recur is a disease of the mind. At any rate it is the sort of disease for which a person should be detained in hospital rather than be given an unqualified acquittal.'

It seems to us that if there is a danger of recurrence that may be an added reason for categorising the condition as a disease of the mind. On the other hand, the absence of the danger of recurrence is not a reason for saying that it cannot be a disease of the mind. Subject to that possible qualification, we respectfully adopt Lord Denning's suggested definition.

There have been several occasions when during the course of judgments in the Court of Appeal and the House of Lords observations have been made, obiter, about the criminal responsibility of sleep-walkers, where sleep-walking has been used as a self-evident illustration of non-insane automatism. For example in the speech of Lord Denning, from which we have already cited an extract, appears this passage, at p.409:

> 'No act is punishable if it is done involuntarily: and an involuntary act in this context—some people nowadays prefer to speak of it as "automatism"—means an act which is done by the muscles without any control by the mind, such as a spasm, a reflex action or a convulsion; or an act done by a person who is not conscious of what he is doing, such as an act done whilst suffering from concussion or whilst sleep-walking. The point was well put by Stephen J in 1889:
> "Can anyone doubt that a man who, though he might be perfectly sane, committed what would otherwise be a crime in a state of somnambulism, would be entitled to be acquitted? And why is this? Simply because he would not know what he was doing." ' . . .

We accept of course that sleep is a normal condition, but the evidence in the instant case indicates that sleep-walking, and particularly violence in sleep, is not normal . . . [I]n none of the other cases where sleep walking has been mentioned, so far as we can discover, has the court had the advantage of the sort of expert medical evidence which was available to the judge here.

One turns then to examine the evidence upon which the judge had to base his decision . . . Dr d'Orban in examination-in-chief said . . . [that]:

> 'Burgess's actions had occurred during the course of a sleep disorder.'

He was asked, 'Assuming this is a sleep associated automatism, is it an internal or external factor?' Answer: 'In this particular case, I think that one would have to see it as an internal factor.'

Then in cross-examination: Question: 'Would you go so far as to say that it was liable to recur?' Answer: 'It is possible for it to recur, yes.' Finally, in answer to a question from the judge, namely, 'Is this a case of automatism associated with a pathological condition or not?' Answer: 'I think the answer would have to be yes, because it is an abnormality of the brain function, so it would be regarded as a pathological condition.'

Dr Eames in cross-examination agreed with Dr d'Orban as to the internal rather than the external factor. He accepted that there is a liability to recurrence of sleep-walking. He could not go so far as to say that there is no liability of recurrence of serious violence but he agreed with the other medical witnesses that there is no recorded case of violence of this sort recurring.

It seems to us that on this evidence the judge was right to conclude that this was an abnormality or disorder, albeit transitory, due to an internal factor, whether functional or organic, which had manifested itself in criminality. It was a disorder or abnormality which might recur, though the possibility of it recurring in the form of serious violence was unlikely. Therefore since this was a legal problem to be answered on legal principles, it seems to us that on those principles the answer was as the judge found it to be."

Appeal dismissed

These two cases are highly significant. They bear witness to the continued development of the distinction between internal and external causes as a basis for determining whether a particular condition is a *"disease of the mind"*. It has long been recognised that psychomotor epilepsy is a disease of the mind but dicta, at least, had placed sleepwalking into the category of non-insane automatism. However, the medical evidence relied on in *Burgess*—that sleepwalking is a "near cousin" of epilepsy—gave the court little choice but to decide that sleep-walking should be perceived as arising from some internal factor. The logic in *Burgess* in this respect can be supported. Nevertheless, its categorisation of sleep-walking as insane automatism has divided the medico-legal community: not all experts agree that it is caused by an internal factor. In Canada, for example, it is held to be sane automatism: what causes the defendant's suspension of mental faculties is falling asleep (a perfectly normal occurrence).[515] Moreover, there have been instances in England where defendants have been acquitted of offences on the basis that they were sleepwalking at the time: for example, in *Thomas*, "a decent man and devoted husband" who strangled his wife during a nightmare in which he believed he was attacking an intruder was acquitted after the prosecution withdrew the case.[516]

However, the problem with the (increasingly contested) categorisation of sleepwalking is illustrative of a much more fundamental problem. The distinction between internal and external causes is fundamentally flawed. "It makes illogical, hair-splitting distinctions inevitable."[517] We are forced to conclude that epileptics (0.5 per cent of the population) will be regarded as insane if they commit offences during epileptic fits.[518] The same is true of some diabetics. Diabetics can experience hyperglycaemic episodes (triggered by too much blood sugar and caused by the diabetic condition itself) or hypoglycaemic episodes (too little blood sugar, arising from the combination of diabetes, insulin, food (or lack of it) and possibly alcohol). In *Quick and Paddison*,[519] the court distinguished these two conditions holding that a transitory malfunctioning of the mind caused by hypoglycaemia due to

---

[515] I.D. Ebrahim, P.B. Fenwick, R.L. Marks and K.W. Peacock, "Violence, Sleepwalking and the Criminal Law: Part 1: The Medical Aspects" [2005] Crim. L.R. 601 at 603. See also R.D. Mackay, "Sleepwalkers are Not Insane" (1992) 55 M.L.R. 714.

[516] (2009) *The Independent*, November 21. In *Bilton, The Independent*, December 20, 2005, the defendant was acquitted of rape; in *Davies, The Times*, February 11, 2006, the defendant was acquitted of sexual assault but in *Lowe, The Times*, March 19, 2005, a plea of insane automatism was accepted. See further, R.D. Mackay and B.J. Mitchell, "Sleepwalking, Automatism and Insanity" [2006] Crim. L.R. 901.

[517] W. Wilson et al., "Violence, Sleepwalking and the Criminal Law: Part 2: The Legal Aspects" [2005] Crim. L.R. 614 at 617.

[518] See further, R.D. Mackay and M. Reuber, "Epilepsy and the Defence of Insanity: Time for Change?" [2007] Crim. L.R. 782.

[519] *R. v Quick (William George); R. v Paddison (William)* [1973] Q.B. 910. See also *R. v Bailey (John Graham)* [1983] 1 W.L.R. 760.

external factors (for example, the taking of insulin) is non-insane automatism entitling the defend-ant to an acquittal. On the other hand, in *Hennessy*,[520] it was held that hyperglycaemia gave rise to insane automatism. In this case the defendant was charged with taking a conveyance and with driving while disqualified. His defence was that at the relevant time he had failed to take his proper dose of insulin due to stress, anxiety and depression and this caused the ensuing state of hyperglycaemia. The Court of Appeal accepted the *Quick and Paddison* distinction between hyper- and hypoglycaemia and rejected the defence argument that stress, anxiety and depression were factors that could count as external for the purposes of non-insane automatism. The court added that they constituted a state of mind that was prone to recur and lacked the feature of novelty or accident traditionally associated with non-insane automatism.

The result of these decisions is that we are left with a law under which some diabetics will be able to secure a complete acquittal while others will be regarded as insane. Such a position is absurd. Moreover, the harshness of these categorisations is hardly tempered by telling defendants (and their families), as Lord Diplock does in *Sullivan* and Lord Lane echoes in *Burgess*, that the label "insanity" is merely a technical one.

The key to evaluating these cases depends upon whether the concept "disease of the mind" requires anything more than a finding that the cause is an internal one. In particular, we need to know whether there is any requirement that the internal cause be associated with violence. Lord Denning in *Bratty* stated that "any mental disorder which has manifested itself in violence and is prone to recur is a disease of the mind".[521] This was cited with approval in *Sullivan* but in *Burgess* Lord Lane said that "the absence of the danger of recurrence is not a reason for saying that it cannot be a disease of the mind". It was this that enabled his Lordship to state that the defendant could be said to have a disease of the mind despite the fact that the experts could point to no reported incident of a sleep-walker being repeatedly violent. This modification of *Bratty* flies in the face of Lord Diplock's statement in *Sullivan* that "the purpose of the legislation relating to the defence of insanity, ever since its origin, has been to protect society against dangerous conduct". However, this social defence argument could not with-stand rigorous scrutiny even before *Burgess*. For example, how can one say that epileptics are more dangerous than diabetics having a hypoglycaemic episode? Can mental disorders that do not mani-fest themselves in violence, for example, kleptomania, never be diseases of the mind? Nevertheless, despite such weaknesses, the social defence argument did have a valuable limiting function. As a result of *Burgess*, all that *"disease of the mind"* seems to mean is any internal factor that has, on one occasion at least, manifested itself in criminality.

This discussion demonstrates that the internal/external factor distinction is unable to bear the weight of distinguishing insanity from non-insane automatism. It highlights the failure of the insan-ity test (and perhaps, any insanity test) to come to terms with the issue of the responsibility of the individual defendant on the one hand, and the protection of the public (and the defendant himself) against harm on the other. We shall return to this question later, once the remaining elements of the test of insanity, and the proposals for reform thereof, have been considered.

(ii) Defect of reason

Assuming that the defendant is suffering from a disease of the mind, the next hurdle to be overcome is that this disease of the mind must induce a *"defect of reason"*. The reasoning ability of the defendant must be affected; it is not enough that he or she simply failed to use powers of reasoning which they

---

[520] *R. v Hennessy (Andrew Michael)* [1989] 1 W.L.R. 287.
[521] *Bratty v Attorney-General of Northern Ireland* [1963] A.C. 386 at 412.

had.[522] This aspect of the insanity test is classically illustrative of one of the basic premises of responsibility in law: guilt cannot be adduced in the absence of the *capacity* to reason.

(iii) Nature and quality of the act; knowledge of wrong

Having passed over the initial hurdles, the defendant may be brought within the ambit of the special verdict if either of two further conditions are satisfied. First, the defendant must not know *"the nature and quality of his acts"*. Kenny provides a vivid example of this: "The madman who cuts a woman's throat under the idea that he is cutting a loaf of bread"[523] does not know the nature and quality of his acts. Alternatively, it must be established that the defendant does not know that his actions are *"wrong"*.[524] The case of *Windle*[525] decided that this means knowledge that the acts are legally (and not merely morally) wrong. It is often thought that this limb adds very little to the insanity test, yet research has shown that it is this part of the test that is most commonly used to secure a special verdict.[526] For example, in one case:

> "A 22 year old male attempted to kill his parents because he believed that they were to be tortured and that he must kill them in order that they would die in a humane way. Two psychiatrists stated that while he knew the nature and quality of the act of stabbing his parents, he did not know that what he was doing was wrong . . . His mind was plagued with delusional perceptions which confused his rational thinking to the extent that the wrongness of his act would not have been a consideration." [527]

Research also shows that a broad-brush approach is taken to this requirement. Little effort is made to distinguish between cases where the defendant does not know that her actions are legally wrong and those where there is a lack of knowledge that the actions are morally wrong.[528] "In so doing, it may be argued that psychiatrists in many respects are adopting a common sense approach and that the courts by accepting this interpretation are, in reality, expanding the scope of the M'Naghten Rules."[529] In *Johnson*,[530] the Court of Appeal acknowledged that there had been occasions when the courts had been prepared to take a more flexible approach, and agreed that there was a persuasive argument for extending the defence, but reaffirmed the law as stated in *Windle*.[531] In concluding, Latham LJ stated:

> "This area, however, is a notorious area for debate and quite rightly so. There is room for reconsideration of the rules and, in particular, rules which have their genesis in the early years of the 19th century."[532]

---

[522]   *R. v Clarke (May)* [1972] 1 All E.R. 219.

[523]   C.S. Kenny, *Outlines of Criminal Law*, 17th edn (Cambridge: OUP, 1958), p.76. *Northern Ireland* [1963] A.C. 386 at 412. *R. v Clarke (May)*, above.

[524]   In *Harris (Darren) v The Queen* [2013] EWCA Crim 223, the defendant was convicted of arson. His conviction was quashed on the basis that although he was affected by a mental disorder he knew what he was doing and that it was wrong, so insanity did not arise, nevertheless, his claim that he did not foresee the risk because of mental disorder (i.e. a claim of lack of mens rea) should have been put to the jury (at [56]).

[525]   *R. v Windle (Francis Wilfred)* [1952] 2 Q.B. 826.

[526]   R.D. Mackay and G. Kearns, "More Fact(s) about the Insanity Defence" [1999] Crim. L.R. 714.

[527]   Mackay, fn.487 above, p.104.

[528]   See fn.516.

[529]   Mackay and Kearns, fn.526 above, p.723.

[530]   *R. v Johnson (Dean)* [2007] EWCA Crim 1978. See D. Ormerod, "Insanity: knowledge of right and wrong—'wrong' meaning against the law" [2008] Crim. L.R. 132 and M. Hathaway, "The Moral Significance of the Insanity Defence" (2009) 73 J. Crim. L. 310.

[531]   The court referred to the Australian decision of *Stapleton* (1952) 86 C.L.R. 358 where *R. v Windle (Francis Wilfred)* [1952] 2 Q.B. 826 was held to be wrongly decided. See further, R.D. Mackay, "Righting the Wrong?—Some Observations on the Second Limb of the M'Naghten Rules" [2009] Crim. L.R. 80 where the retreat from the test is *Windle* in various jurisdictions is discussed.

[532]   *R. v Windle (Francis Wilfred)*, above at [24]. The court also commented that given the genesis of the Rules (as answers to questions) "it has always been recognised that the M'Naghten Rules . . . have to be approached with some caution."

(iv) Role of medical evidence

The courts have made it plain from *M'Naghten* onwards that they regard all these questions as legal ones for their determination. Medical evidence is, in theory, just that—evidence from which decisions can be made. However, there can be little doubt that a large part of the decision-making can rest with the medical expert. Under s.1 of the Criminal Procedure (Insanity and Unfitness to Plead) Act 1991 no verdict of not guilty by reason of insanity can be returned except on the written or oral evidence of two or more registered medical practitioners (at least one of whom has to be approved under s.12 of the Mental Health Act 1983). The reasons advanced for the introduction of this requirement are of interest. In some cases insanity verdicts had been returned without any medical evidence to support the plea.[533] Clearly, giving so little weight to the role of experts was unsatisfactory.[534] The position now, however, is that experts are called upon to do too much *if* the issue is a legal one. Medical experts may not be asked baldly: "Do you think this person is insane?" (The word would be of no medical significance in any event). But they may well be asked: "Do you think this defendant has a disease of the mind?" This intermingling of medical and legal concepts is fraught with danger and the situation is not improved by the decision in *Burgess* where, despite stating that the issues involved were legal ones, considerable reliance was placed upon the expert's statement that the defendant's condition was pathological. Further, not only may medical experts fundamentally disagree amongst themselves about a particular diagnosis but they may, if their sympathies are engaged with their "patient", distort the evidence to fit the "manifest absurdity of the M'Naghten test".[535] One possibility is that it was because neither the judiciary nor the medical experts seemed wholly convinced about their role in the adjudication process that s.1 was passed. It has been argued that it is an "effort to ensure greater congruence between the evidence necessary for a person to be found not guilty by reason of insanity and that necessary for long-term detention under the Mental Health Act 1983 on grounds of mental disorder".[536] If this argument is correct then it would help to rebut a challenge that the *M'Naghten* Rules contravene the European Convention on Human Rights.[537] It is by no means clear, however, that s.1 was meant to be anything more than a procedural change and the Draft Criminal Code expressly rejects the assimilation of the two concepts on the basis that the definition of mental disorder under the Mental Health Act 1983 is too wide and was designed for different purposes.[538]

As matters stand, even if medical experts and judges are clear in their own minds about their respective roles, juries appear to have little role to play in most cases. Research has revealed that in 86 per cent of cases there was agreed expert evidence and the jury was simply directed (with both prosecution and defence agreement) to return a verdict of not guilty by reason of insanity.[539]

---

[533] R.D. Mackay, "Fact and Fiction about the Insanity Defence" [1990] Crim. L.R. 247 at 251; E. Baker, "Human Rights, M'Naghten and the 1991 Act" [1994] Crim. L.R. 84 at 86.

[534] Although see Loughnan, fn.485 above for a discussion of the role that collective, lay knowledge of madness has in understandings of insanity in the criminal trial.

[535] Royal Commission on Capital Punishment, Cmnd. 8932 (1953), p.104.

[536] P. Fennell, "The Criminal Procedure (Insanity and Unfitness to Plead) Act 1991" (1992) 55 M.L.R. 547 at 549.

[537] Below, p.416. See further, Baker, fn.533 above.

[538] Law Com. No.177 (1989), fn.21 above, paras 11.26–11.28.

[539] Mackay and Kearns, fn.526 above. A follow up study, examining the use of the insanity plea in the years 1997–2001, confirmed the finding that juries "have little real deliberative role to play" in such cases: K.D. Mackay, B.J. Mitchell and L. Howe, "Yet More Facts About the Insanity Defence" [2006] Crim. L.R. 399 at 404.

(b) *Criminal Procedure (Insanity and Unfitness to Plead) Act 1991*

Before the 1991 Act, the result of a finding of "not guilty by reason of insanity" was mandatory commitment to such hospital as directed by the Home Secretary (commonly a special hospital such as Broadmoor) without limitation of time. Not unnaturally, defendants faced with this possibility, when their plea had originally been not guilty (because of non-insane automatism), often decided to change their pleas to guilty; indeed, Sullivan did precisely this. Whilst research reveals that defendants did not spend as long in hospital as they feared,[540] this forced change of plea was clearly unacceptable. Further, given the diversity of cases brought within the concept of "disease of the mind" by the development of the internal/external distinction, there was a pressing need for this to be reflected in the methods of disposal available to the court. It was profoundly unsatisfactory that judges could not make an order that distinguished between the treatment appropriate for an epileptic, a diabetic or a schizophrenic.

The Criminal Procedure (Insanity and Unfitness to Plead) Act 1991 (as amended) enables the court to do this. Until 2004, mandatory commitment followed a finding of insanity in cases of murder. However, in all cases the court may now make a hospital order (with or without restriction order), a supervision order or an order for absolute discharge.[541]

It should be stressed that this section does nothing to alter the *M'Naghten* Rules themselves.[542] Indeed, it is possible that by removing mandatory commitment reform may now be less likely than ever, although both the insanity defence and unfitness to plead are currently being considered by the Law Commission as part of its programme of law reform. Despite their limited nature, however, these reforms are welcome and it seems that the judiciary have embraced the new flexibility[543] and that, although still very rare, an increase in the use of the insanity plea has occurred.[544]

(c) *Proposals for reform*

It is possible to support the *M'Naghten* Rules.

American Law Institute, Model Penal Code Tent. Draft. No.4 (1955), comments to s.4.01, pp.156–157:

"The traditional M'Naghten rule resolves the problem solely in regard to the capacity of the individual to know what he was doing and to know that it was wrong. Absent these minimal elements of rationality, condemnation and punishment are obviously both unjust and futile. They are unjust because the individual could not, by hypothesis, have employed reason to restrain the act; he did not and he could not know the facts essential to bring reason into play. On the same ground, they are futile. A madman who believes that he is squeezing lemons when he chokes his wife or thinks that homicide is the command of God is plainly beyond reach of the restraining influence of law; he needs restraint but condemnation is entirely meaningless and ineffective. Thus the attacks on the M'Naghten rule as an inept definition of insanity or as an arbitrary definition in terms of special symptoms are entirely misconceived. The rationale of the position is that these are cases in which reason cannot operate

---

[540] Mackay, fn.533 above, pp.251–255 and Mackay, fn.487 above, pp.104–105.

[541] Criminal Procedure (Insanity) Act 1964 s.5 as amended by the Criminal Procedure (Insanity and Unfitness to Plead) Act 1991 and the Domestic Violence, Crimes and Victims Act 2004. If the charge is one of murder *and* the court has the power to make a hospital order (broadly, because of the nature of the condition of the defendant) a hospital order with a restriction order must be made (s.5(3)).

[542] There is an argument, canvassed earlier, that s.1 of the Act does effect a change. Above, p.413.

[543] Mackay's research (over a 10-year period between 1991–2001) revealed that in over 50% of cases a community-based order was made: Mackay et al., fn.539 above, p.407.

[544] In the first five years of Mackay's research there was an average of 8.8 findings per year of not guilty by reason of insanity; by 1997–2001 this had risen to an average of 14.4 per year: Mackay et al., fn.539 above, p.400. The average is now over 20 per year: Mackay, fn.487 above .

and in which it is totally impossible for individuals to be deterred. Moreover, the category defined by the rule is so extreme that to the ordinary man the exculpation of the person it encompasses bespeaks no weakness in the law" [545]

However, more commonly, the *M'Naghten* Rules have been subjected to intense criticism.

Report of the Committee on Mentally Abnormal Offenders (Butler Committee) (Cmnd.6244, 1975), pp.217–219:

"18.5 Almost throughout their existence the M'Naghten Rules have been criticised, generally as being based on too limited a concept of the nature of mental disorder. The Royal Commission on Capital Punishment in 1953 noted that the interpretation of the rules by the courts had been broadened and stretched to make them fit particular cases, to the point where 'the gap between the natural meaning of the law and the sense in which it is commonly applied has for so long been so wide, it is impossible to escape the conclusion that an amendment of the law, to bring it into closer conformity with the current practice, is long overdue.' The Royal Commission pointed out that many offenders who know what they are doing and that it is wrong are nevertheless undoubtedly insane and should not be held responsible for their actions. Another serious difficulty lies in the outmoded language of the rules which gives rise to problems of interpretation. It is unclear, for example, whether the reference to the knowledge of the accused of the nature and quality of his act should be taken to cover the whole mental element in crime or some narrower concept. Similarly the nineteenth century term 'disease of the mind' raises the question whether the rules are intended to cover severe subnormality, neurosis or psychopathy.

18.6 But the main defect of the M'Naghten test is that it was based on the now obsolete belief in the pre-eminent role of reason in controlling social behaviour. It therefore requires evidence of the cognitive capacity, in particular the knowledge and understanding of the defendant at the time of the act or omission charged. Contemporary psychiatry and psychology emphasise that man's social behaviour is determined more by how he has learned to behave than by what he knows or understands. For many years a number of mental disorders differing in their clinical characteristics have been recognised and distinguished from one another. In some disorders the patient's beliefs are so bizarre or his change of mood is so profound and inexplicable, or he is so changed in manner and conduct, that his condition can only be described as alien, or mad. In such cases it is accepted opinion in civilised countries that he should not be held responsible for his actions.

18.7 Strictly interpreted the M'Naghten Rules would provide that mentally disordered defendant with very limited protection. Just as a person must generally be very mad indeed not to know what he is doing (the nature and quality of his act) when he is killing a man or setting fire to a building, so he must be very mad not to know that these acts attract the unfavourable notice of the police (his knowledge of wrong). For example, if a psychotic patient kills a person whom he believes to be putting thoughts into his mind, or kills him and gives as a reason that the victim is spying on him, or simply kills him because he has an overpowering urge to do so, the M'Naghten Rules, strictly interpreted, will not give him a defence if he admits that he knew that he was killing a man and that murder was a crime.

18.8 The M'Naghten Rules are in part linked with the *mens rea* doctrine, in recognising that evidence of disease of the mind may have the effect of negativing a mental element of the crime. The 'knowledge of wrong' test is not an application of the ordinary rules of *mens rea*, however. 'Wrong' has been held to mean 'legally wrong' and a sane defendant cannot set up a defence of ignorance of the criminal law. Knowledge of the law is hardly an appropriate test on which to base ascription of responsibility to the mentally disordered. It is a very narrow ground of exemption since even persons who are grossly disturbed generally know that murder and arson instances, are crimes. It might seem at first sight more attractive to have regard to the defendant's appreciation of what is morally wrong, but the problems in a test to the mentally disordered would be very great. 'Knowledge of wrong,' as included in M'Naghten, is not therefore a satisfactory test of criminal responsibility."

---

[545] See also Lord Devlin, "Mental Abnormality and the Criminal Law" in St. J. MacDonald (ed.), *Changing Legal Objectives* (Toronto: University of Toronto Press, 1963).

In addition to these criticisms, there is a further problem with the *M'Naghten* Rules. There is still a possibility that they could be found to be incompatible with art.5 of the European Convention on Human Rights. This provision protects the right of individuals to "liberty and security of person" and deprivation of this right has to be "in accordance with a procedure prescribed by law". Further, "persons of unsound mind" can only be detained where proper account of objective medical expertise has been taken. This has been interpreted to mean that there must be a strong relationship between legal and medical criteria used to assess those who are insane.[546] Because of these concerns the forms of disposal following a finding of not guilty by reason of insanity (or a finding of unfitness) were changed, as we have seen, in 2004. However, while in this respect the law is now compatible with art.5, it is not entirely safe from further challenge. Whilst s.1 states that the evidence of two doctors is needed before a finding of not guilty by reason of insanity can be made, the weight to be given to this evidence remains unspecified. Certainly it is not binding because, as we have seen, the test of insanity is regarded as a legal one. The result may be that *M'Naghten* contravenes the Convention.[547]

Further reform has been proposed. The Butler Committee on Mentally Abnormal Offenders[548] reported in 1975 that major reform was necessary but this Report has been ignored by successive governments. The Law Commission has also recommended reform[549] and is currently re-examining the law. Rightly, given the inter-relationship of automatism and insanity, reform of both is being considered. Responses to the Law Commission's Scoping Paper[550] reveal that while criticisms of the law are regarded as justified, both legal and medical practitioners work around the problems and that reform to the fitness to plead test is more urgent.[551] The Law Commission has thus prioritised that work but, nonetheless, regards reform of the law on automatism and insanity as necessary as it is "outmoded, inappropriate and complicated".[552] Its provisional proposals would constitute a radical change.[553] The verdict of not guilty by reason of insanity would be replaced by one of "not criminally responsible by reason of a recognised medical condition", or RMC (reflecting the view, noted earlier, that the true rationale of the defence is a lack of capacity). The phrase "recognised medical condition" is deliberately wide so as to encompass physical as well as mental conditions.[554] A number of implications flow from this: for example, the stigmatising label "insanity" would become even more inappropriate than under the existing law and would be jettisoned. The concept would encompass a wide range of conditions, which might now lead to a finding of automatism; thus the boundary between the two defences would shift. However, in addition to establishing that the defendant was suffering from a recognised medical condition, it would also be necessary to establish that

---

[546]   *Winterwerp v The Netherlands* (1979) 2 E.H.R.R. 387. See further, *R. v Grant (Heather)* [2002] Q.B. 1030, *R (on the application of David Grant Juncal) v Secretary of State for the Home Department et al* [2008] EWCA Civ 869 and P.J. Sutherland and C.A. Gearty, "Insanity and the European Court of Human Rights" [1992] Crim. L.R. 418.

[547]   Indeed, this view was accepted in Jersey at first instance (R.D. Mackay and C.A. Gearty, "On Being Insane in Jersey—the case of *Attorney-General v Jason Prior*" [2001] Crim. L.R. 560). However, the appeal court disagreed (R.D. Mackay, "On Being Insane in Jersey Part Two—the Appeal in *Jason Prior v Attorney-General*" [2002] Crim. L.R. 728).

[548]   Cmnd.6244 (1975).

[549]   Law Com. No.177 (1989), fn.21 above, cll 35–336, largely drawing upon the Butler recommendations.

[550]   Law Commission, *Insanity and Automatism, A Scoping Paper* (2012). See further, J. Peay, "Insanity and Automatism: questions from and about the Law Commission's Scoping Paper" [2012] Crim. L.R. 927.

[551]   Law Commission Discussion Paper (2013), fn.461 above, para.1.10.

[552]   Above, para.1.84.

[553]   Above, para.1.85.

[554]   It would, however, exclude "acute intoxication". See below, p.447.

"the defendant wholly lacked the capacity

(i) rationally to form a judgment about the relevant conduct or circumstances;

(ii) to understand the wrongfulness of what he or she is charged with having done[555]; or

(iii) to control his or her physical acts in relation to the relevant conduct or circumstances."[556]

There is much to commend in the discussion paper, including the proposal that the defence would apply in the magistrates' court as well as the Crown Court and that the defendant would bear only an "elevated evidential burden" rather than have to prove the defence, but there are also justifiable concerns about the proposed defences. As Ashworth has commented:

"How often the new defences would be used is unclear, since the RMC defence will require two expert reports and if successful, may lead to a medical disposal. As now, some defendants may prefer to take their chances with ordinary sentencing powers. Both new defences are narrowly drawn, requiring a total lack of capacity or control, and that may ensure that few cases end in a special verdict or an acquittal on grounds of automatism."[557]

In contrast to England where, despite the compelling case for reform, proposals have thus far been ignored by government, other countries have already acted. Scotland, for example, reformed its law in 2010[558] while the United States has witnessed a remarkable series of reforms.[559] Initially, based upon the formula of the Model Penal Code,[560] the insanity laws were widened to include those who could not control their actions (sometimes referred to as irresistible impulse).[561] The inclusion of this volitional limb in the test was never without its critics: some believed that the test was too broad and others argued that it was simply not possible to identify those who could not control their actions. These doubts, particularly as voiced by the anti-crime, pro-victim lobby, were fuelled by the highly controversial acquittal of John Hinckley on the ground of insanity, after he had attempted to murder President Reagan.[562] The insanity defence was thought to have been misused with expensive defence lawyers hoodwinking juries into false acquittals. It was also said that dangerous persons were being given early release from psychiatric detention after having been "cured", only to commit further serious crimes.[563]

In fact, evidence fails to support either of these criticisms of the operation of the defence.[564] In reality, just as in this country, the insanity defence in the United States is very rarely used and

---

[555] "Wrongfulness" would not be limited to illegality as under the existing law: Law Commission Discussion Paper (2013), fn.461 above, para.4.33.

[556] Above, para.1.93.

[557] A. Ashworth, "Editorial, Insanity and automatism: a discussion paper" [2013] Crim. L.R. 787 at 788.

[558] Criminal Justice and Licensing (Scotland) Act 2010, s.168, inserting a new s.51A into the Criminal Procedure (Scotland) Act 1995.

[559] Other jurisdictions have also amended or rejected the M'Naghten Rules: see, for example, Phillip (Francis) and John (Kim) v The Queen [2007] UKPC 31 where the Privy Council had to consider the reformed law of St. Lucia.

[560] The American Law Institute, Model Penal Code, Proposed Official Draft (1962), s.4.01 was approved by statute in 29 states and all federal courts by 1982. Eighteen states, including New York, currently use the Model Penal Code rule or a variation thereof.

[561] This is still the case in Texas.

[562] USA v Hinckley Criminal No.81, 306 US Dt. Ct. for the District of Columbia, 525 F. Supp. 1342, Nov. 17, 1981.

[563] A.P. Brooks, "The Merits of Abolishing the Insanity Defense" (1985) 477 The Annals 125 at 126.

[564] H.J. Steadman, "Empirical Research on the Insanity Defense" (1985) 477 The Annals 58; M. Perlin, The Jurisprudence of the Insanity Defense (Durham: Carolina Academic Press, 1994).

even more rarely successful.[565] However, the combination of myth and valid criticism led to rapid and widespread reform. In some states, reform has done nothing more than change the description of the verdict to "not responsible by reason of insanity" on the basis that public reaction to the Hinckley verdict was based upon a misunderstanding.[566] Many states shifted the burden of proof from the prosecution to the defence to prove that the defendant was insane. The fact that in the District of Columbia, unlike in England, the prosecution had to prove that Hinckley was sane was thought to be one of the main reasons he was acquitted.[567] Sometimes, in addition to this change, the standard of proof has also been raised.[568] Other states have abandoned the "capacity to conform" test in a remarkable return to a modernised version of the *M'Naghten* Rules.[569] Other states have introduced new verdicts of "guilty but mentally ill" as *alternatives* to the existing verdict.[570] However, as we shall see in the next section, four states have rejected the insanity defence altogether.

(d) *Should the insanity defence be retained?*

There are critics who would still be profoundly dissatisfied even if reforms of the type indicated above were to take place. It is their belief that the insanity defence ought to be completely abolished. Most, although not all, of these attacks have taken place in the United States and the reasoning behind them embraces arguments of principle about the concept of responsibility as well as concerns about mistaken assessments of the danger to which the public are exposed by abuse of the insanity defence.

(1) Procedural criticisms

There are very real problems of procedure in this area: expert evidence often conflicts, trials may be long, the difficulty of sifting through the evidence to assess accountability is immense, but, as Fletcher points out:

"it is curious to argue from these problems to the conclusion that the defence ought to be abolished. Would anyone wish to abolish the defence of duress because it might be difficult to establish whether the accused was fairly capable of resisting pressure exerted against him?"[571]

---

[565] National Advisory Commission, *Myths and Realities: A Report of the National Commission on the Insanity Defense* (1983).
[566] For example, Indiana: Ind. Stat. 35–36–2–3 s.3(3).
[567] About two-thirds of those states which accept the insanity defence now place the burden of proof upon the defendant, normally by a preponderance of the evidence (Mackay, fn.487 above, p.117).
[568] For example, in Arizona the defendant must prove insanity by "clear and convincing evidence" (Ariz. Rev. Stat. An. s.13–502(b) (1984)). The constitutionality of Arizona's test for insanity (which relates to the accused's moral capacity only and not cognitive capacity) was upheld in *Arizona v Clarke* (2006) 548 US 735. See further, Law Commission Scoping Paper (2012), fn.550 above, Appendix C.
[569] Federal law was changed by the Insanity Reform Act 1984 (see Title 18 of the United States Code). In relation to state law see, for example, California Penal Code (supp. 1987), s.25(b). Research has shown that such revised tests had little impact upon the number of successful insanity pleas: H.J. Steadman et al., *Before and After Hinckley: Evaluating Insanity Defense Reform* (New York: Guildford Publications, 1993), p.142.
[570] The additional verdict was introduced to give juries a choice and to reduce the number of acquittals on the basis of insanity.
[571] Fletcher, fn.7 above, p.845.

(2) Therapeutic Criticisms:

A.W.B. Simpson, "The Butler Committee's Report: The Legal Aspects" (1976) 16 Brit. J. Criminol. 175 at 176:

"If one takes the central recommendation of the Butler Committee on the disposal of mentally disordered 'offenders'—'the guiding principle in disposal of mentally disordered offenders by the courts is that they should be sent wherever they can best be given the treatment they need: generally treatment by the health services is appropriate'—one cannot but be struck by the incongruity of involving criminal courts in the matter at all. What are red judges doing performing functions which, in the case of measles or mumps, we assign to general practitioners and supporting medical staff? It is as if a doctor, lighting on a case where a patient contracted a chill whilst stealing, took to prescribing aspirins and six months in the local prison.

This fundamental incongruity makes it extremely difficult, and perhaps impossible, to produce a set of recommendations designed to adapt a penal system to a task utterly out of character with the nature of such a system."

(3) Criminal Law v Mental Health Powers

Commentators have increasingly voiced doubts about the uneasy mixture of the criminal law and its objectives with the power of courts under mental health legislation to confine dangerous people to hospitals. Some critics of the insanity defence have argued that discussion of mental disorder should be limited to the issue of mens rea. If the mental condition of the defendant negated the mens rea required for the offence, then no further criminal questions could arise—the defendant would be entitled to an acquittal. There would, however, remain the separate issue of civil commitment.

J. Goldstein and J. Katz, "Abolish the 'Insanity Defense'—Why Not?" (1963) 72 Yale L.J. 853 at 854–855, 862–864, 865:

"In our efforts to understand the suggested relationship between 'insanity' and 'mens rea' there emerges a purpose for the 'insanity defense' which, though there to be seen, has remained of extremely low visibility. That purpose seems to be obscured because thinking about such a relationship has generally been blocked by unquestioning and disarming references to our collective conscience and our religious and moral traditions. Assuming the existence of the suggested relationship between 'insanity' and 'mens rea,' the defence is not to absolve of criminal responsibility 'sick' persons who would otherwise be subject to criminal sanction. Rather, its real function is to authorize the state to hold those 'who must be found not to possess the guilty mind mens rea,' even though the criminal law demands that no person be held criminally responsible if doubt is cast on any material element of the offense charged . . .

What this discussion indicates, then, is that the insanity defense is not designed, as is the defence of self-defense, to define an exception to criminal liability, but rather to define for sanction and exception from among those who would be free of liability. It is as if the insanity defense were prompted by an affirmative answer to the silently posed question: 'Does mens rea or any essential element of an offense exclude from liability a group of persons whom the community wishes to restrain?' If the suggested relationship between mens rea and 'insanity' means that 'insanity' precludes proof beyond doubt of mens rea then the 'defense' is designed to authorize the holding of persons who have committed no crime. So conceived, the problem really facing the criminal process has been how to obtain authority to sanction the 'insane' who would be excluded from liability by an overall application of the general principles of the criminal law.

Furthermore, even if the relationship between insanity and 'mens rea' is rejected, this same purpose re-emerges when we try to understand why the consequence of this defense, unlike other defenses, is restraint, not release."

Norval Morris, Madness and the Criminal Law (1982), pp.31–32, 61–64:

"It is the overarching theme of this book that injustice and inefficiency invariably flow from any blending of the criminal-law and mental health powers of the state. Each is sufficient unto itself to achieve a just balance between freedom and authority; each has its own interested constituency; when they are mixed together, only the likelihood of injustice is added . . .

My belief is that practice and scholarship have been led astray by the following ambivalent and corruptive reaction: though he has done a criminal act, being mentally abnormal he is less guilty in moral terms; St. Peter may indeed hold him morally faultless or at least less blameworthy and so should we; but also he is different from the rest of us, strange and probably more dangerous, and therefore, since he has committed a crime, we had better for his sake and ours separate him from the community or prolong his separation, for his treatment and our protection. We are at the same time more forgiving and more fearful, less punitive and more self-protective; we wish to have it both ways . . .

[From this position Morris goes on to attack the notion that we seek to identify the truly responsible by means of an insanity defence]. [The central issue is] the question of fairness, the sense that it is unjust and unfair to stigmatize the mentally ill as criminals and to punish them for their crimes. The criminal law exists to deter and to punish those who would or who would choose to do wrong. If they cannot exercise choice, they cannot be deterred and it is a moral outrage to punish them. The argument sounds powerful but its premise is weak.

Choice is neither present nor absent in the typical case where the insanity defense is currently pleaded; what is at issue is the degree of freedom of choice on a continuum from the hypothetically entirely rational to the hypothetically pathologically determined—in states of consciousness neither polar condition exists.

The moral issue sinks into the sands of reality. Certainly it is true that in a situation of total absence of choice it is outrageous to inflict punishment; but the frequency of such situations to the problems of criminal responsibility becomes an issue of fact in which tradition and clinical knowledge and practice are in conflict . . . I think that much of the discussion of the defense of insanity is the discussion of a myth rather than of a reality. It is no minor debating point that in fact we lack a defense of insanity as an operating tool of the criminal law other than in relation to a very few particularly heinous and heavily punished offenses. There is not an operating defense of insanity in relation to burglary or theft, or the broad sweep of index crimes generally; the plea of not guilty on the ground of insanity is rarely to be heard in city courts of first instance which handle the grist of the mill of the criminal law—though a great deal of pathology is to be seen in the parade of accused and convicted persons before these courts. As a practical matter we reserve this defense for a few sensational cases where it may be in the interest of the accused either to escape the possibility of capital punishment (though in cases where serious mental illness is present, the risk of execution is slight) or where the likely punishment is of a sufficient severity to make the indeterminate commitment of the accused a preferable alternative to a criminal conviction. Operationally the defense of insanity is a tribute, it seems to me, to our hypocrisy rather than to our morality.

To be less aggressive about the matter . . . the special defense of insanity may properly be indicted as producing a morally unsatisfactory classification on the continuum between guilt and innocence. It applies in practice to only a few mentally ill criminals, thus omitting many others with guilt-reducing relationships between their mental illness and their crimes; it excludes other powerful pressures on human behaviour, thus giving excessive weight to the psychological over the social. It is a false classification in the sense that if a team of the world's most sensitive and trained psychiatrists and moralists were to select from all those found guilty of felonies and those found not guilty by reason of insanity any given number who should not be stigmatized as criminals, very few of those found not guilty by reason of insanity would be selected."

Morris concludes that the mentally disordered are entitled to be held responsible for their actions, but that their condition may be relevant in sentencing and might result in mitigation on grounds of less moral blameworthiness, or aggravation because of constituting a danger to the public.

(4) Denial of Responsibility:

Baroness Wootton, Crime and the Criminal Law, 2nd edn (1981), pp.90–91:

"At a more fundamental level, acceptance of mental disorder as diminishing or *eliminating* criminal responsibility demands an ability to get inside someone else's mind so completely as to be certain whether he has acted wilfully or knowingly, and also to experience the strength of the temptations to which he is exposed. This, I submit, is beyond the competence of even the most highly qualified expert. Psychiatrists may uncover factors in patients' backgrounds (often in terms of childhood experience) by which they profess to 'explain' why one individual has an urge to strangle young girls and another to rape elderly women: but these 'explanations' are merely predictive of the *likelihood* of such behaviour occurring . . .

I submit, therefore, that the present law, under which offenders must be classified as either mentally disordered or criminally responsible for their actions not only produces anomalies but attempts the impossible . . . In the end it would seem that for practical purposes we are brought to the paradoxical conclusion that, if a person's crimes are by ordinary standards only moderately objectionable, he should be regarded as wicked and liable to appropriate punishment, but if his wickedness goes beyond a certain point (when we cannot comprehend how anyone could commit such a crime) it ceases to be wickedness at all and becomes a medical condition."

At least some of Baroness Wootton's arguments would be supported by those who have secured wide-ranging reform of the insanity laws in the United States following the acquittal of John Hinckley.[572] Indeed, some states have become so disenchanted with the insanity defence that, rather than amend it, they have completely abolished it.[573] Where this reform has taken place, the trend has been to restrict the role of insanity to one of determining whether the defendant lacked the necessary mental state for the definition of the crime. If for this reason the defendant cannot be convicted of an offence, then automatic civil commitment follows.

The effect of this is, of course, to make mens rea even more important and this aspect of reform of the insanity defence would have found no favour at all with Baroness Wootton. Her view (explored in Ch.2), was that the entire assessment of responsibility was a futile one and that questions relating to the mental state of the defendant ought to be reserved for the post-conviction, sentencing stage.

In complete contrast to Baroness Wootton, we may examine the views of Szasz, a psychologist who embraces so whole-heartedly the concept of responsibility that he feels everyone ought to be regarded as sane and accountable for their actions.

T.S. Szasz, "The Myth of Mental Illness" (1960) 15 American Psychologist 113 at 115–118:

"[A] currently prevalent claim [is that] . . . mental illness is just as 'real' and 'objective' as bodily illness . . . This is a confusing claim since it is never known exactly what is meant by such words as 'real' and 'objective.' I suspect, however, that what is intended by the proponents of this view is to create the idea in the popular mind that mental illness is some sort of disease entity, like an infection or a malignancy. If this were true, one could *catch* or *get* a 'mental illness,' one might *have* or harbour it, one might transmit it to others, and finally one could get rid of it. In my opinion there is not a shred of evidence to support this view. To the contrary, all the evidence is the other way and supports the view that what people now call mental illnesses are for the most part communications expressing unacceptable ideas, often framed, moreover in an unusual idiom . . .

[T]he diversity of human values and the methods by means of which they may be realized is so vast . . . that they cannot fail but lead to conflicts in human relations. Indeed, to say that human relations at all levels from mother to child, through husband and wife, to nation and nation—are fraught with stress, strain and disharmony is, once again, making the obvious explicit . . . I submit that the idea of mental illness is now being put to work to obscure certain difficulties which at present may be inherent—not that they need be unmodifiable—in the social intercourse of persons. If this is true, the concept functions as a disguise; for instead of calling attention to conflicting human needs, aspirations and values, the notion of mental illness provides an amoral and impersonal 'thing' (an illness) as an explanation for *problems in living*. We may recall in this connection that not so long ago it was devils and witches who were held responsible for men's problems in social living. The belief in mental illness, as something

---

[572] Above, p.419.

[573] Montana (Mont. Code s.46–14–214 (2001)), Idaho (Idaho Code 181–207 (1997)), Kansas (KSA 22–3220 (1995)) and Utah (Utah Code s.76-2-305 (1999)). In Montana, following the reform, the numbers found unfit to plead increased, one interpretation being that the courts were "trying to compensate for not being able to acquit the accused by diverting him or her from the criminal trial by a procedural mechanism." Law Commission Discussion Paper (2013), fn.461 above, para.2.4, citing P. Appelbaum, *Almost a Revolution: Mental Health Law and the Limits of Change* (Oxford: Oxford University Press, 2004), pp.173–175, 181–183.

other than man's trouble in getting along with his fellow man, is the proper heir to the belief in demonology and witchcraft. Mental illness exists or is 'real' in exactly the same sense in which witches existed or were 'real.'

. . . The myth of mental illness encourages us, moreover, to believe in its logical corollary: that social intercourse would be harmonious, satisfying and the secure basis of a good life were it not for the disrupting influences of mental illness. The potentiality for universal human happiness, in this form at least, seems to me but another example of the I-wish-it-were-true type of fantasy. I do believe that human happiness or well-being on a hitherto unimaginably large scale, and not for a select few, is possible. This goal could be achieved, however, only at the cost of many men, and not just a few being willing and able to tackle their personal, social and ethical conflicts. This means having the courage and integrity to forgo waging battles on false fronts, finding solutions for substitute problems—for instance, fighting the battle of stomach acid and chronic fatigue instead of facing up to a marital conflict . . .

My argument [is] . . . limited to the proposition that mental illness is a myth, whose function it is to disguise and thus render more palatable the bitter pill of moral conflicts in human relations."

One final insight might be considered.

D.L. Rosenhan, "On being Sane in Insane Places" (1973) 179 Science 250 at 250–258:

"If sanity and insanity exist, how shall we know them?

The question is neither capricious nor itself insane. However much we may be personally convinced that we can tell the normal from the abnormal, the evidence is simply not compelling. It is commonplace, for example, to read about murder trials wherein eminent psychiatrists for the defense are contradicted by equally eminent psychiatrists for the prosecution on the matter of the defendant's sanity. More generally, there are a great deal of conflicting data on the reliability, utility and meaning of such terms as 'sanity,' 'insanity,' 'mental illness' and 'schizophrenia' . . . what is viewed as normal in one culture may be seen as quite aberrant in another. Thus, notions of normality and abnormality may not be quite so accurate as people believe they are . . . [this] in no way questions the fact that some behaviours are deviant or odd.

[Rosenhan then goes on to describe the nature of the research he had undertaken; 8 sane people gained secret admission to 12 different hospitals, all complained that they had heard voices, saying in particular, 'thud,' 'hollow and empty.' In all other respects (save their name and if necessary their profession) the pseudo-patients told the truth about their feelings, their background, and their present lives. The aim of the research was to ascertain whether and how the sane people would be detected. If they were, it would be some support at least for the view that sanity and insanity are distinct enough to be recognised wherever they occur. All the pseudo-patients were admitted to hospital, whereupon they ceased simulating any symptoms of abnormality but behaved as they 'normally' behaved.]

Despite their public 'show' of sanity, the pseudo-patients were never detected. Admitted, except in one case, with a diagnosis of schizophrenia each was discharged after hospitalisation of between 7 to 52 days, with a diagnosis of schizophrenia 'in remission.' The label 'in remission' should in no way be dismissed as a mere formality, for at no time during any hospitalisation had any question been raised about any pseudo-patients' simulation. Nor are there any indications in hospital records that the pseudo-patients status was suspect. Rather, the evidence was strong that once labelled schizophrenic, the pseudo-patient was stuck with that label. If the pseudo-patient was to be discharged, he must naturally be 'in remission'; but he was not sane, nor in the institutions' view, had he ever been sane . . .

The facts of the matter are that we have known for a long time that diagnoses are often not useful or reliable, but we have nevertheless continued to use them. We now know that we cannot distinguish insanity from sanity."

How are we to respond to arguments such as these? Do they constitute a persuasive case for abolition that "trumps" the arguments addressed in the introductory discussion of this defence? Fletcher, for example, remains unconvinced.

George P. Fletcher, Rethinking Criminal Law (1978), p.846:

"The criminal law expresses respect for the autonomy of the sane as much as it shows compassion for the insane. The line between the two may shift over time. Our theories of sanity may change. But the line remains. If the criminal law is to be an institution expressing respect as well as compassion, its institutions must be able both to punish the guilty and excuse the weak. These two sentiments depend on each other. Compassion is possible only so far as punishment is the norm. Punishing wrongdoing is possible only so far as we have a concept of accountability for wrongdoing. Respect for autonomy and compassion for the weak are too important to our culture to be easily shaken by the skeptics."

C. Automatism

1. Introduction

In the two preceding sections we have seen that non-insane automatism (commonly termed simply "automatism") entitles a defendant to a complete acquittal and that, fearful of allowing too many such acquittals, the law has rigorously circumscribed the parameters of the defence of automatism. This has been achieved, in particular, by insisting that the defendant be blameless in causing the state of automatism and by adopting a broad definition of "disease of the mind" to ensure that in many cases, where there is the slightest risk of repetition of the conduct, the defendant is adjudged insane giving the courts power to make orders in relation to that person.

There have been two main consequences of this restrictive approach. First, the number of situations in which automatism can be successfully pleaded are few and far between. Apart from hypoglycaemia and the (possibly anomalous) decisions involving sleep-walking, already discussed, it would appear that it is only in cases involving isolated incidents of an external cause prompting the involuntary behaviour that the defence will be available. Examples would include physical compulsion (for example, being pushed over so as to injure another) and reflex actions of external origin (for example, reflexive movements while being attacked by a swarm of bees[574]). More problematic is involuntary action caused by a blow. Clearly, a physical blow which causes concussion will qualify here. But, in some cases, there might be a less immediate connection between the "blow" and the automatic behaviour. In T,[575] the defendant, on a charge of robbery and assault causing actual bodily harm, claimed that she had been raped three days previously and that this caused her to suffer from post-traumatic stress disorder with the result that she was in a state of psychogenic fugue rendering her actions automatic. At her trial it was ruled that she was entitled to have this defence put to the jury as one of non-insane automatism.[576] It is, however, doubtful whether the law would extend this to purely non-physical psychological "blows" such as receiving a shock or distressing news. In such a situation it has been held that the ensuing behaviour has its source in the internal psychological or emotional condition of the defendant thus rendering the case one of insanity.[577] Such distinctions are, however, difficult to sustain. It is unrealistic to conclude that the post-traumatic stress disorder in T was purely the product of the physical impact of the rape; presumably it was the psychological shock thereof that produced this state. Yet given the law's reluctance to expand the category of automatism, it seems unlikely that the approach adopted in T would be approved if directly tested in the appellate courts.[578]

---

[574] *Hill v Baxter* [1958] 1 Q.B. 277.
[575] *R. v T* [1990] Crim. L.R. 256.
[576] She was convicted.
[577] *Rabey* [1980] S.C.R. 513 (Canada).
[578] In *R. v Huckerby (Graham)* [2004] EWCA Crim 3251, the issue was not one of automatism but the Court of Appeal did conclude that a conviction for robbery was unsafe because the trial court had not heard evidence about the full impact (including post-traumatic stress) an earlier robbery upon the defendant might have had upon him.

Another problematic cause of "involuntary" behaviour is hypnotism. There are dicta in *Quick*[579] to the effect that this could give rise to automatism. On the other hand, it seems unlikely that the courts would go so far as to hold that "brainwashing" can lead to automatic behaviour. Such a holding would be dangerously close to concluding that a person's unfortunate upbringing should exempt him from criminal liability.

The second consequence of the courts' restrictive interpretation of automatism and expansive interpretation of insanity has been to force many defendants to plead guilty. The defendants in both *Sullivan* and *Hennessy*, discussed earlier, changed their pleas to guilty as soon as it was ruled that their defence was, in reality, one of insanity. These cases were both decided before the Criminal Procedure (Insanity and Unfitness to Plead) Act 1991, at which time all defendants found not guilty by reason of insanity faced mandatory indefinite commitment. The reforms effected in the 1991 Act have produced a slow increase in the use of the plea; thus it would appear that the fear which induced defendants to change their plea is dissipating as the courts show their willingness to use the more flexible powers given to them under the 1991 Act.[580] Given that mandatory commitment is no longer the only disposal available in murder cases, it may be that, rather than pleading diminished responsibility as defendants have done in the past, a corresponding increase in the plea of automatism has occurred. However, no data is collected which enables this possibility to be confirmed.[581]

There is a great deal of dissatisfaction with the present response of the law to the problem of automatism. Along with proposals to modify the insanity defence, reforms have been suggested to the law of non-insane automatism.[582] As noted in the discussion of insanity, the Law Commission has made provisional recommendations for reform of the law to both insanity and automatism. Automatism would only be a defence, as now, if there was no prior fault,[583] and

"if the jury or magistrates find that the accused raises evidence that at the time of the alleged offence he or she wholly lacked the capacity to control his or her conduct and the loss of capacity was not the result of a recognised medical condition . . . he or she shall be acquitted unless the prosecution disprove this to the criminal standard."[584]

While this would not lead to a different outcome for an epileptic who commits offences during a seizure (because under the current law the condition is regarded as internally caused and thus raising the plea of insanity) it would do so for a diabetic who, to use an example given by the Law Commission, causes death by dangerous driving during a hypoglycaemic episode where there was no warning of the onset of the episode.[585] Without prior fault and with a complete absence of control, such a defendant would currently secure an acquittal. Under the proposed reform, the result would be the new special verdict of "not criminally responsible by reason of a recognised medical condition". While the removal of the hair-splitting internal/external distinction is wholly to be commended, there must be doubt as to whether defendants will wish to risk a special verdict – even one which does not have the negative connotations associated with the label "insanity".

---

[579] *R. v Quick (William George); R. v Paddison (William)* [1973] 1 Q.B. 910.
[580] Mackay et al., fn.539 above, p.400.
[581] Consequently, the Law Commission requested information about the use of the plea of automatism in its scoping paper on insanity and automatism: fn.550 above.
[582] Law Com, No.177 (1989), fn.21 above, cl 33. See further, R.D. Mackay, "Craziness and Codification—Revising the Automatism and Insanity Defences" in I. Dennis (ed.), *Criminal Law and Justice* (London: Sweet & Maxwell, 1987), pp.112–118 and Wilson et al., above, fn.517.
[583] Law Commission Discussion Paper (2013), fn.461 above, para.5.111.
[584] Law Commission Scoping Paper, fn.550 above, para.5.124.
[585] Law Commission Discussion Paper (2013), fn.461 above, para.1.113.

Finally, we need to examine whether this whole approach is sound. Should automatism provide a complete defence?

The result may be open to doubt at two levels.

2. Psychiatry's view of the automaton's true state of mind

R.W. White, The Abnormal Personality (1948), pp.203–205, 288:

"A colour-sergeant was carrying a message, riding his motorcycle through a dangerous section of the front. All at once it was several hours later and he was pushing his motorcycle along the streets of a coastal town nearly a hundred miles away. In utter bewilderment he gave himself up to the military police, but he could tell absolutely nothing of his long trip. The amnesia was ultimately broken by the use of hypnosis. The man then remembered that he was thrown down by a shell explosion, that he picked up himself and his machine, that he started straight for the coastal town, that he studied signs and asked for directions in order to reach this destination.

It is clear, in this case, that the amnesia entailed no loss of competence. The patient's actions were purposive, rational, and intelligent. The amnesia rested only on his sense of personal identity. The conflict was between fear, suddenly intensified by his narrow escape and duty to complete the dangerous mission. The forgetting of personal identity made it possible to give way to his impulse toward flight, now irresistible, without exposing himself to the almost equally unbearable anxiety associated with being a coward, failing his mission, and undergoing arrest as a deserter. When he achieved physical safety the two sides of the conflict resumed their normal proportions and his sense of personal identity suddenly returned . . .

Hypnotism makes a very strong appeal to a man's delight in the marvellous and his desire for omnipotence. So strong is this appeal that many people would rather not be told that hypnotic phenomena are measurable and that they can be explained by straightforward psychological principles. It is more fun to believe that every vestige of the response to pain can be wiped out, or that suggested blindness produces the equivalent of real blindness, than to regard these as limited, measurable changes in the usual organisation of behaviour. As a result of this secret joy in magic and omnipotence, there has tended to be a large and important constant error in all thinking about the nature of hypnotism. This error is the belief that the *hypnotist, rather than the subject produces the phenomena* . . .We should always bear in mind that the subject is still a person, even though he is participating in an unusual experiment and entering an unusual state. He has not become a fool, and it is he who produces the hypnotic behaviour.

. . . [There have been] various experimental investigations in which hypnotized persons were given suggestions to perform criminal acts. These experiments laboured under one great disadvantage. As it was not known whether the subjects would carry out the suggestions, the 'criminal acts' had to be arranged so that a really dangerous outcome was impossible. Rubber daggers and wooden pistols were used, the subjects being assured that they were real weapons. The outcome of all these earlier experiments can be condensed in a single illustration, amusingly described by Janet:

'A number of persons of importance, magistrates and professors, had assembled in the main hall of the Salpetriere museum to witness a great seance of criminal suggestions. Witt, the principal subject, thrown into the somnambulist state, had under the influence of suggestion displayed the most saguinary instincts. At a word or sign, she had stabbed, shot and poisoned; the room was littered with corpses. The notables had withdrawn, greatly impressed, leaving only a few students with the subject, who was still in the somnambulist state. The students, having a fancy to bring the seance to a close by a less bloodcurdling experiment, made a very simple suggestion to Witt. They told her that she was now quite alone in the hall. She was to strip and take a bath. Witt, who had murdered all the magistrats without turning a hair was seized with shame at the thought of undressing. Rather than accede to the suggestion, she had a violent fit of hysteria.' (P. Janet, *Psychological Healing* (1925), Vol. 1, p. 184.)

This example exposes the fallacy that has ruined so much experimental work with hypnotism: the notion that the subject is a helpless fool who has no idea that he is being deceived. It points unmistakably to the conclusion that hypnotized persons will not carry out suggested acts which are repugnant to them—not when they think the consequences are real."

If one accepts the above psychiatric evidence, what should be the law's response to a defendant who, while under a hypnotic influence, commits a crime? Should such persons have a complete defence as "the dependency and helplessness of the hypnotised subject are too pronounced",[586] and that many persons are saved from being criminals by the force of their inhibitions which hypnotism removes?

3. That even if insanity is not an issue, the public interest may not be served by a complete acquittal

Even those who would not go so far as to accept the above view of autonomic acts have sometimes expressed concern that certain automatons have been given absolute acquittals.

R. Cross, "Reflections on Bratty's Case" (1962) 78 L.Q.R. 236 at 238–239:

"Although they are still comparatively rare, pleas of non-insane automatism are becoming increasingly frequent, and questions may be legitimately raised concerning the sufficiency of the courts' powers. Is it right that someone who has been acquitted on the ground of non-insane automatism should inevitably go free? In *R. v Charlson* (1955) 29 Cr.App.R.37 the accused was acquitted on various charges of causing grievous bodily harm to his son because he acted in a state of automatism which may have been due to a cerebral tumour. It is only natural to feel the deepest sympathy for the accused in such a case, but it is equally natural to question the propriety of an unqualified acquittal. One way of dealing with such problems would be to give the judge powers in all cases of a successful plea of automatism, insane or non-insane, to order the detention of the accused pending a medical inquiry, after which the appropriate order could be made."

A similar approach to that advocated by Cross is to be found in the Scottish case of *H.M. Advocate v Fraser*.[587] In this sleepwalking case it was made a condition of discharge that the defendant should not sleep in the same room with anyone else. We have seen that as a result of *Sullivan*, epileptics, sleepwalkers, those suffering from arteriosclerosis and diabetics during hyperglycaemic episodes, may all now be regarded as insane. It has been argued that this is inappropriate. Although mandatory commitment no longer follows a finding of insanity, there is an undeniable stigma attached to such a finding. The Draft Criminal Code would rename the special verdict. However, it is doubtful whether the proposed term "mental disorder" is neutral enough to have the desired effect.[588] Two options, therefore, could be considered. One could continue to include some automatons within the "special verdict" but demedicalise the test and label, or one could deal with all automatons outside the special verdict but qualify the acquittal as and when necessary by appropriate orders. Clearly, there would be problems in empowering courts to make appropriate orders in these cases, for example, such orders would probably be incompatible with art.5 of the European Convention on Human Rights.[589] However, if constructed in such a manner as to ensure compatibility with the Convention, such an approach might well be preferable to including such automatons within the definition of insanity.

VIII. Intoxication

A. Background

A significant proportion of criminal offences are committed by persons who are under the influence of alcohol and/or drugs.

---

[586] The American Law Institute, Model Penal Code, Tent. Draft No.4 (1955), Comments to s.2.01 at p.122.

[587] *H.M. Advocate v Fraser* (1878) 4 Couper 70. But see now *Carmichael v Boyle* [1985] S.L.T. 399.

[588] Griew argues that public education would be necessary. E. Griew, "Let's Implement Butler on Mental Disorder and Crime" [1984] C.L.P. 47 at 52. We would tend to agree with Mackay that this is unlikely to be successful: fn.487 above, p.115.

[589] Baker, fn.533 above, p.90.

John E. Hodge, "Alcohol and Violence" in P.J. Taylor (ed.), Violence in Society (1993), pp.129–130:

"Assault
There is clear evidence of a consistent association with alcohol use in cases of assault . . . Meyer *et al* found that approximately two-thirds of perpetrators of police assault had been drinking just prior to the assault, while in a large study in which data on over 10,000 inmates of American prisons were reviewed, just under two-thirds of those convicted of assault were found to have been drinking at the time of the offence.

Homicide
Lindquist found that two-thirds of the offenders and approximately half their victims had been intoxicated at the time of the offence . . .

Rape
The use of alcohol by rapists and their victims also seems fairly well established. Shupe found 50 per cent of men arrested for rape had been drinking, and 45 per cent could be described as intoxicated . . .

Domestic violence
Pizzey found that alcohol had been involved in about 40 per cent of cases of battered wives and children seeking refuge from domestic violence. Other studies have tended to find rates of alcohol involvement of about 50 per cent."

Research into crimes of violence in Bristol has confirmed this pattern: "we came to regard cases in which drink was *not* a factor as rather remarkable."[590]

The above research is not necessarily claiming that the consumption of alcohol *caused* the criminal acts, but that there is a strong association between the two. Why is this so?

John E. Hodge, "Alcohol and Violence" in P.J. Taylor (ed.), Violence in Society (1993), pp.132–134:

"Moral theory
Probably the first was the pre-scientific 'moral theory', which held that drinking loosens moral restraints, with the result that individuals who drink lose personal control and, as a result, engaged in immoral behaviours, including violence. While this theory has little scientific validity, it is still popular . . . Labelling alcohol as the culprit provides a convenient scapegoat for violent acts.

Disinhibition theory
[B]ehavioural constraints are loosened by the pharmacological action of alcohol, and violence then results. However, the theory appears to imply that aggression is a natural state which is normally held in check . . . which can be released by the pharmacological effects of alcohol . . . [However], there is little evidence that aggression or violence is a normal human state . . . Sobell and Sobell suggested that alcohol may directly act on the inhibitory control of the cerebral cortex over the lower brain centres and thus disinhibit aggressive urges. However, no empirical evidence has been obtained which either supports or refutes this hypothesis.

Stimulation theory
[S]ome . . . have suggested that alcohol may directly stimulate aggression in individuals who may in some way be more biologically sensitive to its effects. A particular example of this is the theory of pathological intoxication, which suggests that a small proportion of individuals are particularly prone to become excessively aggressive under the influence of alcohol . . .

Other factors which may explain the relationship between alcohol and violence
. . . The first is the simple physiological effects of alcohol, such as impaired reaction time. It seems unlikely, though, that these effects will lead directly to violence, although it is possible that poor co-ordination may result in a more extreme violent outcome that was perhaps the original intention. Similarly, Pernanen's hypothesis that cognitive impairment may be important in understanding the relationship between alcohol and violence

---

[590] A. Cretney and G. Davis, *Punishing Violence* (Oxford: Routledge, 1995), p.26. See also, G. Dingwall, *Alcohol and Crime* (Cullompton: Willan Publishing, 2006) and Law Commission, *Intoxication and Criminal Liability*, Law Com. No.314 (Cmnd.7526, 2009), para.1.1.

has little supportive evidence . . . [There are other] situational and psychological variables . . . which help explain the association between alcohol and violence. One of these is the drinking situation itself. In this case, it is fairly clear that situations do influence the association between violence and alcohol. Alcohol use in some situations (for example, at football matches) is more likely to be associated with violence than in others (for example, party going). Cultural factors would also appear to be associated with the levels of violence after drinking . . .

One major factor . . . is the individual's expectancy of the outcome of drinking. If, as seems likely, there is a generally held belief that violence and alcohol are associated, this is likely to affect both the behaviour of the drinker and the interpretations of his/her behaviour by observers."

The problem for the criminal law is one of determining what importance should be attached to the intoxication (whether by drink or drugs or both) of defendants who might claim either that they would never have committed the crime but for their drunkenness which loosened their inhibitions, or, alternatively, that they were so drunk that their did not know what they was doing and thus lacked mens rea. An example of the latter claim can be seen from *Lipman*[591] where the defendant, a drug addict, while on an LSD "trip" had the illusion of descending to the centre of the earth and being attacked by snakes. In his attempt to fight off these reptiles he struck the victim (also a drug addict on an LSD "trip") two blows on the head causing haemorrhage of the brain and crammed some eight inches of sheet into her mouth causing her to die of asphyxia. He claimed to have had "no knowledge of what he was doing and no intention to harm her". A similar example can be found in the Scottish case of *Brennan v H.M. Advocate*,[592] where the defendant consumed between 20 and 25 pints of beer, a glass of sherry and a quantity of the drug LSD He then stabbed his father to death with a knife. In both these cases the defendant claimed that because of drunkenness he was unable to foresee the consequences of his actions and so lacked mens rea.

The law here is faced with a dilemma. On the one hand, strict principle suggests that defendants such as Lipman and Brennan lack mens rea, or perhaps did not even "act" and, accordingly, should escape criminal liability. On the other hand, particularly given the statistics on the close connection between crime and alcohol, the law is concerned with protecting the public (and deterrence) and cannot allow drunken persons to escape criminal liability and punishment. In short, there is a clash between a "strictly logical, subjective approach" and an "absolutist" policy-led approach, "which would focus solely on D's conduct and its effects, but which would disregard D's state of mind where affected by voluntary intoxication".[593] The law has tried to achieve some sort of compromise between the two approaches:

"Given the unattractiveness of both the strictly logical approach to criminal liability and the absolutist alternative, it should come as no surprise that English law has rejected both these extreme approaches in favour of an intermediate position. To put it another way, English law has adopted the purely logical view for some offences, focusing solely on the definitional requirements of the offence charged, but has employed the absolutist approach in relation to other offences."[594]

B. Drunken Intent

As the above cases make clear, the law is *not* concerned with a defendant who has several (or many) drinks that merely "loosen her up" and remove her inhibitions. If at the time of the crime she knows what

---

[591] *R. v Lipman (Robert)* [1970] 1 Q.B. 152.
[592] *Brennan v H.M. Advocate* (1977) S.L.T. 151.
[593] Law Com. No.314 (2009), fn.590 above, para.1.56
[594] Above, para.1.61. See also R. Williams, "Voluntary intoxication – a lost cause?" (2013) 129 L.Q.R. 264 at 288–289.

she is doing, it is irrelevant that she would not have committed the crime, but for the drinks she has consumed. It was stressed in *Sheehan and Moore* that "a drunken intent is nevertheless an intent".[595]

Equally, the law is not concerned with persons who claim that they would not have committed the crime had they not been intoxicated. The loss of self-control was the defendant's fault. At the time of the crime she knew what she was doing and so must be held fully responsible.

Accordingly, the only cases in which the criminal law might consider intoxication to be a relevant issue are those where the defendant is so intoxicated as to lack mens rea or to be in a state of automatism. It is not a matter of whether the defendant was *capable* of forming mens rea. It is a question of whether mens rea was, in fact, formed.[596]

C. Intoxication as a "Defence"

Even in cases where the defendant does lack mens rea, the law is unwilling to allow drunken persons to escape criminal liability and draws a distinction between voluntary and involuntary intoxication, the general rule being that drunkenness is only an answer to a charge in the latter situation.

Being voluntarily intoxicated is usually no answer to a criminal charge. However, this rule is subject to a significant exception. Quite how this exception should be classified, however, has always been a matter of difficulty. Judges and texts commonly refer to voluntary intoxication, in these exceptional circumstances, as providing a partial excuse or defence for the defendant. Certainly, in terms of its effect upon the liability of an intoxicated defendant, charged, say, with murder, and eventually convicted of manslaughter, this is how it appears to operate. But as the Law Commission has recently emphasised, "[t]here is no common law or statutory 'defence' of intoxication. That is to say, the simple fact that D was voluntarily intoxicated at the time he or she allegedly committed the offence charged does not provide D with a 'defence'".[597] So how does intoxication have an impact upon a defendant's liability?

A.P. Simester, "Intoxication is Never a Defence" [2009] Crim. L.R. 3 at 4–5:

"The criminal law does contain an intoxication doctrine, but it is a doctrine of *inculpation*, not exculpation. Whether the intoxication doctrine is evidential or substantive is uncertain . . . Either way, however, it operates for the benefit of the prosecution, not the defence. Wherever the doctrine applies, its function—its sole function—is to treat the defendant as if he acted with mens rea, when in fact, he did not.

The intoxication doctrine is a supplementary device that assists the prosecution to 'prove' mens rea where that does not actually exist . . .

Suppose . . . that D lacked mens rea at the time when he perpetrated the actus reus of the offence charged. Ordinarily, he is then entitled to an acquittal. Yet before we acquit, we need to consider *why* mens rea was missing. If D lacked mens rea because intoxicated (i.e. where D would have foreseen the risk of perpetrating the actus reus had he been sober), the intoxication doctrine then comes into operation. The doctrine holds that, where D lacks mens rea because intoxicated and certain additional criteria are satisfied, D is to be *treated as if* he had mens rea."

This is a persuasive analysis of the approach taken by the law. In effect, as will be seen, it reverses the standard account and, arguably, intoxication becomes a form of constructive liability.[598] But before examining this further the concept of voluntary intoxication requires elaboration.

---

[595] *R. v Sheehan (Michael); R. v Moore (George Allen)* [1975] 1 W.L.R. 739; see further, *R. v Stubbs (Kevin John)* (1989) 88 Cr. App. R. 53.

[596] *R. v Pordage* [1975] Crim. L.R. 575; *Cole* [1993] Crim. L.R. 300; *R. v Hayes (Dennis Francis)* [2002] EWCA Crim 1945.

[597] Law Com. No.314 (2009), fn.590 above, para.1.15.

[598] In the light of this there is an argument for removing the discussion of intoxication from a chapter on defences. However, given that it is has long been referred to as a "defence" and pending enactment of the Law Commission's proposals, it is to be retained in this chapter.

D. Meaning of Voluntary Intoxication

Report of the Committee on Mentally Abnormal Offenders (Butler Committee) (Cmnd.6244, 1975), para.18.56:

"'Voluntary intoxication' would be defined to mean intoxication resulting from the intentional taking of drink or a drug knowing that it is capable in sufficient quantity of having an intoxicating effect; provided that intoxication is not voluntary if it results in part from a fact unknown to the defendant that increases his sensitivity to the drink or drug. The concluding words would provide a defence to a person who suffers from hypoglycaemia, for example, who does not know that in that condition the ingestions of a small amount of alcohol can produce a state of altered consciousness, as well as to a person who has been prescribed a drug on medical grounds without warning of the effect it may produce."

The present law does not appear to go quite as far as the above proposal. In *Allen*,[599] the defendant claimed that he had not realised that wine he had drunk had a high alcohol content. It was held that, where an accused knows he is drinking alcohol, it is irrelevant whether he knows the precise nature or strength of the alcohol. It was a clear case of voluntary intoxication.

R. v Hardie (1985) 80 Cr. App. R. 157 (Court of Appeal, Criminal Division)

PARKER LJ:

"The problem is whether . . . [the taking of] valium . . . should properly be regarded as self-induced intoxication . . .

There can be no doubt that the same rule applies both to self-intoxication by alcohol and intoxication by hallucinatory drugs, but this is because the effects of both are well-known and there is therefore an element of recklessness in the self-administration of the drug . . .

In the present instance the defence was that the valium was taken for the purpose of calming the nerves only, that it was old stock and that the appellant was told it would do him no harm. There was no evidence that it was known to the appellant or even generally known that the taking of valium in the quantity taken would be liable to render a person aggressive or incapable of appreciating risks to others or have other side effects such that its self-administration would itself have an element of recklessness. It is true that valium is a drug and it is true that it was taken deliberately and not taken on medical prescription, but the drug is, in our view, wholly different in kind from drugs which are liable to cause unpredictability or aggressiveness. It may well be that the taking of a sedative or soporific drug will, in certain circumstances, be no answer, for example in a case of reckless driving, but if the effect of a drug is merely soporific or sedative the taking of it, even in some excessive quantity, cannot in the ordinary way raise a *conclusive* presumption against the admission of proof of intoxication for the purpose of disproving *mens rea* in ordinary crimes, such as would be the case with alcoholic intoxication or incapacity or automatism resulting from the self-administration of dangerous drugs."

Thus, the fact that the court thought that the drug was non-dangerous was highly significant. The Law Commission has long regarded it as unsatisfactory that the courts should have to determine whether or not a drug is dangerous on a case-by-case basis.[600] Its original approach was to define intoxication and the circumstances in which it would be held to be involuntary.[601] However, subsequent Government proposals, instead, defined voluntary intoxication and, significantly, inserted a provision that intoxication is presumed to be voluntary.[602] In its latest proposals, the Law Commission has not adopted this strategy. Its current proposals are that neither "intoxicant" nor "voluntary intoxication" should

---

[599] *R. v Allen (Kevin)* [1988] Crim. L.R. 698.
[600] Law Commission, *Legislating the Criminal Code: Intoxication and Criminal Liability*, Law Com. No.229 (1995), para.5.42. See also, Law Com. No.314 (2009), fn.590 above, paras 1.25, 2.85–2.86.
[601] Draft Criminal Law (Intoxication) Bill 1995 cl.4.
[602] Draft Offences Against the Person Bill 1998 cl.19.

be defined. Instead, it recommends "that the concept of involuntary intoxication, at or least the most obvious situations which should be regarded as involuntary intoxication, should be expressly set out."[603]

E. Law on Voluntary Intoxication

1. Specific and basic intent

We are now in a position to examine further the impact voluntary intoxication has upon a defendant's liability for offences. In the leading case of *Majewski*,[604] the House of Lords confirmed a long line of authority[605] that drunkenness was an answer to charges involving crimes of "specific intent" and not to crimes of "basic intent".[606]

This distinction caused little problem at first. A rough list was drawn up by judges: for example, murder and s.18 of the Offences Against the Person Act 1861 were deemed to be crimes of specific intent while manslaughter and s.20 of the Offences Against the Person Act 1861 were held to be crimes of basic intent. This distinction was a functional one aimed at achieving a "compromise between the rigors of denying the relevance of intoxication and allowing it to undercut all liability".[607] Drunken defendants charged with murder and s.18 could instead be convicted of manslaughter and s.20, respectively.

Intoxication could be seen, in effect, to be acting as a mitigating factor and hence operated in a defence-like way. However, Simester has pointed out that this apparent similarity with partial defences is very limited; indeed, he argues that this thinking needs to be abandoned.

A.P. Simester, "Intoxication is Never a Defence" [2009] Crim. L.R. 3 at 13:

"Unlike partial exculpations, intoxication is a doctrine of (partial) inculpation. Structurally speaking, they work in opposite directions.

True partial defences, such as provocation [now loss of control], operate to excuse a defendant's *deliberate choice* to harm the victim. Provocation does not deny that D has the mens rea for murder. Quite the reverse: it explains why he did. It prevents conviction of an offence for which the necessary inculpatory elements are satisfied . . . Disregard provocation, and the case is a culpable murder.

For intoxication, by contrast, it is not the drunkenness that is supplying the exception. It is the lack of mens rea. Indeed, strictly speaking exculpation is not required. The core inculpatory element is missing. This is why, in a specific intent offence, intoxication informs no substantive defence known to the criminal law (and why the defendant bears no burden to establish it). The defendant's submission is like the 'defence' of alibi: that the prosecution has not proved the elements, the actus reus and mens rea, of the offence. Of course, courtroom lawyers frequently call such denials a defence, but we should not confuse this usage with the corresponding substantive-law term. The prosecution bears the burden of proving actus reus and mens rea, It has simply failed to do so.

When we come to basic intent offences, on the other hand, *now* intoxication becomes relevant as a matter of substantive law. The prosecution acquires a supplementary way to establish culpability. It need not, though it may, prove mens rea. Or it may prove that D would have had mens rea but for his voluntary intoxication. Where

---

[603] Law Com. No.314 (2009), fn.590 above, para.3.123.

[604] *DPP v Majewski* [1977] A.C. 443.

[605] *DPP v Beard* [1920] A.C. 479; *Attorney General of Northern Ireland v Gallagher (Patrick)* [1963] A.C. 349; *Bratty v Attorney-General of Northern Ireland* [1963] A.C. 386.

[606] For crimes requiring specific intent, intoxication will be part of all the evidence that the jury must consider in determining whether the prosecution has established that the defendant had the necessary mens rea (earlier dicta in *Beard* [1920] A.C. 479 that the onus of proof is on the defendant cannot now be relied upon). If the issue of intoxication emerges as a material factor at the trial, the judge should direct the jury on it, even if the defendant does not raise the issue themselves: *Bennett* [1995] Crim. L.R. 877; *Groark* [1999] Crim. L.R. 669; *R. v Hayes (Dennis Francis)* [2002] EWCA Crim 1945. However, the key decision as to whether it is "material" rests with the judge and there is some indication that the threshold is being raised: see *R. v Porceddu (Stefano)* [2004] EWCA Crim 1043 and Ormerod, fn.4 above, pp.296–312.

[607] Fletcher, fn.7 above, p.849.

it succeeds in the latter, this is not to conclude that D somehow *had* mens rea in fact, but rather that he evinced the level of culpability that the mens rea requirement is designed to track."

Whichever view of the operation of intoxication upon liability is taken, and Simester's view is compelling, the terms "specific" and "basic" intent are crucially important and need to be explained. However, initially they were concepts without substance. They meant nothing. They were like elephants—the courts knew them when they saw them (i.e. they knew when a defendant's liability could be reduced without escaping all punishment)—but they could not be defined. Difficulties started arising when judges began trying to define these concepts. Attempting to identify a coherent rationale for a practice born out of a compromise between principle and policy considerations was always going to be problematic.

Several views started emerging. For example, Lord Simon in *Majewski* equated specific intent with "direct" intent (i.e. aim or purpose): "the prosecution must in general prove that the purpose for the commission of the act extends to the intent expressed or implied in the definition of the crime".[608] This view, however, never won judicial support and instead the "ulterior intent test" was the first to gain broad acceptance. Under this view, crimes of specific intent are crimes where the mens rea of the offence extends beyond the actus reus, while in crimes of basic intent the mens rea goes no further than extending to the elements of the actus reus itself. An example will illustrate this distinction. Assault is a crime of basic intent: the actus reus is causing apprehension of immediate force; the mens rea is an intention (or recklessness) to cause such apprehension; no mens rea extending beyond the actus reus is required. But assault with intent to resist arrest[609] is a crime of specific intent: the actus reus is the same as that of common assault, namely, causing apprehension of immediate force; the mens rea is two-fold—there must be the mens rea of the assault *and in addition* there must be an intent to resist arrest. This additional intention does not relate to anything in the actus reus of the crime; it extends beyond the actus reus; the crime is thus one of specific intent.

However, an alternative view was also expressed in *Majewski*,[610] and endorsed in the subsequent House of Lords' decision of *Caldwell*, namely, the "recklessness test". According to this, drunkenness can only be relevant to crimes that require proof of intention (such as murder and s.18), and is no answer to crimes that can be committed recklessly (such as manslaughter and s.20). In short, a crime of "specific intent" is one that cannot be committed recklessly. It ought to be stressed that while the decision in *Caldwell* was effectively overruled by the House of Lords in *G and Another*,[611] this latter decision was careful not to overrule anything said in *Caldwell* about self-induced intoxication.

R. v Caldwell [1982] A.C. 341 (House of Lords)

[The facts are set out above, p.174]
(Criminal Damage Act 1971, s.1(2):

"A person who without lawful excuse destroys or damages any property, whether belonging to himself or another—(a) intending to destroy or damage any property or being reckless as to whether any property would be destroyed or damaged; and (b) intending by the destruction or damage to

---

[608]   *DPP v Majewski* [1977] A.C. 443 at 479.
[609]   Offences Against the Person Act 1861 s.38.
[610]   *DPP v Majewski* [1977] A.C. 443 at 475 (Lord Elwyn-Jones).
[611]   *R. v G and Another* [2004] 1 A.C. 1034.

endanger the life of another or being reckless as to whether the life of another would be thereby endangered; shall be guilty of an offence.")

LORD DIPLOCK:

"As respects the charge under section 1(2) the prosecution did not rely upon an actual intent of the respondent to endanger the lives of the residents but relied on his having been reckless whether the lives of any of them would be endangered . . . If the only mental state capable of constituting the necessary *mens rea* for an offence under section 1(2) were that expressed in the words 'intending by the destruction or damage to endanger the life of another', it would have been necessary to consider whether the offence was to be classified as one of 'specific' intent for the purposes of the rule of law which this House affirmed and applied in *R. v Majewski* [1977] A.C. 443; and this it plainly is. But this is not, in my view, a relevant inquiry where 'being reckless as to whether the life of another would be thereby endangered' is an alternative mental state that is capable of constituting the necessary *mens rea* of the offence with which he is charged.

The speech of Lord Elwyn-Jones L.C. in *R. v Majewski* . . . is authority that self-induced intoxication is no defence to a crime in which recklessness is enough to constitute the necessary *mens rea*. The charge in *Majewski* was of assault occasioning actual bodily harm and it was held by the majority of the House, approving *R v Venna*, that recklessness in the use of force was sufficient to satisfy the mental element in the offence of assault. Reducing oneself by drink or drugs to a condition in which the restraints of reason and conscience are cast off was held to be a reckless course of conduct and an integral part of the crime . . . The Lord Chancellor accepted at p. 475 as correctly stating English law the provision in s.2.08(2) of the American Model Penal Code:

'When recklessness establishes an element of the offence, if the actor, due to self-induced intoxication, is unaware of a risk of which he would have been aware had he been sober, such unawareness is immaterial.' . . .

My Lords, the Court of Appeal in the instant case regarded the case as turning on whether the offence under section 1(2) was one of 'specific' intent or 'basic' intent . . . [T]hey held that the offence under section 1(2) was one of 'specific' intent in contrast to the offence under section 1(1) which was of basic intent. This would be right if the only *mens rea* capable of constituting the offence were an actual intention to endanger the life of another. For the reasons I have given, however, classification into offences of 'specific' and 'basic' intent is irrelevant where being reckless as to whether a particular harmful consequence will result from one's act is a sufficient alternative *mens rea*".

LORD EDMUND-DAVIS (DISSENTING):

"Something more must be said . . . having regard to the view expressed by my noble and learned friend, Lord Diplock . . . that the speech of Lord Elwyn-Jones L.C. in *R. v Majewski* 'is authority that self-induced intoxication is no defence to a crime in which recklessness is enough to constitute the necessary *mens rea*'. It is a view which, with respect, I do not share. In common with all the noble and learned Lords hearing that appeal, Lord Elwyn-Jones L.C. adopted the well-established (though not universally favoured) distinction between basic and specific intents. *R. v Majewski* . . . related solely to charges of assault, undoubtedly an offence of basic intent, and the Lord Chancellor made it clear that his observations were confined to offences of that nature . . . My respectful view is that *Majewski* accordingly supplies no support for the proposition that, in relation to crimes of specific intent (such as section 1(2)(b) of the Act of 1971) incapacity to appreciate the degree and nature of the risk created by his action which is attributable to the defendant's self-intoxication is an irrelevance. The Lord Chancellor was dealing simply with crimes of basic intent, and in my judgment it was strictly within that framework that he adopted the view expressed in the American Penal Code . . . and recklessness as an element in crimes of specific intent was, I am convinced, never within his contemplation . . .

My Lords, it was recently predicted that 'There can hardly be any doubt that *all* crimes of recklessness except murder will now be held to be crimes of basic intent within *Majewski*': see *Glanville Williams, Textbook of Criminal Law*, p. 431 [and] that will surely be the effect of the majority decision in this appeal. That I regret, for the consequence is that, however grave the crime charged, if recklessness can constitute its *mens rea* the fact that it was committed in drink can afford no defence. It is a very long time since we had so harsh a law in this country."

Appeal dismissed

R. v Heard [2008] Q.B. 43 (Court of Appeal, Criminal Division)

The defendant was charged with sexual assault, contrary to s.3 of the Sexual Offences Act 2003. The defendant, who had been drinking heavily, claimed he could not remember the sexual assault upon a policeman. He was convicted and appealed on the ground that s.3 created an offence of specific intent and that the jury should have been directed to consider whether the drink he had taken meant he did not have an intention to touch as required under s.3.

HUGHES LJ:

"The first thing to say is that it should not be supposed that every offence can be categorised simply as either one of specific intent or basic intent. So to categorise an offence may conceal the truth that different elements of it may require proof of different states of mind . . . The current legislative practice of itemising separately different elements of offences created by statute, which is much exhibited in the Sexual Offences Act 2003, may occasionally have the potential to complicate matters for a jury, but it demonstrates the impossibility of fitting an offence into a single pigeon-hole, whether it be labelled 'basic intent' or specific intent'.

The offence of sexual assault, with which this case is concerned, is an example . . . [I]t is only the touching which must be intentional, whilst the sexual character of the touching is unless equivocal, to be judged objectively, and a belief in consent must be objectively reasonable . . .

In the present case, what the appellant did and said at the time . . . made it perfectly clear that this was a case of drunken intentional touching. Although the Judge directed the jury that drunkenness was no defence, he also directed the jury that it must be sure that the touching was deliberate. That amounted to a direction that for conviction the appellant's mind (drunken or otherwise) had to have gone with his physical act of touching . . .

[W]e agree that the Judge's direction that the touching must be deliberate was correct . . .

The remaining question is whether the Judge was also correct to direct the jury that drunkenness was not a defence.

We do not agree with [counsel's] submission for the appellant that the fact that reckless touching will not suffice means that voluntary intoxication can be relied upon as defeating intentional touching. We do not read the cases, including *DPP v Majewski*, as establishing any such rule . . . The Judge was accordingly correct, not only to direct the jury that the touching must be deliberate, but also to direct it that the defence that voluntary drunkenness rendered him unable to form the intent to touch was not open to him . . .

[Counsel for the appellant's] proposition that *Majewski* decides that it is only where recklessness suffices that voluntary intoxication cannot be relied upon derives from a part of the speech by Lord Elwyn-Jones LC in *Majewski*, and some observations, obiter of Lord Diplock in the subsequent case of *Caldwell* . . .

There are a number of difficulties about extracting [counsel's] proposition from the [two cases] . . .

(i) Lord Elwyn-Jones was addressing the submission made on behalf of the appellant in *Majewski* that it was unprincipled or unethical to distinguish between the effect of drink upon the mind in some crimes and its effect upon the mind in others. In rejecting that submission, and upholding the distinction between crimes of basic and specific intent, he was drawing attention to the fact that a man who has got himself into a state of voluntary intoxication is not, by ordinary standards, blameless. Both the Lord Chancellor and others of their Lordships made clear their view that to get oneself into such a state is, viewed broadly, as culpable as in any sober defendant convicted of a crime of basic intent, whether because he has the basic intent or because he is reckless as to the relevant consequence or circumstance. Throughout *Majewski* it is clear that their Lordships regarded those two latter states of mind as equivalent to one another for these purposes. It therefore does not follow from the references to recklessness that the same rule (that voluntary intoxication cannot be relied upon) does not apply also to basic intent; on the contrary, it seems to us clear that their Lordships were treating the two as the same.

(ii) The new analysis of recklessness in *Caldwell* may have led readily to the proposition that voluntary intoxication is broadly equivalent to recklessness, thus defined. But that analysis and definition of recklessness have now been reversed by the House of Lords in *R v G* [2004] 1 AC 1034. As now understood, recklessness requires actual foresight of the risk.

(iii) Since the majority in *Caldwell* held that it was enough for recklessness that the risk was obvious objectively (thus, to the sober man) no question of drink providing a defence could arise; it follows that the explanation of *Majewski* which was advanced was plainly obiter.

(iv) Lord Diplock's proposition in *Caldwell* attracted a vigorous dissent from Lord Edmund-Davies . . . [He] dissented not only from the new definition of recklessness, but also from the analysis of *Majewski* . . .

(v) There were, moreover, many difficulties in the proposition that voluntary intoxication actually supplies the *mens rea*, whether on the basis of recklessness as re-defined in *Caldwell* or on the basis of recklessness as now understood; if that were so the drunken man might be guilty simply by becoming drunk and whether or not the risk would be obvious to a sober person, himself or anyone else. That reinforces our opinion that the proposition being advanced was one of broadly equivalent culpability, rather than of drink by itself supplying the *mens rea*.

It is necessary to go back to *Majewski* in order to see the basis for the distinction there upheld between crimes of basic and of specific intent. It is to be found most clearly in the speech of Lord Simon . . . [and] was that crimes of specific intent are those where the offence requires proof of purpose or consequence, which are not confined to, but amongst which are included, those where the purpose goes beyond the *actus reus* (sometimes referred to as cases of 'ulterior intent') . . .

That explanation of the difference is consistent with the view of Lord Edmund-Davies that an offence contrary to s1(2)(b) Criminal Damage Act is one of specific intent in this sense, even though it involves no more than recklessness as to the endangering of life; the offence requires proof of a state of mind addressing something beyond the prohibited act itself, namely its consequences. We regard this as the best explanation of the sometimes elusive distinction between specific and basic intent in the sense used in *Majewski*, and it seems to us that this is the distinction which the Judge in the present case was applying when he referred to the concept of a 'bolted-on' intention . . .

There is a great deal of policy in the decision whether voluntary intoxication can or cannot be relied upon. [There are] several passages in *Majewski* where the rule is firmly grounded upon common sense, whether purely logical or not . . .

[O]ur view is that the Judge's directions were substantially correct."

Appeal dismissed

Everything said in this decision about the distinction between specific and basic intent was technically obiter.[612] It was clear that the defendant had a drunken intent and this has never been a defence. Despite being obiter, the Court of Appeal has, here, disapproved the recklessness test and expressed a strong preference for the "purposive intent" approach and for the ulterior intent test. In doing this, however, the judgment is riddled with ambiguity. It is stated that specific intent *includes* ulterior intent but is "not confined to" such cases. It is far from clear when an offence, which is not one of ulterior intent, would nevertheless be one of specific intent. There are significant problems with this approach. There is abundant precedent that murder and s.18 are crimes of specific intent yet neither of these is generally[613] a crime of ulterior intent. Equally, neither of these crimes requires direct, "purposive" intent; oblique intent suffices. It is unfortunate that the simple "recklessness test" has been disapproved by the Court of Appeal (on some rather selective reading of the House of Lords' decisions); the matter cannot be regarded as resolved. It is submitted that the better view is that drunkenness should be an answer to crimes that can only be committed intentionally. This would not necessarily lead to unmeritorious acquittals. In the above case, for example, there was ample evidence of an intention to touch the policeman.

In *Heard*, it is stated that offences cannot be rigidly categorised as being of specific or basic intent. However, there are clear precedents and judicial pronouncements concerning the specific/basic intent distinction. On the basis of these it would appear that the following are crimes of specific intent:

---

[612]   See further, Williams, fn.594 above, pp.267–274.
[613]   Below, p.438.

(i) Murder

There is no doubt that intoxication leads to an acquittal for the crime of murder; the defendant will instead be found guilty of the lesser included offence of manslaughter.[614] This rule can now be reconciled with the "recklessness test" as since *Moloney* and *Hancock* it is clear that murder is a crime of intention; it cannot be committed recklessly. However, this coincidence between principle and policy is little more than chance. For many years preceding *Moloney* and *Hancock*, murder was a crime that arguably could be committed recklessly,[615] yet during this time it was never doubted that murder was nevertheless a crime of specific intent. The policy reasons underlying this were clear. In murder cases there was always the possibility of a manslaughter conviction operating as a safety-net. Drunken defendants would not escape liability completely so it was "safe" to deem murder to be a crime of specific intent. This had the further advantage that it enabled the judge to avoid the imposition of the mandatory sentence for murder.[616] Drunken killers were blameworthy and deserved punishment, but they were, perhaps, not always as blameworthy as deliberate murderers. Conviction for manslaughter allowed the judge flexibility to assess the degree of blameworthiness and punish appropriately.

(ii) Section 18

The crime of wounding or causing grievous bodily harm with intent to cause grievous bodily harm or with intent to resist apprehension is a crime that cannot be committed recklessly. Drunkenness can lead to the defendant escaping liability for s.18 but the defendant will then be convicted of the lesser basic intent offence of s.20, an offence that can be committed recklessly.[617] However, there is a problem here. While wounding with intent to cause grievous bodily harm, and wounding or causing grievous bodily harm with intent to resist apprehension, are clearly crimes of ulterior intent, the same cannot be said of causing grievous bodily harm with intent to cause grievous bodily harm. Thus if ulterior intent were required, drunkenness would be no answer to such a charge. This view, however, is not consistent with the better "recklessness test" and is not supported by authority which suggests that s.18 is *always* a specific intent offence.[618]

(iii) Theft[619]

This is a crime of intention; recklessness does not suffice; it is also a crime of ulterior intent.

(iv) Robbery[620]

Again, recklessness will not suffice here and it is a crime of ulterior intent.

---

[614] *DPP v Beard* [1920] A.C. 479; *Attorney General of Northern Ireland v Gallagher (Patrick)* [1963] A.C. 349; *DPP v Majewski* [1977] A.C. 443.

[615] This was certainly a plausible interpretation of *Hyam v DPP* [1975] A.C. 55.

[616] J. Sellers, "Mens Rea and the Judicial Approach to 'Bad Excuses' in the Criminal Law" (1978) 41 M.L.R. 245 at 261.

[617] *R. v Pordage* [1975] Crim. L.R. 575; *DPP v Majewski* [1977] A.C. 443; *R. v Bailey (John Graham)* [1983] 1 W.L.R. 760; *R. v Davies* [1991] Crim. L.R. 469.

[618] It is conceded that in none of these cases (above, fn.606) was the charge causing grievous bodily harm with intent to cause grievous bodily harm.

[619] Theft Act 1968 s.1. *Ruse v Read* [1949] 1 K.B. 377; Lord Salmon in *DPP v Majewski* [1977] A.C. 443 at 482.

[620] Theft Act 1968 s.8.

(v) Burglary

While recklessness as to whether entry to a building as a trespasser will suffice, such entry must be accompanied by an intention (only) to commit a listed offence.[621] It would thus appear to be a crime of specific intent, passing the "recklessness test". It is also a crime of ulterior intent.

(vi) Handling stolen goods

In *Durante*,[622] it was accepted that this was an offence of specific intent. This is not an offence of intention at all. The mens rea stipulated by s.22 of the Theft Act 1968 is that the defendant must act dishonestly and must know or believe that the goods are stolen. If one adopts the "recklessness" test it is difficult to see why this should be regarded as a crime of specific intent.

(vii) Attempt

Only intention suffices; further, it is a crime of ulterior intent.[623]

(viii) Assault with intent to resist arrest

As with burglary, while one of the elements, the assault, may be committed recklessly, there must be a further intention to resist arrest.

It must be emphasised that this list does not purport to be exhaustive.

Most other offences are crimes of basic intent. The most prominent on this list are the following: manslaughter, s.20, s.47 and common assault. Occasionally, a statute specifically provides that intoxication cannot be a defence: the Public Order Act 1986 is an example of this.[624] It is also widely accepted that rape was, under the law prior to the Sexual Offences Act 2003, and continues to be, a crime of basic intent.

R. v Fotheringham (1989) 88 Cr. App. R. 206 (Court of Appeal, Criminal Division)

The appellant and his wife went out for the evening leaving a 14-year-old girl to baby-sit. The wife (probably in the appellant's absence) told the girl to sleep in the matrimonial bed. On returning home, the appellant got into the matrimonial bed and had sexual intercourse with the girl without her consent. The wife appeared and the intercourse ceased. The appellant was charged with rape but claimed that because of drunkenness, he had mistaken the girl for his wife. He admitted that he would not have made this mistake if he had been sober. The judge directed the jury to disregard the appellant's self-induced intoxication in considering whether there were reasonable grounds for his believing that he was having sexual intercourse with a consenting woman, namely, his wife. The appellant was convicted and appealed.

WATKINS LJ:

"The point of law . . . [is] whether it is a defence to a charge of rape . . . that a defendant, as a result of self-induced intoxication, has an honest but mistaken belief that he was having conjugal relations . . .

---

[621] Theft Act 1968 s.9.
[622] *R. v Durante (Reginald William)* [1972] 3 All E.R. 962.
[623] In *R. v Durante (Reginald William)*, above, endeavouring to obtain money on a forged instrument was accepted as a crime of specific intent; this is analogous to an *attempt* to commit a crime.
[624] Public Order Act 1986 s.6(5).

Counsel had to recognise, as in fact he did, that where the issue in rape is consent, a defendant's self-induced intoxication is not a relevant matter which a jury are entitled to take into account in deciding whether there were reasonable grounds for the defendant's belief that the woman consented—see *Woods* (1982) 74 Cr.App.R.312. Likewise he had to face the law, which is that 'self-induced intoxication is no defence to a crime in which reckless-ness is enough to constitute the necessary *mens rea*'—see . . . [*Caldwell* where Lord Diplock refers to *Majewski*] where it was held that rape is a crime of basic intent to which self-induced intoxication is no defence . . .

[The appellant's argument] clearly runs counter to authority, which is that in rape self-induced intoxication is no defence, whether the issue be intention, consent or, as here, mistake as to the identity of the victim. We do not doubt that the public would be outraged if the law were to be declared to be otherwise."

Appeal dismissed

At the time of this decision, rape was a crime that could be committed recklessly in that knowledge or recklessness *as to consent* would suffice. (Today, the requirement is that the defendant lacks a reason-able belief as to consent.) But in *Fotheringham*, the mistake was not as to consent but as to whether the defendant was having *unlawful* sexual intercourse. (As the law then stood, if it had been his wife the sexual intercourse would have been lawful.) However, it was also, and is still, the case that the defendant had to *intend* to have sexual intercourse.[625] What was never decided, before the reforms to the law of rape, was whether there had to be an intention to have *unlawful* sexual intercourse (i.e. *knowledge* that it was not his wife) or whether recklessness as to the element sufficed. If the former view was correct, the defendant would have lacked mens rea in respect to an element which could not be satisfied by recklessness. On this basis drunkenness should have been relevant. A literal interpretation in *Fotheringham*, however, means that if *any* element of a crime can be satisfied by proof of recklessness, the crime is always one of basic intent. Acceptance of this view would necessitate a reassessment of the list of crimes of specific intent pre-sented above. In particular, burglary and assault with intent to resist arrest would all have to be regarded as crimes of basic intent because in each of them one element can be satisfied by proof of recklessness.

The alternative interpretation is that, consistent with the general principle, recklessness as to a sur-rounding circumstance (in *Fotheringham*, the "unlawfulness" requirement) suffices and, accordingly, his drunkenness as to this element is irrelevant. Since the abolition of the "marital rape exemption" this particular point is no longer of practical importance but the broader issue still remains. What is the position if a defendant intends to sexually assault a woman in the vaginal area without penetrat-ing her, but, because of his drunkenness, he does penetrate her? Strict principle might suggest that as this element of the crime can only be committed intentionally, drunkenness ought to preclude liability. However, it is almost inconceivable that any court would engage in such an analysis. Policy would almost certainly prevail here and so it can be concluded, especially in the light of *Heard* above, that, irrespective of the nature of the mistake, rape is always a crime of basic intent.

What is the rationale of this "recklessness test"? In *Majewski*, Lord Elwyn-Jones L.C. said:

"If a man of his own volition takes a substance which causes him to cast off the restraints of reason and conscience, no wrong is done to him by holding him answerable criminally for any injury he may do while in that condition. His course of conduct in reducing himself by drugs and drink to that condition in my view supplies the evidence of *mens rea*, of guilty mind certainly sufficient for crimes of basic intent. It is a reckless course of conduct and recklessness is enough to constitute the neces-sary *mens rea* in assault cases . . . The drunkenness is itself an intrinsic, an integral part of the crime, the other part being the evidence of the unlawful use of force against the victim. Together they add up to criminal recklessness."[626]

---

[625] Sexual Offences Act 2003 s.1.
[626] *DPP v Majewski* [1977] A.C. 443 at 474–475. In *R. v Kingston* [1995] 2 A.C. 355 at 369 Lord Mustill stated that he was not

There were two problems with this approach. Suppose a defendant starts drinking at 8 p.m. and by 10 p.m. is no longer aware of his actions. At 11 p.m. he commits the actus reus of the crime. The mens rea of the crime (getting so drunk which is a reckless thing to do) precedes the actus reus. There is no coincidence of actus reus and mens rea, and as Dashwood points out:

"It might be argued that the carry-over of *mens rea* in the present situation would correspond to that in the famous cases of *Thabo-Meli* and *Church* [above, p.201] where the immediate cause of death was not the attack upon the victim but the measures taken to dispose of what was believed to be a dead body. However, an important distinction is that in these cases the attack and the disposal of the supposed corpse represented successive steps in a single criminal transaction, the later act being consciously linked in the mind of the accused with the earlier act; such an analysis would not apply to the case of misconduct following reckless intoxication."[627]

The second problem with Lord Elwyn-Jones' approach is that recklessness does not exist in the abstract. One has to be reckless as to a particular consequence. Thus under the subjective test of recklessness it should have been necessary to establish that when the defendant was getting drunk (the recklessness) he foresaw the possibility of committing the crime.

It is quite clear that the courts were less concerned with fine arguments such as these than with ensuring that a fair and just solution (in terms of balancing the competing interests of protection of society and the rights of the defendant) was achieved. As Lord Simon said:

"One of the prime purposes of the criminal law, with its penal sanctions, is the protection from certain proscribed conduct of persons who are pursuing their lawful lives. Unprovoked violence has, from time immemorial, been a significant part of such proscribed violence. To accede to the argument on behalf of the appellant would leave the citizen legally unprotected from unprovoked violence where such violence was the consequence of drink or drugs having obliterated the capacity of the perpetrator to know what he was doing or what were its consequences."[628]

In *Caldwell*, Lord Diplock was able to avoid these problems by re-casting recklessness in an objective mould. If the risks would have been obvious to an ordinary person at the time of drinking, then the defendant *was* reckless *as to the particular consequence*; it was irrelevant whether the defendant, because of intoxication, foresaw the risk himself.

However, despite the fact that the *Caldwell*-recklessness test was, in this respect, a more principled approach to the issue of intoxication, it has been jettisoned from English law.[629] The clash between principle and policy is marked. When subjective mens rea correlates with ordinary people's notions of fault or blameworthiness (say, cases of sober mistakes or accidents) it can be employed. When it does not (as in cases of drunken violence), the concept of subjective mens rea has to be abandoned. The true basis of mens rea is the attribution of blame, which might, or might not, coincide with a defendant's state of mind. Blame is attributed to persons who render themselves insensible through drink or drugs and then commit a crime.[630] As Lord Russell in *Majewski* said:

---

required to decide how this rationalisation (or that of the defendant being estopped from relying on his self-induced incapacity) stood up to attack.

[627]   A. Dashwood, "Logic and the Lords in Majewski" [1977] Crim. L.R. 532, 591 at 540.

[628]   *DPP v Majewski* [1977] A.C. 443 at 476. See also Hughes LJ in *Coley (Scott) v The Queen; McGhee (Colin) v The Queen; Harris (Darren) v The Queen* [2013] EWCA Crim 223 at [82].

[629]   *R. v G and Another* [2004] 1 A.C. 1034.

[630]   In *Harris (Darren) v The Queen* [2013] EWCA Crim 223, the Crown argued that this should be extended to defendants who

"*Mens rea* has many aspects. If asked to define it in such a case as the present I would say that *the element of guilt or moral turpitude* is supplied by the act of self-intoxication reckless of possible consequences."[631]

Such views were endorsed by Lord Simon in *Majewski*:

"*Mens rea* is therefore on ultimate analysis the state of mind stigmatised as wrongful by the criminal law which, when compounded with the relevant prohibited conduct, constitutes a particular offence. There is no juristic reason why mental incapacity brought about by self-induced intoxication, to realise what one is doing or its probable consequences should not be such a state of mind stigmatised as wrongful by the criminal law."[632]

In *Heard*, the Court of Appeal recognised the fallacy (particularly since *G and Another*) in the reasoning that getting drunk is a reckless thing to do and that this can constitute the mens rea of an offence. Instead, it suggested that the issue was one of "broadly equivalent culpability" rather than the drink by itself supplying the mens rea. Quite what the culpability relates to was left unclear although an answer has since been supplied by the Law Commission:

"[G]iven the culpability associated with knowingly and voluntarily becoming intoxicated, and the associated increase in the known risk of aggressive behaviour . . . the advertent recklessness in voluntarily choosing to become intoxicated, and becoming a greater danger to society, may be equated, morally, with the subjective (advertent) recklessness required for liability."[633]

This is probably the closest we are likely to get to a satisfactory answer. It lends support to Simester's analysis of the intoxication doctrine as a form of constructive liability: "becoming voluntarily drunk supplies a gateway to liability, without further mens rea, for basic intent offences."[634]

Despite the long-standing debate over its rationale, the recklessness test received the following endorsement in 1980.

Criminal Law Revision Committee, 14th Report, Offences Against the Person (Cmnd.7844, 1980), paras 267, 270:

"267(1): . . . evidence of voluntary intoxication should be capable of negating the mental element in murder and the intention required for the commission of any other offence; and

(2) in offences in which recklessness constitutes an element of the offence, if the defendant owing to voluntary intoxication had no appreciation of a risk which he would have appreciated had he been sober, such lack of appreciation is immaterial . . .

270. The test in (2) above is formulated in such a way as to require the court to take into consideration any particular knowledge or any other personal characteristics of the defendant, as for example backwardness. Thus in a case where a gun is discharged killing or injuring another a jury might consider that many people could have

---

commit offences whilst affected by mental disorder brought on by past voluntary drinking even if not intoxicated at the time. Hughes LJ agreed that there while there "is scope for the argument that an illness caused by . . . [D's] own fault ought as a matter of policy to be treated in the same way as drunkenness at the time of the offence . . .. this would represent a significant extension of *DPP v Majewski*." (at [59]).

[631]   *DPP v Majewski* [1977] A.C. 443 at 498 (emphasis added).
[632]   *DPP v Majewski*, above at 478.
[633]   Law Com. No.314 (2009), fn.590 above, paras 1.55, 1.61.
[634]   A.P. Simester, p.431 above.

made a mistake about the risk. But if the defendant was familiar with fire-arms the jury may find that he would have appreciated the risk if he had been sober. For similar reasons it would be unjust that a subnormal person should be judged on the same basis as one of average intelligence."

Whilst the courts and reform bodies have endeavoured to distinguish specific and basic intent, those applying the law suggest that it has caused little difficulty in practice. The Law Commission has acknowledged the importance of this perspective but has stated that the lack of general agreement on the test "must inevitably lead to uncertainty, wasted court time and the unnecessary incurring of legal costs when a new offence is introduced, since, until the matter is decided by the courts, it will not be possible to ascertain into which category it falls".[635] Its latest proposals, to be considered below, are based upon the belief that the distinction between offences of specific and basic intent is "ambiguous, misleading and confusing, and that it should be abandoned."[636]

2. A partial "defence"?

Thus the compromise has developed so that intoxication is an answer to those crimes of intention where there is a lesser included offence for which the defendant can be convicted. As we have seen, one way of looking at this (although not the one argued for so convincingly by Simester) is that intoxication has the practical effect of reducing murder to manslaughter[637] and of reducing s.18 to s.20. However, despite the obvious importance to the development of the law of the existence of a lesser offence, it is clear that intoxication can sometimes, at least in theory, lead to a complete acquittal under English law. As Lord Russell stated in *Majewski*:

"[S]pecial intent cases are not restricted to those crimes in which the absence of a special intent leaves available a lesser crime embodying no special intent, but embraces all cases of special intent even though no alternative lesser criminal charge is available."[638]

The crime of theft is just such a case. Intoxication is an answer to a charge of theft, although there is no lesser included offence of which the defendant can be convicted. This sudden reassertion of principle is somewhat anomalous and, while there are dicta supporting this approach, it is unlikely that the courts actually will take this step and allow a complete defence in such circumstances.[639]

3. Drunken mistake

In most cases a drunken defendant will claim that a mistake has been made with the result that mens rea is missing. For example, there will be a claim that there was no intention to kill; the drunken defendant thought he was shooting at a tree stump. Such a plea will be dealt with under the rules canvassed above. There is evidence that drink can cause persons to make mistakes of a somewhat different nature. One effect of alcohol can be to lead the drinker to interpret the words and actions

---

[635] Law Com. No.229 (1995), fn.600 above, para.3.27. For example, in *DPP v Kellett* [1994] Crim. L.R. 916 the court had to decide whether Dangerous Dogs Act 1991 s.1(7) created an offence of basic or specific intent. It was held to be the former.

[636] Law Com. No.314 (2009), fn.590 above, para.1.28.

[637] See C.M.V. Clarkson, "Drunkenness, Constructive Manslaughter and Specific Intent" (1978) 41 M.L.R. 478.

[638] *DPP v Majewski* [1977] A.C. 443 at 499.

[639] A common circumstance is that of "stealing" a vehicle whilst drunk. Even if the defendant was drunk enough to be acquitted of a charge of theft, he would still be liable for the offence of taking and driving away, contrary to Theft Act 1968 s.12.

of others as threatening, thereby increasing "defensive activity".[640] In other words, a drunken person may act violently, mistakenly believing himself to be under attack.[641] What is the position where such a person makes a mistake as to a "defence"?

With regard to self-defence, it was held in *O'Grady*[642] that a person who makes a drunken mistake in thinking that he is being attacked is not entitled to a defence.[643] This is confirmed by s.76(5) of the Criminal Justice and Immigration Act 2008: a defendant cannot "rely on any mistaken belief attributable to intoxication that was involuntary". The rationale behind this approach can be found in the judgment of Lord Lane CJ in *O'Grady* where he stated:

> "This brings us to the question of public order. There are two competing interests. On the one hand the interest of the defendant who has only acted according to what he believed to be necessary to protect himself, and on the other hand that of the public in general and the victim in particular who, probably through no fault of his own, has been injured or perhaps killed because of the defendant's drunken mistake. Reason recoils from the conclusion that in such circumstances a defendant is entitled to leave the Court without a stain on his character."

It should be stressed that if defendants make reasonable mistakes as to the need for self-defensive action, they will not automatically be denied the defence of self-defence simply because they happened to be intoxicated. Under s.76(5) the mistaken belief must be *"attributable"* to their intoxication. If the belief is only caused by ("attributable to") the intoxication, it could never qualify as a reasonable belief.

This whole approach is, seemingly, at odds with the general rules on intoxication as a (partial) "defence". It is difficult to see any material distinction in culpability between a defendant who makes a drunken mistake about the actus reus and one who makes a similar mistake concerning a defence element. As Dingwall comments on the common law cases:

> "[A]n intoxicated individual who kills in mistaken self-defence is potentially in a worse position than an intoxicated individual who kills without this belief . . . It should be noted that allowing a defendant to rely on intoxicated mistake does not mean that he also has a complete defence to manslaughter . . . [T]here is no reason why he should not be convicted of manslaughter if he was grossly negligent in making the mistake."[644]

The law has adopted a similar approach with regard to other mistakes. In *Fotheringham*,[645] the defendant made a drunken mistake when having non-consensual intercourse with his 14-year-old baby-sitter; he thought she was his wife. It was held that such a drunken mistake was no defence. Presumably, the same approach will be adopted with other drunken mistakes: for example, in duress where the defendant, because of his intoxication, believes he has been subjected to threats of death or grievous bodily harm. For duress there has to be a reasonable belief in the existence of the threats. If the defendant's belief in such threats is because of his intoxication, it is unlikely to be a reasonable belief.

---

[640] R. Gustafson and H. Kallinen, "Changes in the Psychological Defence System as a Function of Alcohol Intoxication in Men" (1989) 84 B.J. Addict. 1515.
[641] Cretney and Davis, fn.590 above, p.27.
[642] *R. v O'Grady (Patrick Gerald)* [1987] Q.B. 995.
[643] See also, *R. v O'Connor* [1991] Crim. L.R. 135; *R. v Hatton (Jonathan)* [2006] 1 Cr. App. R.16. See A. Ashworth, "Self-defence: Murder—Self-induced Intoxication" [2006] Crim. L.R. 353.
[644] G. Dingwall, "Intoxicated Mistakes and the Need for Self-Defence" (2007) 70 M.L.R. 127 at 132.
[645] *R. v Fotheringham* (1989) 88 Cr. App. R. 206.

However, the law in this regard is riddled with inconsistencies. In *Richardson and Irwin*,[646] the defendants, who were students, dropped the victim from a balcony causing him to be seriously injured. The Court of Appeal held that their drunken mistake that the victim was consenting to this "horseplay" could be a defence to inflicting grievous bodily harm contrary to s.20 of the Offences Against the Person Act 1861. Whether one adopts the general rule that intoxication is no answer to basic intent crimes (of which s.20 is undoubtedly one) or one adopts the rule in *O'Grady* that all drunken mistakes are irrelevant, the defendants ought to have been convicted. The authority of this decision must be in serious doubt.

Finally, there are certain statutes that expressly provide that a defendant has a defence if she holds a particular belief. For example, s.5(2) of the Criminal Damage Act 1971 provides that a person has a defence (or a "lawful excuse" as per s.1(1)) to a charge of criminal damage if she believed that she had the consent of the person entitled to give consent and s.5(3) provides that "it is immaterial whether a belief is justified or not if it is honestly held". What is the position where a defendant only holds such a belief because of their drunkenness?

Jaggard v Dickinson [1981] Q.B. 527 (Queens Bench Divisional Court)

The appellant while drunk broke two windows and damaged a curtain in another person's house. She honestly believed that the house belonged to a friend who would have consented to her breaking in and causing the damage.

MUSTILL J.:

"Her defence is founded on the state of belief called for by section 5(2). True, the fact of the appellant's intoxication was relevant to the defence under section 5(2), for it helped to explain what would otherwise have been inexplicable, and hence lent colour to her evidence about the state of her belief. This is not the same as using drunkenness to rebut an inference of intention or recklessness. Belief, like intention or recklessness, is a state of mind: but they are not the same states of mind.

Can it nevertheless be said that, even if the context is different, the principles established by *R. v Majewski* . . . ought to be applied to this new situation? If the basis of the decision in *R. v Majewski* had been that drunkenness does not prevent a person from having an intent or being reckless, then there would be grounds for saying that it should equally be left out of account when deciding on his state of belief. But this is not in our view what *R. v Majewski* decided. The House of Lords did not conclude that intoxication was irrelevant to the fact of the defendant's state of mind, but rather that, whatever might have been his actual state of mind, he should for reasons of policy be precluded from relying on any alteration in that state brought about by self-induced intoxication . . . But these considerations do not apply to a case where Parliament has specifically required the court to consider the defendant's actual state of belief, not the state of belief which ought to have existed. It seems to us that the court is required by section 5(3) to focus on the existence of the belief, not its intellectual soundness; and a belief can be just as much honestly held if it is induced by intoxication as if it stems from stupidity, forgetfulness or inattention . . .

Parliament has specifically isolated one subjective element, in the shape of honest belief, and has given it separate treatment, and its own special gloss in section 5(3). This being so, there is nothing objectionable in giving it special treatment as regards drunkenness, in accordance with the natural meaning of the words."

Appeal allowed

This whole approach does seem distinctly odd. Where a defendant causing criminal damage makes a drunken mistake, her entire criminal liability depends on the precise form of her mistake. For instance, if she makes a mistake and thinks the property is her own, she will be liable as drunkenness is no answer to a charge of criminal damage. If, however, because of her drunkenness she believes

---

[646]   *R. v Richardson (Nigel John) and Irwin (Sean Anthony)* [1999] 1 Cr. App. R. 392.

that the owner would consent to the damage to the property, then s.5(3) applies and, as in *Jaggard v Dickinson*, the defendant will escape liability.

It is interesting to compare s.5(3) with s.8 of the Criminal Justice Act 1967. In *Majewski*, Lord Elwyn-Jones held that drunkenness could not be taken into account under s.8:

> "Its purpose and effect [section 8] was to alter the law of evidence about the presumption of intention to produce the reasonable and probable consequences of one's acts. It was not intended to change the common law rule. In referring to 'all the evidence' it meant all the *relevant* evidence. But if there is a substantive rule of law that in crimes of basic intent, the factor of intoxication is irrelevant (and such I hold to be the substantive law), evidence with regard to it is quite irrelevant."[647]

It has been commented that it "is difficult to see that section 5(3) performs any different function in relation to lawful excuse than section 8 of the Criminal Justice Act 1967 performs in relation to intention and recklessness."[648] If evidence of drunkenness is irrelevant to an ascertainment of intention or foresight, it is difficult to understand why it is relevant to determining whether one believes another has consented to the property being damaged.[649]

F. Involuntary Intoxication

Where a defendant is reduced to a state of intoxication through no fault of his own (because, for example, his drinks were "laced"), he cannot be "blamed" for his actions and will accordingly have a defence to any criminal charge. However, this protection extends only to the defendant who is so intoxicated that he does not form mens rea.

R. v Kingston [1995] 2 A.C. 355 (House of Lords)

The appellant, his drink having been laced with drugs, indecently assaulted a 15-year-old boy. He was convicted after the judge directed the jury that they should acquit if they found that he was so affected by the drugs that he lacked intent, but to convict if he had intent. The defendant appealed, claiming that he would not have committed the offence but for the drugs. The Court of Appeal upheld his appeal on the basis that the "operative fault" was not his. The Crown appealed to the House of Lords.

LORD MUSTILL:

"[T]he general nature of the case is clear enough. In ordinary circumstances the respondent's paedophiliac tendencies would have been kept under control, even in the presence of the sleeping or unconscious boy on the bed. The ingestion of the drug (whatever it was) brought about a temporary change in the mentality or personality of the respondent which lowered his ability to resist temptation so far that his desires overrode his ability to control them. Thus we are concerned with a case of disinhibition . . .

On these facts there are three grounds on which the respondent might be held free from criminal responsibility. First, that his immunity flows from general principles of the criminal law. Secondly, that this immunity is already established by a solid line of authority. Finally, that the court should, when faced with a new problem acknowledge the justice of the case and boldly create a new common law defence.

It is clear . . . that the Court of Appeal adopted the first approach. The decision was explicitly founded on general principle . . .:

---

[647] *DPP v Majewski* [1977] A.C. 443 at 475–476.
[648] C. Wells, "Swatting the Subjectivist Bug" [1982] Crim. L.R. 209.
[649] The Law Commission finds no justification for the anomalous result and recommends that the same rules apply to both statutory and general defences: Law Com. No.314 (2009), fn.590 above, paras 3.81–3.83.

'the law recognises that, exceptionally, an accused person may be entitled to be acquitted if there is a possibility that although his act was intentional, the intent itself arose out of circumstances for which he bears no blame.'. . .

My Lords, with every respect I must suggest that no such principle exists or, until the present case, had ever in modern times been thought to exist. Every offence consists of a prohibited act or omission coupled with whatever state of mind is called for by the statute or rule of the common law which creates the offence. In those offences which are not absolute the state of mind which the prosecution must prove to have underlain the act or omission—the 'mental element'—will in the majority of cases be such as to attract disapproval. The mental element will then be the mark of what may properly be called a 'guilty mind'. . . [His Lordship then surveyed cases both here and in other jurisdictions and concluded that there was no basis] for holding that the defence relied upon is already established by the common law, any more than it can be derived from general principles. Accordingly I agree with the analysis of Professor Griew, *Archbold News*, May 28 1993, pp.4–5:

'What has happened is that the Court of Appeal has recognised a new *defence* to criminal charges in the nature of an exculpatory excuse. It is precisely because the defendant acted in a prohibited way with the intent (the *mens rea*) required by the definition of the offence that he needs this defence.'. . .
To recognise a new defence of this type would be a bold step . . . I can only say that the defence runs into difficulties at every turn. In point of theory, it would be necessary to reconcile a defence of irresistible impulse derived from a combination of innate drives and external disinhibition with the rule that irresistible impulse of a solely internal origin (not necessarily any more the fault of the offender) does not in itself excuse although it may be a symptom of disease of the mind . . . Equally, the state of mind which founds the defence superficially resembles a state of diminished responsibility . . . On the practical side there are serious problems . . .

My Lords, the fact that a new doctrine may require adjustment of existing principles to accommodate it . . . is not of course a ground for refusing to adopt it, if that is what the interests of justice require. Here, however, justice makes no such demands, for the interplay between the wrong done to the victim, the individual characteristics and frailties of the defendant, and the pharmacological effects of whatever drug may be potentially involved can be far better recognised by a tailored choice from the continuum of sentences available to the judge than by the application of a single yea-or-nay jury decision.

. . . I consider that both the ruling and the direction of the judge were correct."

Appeal allowed

Many commentators condemned the Court of Appeal decision in *Kingston* as surprising, dangerous and contrary to principle,[650] and favoured the narrower view of blame adopted by the House of Lords. However, others have argued that a new exculpatory defence should be developed for circumstances such as those in *Kingston*. Many persons might have secret urges to commit criminal acts, but blame is inappropriate if they exercise control and restraint. If the only reason their inhibitions are removed is because someone else has secretly laced their drink, they are no longer able to evaluate their actions[651] and should not be blamed. It has been suggested that such a defence, if it were to be afforded, should depend upon an assessment whether the conduct was "out of character".[652] This would involve comparing the defendant's "settled" character with the defendant's intoxicated character. If the involuntary intoxication "destabilises" his character so that he commits an offence he should have an excuse.[653] Such an approach, however, is perceived by others to be blaming persons for what they are rather than what they have done. Apart from difficulties of proof (for example, establishing whether or not Kingston had abused children on previous occasions), the fact is that the evidence established on this occasion that Kingston only gave way to his desires because of the unforeseen actions of a third party. The real blame should be directed at that third party. Where a person commits a crime because

---

650   For example, J.C. Smith [1993] Crim. L.R. 784; E. Griew, *Archbold News*, May 28, 1993.
651   Horder, fn.460 above . See also, R. Smith and L. Clements, "Involuntary Intoxication, the Threshold of Inhibition and the Instigation of Crime" [1995] 46 N.I.L.Q. 210.
652   See G.R. Sullivan, "Involuntary Intoxication and Beyond" [1994] Crim. L.R. 272 and W. Wilson, "Involuntary Intoxication: Excusing the Inexcusable" [1995] 1 *Res Publica* 25.
653   Sullivan, fn.33 above, p.131. See also Tadros, fn.32 above, pp.502–506.

of threats by another, we blame that other person and allow the defendant a defence of duress. We do not enquire whether the actions were "out of character". The same approach should be adopted to those whose inhibitions are removed by the secret acts of others.

Criminal liability should generally only be imposed upon blameworthy actors who cause prohibited harms. It was seen in Ch.2 that mens rea is increasingly being given a normative meaning, equating it with blameworthiness or culpability—rather than bearing its cognitive meaning as involving intention or foresight. Following this, it is appropriate to blame actors who voluntarily become intoxicated— even though they might lack cognitive mens rea. On this basis, however, we ought not to blame people such as Kingston. As the Court of Appeal put it, "the law should exculpate him because the operative fault is not his".[654] Judicial developments to date, however, suggest that while courts are prepared to expand the concept of mens rea to inculpate blameworthy actors, they are unwilling to restrict mens rea to exclude non-blameworthy actors such as Kingston. Accordingly, an alternative might be to reflect the lack of fault on the part of an actor like Kingston through the creation of a new defence. Lacey, for example, has argued for the creation of a new defence of "blocked evaluation" which, rather than operating on the basis of lapse of character, could be thought of in "terms of temporary lapses of normal conditions of agency, given that the lapse is of the kind which removes or seriously undermines the normal reasoning process."[655] Such a defence might not only be available to those defendants (with mens rea) pleading involuntary intoxication.[656] The House of Lords, has, however, rejected any such approach and, clinging to orthodoxy, proclaimed that Kingston must be liable as he acted with mens rea and no established defence was applicable. It must be seriously doubted whether this severing of the link between moral fault and blame can be justified.

Despite these concerns, the Law Commission has endorsed the rule in *Kingston*, agreeing with their Lordships' reasoning and approach.[657] It believes that the common law position should be retained and "that there should be no defence of reduced inhibitions or blurred perception of morality where D's condition was caused by involuntary intoxication."[658]

In relation to involuntary intoxication more generally, the Law Commission's proposals also restate the common law but do provide a non-exhaustive list of situations which would count as involuntary intoxication, such as where intoxication results from the administration of an intoxicant under duress, or where intoxication results from taking an intoxicant for a proper medical purpose.[659]

G. "Dutch Courage" Intoxication

Where persons deliberately reduce themselves to a state of intoxication to give themselves "Dutch courage" to commit a crime, their intoxication will not be a defence even to crimes that can only be committed with a specific intention. They are to be "blamed" to the same extent as the person who intentionally commits a crime. As Lord Denning stated in *Gallagher*:

"If a man, whilst sane and sober, forms an intention to kill . . . and then gets himself drunk so as to give himself Dutch courage to do the killing . . . he cannot rely on his self-induced drunkenness as a defence to a charge of murder, nor even as reducing it to manslaughter . . . the wickedness of his

---

[654] *R. v Kingston (Barry)* (1993) 97 Cr. App. R. 401.
[655] Lacey, fn.26 above, p.107 at 120.
[656] Lacey discusses whether it could be used in situations of mercy-killing, for example, where the extreme distress or despair edges out the normal processes of reasoning: above, pp.123–125.
[657] Law Com. No.314 (2009), fn.590 above, para.4.25.
[658] Above, para.4.8.
[659] Above, paras 3.121–3.136.

mind before he got drunk is enough to condemn him, coupled with the act which he intended to do and did do."[660]

Law Commission, Legislating the Criminal Code, Intoxication and Criminal Liability (Law Com. No.229) (1995), paras 6.51–6.52:

"[T]he situation is far-fetched in the extreme . . . Lord Denning was concerned with the defendant who becomes intoxicated *in order to give himself courage to carry out his intention*—not in the hope that he will lose all control of his actions but will nevertheless somehow happen to do the very thing that he lacks the courage to do while conscious. If his purpose is to give himself 'Dutch courage' rather than to turn himself into an automaton, we do not think it right that he should be regarded, *at the time when he causes the consequence he desires*, as intending that consequence. He cannot fairly be deemed to have had, at that later time, the intention that he in fact had when he became intoxicated . . . We have considered whether to propose a special rule for the case of the person who becomes intoxicated in order to turn himself into an automaton, hoping that while in that state he will commit the *actus reus* of an offence requiring intention; but we have concluded that such a rule would be of no practical value . . . [I]t is almost inconceivable that the case envisaged could ever arise; certainly we are unaware of any such case."

H. Intoxication Can Cause Insanity or Diminished Responsibility

Drunkenness can cause a disease of the mind sufficient to bring the defendant within the insanity rules.[661] It can cause, for example, a *delirium tremens*. However, the defence is rarely successful in England. In *Burns*,[662] a psychiatrist testified that Burns had a disease of the mind because his brain was damaged by alcohol with the result that on the occasion of the alleged crime he was suffering from "amnesia in the sense that the thing does not register at the time because the brain function is impaired" which meant that Burns did not know what he was doing, or that it was wrong. It was accepted that this defence could result in an insanity verdict, but the jury rejected the psychiatric evidence and concluded that Burns knew what he was doing.

Although the new greater flexibility in sentencing options upon a finding of "not guilty by reason of insanity" has led to an increase in the number of such verdicts, it is not clear whether this has led to insanity caused by drunkenness to be pleaded more frequently.[663] In *Bromley*,[664] the defendant suffered from brain damage which could motivate him into violence upon consuming a small quantity of alcohol. On a charge of attempted rape, it was held that the drink had made him temporarily insane. Pursuant to the court's powers[665] he was given an absolute discharge.

Can alcoholism amount to a disease of the mind for the purposes of the insanity defence? This issue is problematic because the medical and sociological literature is still divided as to whether alcoholism is a disease or learned behaviour.

---

[660] *Attorney General of Northern Ireland v Gallagher (Patrick)* [1963] A.C. 349.

[661] *Davis* (1881) 14 Cox C.C. 563; *DPP v Beard* [1920] A.C. 479; *Attorney General of Northern Ireland v Gallagher (Patrick)* [1963] A.C. 349.

[662] *R. v Burns (Dafydd John)* (1974) 58 Cr. App. R. 364.

[663] Research into the special verdicts between the years 1997 and 2001 revealed only one case where the diagnosis had been delirium tremens: Mackay et al., fn.539 above, p.400.

[664] *Bromley* (1992) 142 N.L.J. 116 (Winchester Crown Court).

[665] Criminal Procedure (Insanity) Act 1964 s.5(2)(b)(iii), as substituted by the Criminal Procedure (Insanity and Unfitness to Plead) Act 1991.

Julia Tolmie, "Alcoholism and Criminal Liability" (2001) 64 M.L.R. 688 at pp.689–708:

"[These] two competing conceptualisations of the phenomenon . . . can be labelled the 'disease model' and the 'habit model'. . .

[T]he disease model views alcoholism as an abnormal mental condition, whereas the habit model views alcoholics as involved in normal human processes but making bad choices . . . [S]ome disease models of alcoholism view the condition as involving a total loss of control over drinking, whereas *some* disease models and *all* habit models view an alcoholic's control over their drinking as impaired rather than totally lost . . . The model of criminal responsibility that purportedly underpins the criminal justice system is premised on the notion that people have free will and rationality . . . Intoxication can impair one's capacity for choice on a number of . . . levels. However, even if it has, as a matter of public policy the defendant is often not exonerated in spite of that impairment. It is considered that their choice to get dangerously intoxicated in the first place is sufficiently morally culpable to supply criminal responsibility in spite of their lack of choice at the time of the crime. The condition of alcoholism is interesting because it challenges this assumption. Unlike other people who choose to get drunk, alcoholics belong to a category of people who have impaired choice around even the decision to get intoxicated.

How the defendant's alcoholism should shift the normal calculation of criminal liability based on their intoxication differs depending on the model of alcoholism that one adopts. For example, if one views alcoholism as a habit that has impaired the defendant's choices to drink but still left them with choice, it is extremely difficult to argue that there should be reduced criminal liability based on the condition. On the other hand if one views alcoholism as an abnormal mental condition which either totally deprives the defendant of the choice to drink, or leaves them with both an impaired choice and disordered thinking around what degree of choice they do have, then there is a strong argument for taking into account the alcoholic's intoxication when considering their criminal liability . . .

If a history of alcoholism produces an independent and recognised pathological condition then it is uncontroversial that this can form the foundation of an insanity defence. Thus delirium tremens and alcohol withdrawal psychosis can be the basis of a successful insanity defence. What is not so clear is whether alcoholism *per se*, along with states of intoxication which result from it, can form the basis of the insanity defence . . .

Once again the strongest argument for alcoholism forming the foundation of the insanity defence applies if the disease model of alcoholism is adopted . . . On the other hand, if the habit model of alcoholism is adopted then there is little argument for alcoholism forming the foundation of an insanity defence . . .

So from a policy point of view it appears to make the most sense to treat an alcoholic defendant within the auspices of the criminal justice system, releasing them if treatment is successful and they are likely to be reintegrated as a contributing and functional member of the community, but requiring them to serve out the standard sentence for their crime if they are not treatable at that point in time. There are two ways of achieving this result.

The first is to deal with the alcoholic's condition at the point of trial and impose treatment in the place of punishment as a matter of liability rather than sentence. Insanity is a defence that effectively achieves this result . . . The second way of dealing with the issue is to hold an alcoholic fully responsible for the crimes that they have committed and then deal with their condition as a sentencing issue."

Although the matter is unresolved in English law, the better approach would be to follow the lead provided in the United States[666] and regard alcoholism as capable of amounting to a disease of the mind—bearing in mind that a defence of insanity will not succeed in such cases unless the other rigorous requirements of the *M'Naghten* Rules have been satisfied.

Can intoxication give rise to a defence of diminished responsibility? In *Tandy*,[667] it was indicated that alcoholism could bring a defendant within the scope of s.2 of the Homicide Act 1957: (i) "if the alcoholism had reached the level at which her brain had been injured by the repeated insult from intoxicants so that there was gross impairment of her judgment and emotional responses";[668] and (ii) if "the appellant's drinking had become involuntary, that is to say she was no longer able to resist the impulse to drink". It has been argued that the court

---

[666] *Salzman v United States*, 405 F.2d 358 (1968).
[667] *R. v Tandy (Linda Mary)* (1988) 87 Cr. App. R. 45.
[668] See also *R. v Inseal* [1992] Crim. L.R. 35.

"effectively required a defendant who wants to base a defence of diminished responsibility on their alcoholism to demonstrate a total impairment of control *at all times* around alcohol. What this means is that the court was setting a requirement that even the most chronic alcoholic will find difficult to meet".[669]

The decision appeared to be inconsistent with s.2 which then required only a substantial, and not total, impairment of mental responsibility.[670]

It is clear that the transient effect of drink or drugs, even if the intoxication is acute, is insufficient.[671] However, more problematic is the situation where the defendant pleads mental abnormality but is also heavily intoxicated at the time of the offence.

R. v Dietschmann [2003] 1 A.C. 1209 (House of Lords)

The defendant was suffering from a mental abnormality (an adjustment disorder which was a depressed grief reaction to a bereavement) but was also heavily intoxicated at the time of the killing.

LORD HUTTON:

"The policy of the criminal law in respect of persons suffering from mental abnormality is to be found in the words of section 2 . . . [A] brain-damaged person who is intoxicated and who commits a killing is not in the same position as a person who is intoxicated, but not brain-damaged, and who commits a killing . . . I consider that the jury should be directed along the following lines:

'Assuming that the defence have established that the defendant was suffering from mental abnormality as described in section 2, the important question is: did that abnormality substantially impair his mental responsibility for his acts in doing the killing? You know that before he carried out the killing the defendant had had a lot to drink. Drink cannot be taken into account as something which contributed to his mental abnormality and to any impairment of mental responsibility arising from that abnormality. But you may take the view that both the defendant's mental abnormality and drink played a part in impairing his mental responsibility for the killing and that he might not have killed if he had not taken drink. If you take that view, then the question for you to decide is this: has the defendant satisfied you that, despite the drink, his mental abnormality substantially impaired his mental responsibility for his fatal acts, or has he failed to satisfy you of that? If he has satisfied you of that, you will find him not guilty of murder but you may find him guilty of manslaughter.'" [672]

While this is clearly in line with other policy decisions in relation to intoxication, this is not an easy exercise for the jury. The fact that the defendant is intoxicated is not to be taken into account. The jury must focus on the pre-existing abnormality of mind and assess whether that abnormality substantially impaired his mental responsibility. But, given the fact that the drink may also have "played a part in impairing his mental responsibility",[673] it is surely far-fetched to expect a jury to be able to

---

[669] J. Tolmie, "Alcoholism and Criminal Liability" (2001) 64 M.L.R. 688 at 699.

[670] Tolmie, p.700. Coroners and Justice Act 2009 s.52 amends s.2 so that the defence no longer requires a substantial impairment of mental responsibility but a substantial impairment of the defendant's ability to understand the nature of their conduct, form a rational judgment or exercise self-control. See below, p.750.

[671] *R. v Di Duca (David Lancelot)* (1959) 43 Cr. App. R. 167; *R. v Fenton (Martin Charles)* (1975) 119 S.J. 695; *R. v Dowds (Stephen Andrew)* [2012] EWCA Crim 281. See N. Wake, "Diminished Responsibility and Acute Intoxication: Raising the Bar?" (2012) 76 J. Crim. L.197. The Law Commission supports the view that acute intoxication, of itself, should not be regarded as a "recognised medical condition": Law Commission Discussion Paper (2013), fn.461 above, para.4.92.

[672] *R. v Hendy (Jason Geoffrey)* [2006] 2 Cr. App. R. 33 confirms that *R. v Dietschmann* [2003] 1 A.C. 1209 merely explained the law in the earlier case of *R. v Gittens (Charlesworth Alexander)* [1984] Q.B. 698 and did not represent a change in the law.

[673] *R. v Dietschmann* [2003] 1 A.C. 1209. In *R. v Wood (Clive)* [2008] EWCA Crim 1305, the court applied the reasoning of *Dietschmann* to a situation where the underlying condition was itself connected to the alcohol abuse. As Ashworth has commented, the task then for the jury is "fearsomely difficult": A. Ashworth, "Diminished Responsibility: defendant

discriminate between the two causes of impairment. The short answer is that juries will continue to do what they normally do when dealing with diminished responsibility in the minority of cases where there is not a guilty plea and simply accept the views of the medical experts.[674] The practical importance of this decision is that it confirms that drunken defendants with mental abnormalities are not barred from pleading diminished responsibility.

I. Reform of the law

As will be clear from the above discussion, the law on intoxication has long been considered to be in need of reform.

George P. Fletcher, Rethinking Criminal Law (1978), pp.847–848:

"His fault in rendering himself non-responsible at the time of the violent act is constant, whether he commits a burglary, a rape, or a murder. To bring the scope of his liability into line with his culpability in getting drunk, the law seeks a compromise. There has to be some accommodation between (1) the principle that if someone gets drunk, he is liable for the violent consequences, and (2) the principle that liability and punishment should be graded in proportion to actual culpability.

German law and American law reveal two different approaches to reconciling these conflicting principles. German law includes intoxication along with mental illness as a basis for denying the capacity to be held accountable for a wrongful act. Deference to the conflicting principle of liability for the risk implicit in getting drunk is found in a special section of the Code, which is here translated in full:

323a(1) Whoever intentionally or negligently becomes intoxicated through the use of alcohol or other intoxicating substances is punishable up to five years in prison, if while in that intoxicated condition he commits a wrongful act and if by virtue of the intoxication is not responsible for that act (or his non-responsibility is a possibility).

(2) In no event may the punishment be greater than that for the wrongful act committed in the state of intoxication.

The concept of negligence underlying this provision is negligence as to the risk of committing a crime while intoxicated. If the suspect takes adequate precautions against committing a crime while intoxicated, there is no negligence. If, for example, he hires someone to supervise his conduct while he is intoxicated and the hired person unexpectedly fails to restrain him, there would be a good case against liability. If he gets drunk in a bar and while in a state of non-responsibility he throws a bottle at a valuable mirror, he is not punished for the wrongful act of intentionally destroying the property of another; rather he is punished for the wrongful act of creating a risk that he would behave non-responsibly and intentionally destroy property . . .

[T]he theory of the provision is not simply that he negligently take the risk that he might do some harm. The requirement of a wrongful act while intoxicated is an important limitation.

Indeed the limitation suggests that the theory underlying the provision is not simply one of negligently endangering other persons. If risk-taking were the essence of the crime, there would be no concern about the wrongfulness of the intoxicated act and indeed it would be hard to explain why the subsequent act should be required at all."

Over the past few decades, English law reform bodies have vacillated between proposals to modify *Majewski* and the more radical proposal of abolishing *Majewski* and replacing it with a separate offence.

---

diagnosed as suffering from alcohol dependency syndrome but having sustained no brain damage as result" [2008] Crim. L.R. 976. See also *R. v Stewart (James)* [2009] EWCA Crim 593, in which the court endeavours to clarify the jury's task and A. Ashworth, "*R v Stewart*: manslaughter—diminished responsibility—alcohol dependency" [2009] Crim. L.R. 807.

[674]   Below, pp.749–751.

Criminal Law Revision Committee, 14th Report, Offences Against the Person (Cmnd.7844, 1980), paras 259–264:

"259. . . . What calls for punishment is getting intoxicated and when in that condition behaving in a way which society cannot, and should not, tolerate. An offence which covers this situation must make some reference to the harm caused, and cannot be expressed simply in terms of getting dangerously intoxicated, however gross the intoxication may have been. Furthermore, the harm needs to be identified to some extent: the drunken man who on arrest punches a police officer should not be labelled with the same offence as the alcoholic who kills a child when trying to interfere with her sexually. It is doubtful whether any solution to the problem based solely upon legal principle would be generally acceptable. Policy has to be taken into account . . .

260. The Butler Committee considered offences committed while voluntarily intoxicated . . . and they proposed the creation of a strict liability offence where a person while voluntarily intoxicated does an act (or makes an omission) that would amount to a dangerous offence if it were done or made with the requisite state of mind for that offence. Their proposal is that the offence should not be charged in the first instance. On indictment the jury would be directed to find on this offence in the event of intoxication being successfully raised as a defence to the offence originally charged . . . On this proposal the jury would have no option but to convict of the dangerous intoxication offence. On conviction of the offence on indictment the maximum penalty suggested is one year's imprisonment for a first offence or three years' imprisonment for a second or subsequent one; on summary trial the maximum sentence of imprisonment would be six months.

261. One of the defects in the Butler Committee proposal is, in our opinion, the problem of the nomenclature of the offence. A conviction of the Butler Committee offence would merely record a conviction of an offence of committing a dangerous act while intoxicated. This is insufficient. The record must indicate the nature of the act committed, for example whether it was an assault or a killing. It would be unfair for a defendant who has committed a relatively minor offence while voluntarily intoxicated to be labelled as having committed the same offence as a defendant who has killed. The penalty suggested is also in our opinion insufficient to deal with serious offences such as killings or rapes while voluntarily intoxicated by drink or drugs.

262. Professors Smith and Glanville Williams support the proposal of a separate offence because in the first place they consider it to be a fundamental principle that a person should not be convicted of an offence requiring recklessness when he was not in fact reckless. In such a case the verdict of the jury and the record of the court do not represent the truth. Secondly, they think it important that the verdict of the jury should distinguish between an offender who was reckless and one who was not because that is relevant to the question of sentence . . .

The majority of us feel, however, that [the Smith and Williams' proposal for a special offence carrying the same punishment as the complete offence] would also create problems. The separate offence would add to the already considerable number of matters which a jury often has to consider when deciding whether the offences charged have been proved, and some of us feel that the separate offence would make the jury's task even more difficult than it is at present in some cases . . . It seems likely moreover, that if the separate offence is created there would be many more trials in which defendants would raise the issue of drunkenness . . . [M]any defendants might seek to plead to the special offence rather than the offence charged, either because they might prefer to be convicted of the special offence rather than the offence charged (as for example rape), or because the special offence might tend to be regarded as a less serious offence . . . We also consider that it is artificial and undesirable to have a separate offence for which conviction is automatic but which carries the same maximum penalty as the offence for which a defendant would have been convicted but for the lack of proof of the required mental element due to intoxication. It is also important to consider the public reaction to the creation of a separate offence: we are of the opinion that they would be confused by it."[675]

The majority of the Criminal Law Revision Committee accordingly rejected the proposal for a special intoxication offence and instead recommended a codification of the law, endorsing the "recklessness test" discussed above, namely, that intoxication should never be a defence to crimes that can be committed recklessly; it could at most negative the mental element of intention required for the commission of an offence. This proposal was reproduced by cl.22 of the Draft Criminal Code Bill 1989[676] and in the Law Commission's proposals in 1995.

---

[675] For a recent analysis favouring a separate offence, see Williams, fn.594 above, pp.274–289.
[676] Law Com. No.177 (1989), fn.21 above.

Law Commission, Legislating the Criminal Code, Intoxication and Criminal Liability (Law Com. No.229) (1995), paras 6.6–6.7:

"6.6 We . . . have concluded that the best way of codifying the present law, whilst avoiding the problems inherent in the present distinction between offences of specific and basic intent, is to confine the *Majewski* principle, broadly speaking, to offences for which proof of recklessness (or awareness of risk) is sufficient . . .

6.7 This policy *may* represent the present law, although it is difficult to state this with any certainty. . . . [I]t has the advantages of simplicity and clarity, both matters of great importance in any system of criminal law. Finally, this change in the law will have a negligible practical effect in relation to crimes already judicially categorised as being of basic or specific intent, since most crimes designated as being of basic intent are capable of reckless commission."

This recommendation (which was substantially adopted in the subsequent Government proposals[677]) has been criticised.

Jeremy Horder, "Sobering Up? The Law Commission on Criminal Intoxication" [1995] 58 M.L.R. 534 at 535–536:

"Despite the radical change of direction since the Consultation Paper, one thing has not changed in the Commission's final Report. This is, ironically, the attitude of uncomprehending hostility towards the common law's attempt to express, in its division of crimes between those of basic and of specific intent, the very distinctions between offences on which the Commission's new proposals are broadly based. Despite the views of those working in the criminal justice system that the current law works *fairly*, as well as without difficulty, the Commission makes little effort to discern any deeper principles underlying the common law that might explain why its rules can be regarded as fair. They endorse the view that 'the designation of crimes as requiring, or not requiring, specific intent is based on no principle at all' (3.27; 5.36). How is it, then, that the Commission has thought it right to track the designation so closely in its own proposals? For the kinds of *mentes reae* mentioned in clause 1(2), allegations of which may be met by leading evidence of voluntary intoxication, bear a striking resemblance to the *mentes reae* of crimes of specific intent, allegations of which can presently be rebutted by such evidence at common law.

The answer is that the Commission regards the case for restricting the ability of a defendant to deny *mens rea* through pleading voluntary intoxication as founded on pure and simple policy considerations. They side with J.C. Smith in taking the view that 'the real reason for punishing [the defendant, by applying *Majewski*] is the outrage that would quite reasonably be felt if serious injury caused to an innocent person by a drunk were to go unpunished' (5.23). In a sense, thus, the Commission's proposals are purely defensive. The main bulk of the provisions are designed to fend off public criticism rather than to provide a principled basis on which the law can operate. If this is true (as it seems to be), then to allow evidence of voluntary intoxication to negative *mens rea* in *any* crime, particularly a serious crime of violence, looks perverse . . . By allowing a concern for policy to dominate its thinking, the Commission simply clears the way for a Government obsessed with 'crime control' to take that concern to its logical conclusion, which is that the Commission's proposals should be ignored and voluntary intoxication should make no impact whatsoever on criminal liability. Yet this is the very conclusion the Commission and its consultees thought most undesirable."[678]

Almost 15 years later, the author of this extract, Jeremy Horder, as Law Commissioner, was in a position to try to identify the principles underlying the common law and to base new proposals upon them. The Law Commission now accepts that its earlier proposals might have been too complex[679] and has "returned to the subject with a stripped down approach".[680] As noted earlier, it believes that the rationale of the law is and ought to be that the subjective recklessness involved in becoming intoxi-

---

677   Draft Offences Against the Person Bill 1998 cl.19.
678   See also, S. Gough, "Intoxication and Criminal Liability" (1996) 112 L.Q.R. 335; J. O'Leary, "Lament for the Intoxication 'Defence'" [1997] 48 N.I.L.Q. 152 and S. Gough, "Surviving without *Majewski*" [2000] Crim. L.R. 719.
679   Law Com. No.314 (2009), fn.590 above, para.1.67.
680   I. Dennis, "Editorial: Intoxication and Criminal Liability" [2009] Crim. L.R. 133.

cated (and thus more dangerous to society) is the moral equivalent of the subjective recklessness usually required for liability. It takes the view now that the concepts of specific and basic intent are "ambiguous, confusing and misleading" and proposes to abandon them.[681] However, the substance of the distinction is retained.

Law Commission, Intoxication and Criminal Liability (Law Com. No.314) (Cmnd.7526, 2009), paras 3.35–3.48:

"**Recommendation 1: the Majewski rule**

3.35 There should be a general rule that:

(1) if D is charged with having committed an offence as a perpetrator;

(2) the fault element of the offence is not an integral fault element (for example, because it merely requires proof of recklessness); and

(3) D was voluntarily intoxicated at the material time;

then, in determining whether or not D is liable for the offence, D should be treated as having been aware of anything which D would have been aware of but for the intoxication.

3.36 The approach we recommend would apply regardless of the degree to which D was intoxicated and regardless of whether D's state of intoxication was caused by alcohol or some other drug or substance (such as a solvent) or any combination of intoxicants.

3.37 We include recklessness within the scope of this general rule as an 'example', but the practical effect of the rule . . . would be to limit the application of the rule to allegations of recklessness . . .

3.38 If the allegation is one of subjective recklessness, D would be treated as having been aware of any risk or circumstance D would have been aware of but for his or her self-induced state of intoxication . . .

Recommendation 2: the rule for integral fault elements

3.42 If the subjective fault element in the definition of the offence, as alleged, is one to which the justification for the *Majewski* rule does not apply, then the prosecution should have to prove that D acted with that relevant state of mind.

3.43 . . . For such fault elements, evidence of D's voluntary intoxication should be taken into consideration by the court when determining whether the prosecution has proved that D acted (or failed to act) with the required state of mind. We list the integral fault elements below under our next recommendation.

3.44 Importantly, it would be *the particular state of mind* alleged by the prosecution, not the offence itself, which would determine whether the general rule applies. Our recommendation would abandon the courts' unhelpful categorisation which distinguishes between *offences* of 'specific intent' and *offence* of 'basic intent' . . .

3.45 If recklessness is alleged then, as explained above, the general rule would apply. But if the prosecution alleges that D acted with an integral fault element, it would be necessary to prove that D had that required state of mind at the relevant time; and the jury would be directed that D's intoxication should be taken into account in determining whether the allegation has been proved.

Recommendation 3: the integral fault elements

3.46 The following subjective fault elements should be excluded from the application of the general rule and should, therefore, always be proved:

(1) intention as to a consequence [but not intention as to conduct];

(2) knowledge as to something;

(3) belief as to something (where the belief is equivalent to knowledge as to something);

(4) fraud; and

(5) dishonesty.

3.47 Two other states of mind we recommend for inclusion . . . [relate to specific recommendations for those who assist or encourage crime].

3.48 The list of integral fault elements we recommend would be exhaustive."

The term "integral fault element" is not perhaps the most felicitous of expressions but otherwise the recommendations bring greater clarity to the underlying rationale of intoxication (very much like

---

[681] Law Com. No.314 (2009), fn.590 above, para.1.28.

the analysis adopted by Simester discussed earlier) and to the law. As Dennis has commented, given the conservative line taken by the Law Commission, "it is hard to see any of the policy in this report being objected to by the government."[682]

IX. Lack of Age

A. Introduction

Crime (particularly less serious forms of crime) is predominantly a youthful phenomenon. Both official statistics and self-report studies confirm that the peak age of offending is in mid-teens and that most such offenders (particularly females) will "grow out of crime".[683] The response of the criminal justice system to crime by children has fluctuated sharply and has been fundamentally affected by political considerations. The pendulum has swung between a punitive approach (which holds a child responsible as if an adult) and one based upon considerations of welfare. As part of an ever-changing uneasy balance between the two, the law does take some account of the different stages of childhood. Of course, in reality, the process of maturation is a gradual one.[684] The criminal law is rather less subtle than this: it recognises that very young children should not be held responsible for their actions and so there is a fixed age limit below which they will be excused liability.

The age of criminal responsibility is currently set at 10.[685] This is considerably lower than many other European countries, where the average age at which responsibility is imposed is 14 years old.[686] There was also a transitional phase between the ages of 10 and 14, during which time the child used to be presumed to be *"doli incapax"*. Only if the prosecution could rebut the presumption by proof that the child knew what she was doing was seriously or gravely wrong and not merely naughty or mischievous could the child be held criminally responsible for her actions.[687] Although entirely sound in relation to the underlying principles of the criminal law, the presumption increasingly came under fire as illogical, lacking in common-sense, out-dated, a serious disservice to the law and unnecessary.[688] In *C v DPP*, the House of Lords urged that the presumption be subject to "parliamentary investigation, deliberation and legislation".[689] With less deliberation than was warranted by the

---

[682]   Dennis, fn.680 above, p.134. See also J. Child, "Drink, Drugs and Law Reform: A Review of the Law Commission Report No.314" [2009] Crim. L.R. 435.

[683]   J. Fionda, *Devils and Angels* (London: Blackwell, 2005), pp.59–69; A. Rutherford, *Growing out of Crime: The New Era* (Winchester: Waterside Press, 2002).

[684]   Civil law reflects this by reference to the test of *"Gillick*-competence": *Gillick v West Norfolk and Wisbech AHA* [1986] A.C. 112. See further, H. Keating, "The Responsibility of Children in the Criminal Law" (2007) 19 C.F.L.Q. 183. The Law Commission favours consideration being given to a defence of "developmental immaturity": Law Commission Discussion Paper (2013), fn.461 above, paras 9.1–9.24.

[685]   Children and Young Persons Act 1933 s.50 as amended by Children and Young Persons Act 1963 s.16. At common law the age of criminal responsibility was seven. Children and Young Persons Act 1969 s.4, raised the age of responsibility to 14 but this was never implemented and was repealed by Criminal Justice Act 1991 s.72. Lord Dholakia has introduced a private member's Bill (The Age of Criminal Responsibility Bill) with the aim of raising the age of criminal responsibility to 12 but the Bill did not proceed beyond initial debate in the House of Lords:: see further H. Keating, "Children's Rights and Children's Criminal Responsibility" in A. Diduck and H. Reece, *Essays in Honour of Michael Freeman* (Cambridge: CUP, 2014)

[686]   In Scotland, the age of criminal responsibility is still eight. However, as a result of legislation in 2010, no child can be prosecuted below the age of 12 although a child may be the subject of a Children's Hearing (Criminal Justice and Licensing Act 2010, s.38). Ireland increased the age of criminal responsibility to 12 in 2006 (Criminal Justice Act 2006, s.52, amending the Children Act 2001) although it remains at 10 for murder, manslaughter, rape or aggravated sexual assault.

[687]   *C (A Minor) v DPP* [1996] A.C. 1.

[688]   These views were not shared by all commentators: see, for example, P. Cavadino, "Goodbye *doli*, Must we Leave You?" (1997) 9 C.F.L.Q. 165 and S. Bandalli, "Abolition of the Presumption of *doli incapax* and the Criminalisation of Children" (1998) 37 *Howard Journal* 114.

[689]   *C (A Minor) v DPP* [1996] A.C. 1 at 40.

significance of the reform, s.34 of the Crime and Disorder Act 1998 was passed. This states that "[t]he rebuttable presumption of criminal law that a child aged 10 or over is incapable of committing an offence is hereby abolished." On a strict reading, this section abolished the *presumption* only and it was thus argued that it was still open to a child between the ages of 10 and 14 to show that she did not understand that what she had done was seriously wrong.[690] In *CPS v P*, Smith LJ expressed the view (obiter) that the defence remained in existence but also flagged up the issue for another court to consider fully.[691] The House of Lords has now done so in *R. v JTB*.[692] Whilst their Lordships acknowledged the ambiguity of the provision, it has ruled that s.34 abolished both the presumption and the defence of *doli incapax* entirely for children aged 10 and over. It is regrettable that such an important change in the law's approach to the criminal responsibility of children should have been achieved in such an ambiguous manner.

This reform is a very significant part of a policy which over the last 20 years or so has sought to make children—even very young children—increasingly liable for their actions.[693] Despite the fact that only a small number of very young children are brought before the courts[694] and that the 1980s saw considerable success in diverting children away from custody and from the courts by use of formal cautioning, etc.[695] the perception has grown that children are out of control. Concerns about the use of multiple cautions[696] and the perceived growth in both the prevalence and gravity of young children's crime, fed, in part, by the highly-publicised killing of James Bulger by two 10-year-olds[697] have led to a flurry of punitive initiatives. "In the space of only five years the young person in the arms of the criminal law has been largely reconstructed within the 'little adult' imagery of the Victorian era."[698] The measures adopted have led to intense criticism both domestically and internationally.[699]

---

[690] N. Walker, "The End of an Old Song" (1999) 149 N.L.J. 64.

[691] *CPS v P* [2007] EWHC 946 (Admin). See also D. Ormerod, "Young person: young person having low IQ" [2008] Crim. L.R. 165.

[692] *R. v JTB* [2009] UKHL 20. See F.A.R. Bennion, "Mens rea and defendants below the age of discretion" [2009] Crim. L.R. 757 and A. Ashworth, "R v T: Children and Young Persons—doli incapax—Crime and Disorder Act 1998 s.34" [2009] Crim. L.R. 581.

[693] Without a corresponding increase in emphasis upon the rights of natural justice such as those pertaining to the trial of adults (M.D.A. Freeman, "The Rights of Children When They Do Wrong" (1981) 21 Brit. J. Criminol. 210).

[694] In 2012, 262 children aged 10 and 11 were proceeded against at court (*Hansard*, HL Deb, Vol.749, col.488 (November 8, 2013)).

[695] Fionda, fn.683 above, pp.88–97.

[696] Crime and Disorder Act 1998 ss.61 and 62 replaced cautioning with a statutory scheme of reprimands and warnings. This scheme was abolished by the Legal Aid, Sentencing and Punishment of Offenders Act 2012, which has introduced a scheme of youth cautions (s.135, inserting s.66ZA into the Crime and Disorder Act 1998).

[697] *R. v Secretary of State for the Home Department, ex parte Venables; Secretary of State for the Home Department, ex parte Thompson* [1997] 3 All E.R. 97. On the issue of child homicides (and their scarcity) see, Justice, *Children and Homicide* (London: Justice, 1996), P. Cavadino, *Children Who Kill: an examination of the treatment of Juveniles* (Winchester: Waterside Press, 1996) and C. McDiarmid, "Children who Murder" [2000] Crim. L.R. 547. See also the debate engendered by the trial of two boys, aged 10 and 11, who were convicted of causing grievous bodily harm with intent contrary to Offences Against the Person Act 1861 s.18 to two other young children: *The Independent*, January 23, 2010 and *The Telegraph*, January 23, 2010.

[698] A. Rutherford, "Young People and the Penal System" (1997) 147 N.L.J. 771 at 772. In addition to other changes identified in this section, the Government has, for example, introduced secure training centres for 12–14 year olds by the Criminal Justice and Public Order Act 1994 and has extended the range of Children and Young Persons Act 1933 s.53(1).

[699] See, for example, Committee on the Rights of the Child, *Concluding Observations: United Kingdom of Great Britain and Northern Ireland* (49th session), (2008), paras 77–80 and Keating, fn.684 above.

B. Below the Age of 10

Children below this age are irrebuttably presumed to be incapable of committing crime. Care proceedings may be brought if it is thought that the child "is suffering or is likely to suffer significant harm and that the care given to him is not what it would be reasonable to expect a parent to give, or the child is beyond parental control".[700] These proceedings are entirely civil and decisions are based upon the welfare of the child.[701] However, over the last decade an increasing number of other measures have been introduced with the aim of controlling the anti-social behaviour of children under the age of 10 (and their parents).[702] Although these measures are said to be to "protect young children from being drawn into crime" and to "help them change their bad behaviour"[703] there can be little doubt that they are experienced as punishment, and are part of a deeply unsatisfactory trend which could render the concept of the age of criminal responsibility meaningless.

C. Above the Age of 10

Between the ages of 10 and 13, offenders are categorised as children, and between 14 and 17 years old as young persons.[704] The sentencing options available to the youth court[705] depend upon this categorisation. A further, transitional category, referred to in the preceding White Paper[706] as "near adults" has been included in the young person category. The courts are given additional sentencing powers for 16–17 year olds whose maturity warrants such treatment. Courts must "have regard to the welfare of the child or young person"[707] but as this is not the only consideration, the court may find persuasive, for example, the need to protect the public.

X. Sundry Defences

In addition to the general defences discussed in this chapter, there are numerous other defences which are beyond the scope of this book. Such defences are more specific: it is, for example, a defence to a charge of unlawful possession of a firearm to show reasonable excuse or lawful authority.[708] Likewise, it is a defence to the offence of failing to provide a specimen of breath or blood or urine (for the purposes of the offence of driving or being in charge of a vehicle with a blood/alcohol concentration above the prescribed limit) to show a reasonable excuse.[709] Another example of a specific defence is that a police officer may use such force as is reasonable in effecting a lawful arrest.[710]

---

[700]   Children Act 1989 s.31(2).
[701]   Care orders in criminal proceedings were abolished by Children Act 1989 Sch.12, para.23, adding s.12AA to the Children and Young Persons Act 1969.
[702]   Under Crime and Disorder Act 1998 ss.8–15, for example, child safety orders, curfews, and parenting orders may be imposed.
[703]   Home Office, *Tackling Youth Crime: A Consultation Paper* (1997), paras 98–99.
[704]   Criminal Justice Act 1991 s.68, Sch.8.
[705]   Criminal Justice Act 1991 s.70(1). The youth court hears all cases involving young offenders except where the offence is homicide or a "grave crime" or where the child is charged jointly with an adult or there is other adult involvement in the crime (see Powers of Criminal Courts Act (Sentencing) Act 2000 ss.90, 91).
[706]   *Crime, Justice and Protecting the Public* (Cmnd.965, 1990), para.8.16.
[707]   Children and Young Persons Act 1933 s.44(1), as amended. This must be read subject to Crime and Disorder Act 1998 s.37, which states that the principal aim of the youth justice system is to prevent offending by children and young persons.
[708]   Firearms Act 1968 s.17.
[709]   Road Traffic Act 1988 s.7(6).
[710]   Criminal Law Act 1967 s.3(1).

5

INCHOATE OFFENCES

I. Introduction

An inchoate crime is one that is "committed by doing an act with the purpose of effecting some other offence".[1] It is committed when the defendant takes certain steps towards the commission of a crime. There are three main inchoate offences in English law—attempt, conspiracy and encouraging or assisting crime (formerly, incitement)—and the nature of the requisite steps that need be taken varies with each. With attempt the defendant must have tried to commit the offence and have got relatively close to achieving the objective. With conspiracy at least two people must have agreed to commit a crime. With encouraging or assisting crime the defendant must have encouraged or assisted another to commit a crime.

An inchoate offence is one that is "relative to the offence-in-chief".[2] It consists of actions falling short of the consummated crime. It is thus not a crime existing in the abstract. One cannot be charged with "conspiracy" or "attempt". The indictment must be drafted with reference to the complete offence, for example, conspiracy to murder or attempt to steal.

There are many other offences in English law that might be thought of as inchoate in the sense that they penalise conduct that might be preparatory to the commission of other offences. For example, under s.5 of the Terrorism Act 2006, there is an offence of preparation of terrorist acts. These offences are, however, "crimes in themselves" and are charged as such without reference to any further offence. Such offences are commonly described as endangerment offences.

Both inchoate and endangerment offences share a common element. No harm is caused, in the ordinary sense of the word; no person need be injured; no proprietary interest is damaged. A crucial question, therefore, running through the analysis of such offences will be: how can one justify the existence of these offences and how should they be punished in comparison with the complete offence?

II. Attempt

A. Criminology of Attempts

Editorial, "The Criminology of Attempts" [1986] Crim. L.R. 769:

"In recent years the law of criminal attempts has been one of the most discussed areas of the criminal law. Over the same period there has also been an increasing criminological interest in the prevention of crime, . . . Both the Home Office and the police have been placing more emphasis on the taking of measures to prevent crime, and

---

[1]   D.J. Baker, *Glanville Williams' Textbook of Criminal Law*, 3rd edn (London: Sweet & Maxwell, 2012), p.351.
[2]   G.P. Fletcher, *Rethinking Criminal Law* (New York: OUP, 1978), p.132.

few would argue with the general proposition that successful prevention is preferable to *post hoc* efforts to reform or deter offenders. If the crime prevention movement has had any success, then one might expect that more criminal endeavours are ending in failure—to be precise, that the proportion of offences which are mere attempts rather than completed crimes is increasing. Has this happened? . . .

Home Office Research Bulletin no. 21 (1986), at pages 10–13, discusses the British Crime Survey findings on attempted burglaries, an area in which crime prevention has received considerable publicity. The general finding is that only about half of all burglaries or attempts are reported to the police, but when the figures were examined further it was found that two-fifths of all burglaries are unsuccessful attempts to gain entry. Only about 20 per cent of attempts are ever reported to the police,[3] and therefore the proportion coming through the courts is much smaller. It is speculated that about half of the attempts failed because of the level of security, and that the proportion of attempts has increased in recent years."

B. Should there be a Law of Attempt?

Generally, criminal liability is imposed upon a *blameworthy* actor who causes a prohibited *harm*. With attempts, the blameworthiness element is clearly satisfied. The person who attempts to commit an offence clearly has the mens rea of that full offence.[4] But no harm has been caused in the usual sense of the word: for instance, the victim has not died or has not lost any property. Are we justified in imposing criminal liability upon an actor who has caused no such harm?

There are two quite distinct ways of answering this question—both leading to the conclusion that criminal liability should be imposed for attempts:

1. In terms of desert, an attempter's "moral culpability is (broadly) comparable to that of a successful offender".[5] As Ashworth puts it:

"A person who tries to cause a prohibited harm and fails is, in terms of moral culpability, not materially different from the person who tries and succeeds: the difference in outcome is determined by chance rather than choice, and a censuring institution like the criminal law should not subordinate itself to the vagaries of fortune by focusing on results rather than culpability."[6]

Further, where a crime is attempted, there *is* a harm, namely, a threat to security. We all have rights to bodily and proprietary security. An attempt to commit a crime represents a danger to these rights. Our right to security has been infringed. This infringement of our rights constitutes, in itself, a harm that the criminal law seeks to punish. Gross expresses the point well:

"Where there is only attempt liability, the conduct itself may usefully be regarded as a second order harm: in itself it is the sort of conduct that normally presents a threat of harm; and that, by itself, is a violation of an interest that concerns the law. The interest is one in security from harm and merely presenting a threat of harm violates that security interest."[7]

2. In utilitarian terms, criminal liability for attempts may be justified in the absence of any harm. A person who attempts to commit a crime is dangerous and needs restraining. Such a person is also in

---

[3]   The reporting rate for some attempted burglaries is much higher for some types of premises than for others; for example, it is 80% for retail premises and 53% for manufacturing premises (C. Mirrlees-Black and A. Ross, *Crime Against Retail Premises in 1993* (H.O.R.S. No.26) (1995); *Crime Against Manufacturing Premises in 1993* (H.O.R.S. No.27) (1995)).

[4]   Indeed, as shall be seen, this mens rea will often have to be of a *greater* degree than that required for the completed offence.

[5]   Law Commission Consultation Paper No.183, *Conspiracy and Attempts: A Consultation Paper* (2007), para.15.7.

[6]   A. Ashworth and J. Horder, *Principles of Criminal Law*, 7th edn (Oxford: OUP, 2013), p.455.

[7]   H. Gross, *A Theory of Criminal Justice* (New York: OUP, 1979), p.125.

need of rehabilitation and punishment for individual deterrence, otherwise they might try to commit the crime again being more careful the next time. There is also a final important instrumental justification here: the police should be given every encouragement to prevent crime, not simply to detect it. On this basis the police should be empowered to arrest and the Crown Prosecution Service to prosecute, for attempts to commit crimes.

Of course, whenever arguments such as these are raised, we find ourselves faced with the same central question: while utilitarian considerations might explain the *purpose* of punishment, are we ever justified in punishing exclusively for such reasons? Or may we only punish offenders who *deserve* punishment? If the latter, then we are back to our starting point that, generally, punishment is only deserved where there is a combination of blame and harm. However, this is not a cast-iron rule. With crimes of strict liability, the law is prepared to dispense with the element of blame in imposing liability. It could be that with crimes of attempt, the utilitarian arguments for punishment are so strong that we are prepared to dispense with the element of harm, and assert that punishment is justified (i.e. deserved) on the basis of the blame element alone.

Thus under either of these explanations it is possible to justify the existence of a law of attempt. The contours of such a law will vary, however, depending on which of the two views is accepted. This is because the first view focuses on attempts as threats to people's interests in security from interference. Thus unless the attempter gets near to completing the crime (and, generally, unless the crime is possible), no interests are threatened and criminal liability is not justified. But the emphasis in the second view is on the mens rea of the attempter: if they have the requisite mens rea, they need not get near to committing the complete offence (and, generally, it will be irrelevant whether the crime is possible). The tensions between these two approaches and their impact upon the law will be explored further when we examine the actus reus of attempt.

Can there be an attempt to commit all crimes? Section 1(4) of the Criminal Attempts Act 1981 provides that there can only be criminal liability for attempts to commit "any offence which, if it were completed, would be triable . . . as an indictable offence". This includes offences "triable either way".[8] So, even if the substantive offence is one that punishes only acts of preparation, there can be liability for attempt to commit such a crime. For example, s.14 of the Sexual Offences Act 2003 creates the offence of *arranging or facilitating* the commission of a child sex offence. In *Robson* it was held that

"although the acts criminalised by s.14 are acts of preparation, it is nonetheless a substantive offence and there is no reason why there should not be an attempt to commit such a substantive offence".[9]

Criminal liability for attempts to commit summary offences was excluded because there is

"no social need to extend the punishment of attempt outside the class of serious crime. The amount of time spent considering complicated questions would be out of all proportion to the advantage accruing from allowing the law to intervene at an early stage."[10]

---

8   An offence is an "indictable offence" even if it is one, such as low value criminal damage, that has to be proceeded with as if it were triable only summarily (*R. v Bristol Magistrates' Court, Ex p. E* [1999] Crim. L.R. 161). In *Nelson* [2013] EWCA Crim 30 the offence of attempted battery was recognised, despite battery being a summary offence; the unconvincing reason being that it is possible to try battery (and common assault) on indictment where it forms part of a series of offences of the same or similar character as an indictable offence.

9   *R. v R* [2008] 2 Cr. App. R. 38 at [11].

10   HC Deb., vol.2, ser.6, col.214 (1981).

It is submitted that such an approach is justifiable. With attempts, criminal liability is imposed in the absence of any direct harm (other than a threat to security). When dealing with serious offences we are arguably justified in dispensing with the requirement of harm. However, when dealing with the lesser summary offences which pose less of a threat to security, we should insist on harm actually occurring as a prerequisite to any criminal liability.[11] The Law Commission has proposed that there should be liability for attempts to commit a summary offence because some summary offences are relatively serious and the demarcation line between indictable and summary offences is somewhat arbitrary.[12] However, after consultation, this proposal has been abandoned. It would have involved an increase in the reach of the substantive criminal law and there was no broad consensus amongst consultees for such an extension of the law.[13]

Section 1(4) of the Act also excludes liability for attempted: (a) conspiracy; (b) aiding, abetting, counselling, procuring or suborning an offence;[14] and (c) offences under s.4(1) (assisting offenders) or s.5(1) (accepting or agreeing to accept consideration for not disclosing information about an arrestable offence) of the Criminal Law Act 1967. In *Goldman*[15] it was held that there could be liability for attempting the (now repealed) offence of incitement. There probably can be liability for attempting the new offences of encouraging or assisting crime.[16] The worrying development of double inchoate liability is considered at the end of this chapter.

It has been suggested that we do not need a *general* law of attempt. Each substantive offence could be defined, or redefined, so as to include attempts to commit that offence.[17] For instance, the crime of handling stolen goods is defined by s.22 of the Theft Act 1968 in the following terms:

"(1) A person handles stolen goods if . . . he receives the goods, or . . . undertakes or assists in their retention, removal, disposal or realisation . . ., *or if he arranges to do so*" (our emphasis added).

Arranging to receive stolen goods is part of the substantive offence. Without this provision many such arrangements would have constituted attempts to commit the offence. If all offences were defined in a comparable manner, a general law of attempt would be unnecessary. Such an approach, however, poses immense problems. First, is it realistic to expect that *all* criminal offences could be defined (and all existing offences redefined) so as to include attempts within their definition? Secondly, and most importantly, if, as will be suggested in the next section, attempts are to be regarded as less serious than completed offences, we surely do not wish to collapse the distinction between the two. One way of avoiding this would be to increase the number of separate offences of ulterior intent, such as committing an offence with intent to commit a sexual offence.[18] This would have the advantage of fair labelling in the sense that it accurately reflected what the defendant did,[19] but it would lead to a plethora of offences. Ulterior intent crimes have their place but a general law of attempt, separate

---

[11]   See above, p.461.
[12]   Law Commission Consultation Paper No.183, *Conspiracy and Attempts* (2007), paras 16.99–16.100.
[13]   Law Commission Paper No.318, *Conspiracy and Attempts* (2009), paras 8.159–8.160.
[14]   See further, M. Bohlander, "The Conflict between the Serious Crime Act 2009 and Section 1(4)(b) Criminal Attempts Act 1981—A Missed Repeal" [2010] Crim. L.R. 483 and J. Child, "The Difference between Attempted Complicity and Inchoate Assisting and Encouraging—A Reply to Professor Bohlander" [2010] Crim. L.R. 924.
[15]   *R. v Goldman (Terence)* [2001] EWCA Crim 1684.
[16]   Law Commission Paper No.300, *Inchoate Liability for Assisting and Encouraging Crime* (2006), para.5.28, n.29.
[17]   P.R. Glazebrook, "Should we have a Law of Attempted Crime?" (1969) 85 L.Q.R. 28.
[18]   Sexual Offences Act 2003 s.62.
[19]   For an example of where an ulterior intent crime might have played such a role, see *R. v Geddes (Gary William)* [1996] Crim. L.R. 894; below, p.478.

from the complete crime, is still needed for reasons of fair labelling—it is an attempt rather than the complete offence—and punishment.[20]

C. Punishment of Attempts

Criminal Attempts Act 1981 s.4(1)

"A person guilty . . . of attempting to commit an offence shall—

(a) if the offence attempted is murder or any other offence the sentence for which is fixed by law, be liable on conviction on indictment to imprisonment for life; and

(b) if the offence attempted is indictable but does not fall within paragraph (a) above, be liable on conviction on indictment to any penalty to which he would have been liable on conviction on indictment of that offence; and

(c) if the offence attempted is triable either way, be liable on summary conviction to any penalty to which he would have been liable on summary conviction of that offence."

California Penal Code s.664

"Every person who attempts to commit any crime, but fails, or is prevented or intercepted in its perpetration shall be punished, where no provision is made by law for the punishment of those attempts, as follows:

(a) If the crime attempted is punishable by imprisonment in the state prison, the person guilty of such attempt shall be punished by imprisonment in the state prison for one-half the term of imprisonment prescribed upon a conviction of the offense so attempted. However, . . . if the crime attempted is any other one in which the maximum sentence is life imprisonment or death, the person guilty of the attempt shall be punished by imprisonment in the state prison for five, seven or nine years . . .

(b) If the crime attempted is punishable by imprisonment in a county jail, the person guilty of the attempt shall be punished by imprisonment in a county jail for a term not exceeding one-half the term of imprisonment prescribed upon a conviction of the offense attempted.

(c) If the offense so attempted is punishable by a fine, the offender convicted of that attempt shall be punished by a fine not exceeding one-half the largest fine which may be imposed upon a conviction of the offense attempted."

The completed crime of theft carries a maximum sentence of seven years' imprisonment in England and Wales and attempted theft can similarly be punished, on conviction on indictment, up to this maximum of seven years' imprisonment. But in California, if theft there carried a presumptive penalty of seven years' imprisonment in the state prison, attempted theft would carry a presumptive penalty of three-and-a-half years' imprisonment. This divergence of approach raises the fundamental question: should attempts be punished to the same, or to a lesser, extent as the completed crime? On what basis can either of these approaches be rationalised?

---

[20]   J. Horder, "Crimes of Ulterior Intent", in A.P. Simester and A.T.H. Smith, *Harm and Culpability* (Oxford: OUP, 1996), pp.153–172.

James Brady, "Punishing Attempts" (1980) 63 The Monist 246 at 247–250:

"2. Equal harm

According to Becker ('Criminal Attempt and the Law of Crimes', Philosophy and Public Affairs, Vol. 3 (Spring, 1974): pp. 262–294), we need to distinguish between the private harm done to the individual, which, of course, is different in the case of attempts and completions, and the 'social' harm to which the criminal law is mainly addressed. The harm which is the concern of the criminal law is that which disrupts social stability and arouses self-defensive reactions within persons in the society. One's assurance that one will not be interfered with is perceived to be threatened equally by an attempt on others and by completed crimes. Thus, in general, attempts and completed crimes are equal in what Becker calls their 'social volatility'; the *criminal* harm is the same . . .

However . . . his claim . . . is unfounded. The fear, resentment, and apprehension occasioned when harm, in its ordinary sense, occurs does appear to be different than when, even by accident, no harm occurs. These attitudes seem to be what Becker has in mind when he talks of the 'social volatility' of conduct. Therefore, on Becker's own theory we should, *contra* his position, treat attempts differently . . .

3. Equal dangerousness

A more plausible claim than the argument that attempts and the completed crime do not differ in the harm done, is the claim that, in general, attempts pose no less danger to the legally protected interest than does the completed crime. If the general purpose in punishing is to prevent harm, the law should identify, at the earliest feasible moment, the dangerous individual who is likely to cause harm. In such a theory, conduct might be required before such intervention is justifiable, but the primary function of the conduct requirement would be evidentiary, serving as proof of the intent which is an index to the dangerousness of the offender.

If the dangerousness of the offender is the key element in grading offenses, then it follows that two equally dangerous offenders should be treated the same. If there is no difference in dangerousness between the successful offender and the person who fails to cause harm because he is prevented by some external circumstance, the law should treat them equally. Being equally dangerous, they are equally in need of treatment and reform.

There is, of course, the chance that the person who attempts a crime might be deterred from completing it if he were to receive a more severe penalty for the successful crime than if the penalty for attempts and the completed crime are the same.[21] If he is already liable to the full penalty for the attempt, then he has no motive to desist from completing the crime. But this does not provide an argument, under an equal dangerousness theory, for punishing attempts, in general, less than the completed crime. To take care of these special and probably rare cases, it would seem to be better to provide, as the Model Penal Code does, an affirmative defense of abandonment or, renunciation of purpose. Such a defense is a defense to the crime of attempt.[22] If the defendant is successful in proving the defense, he receives no punishment at all. Thus, the offender has an even greater motive for not carrying out his purpose than if the law merely provided an across-the-board reduction in punishment for attempts.

[But if this] equal dangerousness argument were to be followed consistently, crimes of unequal culpability should also be treated the same. The focus of a dangerousness approach is on the characteristics of a person which identify him as presenting a threat of harm to society. Negligent or reckless offenders may pose as much of a continuing threat of harm and may require as much treatment and reform to 'neutralize' their dangerousness as the intentional offender. Thus, if we accept the equal dangerousness rationale for punishing attempts, it would appear that we should also accept the premise that offenses should not be ranked according to culpability elements such as intention, recklessness, and negligence. We could, of course, simply accept this conclusion that

---

[21]   Ed: Research from the United States suggests that people generally believe that attempts are punished significantly less than completed crimes (J.M. Darley, C.A. Sanderson and P.S. LaMantia, "Community Standards for Defining Attempt: Inconsistencies with the Model Penal Code" 39 Amer. Behav. Sci. (1996), cited in P.H. Robinson and J.M. Darley, "Does Criminal Law Deter? A Behavioural Science Investigation" (2004) O.J.L.S. 173 at 176, n.3.

[22]   This is the position in the United States, but as shall be seen, not under English law.

intentional offenses should be classified as being of the same criminal 'degree' as reckless or negligent offenses where there is reason to believe that there is no difference in the dangerousness of the offender. But this would entail a radical reform of the criminal law; indeed, to follow a dangerous rationale consistently would be, in effect, to abolish the system of control now known as the criminal law and substitute a system of treatment and prevention.

4. Equal culpability

. . . [This] assumes that the sole determining factor in assessing the degree of blame in attempts is the person's intention. If the offender has done everything in his power to carry out his intention to cause harm and fails through some fortuity, then he should be considered as culpable as if he had succeeded. The first version holds, moreover, that cases of attempts other than the extreme case should also be ranked equally with the extreme case and with the completed offense. After all, what difference in intent is discernible between a person who is apprehended before he has taken the last step towards the commission of the offense, if we are convinced that he had the intention or the 'fixed' intention to commit the offense, and one who has taken that step in furtherance of his intent? On this view, how can there be any difference in culpability between the person apprehended while 'lying in wait', or at an even earlier stage of preparation, and the person who shoots but misses? Under this version, punishment for attempts should be the same whenever we are satisfied that intent or 'fixed' intent is present, the conduct requirement serving as evidence of that intent."

Andrew Ashworth, "Belief, Intent and Criminal Liability", in J. Eekelaar and J. Bell (eds), Oxford Essays in Jurisprudence (1987), pp.16–17:

"Is A, who shoots at X intending to kill him but misses because X unexpectedly moves, any less culpable than B, who shoots at Y intending to kill him and does so? An external description of both sets of events would probably not suggest that they have 'done' the same thing, whereas an account which paid more attention to the actor's point of view and to matters which lay within the actor's control would suggest that they both intended and tried, to the same extent, to do the same thing. The argument here is that, because of the element of uncertainty in the outcome of things which we try to do, it would be wrong for assessments of culpability to depend on the occurrence or non-occurrence of the intended consequences.

'Success or failure . . . makes no difference at all to [an agent's] moral status in relation to his original act. His original act, strictly considered, was simply his trying and *that* is what moral assessment must concern itself with' (Winch, *Ethics and Action*, 1972, p.139).

. . . Moral blame and criminal liability should be based so far as possible on choice and control, on the trying and not on what actually happened thereafter.

What are the reasons for wishing to reduce the influence of chance upon criminal liability? It cannot be doubted that luck plays a considerable part in everyday events. Actual results also play a considerable part in judgments of others, and tend to dominate assessments in such fields as business, sport, and education. Those who try hard but are unsuccessful often receive less recognition than those who achieve goals (no matter how little effort they put into it). But these are not moral assessments of the individuals or their characters. If one turns to moral and social judgments, it is doubtful whether outcomes should be proper criteria. It may be desirable overall to have fewer bad outcomes and more good outcomes in society, but that does not lead to the conclusion that moral praise and blame should be allocated solely according to result. Indeed, a bad outcome stemming from a good intent may be a better predictor of good outcomes than a good outcome born of a bad intent. From time to time we may praise someone for producing a good result, even though it was not what he was trying to do, but this is more a reflection of our pleasure at the outcome than an assessment of his conduct and character. If we turn to blaming, is it not unacceptable to blame people for causing results irrespective of whether they were caused intentionally, negligently, or purely accidentally? Blaming is a moral activity which is surely only appropriate where the individual had some choice or control over the matter. For this reason the criminal law should seek to minimize the effect of luck upon the incidence and scale of criminal liability."

A relatively common view is that punishment for attempts should depend upon the dangerousness of the defendant's actions; this is measured by determining how imminent the threatened harm is and by examining the reason for failure.

Sir Rupert Cross and Andrew Ashworth: The English Sentencing System, 3rd edn (1981), pp.154–155:

"[T]he question whether an attempt should be punished less severely than the completed crime is largely dependent on the reason why the attempt failed. If it failed because the attempter voluntarily abandoned the attempt, he should be punished less because he is less wicked or needs less deterring. If it failed because of his incompetence, either in executing his design clumsily or in choosing a method which, owing to his failure to appreciate the true facts, proved to be impossible, he may be punished less on the ground that he represents less of a social danger than successful criminals. If it failed because of someone's intervention before he had done all he set out to do, he may be treated more leniently than the successful criminal: his wickedness may be less, since (as Blackstone said) it takes more wickedness to carry through a plan than to conceive it, and it may be desirable (on a utilitarian view) to mark each stage of an attempt by a portion of punishment in order to deter the attempter from pursuing his criminal design to its conclusion. There remain difficulties, however, with cases . . . where the attempter has done all the acts he intended and has failed to produce the planned result . . . On principle . . . there is no distinction in point of either wickedness or social danger between the successful criminal and the unsuccessful attempter in this last class. Chance may well be the only explanation of why one attempt succeeded and the other failed, and a sound sentencing policy should take little notice of a factor which lies outside the offender's control. He should be judged on the basis of what he intended to do, believed he was doing or knowingly risked."

Gross pushes the argument to its logical conclusion by asserting:

"In some cases, then, attempt liability will be as extensive as liability for the completed crime, and may even be greater, for sometimes, even though harm does not occur, the conduct of the accused was more dangerous than in a case in which harm does occur. In other cases of attempt the conduct is less dangerous and so liability is less extensive."[23]

It is our submission that it can *never* be justifiable to impose greater punishment for an attempt than for the completed crime. Indeed, it is our submission that attempts should *always* be punished to a lesser extent than the completed crime. This is because the paradigm of criminal liability is the combination of blame and harm and the absence of one of these should be reflected by, at least, less punishment. In relation to the law of attempt there is no harm (or, at most, there is only a second-order harm) so punishment should be lower than for the completed crime.[24] The reasons for this view need to be explored. Why should the causing of harm be regarded as so significant?

Michael Davis, "Why Attempts Deserve Less Punishment than Complete Crimes" 5 Law & Phil. (1986) 1 at 28–29:

"Someone who attempts a crime but fails to do the harm characteristic of success still (ordinarily) risks doing that harm. He deserves punishment for risking that harm because even risking such harm is an advantage the law abiding do not take. He deserves less punishment for the attempt than he would for the complete crime because being able to risk doing harm is not as great an advantage as being able to do it. To attempt murder is,

---

[23] See Gross, fn.7 above at p.460. For a criticism of Gross's views, see J.B. Brady, "Punishing Attempts" (1980) 63 *The Monist* 246 at 251–255.

[24] C.M.V. Clarkson, "Aggravated Endangerment Offences" (2007) 60 C.L.P. 278 at 282.

for example, not worth as much as to succeed. The successful murderer has the advantage of having done what he set out to do. The would-be murderer whose attempt failed has only had the *chance* to do what he set out to do. The difference is substantial."

J.C. Smith, "The Element of Chance in Criminal Liability" [1971] Crim. L.R. 63 at 69–72:

"Ought we then to get rid of the element of harm and base liability purely on fault?. . .

Even the most ardent advocate for the re-introduction of capital punishment did not—so far as I know—want it for *attempted* murder as well as murder. Yet the only difference between the attempt and the full offence is that in the latter the harm which it is the object of the law to prevent is caused, in the former it is not; but it seems to be generally accepted that this justifies a difference in the gravity of the offence and the punishment which may be imposed . . .

[This] suggests that great significance is still attached to the harm done, as distinct from the harm intended or foreseen. Perhaps the significance of the harm done derives from our emotional reaction to the acts of others. If one of my small boys, not looking what he is doing, throws a stone which just misses the dining room window, I shall be very cross with him; but if the stone breaks the dining room window, I shall be absolutely furious. His behaviour is just as bad and just as dangerous in the one case as in the other; but my indignation is much greater in the case where he has caused the harm than in that where he has not . . .

Stephen J. thought . . . there was nothing irrational in basing liability on the harm done:

'If two persons are guilty of the very same act of negligence, and one of them causes thereby a railway accident, involving the death and mutilation of many persons, whereas the other does no injury to anyone, it seems to me that it would be rather pedantic than rational to say that each had committed the same offence, and should be subjected to the same punishment. Both certainly deserve punishment, but it gratifies a natural public feeling to choose out for punishment the one who actually has caused great harm, and the effect in the way of preventing a repetition of the offence is much the same as if both were punished.'"

H.L.A. Hart, Punishment and Responsibility (Essays in the Philosophy of Law) (1968), p.131:

"It is pointed out that in some cases the successful completion of a crime may be a source of gratification, and, in the case of theft, of actual gain, and in such cases to punish the successful criminal more severely may be one way of depriving him of these illicit satisfactions which the unsuccessful have never had . . .

My own belief is that this form of retributive theory appeals to something with deeper instinctive roots than the last mentioned principle. Certainly the resentment felt by a victim actually injured is normally much greater than that felt by the intended victim who has escaped harm because an attempted crime has failed."

James Brady, "Punishing Attempts" (1980) 63 The Monist 246 at 255:

"[F]eelings of guilt and remorse are significantly different in the case where one has actually caused harm than in the case where, acting with the same intent, one has not been the cause of harm. Feelings of guilt and remorse do vary in degree when one has, for example, through reckless driving caused a death and where one has acted with equal recklessness but there has been no victim. In this case, as with the unsuccessful attempt, there is a kind of 'space' in which the person is allowed to express relief that he has not been the cause of harm."

C.M.V. Clarkson, "Aggravated Endangerment Offences" (2007) 60 Current Legal Problems 278 at 282–283:

"If the sole focus were to be on the culpability/wrongdoing of the defendant, one could abolish all result crimes such as murder. People who try to kill should be punished for their endeavors irrespective of whether they succeed. The crime of attempted murder could cover all such cases. The result could be dismissed as irrelevant and the possible product of luck. Such an approach would be totally inconsistent with the whole structure of the criminal law. The criminal law has a communicative function: it communicates what conduct is unacceptably wrong. This communication is both to the public . . . and to the defendant and the victim explaining the nature of the wrong. It is a formal way of saying: '"look what you did" . . . What should be communicated to a successful criminal is not merely that she culpably tried to do some wrongful harm, but that she actually did it . . . what she must repent and be grieved by is the harm she has done' (R.A. Duff, *Criminal Attempts* (1996), p.352)."

R.A. Duff, Criminal Attempts (1996), pp.351–352, 354:

"Our moral responses to an agent and her action, including such responses as blame or reproach, are commonly conditioned partly by her action's actual outcome; rather than seeing this as a regrettably irrational infection of our moral judgments of culpability by our natural concerns for actual outcomes, we should recognise it as an appropriate structuring of the moral responses of people living a human social life . . . [This involves] portraying moral blame as a social, communicative response to another's wrongdoing: an attempt to communicate to him, to persuade him to accept, an adequate moral understanding of the implications of what he has done . . . On a communicative conception of punishment, the punishment which an offender receives should itself aim to communicate to her an appropriate understanding of the wrong that she did: to give forceful and symbolic expression to the message which her conviction itself aimed to communicate. . . . One who tried but failed to do some criminal harm should . . . understand and repent the wrong that she did; if she attempted to commit a serious crime, that wrong was itself serious. Our understanding of her wrongdoing is, however, conditioned by its failure: we are relieved that she has failed. If she is to come to an adequate moral understanding of what she has done, she must therefore come to share that relief . . .

 If the law ignored actual outcomes at the stage of conviction or of sentencing, it would in effect be saying that it does not matter whether the defendant actually caused harm, actually killed his victim, or actually damaged another's property."[25]

Before ending this section it is perhaps worth pausing to consider briefly the concept of "blame" as applied in the field of attempts, and to question the assumption that the blameworthiness of those who attempt and those who succeed is necessarily the same. It is a prerequisite of criminal liability for attempts that the attempter intends to commit the criminal offence. But while many attempters *appear for legal purposes* to possess this necessary intention, closer examination reveals that this might not necessarily be so. As Menninger has written: "[T]he failure to achieve success . . . is apt to express accurately the mathematical resultant of component wishes—conscious and unconscious—acting as vectors."[26] And Freud wrote that:

"Errors . . . are not accidents; they are serious mental acts; they have their meaning; they arise through the concurrence—perhaps better, the mutual interference—of two different intentions."[27]

---

[25]   See also, R.A. Duff, "Whose Luck Is It Anyway?", in C.M.V. Clarkson and S. Cunningham (eds), *Criminal Liability for Non-Aggressive Death* (Aldershot: Ashgate Press, 2008).
[26]   K. Meninger, *Man against Himself* (New York: Harcourt, Brace & Co, 1938), p.22.
[27]   S. Freud, *A General Introduction to Psychoanalysis* (London: Hogarth Press, 1958), p.48.

Stephen J. Schulhofer, "Harm and Punishment: A Critique of Emphasis on the Results of Conduct in the Criminal Law" (1974) 122 University of Pennsylvania L. Rev. 1497 at 1590:

"A slightly different dimension is added by psychological theories concerning the interplay between conscious and unconscious intentions. Freud argued that divergence between an actor's conscious purpose and the results he actually achieves will often be explained by an unconscious intention to further a different purpose. A defendant who attempted to shoot his victim but missed may, of course, have failed because of his inherent lack of skill or because the victim suddenly moved away. But he also may have failed because an unconscious desire not to kill interfered with his conscious purpose, causing him to aim poorly and miss a shot that would have given him no difficulty under other circumstances. And even the first group of explanations is not inconsistent with the possibility that the defendant's intention was ambivalent. If the defendant had always been a poor shot, his decision not to choose a weapon better suited to his talents may have been influenced by an unconscious intention that the plan fail; similarly, the victim may be lucky enough to move out of the way only because the defendant waited unnecessarily long before firing. Even if success is prevented only by police intervention at the last moment, it cannot always be said that the defendant's intention was unequivocal; he may have purposely, though unconsciously, chosen to execute his plan at a time when apprehension was especially likely."[28]

However, while many attempts might have failed as a result of the attempter exercising internal control at the unconscious level (and thus arguably deserving less punishment), it is clear that in some cases the attempt only fails as a result of factors lying outside the attempter's control, namely, chance. Even in that respect it has already been argued that attempts ought *on principle* to be punished to a lesser extent than the completed crime.

It is difficult to establish sentencing levels for attempts because the statistics only cover attempted murder. In 2000, the average sentence for attempted murder was 9.7 years' imprisonment.[29] The Criminal Justice Act 2003 introduced "starting points" or minimum sentences to be served by all persons convicted of murder. In *Ford*,[30] the Court of Appeal broadly endorsed an approach that an attempted murderer should receive a sentence that would result in a term of about one-half of the minimum sentence for the complete crime being served. Sentencing guidelines for attempted murder were issued by the Sentencing Guidelines Council in 2009.[31] These guidelines reflect the fact that for attempted murder there must be an intention to kill (whereas for murder an intention to cause grievous bodily harm will suffice) and so, even when no injury has been caused, "an offence of attempted murder will be extremely serious". The starting points are heavily influenced by whether serious physical or psychological harm is caused. For the worst cases, that would have attracted a starting point of either a whole life order or 30 years' custody had the victim died, the starting point for attempted murder ranges from 15 years' custody (where there is little or no physical or psychological harm) to 30 years' custody (where there is serious and long-lasting physical or psychological harm). Bearing in mind that the minimum terms set for murder must be served in full, while for determinate sentences (such as those for attempt) the defendant will be released on licence after serving one-half of the set term, the net result is that for attempted murders the offender will generally serve less than half the sentence that would have been served had the victim died.

---

[28]   See also F. Picinali, "A Retributive Justification for not Punishing Bare Intentions or: on the Moral Relevance of the 'Now Belief'" [2012] 32 *Law and Philosophy* 385.

[29]   Sentencing Advisory Panel, *Minimum Terms in Murder Cases: The Panel's Advice to the Court of Appeal* (2002). This average excludes those who were given life sentences.

[30]   *R. v Ford (Kevin)* [2006] 1 Cr. App. R. (S.) 36.

[31]   Sentencing Guidelines Council, *Attempted Murder: Definitive Guideline* (2009).

In most of these, and other, attempt cases it ought to be borne in mind that the sentence is reflecting not just the "pure attempt" but the fact that there has usually been very serious injury caused (in attempted murder cases) or severe fear and degradation (in attempted rape cases). Further, in some attempted theft cases it seems that the court is sentencing defendants as "professional pickpockets". The fact that there is only evidence to support a charge of attempt is effectively ignored.[32] One of the few reported cases where there was no other injury, fear or distress (at least at the time of the crime) is *Cooper* where the defendant attempted to rape a drunk girl who was largely unaware of what was happening. A sentence of 18 months' youth custody was imposed on appeal.[33] Had the crime been completed the defendant would have received a sentence more in the region of the three years' youth custody originally imposed.

D. The Law

1. Actus reus

(i) Act must be more than merely preparatory

Criminal Attempts Act 1981 s.1(1)

"If, with intent to commit an offence to which this section applies, a person does an act which is more than merely preparatory to the commission of the offence, he is guilty of attempting to commit the offence."

This is similar to the common law rule as laid down by Baron Parke in *Eagleton* that:

"[S]ome act is required . . . Acts remotely leading towards the commission of the offence are not to be considered as attempts to commit it; but acts immediately connected with it are."[34]

Suppose a defendant wakes up one morning and decides to kill his wife by poisoning her. He walks to a shop where he purchases some rat poison. He returns home and adds the poison to the whisky in his whisky decanter. That evening he offers his wife a drink of whisky; she accepts. He pours the poisoned whisky into a glass and hands it to her. She starts drinking the whisky. At what point in this chain of actions could he be said to have done an act which was "more than merely preparatory to the commission of the offence"? When he handed her the whisky? When he put the poison in the decanter? When he purchased the poison?

Questions such as these cannot be answered in a theoretical vacuum; they, and all the contours of the law of attempt, can only be determined by reference to the underlying justification (and policy) of the law of attempt. Thus if attempts are viewed as being threats to people's interests in security from interference (the "second order harm" discussed earlier), one ought to insist on the attempter getting near to completing the crime. Until he has got near to committing the complete crime, the wife's interests in security from interference are not threatened. On the other hand, if the law of attempt is justified on the utilitarian bases canvassed above, then the emphasis is on the mens rea of the attempter and liability can be imposed at a much earlier stage in the chain of actions. Of course, such an approach still does not tell us exactly when the husband has done enough to threaten the wife's interests; or when his mens rea is sufficiently manifest to justify the imposition of criminal liability for

---

[32]   *R. v Daniel (Gary Michael)* (1988) 10 Cr. App. R. (S.) 341.
[33]   *R. v Cooper (Dennis James)* (1988) 10 Cr. App. R. (S.) 325.
[34]   *Eagleton* (1855) Dears C.C. 515 at 538.

attempt, but adoption of one or other of these views does provide an important indication of *how* to try to answer the question.

Fletcher and Duff suggest another approach, not dissimilar in its effect.

George P. Fletcher, Rethinking Criminal Law (1978), pp.138–139:

"The critical question . . . is the elementary issue whether the act of attempting is a distinct and discernible element of the crime of attempting. To say that the act is a distinct element is to require that the act conform to objective criteria defined in advance. The act must evidence attributes subject to determination independently of the actor's intent. In short, there must be features of the attempt as palpable as the death of the victim in homicide or a trespassory taking in larceny. We shall refer to the set of arguments favoring this approach as the 'objectivist' theory of attempts. Though the term 'objective' may have a different connotation in some contexts, we shall use the term to mean a legal standard for assessing conduct that does not presuppose a prior determination of the actor's intent.

The opposing school is appropriately called 'subjectivist', for it dispenses with the objective criteria of attempting. The act of execution is important so far as it verifies the firmness of the intent. No act of specific contours is necessary to constitute the attempt, for any act will suffice to demonstrate the actor's commitment to carry out his criminal plan.

As we delve more deeply into objectivist and subjectivist theories of liability for criminal attempts, we shall discover that objectivists tend to favor a minimalist approach, subjectivists, a maximalist approach to liability . . . [T]his means that objectivists tend to draw the line of liability as close as possible to consummation of the offense and tend, further, to be sympathetic to claims of impossibility as a bar to liability. This combination of views generates a minimalist approach to liability. Subjectivists, in contrast, tend to push back the threshold of attempting and reject the relevance of impossibility—a stance that yields a maximalist net of liability. In turning to a more detailed study of objectivist and subjectivist theories, we should keep in mind that the watershed between them is the question whether the act of attempting is a distinct element of liability."

Thus there are two competing theories underlying the law of attempt. First, the "objectivist" theory requires the defendant to have come sufficiently close to committing the crime for their conduct to generate apprehension and thus amount to a "second order harm". Duff supports this objectivist approach because, by insisting that conduct comes close to the actual commission of the offence, one is affording intending criminals an opportunity to abandon their criminal enterprise. By doing this, even if we think it unlikely they will desist, we are according the person respect as a responsible agent "who is in principle susceptible to rational persuasion".[35] Secondly, there is the "subjectivist" theory which stresses the mental element of the defendant: if they have mens rea they are dangerous and need restraining. Liability can accordingly be imposed at a much earlier stage (which will facilitate the task of the police and other law enforcement agencies). The only conduct required would be some action that would be corroborative of this intention. The tensions between these two theories is demonstrated by a consideration of the various "tests" employed by English law in its effort to demarcate how much action is required for the actus reus of attempt.

(a) *The common law*

Until 1981 the common law flirted with various tests. One of these was the "equivocality test" under which a defendant had to take sufficient steps towards the crime for their actions clearly and unequivocally to indicate that their purpose was to commit the crime.[36] This was clearly in accord with the "second order harm" view and the objectivist theory. The defendant had to get sufficiently close to committing the offence for their actions to be "manifestly criminal . . . [and] unnerving to the

---

[35]   R.A. Duff, *Criminal Attempts* (Oxford: Clarendon Press, 1996), p.388.
[36]   *Davey v Lee* [1968] 1 Q.B. 366, 371.

community".[37] This test was eventually abandoned because a defendant could be on the point of committing a crime (for example, about to break into a car) but the actions could still be equivocal (for example, were they going to steal the car or vandalise it?).

An alternative test, suggested by the Law Commission in 1973, was the "substantial step test" where the focus was on whether the defendant had taken a substantial step towards the crime, for example, reconnoitring the place contemplated for a burglary.[38] This test, consistent with the subjectivist theory of attempts because the focus was on the action only having to be sufficient to provide evidence of the defendant's intention, was never adopted as it would have amounted to casting the net of liability far too wide in the sequence of actions.[39]

Another test was Stephen's "series of acts" test under which it was necessary to determine whether the defendant had committed an act which was one of a series of acts that would lead to the crime if it were not interrupted. This test was also of little utility: it was too imprecise and could have led to the imposition of liability at an intolerably early state.

The test finally adopted by the common law[40] was the "proximity test". The defendant's actions had to be proximate to the completed offence in the sense of being "immediately and not merely remotely, connected"[41] with the completed offence. In *Robinson* a jeweller, who had insured his stock against burglary, hid the jewellery, tied himself up, called for help and represented to the police that his premises had been burgled. His object was to obtain policy money from his insurance company. It was held that his actions were still merely preparatory; they were "only remotely connected with the commission of the full offence, and not immediately connected with it".[42] He would have needed to have communicated with the insurance company before an attempt could be committed. In *Stonehouse* Lord Diplock stated that in order to have passed the threshold of proximity, the defendant must have "crossed the Rubicon and burnt his boats".[43] All the cases confirming this test emphasised that the defendant had to get very close to committing the offence; in some cases such as *Robinson* it appeared that the defendant would only be liable if he had committed the last act dependent upon himself—although from other cases it is clear that the proximity test did not demand as a matter of law that the defendant go so far.[44] This proximity test was very much in tune with Fletcher's objectivist theory of attempts: the emphasis was on the objective acts and not on the intentions of the defendant.

(b) *Criminal Attempts Act 1981*

Section 1(1) states that the defendant must do "an act which is more than merely preparatory to the commission of the offence". Is this different in any way from the proximity test developed by the common law?

---

[37]   G.P. Fletcher, *Rethinking Criminal Law* (New York: OUP, 1978), pp.142–144.
[38]   Law Commission Working Paper No.50, *Inchoate Offences* (1973), para.75.
[39]   Law Commission Paper No.102 (1980), para.2.32. For a plea for the introduction of the test, see G. Williams, "Wrong Turnings in the Law of Attempt" [1991] Crim. L.R. 416.
[40]   History is in the process of being rewritten with cases since the 1981 Act suggesting that it is not clear which test was applied at common law. However, two House of Lords' decisions, *Haughton v Smith* [1975] A.C. 476 and *DPP v Stonehouse* [1978] A.C. 55 made it plain that the proximity test was the favoured one.
[41]   *Jones v Brooks* (1968) 52 Cr. App. R. 614 at 616; *Davey v Lee* [1968] 1 Q.B. 366 at 371, approved in *Haughton v Smith* [1975] A.C. 476.
[42]   *R. v Robinson (Harry)* [1915] 2 K.B. 342 at 349.
[43]   *Stonehouse* [1978] A.C. 55.
[44]   Again, post-1981 Act cases are rewriting history by suggesting that the proximity test was synonymous with a last act test. It was not. See, e.g. *R. v Harris (Paul Andrew)* (1976) 62 Cr. App. R. 28.

One view is that no real change in the law was intended by the enactment of s.1(1). The government, in the course of the parliamentary proceedings, took the view that the law on this matter was not being altered.[45] The Law Commission, whose Report led to the legislation, felt that it was "undesirable to recommend anything more complex than a rationalisation of the present law".[46] Under *Eagleton* the common law always distinguished between preparatory and non-preparatory acts and non-preparatory acts were simply called "proximate" acts.

However, the Law Commission at the same time did recommend abandoning the phrase "proximate" as its literal meaning was "nearest, next before or after . . . [and] thus would clearly be capable of being interpreted to exclude all but the 'final act'".[47] The Law Commission disapproved of such an approach and felt that the new terminology could open the door to conviction in cases such as *Robinson*. If the Act had not altered the law, reference to the common law cases would presumably be permissible. However, the leading cases since the Act have stressed that discussion of the old cases is impermissible, suggesting that a new test for the actus reus of attempts is being evolved. Further, it can be argued that a change in the law has been brought about by the insertion of the word "merely". Unlike the position at common law, not all preparatory acts are excluded; only *merely* preparatory acts do not suffice.[48] Indeed, in *Tosti*[49] it was stated that the defendants "had committed acts which were preparatory, but not merely so".

Before examining the cases it is important to stress that the ultimate decision here is one for the jury. Section 4(3) of the Criminal Attempts Act 1981 provides:

"Where . . . there is evidence sufficient in law to support a finding that he did an act falling within [section 1(1)] . . ., the question whether or not his act fell within that subsection is a question of fact."

So the judge, using the law about to be outlined, must decide whether there is sufficient evidence that the defendant *could* come within the law of attempt, and then, if so, it must be left to the jury to decide whether the acts did or did not come within the definition of the actus reus provided in s.1(1). Not only will this lead to inconsistency of jury verdicts, with one jury deciding that a defendant like Robinson did commit the actus reus of attempt while another jury decides that he did not, but also it involves the jury having to decide what is essentially a matter of law. Whether certain acts satisfy certain legislative criteria ("more than merely preparatory") so as to amount in law to a crime, is a question of law which ought to be left to the judges to develop.[50] The Law Commission in 2007 recommended that s.4(3) be repealed and that the test become a legal one for the judge to determine.[51] This proposal was not supported strongly enough and the Law Commission has now abandoned it.[52]

The following is the leading case which has been cited in most subsequent decisions.

R. v Gullefer (1990) 91 Cr. App. R. 356 (Court of Appeal, Criminal Division)

During a race at a greyhound racing stadium the appellant climbed on to the track in front of the dogs and attempted to distract them by waving his arms. His efforts were only marginally successful and

[45]   I. Dennis, "The Criminal Attempts Act 1981" [1982] Crim. L.R. 379.
[46]   Law Commission Paper No.102 (1980), para.2.47.
[47]   Law Commission Paper No.102 (1980), para.2.48.
[48]   D. Ormerod, *Smith and Hogan's Criminal Law*, 13th edn (Oxford: OUP, 2011), p.413.
[49]   *R. v Tosti* [1997] Crim. L.R. 746.
[50]   See further, Williams, fn.39 above.
[51]   Law Commission Consultation Paper No.183, *Conspiracy and Attempts* (2007), paras 16.89–16.95.
[52]   Law Commission Paper No.318, *Conspiracy and Attempts* (2009), para.8.184.

the stewards decided it was unnecessary to declare "no race". The appellant told the police he had attempted to stop the race because the dog on which he had staked £18 was losing. He had hoped for a no-race declaration and the recovery of his stake. He was convicted of attempted theft and appealed on the ground that his acts were not "sufficiently proximate to the completed offence of theft to be capable of comprising an attempt to commit theft".

LANE LCJ:

"The first task of the court is to apply the words of the Act of 1981 to the facts of the case. Was the appellant still in the stage of preparation to commit the substantive offence, or was there a basis of fact which would entitle the jury to say that he had embarked on the theft itself? Might it properly be said that when he jumped on to the track he was trying to steal £18 from the bookmaker?

Our view is that it could not properly be said that at that stage he was in the process of committing theft. What he was doing was jumping on to the track in an effort to distract the dogs, which in its turn, he hoped would have the effect of forcing the stewards to declare 'no race', which would in turn give him the opportunity to go back to the bookmaker and demand the £18 he had staked. In our view there was insufficient evidence for it to be said that he had, when he jumped on to the track, gone beyond mere preparation . .

[His Lordship considered the common law proximity test and Stephen's "series of acts" test.]

It seems to us that the words of the Act of 1981 seek to steer a midway course. They do not provide, as they might have done, that the *Eagleton* test is to be followed, or that, as Lord Diplock suggested, the defendant must have reached a point from which it was impossible for him to retreat before the actus reus of an attempt is proved. On the other hand the words give perhaps as clear a guidance as is possible in the circumstances on the point of time at which *Stephen's* "series of acts" begin. It begins when the merely preparatory acts come to an end and the defendant embarks upon the crime proper. When that is will depend of course upon the facts in any particular case."

Appeal allowed

Lord Lane clearly thought he was pushing back the point at which liability could be imposed. In adopting his "midway course" he rejected the "Rubicon test". But what else was there left for the defendant to do? Assuming his efforts had been successful and the race declared void, all that remained for him to do was to claim his refund which would have been his last act, comparable to Robinson filing a claim with his insurance company. Accordingly, the approach adopted in *Gullefer* looks indistinguishable from that adopted in the much-criticised common law decision of *Robinson*.

The test laid down in *Gullefer* is that the defendant must have "embarked on the crime proper". Defendants must have started committing the crime. They must be "on the job".[53] Such a test works well when applied to some cases. In *Boyle and Boyle*[54] the defendants had broken down a door in their effort to commit burglary. Burglary requires an entry as a trespasser. To break down a door means that you have embarked on the process of securing entry to the building and can clearly amount to embarking on committing the crime. This approach was extended in *Tosti*[55] where it was held that a defendant who was merely examining a padlock (having hidden oxyacetylene equipment behind a hedge) was liable for attempted burglary. Similarly, in *Toothill*[56] it was held that a defendant who knocked at the proposed victim's door was in the "executory stage of his plan" and liable for attempted burglary. In *Litholetovs*[57] the defendant was liable for attempted arson when he poured petrol over the door of a house—even though he had not produced or lit the cigarette lighter that he had on him.

---

[53]   D. Ormerod, *Smith and Hogan's Criminal Law*, 13th edn (Oxford: OUP, 2011), p.413, citing Rowlatt J in *Osborn* (1919) 84 J.P. 63.

[54]   *R. v Boyle (George)* (1987) 84 Cr. App. R. 270.

[55]   *Tosti* [1997] Crim. L.R. 746.

[56]   *Toothill* [1998] Crim. L.R. 876.

[57]   *R. v Litholetovs (Mihails)* [2002] EWCA Crim 1154.

In other cases, the application of the test of embarking on the crime proper has not been so straightforward. In *Rowley*[58] the defendant left notes in public places offering money and presents to boys. These notes, which were not indecent in themselves and did not contain any propositions, were designed to lure boys for immoral purposes. On appeal he was found not liable for attempted incitement of a child under the age of 14 years to commit an act of gross indecency. His actions were merely preparatory as they "went no further than to seek to engineer a preliminary meeting". He was "at most preparing the ground for an attempt." It was stated that an attempted incitement would require, for example, a posted letter inviting a boy to commit gross indecency which did not reach the boy.[59]

The problem with this decision is that had he met the boys and said anything suggestive, he would have committed the full offence of incitement. The example of the non-arriving letter is a classic instance of a defendant having performed the last act there was for him to do. Again, it appears that the 1981 Act has not effected any change to the law.

R. v Jones (1990) 91 Cr. App. R. 351 (Court of Appeal, Criminal Division)

The appellant, a married man, had an affair with a woman who then started a relationship with another man, Foreman. When she refused to resume their association the appellant applied for a shotgun certificate and three days later bought some guns. He shortened the barrel of one of them and test fired it twice. Three days later he told his wife he was going to Spain to work on their chalet and left home dressed normally for work. He then changed into a disguise of overalls and a crash helmet with the visor down. He waited outside a school where Foreman dropped his daughter off and then jumped into the rear seat and asked Foreman to drive on. They drove to a grass verge where the appellant took the loaded sawn-off shotgun from a bag and pointed it at Foreman at a range of some 10–12 inches and said: "You are not going to like this." The safety catch of the shotgun was in the on position. Foreman grabbed the end of the gun and after a struggle managed to throw it out of the window and escape. The appellant was convicted of attempted murder and appealed on the ground that he had not yet committed the actus reus of this offence.

TAYLOR LJ:

"[At his trial the defence had argued] that since the appellant would have had to perform at least three more acts before the full offence could have been completed, i.e. remove the safety catch, put his finger on the trigger and pull it, the evidence was insufficient to support the charge . . .

The 1981 Act is a codifying statute. It amends and sets out completely the law relating to attempts and conspiracies. In those circumstances the correct approach is to look first at the natural meaning of the statutory words, not to turn back to earlier case law and seek to fit some previous test to the words of the section . . . [He then cited *Gullefer* with approval.] We respectfully adopt those words. We do not accept . . . [the] contention that section 1(1) of the 1981 Act in effect embodies the 'last act' test derived from *Eagleton*

[T]he 1981 Act followed a report from the Law Commission [No. 102] [which] states:

'. . . the definition must cover those instances where a person has to take some further step to complete the crime, assuming that there is evidence of the necessary mental element on his part to commit it; for example, when the defendant has raised the gun to take aim at another but has not yet squeezed the trigger.'

Clearly, the draftsman of section 1(1) must be taken to have been aware of . . . the Law Commission's report. The words 'an act which is more than merely preparatory to the commission of the offence' would be inapt if they were intended to mean 'the last act which lay in his power towards the commission of the offence.' . . . Clearly his

---

58   *R. v Rowley (Michael)* (1992) 94 Cr. App. R. 95.
59   Citing *Ransford* (1874) 31 L.T. 488. For a similar decision to *Rowley*, see *Nash* [1999] Crim. L.R. 308.

actions in obtaining the gun, in shortening it, in loading it, in putting on his disguise, and in going to the school could only be regarded as preparatory acts. But, in our judgment, once he had got into the car, taken out the loaded gun and pointed it at the victim with the intention of killing him, there was sufficient evidence for the consideration of the jury on the charge of attempted murder."

Appeal dismissed

While, despite the comments in the above case, the common law was not rigidly committed to any "last act" doctrine, on facts not dissimilar to these, a St Helena Court of Appeal decision, applying the English common law, held that there was no liability for attempted murder.[60]

R. v Campbell (1991) 93 Cr. App. R. 350 (Court of Appeal, Criminal Division)

The appellant planned to rob a sub-post office. He drove a motorbike near to the post office, parked it and approached, wearing a disguise of sun glasses and a crash helmet, although he later placed the sunglasses in his pocket. He was carrying an imitation gun and a threatening note which he planned to pass to the cashier in the sub-post office. He was walking down the street and when one yard from the post office door, police, who had been tipped off, grabbed the appellant and arrested him. He was convicted of attempted robbery and appealed.

WATKINS LJ:

"[His Lordship repeated the *Gullefer* test that the 1981 Act was steering a 'midway course' and that preparatory acts ended when the defendant 'embarks on the crime proper'. He endorsed the stance in *Jones* that judges 'should stick to the definition of an attempt in the Act itself' and that it was 'wholly unnecessary' to refer to the common law.]
    Looking at the circumstances here it was beyond dispute that the appellant, at the material time, was carrying an imitation firearm which he made no attempt to remove from his clothing. He was not, as he had done previously that day, wearing, as a form of disguise, sunglasses. It was not suggested that he had, in the course of making his way down the road . . ., moved towards the door of the post office so as to indicate that he intended to enter that place.
    In order to effect the robbery it is equally beyond dispute it would have been quite impossible unless obviously he had entered the post office, gone to the counter and made some kind of hostile act—directed, of course, at whoever was behind the counter and in a position to hand him money. A number of acts remained undone and the series of acts which he had already performed—namely, making his way from his home . . ., dismounting from the cycle and walking towards the post office door—were clearly acts which were, in the judgment of this court, indicative of mere preparation . . . If a person, in circumstances such as this, has not even gained the place where he could be in a position to carry out the offence, it is extremely unlikely that it could ever be said that he had performed an act which could be properly said to be an attempt."

Appeal allowed

There can only be an attempt when the defendant has "embarked on the crime proper" and in this case it is suggested that the defendant could have embarked on the crime of robbery when he entered the sub-post office. Robbery involves the use of force or threatened force.[61] It is difficult to see how someone who has entered a post office, but has not yet reached the counter or issued any threats can be said to have embarked on the crime of robbery. Clearly, the court in *Campbell* was adopting a more flexible approach to the notion of "embarking on the crime proper". This flexibility was reinforced in the following case.

---

[60]   *Stevens v R* [1985] L.R.C. (Crim) 17. See L. Blake (1986) 50 Jo. C.L. 247.
[61]   Theft Act 1968 s.8.

Attorney-General's Reference (No.1 of 1992) (1993) 96 Cr. App. R. 298 (Court of Appeal, Criminal Division)

The defendant, walking a girl home (both of them drunk), pulled her behind a hedge, forced her to the ground and lay on top of her. She lost consciousness. He then dragged her up some nearby steps to a shed. The girl, who had regained consciousness, was crying and trying to scream. The defendant had lowered his trousers and interfered with her private parts but had not actually attempted penetration because his penis was flaccid. He claimed he was unable to have intercourse "cause I was drunk, so I couldn't, could I?" The trial judge directed an acquittal because there was no evidence of an actual physical attempt at penetration. The Attorney-General referred the following point of law for the opinion of the Court of Appeal:

> "Whether, on a charge of attempted rape, it is incumbent upon the prosecution, as a matter of law, to prove that the defendant physically attempted to penetrate the woman's vagina with his penis."

TAYLOR LCJ:

"The words [in the 1981 Act] are not to be interpreted so as to re-introduce either of the earlier common law tests. Indeed one of the objects of the Act was to resolve the uncertainty those tests created . . .

It is not, in our judgment, necessary, in order to raise a prima facie case of attempted rape, to prove that the defendant with the requisite intent had necessarily gone as far as to attempt physical penetration of the vagina. It is sufficient if there is evidence from which the intent can be inferred and there are proved acts which a jury could properly regard as more than merely preparatory to the commission of the offence. For example, and merely as an example, in the present case the evidence of the young woman's distress, of the state of her clothing, and the position in which she was seen, together with the respondent's acts of dragging her up the steps, lowering his trousers and interfering with her private parts, and his answers to the police, left it open to a jury to conclude that the respondent had the necessary intent and had done acts which were more than merely preparatory. In short that he had embarked on committing the offence itself."

Opinion accordingly

Clearly, when the defendant is trying to commit the offence, that is, trying to penetrate the woman, he can be said to have embarked on the crime. However, in this case it is stated that even prior to that the defendant can be held to have "embarked on the crime proper". This decision is understandable in both common sense and policy terms in that the defendant had progressed relatively far in the series of acts that might have culminated in penetration: in particular, he had lowered his trousers and interfered with her private parts. However, in *Patnaik*[62] it was held that it was unnecessary for the defendant to have removed any clothing or to have done "some unequivocal sexual act". In this case the defendant had not undone any of his clothing and had not indecently disarranged the woman's clothing or intimately touched her. It was held that pushing her over a wall, straddling her legs and attempting to kiss her amounted to sufficient evidence to go to the jury that his acts were more than merely preparatory to the crime of rape: "the threshold was essentially a matter for the judge's judgment of the facts of the case". Similarly, in *Dagnall*[63] it was held that by telling a woman that he wanted to "fuck her", pulling her hair and pushing her against a fence and causing her to feel that rape was inevitable, the acts of the defendant were capable of being more than merely preparatory despite the fact that the girl's clothing had not been disarranged and that the defendant might not have touched her in a sexual way.

---

[62]   *Patnaik*, L.T.L. Unreported February 1, 2000.
[63]   *R. v Dagnall (Chris)* [2003] EWCA Crim 2441; (2003) 147 S.J.L.B. 995, CA (Crim. Div.).

Such an approach renders the test of "embarking on the crime" useless. The defendant in *Patnaik* had clearly embarked on the crime of sexual assault in trying to kiss the woman and, in his other actions, had committed several complete offences. Similarly, the defendant in *Dagnall* had committed a common assault (and possibly a sexual assault) on the woman. Such defendants would now clearly be liable for the offence committing an offence with intent to commit a sexual offence contrary to s.62 of the Sexual Offences Act 2003. It is not easy to see, however, that these men had embarked on the crime of rape.

The difficulty of applying this test is revealed by a consideration of two final cases, not involving attempted rape. In *Griffin*,[64] a mother planning to abduct her children and take them out of the country, bought ferry tickets to Ireland and went to the children's school and told the teacher she had come to take them to the dentist. These actions were held to constitute an attempt to abduct children. The full offence here, under the Child Abduction Act 1984 s.1(1), is only committed if the child is taken or sent out of the United Kingdom. The court rejected an argument that the mother would at least have had the children in her custody and have embarked on the journey. In *Geddes*[65] the defendant, with no legitimate purpose for being there, was seen on school premises, equipped with a knife, lengths of rope and masking tape. In quashing the defendant's conviction for attempted false imprisonment, Lord Bingham CJ stated:

> "[T]here is not much room for doubt about the appellant's intention. Furthermore, the evidence is clearly capable of showing that he made preparations, that he equipped himself, that he got ready, that he put himself in a position to commit the offence charged . . . But was the evidence sufficient in law to support a finding that the appellant had actually tried to or attempted to commit the offence of imprisoning someone? Had he moved from the realm of intention, preparation and planning into the area of execution or implementation? . . . [I]t is true that the appellant had entered the school but he had never had any contact or communication with any pupil; he had never confronted any pupil at the school in any way . . . The whole story is one which fills the court with the gravest unease. Nonetheless, . . . we feel bound to conclude that the evidence in law was not sufficient to support a finding that the appellant did an act which was more than merely preparatory . . ."[66]

It is, of course, inevitable that fine distinctions have to be drawn in determining liability for attempt but as a result of these cases it is virtually impossible to predict at what stage the defendant will have passed beyond the point of mere preparation and have "embarked on the crime proper".

Finally, it ought perhaps to be emphasised that, apart from *Gullefer*, all of the above cases concerned attempts to commit offences against the person. In *Qadir and Khan*[67] it was stated that because attempted killing or wounding concentrates on a particular moment, acts earlier in time are more likely to be merely preparatory. On the other hand, with attempts to commit offences involving deception or evasion then there is more likely to be a "stratagem carried on over a period of time" and thus the moment of embarkation on the crime "may be quite remote in time from its final outcome".

---

[64]   *R. v Griffin* [1993] Crim. L.R. 515.
[65]   *Geddes* [1996] Crim. L.R. 894.
[66]   As J.C. Smith points out in his commentary (at p.896) there was no endangerment or ulterior intent crime (such as going equipped with intent to kidnap) with which the defendant could be charged.
[67]   *Qadir and Khan*, *Archbold News*, November 17, 1997.

(c) *Conclusion*

It is almost impossible to extract any clear principles from the cases interpreting s.1(1). Three points can be stated with confidence, although quite where they lead and what they mean in real cases is another matter.

First, the courts are striving at some sort of half-way house between the old proximity test and Stephen's "series of acts" tests. The problem with this is that it is impossible to find a "midway" point between proximity (which meant different things to different judges) and something completely unascertainable (which is all that can be said for Stephen's test). In short, talk about a "midway" point is rhetoric disguising the judges' desire to give themselves maximum flexibility.

Secondly, the "Rubicon test" has been abandoned.[68] A defendant need not have reached the point of no-return. Similarly, the fact that he has reached such a point will not necessarily indicate that his actions are more than merely preparatory. When a defendant climbs on to a race track in front of racing dogs and waves his arms at the animals it would surely be permissible to assert that he has "crossed the Rubicon and burnt his boats". This is what the defendant did in *Gullefer* and yet it was insufficient for liability.

Thirdly, the test now appears to be whether the defendant has "embarked on the crime proper". As seen from the above cases, however, there is no clear view as to what "embarking on the crime proper" means.

A theme uniting many of the cases where there has been liability for attempt is that there has been a "confrontation" with the victim or the property, whereas in the cases where acts have been held to be merely preparatory there has been no such confrontation. For example, in *Geddes* and *Rowley* the defendant had not met any of the children; in *Gullefer*, the defendant, who was charged with attempted theft, had not confronted the bookmakers. In *Campbell* there had been no confrontation with the cashier. On the other hand, in *Jones* and the attempted rape cases there had been such a confrontation and in *Boyle and Boyle* and the other attempted burglary cases there had been a "confrontation" with the building.

However, confrontation can be no more than evidence that acts are more than merely preparatory. In an attempted rape scenario, a man might confront a woman and pull her arm. Even under the broadest approach adopted above, this could never amount to acts more than merely preparatory to the crime of rape.

As the above cases demonstrate, in many instances this test of "embarking on the crime proper" is problematic and appears to be little more than yet another smoke-screen behind which policy can dictate when liability should be imposed.

(ii) Reform

The Law Commission in 2007[69] argued that there are two main defects to the present law of attempt. First, the "more than merely preparatory" test of proximity has proved to be too vague and uncertain.[70] Secondly, many leading decisions such as *Geddes* and *Campbell* have rendered the offence unduly narrow.[71] Too much emphasis has "been placed on the offence's label ('attempt')—and there-

---

[68]   It was never a "test" in the sense that the proximity test was. It was one method for establishing whether the proximity test had been satisfied. Had it ever been a "test" gunmen would not have been guilty of attempted murder until they had pulled the trigger.

[69]   Law Commission Consultation Paper No.183, *Conspiracy and Attempts* (2007).

[70]   At para.12.14.

[71]   At paras 12.17–12.22.

fore on the notion of 'trying' to commit an offence".[72] Accordingly, the Law Commission proposed that the present law of attempt should be repealed and replaced by two separate inchoate offences:

(1) an offence of criminal attempt which would be limited to last acts needed to commit the intended offence; and

(2) an offence of criminal preparation, limited to acts of preparation which are "properly to be regarded as part of the execution of the plan to commit the intended offence".[73]

With regard to the proposed restricted offence of attempt, the Law Commission emphasised that "'last acts' should not be understood to extend only to the very last act that was required".[74] It argued that this new offence would accord with society's understanding of the word and would not involve any narrowing of the offence as "in practice, most cases charged as attempts will have involved a last act or acts needing to be done".[75] The new offence of criminal preparation would not cover mere preparation. The defendant would only be liable if they were "in the process of executing his or her plan to commit an intended offence";[76] there had to be "on the job"[77] preparation.

Recognising that it could be difficult to decide whether a defendant was "on the job" or not, the Commission proposed that guidance in the form of a list of examples should be provided.

Law Commission Consultation Paper No.183, Conspiracy and Attempts (2007), Proposal 17:

"We propose that the new general offence of criminal preparation should encompass at least the following situations:

(1) D gains entry into a building, structure, vehicle or enclosure or (remains therein) with a view to committing the intended offence there and then or as soon as an opportunity presents itself.

(2) D examines or interferes with a door, window, lock or alarm or puts in place a ladder or similar device with a view there and then to gaining unlawful entry into a building, structure or vehicle to commit the intended offence within.

(3) D commits an offence or an act of distraction or deception with a view to committing the intended offence there and then.

(4) D, with a view to committing the intended offence there and then or as soon as an opportunity presents itself:

(a) approaches the intended victim or the object of the intended offence; or

(b) lies in wait for an intended victim; or

(c) follows the intended victim."

The Law Commission proposed that both these new offences should carry the same maximum penalty.[78]

---

[72]   At para.12.15.
[73]   Proposal 15.
[74]   At para.16.17.
[75]   At para.16.11.
[76]   At para.16.41.
[77]   At para.16.19.
[78]   At paras 16.18–16.22.

There were many objections to this proposal to subdivide the present law of attempt into two separate offences.[79] For example, separate offences should capture different wrongs but both the proposed new offences are aimed at the same wrongdoing; the offence of attempt, being restricted to last acts, would become very narrow; there would be immense difficulty in distinguishing attempts from criminal preparation; the new crime of preparation would be too broad and could lead to the risk of over-criminalisation; there is the danger of introducing confusing labels and so on. Accordingly, in its final Report, the Law Commission has abandoned this proposal and, with one exception,[80] is no longer recommending any reform of the conduct element of attempts.[81]

(iii) Abandonment

What is the position if a defendant, with intention to commit the complete offence, does an act which is more than merely preparatory, but then decides to abandon the criminal enterprise? For example, in one US case a man who was about to rape a woman discovered that she was pregnant and, in response to her pleas that he would hurt her baby, abandoned the plan.[82] Should such a defendant be guilty of attempted rape? Would it make any difference if, instead of discovering the woman was pregnant, the defendant had simply been struck by remorse and had desisted saying: "I won't do it; God has stayed my hand"?[83]

It is clear that there is no "defence" of abandonment in English law.

Haughton v Smith [1975] A.C. 476 (House of Lords)

LORD HAILSHAM:

"First [the defendant] may simply change his mind before committing any act sufficiently overt to amount to an attempt. Second, he may change his mind, but too late to deny that he had got so far as an attempt In the first case no criminal attempt is committed. At the relevant time there was no *mens rea* since there had been a change of intention, and the only overt acts relied upon would be preparatory and not immediately connected with the completed offence. In the second case there is both *mens rea* and an act immediately connected with the completed offence . . . It follows that there is a criminal attempt."

The Law Commission (Law Com. No.102), Attempt (1980):

"2.132. There is no authority to suggest that withdrawal from an attempt to commit an offence may at present be raised as a defence. Any interruption of the defendant's acts, whether or not due to his voluntary desistance, is not material to whether there has been an attempt, although it might show that there was not the *mens rea* necessary for liability. As the Working Party pointed out, an attempt is committed as soon as there are proximate acts accompanied by the necessary intent; thus even though withdrawal might result in the completed offence not being committed, it could not undo the fact that at some stage the defendant would have committed the inchoate offence . . . In favour of the defence was the suggestion that it could operate as an inducement to one who had embarked upon criminal conduct to desist from the completion of the offence by enabling him to raise

---

[79] C.M.V. Clarkson, "Attempt: The Conduct Requirement" (2009) 29 O.J.L.S. 25. See also J. Rogers, "The Codification of Attempts and the Case for 'Preparation'" [2008] Crim. L.R. 937.

[80] As there is doubt over the existing law, the Commission proposes clarification to ensure that persons can be convicted of attempted murder by omission (assuming they are under a legal duty to act) (Law Commission Paper No.318, *Conspiracy and Attempts* (2009), para.8.151).

[81] Law Commission Paper No.318, *Conspiracy and Attempts* (2009), para.8.79.

[82] *Le Barron v State*, 32 Wis.2d 294; 145 N.W.2d 79 (1966).

[83] *People v Graham*, 176 App. Div. 38, 162 N.Y.S. 334 (1916).

a complete defence to criminal charges. On the other hand, it was suggested that, since the principal justification for provision of inchoate offences lay in the opportunity they gave for intervention by the police at an early stage in criminal activity, there would be an inherent contradiction in providing a defence when that activity had already reached a stage sufficiently advanced to warrant such intervention. The social danger already manifested by the defendant's conduct made it appropriate that any effort he might make to nullify its effects should instead be reflected by mitigation of penalty.

2.133 . . . We believe that provision of a defence could only be justified if there were decisive arguments in its favour; particularly in the context of attempt, the defence could raise difficulties for law enforcement authorities still greater than those which already exist in deciding where the law may impose criminal sanctions.

For these reasons we do not recommend any defence of withdrawal in relation to attempt."

Such a defence, however, is widely accepted in the United States.

American Law Institute, Model Penal Code, Proposed Official Draft s.5.01(4):

"*Renunciation of criminal purpose.* When the actor's conduct would otherwise constitute an attempt . . . It is an affirmative defence that he abandoned his effort to commit the crime or otherwise prevented its commission, under circumstances manifesting complete and voluntary renunciation of his criminal purpose . . .

Within the meaning of this Article, renunciation of criminal purpose is not voluntary if it is motivated, in whole or in part, by circumstances, not present or apparent at the inception of the actor's course of conduct, which increase the probability of detection or apprehension or which make more difficult the accomplishment of the criminal purpose. Renunciation is not complete if it is motivated by a decision to postpone the criminal conduct until a more advantageous time or to transfer the criminal effort to another but similar objective or victim."

Should English law follow this lead and allow such a defence?

Martin Wasik, "Abandoning Criminal Intent" [1980] Crim. L.R. 785 at 787– 788, 790–794:

"It is clear that the *voluntary* nature of the abandonment is an essential requirement for the success of any excuse in this area . . . [T]wo reasons [are put forward] for the central importance of the requirement of voluntariness. Sometimes it is argued that voluntary desistance provides clear evidence that the actor lacked the resolve to carry out the crime, and hence was not truly dangerous, and sometimes it is said that voluntary desistance is a 'good act' which somehow compensates for or erases the initial criminal act, thus making an acquittal appropriate.[84]

. . . One argument in favour of excusing the defendant who renounces a criminal purpose is in terms of negation of *mens rea*. According to Glanville Williams (*Criminal Law: The General Part* (1961), pp. 620–621) 'where the accused has changed his mind, it would only be just to interpret his previous intention where possible as only half-formed or provisional, and hold it to be an insufficient *mens rea*' . . . Any [such] suggestion . . . would greatly undermine the law of attempt. There must be few cases where the defendant would not accept the need to give up the attempt in certain circumstances . . . [Also] the problems of proof would be considerable . . .

[W]hat other reasons exist for allowing [the excuse] to relieve the defendant of responsibility? First, it is argued that any dangerousness of character is negatived by clear evidence of abandonment. An acceptance of abandonment as an excuse would . . . show that the psychological barrier had not been crossed. Under English law, as we have seen, such late abandonment could not amount to an excuse because a proximate act has already been committed. On the other hand such questions of individual psychology and relative dangerousness are the very stuff of mitigation and sentencing policy . . .

The second reason often advanced for allowing a defence of withdrawal is one of legal policy. It is claimed that since it is a prime purpose of the criminal law to prevent the occurrence of harm, it makes sense to provide a rea-

---

[84] If this latter view is adopted, must the abandonment be prompted by a commendable motive? cf. G.P. Fletcher, *Rethinking Criminal Law* (New York: OUP, 1978), pp.193–194.

sonable inducement for the attempter to desist before any real harm is done . . . The importance of the argument turns upon how realistic it is. How likely is it that a man who is sufficiently far along the path towards committing a criminal offence, that he would be guilty of an attempt if stopped, and who then decides not to commit it, would change his mind again and decide to carry on, since he realises he is guilty of the attempt anyway? The argument is far-fetched.[85] . . .

It has been strongly argued, then, that mitigation is not enough in cases of voluntary abandonment and that 'No argument of deterrence, reformation or prevention seems to require the punishment of one who is truly repentant and has done no harm.'

[Wasik, nevertheless, concludes that abandonment should only be relevant in mitigation of sentence.]"

R.A. Duff, Criminal Attempts (1996), pp.395–396:

"The intending rapist, murderer, or wounder who voluntarily abandons his attempt at the last moment has already attacked his victim, even if he aborted the attack himself . . . Surely he should not be able to escape all criminal liability by his abandonment? . . . [W]e should retain a narrow general law of attempts, supplemented (when necessary) by more specific offences capturing particularly wrongful kinds of conduct which fall outside its scope."

Thus, Duff's objectivist account would not necessarily lead to the complete acquittal of those who abandon their attempts (as they would be guilty of other offences) but would restrict the crime of attempt itself. Is such an approach preferable to that of the current law's reliance upon judicial discretion at the sentencing stage?

2. Mens rea

Section 1(1) of the Criminal Attempts Act 1981 provides that the defendant must act "with intent to commit an offence".

Merrit v Commonwealth, 164 Va. 653, 180 S.E. 395 (1935) (Supreme Court of Appeals of Virginia)

"[W]hile a person may be guilty of murder though there was no actual intent to kill, he cannot be guilty of an attempt to commit murder unless he has a specific intent to kill . . .

When we say that a man attempted to do a given wrong, we mean that he intended to do it specifically; and proceeded a certain way in the doing. The intent in the mind covers the thing in full; the act covers it only in part. . . . To commit murder, one need not intend to take life; but to be guilty of an attempt to murder, he must so intend. It is not sufficient that his act, had it proved fatal, would have been murder."

In *Whybrow*[86] the defendant constructed a device and administered an electric shock to his wife while she was taking a bath. The Court of Appeal held that while an intention to kill or to cause grievous bodily harm would suffice for the completed crime of murder, for attempted murder an intention to

---

[85]   cf. H. Wechsler, "The Treatment in Inchoate Crimes in the Model Penal Code" (1961) 61 Col. L.R. 571 at 617–618: "It is possible, of course, that the defense of renunciation of criminal purpose may add to the incentives to take the first steps towards crime. Knowledge that criminal endeavours can be undone with impunity may encourage preliminary steps that would not be undertaken if liability inevitably attached to every abortive criminal undertaking that proceeded beyond preparation. But this is not a serious problem . . . [A]ny consolation the actor might draw from the abandonment defense would have to be tempered with the knowledge that the defense would be unavailable if the actor's purposes were frustrated by external forces before he had an opportunity to abandon his efforts."

[86]   *R. v Whybrow (Arthur George)* (1951) 35 Cr. App. R. 141. See also *R. v Pond* [1984] Crim. L.R.164.

kill was necessary. This was because for attempted murder "the intent becomes the principal ingredient of the crime". In O'Toole[87] the defendant was charged with attempted arson (causing criminal damage by fire). It was held that while recklessness would suffice for the completed offence,[88] there had to be intention for the attempted offence.

If the complete crime can be committed recklessly or negligently, why does this same mens rea not suffice for an attempt to commit the crime?

R. v Mohan [1976] Q.B. 1 (Court of Appeal, Criminal Division)

JAMES LJ:

"In our judgment it is well established law that intent (mens rea) is an essential ingredient of the offence of attempt . . .

An attempt to commit crime is itself an offence. Often it is a grave offence. Often it is as morally culpable as the completed offence which is attempted but not in fact committed. Nevertheless it falls within the class of conduct which is preparatory to the commission of a crime and is one step removed from the offence which is attempted. The court must not strain to bring within the offence of attempt, conduct which does not fall within the well-established bounds of the offence. On the contrary, the court must safeguard against extension of those bounds save by the authority of Parliament."

Donald Stuart, "Mens Rea, Negligence and Attempts" [1968] Crim. L.R. 647 at 656, 658–659, 661–662:

"Many writers rely heavily on the fact that the word 'attempt' refers to an endeavour or an effort to commit a crime. It is argued that there cannot be an attempt unless the defendant was trying to commit the crime and that, in legal terms, this necessarily means that there must have been an intention of the 'purpose' type to commit the crime. Even Howard (Australian Criminal Law (1965) 253) says:

'Attempt implies purpose. To say that D is attempting to do something means that he is acting with the purpose of accomplishing that which he is said to be attempting. There is no disagreement that purpose must be proved for conviction of attempts but different views have been expressed on the scope of the purpose.'

It is, however, difficult to see why there is such magic in the popular meaning of the word 'attempt' but not in the words 'murder', 'assault' or 'rape'—crimes for which recklessness is now sufficient mens rea. . .

Do any of the theories of punishment offer an explanation of why it is that only direct intention will suffice in these cases of attempt? . . . It is difficult to challenge Professor Hart's (Punishment and Responsibility, p.127) assertion that

'No calculation of the efficacy of deterrence or reforming measures, and nothing that would ordinarily be called retribution seems to justify this distinction. In the attempt case, for example, the variant where the intention is indirect seems equally wicked, equally harmful, and equally in need of discouragement by the law.'

There seems, furthermore, to be every reason to apply the full notion of mens rea (embracing intention and recklessness) . . . to attempts . . .

If a fanatical punter contrives to half-sever the stirrup on the saddle of the favourite horse before a race he would be guilty of recklessly assaulting the jockey if the stirrup broke during the race and the jockey fell and was trampled. If, however, the mischief was unearthed before the race was run the punter should surely be guilty of recklessly attempting an assault even though he was aiming, not to injure the jockey, but merely to stop the horse from winning . . .

Further there is much to be said for . . . [the] suggestion that a negligent attempt to commit a crime of neg-

---

[87]   R. v O'Toole (Michael) [1987] Crim. L.R. 759.
[88]   Criminal Damage Act 1971 s.1(2).

ligence should be punished. Negligence is a failure to measure up to a standard and if this failure occurs or is stopped short of the completed offence there seems to be no reason of policy why it should escape punishment. This would lead to the view, at present widely rejected, that it is possible to attempt to commit the crime of involuntary manslaughter. If a pharmacist is grossly negligent in making up a prescription and the patient dies as a result of taking the dosage on the bottle the pharmacist is clearly guilty of manslaughter. Surely the policy considerations which dictate such a conviction apply equally if, through chance, the negligent error is discovered before any damage is done. There seems to be every reason for a verdict of attempted manslaughter.

If, in the Code of the Brave New World, the codifiers are prepared to cast off the traditional misplaced fear of liability based on negligence, there is, then, a strong case for declaring that the mental element for an attempt may consist in the mental element—here including negligence—required for the completed crime."

In some jurisdictions, this approach is followed. For example, in Colorado persons can be liable for a criminal attempt if they act "with the kind of culpability otherwise required for commission of an offence".[89] Such an approach is, however, unacceptable. Apart from the semantic argument that it is linguistic nonsense to speak of someone attempting to commit a crime unless He is trying to commit that crime, there is a more important argument of principle. With attempts we are punishing in the absence of any harm (or "first order harm"). While such an approach can be justified, it is surely only permissible when dealing with the highest degree of blame. Exceptions to the paradigm of criminal liability involve extensions of liability and should be rigidly controlled. As attempt is essentially a crime of mens rea, with the actus reus performing only a secondary or subsidiary role, only the clearest form of mens rea should suffice, namely, intention.

This latter reasoning was given statutory force by s.1(1) of the Criminal Attempts Act 1981. It is now clear that even for attempting a crime of strict liability, the defendant must intend to produce the prohibited consequence.[90]

What meaning is to be attributed to the word "intention" in s.1(1)? In *Mohan*,[91] it was held that this involved "proof of specific intent, a decision to bring about, in so far as it lies within the accused's power, the commission of the offence which it is alleged the accused attempted to commit, no matter whether the accused desired that consequence of his act or not". This was approved, after the coming into force of the Criminal Attempts Act 1981, in *Millard and Vernon*,[92] where it was stated that a direct or purposive intention was required. Intention had to bear its "ordinary meaning", namely, that the defendant must have "decided, so far as in him lay, to bring about" the result. It would, of course, be possible (albeit messy) for intention to bear different meanings in different contexts and for direct intent to be required here as the concept of an "attempt" connotes trying or meaning to achieve a result. However, the courts have rejected such an approach holding that "intention" bears the same meaning, whether for a completed crime or an attempt.

R. v Pearman (1984) 80 Cr. App. R. 259 (Court of Appeal, Criminal Division)

STUART-SMITH J:

"We see no reason why the passing of the 1981 Act should have altered the law as to what is meant by the word 'intent'. The purpose of the Act was to deal with other matters rather than the content of the word 'intent'. We can see no reason why the judgment of the court in that case [*Mohan*] should not still be binding upon this court.

---

89   Col. Rev. Stat. art.18–2–101(1).
90   This was probably the position at common law: *Gardner v Akeroyd* [1952] 2 Q.B. 743; cf. *R. v Collier* [1960] Crim. L.R. 204. It should, however, be borne in mind that most strict liability offences are summary offences which cannot be attempted.
91   *R. v Mohan (John Patrick)* [1976] Q.B. 1.
92   *R. v Millard and Vernon* [1987] Crim. L.R. 393.

The words of James L.J. [in *Mohan*] which he used at the end of that passage, namely 'no matter whether the accused desired that consequence of his act or not', are probably designed to deal with a case where the accused has, as a primary purpose, some other object, for example, a man who plants a bomb in an aeroplane, which he knows is going to take off, it being his primary intention that he should claim the insurance on the aeroplane when the freight goes down into the sea. The jury would not be put off from saying that he intended to murder the crew simply by saying that he did not want or desire to kill the crew, but that was something that he inevitably intended to do. Similarly, for example, a man who is cornered by the police when he is in a car may have the primary purpose of simply escaping from that situation. If he drives straight at the police officers at high speed, a jury is likely to conclude that he intended to injure a police officer and maybe cause him serious grievous bodily harm."

R. v Walker and Hayles (1990) 90 Cr. App. R. 226 (Court of Appeal, Criminal Division)

The defendants threw the victim from a third floor balcony. At their trial for attempted murder the judge directed the jury that they had to be sure that the defendant intended and tried to kill. The jury asked for clarification and the judge directed them in *Moloney/Hancock* terms (the appropriate test before *Woollin*) that if:

(1)   there was a very high degree of probability that the victim would be killed, and

(2)   the defendant knew there was such a high risk, then

(3)   they were entitled to draw the inference that the defendants intended to kill.

The defendants appealed against this direction.

LLOYD LJ:

"By the use of the word 'entitled' [the recorder] was making it sufficiently clear to the jury that the question whether they drew the inference or not was a question for them . . . [He was not] equating foresight with intent . . . He was perfectly properly saying that foresight was something from which the jury could infer intent. He was treating the question as part of the law of evidence, not as part of the substantive law of attempted murder . . .

[I]n the great majority of cases of attempted murder, as in murder, the simple direction will suffice, without any reference to foresight. In the rare case where an expanded direction is required in terms of foresight, courts should continue to use virtual certainty as the test, rather than high probability."

Appeals dismissed

This case must now be read in the light of *Woollin* under which an inference of intention can only be drawn if the consequence is foreseen as virtually certain (or, under the alternative interpretation, foresight of a virtual certainty is intention).[93] In *Hales*[94] it was accepted that the *Woollin* test of intention applied to attempted murder but, on the facts, a *Woollin* direction was not necessary. Accordingly, it seems clear now that the concept "intention" bears the same meaning here as elsewhere in the criminal law. The Law Commission has endorsed this approach stating that it would be inappropriate to have a special test for "intent" that differed from that applied to all other criminal offences. Intention "should not be limited to purpose but should encompass '*Woollin*' intent".[95]

---

[93]   Technically, *Woollin* only applies to the crime of murder. However, even if this is so, the test in *Nedrick* would apply as this represents a synthesis of the tests in *Moloney* and *Hancock* which were approved in *Walker and Hayles*. The test in *Nedrick* is arguably the same as that in *Woollin*.

[94]   *R. v Hales (Ricky)* [2005] EWCA Crim 1118.

[95]   Law Commission Paper No.318, *Conspiracy and Attempts* (2009), para.8.91.

What mens rea is required with regard to relevant surrounding circumstances? The position at common law appears to have been that while the consequence had to be intended, recklessness with regard to circumstances would suffice for attempt, provided such recklessness would suffice for the completed offence.[96] Thus if a defendant, being reckless as to whether his first wife was alive, were about to go through a second marriage ceremony, he could be convicted of attempted bigamy. The 1981 Act draws no distinction between consequences and circumstances, but simply states that the defendant must act "with intent to commit an offence". Despite the wording of this statute, the common law approach was confirmed in the following decision.

R. v Khan [1990] 2 All E.R. 783 (Court of Appeal, Criminal Division)

The appellant attempted to have sexual intercourse with a non-consenting girl, but failed. The trial judge directed the jury that recklessness as to whether the girl consented was sufficient for attempted rape. The appellant appealed on this point.

RUSSELL LJ:

"The only difference between the two offences is that in rape sexual intercourse takes place whereas in attempted rape it does not, although there has to be some act which is more than preparatory to sexual intercourse. Considered in that way, the intent of the defendant is precisely the same in rape and in attempted rape and the mens rea is identical, namely an intention to have intercourse plus a knowledge of or recklessness as to the woman's absence of consent. No question of attempting to achieve a reckless state of mind arises; the attempt relates to the physical activity; the mental state of the defendant is the same. A man does not recklessly have sexual intercourse, nor does he recklessly attempt it. Recklessness in rape and attempted rape arises not in relation to the physical act of the accused but only in his state of mind when engaged in the activity of having or attempting to have sexual intercourse.

If this is the true analysis, as we believe it is, the attempt does not require any different intention on the part of the accused from that for the full offence of rape. We believe this to be a desirable result which in the instant case did not require the jury to be burdened with different directions as to the accused's state of mind, dependent on whether the individual achieved or failed to achieve sexual intercourse.

We recognise, of course, that our reasoning cannot apply to all offences and all attempts. Where, for example as in causing death by reckless driving or reckless arson, no state of mind other than recklessness is involved in the offence, there can be no attempt to commit it.

In our judgment, however, the words 'with intent to commit an offence' to be found in s.1 of the 1981 Act mean, when applied to rape, 'with intent to have sexual intercourse with a woman in circumstances where she does not consent and the defendant knows or could not care less about her absence of consent'. The only 'intent', giving that word its natural and ordinary meaning, of the rapist is to have sexual intercourse. He commits the offence because of the circumstances in which he manifests that intent, ie when the woman is not consenting and he either knows it or could not care less about the absence of consent."

Appeal dismissed

It is possible to support such an approach. If recklessness as to surrounding circumstances suffices for the complete offence it should also suffice for an attempt, as "the mens rea of the complete crime should be modified only in so far as it is necessary in order to accommodate the concept of attempt".[97]

The approach adopted in *Khan* was followed in *Attorney General's Reference (No.3 of 1992)*[98] where it was held that on a charge of attempted arson contrary to s.1(2) of the Criminal Damage Act 1971 it

---

[96] *R. v Pigg (Stephen)* (1982) 74 Cr. App. R. 352; R. Buxton, "Inchoate Offences: Incitement and Attempt" [1973] Crim. L.R. 656 at 661–664.

[97] D. Ormerod, *Smith and Hogan's Criminal Law*, 13th edn (Oxford: OUP, 2011), p.406. It should be noted that recklessness is no longer part of the mens rea for rape.

[98] *Re Attorney General's Reference (No.3 of 1992)* (1994) 98 Cr. App. R. 383.

was sufficient to prove an intention to cause damage by fire and that the defendant was reckless as to whether life would thereby be endangered. It was stated that for an attempt "it must be shown that the defendant intended to achieve that which was missing from the full offence". In *Khan* what was missing was sexual intercourse. In *Attorney-General's Reference (No.3 of 1992)* what was missing was damage to property. Intention must be proved in relation to these missing elements but beyond that only the same mens rea as for the full crime need be proved.

However, *Khan* and *Attorney-General's Reference (No.3 of 1992)* are distinguishable from each other. *Khan* was clearly dealing with a surrounding circumstance: whether the woman was consenting. In *Attorney-General's Reference (No.3 of 1992)* the offence element of "whether the life of another would be thereby endangered" can be viewed as a consequence. Under s.1(2), two consequences need to be achieved: damage to property and a state of affairs perceived to be life-threatening by an ordinary prudent person. While intention is required for the first consequence (damage to property) because that was what was "missing", recklessness with regard to the second consequence (creating a life-threatening situation) suffices. This marks an important extension of the law and it has been argued that the ratio of *Attorney-General's Reference (No.3 of 1992)* should be confined to "state-of-affairs consequences that do not comprise realised harms".[99]

What mens rea is required for surrounding circumstances in offences of negligence (for example, rape) or strict liability (for example, rape of a child under 13)? On a "simplistic"[100] reading of *Attorney-General's Reference (No.3 of 1992)* there only need be intent with regard to "what is missing" and, beyond that, only that mens rea (or lack of it) required for the full offence need be established. So, for attempted rape the defendant would need to intend penetration but negligence as to consent would suffice. For attempted rape of a child under 13, the defendant would need to intend penetration but his honest and reasonable belief that the child was 16 would not exculpate. The Law Commission proposes that for crimes that require recklessness or negligence or strict liability a defendant should only be liable for an attempt to commit that crime if he was subjectively reckless as to the circumstances:

> "[T]here may be very good reasons for defining a substantive offence with a requirement of objective fault, or with no fault at all, but the justification may be substantially weaker when applied to an inchoate offence of attempt".[101]

On the other hand, it can be argued that recklessness should not suffice even for clear circumstances such as those in *Khan*. The 1981 Act specifies very clearly that the defendant must act "with intent to commit an offence" and thus for surrounding circumstances, knowledge (the general equivalent to intention when dealing with surrounding circumstances).[102] This is the approach which has been taken in the following recent decision.

Pace [2014] EWCA Crim 186 (Court of Appeal, Criminal Division)

The defendants, who were scrap metal dealers, received a series of visits from undercover police officers in pursuance of a police operation to test whether scrap metal yards would accept purportedly

---

[99]   A.P. Simester, J. R. Spencer, G.R. Sullivan and G.J. Virgo, *Simester and Sullivan's Criminal Law: Theory and Doctrine*, 5th edn (Oxford: Hart, 2013), p.351.

[100] Law Commission Consultation Paper No.183, *Conspiracy and Attempts* (2007), para.14.48.

[101] Law Commission Paper No.318, *Conspiracy and Attempts* (2009), para.8.128.

[102] An earlier Law Commission Paper (No.102, 1980) stated that an intention as to every element of the offence was required (although in practice knowledge of surrounding circumstances would suffice to establish the necessary intent) (para.2.15).

stolen items. The defendants bought metal items such as earthing tape and power cables described to them by the officers as "having been stolen from the back of a van". It was an agreed fact that the property was not stolen but belonged to the police. The defendants were charged with attempting to convert criminal property contrary to s.327 of Part 7 (Money Laundering) of the Proceeds of Crime Act 2002, the state of mind applicable to the substantive offence being knowledge or suspicion (s. 340(3)). The defendants were convicted and appealed.

DAVIS LJ:

"1. The principal issue raised on these two appeals relates to the mental element required for criminal attempt. It is one that, albeit in the context of differing underlying substantive criminal offences, has caused difficulties over the years. Various decisions of the courts in those years do not always reveal a consistency in approach and sometimes, it has to be said, reveal a possible inconsistency in approach. It is also an area which has attracted much academic debate; and there too considerable divergences in approach have been manifested.

2. This issue requires consideration of the meaning and effect of s.1 of the Criminal Attempts Act 1981 ('the 1981 Act'): a section which in the past has been judicially described as 'winning no prize for lucidity' . . .

3. The trial judge decided that in this case the applicable mens rea for the offences of [attempting to conceal, disguise or convert criminal property] . . . was capable of being suspicion. . . .

21. . . . [The trial judge told the jury]

'The law is clear: the prosecution must prove against each defendant on each count in which they are allegedly involved that at the time of accepting, checking, weighing or paying for the goods he either knew or suspected that they were stolen or had otherwise been obtained dishonestly'. . .

He went on to explain to the jury, among other things, that 'suspicion . . . falls below knowledge or belief'. He further instructed them that the suspicion did not need to be firmly grounded or even based on reasonable grounds.

22. Complaint is made by the appellants with regard to these directions . . .

35. That, then, leads to what is at the heart of these appeals: the mens rea which the prosecution was, in law, required to prove if it could make out its case of attempting to conceal, disguise or convert criminal property. (For shorthand, we will hereafter describe it as attempting to convert criminal property) . . .

46. A convenient starting point is this. Where the substantive criminal offence specifically requires the consequence of an act, it is well established that an attempt to commit that offence ordinarily requires proof of intent as to that consequence. To take a familiar example, the required intent for murder is either an intent to kill or an intent to cause really serious injury. The required consequence of the act is, of course, death. Accordingly, for a charge of attempted murder to be made out the intent which must be proved is an intent to kill: see *Whybrow* (1951) 35 Cr App R 141. That remains the case since the 1981 Act. Of course, that is an offence different from the present case. But . . . [counsel for the appellants] is at least entitled to make the point that that case is an illustration of the proposition that the mental element required to make a person guilty of an attempted offence may well be different from, and at a higher level than, that applicable to the substantive offence itself . . .

48. We next turn to the decision in *Khan*, which did post-date the Act . . .

52. One can see the potential support for [counsel for the Crown's] argument that *Khan* affords. He would thus seek to derive from it the proposition that, assuming the acts here were more than preparatory, in the present cases the intention here was to convert the scrap metal (the act) and the required mental state was knowledge or suspicion that the scrap metal was stolen. But the authority of *Khan* is not decisive for present purposes . . . In *Khan*, the substantive offence admitted of recklessness as the mens rea: which is not the case here. In *Khan*, moreover, the appellants were charged with attempted rape solely because they had not succeeded in penetrating the victim, which is what they had intended to do. Had they succeeded in that act, as they had intended, the full offence of rape would have been made out. But that is not so in the present case. The two appellants here could never have been guilty of the substantive offence of converting criminal property: just because the property in question did not constitute or represent benefit from criminal conduct. Furthermore, the court in *Khan* had been careful to say (at p.35):

'We recognise, of course, that our reasoning cannot apply to all offences and all attempts. Where, for example, as in causing death by reckless driving or reckless arson, no state of mind other than recklessness is involved in the offence, there can be no attempt to commit it.'

53. We were also referred to . . . the decision of another constitution of this court in *AG's Reference (No 3 of 1992)* (1994) 98 Cr App R 383, which adopted broadly the same approach as in *Khan*. That too was a decision in a context different from the present case. It related to attempted arson being reckless whether life be endangered, contrary to s.l(2) of the Criminal Damage Act 1971. We have to say that we found, with respect, some of the passages in the judgment somewhat elliptical, if not self-contradictory . . . We do not, at all events, *think* that it materially advances the Crown's argument. It is true that, in giving the judgment of the court, Schiemann J said (somewhat tentatively, on one view) at page 390:

'One way of analysing the situation is to say that a defendant, in order to be guilty of an attempt, must be in one of the states of *mind* required for the commission of the full offence and did his best, as far as he could, to supply what was missing from the offence.'

But [counsel for the appellants] was in a position to seek to cull from the decision at least some support for his own argument. For at page 390 Schiemann J then went on to say this:

'If the facts are that, although the defendant has one of the appropriate states of mind required for the complete offence, but the physical element required for the commission of the complete offence is missing, the defendant is not to be convicted unless it can be shown that he intended to supply the physical elements.'. .

[Counsel for the appellants'] submission was that the 'physical element' in the present case which was missing was conversion of criminal property: and it was the 'supply' of that which had to be shown to be intended.

54. This, at all events, leads on to another line of authority which also bears on the present problem. That relates to cases where the attempt is to commit the 'impossible'—the position here . . . [His Lordship then reviewed the leading cases, considered below at pp.496–498.]

60. Against that citation of authority we turn to the disposal of these two appeals . . .

62. Turning, then, to s.1(1) [of the 1981 Act] we consider that, as a matter of ordinary language and in accordance with principle, an 'intent to commit an offence' connotes an intent to commit all the elements of the offence. We can see no sufficient basis, whether linguistic or purposive, for construing it otherwise.

63. Once that is appreciated, the fault line in the Crown's argument is revealed. A constituent element of the offence of converting criminal property is, as we have said, that the property in question *is* criminal property. That is an essential part of the offence. Accordingly, an intent to commit the offence involves, in the present case, an intent to convert criminal property: and that connotes an intent that the property should *be* criminal property. But the Crown's argument glosses over that. Its argument connotes that the property in question which it is intended to be converted is *property* known or suspected to constitute or represent benefit from criminal conduct. It ignores the requirement for the substantive offence that the property concerned must be *criminal property* (as defined). The Crown, in effect, thus seeks to make it a criminal offence to intend to convert property suspecting, if not knowing, that it is stolen. But that is not what s.327, read with s.340(3), provides.

64. Reflecting this difficulty in the Crown's argument, there is this further point to be made. For the purpose of the substantive offence, a person may in point of fact convert property intending and believing that it is criminal property: yet he will not be guilty of the substantive offence if, in fact, it is not criminal property (*Montila* [2004] UKHL 50). It is most odd that, on the Crown's case, such a person who cannot on such a scenario be liable for the substantive offence can nevertheless be made liable, where his state of mind is one of suspicion only, if what is charged is, instead, an attempt to commit the offence. We have the greatest difficulty in seeing that the provisions of s.1 of the 1981 Act were designed to bring about such a result.

65. We further consider . . . that such a conclusion is supported by the approach of Parliament taken to conspiracy cases as enunciated in s.1 of the 1977 Act, as amended, and as interpreted by the courts. . .

66. We say that for the following reasons.

i) First, the provisions of s.1 of the 1977 Act, as amended, were introduced by the 1981 Act itself. One would therefore be predisposed to anticipate a coherence of approach in the relevant provisions of the two statutes in this regard.

ii) Second, offences of criminal attempt and offences of criminal conspiracy are both inchoate offences. Both have in common that they are looking to what is planned for the future. That remains so even if counts formulated as conspiracy counts are commonly sought to be proved by proof of the commission of substantive offences.

iii) Third, it is not difficult to envisage scenarios—not least, as it happens, in money laundering cases – where what may be charged as an attempt would be capable of being charged as conspiracy, and vice versa.

67. In this regard, we think that the approach taken by the courts to s.1 of the 1977 Act is most revealing. [His lordship then reviewed the case- law, including *Saik*, discussed above at p.512] . . .

74. [T]his authority establishes that a conspiracy to commit an offence under s.327 of the 2002 Act . . . can require a higher level of mens rea than that applicable to the actual commission of the substantive offence itself. True it is that the language of s.1 of the 1977 Act is not precisely the same as s.1 of the 1981 Act. Even so . . . s.1 of the 1977 Act can properly be read so as to take account of the 1981 Act, and vice versa. Accordingly it makes it, in our view, all the more principled to conclude that likewise in the case of attempt a higher level of mens rea may be required under s.1(1) than is applicable to the substantive offence itself: and thus that, in the present case, proof of suspicion will not suffice on a count of attempted money laundering . . .

78. For the reasons we have given, we conclude that the appeals must be allowed. For the purposes of a count of attempted money laundering proof of a mental element of suspicion (only) does not suffice . . .

79. We do appreciate the anxieties of the Crown in the context of money laundering. Such cases are not always easy of proof . . . But, . . . the policy behind the substantive offences of money laundering cannot be allowed to distort the meaning of s.1 of the 1981 Act . . .

81. That may or may not create problems for prosecutors. However, we observe that there in any event may well be . . . other charges potentially available[103] . . . [Further] the margin between knowledge and suspicion is perhaps not all that great, at all events where the person has reasonable grounds for suspicion. Where a defendant can be shown deliberately to have turned a blind eye to the provenance of goods and deliberately to have failed to ask obvious questions, that can be capable, depending on the circumstances, of providing evidence going to prove knowledge or belief . . ."

Appeal allowed

Attempt is essentially a crime of mens rea. Given this, there is a strong argument that it ought to be restricted to those who act with intent (or its equivalent, knowledge or, it seems, according to Pace, belief)) in relation to all the elements of the offence. Thus, the decision in *Pace*, that a conviction for attempt cannot be based upon suspicion is to be supported. However, although the Court of Appeal was critical of aspects of the decision in *Khan* it did not overrule it. Instead, it was distinguished on the questionable basis that, unlike *Khan*, the case before it concerned impossibility. It may well be that *Pace* will be appealed to the Supreme Court, but in the meantime we are in the difficult position of having competing Court of Appeal authorities, one dealing with possible attempts and the other with those which are impossible.[104] Further, as *Attorney-General's Reference (No.3 of 1992)* demonstrates, it is difficult to draw a clear distinction between consequences and circumstances. For example, it could be argued that s.1(2) requires the causing of criminal damage to be committed in the circumstances of it being life-endangering. It is highly inappropriate to make criminal liability hinge on such fine distinctions that have no bearing on culpability.

A final problem remains: will a so-called "conditional intention" suffice for attempt? If a defendant opens a suitcase, intending to steal its contents "on condition they are of some value", can she be convicted of attempted theft?

---

103   In this instance, the defendants could have been charged with assisting or encouraging crime, believing it would be committed under the Serious Crime Act 2007, s.45 (below p.527). See further, F. Stark, "The Mens Rea of Criminal Attempt" [2014] *Archbold Review* 7 at 9.

104   See further, Stark, "The Mens Rea of Criminal Attempt" [2014] *Archbold Review* 7 at 9, who argues that the Court of Appeal reached the right decision but for the wrong reasons and, in particular, that the criticism of *Khan* was misplaced.

The Law Commission (Law Com. No.102) Attempt, 1980, Appendix E, "'Conditional Intent' and R. v Husseyn":

"4. In delivering the judgment of the Court of Appeal in the attempted theft case of *R. v Husseyn*, Lord Scarman stated ((1978) 67 Cr.App.R.131, at p. 132) 'it cannot be said that one who has it in mind to steal only if what he finds is worth stealing has a present intention to steal'.

5. This simple statement, taken by itself and out of context, was the origin of the difficulties. It gave rise to the doctrine that 'conditional intent' in the sense of 'intending to steal whatever one might find of value or worth stealing' was not a sufficient mental element in these theft-related offences; the prosecution must aver and prove that at the time of attempting, entering as a trespasser, etc., the accused had a settled intention to steal some particular and specified object existing or believed by him to exist in his target area.

6. In such a form, the doctrine was obviously capable of mischievous results. In particular, it excluded from criminal liability the large majority of sneak thieves and burglars who conduct their operations 'on spec'. Without knowing what a handbag, a package left in a car, or a house contains, they nevertheless proceed in the hope or expectation that they will find something of value or worth stealing there, and intend, in that event, to steal it. As Geoffrey Lane L.J. pungently remarked (*R. v Walkington* [1979] 1 W.L.R. 1169, 1179), after setting out the reasoning that led to the acquittal of one burglar, 'a reading of that would make the layman wonder if the law had taken leave of its senses . . . Nearly every prospective burglar could no doubt truthfully say that he only intended to steal if he found something in the building worth stealing.'

7. Unfortunately, several factors obscured the clarity of the issue. As reported, *R. v Husseyn* gave no indication that the charge of attempted theft in that case had related to specific identifiable objects, and although Lawton L.J. did stress that the indictment in the subsequent case of *R. v Hector* ((1978) 67 Cr.App.R.224) also charged attempted theft of particular objects, the report was headed 'Whether conditional intention enough', a phrase not used in the judgment. So it was not realised that Lord Scarman's statement related only to the facts of the case before him or that the decision in both cases rested on the basic rule of criminal pleading that an allegation that the accused attempted to steal a particular item involves proof that that item was what he intended to steal; in such a case it is not enough to show that he intended to steal whatever he found worth stealing . . .

8. Whatever the reasons, within a few months of the decision in *R. v Husseyn*, submissions that 'conditional intent is not enough' were being accepted by magistrates and Crown Court judges in all these theft-related offences, causing frustration and perplexity to prosecuting authorities and bringing the criminal law into disrepute . . .

9. Study of the relevant indictments and transcripts convinced us that, once the complications mentioned in paragraph 7 had been cleared out of the way, the matter could be put right without recourse to legislation and that the appropriate way to proceed was by way of Attorney General's References to the Court of Appeal under section 36 of the Criminal Justice Act 1972 . . .

10. The two References were decided by the Court of Appeal as *Attorney General's References (Nos 1 and 2 of 1979)* ([1979] 3 W.L.R. 577) . . . and . . . restore clarity and common sense to the law. Where the accused's state of mind is that of intending to steal whatever he may find worth stealing in his target area, there is no need to charge him with attempting to steal specific objects. In appropriate cases of attempted theft a charge of attempting to steal some or all of the contents of (for example) a car or a handbag will suffice. In cases where the substantive offence does not require anything to be stolen, it is not necessary to allege more than 'with intent to steal'. The important point is that the indictment should correctly reflect that which it is alleged the accused did and that the accused should know with adequate detail what he is alleged to have done (at 590). The result, in the Commission's view, is that it is now possible to state with confidence that in cases where an intention to steal anything of value or worth stealing accurately reflects the accused's state of mind at the time of the actus reus, this is sufficient to constitute 'an intention to steal' and applies equally to all the theft-related offences."

The law on this point is unaffected by the Criminal Attempts Act 1981, which abolishes "the offence of attempt at common law" (s.6(1)). These developments on "conditional intention" are best regarded as part of the "common law of intention"; some of the important decisions on this point were not delivered in the context of attempted crime at all.[105] It is simply that the point is of particular importance when dealing with attempts.

---

[105]   *R. v Greenhof* [1979] Crim. L.R. 108, *R. v Bozickovic* [1978] Crim. L.R. 686 and *R. v Walkington (Terence John)* [1979] 1 W.L.R. 1169 were all decisions on burglary.

The Law Commission has proposed that an "intention to commit an offence includes a conditional intent to commit it".[106] As they state:

"If D breaks into a car intending to steal if he or she finds something worth stealing, that is intention to steal. Such an intention is functionally equivalent to the intention of someone who drops a stone off a tall building, saying, 'I intend this stone to hit anyone who happens to be passing below'. Such a person intends to strike someone with the stone."[107]

(iv) Impossibility

(a) *Introduction*

Can there be criminal liability for attempting the impossible? If a defendant shoots at his victim trying to kill her but unknown to him the victim has had a heart attack and is already dead, can the defendant be liable for attempted murder?

Before exploring the present law, it is helpful briefly to outline the position at common law before the enactment of the Criminal Attempts Act 1981.

(b) *The common law*

The common law utilised a three-fold classification:

1. Legal impossibility

This is where the defendant performs all the physical actions he intends to perform, but, unknown to him, what he has done does not amount to a crime. For example, he intends to steal an umbrella but unknown to him, the umbrella turns out to be his own.

In *Haughton v Smith*[108] the defendant was charged with attempting to handle stolen goods contrary to s.22 of the Theft Act 1968. The defendant had actually handled the goods but, unknown to them, they were not stolen goods.[109] The House of Lords unanimously held that there could be no liability for attempt in such circumstances. Lord Hailsham stated:

"there must be an overt act of such a kind that it is intended to form and does form part of a series of acts which would constitute the actual commission of the offence if it were not interrupted. In the present case the series of acts would never have constituted and in fact did not constitute an actual commission of the offence, because at the time of the handling the goods were no longer stolen goods."[110]

Lord Reid:

"The crime is impossible in the circumstances, so no acts could be proximate to it. [H]e took no step towards the commission of a crime because there was no crime to commit."[111]

---

[106] Law Commission Paper No.318, *Conspiracy and Attempts* (2009), para.8.106.
[107] Law Commission Consultation Paper No.183, *Conspiracy and Attempts* (2007), para.16.74.
[108] *Haughton v Smith* [1975] A.C. 476.
[109] The goods had been stolen, but when the police commandeered the van in which the goods were travelling, the goods ceased to be "stolen" by virtue of s.24(3) of the Theft Act 1968 as they had been "restored to lawful custody".
[110] *Haughton v Smith* [1975] A.C. 476 at 492.
[111] *Haughton v Smith* [1975] A.C. 476 at 499–500.

Lord Morris:

"His belief that the goods were stolen did not make them stolen goods . . . To convict him of attempting to handle stolen goods would be to convict him not for what he did but simply because he had had a guilty intention."[112]

2. Physical impossibility

This is where it is physically impossible for the defendant to commit the complete crime, whatever means he adopts. For example, he intends to pick a pocket and places his hand in the victim's pocket, but it is empty; there is nothing to steal. In *Partington v Williams* it was held that there could be no liability in such cases because the commission of the substantive offence was, in the circumstances, impossible.[113]

The House of Lords in *DPP v Nock*,[114] a conspiracy case, considered obiter "the proper limits" of *Haughton v Smith* and attempts to commit the impossible, and held that liability depended on the manner in which the particular indictment was framed. If, in an attempted theft case, the indictment was limited to an attempt to steal specific property or property from a specific place, then if the property was not there, the actus reus of the complete crime, namely, the appropriation of the *specific* property belonging to another, would be incapable of proof. The defendant would escape liability. On the other hand, if the indictment alleged an attempt to steal from the person generally, then the pickpocket who puts his hand in an empty pocket could be liable for attempted theft. This would be a mere "transient frustration". The crime would still be possible; the pickpocket, if undetected, would continue his attempts until successful.

This purported limitation of the *Haughton v Smith* principle does not stand up to close analysis. First, it ignores the immense difficulties involved in proving the requisite general intent to continue until the crime is eventually completed successfully, and, secondly, it overlooks the necessity to prove that the defendant's actions were more than merely preparatory to the complete offence.

This whole approach towards attempts to commit the physically impossible caused other problems. What was meant by an empty pocket or an empty box? What if the pocket contained only a dirty handkerchief or a broken match? Was the test of emptiness a purely objective one, or was it relative to the defendant, namely, whether there was something there that they would (or might) have stolen? For instance, the Law Commission[115] cites an unreported case in which a suitcase full of luggage was effectively held to be "empty" because it contained nothing the defendant wanted. In *Bayley and Easterbrook*[116] the defendants opened a box hoping to steal from it; the box contained "a Pammex Model 60 rail and flange lubricator"—a valuable article, but useless to the defendants so they returned the box and its contents. Their conviction for "attempting to steal the contents of a box belonging to the British Railways Board" was upheld, but as Smith points out:

"It is clear then that the defendants were convicted of attempting to steal not the actual contents but something, unidentified, that was not in the box . . . Apart from the Pammex Model 60 rail and flange lubricator, this was an empty box. The presence of those articles was clearly totally irrelevant. They were of no more significance than, say, pieces of straw in which they had been packed."[117]

---

[112] *Haughton* [1975] A.C. 476 at 501.
[113] *Partington v Williams* (1975) 62 Cr. App. R. 220.
[114] *DPP v Nock* [1978] A.C. 979.
[115] Law Commission Paper No.102 (1980), para.2.62.
[116] *R. v Bayley and Easterbrook* [1980] Crim. L.R. 503.
[117] *Bayley and Easterbrook* [1980] Crim. L.R. 503. On this problem, see generally, G. Williams, "Three Rogues' Charters" [1980] Crim. L.R. 263.

3. Impossibility through ineptitude

This is where the crime is impossible in the circumstances because of the defendant's ineptitude, inefficiency or the adoption of insufficient means. For example, he tries to force open a door with an iron bar, but the iron bar is too weak ever to do so. Here the common law took a different approach from that adopted in relation to the above two categories of impossibility and held that there could be criminal liability for attempt. The reasoning was that such crimes were not really "impossible" because the crime *was* possible with different means. The defendant could open the door; he simply needed to fetch and use a stronger iron bar.[118]

In *Farrance*[119] the defendant had been convicted of attempting to drive with a blood alcohol concentration above the prescribed limit contrary to s.6(1) of the Road Traffic Act 1972. The clutch of his car had burnt out so that he could not drive the car. The Court of Appeal upheld his conviction on the ground that a burnt out clutch was only an impediment to the commission of a crime similar to the inadequate burglar's tool or the poisoner's insufficient dose. In the Brunei case of *Zainal Abidin b Ismail*[120] the defendant's impotence prevented him from raping a woman. This was regarded as an instance of impossibility by ineptitude and the defendant was convicted of attempted rape.

Holding that there could be liability in these cases, but not in cases of attempting the physically impossible, posed immense problems. Suppose a defendant fired their gun at a victim who was out of range. Was this ineptitude or physical impossibility? Did it matter whether his victim was only just out of range or miles out of range? Or suppose that a defendant tried to kill his victim with a weak solution of poison; this was presumably ineptitude, but what if the solution was so weak that it could cause no harm at all? Or if the solution was entirely innocent, as where water was administered in mistake for cyanide? At what point did ineptitude become transformed into impossibility?

(c) *Criminal Attempts Act 1981*

Criminal Attempts Act 1981 s.1

"(2) A person may be guilty of attempting to commit an offence to which this section applies even though the facts are such that the commission of the offence is impossible.

(3) In any case where—

(a) apart from this subsection a person's intention would not be regarded as having amounted to an intent to commit an offence; but

(b) if the facts of the case had been as he believed them to be, his intention would be so regarded,

then, for the purposes of subsection (1) above, he shall be regarded as having had an intent to commit that offence.

(4) This section applies to any offence which, if it were completed, would be triable in England and Wales as an indictable offence . . ."

Section 1(2) provides that there can be liability for attempting the impossible, irrespective of the category of impossibility. Section 1(3) purports to confirm the self-evident proposition that where a person believes the facts to be such that they would be committing a crime, they are to be regarded as having the necessary intention to commit the offence. This means that a defendant who intends to handle a particular radio believing it to be stolen, when in fact it is not stolen, cannot argue that he intended

---

[118]   *Haughton* [1975] A.C. 476 at 500.
[119]   (1977) 67 Cr. App. R. 136.
[120]   *Zainal Abidin b Ismail* [1987] 2 M.L.J. 741. For a discussion of this case, see C.M.V. Clarkson, "Rape: Emasculation of the Penal Code" [1988] 1 M.L.J. cxiii.

to handle a "non-stolen radio". Section 1(3) makes it plain that if he believed the radio was stolen, he intended to handle a "stolen radio". This provision is actually completely redundant. Intention relates purely to a defendant's subjective state of mind. An intention to handle a stolen radio is just that: an intention to handle a radio believed to be stolen. The objective status of the goods (stolen or not stolen) has no bearing upon the defendant's intention.

These provisions represent a clear and emphatic victory for the "subjectivist" theory of attempts where emphasis is placed on the intention of the defendant and the firmness of that intention. However, the House of Lords was initially not prepared to accept such blatant subjectivism and, in an extraordinary judgment, declared that the statute would lead to "asinine" results and proceeded to subvert the legislation from its original purpose.

Anderton v Ryan [1985] A.C. 560 (House of Lords)

The defendant was convicted of dishonestly attempting to handle a stolen video recorder. She had purchased the recorder believing it was stolen and had confessed this to police investigating a burglary at her home. There was, however, no evidence that the recorder had been stolen and it therefore had to be treated as if it were not stolen. She appealed against her conviction.

LORD BRIDGE:

"Does section 1 of the Act of 1981 create a new offence of attempt where a person embarks on and completes a course of conduct which is objectively innocent, solely on the ground that the person mistakenly believes facts which, if true, would make that course of conduct a complete crime? If the question must be answered affirmatively it requires convictions in a number of surprising cases: the classic case . . . of the man who takes away his own umbrella from a stand, believing it not to be his own and with intent to steal it; the case of the man who has consensual intercourse with a girl over 16 believing her to be under that age; the case of the art dealer who sells a picture which he represents to be and which is in fact a genuine Picasso, but which the dealer mistakenly believes to be a fake.

The common feature of all these cases, including that under appeal, is that the mind alone is guilty, the act is innocent. I should find it surprising that Parliament, if intending to make this purely subjective guilt criminally punishable, should have done so by anything less than the clearest express language, and, in particular, should have done so in a section aimed specifically at inchoate offences.

. . . [S]ection 1(1) and (4) of the Act of 1981 provide a statutory substitute for the common law offence of attempt . . .

It is sufficient to say of subsection (2) that it is plainly intended to reverse the law . . . that the pickpocket who puts his hand in an empty pocket commits no offence. Putting the hand in the pocket is the guilty act, the intent to steal is the guilty mind, the offence is appropriately dealt with as an attempt, and the impossibility of committing the full offence for want of anything in the pocket to steal is declared by the subsection to be no obstacle to conviction . . .

It seems to me that subsections (2) and (3) are in a sense complementary to each other. Subsection (2) covers the case of a person acting in a criminal way with a general intent to commit a crime in circumstances where no crime is possible. Subsection (3) covers the case of a person acting in a criminal way with a specific intent to commit a particular crime which he erroneously believes to be, but which is not in fact, possible. Given the criminal action, the appropriate subsection allows the actor's guilty intention to be supplied by his subjective but mistaken state of mind, notwithstanding that on the true facts that intention is incapable of fulfilment. But if the action is throughout innocent and the actor has done everything he intended to do, I can find nothing in either subsection which requires me to hold that his erroneous belief in facts which, if true, would have made the action a crime makes him guilty of an attempt to commit that crime."

Appeal allowed

C.M.V. Clarkson, Understanding Criminal Law, 4th edn (2005), pp.171–172:

"This distinction between 'objectively innocent' acts, on the one hand, and 'criminal' or 'guilty' acts on the other is particularly interesting. It would appear that a 'criminal' or 'guilty' act is one that looks *manifestly criminal*. (This cannot refer to actual crimes. The defendant stabbing the pillow believing he is stabbing his victim commits no offence if it is his own bedding and pillow that he is damaging. Yet Lord Roskill clearly held that there would be liability for attempt in such a situation.) Fletcher (1978) states that 'manifestly criminal' activities must exhibit at least the following essential features. First, the criminal act must manifest, on its face, the actor's criminal purpose. Secondly, the conduct should be 'of a type that is unnerving and disturbing to the community as a whole'. These requirements are clearly satisfied in the pickpocket and defendant stabbing the pillow cases. The actions manifest the defendant's unlawful purpose and are 'unnerving and disturbing' to the community. This requirement of manifest criminality is, of course, one that lays emphasis on *harm*, albeit of a second-order nature. It insists that actions infringe another's security interests; they must seemingly pose real and objective threats of harm.

On the other hand, 'objectively innocent' activities such as those of Mrs. Ryan or the defendant having sexual intercourse with the 16-year-old girl believing her to be under 16 pose no threat of harm to anyone. Nobody's security interests are being violated thereby. At most, he is manifesting a generalised dangerousness, in the sense that he has shown that he could perhaps commit the crime at another time and place. If criminal liability were to be imposed in such cases it would be in the complete absence of any degree of harm, however defined. On this basis it can be suggested that the House of Lords in *Anderton v Ryan* (1985), despite blatantly ignoring Parliament's intentions and creating confused distinctions, did lend its weight to the view . . . that the causing of harm is an essential prerequisite in the general formula for the construction of criminal liability."

In one of the most dramatic about-turns in English law, the House of Lords within months overruled itself and held that there could be criminal liability in all cases of attempting the impossible.

R. v Shivpuri [1987] A.C. 1 (House of Lords)

The defendant thought he was dealing in prohibited drugs but it transpired that the substance in his possession was only snuff or similarly harmless vegetable matter. He was convicted of attempting to be knowingly concerned in dealing with prohibited drugs, contrary to s.1(1) of the Criminal Attempts Act 1981 and s.170(1)(b) of the Customs and Excise Management Act 1979. He appealed against his conviction.

LORD BRIDGE:

"[T]he first question to be asked is whether the appellant intended to commit the offences of being knowingly concerned in dealing with and harbouring drugs of Class A or Class B with intent to evade the prohibition on their importation. Translated into more homely language the question may be rephrased, without in any way altering its legal significance, in the following terms: did the appellant intend to receive and store (harbour) and in due course pass on to third parties (deal with) packages of heroin or cannabis which he knew had been smuggled into England from India? The answer is plainly yes, he did. Next, did he in relation to each offence, do an act which was more than merely preparatory to the commission of the offence? The act relied on in relation to harbouring was the receipt and retention of the packages found in the lining of the suitcase. The act relied on in relation to dealing was the meeting at Southall station with the intended recipient of one of the packages. In each case the act was clearly more than preparatory to the commission of the *intended* offence; it was not and could not be more than merely preparatory to the commission of the *actual* offence, because the facts were such that the commission of the actual offence was impossible. Here then is the nub of the matter. Does the 'act which is more than merely preparatory to the commission of the offence' in section 1(1) of the Act of 1981 (the *actus reus* of the statutory offence of attempt) require any more than an act which is more than merely preparatory to the commission of the offence which the defendant intended to commit? Section 1(2) must surely indicate a negative answer; if it were otherwise, whenever the facts were such that the commission of the actual offence was impossible, it would be impossible to prove an act more than merely preparatory to the commission of that offence and subsections (1) and (2) would contradict each other.

This very simple, perhaps over simple, analysis leads me to the provisional conclusion that the appellant was rightly convicted of the two offences of attempt with which he was charged. But can this conclusion stand with *Anderton v Ryan*? . . .

Running through Lord Roskill's speech and my own in *Anderton v Ryan* is the concept of 'objectively innocent' acts which, in my speech certainly, are contrasted with 'guilty acts'.

I am satisfied on further consideration that the concept of 'objective innocence' is incapable of sensible application in relation to the law of criminal attempts. The reason for this is that any attempt to commit an offence which involves 'an act which is more than merely preparatory to the commission of the offence' but for any reason fails, so that in the event no offence is committed, must ex hypothesi, from the point of view of the criminal law, be 'objectively innocent'. What turns what would otherwise, from the point of view of the criminal law, be an innocent act into a crime is the intent of the actor to commit an offence . . . A puts his hand into B's pocket. Whether or not there is anything in the pocket capable of being stolen, if A intends to steal, his act is a criminal attempt; if he does not so intend, his act is innocent. A plunges a knife into a bolster in a bed. To avoid the complication of an offence of criminal damage, assume it to be A's bolster. If A believes the bolster to be his enemy, B, and intends to kill him, his act is an attempt to murder B; if he knows the bolster is only a bolster, his act is innocent. These considerations lead me to the conclusion that the distinction sought to be drawn in *Anderton v Ryan* between innocent and guilty acts considered 'objectively' and independently of the state of mind of the actor cannot be sensibly maintained.

Another conceivable ground of distinction which was to some extent canvassed in argument, both in *Anderton v Ryan* and in the instant case, though no trace of it appears in the speeches in *Anderton v Ryan*, is a distinction which would make guilt or innocence of the crime of attempt in a case of mistaken belief dependent on what, for want of a better phrase, I will call the defendant's dominant intention. According to the theory necessary to sustain this distinction, the appellant's dominant intention in *Anderton v Ryan* was to buy a cheap video recorder; her belief that it was stolen was merely incidental. Likewise in the hypothetical case of attempted unlawful sexual intercourse, the young man's dominant intention was to have intercourse with the particular girl; his mistaken belief that she was under 16 was merely incidental. By contrast, in the instant case, the appellant's dominant intention was to receive and distribute illegally imported heroin or cannabis.

Whilst I see the superficial attraction of this suggested ground of distinction, I also see formidable practical difficulties in its application. By what test is a jury to be told that a defendant's dominant intention is to be recognised and distinguished from his incidental but mistaken belief? But there is perhaps a more formidable theoretical difficulty. If this ground of distinction is relied on to support the acquittal of the appellant in *Anderton v Ryan*, it can only do so on the basis that her mistaken belief that the video recorder was stolen played no significant part in her decision to buy it and therefore she may be acquitted of the intent to handle stolen goods. But this line of reasoning runs into head-on collision with section 1(3) of the Act of 1981. The theory produces a situation where, apart from the subsection, her intention would not be regarded as having amounted to any intent to commit an offence. Section 1(3) (b) then requires one to ask whether, if the video recorder had in fact been stolen, her intention would have been regarded as an intent to handle stolen goods. The answer must clearly be yes, it would. If she had bought the video recorder knowing it to be stolen, when in fact it was, it would have availed her nothing to say that her dominant intention was to buy a video recorder because it was cheap and that her knowledge that it was stolen was merely incidental. This seems to me fatal to the dominant intention theory.[121]

I am thus led to the conclusion that there is no valid ground on which *Anderton v Ryan* can be distinguished. I have made clear my own conviction . . . that the decision was wrong."

Appeal dismissed

The law is now clear. There can be liability in all cases of attempting the impossible. In *Attorney General's Reference (Nos.3 and 4 of 2005)*[122] the defendant was convicted of attempting to cause grievous bodily harm when he kicked a man who was already dead. In *Jones*[123] the defendant was convicted of attempting to incite (by text message) a child under the age of 13 to engage in sexual activity contrary to s.8 of the Sexual Offences Act 2003. On the facts the crime was impossible as the recipient of the message was an adult policewoman pretending to be a child under the age of 13.

Is such an approach justifiable?

---

[121]   For a discussion of this dominant intention theory, see pp.500–501.
[122]   *Re Attorney General's Reference (Nos.3 and 4 of 2005)* [2005] 2 Cr. App. R. (S.) 98.
[123]   *R. v Jones (Ian Anthony)* [2007] EWCA Crim 1118.

The Law Commission (Law Com. No.102), Attempt (1980), paras 2.96–2.98:

"2.96. We think it would be generally accepted that if a man possesses the appropriate *mens rea* and commits acts which are sufficiently proximate to the *actus reus* of a criminal offence, he is guilty of attempting to commit that offence. Where, with that intention, he commits acts which, if the facts were as he believed them to be, would have amounted to the *actus reus* of the full crime or would have been sufficiently proximate to amount to an attempt, we cannot see why his failure to appreciate the true facts should, in principle, relieve him of liability for the attempt. We stress that this solution to the problem does not punish people simply for their intentions. The necessity for proof of proximate acts remains. The fact that the impossibility of committing the full crime reduces the social danger is adequately reflected in the generally milder penalty which an attempt attracts instead of that for the full offence. And even if it is conceded that there may be some reduction in the social danger in cases of impossibility, it has to be borne in mind that a certain social danger undoubtedly remains. Defendants in cases such as *Haughton v Smith* and *Nock and Alsford* are prepared to do all they can to break the criminal law even though in the circumstances their attempts are doomed to failure; and if they go unpunished, they may be encouraged to do better at the next opportunity. Finally, if the solution under consideration is accepted, it makes it possible to dispense with the doctrine of 'inadequate means' and with stained efforts to catch those who might otherwise escape by resort to broadly drawn indictments and an 'inferred general intention'.

2.97. If it is right in principle that an attempt should be chargeable even though the crime which it is sought to commit could not possibly be committed, we do not think that we should be deterred by the consideration that such a change in our law would also cover some extreme and exceptional cases in which a prosecution would be theoretically possible. An example would be where a person is offered goods at such a low price that he believes that they are stolen, when in fact they are not; if he actually purchases them, upon the principles which we have discussed he would be liable for an attempt to handle stolen goods. Another case which has been much debated is that raised in argument by Bramwell B. in *R. v Collins* (1864) 9 Cox C.C. 497. If A takes his own umbrella, mistaking it for one belonging to B and intending to steal B's umbrella, is he guilty of attempted theft? Again, on the principles which we have discussed he would in theory be guilty but in neither case would it be realistic to suppose that a complaint would be made or that a prosecution would ensue. On the other hand, if our recommendations were formulated so as to exclude such cases, then it might well be impossible to obtain convictions in cases such as *Haughton v Smith*, where a defendant handles goods which were originally stolen, intending to handle stolen goods, but where, unknown to him, the goods had meanwhile been restored to lawful custody. Another example of possible difficulty which has been suggested is where a person in the erroneous belief that he can kill by witchcraft or magic takes action such as sticking pins into a model of his enemy—intending thereby to bring about his enemy's death. Could that person be charged with attempted murder? It may be that such conduct could be more than an act of mere preparation on the facts as the defendant believes them to be; and in theory, therefore, it is possible that such a defendant could be found guilty. In the ordinary course, we think that discretion in bringing a prosecution will be sufficient answer to any problems raised by such unusual cases; but even if a prosecution ensued, it may be doubted whether a jury would regard the acts in question as sufficient to amount to an attempt.

2.98. A possible difficulty of another kind which we have considered is the distinction which it will be necessary to draw between impossibility arising from misapprehension as to the facts and impossibility arising from a misapprehension of the law in situations which at first sight appear to be similar. As we have seen, if the defendant believes, because of a mistake of law, that certain conduct constitutes an offence when it is not, he should not be liable for attempt if he acts in accordance with his intent. For example, the defendant intends to smuggle certain goods through the customs in the belief that they are dutiable; under the relevant law those goods are in fact not dutiable. He has made no mistake as to the nature of the goods; his error is solely one of law, and if he imports them he should not be liable for an attempt improperly to import goods without paying duty, since he had no intent to commit an offence known to the law.[124] The position is different if the defendant is asked while abroad to smuggle into the country goods which he is assured by the person making the request are goods which are actually dutiable, but which are not in fact dutiable because they are not what he believes them to be. Here the defendant's error arises solely from his misapprehension as to the nature of the goods; it is a pure error of fact. He has every intention of committing an offence on the facts as he believes them to be, and if he succeeds

---

124   This is illustrated by *Taaffe* [1984] 1 A.C. 539, where the defendant, believing that the importation of currency was prohibited, tried to smuggle several packages of what he (wrongly) believed was currency into the country. Although this made his actions "morally reprehensible", he could not be guilty of an attempt to commit any crime—there is no such crime. He had made a classic mistake of law, which was "irrelevant". See above, pp.209–218, and also pp.220–225.

in importing the goods or in getting sufficiently close to his objective, he must be liable for an attempt upon the principles which we have been considering. Fine as the distinction appears to be in these cases it is one which is in our view vital to make."

Supporters of the objective theory of attempts tend to reject such reasoning and assert that such "subjectivism" amounts to little more than punishing people for their guilty intentions. The Law Commission conceded the absurdity of there being liability in situations where a person buys legitimate goods but at such a low price that she thinks (wrongly) that they are stolen. It concluded that prosecutions would never be brought in such cases. Yet it was on broadly similar facts that a prosecution was brought in *Anderton v Ryan* forcing the House of Lords to adopt some highly innovative techniques to ensure an acquittal.

However, even the hardened "objectivist" concedes the necessity for liability in certain obvious cases. The problem is in isolating such situations.

George P. Fletcher, Rethinking Criminal Law (1978), pp.149–150, 152–154, 161–163, 165–166:

"It is agreed by all supporters of an objectivist approach to attempts that there should be no liability in the case of shooting at a tree stump with the intent to kill. Yet the courts have found liability in closely related situations . . . [A] Missouri court convicted on a charge of attempted murder for shooting at the bed where the intended victim usually slept (*State v Mitchell*, 170 Mo. 633, 71 S.W. 175 (1902)) . . . Shooting at the intended victim's bed and aiming a gun manifest the intent to kill. In shooting at a tree stump, in contrast, there is nothing in the facts to indicate that an attempt is under way. According to objectivist theory, attempting is not just an event of inner experience. It is an effort in the real world to accomplish one's objective. Therefore, when the act is aptly related to that actor's objective, the courts perceive a manifest attempt to commit an offense. Yet when the act is objectively unrelated to the intent, as in the case of shooting at a tree stump, judges and theorists properly balk at positing an act of attempting. The notion of aptness here is obviously closely related to the principle of manifest criminality . . .

[T]he problem of aptness is one of assessing whether in the long run the type of conduct involved is likely to produce harm. If the type of conduct would produce harm in the long run, then the defendant's act is apt and a punishable attempt, even though it is impossible under the circumstances . . .

The principle that inapt efforts should be exempt from liability readily explains why the courts do not discern an act of attempting in the giving of an innocuous substance as an intended poison or abortifacient.

The difficult problem in these cases is drawing the distinction between giving the intended victim an innocuous substance and giving him too small a dosage of a noxious poison. It is the distinction between trying to kill by putting sugar in his coffee and trying to kill by administering a harmless dosage of cyanide. In the latter cases, the courts have been willing to convict, and as a result we are put to the challenge to explain why sugar makes the attempt inapt but a harmless dosage of cyanide makes it apt. As we discovered in our analysis of the shooting cases, the standard of aptness does not apply to isolated events, but rather to types or classes of acts. Apt attempts belong to a class of acts that are likely to generate harm. If the class is defined as administering a dosage of cyanide or other deadly poison, there is no doubt that the class of acts is likely to generate harm, and therefore we can regard every instance of the class as an apt attempt . . .

[Dealing with the empty pocket cases] there is nothing inapt about these efforts. They are well calculated to provide a thief's income, even if it turns out that in the particular situation the bounty is not there . . .

[However for other cases, for example, cases such as *Haughton v Smith*, Fletcher suggests an alternative theory—'the test of rational motivation'.] The thesis is this: mistaken beliefs are relevant to what the actor is trying to do if they affect his incentive in acting. They affect his incentive if knowing of the mistake would give him a good reason for changing his course of conduct . . . Suppose the accused engages in sexual intercourse with a girl he takes to be under the age of consent; in fact, she is over age. Is he guilty of attempted statutory rape? In the normal case it would not be part of the actor's incentive that the girl be underage (again, one could imagine a variation in which the youth of the girl did bear upon the actor's motivation). If he is just as happy to have intercourse with a girl over age, then his mistake would not bear on his incentive and it would be incorrect to describe his act as trying to have intercourse with a girl under the age of consent . . . The thesis is that there should be liability in a case of impossibility only if the actor fails in his purpose. The only way to determine whether the actor is attempting an act that includes a particular circumstance, X, is to inquire: what would the actor do if he knew that X was not so? If he would behave in precisely the same way, we cannot say that his mistaken belief in X bears on his motivation; and if it does not, we cannot say that he is attempting to act with reference to X . . .

If applied to the cases of shooting at stumps and 'poisoning' with sugar, the test of rational motivation leads to convictions where the standard of aptness would favour an acquittal. It is obviously part of the actor's system of incentives that he believes the stump to be a person, or the dosage to be sufficient to kill. If told of the truth, he would presumably change his plans. So far as the standard of incentive is controlling, the person shooting at the stump is undoubtedly attempting to kill. The problem is whether the test of aptness should prevail over the theory of rational motivation in cases involving assaults on the core interests protected by the criminal law . . .

One reason to believe that the principle of aptness is indispensable in a comprehensive theory of attempt liability is that there is no other way to solve one case in which virtually everyone agrees that there should be no liability. That is the case of nominal efforts to inflict harm by superstitious means, say by black magic or witch-craft. The consensus of Western legal systems is that there should be no liability, regardless of the wickedness of intent, for sticking pins in a doll or chanting an incantation to banish one's enemy to the nether world. Against the background of the fears and taboos prevailing in modern Western society, objectivist theorists take these cases to be inapt attempts, therefore exempt from punishment. Yet the theory of rational motivation points in the direc-tion of liability. If the intending party knows the truth about black magic (namely, that it does not work), he would have a good reason to change his plan of attack. To account for the consensus favouring an exemption in this type of case, we need the principle of aptness to offset the implications of the competing theory of rational motivation.

The problem that remains to be resolved is determining the relative scope of these two competing theories."

Duff supports an approach broadly similar to Fletcher's theory of rational motivation. Under his view Mrs Ryan did not intend to handle a stolen video recorder as that played no motivational part in her conduct; her actions were not directed towards handling stolen goods; the fact that the goods were stolen was merely a side-effect.[125] Both of these approaches are similar to the "dominant intention" theory rejected in *Shivpuri*. The problem with these theories is that they boil down to making liabil-ity dependent on motive. This is problematic in evidential terms and questionable in moral terms. Further, as Fletcher points out, it leads to liability in the shooting at the tree-stump case. Duff rejects liability in such cases on the ground that the attack "fails so radically to engage with the world that it does not even amount to a failed attack". Fletcher's theory of aptness would similarly resolve some of these issues, but the real problem with his analysis is the failure to spell out the exact circumstances in which the theory of aptness is applicable and those in which it is appropriate to apply the theory of rational motivation.

English law has rejected the dominant intention (rational motivation) theory. The theory of aptness is broadly similar to the "objectively innocent" v "guilty acts" approach approved in *Anderton v Ryan*. This was rejected in *Shivpuri*. It is, of course, extremely difficult to capture these notions in a practica-ble statutory formulation.[126] However, it must remain questionable whether English law has adopted the right solution in ignoring these important considerations of principle and imposing liability in all these situations and then relying on prosecutorial discretion to avoid injustice.

III. CONSPIRACY

A. Introduction

Conspiracy is an inchoate crime because, like attempt, it penalises steps towards the commission of a crime. In the case of conspiracy, an *agreement* is the essence of the offence. The agreement may be

---

[125] R.A. Duff, *Criminal Attempts* (Oxford: Clarendon Press, 1996), pp.378–379.
[126] Duff, *Criminal Attempts* (1996), p.384.

to commit murder as part of a terrorist plot, to launder money derived from drug trafficking, to cause damage as part of an animal rights campaign or to publish names and information about prostitutes. It is not possible to get accurate figures about the use of conspiracy charges because of the way in which criminal statistics are compiled[127] but, impressionistically, the use of conspiracy laws appears to be increasing. It is frequently used, for example, in relation to organised crime. It is likely that one response to the threat from terrorists will be that the use of conspiracy charges will continue to increase.[128]

The law on conspiracy has been described as "the least systematic, the most irrational branch of English penal law".[129] Whilst some reform has taken place since that statement was made, it is still the case that in terms of its rationale, its content and its use, the crime of conspiracy is highly suspect. In the light of concerns about the offence, in 2006 the Government asked the Law Commission to review the law. Its report[130] recommended some important changes to conspiracy but although they have been accepted they will not be implemented.

B. Should there be a Law of Conspiracy?

Richard Card, "Reform of the Law of Conspiracy" [1973] Crim. L.R. 674 at 675–676:

"It may be asked whether it is desirable that criminal liability should attach to persons who, albeit at the time of the agreement intend to carry it out, never get beyond the stage of agreement. To take an extreme case, suppose that there is a bare agreement, the details remaining to be agreed, and that the next day the parties withdraw from their agreement; is this really conduct deserving of punishment?

It must be admitted that in practice a conviction for conspiracy in such a case will not generally be possible because of the difficulty of proving the agreement. Convictions for conspiracy usually depend on inferences from overt acts said by the prosecution to have been performed in pursuance of the agreement. In practical terms liability often arises by virtue of overt acts done in pursuance of the agreement . . . In such cases, . . . the offence of conspiracy would seem to be in part redundant. If these further acts constitute an attempt the conspirators who commit them can be convicted of attempt (to which any other conspirator would be an accomplice). On the other hand, if the further acts are insufficient to constitute an attempt, the punishment of the conspirators, both those who committed the overt acts and those who did no more than enter the agreement, can only be justified on the basis that it is the combination of persons which aggravates their conduct and produces liability

It is merely suggested that criminal liability should not attach to those who merely agree, . . . where no further steps are taken to effect it. Such a rule has been adopted in part in the Model Penal Code of the American Law Institute. Article 5.03 provides:

'Overt Act. No person may be convicted of conspiracy to commit a crime, other than a felony of the first or second degree, unless an overt act in pursuance of such conspiracy is alleged and proved to have been done by him or by a person with whom he conspired.'

Conspiracy has another rationale besides that of 'nipping crime in the bud'. This is that it is an appropriate offence to charge where a series of crimes have been committed at different times by different people pursuant to a prior agreement. The series of crimes may be so large that there would be great difficulty in indicting for all of them.

---

[127]   Inchoate offences are recorded together with the relevant substantive offence.
[128]   See, for example, *R. v Barot (Dhiren)* [2007] Crim. L.R. 741. Below p.506.
[129]   *DPP v Bhagwan* [1972] A.C. 60 at 79. The development of conspiracy from a narrowly circumscribed crime of agreeing falsely to accuse another to one where agreeing to do any unlawful act fell within its ambit, and its use, in particular, against the early trade union movement has been well documented; see G. Robertson, *Whose Conspiracy?* (Civil Liberties Trust, 1974); R. Hazell, *Conspiracy and Civil Liberties* (Bell (for the Social Administration Research Trust), 1974), pp.13–19, F. Sayre; "Criminal Conspiracy" (1922) 35 Harv. L.R. 402; R. Spicer, *Conspiracy* (London: Lawrence and Wishart, 1981).
[130]   Law Commission Paper No.318 *Conspiracy and Attempts* (2009).

In addition, each offence taken on its own may be relatively trivial but the gravity of the conduct of those involved greatly increased by viewing their acts as part of a larger criminal enterprise. These matters can be dealt with at present by the use of a conspiracy charge. Such situations may well warrant the creation of a crime which specifically deals with such completed criminal enterprises but, it is submitted, they do not justify the continued existence of a crime where liability is based on agreement and no more.

If it was accepted that there should no longer be a crime of conspiracy based on mere agreement to commit a crime, it is submitted that the criminality of acts done pursuant to that agreement (which did not result in the commission of a substantive offence) should be dealt with by the law of attempt."

Phillip Johnson, "The Unnecessary Crime of Conspiracy" (1973) 61 Cal. L. Rev. 1137 at 1157–1158:

"Conspiracy is also an inchoate or preparatory crime, permitting the punishment of persons who agree to commit a crime even if they never carry out their scheme or are apprehended before achieving their objective . . .

The Model Penal Code commentary offers perhaps the most carefully stated justification for a doctrine of conspiracy that 'reaches further back into preparatory conduct than attempt':

First: The Act of agreeing with another to commit a crime, like the act of soliciting, is concrete and unambiguous; it does not present the infinite degrees and variations possible in the general category of attempts. The danger that truly equivocal behaviour may be misinterpreted as preparation to commit a crime is minimized; purpose must be relatively firm before the commitment involved in agreement is assumed.

Second: If the agreement was to aid another to commit a crime or it otherwise encouraged its commission, it would establish complicity in the commission of the substantive offense . . . It would be anomalous to hold that conduct which would suffice to establish criminality, if something else is done by someone else is insufficient if the crime is never consummated. This is a reason, to be sure, which covers less than all the cases of conspiracy, but that it covers many is the point.

Third: In the course of preparation to commit a crime, the act of combining with another is significant both psychologically and practically, the former since it crosses a clear threshold in arousing expectations, the latter since it increases the likelihood that the offense will be committed. Sharing lends fortitude to purpose. The actor knows, moreover, that the future is no longer governed by his will alone; others may complete what he has had a hand in starting, even if he has a change of heart."

Abraham Goldstein, "Conspiracy to Defraud the United States" (1959) 68 Yale L.J. 405 at 414:

"More likely, empirical investigation would disclose that there is as much reason to believe that a large number of participants will increase the prospect that the plan will be leaked as that it will be kept secret; or that the persons involved will share their uncertainties and dissuade each other as that each will stiffen the other's determination."

Note, "The Conspiracy Dilemma: Prosecution of Group Crimes or Protection of Individual Defendants" (1948) 62 Harv. L. Rev. 276 at 283–284:

"Several factors, seldom articulated by the courts, seem to underlie this concept of the unique criminality of group action. Basic is the increased danger to the public welfare and safety that exists in the combination of united wills to effect a harmful object, as contrasted with the menace of the criminal purpose of a single individual. Reliance on the co-operation of co-conspirators and the intent to support and aid them in the future increases the likelihood of criminal conduct on the part of individual conspirators. And it is more difficult to guard against the antisocial designs of a group of persons than those of an individual. Thus, the crucial importance of the conspiracy weapon stems from its effectiveness in reaching organized crime. The advantages of division of labor and complex organization characteristic of modern economic society have their counterparts in many forms of criminal activity. Manufacture or importation and distribution of contraband goods, for example, often demands a complicated organization. The interrelations of the parties in schemes to defraud may be highly complex. Except for the conspiracy device, society would be without protection until the criminal object is actually executed or at least sufficiently approached to become indictable as an attempt; and even then often only the actual perpetrator and perhaps his immediate accessories could be reached. Through the conspiracy dragnet, all participants in gang operations, the catspaw and his principal, those who contribute from afar as well as the immediate actors can be punished often before the evil design has fully matured into the criminal act."

The arguments for retaining a crime of conspiracy can thus be grouped into three main strands:

1. The prevention of crime including, increasingly, the assistance of intelligence-led policing: if these are now regarded as key objectives (the view taken by the Law Commission[131]) then it would seem to follow that the agreement should be to do something that would be *criminal* if completed. As we shall see, the Criminal Law Act 1977 only partially succeeded in reducing conspiracy to this formula. But these justifications depend to a significant degree on the ambit of other inchoate offences. If English law had adopted the substantial step test[132] for determining the extent of action required for an attempt, this justification for conspiracy would have been undermined: in most cases the only evidence of the agreement will be overt acts that could have satisfied the substantial step test. However, this test has not been adopted by English law (instead requiring the defendant to have done acts that are more than merely preparatory to the commission of the offence) and until very recently, therefore, it was possible, in crime prevention terms, to justify a crime of conspiracy. With the introduction of three new inchoate offences dealing with encouraging or assisting crime in the Serious Crime Act 2007[133] the crime prevention rationale has again come under scrutiny, although the Law Commission has rejected the argument that these offences are so broad that conspiracy, as a preventative tool, has become redundant on the ground that it facilitates 'the effective use of intelligence-led policing'.[134] Despite this, the fact that large numbers of conspiracy charges are brought *after* the crime has been completed[135] does support the view that other justifications are increasingly important in responding to serious crime.[136]

2. The "full story" rationale: a conspiracy charge enables a number of crimes, which may or may not be serious in themselves, to be brought before the court in their "true" light.[137] It enables larger numbers of those involved to be held responsible. However, this largely ignores the role of the law relating to complicity and may lead to the conspiracy charge being abused.[138]

3. The "general danger" rationale: that people working in concert with one another are more dangerous than lone actors. Not only are they able to commit more complex crimes but they will be more likely to carry out their intentions. It is this argument which enabled conspiracy to develop so as to embrace an agreement with others to do an act, such as trespass, which was not in itself criminal and while this is no longer the law, this claim remains problematic. However, it is notable that the Law Commission's recent defence of conspiracy is influenced by research which lends some support to this justification: conspiracy may be justified on an economic basis (it permits a specialisation of labour)

---

131   Law Commission Consultation Paper No.183, *Conspiracy and Attempts* (2007), paras 2.4–2.10. See also Law Commission Paper No.76, *Conspiracy and Criminal Law Reform* (1976), para.1.5.

132   Above, p.472.

133   Replacing the common-law offence of incitement, pp.521–535.

134   Law Commission Consultation Paper No.183, *Conspiracy and Attempts* (2007), para.2.9.

135   There is no bar under English law to bringing conspiracy charges when the offence has been completed (they do not "merge"), but it is bad practice: Practice Direction [1977] 2 All E.R. 540. The prosecution has to justify to the judge the inclusion of the conspiracy count and if the judge is not satisfied then the prosecution has to elect to proceed with either the conspiracy or the substantive count.

136   This extends beyond organised or terrorist crimes. In *Skidmore* [2009] Crim. L.R. 42 a conviction for conspiracy was upheld when the substantive offence of preventing a lawful and decent burial of a child had occurred.

137   See, for example, *R. v Dove (Matthew Jonathon)* [2005] EWCA Crim 1982 where 12 robberies were committed by the defendants within a short space of time.

138   In *R. v Barratt (Paul Henry)* [1996] Crim. L.R. 495, for example, the court felt that the evidence fell far short of establishing a single conspiracy extending over two years to burgle houses. As Smith comments (at p.497) the idea was "utterly far-fetched".

and a psychological basis (where a group loyalty and solidarity develops), both of which advance the criminal purpose.[139]

One has to conclude that conspiracy is used as more than an inchoate crime.[140] The reality is that its use, when the crime has been completed, brings substantial advantages for the prosecution. Not only does it provide the prosecution with another chance of securing a conviction where the evidence relating to the completed crime is doubtful, but there are evidential benefits as well.[141] As we shall see, some doubt over the continued attractiveness to prosecutors of conspiracy charges, where the crime has occurred, has been cast by the House of Lords' decision in *Saik*.[142] In this case Lord Hope refers to the device of bringing conspiracy charges where the crime has been completed as "trying to fit a square peg into a round hole"[143]: the crime was not designed to be used in this way.

As with attempts, a conspiracy, if charged when the offence has not been completed, causes no actual harm. Bearing in mind the discussion of the rationale of the law of attempt, two questions need to be considered. Do conspiracies pose a "second order" harm—in the sense of posing a threat to security? Alternatively, is the blameworthiness of a conspirator so great as to justify dispensing with the requirement of harm which is normally required for the imposition of criminal liability? Or are there (and can there ever be) sufficient utilitarian arguments to justify dispensing with the requirement of harm?

C. Punishment of Conspiracies

At common law the punishment of those convicted of conspiracy was at the discretion of the court.[144] In the case of those conspiracies which now fall within s.1 of the Criminal Law Act 1977, punishment is limited to the maximum sentence for the complete crime which the defendants conspired to commit.[145] In the case of common law conspiracies to defraud, the maximum sentence has been reduced to 10 years.[146]

Sir Rupert Cross and Andrew Ashworth; The English Sentencing System, 3rd edn (1981), p.156:

"Conspiracies might, however, be regarded as more serious crimes than attempts. Indeed, at common law it was held in *Verrier v Director of Public Prosecutions* ([1967] 2 A.C. 195) that some conspiracies might call for a greater punishment than could be imposed for the completed offence. Although s.3 of the Criminal Law Act now prohibits courts from exceeding the statutory maximum for the completed offence in conspiracy cases, a court still might wish to visit conspirators with more severe punishment than it would mete out to an individual committing the completed offence, whilst keeping within the statutory maximum. The argument is that the nature of the offence is exceptionally changed by the co-operation of large numbers in its commission, because of the greater

---

[139]   Law Commission Consultation Paper No.183, *Conspiracy and Attempts* (2007), paras 2.11–2.20.

[140]   The Government's White Paper, *One Step Ahead: A 21st Century Strategy to Defeat Organised Crime* (Cmnd.6167, 2004) even contemplated changing the link between conspiracy and certain predicate (underlying) crimes as part of its strategy to respond to organised crime (para.6.1).

[141]   The normal rule of evidence, for example, that prevents the statements of one co-defendant being used against another does not apply in conspiracy trials. See further, Law Commission Consultation Paper No.183, *Conspiracy and Attempts* (2007), paras 2.20–2.21.

[142]   *R. v Saik (Abdulrahman)* [2007] 1 A.C. 18. Note that the Law Commission's recommendations are designed to remove the barrier erected by *Saik*: below p.512.

[143]   *Saik* [2007] 1 A.C. 18 at [41].

[144]   This is still true in relation to the imposition of fines by the Crown Court (Criminal Law Act 1977 s.3(1)).

[145]   Criminal Law Act 1977 s.3(3).

[146]   Criminal Justice Act 1987 s.12.

chance of the occasioning of alarm and of the use of force. In fraud cases, the co-operation of different people in different places may facilitate both the execution and the concealment of the design. These considerations go to show that any offence, whether inchoate or completed, which is committed by a number of people acting in concert may be viewed as presenting a greater social danger than the same offence committed by an individual. On general deterrent grounds the sentence for 'group' offences may therefore be longer. Sentences for rape by gangs are on this account higher than those for rape by an individual."

Consider, again, the discussion of the punishment for attempts and the significance of harm. It can be argued that those considerations have even greater force here if what is being punished is an agreement (that goes no further) to commit a crime. However, although the "dangerousness of col-laboration argument" might be thought to be a weak one, it has certainly become more significant in a post-9/11 world; for example, in *Barot (Dhiren)* the defendant was given a life sentence with a minimum term of 30 years after having pleaded guilty to conspiring to commit mass murder in the United Kingdom and the United States.[147] In relation to conspiracies where the crime has been com-pleted (or where it has failed) there are different concerns. For evidential reasons the prosecution may fail to prove the complete crime but manage to secure a conviction for conspiracy. If the essence of the crime is the *agreement*, tempting though it might be to look beyond it in sentencing, this would amount to punishing somebody for something that has not been proven.

D. The Law

1. Types of conspiracy

At common law a conspiracy was an agreement between two or more persons "to do an unlawful act, or to do a lawful act by unlawful means".[148] Thus it was not necessary to prove that there was an agreement to commit a crime; agreements to commit other "unlawful acts", such as fraud, some torts or corruption of public morals, clearly sufficed. For instance, in *Kamara v DPP*[149] an agreement to commit the tort of trespass to land, if accompanied by an intention to inflict more than merely nominal damage, was held to be a criminal conspiracy. Of course, it was virtually impossible to justify making it a crime to agree to do something that if actually done by one person acting alone would not have been criminal. Accordingly, the Criminal Law Act 1977 sought to limit conspiracy primarily to agreements to commit crimes. However, fearing that gaps might be created, and pending a comprehensive review of the law of fraud, obscenity and indecency, s.5 preserved certain common law conspiracies. We are thus left with the following rather unsatisfactory situation:

(1)   There are agreements to commit a crime. These are termed statutory conspiracies and are governed by the provisions of s.1 of the Criminal Law Act 1977.

(2)   There are common law conspiracies governed by the old common law rules. Under s.5 of the Criminal Law Act 1977, two species of common law conspiracy have been preserved. These are conspiracy to defraud and conspiracy to corrupt public morals or outrage public decency. Commentators have been saying since 1977 that these retentions were designed to be temporary. In 2002, the Law Commission proposed the abolition of the crime of conspiracy to defraud.[150]

---

[147]   *R. v Barot (Dhiren)* [2007] Crim. L.R. 741. The trial judge had imposed a minimum term of 40 years but the Court of Appeal found this to be manifestly excessive, arguing that such sentences were to be reserved for a terrorist convicted "of a serious attempt to commit mass murder by a viable method" (at p.743).

[148]   *Mulcahy* (1868) L.R. 3 H.L. 306.

[149]   *Kamara v DPP* [1974] A.C. 104.

[150]   Law Commission Paper No.276, *Fraud* (2002).

However, the Fraud Act 2006 does not give effect to this recommendation. Moreover, a recent report by the Ministry of Justice concludes that conspiracy to defraud works well alongside the Fraud Act and is an essential tool in combatting fraud.[151] It is now considered to be far too useful a charge to prosecutors where there are multiple offences[152] (especially if more than one jurisdiction is involved) to abolish it.

2. Common law conspiracies

(i) Conspiracy to defraud

Section 5(2) of the Criminal Law Act 1977 provides that common law rules continue to apply "so far as relates to conspiracy to defraud". Two issues need to be addressed: the relationship between this common law conspiracy and statutory conspiracy and the width of this offence.[153]

(a) *Relationship to statutory conspiracy*

Common law conspiracies to defraud will usually involve agreements to commit crimes. At one stage the House of Lords took the view that any conspiracy which involved an agreement to commit a crime had to be dealt with under the Criminal Law Act 1977 rather than the common law.[154] This caused the prosecution considerable difficulties with both indictments and convictions for common law conspiracy being quashed when belatedly it was realised that the agreement was to commit an offence. The position now is that defendants may be charged with either offence in such cases.[155]

(b) *Width of the offence*

In *Scott v Metropolitan Police Commr.*, the leading case on conspiracy to defraud, the House of Lords stated:

> "[I]t is clearly the law that an agreement by two or more by dishonesty to deprive a person of something which is his or to which he is or would be or might be entitled and an agreement by two or more by dishonesty to injure some proprietary right of his, suffices to constitute the offence of conspiracy to defraud."[156]

The following points need to be made in relation to this definition:

As indicated above, it embraces agreements to do an act which would not be an offence if completed. In 2002, the Law Commission provided an extensive list of conduct that could be prosecuted only as conspiracy to defraud.[157] Since then, however, the Fraud Act 2006 has expanded the reach of the law of completed offences. From the original list it would appear that only the following forms of conduct will not amount to the offence of fraud and so can only be prosecuted as conspiracy to defraud:

---

[151] Ministry of Justice, *Post-Legislative Assessment of the Fraud Act 2006, Memorandum to the Justice Select Committee* (2012, Cm. 8372), paras 36–38.

[152] See, for example, *Mba* [2006] All E.R. (D) 73. In this case, the defendants were convicted on a single charge of conspiracy to defraud which involved many transactions, using false identities to obtain loans, withdraw cash or transfer money.

[153] For further details of conspiracy to defraud, see A.T.H. Smith, *Property Offences* (Oxford: OUP, 1994), Ch.19.

[154] *R. v Ayres (David Edward)* [1984] A.C. 447.

[155] Criminal Justice Act 1987 s.12. For guidelines on when to charge conspiracy to defraud, see *http://www.cps.gov.uk/legal/h_to_k/inchoate_offences/* [Accessed June 9, 2014].

[156] *Scott v Commissioner of Police of the Metropolis* [1975] A.C. 819 at 840.

[157] Law Commission Paper No.276, *Fraud* (2002), paras 4.5–4.59.

(i)   dishonestly obtaining a benefit which does not amount to property or services (as defined in the Fraud Act 2006) for example, obtaining confidential information;

(ii) deception without an intention to obtain a gain, or cause a loss, but which prejudices another's financial interests;

(iii) deception for a non-financial purpose; and

(iv) "fixing" an event on which bets have been placed.

In general, there need be no deception or false representation in order for the offence to be committed. In *Scott*, for example, the defendant agreed with employees of cinema owners temporarily to remove films so that he could make pirate copies which could be distributed commercially. There was no deception played on the owners who were unaware of what was happening. The House of Lords rejected the idea that deception was a necessary ingredient of the offence. There must, of course, be dishonesty. However, the offence is so broad that many activities that would otherwise be legitimate can become fraudulent if the conduct is regarded as dishonest. As the Law Commission points out:

> "In a capitalist society, commercial life revolves around the pursuit of gain for oneself and, as a corollary, others may lose out, whether directly or indirectly. Such behaviour is perfectly legitimate. It is only the element of 'dishonesty' which renders it a criminal fraud."[158]

Despite the width of the offence, there are some limits. In *GG (Plc)*, for example, in relation to a prosecution brought by the Serious Fraud Office, the House of Lords refused to accept that a large-scale price-fixing agreement amounted to a conspiracy to defraud even though it had been conducted secretly and, arguably, dishonestly. As a price-fixing agreement (prior to introduction of the cartel offence in s.188 of the Enterprise Act 2002) was not criminal, aggravating factors such as misrepresentation needed to be proved upon which a conspiracy to defraud charge could be based.[159]

It is clear that there is no requirement that actual economic loss be involved as long as the victim's economic interests are put at risk.[160]

> "If the economic or proprietary interests of some other person are imperilled, that is sufficient to constitute fraud even though no loss is actually suffered and even though the fraudsman himself did not desire to bring about any loss."[161]

Theoretically, at least, the agreed offence needs to be one that will be committed by the parties to the agreement,[162] yet in practice it appears to be irrelevant that third parties will effect the defrauding.[163]

It now seems settled that there need be no intent to defraud in the sense of intending to cause another economic loss. The Privy Council has held that it is sufficient if the conspirators have dishonestly agreed to do something

---

158   Law Commission Paper No.276, *Fraud* (2002), para.3.6.
159   *R. v GG Plc* [2008] UKHL 17. See also *Norris v United States* [2008] 1 A.C. 920.
160   *R. v Allsop (Anthony Adward)* (1977) 64 Cr. App. R. 29.
161   *Wai Yu-Tsang v The Queen* [1992] 1 A.C. 269 (trial judge's direction approved on appeal by the Privy Council). See also *Adams v The Queen* [1995] 2 Cr. App. R. 295.
162   The rule contained in s.1(1)(a) is meant to be a restatement of the common law.
163   *R. v Hollinshead (Peter Gordon)* [1985] A.C. 975. This decision is rightly criticised by the Law Commission Paper No.300, *Inchoate Liability for Assisting and Encouraging Crime* (2006), paras 3.15–3.17. The new inchoate offence of encouraging or assisting crime should obviate the need for conspiracy to defraud to be distorted in this way.

"which they realise will or may deceive the victim into so acting, or failing to act, that he will suffer economic loss or his economic interests will be put at risk".[164]

The defendants may not wish to harm the victim (they may even think they are acting with the best of motives)[165] but if they intend to bring about the state of affairs realising that the victim's interests could be put at risk, they will be guilty.

Finally, conspiracy to defraud is not limited to situations where economic loss is involved or risked. It is also a conspiracy to defraud to agree dishonestly to deceive a public official into acting contrary to his public duties.[166]

(ii) Conspiracy to corrupt public morals or outrage public decency

Section 5(3) of the Criminal Law Act 1977 provides that the common law rules continue to apply to conspiracies to corrupt public morals or outrage public decency provided that the object of the agreement does not amount to a crime. At the time it was unclear whether outraging public decency and corrupting public morals were criminal offences in their own right although the Law Commission was of the view that they probably were.[167] The issue is now settled in relation to outraging public decency which is recognised as an offence by s.320 of the Criminal Justice Act 2003. Accordingly, charges of conspiracy to outrage public decency will now be brought under the Criminal Law Act 1977 as statutory conspiracies.

The position is still unclear with regard to conspiracy to corrupt public morals. The House of Lords' decision of *Shaw v DPP*, in which the defendant agreed to (and did) publish a "Ladies' Directory" advertising information about named prostitutes, affirmed the existence of the offence of conspiracy to corrupt public morals.[168] It did not resolve the issue of whether there is a substantive offence of corrupting public morals.[169]

Where does this leave us? Where the agreement involves a criminal offence (for example, under the Obscene Publications Act 1959) statutory conspiracy should be charged rather than conspiracy to corrupt public morals. There may well be gaps, however, where no criminal offence is involved and conspiracy to corrupt public morals currently occupies this space. This could be supported provided its use was confined to circumstances which "the jury might find to be destructive to the very fabric of society"[170] rather than being used for conduct which, by current standards of ordinary decent people, is mildly offensive. On the other hand, it is extremely difficult to justify the criminalisation of an agreement to do something which, if actually done, would not be criminal.

---

[164] *Wai Yu-Tsang* [1992] 1 A.C. 269 at 280.

[165] As in the case of *Wai Yu-Tsang* where one of the conspirators thought he was acting in the defrauded bank's best interests by trying to prevent a run on it.

[166] *Wai Yu-Tsang* [1992] 1 A.C. 269 at 280; *R. v Moses and Ansbro* [1991] Crim. L.R. 617; *DPP v Withers* [1975] A.C. 842; *Board of Trade v Owen* [1957] A.C. 602; *Welham v DPP* [1961] A.C. 103.

[167] Law Commission Paper No.76 (1976), paras 3.21–3.24.

[168] *Shaw v DPP* [1962] A.C. 220. *Shaw* is an important decision for a further reason. Lord Simmonds, in particular, seemed to be of the view that the judiciary had a residual power to create new criminal offences to deal with new situations. This view was firmly rejected in the subsequent decision of *Knuller (Publishing, Printing and Promotions) Ltd v DPP* [1973] A.C. 435.

[169] Although this was the view of the Court of Criminal Appeal, the House of Lords did not decide this point. The case of *R. v Gibson (Richard Norman)* (1990) 91 Cr. App. R. 341 lends some support to the view that there is an offence of corrupting public morals.

[170] Per Lord Simon in *Knuller v DPP* [1973] A.C. 435 at 491.

3. Statutory conspiracy

(i) Definition

Criminal Law Act 1977 s.1

"(1) Subject to the following provisions of this Part of this Act, if a person agrees with any other person or persons that a course of conduct shall be pursued which, if the agreement is carried out in accordance with their intentions, either—

(a) will necessarily amount to or involve the commission of any offence or offences by one or more of the parties to the agreement, or

(b) would do so but for the existence of facts which render the commission of the offence or any of the offences impossible,

he is guilty of conspiracy to commit the offence or offences in question.

(2) Where liability for any offence may be incurred without knowledge on the part of the person committing it of any particular fact or circumstance necessary for the commission of the offence, a person shall nevertheless not be guilty of conspiracy to commit that offence by virtue of subsection (1) above unless he and at least one other party to the agreement intend or know that that fact or circumstances shall or will exist at the time when the conduct constituting the offence is to take place."

(ii) Agreement

There must be an agreement between at least two persons. There must have been a meeting of minds; decisions must have been communicated between the parties[171] although it is not necessary that each conspirator is aware of all the details of the conspiracy as long as there is a shared common purpose.[172]

There must, of course, be at least two parties to the agreement. However, s.2(2) (a) provides that a husband and wife cannot be liable for conspiracy, if they are the only parties to the agreement.[173] This provision was extended to civil partners by the Civil Partnership Act 2004.[174] The Law Commission has proposed abolishing the archaic marital exception.[175] The Act also provides that a person cannot be liable if the only other party to the "agreement" is a person under the age of criminal responsibility (s.2(2)(b)) or is the intended victim of the offence (s.2(2)(c)). 'Victim' is not defined in the Act but its meaning has now been considered by the Supreme Court in *Gnango*[176] where Lord Phillips argued that a narrow interpretation should be given to the word whereby 'victim' is confined to persons of a class the law intends to protect, otherwise:

"If . . . [victim] is given the wide meaning it would seem to produce the surprising result that a conspiracy by two persons that one will commit a terrorist atrocity as a suicide bomber, or set fire to

---

[171] *R. v Scott (Valerie)* (1979) 68 Cr. App. R. 164. Parties does not include someone who is the intended victim of the offence (s.2(1)).

[172] *R. v Fritzl (Jaqueline)* [2011] EWCA Crim 1220; *Griffiths* (1969) 49 Cr. App. R. 279. Even if there is sufficient evidence to point to an agreement having been made, if there is no credible evidence that it is anything other than a "fantasy", there can be no conspiracy: in *R. v G* [2012] EWCA Crim 1756 it stated that an "executory intent" is needed.

[173] This confirms the common law decision of *Mawji v The Queen* [1957] A.C. 126. See *R. v Chrastny (Charlotte Barbara) (No.1)* [1992] 1 All E.R. 189 and *R. v Singh (Harbans)* [2011] EWCA Crim 2992.

[174] Schedule 27. The Marriage (Same Sex Couples) Act 2013 s11 and Sch 3, Part 1, on a date to be appointed, will extend this provision to parties to a same-sex marriage.

[175] Law Commission Paper No.318 *Conspiracy and Attempts* (2009), paras 5.7–5.16.

[176] *Gnango* [2011] UKSC 59.

a house owned by one of them in furtherance of some ulterior motive, would appear not to subject either to criminal liability."[177]

Although obiter, it would seem likely that this approach would be followed if the issue were to come before a court. It also accords with the recommendation of the Law Commission that the exemption should be abolished for the non-victim conspirator but be retained for the victim where the conspiracy is to commit an offence which exists for the protection of a class of persons to which the victim belongs.[178] This would bring the law in line with the provisions in the Serious Crime Act 2007 and complicity.[179]

As the law stands, it would thus appear that there *can* be liability if the defendant conspires with any other person having a defence (say insanity) other than the above, provided that such person is capable of reaching an *agreement* with the defendant.[180] Where a defendant and others are charged with conspiracy and those others are acquitted, s.5(8) provides that the defendant may nevertheless be convicted "unless under all the circumstances of the case his conviction is inconsistent with the acquittal of the other person or persons in question".[181] This is sensible. There may be evidence admissible against the defendant that he conspired with A and B, but that evidence might not be admissible against A or B. Alternatively, it might be clear that he conspired with either A or B, but it is not certain which one it was. A and B must be given the benefit of the doubt and acquitted, but there is no reason why the defendant, whose guilt is beyond doubt, should be offered the same indulgence.[182]

(iii) Object of agreement

There must be an agreement that:

(a) a course of conduct be pursued,

(b) which if carried out in accordance with their intentions,

(c) will necessarily amount to (or involve) a crime.

Each of the phrases will now be examined in turn.

(a) *Course of conduct be pursued*

The phrase "course of conduct" here does not refer purely to physical actions, but must be taken to include intended consequences—in short, the plan. This point is best illustrated with an example. Suppose two persons agree to place a bomb under another's car and detonate the bomb so as to kill the owner. The physical course of conduct agreed to, namely, the physical actions of planting the

---

[177] *Gnango* [2011] UKSC 59 at [49].
[178] Law Commission Paper No.318 *Conspiracy and Attempts* (2009), paras 5.7–5.16.d., paras 5.17–5.35. The Law Commission also recommends retention of the exemption for a child conspirator under the age of 10 (paras 5.36–5.45). However, the other adult co-conspirator could be prosecuted for encouraging the formation of a conspiracy under the Serious Crime Act 2007 s.44.
[179] Section 51. Below p.533 and 590.
[180] This confirms the common law decision of *Duguid* (1906) 75 L.J. K.B. 470.
[181] This was already the position at common law in relation to separate trials (*DPP v Shannon* [1975] A.C. 717), but reverses the common law position in relation to joint trials (*R. v Thompson, Tillotson and Maddock* (1851) 16 Q.B. 832; *R. v Coughlan (Joseph John)* (1977) 64 Cr. App. R. 11).
[182] See, for example, *R. v Testouri (Adel Ben)* [2004] 2 Cr. App. R. 4 and *R. v Austin (Alan Brian)* [2011] EWCA Crim 345. See further, *R. v Mehta (Subhash)* [2012] EWCA Crim 2824 and *R. v Shillam (Wayne Lee)* [2013] EWCA Crim 160.

bomb, will not necessarily amount to the crime because the bomb may never go off. However, if the *plan* is carried out according to their intentions, the bomb will explode and the owner of the car will be killed. This necessarily amounts to a crime; killing someone in such circumstances is murder. The Law Commission has confirmed that this is the correct interpretation of the current law.[183]

To say that the agreed course of conduct includes the planned consequences is also a limiting qualification. Only planned consequences can be included within the agreed course of conduct. Thus, as stated in *Siracusa*,[184] an agreement to cause grievous bodily harm is not sufficient to support a charge of conspiracy to murder even though an intention to cause grievous bodily harm is sufficient to support a charge of murder itself. In *Siracusa* it was held that although a person smuggling heroin could be convicted of a substantive offence if she thought that they were smuggling cannabis, the same was not true on a conspiracy charge: "the essence of the crime of conspiracy was the agreement and, in simple terms, one did not prove an agreement to import heroin by proving an agreement to import cannabis".[185] The basis of this decision is that heroin and cannabis are different class drugs, involving separate offences. In *Broad*[186] it was held to be immaterial that one conspirator thought heroin was to be produced while the other thought it would be cocaine. Both are Class A drugs; they had agreed to commit the same offence. It is further submitted that planned consequences mean intended consequences. If arson is planned between conspirators who are reckless as to whether anyone is killed during their fire, the death of those persons is not part of their plan. One does not plan for and intend an event possibly happening. Intention here, of course, should bear the same meaning as in other areas of law—bearing in mind that such intention may be inferred or established from foresight of a consequence as virtually certain.

The planned course of conduct also includes (and only includes) *intended* or *known* surrounding circumstances.[187] This phrase came under intense scrutiny in relation to conspiracies to traffic drugs[188] or to launder money. Under s.93C(2) of the Criminal Justice Act 1988 defendants could be convicted of money laundering if they knew or *had reasonable grounds to suspect* that the property was the proceeds of crime.[189] Controversially, the Court of Appeal held that where defendants were charged with conspiracy to launder money, the prosecution need only establish that the defendant suspected (rather than knew) that the money was the proceeds of crime in order to convict.[190] This approach was ended by the following important decision.

R. v Saik [2007] 1 A.C. 18 (House of Lords)

The facts appear from the judgment.

LORD NICHOLLS:

"[1] This appeal raises questions about the ingredients of the statutory offence of conspiracy and their application in the circumstances of this case. Shorn of its complexities the context is a charge of conspiracy to launder money

---

[183]   Law Commission Paper No.318 *Conspiracy and Attempts* (2009), para.2.13.
[184]   *Siracusa* (1989) 90 Cr. App. R. 340.
[185]   This was confirmed in *R. v Taylor (Robert John)* [2002] Crim. L.R. 205.
[186]   *Broad* [1997] Crim. L.R. 666.
[187]   Section 1(2). On its actual wording s.1(2) appears to be limited to crimes of strict liability but, as *Saik* [2007] A.C. 18 makes clear, it cannot mean this.
[188]   Drug Trafficking Act 1994 s.49(2).
[189]   Both this provision and s.49(2) of the Drug Trafficking Act 1994 have now been repealed and replaced by the Proceeds of Crime Act 2002. The issue of suspicion does not arise with the new offences under the Act.
[190]   See *Sakavickas* [2005] 1 Cr. App. R. 584; *R. v Singh (Gulbir Rana)* [2003] EWCA Crim 3712; *R. v Rizvi (Zafar)* [2003] EWCA Crim 3575.

brought against the Appellant, Mr Abdulrahman Saik. He operated a bureau de change in London, near Marble Arch. At his trial he pleaded guilty, subject to the qualification that he did not know the money was the proceeds of crime. He only suspected this was so. This qualified plea was accepted. The issue before your Lordships is whether the offence to which the Appellant pleaded guilty is an offence known to law. Reasonable grounds for suspicion are enough for the substantive offence of laundering money. But are they enough for a conspiracy to commit that offence?

[2] The mental ingredient in the statutory offence of conspiracy has given rise to difficulty. Some of the case law is confusing, and the academic commentators do not always speak with one voice . . .

[4] . . . [T]he mental element of the offence, apart from the mental element involved in making an agreement, comprises the intention to pursue a course of conduct which will necessarily involve commission of the crime in question by one or more of the conspirators. The conspirators must intend to do the act prohibited by the substantive offence. The conspirators' state of mind must also satisfy the mental ingredients of the substantive offence. If one of the ingredients of the substantive offence is that the act is done with a specific intent, the conspirators must intend to do the prohibited act and must intend to do the prohibited act with the prescribed intent . . .

[6] Section 1(2) qualifies the scope of the offence created by section 1(1). This subsection is more difficult. Its essential purpose is to ensure that strict liability and recklessness have no place in the offence of conspiracy . . .

[7] Under this subsection conspiracy involves a third mental element: intention or knowledge that a fact or circumstances necessary for the commission of the substantive offence will exist . . .

[8] It follows from this requirement of intention or knowledge that proof of the mental element needed for the commission of the substantive offence will not always suffice on a charge of conspiracy to commit that offence. In respect of a material fact or circumstance conspiracy has its own mental element. In conspiracy this mental element is set as high as 'intend or know' . . . In this respect the mental element of conspiracy is distinct from and supersedes the mental element in the substantive offence . . .

[13] The rationale underlying this approach is that conspiracy imposes criminal liability on the basis of a person's intention. This is a different harm from the commission of the substantive offence. So it is right that the intention which is being criminalized in the offence of conspiracy should itself be blameworthy. This should be so, irrespective of the provisions of the substantive offence.

[14] Against this background I turn to some issues concerning the scope and effect of section 1(2). The starting point is to note that this relieving provision is not confined to substantive offences attracting strict liability. The subsection does not so provide. Nor would such an interpretation of the subsection make sense. It would make no sense for section 1(2) to apply, and only require proof of intention or knowledge, where liability for the substantive offence is absolute but not where the substantive offence has built into it a mental ingredient less than knowledge, such as suspicion.

[15] So much is clear. A more difficult question arises where an ingredient of the substantive offence is that the defendant must know of a material fact or circumstance. On its face section 1(2) does not apply in this case. The opening words of section 1(2), on their face, limit the scope of the subsection to cases where a person may commit an offence without knowledge of a material fact or circumstance.

[16] Plainly Parliament did not intend that a person would be liable for conspiracy where he lacks the knowledge required to commit the substantive offence. That could not be right. Parliament could not have intended such an absurd result. Rather, the assumption underlying section 1(2) is that, where knowledge of a material fact is an ingredient of a substantive offence, knowledge of that fact is also an ingredient of the crime of conspiring to commit the substantive offence.

[17] There are two ways this result might be achieved. One is simply to treat section 1(2) as inapplicable in this type of case . . .

[18] The other route is to adopt the interpretation of section 1(2) suggested by Sir John Smith. The suggestion is that section 1(2) applies despite the opening words of the subsection . . .

[19] The first route accords more easily with the language of section 1(2), but I prefer the second route for the following reason. A conspiracy is looking to the future. It is an agreement about future conduct. When the agreement is made the 'particular fact or circumstance necessary for the commission' of the substantive offence may not have happened. So the conspirator cannot be said to know of the fact or circumstance at that time. Nor, if the happening of the fact or circumstance is beyond his control, can it be said that the conspirator will know of that fact or circumstance.

[20] Section 1(2) expressly caters for this situation. The conspirator must 'intend or know' that this fact or circumstance 'shall or will exist' when the conspiracy is carried into effect. Although not the happiest choice of language, 'intend' is descriptive of a state of mind which is looking to the future . . . Thus on a charge of conspiracy

to handle stolen property where the property has not been identified when the agreement is made, the prosecution must prove that the conspirator intended that the property which was the subject of the conspiracy would be stolen property . . .

[23] . . . [In relation to conspiracy to launder money his Lordship continued] Hence, where the property has not been identified when the conspiracy agreement is reached, the prosecution must prove that the defendant intended that the property would be the proceeds of criminal conduct . . .

[25] What, however, if the property to which the conspiracy relates was specifically identified when the conspirators made their agreement? In that event the prosecution must prove the conspirators 'knew' the property was the proceeds of crime. This is the next point of difficulty with the interpretation of section 1(2). [D]oes 'know' in this context mean 'believe'? . . .

[26] I do not think . . . [this] approach can be accepted. The phrase under consideration ('intend or know') in section 1(2) is a provision of general application to all conspiracies. In this context the word 'know' should be interpreted strictly and not watered down. In this context knowledge means true belief . . .

[30] From what has been said above, it is evident that this conviction cannot stand. Suspicion is not sufficient in respect of a fact to which section 1(2) applies. Knowledge or intention regarding the provenance of the property must be proved or admitted."

Appeal allowed

This decision settles, for now at least, a number of the interpretative difficulties which had plagued s.1(2). We now know that s.1(2) applies to conspiracies to commit all offences. This is clearly right. We also know that mere suspicion will not suffice and that intention or knowledge must be proved. As Ormerod has commented,

"In this respect the offence of conspiracy is stricter than that of attempt where the courts have accepted that recklessness as to circumstances is a sufficient *mens rea* where that would suffice for the substantive crime attempted. This is not objectionable or illogical, it is submitted, since conspiracy is a distinct crime reflecting a different wrong from that involved in attempt."[191]

So much is clear from *Saik*. Beyond this, however, as the Law Commission has commented, their Lordships held different views as to what would constitute "knowledge".[192] Further, although Lord Nicholls distinguished between agreements relating to identified and as yet unidentified property (when in the latter case, the appropriate word for prosecutors to use would be "intend" and not "knowledge"), this distinction could give rise to difficulties.[193]

This more rigorous interpretation of the elements of conspiracy has the potential of reducing its usefulness to prosecutors where the completed crime has taken place.[194] It was to be anticipated, therefore, that in light of *Saik* the Government would ask the Law Commission to review the law of conspiracy.

---

[191] D. Ormerod, "Conspiracy: Conspiracy to Launder Money" [2006] Crim. L.R. 998 at 1001. See more generally, D. Ormerod, "Making Sense of Statutory Conspiracies" (2006) C.L.P. 277.

[192] Law Commission Paper No.318 *Conspiracy and Attempts* (2009), para.2.64. One issue is whether knowledge here can include wilful blindness. For a recent application of *Saik*, see *Ahmed* [2013] EWCA Crim 1755.

[193] need, for example, whether a property's status is to be established objectively or whether the particular conspirators need to have identified the property is unclear.

[194] There was also concern that *Saik* would lead to a large number of appeals by defendants convicted under the old law. However, in *R. v R (Amer)* [2006] EWCA Crim 1974 (where the Court of Appeal heard seven appeals together) it was held that, although such convictions were unsafe in the light of *Saik*, leave to appeal out of time would not be granted as no injustice had been done to any of those convicted. In all cases there was evidence that would have convicted them of the substantive offences. See further, D. Ormerod, "Proceeds of Crime: Conspiracy—Mens Rea" [2007] Crim. L.R. 79 and *R. v Suchedina (Hasnain)* [2007] Crim. L.R. 301 (and commentary thereto).

Law Commission, Conspiracy and Attempts (Consultation Paper No. 183) (2007), paras 4.107-4.108:

"4.107 As a matter of statutory interpretation, on the facts the correct conclusion was reached by the majority of the House of Lords in *Saik*. As Lord Nicholls noted, '[a] decision to deal with money suspected to be the proceeds of crime is not the same as a conscious decision to deal with the proceeds of crime.' Only the latter behaviour is prohibited on the correct construction of section 1(2).

4.108 However, in our view, this reading of section 1(2) renders the offence unacceptably narrow. If the prosecution have to prove in every case that, at the time of the agreement, the parties knew or intended that the relevant facts or circumstance existed, then the law is too generous to those who plan to engage in conduct that may well be criminal. It does not extend to highly blameworthy behaviour that we believe should be encompassed within the offence of conspiracy."

Accordingly, as the law itself is regarded as defective, the Law Commission recommends that it should be changed so that:

"An alleged conspirator must be shown at the time of the agreement to be reckless whether a circumstance element of a substantive offence (or other relevant circumstance) would be present at the relevant time, when the substantive offence requires no proof of fault, or has a requirement for proof only of negligence (or its equivalent), in relation to that circumstance."[195]

The Law Commission's view is that this would

"ensure that defendants such as Mr Saik, those who agree to commit rape believing that the victim 'might not' consent and those who agree to handle stolen goods believing that, should they do so, the goods will be stolen, would all be guilty of statutory conspiracy."[196]

This change would also bring the law in this respect into line with both the law relating to attempt and the new offences of encouraging or assisting crime.

(b) *If carried out in accordance with their intentions*

What is the position if the parties' intentions are equivocal? For example, they might agree to burgle a house if a window has been left open. The better view here is that the "plan" is a plan to burgle a house (albeit subject to a condition) and if that plan is carried out it will necessarily amount to a crime. As Lord Nicholls comments in *Saik*:

"An intention to do a prohibited act is within the scope of section 1(1) even if the intention is expressed to be conditional on the happening, or non-happening, of some particular event. The question always is whether the agreed course of conduct, if carried out in accordance with the parties' intentions, would necessarily involve an offence. A conspiracy to rob a bank tomorrow if the coast is clear when the conspirators reach the bank is not, by reason of this qualification, any less a conspiracy to rob. In the nature of things, every agreement to do something in the future is hedged about with conditions, implicit if not explicit."[197]

---

[195] Law Commission Paper No.318 *Conspiracy and Attempts* (2009), para.2.137. Where the substantive offence has a fault requirement not involving mere negligence (or its equivalent) this fault requirement must also be proved for conspiracy (para.2.146).

[196] Law Commission Consultation Paper No.183, *Conspiracy and Attempts* (2007), para.1.33.

[197] *Saik* [2007] A.C. 18 at [5].

R. v Jackson [1985] Crim. L.R. 442 (Court of Appeal, Criminal Division)

The appellants agreed to shoot their friend, W, in the leg if he was convicted of a burglary for which he was being tried. They thought this would provide mitigation. W was shot and permanently disabled. The appellants appealed against their conviction for conspiracy to pervert the course of justice on the ground that their agreement did not necessarily involve the commission of a crime, as everything depended on a contingency (W's conviction for burglary) which might not have taken place.

Held, "[P]lanning was taking place for a contingency and if that contingency occurred the conspiracy would necessarily involve the commission of an offence. 'Necessarily' is not to be held to mean that there must inevitably be the carrying out of an offence. It means, if the agreement is carried out in accordance with the plan, there must be the commission of the offence referred to in the conspiracy count."

Appeal dismissed

In *O'Hadhmaill*[198] the defendant, a member of the IRA, agreed to a bombing campaign if the cease-fire in Northern Ireland ended. This was held to be sufficient intention for the crime of conspiracy.

The approach adopted in all these cases is defensible. Virtually all agreements are conditional. It is implicit in most agreements to commit a crime that the actions will only be carried out if there is not the metaphoric "policeman at one's elbow" at the scene of the crime. However, there is still some uncertainty about the precise scope of conditional intention in relation to s.1(2) that has been exposed by the decision in *Saik*. What if two defendants agree that they will have sex with a woman and they suspect that she may not consent? Although the issue of conditional intention did not fall to be determined in *Saik* it would appear that this state of mind will not now suffice for liability for conspiracy to rape. However, as Baroness Hale in her dissenting speech argues, the defendants have an intent to rape—they have agreed that they will go ahead even if at the time when they go ahead they know she is not consenting—and this ought to be a conspiracy to commit rape. If recklessness rather than intention or knowledge were required in relation to facts or circumstances, as proposed by the Law Commission, the liability of such defendants would be clear.[199]

The plan must also be carried out "in accordance with their intentions". What does this mean? What is the position of a person who agrees to the commission of a crime and agrees to supply tools for the crime but who thereafter has no interest in what happens and indeed thinks the planned crime is over-ambitious and will never be committed? Or, what is the position of a plain-clothes police officer who, with a view to entrapping the others, "agrees" to a plan to commit a crime, but actually intends to prevent the crime at the last moment? In short, must each conspirator intend that the crime actually be carried out?

R. v Anderson [1986] A.C. 27 (House of Lords)

The defendant agreed for a fee to supply diamond wire to cut through bars in order to enable another person, Andaloussi, to escape from prison. He claimed that he only intended to supply the wire and then go abroad. He believed the plan could never succeed. He appealed against his conviction for conspiring with others to effect the release of one of them from prison claiming that as he did not intend or expect the plan to be carried out, he lacked the necessary mens rea for the offence of conspiracy.

198   *R. v O'Hadhmaill* [1996] Crim. L.R. 509. See also *Reed* [1982] Crim. L.R. 818.
199   See further, Law Commission Paper No.318 *Conspiracy and Attempts* (2009), paras 2.99–2.128.

LORD BRIDGE:

"[I]t is not necessary that more than one of the participants in the agreed course of conduct shall commit a substantive offence. It is, of course, necessary that any party to the agreement shall have assented to play his part in the agreed course of conduct, however innocent in itself, knowing that the part to be played by one or more of the others will amount to or involve the commission of an offence.

. . . The heart of the submission for the appellant is that in order to be convicted of conspiracy to commit a given offence . . . the party charged should not only have agreed that a course of conduct shall be pursued which will necessarily amount to or involve the commission of that offence by himself or one or more other parties to the agreement, but must also be proved himself to have intended that that offence should be committed. Thus, it is submitted here that the appellant's case that he never intended that Andaloussi should be enabled to escape from prison raised an issue to be left to the jury, who should have been directed to convict him only if satisfied that he did so intend . . .

I am clearly driven by consideration of the diversity of roles which parties may agree to play in criminal conspiracies to reject any construction of the statutory language which would require the prosecution to prove an intention on the part of each conspirator that the criminal offence or offences which will necessarily be committed by one or more of the conspirators if the agreed course of conduct is fully carried out should in fact be committed . . . In these days of highly organised crime the most serious statutory conspiracies will frequently involve an elaborate and complex agreed course of conduct in which many will consent to play necessary but subordinate roles, not involving them in any direct participation in the commission of the offence or offences at the centre of the conspiracy. Parliament cannot have intended that such parties should escape conviction of conspiracy on the basis that it cannot be proved against them that they intended that the relevant offence or offences should be committed.

There remains the important question whether a person who has agreed that a course of conduct will be pursued which, if pursued as agreed, will necessarily amount to or involve the commission of an offence is guilty of statutory conspiracy irrespective of his intention, and, if not, what is the *mens rea* of the offence. I have no hesitation in answering the first part of the question in the negative. There may be many situations in which perfectly respectable citizens, more particularly those concerned with law enforcement, may enter into agreements that a course of conduct shall be pursued which will involve commission of a crime without the least intention of playing any part in furtherance of the ostensibly agreed criminal objective, but rather with the purpose of exposing and frustrating the criminal purpose of the other parties to the agreement. To say this is in no way to encourage schemes by which the police act, directly or through the agency of informers, as agents provocateurs for the purpose of entrapment. That is conduct of which the courts have always strongly disapproved. But it may sometimes happen, as most of us with experience in criminal trials well know, that a criminal enterprise is well advanced in the course of preparation when it comes to the notice either of the police or of some honest citizen in such circumstances that the only prospect of exposing and frustrating the criminals is that some innocent person should play the part of an intending collaborator in the course of criminal conduct proposed to be pursued. The *mens rea* implicit in the offence of statutory conspiracy must clearly be such as to recognise the innocence of such a person, notwithstanding that he will, in literal terms, be obliged to agree that a course of conduct be pursued involving the commission of an offence . . .

[B]eyond the mere fact of agreement, the necessary *mens rea* of the crime is, in my opinion, established if, and only if, it is shown that the accused, when he entered into the agreement, intended to play some part in the agreed course of conduct in furtherance of the criminal purpose which the agreed course of conduct was intended to achieve. Nothing less will suffice; nothing more is required.

Applying this test to the facts which, for the purposes of the appeal, we must assume, the appellant, in agreeing that a course of conduct be pursued that would, if successful, necessarily involve the offence of effecting Andaloussi's escape from lawful custody, clearly intended, by providing diamond wire to be smuggled into the prison, to play a part in the agreed course of conduct in furtherance of that criminal objective. Neither the fact that he intended to play no further part in attempting to effect the escape, nor that he believed the escape to be impossible, would, if the jury had supposed they might be true, have afforded him any defence."

Appeal dismissed

One of the major reservations underlying all the inchoate offences is that no (first order) harm has been caused. How do we justify the invocation of the criminal law? We saw that (apart from arguments of there being a second order harm) the main case for criminalisation was on grounds of blameworthiness. With attempted crime the absence of harm is compensated by a requirement that the defendant intended to commit the complete offence; the highest degree of blame is required. An examination of s.1 of the

Criminal Law Act 1977 should lead one to a similar conclusion in relation to conspiracy—as, indeed, it has done in relation to s.1(2). One would have thought that no one could be convicted of an offence if he or she did not intend the consequences comprising the offence. *Anderson* refutes this view with the result that a defendant can be guilty of a serious criminal offence when there has been no conduct beyond a bare agreement and where the defendant never intended that the offence be carried out.

Subsequent decisions have appeared to share this concern and have not all followed *Anderson*. In *McPhillips*[200] a defendant was acquitted of conspiracy to murder because he intended to give a warning before a bomb was exploded. It was held that he could only be liable if he had intended that the plan be carried out. *Anderson* was distinguished on the fairly unconvincing ground that in that case there had been no intention of frustrating the plan. In *Edwards*,[201] the Court of Appeal stated that the trial judge had been right to direct the jury that the defendant could only be guilty of conspiring to supply amphetamine if he had intended to supply amphetamine. *Anderson* was again distinguished in the following Privy Council decision.

Yip Chiu-Cheung v The Queen [1995] 1 A.C. 111 (Privy Council)

The defendant was convicted of conspiracy to traffic in heroin contrary to common law and the Hong Kong Dangerous Drugs Ordinance. He appealed on the basis that his co-conspirator, Needham (who had not been prosecuted), was an undercover drugs enforcement agent who had had no intention that the crime would be committed.

LORD GRIFFITHS:

"[I]t was submitted that the trial judge and the Court of Appeal were wrong to hold that Needham, the undercover agent, could be a conspirator because he lacked the necessary *mens rea* or guilty mind required for the offence of conspiracy. It was urged upon their Lordships that no moral guilt attached to the undercover agent who was at all times acting courageously and with the best of motives in attempting to infiltrate and bring to justice a gang of criminal drug dealers. In these circumstances it was argued that it would be wrong to treat the agent as having any criminal intent, and reliance was placed upon a passage in the speech of Lord Bridge of Harwich [in *Anderson* above]; but in that case Lord Bridge was dealing with a different situation from that which exists in the present case. There may be many cases in which undercover police officers or other law enforcement agents pretend to join a conspiracy in order to gain information about the plans of the criminals, with no intention of taking any part in the planned crime but rather with the intention of providing information that will frustrate it. It was to this situation that Lord Bridge was referring in *R. v Anderson*. The crime of conspiracy requires an agreement between two persons to commit an unlawful act with the intention of carrying it out. It is the intention to carry out the crime that constitutes the necessary *mens rea* for the offence. As Lord Bridge pointed out, the undercover agent who has no intention of committing the crime lacks the necessary *mens rea* to be a conspirator.

The facts of the present case are quite different . . . Needham intended to commit that offence by carrying the heroin through the customs and on to the aeroplane bound for Australia . . . Naturally, Needham never expected to be prosecuted if he carried out the plan as intended. But the fact that in such circumstances the authorities would not prosecute the undercover agent does not mean that he did not commit the crime albeit as part of a wider scheme to combat drug dealing."[202]

Appeal dismissed

---

[200]   *McPhillips* (1990) 6 BNIL (Northern Ireland).
[201]   *R. v Edwards* [1991] Crim. L.R. 45.
[202]   To respond to the problems raised by law enforcement agents working under cover and in furtherance of the justification of conspiracy in assisting intelligence-led policing, the Law Commission has recommended that the defence of acting reasonably under the Serious Crime Act 2007 s.50 be extended to conspiracy: Law Commission Paper No.318 *Conspiracy and Attempts* (2009), para.6.56. See below, p.532.

This decision is, of course, of persuasive authority only and, strictly, applies only to the common law offence of conspiracy. However, it restates the right principle and is the approach that should be adopted. In *Saik*, Lord Nicholls, without referring to *Anderson*, commented that the conspirators must intend to do the act prohibited by the substantive offence.[203]

The defendant in *Anderson* was not truly a conspirator. Had he supplied the diamond wire (he was injured before he could even attempt to do so) it would have been appropriate to charge him with aiding and abetting a conspiracy.[204] In such circumstances it is now possible to use the new inchoate offences of encouraging or assisting crime. As the Law Commission states, this solution addresses the policy concerns identified by Lord Bridge in *Anderson* and means that the approach taken in that case is "no longer appropriate or necessary".[205]

On the facts of *Anderson* there were two or more other conspirators who did intend the offence to be committed, and, although the House of Lords does not seem to have regarded this as significant, it is submitted that this is crucial for a conviction under s.1. If this were not so, one could have a situation where there was a "conspiracy which no one intends to carry out [which would be] an absurdity, if not an impossibility".[206] The solution adopted by the Draft Criminal Code (below) is that it is necessary for the accused and at least one other party to the agreement to intend that the offence be committed. More recently the Law Commission has indicated that each defendant must intend that the conduct and consequence element occur, an approach which would go a long way in restoring clarity to the law.[207]

In addition to these difficulties, *Anderson* created a further problem. Lord Bridge refers to the requirement that each conspirator must have "assented to play his part in the agreed course of conduct". It has never been part of the crime of conspiracy that all conspirators need to agree to play an active role and could place the godfathers of criminal conspiracies even further beyond the reach of the criminal justice system."[208] Fortunately, the Court of Appeal has recently indicated (obiter) that it does not favour Lord Bridge's "controversial" requirement being taken literally.[209]

(c) *Necessarily amount to (or involve) a crime*

We have already examined the meaning of "necessarily". It does not matter whether the actual conduct will in fact amount to a crime. What matters is whether the plan, if successfully carried out, will do so. It therefore follows that it is irrelevant whether the crime is even possible. As shall be seen, this is confirmed by s.1(1)(b) of the Criminal Law Act 1977.

What is meant by "amount to or involve the commission of any offence or offences by one or more of the parties to the agreement"? In *Hollinshead*[210] the Court of Appeal held that this meant that one of the parties had to intend to commit the offence as a principal offender. This means that there cannot be a conspiracy to aid and abet an offence.[211]

---

[203] *Saik* [2007] A.C. 18 at [4].
[204] One can aid and abet any offence, common law or statutory, unless expressly excluded by statute (*R. v Jefferson (Andrew Steven)* [1994] 1 All E.R. 270).
[205] Law Commission Consultation Paper No.183, *Conspiracy and Attempts* (2007), para.4.33.
[206] D. Ormerod, *Smith and Hogan's Criminal Law*, 13th edn (Oxford: OUP, 2011), p.440.
[207] Law Commission Paper No.318 *Conspiracy and Attempts* (2009), para.2.56.
[208] D. Fitzpatrick, "Variations on Conspiracy" (1993) 143 N.L.J. 1180. See also *Siracusa* (1989) 90 Cr. App. R. 340, where the Court of Appeal tried (unsuccessfully) to repair the damage.
[209] *R. v King (Joseph)* [2012] EWCA Crim 805 at [55].
[210] *R. v Hollinshead (Peter Gordon)* [1985] 1 All E.R. 850.
[211] This was confirmed in *Kenning* [2009] EWCA Crim 1534. However, defendants who agree to assist others commit crimes may now be charged under ss.44–46 of the Serious Crime Act 2007: below, p.532.

(iv) Impossibility

At common law the House of Lords in *Nock*[212] followed *Haughton v Smith*[213] and held there could be no liability for a conspiracy to commit the impossible. This decision has now been reversed by the amendment to s.1(1) which states that there can be liability even though there exist facts which render the commission of the offence impossible. Thus if two defendants agree to kill X, but unknown to them X is already dead, they can nevertheless still be liable for conspiracy to murder. This provision is, however, limited to statutory conspiracies. The result is somewhat anomalous: there can be liability for a statutory conspiracy to commit the impossible, but no liability for similar common law conspiracies. In relation to statutory conspiracies, the question must be asked again: when defendants have done no more than agree to commit a crime, and when it is quite impossible in any event for that crime to be committed, are we justified in imposing criminal liability?

(v) Repentance

If a conspirator repents and withdraws immediately after the agreement has been reached, it would appear that he is still guilty of conspiracy.[214] In the light of the material on repentance in the law of attempt,[215] should not a defendant who never gets further than agreeing to commit a crime, and who never does anything in pursuance of that agreement—indeed, who positively disassociates himself from it—be entitled to a defence? Unless one attaches very considerable significance to the "dangerousness of collaboration" argument, liability cannot be justified in such cases. It is disappointing, therefore, that the Law Commission has rejected the idea of withdrawal amounting to a defence.[216]

(vi) Jurisdiction

One of the justifications offered in support of conspiracy is that it is necessary to fight organised crime and, increasingly, organised crime involves trading in drugs. It is, therefore, likely that such conspiracies (and, with growing mobility, others as well) will contain an international element. More recently, there has been significant concern over international conspiracies to commit terrorist acts.

The position now is clear. If the agreement is made in this country and the defendant knows that the substantive offence will be committed in this country (such as the importation of controlled substances) then no problems of jurisdiction arise. If the agreement is made abroad the conspiracy is indictable in this country even though no overt act takes place here before the defendants are caught.[217]

The reverse situation, where there is an agreement in this country to commit a crime abroad, is dealt with by s.1A of the Criminal Law Act 1977.[218] English courts will have jurisdiction over any conspiracy to commit a crime abroad. The agreed acts must amount to a crime in the country where they are to take place and must constitute an offence under English law were they to be committed here. This

---

[212]   *DPP v Nock* [1978] A.C. 979.
[213]   *Haughton* [1975] A.C. 476.
[214]   M. Wasik, above, p.482 at 788; *Barnard* (1979) 70 Cr. App. R. 28.
[215]   Above, p.481.
[216]   Law Commission Consultation Paper No.183, *Conspiracy and Attempts* (2007), paras 2.32–2.44.
[217]   It was formerly the case that some such overt act needed to be proved: *DPP v Doot* [1973] A.C. 807. However, both the Privy Council in *Liangsiriprasert v US Government* (1991) 92 Cr. App. R. 77 and the Court of Appeal in *R. v Sansom (Alec James)* [1991] Crim. L.R. 126 have rejected this. See also *R. v Naini (Jamshid Hashemi)* [1999] 2 Cr. App. R. 398.
[218]   Inserted by the Criminal Justice (Terrorism and Conspiracy) Act 1998 s.5(1).

provision, aimed at terrorist organisations in England planning crimes abroad, is of wide effect and covers agreements to commit any crime abroad, no matter how trivial it might be.[219]

The Law Commission has recommended that all of these provisions be brought into line with the rules for the new offences of encouraging and assisting.[220]

IV. Encouraging or Assisting Crime

A. Introduction

At common law there was an inchoate offence of incitement[221] whereby the defendant persuaded or encouraged another to commit a crime. It could be used, for example, against defendants who encouraged others to view pornographic images of children, to grow cannabis or to attack unbelievers. However, the Law Commission formed the view that the offence of incitement was in need of clarification and reform[222] and in 2007 the common law offence was abolished and replaced with three new inchoate offences dealing with encouraging or assisting crime. These offences, contained within Pt 2 of the Serious Crime Act 2007, were designed as part of the response to serious and organised crime, although they are not limited to such offences. They have been subject to sustained criticism from the beginning by academic commentators and more recently by the House of Commons Justice Committee[223] and the Court of Appeal.[224] The provisions are undeniably complex and raise profound concerns about the breadth of the law.

B. Rationale of Liability and Reform

The need for a crime of incitement (or solicitation as it is commonly named, especially in the United States) was always controversial.

Wayne R. LaFave and Austin W. Scott, Criminal Law, 2nd edn (1986), pp.488–489:

"One view is that a mere solicitation to commit a crime, not accompanied by agreement or action by the person solicited, presents no significant social danger. It is argued, for example, that solicitation is not dangerous because the resisting will of an independent agent is interposed between the solicitor and commission of the crime which is his object. Similarly, it is claimed that the solicitor does not constitute a menace in view of the fact that he has manifested an unwillingness to carry out the criminal scheme himself. There is not the dangerous proximity to success which exists when the crime is actually attempted, for, 'despite the earnestness of the solicitation, the actor is merely engaging in talk which may never be taken seriously' (1 National Commission of Reform of Federal Criminal Laws, Working Papers 370 (1970)).

On the other hand, it is argued

---

[219]   In *R. v Patel (Sophia)* [2009] Crim. L.R. 466 it was made clear that defendants convicted of such foreign conspiracies are liable to the maximum sentence as that available for the substantive offence under English law.

[220]   Law Commission Paper No.318 *Conspiracy and Attempts* (2009), paras 7.71–7.71. For example, it would be sufficient for liability if the defendant knew *or believed* that the substantive offence might be committed in this country. See below, p.534.

[221]   Statute sometimes prohibits certain specific incitements—for example, incitement to racial hatred contrary to s.18(1) of the Public Order Act 1986. These are generally not true inchoate offences in the sense of being steps on the way to the commission of a crime: there is no substantive crime of "racial hatred". See also incitement to sedition contrary to s.3 of the Aliens Restriction (Amendment) Act 1919. These offences are unaffected by the abolition of common law incitement.

[222]   Law Commission Paper No.300, *Inchoate Liability for Assisting and Encouraging Crime* (2006), para.1.5.

[223]   *Post-legislative Scrutiny of Part 2 (Encouraging or Assisting Crime) of the Serious Crime Act 2007, Sixth Report of the Justice Committee* (HC 639, 2013).

[224]   *R. v Sadique (Omar)* [2013] EWCA Crim 1150.

'that a solicitation is, if anything, more dangerous than a direct attempt, because it may give rise to that cooperation among criminals which is a special hazard. Solicitation may, indeed, be thought of as an attempt to conspire. Moreover, the solicitor, working his will through one or more agents, manifests an approach to crime more intelligent and masterful than the effort of his hireling.' (Wechsler, Jones and Korn, 61 Colum. L. Rev. 571 (1961)).

It is noted, for example, that the imposition of liability for criminal solicitation has proved to be an important means by which the leadership of criminal movements may be suppressed.

Without regard to whether it is correct to say that solicitations are more dangerous than attempts, it is fair to conclude that the purposes of the criminal law are well served by inclusion of the crime of solicitation within the substantive criminal law. Providing punishment for solicitation aids in the prevention of the harm which would result should the inducements prove successful, and also aids in protecting the public from being exposed to inducements to commit or join in the commission of crimes. As is true of the law of attempts, the crime of solicitation (a) provides a basis for timely law enforcement intervention to prevent the intended crime, (b) permits the criminal justice process to deal with individuals who have indicated their dangerousness, and (c) avoids inequality of treatment based upon a fortuity (here, withholding of the desired response by the person solicited) beyond the control of the actor.

Objections to making solicitation a crime . . . are sometimes based upon the fear that false charges may readily be brought either out of a misunderstanding as to what the defendant said or for purposes of harassment. This risk is inherent in the punishment of almost all inchoate crimes, although it is perhaps somewhat greater as to the crime of solicitation in that the crime may be committed merely by speaking."

Consider again our earlier discussion of the rationale and punishment of attempts and conspiracies.[225] In relation to conduct that now falls within the description of "encouraging", bear in mind that if the person encouraged agrees to commit the crime there will be a criminal conspiracy. Thus, the offence amounts to no more than an attempted conspiracy (an offence abolished by s.1(4) of the Criminal Attempts Act 1981), and this raises the question of whether the existence of this form of inchoate liability is justified. Such persons clearly have indicated some degree of dangerousness and it is obviously desirable to deter people from encouraging others to commit crime, but, unlike attempt, such actors are far removed from the complete crime. It can be argued that their actions are not *manifestly* dangerous; they constitute no "second order" harm and, unlike conspiracy, there is not necessarily the "dangerousness of combination" argument that can justify the existence of the offence. In short, given the reasons why the law does not punish guilty intentions alone but insists upon a manifestation of those intentions, does the law push back the threshold of criminal liability too far? Or have we reached the point where serious and organised crime represents such a threat to society that liability is justified? Even if the crime could now be justified, surely for the same reasons, it could *never* be justifiable to impose the same sentence (let alone a greater one, as was possible under the common law) as for the completed crime.

That does not, however, conclude the discussion. Unlike the common law offence of incitement, the new offences criminalise the doing of acts which "assist" as well as encourage the commission of offences. Indeed, one of the main catalysts for reform was the absence of an offence of facilitating crime.

Law Commission, Inchoate Liability for Assisting and Encouraging Crime (Law Com. No. 300), (2006), paras 1.3–1.5:

"1.3 [W]e consider [this] to be a major defect of the common law. At common law if D *encourages* P to commit an offence that subsequently P does not commit or attempt to commit, D may nevertheless be criminally liable. By

---

[225] Above, pp.460–463; 502–505.

contrast, if D *assists* P to commit an offence, D incurs no criminal liability at common law if subsequently P, for whatever reason, does not commit or attempt to commit the offence:

Example 1A

D, in return for payment, lends a van to P believing that P will use the van in order to commit a robbery. The police arrest P in connection with another matter before P can even attempt to commit the robbery. D is not criminally liable despite the fact that he or she intended to bring about harm and, by lending the van to P, has manifested that intention. If, however, in addition to giving P the van, D had uttered words encouraging P to rob V, D would be guilty of incitement to commit robbery. The common law appears to treat words more seriously than deeds. Yet, it might be thought that seeking to bring about harm by assisting a person to commit an offence is as culpable as seeking to do so by means of encouragement.

1.4 Increasingly, the police, through the gathering of intelligence, are able to identify preliminary acts of assistance by D before P commits or attempts to commit the principal offence. Yet, the common law only partially reflects this significant development. As a result, if D assists but does not encourage P to commit an offence, the police may have to forego at least some of the advantages of more sophisticated and effective methods of investigation by having to wait until P commits or attempts to commit the offence before they can proceed against D.

1.5 In contrast to acts of assistance, if D encourages P to commit an offence which P does not go on to commit, D will be guilty of incitement provided he or she satisfies the fault element of the offence. However, the offence of incitement has a number of unsatisfactory features:

(1) there is uncertainty as to whether it must be D's purpose that P should commit the offence that D is inciting;

(2) the fault element of the offence has been distorted by decisions of the Court of Appeal. These decisions have focused, wrongly, on the state of mind of P rather than on D's state of mind;

(3) there is uncertainty as to whether and, if so, to what extent it is a defence to act in order to prevent the commission of an offence or to prevent or limit the occurrence of harm;

(4) there is uncertainty as to the circumstances in which D is liable for inciting P to do an act which, if done by P, would not involve P committing an offence, for example because P is under the age of criminal responsibility or lacks a guilty mind;

(5) the rules governing D's liability in cases where D incites P to commit an inchoate offence have resulted in absurd distinctions;

(6) D may have a defence if the offence that he or she incites is impossible to commit whereas impossibility is not a defence to other inchoate offences, apart from common law conspiracies."

Thus, the legislation attempts to remedy the defects of the common law and plug the gaps caused by the lack of a crime of facilitation (the absence of which, in the view of the Law Commission, had led to an unacceptable extension of the law of conspiracy[226]). In relation to the flaws with incitement, it has been commented that even the Law Commission acknowledged that they "rarely troubled the courts"[227] and that although some statutory clarification might have been desirable, none of the reasons above provided "a compelling case for outright abolition of incitement".[228] Further, despite the Law Commission's arguments, views are divided as whether there was a need to criminalise acts of assistance at all or in the way adopted. While some commentators argue that the broad approach is an understandable response to serious, organised and terrorist crime,[229] others remain sceptical

---

[226] Law Commission Paper No.300, *Inchoate Liability for Assisting and Encouraging Crime* (2006), para.3.9.
[227] Law Commission Paper No.305, *Participating in Crime* (2007), para.3.17.
[228] D. Ormerod and R. Fortson, "Serious Crime Act 2007: the Part 2 Offences" [2009] Crim L.R. 389 at 395–396.
[229] G. Sullivan, "Inchoate Liability for Assisting and Encouraging Crime" [2006] Crim L.R. 1047; J.R. Spencer, "Helping Another Person to Commit a Crime", in P. Smith (ed.) *Essays in Honour of J.C. Smith* (London: Butterworths, 1987) and W. Wilson, "A Rational Scheme of Liability for Participating in Crime" [2008] Crim. L.R. 3.

and believe that even if criminalisation might be justified, it could have been achieved in a much more straightforward way[230] by simply creating a new inchoate offence of facilitation.[231]

Finally, it should be noted that the proposals of the Law Commission in relation to incitement went hand in hand with their proposals in relation to complicity. Whilst the Government has taken up the first proposals it has yet to do so in relation to parties to crime. The Law Commission's original proposals were an attempt to introduce a coherent range of measures where the width of the new encouraging and assisting offences was balanced by a narrowing of the law on complicity. It is most unfortunate that as a result of the Government's response we are left with laws which significantly extend the net of liability.

C. The Law

The Serious Crime Act 2007 Pt 2 creates three offences of encouraging and assisting crime.[232] Despite the legislation having been in force since 2008, there is little case-law on the provisions,[233] although the difficulties inherent in s.46 have now, as will be seen below, been subject to judicial scrutiny. However, use is increasingly being made of the provisions[234]—and this is certainly true in relation to prosecutions arising from the riots in August 2011.[235]

1. Common elements

The three offences share certain key words and phrases; notably "encouraging", "assisting" and "capable of". In a piece of legislation in which so much is spelt out one might have anticipated that these terms would have been defined. However, the Act does not define what acts[236] are capable of being encouragement or assistance. In so far as "encouragement" is concerned, the Law Commission's view was that it should carry the same broad meaning that incitement had had at common law[237]; thus, it will include persuading, suggesting, requesting, commanding or goading another person (P) to commit a crime.[238] Section 65(1) does make clear that, just as with the common law, encouragement includes threatening another or otherwise putting pressure on P to commit the offence. Beyond this, the concept will be one for the courts to develop. In relation to "assistance" the term is also undefined although the Law Commission's view was that it "extends to any conduct on the part of D that, as a matter of fact, makes it easier for P to commit the principal offence".[239] It is

---

230 Ormerod and Fortson, "Serious Crime Act 2007: the Part 2 Offences" [2009] Crim L.R. 389 at 397.

231 J.R. Spencer and G. Virgo, "Encouraging and Assisting Crime: Legislate in Haste, Repent at Leisure" (2008) *Archbold News* 7.

232 Section 59 abolishes the common law of incitement.

233 Most decisions to date have related to sentencing: see *Garner-Harris* [2012] EWCA Crim 2996; *Lanphier* [2012] EWCA Crim 731; *Watling* [2012] EWCA Crim 2894.

234 Ministry of Justice, *Post-legislative Scrutiny of the Serious Crime Act 2007, Memorandum to the Home Affairs Committee and Justice Committee* (2012, Cm.8502), para.52: in 2009 there were 13 prosecutions under Part 2 of the Act; in 2011 the number had risen to 121.

235 *Blackshaw* [2011] EWCA Crim 2312: the case involved 10 appeals against sentence. The provisions may also be increasingly used to deal with organised crime: see *Sadique* [2013] EWCA Crim 1150, below at p.530.

236 Care is needed here. Part 2 of the Serious Crime Act 2007 uses the term "act" throughout the provisions. But sometimes it refers to the defendant's act and sometimes to that of P. One notable potential cause for confusion is s.47(8) where it states that reference in s.47 to the "doing of an act" includes a failure to act; the continuation of an act that has already begun; and an attempt to do an act. The phrase "doing of an act" refers to the act of P and not to that of the defendant.

237 Law Commission Paper No.300, *Inchoate Liability for Assisting and Encouraging Crime* (2006), para.5.37.

238 *R. v Goldman (Terence)* [2001] Crim. L.R. 822.

239 Law Commission Consultation Paper No.131, *Assisting and Encouraging Crime* (1993), para.4.48.

also of concern that any act of assistance, however trivial, appears to suffice for liability if it is capable of assisting another.[240]

Under s.65(2), acts that are capable of encouraging or assisting can include "taking steps to reduce the possibility of criminal proceedings being brought in respect of that offence". While the mischief aimed at by inchoate offences is acts done prior to the commission of the substantive offence, there is nothing in the wording of the statute to prevent acts done afterwards being prosecuted. It could be argued, for example, that the provision of a getaway car encourages the offence. Section 65(2)(b) states that the defendant is liable if he fails to take reasonable steps to discharge a duty—but only if the failure is a deliberate one rather than mere forgetfulness.[241] The Law Commission gave, as an example, a security guard who omits to turn on the burglar alarm with the intention of assisting another to burgle the premises.[242]

Further, under s.66 the defendant may be liable where their encouragement or assistance is indirect, for example, a gang leader who instructs a member of the gang to encourage another person to kill the victim would be liable under s.44.[243]

The third common phrase is that the defendant's act must be "capable of" encouraging or assisting another to commit an offence. As the focus is upon the defendant's conduct it is unnecessary for it, in fact to encourage or assist P to commit an offence. Indeed, it seems that it is unnecessary for P to be aware of the defendant's conduct as long as the act "is capable" of assisting or encouraging the commission of a crime.[244] This means that the new offences are wider than the old law of incitement where the acts constituting the incitement had to be communicated to the incitee.[245]

Given these common elements the key difference between the three new offences is in relation to the mens rea requirements.

2. Intentionally encouraging or assisting an offence
Serious Crime Act 2007 s.44

"(1) A person commits an offence if—

(a) he does an act capable of encouraging or assisting the commission of an offence; and

(b) he intends to encourage or assist its commission.

(2) But he is not to be taken to have intended to encourage or assist the commission of an offence merely because such encouragement or assistance was a foreseeable consequence of his act."

By virtue of s.55 the offence is triable in the same way as the "anticipated offence" (the offence which the defendant is encouraging or assisting another to commit).

---

240 Law Commission Paper No.300, *Inchoate Liability for Assisting and Encouraging Crime* (2006), para.5.5.
241 R. Fortson, *Blackstone's Guide to the Serious Crime Act 2007* (London: Blackstone, 2008), p.81. Section 65(3) excludes from this provision a failure to respond to a constable's request for assistance.
242 Law Commission Paper No.300, *Inchoate Liability for Assisting and Encouraging Crime* (2006), para.3.34.
243 Home Office, *Explanatory Notes to the Serious Crime Act 2007* (2007), para.232.
244 Law Commission Paper No.300, *Inchoate Liability for Assisting and Encouraging Crime* (2006), para.5.29.
245 *Banks* (1873) 12 Cox C.C. 393. Although where communication failed it was possible to prosecute for an attempt to incite: *R. v Chelmsford Justices Ex p. Amos (JJ)* [1973] Crim. L.R. 437.

(i) Actus reus

The defendant's acts must be capable of encouraging or assisting the commission of an offence and may include a "course of conduct".[246] As noted above, the focus is very much upon the acts of the defendant and not upon the impact it has upon P. Unlike ss.45 and 46 below, the offence encouraged or assisted can be the other inchoate offences of conspiracy or attempt; thus the defendant could be found liable for encouraging P to enter into a conspiracy if she possesses the necessary mens rea. The existence of this double inchoate liability is a worrying illustration of the width of this offence.

(ii) Mens rea

At first sight, the mens rea requirement under s.44 appears straightforward: the defendant must intend by his act to assist or encourage the commission of the offence. Section 44(2) states that such a defendant cannot be taken to have intended to encourage or assist merely because such encouragement or assistance was a foreseeable consequence of his conduct. Thus, only intention suffices.[247] However, beyond this the provisions become much more complex.

Serious Crime Act 2007 s.47

"47 Proving an offence under this Part
   (1) Sections 44, 45, and 46 are to be read in accordance with this section.
   (5) In proving for the purposes of this section whether an act is one which, if done, would amount to the commission of an offence—

  (a) if the offence is one requiring proof of fault, it must be proved that—

     (i)   D believed that, were the act to be done, it would be done with that fault;

     (ii) D was reckless as to whether or not it would be done with that fault; or

     (iii) D's state of mind was such that, were he to do it, it would be done with that fault; and

  (b) if the offence is one requiring proof of particular circumstances or consequences (or both), it must be proved that—

     (i)   D believed that, were the act to be done, it would be done in those circumstances or with those consequences; or

     (ii) D was reckless as to whether or not it would be done in those circumstances or with those consequences."

Section 44 penalises the encouragement or assistance of *an offence*; thus, where that offence requires proof of fault the defendant must also have mens rea in relation to it. By virtue of s.47(5)(a), for offences requiring proof of fault, it must be proved that: (i) the defendant intended[248] or believed that the act would be done with the necessary fault, (ii) was reckless whether it would be done with that fault, or (iii) that the defendant's state of mind was such that, were they to do it, it would be done with that fault.

---

[246] Serious Crime Act 2007 s.67.
[247] It is not clear whether oblique intention suffices here. The *Woollin* test requiring foresight of virtual certainty could well be applicable as this involves a far greater degree of foresight than merely being a "foreseeable consequence".
[248] Section 47(7)(a).

Further, if the offence is one that requires proof of consequences or circumstances or both, s.47(5)(b) requires that the defendant believed or was reckless as to whether P's conduct would have those consequences or be done in those circumstances. The relationship between these two provisions is important. Suppose the defendant provides P with a baseball bat, intending that P use it to cause grievous bodily harm to the victim but P uses it intentionally to kill the victim. Under s.47(5)(a) the defendant has the requisite mens rea for encouraging murder but under s.47(5)(b) the defendant does not believe and is not reckless as to the consequence (death) and so cannot be liable for encouraging murder. Equally, he cannot be liable for encouraging manslaughter. While P (if he had a lesser mens rea) can be liable for constructive manslaughter if he performs a dangerous unlawful act which causes death, the defendant must foresee the consequence (death). There is no room for constructive liability here. In the baseball bat example, it is possible, however, that the defendant could be liable for encouraging grievous bodily harm, contrary to s.18 of the Offences Against the Person Act 1861—provided this offence was specified in the indictment. According to the Explanatory Notes to the Act, it would be unfair to hold the defendant liable for encouraging and assisting murder, unless he also believed or was reckless as to whether the victim was killed.[249] While this is a useful safeguard (and in the context of strict liability offences means rightly that the defendant cannot be liable without belief or recklessness as to circumstances), it does demonstrate how much overlap there now is between these inchoate offences and participatory liability: this example clearly suggests that the fact that the crime has been committed is no bar to bringing a prosecution for an inchoate offence.[250]

Finally, if the defendant's act is capable of encouraging or assisting the commission of more than one offence, under s.49(2) he can be charged with s.44 in relation to each of the offences he intends to encourage or assist to be committed.

3. Encouraging or assisting an offence believing it will be committed

Serious Crime Act 2007 s.45

"A person commits an offence if—

(a) he does an act capable of encouraging or assisting the commission of an offence; and

(b) he believes—

(i) that the offence will be committed; and

(ii) that his act will encourage or assist its commission."

As with s.44, by virtue of s.55, the offence is triable in the same way as the "anticipated offence" (the offence which the defendant is encouraging or assisting another to commit).

(i) Actus reus

As with s.44, the defendant must do an act capable of encouraging or assisting the commission of an offence. Reference should be made to the discussion above of common elements.

---

[249] Home Office, *Explanatory Notes to the Serious Crime Act 2007* (2007), para.157.
[250] See further, J. Child, "The Differences Between Attempted Complicity and Inchoate Assisting and Encoraging—A Reply to Professor Bohlander" [2010] Crim. L.R.924 and J. Child, "Exploring the Mens Rea Requirements of the Serious Crime Act 2007 Assisting and Encouraging Offences" [2012] 76 Jo. Cr. L. 220.

If the defendant's act is capable of encouraging or assisting the commission or more than one offence, by virtue of s.49(2) he can be charged with s.45 in relation to each of the offences he believes will be encouraged or assisted.

Finally, while it is possible for defendants to be charged under s.44 when they *intend* to encourage or assist in the commission of an inchoate offence, liability does not extend under s.45 to acts which a defendant merely *believes* will encourage or assist another inchoate offence.[251]

(ii) Mens rea

Two main features distinguish this offence from the offence in s.44. First, s.44 requires the defendant to have acted with the purpose of encouraging or assisting the commission of an offence. Whether she believes that her endeavours will be successful is irrelevant. Under s.45, on the other hand, the defendant must believe that the offence that she is encouraging or assisting will be committed. If a person sells a gun to another (purely because she needs the money and hoping that the gun will not be used) she cannot be liable under s.44, but will be liable under s.45 if she believes the offence will be committed.

The second distinguishing feature is that, for an offence under s.45, the defendant must believe that her act will encourage or assist P to commit the offence. Under s.44, in contrast, as long as the defendant intends to encourage or assist the commission of the offence, it is irrelevant whether she believes that her acts will actually be successful in encouraging or assisting the commission of the crime.

The term "believes" is not defined by the Act and, as commentators have said, "its boundaries remain ambiguous, lying as it does between the equally vague concepts of suspicion and knowledge".[252] However, it is much closer to knowledge than mere suspicion and when coupled with the word *will*, "indicates a high level of confidence in D's mind that P is going to commit the anticipated offence".[253] Where the offence is one involving fault, s.47(5) applies just as it does in relation to s.44.

4. Encouraging or assisting offences believing one or more will be committed

This offence is the

"broadest, most complex and most controversial of the new offences. It is introduced to deal with the problem encountered in secondary liability where D gives assistance and D is aware that P is likely to commit one of a number of offences, but is unsure which. For example, D drives P to a public house, being unsure whether P is likely to commit robbery, murder, explosives offences or offences against the person."[254]

---

[251] Section 49(4); Sch.3.
[252] Ormerod and Fortson, "Serious Crime Act 2007: the Part 2 Offences" [2009] Crim L.R. 389 at 405.
[253] A. Ashworth and J. Horder, *Principles of Criminal Law* (Oxford: OUP, 2013), p.480.
[254] Ormerod and Fortson, "Serious Crime Act 2007: the Part 2 Offences" [2009] Crim L.R. 389 referring to *DPP v Maxwell* [1978] 1 W.L.R. 1350 (below p.572).

Serious Crime Act 2007 s.46

"(1) A person commits an offence if—

(a) he does an act capable of encouraging or assisting the commission of one or more of a number of offences; and

(b) he believes—

(i) that one or more of those offences will be committed (but has no belief as to which); and

(ii) that his act will encourage or assist the commission of one or more of them.

It is immaterial for the purposes of subsection (1)(b)(ii) whether the person has any belief as to which offence will be encouraged or assisted."

Under s.55(5) this offence is triable only on indictment.

(i) Actus reus

The defendant must do an act capable of encouraging or assisting the commission of one or more offences. The only difference between this and the earlier sections is the need to establish that the act was capable of encouraging or assisting more than one offence (which the prosecution must specify in the indictment[255]). Other than this, reference should be had to the discussion above of common elements.

As with s.45, under Sch.3 a defendant cannot be found liable for acts which he believes will encourage or assist another inchoate offence such a conspiracy or attempt.

(ii) Mens rea

As with s.45 the mens rea is two-fold: the defendant must both believe that one or more offences will be committed (including reference to s.47(5)) and that his act will encourage or assist the commission of one or more of them. However, he need not have any belief as to which of the offences will be committed in fact. In *Blackshaw* a defendant was convicted of this offence, having posted messages on Facebook encouraging both associates and the public to meet at a particular place and time. He believed that a number of different offences, including burglary, criminal damage and riot might be committed and that at least one would be committed.[256]

The offence has twice come under close scrutiny by the Court of Appeal in the case of *Sadique*. The defendant was alleged to have been involved in a national distribution business supplying chemical cutting agents (such as benzocaine) both to regional distributors of chemical cutting agents and to drug dealers. This supply was alleged to have been capable of encouraging or assisting one or more offences of supplying or being concerned in the supply of Class A or Class B drugs; that Sadique believed that one or more of these offences would be committed and that his act would assist the commission of one or more of the offences. He was charged with one count under s.46: that he assisted in the supply of Class A or Class B drugs. In an interlocutory appeal before the Court of Appeal, Sadique claimed that the offence was so vague as to be incompatible with art.7 of the ECHR. This argument was rejected. However, the reasoning which the court then adopted, interpreting the

---

[255] Serious Crime Act 2007 s.48(3).
[256] *R. v Blackshaw (Jordan Philip)* [2011] EWCA Crim 2312.

elements of the s.46 offence and providing guidance on the framing of indictments, divided com-menters.[257] It has now been found to have been flawed by a differently constituted Court of Appeal which heard Sadique's appeal against conviction.

Sadique (Omar) (No.2) [2013] EWCA Crim 1195 (Court of Appeal)

JUDGE CJ:

"[18] . . . [In the first case of *Sadique*] the court observed that s 46 'should only be used when the prosecution allege that D's act is capable of encouraging or assisting more than one offence', and continued that '. . . the indictment need only specify two offences and could specify any number greater than two'. The court then explained s 46 in the context of a case in which it was alleged that the count in the indictment specified offence X, punishable by life imprisonment, Y, punishable by 14 years imprisonment, and Z, punishable by ten years imprisonment. In that context the court observed that:

> "section 46 should only be used, and needs only to be used, when it may be that D, at the time of doing the act, believes that one or more of either offence X, or offence Y or offence Z will be committed, but has no belief as to which of one or ones of the three will be committed.'

In the case of a trial involving these issues, the court agreed with the prosecution that it would be better practice to have a separate s 46 count for X, Y and Z, and indeed went on to say 'that there should always be separate counts if D pleads not guilty' adding, however, that the failure to do so (that is to produce separate counts) 'would not of itself affect the safety of the conviction'. On this basis the observations of the court were directed not to issues of substantive law, but to process.

[19] According to Professor Virgo, *Encouraging or Assisting More Than One Offence* (Archbold Review, 13 March 2012) the effect of the judgment, which was addressing the issue of vagueness and uncertainty has, 'if anything made the offence vague, uncertain and effectively redundant'. The offence in s 46 was rendered 'practically obso-lete'. In issue 3 dated 12 April 2013 of Archbold News—*Enough is Enough'* Professor Virgo returned to the impact of the decision which, he suggests:

> '. . . drives a coach and horses through the s 46 offence, bears out my concerns about the drafting and com-prehensibility of the legislation, which has made the task of the senior judiciary very difficult in making sense of the law . . . The effect of their (the judges') decision is to render that offence otiose. Since each contemplated offence must now be charged as a separate count, the Defendant can only be convicted if he or she believed that a specific offence would be committed; that is the same as the conditions for conviction under s 45. It follows that a Defendant who contemplates a number of offences being committed but does not believe any specific crime would be committed, cannot be guilty of assisting or encouraging an offence. That is an unfor-tunate restriction on the ambit of liability and will cause problems in future . . .'.

[20] The problem, if we may say so, rightly identified by Professor Virgo arises, as it seems to us, from the start-ing point in the reasoning of the court, found at para 49 of the judgment:

> 'D cannot be convicted of count 1 (the other ingredients being satisfied) unless at the time of doing the act:

(a) Either

   (i)   D believes that X will be committed; or

---

257   See, for example, R. Fortson, "R v S and H: Assisting and Encouraging—Trial—Indictment" [2012] Crim. L.R. 449 (support-ing the decision) and G. Virgo. "Encouraging or Assisting More than One Offence", *Archbold Review*, March 13, 2012 and G. Virgo, "Enough is Enough", *Archbold News*, April 12, 2013 (criticising the decision).

(ii) D believes that one or more of the offences specified in the indictment (X, Y and Z) will be committed but has no belief as to which; and

(b) D believes that his act will encourage or assist the commission of X; and

(c) D believes that X will be committed with the necessary fault for X.'

[21] We are concerned that in this analysis it appears that a reference to the offence created by s 45 of the Act has been included as an ingredient of the offence created by s 46. In this paragraph of the judgment (a) (i) 'D believes that X will be committed'; repeats the precise language in s 45(b)(i) that D believes that the offence will be committed. Section 45, of course, is directed to 'an offence' or 'the offence'. However the entire thrust of s 46 is directed to the encouragement or assistance of offences in the belief that one or more of a number of offences will be committed. As the offences created by ss, 44, 45 and 46 are distinct offences, we have concluded that the foundation for the analysis was flawed, and that we are not bound by obiter observations of the court directed to procedural matters relating to the indictment rather than the full ambit of the offence. . . .

[30] As we have already explained, the 2007 Act created three distinct offences. It is not open to the court to set one or other of them aside and the legislation must be interpreted to give effect to the creation by statute of the three offences. It may well be that the common law offence of inciting someone else to commit an offence was less complex. It may equally be that the purpose of the legislation could have been achieved in less tortuous fashion. Nevertheless these three distinct offences were created by the 2007 Act, with none taking priority over the other two. Section 46 creates the offence of encouraging or assisting the commission of one or more offences. Its specific ingredients and the subsequent legislative provisions underline that an indictment charging a s 46 offence of encouraging one or more offences is permissible.

[31] This has the advantage of reflecting practical reality. A Defendant may very well believe that his conduct will assist in the commission of one or more of a variety of different offences by another individual without knowing or being able to identify the precise offence or offences which the person to whom he offers encouragement or assistance intends to commit, or will actually commit. As Professor Virgo explains in his most recent article, the purpose of the s 46 was 'to provide for the relatively common case where a Defendant contemplates that one of a variety of offences might be committed as a result of his or her encouragement'. We entirely agree . . .

[34] In our judgment the ingredients of the s 46 offence, and the ancillary provisions, and s 58(4)–(7) in particular, underline that an indictment charging a s 46 offence by reference to one or more offences is permissible, and covers the precise situation for which the legislation provides. Before the Appellant in the present case could be convicted, the jury had to be satisfied that:

(a) he was involved in the supply of the relevant chemicals and

(b) that, if misused criminally, the chemicals were capable of misuse by others to commit offences of supplying or being concerned in the supply of, or being in possession with intent to supply class A and/or class B drugs. None of this would be criminal unless it was also proved

(c) that at the time when the relevant chemicals were being supplied, the Appellant believed that what he was doing would encourage or assist the commission of one or more of these drug related offences and

(d) that he also believed that this was the purpose, or one of the purposes, for which the chemicals would be used by those to whom he supplied them. If those ingredients were established, as the chemicals could be used for cutting agents for class A drugs or class B drugs, or both, it was not necessary for the Crown to prove that he had a specific belief about the particular drug related offence which those he was encouraging or assisting would or did commit . . .

[36] In our judgment count 1 of the indictment was appropriately charged and fell within the proper ambit of the s 46 offence created by the 2007 Act . . .

[40] The Appellant was properly convicted of this offence. The appeal against conviction will therefore be dismissed . . ."

Appeal dismissed

As has been commented, the fact that two differently constituted Court of Appeals could come to different interpretations of s.46 is not the fault of the judiciary.[258] It illustrates the profound difficulties inherent with this provision. Whilst the second appeal restores purpose to the provision, not only are we left with a very wide offence, but also the interpretative difficulties have not been fully resolved: prosecutors are still likely to encounter difficulties in framing appropriate indictments.

5. Defences

As the three offences are inchoate it is, of course, no defence to put forward a defence that P did not actually commit an offence.[259] But Pt 2 of the Serious Crime Act 2007 does create two special defences to the three offences.

(i) The defence of acting reasonably

Serious Crime Act 2007 s.50

"(1) A person is not guilty of an offence under this Part if he proves—

(a) that he knew certain circumstances existed; and

(b) that it was reasonable for him to act as he did in those circumstances.

(2) A person is not guilty of an offence under this Part if he proves—

(a) that he believed certain circumstances to exist;

(b) that his belief was reasonable; and

(c) that it was reasonable for him to act as he did in the circumstances as he believed them to be.

(3) Factors to be considered in determining whether it was reasonable for a person to act as he did include—

(a) the seriousness of the anticipated offence (or, in the case of an offence under section 46, the offences specified in the indictment);

(b) any purpose for which he claims to have been acting;

(c) any authority by which he claims to have been acting."

Two points must be noted. First, the question of whether the defendant's belief is reasonable is one to be determined by a jury; it is not enough that the defendant believes his acts to be reasonable. Secondly, the burden of proof rests with the defence to prove reasonableness.

This defence applies to all three of the offences despite the Law Commission's view that it should not be available to s.44. However, given that s.44 requires intention it is most unlikely that the defence will be available in any event. The Law Commission provided illustrations of when the defence might operate: for example, the defendant, a motorist, who moves into an inside lane to allow P, another

---

[258] R. Fortson, "*R v Sadique (Omar)*: Assisting and Encouraging—Trial—Indictment' [2014] Crim. L.R. 61 at 66.
[259] Serious Crime Act 2007 s.49(1). By virtue of s.47(2) it is also no defence for the defendant to claim that he did not know that the conduct that he was encouraging or assisting P to commit was a criminal offence. Ignorance of the law is no defence.

motorist to overtake, even though the defendant is aware that P is exceeding the speed limit, could use the defence of acting reasonably in answer to a charge under s.45.[260]

(ii) Defence for the victim assister

Serious Crime Act 2007 s.51

"(1) In the case of protective offences, a person does not commit an offence under this Part by reference to such an offence if—

(a) he falls within the protected category; and

(b) he is the person in respect of whom the protective offence was committed or would have been if it had been committed.

(2) 'Protective offence' means an offence that exists (wholly or in part) for the protection of a particular category of persons ('the protected category')."

This section codifies the principle established in the case of *Tyrrell*.[261] The effect of the section is to make it clear that defendants cannot be liable for encouraging or assisting offences which are designed to protect them. For example, if a 12-year-old girl intentionally encourages P, a man of 21, to have sex with her and he declines, s.51 prevents her being liable for the offence of encouraging child rape because the offence of child rape was created to protect children under 13 years old.

6. Impossibility

Originally, under the common law of incitement it had been held in *McDonough*[262] that there could be liability for an incitement to commit the impossible. This was approved obiter by the House of Lords in *Nock*.[263] However, in *Fitzmaurice*[264] it was held that in many cases there could be no liability for incitement to commit the impossible.[265]

In proposing the new offences the Law Commission stated:

"We believe that impossibility should not be a defence to the new offences that we are recommending. D's state of mind and, therefore, his or her culpability, is unaffected by the unknown impossibility of the principal offence being committed. Further, if D can be liable notwithstanding that, contrary to D's belief, P never intends to commit the principal offence, it would be illogical if D was able to plead that it would have been impossible to commit the principal offence."[266]

The Serious Crime Act 2007 has not addressed this point directly. However, for all three offences the defendant's acts must be capable of encouraging or assisting the commission of an offence. So if the defendant encourages or does an act to assist P to kill X, but X is already dead (one of the classic

---

[260] Law Commission Paper No.300, *Inchoate Liability for Assisting and Encouraging Crime* (2006), para.A.63.
[261] *R. v Tyrrell* [1894] 1 Q.B. 710.
[262] *McDonough* (1962) 47 Cr. App. R. 37.
[263] *Nock* [1978] A.C. 979.
[264] *R. v Fitzmaurice (Robert)* [1983] Q.B. 1083.
[265] See the 6th edition of this book, pp.538–539.
[266] Law Commission Paper No.300, *Inchoate Liability for Assisting and Encouraging Crime* (2006), para.6.61.

examples of impossibility), the defendant has not done an act capable of encouraging or assisting the murder of X. Because of the impossibility of the crime, there can be no liability.

Such an approach would, however, place the law here at odds with the law on attempting the impossible and statutory conspiracies to commit the impossible. One can, therefore, predict that the courts will follow the approach in these other areas of law and simply require that the acts be capable of encouraging or assisting the commission of the *anticipated* offence (the murder of X). For oblique support, the courts could draw on s.49(7) which provides that for the purposes of s.45(b)(i) and s.46(1)(b)(i) (believing that the offence will be committed), it is sufficient for the defendant to believe that the offence will be committed if certain conditions are met. One of these conditions could be that X is alive.

It is unfortunate, given the length and complexities of Pt 2 of the Serious Crime Act 2007, that nothing explicit has been stated about the issue of impossibility.[267]

7. Jurisdiction

As noted in relation to conspiracy, the issue of jurisdiction has become increasingly important and it is not surprising given the framework of the Serious Crime Act within which the new offences sit that the courts are given wide jurisdiction. If a defendant "knows or believes that what he anticipates might take place wholly or partly in England and Wales" he may be liable under ss.44–46 no matter where in the world his relevant conduct occurred.[268]

If the prosecution cannot prove that a defendant believed that the offence being encouraged or assisted might be committed wholly or partly in England, the defendant can still be convicted if certain conditions are met under s.52(2) or Sch.4. First, para.1 provides jurisdiction if the defendant's conduct occurred wholly or partly in England; the defendant knew or believed that the offence might occur wholly or partly outside England; and that offence would be triable under the law of England if committed in that place (such as murder by a British citizen anywhere in the world[269]). If the above paragraph is inapplicable then under para.2 a defendant can still be tried in this country if his conduct occurred wholly or partly in this country; he knew or believed that the offence might occur wholly or partly in a place outside England; and the offence would also be an offence under the law in force in that place. Finally, under para.3, a defendant can be tried here if his conduct occurred wholly outside England; he knew or believed that the offence might occur wholly or partly outside England; and the defendant could be tried here (as the perpetrator) if he committed the offence in that place. In other words, liability may arise where both the defendant and P are outside England but the courts in England would have had jurisdiction if the defendant had committed the offence himself.[270] In cases where proceedings are sought under Sch.4 the consent of the Attorney General is needed.[271]

8. Punishment

Section 58 provides the penalties that apply to the three new offences. Where the offence encouraged or assisted is murder, s.58(2) states that the maximum penalty is imprisonment for life. Section 58(3)

---

[267] For one instance where impossibility has been provided for, see s.47(6) (where the defendant is *assumed* to be able to do the relevant act) and Home Office, *Explanatory Notes to the Serious Crime Act 2007* (2007), para.159.

[268] Serious Crime Act 2007 s.52(1). References to England include Wales hereafter.

[269] See the Offences Against the Person Act 1861 s.9.

[270] See further, Home Office, *Explanatory Notes to the Serious Crime Act 2007* (2007), paras 181–193.

[271] Serious Crime Act 2007 s.53.

provides that, other than for murder, the maximum penalty available for an offence under s.44 or s.45 is the same as the maximum available on conviction for the full offence. This rule also applies to s.46 but is restricted to where the defendant is found guilty in relation to one offence only:

> "For example D lends P a van, false number plates and a gun. The prosecution argue that he believed that either burglary or murder would be committed. The jury find D guilty in relation to burglary but not guilty in relation to murder. The maximum sentence available for the conviction under section 46 will be the maximum sentence available for the offence of burglary (14 years)."[272]

The situation where a defendant is convicted of more than one offence under s.46 is provided for under s.58(5) and (7). Where one of the offences is murder the maximum available penalty is imprisonment for life. Where none of the full offences is murder, but one or more of them is punishable by imprisonment, the maximum sentence is limited to the offence that carries the highest penalty. If none of the offences is punishable by imprisonment the maximum penalty is a fine.[273]

9. Conclusion

The offences contained within Pt 2 of the Serious Crime Act 2007 were created to remedy defects in the old common law of incitement despite the fact that the case for abolition was far from overwhelming and to remove the gap caused by the lack of a crime of facilitation—and doubts still exist as to whether this was a real lacuna. Even if a lacuna existed, reform could have been much more straightforward. Instead, the legislation is "over-detailed, convoluted and unreadable"[274] amply demonstrated by the differing interpretations of s.46 in *Sadique*. While the Ministry of Justice is relatively sanguine about the operation of Pt 2 of the Act in its post-legislative scrutiny, the Justice Committee is much more concerned by the 'trenchant' criticism the provisions have received. It recommends a further full review in 2016 but also states:

> "If, in the meantime, the number of appeals on Part 2 increases, we expect the Ministry to consider bringing forward legislative proposals for revising, or even replacing, Part 2 to meet the purpose of the legislation in a less tortuous fashion."[275]

A better course of action would be to initiate reform now.[276]

V. DOUBLE INCHOATE LIABILITY

Double inchoate liability arises when the defendant is convicted of committing an inchoate offence that relates to another inchoate offence. Under the old common law of incitement, for example, it was an offence to incite someone to incite a crime.[277] In view of the issues considered at the beginning of

---

272 Ministry of Justice, *Serious Crime Act 2007: Implementation of Part 2* (2008), para.70.
273 Section 58(7).
274 J.R. Spencer and G. Virgo, "Encouraging and Assisting Crime: Legislate in Haste, Repent at Leisure" (2008) *Archbold News* 7 at 8.
275 House of Commons Justice Committee, *Post-legislative Scrutiny of Part 2 (Encouraging or Assisting Crime) of the Serious Crime Act 2007* (HC 639, 2013).
276 See, for example, the comments by F. Stark, "Encouraging or Assisting Clarity" [2013] 72 Cambridge L.J. 497 at 501.
277 *Sirat* (1985) 83 Cr. App. R. 41. See Law Commission Paper No.300, *Inchoate Liability for Assisting and Encouraging Crime* (2006), para.3.36.

this chapter any such liability should be viewed with considerable caution. It is far from clear that there is a need for criminal liability in circumstances where the defendant's actions are so far removed from a substantive offence. However, the trend in recent years has been to expand the reach of the criminal law to cover such cases.

As the law stands, the following double inchoate crimes may be prosecuted:

- It is an offence to intentionally encourage or assist an act of encouragement or assistance in relation to an offence.[278]

- It is an offence to intentionally encourage or assist a conspiracy.[279]

- It is an offence to intentionally encourage or assist an attempt.[280]

In none of the above three situations is it an offence to encourage or assist the commission of an inchoate offence if the defendant merely believes that his acts will encourage or assist the commission of an offence.[281]

- It is an offence to attempt to encourage or assist the commission of an offence.[282]

- Further, as already seen, it is possible to attempt any indictable offence (other than those excluded by s.1(4) of the Criminal Attempts Act 1981) even if that offence is one that only punishes acts of preparation.[283]

The Law Commission had favoured making it an offence to attempt to conspire[284] in the interests of consistency in this area of law, but the strength of opposition to the proposal resulted in it being abandoned.[285] The argument that the "ultimate harm would be too remote and that [it] would therefore result in an unjustified expansion of the law"[286] is persuasive and it is to be hoped that this will act as a brake upon further development of double inchoate liability.

VI. ENDANGERMENT OFFENCES

R.A. Duff, "Intentions Legal and Philosophical" (1989) 9 O.J.L.S. 76 at 86:

"What harms should the criminal law aim to prevent? Death, bodily injury and the loss of property may seem to be three obvious 'primary harms' (each primary harm will generate a range of 'secondary harms', which take their character as harms from their relation to a primary harm; if death is a primary harm, then being subjected to the threat, risk or fear of death is a secondary and derivative harm);

Though these harms are initially identified without reference to human actions as their causes, the criminal

---

[278] Serious Crime Act 2007 s.49(4). This applies to intentional encouragement or assistance only, i.e. the s.44 offence.
[279] By virtue of the repeal of the Criminal Law Act 1977 s.5(7) (which stated that it is not an offence to incite a conspiracy) by the Serious Crime Act 2007 Sch.14.
[280] By virtue of the Serious Crime Act 2007 ss.44, 49(4) and Sch.3.
[281] i.e. Offences under the Serious Crime Act 2007 ss.45 and 46 are excluded by s.49(4) and Sch.3.
[282] Criminal Attempts Act 1981 s.1(4) (see above p.462) excludes certain forms of liability, such as attempted conspiracy and attempts to aid and abet a crime, from its ambit, but does not exclude the possibility of an attempt to encourage or assist a crime. As it was technically possible to conspire to incite under the common law it is possibly unlawful to conspire to encourage or assist. See A. Ashworth and J. Horder, *Principles of Criminal Law*, 7th edn (Oxford: OUP, 2013), p.486.
[283] *R. v R* [2008] 2 Cr. App. R. 38. See p.461.
[284] By repealing the Criminal Attempts Act 1981 s.1(4)(a).
[285] Law Commission Paper No.318 *Conspiracy and Attempts* (2009), paras 3.1–3.23.
[286] Law Commission Paper No.318 *Conspiracy and Attempts* (2009), para.3.16.

law, as a set of sanction-backed prohibitions, can help to prevent them by prohibiting and thus preventing actions which cause them. It can do this in various ways: by directly prohibiting actions which cause such harms ('killing', 'wounding and causing grievous bodily harm', 'damaging or destroying property' or 'depriving another of his property'); by prohibiting actions which are likely to cause such harms, under descriptions which refer directly to those harms ('attempting to kill'; 'reckless driving', defined in terms of the creation of an 'obvious and serious risk of causing physical injury'; or 'causing danger to the lieges by culpable recklessness'); by prohibiting conduct which is likely to cause such harms, but under descriptions which make no *direct* reference to those harms ('driving with excess alcohol in the blood,' or offences under s.19 and s.20 of the Firearms Act 1968)."

The term "endangerment offences" is used here to describe those offences that are complete in themselves and not dependent upon proof that any further offence was intended.[287] Some of these offences have the same rationale as inchoate offences; they are conceived of as being steps to the commission of further offences. For example, people who carry offensive weapons in public places could well use those weapons. As Bazelon J reasoned in *Benton v United States*,[288] such possession gives "rise to sinister implications". More commonly, however, conduct is criminalised simply because of its potential to cause harm. For example, dangerous driving is conduct that is likely to cause harm and is criminalised, again, for reasons similar to the criminalisation of inchoate offences, namely, in the hope of preventing the materialisation of the harm. The seriousness of endangerment offences is loosely linked to the likelihood (and potential gravity) of the harm materialising. For example, dangerous driving is more likely to cause harm than careless driving and accordingly carries a heavier penalty.

English law abounds with a wide variety of such offences and the number of them continues to increase. There are many offences of possessing prohibited articles, such as possessing explosives,[289] firearms,[290] or counterfeiting tools.[291] The object of the legislation prohibiting such possession is "frequently to prevent the articles being used for criminal purposes".[292] The Road Traffic Act 1988 penalises various forms of bad driving: for example, dangerous driving, careless driving and driving when under the influence of drink or drugs.[293] The Criminal Attempts Act 1981 s.9, creates the offence of interfering with vehicles; such conduct again has "sinister implications" as being indicative that theft or a similar offence is likely to be committed. Under the Criminal Damage Act 1971 it is an offence to cause criminal damage "intending . . . or being reckless as to whether the life of another would be thereby endangered".[294] The Sexual Offences Act 2003 creates an offence of meeting following grooming to try to deal with the dangers posed by adults using internet chat-rooms to seduce children.[295] Finally, by way of example, new terrorism offences have also been created: s.58(1)(b) of the Terrorism Act 2000 creates an offence of possessing information likely to be useful to a person committing or preparing an act of terrorism.[296]

With endangerment offences, particularly the driving offences, research suggests that in practice a prosecution is usually only brought when the danger has materialised: for example, when there

---

[287] See generally, R.A. Duff, "Criminalizing Endangerment", in R.A. Duff and S. Green (eds), *Defining Crimes* (Oxford: OUP, 2005).

[288] *Benton v United States* 232 F.2d 341 at 344–345 (D.C. Cir. 1956).

[289] Explosive Substances Act 1883 s.4(1).

[290] Firearms Act 1968 ss.16–22.

[291] Forgery and Counterfeiting Act 1981 s.17.

[292] D.J. Baker, *Glanville Williams Textbook of Criminal Law*, 3rd edn (London: Sweet & Maxwell, 2013), p.636.

[293] Sections 1, 3 and 4 respectively.

[294] Criminal Damage Act 1971 s.1(2).

[295] Section 15. See further B. Gallagher et al., *International and Internet Child Sexual Abuse and Exploitation* (Huddersfield: Huddersfield University, 2006).

[296] For a list of offences under the Offences Against the Person Act 1861 involving danger to life or bodily harm, see Criminal Law Revision Committee, 14th Report, *Offences Against the Person*, Cmnd.7844, (1980) paras 192–214. See generally, K.J.M. Smith, "Liability for Endangerment: English *Ad Hoc* Pragmatism and American Innovation" [1983] Crim. L.R. 127.

has been a car crash and someone is injured.[297] In cases where a death has resulted, English law has several aggravated endangerment offences such as causing death by dangerous driving.[298] In other cases where the harm has materialised the defendant is simply convicted of the endangerment offence but is given an increased punishment to reflect the causing of the harm. For example, under s.3(1) of the Dangerous Dogs Act 1991 a person is liable for a basic endangerment offence if his dog is dangerously out of control in a public place; this offence is punishable with a maximum of six months' imprisonment. If that dog injures any person, an aggravated offence is committed which is punishable by a maximum of two years' imprisonment on conviction on indictment. This has been the usual way of dealing with cases where a death has resulted at work as a result of a breach of the endangerment offences contained in the Health and Safety at Work etc. Act 1974 ss.2–4. Greater punishment is imposed to reflect that death or other serious injury has occurred.[299]

In evaluating these endangerment offences, it is important to remember that, unlike the inchoate offences, they are all complete crimes in themselves and each carries its own penalty. Indeed, if they are indictable offences, there may be liability for attempting to commit them,[300] or for conspiracy or for encouraging or assisting someone to commit them. Can one ever justify liability for an inchoate offence when the offence-in-chief is itself only an endangerment offence?

With these offences there is a harm, albeit a second-order harm. For example, the harm involved in unauthorised possession of a firearm or other offensive weapons is the violation of society's interests in security and freedom from alarm. Firearms are inherently dangerous and their widespread, unlicensed possession could lead to an increase in their usage. Whether conduct that has the potential for causing harm is criminalised depends on balancing the seriousness of the possible harm and the likelihood of its occurrence against the social value of the conduct. So possession of firearms is prohibited while possession of other dangerous weapons with greater social value, such as kitchen knives, is not criminalised.[301]

Following this reasoning, it is possible to justify the existence of these offences on the basis of there being a secondary harm. However, it is disturbing that many of these offences are ones of strict liability. For example, in *Hussain*[302] the defendant was convicted of possessing a firearm which he believed was his son's toy. With attempts, the second-order harm has to be backed up by "first degree blameworthiness" in the form of intention. With endangerment offences, such as possession of a firearm, the second-order harm need be accompanied by no blameworthiness at all. This hardly seems justifiable. In such cases there ought to be a "due-diligence defence" to enable defendants such as Hussain to escape liability.

In the United States many states have general offences of "reckless endangerment". Section 211.2 of the Model Penal Code provides the following definition of such an offence:

"A person commits a misdemeanour if he recklessly engages in conduct which places or may place another person in danger of death or serious bodily injury. Recklessness and danger shall be pre-

---

[297]   In interview many police officers and Crown prosecutors stated that it was "virtually impossible" to get a charge of dangerous driving where there had not been a collision: L.M. Pearce et al., *Dangerous Driving and the Law*, Road Safety Research Report No.26 (2002).

[298]   Road Traffic Act 1988 s.1. See, generally, C.M.V. Clarkson, "Aggravated Endangerment Offences" (2007) 60 C.L.P. 278.

[299]   Above, pp.284–290.

[300]   For example, *R v R* [2008] EWCA Crim 619.

[301]   See, generally, A. von Hirsch, "Extending the Harm Principle: 'Remote' Harm and Fair Imputation", in A.P. Simester and A.T.H. Smith (eds), *Harm and Culpability* (Oxford: Clarendon Press, 1996).

[302]   *Hussain* (1981) 47 Cr. App. R. 143. See also *R. v Bradish (Liam Christopher)* [1990] Crim. L.R. 723; *R. v Waller* [1991] Crim. L.R. 381; *Steele* [1993] Crim. L.R. 298.

sumed where a person knowingly points a firearm at or in the direction of another, whether or not the actor believed the firearm to be loaded."[303]

English law has no such general counterpart, preferring to focus instead on specific areas of risk-creation as instanced above. Is this English ad hoc approach justifiable?

C.M.V. Clarkson, "General Endangerment Offences: The Way Forward?" (2005) 32(2) University of Western Australia Law Review 131 at 135–137, 141–143:

"**CASE FOR A GENERAL ENDANGERMENT OFFENCE**

There is no particular reason why certain dangerous activities have been criminalised but others have not. For example, in English law why is reckless endangerment[304] a criminal offence (carrying a maximum penalty of life imprisonment) when the defendant is damaging another person's property but no offence when he or she is engaging in some other activity?

One of the main reasons for having a general endangerment offence is to ensure that there are no gaps, which might exist if there were only specific endangerment offences . . . While specific endangerment offences can be tailored to certain dangerous activities such as driving motor vehicles or running factories, there are a host of other everyday activities where we depend on others to perform their actions safely (eg, electricians and builders working in our houses, or child carers looking after our children, or doctors caring for our health). It is almost impossible to cater in advance, through specific offences, for all such persons who might act in a manner dangerous to our lives or safety. Only a general offence is capable of covering all such cases.

CASE AGAINST A GENERAL ENDANGERMENT OFFENCE

When the general endangerment offence was introduced in Western Australia . . . many specific offences [were retained] . . . The result is too many overlapping offences. This is undesirable. One of the main functions of the criminal law is to communicate clearly with citizens exactly what conduct is prohibited and the consequences of a violation of that law. If any individual action can give rise to a myriad of offences, that communication will necessarily be obscured. A further and very significant objection to having too many overlapping offences is that this confers too much discretion on the prosecution as to which charge(s) to bring . . . [T]the result is that defendants may feel pressured into pleading guilty to lesser offences rather than face the more serious charges . . .

[Another] . . . objection to the introduction of a general endangerment offence is that it could lead to over-criminalisation and offend the minimalism principle (ie, the last resort principle) . . . A potential problem with a general endangerment offence is that it can be so broad as to sweep conduct within its ambit that would not warrant criminalisation under these strict criteria. Controversial examples that have been cited include the following: the solo yachtsman sailing around the world, or the mountain climber who causes someone to undertake a dangerous rescue, or firemen going on strike. Given the much publicised dangers of passive smoking it could well be argued that smoking in public threatens the life, health and safety of those around the smoker. Such conduct could presumably be swept within the ambit of a general endangerment offence . . .

Decisions to make it an offence to be drunk in the street or to smoke in the presence of others or to engage in sexual activity while HIV positive (bearing in mind that in Australia the general endangerment offences are relatively serious offences) require careful debate before being swept within the ambit of a broad new offence. The existence of a general endangerment offence means that full discussion of whether such conduct should be criminalised is avoided. One of the fundamental principles underpinning the criminal law is that of fair warning. People should know in advance what conduct is impermissible. In all these above scenarios this principle is violated."

---

[303] In Australia many states have separate endangerment offences relating to death and to serious injury. See D. Lanham, "Danger Down Under" [1999] Crim. L.R. 960.

[304] Recklessly endangering the life of another (Criminal Damage Act 1971 s.1(2)).

6

PARTICIPATION IN CRIME

I. Introduction

So far in our analysis of the criminal law, we have assumed that only one defendant is involved, and we have considered that person's liability for acting alone. This may well be the case but it is also likely that at some stage either in the planning or commission of the crime other persons have become involved.[1] They may have supplied tools, information, advice, kept a look-out or even instigated the crime. In many cases, however, the crime may have been unplanned and spontaneous, brought about on the spur of the moment when a suggestion from one member of a group is taken up by others and acted upon. Where crime is a group activity it is arguable that a distinct set of problems arise in relation to using punishment to deter criminal activity.

Paul H. Robinson and John M. Darley, "Does Criminal Law Deter? A Behavioural Science Investigation" (2004) 24 O.J.L.S. 173–205 at pp.180–181:

"[B]oth the ability and the motivation to make the calculations required for deterrence can be influenced by a variety of contextual effects, . . . Perhaps the most important of these stems from the fact that crimes are often committed by groups. When offenders commit crimes in street gangs, for instance, several effects can temporarily reduce the possible impact of a threatened future prison term on current law-breaking activities: an 'arousal effect' leads to sprees and reduced sensitivity to risk, and an increase in the immediate rewards can arise from an increase in esteem in which the group holds the member who boldly breaks the law.

Of exacerbating effect is the fact of differential association . . . Interviews with criminals consistently show that the individual feels 'led to' the commission of the crime by the confidence that other gang members give them that 'they will not get caught' . . . Behavioural scientists will recognize this as an instance of the well-known 'risky shift' phenomenon, in which a group that comes to a collective decision after discussion comes to a decision that is often more risky than the average of the decisions that individuals held prior to the discussion. This means that the group tends to badly underestimate the risk of being caught.

Yet another process likely to lead groups toward crime commission is the phenomenon called 'deindividuation' in which the individual is 'lost in a crowd'; he perceives a loss of accountability for his individual actions when those actions are taken in a crowd or mob and thus engages in many more anti-social acts. The effect is illustrated most dramatically by gangs of teenagers or soccer crowds who sweep through neighbourhoods, breaking windows, assaulting those unlucky enough to be in their paths, but is at work in most groups of potential offenders.

---

[1] Between 1990 and 2000, 22% of murders and 15% of involuntary manslaughters involved multiple parties (Weston, *Criminal Complicity: A Comparative Analysis of Homicide Liability*, 2002, PhD thesis, University of Wales, Swansea). Although only looking at joint enterprise, a recent report revealing that between 2005 and 2013 there were 4,590 prosecutions for homicide involving two or more defendants also gives an indication of the scale of offending involving more than one party: the Bureau of Investigative Journalism, *Joint Enterprise: An Investigation into the Legal Doctrine of Joint Enterprise in Criminal Convictions* (London: The Bureau of Investigative Journalism, 2014), p.7.

Available data suggests that a significant proportion of offences are committed by offenders in groups. Except in cases of murders and rapes without theft, which are crimes in which offenders usually know their victim, 'the majority of offenders commit their offences with accomplices'. To sum up, . . . individual pathologies are likely to be extended and amplified by the fact that the decision to commit a crime is often a group rather than an individual decision, and the group processes shift its members toward taking more risky actions, and deindividuates them, facilitating the commission of destructive behaviours. It is difficult to fit this to the image of a person who is affected by complex rational deterrence considerations."[2]

In addition to questions of deterrence there is also the issue of desert requiring separate consideration in relation to group criminality. If several group members encouraged the offence, but only one individual actually carried out the actus reus, the need arises to find some way of measuring the blameworthiness of the other group members and the degree to which the end result can be attributed to them. How does the law respond to such group criminality? The approach taken by the English law of complicity is to make those individuals who help in the commission of offences liable for the full crime. Such secondary parties[3] are "liable to be tried, indicted and punished"[4] as if they had committed the crime themselves. This means, for example, that a defendant who assisted another to rape a woman (say, by blocking any entrance to the room) is guilty of rape, even though he never touched the woman. Unlike the inchoate offences, there is no crime of "aiding and abetting rape" or any other offence. References to "aiding and abetting rape" or other offences are simply a shorthand way of describing *how* the defendant came to be liable for the offence. Another consequence of this approach is that an accessory can plead common law defences such as duress or self-defence. Also, it means accessories are sentenced as if they were principals in cases where fixed or automatic sentences apply.[5] Whether it is appropriate to regard all of those involved in crimes as equally blameworthy is a question which can only be considered once the law has been examined. But what needs to be explored now is *how* the law is able to come to a conclusion that such parties are guilty of the same offence as the principal offender.

There are two stumbling-blocks to the imposition of full liability. The first is that it may be difficult to say that the secondary offender's conduct *caused* the crime, particularly where she was not even present at the scene. The second is that the secondary party may lack the mens rea of the offence. Thus whatever links the defendant with the crime, it cannot be the same actus reus and mens rea as that required for the principal offender. The question then becomes one of ascertaining what the different requirements are.

Present English law on participation is committed to the principle of *derivative liability*. The liability of the secondary party derives from, and is dependent on, the commission of an offence by the principal

---

2   See also, B. Livings and E. Smith, "Locating Complicity: Choice, Character, Participation, Dangerousness and the Liberal Subjectivist", in A. Reed and M. Bohlander (eds), *Participation in Crime: Domestic and Comparative Perspectives* (Farnham: Ashgate, 2013),

3   Whilst the terms "secondary offenders", "accomplices" and "accessories" are often used interchangeably, the Court of Appeal has expressed the view that the term "secondary parties" is preferable because it emphasises that secondary liability is derivative from the liability of the principal offender: *R. v Bryce (Craig Brian)* [2004] 2 Cr. App. R. 35 at [38].

4   Accessories and Abettors Act 1861 s.8. It is also possible to aid and abet a summary offence: Magistrates' Courts Act 1980 s.44.

5   *Attorney-General's Reference (No.71 of 1998) (Anderson)* [1999] 2 Cr. App. R. (S.) 369. The mandatory life sentence for murder applies to secondary parties in the same way as it applies to principal offenders. In *R. v Height (John)* [2009] 1 Cr. App. R. (S.) 117 it was held that although no reference was made to secondary parties in paras (4) and (5) of Sch.21 to the Criminal Justice Act 2003, those guidelines could be applied to secondary parties in the same way as they applied to principal offenders, and it would be wrong in the present case for the starting point for the secondary party's minimum term of imprisonment for murder to be lower than that of the principal offender, given that the former had arranged for his wife to be killed.

offender. Unlike the law of attempt where the focus is forward-looking on the defendant's actions and endeavours towards the commission of a crime, accessorial liability is backwards-looking. A crime must have been committed.[6] The issue is one of determining which persons participated sufficiently in that crime to be held liable for it. How is one to determine whether there has been "sufficient participation"?

K.J.M. Smith, A Modern Treatise on the Law of Complicity (1991), p.5:

"[I]t is tempting to view complicity as a shadow variety of principal liability, following as far as possible, both its *actus reus* and *mens rea* contours. As a starting-point, paradigmatic principal liability could be taken as involving a voluntary actor, with appropriate fault, engaging in harmful conduct or causing harm. An equivalence or parallel liability theory of complicity would demand a variable level of culpability as dictated by the principal offence's fault requirements. Such a shadowing process would, though, require the accessory's mental state to be an amalgam of purpose, perception, etc. in respect of both his own and the principal's actions. Paralleling the requirements of principal liability becomes even more difficult in respect of the principal's *actus reus*. While there is some level of plausibility in maintaining that an accessory must have a similar level of mental culpability to the perpetrator, this is not possible in respect of *actus reus* demands. Whether the principal offence is one based on the actor's conduct or the result of such conduct, the accessory's involvement (depending on the offence) cannot always be that stipulated by the offence's definition."

As the secondary party is fully liable for the offence committed, logic dictates that there should be a high degree of mens rea as well as a substantial contribution (actus reus) towards the offence. However, because the accessory's liability is based not only on his own acts, but also on his involvement or participation in the offence committed by another, the actus reus and mens rea required for secondary liability have to be assessed, not in isolation, but also in relation to the actus reus and mens rea of the principal offender.

Hardly surprisingly, this task of specifying the appropriate level of contribution and the required mental element for the accessory has proved highly problematic. Ashworth accuses the common law of

"running wild—there are too many decisions on complicity, so that courts (and/or counsel) tend to pick and choose among the many precedents; and there is no settled set of principles, which means that judicial development of the law does not always conduce to coherence."[7]

II. THE LAW

A. Principal Offenders

Despite the fact that all parties to a crime may, by virtue of s.8 of the Accessories and Abettors Act 1861, be tried, indicted and punished in the same way,[8] it is common[9] to distinguish between the principal offender and secondary parties.[10] The principal offender is usually described as the one whose

---

[6]   This is the key to distinguishing secondary liability from the new offences of encouraging or assisting crime under ss.44, 45 and 46 of the Serious Crime Act 2007, which do not require that the offence that is encouraged or assisted actually be committed.

[7]   Ashworth's commentary on *Bryce* [2004] Crim. L.R. 936 at 937.

[8]   Until 1967, principals were known as principals in the first degree and secondary parties as principals in the second degree if they were present at the crime and accessories if they were not. The Criminal Law Act 1967 effectively abolished the need for that distinction to be drawn.

[9]   There is no legal obligation to draw this distinction in an indictment. See fnn.21–25 below.

[10]   Not least because strict liability does not extend to accessories (*Callow v Tillstone* (1900) 8 L.T. 411). Even if a principal can be convicted without proof of mens rea, secondary parties must act with the requisite mental element.

act is the most immediate cause of the actus reus.[11] It is the principal offender who shoots and kills the victim in a crime of murder or who snatches the bag in the crime of theft or robbery.[12] Clearly, there may be more than one principal offender: two or more defendants may fatally stab a victim.

There is one exception to the rule that the principal offender is the one whose act is the most immediate cause of the actus reus. Where a defendant acts through an intermediary who is an "innocent agent" because, for example, she is below the age of criminal responsibility, it will be the instigator who will be regarded as the principal offender. The same result will apply if the defendant acts through someone who has no mens rea, as in the situation where the agent is instructed to put what is described as a harmless substance into someone's food, which the defendant knows will kill.[13]

B. Secondary Parties

1. Distinct modes of participation?

The liability of secondary parties is governed by s.8 of the Accessories and Abettors Act 1861:

"whosoever shall aid, abet, counsel or procure the commission of any indictable offence shall be liable to be tried, indicted and punished as a principal offender."

Prior to 1975

"the received view was that the particular words used in s.8 [aid, abet, counsel or procure] . . . had no special implications, and certainly were not to be taken in their literal or natural meaning as coercing any particular conclusion as to the type of conduct that amounts in law to complicity."[14]

In that year, however, the Court of Appeal stated that:

"We approach s.8 of the 1861 Act on the basis that the words should be given their ordinary meaning, if possible. We approach the section on the basis also that if four words are employed here 'aid, abet, counsel or procure', the probability is that there is a difference between each of those four words and the other three, because, if there were no difference, then Parliament would be wasting time in using four words where two or three would do."[15]

It is, however, extremely difficult to give these archaic words their "ordinary meaning". At a simplistic level, "aid" means help or assistance. While "abet" is generally regarded as largely synonymous with "aid", there have been suggestions that while "aid" is a neutral term, "abet" suggests wrongdoing: "'abet' clearly imports mens rea, which 'aid' may not".[16] "Counsel" suggests advice or encouragement

---

[11] D. Ormerod, *Smith and Hogan's Criminal Law*, 13th edn (Oxford: OUP, 2011), p.187.

[12] Unfortunately, comments by, for example, Lords Brown and Clark in *Gnango* [2011] UKSC 59 at [71] and [81] that the defendant was guilty of murder as a principal give insufficient weight to this key point: this decision is considered below at p.560.

[13] See *R. v Stringer (Neil Bancroft)* (1992) 94 Cr. App. R. 13 where the defendant, a business manager of a company, signed false invoices with the intention that innocent company employees would pass them for payment. When the company's bank account was duly debited, the defendant was convicted of theft of the money involved, through innocent agents.

[14] Law Commission Consultation Paper No.131, *Assisting and Encouraging Crime* (1993), para.2.10.

[15] *Attorney-General's Reference (No.1 of 1975)* [1975] Q.B. 773 at 779.

[16] *DPP for Northern Ireland v Lynch* [1975] A.C. 653 at 698.

while "procure" means "produce by endeavour".[17] This terminology was, perhaps, apt before 1967 when a distinction had been drawn between those present at the crime (aiders and abetters) and those not present (counsellors and procurers).[18] However, this distinction is no longer part of the law[19] and in more recent years it has become clear that, with the possible exception of "procure", these words are mere synonyms for assisting or helping or encouraging.[20]

That there is no critical distinction between these terms is emphasised by the fact that it is possible for an indictment to be framed in language which embraces all four terms[21] or for the defendant to be charged with committing the crime without any reference to the terms in s.8.[22] While the House of Lords in *Maxwell*[23] stressed that it was desirable that the true nature of the case against the defendant should be made clear in the indictment, it appears this recommendation has been almost "universally ignored".[24] There is no legal obligation to make such a specification and a failure to spell out the precise role of a person in an enterprise is not a breach of art.6 of the European Convention on Human Rights.[25]

To conclude, therefore, it is almost certain that no real conceptual distinctions can be drawn between most of the terms. Between them they embrace conduct which encourages or influences the principal offender or helps her in the commission of the crime. Accordingly, the following analysis of the law will not focus on its antiquated terminology but will concentrate on the different ways in which persons can be said to participate in the commission of a crime. However, as there might still be some justification for regarding procuring as distinct, this form of complicity is discussed later in the chapter.

2. Causation

English law on participation in crime is theoretically underpinned by the doctrine of derivative liability. As seen, this means accessories are held responsible for the result (the crime) that occurs. Unlike an inchoate model of liability, the focus is not simply on their contribution. If they are being blamed for the end result, it would follow logically that their actions should have had a role in *causing* that result. This view has support. K.J.M. Smith argues that a "broad causal account of complicity offers the most internal coherence alongside the greatest consistency with general principles of criminal responsibility that touch and concern complicity"[26] and that "it has always been implied in the concept of complicity that an accessory's involvement (whether as an 'assister' or 'encourager') did make some difference to the outcome".[27] In the recent decision of *Mendes*[28] Tolson LJ was also of this view.

However, causation is difficult to establish here because of the central principle that a causal chain

---

17   *Attorney-General's Reference (No.1 of 1975)* [1975] Q.B. 773.
18   See fn.8 above.
19   In *Stringer* [2011] EWCA Crim 1396 the Court of Appeal reaffirmed this, rejecting an argument that in order to aid and abet the defendant had to be present at the time of the commission of the crime.
20   For example, in *Attorney-General v Able* [1984] Q.B. 795 all the words were regarded as synonyms for "helping".
21   In *Bryce* the Court of Appeal stated that in charging secondary parties "it is frequently advisable (as was done in this case) to use the 'catch-all' phrase 'aid, abet, counsel or procure' because the shades of difference between them are far from clear": *Bryce* [2004] 2 Cr. App. R. 35 at [39].
22   *R. v Forman and Ford* [1988] Crim. L.R. 677. This avoids prosecution problems where uncertainty exists as to who is the principal.
23   *DPP of Northern Ireland v Maxwell* (1979) 68 Cr. App. R. 128.
24   *Taylor, Harrison and Taylor* [1998] Crim. L.R. 582. The citing in *R. v Montague (Damian John)* [2013] EWCA Crim 1781 of the passage in *Maxwell* which stressed the need for clarity is, therefore, welcome.
25   *R. v Mercer (Mark John) (Retrial)* [2001] EWCA Crim 638. Article 6(3)(a) states that everyone charged with a criminal offence has the right to be informed "in detail, of the nature and cause of the accusation against him".
26   K.J.M. Smith, *A Modern Treatise on the Law of Complicity* (Oxford: Clarendon Press, 1991), p.7.
27   Smith, *A Modern Treatise on the Law of Complicity* (1991), p.246.
28   *R. v Mendez (Reece)* [2010] EWCA Crim 516.

is generally broken by voluntary, willed human action. In participation cases this means that the voluntary, willed actions of the principal offender would normally be regarded as breaking the causal chain. As Kadish says:

> "Causation applies where results of a person's actions happen in the physical world. Complicity applies where results take the form of another person's voluntary action. Complicity emerges as a separate ground of liability because causation doctrine cannot satisfactorily deal with results that take the form of another's voluntary action."[29]

English law has largely accepted this view, rather than that expressed by Tolson J.

R. v Calhaem [1985] 1 Q.B. 808 (Court of Appeal, Criminal Division)

The defendant, Mrs Calhaem, was infatuated with her solicitor. She was charged with the murder of a woman who was having an affair with her solicitor. She had instructed one Zajac to commit the murder. He pleaded guilty to the murder but said in evidence that up to the point when he went berserk and killed the woman, he had come to a decision not to go through with the plan. The defendant appealed against her conviction for murder on the basis that counselling required a substantial causal connection between the acts of the counsellor and the commission of the offence and that none existed on the facts.

PARKER LJ:

"We must therefore approach the question raised on the basis that we should give to the word 'counsel' its ordinary meaning, which is as the judge said, 'advise', 'solicit', or something of that sort. There is no implication in the word itself that there should be any causal connection between the counselling and the offence. It is true that, unlike the offence of incitement at common law, the actual offence must have been committed and by the person counselled. To this extent there must clearly be, first, contact between the parties, and secondly, a connection between the counselling and the murder. Equally, the act done must, we think, be done within the scope of the authority or advice, and not, for example, accidentally when the mind of the final murderer did not go with his actions. For example, if the principal offender happened to be involved in a football riot in the course of which he laid about him with a weapon of some sort and killed someone, who, unknown to him, was the person whom he had been counselled to kill, he would not, in our view, have been acting within the scope of his authority; he would have been acting entirely outside it, albeit what he had done was what he had been counselled to do.
    We see, however, no need to import anything further into the meaning of the word."

Appeal dismissed

Subsequently, the Court of Appeal has followed this decision, in a case involving similar facts. In *Luffman*[30] the principal offender, who had been paid to kill the deceased and been given a sawn-off shotgun for that purpose by the secondary parties, claimed that he never intended to go through with the plan but met with the victim with the intention of robbing him, and shot him when the robbery went wrong. The secondary parties argued that there was no causal connection between their encouragement and the murder and so they should not be liable. The Court of Appeal, whilst resisting the invitation to provide more guidance as to how strong a connection was needed for aiding, abetting or counselling an offence,[31] was content that sufficient connection was proved in the present case and

---

[29]   S.H. Kadish, "Complicity, Cause and Blame: A Study in the Interpretation of Doctrine" (1985) 73 Cal. L. Rev. 324 at 327. See also, G. Williams, "Complicity, Purpose and the Draft Code—I" [1990] Crim. L.R. 4 at 6.

[30]   *R. v Luffman* [2008] EWCA Crim 1739.

[31]   The court accepted that causation would be important in a case of procuring (see fn.39 above), but treated the present case as one that involved aiding, abetting or counselling, but not procuring.

that the principal offender had not acted outside the scope of his authority, given that he did exactly what he had been contracted to do. Some further guidance as to what constitutes a "connecting link" is provided by Toulson LJ in the recent decision of *Stringer*:[32]

> "[E]ncouragement by its nature involves some form of transmission by words or conduct, whether directly or via an intermediary. An un-posted letter of encouragement would not be encouragement unless P chanced to discover it and read it. Similarly, it would be unreal to regard P as acting with the . . . encouragement of D if the only encouragement took the form of words spoken by D out of P's earshot."[33]

As long as the encouragement has "the capacity to act on P's mind"[34] it seems clear that liability is not restricted to situations where there is a causal relationship between the accessory's and principal's acts. This was underlined in *Giannetto*[35] where the court was of the view that liability would follow if a husband merely said "Oh goody" to a plan already in existence to kill his wife.[36] In such a case it cannot be asserted that the accessory's acts made any causal contribution to the end result.

In so far as assistance, rather than encouragement, is concerned, far from a causal connection being required,[37] it is possible that one could aid a crime without the principal even being aware that assistance is being provided.[38] However, with regard to "procuring", it has been held that causation is necessary[39] although consensus is not required. This, again, underlines the need for procuring to be dealt with separately.

3. Assistance and encouragement

Whether conduct amounts to assistance or encouragement is a question of fact.[40] Although the following are not distinct legal categories, it is useful, for purposes of exposition, to group the types of assistance and encouragement that may be provided as follows:

(i) Unplanned presence at the crime

Generally, being present[41] when a crime is committed does not, of course, implicate one in the crime. But, what if a fight starts in a pub and those present start to "egg on" the participants? The following is the leading decision on this point.

---

[32]   *Stringer* [2011] EWCA Crim 1396.
[33]   *Stringer* [2011] EWCA Crim 1396 at [49].
[34]   *Stringer* [2011] EWCA Crim 1396, per Toulson LJ, citing the words of the Law Commission: Law Com. No.300, *Inchoate Liability for Assisting and Encouraging Crime* (2006), para 2.36.
[35]   *Giannetto* [1997] 1 Cr. App. R. 1.
[36]   See further, J.C. Smith, "Criminal Liability of Accessories: Law and Law Reform" (1997) 113 L.Q.R. 453 at 458. See also *Attorney-General v Able* [1984] 1 Q.B. 795 where it was stated that it "does not make any difference" whether the person counselled would have acted anyway.
[37]   In *Bryce* [2004] 2 Cr. App. R. 35 at [75] the court concluded that as long as there is no "overwhelming supervening event" between the defendant's act of assistance and the commission of the offence then liability will be established. The position is different with regard to procuring.
[38]   D. Ormerod, *Smith and Hogan's Criminal Law*, 13th edn (Oxford: OUP, 2011), p.194. One may certainly procure an offence without the principal's knowledge.
[39]   *Attorney-General's Reference (No.1 of 1975)* [1975] Q.B. 773.
[40]   *Stringer* [2011] EWCA Crim 1396 at [51].
[41]   The term "presence" is broadly interpreted so as to include, for example, the look-out person standing outside: *Betts and Ridley* (1930) 22 Cr. App. R. 148.

R. v Clarkson (1971) 55 Cr. App. R. 445 (Courts-Martial Appeal Court)

The defendant was convicted of aiding and abetting the rape of a woman in an army barracks. He and another defendant, Carroll, appealed.

MEGAW LJ:

"[T]he presence of those two appellants in the room where the offence was taking place was not accidental in any sense and it was not by chance, unconnected with the crime, that they were there. Let it be accepted that they entered the room when the crime was committed because of what they had heard, which indicated that a woman was being raped, and they remained there.

Coney (1882) 8 Q.B.D. 534 decides that non-accidental presence at the scene of the crime is not conclusive of aiding and abetting . . .

What has to be proved is stated by Hawkins J. in a well-known passage in his judgment in *Coney* at p. 557 of the report. What he said was this:

'. . . In my opinion, to constitute an aider and abettor some active steps must be taken by word, or action, with the intent to instigate the principal, or principals. Encouragement does not of necessity amount to aiding and abetting, it may be intentional or unintentional, a man may unwittingly encourage another in fact by his presence, by misinterpreted words, or gestures, or by his silence, or non-interference, or he may encourage intentionally by expressions, gestures, or actions intended to signify approval. In the latter case he aids and abets, in the former he does not. It is no criminal offence to stand by, a mere passive spectator of a crime, even of a murder. Non-interference to prevent a crime is not itself a crime. But the fact that a person was voluntarily and purposely present witnessing the commission of a crime, and offered no opposition to it, though he might reasonably be expected to prevent and had the power so to do, or at least to express his dissent, might, under some circumstances, afford cogent evidence upon which a jury would be justified in finding that he wilfully encouraged and so aided and abetted. But it would be purely a question for the jury whether he did so or not.'

It is not enough, then, that the presence of the accused person has, in fact, given encouragement. It must be proved that he intended to give encouragement; that he *wilfully* encouraged. In a case such as the present, more than in many other cases where aiding and abetting is alleged, it was essential that that element should be stressed; for there was here at least the possibility that a drunken man with his self-discipline loosened by drink, being aware that a woman was being raped, might be attracted to the scene and might stay on the scene in the capacity of what is known as a voyeur; and, while his presence and the presence of others might in fact encourage the rapers or discourage the victim, he himself, enjoying the scene or at least standing by assenting, might not intend that his presence should offer encouragement to rapers and would-be rapers or discouragement to the victim; he might not realise that he was giving encouragement; so that, while encouragement there might be, it would not be a case in which, to use the words of Hawkins J., the accused person 'wilfully encouraged'.

A further point is emphasized in passages in the judgment of the Court of Criminal Appeal in *Allan* [1965] 1 Q.B. 130, at 135 and 138. That was a case concerned with participation in an affray. On page 135 the Court said this:

'In effect, it amounts to this: that the judge thereby directed the jury that they were in duty bound to convict an accused who was proved to have been present and witnessing an affray, if it was also proved that he nursed an intention to join in if help was needed by the side he favoured and this notwithstanding that he did nothing by words or deeds to evince his intention and outwardly played the role of a purely passive spectator. It was said that, if that direction is right, where A and B behave themselves to all outward appearances in an exactly similar manner, but it be proved that A had the intention to participate if needs be, whereas B had no such intention, then A must be convicted of being a principal in the second degree to the affray, whereas B should be acquitted. To do that, it is objected, would be to convict A on his thoughts, even though they found no reflection in his action.'. . .

From that it follows that mere intention is not in itself enough. There must be an intention to encourage; and there must also be encouragement in fact in cases such as the present case."

Appeal allowed[42]

---

[42]   See also *Wilcox R. v Jeffrey* [1951] 1 All E.R. 464 and *R. v Bland* [1988] Crim. L.R. 41.

In *Tait*[43] the Court of Appeal confirmed that both an intention to encourage and encouragement in fact must be established. Fletcher, however, has questioned the necessity for such a psychological effect on the principal:

"After all, whether the aid is actually rendered is fortuitous; the actor is equally culpable and his dangerousness is equally great if the perpetrator never receives the aid."[44]

Such an argument provides a justification for the new inchoate offences of encouraging or assisting crime under the Serious Crime Act 2007, leaving the law on complicity to punish those who in fact encourage a completed offence. While causal explanations of complicity have been generally rejected by English law (except in relation to procuring), it would seem that in these cases of unplanned presence at the scene of the crime, the law's insistence upon actual encouragement does manifest vestiges of a causal theory of complicity. This can best be explained by looking at the problem from another perspective. If, in these cases, liability were imposed in the absence of actual encouragement, this would be tantamount to punishing persons for an omission to act in situations where there was no pre-existing duty to act.[45]

(ii) Failure to exercise control

Exceptionally, presence without intended and actual encouragement may give rise to liability if the defendant has a right to control the actions of the principal offender. If, for instance, the owner of a vehicle sits in the passenger seat and does nothing whilst the principal offender behind the wheel drives dangerously, his omission may inculpate him.[46] Perhaps because visions of owners grabbing the steering wheel from the dangerous driver (and exacerbating the situation) arose before the judges' eyes, the rule of control being the legal equivalent of actual encouragement is now regarded as *evidence* only that the owner may have encouraged the commission of the crime.[47] If a prosecution for dangerous driving is to be based on the car owner's omission to intervene upon the principal offender's commission of the offence, it must be shown that the owner had the opportunity to do so.[48] In *Alford Transport Ltd*[49] it was held that actual presence at the scene of the crime was not necessary. Where a transport manager or the managing director of a company who had a right to control the actions of its employees deliberately refrained from exercising control, it could be inferred that there was positive encouragement. The mens rea of this species of complicity will be considered later.

(iii) Counselling

Counselling normally (although not invariably) refers to help given before the commission of the crime. It may take a wide variety of forms but includes advice, encouragement or the supply of information or equipment. The mens rea of counselling is discussed below.

---

43   *R. v Tait* [1993] Crim. L.R. 538. See also the Privy Council decision in *Robinson v The Queen* [2011] UKPC 3.
44   G.P. Fletcher, *Rethinking Criminal Law* (New York: OUP, 1978), p.679.
45   Such persons could be liable for encouraging crime under the Serious Crime Act 2007, provided that they either intended to encourage the commission of an offence or believed that their act would encourage its commission.
46   *Du Cros v Lambourne* [1907] 1 K.B. 40; cf. *R. v Harris* [1964] Crim. L.R. 54 where the supervisor of a learner-driver was convicted as an accessory to the learner-driver's traffic offences because he knowingly failed to take steps to stop them.
47   *Cassady v Morris (Reg.) (Transport)* [1975] R.T.R. 470; *Forman and Ford* [1988] Crim. L.R. 677.
48   *R. v Webster (Peter David)* [2006] 2 Cr. App. R. 6.
49   *R. v JF Alford Transport Ltd* [1997] 2 Cr. App. R. 326.

(iv) Joint enterprise

Where two or more people embark on a joint unlawful enterprise, for example a burglary or an attack on someone, the law has long adopted the view that all the parties should be liable for the direct and agreed consequences of that joint enterprise. Where the co-defendants merely commit the planned offence—the type of joint enterprise that Lord Hoffmann has described as a "plain vanilla" version of joint enterprise[50]—the finding of guilt for each co-defendant involved in the plan is straightforward. However, problems arise in cases other than the "plain vanilla" variety (cases which could perhaps be termed the "tutti frutti" variety), where the principal offender goes beyond what was agreed and commits a second offence, sometimes referred to as the "collateral" offence.[51] For example, in *Slack*[52] the defendant handed a knife to the principal offender during a burglary so that he could threaten the occupier if she started screaming. While the defendant was out of the room, the principal offender stabbed and killed the occupier. Is the accessory guilty of the collateral offence of murder in such a case?

R. v Powell; R. v English [1999] 1 A.C. 1 (House of Lords)

In the first appeal Powell and Daniels went with another man to a drug dealer's house to purchase drugs. The drug dealer was shot dead when he came to the door. The Crown case was that if the other man fired the gun, Powell and Daniels were guilty of murder because they knew the other man was armed with a gun and realised he might use it to kill or cause really serious injury to the drug dealer. They were convicted of murder and appealed.

In the second appeal, English and another man took part in a joint enterprise to attack and cause injury with wooden posts to a police officer. During the attack the other man used a knife and stabbed the officer to death. English had no knowledge that the other man was carrying a knife but was convicted of murder on the basis that he realised there was a substantial risk that the other man might kill or cause really serious injury to the police officer with the wooden post. He appealed.

LORD HUTTON:

"[T]he two questions certified for the opinion of the House are as follows:

'(i) Is it sufficient to found a conviction for murder for a secondary party to a killing to have realised that the primary party might kill with intent to do so or with intent to cause grievous bodily harm or must the secondary party have held such an intention himself?
    (ii) Is it sufficient for murder that the secondary party intends or foresees that the primary party would or may act with intent to cause grievous bodily harm, if the lethal act carried out by the primary party is fundamentally different from the acts foreseen or intended by the secondary party?'. . .

My Lords, I consider that there is a strong line of authority that where two parties embark on a joint enterprise to commit a crime, and one party foresees that in the course of the enterprise the other party may carry out, with the requisite *mens rea*, an act constituting another crime, the former is liable for that crime if committed by the latter in the course of the enterprise.

In *R. v Anderson and Morris* [1966] 2 Q.B. 110 the primary party (Anderson) killed the victim with a knife. The defence of the secondary party (Morris) was that even though he may have taken part in a joint attack with Anderson to beat up the victim, he did not know that Anderson was armed with a knife . . .

In delivering the judgment of the Court of Appeal Lord Parker C.J. accepted the principle [that]

---

50   *Brown v The State* [2003] UKPC 10 at [13].
51   See, for example, Law Commission Paper No.300, *Inchoate Liability for Assisting and Encouraging Crime* (2006), para.2.3; R. Buxton, "Joint Enterprise" [2009] Crim. L.R. 233.
52   *R. v Slack (Martin Andrew)* [1989] Q.B. 775.

'. . . where two persons embark on a joint enterprise, each is liable for the acts done in pursuance of that joint enterprise, that that includes liability for unusual consequences if they arise from the execution of the agreed joint enterprise but (and this is the crux of the matter) that if one of the adventurers goes beyond what has been tacitly agreed as part of the common enterprise, his co-adventurer is not liable for the consequences of that unauthorised act. Finally, he says it is for the jury in every case to decide whether what was done was part of the joint enterprise, or went beyond it and was in fact an act unauthorised by that joint enterprise.'

As a matter of strict analysis there is . . . a distinction between a party to a common enterprise contemplating that in the course of the enterprise another party may use a gun or knife and a party tacitly agreeing that in the course of the enterprise another party may use such a weapon. In many cases the distinction will in practice be of little importance because as Lord Lane C.J. observed in *R. v Wakely* with reference to the use of a pickaxe handle in a burglary, 'forseeability that the pickaxe handle might be used as a weapon of violence was practically indistinguishable from tacit agreement that the weapon should be used for that purpose'. Nevertheless, it is possible that a case might arise where a party knows that another party to the common enterprise is carrying a deadly weapon and contemplates that he may use it in the course of the enterprise, but whilst making it clear to the other party that he is opposed to the weapon being used, nevertheless continues with the plan. In such a case, it would be unrealistic to say that, if used, the weapon would be used with his tacit agreement. However, it is clear from a number of decisions . . . that as stated by the High Court of Australia in *McAuliffe v R.* (1995) 130 A.L.R. 26 at 30 . . . 'the scope of the common purpose is to be determined by what was contemplated by the parties sharing that purpose'. Therefore, when two parties embark on a joint criminal enterprise one party will be liable for an act which he contemplates may be carried out by the other party in the course of the enterprise even if he has not tacitly agreed to that act.

The principle . . . was applied by the Privy Council in *Chan Wing-siu v R.* [1985] A.C. 168 at 175 in the judgment delivered by Sir Robin Cooke, who stated:

"The case must depend rather on the wider principle whereby a secondary party is criminally liable for acts by the primary offender of a type which the former foresees but does not necessarily intend. That there is such a principle is not in doubt. It turns on contemplation or, putting the same idea in other words, authorisation, which may be express but is more usually implied. It meets the case of a crime foreseen as a possible incident of the common unlawful enterprise. The criminal culpability lies in participating in the venture with that foresight.'
. . .

In *Hui Chi-ming v R.* [1992] 1 A.C. 34 at 53 the Privy Council [agreed and] . . . Lord Lowry stated:

"The appellant's second point relies on Sir Robin Cooke's use of the word "authorisation" as a synonym for contemplation . . . Their Lordships consider that Sir Robin Cooke used this word . . . to emphasise the fact that mere foresight is not enough: the accessory, in order to be guilty, must have foreseen the relevant offence which the principal may commit *as a possible incident of the common unlawful enterprise* and must, with such foresight, still have participated in the enterprise. The word "authorisation" explains what is meant by contemplation, but does not add a new ingredient . . .'

In *McAuliffe v R.* the High Court of Australia has recently stated that the test for determining whether a crime falls within the scope of a joint enterprise is now the subjective test of contemplation and the court stated:

'. . . the test has become a subjective one and the scope of the common purpose is to be determined by what was contemplated by the parties sharing that purpose.'

There is therefore a strong line of authority that participation in a joint criminal enterprise with foresight or contemplation of an act as a possible incident of that enterprise is sufficient to impose criminal liability for that act carried out by another participant in the enterprise . . .

I consider that Lord Parker C.J. [in *Anderson and Morris*] applied the test of foresight when he stated:

'It seems to this court that to say that adventurers are guilty of manslaughter when one of them has departed completely from the concerted action of the common design and has suddenly formed an intent to kill and has used a weapon and acted in a way which no party to that common design could suspect is something which would revolt the conscience of people today.' . . .

In reliance upon *R. v Moloney* and *R. v Hancock* Mr Feinberg, on behalf of the appellants Powell and Daniels, submitted to this House . . . that as a matter of principle there is an anomaly in requiring proof against a secondary party of a lesser mens rea than needs to be proved against the principal who commits the actus reus of murder. If foreseeability of risk is insufficient to found the mens rea of murder for a principal then the same test of liability should apply in the case of a secondary party to the joint enterprise. Mr Feinberg further submitted that it is wrong for the present distinction in mental culpability to operate to the disadvantage of a party who does not commit the actus reus and that there is a manifest anomaly where there is one test for a principal and a lesser test for a secondary party . . .

My Lords, I recognise that as a matter of logic there is force in the argument . . . But the rules of the common law are not based solely on logic but relate to practical concerns and, in relation to crimes committed in the course of joint enterprises, to the need to give effective protection to the public against criminals operating in gangs . . .

A further consideration is that, unlike the principal party who carries out the killing with a deadly weapon, the secondary party will not be placed in the situation in which he suddenly has to decide whether to shoot or stab the third person with intent to kill or cause really serious harm. There is, in my opinion, an argument of considerable force that the secondary party who takes part in a criminal enterprise (for example the robbery of a bank) with foresight that a deadly weapon may be used, should not escape liability for murder because he, unlike the principal party, is not suddenly confronted by the security officer so that he has to decide whether to use the gun or knife or have the enterprise thwarted and face arrest. This point has been referred to in cases where the question has been discussed whether in order for criminal liability to attach the secondary party must foresee an act as more likely than not or whether it suffices if the secondary party foresees the act only as a possibility.

In *Chan Wing-siu v R.* counsel for the Crown submitted:

'Regard must be had to public policy considerations. Public policy requires that when a man lends himself to a criminal enterprise knowing it involves the possession of potentially murderous weapons which in fact are used by his partners with murderous intent, he should not escape the consequences to him of their conduct by reliance upon the nuances of prior assessment of the likelihood that such conduct will take place. In these circumstances an accomplice who knowingly takes the risk that such conduct might, or might well, take place in the course of that joint enterprise should bear the same responsibility for that conduct as those who use the weapons with the murderous intent.' . . .

Therefore, for the reasons which I have given I would answer the [first] certified question of law . . . by stating that it is sufficient to found a conviction for murder for a secondary party to have realised that in the course of the joint enterprise the primary party might kill with intent to do so or with intent to cause grievous bodily harm. . . .

The problem raised by the second certified question is [whether] there will be liability for murder on the part of the secondary party if he foresees the possibility that the other party in the criminal venture will cause really serious harm by kicking or striking a blow with a wooden post, but the other party suddenly produces a knife or a gun, which the secondary party did not know he was carrying, and kills the victim with it.

[Counsel] for the appellant . . . [argued that] where the primary party kills with a deadly weapon, which the secondary party did not know that he had and therefore did not foresee his use of it, the secondary party should not be guilty of murder. He submitted that to be guilty under the principle stated in *Chan Wing-siu v R.* the secondary party must foresee an act of the type which the principal party committed, and that in the present case the use of a knife was fundamentally different to the use of a wooden post.

My Lords, I consider that this submission is correct . . .

Accordingly, in the appeal of English, I consider that the direction of the learned trial judge was defective . . . [because] he did not qualify his direction on foresight of really serious injury by stating that if the jury considered that the use of the knife by Weddle was the use of a weapon and an action on Weddle's part which English did not foresee as a possibility, then English should not be convicted of murder. As the unforeseen use of the knife would take the killing outside the scope of the joint venture the jury should also have been directed, as the Court of Appeal held in *R. v Anderson and Morris*, that English should not be found guilty of manslaughter . . .

However, I would wish to make this observation: if the weapon used by the primary party is different to, but as dangerous as, the weapon which the secondary party contemplated he might use, the secondary party should not escape liability for murder because of the difference in the weapon, for example, if he foresaw that the primary party might use a gun to kill and the latter used a knife to kill, or vice versa . . .

[With regard to] the degree of foresight required to impose liability . . . the secondary party is subject to criminal liability if he contemplated the act causing the death as a possible incident of the joint venture, unless the risk was so remote that the jury take the view that the secondary party genuinely dismissed it as altogether negligible . . .

I consider that the test of foresight is a simpler and more practicable test for a jury to apply than the test of whether the act causing the death goes beyond what had been tacitly agreed as part of the joint enterprise. Therefore, in cases where an issue arises as to whether an action was within the scope of the joint venture, I would suggest that it might be preferable for a trial judge in charging a jury to base his direction on the test of foresight rather than on the test set out in the first passage in *R. v Anderson and Morris* [above, p.551]. But in a case where, although the secondary party may have foreseen grievous bodily harm, he may not have foreseen the use of the weapon employed by the primary party or the manner in which the primary party acted, the trial judge should qualify the test of foresight . . . in the manner stated by Lord Parker C.J. in the second passage in *R. v Anderson and Morris* [above, pp.551–552]."

LORD STEYN:

"I would reject the argument that the accessory principle *as such* imposes a form of constructive liability. The accessory principle requires proof of a subjective state of mind on the part of a participant in a criminal enterprise, *viz* foresight that the primary offender might commit a different and more serious offence. Professor Sir John Smith explained how the principle applies in the case of murder ((1997) 113 L.Q.R. 453 at 464):

'Nevertheless, as the critics point out it is enough that the accessory is reckless, whereas, in the case of the principal, intention must be proved. Recklessness whether death be caused is a sufficient *mens rea* for a principal offender in manslaughter, but not murder. The accessory to murder, however, must be proved to have been reckless, not merely whether death might be caused but whether murder might be committed; *he must have been aware, not merely that death or grievous bodily harm might be caused, but that it might be caused intentionally, by a person whom he was assisting or encouraging to commit a crime.* Recklessness whether murder be committed is different from, and more serious than, recklessness whether death be caused by an accident.' (My emphasis.)

. . . [There is an] argument that it is anomalous that the secondary party can be guilty of murder if he foresees the possibility of such a crime being committed while the primary can only be guilty if he has an intent to kill or cause really serious injury. Recklessness may suffice in the case of the secondary party but it does not in the case of the primary offender. The answer to this supposed anomaly, and other similar cases across the spectrum of criminal law, is to be found in practical and policy considerations. If the law required proof of the specific intention on the part of a secondary party, the utility of the accessory principle would be gravely undermined. It is just that a secondary party who foresees that the primary offender might kill with the intent sufficient for murder, and assists and encourages the primary offender in the criminal enterprise on this basis, should be guilty of murder. He ought to be criminally liable for harm which he foresaw and which in fact resulted from the crime he assisted and encouraged. But it would in practice almost invariably be impossible for a jury to say that the secondary party wanted death to be caused or that he regarded it as virtually certain. In the real world proof of an intention sufficient for murder would be well nigh impossible in the vast majority of joint enterprise cases. Moreover, the proposed change in the law must be put in context. The criminal justice system exists to control crime. A prime function of that system must be to deal justly but effectively with those who join with others in criminal enterprises. Experience has shown that joint criminal enterprises only too readily escalate into the commission of greater offences. In order to deal with this important social problem the accessory principle is needed and cannot be abolished or relaxed."

Powell and Daniels' appeals dismissed. English's appeal allowed

From this decision it is clear that an accessory will only be liable for acts done within the scope of the joint enterprise. Each party to a joint enterprise is liable for any act done pursuant to that venture.

Where there is a shared joint enterprise, each member of the group assumes responsibility for the actions of other members of the group, the basis for the liability of those participating with foresight of how other parties may act being described as "parasitic accessorial liability" by Smith.[53]

However, one is only a "member of a group" with regard to "group actions", that is, acts done in accordance with the joint enterprise. If the principal offender departs from the joint enterprise in a material manner, for example, produces a gun and kills, when the enterprise was to beat the victim with sticks, the defendant escapes liability. The question then becomes one of determining the scope of the joint enterprise. In *Hui Chi-ming* this was defined as the "contemplated area of guilty conduct" and in *McAuliffe* as being "determined by what was contemplated by parties sharing that purpose". Both decisions were approved in *Powell*. Accordingly, if two parties embark on a burglary and one contemplates that the other might have a knife, the joint enterprise is burglary armed with a knife. The joint enterprise is defined by reference to the type of activity and the degree of dangerousness involved. Lord Hutton stated that if the weapon used was different to, but just as dangerous as, the contemplated weapon, for example, a gun as opposed to a knife, the act would still be within the joint enterprise.

R. v Greatrex [1999] 1 Cr. App. R. 126 (Court of Appeal, Criminal Division)

A group of youths, including the defendant, were violently kicking a victim when the principal offender produced a bar or spanner and struck the victim killing him. The defendant was convicted of murder and appealed.

BELDAM LJ:

"In deciding whether the actions of one participant are so fundamentally different the jury will have regard to all the circumstances and of course where one participant unknown to the others is carrying a lethal weapon such as a knife or revolver and uses it in a way which indicates that his actions go entirely beyond actions which were foreseen by the others, that is cogent evidence that what was done was substantially different from actions within the common purpose . . . Whilst it would have been open to the jury to conclude that the shod foot is as much a weapon as a bar, and equally dangerous in the sense of being capable of inflicting really serious injury and so not beyond the contemplation or foresight of Greatrex when he joined in the attack, it was for the jury to decide whether that was so or whether the actions of Bates in using the bar were not foreseen by Greatrex at the time when the fatal blow was struck and so were outside the combined purpose . . .

As these questions were not left to the jury, we consider that the conviction of Greatrex cannot be upheld."

Appeal of Greatrex allowed

In *Powell; English* Lord Hutton was of the view that a gun was intrinsically more dangerous than a stick or post.

R. v Yemoh [2009] EWCA Crim 930 (Court of Appeal, Criminal Division)

The defendants were members of a gang involved in the stabbing of the deceased. The principal offender was never identified, and they were all convicted on the basis of their participation in a joint enterprise. On appeal, the defendants argued that although some of them had known that a member of their group had been in possession of a Stanley knife, they had not known that any other sort of knife might be used. The forensic evidence suggested that the fatal wounds were inflicted with a blade much longer than that of a Stanley knife, and the defendants sought to argue that the knife that was

---

[53]   J.C. Smith, "Criminal Liability of Accessories: Law and Law Reform" [1997] 113 L.Q.R. 453 at 455. This terminology was adopted by the Supreme Court in *R. v Gnango (Armel)* [2011] UKSC 59, below at p.560.

used was of such a different type as to make it fundamentally different and take the act of the principal outside the scope of the joint enterprise. The Court of Appeal rejected this argument.

LORD JUSTICE HOOPER:

"[149] It is common knowledge that a Stanley knife can be used to stab albeit not very deeply and not very efficiently. But a Stanley knife can also be used to cause serious injury or death when used in a slashing motion. In our view the difference between the infliction of death or serious injury by means of a Stanley knife, on the one hand, and by means of a knife of the kind used in this case, on the other hand, is not of itself enough to enable the factual issue of 'fundamental difference' to be left to the jury. If left to the jury, the issue could only properly be decided one way. In that sense, given that the two knives with which we are concerned in this case are sufficiently similar in their capacity to cause death or serious injury (albeit one primarily by stabbing and one primarily by slashing) it cannot be said, as a matter of law, that the knife used to kill in this case is more lethal than a Stanley knife, to adopt the words of Lord Hutton in *Powell* and *English*. We therefore reject this submission also."

Appeal dismissed

This decision seems correct. If the law were to recognise the difference between a Stanley knife and a kitchen knife, where would the distinctions end?[54] In *Jackson*,[55] however, the Privy Council seemed to suggest that a long-bladed knife could be seen as fundamentally different to a machete or cutlass. This appeal from Jamaica dealt with a case in which a number of defendants had taken part in beating the victim with the flat sides of their machetes. The Privy Council suggested that the principal offender's decision to use the sharp point of a knife to stab the victim might take his act outside the scope of the joint enterprise. Although this suggestion was obiter, the Privy Council held that the issue should have been left to the jury.

Jackson illustrates that it is not simply the nature of the weapon that matters. It is the use to which it is to be put that determines the scope of the enterprise. In *Attorney-General's Reference No.3 of 2004*[56] there was a joint enterprise to terrorise the victim with the use of a loaded gun. The defendant recruited two others, one of whom was the principal offender and both of whom were convicted of murder, to put pressure on the victim. The assumed facts were that the defendant knew that the principal might discharge the gun near the victim in order to frighten him, but the defendant did not intend the victim to die or to suffer harm, and had not foreseen death or physical injury. The Court of Appeal held that the principal's use of the gun to shoot the victim at point-blank range took his acts outside the scope of the joint unlawful enterprise and that, as a result, the defendant would not be liable for manslaughter. The act done by the principal was of a fundamentally different character from any act contemplated by the defendant. The obvious anomaly here is that if, rather than shooting the victim deliberately, the principal had discharged the gun in order to frighten the victim and it had accidentally killed him, the defendant would have in those circumstances been liable for manslaughter. His state of mind would have been the same but because of events beyond his control (i.e. the acts of the principal) his liability would be quite different. In this case the court highlighted the need for the prosecution to provide appropriate alternative counts on the indictment (for non-fatal offences) to ensure that a secondary party in the defendant's position did not escape criminal liability altogether.

Given the harshness of the law on joint enterprise, it is unsurprising that some secondary parties have been forced to raise some rather inventive defences. In *Rahman*,[57] the defendants knew that

---

54 In *R. v Lewis (Rhys Thomas)* [2010] EWCA Crim 496 no material difference was found where a particularly ferocious blow killed in a joint enterprise involving the use of fists and feet.
55 *The Queen v Jackson* [2009] UKPC 28.
56 *Attorney-General's Reference (No.3 of 2004)* [2006] Crim. L.R. 63.
57 *R. v Rahman (Islamur)* [2009] 1 A.C. 129.

one of their members might have a knife, and that it might be used to stab and cause grievous bodily harm to the deceased. However, their novel argument was that the principal offender's state of mind, in intending to kill, took his act outside the scope of the joint enterprise. How did the House of Lords respond to this argument?

R. v Rahman [2009] 1 A.C. 129 (House of Lords)

A number of young men, including the defendants, gathered with various weapons (blunt instruments such as baseball bats, a metal bar, table leg) and attacked the deceased and his friend. The deceased died of three knife wounds. Only some of the defendants' group were apprehended, and the knifeman was never found. The Crown's case for murder was that the role of each of the defendants in the attack involved either the deliberate and intentional infliction of serious physical harm or, by their conduct, the intentional encouragement of others to do likewise. The defendants argued that they had joined in the joint enterprise with, at most, an intent to do serious bodily harm without knowledge or foresight that anyone else involved intended to kill. The results of the post mortem suggested that the fatal stab wounds, because of the force with which they must have been inflicted, the site of the wound and the angle of the blade, might have been inflicted with intent to kill. If the principal offender had acted with such intent, that intent, they argued, would take his acts outside the scope of the common design and render them fundamentally different to anything they had foreseen or contemplated. The judge declined to direct the jury along these lines and the defendants were convicted of murder and appealed unsuccessfully to the Court of Appeal who certified the following point of law of general public importance for the House of Lords:

> "If in the course of a joint enterprise to inflict unlawful violence the principal party kills with an intention to kill which is unknown to and unforeseen by a secondary party, is the principal's intention relevant, (i) to whether the killing was within the scope of a common purpose to which the secondary party was an accessory? (ii) to whether the principal's act was fundamentally different from the act or acts which the secondary party foresaw as part of the joint enterprise?"

Lord Bingham:

"[21] It was, inevitably, common ground between the parties that an accessory may only be criminally liable for a crime which the principal has committed, in murder unlawful killing with intent to kill or cause really serious injury. It was also common ground that the test of an accessory's liability under the wider principle explored in *R. v Powell (Anthony), R. v English* is one of foresight. The crucial divide between the parties was: foresight of what? The appellants' answer . . . would include foresight of the principal's intention. The respondent's answer . . . was: foresight of what the principal might do. On the Crown's analysis the principal's undisclosed intention is beside the point. It is his acts which matter.

[22] The appellants' argument derives little assistance, in my opinion, from authority. In *Anderson and Morris* (1966) 50 Cr.App.R.216, the principle . . . accepted by the court . . . concentrated on the unauthorised act of the principal and on 'what was done'. The case turned on the use of a knife, which the successful appellant denied knowing his associate had. In *Uddin* . . . the facts were somewhat similar: the case did not turn on the intention with which the knife was used but on its unforeseen production and use. It is, with respect, clearly inappropriate to speak of a weapon's 'propensity to cause death', since an inanimate object can have no propensity to do anything. But of course it is clear that some weapons are more dangerous than others and have the potential to cause more serious injury, as a sawn-off shotgun is more dangerous than a child's catapult . . . . In *Attorney General's Reference (No.3 of 2004)* . . . it was the radically different nature of the act, not the principal's change of intention, which dictated the result.

[23] I regard the respondent's submission as consistent with existing authority. In describing the wider principle in *Chan Wing-Siu* Sir Robin Cooke referred to 'acts by the primary offender of a type which the former foresees

but does not necessarily intend'. In *Gamble* [1989] N.I. 268, at 282, Carswell J. emphasised the need to have regard to 'the nature of the act contemplated and that which was in fact committed'. In *English* the submission of counsel which Lord Hutton accepted was that 'the secondary party must foresee an act of the type which the principal party committed . . . ', and the judge's direction was defective in failing to invite the jury's attention to the use of the knife by Weddle and the action on his part. As Laws L.J. pithily observed in *R. v Roberts, Day and Day* [2001] EWCA Crim 1594 at [52]:

> 'The subject matter of a joint enterprise is not a state of mind or intention but an objective act which it is contemplated will or might be done.'

[24] Authority apart, there are in my view two strong reasons, one practical, the other theoretical, for preferring the respondent's contention. The first is that the law of joint enterprise in a situation such as this is already very complex, and the appellants' submission, if accepted, would introduce a new and highly undesirable level of complexity. Given the fluid, fast-moving course of events in incidents such as that which culminated in the killing of the deceased, incidents which are unhappily not rare, it must often be very hard for jurors to make a reliable assessment of what a particular defendant foresaw as likely or possible acts on the part of his associates. It would be even harder, and would border on speculation, to judge what a particular defendant foresaw as the intention with which his associates might perform such acts. It is safer to focus on the defendant's foresight of what an associate might do, an issue to which knowledge of the associate's possession of an obviously lethal weapon such as a gun or a knife would usually be very relevant.

[25] Secondly, the appellants' submission, as it seems to me, undermines the principle on which, for better or worse, our law of murder is based. In the prosecution of a principal offender for murder, it is not necessary for the prosecution to prove or the jury to consider whether the defendant intended on the one hand to kill or on the other to cause really serious injury. That is legally irrelevant to guilt. The rationale of that principle plainly is that if a person unlawfully assaults another with intent to cause him really serious injury, and death results, he should be held criminally responsible for that fatality, even though he did not intend it. If he had not embarked on a course of deliberate violence, the fatality would not have occurred. This rationale may lack logical purity, but it is underpinned by a quality of earthy realism. To rule that an undisclosed and unforeseen intention to kill on the part of the primary offender may take a killing outside the scope of a common purpose to cause really serious injury, calling for a distinction irrelevant in the case of the primary offender, is in my view to subvert the rationale which underlies our law of murder.

[26] I would accordingly reject the appellants' submission on this point. I would also reject a subsidiary submission that the judge should have explained to the jury what was meant by 'fundamentally different'. This is not a term of art. It may, or may not, be regarded as a helpful turn of phrase, but its meaning is plain and cannot be misunderstood by a jury to whom the governing principle has been explained, as it was here. In any event, it is hard to see how the judge could have explained his meaning more clearly than when he said:

> 'But if you conclude that to stab with a knife in the back was in a different league to the kind of battering to which the attackers implicitly agreed upon by the use of those other weapons, then the others are not responsible for the consequences of the use of the knife unless in the case of the Defendant whose case you are considering he actually foresaw the use of a knife to kill Tyrone Clarke.' . . .

[28] The Court of Appeal certified the following point of law of general public importance as involved in its decision:

> 'If in the course of a joint enterprise to inflict unlawful violence the principal party kills with an intention to kill which is unknown to and unforeseen by a secondary party, is the principal's intention relevant,
>
> (i) to whether the killing was within the scope of a common purpose to which the secondary party was an accessory?
>
> (ii) to whether the principal's act was fundamentally different from the act or acts which the secondary party foresaw as part of the joint enterprise?'

I would answer both parts of the question in the negative, and would accordingly dismiss these appeals."

LORD BROWN:

"[63] As it seems to me, the first question is misconceived. If the principal (the killer) was at all times intent on killing the victim and the secondary party was not, then it is simply unrealistic to talk in terms of their sharing a common purpose. But that matters nothing. Once the wider principle was recognised (or established), as it was in *Chan Wing-Siu* and *Hyde*, namely that criminal liability is imposed on anyone assisting or encouraging the principal in his wrongdoing who realises that the principal may commit a more serious crime than the secondary party himself ever intended or wanted or agreed to, then the whole concept of common purpose became superfluous. There really is no longer any need for judges to direct juries by reference both to whether the relevant actions were within the scope of the common purpose of those concerned and also by reference to whether the secondary party realised that the principal might commit the acts constituting the more serious offence. The second limb of such a direction effectively subsumes the first. If the relevant acts were within the scope of the principal's and accessory's common purpose, necessarily the secondary party would realise that the principal might thereby commit the more serious offence. And if the secondary party did not foresee even the possibility of the more serious offence, such could hardly have been within the scope of any shared purpose.

[66] Of course the secondary party can say in evidence that he was ignorant not merely of the principal's possession of a knife or gun or whatever it was but also of his murderous intent. But if the jury conclude that he knew about the weapon and foresaw the possibility of its use to cause at least grievous bodily harm then they must convict him of murder whether he knew of the killer's murderous intent or not. *Powell* itself is surely directly in point on this issue: no one suggested there that it mattered whether the appellants realised that the third man was intent on killing the drug dealer; it was sufficient and fatal to their defence that they knew he had a gun and foresaw he might use it at least to cause gbh . . .

[68] . . . [The *Hyde* principle, as qualified in *English*] can surely be restated thus:

'If B realises (without agreeing to such conduct being used) that A may kill or intentionally inflict serious injury, but nevertheless continues to participate with A in the venture, that will amount to a sufficient mental element for B to be guilty of murder if A, with the requisite intent, kills in the course of the venture *unless (i) A suddenly produces and uses a weapon of which B knows nothing and which is more lethal than any weapon which B contemplates that A or any other participant may be carrying and (ii) for that reason A's act is to be regarded as fundamentally different from anything foreseen by B.*' (The italicised words are designed to reflect the *English* qualification)."

Appeals dismissed

This is, in some respects, a troubling decision and it is worthwhile exploring the two grounds for appeal separately. In relation to the first ground—the question of whether the principal's intention is relevant to whether the killing was within the scope of a joint enterprise—the House of Lords' decision was unanimous. It is clear that it is irrelevant that the secondary party only foresaw that the principal offender would intend to cause grievous bodily harm. The fact that the principal offender intended to kill does not take the action outside the scope of the joint enterprise. This is understandable because, as Lord Bingham stated, for murder it does not matter whether the principal offender intended to kill or to cause grievous bodily harm—and, further, it would be impracticable for a jury to determine whether the secondary party foresaw that the principal offender intended to kill or cause grievous bodily harm.

Rahman has arguably modified the *Powell; English* rules relating to the mens rea of the secondary party. This will be discussed in the next section.

It is in relation to the second ground of appeal that the decision is more problematic. The House of Lords was asked to consider if the principal's intention was also irrelevant when his act was fundamentally different from what the secondary party foresaw as part of the joint enterprise. The rule in *English* was one that involved assessing not just the weapon used but also the intent with which the principal used it. Both had to be considered in deciding whether the act was "fundamentally different". In *Rahman* both Lord Bingham and Lord Rodger took the view that no change was required to the rule in *English*: Lord Bingham thought the term "fundamentally different" had a "plain meaning" and was not a term of art.[58] However, the certified question (whether, if in the course of a joint enterprise to inflict unlawful violence the principal party kills with an intention to kill which is unknown to and unforeseen by a secondary party, is the principal's intention relevant to whether the act was fundamentally different from the act or acts which the secondary party foresaw as part of the joint enterprise?) is answered in the negative, even by Lord Bingham, and Lord Brown's reformulation reduces the rule to a consideration of the relative lethal qualities of the weapon. Moreover, it only seems to apply where the principal offender "suddenly produces" a weapon of which the secondary party knows nothing. The restrictions placed upon the rule in *English* are both unfortunate and unclear.

Not surprisingly, the courts have sought to clarify the effect of *Rahman*. In *Yemoh*[59] the Court of Appeal interpreted *Rahman* as restricting the *Powell; English* principle (about more lethal weapons) to murder cases where "the defendant's state of mind was less culpable than *intending the victim to be killed*". According to this, where the secondary party intends that the victim be killed by way of being beaten with blunt instruments, but the principal pulls out a knife and uses it to kill instead, the secondary party will be liable, since the agreed joint enterprise was to kill and it should make no difference how that aim is achieved.[60] According to *Yemoh*:

> "The [*Powell; English*] principle [that the production of a more lethal weapon will relieve the secondary party of liability] now only comes into play if the defendant:
>
> a) realised that one of the attackers might kill with intent to kill or cause really serious bodily harm; or
>
> b) intended that really serious bodily harm would be caused; or
>
> c) realised that one of the attackers might cause really serious bodily harm with intent to cause such harm."[61]

The latest reformulation of the ruling in *Rahman* by the Court of Appeal in *Mendes* states that:

> "In cases where the common purpose is not to kill but to cause serious harm, D is not liable for the murder of V if the direct cause of V's death was a deliberate act by P which was of a kind (a) unforeseen by D and (b) likely to be altogether more life-threatening than acts of the kind intended or foreseen by D. The reference to a 'deliberate act' is to the quality of the act—deliberate and not by chance—rather than to any consideration of P's intention as to the consequences."[62]

The court also states that what matters is not simply the difference in weapons but the way in which it is likely to be used and the degree of injury which it is likely to cause.[63]

This is a welcome attempt by the Court of Appeal to state the law as straightforwardly as possible and, if followed, would mitigate some of the difficulties associated with *Rahman* (where the issue was reduced to the relative lethal qualities of the weapon). However, the matter cannot be regarded as settled: *Rahman* is a decision of the House of Lords.

---

58 *R. v Rahman (Islamur)* [2009] 1 A.C. 129 at [26].
59 *R. v Yemoh (Kurtis)* [2009] EWCA Crim 930. For the facts, see above at p.554.
60 This was the view expressed by Lord Roger in *Rahman* [2009] 1 A.C. 129 at [33]. It has been endorsed in *Mendes* [2010] EWCA Crim 516 at [44].
61 *Yemoh* [2009] EWCA Crim 930 at [135]–[136].
62 *Mendes* [2010] EWCA Crim 516 at [45].
63 *Mendes* [2010] EWCA Crim 516 at [42].

As matters stand, where the secondary party only *intends serious injury* or only realises that the principal offender *might* kill or cause serious injury, then the production of a more lethal weapon will relieve him of liability.

This is surely an improvement on the position in *Powell; English*. As stated in previous editions of this book, there can be no justification for an approach which allows a secondary party to escape liability because although he intends that the principal will be killed he is mistaken about the weapon that the principal will use to do so. While, of course, a gun is intrinsically more dangerous than a wooden post (for example), nevertheless, if the secondary party intends that the victim be killed, it is difficult to see why the method of killing, or the instrument used, should make any difference. Yet, Lord Brown's reformulation of the *English* qualification as interpreted in *Yemoh* appears to open up the prospect of the secondary party escaping liability by claiming that although all parties intended grievous bodily harm (rather than *death*) to result he thought that this was by using, say, fists rather than the knife the principal in fact used. In an area of law which takes a very robust approach to liability, this is indeed liberal.

In most cases of group violence involving fighting there has seldom been planning. As stated in *Greatrex*:

> "[A]s the participants rush to take part in the attack, they give no thought to the means by which they will overwhelm the victim nor do they have any particular foresight whether one or other of them may in the course of the ensuing violence pick up or use any weapon which may conveniently come to hand."[64]

Thus, in *O'Flaherty*[65] it was held that in a case of spontaneous violence where there was no prior agreement as to what would happen, the question of whether the principal offenders acted within the scope of the joint enterprise was a matter which the jury must infer from the knowledge and actions of the individual participants. In *Uddin*[66] it was held that the scope of an unlawful enterprise can change if, after the production of an unforeseen weapon, the others continue with their attack:

> "If in the course of the concerted attack a weapon is produced by one of the participants and the others knowing that he has it in circumstances where he may use it in the course of the attack participate or continue to participate in the attack, they will be guilty of murder if the weapon is used to inflict a fatal wound."

While the ratio of *Powell* only extends to murder, the principle underlying this case is broader and applies to all crimes.[67]

The final case to consider at this point is the recent, troubling, decision of the Supreme Court in *Gnango*:

R. v Gnango [2011] UKSC 59 (Supreme Court)

The defendant voluntarily exchanged gunfire with an opponent, B, referred to as "Bandana Man", in a public car park. A shot by B killed an innocent passer-by. A man thought to be B was arrested but

---

64   *R. v Greatrex (David Anthony)* [1999] 1 Cr. App. R. 126 at 139.
65   *R. v O'Flaherty (Errol Carlton)* [2004] 2 Cr. App. R. 20.
66   *R. v Uddin (Rejan)* [1998] 2 All E.R. 744.
67   In *Yemoh* these principles were applied to manslaughter.

there was insufficient evidence to charge him. The defendant was charged with the victim's murder. At trial the judge held that it was not relevant that the defendant and B had reciprocally opposing intentions to shoot each other. He rejected the Crown's argument that the defendant could be liable for aiding and abetting the killing, directing the jury that the defendant would be guilty of murder if they were sure that he and B had been in a joint enterprise (whether planned or spontaneous) to use unlawful violence against each other, and that in the course of that joint enterprise fight, the victim had been murdered by B on the basis of transferred malice. The defendant was convicted and appealed. The Court of Appeal allowed the appeal, holding that there was no evidence of a shared common purpose. The Crown appealed to the Supreme Court, contending, inter alia, that the defendant's conviction could be justified on the basis that the defendant had aided and abetted the commission of the murder by actively encouraging B to shoot at him.

LORD PHILLIPS P and LORD JUDGE CJ (with whom Lord Wilson agreed).

"[1] Permission to appeal was granted in this case in order to enable this court to consider the following point of law, certified by the Court of Appeal as being of general public importance:

> If (1) D1 and D2 voluntarily engage in fighting each other, each intending to kill or cause grievous bodily harm to the other and each foreseeing that the other has the reciprocal intention, and if (2) D1 mistakenly kills V in the course of the fight, in what circumstances, if any, is D2 guilty of the offence of murdering V?'

The facts of this case are unusual, but the importance of the point of law lies in the implications that it may have in respect of the scope of potential liability of those who permit themselves to become involved in public order offences.

[2] No previous decision in this jurisdiction provides a clear indication of how the point of law should be resolved . . . In resolving the point of law it will be appropriate to have regard to policy . . .

[13] [S]ection [8] does not specify what is encompassed by the words 'aid, abet, counsel, or procure'. That question is determined by the common law . . . Having regard to the facts of this case we can start with this simple proposition. Where two persons, D1 and D2, agree to the commission of an indictable offence, where both are present at the place where the criminal act is to be performed and where one of them, D1, commits that act, both will be jointly liable for the crime. The act will have taken place pursuant to their joint criminal purpose and D2 will be equally guilty with D1, having aided, abetted, counselled or procured D1 to commit the crime.

[14] The law becomes more complicated where, in the course of committing, or attempting to commit the criminal act which is their common purpose, D1 commits a further criminal act which goes beyond that purpose . . .

[Their Lordships endorse the following passage from *R. v A* [2010] EWCA Crim 1622 at [27]]:

> '. . . the liability of D2 . . . rests, as all these citations show, on his having continued in the common venture of crime A when he realises (even if he does not desire) that crime B may be committed in the course of it. Where crime B is murder, that means that he can properly be held guilty if he foresees that D1 will cause death by acting with murderous intent (viz either the intent to kill or the intent to do GBH). He has associated himself with a foreseen murder . . .'

[15] Professor Sir John Smith coined the phrase 'parasitic accessory liability' to describe this form of liability arising out of participation in a joint criminal enterprise. While this is not the most elegant phraseology we propose to adopt it in this judgment by way of convenient shorthand. . . .

[22] [The trial judge dismissed aiding and abetting as the source of liability on the basis that the defendant had not actively encouraged 'Bandana Man' to shoot him]. The alternative [prosecution] case . . . advanced was one of parasitic accessory liability. The judge accepted that this alternative was viable. He held that it was open to the jury to find that the respondent and Bandana Man were subject to a joint enterprise to commit an affray and that, if the jury then found that the respondent foresaw and envisaged that Bandana Man might shoot and kill an innocent passer-by this would found a verdict of murder on the part of the respondent [he subsequently so directed the jury who found the defendant guilty of murder]. . .

[24] Before the Court of Appeal . . . [the Crown did not revive the aiding and abetting argument but] sought to uphold the judge's direction on the basis of parasitic accessory liability . . .

[25] The Court of Appeal . . . [rejected] this argument . . . [W]e believe that we can summarise . . . [its reasons] quite shortly. Parasitic accessory liability has to arise out of a joint enterprise that involves the two parties acting together, or in concert, or for a common purpose. Where an affray is alleged to have arisen from a fight between two people it does not ordinarily involve a joint enterprise or common purpose. Ordinarily the purpose of each protagonist to such an affray is the individual purpose of striking the other and avoiding being struck himself. Such purposes are not shared by the two protagonists, they are reciprocal, or equal and opposite purposes. It was none the less possible to envisage a scenario in which two persons shared a common purpose to strike *and be struck*—a prize fight or a duel were examples of this. On the facts of the present case there might have been a common purpose to shoot *and be shot at*, as in a duel, but the judge had never asked the jury to consider that possibility [so it could form the basis of D's conviction] . . .

[29] Before this court . . . the Crown has sought to revive the case . . . that the respondent had been an accessory to Bandana Man's attempt to kill him and thus shared Bandana Man's liability, as a result of the doctrine of transferred malice, for the murder. . . [relying upon parasitic accessory liability in the alternative].

[31] We propose to start by considering . . . [the] attempt to rely upon the doctrine of parasitic accessory liability . . .

[42] Parasitic accessory liability arises where (i) D1 and D2 have a common intention to commit crime *A*, (ii) D1, as an incident of committing crime *A*, commits crime *B*, and (iii) D2 had foreseen the possibility that he might do so. Here there was no crime *A* and crime *B*. It cannot be said that the two protagonists had a joint intention to commit violence of a type that fell short of the violence committed. Either Bandana Man and the respondent had no common intention, or there was a common intention to have a shoot-out. If they intended to have a shoot-out, then each necessarily accepted that the other would shoot at him with the intention to kill or cause serious injury. Neither intended that the other should kill him but each accepted the risk that he might do so.

[43] The Crown sought to suggest that there was a joint intention to have an affray, which was crime *A*, and that the killing by Bandana Man was crime *B*, for which the respondent was liable as an accessory because it was within his contemplation as a possible, albeit unintended, incident of crime *A*. The fallacy of this argument is that, if there was a joint intention to have an affray, that intention was to have an affray by shooting at each other with homicidal intent. It is artificial to treat the intention to have an affray as a separate intention from the intention to have a potentially homicidal shooting match . . .

[44] Why was the Crown so keen to establish liability under the doctrine of parasitic accessory liability? The answer is, we believe, that the Crown believed that this route would enable it to by-pass what was perceived to be a barrier to the direct route to the respondent's liability for murder. The direct route was as follows: (i) Bandana Man attempted to kill the respondent; (ii) by agreeing to the shoot-out, the respondent aided and abetted Bandana Man in this attempted murder; (iii) Bandana Man accidentally killed Ms Pniewska instead of the respondent. Under the doctrine of transferred malice he was guilty of her murder; (iv) the doctrine of transferred malice applied equally to the respondent as aider and abetter of Bandana Man's attempted murder. He also was guilty of Ms Pniewska's murder.

[45] The Crown believed that there was a barrier to this direct route to the respondent's liability for murder. This was the application of the victim rule . . . the respondent could not aid and abet his own attempted murder. If this proposition correctly represents the law, we do not see how the Crown can avoid its effect by invoking the doctrine of parasitic accessory liability. Parasitic accessory liability does not differ in principle from the more common basis for finding someone guilty of aiding, abetting, counselling or procuring the commission of a crime. In so far as the law precludes conviction for aiding and abetting a crime in respect of which the defendant is the victim, it must surely do so whatever the route by which the defendant would otherwise be held to have been an accomplice . . .

[Their Lordships decided that, in fact, the victim rule was not a bar here: see below p.591.]

[55] If the respondent aided, abetted, counselled and procured Bandana Man to shoot at him he was, on my analysis, guilty of aiding and abetting the attempted murder of himself. Had he been killed by Bandana Man, he would have been a party to his own murder. Although he had not intended that Bandana Man should succeed in hitting him, complicity in his attempt to do so would have rendered him a party to the successful achievement of that attempt. As it was, Bandana Man accidentally shot Ms Pniewska. Under the doctrine of transferred malice he was liable for her murder. Under the same doctrine, the respondent, if he had aided, abetted, counselled and procured the attempt, was party to the murder that resulted. Does it follow that, having regard to the terms of the judge's directions, the jury must have been satisfied that the respondent had aided, abetted, counselled and procured Bandana Man to shoot at him with murderous intent? If so, his conviction can stand. If not, the Court of Appeal correctly quashed it . . .

[58] . . . Contrary to the finding of the Court of Appeal, [our view is that] the direction of the judge required the jury to consider whether they were satisfied that the respondent and Bandana Man had a common plan or agree-

ment to shoot at each other and be shot at. If they were so satisfied, and their verdict indicates that they were, this was a proper basis for finding that the respondent was guilty of murder . . .

[60] A guilty verdict in this case involves a combination of common law principles in relation to aiding and abetting and the common law doctrine of transferred malice . . .

[61] We have considered whether to hold the respondent guilty of murder would be so far at odds with what the public would be likely to consider the requirements of justice as to call for a reappraisal of the application of the doctrine in this case. We have concluded to the contrary. On the jury's verdict the respondent and Bandana Man had chosen to indulge in a gunfight in a public place, each intending to kill or cause serious injury to the other, in circumstances where there was a foreseeable risk that this result would be suffered by an innocent bystander. It was a matter of fortuity which of the two fired what proved to be the fatal shot. In other circumstances it might have been impossible to deduce which of the two had done so. In these circumstances it seems to us to accord with the demands of justice rather than to conflict with them that the two gunmen should each be liable for Ms Pniewska's murder.

[62] We have considered the judgments of Lord Brown and Lord Clarke. They essentially agree with our conclusions. Each, however, considers that the defendant was liable as a principal to the agreed joint activity of shooting with intent to kill or cause serious injury, rather than as an accessory to the act of firing the shot. This is not a difference of substance . . . Whether the respondent is correctly described as a principal or an accessory is irrelevant to his guilt . . .

[63] . . . [T]he reality [is] that whether an offence is committed as a principal or as an accessory, the offence is the same offence and the defendant is guilty of it. There may be many situations in which it will be important to distinguish between the principal and the accessory, but this is not such a case.

[64] On the jury's verdict, both men agreed to the joint enterprise of having a shoot-out. Whether, on strict analysis, that made the respondent guilty as a principal to Bandana Man's actus reus of firing the fatal shot, or guilty as one who had 'aided, abetted, counselled, or procured' his firing of that shot creates no practical difficulty on the facts of this case and does not affect the result.

[65] For these reasons we would answer the certified question in the affirmative, allow this appeal and restore the respondent's conviction for murder."

LORD KERR SCJ (dissenting)

". . . [114] . . . [F]or parasitic accessory liability to arise, Gnango and B *would have to have a common intention* to commit an affray, if affray is the crime on which Gnango and B are to be said to have jointly embarked. Whether or not a common intention is required for a joint offence of affray, it is most certainly required for parasitic accessory liability . . . The essence of parasitic accessory liability is that there is a common purpose and in the course of furthering that common purpose, the principal goes beyond what was agreed but the secondary participant foresaw the possibility of this occurring . . .

[115] Lord Phillips, Lord Judge and Lord Dyson have concluded that, although it was not left to the jury by the trial judge, the effect of their verdict is that Gnango was guilty because he aided and abetted B to fire at him. This was on the basis that both shared a common intention to shoot at one another. In particular, each intended to shoot at the other and to be shot at by him. The Court of Appeal concluded that the jury was 'never asked to confront the question whether the shared common purpose was not only to shoot, but to be shot at' (para [59]) . . . This is unquestionably correct. The jury was not invited at any time . . . to address the question whether the shared intention included what seems to be the supremely important element of the avowed aiding and abetting of this offence—the agreement to be shot at.

[116] The judge had refused to allow aiding and abetting to go to the jury because he considered that it could not reasonably be concluded that Gnango had encouraged B to fire at him. The mens rea of aiding and abetting is an *intention* by one's act to assist the principal in the commission of his offence . . .

[117] Since mere presence at the scene of a crime can in certain circumstances be enough to justify a finding of guilt, it is perhaps difficult to see why Gnango's remaining at the scene and firing the gun at B could not amount, in law, to encouragement. It seems likely, however, that the judge considered that the notion of someone encouraging another to fire at him was so at odds with common experience as to be unbefitting of the jury's consideration as a possible basis of liability . . . If the jury was not invited to consider whether Gnango had that intention, the conclusion that their verdict admits of no view other than that Gnango intended to assist B in firing at him is somewhat startling and one which could only be reached after very careful examination of possible alternative explanations for the verdict . . .

[121] The terms of any 'plan' are critical to any conclusion that the parties to it must be taken to have encouraged each other to shoot. But an anterior question must be addressed. Can it be said that solely because there

was an exchange of fire, this must be on foot of a plan? . . . I do not consider that because there was a shoot-out (whatever that term may mean) and because the jury were asked to consider that Gnango and B 'joined together . . . to commit . . . unlawful violence', by returning a verdict of guilty, the jury must be taken to have concluded that there was a plan in the sense of an agreement between them.

[Lord Kerr then stated that even if there was a plan there was no basis upon which the jury's decision implied that they thought there was a plan to shoot and *be shot at*.] . . .

[123] Even if it were possible so to conclude, however, it does not follow that this amounted to an intention on the part of Gnango or B to assist or encourage each other to shoot. One might be alive to the very real risk that firing, if the target was not hit, would prompt return fire, but that is a significantly different thing from saying that this was encouragement to fire back. Being prepared to run the risk does not equate with encouraging an opponent to fire at you. Before, therefore, one could be confident that the jury's verdict meant that they had found it established that Gnango had intended to encourage B to fire, it would have been necessary for them to receive directions about that vital component of aiding and abetting. As the judge said, when ruling that he would not allow this to go to the jury as a possible basis of liability, 'on the evidence, the defendant fired at Bandana Man in the hope of killing him or causing him grievous bodily harm, frightening him, or arguably, in self-defence'. Being shot at was hardly likely to have been a desired outcome on the part of Gnango. Intending to encourage B to fire at him was even less likely . . .

[125] . . . In the absence of a specific direction on Gnango's intention [including a reference to foresight of virtually certain consequences by the defendant] to encourage B to shoot at him, I do not consider that the verdict of the jury can be upheld on the basis that it was founded on their conclusion that he either had the requisite intention or that the virtually certain result of his firing at B was that he would return fire and that Gnango knew that this was virtually certain to occur.

[126] This is particularly so because there is an obvious explanation for the jury's verdict other than that they concluded that there had been a plan which included an intention on the part of Gnango and B to encourage the other to shoot at him. The judge had put to the jury that if they were satisfied that Gnango and B had participated by agreement in an affray, in the course of which Gnango foresaw that B might commit intentional grievous bodily harm or kill, he could be found guilty on that account. For the reasons given by Lord Phillips, Lord Judge and Lord Dyson, with which I agree, this form of parasitic accessory liability was not a basis on which the jury could convict. But it seems to be likely in the extreme that this is the basis on which they did convict. That being so, there was no occasion for them to consider whether the requisite intention on the part of Gnango to found a verdict of guilty on the basis of aiding and abetting was present. Nor can their verdict be considered to supply the necessary ingredients of liability on that basis . . .

[133] I would dismiss the appeal."

Appeal allowed

By a majority of six to one, the Supreme Court restored the defendant's conviction for murder. Beyond this, however, there are fundamental differences of view among the majority which make it difficult to assess the likely impact of this controversial decision. Lords Phillips and Judge (with whom Lord Wilson agrees) and Lord Dyson adopt one approach:

1. that the defendant was guilty of murder;

2. not on the basis of joint enterprise or "parasitical accessorial liability", because, put simply, there was no crime A or B (see paras [42] and [43] above); but

3. on the basis that he had aided and abetted the murder by encouraging "Bandana Man" to shoot back at him, foreseeing that he might do so; and

4. applying the doctrine of transferred malice so that the defendant's intention towards "Bandana Man" was transferred to the victim.[68]

---

68   See below pp.592–594.

They come to this conclusion despite the fact that the trial judge had rejected this mode of analysis and the profound difficulties with this approach exposed by Lord Kerr in his persuasive dissent. Two of the remaining Supreme Court judges in the majority, Lords Brown and Clarke, on the other hand, find the defendant guilty of murder as a principal, despite the difficulties in establishing causation given the voluntary actions of "Bandana Man" which would ordinarily break the chain of causation between the defendant's actions and the death of the passer-by.[69]

In trying to make sense of this decision one fact stands out as significant: "Bandana Man" was arrested but not charged and subsequently disappeared. Had he been charged it seems unlikely that the convoluted prosecution of Gnango for murder (as opposed to the appropriate charge of attempted murder of "Bandana Man") would have been pursued. Policy or the desire that someone should be brought to justice for the death of the innocent passer-by[70] are important considerations in this Supreme Court decision, as is evident by Lord Brown's comment:

> "[T]o my mind the all-important consideration here is that both A and B were intentionally engaged in a potentially lethal unlawful gunfight (a 'shoot-out' as it has also been described) in the course of which an innocent passer-by was killed. The general public would in my opinion be astonished and appalled if in those circumstances the law attached liability for the death only to the gunman who actually fired the fatal shot (which, indeed, it would not always be possible to determine). Is he alone to be regarded as guilty of the victim's murder? Is the other gunman really to be regarded as blameless and exonerated from all criminal liability for that killing? Does the decision of the Court of Appeal here, allowing A's appeal against his conviction for murder, really represent the law of the land? . . .
> To my mind the answer to these questions is a plain 'No'."[71]

Regrettably this decision does nothing to clarify the complexities[72] of the law pertaining to joint enterprise, which the House of Commons Justice Committee has condemned as "unacceptable for such an important aspect of the criminal law".[73] The most which can be said for *Gnango* is that it lends weight to the view that joint enterprise is merely part of the ordinary rules of accessorial liability rather than a separate doctrine.[74] This issue will be considered further in the following discussion of the mens rea of accessories.

---

[69]   See above p.100.

[70]   E. Freer, "R. v. Gnango: The Curious Case of Bandana Man" (2012) 176 Crim. Law and Justice Weekly 218.

[71]   *Gnango* [2011] UKSC 59 at [68]–[69]. See further, D. Ormerod, "Worth the Wait?" [2012] Crim. L.R. 79 at 80.

[72]   For further commentary, see R. Buxton, "Being an Accessory to One's Own Murder" [2012] Crim. L.R. 275; G. Virgo, "Joint Enterprise Liability is Dead: Long Live Accessorial Liability" [2012] Crim. L.R. 850; P. Mirfield, "Guilt by Association: A Reply to Professor Virgo" [2012] Crim. L.R. 577; G. Virgo, "Guilt by Association: A Reply to Peter Mirfield" [2013] Crim L.R. 584 and B. Sullivan, "Accessories and Principals after *Gnango*", in A. Reed and M. Bohlander (eds), *Participation in Crime: Domestic and Comparative Perspectives* (Farnham: Ashgate, 2013).

[73]   House of Commons Justice Committee, *Joint Enterprise* (Eleventh Report of Session 2010–2012 (2012, HC Paper No. 1597 at [36])).

[74]   Although the difficulty surrounding this decision is such that Simester and Sullivan argue that it supports their view that it is a separate ground of liability: A.P. Simester et al., *Simester and Sullivan's Criminal Law: Theory and Doctrine*, 5th edn (Oxford: Hart, 2013), p.245.

4. Mens rea of accessories

(i) Introduction

The extracts from the above cases (*Clarkson, Powell; English, Rahman* and *Gnango*) considered not only the extent of conduct required for accessorial liability (actus reus) but also the mens rea needed by the accessory. In assessing the following section, reference should again be made to these cases.

Accessorial liability involves a "two-fold structure".[75] The accessory who is assisting or encouraging the crime must have mens rea in relation to his own conduct. For example, in *Clarkson* it was said there must be an "intention to encourage". It is implicit in the notion of counselling that one can only encourage or influence another to do something if it is one's intention to encourage. This was confirmed in *Bryce* where Potter LJ stated:

> "[I]t is necessary to show firstly that the act which constitutes the aiding, abetting [counselling] etc was done intentionally in the sense of deliberately and not accidentally and secondly that the accused knew it to be an act capable of assisting or encouraging the crime"[76]

In *Gnango* as we have just seen, the defendant was taken by the majority to have encouraged the principal to shoot by firing at him. With joint enterprise cases, participation in the enterprise is deemed to be intentional assistance. However, because the accessory is liable for the crime committed by the principal (as opposed to being simply liable for his own acts of encouragement, etc.), the accessory also needs mens rea in relation to that crime.

The common theme of all these forms of assistance and encouragement is that the accessory is knowingly and deliberately providing help to a criminal enterprise. The point has already been made that no real conceptual distinctions can be drawn between most of the terms. Arguably, therefore, it is irrelevant whether the accessory is described as a party to a joint unlawful enterprise or a counsellor. Nothing should hinge upon the term adopted in a particular case. The judgment in *Powell; English* can certainly be read as applying to all cases of consensual accessorial liability. Other cases confirm this approach. In *Rook*,[77] for example, the accessory helped plan the crime but failed to turn up for the execution of the crime. A person who provides advice and helps plan a crime in advance traditionally has been described as a counsellor. Equally, such a person can be regarded as a party to a joint enterprise, albeit one who was absent from the actual scene of the crime—and this was how the case was dealt with. Similarly, in *Reardon*,[78] which was a classic case of counselling in that a knife was provided by an accessory who was not involved in any enterprise with the principal offender, the joint enterprise principles established in *Powell; English* were applied. Finally, a number of recent Court of Appeal decisions have stressed that joint enterprise is not a separate form of liability: in *Stringer*, for example, it was stated that "joint enterprise" is not a legal term of art but involves the application of ordinary principles of secondary liability.[79]

While this approach of treating all accessories as subject to the same mens rea rules would appear to represent the present law, the matter is not completely beyond doubt. Virgo,[80] Smith[81] and

---

[75]   Law Commission Consultation Paper No.131, *Assisting and Encouraging Crime* (1993), para.2.49.

[76]   *Bryce* [2004] 2 Cr. App. R. 35 at [42].

[77]   *R. v Rook (Adrian)* (1993) 97 Cr. App. R. 327.

[78]   *Reardon* [1999] Crim. L.R. 392.

[79]   *Stringer* [2011] EWCA 1361 Crim at [57]. See also *Mendes* [2010] EWCA Crim 516 at [17]; *R. v A* [2010] EWCA Crim 1622 and *Montague* [2013] EWCA Crim 1781.

[80]   G. Virgo, "Clarifying Accessorial Liability" (1998) 57 C.L.J. 13 at 15: "It is to be hoped that in future joint enterprise liability can be treated simply as a historical footnote and not as a distinct part of accessorial liability".

[81]   Commentary to *Marks* [1998] Crim. L.R. 676: "it is unfortunate that the phrase 'joint enterprise' has been given a special status for which there is no proper foundation" (at 677).

Buxton[82] all express the opinion that joint enterprise is not distinct from other modes of accessorial liability. Simester and Sullivan, on the other hand, "think that joint enterprise is a special case of secondary participation and not merely a sub-species of assistance and encouragement". [83] The Law Commission favour Simester's views, arguing that a secondary party to a joint enterprise is different to an aider or abettor because he need not have contributed to the commission of the principal's offence, but has condoned it by changing his normative position in choosing to take part in the joint enterprise.[84] As noted above, however, the law relating to aiding and abetting does not require causation in the strict sense between a secondary party's assistance or encouragement and the commission of the offence by the principal. All in all, it is prudent to be cautious in this complex area of law, not least because Lord Hutton, in answering the certified questions in *Powell; English*, limited himself to cases arising "in the course of the joint enterprise" and the recent decision of *Gnango* has been interpreted by some as supporting joint liability as a separate form of liability.[85] For this reason, and for simplicity of exposition, the mens rea requirement in joint unlawful enterprises will be examined separately from that requirement in other cases.

(ii) Joint enterprise

Powell affirms that an accessory who foresees a risk that the principal offender might, with the mens rea of murder, kill the victim is liable for murder even if she did not want this result to occur and might even have urged the principal offender not to kill. The accessory joined an enterprise knowing this could occur and, for policy reasons, is held responsible for the foreseen result. She must, though, have foreseen *death*. However, in *Rahman* the House of Lords restated the mens rea requirement:

"If B realises (without agreeing to such conduct being used) that A may kill or intentionally inflict serious injury, but nevertheless continues to participate with A in the venture, that will amount to a sufficient mental element for B to be guilty of murder if A, with the requisite intent, kills in the course of the venture."[86]

According to this, the secondary party need not foresee death. It is sufficient if she foresees that the principal offender may intentionally inflict serious injury.[87] This is an extension of the common understanding of *Powell; English*.

As the crime of murder requires an intention to kill or cause grievous bodily harm, the accessory need only foresee a risk of the principal offender (intentionally) causing death or grievous bodily harm. At first glance this looks like classic *Cunningham* recklessness. What degree of risk must the accessory foresee? Lord Hutton's answer in *Powell; English* was plain. The defendant need only foresee the principal acting in such a manner as a "possible incident" of the venture unless the risk was so remote that the jury believe the accessory had "genuinely dismissed it as altogether negligible". In the case of *Bryce*[88] the defendant drove the principal, with a gun, to a caravan near the victim's home where

---

82   R. Buxton, "Joint Enterprise" [2009] Crim. L.R. 233 at 238.
83   A.P. Simester et al., *Simester and Sullivan's Criminal Law: Theory and Doctrine*, 5th edn (Oxford: Hart, 2013), p.245. See also A.P. Simester, "The Mental Element in Complicity" (2006) 122 L.Q.R. 578–601 and B. Kreb, "Joint Criminal Enterprise" [2010] 73 M.L.R. 578.
84   Law Commission Report No.305, *Participating in Crime* (2007), para.3.52.
85   Above fn.74.
86   *Rahman* [2009] 1 A.C. 129 at [68].
87   The requirement that the principal must act *with intent* was strongly re-affirmed in the decision of *R. v A* [2010] EWCA Crim 1622.
88   *Bryce* [2004] 2 Cr. App. R. 35.

he dropped him off to wait for an opportunity to commit murder. The principal shot and killed the victim 12 hours later. The defendant was convicted of murder and appealed against his conviction on the basis that at the time when he left the principal at the caravan, the principal had not yet decided whether he was going to commit murder or not. The crime was therefore too remote from the defendant's actions for him to be responsible as an accessory. The Court of Appeal rejected this argument, however, on the basis that he had foreseen murder as a real possibility.

It is worth repeating that the principle in *Powell* applies to all crimes that can be committed by accessories and not just to murder. Thus, for example, if the principal were charged with constructive manslaughter, a crime which only requires that the defendant commit an unlawful act (say, a battery) which is objectively likely to cause some physical injury, the accessory will also be liable for manslaughter if he foresees a risk that the principal offender might intentionally or recklessly (the mens rea of battery) hit the victim.

But what of secondary parties in a case where the principal offender is guilty of murder but the accomplices only foresaw that some injury, not serious injury or death, would be inflicted? In the *English* appeal the joint enterprise was to inflict blows with wooden posts. English was not liable because the principal's use of a knife took his acts outside the scope of the joint enterprise. But what would have been the position if the victim had died from blows inflicted by the posts but the accessory had not foreseen death or serious harm? If the principal offender (unknown to the defendant) inflicted the blows with intent to kill or cause grievous bodily harm and was convicted of murder, would the defendant escape all liability for the death? Both policy and principle would suggest that the answer should be no. The first stage would be for the jury to find that the act was within the scope of the joint unlawful enterprise. Precise liability should then be determined by the defendant's mens rea. The accessory lacks the mens rea for murder as defined by *Powell* and *Rahman* but clearly satisfies all the requirements for constructive manslaughter and should be liable for that offence.

This was also the approach adopted in the pre-*Powell* case of *Stewart*[89] where the joint unlawful enterprise was to rob a shop while armed with a scaffolding bar to inflict only moderate injury. The principal offender, motivated by racial hatred, beat the victim to death. This act was found to be within the scope of the joint enterprise and the principal was liable for murder.[90] The accessory, who had not foreseen this result, was nevertheless liable for constructive manslaughter. This approach was adopted in the following post-*Powell* case.

R. v Gilmour [2000] 2 Cr. App. R. 407 (Court of Appeal of Northern Ireland)

The defendant drove the principal offenders to a house knowing that it was going to be petrol-bombed. Three people died in the fire. The defendant was convicted of murder. On appeal, it was found that the defendant had not realised the principals intended to inflict grievous bodily harm. He thought they intended to start a fire to put the occupants in fear and intimidate them. Accordingly, the murder conviction was quashed. The issue then was whether he could be found guilty of manslaughter.

---

[89]   *R. v Stewart (Heather)* [1995] 1 Cr. App. R. 441.

[90]   The Law Commission has suggested that this case would be decided differently since *Powell* on the basis that a racially aggravated assault is "fundamentally different" to a "mild" assault and would therefore lie outside the scope of the joint enterprise, meaning that the defendant would not be liable for either murder or manslaughter: Law Commission Consultation Paper No.177, *A New Homicide Act for England and Wales?* (2005), para.5.37(6)(e). Following *Rahman*, however, it is not clear that the law would make such a distinction, since the "fundamentally different" rule seems to be limited to the type of weapon used.

CARSWELL LCJ:

"The appellant foresaw that the principals would carry out the act of throwing a petrol bomb into the house, but did not realise that in so doing they intended to kill or do grievous bodily harm to the occupants . . . The line of authority represented by such cases as *Anderson* and *Morris*, approved in *R. v Powell and English*, deals with situations where the principal departs from the contemplated joint enterprise and perpetrates a more serious act of a different kind unforeseen by the accessory. In such cases it is established that the accessory is not liable at all for such unforeseen acts. It does not follow that the same result should follow where the principal carries out the very act contemplated by the accessory, though the latter does not realise that the principal intends a more serious consequence from the act.

We do not consider that we are obliged by authority to hold that the accessory in such a case must be acquitted of manslaughter as well as murder. The cases in which an accessory has been found not guilty both of murder and manslaughter all concern a departure by the principal from the actus reus contemplated by the accessory, not a difference between the parties in respect of the mens rea of each. In such cases the view has prevailed that it would be wrong to hold the accessory liable when the principal committed an act which the accessory did not contemplate or authorise. We do not, however, see any convincing policy reason why a person acting as an accessory to a principal who carries out the very deed contemplated by both should not be guilty of the degree of offence appropriate to the intent with which he so acted."

Appeal allowed; verdict of guilty of manslaughter substituted

This approach was followed again in *Roberts*,[91] where the deceased was killed in the course of a fight during which he suffered a kick to the head. Whilst the principal offender may have had an intention to kill or cause grievous bodily harm, the secondary parties had joined in the fight with no such intention and were held to be liable for manslaughter. Despite these Court of Appeal decisions, there was nevertheless still some doubt before *Rahman* as to whether this was the correct approach. However, the view that a secondary party should be liable for manslaughter when he lacked the foresight that the principal might kill or cause grievous bodily harm was again confirmed post-*Rahman* by the Court of Appeal's decisions in *Yemoh* and *Parsons*.[92] In such a case where the principals have "larger intentions" than the accessory, "there is no reason why the participants should not be convicted and sentenced appropriately as their several states of mind dictate".[93]

The situation is different when, unlike the above cases, the principal offender's acts take him outside the scope of the joint enterprise. This is what happened in the *English* appeal. The House of Lords indicated that English fully deserved punishment for the attack but as he had already spent a number of years in detention, no further consideration was given to the matter. However, in quashing his conviction, the House of Lords did not substitute a manslaughter verdict and, indeed, indicated that he should not be liable for manslaughter. Despite this, even in this situation there is a strong argument that the accessory should be liable for manslaughter. The defendant in the *English* appeal could easily have been charged with assault or conspiracy to commit an aggravated assault, but the principle of fair labelling surely dictates that he should have been liable for manslaughter. While he was no longer a party to a murderous joint enterprise, he was, at the very least, a party to a joint enterprise involving a battery which was objectively likely to cause some physical harm. He should have been convicted of constructive manslaughter.[94]

Finally, one must question whether their Lordships were right in both *Powell* and *Rahman* to conclude that while the principal offender is only guilty of murder if he intended to kill or cause grievous

---

[91]   *R. v Roberts (Stephen)* [2001] Crim. L.R. 984.

[92]   *R. v Parsons (Anthony John)* [2009] EWCA Crim 64. See also *R. v Carpenter (Tracy Maureen)* [2011] EWCA Crim 2568.

[93]   Cited in Commentary to *Roberts* [2001] Crim. L.R. 984 at 985.

[94]   C.M.V. Clarkson, "Complicity, *Powell* and Manslaughter" [1998] Crim. L.R. 556. cf. "Complicity and *R. v Powell*" J.C. Smith [1998] Crim. L.R. 232.

bodily harm, the secondary party, who might not even have been present at the scene of the crime, is guilty of murder on the basis of merely foreseeing a risk that the principal offender might kill or cause serious bodily harm. While it has been held not to be contrary to art.6 of the European Convention on Human Rights for an accessory to be convicted of murder with a lesser mens rea than the principal offender,[95] the question still remains as to whether this is the right approach in terms of principle and policy.

The argument in favour of the *Powell* and *Rahman* approach is that because of the dangerousness of collaborative ventures and group violence, policy dictates that anyone who goes along with a venture knowing that death or serious harm might occur, ought to be counted a murderer when that level of violence is committed. On the other hand, it can be argued that an accessory should not be guilty of the same offence as the principal offender if she has a lesser mens rea. As has been said:

> "Since the act and cause requirements of accomplice liability are so minimal, and since an accomplice [can be punished] the same as the perpetrator of the substantive offence, the *mens rea* requirement becomes more significant. Accomplice liability hinges upon the *mens rea* element."[96]

It is accordingly submitted that in such cases the extent of the accessory's liability should be dependent upon mens rea. If the accessory *intends* death or grievous bodily harm (bearing in mind that intention can be inferred in cases where the consequence is foreseen as virtually certain) a murder verdict is appropriate. However, if the accessory only foresees a risk that the principal will cause death or serious harm, this is only a species of recklessness and the accessory should only be convicted of manslaughter.[97] It is a matter of regret that the House of Lords firmly rejected such a view.

Not only are there strong reasons of principle to reject the approach taken in *Powell* and subsequent cases, but there are also practical problems with the law as it currently stands. Juries in cases involving multiple defendants are faced with an extremely complicated task in reaching their verdict as to the guilt of the various participants. The Judicial Studies Board has tried to simplify the guidance given to juries in such cases by providing specimen directions, but they are, however, far from "simple".[98] The Court of Appeal has complained that the law in relation to murder in joint enterprise cases is immensely complex, and that pending any reform of the law which would hopefully simplify the rules to be applied, the courts should approve a much simpler approach to giving directions in such cases.[99]

(iii) Counselling

Before *Powell* it was relatively clear that it was only necessary to prove that the accessory knew that the offence was to be committed. It was enough that they foresaw a real or substantial risk of the principal committing the offence.[100] The leading, and much cited, case is *NCB v Gamble*[101] where a weigh-bridge operator, in the course of his job, issued a ticket to a driver leaving the colliery premises, knowing that the lorry was over-loaded. The Coal Board (as the weigh-bridge operator's employer)

---

95   Ashworth, "A Decade of Human Rights in Criminal Justice" [2014] Criminal Law Review 325 at 327.
96   G.E. Mueller, "The Mens Rea of Accomplice Liability" (1988) 61 South. Calif. L.R. 2169 at 2172.
97   This used to be the position in English law. See e.g. *Reid* (1975) 62 Cr. App. R. 109.
98   See *JSB Crown Court Benchbook* (Judicial Studies Board, 2010).
99   *Mitchell* [2008] EWCA Crim 2552. See also *Mendes* [2010] EWCA Crim 516 at [48]
100   *Rook* (1993) 97 Cr. App. R. 327.
101   *NCB v Gamble* [1959] 1 Q.B. 11. See also *DPP v Lynch* [1975] A.C. 653.

was convicted of being an accessory to the offence of using a lorry on the road with a load weighing more than that permitted.[102] It was held that the only mens rea required was knowledge of the circumstances rendering the act criminal. Devlin J concluded that:

> "an indifference to the result of crime does not of itself negative abetting. If one man deliberately sells to another a gun to be used for murdering a third, he may be indifferent about whether the third man lives or dies and interested only in the cash profit to be made out of the sale, but he can still be an aider and abettor."[103]

This approach has been criticised by Williams:

> "It seems a strong thing to hold that a man who is simply pursuing his ordinary and lawful vocation, and takes no special steps to assist illegalities, becomes involved as a party to crime committed by the customer merely because he realises that his customer will be enabled by what he himself does to commit such a crime."[104]

On the other hand, it is possible to defend the approach adopted in *Gamble*. If the defendant knows that a crime is to be committed, why should he be allowed to shelter behind a shield that he was "just doing his job"? Legitimate business enterprise should not be permitted to extend to the knowing provision of tools for the commission of crime.

The central question, however, is whether these rules have been affected by *Powell* and *Rahman*. The principle in *Powell* was applied in *Webster*,[105] a case of causing death by dangerous driving. Here, the defendant had allowed the principal, who had been drinking, to drive his car. It was held that the defendant, in allowing the principal to drive, would be liable if he foresaw that the principal was likely to drive dangerously.[106] In reaching this conclusion the court cited *Powell* and *Blakely; Sutton*.[107] But the same conclusion could have been reached by applying the test in *Gamble*: whether the secondary party foresaw the risk of the crime occurring. Given that joint enterprise is rejected by many as being a separate doctrine of accessorial liability, the cases that apply should be interchangeable as between different modes of participation. A practical reason why the same rules should apply is that, as argued earlier, it is impossible in practice, and pointless in principle, to draw sharp distinctions between counsellors and parties to joint unlawful enterprises. Returning to the case of *Rook*[108] there seems no difference in culpability whether the defendant is classed as a counsellor or a member of a joint enterprise. In an area of law renowned for its complexity, there would be much to be gained from the development of a single rule applicable to most cases of complicity.

The test in *Powell* works well in cases where encouragement or assistance is given before the commission of the actus reus. In cases where assistance is given during the commission of the actus reus, the foresight test is less realistic and a test based on knowledge seems more appropriate. This was the approach adopted in the joint enterprise case of *Uddin*[109]:

---

102 Contrary to the Motor Vehicles (Construction and Use) Regulations 1955 (SI 1955/990) regs 68 and 104.
103 *Gamble* [1959] 1 Q.B. 11 at 23.
104 D.J. Baker, *Glanville Williams' Textbook of Criminal Law*, 3rd edn (London: Sweet & Maxwell, 2012), p.465.
105 *R. v Webster (Peter David)* [2006] 2 Cr. App. R. 6.
106 It was said that knowledge of the principal's intoxication was powerful evidence that the secondary party foresaw that the principal was likely to drive in a dangerous manner; the more drunk the principal appeared to be, the easier it would be for the prosecution to prove that the defendant foresaw that he was likely to drive dangerously.
107 See below, p.574.
108 See above, p.566.
109 *R. v Uddin (Rejan)* [1999] Q.B. 431.

"[I]f in the course of the concerted attack a weapon is produced by one of the participants and the others *knowing* that he has it in circumstances where he may use it in the course of the attack participate or continue to participate in the attack, they will be guilty of murder if the weapon is used to inflict a fatal wound."[110]

This approach was also used as an alternative basis for the imposition of liability in *Webster* (discussed above). In relation to the prosecution case that, having let the principal take the wheel the secondary party should have intervened to stop him driving in a dangerous manner during the commission of that offence, it was ruled that the test was not foresight as to what was likely to happen but rather knowledge of what was happening at the time.[111]

One final question remains. To what extent must the counsellor know the details of the principal's intended offence? Is it enough that he knows that some sort of property offence is being planned or does he need to have a fair idea of when or how or where? In *Bainbridge*[112] it was held that as long as the defendant was aware of the type of offence to be committed, that would be enough to incriminate him. The "type of offence" formula was not without difficulties (establishing, for example, whether one offence was of a similar type to another) and so the issue was re-examined by the House of Lords in the following case.

Maxwell v DPP for Northern Ireland (1979) 68 Cr. App. R. 128 (House of Lords)

LORD SCARMAN:

"I think *Bainbridge* . . . was correctly decided. But I agree with counsel for the appellant that in the instant case the Court of Criminal Appeal in Northern Ireland has gone further than the Court of Criminal Appeal for England and Wales found it necessary to go in *Bainbridge*. It is not possible in the present case to declare that it is proved, beyond reasonable doubt, that the appellant knew a bomb attack upon the Inn was intended by those whom he was assisting. It is not established, therefore, that he knew the particular type of crime intended. The Court, however, refused to limit criminal responsibility by reference to knowledge by the accused of the type or class of crime intended by those whom he assisted. Instead, the Court has formulated a principle which avoids the uncertainties and ambiguities of classification. The guilt of an accessory springs, according to the Court's formulation, 'from the fact that he contemplates the commission of one (or more) of a number of crimes by the principal and he intentionally lends his assistance in order that such a crime will be committed': *per* Sir Robert Lowry C.J. 'The relevant crime', the Lord Chief Justice continues,

'must be within the contemplation of the accomplice and only exceptionally would evidence be found to support the allegation that the accomplice had given the principal a completely blank cheque.'

The principle thus formulated has great merit. It directs attention to the state of mind of the accused—not what he ought to have in contemplation, but what he did have: it avoids definition and classification, while ensuring that a man will not be convicted of aiding and abetting any offence his principal may commit, but only one which is within his contemplation. He may have in contemplation only one offence, or several: and the several which he contemplates he may see as alternatives. An accessory who leaves it to his principal to choose is liable, provided always the choice is made from the range of offences from which the accessory contemplates the choice will be made. Although the court's formulation of the principle goes further than the earlier cases, it is a sound development of the law and in no way inconsistent with them. I accept it as good judge-made law in a field where there is no statute to offer guidance."

---

[110] *Uddin* [1999] Q.B. 431 at 441. Emphasis added.
[111] The Law Commission prefer a test of "knowledge or belief" in such cases (Law Commission Consultation Paper No.177, *A New Homicide Act for England and Wales?* (2005), para.5.20).
[112] *R. v Bainbridge (Alan)* [1960] 1 Q.B. 129.

It should be noted, first, that *Maxwell* is the kind of case which the Law Commission had in mind when drafting the new offences of assisting and encouraging crime. A defendant such as *Maxwell* would now be liable for one of the inchoate offences under the Serious Crime Act 2007 although, unless and until the Law Commission's recommendations relating to secondary liability are enacted, he could also remain liable for the substantive offences as an accomplice.

Assuming the earlier argument that *Powell* and *Rahman* apply in all such cases is accepted, these cases must be read in the light of those decisions. Arguably, having a crime within one's contemplation is just another way of saying that it must be foreseen as a possibility, the relevant question posed in *Powell*. In a case of counselling murder, an accomplice who provided the knife used in a murder might have had murder, manslaughter, wounding and robbery on their shopping list. That in itself would provide her with the necessary mens rea whether one applied *Maxwell* or *Powell* and *Rahman*.

Maxwell left one question unresolved. Does the accessory continue to be liable for the crimes of the principal so long as they continue to be on their "shopping list" of crimes? One could imagine the well-worn and well-used jemmy being the source of endless liability for the supplier of it. There is nothing in the law as it presently stands, which prevents the accessory being implicated every time the tool is used for one of the "shopping list" crimes—although it does not appear to have been a problem in practice.

5. Procuring

Attorney-General's Reference (No.1 of 1975) [1975] Q.B. 773 (Court of Appeal, Criminal Division)

The defendant surreptitiously laced a friend's drinks with double measures of spirits when he knew his friend would be driving home. He was charged with aiding, abetting, counselling and procuring the offence of driving with an excess quantity of alcohol in the blood under s.6(1) of the Road Traffic Act 1972. The reference concerned the question of whether there had to be a shared intention between the parties or encouragement of the offence.

LORD WIDGERY CJ:

"Of course it is the fact that in the great majority of instances where a secondary party is sought to be convicted of an offence there has been a contact between the principal offender and the secondary party. Aiding and abetting almost inevitably involves a situation in which the secondary party and the main offender are together at some stage discussing the plans which they may be making in respect of the alleged offence, and are in contact so that each knows what is passing through the mind of the other.

In the same way it seems to us that a person, who counsels the commission of a crime by another, almost inevitably comes to a moment when he is in contact with the other, when he is discussing the offence with that other and when, to use the words of the statute, he counsels the other to commit the offence.

The fact that so often the relationship between the secondary party and the principal will be such that there is a meeting of minds between them caused the trial judge in the case from which this reference is derived to think that this was really an essential feature of proving or establishing the guilt of the secondary party and, as we understand his judgment, he took the view that in the absence of some sort of meeting of minds, some sort of mental link between the secondary party and the principal, there could be no aiding, abetting or counselling of the offence within the meaning of the section.

So far as aiding, abetting and counselling is concerned we would go a long way with that conclusion. It may very well be, as I said a moment ago, difficult to think of a case of aiding, abetting or counselling when the parties have not met and have not discussed in some respects the terms of the offence which they have in mind. But we do not see why a similar principle should apply to procuring. We approach section 8 of the Act of 1861 on the basis that the words should be given their ordinary meaning, if possible. We approach the section on the basis also that if four words are employed here, 'aid, abet, counsel or procure', the probability is that there is a difference between each of those four words and the other three, because, if there were no such difference, then Parliament would be wasting time in using four words where two or three would do. Thus, in deciding whether that which is assumed to be done under our reference was a criminal offence we approach the section on the footing that each word must be given its ordinary meaning.

To procure means to produce by endeavour. You procure a thing by setting out to see that it happens and taking the appropriate steps to produce that happening. We think that there are plenty of instances in which a person may be said to procure the commission of a crime by another even though there is no sort of conspiracy between the two, even though there is no attempt at agreement or discussion as to the form which the offence should take. In our judgment the offence described in this reference is such a case.

If one looks back at the facts of the reference: the accused surreptitiously laced his friend's drink. This is an important element and, although we are not going to decide today anything other than the problem posed to us, it may well be that, in similar cases where the lacing of the drink or the introduction of the extra alcohol is known to the driver, quite different considerations may apply. We say that because, where the driver has no knowledge of what is happening, in most instances he would have no means of preventing the offence from being committed. If the driver is unaware of what has happened, he will not be taking precautions. He will get into his car seat, switch on the ignition and drive home and, consequently, the conception of another procuring the commission of the offence by the driver is very much stronger where the driver is innocent of all knowledge of what is happening, as in the present case where the lacing of the drink was surreptitious.

The second thing which is important in the facts set out in our reference is that, following and in consequence of the introduction of the extra alcohol, the friend drove with an excess quantity of alcohol in his blood. Causation here is important. You cannot procure an offence unless there is a causal link between what you do and the commission of the offence, and here we are told that in consequence of the addition of this alcohol the driver, when he drove home, drove with an excess quantity of alcohol in his body.

Giving the words their ordinary meaning in English, and asking oneself whether in those circumstances the offence has been procured, we are in no doubt that the answer is that it has. It has been procured because, unknown to the driver and without his collaboration, he has been put in a position in which in fact he has committed an offence which he never would have committed otherwise."

Opinion accordingly

This case was followed a number of years later by another, more bizarre, case of lacing. In *Blakely, Sutton*[113] the defendants laced the principal's tonic water with vodka. They intended to tell him before he left to drive home so that he would stay the night. In other words, they gave him the alcohol so that he would *not* drive. Unfortunately, the principal left before they could tell him and was subsequently found to be over the legal limit when breathalysed. The defendants' evidence ensured that the principal was given an absolute discharge to the charge of drink-driving but they were then charged with "aiding, abetting, counselling, procuring and commanding" that offence. In fact, as only procuring was alleged, the case proceeded on this footing. They appealed against their conviction, the question being whether procuring could be committed recklessly.

The Court of Appeal was somewhat tentative in its response, stating that it

"must, at least, be shown that the accused contemplated that his act would or might bring about or assist the commission of the principal offence: he must have been prepared nevertheless to do his own act, and he must have done that act intentionally."

But it was further stated that in relation to those

"accused only of procuring and perhaps also those accused only of counselling and commanding, it might be that it was necessary to prove that the accused intended to bring about the principal offence".

---

[113]   *Blakely v DPP* [1991] Crim. L.R. 763.

The appeal was allowed.

It is submitted that if one accepts that to procure is "to produce by endeavour" then it is impossible to avoid the conclusion that intention is required and that there is some merit in continuing to regard procuring in this way. If this is the case, there is also an argument that "procuring" an offence ought to be treated in law as a more serious form of participation than others such as counselling, which only require foresight of the offence. Take the example of the generous host who makes drink available for her guests but leaves them to decide whether they will drink, walk home or drive. If charged with procuring the principal's offence of drunken driving, then, following *Attorney-General's Reference (No.1 of 1975)*, she should be acquitted. But, if the case is argued on the basis of counselling which can be satisfied by mere contemplation, then generous hosts (and publicans) would be convicted.[114] The offence for which they would be convicted is that of drunken driving, whether or not the case succeeds on the basis of procuring (requiring intention) or counselling (where foresight suffices). Does this satisfactorily identify those who are truly deserving of blame?

6. Reform proposals

The Law Commission in 1993 proposed a radical rethink of the law relating to complicity.[115] Under these proposals, the terms "aid, abet, counsel or procure" would be jettisoned as would the derivative principle of liability for the full offence. Instead, two new inchoate offences would be created: assisting crime and encouraging crime. Whilst the Law Commission's analysis of complicity as consisting of either encouraging or assisting was generally welcomed, there was much less support for the radical proposal to abandon derivative liability.[116]

The Law Commission has now abandoned the proposal to abolish secondary liability, although its proposals concerning inchoate liability have been enacted, with some amendment, under the Serious Crime Act 2007 (see Ch.5). The most recent report on participation in crime recommends further offences of assisting or encouraging crime, which would follow the current law in enabling secondary parties to be convicted of the same offence as the principal offender. The Law Commission produced this report a year after the report on inchoate liability and clearly had in mind that the two reports should make a package of reform:

> "Taken together, the recommendations contained in both reports would, if implemented, result in a scheme whereby inchoate and secondary liability will support and supplement each other in a way that is rational and fair".[117]

---

[114] The Law Commission states that a generous host is liable for drunken driving even if she is indifferent to whether the principal commits the offence, and that it is enough that she believes that they will commit the offence as a result of the alcohol she supplies. In a footnote, the Law Commission further admits that, following *Blakely*, *Sutton* and *Webster* it is enough that they foresee that the principal might, or was likely to, commit the offence: Law Commission Paper No.300, *Inchoate Liability for Assisting and Encouraging Crime* (2006), para.4.17.

[115] Law Commission Consultation Paper No.131, *Assisting and Encouraging Crime* (1993). For a recent argument that complicity ought to be abolished, see G. Sullivan, "Doing without Complicity" [2012] J. of Commonwealth Crim. Law 199.

[116] J.C. Smith, "Criminal Liability of Accessories: Law and Law Reform" (1997) 113 L.Q.R. 453 at 463 and K.J.M. Smith, "The Law Commission Consultation Paper on Complicity: (1) A Blueprint for Rationalisation" [1994] Crim. L.R. 239 at 250.

[117] Law Commission Report No.305, *Participating in Crime* (2007), para.1.4. Before the Law Commission completed its report on secondary liability it had already, however, made recommendations relating to secondary liability in cases of homicide (Law Commission Paper No.304, *Murder, Manslaughter and Infanticide* (2006)). These recommendations were originally adopted in part by the Government in drafting the Coroners and Justice Bill. However, following the consultation process they were dropped from the Bill on the basis that secondary liability needs to be reformed as a whole rather than in parts: Ministry of Justice, *Murder, Manslaughter and Infanticide: Proposals for Reform of the Law: Summary of Responses and Government Position*, CP(R) August 19, 2009, paras 105–106.

As the law currently stands, however, there is considerable overlap between the new inchoate offences of assisting or encouraging crime and secondary liability. This was recognised by the Law Commission in its report on inchoate liability.

Law Commission, Inchoate Liability for Assisting and Encouraging Crime (Law Com. No.300), (2006) paras 5.8–5.9:

"Potential overlap with secondary liability

5.8 The new offences can be committed whether or not the principal offence is committed. In Part 2, we said that we were persuaded that secondary liability should be retained to cater for cases where D encourages or assists P to commit an offence intending that P should commit the offence. Accordingly, there is a potential overlap between secondary liability and the clause 1 offence [see below, p.577]:

Example 5C

D encourages P to set fire to the local tax office.

If P decides not to set fire to the tax office, D can only be guilty of the clause 1 offence. D would not be an accessory to arson because P had not even attempted to commit the offence. On the other hand, were P to set fire to the premises, D, as well as committing the clause 1 offence, would be an accessory to arson because it was D's intention that P should commit arson. The prosecution could choose to charge D with the clause 1 offence but we would expect that they would wish to charge D with arson.

5.9 By contrast, under our forthcoming proposals for reform of secondary liability, there is limited scope for overlap between secondary liability and the clause 2(1) offence because, subject to one exception, D will not be secondarily liable in cases where it was not his or her intention that P should commit the principal offence or be encouraged or assisted to commit it:

Example 5D

D, a shopkeeper, sells petrol to P believing that P will use it to make a petrol bomb with which to commit arson. D is indifferent as to what P does with the petrol. P, as D anticipated, makes a petrol bomb and uses it to set fire to the tax office.

D is guilty of the clause 2(1) offence but is not an accessory to and guilty of arson."

Arguably, this overlap raises questions of fair labelling, given that where D has assisted in the commission of an offence which has actually been committed by P, there is nothing to stop the Crown charging one of the inchoate offences rather than trying to prove liability under the 1861 Act.

David Ormerod and Rudi Fortson, "Serious Crime Act 2007: The Part 2 Offences" [2009] Crim. L.R. 389, p.393:

"In principle, the Act might be criticised for creating a degree of incoherence, by overlaying such a scheme of broad inchoate liability (SCA 2007) on the existing common law regime of derivative liability (common law and Accessories and Abettors Act 1861, s.8). The two schemes now overlap much more than common law incitement. This results once again in broad discretion for the prosecutor. In many cases there will be an option of charging D with aiding and abetting a less serious offence, or assisting and encouraging a more serious one. For example, D will be liable under s.44 [SCA 2007] in relation to the criminal act that he *intended* (say murder) rather than as an accessory to the actual offence committed by P (perhaps only a firearms offence). Practitioners will need to give careful thought to the counts which should be left to the jury (and how the jury ought to be directed) where the facts disclose the commission of secondary liability for a substantive offence applying s.8 of the 1861 Act, and inchoate liability under Pt 2 of the SCA 2007.

This is not simply analogous to the numerous instances in which the prosecution have been provided with a choice between overlapping substantive offences (such as wounding or grievous bodily harm; blackmail or robbery). In this instance the prosecution are left with a choice between distinct schemes of criminal responsibility. Criminal liability imposed for secondary participation reflects a distinctive type of wrong from that of inchoate liability. The focus in an inquiry into secondary liability is on the harm caused by P and on D's playing a culpable part in that harm by his acts of knowing assistance or encouragement. With inchoate liability, the focus is on the conduct of D and the prospect of harm—albeit remote—that his culpable behaviour might generate. There is a fundamental shift to looking at the harm threatened instead of the harm caused."

Ormerod and Forston warn that

"because of the breadth of inchoate offences . . . it is questionable to what extent the inchoate scheme will completely supersede existing or proposed offences of secondary liability".[118]

Whilst there may be considerable overlap between the inchoate offences and the Law Commission's recommendations in relation to secondary liability, as well as overlap between the inchoate offences and the current law, it is worthwhile considering the Law Commission's recommendations as to secondary liability. Given that the law has become so complex, it would be unfortunate if the programme of reform was abandoned now that the inchoate offences have been enacted.

The Law Commission's proposals are for two separate statutory provisions to replace the law of aiding, abetting, counselling and procuring. The first of these would create an offence of "intentional encouraging or assisting" crime, whilst the second provides a separate route to liability for participants of joint enterprises (or "joint criminal ventures"). As noted above, there is disagreement over whether the rules relating to joint enterprise liability form a separate doctrine of accessory liability. The Law Commission, in its consultation paper, took the same view as Simester and others that it is a separate doctrine.[119] In the Report, however, the Commission is more hesitant and ambiguous, stating that the different approaches taken by commentators "do not produce sufficiently significant differences in practice for it to be important for us to choose between them".[120] However, it agreed that offences committed as part of a joint enterprise can be committed without any actual assistance or encouragement on the part of the secondary party.[121] It is the Commission's view that "D's liability for a collateral offence should not be dependent on whether his or her conduct is classified as 'assistance' or 'encouragement'" which has led to its recommendation for a separate offence under cl.2 of the draft bill, discussed below.

(i) Clause 1: assisting or encouraging an offence

Law Commission No.305, Participating in Crime (2007), Appendix A: Draft Participating in Crime Bill:

"1 Assisting or encouraging an offence
(1) Where a person (P) has committed an offence, another person (D) is also guilty of the offence if—
(a) D did an act with the intention that one or more of a number of other acts would be done by another person,
(b) P's criminal act was one of those acts,

118   D. Ormerod and R. Fortson, "Serious Crime Act 2007: The Part 2 Offences" [2009] Crim. L.R. 389 at 394.
119   Law Commission Consultation Paper No.131 Assisting and Encouraging Crime (1993), para.2.120.
120   Law Commission Report No.305 Participating in Crime (2007), para.3.56.
121   Law Commission Report No.305 Participating in Crime (2007), para.3.56.

(c) D's behaviour assisted or encouraged P to do his criminal act, and
(d) subsection (2) or (3) is satisfied.
(2) This subsection is satisfied if D believed that a person doing the act would commit the offence.
(3) This subsection is satisfied if D's state of mind was such that had he done the act he would have committed the offence."

In drafting this provision the Law Commission wished to preserve the forensic advantages of secondary liability, by which the prosecution is under no duty to prove which of a number of participants was the principal offender, and to reflect the derivative theory of secondary liability. However, in attempting to introduce "parity of culpability" it has sought to narrow the scope of liability for secondary parties. The means by which this is achieved, and what distinguishes it from the current law, is the requirement that D *intended* that the offence charged be committed, either by P, or some other person. This departs from the current law where mere foresight of the offence being committed suffices. It does not require that D and P are in agreement, however, and this is what distinguishes liability under cl.1 from liability from participating in a joint criminal venture under cl.2.[122]

The result is that those who might be guilty of counselling an offence under current law because they provided the principal offender with the weapon ultimately used to commit the offence and foresaw the type of offence committed, would escape liability for the offence itself but would be liable for the inchoate offence of assisting or encouraging crime. The sales assistant who sells a baseball bat to a customer, overhearing that the customer is contemplating using the bat to commit assault, should not be liable for the assault eventually committed by the customer, since the sales assistant does not share parity of culpability with the customer and their culpability is clearly of a lesser degree. Unlike the customer, they did not intend that assault be committed.[123]

There is no recommended definition of what amounts to "assisting or encouraging", but cl.8 states that encouraging includes threatening or otherwise putting pressure on P to commit the offence. It also covers "taking steps to reduce the possibility of criminal proceedings being brought in respect of the act's being done" and "failing to take reasonable steps to discharge a duty". The latter would support the conviction of a disgruntled security guard who failed to turn on a burglar alarm in order to assist a burglar.[124] In addition to the guidance provided in cl.8, the Law Commission suggests that "encouraging" should also mean "emboldening".[125] This follows the recommendations made in relation to liability for the inchoate offence of "assisting or encouraging" crime, where "emboldening" is presumed to mean the same thing as "inciting".[126] It is rather odd, however, that the Commission's wishes in this regard were not incorporated within the draft bill,

Before assessing the desirability of enacting the Law Commission's recommendation, the second offence must be considered.

---

[122] Law Commission Report No.305 *Participating in Crime* (2007), para.3.7.
[123] Law Commission Report No.305 *Participating in Crime* (2007), para.1.9.
[124] Law Commission Report No.305 *Participating in Crime* (2007), para.3.34.
[125] Law Commission Report No.305 *Participating in Crime* (2007), para.3.15.
[126] Law Commission Report No.305 *Participating in Crime* (2007), para.3.12.

(ii) Clause 2: participating in a joint criminal venture

Law Commission No.305, Participating in Crime (2007), Appendix A: Draft Participating in Crime Bill:

"2 Participating in a joint criminal venture
(1) This section applies where two or more persons participate in a joint criminal venture.

(2) If one of them (P) commits an offence, another participant (D) is also guilty of the offence if P's criminal act falls within the scope of the venture.

(3) The existence or scope of a joint criminal venture may be inferred from the conduct of the participants (whether or not there is an express agreement).

(4) D does not escape liability under this section for an offence committed by P at a time when D is a participant in the venture merely because D is at that time—

(a) absent,

(b) against the venture's being carried out, or

(c) indifferent as to whether it is carried out."

This provides liability both in cases of the "plain vanilla" variety of joint enterprises (where P commits the agreed offence) and the "tutti frutti" variety (where P commits a collateral offence). It is an attempt to codify the current law applicable to joint enterprise liability.[127] As seen above, the two issues presenting challenges for the courts in joint enterprises have been the question of what mens rea should be required of a secondary party, and the question of when the principal's act goes beyond the scope of the joint enterprise, providing the secondary party with a defence. How has the Law Commission tackled these issues?

In relation to the first issue, there are no mens rea terms appearing in the draft offence. In the Report, the Law Commission recommends the following alternate fault requirements:

"(1)   D intended that P (or another party to the venture) should commit the conduct element;
(2)   D believed that P (or another party to the venture) would commit the conduct element; or
(3)   D believed that P (or another party to the venture) might commit the conduct element."[128]

None of this appears in the draft bill, however, on the basis that the Law Commission wished to draft an "open textured" bill, focusing on general principles and leaving it to the courts and Judicial Studies Board, in drafting model directions to juries, to fill in the details.[129] This approach has met with opposition, with Buxton describing it as "contrary to principle: it is Parliament, not the Judicial Studies Board, that should make the law".[130] Buxton also criticises the substance of the Law Commission's recommendation in relation to the fault element, pointing out that requiring that D foresaw that P might commit the *conduct element* of the offence is treating parties to a joint criminal venture more harshly than those liable under the cl.1 offence, who must believe that P would commit *the offence*.[131]

---

[127]   G.R. Sullivan, "Participating in Crime: Law Com No.305—Joint Criminal Ventures" [2008] Crim. L.R. 19.
[128]   Law Commission Report No.305 *Participating in Crime* (2007), para.3.151.
[129]   Law Commission Report No.305 *Participating in Crime* (2007), Appendix A, para.A.15. For a defence of this approach, see J. Horder and D. Hughes, "Joint Criminal Ventures and Murder: The Prospects for Law Reform" (2009) 20 K.L.J. 379–401.
[130]   R. Buxton, "Joint Enterprise" [2009] Crim. L.R. 233 at 240. But see also the response by Jeremy Horder, Law Commissioner at the time of the proposals in J. Horder, *Homicide and the Politics of Law Reform* (Oxford: OUP, 2012), p.165.
[131]   R. Buxton, "Joint Enterprise" [2009] Crim. L.R. 233 at 240.

In relation to the second issue, the draft section requires that P act within the scope of the venture and that what was within the scope of the venture can be inferred from the conduct of the participants. The Law Commission describes this as opting for the "simplest course":

> "The question for the jury will be one of fact and degree: have the prosecution shown that the act fell within the scope of the joint criminal venture? This test should not be made more complex by additional legal tests being superimposed upon it."[132]

It appears more than a little naïve, or perhaps just unreasonable, that the law should be expected to develop without further guidance, given the problems faced by the courts under the current law.

G.R. Sullivan, "Participating in Crime: Law Com No.305—Joint Criminal Ventures" [2008] Crim. L.R. 19 at 31:

"Law Com No.305 is a disappointment in terms of its discussion and proposals relating to the joint venture doctrine. First, and perhaps most importantly, cl.2, put forward on its face as the embodiment of the new law is no such thing, merely a signifier of change rather a clear statement of the content of change. This will cause considerable uncertainty from the outset: it remains to be seen if judges will confine themselves to an interpretation of the clause or go beyond the clause in the manner specified by the Commission. If judges do as the Commission advises, we will be left, in broad terms, with the status quo. The Commission fails to provide sufficient justification, doctrinally or in terms of policy for this decision. The most favourable argument in favour of the current law of criminal joint ventures is that it is a well-established and integrated part of the general law of complicity. But that is an argument which is very hard to sustain and no attempt is made to do so in Law Com 305. The better view is that the joint venture doctrine goes beyond the doctrines of complicity and is only sustainable in conceptual and moral terms if liability on the basis of that doctrine is confined to crimes the parties have agreed."

Those who disagree that the doctrine of joint enterprise is separate to other principles of complicity will no doubt be equally disappointed by the recommendations, however. It may be that a separate provision is needed in order to retain the "forensic advantage" in cases of joint enterprise that the principal offender need not be identified. If it were impossible for the prosecution to prove which party committed the actus reus of an offence, the prosecution would find it difficult to prove the liability of each party under cl.1. That problem could, however, be rectified by drafting an appropriate clause.

(iii) Clause 5: causing a no-fault offence

Law Commission No.305, Participating in Crime (2007), Appendix A: Draft Participating in Crime Bill:

"5 Offence of causing a no-fault offence
    (1) A person commits an offence if he causes another person to commit a no-fault offence, and
    (a)   it is his intention that a person should commit the offence, or
    (b)   he knows or believes that his behaviour will cause a person to commit it.
    (2) 'No-fault offence' means an offence that does not require proof of fault."

---

[132] Law Commission Report No.305 *Participating in Crime* (2007), para.3.159.

As noted above, whilst "aiding", "abetting" and "counselling" can all be synonyms for "helping", "procuring" has been interpreted to mean something very specific: to "produce by endeavour". The Law Commission decided against an additional offence of "procurement", and thought that most cases of procuring would be covered by "assisting or encouraging", but thought that a separate offence of some kind was needed, given that it is inappropriate to describe D's conduct in causing P to commit a no-fault offence as assisting or encouraging P to commit that offence.[133] This offence would cover the kind of situation which arose in *Attorney-General's Reference (No.1 of 1975)*, and it is arguably a valuable addition to the Law Commission's recommendations.[134]

The House of Commons Justice Committee has recommended that the government should consult on moving forward with these recommendations.[135] Whilst, the Government has announced that no such consultation will take place at least during the current parliament,[136] in response to the report, the DPP issued guidance to the CPS on when to use joint enterprise charges.[137]

III. The Limits of Accessorial Liability

A. No Principal Offender

As we have seen, complicity is a form of derivative liability. It presupposes the existence of a crime. "There is one crime and that it has been committed must be established before there can be any question of criminal guilt or participation in it."[138] This simple proposition requires qualification:

(a) The principal may be acquitted through lack of evidence or because of some procedural defect that applies to them. Secondary parties may nevertheless be convicted if the evidence shows clearly that there was a crime.

(b) The principal may be acquitted and the court can apply the doctrine of innocent agency to justify the conviction of the secondary party. In such a case the secondary party is in fact deemed to be the principal offender.

(c) In situations where the doctrine of innocent agency is inapplicable but where the actus reus has been committed, the accessory may be convicted even though the principal offender is acquitted because of lack of mens rea or the existence of a defence.

The relationship between the last two propositions needs to be examined.

R. v Bourne (1952) 36 Cr. App. R. 125 (Court of Criminal Appeal)

The defendant terrorised his wife into committing buggery with a dog. He was convicted of aiding and abetting his wife to commit buggery with a dog. He appealed.

---

[133] Law Commission Report No.305 *Participating in Crime* (2007), para.4.29.
[134] The Law Commission propose one further offence, considered below at p.585.
[135] House of Commons Justice Committee, *Joint Enterprise* (Eleventh Report of Session 2010–2012) (2012) HC Paper No.1507).
[136] House of Commons Justice Committee, *Joint Enterprise: Government Response to the Committee's Eleventh Report of Session 2010–2012*, (2012) HC Paper No. 901. p.2.
[137] *CPS Guidance on: Joint Enterprise Charging Decisions* (issued December 2012), available at *http://www.cps.gov.uk/legal/assets/uploads/files/Joint_Enerprise.pdf* [Accessed March 31, 2014].
[138] J.W.C. Turner, *Russell on Crime*, 12th edn (London: Stevens & Sons, 1964), p.128; affirmed in *Surujpaul v The Queen* [1958] 3 All E.R. 300 at 301.

LORD GODDARD CJ:

"I am willing to assume for the purpose of this case . . . that if this woman had been charged herself with committing the offence, she could have set up the plea of duress, not as showing that no offence had been committed, but as showing that she had no *mens rea* because her will was overborne by threats of imprisonment or violence so that she would be excused from punishment . . . [T]he offence of buggery . . . depends on the act, and if an act of buggery is committed, the felony is committed . . .

The evidence was . . . that he caused his wife to have connection with a dog, and . . . he is guilty, whether you call him an aider and abettor or an accessory, as a principal in the second degree."

Appeal dismissed

R. v Cogan and Leak [1976] Q.B. 217 (Court of Appeal, Criminal Division)

Leak compelled his wife to have sexual intercourse with Cogan, who believed that she consented. As Cogan's conviction was quashed on the strength of his belief, it became necessary to decide whether Leak's conviction as aider and abettor could stand.

LAWTON LJ:

"Leak's appeal against conviction was based on the proposition that he could not be found guilty of aiding and abetting Cogan to rape his wife if Cogan was acquitted of that offence as he was deemed in law to have been when his conviction was quashed . . .

[A]s was said by this court in *R. v Quick* [1973] Q.B. 910, 923, when considering this kind of problem:

'The facts of each case . . . have to be considered and in particular what is alleged to have been done by way of aiding and abetting.'

The only case which counsel for Leak submitted had a direct bearing on the problem of Leak's guilt was *Walters v Lunt* [1951] 2 All E.R. 645. In that case the respondents had been charged under the Larceny Act 1916, s.33(1), with receiving from a child aged seven years, certain articles knowing them to have been stolen. In 1951 a child under eight years was deemed in law to be incapable of committing a crime: it followed that at the time of receipt by the respondents the articles had not been stolen and that the charges had not been proved. That case is very different from this because here one fact is clear—the wife had been raped.

Cogan had had sexual intercourse with her without her consent. The fact that Cogan was innocent of rape because he believed that she was consenting does not affect the position that she was raped.

Her ravishment had come about because Leak had wanted it to happen and had taken action to see that it did by persuading Cogan to use his body as the instrument for the necessary physical act. In the language of the law the act of sexual intercourse without the wife's consent was the *actus reus*; it had been procured by Leak who had the appropriate *mens rea*, namely his intention that Cogan should have sexual intercourse with her without her consent. In our judgment it is irrelevant that the man whom Leak had procured to do the physical act himself did not intend to have sexual intercourse with the wife without her consent. Leak was using him as a means to procure a criminal purpose . . .

Had Leak been indicted as a principal offender, the case against him would have been clear beyond argument. Should he be allowed to go free because he was charged with 'being aider and abettor to the same offence'? If we are right in our opinion that the wife had been raped (and no one outside a court of law would say that she had not been), then the particulars of offence accurately stated what Leak had done, namely he had procured Cogan to commit the offence. This would suffice to uphold the conviction. We would prefer, however, to uphold it on a wider basis. In our judgment convictions should not be upset because of mere technicalities of pleading in an indictment. Leak knew what the case against him was and the facts in support of that case were proved. But for the fact that the jury thought that Cogan in his intoxicated condition might have mistaken the wife's sobs and distress for expressions of her consent, no question of any kind would have arisen about the form of pleading. By his written statement Leak virtually admitted what he had done. As Judge Chapman said in *R. v Humphreys* [1965] 3 All E.R. 689, 692:

'It would be anomalous if a person who admitted to a substantial part in the perpetration of a misdemeanour as aider and abettor could not be convicted on his own admission merely because the person alleged to have been aided and abetted was not or could not be convicted.'

In the circumstances of this case it would be more than anomalous: it would be an affront to justice and to the common sense of ordinary folk. It was for these reasons that we dismissed the appeal against conviction."

Appeal dismissed

Two main arguments were advanced in *Cogan and Leak*. The first concerned the doctrine of innocent agency. It is quite clear that crimes may be committed through an innocent agent but to employ it in *Cogan and Leak* would be to stretch the doctrine to implausible lengths. Even if one accepts the abuse of language involved in saying that Leak raped his wife when he committed no such act against her, Williams has demonstrated the fundamental flaw with its use in this context:

"The decision was rendered possible by the fact that the defendant happened to be a man. Rape can only be perpetrated by a man; the statute says so . . . if the duress is applied by a woman it would need an even greater degree of hawkishness than that displayed by the court in *Cogan* to call her a constructive man. Yet it is highly illogical that a man can commit rape through an innocent agent when a woman cannot."[139]

Fletcher adds that cases of innocent agency or "perpetrator-by-means" ought to be restricted to situations where "the party behind the scenes in fact dominates and controls his agent".[140] Finally, if the doctrine was thought to be applicable in *Cogan and Leak* it is difficult to see why it was not invoked in *Bourne*.

If the doctrine of innocent agency is, therefore, inappropriate in some circumstances, an alternative basis for liability has to be found. This can be derived from the assertion by Lawton LJ that it was clear that "the wife had been raped" and that Leak had procured the rape (a similar view is implicit in *Bourne*). However, a finding of rape could only follow if both actus reus and mens rea were established and the argument is, thus, of doubtful validity. However, it has been refined and developed in subsequent cases. In *Millward*[141] it was held that the defendant could be liable for procuring a driving offence provided there is an actus reus even though the principal offender is acquitted.[142] There are doubts about whether there was an actus reus on the facts of *Millward*[143] but the principle itself appears to be gaining momentum.

DPP v K and B [1997] 1 Cr. App. R. 36 (Court of Appeal, Criminal Division)

Two girls, aged 14 and 11, were alleged to have procured the rape of another girl by the principal offender, a boy (never traced) aged between 10 and 14. The magistrates acquitted the girls on the basis (inter alia) that the prosecution had failed to rebut the presumption of doli incapax in relation to the boy. The prosecution appealed by way of case stated.

---

[139] D.J. Baker, *Glanville Williams, Textbook of Criminal Law*, 3rd edn (London: Stevens & Sons, 2012), p.518.

[140] Fletcher, *Rethinking Criminal Law* (1978), pp.665–667. cf. *Stringer* (1992) 94 Cr. App. R. 13.

[141] *R. v Millward (Sidney Booth)* [1994] Crim. L.R. 527.

[142] *Wheelhouse* [1994] Crim. L.R. 756 followed *Millward* although it was unnecessary to do so on the facts since the doctrine of innocent agency applied.

[143] See, for example, commentary to *R. v Loukes (Noel Martyn)* [1996] Crim. L.R. 341 at 343; and R. Taylor, "Complicity, Legal Scholarship and the Law of Unintended Consequences" (2009) 29 L.S. 1 at 7.

RUSSELL LJ:

"In my judgment, the decision of the magistrate in this appeal cannot be supported. There is no doubt whatever that 'W' was the victim of unlawful sexual intercourse without her consent; such was not disputed. The *actus reus* was proved. The respondents procured the situation which included the sexual intercourse. It would, in my view, be singularly unattractive to find that because of the absence of a mental element on the part of the principal, the procurers could thereby escape conviction when, as the magistrate found, K and B had the requisite *mens rea* namely, the desire that rape should take place and the procuring of it.

In my judgment, neither authority nor common sense nor justice compels this Court to support the finding of the magistrates."

Appeal allowed

Two points must be stressed. First, there must be an actus reus. If there is no actus reus, the secondary party cannot be found liable. So, for example, in *Loukes*,[144] a case involving causing death by dangerous driving,[145] the principal was acquitted because there was insufficient evidence that he knew of the dangerous condition of the vehicle or that it was so obvious that he ought to have known (an objective standard of driving). There was, therefore, no evidence of dangerous driving on his part, and thus no actus reus. In such circumstances the defendant, whose business it was to oversee the condition of the vehicles, could not be convicted of procuring the offence.

The underlying rationale of these developments can be accepted in relation to the procuring of offences where, as we have seen, it is causation and not consensus that is material and the principal need not even be aware that a crime is being committed. However, the application of the principle in cases such as *Loukes* is more questionable. In this case, and in *Roberts and George*,[146] the offence of causing death by dangerous driving was described as being a strict liability offence. As there was insufficient evidence of dangerous driving by the principal offender, there was no actus reus. However, this offence could be regarded as one of negligence. Culpability is required in that the driving must be dangerous.[147] Taylor notes that dangerous driving can be interpreted as having two alternative modes of commission, one requiring attitudinally defined conduct and the other requiring factually defined conduct.[148] By this he means that dangerous driving is committed either due to the manner in which the vehicle was driven by the driver, or alternatively where the driving is dangerous because the condition of the vehicle is dangerous. It is the latter mode which was in issue in cases such as *Loukes*, where objective mens rea must be established (the defendant either knew that the condition of the vehicle was dangerous, or *ought* to have known because it would have been obvious to a competent and careful driver). In these cases, the principle derived from *Cogan and Leak* can be applied. According to this latter analysis, there was an actus reus in these cases and the procurer, assuming his mens rea was established, should have been liable.

The second point to stress is that the principle that the accessory can be liable if there is an actus reus has only been applied in cases of procuring. Assuming the *Powell* principle does extend to all other situations of complicity, it is difficult to see how, in principle, an accessory could be liable if the principal offender is not liable. Under *Powell* the accessory must realise that there is a risk that the principal offender will commit the offence with the mens rea of that offence. The accessory's liability is, thus, dependent upon that of the principal.

---

144 *Loukes* [1996] 1 Cr. App. R. 444; see also *Thornton v Mitchell* [1940] 1 All E.R. 339 and *R. v Roberts (David Geraint)* [1997] Crim. L.R. 209.
145 Contrary to the Road Traffic Act 1988 ss.1 and 2A.
146 *Roberts* [1997] Crim. L.R. 209.
147 Smith, Commentary to *Roberts* [1997] Crim. L.R. 209 at 211.
148 Taylor, "Complicity, Legal Scholarship and the Law of Unintended Consequences" (2009) 29 L.S 1 at 9.

This does, at first sight, seem anomalous. There appears to be one rule for procuring and another for other forms of complicity. This is compounded when one considers that the prosecution does not even have to specify the form of complicity in the charge. However, the problem may not, in fact, be as significant as it seems. If the accessory does have the appropriate mens rea and the crime is committed by a principal offender who lacks mens rea or who has a defence such as duress, the situation would almost certainly be regarded as one of procuring or innocent agency. Liability could then be imposed under the above principles.

In its Report on *Participating in Crime*, the Law Commission recommends creating a statutory offence of using an innocent agent:

Law Commission No.305, Participating in Crime (2007), Appendix A: Draft Participating in Crime Bill:

"4 Using an innocent agent
(1) If a person (D) uses an innocent agent (P) to commit an offence, D is guilty of that offence.
(2) P is an innocent agent in relation to an offence if
(a) he does a criminal act, and
(b) he does not commit the offence itself for one of the following reasons.
 (i) he is under the age of 10,
(ii) he has a defence of insanity, or
(iii) he acts without the fault required for conviction, and there is no other reason why he does not commit it.
(3) D uses P to commit an offence if—
(a) D intends to cause a person (whether or not P) to do a criminal act in relation to the offence,
(b) D causes P to do the criminal act, and
(c) subsection (4) or (5) is satisfied.
(4) If a particular state of mind requires to be proved for conviction of the offence that D uses P to commit, D's state of mind must be such that, were he to do the act that he intends to cause to be done, he would do it with the state of mind required for conviction of the offence.
(5) If the offence which D uses P to commit is a no-fault offence, D must know or believe that, were a person to do the act that D intends to cause to be done, that person would do it—
(a) in the circumstances (if any), and
(b)   with the consequences (if any), proof of which is required for conviction of the offence."

Taylor has described the Law Commission's proposals as taking a "twin-track" approach.[149] In cases where P is incapable (due to a defence of infancy or insanity) or non-culpable (where P does not have mens rea, as in *Cogan*), D is liable due to innocent agency, and D is treated as the principal offender. But where P is not liable due to being excused (due to a defence such as duress or, in murder cases, loss of control) D remains the secondary party rather than acting as a P through an innocent agent, because P is not a truly "innocent" agent in such cases. Taylor questions whether there is any reason for taking this "twin-track" approach, and points out that it could lead to difficult cases where P is both incapable and has an excusatory defence, in which case P would escape liability on both tracks.[150] Taylor concludes that there was no need to propose this additional offence and that with a little

---

149 R. Taylor, "Procuring, Causation, Innocent Agency and the Law Commission" [2008] Crim. L.R. 32 at 36.
150 Taylor, "Procuring, Causation, Innocent Agency and the Law Commission" [2008] Crim. L.R. 32 at 40. D would avoid liability under cl.4 because subs.(2) would require that there were no additional reasons why P did not commit the offence, other than his being under the age of 10, having the defence of insanity, or acting without the fault requirement. If he was acting under duress there *would* be another reason.

amendment to cl.1, cases falling within the doctrine of innocent agency could have been dealt with more appropriately through derivative liability.[151]

B. Accessory can be Guilty of Graver Offence than the One Committed

Until the following decision in *Howe*, the law was that if the principal had the mens rea of one offence, such as manslaughter, it was not possible for an accessory not present at the scene of the crime to be guilty of the graver offence of murder.[152] The reason for this rule was "that one could [not] say that that which was done can be said to be done with the intention of the defendant who was not present at the time". Without, it must be said, much discussion of the merits or demerits of this approach, the law has now changed.

R. v Howe [1987] 1 A.C. 417 (House of Lords)

(The facts and a fuller extract appear, above, p.376.)

LORD MACKAY OF CLASHFERN:

"I turn now to the second certified question [whether a secondary party can be convicted of murder despite the conviction of the principal for manslaughter] . . . I am of the opinion that the Court of Appeal reached the correct conclusion upon it as a matter of principle.

Giving the judgment of the Court of Appeal Lord Lane C.J. said [1986] Q.B. 626, 641–642:

'The judge based himself on a decision of this court in *R. v Richards*. The facts in that case were that Mrs Richards paid two men to inflict injuries on her husband which she intended should "put him in hospital for a month". The two men wounded the husband but not seriously. They were acquitted of wounding with intent but convicted of unlawful wounding. Mrs Richards herself was convicted of wounding with intent, the jury plainly, and not surprisingly, believing that she had the necessary intent, though the two men had not. She appealed against her conviction on the ground that she could not properly be convicted as accessory before the fact to a crime more serious than that committed by the principals in the first degree. The appeal was allowed and the conviction for unlawful wounding was substituted. The court followed a passage from Hawkins' Pleas of the Crown, vol. 2. c. 29, para. 15: "I take it to be an uncontroverted rule that [the offence of the accessory can never rise higher than that of the principal]; it seeming incongruous and absurd that he who is punished only as a partaker of the guilt of another, should be adjudged guilty of a higher crime than the other."'

James LJ delivering the judgment in *R. v Richards* said:

'If there is only one offence committed, and that is the offence of unlawful wounding, then the person who has requested that offence to be committed, or advised that that offence be committed, cannot be guilty of a graver offence than that in fact which was committed.'

The decision in *R. v Richards* has been the subject of some criticism . . . Counsel before us posed the situation where A hands a gun to D informing him that it is loaded with blank ammunition only and telling him to go and scare X by discharging it. The ammunition is in fact live, as A knows, and X is killed. D is convicted only of manslaughter, as he might be on those facts. It would seem absurd that A should thereby escape conviction for murder. We take the view that *R. v Richards* was incorrectly decided, but it seems to us that it cannot properly be distinguished from the instant case.

---

[151]   Taylor, "Procuring, Causation, Innocent Agency and the Law Commission" [2008] Crim. L.R. 32 at 49.
[152]   *R. v Richards (Isabelle Christina)* [1974] Q.B. 776.

I consider that the reasoning of Lord Lane C.J. is entirely correct and I would affirm his view that where a person has been killed and that result is the result intended by another participant, the mere fact that the actual killer may be convicted only of the reduced charge of manslaughter for some reason special to himself does not, in my opinion in any way, result in a compulsory reduction for the other participant."

Appeal dismissed

It has been pointed out that in neither *Howe* nor *Richards* was any real attempt made to understand the theoretical underpinnings of the two positions.[153] Since it has long been possible to convict those present at the scene of the crime of a more serious offence than the principal, at one level, *Howe* merely reflects the increasing trend of regarding presence as not determinative of anything. However, it is a departure "from orthodox complicity theory that insists on the parties' sharing in liability for *one* offence".[154] In other words, this may be a departure from derivative liability similar to that in cases such as *Cogan*. Further, despite all the criticism of *Richards* there may have been a sound principle underlying it: that of control. Mrs Richards lacked control over the principal offender and should not have been guilty of a more serious offence despite her greater mens rea. We will return to this issue in the final section of this chapter.

C. Withdrawal of Accessories

A withdrawal from a criminal enterprise may amount to a claim that there is no actus reus or mens rea of complicity. For example, a person may lend a gun to the principal offender to commit murder, but later take the gun back. If the principal offender shoots the victim with a different gun, the original provider of the gun will not be liable as there will be no actus reus of complicity.[155] However, in other cases the accessory's involvement might clearly satisfy the actus reus and mens rea requirements of complicity but there might be a "withdrawal" before the commission of the offence.[156] This latter scenario is exemplified by the following leading case.

R. v Becerra and Cooper (1975) 62 Cr. App. R. 212 (Court of Appeal, Criminal Division)

Becerra broke into a house with Cooper and another. They intended to steal but Becerra gave a knife to Cooper which he was to use if anyone interrupted them. Lewis, an upstairs tenant, came to investigate the noise, at which Becerra said, "There's a bloke coming. Let's go," and jumped out of a window. As he ran away Cooper stabbed and killed Lewis with the knife. Becerra was convicted with Cooper of murder, and appealed.

ROSKILL LJ:

"It was argued in the alternative on behalf of Becerra, that even if there were this common design, nonetheless Becerra had open to him a second line of defence, namely that . . . —whatever Cooper did immediately before

---

[153] K.J.M. Smith, *A Modern Treatise on the Law of Complicity* (Oxford: Clarendon Press, 1991), p.130.
[154] Law Commission Consultation Paper No.131, *Assisting and Encouraging Crime* (1993), para.2.38. See also Smith, *A Modern Treatise on the Law of Complicity* (1991), pp.127–133.
[155] K.J.M. Smith, "Withdrawal in Complicity: A Restatement of Principles" [2001] Crim. L.R. 769.
[156] Smith (see fn.155) argues that the nature and scope of a withdrawal defence should depend on the rationale for having such a defence: whether it is an incentive for the accessory to desist or whether it is evidence of the accessory's lack of (or diminished) culpability or future dangerousness.

and at the time of the killing of Lewis, Becerra had by then withdrawn from that common design and so should not be convicted of the murder of Lewis, even though the common design had previously been that which I have stated . . .

It is necessary, before dealing with that argument in more detail, to say a word or two about the relevant law. [Roskill L.J. then cited a decision of the Court of Appeal of British Columbia in *Whitehouse (alias Savage)* (1941) 1 W.W.R. 112, at pp. 115 and 116.]

> 'Can it be said on the facts of this case that a mere change of mental intention and a quitting of the scene of the crime just immediately prior to the striking of the fatal blow will absolve those who participate in the commission of the crime by overt acts up to that moment from all the consequences of its accomplishment by the one who strikes in ignorance of his companion's change of heart? I think not. After a crime has been committed and before a prior abandonment of the common enterprise may be found by a jury there must be, in my view, in the absence of exceptional circumstances, something more than a mere mental change of intention and physical change of place by those associates who wish to dissociate themselves from the consequences attendant upon their willing assistance up to the moment of the actual commission of that crime. I would not attempt to define too closely what must be done in criminal matters involving participation in a common unlawful purpose to break the chain of causation and responsibility. That must depend upon the circumstances of each case but it seems to me that one essential element ought to be established in a case of this kind. Where practicable and reasonable there must be timely communication of the intention to abandon the common purpose from those who wish to dissociate themselves from the contemplated crime to those who desire to continue in it. What is "timely communication" must be determined by the facts of each case but where practicable and reasonable it ought to be such communication, verbal or otherwise, that will serve unequivocal notice upon the other party to the common unlawful cause that if he proceeds upon it he does so without the further aid and assistance of those who withdraw. The unlawful purpose of him who continues alone is then his own and not one in common with those who are no longer parties to it nor liable to its full and final consequences.' . . .

In the view of each member of this Court, that passage, if we may respectfully say so, could not be improved upon and we venture to adopt it in its entirety as a correct statement of the law which is to be applied in this case . . .

We therefore turn back to consider the direction which the learned judge gave in the present case to the jury and what was the suggested evidence that Becerra had withdrawn from the common agreement. The suggested evidence is the use by Becerra of the words 'Come on let's go', coupled with his act in going out through the window. The evidence, as the judge pointed out, was that Cooper never heard that nor did the third man. But let it be supposed that that was said and the jury took the view that it was said.

On the facts of this case, in the circumstances then prevailing, the knife having already been used and being contemplated for further use when it was handed over by Becerra to Cooper for the purpose of avoiding (if necessary) by violent means the hazards of identification, if Becerra wanted to withdraw at that stage, he would have to 'countermand,' to use the word that is used in some of the cases or 'repent' to use another word so used, in some manner vastly different and vastly more effective than merely to say 'Come on, let's go' and go out through the window.

It is not necessary, on this application, to decide whether the point of time had arrived at which the only way in which he could effectively withdraw, so as to free himself from joint responsibility for any act Cooper thereafter did in furtherance of the common design, would be physically to intervene so as to stop Cooper attacking Lewis, as the judge suggested, by interposing his own body between them or somehow getting in between them or whether some other action might suffice. That does not arise for decision here. Nor is it necessary to decide whether or not the learned judge was right or wrong, on the facts of this case, . . . [to say] 'and at least take all reasonable steps to prevent the commission of the crime which he had agreed the others should commit'. It is enough for the purposes of deciding this application to say that under the law of this country as it stands, and on the facts (taking them at their highest in favour of Becerra), that which was urged as amounting to withdrawal from the common design was not capable of amounting to such withdrawal. Accordingly Becerra remains responsible, in the eyes of the law, for everything that Cooper did and continued to do after Becerra's disappearance through the window as much as if he had done them himself."

Appeal dismissed

Accordingly, there must be, at least, a "timely communication" of the decision to withdraw. This was confirmed in *Rook*[157] where the appellant tried to disassociate himself from the planned murder by simply not being around when the others came to collect him on the way to the crime.

> "[T]he appellant never told the others that he was not going ahead with the crime. His absence on the day could not possibly amount to 'unequivocal communication' of his withdrawal . . . he had made it quite clear to himself that he did not want to be there on the day. But he did not make it clear to the others."

However, in *Mitchell*[158] it was held that the requirement of communication of withdrawal only applies in cases of pre-planned violence and not to cases of spontaneous violence, although in these latter cases it would be more difficult evidentially to establish withdrawal if there had been no communication. This was followed in *O'Flaherty*[159] where it was held that the question of whether or not the defendant had withdrawn is no more than a consideration of whether the principal had departed from the joint enterprise.[160] This was another case of spontaneous violence in which, as pointed out by Ashworth,[161] the principals may have been as unaware of the defendants' participation in the joint enterprise as they were of their withdrawal. Three appellants, O'F, R and T, joined in an attack on the victim with various weapons. Subsequently, the victim was chased by a group of individuals, including O'F, but R and T did not join the group and instead chose to leave. The victim sustained fatal injuries during a second attack. O'F did not take part in the second attack but was present at the scene, and looked on whilst holding a cricket bat. R and T had not communicated their withdrawal from the attack but it was held that they did not need to do so as the second attack could not be said to be part of the joint enterprise to which they were party, and their appeal against conviction for murder was allowed. O'F's presence at the scene of the second attack was, however, enough to show that he had aided and abetted the crime of murder. *O'Flaherty* has been followed, post-*Rahman*, in the case of *Mitchell*,[162] where D's argument that there were two distinct joint enterprises and that her presence at the second was only to look for her shoes and not to encourage further violence was rejected by the Court of Appeal. In its judgment the court stated that there was ample evidence that D had not withdrawn from the joint enterprise and that the jury was entitled to conclude that she had become party to an enterprise in which she had foreseen or contemplated that one of the other parties might kill with the intention of inflicting really serious bodily injury.

In some cases, depending on the circumstances,[163] it may be that timely communication alone is not enough and that some further action is required. In *Rook*, for example, the Court of Appeal stated that a suggestion that "a declared intent to withdraw from a conspiracy to dynamite a building is not enough, if the fuse has been set; he must step on the fuse" went too far. "It may be enough that he should have done his best to step on the fuse." Presumably in such cases

---

[157] *Rook* (1993) 97 Cr. App. R. 327. See also *R. v Grundy* [1977] Crim. L.R. 543, where the party also sought (successfully) to withdraw before the commission of the crime (some two weeks hence); see also *R. v Croft (William James)* (1944) 29 Cr. App. R. 169, *R. v Whitefield (Arthur Armour)* (1984) 79 Cr. App. R. 36 and *R. v Baker* [1994] Crim. L.R. 444.

[158] *R. v Mitchell (Frank)* [1999] Crim. L.R. 496.

[159] *O'Flaherty* [2004] 2 Cr. App. R. 20.

[160] This was also the approach taken in *R. v D* [2005] EWCA Crim 1981.

[161] *R. v O'Flaherty (Errol Carlton)* [2004] Crim. L.R. 751 at 752.

[162] *Mitchell* [2008] EWCA Crim 2552; [2009] Crim L.R. 287.

[163] In a case of spontaneous violence it is clear that it is not necessary for the accessory to take reasonable steps to prevent crime: *O'Flaherty* [2004] 2 Cr. App. R. 20 at [61].

"some form of correlation [should] exist between the nature or form of the defendant's complicitous behaviour and the nature or form of his required exculpatory action. In crude terms: the greater the extent of inculpatory behaviour the more demanding will be the price of exculpation."[164]

The Law Commission has recommended that in certain circumstances a secondary party ought to have a specific defence where he made efforts to undo some of the work of the principal offender:

Law Commission No.305, Participating in Crime (2007), Appendix A: Draft Participating in Crime Bill:

"7 Defence of acting to prevent commission of offence etc.

(1) In proceedings for an offence to which this section applies, a person is not guilty of the offence if he proves on the balance of probabilities that—
  (a) he acted for the purpose of—
  (i)   preventing the commission of that offence or another offence, or
  (ii) preventing, or limiting, the occurrence of harm, and
  (b) it was reasonable for him to act as he did."

D. Victims Cannot be Accessories

The case of *Tyrell*[165] established a general principle that where a statutory offence exists in order to protect a particular class of victim, such a victim cannot be held liable for participating in the offence as an accessory. This, and subsequent cases,[166] concerned sexual offences such as incest and underage sexual intercourse. If a principal offender has sexual intercourse in a situation where to do so is an offence by virtue of the identity of the other party (because of her age or relationship with the principal), that victim cannot be said to have aided, abetted, counselled or procured the offence.[167]

While the *Tyrell* principle has, to date, only been applied to sexual offences, there is no reason why it should not be applied to other offences.[168] However, the principle is uncertain and interpretative difficulty surrounds the notion of "victim". For example, the notion of "victim" appeared to take on different meanings in *Brown*.[169] Prior to the prosecution 26 people were cautioned for aiding and abetting offences against themselves.[170] It thus seems that the passive participants in the sado-masochistic activities in *Brown* were not "victims" for the purpose of the protection afforded by the rules on accessorial liability but, of course, were regarded as "victims" for the purpose of assessing the criminal

---

[164] "Withdrawal in Complicity: A Restatement of Principles" [201] C.L.R. 769 at 776.
[165] *R. v Tyrell* [1894] 1 Q.B. 710.
[166] e.g. *R. v Whitehouse (Arthur)* [1977] Q.B. 868.
[167] Although this principle has not been repealed by legislation, it has been argued that certain provisions under the Sexual Offences Act 2003 manage to circumvent its application, thereby criminalising victims one would expect to see protected by the law (M. Bohlander, "The Sexual Offences Act 2003 and the *Tyrell* Principle—Criminalising the Victims?" [2005] Crim. L.R. 701). The Law Commission considered the point at some length in its most recent report on secondary liability: Law Commission Report No.305, *Participating in Crime* (2007), paras 5.24–5.38.
[168] Section 51 of the Serious Crime Act 2007 codifies *Tyrell* and excludes liability for encouraging or assisting crime for victims in cases of any "protective offence". See above, Ch.5. A similar draft provision is included in cl.6 of the draft Participating in Crime Bill, appended to Law Commission Report No.305, *Participating in Crime* (2007).
[169] *R. v Brown (Anthony Joseph)* [1994] 1 A.C. 212.
[170] *The Guardian*, February 8, 1992.

liability of the principal offender.[171] The following decision drew upon *Brown* (even though, as Herring points out, the "victims" were not actually prosecuted but only those who inflicted harm[172]) in reaching its conclusion that a narrow interpretation should be given to the victim rule.

R v Gnango [2011] UKSC 59 (Supreme Court)

(The facts appear above, p.560)

LORD PHILLIPS P and LORD JUDGE CJ:

"[46] . . . (i) Does the victim rule preclude the conviction of a defendant for aiding and abetting a crime in respect of which he is the victim, even where the crime is not designed to protect a particular class of which the victim is a member? If yes, (ii) does the victim rule preclude the conviction of a defendant for aiding and abetting a crime in respect of which he was the intended victim, but where the actual victim is a third party? . . .

[51] [T]here is no applicable statutory victim rule that precludes conviction of the respondent on the basis that he aided and abetted Bandana Man's attempt to kill him or cause him serious injury. Is there, or should there be, a common law rule that does so?

[52] The fact that Parliament found it necessary to enact s 2(1) of the [Criminal Law Act] 1977[173] Act and s 51 of the [Serious Crime Act] 2007 Act[174] is cogent indication that there is no common law rule that precludes conviction of a defendant of being party to a crime of which he was the actual or intended victim. We are satisfied that there is no such rule. This is evident from the fact that, under common law, attempted suicide was a crime, as was aiding and abetting suicide . . .

[53] We can see no reason why this court should consider extending the common law so as to protect from conviction any defendant who is, or is intended to be, harmed by the crime that he commits, or attempts to commit. Such an extension would defeat the intention of Parliament in circumscribing the victim rule in s 51 of the 2007 Act. In *R v Brown* [1993] 2 All ER 75, [1994] 1 AC 212 sado-masochists were held to have been rightly convicted of causing injury to others who willingly consented to the injuries that they received. There would have been no bar to conviction of the latter of having aided and abetted the infliction of those injuries upon themselves. It is no doubt appropriate for prosecuting authorities to consider carefully whether there is justification for prosecuting anyone as party to a crime where he is the victim, or intended victim of that crime, but that is not to say that the actual or intended victim of a crime should on that ground alone be absolved from criminal responsibility in relation to it . . ."

The decision is controversial:

Jonathan Herring, "Victims as Defendants: When Victims Participate in Crimes against Themselves", in Alan Reed and Michael Bohlander (eds), Participation in Crime: Domestic and Comparative Perspectives (Farnham: Ashgate, 2013), pp.84, 90–91:

"[T]heir Lordships' argument is that [statutory provisions in relation to victims such as in s.51 of the Serious Crime Act 2007] would not be necessary if there was a general rule that victims could not be liable as accomplices. However, it is always dangerous to assume a common law principle from a statute. The mere fact that a statute creates a particular offence or defence does not necessarily amend the common law as it applies in similar situations . . .

The discussion of this issue in *Gnango* was *obiter* and . . . there was no precedent to support it. A deeper consideration of the issues might have explained why no prosecutions have been brought . . .

---

[171]   L. Bibbings and P. Alldridge, "Sexual Expression, Body Alteration, and the Defence of Consent" (1993) 20 J.L. and Soc. 356 at 364.

[172]   J. Herring, "Victims as Defendants: When Victims Participate in Crimes Against Themselves", in A. Reed and M. Bohlander (ed.), *Participation in Crime: Domestic and Comparative Perspectives* (Farnham: Ashgate, 2013), p.83.

[173]   See above p.510.

[174]   See above p. 533.

The best arguments against [victims'] accessorial liability require us to return to the arguments generally against criminalising self-harm. The first concerns autonomy. If there is respect for the principles . . . that people should be entitled to shape their lives . . . as they wish, the criminal law should be reluctant to criminalise what is done. Where the actors only harm themselves it is not clear that the harm is sufficient to justify criminal liability, save, maybe, in cases of serious harm. That argument is as powerful in cases where the defendant has harmed him or herself as it is in cases where the defendant has persuaded another to harm him.

. . . [T]here will be cases which arguably are not protected by the principle of autonomy. There are cases where serious harm is done or the behaviour is seen as showing a particular lack of respect for the dignity of the individual. But . . . these are likely to be cases where the individual is in a sorry state and needs support and help, rather than punishment . . .

There may be a small band of cases where the individual has encouraged or helped in causing themselves a serious injury, but there is no therapeutic case for intervening. Perhaps the *Wright* [(1603) 1 Co. Lit. 127a] case, in which the person had their arm removed to assist in begging, is an example. But these will be very rare indeed."

E. Accomplices and Transferred Malice

David Lanham, "Accomplices and Transferred Malice" (1980) 96 L.Q.R. 110 at 110–111:

"An accomplice (A) instigates a principal offender (PO) to commit a specific crime. PO commits a crime of the same description but against a different victim or subject-matter or in a different manner. In what circumstances is A criminally liable for the crime committed by PO? The law in this area has become incoherent for two reasons. First, opinions differ on the nature of the link required between A and the crime actually committed. There are four theories running through the authorities. First, the direct consequences theory. Under this theory it is enough that the crime committed by PO flows directly from PO's attempt to commit the crime suggested. The second theory is the probable consequence theory. A is liable only if the crime actually committed is a probable consequence of the crime suggested by A. This has been held to mean that A is liable if he ought to have foreseen the likelihood of the crime actually committed by PO. The third theory is that of recklessness. A will be liable only if he actually foresees the possibility that the crime actually committed will occur. Finally, there is the express authority theory. A will be liable only if he has expressly authorised the crime which is actually committed.

These four approaches would be enough in themselves to lead to confusion but the law is complicated still further by the fact that some authorities appear to apply different principles to different aspects of the problem. While the problem is basically one of transferred malice, the situations requiring the transfer can arise in various different ways. First, PO may attempt to harm the right victim (X) but harm another (V) by accident. Secondly, he may believe that V is X and so harm the wrong victim by mistake. Thirdly, he may do more harm than A ordered, *e.g.* injuring V (an unintended victim) as well as X (the intended victim). Fourthly, he may deliberately depart from A's orders and injure V even though he knows that V is not X. Fifthly, he may commit the crime ordered by A against the correct victim but at a different time, place or in a different manner from that ordered or advised by A. Finally, he may commit the crime ordered but against the wrong subject-matter."

Authority on this problem is scarce with most of the controversy revolving around the following case.

R. v Saunders and Archer (1573) 2 Plowden 473; 75 E.R. 706 (Warwick Assizes)

Saunders wished to kill his wife so that he could marry another woman. He explained his plans to Archer who advised him to kill her by poison. Archer bought the poison and gave it to Saunders to give to his wife. Saunders mixed the poison with two pieces of roasted apple and gave it to his wife. After tasting it the wife handed the rest of the apple to Eleanor, their three-year-old daughter. Saunders, on seeing this, merely said that "apples were not good for such infants" but when his wife persisted he simply watched his daughter eat the apple and did nothing "lest he be suspected". The daughter died of the poison. Saunders was found guilty of murder but the question remained as to the liability of Archer.

LORD DYER CJ:

"But the most difficult point in this case . . . was whether or not Archer should be adjudged accessory to the murder. For the offence which Archer committed was the aid and advice which he gave to Saunders, and that was only to kill his wife, and no other, for there was no parol communication between them concerning the daughter, and although by the consequences which followed from the giving of the poison by Saunders the principal, it so happened that the daughter was killed, yet Archer did not precisely procure her death, nor advise him to kill her, and therefore whether or not he should be accessory to this murder which happened by a thing consequential to the first act, seemed to them to be doubtful. For which reason they thought proper to advise and consider of it until the next gaol delivery, and in the meantime to consult with the justices in the term . . . [It was finally agreed] that they ought not to give judgment against the said Alexander Archer, because they took the law to be that he could not be adjudged accessory to the said offence of murder, for that he did not assent that the daughter should be poisoned, but only that the wife should be poisoned, which assent cannot be drawn further than he gave it, for the poisoning of the daughter is a distinct thing from that to which he was privy, and therefore he shall not be adjudged accessory to it; and so they were resolved before this time."

The judges took two years to decide that Archer was not liable as accessory to the crime of murder.[175] Many times that number of years have been spent interpreting this decision. A broad interpretation is that the accomplice will only be liable if they expressly authorise or foresee the harm which occurs. In *Reardon*[176] the principal offender shot two victims who were carried into the garden of a bar. The principal offender returned to the bar and asked for a knife because one of the victims was still alive. The defendant handed over a knife. The principal offender stabbed both victims to death. It was held that the defendant would be liable if he foresaw the type of act the principal offender committed. He would have

"foreseen at least the strong possibility that if [the principal] found that the other deceased was still breathing and alive, he might use the knife in the same way, and therefore that was an act by [the principal offender] of a type which the appellant had foreseen even though he might not necessarily have intended that use."

A narrower interpretation of *Saunders and Archer* suggests that secondary parties will not be liable if the principal *deliberately* chooses another victim; effectively this is what Saunders did. He chose to let a different victim die, rather than step in to prevent it. On the other hand, if Saunders had not been present when his daughter ate the apple, he would not have deliberately changed the plan and the doctrine of transferred malice could apply and Archer would have been liable. The first case to arise on similar facts in more recent times is *Leahy*.[177] In this case, where a deliberate wounding of a different victim took place, the defendant was held not to have aided and abetted the principal's offence.

In the recent decision of *Gnango*, where, very unusually, the mens rea of the principal *towards* the defendant (with whom he was engaged in a shoot-out) was transferred to the killing of an innocent passer-by, leaving the defendant liable for murder as an accessory, Lords Phillips and Judge stated that:

---

175   Even then, his release was not immediately ordered; he was kept in prison until he could purchase his pardon.
176   *Reardon* [1999] Crim. L.R. 392.
177   *R. v Leahy* [1985] Crim. L.R. 99.

"The doctrine applies to secondary parties as it does to principal offenders. Thus if D2 attempts to aid, abet, counsel or procure D1 to murder V1 but D1, intending to kill V1, accidentally kills V2 instead, D2 will be guilty of the murder of V2."[178]

The Draft Criminal Code Bill 1989 proposes that the accessory be liable where the intended offence takes place on an unintended victim or property, but not liable, as in *Leahy*, for "an offence intentionally committed by the principal in respect of some other person or thing".[179] The Law Commission's current recommendations take a similar approach when looking at the "scope of the venture" test for joint criminal ventures.[180] The following example is provided to illustrate how a secondary party would escape liability for murder, although she would be liable for the inchoate offence of assisting or encouraging crime:

"D agrees with P, a professional assassin, to provide P with a gun to murder D's wife. P is then paid a large sum of money by X to murder X's wife, V. P murders V with D's gun. P does not shoot D's wife."[181]

However, the transferred malice doctrine would apply to enable the conviction of the secondary party in this second example:

"D encourages P to hit X and gives P a stick with which to do it. D takes a swing at X but X ducks and the blow strikes and injures V."[182]

IV. Conclusion

We have seen that underpinning the present law are two assumptions. The first is that complicity is a form of derivative liability—there is only one offence, that of the principal—and the second is that accessories are as blameworthy as principal offenders. They are liable to the same extent and deserve comparable punishment.

Despite commitment to the first assumption, it is necessary to question the second assumption that accessories are as blameworthy as principal offenders and deserve comparable punishment. At a superficial level, of course, the rationale for this is obvious: the accessory's role may have greatly facilitated the commission of the crime; he "may sometimes be more guilty than the perpetrator. Lady Macbeth was worse than Macbeth".[183] English law currently allows for maximum flexibility: where the contribution of the secondary party is greater than that of the principal he can receive greater punishment, where the contribution is minor, he can receive less punishment.

It should now be apparent (particularly from the chapter on inchoate offences) that a basic theme of this book is that criminal liability ought generally to be imposed only when a blameworthy actor has

---

[178] *Gnango* [2011] UKSC 59 at [16].
[179] Law Commission No.177 (1989) cl.27(5). This is the approach taken in the CPS guidance on charging joint enterprise cases: *CPS Guidance on: Joint Enterprise Charging Decisions* (issued December 2012), available at *http://www.cps.gov.uk/legal/assets/uploads/files/Joint_Enterprise.pdf* [Accessed 31 March 31, 2014] at [15].
[180] The Law Commission is of the opinion that the issue would not arise in cases of complicity other than those involving a joint criminal venture: Law Commission Report No.305, *Participating in Crime* (2007), para.3.165.
[181] Law Commission Report No.305, *Participating in Crime* (2007), para.3.163.
[182] Law Commission Report No.305, *Participating in Crime* (2007), para.3.164.
[183] G. Williams, *Textbook of Criminal Law*, 1st edn (London: Stevens & Sons, 1978), p.287; see also J.C. Smith, "A Note on Duress" [1974] Crim. L.R. 349 at 351, cited with approval by Lord Edmund-Davies in *Lynch v DPP* [1975] A.C. 653 at 709. Lord Simon in *Lynch* and Lords Wilberforce and Edmund-Davies in *Abbott v The Queen* [1977] A.C. 755, all opined that no distinction could be based on the degree of participation in a crime.

caused a specified harm. This is only a general proposition, not a necessary rule. Thus, as we have seen, one *might* be justified in imposing criminal liability in the absence of blameworthiness (as in crimes of strict liability) or in the absence of obvious harm, or "first order harm" (as with inchoate offences). However, where one of these elements is missing and liability is nevertheless justified, the equation ought only to be balanced by imposing *less* criminal liability. This model provides the key for the structuring of all criminal offences and ascertaining appropriate levels of punishment. Thus there can be degrees of blameworthiness (for instance, intentionally causing harm being regarded as worse than recklessly causing harm), and, of course, there are degrees of harm (for instance, killing one's victim is worse than injuring them). The correlation of the degree of blameworthiness with the degree of harm ought to provide a fairly precise level of criminal liability with appropriate level(s) of punishment.

How does accessorial liability fit into such a model of criminal liability and punishment? The answer is clear. If an accessory is less blameworthy or causes less harm than the principal offender, then they deserve less criminal liability. If they are *both* less blameworthy *and* cause less harm, then they deserve *even less* criminal liability and punishment. So the central questions become:

1. is the accessory less blameworthy, and/or

2. do they cause less harm than the principal offender?

A. Blameworthiness

The liability of the accessory is derivative; it stems from the offence committed by the principal.

"Since the source of culpability as an accessory is not the offence definition, there is no logical imperative that the mental element for an accessory should be the same as that required for a principal."[184]

As we have seen, the courts appear now to have accepted this proposition, but not its implications. If it were accepted that the concept of mens rea presupposes a capacity to control one's actions and to choose between alternative courses of conduct, then the implications become clear. An accessory lacks control over the principal offender; she cannot make choices for that principal. (If she could we should classify her as a principal acting through an innocent agent, or as a co-principal.) The principal is

"always the dominant party in the transaction. In criminal schemes, the principal is the actor-on-stage, who makes the final determination whether to commit the discrete criminal act."[185]

The principal can have the mens rea of the actual offence because of his hegemony and control. The accessory, at most, has choice and control over *her own actions, namely, her acts of assistance or encouragement.* Once it is realised that this mens rea of the accessory is not the mens rea of the offence itself, that it is, in a sense, a step removed from the offence, we can then focus on the real question: is this mens rea of assisting as reprehensible as the mens rea of the principal who actually commits the offence? The answer to this question must be delayed until we have considered the next problem.

---

[184]   I. Dennis, "The Mental Element for Accessories", in P. Smith (ed.), *Essays in Honour of J.C. Smith* (London: Butterworths, 1987), p.40.
[185]   Fletcher, *Rethinking Criminal Law* (1978), p.656.

B. Causing Harm

Except in cases of procuring, an accessory, by definition, does not cause the ultimate harm. He contributes to the crime by his assistance or encouragement, but he does not actually cause the ultimate harm if it is inflicted by a responsible principal. So, in *Lynch v DPP*,[186] for example, Lynch drove some IRA gunmen to a place where they killed a policeman. By his driving, Lynch assisted in the commission of the crime, but his actions clearly did not "cause" the death of the policeman. Indeed, the rules of accessorial liability only exist because such an accessory does not cause the prohibited harm; if he did, he would be a principal offender (or co-principal) and such rules would be unnecessary.[187]

David Lanham, "Accomplices, Principals and Causation" (1980) 12 Melbourne University L. Rev. 490 at 510–511:

"*Assistance or permission*: neither assistance nor permission should be sufficient to amount to cause. If this is all that can be proved against A, it seems plain that the main motivation for the deed has come from B or elsewhere. Assistance or permission may be enough to make A liable as a secondary party where the other conditions for such liability have been met but they should not be sufficient to make A a principal on the basis of causation . . .

   Advice or counselling: These should arguably be enough where A knows the facts which make B's conduct criminal and B does not. They should not amount to causation where B knows that his conduct is criminal. In this latter situation it is reasonable to regard B, the immediate actor, as the principal offender and to relegate A's position to that of secondary party."

So causation is not established in such cases. But why is this so? In the case of *Richards*,[188] Mrs Richards paid two men to inflict injuries on her husband which she intended should "put him in hospital for a month". The two men wounded the husband but not seriously. Mrs Richards was convicted of wounding with intent, although this was substituted by a conviction for unlawful wounding on appeal. Mrs Richard's actions, in arranging for her husband to be beaten up badly enough to "put him in hospital for a month", were clearly *a* cause of her husband's ultimate injuries.[189] Why can they not be regarded as the *legal* cause? Unless one adopts the "policy approach" or the "mens rea approach" to causation the answer would appear to be as follows: an accessory cannot cause that over which they have no control[190] and the causal link cannot be traced through the actions of a responsible actor.[191] Mrs Richards caused the principal to act,[192] but, by being a responsible actor not subject to the control or dominance of Mrs Richards, the principal's actions broke the chain of causation between Mrs Richards' actions and the injuries sustained by her husband. The principal caused the injuries.[193]

---

[186]   *Lynch* [1975] A.C. 653.
[187]   But see Smith, *A Modern Treatise on the Law of Complicity* (Oxford: Clarendon Press, 1991), pp.54–93 where he explores causation's role in complicity and concludes that "narrowing complicity's coverage to cases of provable causal contribution would offer a basis of liability which was more intuitively appealing and morally consistent (with that of a principal)" (p.90).
[188]   *R. v Richards (Isabelle Christina)* [1974] Q.B. 776 (cited in the extract of *Howe*, above, p.586).
[189]   Above, p.586.
[190]   Fletcher, *Rethinking Criminal Law* (1978), p.656; D. Lanham, "Accomplices, Principals and Causation" [1980] 12 Melbourne University Law Review 490 at 50, p.506.
[191]   Above, pp.114–118.
[192]   H.L.A. Hart and T. Honoré would dispute even this. Where the actions of the principal offender are fully voluntary "it will not strictly be correct to say that the instigator has caused the principal to act as he does". They argue, however, that the actions of the principal "may, in a sense, be described as the *consequence* of the instigator"—this they describe as a different variety of causal connection (H.L.A. Hart and T. Honoré, *Causation in the Law*, 2nd edn (Oxford: Clarendon Press, 1985), p.381).
[193]   Gardner argues, however, that to say that the secondary party (in our example, Mrs Richards) does indeed "cause" the harm or death does not wipe out the hitman's part in the story as a responsible agent. In his view, accomplices do make a causal contribution to the end crime but the nature of their causal contribution is different to that of a principal offender: "The

In some cases, particularly those of aiding and abetting, it might be difficult even to establish that the accessory's actions were *a* cause of the ultimate harm. Thus in *State v Tally*[194] it was stated:

"The assistance given, however, need not contribute to the criminal result in the sense that, but for it, the result would not have ensued. It is quite sufficient if it facilitated a result that would have transpired without it. It is quite enough if the aid merely renders it easier for the principal actor to accomplish the end intended by him and the aider and abettor, though in all human probability the end would have been attained without it."[195]

Dressler argues that the law should distinguish between those accomplices who can be described as "causal" and those that are "non-causal". A "causal" accomplice would be a person but for whose assistance the offence would not have occurred, who should be liable for the same offence as the principal offender, whilst "non-causal" accomplices would be liable for a lesser offence and punished accordingly.[196] Wilson has suggested something similar.

William Wilson, "A Rational Scheme of Liability for Participating in Crime" [2008] Crim. L.R. 3 at 5:

"Of course, agreeing with this latter view [that accomplices should be liable for the same crime as the principal offender] does not commit us to a structure of offenders comprising principals, accessories and inchoate offenders. An attractive alternative . . . is to abandon the idea that participation in crime takes the form of physical perpetration on the one hand, or secondary participation on the other. In its place we could extend the scope of principal liability to include all those such as instigators and partners, who 'cause' or otherwise control the occurrence of a criminal act, without necessarily physically perpetrating it, relegating other forms of participation. This solution could engender the necessary moral and systemic clarity in relation to the imposition of liability for those who help or encourage criminal activities. And it would solve at a stroke most of the doctrinal tensions arising from the theory of derivative liability, such as those occurring in the fields of joint enterprise liability and innocent agency and related cases."

As Dressler concedes, however, the problem would be in defining the causation test. Dressler himself opts for a wide interpretation of the "but-for" test, and is happy to leave it to a jury to decide whether, in a case where an accomplice's lack of assistance would have delayed but not prevented the commission of the principal's crime, a delay of minutes, hours or weeks would prevent the finding of causation in relation to the secondary party's liability.[197] Whilst Dressler's and Wilson's instinct that the law ought to distinguish between those who are critical parties to a crime and those whose involvement is peripheral is an understandable one, it is not clear that this causal thesis is workable. Arguably, English law now makes a similar distinction, having created the inchoate offences of encouraging or assisting crime. These inchoate offences would catch Dressler's "non-causal" accomplices and punish

---

essential difference between them is that accomplices make their difference through principals, in other words by making a difference to the difference that principals make", J. Gardner, "Complicity and Causality" (2007) Crim. Law and Philos. 1, 127–141 at 128.

[194] *State v Tally* (1894) 102 Ala. 25.

[195] Hart and Honoré, *Causation in the Law*, 2nd edn (1985),: "When the participant merely assists he neither 'causes' the principal to act nor does the latter act 'in consequence' of his assistance. Probably the assistance need not even be a *sine qua non* of success" (p.388).

[196] J. Dressler, "Reassessing the Theoretical Underpinnings of Accomplice Liability: New Solutions to an Old Problem" (1985) 37 Hastings L.J. 91; J. Dressler, "Reforming Complicity Law: Trivial Assistance as a Lesser Offence?" (2008) 5 *Ohio State Journal of Criminal Law* 427–448.

[197] Dressler, "Reforming Complicity Law: Trivial Assistance as a Lesser Offence?" (2008) 5 *Ohio State Journal of Criminal Law* 427–448 at 442.

them less harshly than full accomplices. However, under the current law there is nothing to prevent "non-causal" accomplices from also being convicted of the full offence committed by the principal offender. An example will help to illustrate these points.

William Wilson, "A Rational Scheme of Liability for Participating in Crime" [2008] Crim. L.R. 3 at 6, 7:

"John and Anne wish to kill Mark. Anne suggests to John that he invites Mark over to swim in his swimming pool and then drown him. They are overheard by two friends, Philip and Jane. Philip says 'Great idea. I never liked Mark'. On hearing John doubt the cogency of the drowning plan, Jane, a busybody but with no other interest in the outcome, remarks that a good way of drowning Mark, who was not a strong swimmer, would be to throw a heavy jute net over the pool so that he could not get out. John and Anne go to Stephen's chandlery to buy a heavy jute net. Stephen overhears John and Anne talking about their intentions while he is in the stock room. He nevertheless sells them the net, unwilling to sacrifice a sale.

Under the present scheme of liability, if John does commit the principal offence, he is guilty of murder as principal, having the intention to kill Mark. Although it would not be doing violence to the nature of her participation to denote her a principal offender, sharing both *mens rea* and causal influence, Anne, as a participant in a joint venture to kill Mark, is guilty of murder as secondary party. She is guilty by virtue of her own intention to kill. Philip, although not a party to the venture, and although having no causal influence on the outcome, is guilty of murder as secondary party by virtue of his words of encouragement and his belief that John would attack Mark with the necessary intention for murder. Jane is guilty of murder as secondary party by virtue of her assistance and her belief that John would attack Mark with the necessary intention for murder. Stephen is guilty of murder as secondary party by virtue of his assistance, believing that the net was to be used to commit murder."

Wilson notes that all of the participants will be liable for the crime of murder under the current rules of secondary liability, but what difference would it make if his suggestion that the law should differentiate between causal and non-causal accomplices were employed? Presumably all but Philip would remain liable for murder. Philip would escape liability for murder, since Wilson states he has no causal influence over the outcome. However, Philip would be liable for the inchoate offence of assisting or encouraging crime under the Serious Crime Act 2007, which does not require any such causal link. But what of Stephen? Would he be seen as a causal accomplice? But for him providing the jute net then John would not have killed Mark as he did, but perhaps John could have purchased a net from elsewhere. Wilson notes that Stephen was in a position to thwart John's endeavour,[198] which would suggest that he would fall into the category of "causal" accomplice. However, Wilson suggests that, while defendants like Stephen may be culpable for their failure to prevent the crime, it is unfair to punish them for murder. However, given that Stephen is a "mechanical" assister providing the tools for the offence it is difficult to see how he would not be classified as a "causal" accomplice, thus undermining the suggestion that the distinction between causal and non-causal accomplices can do the work of selecting which are the most blameworthy participants in crime. If that distinction were coupled with a more rigorous mens rea requirement, an improvement on the current law could be achieved. Thus, if the law of secondary liability required the secondary party to be a causal player in the offence *and* to intend that the crime be committed, defendants such as Stephen would avoid liability for murder and instead be liable for the inchoate offence of assisting or encouraging crime.

Even though accessories do not cause the ultimate harm, it is clear that they do cause a "harm", namely, the harm of assisting or encouraging the principal offender. The harm involved in assisting

---

[198]   W. Wilson, "A Rational Scheme of Liability for Participating in Crime" [2008] Crim. L.R. 3 at 8.

or encouraging other criminals, like the "harm" in endangerment offences, is quite different from the ultimate harm actually inflicted and does not necessarily deserve the same level of criminal liability and punishment.

C. Lesser Liability and Punishment

A secondary party causes a different harm from the principal (the harm of assisting or encouraging a criminal act); she has a different mens rea from the principal (the mens rea of assisting or encouraging). If this is a lesser (as well as different) degree of blameworthiness and harm, this should result in a lesser level of criminal liability and punishment.

There is one context in which the courts have had to face questions similar to these and that is in relation to whether the defence of duress should be made available to an accessory to murder, but withheld from the principal. In the case of *Lynch v DPP*[199] the House of Lords held that duress was a defence to an accessory to murder. In *Abbott*[200] the Privy Council held that duress was no defence to a principal offender to murder. Lord Morris in *Lynch v DPP* felt there was a material difference between the role of the principal and that of the accessory. An accessory

"may cling to the hope that perhaps X will not be found at the place or that there will be a change of intention before the purpose is carried out or that in some unforeseen way the dire event of a killing will be averted. The final and fatal moment of decision has not arrived. He saves his own life at a time when the loss of another life is not a certainty . . . [But the principal offender] must personally there and then take an innocent life. It is for him to pull the trigger or otherwise personally to do the act of killing."[201]

Lynch has now been overruled by the decision of *Howe*,[202] partly on the basis of finding the weight of previous authority to have been against extending the defence of duress to any party to murder, but also partly as a disavowal of there necessarily being a distinction between the killer and a secondary party:

"I can, of course see that as a matter of commonsense one participant in a murder may be considered less morally at fault than another. The youth who hero-worships the gang-leader and acts as a look-out man whilst the gang enter a jeweller's shop and kill the owner in order to steal is an obvious example. In the eyes of the law they are all guilty of murder, but justice will be served by requiring those who did the killing to serve a longer period in prison before being released on licence than the youth who acted as look-out. However, it is not difficult to give examples where more moral fault may be thought to attach to a participant in murder who was not the actual killer; I have already mentioned the example of a contract killing, when the murder would never have taken place if a contract had not been placed to take the life of the victim. Another example would be an intelligent man goading a weakminded individual into a killing he would not otherwise commit."[203]

Are these arguments convincing? Or do the views of Lord Morris in *Lynch* reflect the way most people think?[204] The Law Commission has recommended that duress ought to be a full defence to first

---

[199]   *Lynch* [1975] A.C. 653.
[200]   *Abbott* [1977] A.C. 755.
[201]   The opposite view was expressed by Lords Wilberforce and Edmund-Davies, dissenting in *Abbott*.
[202]   *Howe* [1987] 1 A.C. 417.
[203]   *Howe* [1987] 1 A.C. 417 at 444–445.
[204]   The respondents to a survey on public opinion by R.H. Robinson and J.M. Darley, "Objectivist Versus Subjectivist Views of

degree murder, and should be available to both principal and secondary parties,[205] providing the following example of how the current law may prove unfair to accessories:

> "For example, many people would be disturbed if they knew that at present D, an otherwise innocent taxi driver, could be convicted of murder on account of his having driven P to the victim's address, at gunpoint, on the mere basis that D was aware that murder would be committed there."[206]

The accessory who provides assistance or encouragement is clearly blameworthy, but not as blameworthy as the principal who actually pulls the trigger, stabs with the knife or takes the property. It is the principal who is the dominant party who has to make the final decision to commit the crime. It is the principal who is in control and has the power to choose whether to commit the crime or not. In moral terms this makes his actions "worse" than those of the accessory. The principal is "tainted",[207] contaminated by being the direct instrument of the crime; he is the one with the "blood on his hands". The accessory is likewise tainted or contaminated—but for what she has done, namely his lesser role of assistance or encouragement. German law, for example, recognises the different levels of culpability between principal and accessory by providing that punishment for the latter is reduced as follows:

"1. Instead of life imprisonment, the punishment is imprisonment for not less than three years.
  2. In cases of prescribed terms of imprisonment, the maximum term may be reduced to three-fourths of the prescribed maximum. The same reduction applies to monetary penalties.
  3. The minimum term of imprisonment is mitigated as follows:
  A. From a minimum of ten or five years to a minimum of two years.
  B. From a minimum of three or two years to a minimum of six months.
  C. From a minimum of one year to a minimum of three months.
  D. In other cases the statutory minimum is retained."[208]

However, it does not follow that all secondary parties should be treated the same. One might wish to distinguish between different classes of accessories in terms of their liability and punishment. The actions of the instigator or mastermind behind the crime are generally more reprehensible than those of an accessory simply assisting the principal at the scene of the crime; the causal contribution of such an instigator towards the ultimate crime is certainly greater; he may thus deserve greater punishment.

Even if not all the ideas expressed in this section are fully accepted, it is nevertheless hoped that one fact has clearly emerged. Rules of criminal liability should not be rationalised or reformed in a vacuum. This should only be done by reference to a coherent theory of criminal liability, and such a theory should only be constructed by ultimate reference to the punishment to be meted out to offenders. The Law Commission's proposals in its second report on secondary liability fail to feature this reference point as a basis for reform, and as such are to be lamented.

Criminality: A Study in the Role of Social Sciences in Criminal Law Theory" (1998) 18 O.J.L.S. 409 assigned significantly less liability (and punishment) to accomplices compared to the perpetrators of crime.
[205] Law Commission Paper No.304, *Murder, Manslaughter and Infanticide* (2006), para.4.39.
[206] Law Commission Consultation Paper No.177, *A New Homicide Act for England and Wales?* (2005), para.5.68.
[207] Fletcher, *Rethinking Criminal Law* (1978), pp.345–347.
[208] StGB art.49(1). See Fletcher, *Rethinking Criminal Law* (1978), p.650.

7

NON-FATAL OFFENCES AGAINST THE PERSON

I. Offences against the Person (Non-Sexual)

A. The Extent and Context of Violence

There are many reasons why people commit crimes of violence. Criminological explanations of this type of offending have drawn upon biological and genetic theories, psychological and social psychological theories, and various sociological theories.[1] Discussion of these theories is beyond the scope of this book. However, an understanding of the law is assisted by an appreciation of the context in which violence occurs and the extent to which the law is utilised as a response to violence.

Offences of violence comprise a relatively small proportion of recorded crime. In 2012/13 such offences accounted for 19 per cent of the 3.7 million crimes recorded by the police.[2] Of these violent offences, 47 per cent did not result in any injury to the person.[3] There has been a significant reduction in the number of violent offences reported to the police over the past 5–6 years with official statistics showing the number of crimes falling by 19 per cent from 2007/08.[4]

However, these official figures do not reveal the true extent of violence, often called the "dark figure" of crime. This is because large numbers of violent incidents are never reported to the police. The Crime Survey for England and Wales (CSEW), which is based on around 50,000 interviews with persons aged 16 or over living in private households,[5] estimated that there were 1.68 million offences of violence in 2012/13.[6] In line with recorded offences, the estimated number of violent offences has reduced by 24 per cent over the past five to six years.

Many of the "violent" incidents counted by the survey amount to common assaults, often involving scuffles at school and in and around pubs and clubs when little or no injury has been caused. In fact, the CSEW found that 46 per cent of all CSEW violent incidents involved no injury to the victim.[7] However, it would be a mistake to conclude that there was a clear correlation between seriousness

---

[1] For a good overview of these explanations, see S. Jones, *Understanding Violent Crime* (Buckingham: Open University Press, 2000) and F. Brookman and A. Robinson, "Violent Crime", in M. Maguire, R. Morgan and R. Reiner, *The Oxford Handbook of Criminology*, 5th edn (Oxford: OUP, 2012).

[2] Office of National Statistics, *Crime in England and Wales, Year Ending September 2013* (2014).

[3] Office of National Statistics, *Crime in England and Wales, Year Ending September 2013* (2014).

[4] Office of National Statistics, *Crime in England and Wales, Year Ending September 2013* (2014).

[5] From 2009 the survey has included a separate survey to record the experiences of young people aged 10–15.

[6] See fn.2 above. Note there is a difference between the definition of violence used in the CSEW and that used by the police. For example, the offence of robbery is included within the CSEW definition of violence but it is not counted by the police as a "violent crime", instead it is reported as a separate stand-alone category.

[7] See fn.2 above.

of injury and the reporting of such offences. Many serious attacks resulting in stab wounds, broken cheekbones, noses and ribs are also not reported.[8]

There are various reasons, apart from the triviality of the incident and injury, why offences are not reported. Factors associated with the decision not to report include: an assessment that the police will not be able to do anything about it; the victim's habituation to violence; an unwillingness to have their own conduct exposed to scrutiny; hostility towards the police; fear of reprisal; and the impact such reporting might have upon continuing relationships with the assailant and others.[9] Survey results from 2010/11 found that a significant reason for not reporting violent crime (in 33 per cent of cases) was that victims considered the issue as a private matter best dealt with by themselves.[10] This last reason helps to explain why cases of domestic violence are reported even less frequently than other cases, although the difference in reporting rates between the official statistics and the CSEW is no longer as great as it was.

A further important factor to consider is that, even if the violent incident has been reported to the police, they may not record it because they regard the alleged offence as too trivial or perhaps disbelieve the person reporting the crime, especially if that person comes from a section of society perceived as unreliable as witnesses.[11] It has been estimated that 68 per cent of all offences of violence reported to the police are recorded with only 55 per cent of reported common assaults ending up in the police records.[12] Further, even if an offence is recorded it may be under a different classification, such as drunk and disorderly conduct or criminal damage.[13] And, of course, the fact that a crime has been recorded does not mean that it will be followed by a prosecution. In many cases the CPS will refuse to prosecute, mainly on the basis of the unreliability of victims/witnesses or their unwillingness to testify.

In recent years research has begun to focus on the characteristics of victims of crime. One of the most significant factors affecting the risk of violence is that of ethnic origin. Since separate records were kept, the number of racial assaults has been increasing every year. According to CSEW data there are an estimated 154,000 race "hate crimes" committed each year, with just under 50 per cent of these incidents involving violence against the person.[14] Concern over such assaults, fuelled by media coverage of a few high-profile cases, led to the enactment of the Crime and Disorder Act 1998 increasing the maximum sentence for most of the offences against the person where the offence is "racially aggravated".[15] Fear after September 11 that there could be an increase in attacks on members of religious groups led to the Anti-terrorism, Crime and Security Act 2001 s.39, making similar increases in maximum sentence where the offence is "religiously aggravated". The Criminal Justice Act 2003 s.146 additionally provides that for sentencing purposes the court must treat as an aggravating factor the fact that the offender demonstrated, or was (partly) motivated by, hostility to the victim based on the victim's (actual or presumed) sexual orientation, disability or transgender identity.

Women are also more likely to be victims of crime than they are to be offenders and are more likely than men to be assaulted by someone they know. As Cretney and Davis say:

---

8   C.M.V. Clarkson et al., "Assaults: the Relationship between Seriousness, Criminalisation and Punishment" [1994] Crim. L.R. 4.
9   Clarkson et al., "Assaults: the Relationship between Seriousness, Criminalisation and Punishment" [1994] Crim. L.R. 4.
10   These are the most recent reported reasons. Home Office, *Crime in England and Wales 2010/11* (2011).
11   S. Jones, *Understanding Violent Crime* (Buckingham: Open University Press, 2000), p.16.
12   A. Walker, C. Kershaw and S. Nicholas, *Crime in England and Wales 2005/06 (Home Office Statistical Bulletin, 2006)*, pp.52, 57.
13   T. Jones, B. Maclean and J. Young, *The Islington Crime Survey* (Aldershot: Gower, 1986), p.61.
14   Home Office, Office for National Statistics and Ministry of Justice, *An Overview of Hate Crime in England and Wales* (2013).
15   Section 29. This applies to common assault and ss.47 and 20 of the Offences Against the Person Act 1861. See further discussion in section iv below.

"Assaults are overwhelmingly perpetrated by men. Men in public use violence against other males, whom they may not know. In private they assault women, whom they *do* know."[16]

In 2011/12, women were most commonly victimised by an acquaintance, while men most commonly experienced stranger violence.[17] A higher proportion of women (7 per cent) are victims of domestic violence (often referred to as "intimate violence" which involves partner or family non-physical abuse, threats, force, sexual assault or stalking) than men (5 per cent).[18] Overall, males, especially those aged between 16 and 24, are most likely to be the victims of violence. Much of this violence is associated with the lifestyles of the persons concerned. Younger people are more likely to go to pubs and clubs and other places of entertainment where alcohol is consumed[19] and spend some time on the streets at night, these factors being well-documented predictors of victimisation.[20] Many such cases involve fighting where there might have been victim precipitation of the assault. The reporting and prosecution rate for such violence is particularly low.[21] The CSEW reveals a similar profile for offenders committing acts of violence. In 2012/13, 49 per cent of offenders in violent incidents were believed to be aged 16–24 and 81 per cent were male.[22]

It is often stated that society is becoming more violent but there is little evidence to show that this is true. In fact, the official statistics show that there has been a 16 per cent decrease in the number of recorded violent offences which result in injury over the past decade.[23] The CSEW has also shown that crimes of violence have been declining consistently since 1995. The survey estimates that there is now 60 per cent less violent crime in 2012/13 than in 1995; this being lower than when the crime survey began in 1982.[24] This means that both recorded crime and estimations of the dark figure of violence concur in showing that we are living in a less violent society than the generation before us. Such statistics do not mean, however, that violence is becoming a thing of the past. It is therefore important that the criminal law remains responsive to the differing forms of violence that continue to pervade our ever-expanding society.

B. The Law

1. Introduction

There are many offences involving personal violence, ranging from "mainstream" offences such as causing grievous bodily harm, through kidnapping and administering poison to those such as assaulting a clergyman in the execution of his duties. The main offences, which are mostly statutory, will be considered as these represent an ideal forum for considering how the law deals with the various configurations of degrees of harm and levels of mens rea. The offences are ranked in some sort of hierarchy of seriousness: the extent to which this ordering is based on principle will emerge as the offences are examined. As we shall see, they range from "the merest touching of another in anger",[25]

---

16 A. Cretney and G. Davis, *Punishing Violence* (London: Routledge, 1995), p.18.
17 Ministry of Justice, *Statistics on Women and the Criminal Justice System 2011* (2012).
18 Ministry of Justice, *Statistics on Women and the Criminal Justice System 2011* (2012), p.19.
19 According to the 2012/13 CSEW, victims believed the offender(s) to be under the influence of alcohol in around half (49%) of all violent incidents, Office for National Statistics, *Focus on Violent Crime and Sexual Offences, 2012/13* (2014).
20 Cretney and Davis, *Punishing Violence* (London: Routledge, 1995), pp.23–32.
21 Cretney and Davis, *Punishing Violence* (London: Routledge, 1995), p.39.
22 See fn.19 above.
23 Office of National Statistics, *Crime in England and Wales, Year Ending September 2013* (2014), p.34.
24 Office of National Statistics, *Crime in England and Wales, Year Ending September 2013* (2014), p.28.
25 *Cole v Turner* (1705) 6 Mod. 149, 87 E.R. 907.

to injuries which fall only just short of death. As several of the offences contain the basic element of assault, and as it constitutes the lowest rung in the hierarchy of seriousness, this will be examined first.

2. Common assault and battery

The terms "common assault", "assault" and "battery" are often used interchangeably by laymen and even lawyers. This terminological confusion which causes "angels [to] prepare to dance on needles and legal pedants [to] sharpen their quill pens"[26] is compounded by statute. Section 39 of the Criminal Justice Act 1988 refers to "common assault and battery" as two separate offences while s.40(3) refers only to a "common assault". In *Lynsey*[27] it was held that this latter phrase includes a battery and in *Ireland; Burstow*[28] it was held that the term "assault" in s.47 of the Offences against the Person Act 1861 includes both a common assault and battery.

It is thus clear that there are two separate crimes[29]: common assault and battery. While these are both statutory offences,[30] the statute contains no definition and one has to turn to the common law to discover their constituent elements.[31] A common assault is putting someone in fear of immediate force; a battery is the actual infliction of force on a person. To avoid confusion in this book, the term "assault" is used in its broad generic sense as encompassing either of these specific crimes and the two specific offences will be referred to as "technical assault" and "battery".

Both these offences are only triable summarily (in the magistrates' court) and subject to a maximum penalty of six months' imprisonment.[32] These offences can be used in many cases where injury has resulted and a more serious charge could have been brought. The CPS *Charging Standards* state that where there is no injury or where injuries are not serious, the offence charged should generally be common assault. Where there is serious injury and the likely sentence is clearly more than six months' imprisonment a more serious charge should be brought.[33] There are significant advantages to trial in the magistrates' court instead of the Crown Court; the CPS perceives this as being quicker and cheaper, more likely to result in conviction and, particularly in the context of domestic violence, involving a less onerous task for the victim/witness.[34]

Under s.11 of the Domestic Violence, Crime and Victims Act 2004, common assault is an alternative verdict to more serious charges of aggravated assault even if the count has not been included in the indictment.

(i) Technical assault

This offence is committed when the defendant intentionally or recklessly causes the victim to apprehend imminent force.

---

[26]   *R. v Lynsey (Jonathan Simon)* [1995] 2 Cr. App. R. 667 at 671.
[27]   *Lynsey* [1995] 2 Cr. App. R. 667 at 671.
[28]   *R. v Ireland; R. v Burstow* [1998] A.C. 147 at 161. See also *DPP v Taylor (Keith Richard)* (1992) 95 Cr. App. R. 28.
[29]   *Taylor* (1992) 95 Cr. App. R. 28.
[30]   Criminal Justice Act 1988 s.39; *Taylor* (1992) 95 Cr. App. R. 28.
[31]   In *Haystead v Chief Constable of Derbyshire* [2000] Cr. App. R. 339 it was stated that while charges refer to s.39 "in truth, common assault . . . remains a common law offence" (at 340).
[32]   Under the Crime and Disorder Act 1998 if the offence is "racially or religiously aggravated" it can be tried on indictment and carries a maximum term of two years' imprisonment (s.29(3)).
[33]   CPS, *Offences Against the Person, Incorporating the Charging Standard*, available at *http://www.cps.gov.uk/legal/l_to_o/ offences_against_the_person/index.html#a24* [Accessed April 30, 2014].
[34]   A. Cretney and G. Davis, "Prosecuting Domestic Assault: Victims Failing Courts, or Courts Failing Victims" (1997) 36 *Howard Journal of Criminal Justice* 146.

(a) *Actus reus*

The defendant must do something to make the victim apprehend imminent force. It is often stated that the victim must fear an immediate attack. This latter formulation, while descriptive of most situations of technical assault, is deceptive for two reasons. First, the victim need not be placed in "fear" in the sense of being frightened; he might be confident of their ability to repel the attack. They are nevertheless assaulted as they are made to apprehend the force. Secondly, they need not apprehend an "attack" in the sense of a severe measure of aggressive or destructive force; they need only apprehend any degree of force, which, as we shall see, in some circumstances need amount to little more than an unlawful touching.

Can mere words amount to an assault? While it has always been clear that physical gestures such as shaking a fist or pointing a gun at the victim would suffice, there used to be doubt as to whether words could constitute an assault. This issue has been resolved in the following decision.

R. v Ireland; R. v Burstow [1998] A.C. 147 (House of Lords)

In the first appeal the defendant made repeated silent telephone calls, mostly at night, to three women. Sometimes, he resorted to heavy breathing. As a result, the women suffered psychiatric illness. He was charged with assault occasioning actual bodily harm, contrary to s.47 of the Offences against the Person Act 1861. One of the issues on appeal was whether such conduct could amount to an assault.

LORD STEYN:

"The proposition that a gesture may amount to an assault, but that words can never suffice, is unrealistic and indefensible. A thing said is also a thing done. There is no reason why something said should be incapable of causing an apprehension of immediate personal violence, *e.g.* a man accosting a woman in a dark alley saying 'come with me or I will stab you'. I would, therefore, reject the proposition that an assault can never be committed by words."

LORD HOPE OF CRAIGHEAD:

"[I]t is not true to say that mere words or gestures can never constitute an assault. It all depends on the circumstances . . . The words or gestures must be seen in their whole context.

In this case the means which the appellant used to communicate with his victims was the telephone. While he remained silent, there can be no doubt that he was intentionally communicating with them as directly as if he was present with them in the same room. But whereas for him merely to remain silent with them in the same room, where they could see him and assess his demeanour, would have been unlikely to give rise to any feelings of apprehension on their part, his silence when using the telephone in calls made to them repeatedly was an act of an entirely different character. He was using his silence as a means of conveying a message to his victims. This was that he knew who and where they were, and that his purpose in making contact with them was as malicious as it was deliberate. In my opinion silent telephone calls of this nature are just as capable as words or gestures, said or made in the presence of the victim, of causing an apprehension of immediate and unlawful violence."

Appeals dismissed

Another rule has long been beyond doubt: words may negate an assault. In *Tuberville v Savage*[35] the defendant placed his hand on his sword hilt and told the victim: "If it were not assize-time, I would not take such language from you." This was held not to be an assault. The words accompanying the action (of placing the hand on the sword) clearly demonstrated that because the assize judge was in town, the defendant was *not* going to use his sword. There could thus be no apprehension of immediate

---

[35]   *Tuberville v Savage* (1669) 1 Mod. Rep. 3; 86 E.R. 684.

force. This case must be carefully distinguished from cases involving a conditional threat, such as *Read v Coker*[36] where it was held to be an assault to threaten to break the victim's neck if he did not leave the premises. In such a case there is a threat to use immediate force; the victim *does* apprehend immediate force and the onus is on him to do something to avert that force. If the rule were otherwise it would mean there could be no assault where a robber says "Your money or your life"; such a position would be intolerable.

Another point to be considered is the stance that the law takes in relation to empty threats. For example, a victim might be threatened with a toy gun or an unloaded gun. In *Bentham* the defendant placed his hand inside his jacket causing a bulge to give the impression he had a gun and threatened to shoot unless the victim handed over money and jewellery.[37] Understandably, the law regards this fact as immaterial as long as the victim is made to fear an attack[38]; after all, the victim cannot be expected to know whether the threat is real or not.

The victim must apprehend the imminent use of force. It is a serious gap in the law that it is no offence whatsoever to tell someone that you intend to break both their legs the next day rather than there and then.[39] One of the provisions in the Draft Offences against the Person Bill 1998 was that the existing offence of threatening to kill should be extended to include non-immediate threats to cause serious injury.[40] One of the consequences of this present gap has been the development by the courts of a broad interpretation of "imminence" or "immediacy". In *Smith*[41] it was held that a woman had been assaulted when she saw a man looking through her closed bedsitting room window at night. Although he was outside her room and would have had to break or force open her window and climb in before he could have actually inflicted violence upon her, it was held that she had apprehended a sufficiently immediate application of force. In *Siadatan*[42] it was stated that "immediate" (for purposes of s.4 of the Public Order Act 1986) "connotes proximity in time and proximity in causation; that it is likely that violence will result within a reasonably short period of time and without any other intervening occurrence". This problem of imminence or immediacy is of particular importance in cases where the defendant makes silent or verbally threatening telephone calls.

R. v Ireland; R. v Burstow [1998] A.C. 147 (House of Lords)

LORD STEYN:

"That brings me to the critical question whether a silent caller may be guilty of an assault. The answer to this question seems to me to be 'Yes, depending on the facts'. It involves questions of fact within the province of the jury. After all, there is no reason why a telephone caller who says to a woman in a menacing way 'I will be at your door in a minute or two' may not be guilty of an assault if he causes his victim to apprehend immediate personal violence. Take now the case of the silent caller. He intends by his silence to cause fear and is so understood. The victim is assailed by uncertainty about his intentions. Fear may dominate her emotions, and it may be the fear that the caller's arrival at her door may be imminent. She may fear the *possibility* of immediate personal violence. As a matter of law the caller may be guilty of an assault: whether he is or not will depend on the circumstance and in particular on the impact of the caller's potentially menacing call or calls on the victim. Such a prosecution

---

[36]   *Read v Coker* (1853) 13 C.B. 850. See also *Ansell v Thomas* [1974] Crim. L.R. 31.
[37]   *R. v Bentham (Peter)* [2005] 2 Cr. App. R. 11. In this case the charge was robbery and possession of an imitation firearm contrary to the Firearms Act 1968 s.17(2). The House of Lords held there could be no liability for the latter offence as one could not possess one's hand or fingers. On these facts, there would clearly have been an assault.
[38]   *Logdon v DPP* [1976] Crim. L.R. 121; *R. v St. George* (1840) 9 C. & P. 483; 173 E.R. 921.
[39]   See, generally, P. Alldridge, "Threats Offences—A Case for Reform" [1994] Crim. L.R. 176.
[40]   Clause 10 (Home Office, *Violence: Reforming the Offences Against the Person Act 1861* (1998)).
[41]   *Smith v Chief Superintendent, Woking Police Station* (1983) 76 Cr. App. R. 234.
[42]   *R. v Horseferry Road Magistrates' Court, Ex p. Siadatan* (1991) 92 Cr. App. R. 257.

case under section 47 may be fit to leave to the jury. And a trial judge may, depending on the circumstances, put a commonsense consideration before jury, namely what, if not the possibility of imminent personal violence, was the victim terrified about? I conclude that an assault may be committed in the particular factual circumstances which I have envisaged."

Appeals dismissed

This decision is best understood in the context of events leading up to the appeal. For at least two years prior to the House of Lords' judgment the media had been conducting a high-profile campaign against stalking.

Home Office, Stalking—The Solutions: A Consultation Paper (1996):

"1.2 Stalking . . . can be broadly described as a series of acts which are intended to, or in fact, cause harassment to another person.

1.4 Stalkers can have a devastating effect on the lives of their victims, who can be subjected to constant harassment at home, in public places, and at work, to the extent that they can feel that they are no longer in control of their lives . . .

1.6 The methods employed by stalkers can take many forms . . . [such as] making obscene telephone calls, using abusive and threatening language, or committing acts of violence . . . However, frequently stalkers do not overtly threaten their victims but use behaviour which is ostensibly routine and harmless and therefore not caught by existing laws. But even apparently innocuous behaviour, such as following someone down the street, or sending them flowers, can be intimidating if it is persistently inflicted on a victim against their will. This is one of the defining characteristics of stalking: irrespective of the nature of its component acts, stalking can be distressing and threatening to a victim because of its sheer, oppressive persistence . . .

1.8 . . . The National Anti-Stalking and Harassment campaign (NASH) report that over 7,000 victims of stalking telephoned their helpline between January 1994 and November 1995. Stalking affects both women and men, although NASH estimates that about 95 per cent of victims are women."

Responding to the media clamour for more effective criminal laws against stalking, the Government enacted the Protection from Harassment Act 1997 which introduced two criminal offences of harassment.[43] Section 2 creates the offence of harassment which is committed where a person pursues a course of conduct (in breach of s.1(1) or 1(A)) on at least two occasions which amounts to harassment of another and which the defendant knows or ought to know amounts to harassment. This offence carries a maximum penalty of six months' imprisonment. The emphasis in this crime is upon the defendant's conduct and pursuit of the victim and not upon an impending attack on the victim. The Act does not define harassment specifically. In *Tuppen*,[44] Douglas Brown J held that as the Act does not define "harassment" it was legitimate for the court to have recourse to Parliamentary records on the matter. Such records made it clear that the behaviour sought to be controlled was conduct such as stalking, antisocial behaviour by neighbours and racial harassment. In *Dowson*,[45] Simon J held, after an extensive review of the relevant authorities, that for conduct to constitute harassment within the Act:

---

[43]   There were also already several laws, both civil and criminal, in existence capable of being utilised against many stalkers. For example, s.43(1) of the Telecommunications Act 1984 makes it an offence to make an indecent, obscene or menacing telephone call or persistently to use a telephone to cause annoyance, inconvenience or needless anxiety. Section 1(1) of the Malicious Communications Act 1988 prohibits the sending of an indecent, offensive or threatening letter with the intention of causing distress or anxiety to the recipient. Sections 4, 4A and 5 of the Public Order Act 1986 can also be utilised against persons who stalk their victims in public. For example, under s.4A an offence is committed if a person intentionally causes harassment, alarm or distress by using threatening, abusive or insulting words or behaviour. The maximum penalty for this offence is six months' imprisonment.

[44]   *Tuppen v Microsoft Corporation Ltd, The Times*, November 15, 2000, QBD.

[45]   *Dowson v Northumbria Police* [2010] EWHC 2612 (QB).

"A line is to be drawn between conduct which is unattractive and unreasonable, and conduct which has been described in various ways: 'torment' of the victim, 'of an order which would sustain criminal liability'" ...

Such conduct must also be "objectively judged to be oppressive and unacceptable". What is deemed to be oppressive and unacceptable may "depend on the social or working context in which the conduct occurs".[46]

Section 4(1) of the Act also creates the more serious offence of pursuing a course of conduct (on at least two occasions) which causes another to fear, on at least two occasions, that violence *will* be used against them. The defendant will be liable if he knows or ought to know that his course of conduct will cause the other so to fear on each of those occasions. The maximum penalty is five years' imprisonment.[47]

The Act was more recently amended in 2012[48] to include the new offence of stalking, largely the result of a Stalking Law Reform Campaign that was launched in July 2011.[49] Under s.2A of the Act, a person is now guilty of an offence if the person pursues a course of conduct in breach of s.1(1) *and* the course of conduct amounts to stalking. The section does not define "stalking" but does provide a list of examples of acts and omissions which are associated with it, including: following a person; contacting, or attempting to contact, a person by any means; publishing any statement or other material relating or purporting to relate to a person, or purporting to originate from a person; monitoring the use by a person of the internet, email or any other form of electronic communication; loitering in any place (whether public or private); interfering with any property in the possession of a person; watching or spying on a person.[50] Section 4A also creates the offence of "stalking involving fear of violence or serious alarm or distress". The defendant's course of conduct must amount to stalking, and either cause another to fear, on at least two occasions, that violence will be used against another, or causes another serious alarm or distress which has a substantial adverse effect on his or her usual day-to-day activities. The defendant will only be guilty of such an offence if he knows or ought to know that his course of conduct will cause the victim to fear violence on each of those occasions, or, as the case may be, that his actions will cause alarm or distress.[51] The defendant ought to know his conduct will cause fear or alarm or distress if a reasonable person in possession of the same information would think the course of conduct would cause the victim fear, or alarm or distress which has a substantial adverse effect on the victim's usual day-to-day activities.[52]

It is likely that offenders such as *Ireland* would now be pursued either under the harassment or stalking offences. However, the Protection from Harassment Act 1997 was not in force at the time of the *Ireland* prosecution and, in any event, Lord Steyn described the original harassment offences as "not ideally suited" to deal with the case before him where the victim only feared that violence *might* be used against her. Under s.4 of the Act there has to be fear that violence *will* be used.[53] It was

---

46   *Dowson* [2010] EWHC 2612 (QB) at [142].
47   Discussion of these provisions is beyond the scope of this book. See, generally, D. Ormerod, *Smith and Hogan: Criminal Law*, 13th edn (Oxford: OUP, 2011), pp.695–705.
48   Added by Protection of Freedoms Act 2012 s.111(1).
49   See Home Office, *Consultation on Stalking* (2011). For an overview of the new offences, see J.Gowland, "Protection from Harassment Act 1997: The 'New' Stalking Offences" (2013) 77 J. Crim. L. 387.
50   Section 2A(3).
51   Section 4A(1).
52   Section 4A(2) and (3).
53   As noted above, this is not the case under the newer s.4A where an offence will be committed where the defendant has pursued a course of conduct that has caused the victim "serious alarm or distress which has a substantial adverse effect on the victim's usual day-to-day activities".

against this background that the appeal in *Ireland* was heard. Lord Steyn commenced his judgment by outlining the "significant social problem" of harassment of women by repeated silent telephone calls and immediately pronounced that it was "self-evident" that the criminal law had to be capable of dealing with the problem. His stance was clear. If the law of assault had to be stretched beyond all previously recognised limits, then so be it. Ireland's appeal was doomed from the start. However, as shall be explained, the law has not been radically altered and securing a conviction of similar telephone callers is still no simple matter.

As seen in the *Ireland* extract above, Lord Steyn accepted the basic definition of an assault involving the apprehension of imminent personal violence—with "violence" meaning physical violence. The only extension of the law was his ruling that the victim need only fear the *possibility* of immediate personal violence. She needs only fear that "the caller's arrival at her door may be imminent". On the facts of the particular appeal, the House of Lords was able to side-step the problem of immediacy on the basis that Ireland had pleaded guilty at his trial.[54] In other cases, however, this problem will not be easily overcome. If a victim has received hundreds of phone calls and none of them has been followed by "the caller's arrival at her door", it will be extremely difficult to establish that the victim genuinely feared the possibility of immediate personal violence. In *Ramos*[55] it was held that it was "the state of mind of the victims which is crucial rather than the statistical risk of violence actively occurring within a short space of time". Nevertheless, the more incidents that have not been followed up by violence, the less plausible the claimed apprehension becomes. Further, even in extreme cases where the seriousness of the threats increases, such as *Cox*[56] where after "hundreds of incidents" the caller told the victim that before she went on holiday, she was "going to her death", it is going to be no less difficult to establish that she feared *there and then* the possibility of immediate personal violence—as opposed to fearing violence at some time and at some place in the future. These difficulties were conceded by Lord Steyn when he concluded:

"I nevertheless accept that the concept of an assault involving immediate personal violence as an ingredient of the section 47 offence is a considerable complicating factor in bringing prosecutions under it in respect of silent telephone callers and stalkers. That the least serious of the ladder of offences is difficult to apply in such cases is unfortunate."

A similar unduly broad approach was adopted by the Court of Appeal in *Constanza*[57] (a case decided a few months before, and not referred to in, *Ireland*). This case involved a stalker who made repeated silent telephone calls and sent 800 letters culminating in two further letters which the victim interpreted as clear threats. It was held that the assault was committed when the victim read these latter letters as there was a "fear of violence at some time *not excluding the immediate future*". This is similar to Lord Steyn's test that the victim need only fear the *possibility* of immediate personal violence. This is surely going too far. While the recipient of a telephone call might well fear that the call is from a mobile phone and that the caller will be at her door "in a minute or two",[58] it seems inconceivable that she would apprehend such *immediate* violence upon receipt of a letter.

This whole approach adopted by the House of Lords is misguided and involves stretching the existing concept of assault too far. The central problem with these cases is that they failed to capture the

54   See Lord Steyn at 163 and Lord Hope at 167.
55   *DPP v Ramos* [2000] Crim. L.R. 768.
56   *Cox* [1998] Crim. L.R. 810.
57   *R. v Constanza (Gaetano)* [1997] 2 Cr. App. R. 492.
58   *Ireland* [1998] A.C. 147 at 162.

essence of the wrongdoing involved.[59] Lord Steyn comes close when he posed the right question: "what . . . was the victim terrified of?" However, his answer—"imminent personal violence"—misses the point for most cases. Many recipients of silent or menacing telephone calls will probably not be afraid that the caller will arrive soon at the front door to inflict violence upon them. The fear is more likely to be one of future physical violence, future harassment and similar future calls increasing tension and anxiety. In short, the relentless pressure combined with fear of the unknown causes continuing psychological trauma. The Court of Appeal in *Ireland*[60] recognised this by reformulating an assault as the apprehension of immediate violence with "violence" including psychological damage. In the Court of Appeal Swinton Thomas LJ stated:

> "[W]hen a telephone call is made by the appellant and the victim lifts the telephone and then knows that the man is telephoning them yet again, they will be apprehensive of suffering the very psychological damage from which they did suffer, namely palpitations, difficulty in breathing, cold sweats, anxiety, inability to sleep, dizziness, stress and the like . . . [T]he fact that the violence is inflicted indirectly, causing psychological harm, does not render the act to be any less an act of violence."

Although Lord Hope rejected this view in the House of Lords. it does not mean such phone calls will fall outside the offence of assault. He notes:

> "In my opinion silent telephone calls of this nature are . . . capable . . . of causing an apprehension of immediate and unlawful violence . . . Whether this requirement, and in particular that of immediacy, is in fact satisfied will depend on the circumstances. This will need in each case, if it is disputed, to be explored in evidence"[61].

(b) *Mens rea*

The defendant must intentionally or recklessly cause his victim to apprehend the infliction of immediate force.[62] Thus if he intends to alarm his victim, or is reckless thereto, the mens rea requirement is satisfied, even if he never intended to carry out the threat.

What is meant by recklessness here? In *DPP v K*[63] it was held that the *Caldwell* meaning applied. However, this was disapproved in *Spratt*[64] where it was held that the subjective *Cunningham* test of recklessness applied. The House of Lords, in the leading case of *Savage; Parmenter*,[65] did not deal with this issue, possibly indicating an acceptance that the *Spratt* line of cases represents the law and that *Cunningham* recklessness is required.[66] Although the leading House of Lords' decision in *G*[67] restricts itself to criminal damage, it is widely accepted that the subjective meaning of recklessness there endorsed will be applicable throughout the criminal law.[68]

---

59   J. Horder ("Reconsidering Psychic Assault" [1998] Crim. L.R. 392) argues that the essential wrong in assault is causing fear: "a psychic assault is the sensory and contemporaneous experience that induces a fear of physical interference—whether or not to be inflicted immediately—being done by the threatener" (at 401).
60   [1997] Q.B. 114 at 122.
61   [1998] A.C. 147 at 166-167.
62   *R. v Venna (Henson George)* [1976] Q.B. 421.
63   *DPP v K* (1990) 91 Cr. App. R. 23. The Court of Appeal in *R. v Savage (Susan)* [1991] 2 W.L.R. 418 adopted a similar view.
64   *R. v Spratt (Robert Michael)* [1990] 1 W.L.R. 1073. This same view was adopted in *R. v Nash (Lee)* [1991] Crim. L.R. 768 and by the Court of Appeal in *Parmenter* [1991] 2 All E.R. 225.
65   [1992] 1 A.C. 699.
66   This point was conceded on appeal in *Haystead v Chief Constable of Derbyshire* [2000] 2 Cr. App. R. 339.
67   *R. v G* [2004] 1 A.C. 1034.
68   *R. v Brady (Philip)* [2006] EWCA Crim 2413: "many of their Lordships observations [in *G*] have a much wider application" than merely to criminal damage.

(ii) Battery

A battery is the intentional or reckless infliction of unlawful personal force by one person upon another. While a technical assault is the *threatening* of such force, a battery is the actual infliction of the force.

(a) *Actus reus*

The defendant must inflict unlawful personal force. The meaning of "force" was considered in the following case.

Wilson v Pringle [1986] 2 All E.R. 440 (Court of Appeal, Civil Division)

CROOM-JOHNSON LJ:

"In our view the authorities lead to the conclusion that in a battery there must be an intentional touching or contact in one form or another of the plaintiff by the defendant. That touching must be proved to be a hostile touching. That still leaves unanswered the question, when is a touching to be called hostile? Hostility cannot be equated with ill-will or malevolence. It cannot be governed by the obvious intention shown in acts like punching, stabbing or shooting. It cannot be solely governed by an expressed intention, although that may be strong evidence. But the element of hostility, in the sense in which it is now to be considered, must be a question of fact for the tribunal of fact . . .

Although we are all entitled to protection from physical molestation, we live in a crowded world in which people must be considered as taking on themselves some risk of injury (where it occurs) from the acts of others which are not in themselves unlawful."

This was approved by the House of Lords in *Brown*.[69] Lord Jauncey, however, unhelpfully added that if the defendant's actions are unlawful they are necessarily hostile. Thus because it is unlawful to cause injuries in the course of sado-masochistic activities, the element of hostility is satisfied. Such circular reasoning defies explanation. To say that injuries are inflicted with hostility when they have been consented to is to deprive the word "hostility" of any real meaning. A better approach was adopted by Lord Mustill, dissenting in *Brown*, who stated that hostility was not a crucial matter in determining guilt or innocence, "although its presence or absence may be relevant when the court has to decide as a matter of policy how to react to a new situation".[70]

Several further matters need consideration. First, while many of the cases speak of "force" or "violence", it is clear that any unlawful touching suffices. So, taking a person's arm firmly to escort them out of a garden is capable of amounting to a battery.[71] Secondly, in the "crowded world" (*Wilson v Pringle*) of today where there is much pushing or jostling in queues, etc. there is a "general exception embracing all physical contact which is generally acceptable in the ordinary conduct of daily life".[72] Thirdly, a battery involves the application of physical force upon the victim. Actual touching is not necessary. For example, in *Lynsey*[73] there was a battery when the defendant spat in the face of a police officer. However, the force must be physical. In *Ireland; Burstow* it was held that silent telephone calls resulting in psychiatric injury could not constitute a battery.[74]

---

69   *R. v Brown (Anthony Joseph)* [1994] 1 A.C. 212. See also *Faulkner v Talbot* [1981] 1 W.L.R. 1528. On the issue of the amount of everyday contact to which we are deemed to consent, see *R. v Sutton (Terence)* [1977] 3 All E.R. 476.
70   *Brown* [1994] 1 A.C. 212 at 261.
71   *McMillan v CPS* [2008] EWHC 1457 (Admin).
72   *Collins v Willcock* [1984] 1 W.L.R. 1172.
73   *Lynsey* [1995] 2 Cr. App. R. 667. See also *Pursell v Horn* (1838) 112 E.R. 966 where the defendant threw boiling water scalding the victim. The majority of the court accepted that a battery was not limited to body-to-body contact.
74   *Ireland; Burstow* [1998] A.C. 147 at 161.

Fourthly, it used to be thought that a battery could not be committed by omission.[75] However, in *Santana-Bermudez* a defendant was held liable when he failed to warn a police officer searching him that he had hypodermic needles in his pockets and her finger was pierced by a needle. Maurice Kay J was critical of the "undesirable complexity [that] has bedevilled our criminal law as a result of quasi-theological distinctions between acts and omissions" and simply ruled that:

"[W]here someone (by act or word or by a combination of the two) creates a danger and thereby exposes another to a reasonably foreseeable risk of injury which materialises, there is an evidential basis for the *actus reus* of an assault occasioning actual bodily harm ..."[76]

However, it is unclear from this whether liability was based on his omission (with him being under a duty to tell her about the needles because he had created a dangerous situation) or on the fiction of a continuing act (putting the needles in his pocket was an act which continued until the police officer injured herself). The rather limited ratio of the case seems to suggest that there will be no liability for an omission in other situations where there is a duty to act: for example, where a mother (who did not create the dangerous situation) fails to rescue her child who suffers actual bodily harm as a consequence.

A final issue is whether the force need be applied directly. Is it necessary, for example, that the defendant physically come into contact with the victim with his fist, spittle or some weapon? Older authorities[77] suggest that this was indeed the case (although "direct" was interpreted with a certain amount of flexibility). However, the case of *Martin*[78] can be read as dispensing with the requirement of direct force. In this case the defendant barred the exit to a theatre with an iron bar, turned off the lights and shouted "fire". Some people subsequently were injured when they were crushed against the exit in the panic to escape. The defendant was convicted under s.20 of the Offences against the Person Act 1861 of inflicting grievous bodily harm (an offence then thought to require proof of an assault).

The decision of *Wilson*,[79] however, interpreted *Martin* somewhat differently as supporting the view that "to inflict" grievous bodily harm under s.20 does not necessitate an assault taking place. On the issue of whether an assault itself necessitates direct force, Lord Roskill in *Wilson* approved a passage from the Australian decision of *Salisbury*[80] where a distinction was drawn between "directly and violently" inflicting a harm (an assault) and inflicting harm that was "not itself a direct application of force to the body of the victim, [but] does directly result in force being applied violently to the body of the victim" (not an assault). The House of Lords in *Savage; Parmenter*, albeit obiter, endorsed this approach in holding that there would be no assault in cases like *Martin* or where a defendant had interfered with the breaking mechanism of a car thereby causing an accident and injuries to the driver. Further, in *Ireland; Burstow*[81] Lord Hope stated that a battery could not be committed over the telephone because there was no physical contact between the defendant and the victim.

On the other hand, the following case clearly suggests that a battery can be committed even if the force is applied indirectly.[82]

---

[75]   M. Hirst, "Assault, Battery and Indirect Violence" [1999] Crim. L.R. 577.
[76]   *DPP v Santana-Bermudez* [2003] EWHC 2908 at [10].
[77]   See D. Baker, *Glanville Williams' Textbook of Criminal Law*, 3rd edn (London: Sweet & Maxwell, 2012), pp.247ff where he cites authorities such as *Scott v Sheppherd* (1773) 96 E.R. 525.
[78]   *R. v Martin* (1881) 8 Q.B.D. 54.
[79]   *R. v Wilson (Clarence George)* [1984] A.C. 242.
[80]   *Salisbury* [1976] V.R. 452 at 461.
[81]   *Ireland; Burstow* [1998] A.C. 147 at 165.
[82]   For a view that this case was decided *per incuriam* and that a battery does require a direct physical attack, see M. Hirst, "Assault, Battery and Indirect Violence" [1999] Crim. L.R. 557.

DPP v K (a minor) (1990) 91 Cr. App. R. 23 (Queen's Bench Divisional Court)

The defendant, a 15-year-old schoolboy, was carrying out an experiment using concentrated sulphuric acid in a chemistry class at school when he splashed some of the acid on his hand. He was given permission to go to the toilet to wash it off and without his teacher's knowledge, took a test-tube of the acid with him to test its reaction on some toilet paper. While he was in the toilet he heard footsteps in the corridor and in a panic poured the acid into a hot air drier to conceal it. He returned to his class intending to return later to remove it and wash out the drier. Before he could do so another pupil used the drier. Acid squirted onto his face causing a permanent scar. The defendant was charged with assault occasioning actual bodily harm but was acquitted because he had not intended to harm anyone. The prosecution appealed by way of case stated.

PARKER LJ:

"[I]n my judgment there can be no doubt that if a defendant places acid into a machine with the intent that it shall, when the next user switches the machine on, be ejected onto him and do him harm there is an assault when the harm is done. The position was correctly and simply stated by Stephen J. in *R. v Clarence* (1888) 22 Q.B.D. 23 at 45, where he said:

'If a man laid a trap for another into which he fell after an interval, the man who laid it would during the interval be guilty of an attempt to assault, and of an actual assault as soon as the man fell in.'

This illustration was also referred to by Wills J. in the same case in relation to s.20 of the 1861 Act. Wills J. there also referred to *R. v Martin* (1881) 8 Q.B.D. 54, saying:

'The prisoner in that case did what was certain to make people crush one another, perhaps to death, and the grievous bodily harm was as truly inflicted by him as if he had hurled a stone at somebody's head.'

In the same way a defendant who pours a dangerous substance into a machine just as truly assaults the next user of the machine as if he had himself switched the machine on."

Appeal allowed

In *Haystead* the defendant punched a woman who was holding a child. The child fell from her arms and hit his head on the floor. The main argument on appeal was whether there could be a battery when force was indirectly applied. In a highly ambiguous judgment it was indicated that this "may well be" so, but it was unnecessary to decide as, on the facts, there was a direct application of force even though there was no physical contact with the child:

"[dropping] the child was entirely and immediately the result of the appellant's action in punching her. There is no difference in logic or good sense between the facts of this case and one where the defendant might have used a weapon to fell the child to the floor."[83]

It is to be hoped that the decision in *DPP v K* will be followed. The actions of a person who leaves acid in a hot air drier (which will inevitably be used by someone) seem morally indistinguishable from those of a person who throws acid directly at another.

---

[83]   *Haystead v Chief Constable of Derbyshire* [2000] 2 Cr. App. R. 339 at 346.

(b) *Mens rea*

R. v Venna [1976] Q.B. 421 (Court of Appeal, Criminal Division)

JAMES LJ:

"In our view the element of mens rea in the offence of battery is satisfied by proof that the defendant intentionally or recklessly applied force to the person of another . . .

   We see no reason in logic or in law why a person who recklessly applies physical force to the person of another should be outside the criminal law of assault. In many cases the dividing line between intention and recklessness is barely distinguishable."

The same arguments considered in relation to technical assault apply here with the prevailing consensus being that recklessness bears its "subjective" *Cunningham* meaning. In *D v DPP*[84] it was stated that recklessness involves foresight of the risk of unlawful force and the taking of that risk.

(iii) Punishment

A common assault is punishable upon summary conviction by a fine of up to (currently) £5,000 and/or six months' imprisonment. The offence is no longer triable upon indictment.[85] The Magistrates' Courts Sentencing Guidelines provide that the starting point where no injury is caused is a fine. This is increased to a community order where one (listed) aggravating factor is present and to 26 weeks' custody where two or more aggravating factors are present.[86]

3. Aggravated assaults

The more serious offences of violence are commonly termed "aggravated assaults" although, as we shall see, for some of these offences it is not necessary to prove the existence of an assault. Some assaults are aggravated because of the circumstances in which they are committed, for example, assault with intent to resist arrest[87] or because of the identity of the victim, for example, assault on a police constable in the execution of his duty[88] or assault on an Immigration Officer.[89] The following three sections deal with the core aggravated assaults which can be committed in any circumstances and against any victim; the chapter then examines the law dealing with "racially or religiously aggravated" assaults and finally the causing of serious injury by dangerous driving.

(i) Assault occasioning actual bodily harm

Offences against the Person Act 1861 s.47

"Whosoever shall be convicted on indictment[90] of any assault occasioning actual bodily harm shall be liable . . . to be imprisoned for any term not exceeding five years."

---

[84]   *D v DPP* [2005] EWHC 967.
[85]   Criminal Justice Act 1988 s.39. Exceptionally, common assault can still be tried on indictment if it is founded on the same facts as an indictable offence which is charged, or if it forms part of a series of offences of a similar character to an indictable offence charged (Criminal Justice Act 1988 s.40).
[86]   Sentencing Guidelines Council, *Magistrates' Courts Sentencing Guidelines: Definitive Guideline* (2009).
[87]   Offences Against the Person Act 1861 s.38.
[88]   Police Act 1996 s.89.
[89]   UK Borders Act 2007 s.22.
[90]   The offence is also triable summarily by virtue of the Magistrates' Courts Act 1952 s.19, Sch.1 and punishable by a maximum of six months' imprisonment or £5,000 fine, or both.

(a) *Actus reus*

Three conditions need to be satisfied here. First, there must be an "assault". This means there must be either a technical assault or a battery.[91] Secondly, this assault must "occasion" or *cause* actual bodily harm. For example, in *Roberts*[92] the defendant tried to pull a girl's coat off in a moving car. She jumped out of the car and was injured. Here there was a common assault and she had suffered actual bodily harm. The sole issue in this case was whether causation had been established.[93] Where it is alleged that the actual bodily harm has been caused by a technical assault (as opposed to a battery) it must be established that it was the apprehension of imminent force—as opposed to general fear and upset—that caused the actual bodily harm.[94]

Thirdly, the assault must cause "actual bodily harm". With regard to physical injuries this includes "any hurt or injury calculated to interfere with health or comfort".[95] In *Chan-Fook* it was held that the words "actual bodily harm" were ordinary words generally requiring no elaboration:

"The word 'harm' is a synonym for injury. The word 'actual' indicates that the injury (although there is no need for it to be permanent) should not be so trivial as to be wholly insignificant."[96]

Accordingly, as long as it is not "wholly insignificant", almost any injury will suffice and indeed may simply be inferred from the facts of the case as in *Taylor v Granville*.[97] The evidence established that the defendant had struck the victim on the face and it was held that bruising must, at the least, have been thereby caused; such a finding clearly fell within the definition of actual bodily harm. In *R. (on the application of T) v DPP*[98] it was held that a momentary loss of consciousness could amount to actual bodily harm as it involved an injurious impairment to the victim's sensory functions.

DPP v Smith [2006] 2 Cr. App. R. 1 (Queen's Bench Divisional Court)

The defendant cut off a girl's pony tail without her consent. The justices accepted that this could not amount to actual bodily harm. The prosecution appealed by way of case stated.

SIR IGOR JUDGE P:

"16 . . . In ordinary language, 'harm' is not limited to 'injury', and according to the Concise Oxford English Dictionary extends to 'hurt' or 'damage'. According to the same dictionary, 'bodily', whether used as an adjective or an adverb, is 'concerned with the body'. 'Actual', as defined in the authorities, means that the bodily harm should not be so trivial or trifling as to be effectively without significance.

17. Recent authority shows that evidence of external bodily injury, or a break in or bruise to the surface of the skin, is not required . . . It follows that physical pain consequent on an assault is not a necessary ingredient of this offence.

18. In my judgment, whether it is alive beneath the surface of the skin or dead tissue above the surface of the skin, the hair is an attribute and part of the human body. It is intrinsic to each individual and to the identity of each individual. Although it is not essential to my decision, I note that an individual's hair is relevant to his or her autonomy. Some regard it as their crowning glory. Admirers may so regard it in the object of their affections. Even if, medically and scientifically speaking, the hair above the surface of the scalp is no more than dead tissue, it

---

91   *Ireland; Burstow* [1998] A.C. 147 at 161.
92   *R. v Roberts (Kenneth Joseph)* (1972) 56 Cr. App. R. 95.
93   See pp.130–131.
94   J.C. Smith, Commentary to *Cox* [1998] Crim. L.R. 810.
95   *R. v Miller (Peter)* [1954] 2 Q.B. 282.
96   *R. v Chan-Fook (Mike)* [1994] 1 W.L.R. 689 at 694.
97   *Taylor v Granville* [1978] Crim. L.R. 482. cf. *Reigate Justices Ex p. Counsell* (1984) 148 J.P. 193.
98   *R. (on the application of T) v DPP* [2003] EWHC 266.

remains part of the body and is attached to it. While it is so attached, in my judgment it falls within the meaning of 'bodily' in the phrase 'actual bodily harm'. It is concerned with the body of the individual victim.

19. In my judgment, the defendant's actions in cutting of a substantial part of the victim's hair in the course of an assault on her—like putting paint on it or some unpleasant substance which marked or damaged it without causing injury elsewhere—is capable of amounting to an assault which occasions actual bodily harm."

Appeal allowed

While there is much to be said for the court's reasoning in this case, it is extraordinary that the charge here was for s.47 rather than for common assault. This case demonstrates the ease with which a common assault (punishable by a maximum of six months' imprisonment) can be transformed into an offence punishable by up to five years' imprisonment. The CPS *Charging Standard* states that

"In determining whether or not the injuries are serious, relevant factors may include, for example, the fact that there has been significant medical intervention and/or permanent effects have resulted. Examples may include cases where there is the need for a number of stitches (but not the superficial application of steri-strips) or a hospital procedure under anaesthetic."[99]

The cutting off of a pony tail, while perhaps very upsetting, cannot possibly be regarded as requiring significant medical intervention.

What is the position where the defendant's conduct causes psychiatric illness? Previously the test of "any hurt or injury calculated to interfere with health or comfort" was thought to include hysterical and nervous conditions and shock. This position has now been qualified.

R. v Ireland; R. v Burstow [1998] A.C. 147 (House of Lords)

In *Ireland* the victims of repeated silent telephone calls suffered psychiatric illness. The defendant was charged with an assault occasioning actual bodily harm under s.47. In *Burstow* the victim of an eight-month stalking campaign suffered from a severe depressive illness. The defendant was charged with unlawfully and maliciously inflicting grievous bodily harm contrary to s.20 of the Offences against the Person Act 1861. Both were convicted and appealed.

LORD STEYN:

"The appeals under consideration do not involve structural injuries to the brain such as might require the intervention of a neurologist. One is also not considering either psychotic illness or personality disorders . . . The case was that they developed mental disturbances of a lesser order, namely neurotic disorders. For present purposes the relevant forms of neurosis are anxiety disorders and depressive disorders. Neuroses must be distinguished from simple states of fear, or problems in coping with everyday life. Where the line is to be drawn must be a matter of psychiatric judgment. But for present purposes it is important to note that modern psychiatry treats neuroses as recognisable psychiatric illnesses . . . [N]eurotic illnesses affect the central nervous system of the body, because emotions such as fear and anxiety are brain functions . . .

[I]n *Chan-Fook* the Court of Appeal squarely addressed the question whether psychiatric injury may amount to bodily harm under section 47 of the 1861 Act . . . Hobhouse L.J. stated:

'The first question . . . is whether the inclusion of the word "bodily" in the phrase "actual bodily harm" limits harm to harm to the skin, flesh and bones of the victim . . . The body of the victim includes all parts of the body, including his organs, his nervous system and his brain. Bodily injury therefore may include injury to any of those parts of his body responsible for his mental and other faculties.'

---

[99]   CPS, *Offences Against the Person, Incorporating the Charging Standard*, see fn.33 above.

In concluding that 'actual bodily harm' is capable of including psychiatric injury Hobhouse L.J. emphasised that

'it does not include mere emotions such as fear or distress or panic nor does it include, as such, states of mind that are not themselves evidence of some identifiable clinical condition.'

He observed that in the absence of psychiatric evidence a question whether or not an assault occasioned psychiatric injury should not be left to the jury . . .

In my view the ruling in [*Chan-Fook*] was based on principled and cogent reasoning and it marked a sound and essential clarification of the law. I would hold that 'bodily harm' in ss.18, 20 and 47 must be interpreted so as to include recognisable psychiatric illness."

In *Morris*,[100] the conviction of a stalker, who had allegedly caused his victim to suffer pains, sleeplessness, tension and fear of being alone, was quashed because the trial judge had allowed the issue of whether the assault had occasioned psychiatric injury to be left to the jury without expert evidence. Even with respect to her physical pains, psychiatric evidence should have been adduced to testify that they were the result of the defendant's non-physical attack.

In *Dhaliwal*,[101] a clear distinction was drawn between psychological injury (for example, palpitations, breathing difficulties, cold sweats, anxiety, inability to sleep and so on) and recognisable psychiatric illness. Only the latter can constitute bodily harm. It was stated that any blurring of this distinction would introduce uncertainty into the law. As Horder and McGowan state:

"[This is] the serious difficulty . . . of drawing a distinction in any given case between genuine psychological harm, and the normal human emotions of grief, anxiety, fear, and so forth (even if relatively severe). It seems unlikely that we have yet reached a stage where, in the absence of some further consideration such as a threat to public order, unjustifiably and culpably to cause another to experience severe emotional disturbance should be regarded as a criminal wrong."[102]

(b) *Mens rea*

Section 47 makes no express reference to any mens rea requirement, but it is settled that liability is established if the defendant has the mens rea of common assault.

R. v Savage; DPP v Parmenter [1992] 1 A.C. 699 (House of Lords)

In the first appeal, the appellant, Mrs Savage, threw a pint glass full of beer over Miss Beal. The glass slipped out of her hand, broke, and a piece of it cut Miss Beal's wrist. Savage was convicted of unlawful wounding contrary to s.20 of the Offences against the Person Act 1861. The Court of Appeal partially allowed her appeal substituting a verdict of assault occasioning actual bodily harm contrary to s.47 of the Act. She appealed to the House of Lords.

LORD ACKNER:

"[Mrs Savage assaulted Miss Beal when she threw beer over her. Her actions also caused actual bodily harm: the cut wrist.] Was the offence thus established or is there a further mental state that has to be established in relation to the bodily harm element of the offence? Clearly the section, by its terms, expressly imposes no such

---

[100]   *R. v Morris (Clarence Barrington)* [1998] 1 Cr. App. R. 386.
[101]   *R. v D* [2006] 2 Cr. App. R. 24.
[102]   "Manslaughter by Causing Another's Suicide" [2006] Crim. L.R. 1035 at 1038.

requirement. Does it do so by necessary implication? It uses neither the word 'intentionally' or 'maliciously'. The words 'occasioning actual bodily harm' are descriptive of the word 'assault', by reference to a particular kind of consequence . . .

[His Lordship then discussed *Roberts* (*above*, p.117) where it was held that] once the assault was established, the only remaining question was whether the victim's conduct was the natural consequence of that assault. The word 'occasioning' raised solely a question of causation, an objective question which does not involve inquiring into the accused's state of mind. In *R. v Spratt* [1990] 1 W.L.R. 1073 McCowan L.J. said, at p. 1082:

'However, the history of the interpretation of the Act of 1861 shows that, whether or not the word "maliciously" appears in the section in question, the courts have consistently held that the mens rea of every type of offence against the person covers both actual intent and recklessness, in the sense of taking the risk of harm ensuing with foresight that it might happen.'

McCowan L.J. then quotes a number of authorities for that proposition . . . [However] none of the cases cited were concerned with the mental element required in s.47 cases. Nevertheless, the Court of Appeal in *R. v Parmenter* [1991] 2 W.L.R. 408 [approved] the decision in *R. v Spratt* [1990] 1 W.L.R. 1073 . . .

My Lords, in my respectful view, the Court of Appeal in *Parmenter* were wrong in approving the decision in *Spratt's* case. The decision in *Roberts's* case was correct. The verdict of assault occasioning actual bodily harm may be returned upon proof of an assault together with proof of the fact that actual bodily harm was occasioned by the assault. The prosecution are not obliged to prove that the defendant intended to cause some actual bodily harm or was reckless as to whether such harm would be caused."

Appeal in R. v Savage dismissed

There is thus no requirement that defendants foresee actual bodily harm. All that is required is that they have the mens rea of the assault, namely, intention or recklessness to cause force or apprehension of force. Recklessness here bears the same meaning as in assault. The result is that the degree of moral culpability required for s.47 and for assault is the same despite the maximum penalties for the two offences being five years' and six months' imprisonment respectively.

The effect is that s.47 is a constructive crime of "half mens rea" where the mens rea requirement does not correspond with the actus reus. Whether constructive liability is justified is a controversial matter.[103] What is unfortunate is that the House of Lords should simply reach this decision with no reasoning at all. Surely, we are entitled to expect their Lordships to tell us why *Roberts* was correct but *Spratt* and *Parmenter* (Court of Appeal) were wrong.

(c) Punishment

The maximum punishment is five years' imprisonment. The offence is triable either way. If a defendant is tried on indictment in the Crown Court the jury can return an alternative verdict of guilty of assault even if such a charge was not included in the indictment. As seen earlier, many offences that could have been charged under s.47 are in fact charged as common assault, ensuring trial in the magistrates' court. The Magistrates' Courts Sentencing Guidelines provide that the starting point for assault occasioning actual bodily harm that has been categorised as lesser harm and lower culpability is a medium level community order with a sentencing range of a Band A fine—High level community order.[104] For Crown Courts, the Sentencing Guidelines state that if the assault is pre-meditated and causes relatively serious injury (greater harm and higher culpability) the starting point is 1 year 6 months' custody with a sentencing range of 1–3 years' custody.[105]

---

[103]   The arguments are considered at pp.720–725 in relation to constructive manslaughter.
[104]   Sentencing Guidelines Council, *Magistrates' Court Sentencing Guidelines: Definitive Guideline* (2009).
[105]   Sentencing Council, *Assault: Definitive Guideline* (2011), p.12.

(ii) Malicious wounding and inflicting grievous bodily harm

Offences against the Person Act 1861 s.20

"Whosoever shall unlawfully and maliciously wound or inflict any grievous bodily harm upon any other person, either with or without any weapon or instrument, shall be guilty of [an offence punishable up to a term not exceeding five years' imprisonment]."

(a) *Actus reus*

There must be a wounding or infliction of grievous bodily harm. A *wound* necessitates that the continuity of the whole of the outer skin, or the inner skin within the cheek or lip.[106] It does not include the rupturing of internal blood vessels.[107] Given medical advances it is highly questionable whether minor wounds, for example, a slight cut, should be capable of forming the basis for so serious a charge. The CPS *Charging Standard* states that this offence should only be charged when the wounding is considered to be "really serious".[108] *Grievous bodily harm* means nothing more technical than "really serious bodily harm".[109] The CPS *Charging Standard* lists the following as examples of such serious harm:

"injury resulting in permanent disability, loss of sensory function or visible disfigurement; broken or displaced limbs or bones, including fractured skull, compound fractures, broken cheek bone, jaw, ribs, etc; injuries which cause substantial loss of blood, usually necessitating a transfusion or result in lengthy treatment or incapacity; serious psychiatric injury."[110]

It is clear that internal injuries and infecting a person with a virus such as HIV can also amount to grievous bodily harm.[111] Whether an injury amounts to really serious bodily harm can depend on the vulnerability of the victim. In *Bollom*[112] it was held that bruising and abrasions could amount to grievous bodily harm for an infant, an elderly or unwell person even if they would not be so regarded for a fit adult.

Whether any particular injury amounts to grievous bodily harm is a question of fact to be determined by the jury which means that one jury could find that, say, a broken thumb was grievous bodily harm while another jury could decide it was not.

The grievous bodily harm has to be "inflicted". Until 1983 the word "inflict" was generally interpreted[113] to mean that it was necessary to prove that there had been an assault (a technical assault or a battery). Section 20 was truly an "aggravated assault". For example, in *Clarence*[114] the defendant, knowing he was suffering from venereal disease, had sexual intercourse with his wife and transmitted the disease to her. It was held that because of the wife's consent there had been no battery and, accordingly, he could not be liable under s.20. However, the House of Lords in *Wilson*[115] held that while most cases of inflicting grievous bodily harm would involve an assault, this was not a prerequisite. There could be an infliction of grievous bodily harm contrary to s.20 without

---

[106] Both the dermis and the epidermis must be broken (*Moriarty v Brooks* (1834) 6 C. & P. 684). Thus a scratch or break to the outer skin is not sufficient if the inner skin remains intact (*M'Loughlin* (1838) 8 C. & P. 635).
[107] *JJC (A Minor) v Eisenhower* (1984) 78 Cr. App. R. 48.
[108] CPS, *Offences against the Person, Incorporating the Charging Standard*, see fn.33 above.
[109] *DPP v Smith* [1961] A.C. 290. It has been held that it is not necessary to include the word "really" in the summing up to the jury (*R. v Saunders (Ian)* [1985] Crim. L.R. 230; *R. v Janjua (Nadeem Ahmed)* [1999] 1 Cr. App. R. 91).
[110] CPS, *Offences against the Person, Incorporating the Charging Standard*, see fn.33 above.
[111] *R. v Dica (Mohammed)* [2004] 3 All E.R. 593.
[112] *R. v Bollom (Stephen Clayton)* [2004] 2 Cr. App. R. 6.
[113] *R. v Clarence (Charles James)* (1888) 22 Q.B.D. 23; *Halliday* (1889) 61 L.T. 701; *R. v Lewis* [1970] Crim. L.R. 647 and *Cartledge v Allen* [1973] Crim. L.R. 530.
[114] *R. v Clarence (Charles James)* (1888) 22 Q.B.D. 23.
[115] *R. v Wilson (Clarence George)* [1984] A.C. 242.

an assault being committed. This same reasoning was applied in *Savage; Parmenter* to cases of unlawful wounding where, although it would require "quite extraordinary facts", one can have an unlawful wounding for the purposes of s.20 without the necessity of proving an assault. It was, however, implicit in *Wilson* that one could only "inflict" grievous bodily harm if there were a direct or indirect application of force to the victim's body. With regard to psychiatric injuries, this view has now been rejected.

R. v Ireland; R. v Burstow [1998] A.C. 147 (House of Lords)

The facts are given above at p.616.

LORD STEYN:

"Counsel argued that the difference in wording [between 'causing' in s.18 and 'inflicting' in s.20] reveals a difference in legislative intent: inflict is a narrower concept than cause. This argument loses sight of the genesis of ss.18 and 20 [as the various sections in the 1861 Act were taken from different Acts passed at different times] . . . The difference in language is therefore not a significant factor . . .

[C]ounsel . . . submitted that it is inherent in the word 'inflict' that there must be a direct or indirect application of force to the body . . . [I]n *Mandair* [1995] 1 A.C. 208 at 215 Lord Mackay of Clashfern L.C. observed . . .: 'In my opinion . . . the word "cause" is wider or at least not narrower than the word "inflict".' . . . I regard this observation as making clear that in the context of the 1861 Act there is no radical divergence between the meaning of the two words.

. . . [With regard to *R. v Clarence*] it must be accepted that in a case where there was direct physical contact the majority ruled that the requirement of infliction was not satisfied. This decision was never overruled. It assists counsel's argument. But it seems to me that what detracts from the weight to be given to the dicta in *R. v Clarence* is that none of the judges in that case had before them the possibility of the inflicting, or causing, of psychiatric injury. The criminal law has moved on in the light of a developing understanding of the link between the body and psychiatric injury. In my judgment *R. v Clarence* no longer assists.

The problem is one of construction. The question is whether as a matter of current usage the contextual interpretation of 'inflict' can embrace the idea of one person inflicting psychiatric injury on another. One can without straining the language in any way answer that question in the affirmative. I am not saying that the words cause and inflict are exactly synonymous. They are not. What I am saying is that in the context of the 1861 Act one can nowadays quite naturally speak of inflicting psychiatric injury. Moreover, there is internal contextual support in the statute for this view. It would be absurd to differentiate between ss. 18 and 20 in the way argued . . . The interpretation and approach should so far as possible be adopted which treats the ladder of offences as a coherent body of law."

LORD HOPE OF CRAIGHEAD:

"[*R. v Wilson*, referring with approval to *R. v Salisbury*, does] not wholly resolve the issue which arises in this case, in the context of grievous bodily harm which consists only of psychiatric injury.

The question is whether there is any difference, in this context, between the word 'cause' and the word 'inflict' . . . [F]or all practical purposes there is, in my opinion, no difference between these two words. [He then cited *Mandair* (above) with approval.] But I would add that there is this difference, that the word 'inflict' implies that the consequence of the act is something which the victim is likely to find unpleasant or harmful. The relationship between cause and effect, when the word 'cause' is used, is neutral. It may embrace pleasure as well as pain. The relationship when the word 'inflict' is used is more precise, because it invariably implies detriment to the victim of some kind.

In the context of a criminal act therefore the words 'cause' and 'inflict' may be taken to be interchangeable. As the Supreme Court of Victoria held in *R. v Salisbury*, it is not a necessary ingredient of the word 'inflict' that whatever causes the harm must be applied directly to the victim. It may be applied indirectly, so long as the result is that the harm is caused by what has been done. In my opinion it is entirely consistent with the ordinary use of the word 'inflict' in the English language to say that the appellant's actions 'inflicted' the psychiatric harm from which the victim has admittedly suffered."

Appeals dismissed

This reasoning has been extended to the causing of physical injuries.

R. v Dica [2004] 2 Cr. App. R. 28 (Court of Appeal, Criminal Division)

The defendant, who was HIV positive, had unprotected sexual intercourse with two women as a result of which they contracted HIV. The defendant was convicted of inflicting grievous bodily harm on them contrary to s.20.

JUDGE LJ:

"Such differences as may be discerned in the language used by Lord Steyn and Lord Hope respectively do not obscure the fact that this decision confirmed that even when no physical violence has been applied, directly or indirectly to the victim's body, an offence under s.20 may be committed. Putting it another way, if the remaining ingredients of s.20 are established, the charge is not answered simply because the grievous bodily harm suffered by the victim did not result from direct or indirect physical violence. Whether the consequences suffered by the victim are physical injuries or psychiatric injuries, or a combination of the two, the ingredients of the offence pre-scribed by s.20 are identical. If psychiatric injury can be inflicted without direct or indirect violence, or an assault, for the purposes of s.20 physical injury may be similarly inflicted."

In *Brady*[116] the defendant was perched on a balcony railing and either lost his balance (his version of events) or jumped deliberately and landed on a woman below causing her serious injuries. The Court of Appeal affirmed that, as a result of *Ireland; Burstow*, "even when no physical force has been applied, directly or indirectly to the victim's body, an offence under s.20 may be committed" (a somewhat unnecessary ruling given that physical force had been directly applied to the woman). The defence further argued that (on the defendant's account) the injuries had not been "inflicted" because there had not been "deliberate, non-accidental conduct" by the defendant (i.e. he had accidentally fallen). The Court was "reluctant to come to a concluded view" on this but, on the facts, stated that the deliberate and precarious perching on the railing was a deliberate act. This defence argument seems misplaced. Any act suffices for the actus reus of s.20 provided it causes the result and was not the product of automatism, as would have been the case if he had been pushed off the balcony. Of course, in most cases where the act was accidental, no mens rea will be established. However, if mens rea is present, there should be no requirement of "deliberate, non-accidental conduct".

In *Stranney*[117] the defendant was convicted of inflicting grievous bodily harm when, as a result of very bad dangerous driving, two of the passengers in his car sustained grievous bodily harm. There was no assault in this case and the force was, at most, indirectly applied.

It is clear from all these cases that both psychiatric injury and physical injury may be inflicted without an assault and without direct or indirect force. What, then, is the difference between "inflict" in s.20 and "cause" in s.18?

Lord Steyn in *Ireland; Burstow* was careful to state that he was "not saying that the words cause and inflict are exactly synonymous. They are not." The only hint as to what the difference might be is provided by Lord Hope when he stated that the word "inflict" implies that "the consequence of the act is something which the victim is likely to find unpleasant or harmful". This is extraordinary. The word "harmful" here must refer to the victim subjectively interpreting the injury as harmful because objectively there must, of course, be grievous bodily harm; the word thus adds nothing to the word "unpleasant". Taken literally, this seems to suggest that sado-masochistic activities such as those in *Brown*[118] cannot be prosecuted under s.20 because the victims do not find their injuries unpleasant

[116]   *R. v Brady (Philip)* [2006] EWCA Crim 2413.
[117]   *R. v Stranney (Andrew Paul)* [2008] 1 Cr. App. R. (S.) 104.
[118]   *Brown* [1994] 1 A.C. 212.

and do not suffer "detriment". On the contrary, they find the pain and injury pleasant and to their benefit as an expression of their sexuality. While, for rather different reasons,[119] such an approach could be welcomed, these dicta can hardly be taken to cast doubt on the well-established principles laid down in *Brown*. It follows that the difference between the words "cause" in s.18 and "inflict" in s.20 remains something of a mystery.

The broader implications of the decision in *Ireland; Burstow* are disturbing. The fact that psychiatric injury can constitute grievous bodily harm combined with the fact that no assault, nor any direct or indirect application of force, is required for s.20 raises the potential for liability in situations far removed from those traditionally associated with s.20. For example, if I fail a student's essay with the result that he suffers a psychiatric illness, I have committed the actus reus of s.20, and if I know of his mental instability and foresee him sustaining some psychiatric injury, I have mens rea and could be liable. This is removing s.20 too far from its paradigm. While one can understand that the seriousness of psychiatric illnesses can be such that it is justifiable to conclude that they are the equivalent of serious bodily harm, liability for s.20 should be limited to cases where there has been an assault or the application of some force. This, however, is not the law since *Ireland; Burstow* and *Dica*.

Where a defendant has been charged with a s.20 offence, it has long been possible for a jury, where they were not satisfied that all the elements of s.20 have been proven, to return a verdict of guilty of s.47 as this was a "lesser included offence",[120] that is, all the elements of the lesser offence, s.47 (an assault causing actual bodily harm), were included in the greater offence, s.20 (an assault causing grievous bodily harm). However, if the greater offence, s.20, no longer requires proof of an assault, how could the jury convict of s.47 which does require an assault? Lord Roskill in *Wilson* answered this by stating that while it was not necessarily so, most s.20 cases would involve an assault. "Inflicting" therefore impliedly *includes* "inflicting by assault" and therefore s.47 could be a lesser included offence. This was endorsed in *Savage; Parmenter*. Such an approach is not surprising. Without the power to convict of lesser offences many defendants would escape liability altogether. However, the result is that in some cases a defendant can be convicted of an offence (s.47) when one of the elements of that offence (an assault) has not been proved to exist. Given the broad interpretation of assault in *Ireland* this is unlikely to be a common occurrence. However, as the appeal in *Burstow* itself demonstrates, there can be cases, particularly concerning stalking, when grievous bodily harm is inflicted without an assault. Further, serious injury can be inflicted without an assault in cases where a disease (say gonorrhoea or HIV) is transmitted as a result of consensual sexual intercourse; because of consent there would be no battery. Such situations demonstrate that it is not always appropriate to stretch the present offences against the person to cover inappropriate cases. In cases of stalking, utilisation of the Protection from Harassment Act 1997 will generally be more appropriate.

(b) *Mens rea*

The mens rea element of s.20 is supplied by the inclusion of the word "maliciously" within the section. It has long been accepted that the terms "maliciously" and "recklessly" are synonymous. In *Savage; Parmenter* (below) the House of Lords endorsed the view of Professor Kenny[121] that "malice" includes

---

[119]   Above, pp.23–26; 313–323.
[120]   Criminal Law Act 1967 s.6(3). Of course, s.47 is not actually a lesser offence as it carries the same maximum penalty as s.20. It is nevertheless treated as a lesser offence in sentencing practice.
[121]   C.S. Kenny and J.W.C. Turner, *Outlines of Criminal Law*, 1st edn (Cambridge: CUP, 1902).

"recklessness as to whether such harm should occur or not (i.e. the accused has foreseen that the particular kind of harm might be done and yet has gone on to take the risk of it)".[122]

It was further ruled in this case that this subjective meaning of maliciously was not affected by *Caldwell* which had (for a period) introduced an objective test of recklessness. This was because "the word 'maliciously' in that statute was a term of legal art which imported into the concept of recklessness a special restricted meaning". Since the overruling of *Caldwell* in *G*, it is irrelevant whether maliciously imports a special meaning to recklessness. Both clearly involve subjective foresight.

What is it that must be foreseen? In the case of *Cunningham*,[123] where the charge concerned the malicious administration of a noxious thing under s.23 of the Act, the Court of Criminal Appeal interpreted "maliciously" to mean that the defendant had to foresee the particular kind of harm that might be done and that he nevertheless went on to take the risk of it occurring. It was held that the defendant had to foresee that the victim might inhale gas which the defendant knew was, or might be, noxious. In other words, the crime was one of "full *mens rea*", where the mens rea "matched" or corresponded with the actus reus.

Since then, however, this principle has been considerably whittled away. In *Mowatt*[124] it was held that it was unnecessary for the defendant to foresee a wound or grievous bodily harm. It was enough that *some* physical harm, albeit of a minor character, was foreseen. This approach has been endorsed by the House of Lords.

R. v Savage; DPP v Parmenter [1992] 1 A.C. 699 (House of Lords)

LORD ACKNER:

"4. *In order to establish an offence under section 20 is it sufficient to prove that the defendant intended or foresaw the risk of some physical harm or must he intend or foresee either wounding or grievous bodily harm?*
It is convenient to set out once again the relevant part of the judgment of Diplock L.J. in *R. v Mowatt* . . .

'In the offence under section 20 . . . for . . . which [no] specific intent is required, the word "maliciously" does import . . . an awareness that his act may have the consequence of causing some physical harm to some other person. That is what is meant by "the particular kind of harm" in the citation from Professor Kenny. It is quite unnecessary that the accused should have foreseen that his unlawful act might cause physical harm of the gravity described in the section, i.e. a wound or serious physical injury. It is enough that he should have foreseen that some physical harm to some person, albeit of a minor character, might result.' (Emphasis in original.)

Mr Sedley submits that this statement of the law is wrong. He contends that properly construed, the section requires foresight of a wounding or grievous bodily harm . . .

The contention is apparently based on the proposition that as the actus reus of a section 20 offence is the wounding or the infliction of grievous bodily harm, the mens rea must consist of foreseeing such wounding or grievous bodily harm. But there is no such hard and fast principle. To take but two examples, the actus reus of murder is the killing of the victim, but foresight of grievous bodily harm is sufficient and indeed, such bodily harm, need not be such as to be dangerous to life. Again, in the case of manslaughter, death is frequently the unforeseen consequence of the violence used.

---

[122]   *R. v Savage (Susan)* [1992] 1 A.C. 699 at 705.
[123]   *R. v Cunningham (Roy)* [1957] 2 Q.B. 396.
[124]   *R. v Mowatt* [1967] 1 Q.B. 421.

The argument that as section 20 and section 47 have both the same penalty, this somehow supports the proposition that the foreseen consequences must coincide with the harm actually done, overlooks the oft repeated statement that this is the irrational result of this piece-meal legislation. The Act 'is a rag-bag of offences brought together from a wide variety of sources with no attempt, as the draftsman frankly acknowledged, to introduce consistency as to substance or as to form': Professor Smith in his commentary on *R. v Parmenter* [1991] Crim.L.R.43.

If section 20 was to be limited to cases where the accused does not desire but does foresee wounding or grievous bodily harm, it would have a very limited scope. The mens rea in a section 20 crime is comprised in the word 'maliciously'. As was pointed out by Lord Lane C.J., giving the judgment of the Court of Appeal in *R. v Sullivan* . . . ([1981] Crim.L.R.46), the 'particular kind of harm' in the citation from Professor Kenny was directed to 'harm to the person' as opposed to 'harm to property'. Thus it was not concerned with the degree of the harm foreseen. It is accordingly in my judgment wrong to look upon the decision in *Mowatt* as being in any way inconsistent with the decision in *Cunningham*.

My Lords, I am satisfied that the decision in *Mowatt* was correct and that it is quite unnecessary that the accused should either have intended or have foreseen that his unlawful act might cause physical harm of the gravity described in section 20, i.e. a wound or serious physical injury. It is enough that he should have foreseen that some physical harm to some person, albeit of a minor character, might result."

In *Brady*[125] the Court of Appeal rejected an argument that the defendant needed to foresee an "obvious and significant" risk of some injury. All that is required is awareness of *a risk* of injury.

Was the House of Lords justified in holding that the defendant need only foresee *some harm*? If the defendant only foresees some harm resulting, but is then convicted and punished for ensuing serious harm, is this not making liability and punishment dependent on luck? Horder argues that one should distinguish between "pure" luck and making one's own luck and in the latter situation:

"[B]y doing something intended to harm V, D changes her own normative position, making the bad luck of V's serious injury her (D's) own. There is nothing inappropriate in holding D criminally liable for the serious injury actually inflicted, if there was any risk of such injury resulting from D's intended conduct".[126]

Issues such as these, however, were not considered by the House of Lords. No serious attempt to justify its position was made. Simply pointing out that anomalies also exist in other areas of law is not a justification, nor is it enough for them metaphorically to shrug their shoulders by stating that the 1861 Act is simply "a rag-bag of offences" with no consistency. Such platitudes reinforce the need for statutory intervention—a matter to be dealt with shortly.

(c) *Punishment*

The maximum penalty is five years' imprisonment, the same penalty as s.47. While this is irrational and seemingly distorts any structure of offences based on seriousness, in practice it is treated as a more serious offence with longer prison sentences (on average) being imposed for s.20 compared with s.47. The Magistrates' Courts Sentencing Guidelines provide that where there is a lower level of harm and culpability (such as where the act was not premeditated) the starting point is Community Order (High), with a sentencing range of Community Order (Low)—Crown Court (51 weeks' custody).[127] For Crown Courts the Sentencing Guidelines provides the same starting point of

---

[125] *Brady* [2006] EWCA Crim 2413.

[126] J. Horder, "A Critique of the Correspondence Principle" [1995] Crim. L.R. 759 at 765. See also J. Gardner, "Rationality and the Rule of Law in Offences against the Person" [1994] C.L.J. 502 at 508–509. This approach is criticised in A. Ashworth, "A Change of Normative Position: Determining the Contours of Culpability in Criminal Law" (2008) 11 New Criminal L. Rev. 232.

[127] Sentencing Guidelines Council, *Magistrates' Court Sentencing Guidelines: Definitive Guideline* (2009).

Community Order (High). However, if the offence is categorised as high level harm and high level culpability a starting point of three years is given, with a sentencing range of two years six months to four years' custody.[128]

(iii) Wounding and causing grievous bodily harm with intent

Offences against the Person Act 1861 s.18

"Whosoever shall unlawfully and maliciously by any means whatsoever wound or cause any grievous bodily harm to any person, with intent . . . to do some grievous bodily harm to any person, or with intent to resist or prevent the lawful apprehension or detainer of any person, shall be guilty of [an offence and shall be liable . . . to imprisonment for life]."

(a) *Actus reus*

The terms "wound" and "grievous bodily harm" bear the same meaning as in s.20. "Cause", however, has never been held to imply that the injury need be the result of a common assault. Until the decision of *Wilson*[129] it was, therefore, true to say that "cause" was wider than "inflict" with the paradoxical result that it was easier to prove the actus reus of the more serious offence, s.18, than that of s.20. In *Mandair*[130] the House of Lords held that "causing" was "wider or at least not narrower than the word 'inflict'". This statement was approved in *Ireland; Burstow* where it was added that there was "no radical divergence between the meaning of the two words". Accordingly, on a s.18 charge the jury can instead convict a defendant of an offence contrary to s.20.[131] Research reveals that only 23 per cent of offenders indicted under s.18 are eventually convicted of that offence, with most of the remainder being convicted of lesser offences, particularly s.20.[132]

(b) *Mens rea*

Two mens rea elements are contained within s.18; the offence must be committed "maliciously" and "with intent".

1. Maliciously

In order to appreciate the significance of this term in s.18, it is necessary to dismantle the section to find the possible charges contained within it. If one is charged with maliciously causing grievous bodily harm with intent to cause grievous bodily harm, then *Mowatt*[133] is right in suggesting that the word "maliciously" adds nothing that is not already present in the requirement of intent.

On the other hand, if the defendant is charged with maliciously causing grievous bodily harm with intent to resist or prevent arrest, the inclusion of the term "malicious" may be crucial. If, for example, the defendant intends only to resist arrest and has no state of mind at all in relation to the possibility of harm, they cannot be convicted because they are not malicious. They must, at least, foresee the possibility of some harm.[134]

---

[128] Factors indicating greater harm include: Injury which is serious in the context of the offence; Victim is particularly vulnerable because of personal circumstances; Sustained or repeated assault on the same victim. Factors indicating higher culpability include (amongst others): Use of weapon; Deliberate targeting of vulnerable victim; Leading role in group or gang. Sentencing Council, *Assault: Definitive Guideline* (2011), p.8.

[129] *R. v Wilson (Clarence George)* [1984] A.C. 242.

[130] *R. v Mandair (Singh Mandair)* [1995] 1 A.C. 208.

[131] Criminal Law Act 1967 s.6(3). This is so even if s.20 has not been charged as an alternative: *R. v Lahaye (Dean John)* [2006] 1 Cr. App. R. 11.

[132] E. Genders, "Reform of the Offences against the Person Act: Lessons from the Law in Action" [1999] Crim. L.R. 689.

[133] *Mowatt* [1967] 1 Q.B. 421.

[134] *Morrison* (1989) 89 Cr. App. R. 17.

2. With intent

The defendant must either intend grievous bodily harm or intend to resist arrest.

It has been held that "intent" here bears the same meaning as in *Nedrick*.[135] Whether the House of Lords' decision in *Woollin* apples to crimes other than murder is a moot point discussed elsewhere.[136] The better view is that *Woollin* (to the extent that it may have modified *Nedrick*) should apply to s.18. It would be unfortunate if intention in "intention to cause grievous bodily harm" bore different meanings for s.18 and for murder. It is perhaps because of the difficulty of establishing this requisite intention that so few of those indicted under s.18 are actually convicted of the offence. The cases in which offenders are finally convicted under s.18 tend to be those where there is some objective evidence of premeditation, such as when a weapon has been taken to the scene of the crime.[137]

The CPS *Charging Standard* states that the following factors may indicate a specific intent: a repeated or planned attack; deliberate selection of a weapon or adaptation of an article to cause injury, such as breaking a glass before an attack; making prior threats; and using an offensive weapon against, or kicking the victim's head.[138]

(c) *Punishment*

Section 18 carries a maximum sentence of life imprisonment. The sentences imposed under the guidelines depend on the seriousness of the injury, whether the offence was premeditated and whether a weapon was used. When the injury is life-threatening or particularly grave and was pre-meditated or involved the use of a weapon, the starting point is 12 years' custody, with a sentencing range of 9–16 years' custody. Where similar injuries are caused without premeditation (or where there is premeditation or use of a weapon, but not life-threatening or particularly grave injury), the starting point is six years' custody, with a sentencing range of five to nine years' custody. Where the victim's injuries are considered to be less serious in the context of the offence (or where the offence is not premeditated, or there was a greater degree of provocation from the victim), the starting point is four years' custody with a sentencing range of three to five years' custody.[139]

(iv) Racially and religiously aggravated assaults

Before 1998 there was no specific offence of racially and religiously aggravated assault. During the 1970s and 1980s there was a growing concern over the number of violent offences that were motivated by racial hostilities against black and minority ethnic (BME) communities. In response to this the Government set up the 1980 Joint Committee Against Racialism (JCAR) to investigate the problem of racial violence. Directly afterwards, the Government commissioned its first study into racial violence and harassment.[140] The report highlighted the widespread problem of racial attacks (known more commonly as "hate crimes") in the United Kingdom. It finally gave validity to the concern, consistently vocalised by lobby groups, that racially motivated violence was a social problem that was in need of government attention. However, it was not until the brutal murder of the teenager Stephen Lawrence in 1993 by a group of racially motivated offenders and the prolonged media attention that this single case garnered, that the Government would finally give its support to the introduction of new racially

---

135 *Purcell* (1986) 83 Cr. App. R. 45.
136 See pp.163.
137 Genders, "Reform of the Offences against the Person Act: Lessons from the Law in Action" [1999] Crim. L.R. 689.
138 CPS, *Offences against the Person, Incorporating the Charging Standard*, see fn.33 above.
139 Sentencing Council, *Assault: Definitive Guideline* (2011), pp.4–5.
140 Home Office, *Racial Attacks* (1981).

aggravated offences.[141] In 1998 the then New Labour Government introduced the Crime and Disorder Act 1998 which set out the new offences of "racially aggravated" assault, assault occasioning actual bodily harm and s.20 grievous bodily harm.[142] Three years later, the Act was amended to include "religiously aggravated" offences.[143] The purpose of these offences is to significantly increase the penalty for racially or religiously motivated offences in order to recognise the enhanced level of harm that such crimes are likely to cause; not only to individual victims, but to entire minority ethnic communities.[144]

R. v Rogers [2007] 2 A.C. 62 (House of Lords)

BARONESS HALE:

"The mischiefs attacked by the aggravated versions of these offences are racism and xenophobia. Their essence is the denial of equal respect and dignity to people who are seen as somehow other. This is more deeply hurtful, damaging and disrespectful to the victims than the simple version of these offences. It is also more damaging to the community as a whole, by denying acceptance to members of certain groups not for their own sake but for the sake of something they can do nothing about."

The police now report the number of racially and religiously aggravated offences recorded each year. In 2012/13 there were 6,474 racially and/or religiously assaults recorded by the police.[145] The CSEW estimated that there were 224,000 racially and religiously motivated hate crimes in 2012/13.[146] The survey reports that 49 per cent of the total of all hate crime relates to assault (with or without injury) and wounding.

(a) *Meaning of "racially or religiously aggravated"*

Crime and Disorder Act 1998 s.28

"(1) An offence is racially or religiously aggravated for the purposes of sections 29 to 32 below if—

  (a) at the time of committing the offence, or immediately before or after doing so, the offender demonstrates towards the victim of the offence hostility based on the victim's membership (or presumed membership) of a racial or religious group; or

  (b) the offence is motivated (wholly or partly) by hostility towards members of a racial or religious group based on their membership of that group."

For an assault to be aggravated by either racial or religious hostility the defendant must first commit the basic offence of assault, assault occasioning actual bodily harm or s.20 grievous bodily harm. In addition, the prosecution must then prove either that the defendant "demonstrated" hostility (s.28(1)(a)) or that he was (partly) motivated by it (s.28(1)(b)). The difference between (1)(a) and (1)(b) has caused some confusion within the lower courts who have frequently failed to differentiate

[141] M. Malik, "'Racist Crime': Racially Aggravated Offences in the Crime and Disorder Act 1998 Part II' (1999) 62 M.L.R 409.

[142] Section 29. Assaults aggravated by hostilities demonstrated towards the victim's sexual orientation, disability and/or transgender identity are dealt with at sentencing, Criminal Justice Act 2003 s.146. As to whether these characteristics should be included within the Crime and Disorder Act, see Law Commission Paper No.213, *Hate Crime: The Case for Extending the Existing Offences* (2013).

[143] Amended by the Anti-terrorism, Crime and Security Act 2001 s.39.

[144] As evidenced by a number of empirical studies see, inter alia, G. Herek et al., "Hate Crime Victimization Among Lesbian, Gay and Bisexual Adults: Prevalence, Psychology Correlates and Methodological Issues" (1997) 12 *Journal of Interpersonal Violence* 195; J. McDevitt et al., "Consequences for Victims: A Comparison of Bias- and Non-bias-Motivated Assaults" (2001) 45 *American Behavioural Scientist* 697; P. Iganski, *Hate Crime and the City* (Bristol: The Policy Press, 2008); see also Home Office, fn.14 above.

[145] Home Office, fn.14 above.

[146] Home Office, fn.14 above.

between the two subsections.[147] Such confusion led Baroness Hale in *Rogers* to clarify the distinction by stating that s.28(1)(a) is concerned with the 'outward manifestation . . . of racial hostility' (a largely objective test), while section 28(1)(b) is concerned with the 'inner motivation of the offender' (a subjective test). The distinction will often be reduced to whether a defendant has used certain racist or anti-religious slurs during the commission of the assault (an objective demonstration of hostility) or whether there is evidence of premeditation based on his dislike of the victim's ethnic or religious identity (motivation).[148]

The legislation does not define "hostility" and thus whether a defendant demonstrates, or is motivated by it, is a question of fact for the magistrate or jury to determine.[149] Even where a defendant has admitted to using racial expletives during the commission of an assault, uncertainty has arisen as to whether the defendant's words must be *intended* by him to demonstrate racial or religious hostility or whether his words objectively express hostility in the eyes of the jury; regardless of whether the defendant actually meant his actions to express racial or religious hostility or not.

DPP v Woods [2002] EWHC 85 (Admin) (Queen's Bench Division, Administrative Court)

In this case the defendant assaulted a doorman at a nightclub out of frustration when his friend was refused entry. During the assault, D called the doorman a "black bastard".

MAURICE KAY J:

"The conclusions of the [trial] Justices are set out in these paragraphs from the case stated:

'. . . We found the Respondent's hostility to be borne out of his frustration and annoyance as a result of his companion being denied entry to the premises, and whilst he may have intended to cause offence by the words, this was not "hostility based on the victim's membership (or presumed membership) of a racial group". We believed that the Respondent's frame of mind was such that he would have abused any person standing in [D's] shoes by reference to an obvious physical characteristic had that individual happened to possess one . . .'

The case stated poses the single question: 'Did we err in law in concluding that, in all the circumstances of this case, the words "you black bastard" uttered a few moments before the assault were not such to prove that the Respondent had demonstrated hostility towards the victim based upon his membership of a racial group?'. . .

Section 28(1)(a) was not intended to apply only to those cases in which the offender is motivated solely, or even mainly, by racial malevolence. It is designed to extend to cases which may have a racially neutral gravamen but in the course of which there is demonstrated towards the victim hostility based on the victim's membership of a racial group. Any contrary construction would emasculate section 28(1)(a)."

Remitted to the Justices with a direction to convict

The result of *Woods* is that even where a defendant demonstrates hostility unthinkingly in the "heat of the moment", it matters not that the defendant felt no genuine hostility towards the victim's racial

---

[147] See M.A. Walters, "Conceptualizing 'Hostility' for Hate Crime Law: Minding 'the Minutiae' when Interpreting Section 28(1) (a) of the Crime and Disorder Act 1998" (2014) 34 Oxford J Legal Studies 47.

[148] E. Burney and G. Rose, *Racist Offences: How is the Law Working?* (2002). Note the offender need not be solely motivated by racial hostility, see s.28(3); *DPP v Green* [2004] EWHC QB 1225.

[149] Though the CPS does provide some guidance on this issue stating: "In the absence of a precise legal definition of hostility, consideration should be given to ordinary dictionary definitions, which include ill-will, ill-feeling, spite, contempt, prejudice, unfriendliness, antagonism, resentment, and dislike." Crown Prosecution Service, "Disability Hate Crime—Guidance on the Distinction Between Vulnerability and Hostility in the Context of Crimes Committed Against Disabled People" (2010) *http://www.cps.gov.uk/legal/d_to_g/disability_hate_crime_/*. [Accessed 30 April 30, 2014].

or religious group, only that he has demonstrated hostility (objectively) towards the victim during the commission of the offence, or immediately before or after.[150] One might question whether this is a fair outcome, especially if we consider that the offender will be labelled as a "racist" and be subject to a more severe punishment.

(b) *The meaning of "racial or religious group"*

Crime and Disorder Act 1998 s.28

"(4) In this section "racial group" means a group of persons defined by reference to race, colour, nationality (including citizenship) or ethnic or national origins.

(5) In this section 'religious group' means a group of persons defined by reference to religious belief or lack of religious belief."

The demonstration of hostility must be towards a victim's (presumed) membership of a racial or religious group. But what if the offender's demonstration does not refer explicitly to a specific racial, ethnic or national group? In the case of *Pal*[151] the defendant, a young Asian male, was ejected from a community centre by the caretaker, who was described as of "Asian appearance". In response, the defendant called the caretaker a "White man's arse licker" and a "brown Englishman" and later physically attacked him. Pal was charged with racially aggravated common assault under the Crime and Disorder Act 1998 s.29(1)(c). On appeal the Divisional Court held that the offence was not racially aggravated because his remarks were motivated by his anger at being ejected from the building and referred not to the victim's racial group but to his relationship with white people. Interestingly, the court was not convinced of the applicability of s.28(2) of the Act which states that "'membership', in relation to a racial or religious group, includes association with members of that group". The court noting instead that "it is quite unreal to suggest on the basis of the facts found that the Respondent is anti white men". The facts being that Pal had been with a group including white youths.[152]

In *Rogers*,[153] the defendant who was incapacitated by arthritis, was riding his mobility scooter along the pavement on his way home from a pub. Three women were walking back to their home after a birthday party in a local restaurant. An altercation took place as Rogers tried to get past them on the pavement. He then pursued them in an aggressive manner into a local kebab house where they had taken refuge, as they hid from him he shouted at them "bloody foreigners" as well as telling them to "go back to your own country". The appellant, who had been convicted of a racially aggravated public order offence, appealed on the basis that his comments had not been directed at a specific racial group. The House of Lords held that it did not matter that the phrase used did not refer to a specific race or nationality as it was necessary to take a "flexible, non-technical approach" when interpreting s.28(4).[154] As such, language that refers to the victim being from some *other* race or nationality should fall within the meaning of "racial group" under the Act.[155] As is the case with determining the presence of "hostility", decisions about whether words spoken by the defendant fall within the meaning of s.28(4) are questions of fact for the jury to determine.[156]

---

[150] In *DPP v Green* [2004] EWHC QB 1225, Rafferty J similarly held that "Section 28(1)(a), as distinct from (b), creates a racially aggravated offence without the requirement to prove racist motive. Disposition at the time is irrelevant" at [16]).

[151] *DPP v Pal* [2000] Crim. L.R 756.

[152] *Pal* has since been said to be heavily dependent upon its facts and it is likely that such demonstrations of hostility would fall within s.28(1) of the Act, *DPP v McFarlene* [2002] EWHC 485 (Admin); *Rogers* [2007] 2 A.C. 62.

[153] *R. v Rogers (Philip)* [2007] 2 A.C. 62.

[154] *Rogers* [2007] 2 A.C. 62 at [12].

[155] Other ambiguous phrases which have fallen within the meaning of "racial group" have included "immigrant doctor", central to the case of *AG ref (No.4 of 2004)* [2005] Crim L.R. 799 (CA) and "a monkey" *R. v SH* [2010] EWCA Crim 1931.

[156] Note that an offender can commit a racially aggravated offence against someone of the (presumed) same racial group,

(c) *Immediately before or after the commission of the offence*

Most racially and religiously aggravated assaults are committed where the defendant exclaims racist of anti-religious words *during* the commission of the offence. However, s.28(1)(a) also states the demonstration of hostility can be "immediately" before or after the commission of the offence. This has led to questions on how contemporaneous the hostility has to be to the actual basic offence. In *Parry*[157] the defendant referred to his victims as "Irish cunts" to the police some 20 minutes after the basic offence was committed. The Crown Court held that this amounted to a demonstration of racial hostility immediately after the offence was committed. On appeal the Divisional Court held that the words immediately before or after had to be given L

"[T]heir plain and ordinary meaning and consequently their effect was to make the subsection strike at words uttered or acts done in the immediate context of the substantive offence".[158]

The court found that the offence could not be racially aggravated given that the appellant had left the scene and had been sitting in his own home when he expressed racial hostility.

A very different decision was given in the case of *Babbs*[159] where the defendant had been verbally abusive towards the victim and his companion calling them "fucking foreigners" whilst they were queuing in a fast food restaurant. This resulted in a scuffle and an argument which was quelled by the staff manager. Between 5–15 minutes passed when the defendant gestured to the victim that they should leave the restaurant in order to fight, the victim then responded by calling the defendant "white trash", immediately after which the defendant headbutted the victim. Lord Latham held that the judge had been entitled to leave the matter of whether the hostility was demonstrated immediately before the assault to the jury. This was because the words used by the defendant at the initial confrontation "were capable of colouring the behaviour of the defendant throughout the subsequent events".

It appears thus that where hostility is demonstrated some 15 minutes before an assault it may be considered as part of a continuum of violence depending on the context of the altercation. Whereas if the hostility is demonstrated 20 minutes after the offence and it falls outside the original context of the altercation the hostility will become detached from the assault. As with almost all aspects of racially and religiously aggravated offences, context is everything.

(d) *Punishment*

If a common assault is "racially or religiously aggravated", the maximum sentence is two years' imprisonment—four times higher than the maximum for a non-aggravated assault. If an assault occasioning actual bodily harm is "racially or religiously aggravated" the maximum penalty is increased from five years' to seven years' imprisonment.[160] "Racially or religiously aggravated" s.20 grievous bodily harm is also increased to seven years' imprisonment.[161] Note that s.18 grievous bodily harm is not covered by the Crime and Disorder Act 1998. With the maximum penalty for this offence already set at life imprisonment there is no reason to aggravate the offence in law. In practice, the vast majority of sentences fall well below this maximum.

R. v White (Anthony Delroy) [2001] 1 W.L.R. 1352. Defendants from minority ethnic backgrounds can also commit racially aggravated offences against victims from the majority white population, see *Johnson v DPP* [2008] EWHC 509 (Admin).

[157] *Parry v DPP* [2005] A.C.D. 64.
[158] *Parry v DPP* [2005] A.C.D. 64 at [13].
[159] *R. v Babbs (Richard John)* [2007] EWCA Crim 2737.
[160] Crime and Disorder Act 1998 s.29, as amended by the Anti-Terrorism, Crime and Security Act 2001 s.39.
[161] Crime and Disorder Act 1998 s.29.

(v) Causing serious injury by dangerous driving

Road Traffic Act 1988 s.1A

"(1) A person who causes serious injury to another person by driving a mechanically propelled vehicle dangerously on a road or other public place is guilty of an offence." [162]

This new offence creates a constructive crime, much in the same way as the offence of causing death by dangerous driving does. The defendant must have been driving dangerously and as a result of this serious injury is caused. Section 1A states that "'serious injury' means . . . physical harm which amounts to grievous bodily harm for the purposes of the Offences against the Person Act 1861". This means that when determining what amounts to a serious injury the same case-law will apply to the Act that applies to ss.18 and 20 of the Offences against the Person Act (explored earlier in this chapter). It should be noted, however, that dangerous driving that causes serious psychological harm will not fall within the ambit of this offence. Cunningham has remarked that reference to grievous bodily harm in the Act is a missed opportunity and leaves us with an offence which suffers from the same lack of precision in meaning as the 1861 Act.[163]

Section 1A(3) applies the existing definition of dangerous driving in the Road Traffic Act to the new offence (below p.775). Section 2A states that:

"a person is to be regarded as driving dangerously if:

(a) the way he drives falls far below what would be expected of a competent and careful driver, and

(b) it would be obvious to a competent and careful driver that driving in that way would be dangerous."

The offence was created after campaigners sought to reduce the disparity between the law on causing death by dangerous driving and those cases where serious injury was caused.

The Parliamentary Under-Secretary of State for Justice (Mr Crispin Blunt), Hansard, HC Public Bill Committee, 18th Sitting, col.816 (October 13, 2011)

"The Government believe that it is vital to ensure that the criminal law is fully effective in addressing dangerous driving and its all too often appalling consequences. New clause 15 fills a long recognised gap by introducing a new offence of causing serious injury by dangerous driving. Causing death by dangerous driving is rightly considered a very serious crime, and that is reflected in the maximum penalty of 14 years imprisonment. Our law has always regarded cases where death results from criminality to be uniquely serious. That is why death by dangerous driving carries such a high maximum penalty . . .

For the vast majority of other dangerous driving cases, the maximum penalty of two years imprisonment provides the court with sufficient and proportionate powers to punish offenders. The Government do not agree with those who consider that the maximum penalty for dangerous driving should be raised at large. However, we are aware of the strong feelings about sentencing for dangerous driving cases that cause very severe injuries . . .

The issue is emotive. Campaigners have long suggested that the gap between the current maximum penalty of two years for dangerous driving and 14 years for death by dangerous driving is too wide. They believe that the

---

[162] Added by the Legal Aid, Sentencing and Punishment of Offenders Act 2012 s.143(2).
[163] S. Cunningham, "Taking 'Causing Serious Injury by Dangerous Driving' Seriously" [2012] Crim. LR. 261.

current two-year maximum for dangerous driving does not adequately reflect or address the serious injuries that can result from such driving. A victim can receive very serious life-changing injuries, but the maximum penalty remains at two years. We have therefore decided to target directly the offences where there is a clear and obvious gap in the law. We believe the new offence will enable the courts to deal appropriately with people convicted in these more serious cases. It will enable them to sentence more severely at the most serious and damaging end of the spectrum of dangerous driving incidents . . .

Some people maintain that the courts should focus on the standard of the driving rather than the consequences. They say that whether death or serious injuries result from a piece of bad driving is a matter of chance, however serious the result. I appreciate that argument, but only to a degree. While it is certainly true that the standard of driving must be the most important factor in judging culpability, the Government believe it important to ensure that we strike a balance between the level of criminal fault on the part of dangerous drivers and the consequences of that criminal fault for the victim. We believe that the maximum sentence of five years for the new offence will give the courts the ability better to address that balance."

(a) Punishment

It is clear from the above excerpt that the purpose of s.1A is not to extend the reach of the criminal law but to simply increase the penalties available to the courts when dealing with such cases. Previous to the enactment of s.1A, s.20 or s.35[164] of the Offences against the Person Act 1861 usually applied. Cunningham notes that:

"Anyone who drives dangerously prior to the coming into force of this offence is liable for dangerous driving. The key perceived benefit of the offence . . . is to allow courts access to greater sentencing powers to reflect the more serious consequences of a driver's actions, where those consequences are serious but fall short of death."[165]

Schedule 2 to the Road Traffic Offenders Act 1988 makes provision for the offence to be triable either way and sets out the maximum penalties available on summary conviction, this is six months' imprisonment or a fine of £5,000, or both and on indictment five years' imprisonment or a fine or both. In both cases a mandatory two-year minimum period of disqualification applies (unless special reasons are found not to disqualify) and endorsement.

C. Evaluation

The present structure of these offences, both in terms of substance and penalty structure, is little short of chaotic. Given the large difference in penalty, it is highly anomalous that the same mens rea suffices for both common assault and s.47 and that the difference in harm caused in these two offences need only be slight.[166] Section 20 is supposed to be a far more serious offence than s.47,[167] yet both carry the same maximum penalty (although, in practice, heavier sentences are imposed for s.20). Both s.18 and s.20 cover the same harm—grievous bodily harm; can the difference in their maximum penalties (life imprisonment and five years' imprisonment respectively) be justified exclusively in terms of their differing mens rea requirements?

It is clear that both the substance of these offences and their scale of punishments should be restructured so as to represent a true hierarchy of seriousness. Failure to do this "might either confuse

---

164   The offence of "injuring persons by furious driving".
165   Cunningham, "Taking 'Causing Serious Injury by Dangerous Driving' Seriously" [2012] Crim. LR. 261 at 265.
166   This situation has been exacerbated by the decision in *Brown* [1994] 1 A.C. 212 where it was held that consent could be a defence to common assault but not to assault occasioning actual bodily harm.
167   M. Cavadino and P. Wiles, "Seriousness of Offences: The Perceptions of Practitioners" [1994] Crim. L.R. 489.

moral judgments or bring the law into disrepute, or both".[168] Further, "principles of justice or fairness between different offenders require morally distinguishable offences to be treated differently and morally similar offences to be treated alike".[169]

How should this relative seriousness of the offences be determined? The present unhappy distinction between offences rests on a confused conjunction of mens rea and harm done. Law reform efforts in England have been mainly aimed at achieving a more rational combination of these two elements. Drawing on the work of the Law Commission,[170] the Government published a Consultation Document containing a Draft Bill with the following provisions.

Home Office, Violence: Reforming the Offences against the Person Act 1861, Draft Offences against the Person Bill 1998:

"1(1) A person is guilty of an offence if he intentionally causes serious injury to another. (Max: life imprisonment)

2(1) A person is guilty of an offence if he recklessly causes serious injury to another. (Max: seven years' imprisonment)

3(1) A person is guilty of an offence if he intentionally or recklessly causes injury to another. (Max: five years' imprisonment) . . .

4(1) A person is guilty of an offence if—

(a) he intentionally or recklessly applies force to or causes an impact on the body of another, or

(b) he intentionally or recklessly causes the other to believe that any such force or impact is imminent.

(2) No such offence is committed if the force or impact, not being intended or likely to cause injury, is in the circumstances such as is generally acceptable in the ordinary conduct of daily life and the defendant does not know or believe that it is in fact unacceptable to the other person. (Max: six months' imprisonment) . . .

10(1) A person is guilty of an offence if he makes to another a threat to cause the death of, or serious injury to, that other or a third person, intending that other to believe that it will be carried out. (Max: ten years' imprisonment) . . .

15(1) In this Act 'injury' means—

(a) physical injury, or

(b) mental injury.

(2) Physical injury does not include anything caused by disease but (subject to that) it includes pain, unconsciousness and any other impairment of a person's physical condition.

(3) Mental injury does not include anything caused by disease but (subject to that) it includes any impairment of a person's mental health.

(4) In its application to section 1 this section applies without the exceptions relating to things caused by disease.

[The Bill contains a definition of both intention (cl.14(1)) and recklessness (cl.14(2)), the latter being defined in terms of subjective awareness (*Cunningham* recklessness).]"

Such a restructuring represents an improvement on the present law. It does, however, raise several important questions. First, the distinction between intention and recklessness is thought to be so significant as to justify a maximum of life imprisonment for intentionally causing serious injury as opposed to seven years' imprisonment for recklessly causing serious injury. This is because there is "a definite moral and psychological difference between the two offences which it is appropriate for

[168] H.L.A. Hart, *Law, Liberty and Morality* (Palo Alto: Stanford University Press, 1963), p.36.
[169] Hart, *Law, Liberty and Morality* (1963), p.37.
[170] Law Commission Paper No.218, *Legislating the Criminal Code: Offences against the Person and General Principles* (1993).

the criminal law to reflect".[171] However, when it comes to causing lesser injuries, these concerns have evaporated into thin air and no distinction is drawn between intention and recklessness. It seems odd that the difference in moral blame between intention and recklessness should be regarded as sufficiently significant to warrant such a huge difference in sentencing maxima for serious injury and yet simply be dismissed as inconsequential for lesser injuries.

Secondly, there is the problem of defining injury. "Injury" includes pain. A slap across the face hurts; it causes pain. If that is so (and the defendant becomes liable for an offence carrying a maximum of five years' imprisonment), it would appear that assault will only cover the most trivial cases of force being applied. The Law Commission decided not to exclude minor injuries arguing, inter alia, that the level of injury would be taken into account by prosecutors in deciding the level of charge. However, research has revealed that the seriousness of the injury does not play a significant role in the decision to charge and prosecute.[172] While the CPS *Charging Standard* now emphasises that the degree of injury will determine the level of the charge in most cases,[173] it is not yet known to what extent this is followed in practice.

Thirdly, the definition of "injury" includes "impairment of a person's mental health". This is potentially extremely broad and could encompass many forms of psychological injury currently excluded, such as anxiety and palpitations. The Law Commission felt that this would cover serious mental injury, such as post-traumatic stress disorder that is a medically recognised illness, but will exclude mere anxiety or distress.[174] There is, however, nothing in the Draft Bill to suggest that such a limitation need be imposed. Further, if the Law Commission felt that minor mental impairments should not qualify, it is odd that minor physical injuries were not similarly excluded.

Fourthly, the Bill only draws a distinction between serious injury and injury and leaves the former undefined. In the United States the Model Penal Code has defined "serious injury" as "bodily injury which creates a substantial risk of death or which causes serious, permanent disfigurement, or protracted loss or impairment of the function of any bodily member or organ".[175] There is a case that the difference between serious injury which is of a temporary nature (such as a broken limb) and injuries which are permanently disfiguring or leave the victim in a permanent vegetative state[176] is so fundamental that it should be reflected at the substantive, rather than at the sentencing, stage.

A final question needs to be asked: must the restructuring of these offences be based *entirely* on new combinations of mens rea and harm? Could not other factors also be utilised in informing our moral assessments (to be translated into legal judgments) of the relative seriousness of offences? For instance, Gardner[177] rejects the Law Commission's view that the structure of these offences should be restricted to variations in the configuration of mens rea and resulting harm as this "does not capture all that is interesting, or rationally significant, about the wrong".[178] What matters is the *wrong* involved and not just the harm caused and "the wrong is that of bringing the harm about in that way. In morality, as in law, it matters how one brings things about."[179] Gardner argues that ss.20 and 47

---

[171]   Law Commission Paper No.218, *Legislating the Criminal Code: Offences against the Person and General Principles* (1993), para.8.3, citing the Criminal Law Revision Committee, 14th Report, *Offences against the Person* (1980), para.152.

[172]   C.M.V. Clarkson et al., "Assaults: The Relationship between Seriousness, Criminalisation and Punishment" [1994] Crim. L.R. 4.

[173]   CPS, *Offences against the Person, Incorporating the Charging Standard*, see fn.33 above.

[174]   Law Commission Paper No.218, *Legislating the Criminal Code: Offences against the Person and General Principles* (1993), paras 15.26–15.29. This result has now been broadly achieved by *Ireland* [1997] 4 All E.R. 225.

[175]   Proposed Official Draft s.210.0(3).

[176]   As in *R. v Cross (Adam Stuart)* [2009] 1 Cr. App. R. (S.) 34 where it was stated of the victim that "in practical terms . . . his life was really ended".

[177]   Gardner, "Rationality and the Rule of Law in Offences against the Person" [1994] C.L.J. 502.

[178]   Gardner, "Rationality and the Rule of Law in Offences against the Person" [1994] C.L.J. 502 at 511.

[179]   Gardner, "Rationality and the Rule of Law in Offences against the Person" [1994] C.L.J. 502 at 505.

are neither more serious nor less serious than each other, but rather each belongs to its "own family of offences"[180]: s.20 is a crime of violence; s.47 is a crime of assault which is "not a crime of violence. Its essential quality lies in the invasion by one person of another's body space."[181] Drawing an analogy with the Theft Acts where theft, obtaining by deception (now replaced by fraud), false accounting, making off without payment, etc. are differentiated, not by the harm done (the same property might have been lost), but by the different mode of wrongdoing, he points to lesser known provisions of the Offences against the Person Act 1861 where distinctions are drawn between different modes of violence. For example:

> "Section 21 deals with choking, suffocating, or strangling; section 22 deals with the use of stupefacients and overpowering substances, sections 23 and 24 with poisoning, section 26 with starving and exposing to the elements; sections 28 to 30 deal with burning, maiming, disfiguring and disabling by use of explosives . . ."

Such offences, he claims "are notable for the moral clarity with which they are differentiated".[182] In much the same vein, Horder argues that in terms of fair labelling the Law Commission's recommendations amount to "a slide into the vice of moral vacuity".[183] There are "important qualitative moral distinctions" between deliberately punching someone hard and breaking his nose and castrating a person; these distinctions should be marked in the offence committed.[184]

It would be possible to structure offences not only by the degree and type of harm involved, but also by *how* the harm is caused or the context in which it is caused. Such an approach, however, can only be accepted if there is something *morally significant* (as opposed to just different) about the method by which the harm is caused or the context in which it is caused. As has been stated:

> "One may question, however, whether the awful details of the worst forms of violence need to feature in the *definition* of offences . . . The moral resonance of an offence need not require details of the *modus operandi*."[185]

When would the context or method of committing the crime be sufficiently morally significant to justify the creation of a specific offence? The following are possible examples. Use of a firearm could justify special offence status because of the great fear such use generates and because firearms are so dangerous rendering victims especially vulnerable. There is an offence of torture under the Criminal Justice Act 1988 s.134 but only if committed by a public official or person acting in an official capacity. There is an argument that the use of torture involves a sufficiently significant wrong to justify broadening this offence to covers all instances of torture. The willingness of the torturer to inflict such pain (along with whatever injury is caused) demonstrates greater culpability. The actual pain caused (along with the actual injury) constitutes a morally significant harm. Recently, there have been calls for the introduction of a special offence of domestic violence on the basis that the distinctive wrong in this context is the systematic nature of such violence (usually), the breach of trust involved and that it might shape public attitudes and police policies towards such violence.[186]

---

[180]   Gardner, "Rationality and the Rule of Law in Offences against the Person" [1994] C.L.J. 502 at 507.
[181]   Gardner, "Rationality and the Rule of Law in Offences against the Person" [1994] C.L.J. 502 at 507–508.
[182]   Gardner, "Rationality and the Rule of Law in Offences against the Person" [1994] C.L.J. 502 at 515.
[183]   J. Horder, "Rethinking Non-Fatal Offences against the Person" (1994) 14 O.J.L.S. 335 at 340.
[184]   Horder, "Rethinking Non-Fatal Offences against the Person" (1994) 14 O.J.L.S. 335 at 342.
[185]   A.P. Simester, J.R. Spencer, G.R. Sullivan and G.J. Virgo, *Criminal Law: Theory and Doctrine*, 5th edn (Oxford: Hart Publishing, 2013), p.461.
[186]   V. Tadros, "The Distinctiveness of Domestic Abuse: A Freedom Based Account", in R. A. Duff and S. Green (eds), *Defining*

One could go even further and argue that other factors such as the identity of the victim or defend-ant or the motive underlying the crime could significantly mark out the wrong involved. Examples of such an approach under the current law include assault on a police constable contrary to s.89 of the Police Act 1996[187] and racially or religiously aggravated assault under the Crime and Disorder Act 1998. Taking racial assault as an example, the distinctive wrong here is that the assault is not simply against a person as an individual but constitutes an attack on them as a member of a racial group. Not only is injury caused to the individual, but the assault also expresses hatred or contempt of an entire racial group. The victim is particularly vulnerable. The normal assault-prevention mechanisms commonly employed (looking away; doing nothing to precipitate the assault) are worthless if one is attacked simply because of one's race. This distinctive wrong needs to be marked out by a separate offence with a different sentencing maximum. It is difficult to explain, therefore, why only racial and religious aggravated offences are specifically proscribed under the criminal law, while offences aggravated by sexual orientation, disability and transgender identity hostility remain within sentenc-ing provisions only. Indeed the Law Commission 2013 consultation paper on hate crime law reform explores whether these three latter characteristics should be included under the Crime and Disorder Act 1998.[188] The consultation paper explains:

"In the present context, the 'racially/religiously aggravated' label carries a strong stigma which reflects the fact that hate crimes are considered to be more serious, and different in kind, to basic offences . . . By contrast, under the present law, a defendant who demonstrates hostility on the basis of disability while carrying out an assault will simply be convicted of assault. While the hostility can be taken into account at sentencing—and discussed in open court during the sentencing hearing— the label attaching to the offending behaviour will be silent as to the element of aggravation."[189]

A major problem with this whole approach is that it can lead to over-specificity. One could be left with a bewildering array of offences—the vice of "particularism"[190]—each marking a separate wrong but with a failure to distinguish the offences *in terms of seriousness*. Fair labelling should involve not only capturing the essential wrong involved but also communicating the relative seriousness of that wrongdoing.[191] One response to this is that all these various factors should be dealt with at the sentencing stage rather than through the creation of specific offences. The present Sentencing Guidelines list a wide range of general aggravating factors, including the use of a weapon, a signifi-cant degree of premeditation, and whether the defendant demonstrated hostility against the victim's identity characteristic:

Crimes: Essays on the Special Part of the Criminal Law (Oxford: OUP, 2005). For a critique of Tadros' view, see M. Burton, *Legal Responses to Domestic Violence* (Abingdon: Routledge, 2008), pp.67–68. Burton finds the practical arguments for a separate offence "unconvincing" and doubts that having a separate offence "can effectively communicate a message that domestic violence is a serious form of misconduct" (p.68). The recently introduced Domestic Violence (Legal Framework) Bill 2013–14 makes provision for the investigation of allegations of domestic violence, for duties on the police in respect of domestic violence, for risk assessment and training in connection with related criminal proceedings in England and Wales.

[187] See also: assaulting a clergyman in the discharge of his duties (Offences against the Person Act 1861 s.36); assaulting a magistrate in the exercise of his duty concerning the preservation of a vessel in distress or a wreck (s.37). These offences would be abolished under the Draft Criminal Code, in line with the thinking of the Criminal Law Revision Committee that the victim's identity should generally be relevant to sentencing only and not to the definition of the offence (14th Report, para.162).

[188] Law Commission Paper No.213, *Hate Crime: The Case for Extending the Existing Offences* (2013).

[189] Law Commission Paper No.213, *Hate Crime: The Case for Extending the Existing Offences* (2013), pp.79–80.

[190] Horder, "Rethinking Non-Fatal Offences against the Person" (1994) 14 O.J.L.S. 335 at 340 at 338.

[191] Gardner does not accept that fair labelling is concerned with marking relative seriousness between offences. See, further, C.M.V. Clarkson, *Understanding Criminal Law*, 4th edn (London: Sweet & Maxwell, 2005), p.191.

The Law Commission is set to re-review the law on offences against the person in 2014. If and when a decision is made to restructure the various offences of violence, the issues raised in this section need careful consideration. When are the circumstances/context of the crime sufficiently morally signifi-cant to justify the creation of a dedicated offence—as opposed to being dealt with at the sentencing stage? In implementing such reforms, it is important to remember that individual criminal offences should communicate the essence of the wrongdoing involved. It is also important that the relative seriousness of such offences be communicated and that the criminal law as a whole convey a morally-informative set of messages.

II. Sexual Offences

A. Introduction

There is a large and increasing number of offences that proscribe certain forms of sexual behaviour. They vary widely in the type of harm encompassed, from the very serious (such as rape) to the less significant (such as exposure). Prior to 2003, the law was condemned as "archaic, incoherent and discriminatory".[192] The Sexual Offences Act 2003 resulted from a process of consultation that lasted over three years and had as its objectives the need to modernise the law to reflect "changes in society and social attitudes";[193] to clarify the law, in particular in relation to core concepts such as consent; to improve protection for vulnerable groups, such as children; to ensure that the penalties available were commensurate with the gravity of the offence; and to improve the conviction rate for the offence of rape. It constituted a fundamental reform of the law relating to sexual offences. Many of the changes made were very welcome but concern has remained that the criminalisation of some behaviour is unwarranted and that there is a good deal of complexity in and overlap between the 52 offences contained within the Act. Moreover, as will be seen, conviction rates have largely been unaffected by the changes. This section will focus upon the crime of rape but it will also consider assault by penetra-tion, sexual assault, causing someone to engage in sexual activity and offences against children to illustrate both the strengths and weaknesses of the law.

1. The level of offending

It is extremely difficult to assess the extent of offending in this area. What is clear is that, whether one is talking about consensual but unlawful under-age sexual intercourse, familial sex offences, sexual assault or rape, the official statistics reveal only a tiny proportion of offending. According to such sta-tistics, 59,466 sexual offences were recorded by the police in 2012/13, of which 18,293 were rapes.[194] Both rape and other sexual offences showed a 17 per cent increase for the year ending September 2013 compared with the previous year.[195] The current levels of reported sexual offences now stand in stark contrast to the number of offences reported 60–70 years ago, for example in 1947 just 240 rapes were recorded by the police.[196] Whilst some of this may be explicable in terms of increasing levels of

---

192 *Protecting the Public, Strengthening Protection against Sexual Offenders and Reforming the Law on Sexual Offences* (Cmnd.5668, 2002), para.8.
193 *Protecting the Public, Strengthening Protection against Sexual Offenders and Reforming the Law on Sexual Offences* (Cmnd.5668, 2002), para.4.
194 Office of National Statistics, *Crime in England and Wales, Year Ending September 2013* (2014), p.38.
195 The survey reports that "[e]vidence suggests some of this increase is likely to be a result of Operation Yewtree, connected to the Jimmy Savile inquiry", Office of National Statistics, *Crime in England and Wales, Year Ending September 2013* (2014), p.39.
196 Cambridge Department of Science Report, *Sexual Offences*, (1957), p.12.

violence, much more is due to an increased willingness to report rape. Despite the fact that reporting and recording rates for rape have gone up, at the same time the level of convictions has fallen.[197]

(i) The dark figure of offending

Over the last two decades research has done much to shed some light, generally, on the dark figures of crime. Although no national random sample study of either the incidence or prevalence of rape has taken place, wider surveys of victimisation have provided some insight.[198] Analysis of CSEW data in 2013 found that 2.5 per cent of females and 0.4 per cent of males had reported experiencing some form of sexual offence in the previous 12 months.[199] Based on these prevalence rates, it has been estimated that are between 430,000 and 517,000 adult victims of sexual offences each year.[200] In the vast majority of serious sexual offences the offender is known to the victim. Data gathered between 2007 and 2012 found that 56 per cent of these offences were committed by the victim's partner or former partner, 33 per cent of offenders were known[201] to the victim, leaving only 10 per cent of serious sexual offences that were committed by a stranger.[202] It is also estimated that only about 15 per cent of all rapes are reported to the police; further, 28 per cent of those who had been raped had told no-one about it.[203] While it is clear that females are at the greatest risk of sexual offences, it is probable that male rape is even more under-reported than that upon females.[204]

Victim surveys, as well as providing an insight into the amount of crime, also enable a picture to be built up about the way crime, and, in particular, the fear of crime, affects people's lives. All the evidence supports the view that women's lives and freedom of movement are curtailed by the fear of violence and, in particular, the fear of rape. Carole Sheffield describes this as a form of "sexual terrorism" arguing that "all females, irrespective of race, class, physical or mental abilities, and sexual orientation, are potential victims—at any age, at any time, or in any place".[205] The impacts of sexual violence can also be severe, for example over half (56 per cent) of victims surveyed by the CSEW experienced mental or emotional problems.[206] A further 25 per cent of victims reported having problems trusting people or having difficulty in other relationships, and of particular concern was that 4 per cent of victims attempted suicide.

There is one last insight provided by victim studies that needs to be considered: why are rape and other sexual assaults so under-reported? The most frequently cited reason why victims do not report incidents include: feeling that it would be "embarrassing", that they "didn't think the police could do much to help", that the incident was "too trivial/not worth reporting", or that they saw it as a "private/

---

[197]   Office for Criminal Justice Reform, *Convicting Rapists and Protecting Victims—Justice for Victims of Rape* (2006), p.8.

[198]   L. Kelly, J. Lovatt and L. Regan, *A Gap or a Chasm? Attrition in Reported Rape Cases* (2005) (HORS No.293), p.14. As the authors state, findings from these wider surveys have been subject to criticism and may understate the extent of sexual offending.

[199]   Ministry of Justice, Home Office and the Office for National Statistics, *An Overview of Sexual Offending in England and Wales* (2013) p.11.

[200]   Ministry of Justice, Home Office and the Office for National Statistics, *An Overview of Sexual Offending in England and Wales* (2013) p.11.

[201]   The "known" category includes: a date, friend, neighbour, an acquaintance (outside work or school/college/university), colleague/peer from work or school/college/university, or a person in a position of trust or authority.

[202]   Ministry of Justice, Home Office and the Office for National Statistics, *An Overview of Sexual Offending in England and Wales* (2013), p.16.

[203]   Ministry of Justice, Home Office and the Office for National Statistics, *An Overview of Sexual Offending in England and Wales* (2013), p.17.

[204]   See A.W. Coxall et al., "Lifetime Prevalence, Characteristics, and Associated Problems of Non-Consensual Sex in Men: Cross Sectional Survey" (1999) 318 *British Medical Journal* 846.

[205]   C.J. Sheffield, "Hate Violence", in P.S. Rothenberg (ed.), *Race, Class, and Gender in the United States: An Integrated Study* (New York: St Martins, 1995), p.393.

[206]   Office for National Statistics, *Focus on: Violent Crime and Sexual Offences*, 2011/12 (2013), p.75.

family matter and not police business".[207] Research has also indicated that complainants fear they may receive unsympathetic and even hostile, humiliating treatment, at the hands of the police—at a time when they are at their most vulnerable—and then by the courts.[208] Victims may well be put off reporting where they know that defence barristers or the defendant may take them, stage by detailed stage, through the offence.[209] Both male and female victims have likened this to being raped again,[210] although there is now some evidence to suggest that the experience of giving evidence has improved.[211] Women believe that the courts accept myths about male behaviour; that, once aroused by women, men get "carried away"[212] and, in addition, younger women may fear that they might be blamed, especially if alcohol or drugs were involved.[213] In short, many victims of rape feel that they will be the ones on trial.[214] Further, victims of familial and marital rape are often put under severe emotional, as well as physical, pressure not to report and may feel divided loyalties. In the case of rape by partners or husbands, many will not even define what has happened to them as rape "until the assaults reache[s] a level of brutality associated with stranger rape".[215] Thus, it would be dangerously wrong to conclude that the crime is not reported because there had, in fact, been consent or that the rape had had no serious or lasting impact upon the victim.

(ii) From reporting to conviction

Even if a rape is reported, the chances of securing a conviction are very low. Very large numbers of cases continue to "drop out" of the criminal process or are lost from the system before trial.

L. Kelly, J. Lovett and L. Regan, A Gap or a Chasm? Attrition Rates in Reported Rape Cases (Home Office Research Study No.293) (2005), pp.30–31:

"Research to date in adversarial legal systems has identified four key points at which attrition occurs. The first point is the decision to report itself; estimates of the reporting rate range from 5 to 25 per cent. Even using the highest reporting rate estimate, three quarters of cases never reach the first hurdle within the CJS.[216] The second

---

207   Ministry of Justice, Home Office and the Office for National Statistics, *An Overview of Sexual Offending in England and Wales* (2013), p.17.

208   J. Temkin, *Rape and the Legal Process*, 2nd edn (Oxford: OUP, 2002), pp.3–4, 17–19. Research suggests that improvements have been made to police practice and are continuing to be made by the provision of guidance and training for police and rape prosecutors. However, good practice is not universal: see further, Her Majesty's Crown Prosecution Service Inspectorate and Her Majesty's Inspectorate of Constabulary, *Without Consent: A Report on the Joint Review of the Investigation and Prosecution of Rape Offences* (2007).

209   See further, J. Temkin, "Prosecuting and Defending Rape: Perspectives from the Bar" (2000) 27 J. Law and Society 219.

210   A statement made by, for example, Julia Mason who in 1996 was cross-examined for six days by the defendant, Ralston Edwards (who wore the same clothes that he had worn on the night of the attack). He was later given two life sentences. Partly as a consequence of the outcry surrounding this trial, the automatic right of defendants to conduct their own defence was ended: Youth Justice and Criminal Evidence Act 1999 s.34. See further, Temkin, "Prosecuting and Defending Rape: Perspectives from the Bar" (2000) 27 J. Law and Society 219 at 320–324; M.W. Stewart, S.A. Dobbin and S.I. Gatowski, "'Real Rapes' and 'Real Victims': The Shared Reliance on Common Cultural Definitions of Rape" [1996] IV *Feminist Legal Studies* 159 and P. Rumney "Male Rape in the Courtroom: Issues and Concerns" [2001] Crim. L.R. 205.

211   M.R. Kebbell, C.M.F. O'Kelly and E. Gilchrist, "Rape Victims' Experiences of Giving Evidence in English Courts" (2007) 14 *Psychiatry, Psychology and the Law* 111.

212   Judicial Studies Board, *Equal Treatment Bench Book* (2004), para.6.1.7.

213   Kelly, Lovatt and Regan, *A Gap or a Chasm? Attrition in Reported Rape Cases* (2005) (HORS No.293), p.32.

214   See further, Fawcett Society, *Interim Report on Women and Offending, The Commission on Women and the Criminal Justice System* (2003).

215   Kelly, Lovatt and Regan, *A Gap or a Chasm? Attrition in Reported Rape Cases* (2005) (HORS No.293), p.34.

216   Research identifies, as a cause for the concern, the inflated rate of "no criming" at this stage by the police as a result, in part, of prejudices concerning false allegations: Her Majesty's Crown Prosecution Service Inspectorate and Her Majesty's Inspectorate of Constabulary, *Without Consent: A Report on the Joint Review of the Investigation and Prosecution of Rape*

involves the police investigation stage—the initial response, forensic examination, statement taking, evidence gathering and arrest and/or interviewing of suspects—between half and three-quarters of reported cases are lost here. The third point relates to the minority of cases that are referred through to prosecution, where a proportion are discontinued. The final point is the even smaller number of cases that reach court, where between one-third and over one-half of those involving adults result in acquittals. At each of the points the possibility of withdrawal by the victim exists, although the largest number of these occur during the reporting and investigative stages . . .

This is only part of the story, however, since attrition varies according to the characteristics of the case. The most recent studies in England, Wales and Scotland concur that cases involving children are more likely to be prosecuted and to result in convictions. Adult rape cases have higher attrition rates, especially if they depart from the 'real rape' template."[217]

It is clear that the nature of cases being reported to the police has changed (not least, as we shall see, because the definition of rape has been widened) and that many instances involve people who knew each other (either as acquaintances or intimates) prior to the incident giving rise to the complaint. However, some caution should be exercised in relying upon this as the explanation of low conviction rates. The old category of "acquaintance" rape had included those who have met within the previous 24 hours and even included a complainant who was stopped by her assailant to give directions.[218] Such cases are hardly any different from stranger rape cases and mean that there can be no straight-forward explanation for low conviction rates based on prior relationship. The presence or absence of violence may well be as significant as any prior relationship.[219] Also important, for example, are the time between offence and report, the quality of medical examination, the police force area and whether the offence is linked to other investigations of sexual assault against another victim.[220]

Given the differences that exist between sexual offences that can be recorded and those which can be prosecuted under the Sexual Offences Act, and the effect of various other factors mentioned above, the Office for National Statistics has recently stated that calculating convictions rates as the number of people convicted of rape as a proportion of all rape crimes recorded is "incorrect and misleading in terms of presenting evidence on convictions for rape".[221] Perhaps more reliable then is to examine the conviction rates for cases that come before the Crown Court. The conviction rate in 2011 for completed trials for sexual offences in the Crown Court was 61.6 per cent.[222] In cases involving rape of a female the conviction rate is lower at 51.1 per cent in 2011; though this represents an increase of 9.9 percent-age points since 2005.[223]

While the increased conviction rate is to be welcomed, there is still much to be done by way of encouraging victims to report sexual offences, improving upon the way the police process cases, and

---

Offences (2007), pp.9–10. See also J.M. Brown, C. Hamilton and D. O'Neill, "Characteristics Associated With Rape Attrition and the Role Played by Scepticism or Legal Rationality by Investigators and Prosecutors" (2007) 13 *Psychology, Crime and Law* 355.

[217] See further, L. Kelly and J. Lovett, *Different Systems, Similar Outcomes? Tracking Attrition in Reported Rape Cases in Eleven Countries: European Briefing* (2009).

[218] In one study of the 194 cases concerning acquaintances, 102 had met within this period: J. Harris and S. Grace, *A Question of Evidence? Investigating and Prosecuting Rape in the 1990s* (London: Routledge, 1999); see also J. Gregory and S. Lees, *Policing Sexual Assault* (London: Home Office, 1999).

[219] Harris and Grace, *A Question of Evidence? Investigating and Prosecuting Rape in the 1990s* (1999), and see further, Temkin, *Rape and the Legal Process*, 2nd edn (Oxford: OUP, 2002), pp.25–30.

[220] HMCPSI and HMIC, above fn.208, p.iv. See also Fawcett Society, *Regional Rape Conviction Rates 2007* (2009).The report highlights alarming differences between the conviction rates of different police forces. See further, M. Coy, C. Kelly and J. Foord, *Maps of Gaps 2: the Postcode Lottery of Violence Against Women Services in Britain* (London: End Violence Against Women Coalition, 2009).

[221] Ministry of Justice, above fn.199, p.4.

[222] Ministry of Justice, above fn.199, p.34.

[223] Ministry of Justice, above fn.199, p.34.

increasing conviction rates.[224] Baroness Stern in her review into how rape complaints are handled by public authorities concluded that the policies and laws enacted since 2003 are the "rights ones", however the real failure remains with their implementation.[225] In 2006 the Government consulted on measures that could further strengthen the legal framework and improve the care that victims receive.[226] One significant change which was considered, which would permit expert evidence to be given on the *general* impact sexual assaults may have upon victims (explaining why, for example, victims may not resist, why they may delay in reporting the incident or why they may present a calm demeanour in court[227]), met with a mixed response and has led the Government to conclude merely that it will continue to look for ways in which it might be done.[228] It seems that reform is unlikely in the short term. In the meantime, a trial judge has been criticised by the Court of Appeal for going too far in trying to explain why a victim might delay reporting the offence without also providing an explanation that some women fabricate allegations.[229] Permitting the defence to admit general expert evidence might help to offset concerns about possible lack of balance in judges' summing up and would be a welcome reform, but by itself it would not be enough to change deep-rooted popular understandings of rape.[230] As the myths surrounding rape have been persuasively argued to be at the heart of the attrition rate and low conviction rates, affecting the attitudes not just of the public but of police, legal professionals and jurors, it is to this subject we now turn.[231]

2. Rape in context

Whether the crime involves so-called date rape, rape by a stranger or by a partner or friend, the rhetoric of the law and its reality can only be truly understood against the backdrop of societal attitudes to women and rape generally.

Allison Morris, Women, Crime and Criminal Justice (1987), pp.165–181:

"Most of us believe we know what rape is, but our knowledge is derived from social not legal definitions. 'True' rape in popular imagination involves the use of weapons, the infliction of serious injury and occurs in a lonely place late at night. The 'true' rapist is over-sexed, sexually frustrated or mentally ill, and is a stranger. The

---

[224] Home Office, *The Sexual Offences Act 2003: A Stocktake of the Effectiveness of the Act since its Implementation* (2006), p.3. The report by HMCPSI and HMI concludes that in so far as investigation and prosecution is concerned the key challenge is to ensure that practice is uniformly of a high standard rather than making fundamental changes to procedures; above fn.208, p.161.

[225] Baroness A. Stern, *A report by Baroness Vivien Stern CBE of an independent review into how rape complaints are handled by public authorities in England and Wales* (London: Home Office, 2010).

[226] Office for Criminal Justice Reform, above fn.197, p.4.

[227] In one study of reported rapes less than half were reported on the same day as the offence, A. Feist et al., *Investigating and Detecting Recorded Offences of* Rape (2007) (Home Office Online Report 18/07), p.24. See further, L. Ellison and V.E. Munro, "Reacting to Rape: Exploring Mock Jurors' Assessments of Complainant Credibility" (2009) 49 Brit. J. Criminol. 202 and L. Ellison and V.E. Munro, "Turning Mirrors in Windows? Assessing the Impact of (Mock) Juror Education in Rape Trials" (2009) 49 Brit. J. Criminol. 363.

[228] Office for Criminal Justice Reform, *Convicting Rapists and Protecting Victims—Justice for Victims of Rape: Response to Consultation* (2007), p.21. See further, J. Temkin and B. Krahé, *Sexual Assault and the Justice Gap: A Question of Attrition* (Oxford: Hart Publishing, 2008), pp.57–62, 161–167 and L. Ellison, "Promoting Effective Case-building in Rape Cases: A Comparative Perspective" (2007) Crim. L.R. 691.

[229] *R. v D* [2008] EWCA Crim 2557. The Court of Appeal also found it unnecessary for the judge to explain that rape within a relationship could be as traumatic as stranger rape because of the breach of trust involved. See N. Kibble, "*R v D*: Rape Within a Relationship—Delayed Allegations—Summing Up" (2009) Crim. L.R. 591.

[230] Centre for Law, Gender and Sexuality, *Response to the Office for Criminal Justice Reform's Consultation Paper: Convicting Rapists and Protecting Victims of Rape—Justice for Victims of Rape* (2006).

[231] Temkin and Krahé, *Sexual Assault and the Justice Gap: A Question of Attrition* (Oxford: Hart Publishing, 2008).

'true' rape victim is a virgin (or has had no extra-marital affairs), was not voluntarily in the place where the act took place, fought to the end and has bruises to show for it . . . [T]he reason [other] kinds of situations are not seen as rape is the strength of the assumptions we hold about rape . . . I will now examine some of these assumptions . . .

'Rape is impossible'
. . . [Some] criminologists have argued that to force a woman into intercourse is an impossible task in most cases if the woman is conscious and extreme pain is not inflicted. These beliefs have become part of rape folklore (. . . 'a woman with her skirt up can run faster than a man with his trousers down' and the like) and embedded in the practice of criminal justice professionals . . .

'Women want to be raped'
This assumption has its roots in Freudian beliefs about the masochistic nature of female sexuality . . . rape is believed to dominate women's sexual fantasies . . .

'"No" means "Yes"'
Nineteenth-century women—or, at least ladies—were seen as asexual and presumed not to enjoy sex. Whereas they were passive and submitted (rather than consented) to the sex act, men were viewed as the aggressors and the initiators, and as having sexual needs. These beliefs have resonances today . . . Men are expected to make advances (otherwise the woman thinks she is unattractive) and women are expected to be sexually attractive and, at the same time, both coy and flirtatious. They are expected to play hard to get, to need to be seduced . . . A judge in a recent rape trial in Cambridge told the jury that women sometimes say 'no' when they mean 'yes' and to remember the expression 'Stop it. I like it'[232] . . .

'"Yes" to one, then "yes" to all.'[233]

'The victim was asking for it'
In essence, this assumption implies that the victim should not have dressed like that (*e.g.* with no bra), behaved like that (*e.g.* hitch-hiked), gone to places like that (*e.g.* singles' bars) . . . Amir, in his study of rape, developed the notion of victim precipitation. His definition is both extremely broad and stresses the offender's interpretation of the victim's behaviour, not the victim's. 'The victim actually—or so it was interpreted by the offender—agreed to sexual relations but retracted . . . or did not resist strongly enough when the suggestion was made by the offender.' The term applies also to cases in which the victim enters vulnerable situations charged sexually (*Patterns in Forcible Rape* (1971), p. 266). Earlier, he seems to define any form of female behaviour as rape-precipitating . . . Despite this, only 19 per cent of the rapes in Amir's sample could be so 'explained'. . .

'Rape is a cry for vengeance'
. . . Standard legal texts on evidence and procedure . . . warn of the danger of women contriving false charges of sexual offences.[234] And as recently as 1984, the Criminal Law Revision Committee prefaced its report on sex offences with the words that 'by no means every accusation of rape is true' (15th Report, Sexual Offences, Cmnd.9213, p.5). . . [235]

'Rape is a sexual act'
. . . The popular conception now is that rape is sexually motivated: this is most apparent in accounts offered to excuse rape. Smart and Smart (*Women, Sexuality and Social Control* (1978), pp.98–99) provide examples of this from media coverage of rape:

---

[232] See further, S. Lees, *Ruling Passions: Sexual Violence, Reputation and the Law* (Buckingham: Open University Press, 1997), pp.75–78 and S. Schulhofer, *Unwanted Sex: The Culture of Intimidation and the Failure of the Law* (Cambridge: Harvard College, 1998), pp.47–68.

[233] For discussion of the extent to which evidence of past sexual experience can be introduced, see pp.646–647.

[234] The Court of Appeal has recently commented that every false allegation increases the plight of women who have been victims of rape by making the offence harder to prove and affecting the confidence of a jury to return a verdict of guilty: *R. v McKenning (Zara Louise)* [2008] EWCA Crim 2301. Where prosecutions for perverting the course of justice are made as a consequence of false allegations of rape, a custodial sentence is almost inevitable: *R. v Beeton (Elizabeth)* [2008] EWCA Crim 1421.

[235] This distrust of complainants resulted in the development of rules of corroboration. It was not until 1994 that it ceased to be mandatory to give a warning as to the danger of uncorroborated evidence: below p.646.

'The pregnancy of B's wife may have been one of the reasons for his committing the offence.'
'R attacked her five days before his wife gave birth to their first child.' "

Sexual gratification, however, may not be the major reason for rape. As Brownmiller says, "the penis is deployed as a weapon",[236] and research conducted amongst convicted rapists suggests that the desire to dominate and humiliate the rape victim (often coupled with revenge motives) features most commonly.[237] In furtherance of this motive the attractiveness of the victim is not a vital ingredient, although it is a paradox in a society demanding its females to make themselves attractive that if the rape victim has done so, she may well be condemned for it. Whilst most rape victims are young,[238] what matters more than physical appearance is vulnerability. As one rape victim said:

"[W]hat I exuded that night was not sexuality . . . but vulnerability . . . I, by virtue of my size and gender . . . was recognisable to the rapist as easy game and an exemplary target for his generalised misogyny."[239]

It has been asserted in the past that rapists are pathological individuals; they are "victims of a disease from which many of them suffer more than their victims";[240] they are "sexual psychopaths". Whilst there are undoubtedly rapists who are psychologically disturbed, research has shown how rare this is.[241] The better view, it is submitted, is that rape is about inequalities of power, whether the victim is female or male. The stereotypical rape is depicted as an act committed by a stranger, probably outside the home, at night and where violence is employed. In reality, most victims know their assailants and the home may well be the location for rape.[242]

Much attention has been focused on two different types of rape, both of which have been contrasted with the supposed paradigm of stranger rape. The first is that of relationship rape. It has been suggested that this is a less serious form of sexual assault than stranger rape.[243] In contrast, however, rapes committed by partners may have the greatest of psychological impacts on the victim. One can point to accounts of rape given by those who have been or are in relationships with their assailant to illustrate this point:

"Linda, 41, has to walk with crutches after being violently raped and battered by her husband . . . Her husband began attacking her when she was pregnant . . . The rapes began after her son was born . . . 'He used to tell me that I was supposed to enjoy it—he actually thought women liked being raped. He said it was what all his mates talked about at work. In the end I just hated him. Sex could never be normal—how can you like someone who's beating you up and telling you you should be liking it?'"[244]

---

[236] S. Brownmiller, *Against Our Will* (New York: Simon & Schuster, 1975), p.11. In *Attorney-General's Reference (No.66 of 2008)* [2009] EWCA Crim 87, the Court of Appeal increased a sentence from six to 10 years' imprisonment upon a defendant who had "used sex as a weapon" against his former wife to dominate and humiliate her.

[237] Queen's Bench Foundation, *Rape—Prevention and Resistance* (1976), p.80; contra M. Amir, *Patterns in Forcible Rape* (Chicago: University of Chicago Press, 1971), p.131 who concluded, without much supportive evidence, that strong sexual emotion was the dominant motive.

[238] The ages most at risk are between 16 and 19, Ministry of Justice, above fn.199, p.14. Other studies report ranges between 1 and 82 years (Brownmiller, *Against Our Will* (1975), p.272).

[239] Anonymous letter to *The Observer*, January 10, 1982.

[240] B. Karpman, *The Sexual Offender and his Offenses* (New York: Julian Press, 1954), p.482.

[241] For example, S.D. Smithyman in W.H. Parsonage (ed.), *Perspectives on Victimology* (London: Sage, 1979), pp.99–120. See also Howard League Working Party, *Unlawful Sex* (1985), pp.47ff.

[242] In Harris and Grace's study, above fn.218, 88% of victims were, at least, acquainted with the suspect and that the offence took place in either their joint home or the victim's home in 35% of cases. See further, D.W. Selfe and V. Burke, *Perspectives on Sex Crime and Society* (London: Cavendish, 2001).

[243] G. Williams, "Rape is Rape" (1992) 142 N.L.J. 11.

[244] *The Independent*, February 23, 1990.

The second type is that of "date-rape", perhaps better described as acquaintance rape.[245] Suggesting that such rapes are less serious brings into sharp focus many of the assumptions which may be implicit in relationships between men and women. Does a man who buys a woman a meal have a right to have intercourse with her? Does a woman who gets drunk at a party ask for it? If the disturbing findings of an ICM poll in 2005 are anything to go by, many people, it seems, would answer that she does: 34 per cent of those questioned thought that a woman who behaved flirtatiously was partially or totally responsible if she was raped and 26 per cent thought the same would be true if she wore sexy or revealing clothing.[246] On this basis,

> "it is not difficult to see why changes in law produce such limited results . . . The problem of rape is so deeply embedded in social and cultural constructions of (hetero)sexuality, so closely allied with core dimensions of what we understand as masculinity and femininity, that any steps which do not confront this fundamental aspect of the rape problem are likely to be, at best, modest."[247]

3. What is rape?

Many of the issues highlighted above have had very significant consequences for the shape the law has taken (for example, in relation to the concept of consent) as well as how it has operated in practice. However, before turning to that discussion, it is important to try to identify the "essence" of rape and other sexual offences such as assault by penetration or sexual assault. Such offences are sometimes associated with gross violence. For some, such crimes are always and essentially crimes of violence. One effect of this could be that the offence of rape should be defined so that it only occurs where the victim has shown physical resistance.[248] However, it is not true that all "rapes" are accompanied by violence.[249] Does this mean that there has been no rape? One answer increasingly given is that rape and other sexual assaults are crimes against sexual autonomy and that what matters is whether there was consent.[250] There are difficulties with both approaches.

Victor Tadros, "Rape Without Consent" [2006] 26 O.J.L.S. 515 at 515–516:

"In some jurisdictions, for example, Canada, Michigan and New South Wales, the focus is primarily on force. The will of the complainant plays a subsidiary role or no role at all. Reforms of this kind were motivated by three feminist concerns. First, rape is to be considered a crime of violence. That ought to be reflected in the definition of the offence. Second, defining rape around the will of the victim tends to encourage criminal trials to focus problematically on the conduct and sexual history of the complainant rather than the conduct of the accused. Third, sexual offences ought to be defined with precision to prevent them being manipulated by defence counsel

---

[245] The phrase date-rape is thought to have been coined by American psychologist, Mary Koss, in 1985 but it can be argued that the very description belittles the seriousness of the offence.

[246] Amnesty International, *Sexual Assaults Research* (2005). See also A. Clarke, J. Moran-Ellis and J. Sleney, *Attitudes to Date-rape and Relationship Rape: A Qualitative Study (Sentencing Advisory Panel Research Report No.2)* (2002).

[247] Centre for Law, Gender and Sexuality, above fn.230, p.4. See further, C. Mackinnon, *Toward a Feminist Theory of the State* (Cambridge: Harvard University Press, 1989), p.174 who argues that it is difficult for women to distinguish between rape and intercourse under current conditions of male dominance. See also M.A. Walters and J. Tumath, "Gender 'Hostility', Rape, and the Hate Crime Paradigm" (2014) 77 M.L.R. 563, who argue that the inclusion of "gender" hostility in hate crime policy and legislation may help to reorientate social understandings about what motivates sexual offenders.

[248] In the United States many states used to require a woman to show utmost resistance; even now rape may be defined as non-consensual and forced sexual intercourse. See R. West, "A Comment on Consent, Sex and Rape" (1996) 2 *Legal Theory* 232.

[249] See Temkin, *Rape and the Legal Process*, 2nd edn (Oxford: OUP, 2002), pp.167–168.

[250] For an argument that sexual penetration is itself a prima facie wrong, see M.M. Dempsey and J. Herring, "Why Sexual Penetration Requires Justification" (2007) 27 O.J.L.S. 467.

or subject to problematic interpretation in the light of the prejudices of participants in the criminal process, and in particular judges and juries . . .

In other jurisdictions, the focus is primarily on the will, or rather consent, of the victim, relegating force to a subsidiary role. This is true of England and Wales . . . Such [laws] reflect a fourth feminist concern: undermining the sexual autonomy of the victim need not involve violence or the threat of violence . . .

Meeting the fourth concern . . . appears to involve failing properly to reflect the first three."

Perceiving rape as a crime of violence makes for a relatively straightforward offence but ignores the dynamics of sexual relationships and enables husbands, partners and "date-rapists" to deny that what they do is rape. However, making consent the pivotal concept "does not mark out the offence as a crime of violence even where there has been violence"[251] and has proved to be deeply problematic. Nevertheless, if one conceives of a hypothetical scenario as Gardner and Shute do, in which the victim is unconscious, unharmed and never learns that sexual intercourse (with a condom) has taken place, it is still right to state that the victim has been raped. Indeed, this "pure" case of rape enables one to identify what they describe as "the wrongness of rape":

"Rape, in the pure case, is the sheer use of a person . . . Rape is humiliating even when unaccompanied by further affronts because the sheer use of a person, and in that sense the objectification of a person, is a denial of their personhood. It is literally dehumanizing."[252]

If one views rape as the sheer use of a person as an object[253] there is no case for its being subdivided into more or less serious offences depending upon whether a relationship or acquaintance existed between the victim and the offender. As well as denying the autonomy of the victim it has been further argued that the rape of a woman amounts to a moral harm, not only against the victim, but also against women as a group.

Joan McGregor, Is it Rape? (2005), pp.230–232:

"Rapes express very clearly the inferiority of women. The rapist, whether the violent rapist or the subtler 'date rapist', sends the message that this woman is for his enjoyment, an object to be used for his pleasure. His actions express her inferiority to him since he does not feel the need to bother to investigate whether she was really consenting even in the face of evidence that she was not or may not be. Her physical and verbal rejections are not worth investigating as to whether they were 'real' since her interests do not really matter. For him, her wishes and desires are irrelevant. He is superior to her, his desires matter and hers do not, making her an object rather than an equal person. Sending this message is the expressive moral injury of rape. The message of inferiority is received by all women, not merely the woman who experiences the rape. Not wanting to diminish the real physical and psychological harms to rape victims, I am not claiming that all women experience those harms, which are very real and serious. But there is something peculiar to rape and the response that women have to other women being raped. . . .

The meaning of rape involves the victim's worth and the wrongdoer's worth and we can 'read off' the expression of the offender's superiority. In the case of rape, the diminishment in the victim's worth is tied to group membership. Women are the target of rape in society and women get the message that the rapist sends. In this sense, the moral injury of rape is shared by women as a group."

---

[251] V. Tadros, "Rape Without Consent" [2006] 26 O.J.L.S. 515 at 517.

[252] "The Wrongness of Rape" in J. Horder (ed.), *Oxford Essays in Jurisprudence* (Oxford: OUP, 2000), p.205. Contra, A.P. Simester and G.R. Sullivan, *Criminal Law: Theory and Doctrine*, 3rd edn (Oxford: OUP, 2007), p.467 who argue that psychological trauma, together with physical injury, risk of unwanted pregnancy and infection are very much part of our conception of rape and mean that rape is appropriately characterised as a form of violence as well as a wrong of disregard of the victim's autonomy.

[253] See also, J. Herring, "Mistaken Sex" [2005] Crim. L. R. 511 at 515–617.

One further consequence of seeing sexual offences in terms of sexual autonomy will be considered later in relation to child offences. Respecting a person's right to choose to engage in sexual intercourse has another dimension: the extent to which the law does or should respect a (young) person's right to engage in sexual exploration.

B. The Law

1. Consent

The issue of consent is fundamental to many of the sexual offences contained within the Sexual Offences Act 2003. It has also proved to be a highly problematic concept to define and one of the key objectives of the reform was to clarify this concept. Indeed, as the majority of victims know their assailant, the issue of consent is, in many trials, the pivotal issue.

However, before exploring this contested concept, one matter can be settled: what is required in law is a lack of consent and not positive dissent.[254] English law does not define rape as sexual intercourse by force. It thus absolves the victim from having to make a show of resistance. Thus, in theory, responsibility rests with the instigator to secure consent. That said, it is clear that in the absence of marks or injuries the victim's claim not to have consented may not be believed.[255] Evidentially, there is real pressure on rape victims to struggle and further endanger themselves. Moreover, although changes to legislation mean judges are no longer obliged to warn the jury of the dangers of accepting the victim's uncorroborated story, they have discretion still to do so.[256] One further related question is relevant at this point. The defence in seeking to show that the victim did, in fact, consent to sexual intercourse may wish to adduce evidence, for example, of prior relationships with the defendant or with other men. May evidence of this type be introduced at the trial?

Zsuzsanna Adler, "Rape—the Intention of Parliament and the Practice of the Courts" (1982) 45 M.L.R. 664 at 666–667:

"Before 1976, the defence in a rape trial were free to cross-examine about any prior sexual behaviour, whether with the defendant or anyone else. Her experience with a third party was thought to be relevant to her credibility: the law of evidence seemed to reflect an assumption that women involved in rape cases were likely to be untruthful as a direct result of their sexual 'immorality' . . . [It] gave the defence a virtually unconstrained licence to sling sexual mud . . .

The Advisory Group on the Law of Rape . . . expressed particular anxiety about the humiliation and distress suffered by complainants during cross-examination and argued that the procedure was in need of urgent reform. 'We have reached the conclusion that the previous sexual history of the alleged victim with third parties is of no significance so far as credibility is concerned, and is only rarely likely to be relevant to the issues directly before the jury.' (Report of the Advisory Council on the Law of Rape, 1975, para. 131.)"

As a result of such reasoning, the law was changed to give the trial judge complete discretion as to whether general or specific past history and reputation of the victim might be introduced.[257] However,

---

[254] *Lang* (1975) 62 Cr. App. R. 50; *Olugboja* (1981) 73 Cr. App. R. 344; *Malone* [1998] 2 Cr. App. R. 454.
[255] There are higher conviction rates where violence is established: Harris and Grace, *A Question of Evidence? Investigating and Prosecuting Rape in the 1990s* (1999).
[256] Criminal Justice and Public Order Act 1994 s.32.
[257] Sexual Offences (Amendment) Act 1976 s.2. In Adler's study, the defence applied for leave in 40% of cases and were successful (in part or wholly) in some 75% of applications. Adler believes that any scheme based on judicial discretion controlling sexual history evidence is doomed to fail, because judges will have to fall back on their own beliefs and attitudes (Z. Adler, *Rape on Trial* (London: Routledge & Kegan Paul, 1987), p.154).

studies subsequently concluded that courts were far too ready to allow evidence to be admitted[258] and the report *Speaking up for Justice* concluded that there was "overwhelming evidence that the . . . practice in the courts [was] unsatisfactory and that the existing law [was] not achieving its purpose".[259] As a consequence, a much tighter scheme governing sexual history evidence has been introduced by the Youth Justice and Criminal Evidence Act 1999.[260] No such evidence can be adduced unless certain statutory criteria are satisfied: for example, that the issue is one of consent and the sexual behaviour of the complainant to which the evidence relates is alleged to have taken place at about the same time as the event which is the subject matter of the charge.[261] The court must also believe that a failure to admit the evidence would render the conviction unsafe.[262] One basis for admitting evidence or permitting cross-examination about sexual history might be where the complainant is biased against the defendant or has a motive for fabricating the evidence.[263] An application to introduce evidence should be made in advance of the trial but research has shown that this safeguard is not observed in the vast majority of cases.[264] The provisions have continued to attract criticism, with some commentators arguing that only a complete ban on such history will solve the problem.[265]

Against this background we can now consider what it means to say that someone has consented to sex. There have been numerous attempts to answer these questions, both philosophically and legally.[266] For the first time, however, the Sexual Offences Act 2003 provides a statutory definition which, as we shall see, is supplemented by presumptions as to the absence of consent.

Sexual Offences Act 2003 ss.74, 75 and 76

"74. 'Consent'

For the purposes of this Part, a person consents if he agrees by choice, and has the freedom and capacity to make that choice.

75. Evidential Presumptions about consent

(1) If in proceedings for an offence to which this section applies it is proved—

---

258 J. Temkin, "Sexual History Evidence—the Ravishment of Section 2" [1993] Crim.L.R. 3. See also, A. McColgan, "Common Law and the Relevance of Sexual History Evidence" [1996] 15 O.J.L.S. 275 and G. Durston, "Cross-examination of Rape Complainants: Ongoing Tensions between Conflicting Priorities of the Criminal Justice System" (1998) 62 Jo.C.L. 91.

259 Home Office, *Speaking Up for Justice: Report of the Interdepartmental Working Group on the Treatment of Vulnerable and Intimidated Witnesses in the Criminal Justice System* (1998), para.9.64.

260 Sections 41–43. In addition, the Criminal Justice Act 2003 s.100 requires the defendant to obtain leave from the judge when he wishes to introduce evidence that amounts to an attack upon the victim's character. See further, C. Withey, "Female Rape—an Ongoing Concern: Strategies for Improving Reporting and Conviction Levels" [2007] 74 Jo. C.L. 54.

261 Section 41(3)(b).

262 For recent illustrations of where leave was denied see, for example, *Beedall* [2007] EWCA Crim 23 (defence wished to ask the victim if he was homosexual) and *Winter* [2008] EWCA Crim 3 (defence wished to ask the victim—who was in a long-term relationship with one man—about her relationship with another man).

263 *R. v A (Complainant's Sexual History)* [2002] 1 A.C. 45 at [79] per Lord Hope.

264 L. Kelly, J. Temkin and S. Griffiths, *Section 41: An Evaluation of New Legislation Regarding Sexual History Evidence in Rape Trials* (2006) (Home Office Online Report 20/06).

265 J. McEwan, "The Rape Shield Askew? R v A" [2001] 5 International J. of Evidence and Proof 267. Others have, conversely, commented that the provisions are so tightly drawn as to prevent the court hearing evidence which is relevant. See further, D.J. Birch, "A Fairer Deal for Vulnerable Witnesses" [2000] Crim L.R. 223; N. Kibble, "The Sexual History Provisions: Charting a Course Between Inflexible Legislative Rules and Wholly Untrammelled Judicial Discretion?" [2000] Crim. L.R. 274. See further, *R. v A (No.2)* [2002] 1 A.C. 45 and J.R. Spencer, "'Rape Shields' and the Right to a Fair Trial" (2001) 60 C.L.J. 26.

266 See, for example, L. Alexander, "The Moral Magic of Consent" (1996) 2 *Legal Theory* 165; S. Estrich, *Real Rape* (Cambridge: Harvard University Press, 1987); D.A. Dripps, "Beyond Rape: An Essay on the Difference Between the Presence of Force and the Absence of Consent" (1992) 92 Colum. L.R. 1780; Temkin, *Rape and the Legal Process*, 2nd edn (Oxford: OUP, 2002); S. Lees, *Sexual Violence, Reputation and the Law* (Buckingham: Open University Press, 1997); A. Wertheimer, *Consent to Sexual Relations* (Cambridge: CUP, 2003).

(a) that the defendant did the relevant act,

(b) that any of the circumstances specified in subsection 2 existed, and

(c) that the defendant knew that those circumstances existed—

the complainant is to be taken not to have consented to the relevant act unless sufficient evidence is adduced to raise an issue as to whether he consented and

the defendant is to be taken not to have reasonably believed that the complainant consented unless sufficient evidence is adduced to raise an issue as to whether he reasonably believed it.

(2) The circumstances are that—

(a) any person was, at the time of the relevant act or immediately before it began, using violence against the complainant or causing the complainant to fear that immediate violence would be used against him;

(b) any person was, at the time of the relevant act or immediately before it began, causing the victim to fear that violence was being used, or that immediate violence would be used, against another person;

(c) the complainant was, and the defendant was not, unlawfully detained at the time of the relevant act;

(d) the complainant was asleep or otherwise unconscious at the time of the relevant act;

(e) because of the complainant's physical disability, the complainant would not have been able at the time of the relevant act to communicate to the defendant whether the complainant consented.

(f) any person had administered to or caused to be taken by the complainant, without the complainant's consent, a substance which, having regard to when it was administered or taken was capable of causing or enabling the complainant to be stupefied or overpowered at the time of the relevant act.

76. Conclusive Presumptions about consent
(1) If in proceedings for an offence to which this section applies it is proved that the defendant did the relevant act, that any of the circumstances specified in subsection (2) existed, it is to be conclusively presumed—
that the complainant did not consent to the relevant act, and
that the defendant did not believe that the complainant consented to the relevant act.
(2) The circumstances are that—

(a) the defendant intentionally deceived the complainant as to the nature or purpose of the relevant act;

(b) the defendant intentionally induced the complainant to consent to the relevant act by impersonating a person known personally to the complainant."

(i) The general definition

(a) Freedom

Basing consent upon freedom might, at first sight, appear to be an obvious good. Sexual intercourse ought to occur when it is wanted: when both participants regard it as welcome and it is an encounter which either party might have initiated.[267] Yet the notion of "freedom" is far from uncontroversial. Some feminists, such as MacKinnon, have argued that any attempt to distinguish rape from sexual intercourse on the basis of choice and thus consent is naïve. In a society in which women are socialised to passive receptivity, where sex is something men do to women, there is no clear distinction that can be drawn.[268]

---

[267] M. Chamallas, "Consent, Equality and the Legal Control of Sexual Conduct" (1988) 61 Southern Calif. L. Rev. 777.
[268] C. McKinnon, *Towards a Feminist Theory of the State* (Cambridge: Harvard University Press, 1989).

S. Schulhofer, Unwanted Sex: The Culture of Intimidation and the Failure of the Law (1998), pp.56–57:

"MacKinnon's far-reaching claims about cultural pressure have opened many eyes to the multiple constraints on women's freedom to make independent sexual choices. At the same time, by collapsing the distinctions *between* kinds of sexual pressure, feminism of this sort doesn't advance the effort to draw workable legal lines. Sometimes this strand of feminism even seems to impede the legal reform effort, because it tends to obliterate differences between the kinds of pressure that society will inevitably tolerate and the kinds that it might plausibly forbid . . . The refusal of some leading theorists to draw moral distinctions among the many forms of pressure women face maintains a certain purism for these feminist projects, but it vastly oversimplifies the give-and-take of social power in a complex, imperfect, but not uniformly oppressive society."

Even if one eschews the more far-reaching critique of the use of the concept of freedom within the context of consent, it is obvious that not all sexual choices are completely freely made and yet consent may well have been given. An individual's choice may be constrained for all sorts of reasons: it may be a desire to avoid the row that will follow if sex is not forthcoming; a need for cash; a need to keep one's job; a fear of being beaten or killed. If a person says "yes" in any of these scenarios—or if she permits intercourse after persuading the assailant to wear a condom[269]—is this consent real? The difficult task for the law has been to determine which such constraints operate to nullify consent and which do not. As long as rape is viewed predominantly as a crime of violence the answer is relatively unproblematic. Traditionally, therefore, only threats of death or serious harm vitiate an apparent consent. However, the more rape is perceived as an offence against sexual autonomy, the more the wrong is perceived to be the objectification of a person, the more open-ended become the types of constraints which may nullify consent.[270]

In *Olugboja*,[271] a case decided under the old law, the victim had intercourse with the defendant after his companion had raped her and her friend. The defendant claimed that these circumstances did not nullify her consent since only a threat of death or serious harm would suffice. The Court of Appeal held that, using the "ordinary meaning" of the word, the victim could not be said to have consented to sexual intercourse. The court held that there was a difference between the state of mind of real consent and that of mere submission. The difference between the two was a matter of degree and it was for the jury to decide which side of the line a particular sequence of events falls. For example, a jury would almost inevitably decide that a wife who "reluctantly acquiesced" to intercourse to avoid a sulking husband had, nevertheless, consented.

However, there were difficulties with *Olugboja*. Although the flexibility of its approach had its merits, the distinction between mere submission and real consent was not able to bear close scrutiny.[272] It was rejected as the way forward for reform because it had "led to confusion and [risked] very different conclusions being drawn on similar facts in different cases".[273] Instead, in an attempt to be clear and unambiguous,[274] a statutory definition of consent was preferred. However, the issues discussed above have not been swept away by the definition. It is necessarily vague—but this means that a jury's preconceptions about sexual behaviour and consent may well still affect their interpretation of whether a "free choice" has been made.

---

[269] In 1992, in Texas, a grand jury refused to indict a man who had broken into a house at night, held a knife to a woman's throat and then had intercourse with her on the ground that, because she had begged him to put on a condom, she had consented: *The Washington Post*, October 31, 1992.

[270] J. Gardner, "Appreciating Olugboja" [1996] 16 *Legal Studies* 275 at 277–282.

[271] *R. v Olugboja (Stephen)* [1982] Q.B. 320.

[272] In *McAllister* [1997] Crim. L.R. 233 the jury, for example, asked for an explanation of the difference between the two phrases.

[273] Home Office, *Setting the Boundaries: Reforming the Law on Sexual Offences* (2000), para.2.2.3. See also *R. v (1)PK (2)TK* [2008] EWCA Crim 434, below pp.657–658

[274] *Protecting the Public*, above fn.192, para.30.

(b) *Capacity*

The statutory definition also refers to the capacity of the victim to choose. Capacity is undefined in the Act but must relate to awareness, knowledge and understanding. A person may be incapable of giving consent, because, say, she has been knocked unconscious or because she is suffering from a mental disorder that precludes understanding.[275] However, it is in the context of intoxication that the issue of capacity to consent has become a matter of concern and it is here that societal attitudes towards rape and drinking have the very real potential to influence the outcome of proceedings. Research has shown the existence of a double standard whereby "intoxicated defendants tend to be held *less* responsible than their sober counterparts while intoxicated complainants tend to be held *more* responsible".[276] Indeed, given the publicity surrounding the increase in "binge" drinking among young women, this attitude could harden further.[277] In the much publicised survey conducted for Amnesty International, 30 per cent of respondents thought that a woman was either partly or wholly responsible for being raped if she was drunk.[278] As research reveals that alcohol has been ingested by a significant proportion of victims and defendants in rape cases, this is deeply worrying.[279]

In 2005 a case involving an alleged rape upon a female student who was drunk but conscious at the time of the offence collapsed.[280] Had she been unconscious at the time of the intercourse, the evidential presumption in s.75(2)(d) would have been invoked.[281] The judge directed the jury to return a verdict of "not guilty" when the prosecution revealed that they were unable to proceed further because they could not prove that the complainant had not given consent because of her level of intoxication. It has been argued that the judge could have put the matter to the jury to consider in terms of the complainant's capacity to consent.[282] This issue arose for reconsideration in the following decision.

---

[275] The Sexual Offences Act 2003 creates a number of offences specifically to protect people suffering from mental disorder: ss.30–41. In *R. v C* [2009] UKHL 42 the House of Lords considered the issue of capacity in relation to the offence of sexual activity with a person with a mental disorder under s.30. Baroness Hale concluded that in order to have capacity a person must be able to understand the information relevant to making a decision and must also be able to weigh that information to arrive at a choice. A mentally disordered person might be able to appreciate that the act was sexual but not be able to weigh it in order to arrive at a choice [24]. Whilst, strictly, this decision relates to s.30 only, there will be situations involving mentally disordered victims when charges under ss.1–4 could be brought and, it is submitted, this explanation of capacity should be adopted. For a discussion on how the notion of consent to sexual activity for persons with mental disabilities is interpreted by health professionals and lawyers, see S. Doyle, "The Notion of Consent to Sexual Activity for Persons With Mental Disabilities" (2010) 31 Liverpool L.R. 111.

[276] E. Finch and V. Munro, "The Demon Drink and the Demonised Woman: Socio-sexual Stereotypes and Responsibility Attribution in Rape Trials involving Intoxicants" (2007) 16 *Social and Legal Studies* 591 at 591.

[277] M.A.H. Horvath and J. Brown, "Alcohol as Drug of Choice; Is Drug-Assisted Rape a Misnomer?" (2007) 13 *Psychology, Crime and Law* 417 at 420.

[278] Above fn.246.

[279] See further, Advisory Council on the Misuse of Drugs, *Drug Facilitated Sexual Assault* (2007). The concept of DAR (drug assisted rape) includes both alcohol and drugs such as Rohypnol. The evidence suggests that alcohol is the most common weapon in DAR while the incidence of drug facilitated sexual assault is unclear (paras 5.2–5.3). For a critique of the concept of DAR, see Horvath and Brown, "Alcohol as Drug of Choice; Is Drug-Assisted Rape a Misnomer?" (2007) 13 *Psychology, Crime and Law* 417.

[280] *R v Dougal*, unreported, November 2005, Swansea Crown Court.

[281] The original proposals in the Home Office's consultation paper, *Setting the Boundaries: Reforming the Law on Sexual Offences* (2000), specifically included a presumption about consent that covered cases where "a person is asleep, unconscious or too affected by alcohol or drugs to give consent". This recommendation was dropped in *Protecting the Public*, above, fn.192. See further, E. Finch and V. Munro, "The Sexual Offences Act 2003: Intoxicated Consent and Drug Assisted Rape Revisited" [2004] Crim. L.R. 789 at 793.

[282] Office for Criminal Justice Reform, above, fn.197, p.13. The Centre for Law, Gender and Sexuality response, above fn.230, suggests that the prosecution decision not to proceed might have been in breach of the CPS guidance on capacity and consent (at p.6).

R. v Bree [2007] 3 W.L.R. 600 (Court of Appeal, Criminal Division)

The defendant and M spent the evening together, drinking heavily before returning to the defendant's flat where they had sexual intercourse. Initially the prosecution alleged that M was unconscious throughout most of the activity and thus lacked capacity to consent. Following evidence by M at the trial, the prosecution changed its stance and alleged that M's ability to resist had been hampered by the effects of alcohol but that she had had the capacity to consent. M accepted that her memory of the evening was very patchy; however, she maintained that she had made it clear, in so far as she could, that she did not consent. The defendant claimed that M had been conscious throughout and that he reasonably believed she was consenting. The defendant was convicted of rape and appealed.

SIR IGOR JUDGE P:

"[26] In cases which are said to arise after voluntary consumption of alcohol the question is not whether the alcohol made either or both less inhibited than they would have been if sober, nor whether either or both might afterwards have regretted what had happened, and indeed wished that it had not. If the Complainant consents, her consent cannot be revoked. Moreover it is not a question whether either or both may have had very poor recollection of precisely what had happened. That may be relevant to the reliability of their evidence. Finally, and certainly, it is not a question whether either or both was behaving irresponsibly. As they were both autonomous adults, the essential question for decision is, as it always is, whether the evidence proved that the Appellant had sexual intercourse with the Complainant without her consent . . .

[30] We are not aware of any reported decisions which deal with this aspect of [capacity in] the new legislation. We should however refer to the much publicised case of *R v Dougal*, heard in Swansea Crown Court, in November 2005 . . .

[33] Some of the hugely critical discussion arising after *Dougal* missed the essential point. Neither counsel for the Crown, nor for that matter the judge, was saying or coming anywhere near saying, either that a Complainant who through drink is incapable of consenting to intercourse must nevertheless be deemed to have consented to it, or that a man is at liberty to have sexual intercourse with a woman who happens to be drunk, on the basis that her drunkenness deprives her of her right to choose whether to have intercourse or not. Such ideas are wrong in law, and indeed, offensive. All that was being said in *Dougal* was that when someone who has had a lot to drink is in fact consenting to intercourse, then that is what she is doing, consenting: equally, if after taking drink, she is not consenting, then by definition intercourse is taking place without her consent. This is unexceptionable.

[34] In our judgment, the proper construction of s 74 of the 2003 Act, as applied to the problem now under discussion, leads to clear conclusions. If, through drink (or for any other reason) the Complainant has temporarily lost her capacity to choose whether to have intercourse on the relevant occasion, she is not consenting, and subject to questions about the Defendant's state of mind, if intercourse takes place, this would be rape. However, where the Complainant has voluntarily consumed even substantial quantities of alcohol, but nevertheless remains capable of choosing whether or not to have intercourse, and in drink agrees to do so, this would not be rape. We should perhaps underline that, as a matter of practical reality, capacity to consent may evaporate well before a Complainant becomes unconscious. Whether this is so or not, however, is fact specific, or more accurately, depends on the actual state of mind of the individuals involved on the particular occasion.

[35] Considerations like these underline the fact that it would be unrealistic to endeavour to create some kind of grid system which would enable the answer to these questions to be related to some prescribed level of alcohol consumption. Experience shows that different individuals have a greater or lesser capacity to cope with alcohol than others, and indeed the ability of a single individual to do so may vary from day to day. The practical reality is that there are some areas of human behaviour which are inapt for detailed legislative structures. In this context, provisions intended to protect women from sexual assaults might very well be conflated into a system which would provide patronising interference with the right of autonomous adults to make personal decisions for themselves.

[36] For these reasons, notwithstanding criticisms of the statutory provisions, in our view the 2003 Act provides a clear definition of "consent" for the purposes of the law of rape, and by defining it with reference to "capacity to make that choice", sufficiently addresses the issue of consent in the context of voluntary consumption of alcohol by the Complainant. The problems do not arise from the legal principles. They lie with infinite circumstances of human behaviour, usually taking place in private without independent evidence, and the consequent difficulties of proving this very serious offence . . .

[39] In this case the jury should have been given some assistance with the meaning of "capacity" in circumstances where the Complainant was affected by her own voluntarily induced intoxication, and also whether, and to what extent they could take that into account in deciding whether she had consented.[283] . . .

[43] . . . In a trial in which the issues of consent and voluntary intoxication were fundamental to the outcome, the jury were given no or no sufficient directions to enable the verdict which they reached to be regarded as safe.[284] Accordingly the conviction is quashed."

Appeal allowed

The Government (which had been consulting on ways to remove the barriers to successful prosecutions) subsequently commented that this decision provided vital guidance and that there was, therefore, no need for capacity to be defined for the purposes of the Sexual Offences Act.[285] Both the decision in *Bree* and the Government's response has divided opinion. While it is true that attempting to determine capacity using a grid system based on blood-alcohol levels would be unhelpful for the reasons given by the Court of Appeal, the idea that there need be no further attempts to clarify capacity in the context of intoxication is open to challenge:

"what appears to be part of a liberal non-interventionist approach to regulating private sexual behaviour, in reality can also be seen as a means by which some men's disregard for the sexual autonomy of women is maintained."[286]

Given, as we have seen, the deep-rooted nature of attitudes towards drink and rape, it is unlikely that further guidance or a definition of capacity would be enough to effect a sea-change by themselves but, at least the chances of juries being given the opportunity to consider the relevant issues would be higher if there was a clear definition of capacity.[287]

(ii) The presumptions

The new law distinguishes between two types of presumptions: those that are conclusive and those that raise an evidential presumption that consent was absent.[288] Both types of presumptions apply not only to the issue of consent as an element of the actus reus but also apply to the question of whether the defendant had mens rea.[289]

---

[283] See *R. v Wright (Nathan)* [2007] EWCA Crim 3473 where it was held that it was unnecessary to give a studied direction on capacity to consent as, if the jury accepted the victim's version of events, she was "as good as unconscious". See also *R. v H* [2007] where it was held that it was for the jury and *not* the judge to decide, based on the evidence, whether the victim had the capacity to consent and/or in fact consented to intercourse or not.

[284] In *R. v Kamki* [2013] EWCA Crim 2335 the defendant had been convicted of raping the victim who at the time had been heavily intoxicated. The defendant appealed arguing that the important point that a sexual encounter that was drunken and regretted did not make it non-consensual was not addressed by the trial judge. The Court of Appeal held that where the elements of capacity to consent had been fully dealt with, it was not necessary for the judge to state in every case the simple words that a drunken consent remained a consent.

[285] Office for Criminal Justice Reform, above fn.197, pp.10–11. The government did state that it would keep the issue under review and invite the Judicial Studies Board to consider whether a specimen direction on capacity and consent would assist judges. No such direction has been issued. In *Hysa* [2007] EWCA Crim 2056 the Court of Appeal stressed that the issue of capacity to consent should normally be left to the jury to determine.

[286] P.N.S. Rumney and R. A. Fenton, "Intoxicated Consent in Rape: *Bree* and Juror Decision-making" (2008) 71 M.L.R. 279 at 289. See also, A. Ashworth, "Rape: Consent—Intoxication" [2007] Crim. L.R. 901 and J. Elvin, "The Concept of Consent under the Sexual Offences Act 2003" (2008) 72 J. Crim. L. 519.

[287] Centre for Law, Gender and Sexuality, above fn.230, pp.7–8.

[288] The presumptions apply to offences under ss.1 (rape), 2 (assault by penetration), 3 (sexual assault), and 4 (causing a person to engage in sexual activity without consent).

[289] Judicial Studies Board, *Specimen Directions: 16a* (2007) states that the presumptions do not apply to charges of incitement

(a) *The conclusive presumptions*

In the case of the two conclusive presumptions, once it is proved that the defendant did the relevant act and that either of the circumstances existed, then both consent and lack of belief in consent are conclusively established.[290] Both build upon the previous law. In *Clarence*[291] Stephen J identified two such kinds of fundamental mistake, the first as to the identity of the actor and the second as to the nature of the act, either of which negated the apparent consent of the victim if induced by the deceit of the defendant. The old law only protected victims where the person impersonated was the victim's husband although the Court of Appeal in *Elbekkay*[292] extended this to cover boyfriends as well. The new conclusive presumption applies to the impersonation of anyone known personally to the victim. While this is broader than the old law, it would not, of course, come into operation if the defendant claimed to be, say, Brad Pitt who was only known to the complainant through his films. The other point worth noting is that the impersonation must have induced the complainant to consent.[293]

The second type of fundamental mistake induced by fraud goes to the very nature of the act. In *Flattery*[294] the defendant induced a woman to submit to intercourse by maintaining the deception that he was performing a surgical operation. He was convicted of rape. This was followed in the not dissimilar case of *Williams*[295] where the defendant, who was a singing-master, had intercourse with one of his pupils aged 16. She made no resistance as she believed his claim that he was merely improving her breathing. He too was convicted. The principle upon which both cases were decided was that there had been no consent to sexual intercourse; what had been consented to was a medical or surgical operation.

Prior to the 2003 Act, the courts had generally declined to extend the ambit of the law of rape to cases other than those involving these two types of fundamental mistake. In *Linekar*, for example, the defendant deceived a prostitute into having intercourse with him by claiming (falsely) that he would pay her. Although she would not have had intercourse with him had she known the truth this was, rightly, held not to be a deception as to the nature or the act.[296] However, the narrowness of this approach was put in doubt by the decision of *Tabassum*.[297] In this case, concerning the former offence of indecent assault but raising the issue of consent, the court took the view that the victims, who had consented to breast examinations for what they thought was medical research, would never have done so had they known that the defendant was not medically qualified. It was held that they had consented to the nature of the act but not to its quality—and that accordingly there was no real consent. This is a controversial distinction yet it is one that is replicated by the language of the conclusive presumption in s.76(2)(a) which refers to both the nature and the *purpose* of the act.

(now abolished), conspiracy or attempt to commit the sexual offences in ss.1–4. Presumably the same rule will apply to the new offences of encouraging and assisting crime under the Serious Crime Act 2007. See also, D.A.H. Rodwell, "Problems with the Sexual Offences Act 2003" [2005] Crim. L.R. 290.

[290] This has led McEwan to conclude that they are not presumptions at all but introduce a substantive rule of law. She also notes that in the United States conclusive presumptions have been declared unconstitutional as derogating from the presumption of innocence: "Proving Consent in Sexual Cases: Legislative Change and Cultural Evolution" [2005] International J. of Evidence and Proof 1.

[291] *R. v Clarence (Charles James)* (1888) 22 Q.B.D. 23.

[292] *Elbekkay* [1995] Crim. L.R. 163.

[293] J. Temkin and A. Ashworth, "The Sexual Offences Act: (1) Rape, Sexual Assaults and the Problems of Consent" [2004] Crim. L.R. 328 at 334–335.

[294] *R. v Flattery (John)* (1877) 2 Q.B.D. 410.

[295] *R. v Williams (Owen Richard)* [1923] 1 K.B. 340.

[296] *R. v Linekar (Gareth)* [1995] 2 Cr. App. R. 49.

[297] *R. v Tabassum (Naveed)* [2000] Crim. L.R. 686. See also, *R. v Green (Peter Donovan)* [2002] EWCA Crim 1501.

R. v Jheeta [2007] 2 Cr. App. R. 34 (Court of Appeal, Criminal Division)

By a series of bizarre and unpleasant lies, including texts from the defendant which purported to come from the police telling her that if she did not sleep with him she would be liable to a fine, the defendant induced the victim to continue to have sexual intercourse with him. When the truth came to light the victim claimed that she had only had intercourse with the defendant because of the texts and that she had not truly consented. The defendant pleaded guilty to rape having been advised that his behaviour fell within s.76(2)(a). He then appealed.

JUDGE P:

"[23] [S]ection 76 raises presumptions conclusive of the issue of consent, and thus where intercourse is proved, conclusive of guilt. They therefore require the most stringent scrutiny.

[24] In our judgment the ambit of section 76 is limited to the 'act' to which it is said to apply. In rape cases the 'act' is vaginal, anal or oral intercourse. Provided this consideration is constantly borne in mind, it will be seen that section 76 (2)(a) is relevant only to the comparatively rare cases where the defendant deliberately deceives the complainant about the *nature or purpose* of one or other form of intercourse. No conclusive presumptions arise merely because the complainant was deceived in some way or other by disingenuous blandishments of or common or garden lies by the defendant. These may well be deceptive and persuasive, but they will rarely go to the nature or purpose of intercourse. Beyond this limited type of case, and assuming that, as here, section 75 has no application, the issue of consent must be addressed in the context of section 74 . . .

[28] With these considerations in mind, we must return to the present case. On the written basis of plea the appellant undoubtedly deceived the complainant. He created a bizarre and fictitious fantasy which, because it was real enough to her, pressurised her to have intercourse with him more frequently than she otherwise would have done. She was not deceived as to the nature or purpose of intercourse, but deceived as to the situation in which she found herself. In our judgment the conclusive presumption in section 76 (2)(a) had no application, and counsel for the appellant below were wrong to advise on the basis that it did. However that is not an end of the matter . . . [The appellant] persuaded the complainant to have intercourse with him more frequently than otherwise, and the persuasion took the form of the pressures imposed on her by the complicated and unpleasant scheme which he had fabricated. This was not a free choice, or consent for the purposes of the Act. In these circumstances we entertain no reservations that on some occasions at least the complainant was not consenting to intercourse for the purposes of section 74, and that the appellant was perfectly well aware of it. His guilty plea reflected these undisputed facts."

Appeal dismissed

This was the first case to examine the meaning of s.76(2)(a) and it is thus of some importance. The approach taken before the Act and highlighted by *Tabassum* has been confirmed. Mere "disingenuous blandishments" or "common or garden lies" will "rarely go to the nature or purpose of the act". However, this does not mean that it will be straightforward to determine whether there has been a material deception as to "purpose" in future cases. Purpose is capable of being interpreted in a limited way, as in *Jheeta*, or more broadly.[298] Some support (albeit limited) for the latter approach comes from the bizarre case of *Devonald*. The male defendant posed as a woman over the internet to entice the victim (who had broken off a relationship with the defendant's teenage daughter) to masturbate in front of a webcam with a view to publishing the pictures so as to embarrass the boy and teach him a lesson. The Court of Appeal held that the defendant had deceived the victim as to the purpose of the act.[299] Oddly, this is an instance of the deception in reverse: the *victim* thought that the act was for

---

[298]   See *R. v Piper (Geoffrey Kenneth)* [2007] EWCA Crim 2151 where a defendant's conviction for sexual assault was upheld on the basis that he had deceived the victims into thinking that they were being measured for bikinis to determine their potential to model when it was for his sexual gratification. See also D. Selfe, "The Meaning of Consent Within the Sexual Offences Act 2003" (2008) *Criminal Lawyer* 174.

[299]   *R. v Devonald (Stephen)* [2008] EWCA Crim 527. The prosecution had sought to rely on s.76(2)(b) as well but the Court of Appeal restricted its judgment to s.76(2)(a).

sexual purposes. While the victim clearly would not have acted as he did had he known the truth the same would also have been true of the victim on *Linekar* and, given that the judgment is both unreserved and brief, it would probably be unwise to place too much reliance on *Devonald*.

Is it appropriate to take a narrow approach as in *Jheeta* or should a broader approach be adopted? Answering this question requires one to weigh two competing considerations. First, it may absolutely be the case that the victim would not have consented had the truth been told. In other words, the deception has operated to remove the possibility of real consent. On the other hand, does a defendant in such cases deserve to be labelled a rapist? When a victim has knowingly consented to the defendant's penetration will she suffer the same degree of emotional and psychological trauma as in other rape cases? Many commentators would argue that such admittedly limited, conditional, and, possibly, naïve consent is still valid and that sexual intercourse in such circumstances is not, therefore, rape.[300] However, it can be argued that consent should be understood in a "richer" sense: as full and truthful understanding of what is involved that is free from all pressures.[301]

R. v McNally [2014] 2 W.L.R. 200 (Court of Appeal, Criminal Division)

In this case the defendant, "who was female", contacted the victim (Y) over a social networking website and had claimed to be a young male.[302] Over a period of three-and-a-half years M and Y developed a romantic relationship. Y considered the defendant, who dressed as a boy, to be her boyfriend. M visited Y on four occasions when M was aged 17 and Y 16. During those visits, there were numerous occasions of oral and digital penetration of Y. Y discovered that M was not in fact biologically male. M was subsequently convicted of assault by penetration. The case for the prosecution was that Y's consent was obtained by fraudulent deception that the defendant was a male and that had she known this she would not have consented to acts of vaginal penetration.

LEVESON LJ:

"[25] In reality, some deceptions (such as, for example, in relation to wealth) will obviously not be sufficient to vitiate consent. In our judgment, Lord Judge CJ's observation that 'the evidence relating to "choice" and the "freedom" to make any particular choice must be approached in a broad commonsense way' identifies the route through the dilemma.

[26] Thus while, in a physical sense, the acts of assault by penetration of the vagina are the same whether perpetrated by a male or a female, the sexual nature of the acts is, on any common sense view, different where the complainant is deliberately deceived by a defendant into believing that the latter is a male. Assuming the facts to be proved as alleged, M chose to have sexual encounters with a boy and her preference (her freedom to choose whether or not to have a sexual encounter with a girl) was removed by the defendant's deception.

[27] It follows from the foregoing analysis that we conclude that, depending on the circumstances, deception as to gender can vitiate consent . . ."

Appeal against conviction dismissed

The Court of Appeal in *McNally* did not interpret whether the appellant's deceit fell within the ambit of s.76(2)(a), as it was never suggested that the conclusive presumptions applied, therefore, the relevance of the deception was restricted to the impact it had on the construction of s.74. This approach is similar to that taken in *Jheeta* in that the courts appear to be willing to utilise the breadth of s.74

---

[300] H. Gross, "Rape, Moralism and Human Rights" [2007] Crim. L.R. 220 and McEwan, "The Rape Shield Askew? *R v A*" [2001] 5 International J. of Evidence and Proof 267.

[301] See further, Herring, "Mistaken Sex" [2005] Crim. L. R. 511 at 515–617 and J.W. Herring, "Human Rights and Rape: A Reply to Hyman Gross" [2007] Crim. L.R. 228.

[302] *R. v McNally (Justine)* [2014] 2 W.L.R. 200.

where a narrow interpretation of s.76 is applied, or as in this case where s.76 is not raised at all. However, we are to some extent left unsure whether deceit as to gender will ever fall under s.76(2)(a), or alternatively whether this is a question of fact that must be left to the jury to determine with reference only to the meaning of freedom of choice under s.74.

Whether such a deceit should conclusively vitiate consent is highly questionable, especially if we consider the fact that the nature and purpose of the act, i.e. to penetrate the vagina, remains the same regardless of the gender of the defendant. Lord Leveson's statement that common sense tells us that the nature of the sexual act changes where there is a deception as to gender may not be as commonsensical as he suggests. It is difficult to see how the nature of an act can change retrospectively when both parties previously understood that act to be sexual. There may well be implications for such a deception to the notions of "free choice" and "agreement", such that the victim was denied a free choice to make an informed agreement about the sexual act, but the nature of the act surely remains unchanged. Sexual acts do not become non-sexual just because they are carried out between people of the same gender. The problem with the reasoning provided in *McNally* is that it may lead to a situation where transgendered individuals must reveal their biological sex to prospective sexual partners or risk being prosecuted and labelled as rapists/sexual offenders.[303] This will surely give rise to potential breaches of art.8 of the European Convention on Human Rights which guarantees the right to respect for a private life.[304] By analogy, and if taken literally, Lord Leveson's assertion could also mean that a heterosexual person will have potentially been raped by a homosexual person, where the homosexual person makes the representation that he is in fact straight. If after a sexual act the former finds out that the homosexual person was not in fact heterosexual but was instead "experimenting", the question arises: does the sexual nature of the act change rendering the homosexual partner a rapist?

Such an approach could also extend to the defendant who fails to inform his sexual partner that he is HIV positive because failing to tell the other person deprives her of the opportunity to give "real" consent. However, this is not the approach the courts have taken: the consent to sexual intercourse has been held to be valid.[305] Instead, the failure to inform the complainant will negate consent for the purposes of, for example, ss.18 or 20 of the Offences against the Person Act 1861 if that person were to become infected with HIV.[306] However, it should be noted that Lord Leveson in *McNally* suggested that the court in *B* did not decide that deception as to HIV status could never vitiate consent. Rather, the court had left it open as to whether consent would be negated, if for example the defendant was asked about his HIV status and actively deceived the complainant. This again leaves upon the possibility that deception as to one's sexual health may in some circumstances lead to the vitiation of consent.

A similar question arose in *Assange*[307] where the Divisional Court was concerned with the question of whether sexual intercourse without a condom, where it had been made clear that consent was conditional on the use of a condom, would vitiate consent. Taking a narrow approach to interpreting s.76(2)(a) Sir John Thomas P held that the conclusive presumption did not apply in such a situation

---

[303]   For a critique of this case and its implications for trans people, see A. Sharpe, "Criminalising Sexual Intimacy: Transgender Defendants and the Legal Construction of Non-consent" [2014] Crim. L.R 207. Sharpe argues that non-disclosure of one's gender identity is neither deceptive nor particularly harmful. The belief that non-disclosure is deceptive and harmful is the result of transphobic and homophobic attitudes which must not be accepted as the norm.

[304]   One might also wish to consider whether the courts were therefore justified in McNally in sentencing a young trans man struggling to come to terms with his transgender identity to three years' custody and to lifetime registration on the Sex Offenders' Register.

[305]   *R. v B* [2006] EWCA Crim 2945.

[306]   *Dica* [2004] Q.B. 1257; *Konzani* [2005] 2 Cr. App. R. 98.

[307]   *Assange v Swedish Prosecution Authority* (2011) 108(44) L.S.G. 17.

but that s.74 could and should be used to determine whether the deliberate removal of the condom restricted the complainants capacity to make a free choice.[308]

(b) *The evidential presumptions*

As well as the conclusive presumptions, s.75 creates six evidential presumptions. This is an exhaustive list; thus additions may only be made to it by Parliament.[309] The content of s.75 changed significantly during the reform process. Threats of harm (other than immediate violence) or other serious detriment to the victim or others and cases where the consent of the victim had only been indicated by a third party were dropped from the list and s.75(2)(f) was added.[310] If the prosecution can prove that the defendant did the relevant act in any of the six circumstances and that he knew of the circumstance, it will be presumed that there was no consent and that he lacked a reasonable belief in consent. The defence will then be under an evidential burden to introduce sufficient evidence to raise the issue of consent or reasonable belief in consent.[311] It might be, for example, that the defendant claims that the couple were engaging in consensual sado-masochistic sexual intercourse. If sufficient evidence is raised, the prosecution will have to prove lack of consent or reasonable belief beyond reasonable doubt.[312] As the Judicial Studies Board has noted, the Act does not specify whether it is for the judge or the jury to decide whether the evidential burden is discharged, but the Board's direction assumes that it is a matter for the judge and that "although each case will turn on its facts, it is thought that in many cases a section 75 direction will not be appropriate".[313] In circumstances when it is necessary to give a direction, the Court of Appeal has urged trial judges to take care so as to avoid the risk of elevating the presumptions to the level of the conclusive presumptions.[314]

(iii) The relationship between the presumptions and the general definition

Jennifer Temkin and Andrew Ashworth, "The Sexual Offences Act 2003: (1) Rape, Sexual Assaults and the Problems of Consent" [2004] Crim. L.R. 328 at 336–337:

"By introducing a three-track approach to matters of consent and belief in consent—irrebuttable presumptions, rebuttable presumptions, and a general definition of consent—the Act raised a number of questions. Are the three

---

[308] See also, *R. (F) v Director of Public Prosecutions* [2014] 2 W.L.R. 190 involving a complainant who agreed to sexual intercourse on the basis that the defendant would not ejaculate into her vagina. The defendant agreed to this knowing that he would in fact ejaculate. The court held that, "if before penetration began the intervener had made up his mind that he would penetrate and ejaculate within the claimant's vagina, or . . . he decided that he would not withdraw at all, just because he deemed the claimant subservient to his control, she was deprived of choice relating to the crucial feature on which her original consent to sexual intercourse was based. Accordingly her consent was negated. Contrary to her wishes, and knowing that she would not have consented, and did not consent to penetration or the continuation of penetration if she had any inkling of his intention, he deliberately ejaculated within her vagina. In law, this combination of circumstances falls within the statutory definition of rape" [26].

[309] Temkin and Ashworth, "The Sexual Offences Act: (1) Rape, Sexual Assaults and the Problems of Consent" [2004] Crim. L.R. 328 at 338. *Setting the Boundaries* (above fn.245) had conceived of the list as a starting point, with further circumstances being added as the case-law developed (para.2.10.7).

[310] See further, Temkin and Ashworth, "The Sexual Offences Act: (1) Rape, Sexual Assaults and the Problems of Consent" [2004] Crim. L.R. 328 at 338–340.

[311] In *R. v Ciccarelli* [2011] 1 Cr. App. R. 15 it was held that before the question of the defendant's reasonable belief in the complainant's consent could be left to the jury, some evidence beyond the fanciful or speculative had to be adduced to support the reasonableness of a belief. The defendant's mere assertion of his belief in her consent was insufficient.

[312] On issues of proof, see Temkin and Ashworth, "The Sexual Offences Act: (1) Rape, Sexual Assaults and the Problems of Consent" [2004] Crim. L.R. 328 at 342–344.

[313] Judicial Studies Board, *Specimen Directions: 16a* (2007).

[314] *R. v Zhang (Shanjil)* [2007] EWCA Crim 2018.

categories intended to reflect some kind of moral hierarchy, so that the most serious cases on non-consent give rise to irrebuttable presumptions and the next serious cases of non-consent to rebuttable presumptions with the remainder falling within the general definition? Or is the organising principle one of clarity and certainty, so that it is the clearest cases (not necessarily the worst) that give rise to irrebuttable presumptions and the next clearest to rebuttable presumptions, with the remainder falling within the general definition? Or is it a mixture of the two, with an added element of common law history? One would have thought that consideration ought to be given to marking out the worst cases of non-consent by means of irrebuttable presumptions, but that appears not to have happened."

It is by no means certain that all the right circumstances have been included in the list of evidential presumptions and it is certainly questionable whether the conclusive presumptions are necessarily the "worst". There is a compelling argument, for example, that the fact that the victim was unconscious at the time of the act should have been included as a conclusive presumption rather than an evidential presumption. Had the presumptions only applied to rape and assault by penetration then this might well have been easier to achieve. As it is, it is appropriate that a conclusive presumption should not be applied to a defendant who sexually touches his sleeping partner, as is their habit, during the course of a night.[315]

What does seem clear is that juries are directed to the presumptions first, but only, of course, if applicable to the facts of the case. In practice it seems that cases falling under s.75 are rare and so it is uncommon for the presumptions to be introduced. The general definition applies in the many cases where the presumptions do not, such as, for example, where there are threats of non-immediate violence or threats of other kinds. It is in such situations that juries will continue to experience difficulties in coming to a conclusion from all the evidence as to the presence or absence of consent. The fact that we now have a definition of consent may focus the jury's attention on the right questions.[316] However, given a definition of consent that "positively sprouts uncertainties"[317] it will not make the answers any easier. Indeed, it seems that judges, in trying to guide juries, are tempted to continue to employ the distinction drawn in *Olugboja*, even though, as we have seen, the Government rejected it.[318]

2. Rape

Sexual Offences Act 2003 s.1

"(1) A person (A) commits an offence if—

(a) he intentionally penetrates the vagina, anus or mouth of another person (B) with his penis,

(b) B does not consent to the penetration, and

(c) A does not reasonably believe that B consents.

(2) Whether a belief is reasonable is to be determined having regard to all the circumstances, including any steps A has taken to ascertain whether B consents."

Rape is punishable by a maximum of life imprisonment.[319]

---

[315]   Temkin and Ashworth, "The Sexual Offences Act: (1) Rape, Sexual Assaults and the Problems of Consent" [2004] Crim. L.R. 328 at 338–339.

[316]   Although this is contested: see Tadros, "Rape Without Consent" [2006] 26 O.J.L.S. 515 at 518–532.

[317]   Temkin and Ashworth, "The Sexual Offences Act: (1) Rape, Sexual Assaults and the Problems of Consent" [2004] Crim. L.R. 328 at 338. See also, C.S. Elliot and C. de Than, "The Case for a Rational Reconstruction of Consent in Criminal Law" (2007) 70 M.L.R. 225 at 236–249.

[318]   See *R. v PK* [2008] EWCA Crim 434 where the trial judge drew a problematic distinction between *"willing* submission" and real consent. The Court of Appeal commented that the expression was not an easy one in the context and was not one that it "would commend for use on other occasions" (at [92]), but given the rest of the judge's direction it would not have misled the jury in the instant case.

[319]   Sexual Offences Act 2003 s.1(4).

(i) Introduction

Two very significant issues had been resolved prior to the passing of the Sexual Offences Act 2003. The bar on bringing prosecutions of rape against husbands had been removed and rape had been redefined so as to include male rape.

(a) *Marital rape*

Historically, the offence of rape contained the phrase "unlawful". This was taken to refer to intercourse outside marriage. The origin of this understanding or rule (whether one regards it as one or the other was a part of the debate, as we shall see) lay not in a statute or a case but in the writings of Sir Matthew Hale:

> "But the husband cannot be guilty of a rape committed by himself upon his lawful wife, for by their mutual matrimonial consent and contract the wife hath given herself in this kind unto her husband, which she cannot retract."[320]

For the following 200 years, Hale's analysis was predominantly accepted. Husbands who used force could be charged with an offence of violence[321] but there was a bar to charges of rape. This marital immunity began to erode, however, from 1949 onwards[322] and was completely rejected by the House of Lords in *R*.[323] Lord Keith of Kinkel held that whatever status Hale's proposition might have had, the common law had to evolve in the light of changing social, economic and cultural developments. He stated that the notion that

> "by marriage a wife gives her irrevocable consent to her husband under all circumstances and irrespective of her health and how she happens to be feeling at the time . . . [is] in modern times . . . quite unacceptable".[324]

He believed that

> "it is clearly unlawful to have sexual intercourse with any woman without her consent, and that the use of the word [unlawful] adds nothing . . . [T]here are no rational grounds for putting the suggested gloss on the word, and it should be treated as mere surplusage in this enactment."[325]

Although most commentators warmly welcomed this result[326] there were doubts as to whether the House of Lords was entitled to act in the way it did. It was described as "blatant" judicial law-making[327] amidst allegations of retrospectivity. The matter is now beyond doubt. First, the European Court of Human Rights decided that the decision had not contravened art.7 of the European Convention on

---

[320]   *History of the Pleas of the Crown* (1736), Vol.1 at p.629.
[321]   He could also be guilty of rape as an aider and abetter: see, e.g. *Cogan and Leek* [1976] Q.B. 217.
[322]   *R. v Clarke (James)* (1949) 33 Cr. App. R. 216; *Miller* [1954] 38 Cr. App. R. 1; *R. v O'Brien (Edward Vincent)* [1974] 3 All E.R. 663; *Steele* (1977) 66 Cr. App. R.; *Roberts* [1986] Crim. L.R. 188. In these cases the court held that the immunity no longer protected the husband if the parties had, for example, formally separated.
[323]   [1992] 1 A.C. 599.
[324]   At [1992] 1 A.C. 599 at 616.
[325]   At [1992] 1 A.C. 599 at 622–623.
[326]   The most notable exception being G. Williams in "Rape is Rape" (1992) 140 N.L.J. 11 where he identified what he described as four "powerful" reasons why rape by husbands (and cohabitees) should be distinguished from that by strangers.
[327]   M. Giles, "Judicial Law-Making in the Criminal Court" [1992] Crim. L.R. 407 at 408.

Human Rights.[328] Secondly, legislative reform in 1994 placed the ruling in *R.* upon a solid statutory footing.[329]

(b) *Male rape*

Although it has become increasingly common to talk about the phenomenon of male rape, the law traditionally dealt with non-consensual anal intercourse as buggery.[330] However, since 1994 rape has included anal or vaginal intercourse and the victim may be male or female.[331] The law has thus moved towards gender-neutrality (although the move is not complete since legally only males are capable of committing the offence). This reform was controversial. It has been argued that it ignores the gendered reality of rape: "It is still men who are raping and women who are being raped."[332] It has also been claimed that gender-specific laws "raise unique and important issues of male and female power. It invokes the differences in male and female ways of understanding force and consent and each other."[333] However, other commentators have supported the extension of the law of rape.

Philip Rumney and Martin Morgan-Taylor, "Recognizing the Male Victim: Gender Neutrality and the Law of Rape" (1997) 26 Anglo-American L. Rev. 198 at 219–234:

"[T]he acts of vaginal and anal penetration are too similar to warrant separate legal classification . . . The motives of the assailant . . . would appear to be similar for the penetrative acts in question, irrespective of the sex of the victim . . . Indeed, it is argued . . . that male rape is an act of violence, committed to assert power, rather than being primarily sexually motivated . . . [T]he trauma and consequences of rape are similar for both men and women. In addition to any physical injury, victims may suffer serious psychological trauma as a consequence of rape. Both male and female victims appear to suffer similar psychological reactions after rape . . .

It is therefore argued that the consequences of either vaginal or anal rape are not sufficiently dispersive to justify an exclusionary gender specific approach to rape, and that, on the evidence, the new law is wholly justifiable."

The changes made to sexual offences by the Act of 2003 continue the trend towards gender-neutral offences but draw back from completing the process in that rape continues to be defined so as to be committed by males only.[334]

(ii) Actus reus

The Sexual Offences Act 2003 further extended the definition of rape. As well as penile penetration of the vagina or anus, penetration of the mouth by the penis is now part of the actus reus, it having been recognised that this is "horrible, as demeaning and as traumatising as other forms of penile penetration".[335] It is clear that full sexual intercourse need not take place for rape to occur; the slight-

---

[328]   It ruled that art.7 which prohibits retrospectivity did not prevent judicial clarification and development of case-law provided that the development could reasonably have been foreseen: *C.R. v United Kingdom; SW v United Kingdom* [1996] 1 F.L.R. 434.

[329]   Criminal Justice and Public Order Act 1994 s.142.

[330]   This was an offence punishable by a maximum of life imprisonment: Sexual Offences Act 1956 s.12.

[331]   Criminal Justice and Public Order Act 1994 s.142.

[332]   N. Nafine, "Possession: Erotic Love in the Law of Rape" [1994] 57 M.L.R. 10 at 24. On this, see further, S.J. Schulhofer, *Unwanted Sex: The Culture of Intimidation and the Failure of the Law* (Cambridge: Harvard University Press, 1998), pp.47–68.

[333]   S. Estrich, "Rape" [1986] 95 Yale L.J. 1086 at 1149.

[334]   For a critique of this, see P. Rumney, "The Review of Sex Offences and Rape Law Reform: Another False Dawn?" [2001] 64 M.L.R. 890 at 894–898.

[335]   *Setting the Boundaries*, above fn.245, para.2.8.4; *Protecting the Public*, above fn.192, para.40. As these are all ways in which

est degree of penetration of the vagina, anus or the mouth with the penis suffices.[336] Further, penetration is a continuing act from entry to withdrawal.[337] Thus, if a sexual partner revokes consent during penetration and the other, aware of this, does not withdraw within a reasonable time, this will be rape.[338] Penetration of the vagina, anus or mouth with other parts of the body or inanimate objects is not rape but instead falls within the new offence under s.2 of assault by penetration.[339] To this extent, rape continues to be a gender-specific offence whilst assault by penetration is not.

As well as establishing penetration, it must be proved, as discussed above, that the victim did not consent to penetration.

(iii) Mens rea

Section 1 provides that the defendant will be liable for rape if:

(1) the penetration is intentional, and

(2) he does not reasonably believe that the victim consents.

It is, by the very nature of the acts involved, unlikely that difficulties will occur in establishing that the penetration was intentional.

However, the issue of the defendant's state of mind in relation to the victim's consent is highly problematic. Under the old law, as well as intending to have sexual intercourse the defendant also had to *know* that the person was not consenting, or be *reckless* as to whether she was consenting.[340] In the House of Lords' decision in *Morgan* it was held that where a defendant honestly believed the woman was consenting he could not be said to have the required mens rea for rape.[341] It is important to remember that *Morgan* was decided, and the Sexual Offences (Amendment) Act 1976 enacted,[342] at a time when recklessness bore only its "subjective" meaning: the defendant had actually to be aware that there was a risk the woman was not consenting. This meant that were a defendant asserted that he was genuinely unaware that there was a risk the woman was not consenting, the prosecution would then have to prove beyond reasonable doubt that he was in fact aware of such a risk. This was without doubt a difficult burden to surpass.

Subsequently, the House of Lords in *Caldwell* and *Lawrence* redefined the concept of recklessness so as to encompass a failure to consider an obvious risk and initially it seemed as if this interpretation would be applied to the mens rea of rape.[343] However, shortly afterwards, mirroring

---

the actus reus of rape may be committed, where the charge concerns one act of penetration and there is doubt as to which orifice was penetrated, the indictment can read "penetration, either vaginally or anally": *R. v K (Robert)* [2008] EWCA Crim 1923. Further, no distinction is drawn between the forms of penetration for sentencing purposes: *R. v Ismail (Abokar Ahmed)* [2005] Crim. L.R. 491.

[336] *Hughes* (1841) 9 C. & P. 752. Vaginal penetration occurs as soon as the vulva has been entered: Sexual Offences Act 2003 s.79(9).

[337] Sexual Offences Act 2003 s.79(2).

[338] See the pre-Act case of *Kaitamaki v The Queen* [1985] A.C. 147 (Privy Council). The issue of what amounts to a reasonable amount of time is left to the jury.

[339] See below, p.666.

[340] Sexual Offences Act 1956 s.1(2)(b) as amended by Sexual Offences (Amendment) Act 1976 s.6A. In deciding whether the defendant believed the victim was consenting, the jury should have regard to the presence or absence of reasonable grounds for such a belief (s.1(2)).

[341] *Morgan* [1976] A.C. 182.

[342] Which statutorily endorsed the decision in *Morgan*.

[343] *R. v Pigg (Stephen)* [1982] 1 W.L.R. 762.

developments elsewhere in the criminal law, the *Caldwell/Lawrence* definition of recklessness was rejected in *R. v S.*[344] As a result, for almost 20 years the mens rea requirement was expressed as whether the defendant was reckless in the sense that he "couldn't care less" whether the victim had consented or not in situations where the claim was not that a genuine mistake had been made. That is to say, if the jury concluded that the defendant could not care less whether the victim wanted to have sexual intercourse or not, but continued regardless, then he would have been reckless and guilty of rape.

The controversy surrounding the decision in *Morgan* did not, however, subside during this time. While some agreed that its conclusions were a matter of "inexorable logic"[345] others believed that, as far as an offence such as rape was concerned, it still left women unacceptably vulnerable.

T. Pickard, "Culpable Mistakes and Rape: Relating Mens Rea to the Crime" (1980) 30 University of Toronto L.J. 75 at 77, 83:

"There can be no doubt that it is a major harm for a woman to be subjected to non-consensual intercourse notwithstanding that the man may believe he has her consent. There can be little doubt that the cost of taking reasonable care is insignificant compared with the harm which can be avoided through its exercise: indeed, the only cost I can identify is the general one of creating some pressure towards greater explicitness in sexual contexts. To accept an honest but unreasonable belief in consent as a sufficient answer in these circumstances is to countenance the doing of a major harm that could have been avoided at no appreciable cost. Therefore, in terms of simple balancing of interest, it is sound policy to require reasonable care, given the capabilities of the actor. It is true, of course, that not all sound policies can be appropriately pursued through the use of criminal law. But considering the disparate weights of the interests involved, a failure to inquire carefully into consent constitutes, in my view, such a lack of minimal concern for the bodily integrity of others that it is good criminal policy to ground liability on it . . . I accept that in many instances, particularly where inadvertence is involved, mistaken wrongdoing may not be bad enough to deserve criminal sanction. But a major part of my effort is to show that there are different kinds of mistakes. In rape, we are dealing not with the kind of mistake that results from the complexity of our endeavours and inevitable human frailty, but with an easily avoided and self-serving mistake produced by the actor's indifference to the separate existence of another. When the harm caused is so great, it seems clear to me that making such a mistake is sufficiently culpable to warrant criminal sanction."

The approach taken by the Sexual Offences Act 2003 represents the success of arguments such as those advanced by Pickard at the expense of the subjectivist principle. This is absolutely the right approach. Thus, the question is now whether the defendant reasonably believed that the victim consented[346] and there is no place for the concept of recklessness within this enquiry. If the factual circumstances of the case fall within either ss.75 or 76 then the presumptions will operate.[347]

However, when considering whether the defendant reasonably believed in consent, s.1(2) comes into play. It is here that the success described above has the potential to become rather hollow. Section 1(2) states:

"Whether a belief is reasonable is to be determined having regard to all the circumstances, including any steps A has taken to ascertain whether B consents."

---

[344]   *R. v S (Satnam)* (1984) 78 Cr. App. R. 149.
[345]   Per Lord Hailsham in *Morgan* [1976] A.C. 182 at 214 and echoed by Smith at [1975] Crim. L.R. 717 at 719.
[346]   In *Taran* [2006] All E.R. (D) 173 the court concluded that a direction as to reasonable belief was only required in cases where the jury might conclude that there had been some misunderstanding. It was not necessary to give the jury "an abstract lesson on the law" by giving the complicated direction in cases where it was unnecessary.
[347]   Above, pp.652–657.

Jennifer Temkin and Andrew Ashworth, "The Sexual Offences Act 2003: (1) Rape, Sexual Assaults and the Problems of Consent" [2004] Crim. L.R. 328 at 341–242:

"This wording discards the 'reasonable person' in favour of a general test of what is reasonable in the circumstances. The Home Affairs Committee applauded the change as avoiding the 'potential injustice' of a test that would operate regardless of individual characteristics: 'by focusing on the individual defendant's belief, the new test will allow the jury to look at characteristics such as learning disability or mental disorder—and take them into account.' . . .

Has Parliament replaced the 'couldn't care less' test with one that is more demanding on the prosecution and more favourable to the defence? Much depends on how the phrase 'all the circumstances' comes to be interpreted. The Government's view was that 'it is for the jury to decide whether any of the attributes of the defendant are relevant to their deliberations, subject to directions from the judge where necessary'. Beverly Hughes [Government Minister] expressed the matter slightly differently, stating that it would be for the judge 'to decide whether it was necessary to introduce consideration of the defendant's characteristics and which characteristics . . . The judge and jury can take into account all or any characteristics and circumstances that they wish to, and it is best that we leave that decision to the judge and jury for each case.' By what standards is it to be decided which characteristics are 'relevant'? Much will depend upon the Specimen Directions[348] and the Court of Appeal . . .

In *Protecting the Public* the Government expressed its concern that the *Morgan* test 'leads many victims who feel that the system will not give them justice, not to report incidents or press for them to be brought to trial'. Accordingly, it decided to alter the test 'to include one of reasonableness under the law'. But the present formulation is unlikely to provide the incentive to report or pursue the case that the Government is seeking. The broad reference to 'all the circumstances' is an invitation to the jury to scrutinise the complainant's behaviour to determine whether there was anything about it which could have induced a reasonable belief in consent. In this respect the Act contains no challenge to society's norms and stereotypes about either the relationship between men and women or other sexual situations, and leaves open the possibility that these stereotypes will determine assessments of reasonableness."

So what "circumstances" are the courts likely to decide are relevant? It might well be that the youth, sexual inexperience or the learning difficulties of defendants would be deemed to be relevant in determining whether their belief in consent was reasonable. In *TS*,[349] for example, when fresh evidence was introduced concerning the diagnosis of the defendant with Asperger's syndrome, the Court of Appeal quashed his conviction and ordered a retrial as his condition could have affected his ability to understand the victim's intentions. Given many judges' strong adherence to subjectivism in the past, taking into account the characteristics of the individual defendant might well be seen to be a "means of ameliorating what they might perceive to be the harshness involved in the objective test".[350] However, it is submitted that the courts must exercise the utmost caution. For instance, what if the defendant has been brought up with the complete conviction that a woman's consent is worthless? Are these attributes that the jury can consider when determining whether the defendant's belief is a reasonable one? Such an issue was raised in the case of *R. v MA* where at sentencing it was asserted by defence counsel that the defendant (who originated from outside the United Kingdom) should have been treated "slightly differently from a man who had been brought up in the United Kingdom . . . to reflect that his offending was based on his belief that he had a right to rape his wife."[351] This submission received short shrift from Mr Griffith Williams J who held that:

---

[348] Specimen Direction 16a states that "the Act does not say whether 'circumstances' include any, and if so what, personal characteristics of D, and the answer to this question will have to await judicial development", Judicial Studies Board, *Specimen Directions* (2007).

[349] *R. v TS* [2008] EWCA Crim 6.

[350] C.M.V. Clarkson, *Understanding Criminal Law*, 4th edn (London: Sweet & Maxwell, 2005), p.201.

[351] *R. v MA* [2012] EWCA Crim 1646 at [20].

"We reject that submission out of hand. No man, whatever his background, whatever his race, whatever his creed, has the right to rape his wife."[352]

Taking such characteristics and circumstances into account would largely subvert the objective test enshrined in the Sexual Offences Act 2003. Although the decision in *R. v MA* relates to sentencing matters, it suggests that the courts will be reluctant to entertain evidence pertaining to a defendant's cultural background which gives rise to a belief that would otherwise be seen "objectively" as unreasonable. However, what if the defendant's belief is based, not on his cultural understandings about consent, but on a delusion caused by a psychiatric condition? Should such a circumstance be considered when determining whether the defendant's belief is reasonable?

R. v B [2013] 1 Cr. App. R. 36 (Court of Appeal, Criminal Division)

The defendant was convicted, inter alia, of the rape of his partner. A medical expert submitted that at the time of the offences the defendant had likely to have been suffering from paranoid schizophrenia which had resulted in a number of delusional beliefs. The expert submitted that the acts of sexual intercourse might have been motivated by the defendant's delusional beliefs that he had sexual healing powers. However, any such delusions had not affected his ability to understand whether the complainant was consenting.

HUGHES LJ:

"[24] The [trial] judge was invited to direct the jury that if and when it came to considering the reasonableness of any belief by the defendant that the complainant was consenting, it was entitled to take into account his mental condition at the time. After argument and careful consideration, he declined to do so. He gave the jury an admirably clear and untechnical direction that the mental condition was not to be taken into account. He said:

'If you are satisfied so that you are sure that she was not consenting on the occasion you are considering, you then go on to consider this issue of reasonable belief. This is where you are focusing on what is in the defendant's mind. You have considered her position as to whether she was consenting. Now let us look at him and what he was or might have been believing . . .

As a matter of public policy the law does not permit defendants suffering from mental illness to avoid the consequences of their crimes by relying upon the explanation: 'I only did it because I was mentally ill'. That may sound harsh but you can see the sense behind it, because if mental illness did operate as an excuse for criminal conduct it would be *carte blanche*. The law is not a total ass, because mental illness may well have a role to play in influencing sentence . . .

If . . . you find that he did have a belief or might have had a belief that she was consenting to the particular act of intercourse, then you have to go on and consider the reasonableness of that belief.

Given the facts in this case it is important to understand that a delusional belief in consent or a belief in consent which is the result of his mental illness cannot be a reasonable belief . . .

Ask yourselves what society would reasonably expect of a person not suffering from mental illness, not suffering from mental illness, who found themselves in the circumstances that pertained on each of the occasions . . .

To try to explain it in simple terms, if you put the mental illness out of the question, were all the signs and signals such that someone who had been in a relationship with her all those years would have picked up on the signals and realised that she was not consenting, or were the signals such that someone would have, or might have, thought "Yes, she is consenting" and have carried on?' . . .

[25] Mr Spence QC submits that this was wrong. The judge ought, he says, to have directed the jury in very general terms that the question of whether the belief was reasonable was whether it was reasonable in the particular circumstances of the defendant, which included his mental illness. The judge should, says Mr Spence, have given no other or more specific guidance, leaving the matter to the jury at large.

---

[352] *R. v MA* [2012] EWCA Crim 1646 at [21].

[26] Mr Cray for the Crown submits that the judge was right. A delusional belief may, he says, be a genuine one, but it is by definition an irrational and thus an unreasonable one . . .

[28] We were taken *de bene esse* to the report of the Home Affairs Committee of the House of Commons at the time that the Bill which became the Sexual Offences Act 2003 was passing through Parliament. At the time there was debate (inter alia) as to the form the consent provisions in the Bill should take. One proposal was that it should require a two-stage determination. The first would be whether a reasonable person would have doubted consent. If yes, then the second stage would be whether the defendant acted in a way that a reasonable person would consider sufficient to resolve the doubt. That was not adopted (and would undoubt-edly have been complex to apply). Nor was a further alternative formulation adopted, namely that the test should be what a reasonable person would have thought, if he shared the characteristics of the defendant. The government's view . . . was reported as being strongly in favour of an objective element in the test for belief in consent, on the grounds that it was not unreasonable to require a person to take care to establish that a sexual event as consensual; the cost to him was very slight whilst the cost to a victim of forced sexual activity was very high indeed . . .

[35] . . . we take the clear view that such delusional beliefs cannot in law render reasonable a belief that his partner was consenting when in fact she was not. The Act does not ask whether it was reasonable (in the sense of being understandable or not his fault) for the defendant to suffer from the mental condition which he did. Normally no doubt, absent at least fault such as self-induced intoxication by drink or drugs, the answer to that in the case of acute illness such as this defendant seems to have suffered will be that it is reasonable. What the answer would be if the condition were an antisocial, borderline or psychopathic personality disorder may be more problematic. But the Act asks a different question: whether the belief in consent was a reasonable one. A delu-sional belief in consent, if entertained, would be, by definition, irrational and thus unreasonable, not reasonable. If such delusional beliefs were capable of being described as reasonable, then the more irrational the belief of the defendant the better would be its prospects of being held reasonable . . .

[40] We conclude that unless and until the state of mind amounts to insanity in law, then under the rule enacted in the Sexual Offences Act 2003 beliefs in consent arising from conditions such as delusional psychotic illness or personality disorders must be judged by objective standards of reasonableness and not by taking into account a mental disorder which induced a belief which could not reasonably arise without it . . .

[41] It does not follow that there will not be cases in which the personality or abilities of the defendant may be relevant to whether his positive belief in consent was reasonable. It may be that cases could arise in which the reasonableness of such belief depends on the reading by the defendant of subtle social signals, and in which his impaired ability to do so is relevant to the reasonableness of his belief. We do not attempt exhaustively to foresee the circumstances which might arise in which a belief might be held which is not in any sense irrational, even though most people would not have held it. Whether (for example) a particular defendant of less than ordinary intelligence or with demonstrated inability to recognise behavioural cues might be such a case, or whether his belief ought properly to be characterised as unreasonable, must await a decision on specific facts. It is possible, we think, that beliefs generated by such factors may not properly be described as irrational and might be judged by a jury not to be unreasonable on their particular facts. But once a belief could be judged reasonable only by a process which labelled a plainly irrational belief as reasonable, it is clear that it cannot be open to the jury so to determine without stepping outside the Act."

Appeal dismissed

Following this decision, it seems clear that psychological disorders which give rise to a delusional belief in consent cannot be considered as part of "all the circumstances" when determining whether the defendant's belief was reasonable. The reasoning for this is twofold. Firstly, is that a delusion is considered to be irrational and as such by its very definition cannot be considered to be reasonable; thereby falling outside the ambit of the section. Secondly, it is a matter of public policy that defendants who are mentally ill are not to be provided with a *carte blanche* excuse for raping others. The decision is also interesting in that it leaves open the possibility for those who miss certain social cues, or who are of low intelligence, to raise such factors when a determination is made about the reasonableness of their belief in consent.[353] What this could mean in practice is that those with learning disabilities may raise

---

[353] Such factors not being considered to be irrational.

their disability during such considerations, while those whose belief is "irrational" based on a psycho-logical disorder will be excluded from doing so. Whether it is fair to treat someone with a psychological disorder as culpable for their acts while potentially exonerating those who miss social cues, is far from incontestable. It remains to be seen what other circumstances of the defendant will be considered.

3. Other non-consensual sexual offences

(i) Assault by penetration

Sexual Offences Act 2003 s.2

"(1) A person (A) commits an offence if—

(a) he intentionally penetrates the vagina or anus of another person (B) with a part of his body or anything else,

(b) the penetration is sexual,

(c) B does not consent to the penetration, and

(d) A does not reasonably believe that B consents."

Assault by penetration is punishable by a maximum of life imprisonment.[354]

This offence, together with sexual assault under s.3, broadly replaces the old law of indecent assault which carried a maximum of 10 years' imprisonment.[355] The offence of assault by penetra-tion is an overdue recognition that penetration by objects other than the penis may be every bit as traumatising and harmful as rape.[356] Thus, non-consensual, sexual penetration of the vagina or anus by, for example, a finger or a bottle or other object carries the same maximum as the offence of rape. This is a broad offence. It might be feared that routine internal medical examinations might fall foul of its provisions. However, two factors preclude this. First, in such cases the doctor or nurse obtains the consent of the patient to conduct the examination. Secondly, the penetration is not "sexual". This term is present in a number of offences in the Act and is considered below in relation to sexual assault where it may be more problematic than in relation to assault by penetration.

The mens rea for assault by penetration is that the defendant intends to penetrate and does not reasonably believe that the victim consents.[357]

(ii) Sexual assault

Sexual Offences Act 2003 s.3

"(1) A person (A) commits and offence if—

(a) he intentionally touches another person (B),

(b) the touching is sexual,

---

[354] Sexual Offences Act 2003 s.2(4).
[355] Sexual Offences Act 1956 ss.14, 15. Some actions, such as oral penetration of the mouth by the penis, formerly charged as indecent assault would now be charged as rape.
[356] See *Setting the Boundaries*, above fn.245, paras 2.3.1, 2.91; *Protecting the Public*, above fn.192, para.44.
[357] The same provisions apply as to rape, discussed immediately above.

(c)   B does not consent to the touching, and

(d)   A does not reasonably believe that B consents."

Sexual assault is punishable by a maximum of 10 years' imprisonment.[358]

   This offence replaces the repealed offence of indecent assault.[359] In *Protecting the Public* the view taken was that "some non-penetrative sexual assaults amount to extremely serious offending and can cause high levels of fear, degradation and trauma".[360] Thus, this offence carries a high maximum penalty but it is also recognised that this is a very broad offence and that less serious instances will receive lower sentences.[361] In addition to establishing that the victim does not consent, there are two key elements to be considered in the actus reus. First, there must be touching (a term used in other offences in the Act as well). Section 78(9) states that this "includes touching (a) with any part of the body, (b) with anything else, (c) through anything and in particular includes touching amounting to penetration". In *H*,[362] the defendant approached a woman who was walking her dog and asked her, "Do you fancy a shag?" He then grabbed her tracksuit bottom and pulled her towards him. She was able to break free and run to safety. His conviction under s.3 was upheld by the Court of Appeal: "Where a person is wearing clothing we consider that touching of the clothing constitutes touching for the purpose of section 3."[363]

   The other matter that has to be established is that the touching is "sexual", a term used in many offences of the Act. In many instances it will be very clear that the touching is sexual. If there is doubt, however, guidance can be given to the jury in accordance with the following provision.

Sexual Offences Act 2003 s.78

"[P]enetration, touching or any other activity is sexual if a reasonable person would consider that—

(a)   whatever its circumstances or any person's purpose in relation to it, it is because of its nature sexual, or

(b)   because of its nature it may be sexual and because of its circumstances or the purpose of any person in relation to it (or both) it is sexual."[364]

Under para.(a) the focus is upon the nature of the act itself, rather than surrounding circumstances: would a reasonable person consider that the act is inherently sexual? Paragraph (b), however, is much broader. If a reasonable person would conclude that the behaviour *might be* sexual, whether

---

[358]   Section 3(4). The offence is triable either way.

[359]   In one sense the new offence is narrower than the old law: the new offence requires a touching to occur; the old offence also occurred when the victim was made to apprehend an (indecent) assault. See further, D. Ormerod, "Sexual Assault: Whether Touching of Complainant's Clothing Without Bringing Pressure Against Complainant's Body 'Touching' for Purposes of Sexual Assault" [2005] Crim. L.R. 734 at 736.

[360]   *Protecting the Public*, above n.192, para.45.

[361]   Below p.674.

[362]   *R. v H (Karl Anthony)* [2005] 2 Cr. App. R. 9.

[363]   Per Woolf C.J. at [24]. The appellant had argued it could not amount to touching because he had not touched the victim's body through the clothing.

[364]   As noted by Temkin and Ashworth, Temkin and Ashworth, "The Sexual Offences Act: (1) Rape, Sexual Assaults and the Problems of Consent" [2004] Crim. L.R. 328, and approved by the court in *H* (above) this "cannot be said to provide a definition of the term, rather it sets out an approach for determining whether the activity in question is sexual where this may be in doubt" (p.331).

it *is* sexual is then decided by looking at the defendant's motive and the surrounding circumstances. In *H* (above), the Court of Appeal had doubts as to whether the removal of shoes by a fetishist[365] satisfied the first part of (b) (that the touching "may be sexual"). If this view was taken by a jury, in theory it would not go on to consider the defendant's purpose or the surrounding circumstances at all. This seems a little unrealistic. Firstly, a jury might well decide that the removal of shoes was by itself capable of being sexual. Secondly, even though (b) requires a jury to separate the two questions, it seems more likely that it would look at the facts holistically in deciding whether what happened was "sexual". There are dangers in leaving such an important concept as "sexual" to be decided by the jury and as the court comments in *H*, it is perhaps over-optimistic to hope that recourse to s.78(b) will be limited to unusual circumstances.[366]

The mens rea of sexual assault is that the defendant touches intentionally and does not reasonably believe that the victim consents.[367]

(iii) Intentionally causing someone to engage in sexual activity

Sexual Offences Act 2003 s.4

"(1) A person (A) commits an offence if—

(a) he intentionally causes another person (B) to engage in an activity,

(b) the activity is sexual,

(c) B does not consent to engaging in the activity, and

(d) A does not reasonably believe that B consents.

(2) Whether a belief is reasonable is to be determined having regard to all the circumstances, including any steps A has taken to ascertain whether B consents."

Where the offence involves penetration of the vagina or anus or mouth (in the latter case by the defendant's penis), the maximum sentence is that of life imprisonment.[368] In other situations the maximum sentence is 10 years' imprisonment.[369] The indictment must specify whether the basic or aggravated offence is being charged.

This is a very broad offence that, like s.3, encompasses behaviour that previously would have been prosecuted as indecent assault. The offence consists of causing another person to engage in sexual activity without consent. Thus, for example, women who force men to penetrate them can be prosecuted under this provision. Further, as *Devonald* demonstrates, a defendant who forces the victim to masturbate falls within this offence irrespective of whether he is present at the time.[370]

---

[365] At [11], referring to the pre-2003 Act decision in *R. v George* [1956] Crim. L.R. 52.

[366] At [4].

[367] As with the offences under ss.1 and 2, the question of whether the defendant reasonably believed the victim consented is determined by reference to all the circumstances, including any steps taken by the defendant to ascertain whether the victim consented (s.3(2)). See further, I. Bantekas, "Can Touching Always be Sexual When There is No Sexual Intent?" (2008) 73 Jo. C.L. 251.

[368] Section 4(4).

[369] Section 4(5). This form of the offence can be tried summarily, in which case the maximum penalty is six months' imprisonment.

[370] Above p.654.

4. Child sexual offences

It is beyond the scope of this book to explore in detail the very large number of offences which have been created to protect children. In addition to the non-consensual offences discussed above, there are three further types of offences involving children: unlawful sexual activity with a child under 13 or under 16; familial offences; and abuse of position of trust offences. The Act has made significant improvements to the old law. It has, for example, removed the discriminatory provisions that distinguished indecent assault upon a girl from that upon a boy[371] in a move towards gender-neutral laws. It has also created new offences, such as meeting following grooming,[372] to protect children from new dangers. However, in determining the question of whether the law "strikes an appropriate balance between sexual abuse and exploitation, on the one hand, and permitting the sexual expression of young persons as they proceed through to adulthood, on the other",[373] a number of commentators have expressed grave reservations.

J.R. Spencer, "The Sexual Offences Act 2003: (2) Child and Family Offences" [2004] Crim. L.R. 347 at 347–352:

"The new offences are too many, and there is needless overlap between them; they are badly drafted in a style that combines an excess of detail on minor matters with a failure to deal with certain major ones; and, most seriously, the new law is exceptionally heavy-handed. It ratchets culpability requirements down, building grave stigmatic offences on negligence or even strict liability. And more fundamentally, it renders theoretically punishable with severe penalties (2, 5, 10 and 14 years, and even life) a range of behaviour for which it is inconceivable that anyone will in practice be prosecuted—and for which it would be scandalous if they were . . .

The age of consent, as under the existing law, remains 16. But the effect of this is watered down by a range of provisions that punish consensual sexual acts where the willing participant is older. Thus, the Act contains a group of 'familial child sex offences' that criminalise all sexual acts where one of the participants was under 18 and the other was of a wide range of relatives or carers . . .

The new child sex offences are open to two obvious criticisms: complexity and obscurity, and 'legislative overkill'."[374]

The following is a list of the main offences designed to protect children:

- Rape of a child under 13.[375]

- Assault of a child under 13 by penetration.[376]

- Sexual assault of a child under 13.[377]

- Causing or inciting a child under 13 to engage in a sexual activity.[378]

- Sexual activity with a child.[379]

---

[371] Sexual Offences Act 1956 ss.5, 6, 14, 15.

[372] Sexual Offences Act 2003 s.15. See further, S. Ost, "Getting to Grips with Sexual Grooming? The New Offence under the Sexual Offences Act 2003" (2004) 26 J. of Social Welfare and Family Law 147; A.A. Gillespie, "Indecent Images, Grooming and the Law" [2006] Crim. L.R. 412.

[373] A. Khan, "Comment: Sexual Offences Act 2003" [2004] 68 Jo. C.L. 220 at 220.

[374] See also H. Keating, "'When the Kissing Has to Stop': Children, Sexual Behaviour and the Criminal Law", in M. Freeman (ed.), Law and Childhood Studies (Oxford: OUP, 2012).

[375] Section 5 (maximum life imprisonment).

[376] Section 6 (maximum life imprisonment).

[377] Section 7 (maximum 14 years' imprisonment).

[378] Section 8 (maximum 14 years' imprisonment).

[379] Section 9 (maximum 14 years' imprisonment).

- Causing or inciting a child to engage in sexual activity.[380]
- Engaging in sexual activity in the presence of a child.[381]
- Causing a child to watch a sexual activity.[382]
- Child sex offences committed by children or young persons.[383]
- Arranging or facilitating commission of a child sex offence.[384]
- Meeting a child following sexual grooming.[385]

The first four offences mirror the core sexual offences (the first three of which were discussed above) but are designed to protect children under the age of 13. In pursuit of this aim the purported consent of a child under the age of 13 is irrelevant. Further, there is no need to prove mens rea on the part of the defendant in relation to the child's age. These offences are thus ones of strict liability. While these provisions were intended to and do catch the adult predator, they also catch much younger persons who engage in sexual activity with the (irrelevant) consent of the child under 13. It is entirely possible from the wording of the offences that a boy of 13 could find himself convicted of causing a child to engage in sexual activity under s.8 for kissing and fondling a girl of 12 with her consent—even if he believed she was aged 13 or over. Research reveals that the average age of first sexual experience is 14 for girls and 13 for boys.[386] We may wish this were not true and we may point to the harmful effects early sexual experience may have, but it can hardly be a proportionate response to hold a 13-year-old liable for an offence that carries a maximum of 14 years' imprisonment for such behaviour. Also if the young couple engage in consensual sexual intercourse, it is absurd—and manifest false labelling—to hold the boy to be a rapist.

The government's response to such concerns is that prosecutorial discretion will prevent such cases occurring.[387] However, as the following case demonstrates there is a danger of disproportionate responses.

R. v G [2009] 1 A.C. 92 (House of Lords)

The defendant, a boy of 15, pleaded guilty to rape of a child under 13 (she was 12). The girl initially alleged that she had not consented to sexual intercourse and it was on this basis that the most serious charge was proceeded with. The boy argued that the girl had consented and told him she was 15, but pleaded guilty when told that neither her consent nor his reasonable belief as to her age was relevant. He was sentenced to a 12-month detention and training order and to the sexual offender notification requirements under the 2003 Act. The Court of Appeal dismissed his appeal against conviction but allowed his appeal against sentence (imposing instead a conditional discharge).

---

[380] Section 10 (maximum 14 years' imprisonment).

[381] Section 11 (maximum 10 years' imprisonment).

[382] Section 12 (maximum 10 years' imprisonment).

[383] Section 13, makes punishable by a maximum of five years anything done by a person under 18 which would have been an offence under ss.9–12 had that person been over 18. This provision, creating a lower maximum penalty, is a very limited recognition of the reality of children and young people's sexual behaviour.

[384] Section 14.

[385] Section 15, punishable by a maximum of 10 years' imprisonment. This list does not include ss.16–19 dealing with abuse of trust provisions, nor ss.25–26 dealing with familial offences.

[386] K. Wellings, J. Field, A. Johnson and J. Wadsworth, *Sexual Behaviour in Britain: the National Survey of Attitudes and Lifestyles* (London: Penguin Publishing, 1994), p.40; K. Wellings, "Sexual Behaviour in Britain: Early Heterosexual Experience" (2001) 358 *The Lancet* 1843.

[387] See, for example, *Hansard* 646, paras 1176/77, April 1, 2003. See further, J. Spencer, "The Sexual Offences Act 2003: (2) Child and Family Offences" [2004] Crim. L.R. 347 at 354–355.

LORD HOFFMANN:

"[2] [The Court of Appeal certified two questions as being of general public importance: '(1) May a criminal offence of strict liability violate article 6(1) and/or 6(2) . . .? (2) Is it compatible with a child's rights under article 8 . . . to convict him of rape contrary to section 5 . . . in circumstances where the agreed basis of plea establishes that his offence fell properly within the ambit of s 13 . . .?'

[3] The mental element of the offence under s 5, as the language and structure of the section makes clear, is that penetration must be intentional but there is no requirement that the accused must have known that the other person was under 13. The policy of the legislation is to protect children. If you have sex with someone who is on any view a child or young person, you take your chance on exactly how old they are. To that extent the offence is one of strict liability and it is no defence that the accused believed the other person to be 13 or over . . .

[7] The other ground of appeal is that the conviction violated the Appellant's right of privacy under art 8.

[8] [Counsel] for the Appellant . . . says that, as he was only 15 at the time of the offence, the Crown acted unduly harshly by prosecuting him under s 5 rather than under s 13, which deals with sexual offences committed by persons under 18 and carries a maximum penalty of imprisonment for five years.

[9] Assuming this to be right, the case has in my opinion nothing to do with art 8 or human rights . . .

[10] Prosecutorial policy and sentencing do not fall under art 8. If the offence in question is a justifiable interference with private life, that is an end of the matter. If the prosecution has been unduly heavy handed, that may be unfair and unjust, but not an infringement of human rights. It is a matter for the ordinary system of criminal justice . . .

[12] In my opinion, therefore, the answers to the certified questions are no and yes respectively. That leaves only the question of whether in the particular circumstances of this case, it was an abuse of process for the Crown to prosecute under s 5. That is not a question which has been certified. For what it is worth, I agree with the Court of Appeal that the Crown was not obliged to withdraw the charge under s 5 when they found themselves having to accept the Appellant's version of events. 'Rape of a child under 13' still accurately described what the Appellant had done. Parliament decided to use this description because children under 13 cannot validly or even meaningfully consent to sexual intercourse. So far as the basis of plea provided mitigation, they were entitled to leave the judge to take it into account. I would dismiss the appeal."

LORD HOPE OF CRAIGHEAD (DISSENTING):

"[13] Section 5 of the Sexual Offences Act 2003, which makes sexual intercourse with a child under 13 a crime of strict liability irrespective of the age of the Defendant and calls it rape, has given rise to some important and difficult questions . . . Section 13 of the same Act, read with s 9(1)(c)(ii), makes it an offence for a person under 18 to have sexual intercourse with a child under 13. Unlike s 5, it does not attach the label of rape to this offence. What behaviour then should the criminal law prohibit, and what should it not? To what extent is it reasonable to leave it to the police and other authorities to decide when to prosecute and, where there is a choice, for which offence? These questions have been brought out into the real world by this case.

[14] There is no doubt that when s 5 of the 2003 Act was enacted the protection of children was one of the primary concerns of the legislature. Furthermore . . . its purpose is to protect children under 13 from themselves as well as from others who are minded to prey upon them. But the creation of an unqualified offence of this kind carries with it the risk of stigmatising as rapists children who engage in a single act of mutual sexual activity. A heavy responsibility has been placed on the prosecuting authorities, where both parties are of a similar young age, to discriminate between cases where the proscribed activity was truly mutual on the one hand and those where the Complainant was subjected to an element of exploitation or undue pressure on the other. In the former case more harm than good may be done by prosecuting. In the latter case the threshold will have been crossed and prosecution is likely to be inevitable. But if in the former case it is decided to prosecute, a decision still has to be made about the section under which the perpetrator is to be prosecuted . . .

[34] Article 8(1) guarantees to everyone the right to respect for his private life, and a teenager has as much to respect for his private life as any other individual. It is unlawful for a prosecutor to act in a way which is inconsistent with a Convention right. So I cannot accept Lord Hoffmann's proposition that the Convention rights have nothing to do with prosecutorial policy . . . The questions then are whether the Appellant's continued prosecution for rape under s 5 was necessary in a democratic society for the protection of any of the interests referred to in art 8(2), and whether it was proportionate. Account must be taken in this assessment of the alternative courses that were open to the prosecutor, including proceeding under s 13 instead of s 5, as well as the sentencing options that are available to the court in the event of a conviction under either alternative and the labels which each of them would attract . . .

[38] . . . There are grounds for thinking that the sanctions that can be imposed under s 13 for mutual sexual activity by a person under 18 with a child under 13 provide all that is needed by way of punishment that is proportionate to the offence. The message that this is an offence can be conveyed to children as well as adults very effectively by the use of these sanctions. . .

[39] Section 5, the rape of a child under 13, on the other hand is designed for a different and much more serious situation . . . The description of the offence as rape, and all the consequences that go with that description, are entirely appropriate where the act has been committed upon a child under 13 by a person over the age of 18. It may also be appropriate where the person who committed it was under that age. But the lower the age, the less appropriate it will be. The question in such a case, given the choice that is available, must be whether in all the circumstances to proceed under s 5 would be proportionate . . .

[40] I would hold that it was unlawful for the prosecutor to continue to prosecute the Appellant under s 5 in view of his acceptance of the basis of the Appellant's plea which was that the Complainant consented to intercourse. This was incompatible with his art 8 Convention right, as the offence fell properly within the ambit of s 13 and not s 5 . . . I would allow the appeal and quash the conviction."

Appeal dismissed

In her speech, Baroness Hale (in the majority) drew attention to the positive obligation of the state under art.8 which might "require the criminal law to provide effective protection for those who cannot protect themselves from the sexual attentions of others". This protection is needed

"whether they like it or not . . . [A]nyone who has practiced in the family courts is only too well aware of the long term and serious harm both physical and psychological, which premature sexual activity can do. And the harm which may be done by premature sexual penetration is not necessarily lessened by the age of the person penetrating."[388]

As Ashworth has commented, this is

"a strong argument, but it is questionable whether it is strong enough to justify convicting of this serious offence a young person of 15 on facts such as those that formed the basis of plea in this case. Important as it is to assert the art.8 rights of the girl of 12, the question in the case also concerns the art.8 rights of the 15-year-old. In very few European countries would this case go to a criminal court at all."[389]

As he rightly comments:

"[T]he question for the courts was whether conviction of this very serious offence, carrying a maximum of life imprisonment, was a disproportionate interference with G's right to respect for his private life. The . . . gross disparity between conviction of a life-carrying offence and the ultimate sentence is a fair indication of the disproportionality involved." [390]

---

[388]   *R. v G* [2009] 1 A.C. 92 at [41] and [49]. Baroness Hale further stated that it could not be wrong to apply the label of rape given that the law disabled a child under 13 giving consent (at [55]).

[389]   A. Ashworth, "Sexual Offences: Sexual Offences Act 2003 s.5—Rape of a Child Under 13—Defendant under 18" [2008] Crim. L.R. 818 at 820. See also A. Ashworth, "Rape: Rape of a Child Under 13—Mental Element—Consent" [2006] Crim. L.R. 930 (commentary to the Court of Appeal decision). Lord Hope was influenced by the approach taken in Scotland whereby consensual sexual activity between children can be dealt with under the (more welfare-orientated) Children's Hearing System. See further, B. Malkani, "Article 8 of the European Convention on Human Rights, and the Decision to Prosecute" [2011] Crim. L.R. 943.

[390]   A. Ashworth, *Principles of Criminal Law*, 6th edn (Oxford: OUP, 2009), p.345.

It is submitted that Lord Hope's reasoning is much to be preferred to that of the majority.

This case illustrates the very real difficulties that the offences create. Moreover, the problems are not confined to the offences concerning victims under 13. The other offences are very broad and overlap. For example, s.9 creates two offences of sexual activity with a child; one of sexual touching and an aggravated offence of sexual activity by penetration. Both carry the same maximum sentence. The offence distinguishes between victims over and under 13: if the victim is over 13 but under 16 it is open to the defendant to show that he had a reasonable belief that the victim was over 16. That possibility is not open to the defendant if the child is under 13.[391] Yet, if the child is less than 13 years old, ss.5–8 (that specifically relate to children younger than 13) could also be charged. This duplication makes the selection of an appropriate charge problematic. More controversial, however, is the fact that all consensual sexual touching between young people under 16 is unlawful. Lord Millett has argued that

> "the age of consent has long ceased to reflect ordinary life, and in this respect Parliament has signally failed to discharge its responsibility for keeping the criminal law in touch with the needs of society".[392]

While setting the age of consent at 16 has much to commend it, as Spencer has commented, the offences "are so far out of line with the sexual behaviour of the young . . . they will eventually make indictable offenders of the whole population".[393] If the offences are not prosecuted, as one would hope would be the case with consensual sexual exploration, children may come to perceive them as empty threats. If offences are prosecuted, not only may individual injustices result, but also other children may be deterred from seeking medical advice or treatment. In the light of G, the CPS has recently issued detailed guidelines for prosecutors and it is to be hoped that this will help to ensure that prosecutions are brought in appropriate circumstances and for the appropriate offence.[394]

C. Sentencing

Rape is punishable by a maximum sentence of life imprisonment as is the new offence of assault by penetration. It is now almost axiomatic that if defendants are convicted, they will serve a period of immediate imprisonment. Twenty years ago, the first sentencing guideline case of *Billam*,[395] made it clear that custodial sentences of five years would be the normal sentence for rape without aggravating features and that only in the most exceptional circumstances would a non-custodial sentence be imposed.[396] This general approach was confirmed by the decision in *Millberry* which also stated that the three dimensions to be considered in sentencing rape offenders were the degree of harm to the victim, the level of culpability of the offender and the degree of risk posed by the offender to society.[397]

---

[391]   Section 9 is, thus, also an offence of strict liability if the victim is under 13.

[392]   *R. v K* [2002] 1 A.C. 462 at [44].

[393]   J. Spencer, "The Sexual Offences Act 2003: (2) Child and Family Offences" [2004] Crim. L.R. 347 at 354 and Keating, "'When the Kissing Has to Stop': Children, Sexual Behaviour and the Criminal Law", in M. Freeman (ed.), *Law and Childhood Studies* (Oxford: Oxford University Press, 2012).

[394]   CPS, *Rape and Sexual Offences: Chapter 11: Youths*, available at *http://www.cps.gov.uk/legal/p_to_r/rape_and_sexual_offences/youths/* [Accessed April 30, 2014].

[395]   *R. v Billam (Keith)* (1986) 8 Cr. App. R. (S.) 48.

[396]   As, for example, in the case of *R. v Taylor (Ross Gordon)* (1983) 5 Cr. App. R. (S.) 241, where the defendant was found to have mental disabilities.

[397]   *R. v Millberry (William Christopher)* [2003] 2 Cr. App. R. (S.) 31. In the joint appeal of *R. v Corran (Ben)* [2005] 2 Cr. App. R. (S.) 73 the Court of Appeal followed *Milberry* in holding that where young offenders are convicted of rape or assault by

The Court of Appeal subsequently extended this approach to sentencing to other categories of sexual offences.[398] However, these cases pre-dated changes made to the law (both before and) by the Sexual Offences Act 2003, which has not only changed the definition of offences but also increased the maximum penalty available for certain key offences. Because of this the Sentencing Guideline Council produced guidelines for sexual offences in 2007.[399] More recently, the Sentencing Council has produced guidelines which focus not just on physical harm but also on the psychological traumas caused by rape. The guidelines state that five years' imprisonment should continue to be the starting point for adult rape where there are no aggravating features (category 3), either in terms of severity of harm or level of culpability.[400] However, for most cases the term of imprisonment is likely to be much higher. For instance, the Court of Appeal has stated that aggravating features, such as a "campaign of rape" or a "terrible breach of trust" will mean that a sentence of 20 years' imprisonment is not regarded as excessive.[401] In *Attorney-General's Reference (No.86 of 2006)* the Court of Appeal confirmed that the fact that rape occurred within a domestic context did not justify a reduction in sentence.[402] In considering the extended definition of rape, the Court of Appeal has also stated:

> "[I]n approaching the question of sentencing no distinction should be made because of the category of rape. One form could be more offensive than another to the victim. It was very much a subjective matter."[403]

Assault by penetration under s.2 is punishable by a maximum of life imprisonment. The sentencing guideline states that in the case of an adult victim (category 3) the starting point should be two years' imprisonment. Where the offence falls into category 1 (for example, where there is severe psychological or physical harm and previous violence has been used against the victim)[404] the starting point is 15 years' imprisonment. [405]

The new offence of sexual assault under s.3 is punishable by a maximum of 10 years or 14 years if the victim is under the age of 13 (s.7). As we have seen, this is an offence that ranges from the very serious to the more minor and the sentencing guideline reflects this.[406] For example, the guideline states that where the touching is *not* of the naked genitalia or breasts and there is no significant planning, abuse of trust, or previous violence against the victim then the starting point should be 26 weeks' imprisonment if the victim was under 13 and a high level Community Order if the victim was older than 13.[407]

---

penetration the sentence should generally be significantly shorter than for an adult. However, where there are aggravating features, long sentences will be imposed on young offenders: *Attorney-General's Reference (Nos 7, 8 and 9 of 2009)* [2009] EWCA Crim 1490.

[398] *Attorney-General's Reference (Nos 91, 119, 120 of 2002)* [2003] 2 Cr. App. R. (S.) 338. The Court of Appeal added the need to deter others from acting in a similar fashion to the factors to be considered.

[399] The Sentencing Guideline Council, *Sexual Offences Act 2003, Definitive Guideline* (2007). The sentencing guideline extended the *Milberry* starting points to all non-consensual offences involving penetration of the anus or vagina or penile penetration of the mouth, p.23.

[400] The Sentencing Council, *Sexual Offences: Definitive Guideline* (2014). For the full list of factors which bring an offence into either category 1 or 2, see p.10. Where there are aggravating factors both in terms of severity of harm and level of culpability, the starting point is 15 years. In the case of a rape of a child under 13 where there are no aggravating factors, the starting point is eight years.

[401] *R. v O* [2008] EWCA Crim 738. See also, *R. v AF* [2009] EWCA Crim 1428.

[402] *Attorney-General's Reference (No.86 of 2006)* [2006] EWCA 3077.

[403] *R. v Ismail (Abokar Ahmed)* [2005] 2 Cr. App. R. (S.) 88.

[404] See the full list of factors, The Sentencing Council, *Sexual Offences: Definitive Guideline* (2014), p.14.

[405] The Sentencing Council, *Sexual Offences: Definitive Guideline* (2014).

[406] The Sentencing Council, *Sexual Offences: Definitive Guideline* (2014), p.32.

[407] The Sentencing Council, *Sexual Offences: Definitive Guideline* (2014), p.33. If there has been contact between the naked

D. Evaluation

The law of sexual offences evokes controversy. There is still much cause for concern in the response of the criminal justice system. Indeed, a study in 2008 concluded:

"As large-scale surveys show, the risk of being sexually assaulted is a tangible threat in women's lives. At the same time, victims of sexual assault can expect little in the way of redress or assistance. A large number of rapes go unreported, and of those that do come to the attention of the police, only a tiny fraction end in conviction. The message from the criminal justice system could not be clearer. Women must put strict limits on their behaviour, must trust no one and take no risks. And, since even this is not a guarantee of safety, they must learn to live with rape."[408]

The decline in the prosecution and conviction rate is alarming. Even if cases proceed to trial, complainants may be exposed to the most humiliating of cross-examinations by defence barristers and if not, now, by defendants themselves. The scheme to prevent previous sexual history being introduced may be in need of further reform and the proposals to permit general expert evidence about the impact of offences upon victims seem increasingly likely to come to nothing. At least in relation to sentencing, the stereotypical image of what is rape, which has in the past led to lenient sentencing, appears to be retreating.

In so far as the substantive law is concerned, there have been very considerable improvements as a result of the Sexual Offences Act 2003. Reform to child sex offences, which had been the subject of piecemeal development over many years, was long overdue. However, it remains to be seen whether prosecutorial discretion will protect children from unwarranted prosecutions. So far, the indications are not good. In relation to the offence of rape, it is absolutely right that no truck has been given to the idea that there should be different levels of rape depending upon whether there was or had been a relationship between the complainant and the defendant. Any such view, based upon the paradigm of the stranger/violent rape, is built upon a false premise. Not only are most victims likely to know their assailant, but also strangers do not have exclusive dominion over the use of violence. With or without violence, relationship or acquaintance rape may destroy the possibility of future relationships. If the wrong in rape is the objectification of a person then those who are made to have sexual intercourse without consent by people they know are raped.

The arguments that the actus reus of rape should be broadened to include penile penetration of the mouth were convincing and were accepted in the revised offence. In addition, there is overdue recognition of the gravity of other forms of penetrative sexual assault by the offence of assault by penetration, punishable by a maximum of life imprisonment. There can be no doubt, hearing evidence from victims, that the trauma and harm involved in these assaults can be as bad as that involved in rape. Whether such penetrative assaults should be included within a broadened definition of rape, as has been done in some other jurisdictions, is a controversial matter. On the one hand, there is the view that if the wrong is the objectification of a person, one should not distinguish between penetration by the penis and penetration by an inanimate object. On the other hand, there is the argument that, for fair labelling reasons, rape should be limited to penetration by the penis.[409]

---

genitalia of the offender and the naked face, mouth or genitalia of the victim the starting point is five years if the victim is under 13 years old and three years if the victim is over 13 years old (p.33).

[408] Temkin and Krahé, *Sexual Assault and the Justice Gap: A Question of Attrition* (Oxford: Oxford University Press, 2008), p.209.

[409] For further argument on this point, see C.M.V. Clarkson, *Understanding Criminal Law*, 4th edn (London: Sweet & Maxwell, 2005), p.206 and D. Warbuton, "The Rape of a Label—Why it Would be Wrong to Follow Canada in Having a Single Offence of Unlawful Sexual Assault" [2004] 68 Jo. C.L. 533.

With regard to the mens rea of rape the rule that the defendant need only make an honest mistake about the victim's consent has been rightly consigned to history. As Gardner and Shute argue, those who wish to have sexual intercourse ought to be "astute" to the consent of the other person.[410] Whether the revised law, which requires a reasonable belief in the victim's consent, will do anything to increase conviction rates for rape will depend upon the approach taken to the rebuttable presumptions and the requirement to consider all the circumstances by both judges and juries. It may be that further consideration needs to be given to difficult questions about the burden of proof in relation to the presumptions. It may be, also, that victims should be encouraged to pursue civil claims against rapists (where the status is one of complainant rather than victim)—although this should be as well as, rather than instead of, resorting to the criminal law.[411]

Some commentators on the rape laws in the United States have concluded that the laws are inherently defective; because they have their origins in a patriarchal society, reform attempts will inevitably be half-baked.[412] According to this view we ought to start again from contemporary liberal and feminist first principles regarding women's equal interests in and rights to sexual autonomy and physical security. This has led some commentators to argue that the law of rape ought to jettison the troublesome concept of consent from the definition (and use force instead) since in an unequal society no woman is in a position to consent freely. This position asserts that "consent is no more than a notion men conveniently employ to characterise women's submission as the product of free choice".[413] Indeed, if views such as "No can mean yes if I persist long enough" linger in the minds of defendants and even some judges, a woman's consent (or lack of it) is meaningless anyway.

As noted earlier, views such as these have been profoundly important in changing attitudes, but it is submitted that any redefinition of rape in terms of force rather than lack of consent would bring its own, arguably much greater, dangers.[414] Continuing to refine the concept of consent is the way forward, not least because it does encapsulate the "wrongness" of rape. Whether this new definition has improved the conviction rate for sexual offences is difficult to determine. As noted above, encouragingly, in 2011, the conviction rate for completed trials at the Crown Court for sexual offences was 61.6 per cent, an increase of 7.1 percentage points since 2005. Conviction rates have increased across all sexual offence groups in the Crown Court, with the highest increases for rape of a female (at 51.1 per cent, an increase of 9.9 percentage points since 2005).[415] This is not to underestimate the difficulty with either the proper definition of consent or the question of how consent is communicated. Defining consent as "free agreement" is still subject to changing attitudes of what makes a free choice and how agreements are made during sexual encounters. Cultural attitudes have proved to be resistant to change; human communication is fraught with the potential for ambiguity and violence is likely to remain an important factor in securing a conviction. However, ultimately, the offence of rape should serve to protect sexual integrity and autonomy.

---

[410]   "The Wrongness of Rape" in J. Horder (ed.), *Oxford Essays in Jurisprudence* (Oxford: OUP, 2000), pp.206, 213.

[411]   J. Conaghan, "Extending the Reach of Human Rights to Encompass Victims of Rape" (2005) 13 *Feminist Legal Studies* 145.

[412]   D.A. Dripps, "Beyond Rape" (1992) 92 Colum. L. Rev. 1780; R. West, "Legitimating the Illegitimate: A Comment on Beyond Rape" (1993) 93 Colum. L. Rev. 1442; D.A. Dripps, "More on Distinguishing Sex, Sexual Assault: A Reply to Professor West" (1993) 93 Colum. L. Rev. 1460.

[413]   E. Sherwin, "Infelicitous Sex" (1996) 2 *Legal Theory* 209 at 214.

[414]   For a proposal that rejects consent in favour of a differentiated offence of rape (one offence that could be committed in different ways: by force, fraud, intoxication, etc.), see Tadros, "Rape Without Consent" [2006] 26 O.J.L.S. 515 at 536–543.

[415]   Ministry of Justice, Home Office and the Office for National Statistics, *An Overview of Sexual Offending in England and Wales* (2013) p.34.

8

HOMICIDE

I. INTRODUCTION

A. The Level of Offending

The most recent statistics show that in England and Wales there are 10 homicides (murder, man-slaughter—including corporate manslaughter—and infanticide) per 1,000,000 population.[1] In the 12-month period up until September 2013, 542 homicides were recorded, compared to 1,047 in the year 2002/03.[2] This can be compared with other causes of death: in 2011/12 there were 553 homicides,[3] while figures for 2011 show that more people were killed as a result of falls (3,885), intentional self-harm (3,644), and transport accidents (1,815), but fewer were killed by exposure to smoke fire and flames (242) or accidental drowning or submersion (175).[4] Whereas official statistics only reveal part of the picture of offending for many offences, for homicide, by virtue of the very nature of the offence, the data is likely to be almost entirely accurate.

B. Homicide in Context

Males are most likely to be both the victims and offenders in homicide. Of the 236 suspects against whom proceedings had concluded in relation to homicides recorded in 2011/12,[5] 89 per cent were male and just 11 per cent were female,[6] whilst 68 per cent of homicide victims were male and 32 per cent were female.[7] At first glance this seems to portray a picture similar to that encountered with non-fatal offences against the person of young males inflicting violence on each other. However, closer analysis of the official statistics reveals a different picture: that homicide is predominantly "domestic" in nature. The victim is likely to have known the killer. In 2011/12, for example, 78 per cent of female victims were killed by persons they knew, and 51 per cent of females were killed by current or former partners. In the same year, men were killed by people they knew in 54 per cent of cases; of these killings, 5 per cent were by current or former partners. In short, fewer women (15 per cent of

---

[1] Office for National Statistics, *Statistical Bulletin: Crime in England and Wales, Year Ending 2013*, (2014), p.32, available at *http://www.ons.gov.uk/ons/dcp171778_349849.pdf* [Accessed June 12, 2014].

[2] Office for National Statistics, *Statistical Bulletin: Crime in England and Wales, Year Ending 2013*, (2014), table 4A. It should be noted, however, that 172 of the homicides recorded in 2002/03 were homicides attributed to Harold Shipman committed in previous years which came to light as the result of the investigation in 2002.

[3] ONS above fn.2, table 4A.

[4] Office for National Statistics, *Statistical Bulletin: Focus on: Violent Crime and Sexual Offences 2011/12*, (2013), p.13, available at *http://www.ons.gov.uk/ons/dcp171778_298904.pdf* [Accessed June 12, 2014].

[5] Court proceedings were pending for another 366 suspects.

[6] ONS, above fn.4, p.39.

[7] ONS, above fn.4, p.26.

female victims) were killed by strangers than men (34 per cent of male victims) and women were killed by a far higher proportion of partners than men.[8]

Of all killings by suspects known to the victim, 68 per cent took place during a quarrel, loss of temper, or were motivated by revenge; of killings by strangers, 43 per cent took place in these circumstances. Of all homicides, only 9 per cent occurred during robberies or burglaries and 6 per cent were attributed to "irrational acts".[9]

All this data is of importance[10] and relevance to the way the law responds, particularly in relation to the development of the partial defences of provocation (or loss of control, as it now is) and diminished responsibility and the general defence of self-defence. Over the past 30 years much has been learned about the extent of domestic violence in some women's lives that eventually leads them to kill. What has emerged is that much law, for example, relating to self-defence and provocation, has been based upon a male typology of anger and violence and that women who kill are more likely to be dealt with "as mad rather than bad".[11] Increased understanding of such issues has been a driving force behind developments in the law reforming provocation and replacing it with a new defence of "loss of control" to incorporate elements of excessive force in self-defence.

The official statistics also reveal another important fact. Children under one year of age have consistently been shown to be most at risk of homicide. For example, in 2011/12 there were 21 children under one-year of age killed per million population in that age group, compared with 15 persons per million for the 16–29 age group (the next highest band).[12] While this figure appears to be falling and is much lower than it previously was when women had little access to birth control or abortion and faced harsh penalties for giving birth to illegitimate children, the figure is nevertheless significant enough to be, at least, a factor in the debate as to whether infanticide should be retained as a separate offence or whether many of such killings should be brought within the ambit of the defence of diminished responsibility.

What is it that makes a person resort to such extremes of violence? Some writers have explored the interaction between victim and offender.

"Murder and assault are not one-sided, mechanical activities, with offenders simply acting out aggressive dispositions and victims serving as mere instigators or passive foils. Rather, they are products of a dynamic interchange. The opponents establish and escalate conflict, reject peaceful or mildly aggressive means for resolving it, and turn to massive force as an effective, perhaps mutually agreed-upon method."[13]

The official statistics lend considerable support to this interpretation. What the official statistics do not reflect, according to Miles however, is the influence that alcohol and drugs may have on fatal violence. She found that data taken from the Home Office Homicide Index revealed only that 18 per cent of homicides in England and Wales between 1995 and 2005 were recorded as "intoxicated-related".

---

[8]   ONS, above fn.4, p.28.

[9]   ONS, above fn.4, p.31.

[10]   The official statistics have been used alongside other criminological research to assist in establishing strategies to decrease lethal violence: F. Brookman and M. Maguire, *Reducing Homicide: A Review of the Possibilities*, Home Office Online Report 01/03.

[11]   There is also a continuing debate as to whether women defendants are treated more or less leniently than men. One argument is that because they "betray" their stereotypical role they are likely to be dealt with more harshly. See S. Bandelli, "Provocation from the Home Office" [1992] Crim. L.R. 716 for an illustration of how difficult it is to unravel the arguments and statistics.

[12]   ONS, above fn.4, table 2.03.

[13]   D.F. Luckenbill, "Murder and Assault", in R.F. Meier, *Major Forms of Crime* (Beverly Hills: Sage Publications, 1984), p.32.

Her analysis of police files and interviews with offenders, on the other hand, led to her recording 67 per cent of cases as intoxicated-related. Not only were many of the homicides fuelled by the consumption of alcohol and/or drugs immediately before the killing took place, but

"the data provide substantial evidence that offenders and victims of intoxication-related homicide have often experienced long-term difficulties and that problematic lifestyles enhance the likelihood of involvement in violent conflict."[14]

There are, of course, many other broader explanations: biological, psychological and sociological. While an exploration of these theories is beyond the scope of this book, that is not to deny their importance in the construction of the law of homicide—for example, in informing the debate on the offence of infanticide and the limits of the defences of self-defence and loss of control.

Homicide is regarded as the most serious offence. Our revulsion against it is embedded deep within us and our reactions to certain killings may be extreme. The following extract attempts to explain the underlying significance of homicide.

George P. Fletcher, Rethinking Criminal Law (1978), pp.235–236, 341:

"What makes homicide unique is, among other things, the uniqueness of causing death. While all personal injuries and destruction of property are irreversible harms, causing death is a harm of a different order. Killing another human being is not only a worldly deprivation; in the Western conception of homicide, killing is an assault on the sacred, natural order. In the Biblical view, the person who slays another was thought to acquire control over the blood—the life force—of the victim . . .

Though we are inclined today to think of homicide as merely the deprivation of a secular interest, the historical background of desecration is essential to an adequate understanding . . . of the current survival of many historic assumptions. For example, consent is not a defense to homicide, as it is in cases of battery and destruction of property. The reason is that the religious conception of human life still prevails against the modern view that life is an interest that the bearer can dispose of at will . . .

There are three prominent starting places for thinking about criminal liability. In the pattern of manifest criminality, the point of departure is an act that threatens the peace and order of community life. In the theory of subjective criminality, the starting place is the actor's intent to violate a protected legal interest. In the law of homicide, the focal point is neither the act nor the intent, but the fact of death. This overpowering fact is the point at which the law begins to draw the radius of liability. From this central point, the perspective is: who can be held accountable, and in what way, for the desecration of the human and divine realms? The question is never where to place the point of the legal compass, but how far the arc should sweep in bringing in persons to stand responsible for the death that has already occurred."

The task of this chapter is to determine who should be swept within the arc of liability for homicide and to assess the bases upon which we grade the liability of such persons. This necessarily raises the question of why we grade homicide offences, whether we should continue to do so and, if so, how.

In England there are three categories of homicide: murder, manslaughter (of which there are several species, including corporate manslaughter) and infanticide. Although not classified as homicide by the official statistics, there are further similar offences of "vehicular homicide" and causing or allowing the death of a child or vulnerable adult, which will also be explored in this chapter. We shall examine each in turn before asking whether such categorisation serves any useful purpose.

---

[14]   C. Miles, "Intoxication and Homicide: A Context-Specific Approach" (2012) 52 Brit. J. Crimiol. 870–888 at 885.

II.   Actus Reus of Murder and Manslaughter

Both these forms of homicide share a common actus reus. Historically, this was "unlawfully killing a reasonable person who is in being and under the King's Peace, the death following within a year and a day".[15]

However, the year and a day rule, developed at a time when medical science was primitive, had increasingly been the subject of criticism and in 1994 the Law Commission recommended its abolition. Amongst the reasons listed in advocating the abolition were that advances in modern medical science make it possible for victims to be kept alive (for example on life support machines) for long periods of time whilst still being able to point to a specific cause of eventual death that may have occurred some years earlier. In such cases the normal principles of causation can be applied to ensure that only those that committed a wrongful act will be subject to a homicide conviction.[16] The recommendation was implemented by the Law Reform (Year and a Day Rule) Act 1996 s.1, which abolished the rule for all purposes. However, because of concerns about prosecutions being brought many years after the infliction of injury, s.2 requires the consent of the Attorney-General to proceedings against a person for a fatal offence[17] if the injury alleged to have caused the death was sustained more than three years before the death occurred. Where there has been a delay between the original attack and death, and the attacker has already been convicted of a non-fatal offence such as wounding with intent prior to the death of the deceased, it has been held that a subsequent prosecution for murder following the death of the victim from her injuries is possible and does not breach art.4 of Protocol 7 of the European Convention on Human Rights (ECHR) (double-jeopardy rule).[18]

The remaining elements of the actus reus are unaffected by the reform:

1. *"unlawfully"*: some killings, such as those in self-defence, may be justified and therefore lawful;

2. *"killing"*: the act (or omission) of the defendant must have killed the victim; it must have been the legal cause of the death of the victim. Causation must be established;

3. *"a reasonable person who is in being"*: the victim must be a human being who was alive at the time of the defendant's actions. This raises problems outside the scope of this book as to the precise moment when life begins and ends. In view of developments with heart transplant operations and life-support machines the problem of determining the exact moment of death has assumed some importance in recent times.

    According to English law a foetus is not a human being for the purposes of the law of homicide. However, it is possible for a charge of manslaughter to be brought against a defendant who causes injury to a mother carrying a child in utero if that child is born alive and then subsequently dies from the injuries.[19] If a miscarriage is intentionally procured, and is not a lawful abortion within the terms of the Abortion Act 1967 s.1, the procurer will be guilty of the offence

---

[15]   Coke, 3 Inst. 47.

[16]   Law Commission, Consultation Paper No.136, *The Year and a Day Rule in Homicide* (1994).

[17]   This term is defined in s.2(3) as murder, manslaughter, infanticide or any other offence of which one of the elements is causing a person's death, or the offence of encouraging or assisting a person's suicide, or the offence under s.5 of the Domestic Violence, Crime and Victims Act 2004 of causing or allowing the death of a child or vulnerable adult.

[18]   *R. v Young (Kerry Rena)* [2005] EWCA Crim 2963.

[19]   In *Attorney-General's Reference (No.3 of 1994)* [1998] A.C. 245 the House of Lords held it was not possible for the defendant to be guilty of murder where the injury was caused to the mother whilst the child was in utero. Their Lordships did not accept the idea that a foetus could be treated as part of the mother's body in the same way as, for example, an arm. As far as unlawful act manslaughter was concerned, however, liability is not negated by the fact that the death of the child is caused as a consequence of injury to the mother rather than as a consequence of direct injury to the foetus. See pp206–207.

of criminal abortion.[20] There is also a separate offence of child destruction covering cases of destroying a foetus that is capable of being born alive.[21] A pregnancy that has lasted 24 weeks provides prima facie proof that the foetus is capable of being born alive.[22] Both these offences—criminal abortion and child destruction—carry the same maximum penalty as manslaughter, namely, life imprisonment; and

4. *"under the King's Peace"*: all human beings are under the "Queen's" peace except an alien enemy "in the heat of war, and in the actual exercise thereof".[23]

III. Murder

Murder is committed when a defendant commits the actus reus of homicide with *malice aforethought*. Murder is the most heinous form of homicide carrying the severest penalty in English law—mandatory life imprisonment. The law reserves this category of homicide for those who kill with the most blameworthy state of mind, known technically as "malice aforethought".[24] Defining the parameters of murder is thus primarily[25] a task of defining malice aforethought, the mens rea of murder.

A. History

The term "malice aforethought" originally[26] bore its literal meaning and it would only be murder if the defendant had thought out, planned or premeditated the killing. In the fifteenth and sixteenth centuries an intentional homicide "on the sudden" was not murder but manslaughter. However, it became clear that this was too narrow a definition for murder. Other types of homicide were just as reprehensible and deserving of the ultimate penalty. Accordingly, the judges started expanding the concept "malice aforethought" and dispensing with the requirement of a premeditated intent, until by the mid-seventeenth century it was clear that malice aforethought could be established in any of the following ways.

1. Intent to kill

The development that an intent to kill, without premeditation, sufficed for murder was initially achieved by resorting to the fiction that where there was a sudden killing without provocation, the defendant must have planned the killing and thus the requisite "aforethought" was inferred. Before

---

[20]   Offences against the Person Act 1861 s.58.

[21]   Infant Life (Preservation) Act 1929 s.1.

[22]   Human Fertilisation and Embryology Act 1990 s.37(1)(a).

[23]   Hale, 1 P.C. 433. Hirst, however, argues that the relevance of "under the Queen's peace" is not to do with whether the killing was in time of war, but rather that the offence of murder must have been committed either in England and Wales or abroad in circumstances where by statute the English law of murder now has extraterritorial application. This, he argues, is fundamental, as it determines to whom the English law of murder applies: M. Hirst, "Murder Under the Queen's Peace" [2008] Crim. L.R. 541.

[24]   This phrase was described in *R. v Moloney (Alistair Baden)* [1985] A.C. 905 at 920 as "anachronistic and now wholly inappropriate".

[25]   In certain cases, such as where there is loss of control, a killing can be committed with malice aforethought but, because of the circumstances of the killing, the crime is reduced to voluntary manslaughter. See p.725.

[26]   For a full discussion of the earliest development of the term "malice aforethought," and of the separation of murder from manslaughter in the late fifteenth century, see E.B. Sayre, "Mens Rea" (1932) 45 Harv. L. Rev. 974; R. Moreland, *The Law of Homicide* (Indianapolis: Bobbs-Merrill, 1952), pp.1–16 (and references cited therein) and J. Horder, "Two Histories and Four Hidden Principles of *Mens Rea*" (1997) 113 L.Q.R. 95 at 100–109.

long, however, judges had abandoned this fictitious reasoning and were clearly stating that malice aforethought was present whenever there was an intent to kill.[27] This is sometimes known as "express malice".

2. Intent to cause grievous bodily harm

This has long been established as a form of malice aforethought.[28] In *Vickers*[29] the Court of Appeal confirmed that this was an independent species of malice aforethought and not merely a particular example of the felony-murder rule (intentionally causing grievous bodily harm was a felony and thus if death resulted would have been murder under the felony-murder rule). In *Smith*[30] the House of Lords held that the words "grievous bodily harm" must bear their ordinary natural meaning: "Bodily harm needs no explanation, and 'grievous' means no more and no less than 'really serious.'" This species of malice aforethought is often called "implied malice".

3. Constructive malice

This covered two situations:

(i) Killing a police officer while resisting arrest.

(ii) Killing in the course of committing a felony: the felony-murder rule.

Until 1967, crimes were classified as either felonies or misdemeanours,[31] the former being the more serious offences. The felony-murder rule still flourishes today in the United States where one of its main rationales is that it is a deterrent to the commission of felonies that create a risk of death. However, both forms of constructive malice under English law were abolished by the Homicide Act 1957 s.1.

B. *Present Law*

The mens rea of murder can now be simply stated. The defendant must either:

1. intend to cause death; or

2. intend to cause grievous bodily harm.

This, of course, does not solve the central problem of determining the meaning of intention. The leading decisions on intention are *Moloney*, *Hancock*, *Nedrick* and *Woollin*, which are extracted and discussed in Ch.2 and to which reference should be made. Whether these cases lay down an appropriate test is discussed later.

---

[27]   Moreland, *The Law of Homicide* (1952), Ch.1; R.M. Perkins, "A Re-examination of Malice Aforethought" (1934) 43 Yale L.J. 537.

[28]   For a full historical discussion, see *Hyam* [1975] A.C. 55 and *Cunningham* [1982] A.C. 566.

[29]   *R. v Vickers (John Willson)* [1957] 2 Q.B. 664.

[30]   *DPP v Smith* [1961] A.C. 290 at 334.

[31]   Or as treason. The Criminal Law Act 1967 s.1 abolished this distinction and substituted the classification of crimes as being either arrestable offences or non-arrestable offences (s.2). This classification has, in turn, been abolished by the Serious Organised Crime and Police Act 2005 s.110.

The validity of the grievous bodily harm rule would appear to be beyond doubt as a result of the House of Lords's decision of *Cunningham*. Prior to that it had been argued that the grievous bodily harm rule was simply a sub-species of the felony-murder rule and was thus also abolished by the Homicide Act 1957. This view, endorsed by a minority in *Hyam*, was rejected in *Cunningham*. It had further been argued in *Hyam* that the reason for the grievous bodily harm rule was that in the last century, because of the poor state of medical knowledge and experience, persons sustaining such injuries were likely to die; such a rationale was unacceptable in modern times with the advances in medical knowledge. If transplanting the grievous bodily harm rule into modern times it would need qualifying so that only grievous bodily harm which endangered life should come within the mens rea of murder. This argument was similarly rejected.

R. v Cunningham [1982] A.C. 566 (House of Lords)

LORD HAILSHAM:

"I . . . genuflect before the miracles of modern surgery and medicine, though I express some doubt whether these may not have been offset to some extent by the increased lethal characteristics of modern weaponry (particularly in the fields of automatic weaponry, explosives and poisons), and the assistance to criminality afforded by the automobile, the motorway and international air transport. I also take leave to doubt whether in the case of injuries to the skull in particular or indeed really serious bodily harm in general these advances have made the difference between inflicting serious bodily harm and endangering life sufficiently striking as to justify judicial legislation on the scale proposed. But, more important than all this, I confess that I view with a certain degree of scepticism the opinion expressed in *R. v Hyam* . . . that the age of our ancestors was so much more violent than our own that we can afford to take a different view of 'concepts of what is right and what is wrong that command general acceptance in contemporary society'. . . "

LORD EDMUND-DAVIES:

"[T]he view I presently favour is . . . that there should be no conviction for murder unless an intent to kill is established, the wide range of punishment for manslaughter being fully adequate to deal with all less heinous forms of homicide. I find it passing strange that a person can be convicted of murder if death results from, say, his intentional breaking of another's arm, an action which, while undoubtedly involving the infliction of 'really serious harm' and, as such, calling for severe punishment, would in most cases be unlikely to kill. And yet, for the lesser offence of attempted murder, nothing less than intent to kill will suffice. But I recognise the force of the contrary view that the outcome of intentionally inflicting serious harm can be so unpredictable that anyone prepared to act so wickedly has little ground for complaint if, where death results, he is convicted and punished as severely as one who intended to kill.

So there are forceful arguments both ways . . . Resolution of that conflict cannot, in my judgment, be a matter for your Lordships' House alone. It is a task for none other than Parliament."

An example of how medical treatment can prolong life when serious harm is caused can be found in the case of *Clift*.[32] Here the defendant attacked the victim in 2000, plunging a screwdriver into the victim's brain and causing a catastrophic brain injury. The victim survived the attack for a number of years, reliant on carers and being fed through a tube. In 2002 the defendant was convicted of causing GBH with intent, and sentenced to ten years' imprisonment, and was released in 2007. In 2009 the victim died after complications developed following a medical procedure to reinsert the feeding tube. The defendant was convicted of murder; the post mortem having concluded that the original attack and the death were connected. The defendant's case was joined with a second case with similar facts, the Court of Appeal confirming that the defendant's conviction for the offence under s.18 of the

---

[32]   *R. v Clift (Leigh George)* [2013] 1 Cr. App. R. 15.

Offences against the Person Act 1861 could be adduced as evidence that the defendant intended to cause GBH, providing him with the necessary mens rea for murder.

Whether this grievous bodily harm rule should be retained is discussed later.

C. Penalty for Murder

The Murder (Abolition of the Death Penalty) Act 1965 abolished capital punishment for murder and substituted a sentence of mandatory life imprisonment. The judge has no discretion as to sentence. A convicted murderer must be sentenced to imprisonment for life.[33]

However, convicted murderers seldom remain in prison for the duration of their lives. They can be released from prison on "licence". This means that the offender does not regain absolute liberty. The licence is subject to conditions: for example, requiring supervision by a probation officer. All such persons released on licence are liable to be recalled to prison at any time during the rest of their lives should there be a breach of the conditions of licence or should their conduct indicate that there is a risk of a serious offence being committed.

Until it was declared incompatible with the ECHR the procedure adopted for determining when murderers could be released on licence involved both the judiciary, in the form of the trial judge and the Lord Chief Justice, and the executive, in the form of the Home Secretary. They each had a role to play in setting the minimum period that should be served for retribution and general deterrence before the offender could be considered for release, known as the "tariff".

In *Anderson*,[34] it was held by the House of Lords that the imposition of a sentence was an integral part of the trial and that fixing a tariff was legally indistinguishable from imposing any other sentence. Article 6(1) of the ECHR guarantees defendants the right to a fair trial by an independent and impartial tribunal. "Independent" means "independent of the parties to the case and also of the executive".[35] As the Home Secretary was not an independent tribunal, his fixing the tariff was incompatible with art.6(1) of the Convention.

The Criminal Justice Act 2003 rectified the situation to bring the law in line with the ECHR. Section 269 of the Act places responsibility for setting the minimum term in murder cases squarely with the sentencing judge, who must take into account the seriousness of the offence when setting the term. In doing so, the judge should have regard to the general principles set out in Sch.21, which provide starting points according to criteria related to seriousness. These starting points may be increased or decreased after taking into account aggravating and mitigating factors. The starting points fall into one of three categories of seriousness: "exceptionally high", "particularly high" and all others.

Criminal Justice Act 2003 Sch.21: Determination of minimum term in relation to mandatory life sentence

"Starting points
    4 (1) If—
    (a) the court considers that the seriousness of the offence (or the combination of the offence and one or more offences associated with it) is exceptionally high, and
    (b) the offender was aged 21 or over when he committed the offence,
the appropriate starting point is a whole life order.

---

[33]   Such a sentence is not incompatible with either art.3 or art.5 of the ECHR (*R. v Lichniak (Daniella Helen)* [2003] 1 A.C. 903).
[34]   *R. (on the application of Anderson) v Secretary of State for the Home Department* [2002] 4 All E.R. 1089 following the European Court decision in *Stafford v United Kingdom* (2002) 13 BHRC 260.
[35]   *V v United Kingdom* (2000) 30 E.H.R.R. 121.

(2) Cases that would normally fall within sub-paragraph (1)(a) include—
(a)   the murder of two or more persons, where each murder involves any of the following—
    (i) a substantial degree of premeditation or planning,
    (ii) the abduction of the victim, or
    (iii) sexual or sadistic conduct,
(b)   the murder of a child if involving the abduction of the child or sexual or sadistic motivation,
(c)   a murder done for the purpose of advancing a political, religious, racial or ideological cause, or
(d)   a murder by an offender previously convicted of murder.
  5 (1) If—
(a)   the case does not fall within paragraph 4(1) but the court considers that the seriousness of the offence (or the combination of the offence and one or more offences associated with it) is particularly high, and
(b)   the offender was aged 18 or over when he committed the offence,
the appropriate starting point, in determining the minimum term, is 30 years.
  (2) Cases that (if not falling within paragraph 4(1)) would normally fall within sub-paragraph (1)(a) include—
(a)   the murder of a police officer or prison officer in the course of his duty,
(b)   a murder involving the use of a firearm or explosive,
(c)   a murder done for gain (such as a murder done in the course or furtherance of robbery or burglary, done for payment or done in the expectation of gain as a result of the death),
(d)   a murder intended to obstruct or interfere with the course of justice,
(e)   a murder involving sexual or sadistic conduct,
(f)   the murder of two or more persons,
(g)   a murder that is racially or religiously aggravated or aggravated by sexual orientation, disability or transgender identity, or
(h)   a murder falling within paragraph 4(2) committed by an offender who was aged under 21 when he committed the offence.
5A.(1) If—
(a)   the case does not fall within paragraph 4(1) or 5(1),
(b)   the offence falls within sub-paragraph (2), and
(c)   the offender was aged 18 or over when the offender committed the offence,
the offence is normally to be regarded as sufficiently serious for the appropriate starting point, in determining the minimum term, to be 25 years.
  (2) The offence falls within this sub-paragraph if the offender took a knife or other weapon to the scene intending to—
(a)   commit any offence, or
(b)   have it available to use as a weapon,
and used that knife or other weapon in committing the murder.
  6 If the offender was aged 18 or over when he committed the offence and the case does not fall within paragraph 4(1), 5(1) or 5A(1), the appropriate starting point, in determining the minimum term, is 15 years.
  7 If the offender was aged under 18 when he committed the offence, the appropriate starting point, in determining the minimum term, is 12 years.

Aggravating and mitigating factors
  8 Having chosen a starting point, the court should take into account any aggravating or mitigating factors, to the extent that it has not allowed for them in its choice of starting point.
  9 Detailed consideration of aggravating or mitigating factors may result in a minimum term of any length (whatever the starting point), or in the making of a whole life order.
  10 Aggravating factors (additional to those mentioned in paragraph 4(2), 5(2) and 5A(2)) that may be relevant to the offence of murder include—
(a)   a significant degree of planning or premeditation,
(b)   the fact that the victim was particularly vulnerable because of age or disability,
(c)   mental or physical suffering inflicted on the victim before death,
(d)   the abuse of a position of trust,
(e)   the use of duress or threats against another person to facilitate the commission of the offence,
(f)   the fact that the victim was providing a public service or performing a public duty, and
(g)   concealment, destruction or dismemberment of the body.
  11 Mitigating factors that may be relevant to the offence of murder include—

(a) an intention to cause serious bodily harm rather than to kill,

(b) lack of premeditation,

(c) the fact that the offender suffered from any mental disorder or mental disability which (although not falling within s. 2(1) of the Homicide Act 1957 (c. 11)), lowered his degree of culpability,

(d) the fact that the offender was provoked (for example, by prolonged stress),

(e) the fact that the offender acted to any extent in self-defence or in fear of violence,

(f) a belief by the offender that the murder was an act of mercy, and

(g) the age of the offender."

These are guidelines rather than prescriptive rules. The lists in paras 10 and 11 provide mere examples of aggravating and mitigating circumstances, and are not exhaustive,[36] and it has been held that the cases set out in paras 4(2) and 5(2) are also only examples of cases falling within the "particularly high" category of murders and do not provide a definitive list.[37] The new category under para.5A inserted by the Legal Aid, Sentencing and Punishment of Offenders Act 2012 to supposedly deal with knife crime, is similarly to be interpreted flexibly and it has been held that it was not the legislative intention that every murder involving the use of a knife or weapon to inflict a fatal injury should normally fall within the 25-year starting point.[38] Further, the Court of Appeal has noted that Sch.21 applies equally whether the defendant is a principal offender or a secondary party,[39] and there is no reason why the starting point should not be the same for both.[40] A Practice Direction[41] notes that the guidance need not be applied if a judge considers there are reasons not to follow it. For example, it might be departed from in order to do justice in a particular case, but in such cases the judge must give reasons for doing so. The Practice Direction gives effect to the decision of the Court of Appeal in *Sullivan*,[42] the first case it heard on this issue following enactment of the statute, in which it was confirmed that the judge retains discretion in sentencing. The Court of Appeal in *Sullivan* also suggested that the majority of cases will fall within the general category of cases in which the starting point is a minimum term of 15 years, and that cases falling in the higher categories will be rare. A whole life order should only be made when the facts of a case leave the judge in no doubt that the offender must be kept in prison for the rest of their life.[43] Whatever the decision, the court is under a duty to state the minimum term it has determined, which of the starting points it has chosen and why, and any mitigating or aggravating factors taken into account in departing from the starting point.[44]

Schedule 21 has not been a complete success, as demonstrated by the number of cases involving appeals against sentence in murder cases, illustrating that it should be interpreted as a framework for judicial discretion and nothing more.[45] It was described by the Ministry of Justice as being "based on ill-thought out and overly prescriptive policy. It seeks to analyse in extraordinary detail each and every type of murder. The result is guidance that is incoherent and unnecessarily complex, and is badly in need of reform so that justice can be done properly in each case".[46] Proposals were made to

---

[36] *R. v Last (Emma)* [2005] Crim. L.R. 407; *R. v Peters (Benjamin)* [2005] Crim. L.R. 492.

[37] *R. v Height (John)* [2009] 1 Cr. App. R. (S.) 117.

[38] *R. v Kelly (Marlon)* [2012] 1 Cr. App. R. (S.) 56.

[39] *Attorney-General's Reference (No.24 of 2008)* [2009] 2 Cr. App. R. (S) 241.

[40] *Height* [2009] 1 Cr. App. R.(S.) 117.

[41] Practice Direction (Sup Ct: Crime: Mandatory Life Sentences) (No.2) [2005] 1 Cr. App. R. 8.

[42] *R. v Sullivan (Melvin Terrence)* [2005] 1 Cr. App. R. 3.

[43] *Re Jones (Setting of Minimum Term)* [2006] Crim. L.R. 262.

[44] Criminal Justice Act 2003 s.270.

[45] See, for example, D. Thomas's commentaries on *R. v Khaleel (Mohamed)* [2013] Crim. L.R. 72, *R. v Griffiths (Lee)* [2013] Crim. L.R. 436 and *AG's Reference (No.73 of 2012)* [2013] Crim. L.R. 440.

[46] Ministry of Justice, *Breaking the Cycle: Effective Punishment, Rehabilitation and Sentencing of Offenders*, Cm.7972 (2010), para.170.

simplify the sentencing framework, but these did not come to fruition in the Legal Aid, Sentencing and Punishment of Offenders Bill. This may be seen as unfortunate, but the cases demonstrate that the courts are able to manoeuvre around the provisions to do justice in a particular case. In *Inglis*,[47] for example, the defendant killed her son by injecting him with heroin in what was described as the first "mercy killing" to reach the Court of Appeal since the Criminal Justice Act 2003 was passed. This was a carefully planned murder, the defendant having failed on the first attempt, motivated by the defendant's wish to put her son, who had suffered severe brain injuries and was reliant on medical care, out of his misery. The Court of Appeal held that the factors listed under para.10(a), (b) and (d) should not operate as aggravating factors in a case such as this, and reduced the minimum term from nine to five years.

The setting of minimum terms means that the sentencing of murderers is not dissimilar to the sentencing of other offenders, and the statutory, more transparent scheme may lead to murderers being encouraged to plead guilty in the hope of securing a discount on the minimum term[48] where, previously, they would have felt there was nothing to lose by pleading not guilty.[49] However, there are important differences in sentencing murderers. First, the length of the minimum term is set in "real-time" to be served. Whilst an offender sentenced to a determinate sentence for some other offence may be released on licence having served half the term, a murderer will not be released before she has served the actual number of years of the minimum term. Secondly, there is never a right to release on parole. Once the murderer has served their minimum term the Parole Board must judge whether it is safe to release her. Thirdly, the released murderer is always on licence and liable to recall to prison. These differences raise the fundamental question whether the mandatory sentence of life imprisonment for murder should be retained.[50]

Report of the Advisory Council on the Penal System, Sentences of Imprisonment (A Review of Maximum Penalties) (1978), paras 235–244:

"237. One of the arguments of those who believe that murder merits a unique penalty is that the mandatory life sentence reflects the retributive view that anyone who murders another must place his life at the disposal of the State to the extent that both his release and his liberty to remain at large will always be subject to executive decision. This view is usually associated with the argument that to sentence murderers in the same way as other offenders would be to devalue murder as an offence and to reduce the deterrent effect of the existing penalty.

238. Another argument in favour of the mandatory element is that acts of murder can arouse a good deal of public passion and indignation which would attract more than usual interest to apparent discrepancies in sentencing decisions and tend to bring the administration of justice into undesirable public controversy. This, it is argued, would be likely to cause particular difficulty in what are considered the less culpable types of homicide, where a judge might think it appropriate to pass a shorter sentence than in a bad case of, for instance, robbery, but would immediately become susceptible to the accusation that the courts care more for property than for lives.

---

47 *R. v Inglis (Frances)* [2011] 2 Cr. App. R. (S.) 13.
48 According to guidelines issued by the Sentencing Guidelines Council, a guilty plea in a murder case should lead to a discount of up to one-sixth of the minimum term or five years, whichever is the lesser. Guilty pleas can generally lead to a discount of up to one-third in cases other than murder, but the Council is of the view that the differences in the sentencing scheme for murder, including the fact that a reduction in the minimum term has double the effect on time served in custody when compared to a determinate sentence, along with the unique seriousness of the offence, warrant a special approach: Sentencing Guidelines Council, *Definitive Guideline Revised 2007: Reduction in Sentence for a Guilty Plea*, Part F.
49 D. Thomas, "Sentencing Murderers" [2004] 3 *Archbold News* 7.
50 See also Criminal Law Revision Committee, 14th Report, *Offences against the Person*, Cmnd.7844, paras 42–74; Criminal Law Revision Committee, 12th Report, *Penalty for Murder*, Cmnd.5184; *Report of the Committee on the Penalties for Homicide* (Scottish Home and Health Department), Cmnd.5137; Prison Reform Trust, *Report of the Committee on the Penalty for Homicide* (1993: Chairman, Lord Lane).

239. It is also argued that the absence of the mandatory element in the penalty for murder might actually lead (as the result of public attitudes to the crime of murder) to a situation in which the least dangerous of murderers might remain in custody longer as a result of relative determinate sentencing than they would have done if sentenced to life imprisonment. A related objection to the abolition of the mandatory sentence is that it would lead to over-long sentences in very serious cases . . .

243 . . . [W]e see a number of positive arguments to justify the abolition of the mandatory element in the penalty for murder. The Criminal Law Revision Committee rightly recognised that the main advantage to be derived from the mandatory life sentence is its flexibility in providing the releasing authorities with the freedom to gauge the public interest and the needs of the offender throughout the period of his imprisonment and after release. The prison service and the Parole Board can take account of continuing observation of the prisoner's development in prison and the Board can monitor his behaviour while on licence and, if necessary, recall him without recourse to the courts. These are powerful considerations in favour of the indeterminacy implicit in the life sentence. We do not, however, consider that they necessarily imply that the life sentence must be imposed indiscriminately on every person convicted of murder. Where the nature of the offence connotes dangerousness and there is evidence of a likely continued threat that it will be repeated, the life sentence may be the appropriate, indeed the only wise, sentence to pass. But for some murderers we think that there are strong reasons for giving courts the power to pass fixed terms of imprisonment.

244. Although murder has been traditionally and distinctively considered the most serious crime, it is not a homogeneous offence but a crime of considerable variety. It ranges from deliberate cold-blooded killing in pursuit of purely selfish ends to what is commonly referred to as 'mercy killing'. Instead of automatically applying a single sentence to such an offence, . . . sentences for murder should reflect this variety with correspondingly variable terms of imprisonment or, in the exceptional case, even with a non-custodial penalty . . . [We] cannot believe that the problems of predicting future behaviour at the time of conviction are inherently more difficult in a murder case than in any other case where there is a measure of instability, or that judges are any less able to make predictions or to assess degrees of culpability in murder cases than in any others . . . [Further] efforts to alleviate the harshness of the mandatory penalty, [provocation and diminished responsibility] have led to complications in legal proceedings for which we believe there can be no proper justification."

However, despite the very substantial body of opinion endorsing the view that the mandatory life sentence for murder should be abolished,[51] two Home Affairs Committee Reports[52] have concluded that, although the issue was "exceptionally finely balanced", the mandatory life sentence ought to be retained:

"This reflects a concern for public safety, and doubts about whether there is a satisfactory solution to the problem of how to protect the public from clearly dangerous prisoners who would have to be released at the end of a determinate sentence."[53]

With the changes made to the law governing the setting of minimum terms contained within the Criminal Justice Act 2003, it seems more unlikely than ever that the abolition of the mandatory life sentence will be placed on the political agenda any time in the near future.[54] However, now that a more rigid sentencing regime has been imposed it is arguably more important than ever that the

---

[51]   Including the House of Lords Select Committee on Murder and Life Imprisonment (Session 1988–89, H.L. Paper 78).

[52]   Home Affairs Committee, *Murder: the Mandatory Life Sentence* (First Report) (Session 1995–96, Paper 111) (1995); *Murder: the Mandatory Life Sentence* (Second Report) (Session 1995–96, Paper 412) (1996).

[53]   First Report, p.xxxv.

[54]   This is confirmed by the terms of reference given to the Law Commission for the purposes of its most recent review of homicide offences. It was made clear that the review should "take account of the continuing existence of the mandatory life sentence for murder": Law Commission, Consultation Paper No.177, *A New Homicide Act for England and Wales?* (2005), para.1.1. An amendment to the Coroners and Justice Bill 2008 was moved by Lord Lloyd Berwick on October 26, 2009 at the request of Professor John Spencer Q.C. to allow for a jury to add a rider to a conviction for murder stating that there were extenuating circumstances. This rider would then have given the judge discretion to choose not to pass a life sentence. The House of Lords rejected the amendment by 155 votes to 113: *Hansard*, House of Lords, October 26, 2009, col.1027.

mandatory life sentence be reserved for the most heinous of killings and that the definition of murder be clear and include only the most culpable of killings: "[t]here are . . . some serious drawbacks to the way the guidelines of the 2003 Act relate starting points to mitigating factors. Without reform of the law of murder, it will be almost impossible to rid the law of these drawbacks."[55]

D. Evaluation

Apart from criticism of the mandatory penalty of life imprisonment for murder, there are two further criticisms of the present law.

(1) Criticism of the grievous bodily harm rule.

(2) Criticism of the *Woollin* test of intention.

1. The grievous bodily harm rule

There are arguments in favour of the retention of the grievous bodily harm rule as a species of malice aforethought. If a defendant intends *really* serious bodily harm to another there is always a probability that death may result from such injuries. Most defendants would know this. Thus people who intend to cause grievous bodily harm have chosen to run a risk of endangering life. They are as dangerous and as blameworthy as those who actually intend to kill. Their excessive risk-taking as to the death should render them liable for murder.

Criminal Law Revision Committee, Working Paper on Offences against the Person, 1976, para.29:

"It is argued that a person who inflicts serious injury on another intentionally must know that by so doing there is a real chance that his victim will die and if death results it is right that he should be convicted of murder. There is force also in the argument that a person who is minded to use violence in achieving an unlawful purpose may take more care to refrain from inflicting serious injury if he knows that he may be convicted of murder if his victim dies. A few of our members are in favour of an intent to cause serious injury, simpliciter, remaining a sufficient intent in murder."

The Law Commission, Imputed Criminal Intent (Director of Public Prosecutions v Smith), 1965, para.13:

"13. The main arguments in favour of retaining the intent to inflict grievous bodily harm as an alternative to the intent to kill in murder are as follows:

(a) It is in accord with the general sense of justice of the community that a man who causes death by the intentional infliction of grievous bodily harm, although not actually intending to kill, should not only be punished as severely as a murderer, but should be treated in law as a murderer.

(b) Grievous bodily harm is a relatively simple concept which can be readily explained to a jury. Any attempt to define 'grievous bodily harm' as, for example, 'harm likely to endanger life,' or further to require that the accused should *know* that the harm inflicted is likely to endanger life, would make the judge's direction more difficult for the jury to follow.

---

55   Law Commission, Consultation Paper No.177, *A New Homicide Act for England and Wales?* (2005), para.1.112.

(c) It is true that, with the suspension of the death sentence, a person who kills while intending to inflict griev-ous bodily harm could, if such an offence were only manslaughter, receive as a maximum the same sen-tence, namely life imprisonment, as that which would remain obligatory for murder. But the judge might face practical difficulties in such a case of manslaughter in ascertaining the intent to inflict grievous bodily harm, which he would require to know in order to fix the appropriate sentence. These difficulties would be most acute if the prosecution had accepted pleas of not guilty of murder but guilty of manslaughter, when the judge would have to rely on depositions; but they would also exist to some extent where the accused had been tried on a count of murder but had been found guilty of manslaughter, in which event the judge would have heard the evidence in the case, but would have no verdict of the jury on the question whether the killing followed an act intended to inflict grievous bodily harm."

Despite the approval of the grievous bodily harm rule in *Hyam* and *Cunningham*, it has been the subject of severe judicial criticism.

Attorney-General's Reference (No.3 of 1994) [1998] A.C. 245 (House of Lords)

LORD MUSTILL:

"Murder is widely thought to be the gravest of crimes. One could expect a developed system to embody a law of murder clear enough to yield an unequivocal result on a given set of facts, a result which conforms with apparent justice and has a sound intellectual base. This is not so in England, where the law of homicide is permeated by anomaly, fiction, misnomer and obsolete reasoning. One conspicuous anomaly is the rule which identifies the 'malice aforethought' (a doubly misleading expression) required for the crime of murder not only with a conscious intention to kill but also with an intention to cause grievous bodily harm . . . Many would doubt the justice of this rule, which is not the popular conception of murder and . . . no longer rests on any intellectual foundation . . . [I]t is, I think, right to recognise that the grievous bodily harm rule is an outcropping of old law from which the surrounding strata of rationalisations have weathered away."

Despite this attack, Lord Mustill recognised that there was no ground upon which the House of Lords could abolish so established a rule. However, law reform bodies have also rejected the grievous bodily harm rule in its present form.

The Law Commission, Imputed Criminal Intent (Director of Public Prosecutions v Smith), 1965, paras 15, 18:

"15. The main arguments for changing the present law, which prescribes intent to inflict grievous bodily harm as an alternative to the intent to kill in murder, are as follows:

(a) Murder is commonly understood to mean the intentional killing of another human being; and, unless there are strong reasons which justify a contrary course, it is generally desirable that legal terms should correspond with their popular meaning.
(b) To limit intent in murder to the intent to kill is not to disregard the very serious nature of causing death by the infliction of grievous bodily harm, but, since the suspension of the death sentence, if such an offence were to be treated as manslaughter only, it could nevertheless be punished by a maximum penalty as severe as the penalty prescribed for murder, namely, imprisonment for life . . .
(c) Furthermore, a man should not be regarded as a murderer if he does not *know* that the bodily harm which he intends to inflict is likely to kill . . . If there is any special deterrent effect in the label 'murder' as distin-guished from manslaughter, it should be attached to an act done with intent to inflict bodily harm which the accused knows is likely to kill . . .

18 . . .
(a) So long as a distinction between murder and manslaughter is to be maintained, there must be a defensible criterion for distinguishing between them. In our view the essential element in murder should be willing-ness to kill, thereby evincing a total lack of respect for human life."

Criminal Law Revision Committee, Working Paper on Offences against the Person, 1976, para.29:

"29. . . The majority of us . . . think that if an intent to cause serious injury is to remain part of the mens rea of murder, it should be limited in some way so that it is related more closely to the fact of death. Some of us take the view that the law should distinguish between a person who, although intending to cause serious injury, inflicts it in such a way that death is not likely to result and the person who intentionally causes serious injury in such a way that death is likely to be caused. These members hope that such a distinction might deter a person from causing serious injury with the likelihood of death resulting. Other members think that the distinction should depend on whether or not the offender realised at the time that he might well cause death."

The Draft Criminal Code followed this last proposal and recommended modification of the grievous bodily harm rule so that it would only be murder in such cases when the defendant acts "intending to cause serious personal harm and being aware that he may cause death".[56] The Law Commission has more recently proposed dividing murder into two degrees and has adopted a similar test for its proposed offence of first degree murder, which would be committed where the defendant killed either intending to kill or intending "to do serious injury where the killer was aware that his or her conduct involved a serious risk of causing death".[57] Beyond this, it was recommended that the meaning of "serious" should remain undefined.[58] Where the defendant intended to cause serious injury without the awareness that it might cause death this would, under the Law Commission's recommendations, amount to second degree murder.[59] Included in the recommendations was the suggestion that the word "harm" be replaced by "injury" in order to clarify that it ought not to be stretched to include severe or persisting emotional states that do not amount to a recognised psychiatric illness or injury.[60]

In the United States the Model Penal Code recommended that no express significance be accorded to an intent to cause grievous bodily harm, but that such cases should be subsumed under the standards of extreme recklessness (murder)[61] or recklessness (manslaughter).[62] Thus the fact that the defendant intended to cause serious injury would simply become a relevant consideration in determining whether they acted with "extreme indifference to the value of human life" (murder) or "recklessly" with respect to the death of another (manslaughter). While many states have given effect to this recommendation,[63] others continue to specify "intent to cause serious injury" as sufficing for murder (generally murder in the second degree).

Whilst current English law continues to classify someone who kills intending to cause grievous bodily harm as a murderer, such a state of mind is at least recognised as a possible mitigating factor for courts in setting the minimum term as part of the mandatory life sentence.[64] Should the law go further? Is a defendant who takes such a clear risk as to death so much less culpable or blameworthy

---

[56]   Law Commission Paper No.177, Draft Criminal Code Bill 1989 cl.54(1). This proposal was endorsed by the House of Lords Select Committee on Murder and Life Imprisonment (Session 1988–89, H.L. Paper 78) (1989), para.71.

[57]   Law Commission Paper No.304, *Murder, Manslaughter and Infanticide* (2006), para.2.50.

[58]   Law Commission Paper No.304, *Murder, Manslaughter and Infanticide* (2006), paras 2.88–2.94.

[59]   Law Commission PaperNo.304, *Murder, Manslaughter and Infanticide* (2006), para.2.70. It would also be second degree murder if there was an intention to cause injury or fear or risk of injury while aware of a serious risk of causing death.

[60]   Law Commission Paper No.304, *Murder, Manslaughter and Infanticide* (2006), para.2.84. Under current law "bodily harm" for the purposes of non-fatal offences has been interpreted to include recognised psychiatric conditions (*R. v Chan-Fook (Mike)* [1994] 1 W.L.R. 689), but not to include a severely depressed state that does not amount to a recognised psychiatric illness (*Dhaliwal* [2006] 2 Cr. App. R. 236).

[61]   Section 210.2(1)(b).

[62]   Section 210.3(1)(a).

[63]   e.g. North Dakota (N.D. Cent. Code ss.12.1–16–01(1)(b)).

[64]   In *R. v Wilby (Christopher Keith)* [2008] 1 Cr. App. R. (S.) 98 the Court of Appeal held, correspondingly, that intent to kill was not an aggravating factor in sentencing for murder.

as to deserve liability for manslaughter only? Perhaps this question cannot be fully answered until the *Woollin* test of intention has been considered.

2. Woollin test of intention

As we have seen, the House of Lords in *Moloney* and *Hancock* ruled that there must be an *intention* to kill or cause grievous bodily harm. These decisions overruled *Hyam* in which it had been held that the mens rea of murder could be *satisfied* by proof that the defendant foresaw death or grievous bodily harm as a likely consequence.

It ought perhaps to be emphasised that in overruling *Hyam* the House was overruling what had in reality been the law for at least 100 years. It is true that there had long been a tendency before *Hyam* to assert that, because murder was the most serious crime, it could only be committed intentionally. This however was

> "really a sort of hypocrisy stemming from the days of capital punishment: a desire to pretend to the public that the law only hanged people for intentional killing, while at the same time hanging people who were felt to deserve hanging whether they killed intentionally or not."[65]

Some of their Lordships in *Hyam* were prepared to admit openly that murder was not a crime of intention alone and that alternative states of mind could suffice. However, the others, desirous of clinging to the false notion that murder was a crime of intention, were forced to place expansive interpretations on the concept of intention so as to encompass the alternative state of mind approved by the others.

Following *Woollin*, there is some uncertainty as to the meaning of intention.[66] One interpretation of this decision is that foresight of a virtual certainty is an alternative species of intention. The other interpretation is that intention remains undefined but the jury is entitled to find intention only where there is such foresight of a virtual certainty. But, while they are "entitled" to find such intention, equally they are entitled to find that the defendant did not intend death or grievous bodily harm.

Under this latter interpretation, where intention is not defined and the jury is allowed "moral elbow-room" to decide whether the defendant deserves to be labelled a murderer, the hypocrisy of the past century is continued. Murder is a "crime of intention", but maximum flexibility is retained by not defining the concept.

Alan Norrie, "After Woollin" [1999] Crim. L.R. 532 at 542–543:

"[T]he five recent murder/intention cases . . . can be divided into two groups of two, with one case, *Hancock*, left by itself. In the first group come *Moloney* and *Woollin*. Both involved domestic killings in which there was evidence of a lack of moral *animus* between the killer and his victim. Moloney felt affection for his stepfather. Woollin had seemingly never harmed his baby before. In both cases the use of the symbolic label 'murder', not to mention the mandatory life sentence, probably seemed inappropriate . . . [I]t is not unreasonable to assume the judges felt some moral sympathy for the accused in these cases . . .

Judges are in a sense like Everyman in that they too participate in a moral community . . . What Everyman might achieve by considering first the nature of Woollin's relationship with his child or Moloney's with his father as the irreducible moral context of judgment, the judges must achieve, ventriloqually, as it were, through the law of indirect intention . . .

Then take *Hyam* and *Nedrick*, both cases involving the introduction of inflammable materials through letter-

---

65   G.H. Gordon, "The Mental Element in Crime" (1971) 16 J.L.S.S. 282 at 285.
66   See Ch.2.

boxes . . . [This] represents . . . a pattern of manifest wrongdoing which may not yet be reflected in the intentions of the accused. Mrs Hyam may genuinely have only intended to frighten, but the action carries with it its own intrinsic dangers. There is also no redeeming aspect in the moral relationship between the parties, indeed the fact that it was the other woman's young daughters that died exacerbates the moral view of Hyam's actions . . . *Hancock* . . . occupies a third moral position in which the accused were probably regarded as lacking in the kind of malice evinced in *Hyam*, but still not regarded with the same sympathy as the accused in *Moloney* or *Woollin*.

(Norrie goes on to point out that while Nedrick in fact escaped liability for murder he was nevertheless convicted of manslaughter and a 15 year prison sentence was imposed—in effect, what he would have served on a murder conviction.)"

Such an approach is, however, a recipe for unpredictability and opens the door to irrelevant factors being taken into consideration. Fair labelling requires an open acknowledgment of what forms of killing are murder. In order to determine this, two questions present themselves for consideration. Was the House of Lords in *Moloney* and *Hancock* justified in overruling *Hyam* and so narrowing the mens rea of murder? Secondly, if so, did they go far enough? Should not the crime of murder have been restricted to those who *directly* intend to kill (or cause grievous bodily harm)?

The argument for limiting the mens rea of murder to a *direct* intention is a two-fold one. Murder is the most serious crime under English law and carries the most severe penalty. It should be reserved for the worst cases which are directly intended killings. In such cases the defendant has acted with a degree of control and deliberation that enhances his responsibility for the outcome of his actions and affects our judgment of him as a moral agent. He is not simply showing indifference to the value of human life; he is actually taking positive and purposeful steps towards the ending of the life of another. This evil aim marks him out as more blameworthy. Also, a person who is trying to achieve a result is usually more likely to succeed than someone who merely foresees that result as a by-product of her actions, and can thus perhaps be regarded as more blameworthy than one who engages in conduct with a lesser chance of harm.

Secondly, such an approach avoids all problems of having to draw fine lines on the continuum of risk-taking—for example, distinguishing between foresight of the virtually certain (murder) and foresight of the extremely probable (manslaughter).

The argument against such a strict limitation is that it would unduly restrict the crime of murder and that many persons, such as the bomber on the aeroplane wanting the insurance money, deserve to be brought within the category of murder. This raises the question as to whether there is a moral distinction between one who wants death to result and one who foresees death as virtually certain—or one who merely foresees death as likely.[67] In short, should murder be expanded beyond intent (as currently understood) to kill (or cause grievous bodily harm)? Should cases of gross recklessness be included within the crime of murder?

Criminal Law Revision Committee, 14th Report, Offences against the Person, Cmnd.7844 (1980), paras 23–31:

"Should all reckless killings be murder?

23. We considered whether to propose a definition of murder in terms of intentional or reckless killing, but it seems to us such a wide offence that it could not be called murder. It would include many killings that are now manslaughter and would not be generally thought to be murder. A builder who uses a method of construction which he knows might, in some circumstances, be dangerous to life, might be guilty of an unlawful homicide if a fatal accident results; but it would be wrong to hold him guilty of the same offence as the deliberate killer and for him to be subject to a mandatory sentence of life imprisonment . . .

---

[67]   See above, Ch.2, for further argument on this point.

Should killing with a high degree of recklessness be murder?
24. If reckless conduct causing death is not enough to make a man guilty of murder, why should there not be a conviction for that offence if the defendant knows that there is a high probability or even a mere probability or a serious risk that death will be caused? . . . What is a high probability? Or a mere probability? Or a serious risk? Some may think that there is a probability if death is more likely than not to result—the 3 to 2 odds on chance—and that there is a high probability if the odds are shorter (but how much shorter?). Others may think that there is a probability when the odds are much longer. Should a man who kills another while playing an adaptation of 'Russian roulette' be guilty of murder if he knows there is a bullet in one of the six chambers of the revolver? Or in two, three, four or five chambers? It has been suggested that, since the outcome of death is so serious, knowledge of a statistically small risk of causing death could be held to be knowledge of probability and even high probability. We do not accept that suggestion, but the fact that it can be made confirms our opinion as to the unsatisfactory nature of the formula.

25. We appreciate that it is difficult to draw the line between what we recommend should be the meaning of intention and the high probability test mentioned in Hyam. To confine intention to wanting a particular result to happen would be too rigid . . .

Should killing ever be murder when death is not intended?
28. We think that murder should be extended beyond intentional killing in one respect. There is one category of reckless killing where we believe there would be general agreement that the stigma of murder is well merited. That is where the killer intended unlawfully to cause serious bodily injury and knew that there was a risk of causing death. The intention to cause serious bodily injury puts this killing into a different class from that of a person who is merely reckless, even gravely reckless. The offender has shot, stabbed or otherwise seriously injured the victim, and the circumstances are so grave that the jury can find that he must have realised that there was a risk of causing death . . . To classify this particular type of risk-taking as murder does not involve the danger of escalation to cases of recklessness in general, since it is tied specifically to circumstances in which the defendant intended to inflict serious injury.

Recommendations
31. We therefore conclude that it should be murder:
(a) if a person, with intent to kill, causes death and
(b) if a person causes death by an unlawful act intended to cause serious injury and known to him to involve a
     risk of causing death.

In addition, if Parliament favours . . . [a further] provision . . . we recommend that it should be on the following lines: that it should be murder if a person causes death by an unlawful act intended to cause fear (of death or serious injury) and known to the defendant to involve a risk of causing death."

Draft Criminal Code Bill 1989 (Law Com. No.177) cl.54(1):

"A person is guilty of murder if he causes the death of another—
(a) intending to cause death; or
(b) intending to cause serious personal harm and being aware that he may cause death."

It should be recalled that this Bill defined intention as including oblique intention: a person acts intentionally with respect to a result when "he acts either in order to bring it about or being aware that it will occur in the ordinary course of events".[68]

There are serious problems with any approach based on foresight of a probability of a consequence occurring. The Draft Criminal Code Bill, in that it endorses a concept of "oblique intention" and links the grievous bodily harm rule to an awareness that death "may" result, is to be treated with caution. This is preserving one species of risk-taking. It is difficult, however, to see why the other forms of

---

[68]   cl.18(b)(ii).

risk-taking are not regarded as equally reprehensible. Surely, being grossly reckless as to *death* is at least on a par morally with intending serious injury and being aware that one "may" cause death—especially if "may" covers knowledge that there is a *chance*, albeit a minute one, of death resulting.[69]

More recently, this point has been recognised by the Law Commission who, in the context of proposing the creation of two degrees of murder, has suggested that second degree murder should require either an intention to cause serious harm or a state of mind of "reckless indifference".

Law Commission, Consultation Paper No.177, A New Homicide Act for England and Wales? (2005) paras 3.21–3.22; 3.56:

"3.21 Reckless killing in any form, however reckless the conduct that caused death, is currently regarded as manslaughter. We believe that it is possible to distinguish between more and less blameworthy kinds of recklessness. The more blameworthy kind—'reckless indifference'—should fall within 'second degree murder', with the less blameworthy kind—'simple' recklessness or 'reckless stupidity'—being regarded as a form of gross negligence, within gross negligence manslaughter.

3.22 For the purposes of 'second degree murder', it would first have to be shown that D foresaw an unjustified risk of death being caused by his or her conduct but went ahead with that conduct and thus caused death. So far, this reflects the law's standard definition of recklessness. However, in deciding whether such 'reckless' conduct amounted to reckless indifference—a 'couldn't care less' attitude—the jury would be instructed to have regard to the defendant's own assessment of the justifiability of taking the risk, in the circumstances. The defendant is not recklessly indifferent unless he goes ahead with the risky conduct, knowing the true nature and level of the risk involved. This is not currently a requirement for proving 'simple' recklessness . . .

3.56 As a fault element, reckless indifference respects both the correspondence and the subjectivity principles, as it relates to the cause of death and is fully subjective. By way of contrast, for the purposes of the law of manslaughter, reckless stupidity respects only the correspondence principle, in that it relates to the causing of death. Reckless stupidity does not fully respect the subjectivity principle. It can, for example, be manifested by taking a risk of causing death that the defendant crassly mistakenly believes to be justified when it is not or by an action that the defendant idiotically regards as posing no more than a remote and insignificant risk of causing death. In that respect, reckless stupidity is not a fully subjective principle of liability. In the homicide context, it is, for labelling purposes, appropriately regarded as justifying nothing higher than a conviction for manslaughter."

Here the Law Commission attempts to utilise general principles of criminal law (the correspondence principle and subjectivism) to distinguish between "reckless indifference", judged subjectively, and "reckless stupidity", judged objectively. The distinction between the two could, it suggested, be where the line ought to be drawn between second degree murder and manslaughter. Following consultation, however, it was thought that the test of reckless indifference was too vague and so it was replaced in the final report with a test of "killing through an intention to cause injury or fear or risk of injury while aware of a serious risk of causing death".[70]

Arguably the Law Commission has had to resort to recommending the creation of a second degree of murder in order to circumvent the problems of drawing a rigid line between murder, conviction for which must lead to a mandatory life sentence, and manslaughter, providing discretion in sentencing. As will be seen towards the end of this chapter, creating a middle offence carrying a label of murder, but avoiding the mandatory life sentence, would allow the law to temper criticisms of the grievous bodily harm rule whilst equating that level of blameworthiness with a high degree of recklessness.[71]

---

[69]   C.M.V. Clarkson and H.M. Keating, "Codification: Offences against the Person under the Draft Criminal Code" (1986) 50 Jo. C.L. 405.

[70]   Law Commission No.304 (2006), para.2.70.

[71]   It has been argued that there is no need for the grievous bodily harm rule to be maintained in addition to a test of recklessness, since it is likely that all those who intend to cause serious harm would also be caught by an appropriately defined test for reckless: V. Tadros, "The Homicide Ladder" (2006) 69 M.L.R. 601.

In this way there would no longer be a need to have one clear line distinguishing the "worst" types of killing (murder) from all others (manslaughter).

Other jurisdictions already draw a line between murder and manslaughter using a test of reck-lessness, although such tests tend not to be defined in the way initially suggested by the Law Commission. The American Model Penal Code defines murder, without dividing it into different degrees, as follows.

American Law Institute, Model Penal Code, Proposed Official Draft, 1962:

"Section 210.3 *Murder*
(1) . . . [C]riminal homicide constitutes murder when:
(a) it is committed purposely or knowingly; or
(b) it is committed recklessly under circumstances manifesting extreme indifference to the value of human life. Such recklessness and indifference are presumed if the actor is engaged or is an accomplice in the commission of, or an attempt to commit, or flight after committing or attempting to commit robbery, rape or deviate sexual intercourse by force or threat of force, arson, burglary, kidnapping or felonious escape.

[Under s.210.3 it is manslaughter when a criminal homicide is 'committed recklessly'.]"

Thus under the Mode Penal Code formulation the distinction between murder and manslaughter is a distinction between extreme recklessness and recklessness. Critics of this formulation ask: When does "reckless" become "extremely reckless"? "It is like drawing the weight line between a 'big bear' and an 'extremely big bear'."[72] The commentary to the Model Penal Code, on the other hand, argues that some reckless homicides are as reprehensible as deliberate homicides and thus need to be classed as murder:

"Since risk, however, is a matter of degree and the motives for risk creation may be infinite in variation, some formula is needed to identify the case where recklessness should be assimilated to purpose or knowledge. The conception that the draft employs is that of extreme indifference to the value of human life. The significance of purpose or knowledge is that, cases of provocation apart, it demonstrates precisely such indifference. Whether recklessness is so extreme that it demonstrates similar indifference is not a question that, in our view, can be further clarified; it must be left directly to the trier of the facts. If recklessness exists but is not so extreme, the homicide is manslaughter."[73]

The Law Commission seems to have tried to do what the Model Penal Code thought to be impossible, in reformulating a specific test for what it originally termed "reckless indifference" as an awareness of a serious risk of causing death.

Recklessness seems successfully to be utilised as a sufficient mens rea requirement for murder in some jurisdictions, even without any real clarification of its meaning. A test commonly employed in the United States is that it is murder "when the circumstances attending the killing show an aban-doned and malignant heart",[74] whereas in Scotland the test is one of "wicked intention to kill" or "wicked recklessness".[75]

---

72   R. Moreland, "A Re-examination of the Law of Homicide in 1971: The Model Penal Code" (1971) 59 Ky. L.J. 788–828 at 798.
73   Commentary to 9th Tent. Draft, p.29.
74   Cal. Penal Code, s.188.
75   *Drury v HM Advocate* 2001 S.L.T. 1013.

Robert Goff, "The Mental Element in the Crime of Murder" (1988) 104 L.Q.R. 30 at 54–58:

"It is on the element commonly known as 'wicked recklessness' that I now wish to concentrate. Sheriff Gordon comments:

'Recklessness is . . . not so much a question of gross negligence as of wickedness. Wicked recklessness is recklessness so gross that it indicates a state of mind which is as wicked and depraved as the state of mind of a deliberate killer.' (*The Criminal Law of Scotland* (2nd ed., 1978) at pp. 735–736) . . .

Now we may not be too happy about the use of the word 'wicked,' which is perhaps rather emotive; but the concept is clear enough—it is the fact that the accused did not care whether the victim lived or died—which can be epitomised as indifference to death.

I think it important to observe that the principle so stated does not necessarily involve a conscious appreciation of the risk of death at the relevant time. This is of importance, because we can think of many cases in which it can be said that the accused acted regardless of the consequences, not caring whether the victim lived or died, and yet did not consciously appreciate the risk of death in his mind at the time—for example, when a man acts in the heat of the moment, as when he lashes out with a knife in the heat of a fight; or when a man acts in panic, or in blind rage. These circumstances may explain why the man has gone to the extent of acting as he did, not caring whether the victim lived or died; but I cannot see that the fact that, in consequence, he did not have the risk of death in his mind at the time should prevent him from being held guilty of murder, and this indeed appears to be the position in Scots law . . .

Cases of intention to cause grievous bodily harm. As I see it, adoption of the concept of 'wicked recklessness' provides a far more just solution than does this form of intent, and indeed renders it surplus to requirements . . .

So it looks as though the concept of 'wicked recklessness' works well in practice. Moreover, having regard to the reactions of judges and juries in some of the decided cases, it appears to produce results which conform to their feelings. It has another advantage, because, with this as an alternative, intention to kill can be confined to its ordinary meaning—did the defendant mean to kill the victim? We do not have to try to expand intention by artificial concepts such as oblique intention. Furthermore, in directing juries on intention to kill, judges should not have to embark on complicated dissertations about foresight of consequences and such like. With the alternative of 'wicked recklessness' open to them, the jury in *Hancock* (the case of the striking miners) should not have been puzzled if they had been told to ask themselves the simple questions—did the defendants mean to kill? Or did they act totally regardless of the consequences, indifferent whether anybody in the convoy died or not?"

The advantage of such a proposal is that it attempts to capture the moral difference between murder and manslaughter, rather than concentrating on the form of the distinction.

The distinction between murder and manslaughter should be based on a policy of discrimination between "ethically extremely blameworthy attitudes on the part of the offender toward the life he took on the one hand and attitudes which are considerably less blameworthy on the other".[76] The distinction need not necessarily be drawn in cognitive terms (what the defendant intended or foresaw) such as the Law Commission's recommendation for a test of intention to cause injury coupled with an awareness of serious risk of death. Rather, as Lord Goff suggests above, it could depend on a moral judgment of the defendant's actions. Such judgment must reflect community values which can be represented by the jury.[77]

Wilson, in a similar vein, has suggested an expansion of the law of murder so that it would cover

---

[76]   G.D.W. Mueller, "Where Murder Begins" (1960) 2 N.H.B.J. 214 at 217. Contra, G. Williams, "The *Mens Rea* for Murder" (1989) 105 L.Q.R. 387.

[77]   Crofts argues that modern accounts of criminal law reduce wrongdoing into components such as act, intention and consequence without explicit normative language, and that we should instead critically evaluate models of *wickedness* which do not rely on the subjective model of criminality. In particular, we should look to the historical use of *malice* as a "resource in the form of a legal template of classic conceptions of wickedness as an absence of goodness, transcending the subjective/objective divide and reminding us of the importance of factors beyond act/intention and consequence in attributions of

"what it is about the 'murderer' which we find so appalling. Murderers, in the focal sense, show themselves to be a peculiar kind of person, uncomprehended by civilized society. Shooting into a train carries a small risk but it is a type of risk-taking which causes us to question the shooter's humanity."

However, to avoid the vagueness associated with the Scottish "wicked recklessness" and American "depraved-heart" approaches, he suggests that there is a distinct wrong involved in cases where death results from an attack. The nature of the "attack" necessary for murder can be defined with some precision.

William Wilson, "Murder and the Structure of Homicide", in A. Ashworth and B. Mitchell (eds), Rethinking English Homicide Law (2000), pp.38–45:

"I shall argue for an extended fault element to take into account two forms of risk-taking . . . each involv[ing], as does GBH-murder, a purposive attack upon a victim's corporal interests . . .

1. Intending to Expose Someone to Mortal Danger
. . . What distinguishes Messrs Hyam and other risk-takers as murderers . . . is that the point of their action is victim-centred or, for want of a better expression, 'aimed at' a victim. Looked at another way, which indicates how distinct in terms of moral responsibility the two attitudes are, the (merely) reckless killer acts despite the risk of death. Mrs Hyam . . . act[ed] because of it. If there was no risk to life attending their conduct they would not have acted in the way they did; they would have changed their behaviour. Taking the risk thus structures their conduct . . . [T]he proposed refined mental element . . . [is] an intention to expose someone to mortal danger. As such it would neatly accommodate cases provided for by the American depraved-heart doctrine without succumbing to its emotionalism and conceptual vagueness . . .

2. Risk-Taking in the Course of Violent Crime.
. . . A proposal for elevating recklessness above the ordinary is to tie risk-taking constitutive of murder into particularly heinous contexts such as the commission of dangerous felonies. In a number of jurisdictions a criminal context aggravates an intentional killing. There is no obvious reason why such a context should not also aggravate a reckless killing such that it is 'pushed' through a higher 'threshold' of blame . . . [Wilson then considers some hypothetical examples, such as a rape victim being thrown into a river to destroy evidence of the rapist's involvement.] Each of these cases involves the defendant in an activity which already involves an attack upon the physical interests of another. It is submitted that it should not be necessary to show further either an intention to cause serious injury or a specific intention to expose the victim to the risk of death. His willingness 'to go the extra distance' should suffice for murder.
   The main problem here is in circumscribing the 'unholy' context . . . The simplest way of doing so, and one which would dovetail satisfactorily with GBH-murder, is to require the unlawful object to be the commission of a crime ordinarily involving an attack on or threat to the autonomy or bodily integrity of another or to involve hostile activity in evading capture or lawful arrest . . . A tentative proposal follows:

Criminal homicide also constitutes murder when—
  1(a) death results from the reckless exposure of another to a serious risk of death; and
   (b) D. acted either
        (i) for the purpose of resisting arrest; or
        (ii) in the execution of and for the purpose of executing any specified offence, or for the purpose of evading capture or detection following the commission or attempted commission of such offence.
   (c) The specified offences are robbery, serious sexual assault, torture, whether or not serious injury was thereby effected or intended, abduction."

The problem with this approach is that, as we shall see, persons who kill while committing dangerous,

---

blameworthiness. This model is a reminder of the intersection of the individual and the social in constructions of wickedness." P. Crofts, *Wickedness and Crime: Laws of Homicide and Malice* (Routledge 2013), p.261.

unlawful acts are guilty of manslaughter. Therefore, all that would distinguish murder (under Wilson's proposal) from manslaughter in these cases is that for murder the death must result from "the reckless exposure of another to the serious risk of death".

3. Conclusion

As long as murder is retained as a separate crime, it must be reserved for the "worst", "most reprehensible" killings. Emotive tests such as those involving criteria of depravity or wantonness must be rejected; judgments must relate to people's actions, not to their characters. The better view is that the test of "worst" or "most reprehensible" can only be determined by reference to current community values as to which killings are morally the most blameworthy. In assessing this, the mental element of the defendant will usually be of primary importance—but not of exclusive importance. Arguably there can be room for a consideration of other important factors, such as the circumstances or methods of the killing and the social utility, if any, of the actions causing death. The Law Commission's test of intention to cause injury along with an awareness of a serious risk of death appears to be a purely cognitive test which does not allow for a consideration of such factors. Defining an appropriate test of gross recklessness is highly problematic. Of the formulations considered in this chapter, perhaps the Model Penal Code's definition of murder (which is not dissimilar to Wilson's proposals) comes closest to allowing room for a wide-ranging assessment of the morality of the deed.

IV. MANSLAUGHTER

The crime of manslaughter is committed when a defendant commits the actus reus of homicide but the killing is not sufficiently blameworthy to warrant liability for murder. This will be so in two situations:

1. where the defendant does not have the necessary mens rea for murder, but can nevertheless be regarded as blameworthy to some extent (involuntary manslaughter); or

2. where the defendant does possess the necessary mens rea for murder, but has killed under certain specific circumstances which the law regards as mitigating the seriousness of the offence (voluntary manslaughter).

The lesser blameworthiness is reflected by an avoidance of both the label and stigma of murder and the mandatory penalty of life imprisonment imposed for murder. The maximum penalty for the crime of manslaughter is life imprisonment, enabling the judge to impose any sentence up to that maximum to reflect the appropriate degree of culpability of the defendant.[78]

A. Involuntary Manslaughter

"[O]f all crimes manslaughter appears to afford most difficulties of definition, for it concerns homicide in so many and so varying conditions."[79]

---

[78]   Offences Against the Person Act 1861 s.5.
[79]   *Andrews v DPP* [1937] A.C. 576, per Lord Atkin.

This is because manslaughters range from killings just short of murder to killings only just above the accidental.[80] This can be represented diagrammatically[81]:

In assessing the parameters of the crime of manslaughter, attention must be focused on two questions:

(a) How is manslaughter distinguished from murder (A)? Despite the minimal discussion of manslaughter in *Woollin* and the other leading cases, the House of Lords, in defining the parameters of the crime of murder was, in essence, focusing on the distinction between murder and manslaughter. The point at which this line was drawn was considered above.

(b) How is manslaughter distinguished from accidental or non-culpable killings (B)? What factors make a killing sufficiently blameworthy to justify liability for manslaughter as opposed to liability for some lesser offence or no liability at all?

It is this question that requires close consideration in this section. It might be useful to note at the outset, however, that many cases of manslaughter start out as cases of murder, only to be reduced to manslaughter either due to acceptance of a guilty plea to that offence, or following trial. In a survey of cases resulting in convictions for involuntary manslaughter, Mitchell and Mackay found that only 13 of the 152 defendants had been indicted for manslaughter (six of those 13 having originally been charged with murder); the majority had been indicted for murder.[82] It seems that in most cases of homicide arising out of violence the prosecution will chance its arm on a murder charge, and it is not clear what factors influence the decision to charge only manslaughter from the outset.

During the last 30 years or so, the law of involuntary manslaughter has been the subject of very considerable change. It is now common to assert that it takes three forms:

(1) (Subjective) reckless manslaughter.

(2) Gross negligence manslaughter.

(3) Constructive or unlawful act manslaughter.

It should be stressed at the outset that these are not three separate crimes. Indeed, there is no discreet crime of "involuntary manslaughter" in the sense that one is charged with or convicted of the offence. The term "involuntary manslaughter" is simply a convenient label to describe those residual unlawful killings not otherwise specifically catered for by the law and the culpability necessary for the offence can be established in one of the above three ways.

---

80   For a flavour of the variations in culpability exhibited by those convicted of involuntary manslaughter, see B. Mitchell and R. Mackay, "Investigating Involuntary Manslaughter: An Empirical Study of 127 Cases" (2011) 31 O.J.L.S. 165–191.

81   Justifiable killings have not been included in this diagram.

82   B. Mitchell and R. Mackay, "Investigating Involuntary Manslaughter: An Empirical Study of 127 Cases" (2011) 31 O.J.L.S. 165-191, at 178.

1. (Subjective) Reckless manslaughter

Where the defendant subjectively foresees a risk of death or serious injury (but the degree of foresight fails to come within the *Woollin* test of intention required for murder), there will be liability for manslaughter.[83] As the law of murder has been progressively narrowed with tighter tests of intention, so this category of manslaughter has been correspondingly broadened to occupy the "area vacated by murder".[84] There is little specific authority on this species of manslaughter because in practice such cases are usually dealt with as constructive manslaughter.[85] This category also covers cases where the defendant is charged with murder but the jury convict of manslaughter,[86] or the appellate courts substitute a verdict of manslaughter,[87] or where the defendant pleads guilty to manslaughter having a plea of not guilty to murder accepted.[88]

2. Gross negligence manslaughter

Most manslaughter cases involve the commission of an unlawful act, usually an assault,[89] and so constructive manslaughter is easier to establish. Accordingly, gross negligence manslaughter is usually utilised where the defendant is engaged in a prima facie lawful activity, such as treating a patient or taking care of an aged aunt, from which death results.[90] Mere negligence does not suffice for manslaughter: gross negligence must be established. The classic statement on gross negligence is that of Lord Hewitt CJ in *Bateman* that

"in order to establish criminal liability the facts must be such that, in the opinion of the jury, the negligence of the accused went beyond a mere matter of compensation between the subjects and showed such disregard for the life and safety of others as to amount to a crime against the state and conduct deserving of punishment."[91]

For a period it was thought that this basis of manslaughter had been subsumed into *Lawrence* recklessness manslaughter.[92] However, in the following case, the House of Lords jettisoned *Lawrence* in the context of manslaughter and reverted to the test of gross negligence.

---

[83] Law Commission Paper No.237, *Legislating the Criminal Code: Involuntary Manslaughter* (1996), para. 5.15. The Law Commission's more recent Consultation Paper on homicide does, however, suggest that what is needed is knowledge of a risk of killing (rather than foresight of death *or* serious injury): Law Commission Consultation Paper No.177, *A New Homicide Act for England and Wales?* (2005), para.1.10. The existence of this category of manslaughter was confirmed in *Lidar* LTL November 12, 1999.

[84] J.C. Smith, Commentary to *Adomako* [1994] Crim. L.R. 758 at 759.

[85] Law Commission Paper No.237 (1996), para.2.27.

[86] See, for example, *R. v Kime (Darren John)* [1999] 2 Cr. App. R. (S.) 3. In *R. v Coutts (Graham James)* [2006] 1 W.L.R. 2154 the House of Lords held that, as a matter of principle, a trial judge in a murder case should always leave an alternative count of manslaughter to the jury, even if the defence case is to rely on a complete defence (such as accident) which, if successful, would lead to complete acquittal.

[87] See for example, *R. v Woollin (Stephen Leslie)* [1999] 1 Cr. App. R. 8.

[88] See, for example, *R. v Jackson (Leslie Joseph)* [1999] 2 Cr. App. R. (S.) 77.

[89] In a survey of 56 involuntary manslaughter sentencing cases there was no unlawful act in only five cases (C.M.V. Clarkson, "Context and Culpability in Involuntary Manslaughter: Principle or Instinct?", in A. Ashworth and B. Mitchell (eds), *Rethinking English Homicide Law* (2000). More recently, in a sample of 127 cases of involuntary manslaughter only one case was identified as having been a clear case of gross negligence manslaughter: B. Mitchell and R. Mackay, "Investigating Involuntary Manslaughter: An Empirical Study of 127 Cases" (2011) 31 O.J.L.S. 165–191 at 171.

[90] But see *R. v Willoughby (Keith Calverley)* [2005] 1 Cr. App. R. 29 where, despite the possibility of proving manslaughter via the unlawful act route, the prosecution chose instead to argue their case based on gross negligence.

[91] *R. v Bateman (Percy)* (1927) 19 Cr. App. R. 8, CCA.

[92] *R. v Seymour (Edward John)* [1983] 2 A.C. 493.

R. v Adomako [1995] 1 A.C. 171 (House of Lords)

The defendant was an anaesthetist in an eye operation which involved paralysing the patient. During the operation a tube became disconnected from the ventilator. The defendant became aware that something was wrong four-and-a-half minutes after the disconnection when an alarm sounded. However, the checks he carried out failed to reveal the disconnection. The patient suffered a cardiac arrest and died. The defendant was convicted of manslaughter and appealed.

LORD MACKAY OF CLASHFERN, LC:

"For the prosecution it was alleged that the appellant was guilty of gross negligence in failing to notice or respond appropriately to obvious signs that a disconnection had occurred and that the patient had ceased to breathe. In particular the prosecution alleged that the appellant had failed to notice at various stages during the period after disconnection and before the arrest either occurred or became inevitable that the patient's chest was not moving, the dials on the mechanical ventilating machine were not operating, the disconnection in the endotracheal tube, that the alarm on the ventilator was not switched on and that the patient was becoming progressively blue. Further the prosecution alleged that the appellant had noticed but failed to understand the significance of the fact that during this period the patient's pulse had dropped and the patient's blood pressure had dropped.

Two expert witnesses gave evidence for the prosecution. Professor Payne described the standard of care as 'abysmal' while Professor Adams stated that in his view a competent anaesthetist should have recognised the signs of disconnection within 15 seconds and that the appellant's conduct amounted to 'a gross dereliction of care'.

On behalf of the appellant it was conceded at his trial that he had been negligent. The issue was therefore whether his conduct was criminal . . .

The jury convicted the appellant of manslaughter . . . The Court of Appeal (Criminal Division) dismissed the appellant's appeal against conviction but certified that a point of law of general public importance was involved in the decision to dismiss the appeal, namely: 'in cases of manslaughter by criminal negligence not involving driving but involving a breach of duty is it a sufficient direction to the jury to adopt the gross negligence test . . . [as in *Bateman*] without reference to the test of recklessness as defined in *R. v Lawrence (Stephen)*?' . . .

[Counsel for the appellant] criticised the concept of gross negligence which was the basis of the judgment of the Court of Appeal submitting that its formulation involved circularity, the jury being told in effect to convict of a crime if they thought a crime had been committed and that accordingly using gross negligence as the conceptual basis for the crime of involuntary manslaughter was unsatisfactory . . .

I begin with *Rex v Bateman*, and the opinion of Lord Hewart C.J., where he said:

'In expounding the law to juries on the trial of indictments for manslaughter by negligence, judges have often referred to the distinction between civil and criminal liability for death by negligence. The law of criminal liability for negligence is conveniently explained in that way. If A has caused the death of B by alleged negligence, then, in order to establish civil liability, the plaintiff must prove (in addition to pecuniary loss caused by the death) that A owed a duty to B to take care, that that duty was not discharged, and that the default caused the death of B. To convict A of manslaughter, the prosecution must prove the three things above mentioned and must satisfy the jury, in addition, that A's negligence amounted to a crime. In the civil action, if it is proved that A fell short of the standard of reasonable care required by law, it matters not how far he fell short of that standard. The extent of his liability depends not on the degree of negligence, but on the amount of damage done. In criminal court, on the contrary, the amount and degree of negligence are the determining question. There must be *mens rea*.'

Later he said:

'In explaining to juries the test which they should apply to determine whether the negligence, in the particular case, amounted or did not amount to a crime, judges have used many epithets, such as "culpable", "criminal", "gross", "wicked", "clear", "complete". But, whatever epithet be used and whether an epithet be used or not, in order to establish criminal liability the facts must be such that, in the opinion of the jury, the negligence of the accused went beyond a mere matter of compensation between subjects and showed such disregard for the life and safety of others as to amount to a crime against the state and conduct deserving punishment.' . . .

Next I turn to *Andrews v Director of Public Prosecutions* [1937] A.C. 576 which was a case of manslaughter through the dangerous driving of a motor car . . . Lord Atkin said:

'. . . Simple lack of care such as will constitute civil liability is not enough: for purposes of the criminal law there are degrees of negligence: and a very high degree of negligence is required to be proved before the felony is established. Probably of all the epithets that can be applied "reckless" most nearly covers the case. It is difficult to visualise a case of death caused by reckless driving in the connotation of that term in ordinary speech which would not justify a conviction for manslaughter: but it is probably not all-embracing, for "reckless" suggests an indifference to risk whereas the accused may have appreciated the risk and intended to avoid it and yet shown such a high degree of negligence in the means adopted to avoid the risk as would justify a conviction. If the principle of *Bateman's* case is observed it will appear that the law of manslaughter has not changed by the introduction of motor vehicles on the road. Death caused by their negligent driving, though unhappily much more frequent, is to be treated in law as death caused by any other form of negligence: and juries should be directed accordingly.'

In my opinion the law as stated in these two authorities is satisfactory as providing a proper basis for describing the crime of involuntary manslaughter. Since the decision in *Andrews* was a decision of your Lordships' House, it remains the most authoritative statement of the present law which I have been able to find . . . On this basis in my opinion the ordinary principles of the law of negligence apply to ascertain whether or not the defendant has been in breach of a duty of care towards the victim who has died. If such breach of duty is established the next question is whether that breach of duty caused the death of the victim. If so, the jury must go on to consider whether that breach of duty should be characterised as gross negligence and therefore as a crime. This will depend on the seriousness of the breach of duty committed by the defendant in all the circumstances in which the defendant was placed when it occurred. The jury will have to consider whether the extent to which the defendant's conduct departed from the proper standard of care incumbent upon him, involving as it must have done a risk of death to the patient, was such that it should be judged criminal.

It is true that to a certain extent this involves an element of circularity, but in this branch of the law I do not believe that is fatal to its being correct as a test of how far conduct must depart from accepted standards to be characterised as criminal. This is necessarily a question of degree and an attempt to specify that degree more closely is I think likely to achieve only a spurious precision. The essence of the matter which is supremely a jury question is whether having regard to the risk of death involved, the conduct of the defendant was so bad in all the circumstances as to amount in their judgment to a criminal act or omission . . .

I consider it perfectly appropriate that the word 'reckless' should be used in cases of involuntary manslaughter, but as Lord Atkin put it 'in the ordinary connotation of that word'. Examples in which this was done, to my mind, with complete accuracy are *R. v Stone [and Dobinson]* [1977] Q.B. 354 and *R. v West London Coroner, ex p. Gray* [1988] Q.B. 467.

In my opinion it is quite unnecessary in the context of gross negligence to give the detailed directions with regard to the meaning of the word 'reckless' associated with *R. v Lawrence* . . .

For these reasons I am of the opinion that this appeal should be dismissed and that the certified question should be answered by saying:

'In cases of manslaughter by criminal negligence involving a breach of duty, it is a sufficient direction to the jury to adopt the gross negligence test set out by the Court of Appeal in the present case following *Rex v Bateman* and *Andrews v Director of Public Prosecutions* and that it is not necessary to refer to the definition of recklessness in *R. v Lawrence*, although it is perfectly open to the trial judge to use the word "reckless" in its ordinary meaning as part of his exposition of the law if he deems it appropriate in the circumstances of the particular case.'"

Appeal dismissed

Following this, there are three conditions to be satisfied for this type of manslaughter:

1. the defendant must owe a duty of care to the victim;

2. the defendant must breach that duty; and

3. the breach must amount to gross negligence.

1. Duty of Care

The first requirement that there be a "duty of care" has the potential to cause confusion. It is simply not helpful to import civil concepts into this area of the criminal law without discrimination. The following decision states that concepts such as "duty of care" and "breach" do not bear the same meaning in the criminal law as under the law of tort.

R. v Wacker [2003] 1 Cr. App. R. 22 (Court of Appeal, Criminal Division)

The appellant attempted to smuggle illegal Chinese immigrants into the country in a lorry. On arrival at Dover one of the containers was found to contain the dead bodies of most of the immigrants. The appellant was convicted of 58 offences of manslaughter and appealed.

KAY LJ:

"[Counsel for the appellant] submitted that the first question to be decided was whether applying 'the ordinary principles of the law of negligence', the appellant owed to those in the container a duty of care. He submitted that one of the general principles of the law of negligence, known by the Latin maxim of *ex turpi causa non oritur actio*, was that the law of negligence did not recognise the relationship between those involved in a criminal enterprise as giving rise to a duty of care owed by one participant to another . . .

We venture to suggest that all right minded people would be astonished if the propositions being advanced on behalf of the appellant correctly represented the law of the land. The concept that one person could be responsible for the death of another in circumstances such as these without the criminal law being able to hold him to account for that death even if he had shown not the slightest regard for the welfare and life of the other is one that would be unacceptable in civilised society . . .

[I]t is clear that the criminal law adopts a different approach to the civil law in this regard [because] . . . the very same public policy that causes the civil courts to refuse the claim points in a quite different direction in considering a criminal offence. The criminal law has as its function the protection of citizens and gives effect to the state's duty to try those who have deprived citizens of their rights of life, limb or property. It may very well step in at the precise moment when civil courts withdraw because of this very different function. The withdrawal of a civil remedy has nothing to do with whether as a matter of public policy the criminal law applies. The criminal law should not be disapplied just because the civil law is disapplied. It has its own public policy aim which may require a different approach to the involvement of the law.

Further, the criminal law will not hesitate to act to prevent serious injury or death even when the persons subjected to such injury or death may have consented to or willingly accepted the risk of actual injury or death. By way of illustration, the criminal law makes the assisting another to commit suicide a criminal offence and denies a defence of consent where significant injury is deliberately caused to another in a sexual context (*Brown* [1994] 1 A.C. 212). The state in such circumstances has an overriding duty to act to prevent such consequences . . .

[W]e can see no justification for concluding that the criminal law should decline to hold a person as criminally responsible for the death of another simply because the two were engaged in some joint unlawful activity at the time or, indeed, because there may have been an element of acceptance of a degree of risk by the victim in order to further the joint unlawful enterprise. Public policy, in our judgment, manifestly points in totally the opposite direction."

Appeal dismissed

Although this case rejects the criminal law's use of the civil law defence of *ex turpi causa*, Herring and Palser argue that, in other regards, whether a duty of care existed was decided on the same basis as a tort case would have been.[93] However, they recognise that there are disadvantages in the criminal law determining whether a duty of care exists on the same basis as the civil law. They note that in the law of tort, if a victim is partly to blame for the resulting harm, this can be recognised in one of three ways: damages can be reduced due to contributory negligence; the principle of *volenti non fit injuria* is

---

93   J. Herring and E. Palser, "The Duty of Care in Gross Negligence Manslaughter" [2007] Crim. L.R. 24 at 33.

applied; or the defendant is given the defence of ex turpi causa. In the criminal law, on the other hand, the victim's role is irrelevant:

"Criminal proceedings are not about balancing the responsibility between the defendant and the victim, but in determining whether the activity engaged in by the defendant is sufficiently harmful and blameworthy in the eyes of the state to justify a criminal conviction."[94]

Despite this recognition, however, they conclude that:

"Though there may be calls for the criminal law to develop its own understanding of the duty of care, distinct from that in tort, we would suggest that use is made of the development of the concept of a duty of care in the law of tort as the normal meaning of 'duty of care' in gross negligence manslaughter but recognising that there may be rare cases where the judge can direct that the tortious duty will not be relied upon. These will be in cases where the blameworthiness of the victim leads to there being no duty of care in tort when it may still be appropriate to impose a criminal liability (e.g. the *ex turpi causa* doctrine) and cases involving omissions, where the court will need to find not only a duty of care, but also a duty to act."[95]

There is something to be said for this suggestion. If the civil law is not to be employed here, it is difficult to see what the *Adomako* requirement of "duty of care" actually means. Possibly the requirement has most significance for the law relating to manslaughter by omission. Herring and Palser list circumstances in which a duty of care arises in tort cases for omissions, showing that generally there is overlap between the criminal law and civil law.[96] As in the criminal law, a duty of care arises in tort where there is a voluntary assumption of responsibility; a special relationship of vulnerability or control between parties; and where the defendant creates a source of danger. An additional source of duty of care in tort is where the defendant's position as occupier gives rise to a duty in respect of the safety of lawful visitors. There is clearly no such duty to act under the criminal law.[97] This raises the question of whether there is a difference between a duty to act (omissions) and a duty of care (manslaughter). In *Evans*[98] these two terms were used interchangeably but, as the example of the occupier demonstrates, there can be cases where there is a duty of care in civil law but no duty to act in criminal law. Further, the application of these principles may differ in tort law. The Law Commission argues that *Adomako* may have changed the law by restricting the scope of duties to act in criminal cases by equating it with that of tort where, generally, liability does not flow if a defendant abandons an effort to care for someone (unless, they cause harm through their own incompetence).[99] For example, the defendants in *Stone and Dobinson* might not have been liable in tort. It would, however, be extremely surprising if Lord Mackay's comments were interpreted as (inadvertently) altering the relatively established body of criminal law rules relating to omissions.

A separate question is that of who it is that decides in a particular case whether a duty of care arose. In *Willoughby*, the Court of Appeal has stressed that "whether a duty of care exists is a matter for the

---

94   Herring and Palser, "The Duty of Care in Gross Negligence Manslaughter" [2007] Crim. L.R. 24 at 37.
95   Herring and Palser, "The Duty of Care in Gross Negligence Manslaughter" [2007] Crim. L.R. 24 at 39–40.
96   Herring and Palser, "The Duty of Care in Gross Negligence Manslaughter" [2007] Crim. L.R. 24 at 32.
97   Herring and Palser, "The Duty of Care in Gross Negligence Manslaughter" [2007] Crim. L.R. 24 at 37. The case of *Willoughby* can be seen as a rejection of this principle in the criminal law.
98   [2009] 2 Cr. App. R. 10.
99   Law Commission Paper No.237, *Legislating the Criminal Code: Involuntary Manslaughter* (1996), paras 3.12–3.13. The Law Commission concludes that the language of tort is best avoided.

jury once the judge has decided that there is evidence capable of establishing a duty".[100] However, the more recent case of *Evans*[101] has now clarified the law on this point. As noted in Ch.2, this case confirmed that a duty of care arises in omissions leading to death where the defendant has created a dangerous situation. It also clearly stated that whether the defendant owes a duty of care is a question of law. The jury should be directed on what the law is, for example whether a duty exists if they find certain facts to be established, and it is for them to decide the facts.

2. Breach of duty

Whether the defendant breached the duty of care she owed to the victim is a question of fact for the jury. The jury must also find that the breach caused the death of the deceased, applying the rules on causation discussed in Ch.2.

3. The breach must amount to gross negligence

Whether civil law concepts are applied or not, it is clear that the critical requirement for this type of manslaughter is that there has been gross negligence. The rejection of *Lawrence* means that there is no longer any scope for an argument that the defendant ruled out the risks. Similarly, the argument that an actual awareness of a risk of death is required for manslaughter in order to bring the law in line with the subjective test applied in *G*[102] was rejected in the case of *Mark*,[103] in which the Court of Appeal made it clear that the case of *G* had no bearing on the test for manslaughter. The test is simply one of determining how far the standard of behaviour of the defendant departs from accepted standards and this is "supremely a jury question".[104] The jury must assess whether, having regard to the risk of death, the conduct was so bad in all the circumstances as to be criminal.

This unanimous decision of the House of Lords in *Adomako* (which applies irrespective of the method of killing[105]) has received a mixed response.[106] There are substantial problems with the decision.

The main criticism is that the test to be employed by juries is circular. They should find the defendant's actions criminal (manslaughter) if they think the conduct falls so far below proper standards of care that it should be judged criminal. This arguably amounts to leaving questions of law to the jury as it is for them to decide whether the conduct amounts to a crime. Further, no guidance is given as to how far below accepted standards of behaviour the defendant's conduct must fall other than that the conduct must be "so bad" in all the circumstances as to warrant criminalisation as manslaughter. This absence of any legally defined criteria renders the law highly uncertain and increases the chances of inconsistency of verdicts.

However, the Court of Appeal has endeavoured to rebuff such criticisms.

---

[100]   *Willoughby* [2004] EWCA Crim 3365. Whether a duty of care exists under the Corporate Manslaughter and Corporate Homicide Act 2007 s.2(5), is a question of law. This is discussed in Ch.3.
[101]   [2009] 2 Cr. App. R. 10.
[102]   *R. v G* [2004] 1 A.C. 1034.
[103]   *R. v Mark (Alan James)* [2004] EWCA Crim 2490. See also *R. v Misra (Amit)* [2005] 1 Cr. App. R. 21.
[104]   Per Lord Mackay in *Adomako*.
[105]   See below, p.770 for the effect of *Adomako* on so-called motor manslaughter.
[106]   J.C. Smith [1994] Crim. L.R. 758; G. Virgo, "Reconstructing Manslaughter on Defective Foundations" [1995] C.L.J. 14 at 15. See also, L.H. Leigh, "Liability for Inadvertence: A Lordly Legacy" [1995] 58 M.L.R. 457; S. Gardner, "Manslaughter by Gross Negligence" (1995) 111 L.Q.R. 22.

R. v Misra and Srivastava [2005] 1 Cr. App. R. 21 (Court of Appeal, Criminal Division)

Two Senior House Officers failed to diagnose and treat a case of toxic shock syndrome in a patient following an operation on his knee. The patient died. On appeal against conviction for manslaughter the appellants argued that the circular test of gross negligence in Adomako breached arts 6 (right to a fair trial) and 7 (no punishment without law) of the ECHR because it leads to lack of certainty.[107]

JUDGE LJ:

"[62] On proper analysis [of the test in *Adomako*] . . . the jury is not deciding whether the particular defendant ought to be convicted on some unprincipled basis. The question for the jury is not whether the defendant's negligence was gross, and whether *additionally*, it was a crime, but whether his behaviour was grossly negligent and *consequently* criminal. This is not a question of law, but one of fact, for decision in the individual case.

[63] On examination, this represents one example, amongst many, of problems which juries are expected to address on a daily basis . . .

[64] In our judgment the law is clear. The ingredients of the offence have been clearly defined, and the principles decided in the House of Lords in *Adomako*. They involve no uncertainty".

Appeal dismissed

In *Misra*, the Court of Appeal also attempted to clear up the second problem with the test in *Adomako*. Following the House of Lords' decision in that case it was perhaps unclear what type of risk was required to be considered. While Lord Mackay referred to the "risk of death", his approval of other authorities such as *Bateman* ("disregard for life and safety"), *Stone* ("disregard of danger to the health and welfare of the infirm person") and *R. v West London Coroner, Ex p. Gray* ("obvious and serious risk to the health and welfare") suggested that a risk of something less than death would suffice. However, Lord Mackay twice emphasised that the risk must be one of death and this view has was confirmed by the Court of Appeal in *Misra*.[108] In this respect the decision in *Adomako* is to be welcomed. Under *Lawrence* and its progeny[109] all that was required was that the defendant create an obvious and serious risk of *injury*. For a crime as serious as manslaughter, this was casting the net of liability too wide.[110]

Finally, the decision in *Adomoko* is problematic in that Lord Mackay endorses the use of the phrase "recklessness" in involuntary manslaughter cases, if appropriate in the circumstances of the particular case, as long as it is given its "ordinary meaning". This is meant to exclude *Caldwell* and *Lawrence* recklessness but little further guidance is given. Its use in the decision of *Stone and Dobinson*,[111] for example, is described as completely accurate. Subsequent cases have suggested that whilst evidence of a defendant's state of mind is not required for gross negligence manslaughter, if such evidence exists it might mean that the jury is more likely to find that there has been gross negligence.[112] In *Misra*, the Court of Appeal attempted some clarification of the issue by stating that "a defendant may properly be convicted of gross negligence manslaughter in the absence of

---

[107]   art.7 provides that "no-one shall be held guilty of any criminal offence on account of any act or omission which did not constitute a criminal offence under national or international law at the time when it was committed nor shall a heavier penalty be imposed than the one that was applicable at the time the criminal offence was committed".

[108]   At [52]. Previous support for this had been given in the cases of *R. v Singh (Gurphal)* [1999] Crim. L.R. 582 and *Lewin v CPS* [2002] EWHC 1049 (Admin.).

[109]   *R. v Goodfellow (Kevin)* (1986) 83 Cr. App. R. 23.

[110]   In *R. v Yaqoob (Mohammed)* [2005] EWCA Crim 2169, it was held that a direction to the jury should refer to the risk of death involved and that in a direction incorporating disregard of the life and safety of others the reference to safety was superfluous.

[111]   *R. v Stone (John Edward)* [1977] Q.B. 354.

[112]   *Attorney-General's Reference (No.2 of 1999)* [2000] Q.B. 796.

evidence as to his state of mind. However when it is available, such evidence is not irrelevant to the issue of gross negligence".[113] It becomes relevant as one of the circumstances to which the jury must have regard when deciding whether the negligence was gross. Judge LJ then went on to confirm that gross negligence is a form of mens rea, despite it not requiring any inquiry into the defendant's state of mind.[114]

Despite these attempts in *Misra* to clarify the law, it is clear that the risk of inconsistent verdicts has increased and that this area of law is in need of reform.[115] The danger is not only that juries are left to decide for themselves with little guidance on whether or not an individual is liable, but also that there will be variations in prosecuting practices. Quick has found that there is a greater propensity to prosecute cases of medical negligence (where death has resulted) in the north-west of England, which he partially attributes to "increased prosecutorial discretion in certain regions which have 'got home' on *Adomako*".[116] He argues that prosecutions of such cases are an exercise in "buck-passing", with the buck stopping with experts drafted in by the CPS.[117] Whether an individual medical practitioner is convicted of manslaughter will depend on the views of such experts, who "effectively *decide* on the vague legal question of whether the conduct is grossly negligent".[118] Surely the decision as to guilt is one that ought to be capable of being made in an informed way by juries, guided by clear legal principles, rather than depending on a postcode lottery or the assessment of a few "expert" witnesses. Quick advocates doing away with gross negligence manslaughter and relying instead on reckless manslaughter in all cases, including cases of medical error leading to death.[119] Griffiths and Sanders have found that the CPS only decides to bring a prosecution in five per cent of cases of medical manslaughter referred to it by the police.[120] In 95 per cent of cases, then, a prosecution is not brought. In 27 per cent of cases this is because no breach of duty of care was found in relation to the individuals prosecuted.[121] In 44 per cent of cases the CPS concluded that they could not prove causation.[122] In 17 per cent of cases the CPS were of the opinion that the negligence displayed failed to reach the "gross" threshold, although on Griffiths and Sanders' assessment there was clear evidence of gross negligence in around half of the cases.[123] They conclude that adopting Quick's suggestion of a test of recklessness rather than gross negligence would have little or no impact on decisions made in the cases to which they had access.[124]

---

[113] At [56].
[114] At [57]. See Ch.2, above.
[115] See further, S. Gardner, "Manslaughter by Gross Negligence" [1995] 111 L.Q.R. 22 and L.H. Leigh, "Liability for Inadvertence: A Lordly Legacy" [1995] 58 M.L.R. 457.
[116] O. Quick, "Prosecuting 'Gross' Medical Negligence: Manslaughter, Discretion, and the Crown Prosecution Service" (2006) 33 J. Law and Society 421 at 438.
[117] Griffiths and Sanders suggest that there has been an increase in the number of cases referred to the CPS for a decision on a manslaughter charge in such cases due to an increase in the number of coronial inquests and police investigations of deaths taking in place under medical care, because of the way the "right to life" under art.2 of the ECHR has been interpreted to mean that public bodies are obliged to conduct investigations to establish who may be responsible for any deaths: D. Griffiths and A. Sanders, "The Road to the Dock: Prosecution Decision-Making in Medical Manslaughter Cases", in Griffiths and Sanders, *Bioethics, Medicine and the Criminal Law, Volume 2, Medicine, Crime and Society* (Cambridge: CUP, 2013).
[118] ibid., at 448.
[119] O. Quick, "Medical Killing, Need for a Special Offence?", in C.M.V. Clarkson and S. Cunningham (eds), *Criminal Liability for Non-Aggressive Death* (Aldershot: Ashgate, 2008).
[120] D. Griffiths and A. Sanders, "The Road to the Dock: Prosecution Decision-Making in Medical Manslaughter Cases", in Griffiths and Sanders, *Bioethics, Medicine and the Criminal Law, Volume 2, Medicine, Crime and Society* (Cambridge: CUP, 2013), p.136.
[121] Griffiths and Sanders, above, fn.117.
[122] Griffiths and Sanders, above, fn.117, p.140.
[123] Griffiths and Sanders, above, fn.117, p.143.
[124] Griffiths and Sanders, above, fn.117, p.148.

3. Constructive manslaughter

As a corollary of the felony-murder rule, the law developed a misdemeanour-manslaughter rule whereby it was manslaughter to kill in the course of committing a misdemeanour. The obvious rigours of such a rule were soon mitigated, and this species of manslaughter survived the abolition of the felony-murder rule and abolition of the distinction between felonies and misdemeanours. The present law may be stated in the following terms:

(i)   the defendant must commit an unlawful act; and

(ii)   the unlawful act must be dangerous, namely, it must expose the victim to the risk of some bodily harm resulting therefrom.

(i) The unlawful act

Not all unlawful acts will suffice for constructive manslaughter. Three limitations upon the earlier rule have been developed:

(a)   The unlawful act must constitute a crime. A tort or other civil wrong will not suffice. In *Franklin*,[125] Field J ruled that

"the mere fact of a civil wrong committed by one person against another ought not to be used as an incident which is a necessary step in a criminal case. I have a great abhorrence of constructive crime."

Further, if the defendant would have a defence (say, self-defence) to the unlawful act, then there is no "crime" for the purposes of constructive manslaughter.[126]

(b)   The act must be criminal for some other reason than that it has been negligently performed. For example, driving a car is a lawful act; driving that car negligently is a criminal offence. Such a crime will not suffice for constructive manslaughter. In *Andrews v DPP* Lord Atkin held:

"There is an obvious difference in the law of manslaughter between doing an unlawful act and doing a lawful act with a degree of carelessness which the legislature makes criminal. If it were otherwise a man who killed another while driving without due care and attention would *ex necessitate* commit manslaughter."[127]

(c)   It is doubtful whether an omission will suffice for constructive manslaughter. In *Lowe* it was held that the mere fact that a parent was guilty of the statutory offence of wilful neglect of a child, did not make that parent liable for manslaughter if the child died in consequence of the neglect.

---

[125]   *Franklin* (1883) 15 Cox C.C. 163.
[126]   *R. v Scarlett (John)* (1994) 98 Cr. App. R. 290.
[127]   *Andrews v DPP* [1937] A.C. 576 at 585.

R. v Lowe [1973] Q.B. 702 (Court of Appeal, Criminal Division)

PHILLIMORE LJ:

"Now in the present case the jury negatived recklessness. How then can mere neglect amount to manslaughter? The court feels that there is something inherently unattractive in a theory of constructive manslaughter. It seems strange that an omission which is willful solely in the sense that it is not inadvertent and the consequences of which are not in fact foreseen by the person who is neglectful should, if death results, automatically give rise to an indeterminate sentence instead of the maximum of two years which would otherwise be the limit imposed.

   We think that there is a clear distinction between an act of omission and an act of commission likely to cause harm. Whatever may be the position with regard to the latter it does not follow that the same is true of the former. In other words, if I strike a child in a manner likely to cause harm it is right that, if the child dies, I may be charged with manslaughter. If, however, I omit to do something with the result that it suffers injury to health which results in its death, we think that a charge of manslaughter should not be the inevitable consequence, even if the omission is deliberate."[128]

Apart from these three limitations it would appear that any unlawful act will suffice. It is irrelevant whether that act previously constituted a felony or a misdemeanour. In practice, however, the majority of constructive manslaughter cases are based on some form of assault as the unlawful act. In a survey of 56 manslaughter sentencing appeals, 51 of the cases involved the commission of an unlawful act. Of these, only five cases did not involve an attack amounting to at least a common assault.[129] In a more recent analysis of 110 cases of unlawful act manslaughter, all but one was found to involve some sort of assault against the deceased (although assault was not the main unlawful act in nine of the cases; where a burglary, robbery or arson occurred, assault was committed as part of that unlawful act).[130]

R. v Lamb [1967] 2 Q.B. 981 (Court of Appeal, Criminal Division)

Lamb, in jest, with no intention of doing any harm, pointed a revolver at his best friend who was similarly treating the incident as a joke. He knew there were two bullets in the chambers but as neither bullet was in the chamber opposite the barrel he did not foresee any danger. He pulled the trigger; this rotated the cylinder and placed a bullet opposite the barrel so that it was struck by the striking pin. The bullet was fired and the friend killed. Three experts agreed that Lamb's mistake was natural for somebody unfamiliar with the way the revolver mechanism worked. Lamb was convicted of manslaughter and appealed.

SACHS J:

"The trial judge took the view that the pointing of the revolver and pulling of the trigger was something which could of itself be unlawful even if there was no attempt to alarm or intent to injure.

   It was no doubt on that basis that he had before commencing his summing-up stated that he was not going to 'involve the jury in any consideration of the niceties of the question whether or not the' action of the 'accused did constitute or did not constitute an assault': and thus he did not refer to the defence of accident or the need for the prosecution to disprove accident before coming to a conclusion that the act was unlawful.

---

[128]   *R. v Lowe (Robert)* [1973] Q.B. 702 at 709. In stating that manslaughter should not be the *inevitable* consequence Phillimore LJ was presumably conceding that, while an omission will not suffice for constructive manslaughter, it can form the basis of a manslaughter conviction if there has been gross negligence or recklessness as discussed above.

[129]   C.M.V. Clarkson, above, fn.89.

[130]   B. Mitchell and R. Mackay, "Investigating Involuntary Manslaughter: An Empirical Study of 127 Cases" (2011) 31 O.J.L.S. 165–191 at 186.

Mr Mathew, [counsel for the Crown] however, had at all times put forward the correct view that for the act to be unlawful it must constitute at least what he then termed 'a technical assault.' In this court moreover he rightly conceded that there was no evidence to go to the jury of any assault of any kind. Nor did he feel able to submit that the acts of the defendant were on any other ground unlawful in the criminal sense of that word. Indeed no such submission could in law be made: if, for instance, the pulling of the trigger had had no effect because the striking mechanism or the ammunition had been defective no offence would have been committed by the defendant.

Another way of putting it is that *mens rea*, being now an essential ingredient in manslaughter (compare *Andrews v Director of Public Prosecutions* and *R. v Church*) that could not in the present case be established in relation to the first ground except by proving that element of intent without which there can be no assault."

[Sachs J went on to rule that, while an appropriately directed jury could have convicted Lamb of manslaughter by gross negligence, the jury had not been so directed and so the verdict could not stand.]

Appeal allowed

This case can be contrasted with that of *Larkin*[131] where the defendant brandished a razor at a man in order to terrify him. His mistress fell against the razor, cut her throat and died. Larkin's conviction for manslaughter was upheld. In this case, unlike *Lamb*, there was clearly an unlawful act, namely, an assault by intentionally terrifying the man.[132]

Where an unlawful act has been committed which can easily be proved, the prosecution will usually rely on this species of manslaughter rather than attempting to prove either reckless manslaughter or gross negligence manslaughter. One exception to this was the case of *Willoughby*[133] in which the defendant was convicted of manslaughter and arson[134] after the person whom he had recruited to help him set fire to his pub in order to collect on the insurance was killed in the resulting explosion. What is surprising about this case is that the prosecution based their case on gross negligence, arguing that the defendant owed the deceased a duty of care and breached that duty in failing to ensure that he was safe during the enterprise of destroying the pub, thereby causing his death. Whilst the issue for the Court of Appeal was whether or not a duty of care was owed to the deceased by the defendant,[135] the court expressed some dismay in relation to the prosecution's tactics: "[i]t would have been preferable and much simpler if this case had been left to the jury on the basis of death caused by an unlawful and dangerous act".[136] The converse of this prosecutorial mistake can be seen in the case of *Meeking*,[137] where the defendant was prosecuted for constructive manslaughter where gross negligence manslaughter would have been more appropriate. Here, the defendant was a passenger in her husband's car, and the pair had been arguing. Without warning, she pulled on the handbrake whilst the car was travelling at 60mph, causing the car to spin out of control and collide with an oncoming vehicle. The defendant's husband was killed in the collision, and she was prosecuted for manslaughter on the basis of committing the unlawful act of interfering with a motor vehicle so as to endanger road users, contrary to s.22A(1)(b) of the Road Traffic Act 1988. The Court of Appeal upheld her conviction,[138] but noted that

---

[131] *R. v Larkin (Henry)* (1944) 29 Cr. App. R. 18.
[132] cf. *R. v Arobieke* [1988] Crim. L.R. 314 where a conviction for manslaughter was quashed on the basis of lack of an unlawful act. The victim, terrified of the defendant, had run away and electrocuted himself. The defendant had, however, done no more than look for the victim which was insufficient to amount to an assault.
[133] *Willoughby* [2004] EWCA Crim 3365.
[134] Contrary to ss.1(2) and (3) of the Criminal Damage Act 1971.
[135] It was held that the defendant did owe the deceased a duty of care. However, this was not because he owned the property in which the deceased died, but because he engaged him to participate in spreading petrol with a view to setting fire to the premises for the defendant's benefit.
[136] At [24].
[137] *R. v Meeking (Caroline)* [2013] R.T.R. 4.
[138] It is not at all clear that it was right to do so. As noted by Ashworth, the unlawful act on which the manslaughter was

"[i]t was perhaps an unnecessary complication for the prosecution to have relied on unlawful act manslaughter in this case, rather than taking what might have seemed the more natural approach of presenting the case as one of gross negligence manslaughter, but on the facts of this case we find it impossible to conclude that the jury could have come to any other verdict than guilty if the case had been prosecuted as one of gross negligence manslaughter."[139]

It was held in *Jennings*[140] that it is necessary to identify the unlawful act upon which a prosecution for constructive manslaughter is based. In this case the Crown had relied on the offence of carrying an offensive weapon, contrary to the Prevention of Crimes Act 1953 s.1, but, as it had not been proved that the knife was an offensive weapon, there was no unlawful act for the purposes of constructive manslaughter.

In the earlier case of *Cato*,[141] the defendant injected his friend, at the friend's request, with a mixture of heroin and water. The friend died. The unlawful act here was administering a noxious thing contrary to s.23 of the Offences against the Person Act 1861. More recently there have been a string of similar cases where the courts have struggled to establish that an unlawful act upon which liability for manslaughter can be constructed has been committed. Whilst it is clear that s.23 of the Offences against the Person Act 1861 can be relied upon where the defendant is the one to actually inject the syringe into the victim,[142] as discussed in Ch.2, principles of causation will usually prevent the supplier of a drug who does not himself inject the deceased from being held liable for the death of the drug-taker. This was confirmed by the House of Lords in *Kennedy (No.2)*,[143] clarifying the law and holding that facilitating or contributing to the administration was not sufficient to amount to "administering" the drug. In this case the appellant had prepared a syringe of heroin and handed it to the deceased, who injected himself and returned the syringe to the appellant, who then left the room. As seen in Ch.2 where this case is extracted, the House of Lords reversed the decision of the Court of Appeal, which had managed to uphold the conviction on the basis that both the appellant and the deceased had acted together in administering the drugs, and quashed the conviction. Lord Bingham conceded that

"It is possible to imagine factual scenarios in which two people could properly be regarded as acting together to administer an injection. But nothing of the kind was the case here."

As noted by Ormerod, it is difficult to imagine a scenario that Lord Bingham had in mind, aside from where the defendant injects the deceased.[144] Whilst *Burgess; Byram*[145] provides the potential for such factual scenario (where the defendant had not only prepared the syringe of heroin but also helped

---

based is primarily one of negligence, and the case should not have been allowed to go ahead on the basis of unlawful act manslaughter, on the authority of *Andrews* [1937] A.C. 576: Ashworth, Commentary to *R. v Meeking (Caroline)* [2013] Crim. L.R. 333.

[139]   At [14].

[140]   *R. v Jennings* [1990] Crim. L.R. 588.

[141]   *R. v Cato (Ronald Philip)* (1976) 62 Cr. App. R. 41.

[142]   It would appear that the deceased's consent to be injected will not provide a defence. Where the drug injected is not unlawful but a prescription drug under the Medicines Act 1968, it is an offence to administer such a drug under s.58(2)(b) and s.67 of that statute unless the person doing so is an appropriate practitioner. It has been held that consent to injection (in this case of insulin) by a non-practitioner is, as a matter of policy, no defence to a charge of manslaughter: *R. v Andrews (Christopher Kenneth)* [2003] Crim. L.R. 477.

[143]   *R. v Kennedy (Simon)* [2008] 1 A.C. 269.

[144]   D. Ormerod, Commentary to *Kennedy (No.2)* [2008] 3 Crim. L.R. 222 at 225.

[145]   *R. v Burgess (Lee)* [2008] EWCA Crim 516.

the deceased locate a vein), the Court of Appeal did not have the opportunity to provide any authority on that issue, and merely quashed the appellant's conviction for the reason that his guilty plea was offered on the basis of a point of law decided erroneously (before the House of Lords' judgment in *Kennedy (No.2)*).[146] What *Kennedy (No.2)* does make clear, however, is that the answer to the question of whether a defendant who supplies drugs to the deceased to self-inject can ever be guilty of manslaughter is "never", so long as the deceased is a fully informed adult making a voluntary decision to self-inject.[147]

Given that *Kennedy (No.2)* confirms that in situations where the defendant has assisted in some way in the taking of drugs, but has not injected the deceased herself, there is in reality no suitable unlawful act to form the basis of a manslaughter prosecution without intractable problems of causation being presented, perhaps a more radical approach is necessary.

Timothy H. Jones, "Causation, Homicide and the Supply of Drugs" (2006) 26 L.S. 139 at 153–154:

"The Scottish courts appear to have concluded that there is a moral case for saying that those who supply illegal drugs should be called to account for deaths resulting from their activities. Similarly, in the USA, there are many examples of relatively harsh statutory schemes imposing constructive liability—for manslaughter or even murder—on drug dealers. Since these are facilitated by the continuing attachment to the felony murder rule, it would be dangerous to draw too much upon this experience. That said, the possibility of a statutory offence in the UK might be worthy of consideration . . . [T]he law forbids the conduct in question (supply of a controlled drug). That is, there is a legal duty *not* to supply a controlled drug. If this is breached and a death ensues, it would not be unprecedented for the criminal law to impose liability for homicide.

. . . The key question is whether homicide should encompass straightforward supply cases . . . A statutory offence could be created, without the necessity to impinge upon either the prevailing common-law principles of causation or the law of manslaughter more generally. This could be achieved by inserting a provision into the Misuse of Drugs Act 1971, creating an offence of causing death by the (production or) supply of a controlled drug."[148]

Some states in the United States already have a separate homicide offence to avoid these problems, sometimes labelled "drug-induced homicide".[149] However, there are also arguments against the creation of such offences.

---

[146] There are a number of convictions for manslaughter that have been quashed on this basis since the House of Lords' decision in *Kennedy (No.2)*: for example *R. v Glover (Peter)* [2008] EWCA Crim 1782; *Keen* [2008] EWCA Crim 1742.

[147] Although it is not possible for such a supplier to be liable under the heading of constructive manslaughter he might, depending on the circumstances, be liable for gross negligence manslaughter. If he was present when the drugs were taken and assumed responsibility for the deceased by taking action to help him, for example by giving mouth to mouth resuscitation or administering adrenalin, but failed to take further action such as calling for an ambulance when the victim's condition failed to improve, he might be liable for gross negligence manslaughter. These are the circumstances in which the defendant in *R. v Phillips (Ben)* [2013] 2 Cr. App. R. (S.) 67 pleaded guilty to gross negligence manslaughter. See also *Evans* [2009] 2 Cr. App. R. 10, where the defendant drug supplier was liable for manslaughter, having created a dangerous situation.

[148] C. Elliott and C. de Than have also suggested that a new statutory homicide offence ought to be created: "Prosecuting the Drug Dealer When a Drug User Dies: *R v Kennedy (No.2)*" (2006) 69 M.L.R. 986.

[149] "Drug-induced homicide" is an offence in Wyoming (where the maximum penalty is 20 years' imprisonment: W.S. 6-2-108) and Illinois (where the penalty is 15–30 years' imprisonment: 720 I.L.C.S./5 35-42-1-4). In Pennsylvania there exists a homicide offence of "drug delivery resulting in death". This equates to murder of the third degree, punishable by a minimum of five years' imprisonment: P.C.S. Title 18 ½2506. In New Jersey there is an offence of "strict liability for drug-induced death" committed by anyone who "manufactures, distributes or dispenses" controlled drugs that result in death. The New Jersey Code of Criminal Justice, 2C:35–9 states that "it shall not be a defense to a prosecution under this section that the decedent contributed to his own death by his purposeful, knowing, reckless or negligent injection, inhalation or ingestion of the substance, or by his consenting to the administration of the substance by another".

William Wilson, "Dealing with Drug-induced Homicide", in C.M.V. Clarkson and S. Cunningham (eds), Criminal Liability for Non-Aggressive Death (2008), pp.194–195:

"The vagaries of context/culpability and accountability might make a specific crime more attractive, particularly when we look more closely at the issue of context. Responsibility for both drug supply and demand is arguably spread too broadly to justify atomizing questions of responsibility in the fashion illustrated in *Kennedy*. In a typical case of death caused by heroin overdose this context may muddy the waters of accountability in a more telling fashion than is usual. We can start with a farmer in Afghanistan who returns to farming opium poppies, following State sponsored invasion to remove the Taliban under whose governance it was banned. Following its removal he restores links with a local distributor, who in turn restores his links with an international distributor. We can continue down the supply line to the organizations who prepare the pure heroin, cut it for onward transmission to wholesalers and retailers, including those small retailers who form part of the alienated community of people to whom the drug has such attraction. Where does responsibility lie here? And who is accountable? Given that taking class A drugs of the nature of heroin is a dangerous pastime, and that all those implicated in supplying people with such drugs bear some responsibility for the consequences if those turn out to be fatal, is there any reason to limit accountability to the person most directly associated with the end user? It is certainly arguable that the special transactional context requires us to abandon the premise that causation should be an all or nothing element in liability and embrace the idea that causal responsibility can be apportioned. This would arguably enable the construction of offence labels with appropriately proportioned punishments to reflect the realities of the defendant's causal contribution. [The following definition of a special homicide offence suggested by] Elliot and de Than . . . only partly reflects this analysis:

1 (a)   A person is liable for an offence if he or she knowingly and unlawfully supplies to the victim a Category A controlled drug, or is an accessory to the supply of the controlled drug or is part of a conspiracy to supply the controlled drug, and the person's conduct causes the death of the victim.
(b)   A person will be held to have caused the death of the victim when:
(i)   he or she does an act which makes a more than merely negligible contribution to its occurrence or
(ii)   he or she omits to do an act which might have prevented its occurrence.
(c)   A person does not cause a result where, after he or she does such an act or makes such an omission, an act or event occurs
(i)   which is the immediate and sufficient cause of the result;
(ii)   which he or she did not foresee, and
(iii)   which could not in the circumstances reasonably have been foreseen.
(d)   A defence to this offence will apply where the defendant has attempted to seek medical assistance for the victim within a reasonable time. [Elliott and de Than, "Prosecuting the Drug Dealer When a Drug User Dies" (2006) 69 M.L.R. 986–995.]

The voluntariness of the deceased's conduct in self administering the drug is air-brushed out of this account, so also the broader context within which individual acts of supply take place. It makes accountability simply a function of the contribution made to the events leading up to the death of the victim by being associated with an act of supply. Although it would spread the net of accountability wider than at present its weakness lies precisely in its failure to acknowledge that responsibility for the harms engendered by the supply of dangerous drugs stretches too far to justify singling out individual suppliers and their associates for liability where death occurs."

(ii) The unlawful act must be dangerous

It is clear that constructive manslaughter requires more than simply an unlawful act which causes death. The unlawful act must be a dangerous one, in the sense that it must expose the victim to the risk of some bodily harm resulting therefrom. The fact that an act is unlawful does not necessarily mean that it is dangerous. The requirement of dangerousness is a separate matter requiring proof.[150]

---

[150]   *Scarlett* (1994) 98 Cr. App. R. 290.

R. v Church [1966] 1 Q.B. 59 (Court of Criminal Appeal)

The appellant knocked a woman unconscious. On failing to revive her he threw her into a river where she drowned. He appealed against his conviction for manslaughter on the ground of a misdirection by the trial judge.

EDMUND-DAVIES LJ:

"In the judgment of this court [the trial judge's direction on unlawful act manslaughter] . . . was a misdirection. It amounted to telling the jury that, whenever any unlawful act is committed in relation to a human being which resulted in death there must be, at least, a conviction for manslaughter. This might at one time have been regarded as good law: . . . But it appears to this court that the passage of years has achieved a transformation in this branch of the law and, even in relation to manslaughter, a degree of *mens rea* has become recognised as essential . . . [T]he conclusion of this court is that an unlawful act causing the death of another cannot, simply because it is an unlawful act, render a manslaughter verdict inevitable. For such a verdict inexorably to follow, the unlawful act must be such as all sober and reasonable people would inevitably recognise must subject the other person to, at least, the risk of some harm resulting therefrom, albeit not serious harm . . .

[However the trial judge's direction was not sufficiently defective to warrant quashing the conviction; further, the defendant might have been convicted on grounds of criminal negligence.]"

Appeal dismissed

DPP v Newbury [1977] A.C. 500 (House of Lords)

The appellants, two boys aged 15, pushed part of a paving stone off the parapet of a railway bridge. The stone struck an oncoming train, went through the glass window of the driver's cab and killed a guard who was sitting next to the driver. The boys were convicted of manslaughter. The Court of Appeal dismissed their appeal but certified the following point of law: "Can a defendant be properly convicted of manslaughter, when his mind is not affected by drink or drugs, if he did not foresee that his act might cause harm to another?"

LORD SALMON:

"In *R. v Larkin*, Humphreys J said:
 'Where the act which a person is engaged in performing is unlawful, then if at the same time it is a dangerous act, that is, an act which is likely to injure another person, and quite inadvertently the doer of the act causes the death of that other person by that act, then he is guilty of manslaughter.'

I agree entirely . . . that that is an admirably clear statement of the law which has been applied many times. It makes it plain (a) that an accused is guilty of manslaughter if it is proved that he intentionally did an act which was unlawful and dangerous and that that act inadvertently caused death and (b) that it is unnecessary to prove that the accused knew that the act was unlawful or dangerous. This is one of the reasons why cases of manslaughter vary so infinitely in their gravity. They may amount to little more than pure inadvertence and sometimes to little less than murder . . .

The test is still the objective test. In judging whether the act was dangerous the test is not did the accused recognise that it was dangerous but would all sober and reasonable people recognise its danger."

Appeal dismissed

It is not entirely clear what the unlawful act was that formed the basis of the manslaughter charge and conviction in *Newbury*. Was it criminal damage, common assault or the offence of "endangering the safety of any person conveyed upon a railway" contrary to the Offences Against the Person Act 1861 s.34? Since *Jennings*,[151] it is necessary for the prosecution to identify the wrongful act. As one is

---

[151]   Above, fn.140.

dealing here with what is often termed "unlawful act manslaughter", the requirement that the unlaw-ful act be specified is to be welcomed.

In *Watson*,[152] it was held that the "sober and reasonable" bystander was to be endowed with what-ever knowledge the defendant possessed. In this case the defendant and another burgled an elderly man's house and verbally abused him. The victim was suffering from a serious heart condition and died an hour-and-a-half later. It was held that the unlawful act, the burglary, lasted throughout the time the appellant was on the premises and during that time the defendant must have become aware of the victim's frailty and age. The question then was whether a sober and reasonable bystander, armed with this knowledge, would have recognised that the burglary was likely to expose that elderly man to the risk of some harm. In *Ball*,[153] however, it was emphasised that the sober and reasonable bystander could *not* be endowed with any mistaken belief held by the defendant. In this case the defendant fired at his victim thinking his gun contained blanks (he kept live and blank cartridges together and had grabbed a handful when picking up his gun). Such an act was unquestionably dangerous from the required objective point of view. In *Dawson*[154] it was held that the unlawful act must expose the victim to the risk of some physical harm. Shock or pure emotional disturbance produced by terror would not suffice. However, there could be liability for manslaughter if it was likely that the shock would cause a physical injury, for example, cause a heart attack.[155] Further, in *R. v M*[156] it was made clear that the sober and reasonable bystander does not have to foresee the specific sort of physical harm caused. In that case, a seemingly fit doorman died after suffering from an aneurysm following his dealings with an affray committed by the defendants. It was held by the Court of Appeal that the judge was wrong to rule that a jury could not reasonably conclude that any sober and reasonable person, having knowledge that the defendants had during the incident, would realise there was a risk of the victim suffering an aneurysm rather than some other injury from a fall or blow. The test, as set out in *Church*, was only whether "some harm" was foreseeable.

It is important to note that the question is not whether the offence on which the manslaughter charge is based is dangerous generally, but whether it was dangerous in the particular circumstances of the case. In *Bristow*[157] the defendants burgled a vehicle-repair business located down a private track on a farm, the plan being to steal a number of vehicles. The owner of the business disturbed the defendants and was killed as the defendants escaped in their own vehicle and a stolen vehicle, running him over. In the Court of Appeal, Treacy LJ noted that:

> "This is not a case like *Dawson* or *Watson* where the circumstances demonstrating the risk of harm to the occupier of property did not arise until a point during the burglary or at all. Whilst burglary of itself is not a dangerous crime, a particular burglary may be dangerous because of the circum-stances surrounding its commission."[158]

The relevant circumstances of the case were that the only means of escape from the scene of the crime involved a single track road, passing the victim's home and another property. It was clear that the burglary involved a risk of being interrupted and, if that happened, the means of escape (driving at speed down a single track road) created the risk of harm to any person intervening.

---

[152]   *R. v Watson (Clarence Archibald)* [1989] 1 W.L.R. 684.
[153]   *R. v Ball* [1989] Crim. L.R. 730.
[154]   *R. v Dawson (Brian)* (1985) 81 Cr. App. R. 150.
[155]   *R. v Williams (Barry Anthony)* [1992] 2 All E.R. 183 at 191.
[156]   *R. v M* [2013] 1 Cr. App. R. 10.
[157]   *R. v Bristow (Terrence)* [2013] EWCA Crim 1540.
[158]   At [34].

(iii) The unlawful act must cause the death of the victim

This last point can again be illustrated by contrasting the decision in two cases involving the unlawful act of affray: *R. v M*, above, and *Carey*. In *Carey*,[159] it was stressed that the dangerousness of the act must correspond with its unlawfulness. In this case one group of young people attacked another at a local beauty spot. The deceased was punched in the face and suffered only minor bruises, but in running away from the scene she suffered a heart attack from which she died. It was found that she suffered from a severely diseased heart and the doctors were of the view that the precipitating factor which led to her death was her running away from the incident. At trial the defendants were convicted of affray and manslaughter. The unlawful act upon which manslaughter was based was that of affray. On appeal, although the convictions for affray were upheld, the convictions for manslaughter were quashed. The court took the view that the only unlawful and *dangerous* act upon which the appellants could have been convicted was that of assault. However, in this case, although it could be said that the act of assault was dangerous, it was not the cause of death. The conviction for manslaughter could not be based on the unlawful act of affray, which was not dangerous "in the relevant sense" on the facts of the case. However, the affray in *R. v M* was seen to be dangerous in the relevant sense. In his commentary on *Carey*,[160] Ormerod argues that it seems entirely possible that a conviction for manslaughter could have been founded upon an unlawful and dangerous act of assault (rather than affray) on the basis that the defendant caused the victim to die by triggering a previously undiagnosed medical condition, since the defendant must take their victim as they find them.[161]

However, the approach taken in *Carey* was replicated by the Court of Appeal in the case of *R. v DJ*.[162] In this case a group of young boys shouted abuse and spat at an elderly man who was playing cricket with his son. They also threw stones, one of which hit the man. The man, who had suffered from coronary heart disease, had a heart attack and died. The unlawful and dangerous act relied on was the throwing of stones (a battery) rather than the abuse, given that, as noted by Lord Justice Gage: "insults and spittle can hardly be described as dangerous acts".[163] The difficulty for the prosecution at this point, however, was that it was not clear what the factual cause of the heart attack was. From the expert evidence, although it was possible that it was the incident as a whole, including the battery, which caused the heart attack, "it was impossible . . . for the jury to exclude the insults and spitting as the sole cause of . . . death".[164] Since it was impossible to establish that the battery, as the unlawful and dangerous act, was a cause of death, the appellant's conviction for manslaughter was quashed.

(iv) The unlawful act need not be directed at the victim

It used to be thought that because the unlawful act must expose the victim to the risk of some bodily harm, it had to be aimed at that victim. This was seen in the case of *Dalby*,[165] where the defendant's conviction for manslaughter arising out of the supply of prescription drugs to his friend, the deceased, was quashed on the basis that the unlawful act of supplying the drug must be "directed at the victim". However, that approach was subsequently disapproved. In *Mitchell*,[166] it was held that the only issue in

---

[159] *R. v Carey (Claire Anne)* [2006] EWCA Crim 17.
[160] *Carey* [2006] Crim. L.R. 842.
[161] Ormerod cites *Hayward* (1908) 21 Cox C.C. 692 in support of this argument.
[162] *R. v DJ* [2007] EWCA Crim 3133.
[163] *R. v DJ* [2007] EWCA Crim 3133 at [33].
[164] *R. v DJ* [2007] EWCA Crim 3133 at [53].
[165] *R. v Dalby (Derek Shaun)* (1982) 74 Cr. App. R. 348.
[166] *R. v Mitchell (Ronald James)* (1983) 76 Cr. App. R. 293.

such cases was one of causation and that in *Dalby* there had been "no sufficient link between Dalby's wrongful act (supplying the drug) and his friend's death".[167]

Attorney-General's Reference (No. 3 of 1994) [1998] A.C. 245 (House of Lords)

[For facts see above, p.206.]

LORD HOPE:

"[It is not] necessary, in order to constitute manslaughter, that the death resulted from an unlawful and dangerous act which was done with the intention to cause the victim to sustain harm. This is because it is clear from the authorities that, although the defendant must be proved to have intended to do what he did, it is not necessary to prove that he knew that his act was unlawful or dangerous. So it must follow that it is unnecessary to prove that he knew his act was likely to injure the person who died as a result of it. All that need be proved is that he intentionally did what he did, that the death was caused by it and that, applying an objective test, all sober and reasonable people would recognise the risk that some harm would result . . . [Certain cases] suggest that the defendant cannot be found guilty of this crime unless his unlawful and dangerous act was directed at the person who was the ultimate victim of it. I am not persuaded that . . . [this] proposition is borne out by the authorities. In *R. v Mitchell* . . . [it] was rejected . . .

In this case the act which had to be shown to be an unlawful and dangerous act was the stabbing of the child's mother. There can be no doubt that all sober and reasonable people would regard that act . . . as dangerous. It is plain that it was unlawful as it was done with the intention of causing her injury. As the defendant intended to commit that act, all the ingredients necessary for *mens rea* in regard to the crime of manslaughter were established, irrespective of who was the ultimate victim of it . . . The question, once all the other elements are satisfied, is simply one of causation."

Reference answered accordingly

Following this decision, it seems clear that generally there is no requirement that the act be aimed at the victim and the issue is one of causation. Subsequent, and more recent, cases make no reference to any such requirement. Nevertheless, some commentators support the requirement that the act should be aimed at the victim on the grounds that the approach in *Dalby* "at least introduces a subjective element . . . An act can only be 'directed at the victim' if there is an intention so to direct it" and because the "second qualification stated, that the act must be likely to cause immediate injury also seems to be new, significant and appropriate".[168]

4. Sentencing involuntary manslaughter

As noted above, involuntary manslaughter of any species carries a maximum life sentence, leaving the sentencing judge with a wide ranging discretion to do justice in a particular case, unfettered by any sentencing guidelines set down by the Sentencing Council. Because of the gap between the blameworthiness of the defendant and the outcome of his act, discussed in the next section, cases of constructive manslaughter lead to difficult sentencing decisions for judges. Lord Judge considered the issue in *Attorney-General's Reference (Nos 60, 62 and 63 of 2009) (Appleby)*,[169] involving a number of cases relating to sentences for homicides resulting from street fights where fists and feet were the weapons used, and concluded that the result of death is important in such cases. He was of the

---

[167]   *Dalby* was decided before *Kennedy No.2*. There is now no doubt that the self-injection of the drugs would break the chain of causation.

[168]   J.C. Smith, [1982] Crim. L.R. 440.

[169]   *Re Attorney General's Reference (Nos 60, 62 and 63 of 2009)* [2010] 2 Cr. App. R. (S.) 46.

opinion that the earlier sentencing case of *Coleman*,[170] where the death resulting from an assault was described as "accidental", should no longer be referred to because the public impact of violence on the streets was more of a concern since that case was decided and was a significant aggravating feature. *Coleman* had focused on the actions of the defendant and his intentions at the time of the crime rather than its consequences. Lord Judge concluded that that approach to sentencing was no longer appropriate and that, following the Criminal Justice Act 2003 s.143(1),[171] specific attention should be paid to the consequences of the crime. The description "one-punch manslaughter" should be confined to cases where death resulted from a single blow with a bare hand or fist such as the case of *Furby*,[172] where the starting point for sentence following a guilty plea was 12 months' imprisonment.

Following *Appleby* the question became whether the approach taken in that case to sentencing unlawful act manslaughters, with a focus on the harm caused, should apply equally to other forms of involuntary manslaughter. In *Holtom*[173] the Court of Appeal considered *Appleby* in determining the appropriate sentence for a case of gross negligence manslaughter arising out of a workplace incident, where a 15-year-old assisting a builder had been working unsupervised and was crushed by a wall. A sentence of three years' imprisonment was upheld (the defendant pleaded guilty). Following this, *Appleby* was interpreted in *Barrass*[174] as creating

"a step change in the tariff of sentencing in cases of unlawful act manslaughter and gross negligence manslaughter, each of which ultimately rested on its own facts and by reference to a proper consideration of the fatal consequences of the offence."

The defendant's sentence of two years and eight months' imprisonment, following a guilty plea to manslaughter after he left his vulnerable sister for two-and-a-half weeks on her bedroom floor following a fall, was upheld. Finally, in *Garg*,[175] the Court of Appeal took *Holtom* and *Barrass* as demonstrating that sentencing principles enunciated in *Appleby* applied equally to gross negligence manslaughter, and went on to apply them in a case of manslaughter arising out of gross medical negligence, upholding a sentence of two years' imprisonment following a guilty plea. Quirk has questioned the wisdom of this approach to sentencing medical manslaughter:

"[i]f the men and women in white coats are going to be put away, given the costs to them, the criminal justice system and the National Health Service against the questionable benefits of imprisonment, there needs to be calibrated guidelines and a coherent rationale, not a one-size fits all increase in sentences for all manslaughter cases."[176]

The result of this line of cases is, though, that sentences for all types of involuntary manslaughter have increased. It is about time that the Sentencing Council addressed the issue by providing a definitive guideline for involuntary manslaughter. One imagines, however, that the idea of the task might appear insurmountable, given the wide ranging culpability which involuntary manslaughter covers.

---

170   *R. v Coleman (Anthony Neville)* (1992) 95 Cr. App. R. 159.
171   "In considering the seriousness of any offence, the court must consider the offender's culpability in committing the offence and any harm which the offence caused, was intended to cause or might forseeably have caused."
172   *R. v Furby (Andrew)* [2006] 2 Cr. App. R. (S.) 8.
173   *R. v Holtom (Colin Charles)* [2011] 1 Cr. App. R. (S.) 18.
174   *R. v Barrass (John Morris)* [2012] 1 Cr. App. R. (S.) 80.
175   *R. v Garg (Sudhanshu)* [2013] 2 Cr. App. R. (S.) 30.
176   H. Quirk, "Sentencing White Coat Crime: The Need for Guidance in Medical Manslaughter Cases" [2013] Crim. L.R. 871–888 at 888.

The question then arises as to whether the substantive law ought to be reformed to assist the task of importing consistency at the sentencing stage?

5. Rationale and reform

In cases where a charge of manslaughter is brought, the law here raises, yet again, the fundamental question of what importance should be attached to the actual harm done. If a defendant has acted with gross negligence, or has committed an unlawful act, why should they not simply be punished for that gross negligence or for that unlawful act? Why should they be punished for the more serious crime of manslaughter merely because their actions cause death—if that death was not within their range of contemplation? Take *Larkin* for example. He committed an unlawful act, an assault. Why was he not simply punished for that unlawful act? Why should he be guilty of the much more serious offence of manslaughter merely because his drunk mistress happened to fall against his razor? Was not his blameworthiness the same, whether she fell against the razor or whether she fell to the ground, missing his razor and not injuring herself?

Criminal Law Revision Committee, 14th Report, Offences Against the Person, 1980, Cmnd.7844, paras 120–121, 124:

"120 . . . Suppose that A strikes B and gives him a bleeding nose; B, unknown to A, is a haemophiliac and bleeds to death. Or, A strikes B who falls and unluckily hits his head against a sharp projection and dies. Or A chases B with the object of chastising him; B runs away, trips and falls into a river in which he drowns. In each of these cases, although A is at fault and is guilty of an assault or of causing injury, his fault does not extend to the causing of death or to the causing of serious injury which he did not foresee and in some cases could not reasonably have foreseen. In our opinion, they should not be treated as manslaughter because the offender's fault falls too far short of the unlucky result. So serious an offence as manslaughter should not be a lottery . . . [T]here seems to be no reason for calling it manslaughter. Indeed, the name is positively objectionable for several reasons, among which are the fact that it gives a false idea of the gravity of the defendant's moral offence and that there is always the possibility that it may receive a punishment going beyond that appropriate to the assault.

121 The second instance is causing death by an act of gross negligence. Evidence of this will often be sufficient to enable the jury to draw an inference of recklessness as to the causing of death or serious injury, in which case the act will amount to manslaughter under our recommendation . . . But sometimes the jury may not be able to find more than that the defendant was extremely foolish; and although the foolishness may amount to gross negligence we do not think that it should be sufficient for manslaughter in the absence of advertence to the risk of death or serious injury. It seems that in fact prosecutions falling exclusively under this heading of manslaughter are very rare."[177]

There is, however, another view that weight should be attached to the resulting harm in assessing the extent of criminal liability. The fact that death has been caused is, under this view, crucial in justifying increased liability and punishment.

C.M.V. Clarkson and H. M. Keating, "Codification: Offences against the Person under the Draft Criminal Code" (1986) 50 Jo. C.L. 405 at 422–423:

"Criminal liability cannot and should not be based exclusively on mental elements. The significance of the harm caused, in this case, death, is critical in the construction of criminal liability. We do not judge people solely on the basis of the quality of their actions and their exertions, but also by the *results* of those actions. The fact that

---

[177] It is true that prosecutions for gross negligence manslaughter have been quite rare in the past. However, they are becoming more common. Quick has found that since the mid-1980s the number of investigations of medical gross negligence manslaughter have increased considerably. In the period 1976–1985 only seven cases were investigated. In the following decade (1986–1995) this number almost doubled (13), whilst in the 10-year period 1996–2005 there were 40 incidents that were investigated: Quick, above, fn.116.

a person's negligent or unlawful actions have resulted in the death of a human being totally alters our moral judgment; it arouses resentment in society (quite apart from the bitterness and pain caused to the relatives and friends of the deceased). Imagine a workman high on a building who negligently tosses a brick to the street below where it strikes and kills a passer-by. The response of the C.L.R.C . . . is that this death is 'pure chance.' It is simply 'bad luck.' The workman's actions must be judged *totally* on the basis of his *subjective mens rea*.

It is strongly submitted that this view is unacceptable. Those observing the above incidents would respond with horror. The workman has *killed* the passer-by. His actions were not just dangerous, that is, likely to cause danger. The danger has materialised and someone lies dead. This resultant harm makes its mark and leaves a lasting impression. If the workman tried to run away, we would chase him and attempt his detention.

George P. Fletcher, Rethinking Criminal Law (1978), p. 482:

A totally different approach begins with the observation that persons who inadvertently cause harm feel greater remorse than those who have 'close calls.' If a reckless driver goes into a skid and collides with another car, he is likely to feel different from another driver, equally reckless, whose car merely slides into an embankment. If an assassin aims, shoots and hits her intended victim, she is likely to feel different about her act than she would if the bullet has gone astray. Feelings of guilt, and remorse are appropriate when harm is done, but if all is the same after as before the act, there would be nothing to be remorseful about, and the actor's feelings of guilt would make us wonder why he wanted to suffer inappropriate anguish. Feelings of remorse and guilt are closely connected with causing harm, for these feelings are part of a broader pattern of human interaction. The notions of causing harm, injuring others, feeling guilt and making amends are all part of the patterns by which human relationships are disturbed and then restored. The notion of guilt cannot be lifted out of context and fitted to cases where there is merely a risk of harm, but no concrete impact on the lives of others."

C.M.V. Clarkson, "Context and Culpability in Involuntary Manslaughter: Principle or Instinct", in A. Ashworth and B. Mitchell, Rethinking English Homicide Law (2000), pp.154–155, 158–160:

"*Grossly careless killings*
. . . The Law Commission has long been committed to subjectivism in the criminal law on the basis that criminal liability and punishment should be linked to moral guilt which involves blaming only those who have chosen to cause harm in the sense of intending or knowing that harm could occur. However, while such cognition clearly does involve moral guilt, it is not obvious that moral guilt **must** be linked to cognition. We can blame people for making choices even when the possibility of harm is not in the forefront of their minds. As Duff has argued: a failure to consider obvious risks to others demonstrates an attitude of indifference. Assuming the person is capable of foresight, failing to recognise obvious risks when choosing to act demonstrates that s/he regards them as unimportant or 'couldn't care less'. Students almost never forget a final exam; some students forget tutorials. Exams are of critical importance and care is taken not to oversleep etc.; attendance at tutorials, to some students, is not important and careful precautions (setting the alarm clock etc.) are not taken.

Such uncaring indifference could be condemned even more strongly than the choices of the classically subjective risk-taker who recognises a small chance of a risk occurring, hopes it will not materialise, but nevertheless goes ahead and acts. This indifference is a state of mind, albeit an affective one rather than a cognitive one.

In many situations Duff's account is 'easy'. For example, the boorish man who assumes that all women would consent to intercourse with him clearly demonstrates indifference when having intercourse without consent. But some cases are 'harder'. Horder, ('Gross Negligence and Criminal Culpability' (1997) 47 University of Toronto Law Journal 495) has argued that there are two forms of gross negligence: indifference and a great departure from expected standards. However, assuming a capacity to choose otherwise had all the relevant facts been brought to the actor's attention, the latter is better regarded as evidence of the former. For example, doctors because of their training and rules of conduct regarding their profession are expected to act in the best interests of their patients and achieve a basic level of competence. If, through inattentiveness or tiredness, they make a slight error (not a **great** departure from expected standards) we would probably not conclude that their actions demonstrated uncaring indifference sufficient for criminal liability. But where there is a gross or substantial departure from **expected** standards (bearing in mind that what is expected could vary depending on working conditions) indifference (given the doctor's situation) can more easily be inferred. The fact that s/he is overworked by a stretched NHS will not serve to exculpate. Unless so tired as to be an effective automaton the doctor chose to act knowing of the fatigue. While the primary motivation in acting might be concern for the care of the patient, ultimately other secondary concerns (career prospects, willingness to obey superior's orders etc.) prevailed thereby demonstrating an attitude of indifference to the patient's interests. For instance, the conduct and attitude of the anaesthetist in *Adomako* was described by an expert witness as 'a gross dereliction of care'. Such a choice can be condemned (although we might also wish to blame others for putting the doctor in such a situation) . . .

Killings resulting from dangerous unlawful acts:
    . . . It is my argument that in appropriate cases the requisite culpability can be found in the circumstances/ context in which the defendant acted without any necessary correspondence to the death. The notion that culpability can be established without the fault element corresponding to the prohibited harm is hardly a novel one in English law. For example, cases on intoxication clearly establish that the requisite culpability lies in the excessive consumption of drink or drugs . . .
    However, once one has severed the connection between fault and result, the problem is one of identifying what sort of fault should suffice for manslaughter. It is submitted that when death has been caused departure from the paradigm is permissible as long as the actions are within the same family of offence, namely violence. The essential point about constructive manslaughter is that the defendant has chosen to engage in criminal, dangerous activity: usually violence. Such a person is deliberately engaging in a morally different course of action compared to those who act lawfully and inadvertently cause death. As Horder puts it:

> 'The fact that I *deliberately* wrong V arguably changes my normative position *vis a vis* the risk of adverse consequences of that wrongdoing to V, whether or not foreseen or reasonably foreseeable . . . if . . . my unlawful act is meant to wrong V . . . its deliberateness changes my relationship with the risk of adverse consequences stemming therefrom.' ("A Critique of the Correspondence Principle in Criminal Law" [1995] Crim. L.R. 759.)

This change in normative position is, of course, morally interesting. But is it enough for the fault element for manslaughter? The answer is yes—provided the change in normative position is one involving an attack upon the victim. The moral quality of a deliberate attack upon a person brings the assailant within the family of violence. A defendant who attacks another and risks injury cannot complain when criminal liability is imposed in relation to injuries—even death—resulting from the attack. Horder distinguishes between 'pure luck' (where a fortuitous result unconnected to one's endeavours occurs) and 'making one's own luck' (where the consequence is directly connected to one's endeavours). Where a death results from an unlawful attack on a victim, the defendant 'by directing [his/her] efforts towards harming V' is responsible for the bad luck that s/he has created.
    Take, for example, the case of *Williams* ([1996] 2 Cr.App.R.(S) 72) which is a classic example of the sort of constructive manslaughter objected to by the Law Commission and many commentators. The defendant gave a young woman two pushes and one slap. As a result she fell back, caught her head on a wall-mounted heater, damaged her neck and died. Sacks J., in substituting a sentence of two-and-a-half years' imprisonment, agreed with the trial sentencing judge that this death was 'in a sense, accidental' but stressed that 'we do bear well in mind that this was an assault on a woman' and that he 'set about her . . . with terrible consequences'. Such, admittedly rather generalised, statements are an acceptance of the above proposition that when the defendant, instead of merely quarrelling with the woman as he had been, chose to attack her, he deliberately changed his normative stance to become a violent actor who should bear responsibility for the consequences of his violence. His actions were simply not of the same moral order as those of a person who swears at a woman who in distress turns away and hits her head on a wall-heater and dies.
    This line of reasoning, however, suggests that it is only those who attack their victims in the sense of **assaulting** them **intending or foreseeing some injury** who alter their normative position relevantly to bring themselves within the family of violence. From this it follows that not every unlawful act should suffice for constructive manslaughter as it does under the present law (as long as it is dangerous). Accordingly, there should be no liability for manslaughter in some of the well-known cases such as *Newbury* and the drug-injection or drug-supply cases such as *Cato*. Such offenders have of course engaged in actions of a certain moral quality and there might indeed be risks of adverse consequences flowing from their wrongdoing. They could possibly be liable for killing by gross carelessness. But, by not attacking their victims, they have not chosen to embark on a violent course of action. They have departed too far from the family of violence: the connection between their fault and the death is too tenuous.
    From this it follows that some sort of constructive manslaughter should be retained but only unlawful acts of personal violence involving at least a common assault with intention or foresight of some injury should suffice."

The significance of a defendant changing their "normative position" towards their victim has come under question by Ashworth in the following extract. The concept of a change in normative position can be attributed not just to Horder, who is cited in the above extract, but originally to Gardner.[178] Ashworth points out that it is assumed that a change in normative position should make a defendant who engaged in a violent attack liable for a more serious offence than he foresaw, but we are not told why this is. One of the issues to be addressed is to know what the relevant normative position is. Ashworth suggests that it might be that "there is a duty not knowingly to wrong another by injuring their protected interests, either by way of an attack (which is essentially harmful) or by way of endangerment (which is potentially harmful)". However, it is not enough, on Clarkson's view, that the defendant has intentionally committed any offence; to be liable for manslaughter he must have committed an offence within the family of violence. Ashworth warns, however, that there is a danger of relying on a principle such as "family of offences" in that "it is open to manipulation on other grounds: there can be nuclear and extended families".

In the above extract, Clarkson uses the case of *Williams* as an example of a defendant changing his normative position towards his victim and having to face the consequences of a conviction for manslaughter. Ashworth explores the application of the principle of change of normative position in the context of this case in more detail.

Andrew Ashworth, "Change of Normative Position: Determining the Contours of Culpability in Criminal Law" (2008) 11 New Criminal L. Rev. 232–256 at pp.250–252:

"There is, in principle, a whole range of possible fault elements in such a case. To take four, D could have been (i) walking past V when he tripped over, pushing her against the heater; (ii) leaving the house after burgling it when he encountered V and in his surprise tripped over, pushing her against the heater; (iii) assaulting V by pushing and slapping her once, as in *Williams* itself; or (iv) attacking her with punches and kicking her in the abdomen, causing her to fall against the heater. In which of these scenarios does D change his normative position, or cross a moral threshold, sufficiently for liability for manslaughter? Of course there is a labelling issue here, and we should assume that the crime of manslaughter is understood to be a lower grade of homicide than murder, requiring a lesser degree of fault. Case (i) can be eliminated swiftly, on the ground that D did not intend to assault V or indeed to commit any wrong against V. Perhaps, in order to retain our focus, we can also deal swiftly with case (iv): kicking V in the abdomen suggests an intention to cause at least moderate injury, if not serious injury, and might therefore be regarded as a sufficient fault element for a crime of manslaughter. But what about cases (ii) and (iii)? Is it satisfactory to say that case (iii) ought to be sufficient for manslaughter because D has intentionally assaulted V, thereby changing his normative position in relation to harms that might result to V (including death)? . . . [W]hen Gardner considered the distinction between the offenses of common assault and assault occasioning bodily harm, he argued that committing an assault was a sufficient change of normative position to justify holding D liable for any actual bodily harm that might result, and that the law puts people on notice about that. Can that argument be extended to manslaughter, even if, to adopt Gardner's imagery, one asks the question by travelling 'downhill' from D's responsibility for causing V's death?

In relation to case (ii), can one say that D has sufficiently changed his normative position by intentionally committing a crime against V (burglary), so that it is fair to hold him criminally liable for any resulting harms? One obvious difference between cases (ii) and (iii) is that the crimes of burglary and assault form part of different families of offences. That is a restrictive consideration that points away from the unlawful act approach, which allows the intentional commission of *any* crime to constitute a sufficient change of normative position or crossing of a moral threshold, and we [can see] that Horder's formulation of the malice principle restricts it to conduct wrongfully directed at a particular type of interest. So, if we return to case (iii), the key question is how the moral connection between a death caused by D and D's intentional assault on V is to be established. If D intended nothing more than a common assault, and if the possibility of causing death was statistically

---

178   J. Gardner, "Rationality and the Rule of Law in Offences against the Person" (1994) 53 C.L.J. 502.

very low (as it must be if a simple assault is intended), is it merely a question of putting D on notice of the risk of a manslaughter conviction if death should by mischance ensue? If notice alone were sufficient, that would raise the question whether due notice could convert case (ii) into a morally satisfactory foundation for a manslaughter conviction."

Mitchell similarly challenges the use of *Williams* as providing an effective defence of the change of normative position principle:

"But what is crucial about the distinction between swearing at the woman and attacking her is not that they reflect different families of wrongdoing: rather it is that one carries an intrinsic risk (albeit a very remote risk) of causing serious, possibly fatal, harm, whereas the other does not."[179]

Clearly, there are at least two factions on either side of the argument but, as will be seen, the Law Commission has sided with Gardner, Horder and Clarkson in its proposals for changing the law on manslaughter.[180]

The Law Commission, in a Consultation Paper in 1994,[181] was critical of the (then) law on gross negligence manslaughter and was of the view that constructive manslaughter should be completely abolished. However, in its Final Report in 1996,[182] the Commission conceded that the arguments in favour of gross negligence were formidable—where the harm risked was very serious, namely, death or serious injury: "We may plead that we trod on the snail inadvertently: but not on the baby—you ought to look where you are putting your great feet".[183] Secondly, in response to strong comments favouring retention, in some form, of constructive manslaughter, the Law Commission included a modified form of unlawful act manslaughter in its proposals. In 2000, the Home Office largely accepted these recommendations and, in place of the present broad offence of manslaughter, proposed the creation of new separate offences of reckless killing and killing by gross carelessness in a Draft Involuntary Homicide Bill.[184] Following criticisms of the draft bill, the Law Commission revisited the issue and its proposals are now slightly different. Rather than creating two offences of reckless killing and killing by gross carelessness to replace manslaughter it has recommended that the label of manslaughter should remain and that the offence could be committed in one of two ways.

Law Commission, No.304, Murder, Manslaughter and Infanticide (2006), para.2.163:

"We recommend that manslaughter should encompass:

(1) killing another person through gross negligence ('gross negligence manslaughter'); or

(2) killing another person

---

[179] B. Mitchell, "More Thoughts about Unlawful and Dangerous Act Manslaughter and the One-punch Killer" [2009] Crim. L.R. 502 at 506.

[180] This is of little surprise, given Horder's position in the Law Commission at the time of the Law Commission's report in 2006. For further arguments in support of the Law Commission's approach, see J. Horder, *Homicide and the Politics of Law Reform* (Oxford: OUP, 2012), Ch.5.

[181] Law Commission Consultation Paper No.135, *Involuntary Manslaughter* (1994).

[182] Law Commission Paper No.237, *Legislating the Criminal Code: Involuntary Manslaughter* (1996).

[183] At para.4.23, citing J. Austin, "A Plea for Excuses" in *Proceedings of the Aristotelian Society*, New Series, vol. 57 (1956–7), p.1.

[184] Home Office, *Reforming the Law on Involuntary Manslaughter: The Government's Proposals* (2000).

(a) through the commission of a criminal act intended by the defendant to cause injury, or
(b) through the commission of a criminal act that the defendant was aware involved a serious risk of causing some injury ('criminal act manslaughter')."

These recommendations arguably constitute an improvement on the previous proposals and allow the two forms of killing (gross negligence manslaughter and criminal act manslaughter) to remain separate to some degree. It is right that this should be the case, since killers within the first category are normally engaged in lawful activities, often simply performing their job. Causing injury is not part of their reason for acting. The moral culpability of those who choose to engage in a violent attack, and thus fall within the second category, is aggravated by their crossing a moral threshold and engaging in violence. Fair labelling suggests that this difference in the context and culpability associated with the killing should be marked by a separate offence. That both forms of killing would carry the same offence label (manslaughter) may be a residual objection to the proposals.[185]

B. Voluntary Manslaughter

A defendant who possesses malice aforethought may, when charged with murder, be convicted of the lesser crime of manslaughter if she satisfies one of three mitigating criteria. At common law there was only one such mitigating criterion: killing under provocation. Two further partial defences were added by statute: diminished responsibility[186] and killing in pursuance of a suicide pact.[187] The main reason for the existence of these partial defences is the mandatory life sentence for murder and the need to provide the judge with discretion in sentencing in cases where the killer's blameworthiness is reduced due to some factor personal to her or the surrounding circumstances of the killing. The term voluntary manslaughter is nothing more than a convenient label for these forms of killing. Most recently, the defence of "provocation" has been abolished and replaced with a new statutory partial defence of "loss of control".[188]

1. Loss of control

(i) Introduction

In *Duffy*,[189] a young woman killed her husband after having been savagely beaten by him; in *Camplin*,[190] a 15-year-old boy who had been buggered killed his assailant; in *Bedder*,[191] a man, who knew himself to be impotent, stabbed to death a prostitute who had jeered at him and kicked him in the groin after he had unsuccessfully tried to have intercourse with her. All claimed that they had been provoked into losing their self-control and killing their "victims".

To what extent should we blame such persons for their actions and hold them criminally responsible? If we can envisage situations in which violence of this sort would be a natural response to their

---

[185] It should be noted, however, that these proposals form part of a package of reforms to homicide, in which a "ladder" of offences would be created. Whilst "manslaughter" would remain a fairly broad offence at the bottom of the ladder, it would be narrower than the current offence of manslaughter since some reckless killings and those killings which currently fall within the law of voluntary manslaughter would amount to murder in the second degree.
[186] Homicide Act 1957 s.2.
[187] Homicide Act 1957 s.4.
[188] Coroners and Justice Act 2009 s.56.
[189] *R. v Duffy* [1949] 1 All E.R. 932.
[190] *R. v Camplin (Paul)* [1978] A.C. 705.
[191] *Bedder v DPP* (1954) 38 Cr. App. R.133.

suffering, how is our understanding of their plight to be reflected in the law? By no punishment? By less punishment?

The law has traditionally accepted claims of provocation affecting liability in one area only. Provocation has allowed murder to be reduced to manslaughter[192] because it has been felt unjust to subject the defendant to the full rigour of a conviction for murder; in other words, the courts have wished to avoid the mandatory life sentence. A conviction for manslaughter, on the other hand, gives the courts the necessary flexibility to impose whatever sentence is deemed appropriate.[193] Loss of control, or its predecessor provocation, is not a defence to any other crime as no other serious offence in England carries a fixed penalty. For other crimes, provocation can be taken into account as a mitigating factor, lessening the severity of the sentence.

Under the common law of provocation, a defendant to a charge of murder was provided with a partial defence if the killing could be attributed to the defendant's angry response to some act of provocation from the deceased or from a third party. The test for the jury in such cases was elaborated on in statute.

Homicide Act 1957 s.3

"Where on a charge of murder there is evidence on which the jury can find that the person charged was provoked (whether by things done or by things said or by both together) to lose his self-control, the question whether the provocation was enough to make a reasonable man do as he did shall be left to be determined by the jury; and in determining that question the jury shall take into account everything both done and said according to the effect which, in their opinion, it would have on a reasonable man."

The defence was traditionally divided into two tests: (i) a subjective test that the defendant must have lost their self-control; and (ii) an objective test that the defendant must have responded in a way that the reasonable man would have responded. The law proved troublesome and controversial in respect to both of these tests, and led to a great deal of instability in the case law. Some called for complete abolition of the defence, whilst others argued for reform. The Law Commission sought to widen the ambit of the provocation defence by allowing emotions other than anger, namely fear, to form the basis of the defence, whilst at the same time attempting to narrow the defence in other ways.[194] The view it took was that so long as the Government resists calls for the abolition of the mandatory life sentence for murder, it is pointless to consider the arguments for and against complete abolition.[195]

(ii) Rationale of the law

In reviewing the law of provocation and making recommendations for its reform, the Law Commission naturally attempted to identify the rationale of the law's response, so that it could identify the aims

---

[192]   In *Marks* [1998] Crim. L.R. 676 the Court of Appeal accepted that the defence of provocation was available to an accomplice to murder.

[193]   The Sentencing Guidelines Council provided guidelines for sentencing in provocation cases. There are three starting points depending on whether the degree of provocation is high (starting point of three years' custody), substantial (starting point of eight years' custody) or low (starting point of 12 years' custody). These are based on the provocation taking place over a short period but previous experience of abuse or domestic violence operates as a mitigating factor: Sentencing Guidelines Council, *Manslaughter by Reason of Provocation: Guideline* (2005). A new set of sentencing guidelines is required to take account of changes made to the law by the Coroners and Justice Act 2009.

[194]   Law Commission Paper No.290, *Partial Defences to Murder* (2004).

[195]   Law Commission Paper No.290, *Partial Defences to Murder* (2004), para.3.35.

of the law, all the better to develop improvements. However, the Law Commission described the rationale underlying the defence as "elusive".[196] One possible rationale of the law's response historically is that in weighing the competing interests of the eventual victim against those of the defendant it decides that the victim, by participating in the chain of events, is to *some* extent responsible for his own demise. The victim, therefore, loses some of his claim to be protected by the law. Viewed in this light one could regard provocation as a partial justification for the defendant's actions and an historical analysis of the defence affords considerable support for this. The common-law defence of provocation was of ancient origin but:

> "it emerged in recognisably modern form in the late seventeenth and early eighteenth centuries. It comes from a world of Restoration gallantry in which gentlemen . . . acted in accordance with a code of honour which required insult to be personally avenged by instant angry retaliation . . . To show anger 'in hot blood' for a proper reason by an appropriate response was not only permissible but the badge of a man of honour. The human frailty to which the defence of provocation made allowance was the possibility that the man of honour might overreact and kill when a lesser retaliation would have been appropriate. Provided that he did not grossly overreact in the extent or manner of his retaliation, the offence would be manslaughter."[197]

Thus, an important feature of the law at this time was that of proportionality.[198]

However, while it may well be that for at least some of its history the defence of provocation was a partial justification,[199] the law, by the nineteenth century had already begun to shift in emphasis. Rather than focusing upon the rightfulness of anger, judges "preferred to look upon provocation as something which temporarily deprived the accused of his reason"[200] and were concerned with whether there had been a loss of control. However, this loss of control had to manifest itself in a particular way: extreme anger. This trend continued and the law, especially since the Homicide Act 1957 s.3, seems to have regarded the defence as a "partial excuse". The law ceased to be solely concerned with the victim-offender relationship. Provocation could be pleaded even if the victim was not the provoking agent[201] (in other words, was entirely innocent in the affair). The victim need not have committed an "unlawful act"[202]; indeed, the victim may have been far too young to appreciate the quality of her actions at all.[203] In short, the thrust of the inquiry shifted from the victim (and her provocative acts) to the defendant (and his loss of self-control)[204] and the rationale of the defence became "compassion for human infirmity".[205] As in cases of diminished responsibility and duress, the law recognised that people are not in perfect control of their emotions and actions, particularly when subject to great pressure.

---

[196] Law Commission Paper No.290, *Partial Defences to Murder* (2004), para.3.21.

[197] *R. v Smith (Morgan James)* [2001] 1 A.C. 146 at 159–160 per Lord Hoffmann, drawing upon the work of J. Horder, *Provocation and Responsibility* (Oxford: OUP, 1992).

[198] See further, S. Gough, "Taking the Heat out of Provocation" [1999] 19 O.J.L.S. 481.

[199] See A. Ashworth, "The Doctrine of Provocation" [1976] C.L.J. 292; P. Alldridge, "The Coherence of Defences" [1983] Crim. L.R. 665.

[200] *Smith* [2001] 1 A.C. 146, per Lord Hoffmann at 160.

[201] e.g. *Davies* [1975] Q.B. 691. The requirement in s.3 that the provocation resulted from "things done or said" does, however, suggest that human activity must have been involved: the defendant could not plead, for example, that he was provoked by bad weather.

[202] See Alldridge, "The Coherence of Defences" [1983] Crim. L.R. 665.

[203] As in *R. v Doughty (Stephen Clifford)* (1986) 83 Cr. App. R. 319.

[204] See, generally, on this transmutation of provocation from a partial justification to a partial excuse, Alldridge, "The Coherence of Defences" [1983] Crim. L.R. 665 at 669–672.

[205] *Hayward* (1908) 21 Cox C.C. 692 at 694, per Lord Tindal CJ.

George P. Fletcher, Rethinking Criminal Law (1978), pp.246–247:

"The primary source of difficulty in the analysis of provocation derives from the failure of the courts and commentators to face the underlying normative issue whether the accused may be fairly expected to control an impulse to kill under the circumstances. Obviously there are some impulses such as anger and even mercy . . . that we do expect people to control. If they fail to control these impulses and they kill another intentionally, they are liable for unmitigated homicide or murder. The basic moral question in the law of homicide is distinguishing between those impulses to kill as to which we as a society demand self-control, and those as to which we relax our inhibitions."

It may be that the underlying rationale of the new defence of loss of control still contains elements of both excuse and justification. The new law requires that the defendant lost control and this can be categorised as an excusatory element. Further, it also insists that she did so in circumstances in which a person with a normal degree of tolerance and self-restraint might well have done the same. This latter requirement mirrors the objective test developed under the common law, in relation to which it has been suggested that it retains an element of justification in the defence.[206] Further, it has been suggested that a loss of control should be perceived as justified because it is not only natural, but right to become angry in some circumstances. The new law, however, also recognises that it is sometimes natural to react to a threat of serious violence through the use of excessive, pre-emptive violence, brought on by a state of fear.

(iii) The law

Coroners and Justice Act 2009 s.54: Partial defence to murder: loss of control

"(1) Where a person ('D') kills or is a party to the killing of another ('V'), D is not to be convicted of murder if—
  (a) D's acts and omissions in doing or being a party to the killing resulted from D's loss of self-control,
  (b) the loss of self-control had a qualifying trigger, and
  (c) a person of D's sex and age, with a normal degree of tolerance and self-restraint and in the circumstances of D, might have reacted in the same or in a similar way to D.
(2) For the purposes of subsection (1)(a), it does not matter whether or not the loss of control was sudden.
(3) In subsection (1)(c) the reference to "the circumstances of D" is a reference to all of D's circumstances other than those whose only relevance to D's conduct is that they bear on D's general capacity for tolerance or self-restraint.
(4) Subsection (1) does not apply if, in doing or being a party to the killing, D acted in a considered desire for revenge.
(5) On a charge of murder, if sufficient evidence is adduced to raise an issue with respect to the defence under subsection (1), the jury must assume that the defence is satisfied unless the prosecution proves beyond reasonable doubt that it is not.
(6) For the purposes of subsection (5), sufficient evidence is adduced to raise an issue with respect to the defence if evidence is adduced on which, in the opinion of the trial judge, a jury, properly directed, could reasonably conclude that the defence might apply.
(7) A person who, but for this section, would be liable to be convicted of murder is liable instead to be convicted of manslaughter.
(8) The fact that one party to a killing is by virtue of this section not liable to be convicted of murder does not affect the question whether the killing amounted to murder in the case of any other party to it."

The common law defence of provocation is abolished by s.56 of the 2009 Act. Whilst the Law Commission's recommendations for change had retained the label for the partial defence as "provocation", this was dropped by the Government on the basis that conversations with stakeholders had

---

[206] See further, A. Ashworth, "The Doctrine of Provocation" [1976] C.L.J. 292; J. Horder, "Autonomy, Provocation and Duress" [1992] Crim. L.R. 706 at 707–711; Horder, *Provocation and Responsibility* (1992).

revealed that the term carries "negative connotations".[207] As under the common law, the burden of proof is on the prosecution to prove that the defence is not satisfied (s.54(5)) once the judge is satisfied that there is sufficient evidence that would enable a jury to decide that the defence might apply (s.54(6)).[208]

In comparison to s.3 of the Homicide Act 1957, the new provision provides far more detail, and the elements of the defence are further clarified in s.55, as discussed below. The defence can no longer be separated into a neat "subjective" test and an "objective" test. However, when looking at the section more closely it can be seen that it is very much based on the common law defence of provocation and retains many of its characteristics, whilst at the same time attempting to ensure that it is made available in cases of murder that merit reduction to manslaughter.

(a) *Loss of self-control*

This first requirement mirrors that under the common law defence of provocation, which was meant to exclude from the ambit of the defence planned or revenge killings. No matter how severe the provocation, if the defendant was in control at the time of the killing, there was no evidence upon which the defence could be based.[209] Although the new law now explicitly excludes pure revenge killings through s.54(4), the loss of control requirement is retained, since it is the law's desire to make concessions to "human frailty" which provides a great deal of rationale for the defence. This is despite the Law Commission having recommended that a reformed version of provocation jettison the need for a loss of control.[210] The question that remains, however, is what is meant by "loss of self-control"? It is clearly a subjective test: the issue is whether the defendant lost his self-control, causing him to kill.

Under the common law, in the majority of cases where a sudden killing followed on from a highly provocative incident, it was more or less assumed that the defendant had lost control. However, in some cases it was more problematic and the case-law was disappointing in explaining what "loss of self-control" meant. Cases referred to the defendant not being "master of his own understanding",[211] although beyond using phrases such as "snapping", or "exploding into anger", little further attention was generally paid to this element.[212] It does not mean that it is necessary for the defendant to have "gone berserk"[213]: such an extreme (and rare) condition might even be inconsistent with a finding that the defendant acted with an intention to kill.[214] In *Richens*,[215] it was stressed that there did not need to be a complete loss of control so that the defendant did not know what he was doing; what was required was that the defendant be so angry as to be unable to restrain himself. It is unclear the extent

---

207   Ministry of Justice, *Murder, Manslaughter and Infanticide: Proposals for Reform of the Law*, CP 19/08, 2008, para.34.
208   In *Dawes* [2013] 2 Cr. App. R. 3 the Court of Appeal emphasised the need for there to be sufficient evidence of all three elements of the defence (loss of self-control, qualifying trigger and reaction of a person of normal tolerance and self-restraint) before the judge is required to leave the defence to the jury.
209   As in *R. v Cocker* [1989] Crim. L.R. 740 where the undeniably provocative behaviour of his terminally-ill wife did *not* cause the defendant to lose control (as it could have done) but led him *calmly* to accede to her requests to die.
210   For a discussion of the Law Commission's reasoning, and arguments that the Government was mistaken to reject it, see J. Horder, *Homicide and the Politics of Law Reform* (Oxford: OUP, 2012), Ch.8.
211   Per Tindal CJ in *Hayward* (1833) 6 C. & P. 157, 159, repeated in *Ahluwalia* (1993) 96 Cr. App. R. 133 at 138 by Taylor LCJ.
212   J. Horder, *Provocation and Responsibility* (Oxford: OUP, 1992), p.109; A. Ashworth, *Principles of Criminal Law*, 5th edn (Oxford: OUP, 2006), pp.265–266.
213   Horder, *Provocation and Responsibility* (1992), pp.101–102.
214   It has sometimes been claimed (*Holmes* [1946] A.C. 588) that provocation negates malice aforethought. Both *Lee Chun-Chuen* [1963] A.C. 220 and the Royal Commission on Capital Punishment, Cmnd.8932 (1953), p.51, point out that this is wrong if it means that the prosecution do not have to establish mens rea. If it did, one would not need a special defence of provocation or loss of control. See also J. Horder, "Autonomy, Provocation and Duress" [1992] Crim. L.R.706 at 712–715.
215   *R. v Richens (Andrew Ronald)* (1994) 98 Cr. App. R. 43.

to which this will be relied upon to interpret the new statutory defence, but three years after the new defence came into force, Ashworth commented that

> "what amounts to the loss of self-control required by s.54(1)(a) of the Coroners and Justice Act 2009 remains clouded . . . One can say that a mere loss of temper is not enough, but that does not greatly advance the explanation."[216]

In exploring the concept of loss of self-control Holton and Shute have argued that this subjective limb of the test for provocation (and consequently, one assumes, the test under the new law) might do a far more important job than it has thus far been credited with. Their main point is that before judging whether the defendant lost her self-control, it is important first to establish that she once possessed it: "To borrow Muddy Water's words, 'you can't lose what you ain't never had'; nor, we might add, can you lose what you have already lost".[217] Of three main accounts of lack of control that they identify from the philosophical and psychological literatures, they prefer the following, adapted for their purposes:

> "Self-control consists of the ability to bring one's actions into line with one's considered judgments about what it would be best to do, where these judgments depart from one's desires."[218]

Or, put another way, what one loses is one's control over which of one's mental elements drive one's actions.[219] The importance of this point is that it assumes that we all have certain resolutions by which we choose to live, and we try to stick to those in the face of temptation to do otherwise (when we lose our tempers, for example). Anger may undermine an individual's ability to retain self-control, leading him to lose that ability. Holton and Shute argue that it is right in such cases that the defendant ought always to benefit from a partial defence of provocation, but that in cases where the defendant's self-control was insufficiently strong to restrain him, he should have no defence as he has not "lost" his self-control.[220] Thus, they argue that the defence of provocation (or loss of control) ought to start with a test establishing whether the defendant had self-control prior to the provocation, before requiring that it was lost and that such a loss led to the defendant killing the deceased. This is a novel approach that has much to commend it, particularly in relation to the significance it has for the objective test, to be considered below.

A fundamental change in the law has been introduced by s.54(2) which states that "it does not matter whether or not the loss of control was sudden". Under the common law, in the case of *Duffy*,[221] it was established that the loss of self-control suffered by the defendant had to be of a "sudden and temporary" nature. Thus, loss of self-control was equated with anger and not with fear or despair or other strong emotions. The person who killed through terror of what might happen to her was traditionally excluded from the ambit of the provocation defence if this terror did not express itself in anger.

This concept of anger requires further consideration. Horder has suggested that loss of self-control is one of the forms that anger may take.[222] For example, a lecturer may be so enraged by a late-comer

---

216   A. Ashworth, Commentary to *Dawes* [2013] Crim. L.R. 770 at 772.
217   R. Holton and S. Shute, "Self-Control in the Modern Provocation Defence" (2007) O.J.L.S. 27(1) 49 at 50.
218   Holton and Shute, "Self-Control in the Modern Provocation Defence" (2007) O.J.L.S. 27(1) 49 at 54.
219   Holton and Shute, "Self-Control in the Modern Provocation Defence" (2007) O.J.L.S. 27(1) 49 at 52.
220   Holton and Shute, "Self-Control in the Modern Provocation Defence" (2007) O.J.L.S. 27(1) 49 at 58.
221   *Duffy* [1949] 1 All E.R. 932.
222   J. Horder, *Provocation and Responsibility* (Oxford: Clarendon Press, 1992), pp.72–110. The other form Horder identifies is that of "anger as outrage" which has been lost to modern law: see further, pp.59–71.

to her lecture that her response is to take out a gun and shoot the unfortunate student. Taking this sequence of events apart, the late arrival of the student leads to a judgement being made by the lecturer that wrong has been done to her. This generates anger in the form of loss of control so that the lecturer responds "impetuously", without stopping to determine the appropriate response to the provocative event. She is so carried away that she does not pause to reflect that a verbal rebuke might have suited the occasion rather better.[223]

If, as Horder suggests, the modern law of provocation was based upon such a conception of anger, one can see why the law insisted that the loss of self-control be "sudden and temporary". However, there remained the question of what *precisely* the phrase "sudden and temporary" meant? The courts often stated that the more time "to cool down", the less likely it was that the defendant could be regarded as acting in anger, and the more likely it was that it would be seen as "planned" or "revenge".[224] However, in re-examining the requirement that there be a sudden and temporary loss of control in cases of cumulative provocation, the courts relaxed the requirement somewhat. In *Ahluwalia*[225] the Court of Appeal was faced with deciding what the requirement was in the context of a defendant who had endured 10 years of violence and humiliation from her husband and threw petrol in his bedroom and set it alight. He sustained severe burns and died six days later and she was convicted of murder. On appeal, it was argued that the direction that there be a sudden and temporary loss of control was wrong, with counsel for the appellant suggesting that women who have been subjected frequently over a period to violent treatment may react to the final act or words by a "slow-burn" reaction rather than by immediate loss of self-control. Without accepting this argument in full, the Court of Appeal conceded that a delayed reaction would not necessarily rule out that there was a "sudden and temporary" loss of self-control.[226]

The appellant in *Ahluwalia* failed in her defence of provocation but was afforded the partial defence of diminished responsibility, based on depression caused by her being a battered woman. Thus, whilst the stringency of the requirement of "sudden and temporary" loss of self-control was lessened somewhat by the courts, it still remained an obstacle to certain classes of defendant successfully pleading provocation. The Government saw the abandonment of the sudden and temporary requirement under the Coroners and Justice Act as "a fresh approach which builds on the common law" and "allows for situations where the defendant's reaction has been delayed or builds gradually.[227]

The omission of the "sudden and temporary" requirement means that defendants suffering from domestic violence such as Ahluwalia might now be more likely to plead "loss of control" successfully. This is a matter to which we return below.

(b) *Qualifying trigger*

Under the common law defence of provocation, the defendant was required to have lost her self-control due to things said or done. Although, as has been discussed, the defence developed historically on the basis that the victim, having provoked the defendant, lost some of his claim to be protected by the law, the modern law of provocation did not require that the victim was to blame for the defendant's loss of control, nor that he was even the cause of it. The extent to which the law

---

[223]   Despite the clear over-reaction in this example, it will not necessarily be the case that a hasty reaction is an excessive one. See further, Horder, *Provocation and Responsibility* (1992), pp.107–109.

[224]   The issue could be withdrawn from the jury if the delay was considerable. See, for example, *R. v Ibrams (James David)* (1982) 74 Cr. App. R. 154 in which the Court of Appeal upheld the withdrawal of the defence from the jury in the case of two appellants who had delayed several days before retaliating.

[225]   *R. v Ahluwalia (Kiranjit)* (1993) 96 Cr. App. R. 133.

[226]   *Ahluwalia* (1993) 96 Cr. App. R. 133 at 139.

[227]   Ministry of Justice, *Murder, Manslaughter And Infanticide: Proposals for Reform of the Law*, CP 19/08, 2008, para.37.

rejected this rationale of the defence can be seen in the case of *Doughty*[228] where the defendant killed his 17-day-old son in circumstances where the defendant had had to look after both his wife (after a caesarian operation) and the baby since their return from the hospital. The baby was extremely restless and cried persistently, leading to the defendant finally trying to stop the crying by placing a cushion over the baby's head and then kneeling on it. The trial judge ruled that the perfectly natural episodes of crying or restlessness by a young baby could not constitute evidence of provocation. The defendant appealed against the conviction and the Court of Appeal held that the judge was wrong not to have left the defence of provocation to the jury on the basis that the defendant had lost control because of things said or done. The issue for the jury would then have been, in applying the objective test, whether it was reasonable for the defendant to have done so.

The new law, however, attempts to avoid such controversies by setting out in more detail what it is that must have caused the defendant to lose her self-control.

Coroners and Justice Act 2009 s.55: Meaning of "qualifying trigger"

"(1) This section applies for the purposes of section 54.

(2) A loss of self-control had a qualifying trigger if subsection (3), (4) or (5) applies.

(3) This subsection applies if D's loss of self-control was attributable to D's fear of serious violence from V against D or another identified person.

(4) This subsection applies if D's loss of self-control was attributable to a thing or things done or said (or both) which—

(a) constituted circumstances of an extremely grave character, and

(b) caused D to have a justifiable sense of being seriously wronged.

(5) This subsection applies if D's loss of self-control was attributable to a combination of the matters mentioned in subsections (3) and (4).

(6) In determining whether a loss of self-control had a qualifying trigger—

(a) D's fear of serious violence is to be disregarded to the extent that it was caused by a thing which D incited to be done or said for the purpose of providing an excuse to use violence;

(b) a sense of being seriously wronged by a thing done or said is not justifiable if D incited the thing to be done or said for the purpose of providing an excuse to use violence;

(c) the fact that a thing done or said constituted sexual infidelity is to be disregarded.

(7) In this section references to 'D' and 'V' are to be construed in accordance with section 54."

Essentially the loss of self-control must be attributable to one of two specified "qualifying triggers":

1. fear of serious violence, or

2. something done or said in the circumstances specified in s.55(4)(a) and (b).

Section 55(6) provides for exclusions in particular cases, which will be discussed below.

1. Fear of serious violence

This is an entirely new basis of a partial defence to murder. It allows for defendants who are likely to fail in a plea of self-defence because they have reacted disproportionately to a threat from the deceased to avoid a murder conviction and be convicted of the lesser offence of manslaughter. The Law Commission, in recommending this addition, was of the view that: "D should not be prejudiced

---

[228]   *R. v Doughty (Stephen Clifford)* (1986) 83 Cr. App. R. 319.

because he or she over-reacted in fear or panic, instead of overreacting due to an angry loss of self-control".[229]

The Government envisages that the new defence of loss of control as a response to fear of serious violence will cover two scenarios: (i) where a victim of sustained abuse kills their abuser in order to thwart an attack which is anticipated but not immediately imminent; and (ii) where someone over-reacts to what they perceive as an imminent threat.[230] This approach can be supported. It is right that emotions other than anger should allow for mitigation in homicide cases where warranted as a con-cession to human frailty. Just because one can trace the law back to much earlier notions of outraged honour does not mean that anger should continue to be a privileged emotion. Put simply, why should someone who kills out of (uncontrolled) anger be regarded today as morally more excusable than someone who kills through fear or despair of what has happened or may happen to them? The House of Lords' decision in *Smith* appeared to recognise this with Lord Hoffmann stating:

> "There are people (such as battered wives) who would reject any suggestion that they were 'dif-ferent from ordinary human beings' but have undergone experiences which, without any fault or defect of character on their part, have affected their powers of self-control. In such cases the law now recognises that the emotions which may cause loss of self-control are not confined to anger but may include fear and despair."[231]

Lord Hoffmann's view is one that has been shared by many for some time. Battered women have for a long time fallen between a number of stools, unable to plead provocation due to the requirement of a "sudden" loss of self-control and also unable to plead self-defence because that defence requires that the defendant respond to an imminent threat of violence. Accordingly, all they were left with was the unpalatable option of admitting an "abnormality of mind" and pleading diminished responsibility. Not only does this hamper the law in doing justice in a particular case, but it is also one of the sources of "the sexual asymmetry in the matter of who kills whom and who pleads passion/provocation".[232] The very case which established the modern test for provocation, with its requirement for a "sudden and temporary" loss of self-control,[233] was in fact a case of a battered woman who killed her sleeping (or resting) husband after a long history of domestic violence. She failed in her defence of provocation, but was "more desperate and fearful than angry".[234] Howe notes that "in the far more common wife-killing case . . . the victim is always blamed, always judged for her failings as a wife, her nagging and shagging".[235] The jury in Duffy's trial, on the other hand, were told by Judge Devlin that they were not concerned with the blame attaching to the dead man. Allowing for fear as well as anger to trigger the loss of control defence might go some way to rebalancing the law against such "sexual asymmetry", although Edwards remains unconvinced of this, arguing that "the law continues by lending legitimacy to some conduct to sustain a gendered normative universe".[236]

There is, then, a problem with this new provision. The mere fear of serious violence is not sufficient

---

[229] Law Commission *Murder, Manslaughter and Infanticide* (LC 304) (2006), para.5.54.

[230] Ministry of Justice, CP 19/08, para.28.

[231] *R. v Smith (Morgan James)* [2001] 1 A.C. 146 at 168.

[232] A. Howe, "Mastering Emotions or Still Losing Control? Seeking Public Engagement with 'Sexual Infidelity' Homicide" (2013) 21 Fem. Leg. Stud. 141–161 at 146.

[233] *Duffy* (1949) 1 All E.R. 932.

[234] S. Edwards, "Justice Devlin's Legacy: Duffy—A Battered Woman 'Caught' in Time" [2009] Crim. L.R. 851–869 at 869.

[235] Howe, above fn.232 at 146.

[236] S. Edwards, "Loss of Self-Control: When His Anger is Worth More than Her Fear", in Reed and Bohlander, *Loss of Control and Diminished Responsibility: Domestic, Comparative and International Perspectives* (Ashgate, 2011), p.79.

to trigger the new defence. The fear of serious violence must cause a loss of self-control. While it is plausible that some battered women, such as Ahluwalia, might be continuously in such fear that they do lose self-control, this is implausible in many cases of excessive self-defence where the defendant overreacts.[237] As seen in Ch.4 there have been calls for the introduction of a partial defence of excessive self-defence to cover defendants such as those in *Martin* and *Clegg*.[238] The new defence of loss of control will not cover either of the defendants both of whom, calmly and rationally, used more force than was necessary. The new defence will only be available to those who are so fearful of serious violence that they panic and lose self-control. Horder argues that the loss of self-control requirement may in some cases wrongly sideline the underlying normative argument that, in some situations (when people are performing certain roles, such as that of the defendant in *Clegg*), self-control should never be lost.[239]

The fear must be one of "serious" violence. This is not defined. Although responses to the Government's consultation paper provided suggestions for greater clarity of the distinction between serious and non-serious violence, the Government did not feel it was desirable to be more specific in the statute, since this might depend on the circumstances of the victim and the perpetrator, and concluded that it is a question for the jury to decide based on the individual facts of a case.[240] This is the kind of question that juries are often given the task of determining, and it is right that the Act avoids the thorny issue of defining further what exactly is required.

2. Circumstances of an extremely grave character causing the defendant to have a justifiable sense of being seriously wronged

Section 3 of the Homicide Act 1957 made reference to provocation "whether by things done or by things said or by both together" and the Law Commission's recommendations retained this, to a certain extent, by suggesting that a partial defence be available to someone who reacted to "gross provocation (meaning words or conduct or a combination of words and conduct) which caused the defendant to have a justifiable sense of being seriously wronged".[241] Whilst doing away with the term "gross provocation", primarily because the term "provocation" was being jettisoned in its entirety, the Government initially also planned to retain the element of the defendant responding to "a thing or things done or said (or both) which: (a) amounted to an exceptional happening; and (b) caused D to have a justifiable sense of being seriously wronged".[242] The addition of "an exceptional happening" was intended to convey the idea that the trigger leading to the loss of control might not be a single event, but could amount to a series of words or conduct. Following consultation, as a result of which the obvious difficulties in employing such a woolly term were pointed out, the Government replaced the term with "circumstances of an extremely grave character".

---

[237] On this point, see also B. Mitchell, "Loss of Self-control under the Coroners and Justice Act 2009: Oh No!", in Reed and Bohlander, *Loss of Control and Diminished Responsibility: Domestic, Comparative and International Perspectives*" (Ashgate, 2011). See also comments by respondents in the form of policy stakeholders to interview questions in Fitz-Gibbon, "Replacing Provocation in England and Wales: Examining the Partial Defence of Loss of Control" (2013) 40 Journal of Law and Soc. 280–305 at 291.

[238] See pp.347–351. Whilst such a partial defence has not been created, s.76(5A) of the Criminal Justice and Immigration Act 2008 now allows householders, at least, to use force which may be seen to be disproportionate, so long as it is not *grossly* disproportionate

[239] J. Horder, *Homicide and the Politics of Law Reform* (Oxford: OUP, 2012), p.222.

[240] Ministry of Justice, *Murder, Manslaughter and Infanticide: Proposals for Reform of the Law: Summary of Responses and Government Position*, CP(R) 19/08 (2009), para.28.

[241] Law Commission Paper No.304, *Murder, Manslaughter and Infanticide* (2006), para.5.11.

[242] Ministry of Justice, *Murder, Manslaughter and Infanticide: Proposals for Reform of the Law*, CP 19/08 (2008), Annex A.

Accordingly, it must be established that the loss of control was attributable to a thing/things done or said (or both) which:

(a) constituted circumstances of an extremely grave character, and

(b) caused D to have a justifiable sense of being seriously wronged.

a) Circumstances of an extremely grave character

This term is an improvement on the original proposals but is still bound to generate interpretative problems. The Government has perhaps been a little optimistic in stating that:

> "this formulation should ensure that the defence is only available in a very narrow set of circumstances in which a killing in response to things said or done should rightly be classified as manslaughter rather than murder."[243]

After all, if this were right, there would be no need for the statutory exclusions, discussed below.

It is not clear how the jury is to assess whether there are "circumstances of an extremely grave character". Is this an objective test or is it a question of whether the defendant regards the circumstances as being of an extremely grave character? Lord Judge CJ in *Dawes* suggested that the trigger is

> "much more limited than the equivalent provisions in the former provocation defence. The result is that some of the more absurd trivia which nevertheless required the judge to leave the provocation defence to the jury will no longer fall within the ambit of the qualifying triggers defined in the new defence."[244]

b) Caused a justifiable sense of being seriously wronged

These circumstances of an extremely grave character must cause the defendant to have a justifiable sense of being seriously wronged. This term was adopted from the Law Commission's proposals, and was believed by the Government to be so obviously objective in nature that the statute need not confirm this.[245] Clearly, whether the defendant has a sense of being seriously wronged is a subjective matter. Presumably the word "justifiable" imports an objective quality to the test, implying that if called upon to justify their sense of being seriously wronged to a group of his peers, the defendant would be capable of doing so. If it were otherwise, an extremely sensitive person who was insulted and who regarded the insult as extremely grave (even though reasonable people would not) might be able to rely on the defence. This was the approach taken by Lord Judge CJ in *Dawes*, where he stated that "the presence, or otherwise, of a qualifying trigger is not defined or decided by the defendant", and emphasised the word *justifiable*.[246] It is not for the defendant to be able to say "the circumstances were extremely grave to me and caused me to have what I believed to be a justifiable sense that I had been seriously wronged". In *Hatter*, a case heard alongside *Dawes*, the Court of Appeal was of

---

243 Ministry of Justice, CP(R) 19/08, para.40.
244 *R. v Dawes (Carlos)* [2013] EWCA Crim 322 at [60].
245 Ministry of Justice, CP(R) 19/08, para.45.
246 *Dawes* [2013] EWCA Crim 322 at [61].

the opinion that the fact of the break-up of a relationship, of itself, will not normally constituted such circumstances.[247] In *Bowyer*, in the same case, the defendant was a burglar who attacked the occupier on his return home. The Court of Appeal said it was absurd to suggest that

> "the entirely understandable response of the deceased to finding a burglar in his home provided the appellant with the remotest beginnings of a basis for suggesting that he had any justifiable sense of being wronged, let alone seriously wronged."[248]

These are examples of what do not constitute the trigger, so what *would* amount to circumstances of an extremely grave nature giving a justifiable sense of being seriously wronged? In recommending the test, the Law Commission gave the following example as one which ought to fall within such a defence:

> "An Asian woman returned home to find two white men attempting to rape her 15-year-old daughter. She got a knife from the kitchen. The men shouted racist abuse at her and started to run away. She chased after them and stabbed one of them several times in the back, killing him."[249]

Such a scenario is one that would no doubt attract much sympathy for the killer, and perhaps provides the prime example of conduct warranting an escape from the label of murder and mandatory life sentence. But beyond this, what might amount to a "justifiable sense of being seriously wronged"? Perhaps an examination of the previous writing of Horder (one of the Law Commissioners) on the subject of battered women who kill can help us understand the reasons why this particular terminology was adopted.

Jeremy Horder, Provocation and Responsibility (1992), p.190:

"Ironically, until the hardening of attitudes towards loss of self-control from the time of *Duffy* onwards, no real extension or relaxation of the law would have been required to incorporate such 'slow-burn' cases within the scope of the defence. The root of the trouble and misunderstanding has been the recent failure to recognise that the law's conception of anger has never always been loss of self-control alone, but has historically included outrage. Someone who acts in outrage acts on a principle of retributive justice, and may not be responding to a proximate triggering event in quite the way a tennis player responds to an opponent's shot with a 'reflex' volley. The person who boils up when her long-term violent abuser is asleep in his chair may well be acting out of provoked outrage, despite the absence of immediate provocation. Such a person's anger would historically have fallen within the scope of the defence. What is required is a restatement of this legal position, through substitution of references to provoked angry retaliation in place of references to provoked loss of self-control in the Homicide Act 1957, section 3."[250]

Thus, the "justifiable sense of feeling seriously wronged" clause can be seen as yet another in the package designed to provide abused women with more scope for employing the partial defence to murder in future. Herring has argued that domestic abuse is typically a serious wrong to the woman and that such serious wrong includes, in addition to physical abuse, four elements: "the coercive

---

247   *Dawes* [2013] EWCA Crim 322 at at [65].
248   *Dawes* [2013] EWCA Crim 322 at at [66].
249   This example was used in a public opinion survey conducted by Barry Mitchell for the Law Commission: *Partial Defences to Murder*, Law Com. No.290, Appendix C.
250   See also, J. Horder, "Provocation and Loss of Self-Control" (1992) 108 L.Q.R. 191. Here Horder calls for the abolition of the defence. However, he has later put forward proposals for extension of the law: J. Horder, "Reshaping the Subjective Element in the Provocation Defence (2005) 25 O.J.L.S. 123.

effect of domestic abuse; the breach of trust involved; the impact of children; and its contribution to patriarchy".[251] However, it can be seen that the trigger of being seriously wronged is equally designed to bring within its ambit other cases where the defendant reacts in outrage to something said or done, whilst excluding unmeritorious cases such as parents killing their young babies to shut them up (as in *Doughty*).

3. Qualifying trigger: exclusions

Section 55(6) provides three exceptions to cases which would otherwise amount to a qualifying trigger. The first and second of these find their origins in the Law Commission's recommendations, which sought to provide a bar to the defence where "the provocation was itself incited by the defendant for the purpose of providing an excuse to use violence". The Law Commission was of the view that this provision was unproblematic, on the basis that "self-induced" provocation was not sufficient to found a provocation plea under common law.[252]

The Court of Appeal has had the opportunity to consider the contours of this exclusion in the case of *Dawes*. Lord Judge CJ noted that

"as a matter of statutory construction, the mere fact that in some general way the defendant was behaving badly and looking for and provoking trouble does not of itself lead to the disapplication of the qualifying triggers based on s.55(3), (4) and (5) unless his actions were intended to provide him with the excuse or opportunity to use violence."[253]

The last exclusion, that where the thing causing a loss of control constituted sexual infidelity it is to be disregarded, did not appear in the Law Commission's recommendations but was added by the Government, surviving a challenge to it by the House of Lords during the parliamentary process.[254] Although historically sexual infidelity has been a typical example providing a defendant with something "said or done" giving rise to provocation, the Government was clear that times have changed:

"It is quite unacceptable for a defendant who has killed an unfaithful partner to seek to blame the victim for what occurred. We want to make it absolutely clear that sexual infidelity on the part of the victim can never justify reducing a murder charge to manslaughter. This should be the case even if sexual infidelity is present in combination with a range of other trivial and commonplace factors."[255]

The exclusion has been controversial, however.[256] In interviews with policy stakeholders, barristers and judges, Fitz-Gibbon reported that:

"rather than welcoming the exclusion of such cases from the new partial defence, respondents across all samples interviewed were overwhelmingly critical of this provision in the formulation of the new defence. Legal counsel respondents described the exclusion as 'incredibly convoluted'

---

251   J. Herring, "The Serious Wrong of Domestic Abuse and the Loss of Control Defence", in Reed and Bohlander, *Loss of Control and Diminished Responsibility: Domestic, Comparative and International Perspectives* (Aldershot: Ashgate, 2011), p.78.
252   Law Commission Paper No.304, para.5.79.
253   *Dawes* [2013] 2 Cr. App. R. 3 at [58].
254   *Hansard*, House of Lords, November 11, 2009, col.836.
255   Ministry of Justice, CP 19/08, para.32.
256   A. Howe, "'Red Mist' Homicide: Sexual Infidelity and the English Law of Murder (glossing *Titus Andronicus*)" (2013) 33 *Legal Studies* 407–430.

(UKCounselE) and 'barmy' (UKCounselQ), while one judicial respondent posed that it was 'ill-advised' and 'bad law' (UKJudgeB). Similarly, policy respondents described the sexual infidelity provision as 'very problematic' (UKPolicyA), 'dire' (UKPolicyB), and 'really unnecessary' (UKPolicyC). These criticisms were often based upon respondents' belief that the exclusion of a particular situation was not conducive to good law-making and that it would lead to significant questions surrounding the situations in which the new partial defence would and would not apply."[257]

Reed and Wake have also predicted that the exclusion would create interpretational difficulties, and would be "up for debate in terms of disentanglement of 'infidelity' from other circumstances of taunts regarding inadequacy and disaffection".[258] It was not long until the Court of Appeal were given the opportunity to consider these matters.

R. v Clinton [2013] Q.B. 1

The defendant killed his wife by beating her about the head with a wooden baton, strangling her with a belt, and then tightening a piece of rope around her neck with the aid of the baton. She had admitted to him that she had been having an affair and the defendant claimed that, just prior to the killing, his wife had taunted him about a range of matters including her sexual infidelity to him, that he did not have the courage to kill himself and that she did not care about their children. The trial judge withdrew the defence of loss of self-control from the jury for three reasons: the taunts as to fidelity were excluded as a trigger because they fell into the category of things said or done which "constituted sexual infidelity" within the meaning of s.55(4) of the Coroners and Justice Act 2009; the other matters could not constitute circumstances of an extremely grave character; and they could not have caused the defendant to have a justifiable sense of being seriously wronged. The defendant appealed against his conviction for murder.

LORD JUDGE CJ

"16 We immediately acknowledge that the exclusion of sexual infidelity as a potential qualifying trigger is consistent with the concept of the autonomy of each individual. Of course, whatever the position may have been in times past, it is now clearly understood, and in the present context the law underlines, that no one (male or female) owns or possesses his or her spouse or partner. Nevertheless daily experience in both criminal and family courts demonstrates that the breakdown of relationships, whenever they occur, and for whatever reason, is always fraught with tension and difficulty, with the possibility of misunderstanding and the potential for apparently irrational fury. Meanwhile experience over many generations has shown that, however it may become apparent, when it does, sexual infidelity has the potential to create a highly emotional situation or to exacerbate a fraught situation, and to produce a completely unpredictable, and sometimes violent response. This may have nothing to do with any notional 'rights' that the one may believe that he or she has over the other, and often stems from a sense of betrayal and heartbreak, and crushed dreams.

17 [Counsel for the defendant] drew attention to and adopted much of the illuminating and critical commentary by Professor Ormerod in *Smith & Hogan's Criminal Law*, 13th ed, at pp 520–522. To begin with, there is no definition of 'sexual infidelity'. Who and what is embraced in this concept? Is sexual infidelity to be construed narrowly so as to refer only to conduct which is related directly and exclusively to sexual activity? Only the words and acts constituting sexual activity are to be disregarded: on one construction, therefore, the effects are not. What acts relating to infidelity, but distinguishable from it on the basis that they are not 'sexual', may be taken

---

[257]   K. Fitz-Gibbon, "Replacing Provocation in England and Wales: Examining the Partial Defence of Loss of Control" (2013) 40 J. of Law and Society 280–305 at 293.

[258]   A. Reed and N. Wake, "Sexual Infidelity Killings: Contemporary Standardisations and Comparative Stereotypes", in Reed and Bohlander, *Loss of Control and Diminished Responsibility: Domestic, Comparative and International Perspectives* (Aldershot: Ashgate, 2011), p.133.

into account? Is the provision directly concerned with sexual infidelity, or with envy and jealousy and possessive-ness, the sort of obsession that leads to violence against the victim on the basis expressed in the sadly familiar language, 'if I cannot have him/her, then no one else will/can'? The notion of infidelity appears to involve a relationship between the two people to which one party may be unfaithful. Is a one-night-stand sufficient for this purpose?

18 Take a case like *Stingel v The Queen* (1990) 171 CLR 312, an Australian case where a jealous stalker, who stabbed his quarry when he found her, on his account, having sexual intercourse. He does not face any difficulty with this element of the offence, just because, so far as the stalker was concerned, there was no sexual infidelity by his victim at all. Is the jealous spouse to be excluded when the stalker is not? In *Lewis v State of Trinidad and Tobago* [2011] UKPC 15 an 18-year-old Jehovah's Witness killed his lover, a 63-year-old co-religionist, because, on one view, he was ashamed of the consequences if she carried out her threat to reveal their affair to the com-munity. She was not sexually unfaithful to him, but he killed her because he feared that she would betray him, not sexually, but by revealing their secret. [W]hy should the law exclude one kind of betrayal by a lover but not another?

. . .

20 [Counsel] could readily have identified a large number of situations arising in the real world which, as a result of the statutory provision, would be productive of surprising anomalies. We cannot resolve them in advance. Whatever the anomalies to which it may give rise, the statutory provision is unequivocal: loss of control triggered by sexual infidelity cannot, on its own, qualify as a trigger for the purposes of the second component of this defence. This is the clear effect of the legislation.

. . .

26 We are required to make sense of this provision. It would be illogical for a defendant to be able to rely on an untrue statement about the victim's sexual infidelity as a qualifying trigger in support of the defence, but not on a truthful one. Equally, it would be quite unrealistic to limit its ambit to words spoken to his or her lover by the unfaithful spouse or partner during sexual activity. In our judgment things 'said' include admissions of sexual infidelity (even if untrue) as well as reports (by others) of sexual infidelity. Such admissions or reports will rarely if ever be uttered without a context, and almost certainly a painful one. In short, the words will almost invariably be spoken as part of a highly charged discussion in which many disturbing comments will be uttered, often on both sides.

. . .

34 We must now address the full extent of the prohibition against 'sexual infidelity' as a qualifying trigger for the purposes of the loss of control defence. The question is whether or not sexual infidelity is wholly excluded from consideration in the context of features of the individual case which constitute a permissible qualifying trigger or triggers within section 55(3)(4) .

35 We have examined the legislative structure as a whole. The legislation was designed to prohibit the misuse of sexual infidelity as a potential trigger for loss of control in circumstances in which it was thought to have been misused in the former defence of provocation. Where there is no other potential trigger, the prohibition must, notwithstanding the difficulties identified earlier in the judgment, be applied.

36 The starting point is that it has been recognised for centuries that sexual infidelity may produce a loss of control in men, and, more recently, in women as well as men, who are confronted with sexual infidelity. The exclusion created by section 55(6) cannot and does not eradicate the fact that on occasions sexual infidelity and loss of control are linked, often with the one followed immediately by the other. Indeed on one view if it did not recognise the existence of this link, the policy decision expressly to exclude sexual infidelity as a qualifying trigger would be unnecessary.

37 In section 54(1)(c)(3) the legislation further acknowledges the impact of sexual infidelity as a potential ingredient of the third component of the defence, when all the defendant's circumstances fall for consideration, and when, although express provision is made for the exclusion of some features of the defendant's situation, the fact that he/she has been sexually betrayed is not. In short, sexual infidelity is not subject to a blanket exclu-sion when the loss of control defence is under consideration. Evidence of these matters may be deployed by the defendant and therefore the legislation proceeds on the basis that sexual infidelity is a permissible feature of the loss of control defence.

38 The ambit of section 55(3)(4)—the second component, the qualifying triggers—is clearly defined. Any quali-fying trigger is subject to clear statutory criteria. Dealing with it broadly, to qualify as a trigger for the defendant's loss of control, the circumstances must be extremely grave and the defendant must be subject to a justifiable sense of having been seriously wronged. These are fact specific questions requiring careful assessment, not least to ensure that the loss of control defence does not have the effect of minimising the seriousness of the infliction of

fatal injury. Objective evaluation is required and a judgment must be made about the gravity of the circumstances and the extent to which the defendant was seriously wronged, and whether he had a justifiable sense that he had been seriously wronged.

39 Our approach has . . . been influenced by the simple reality that in relation to the day to day working of the criminal justice system events cannot be isolated from their context. We have provided a number of examples in the judgment. Perhaps expressed most simply, the man who admits, 'I killed him accidentally', is never to be treated as if he had said 'I killed him'. That would be absurd. It may not be unduly burdensome to compartmentalise sexual infidelity where it is the only element relied on in support of a qualifying trigger, and, having compartmentalised it in this way, to disregard it. Whether this is so or not, the legislation imposes that exclusionary obligation on the court. However, to seek to compartmentalise sexual infidelity and exclude it when it is integral to the facts as a whole is not only much more difficult, but is unrealistic and carries with it the potential for injustice. In the examples we have given . . . , we do not see how any sensible evaluation of the gravity of the circumstances or their impact on the defendant could be made if the jury, having, in accordance with the legislation, heard the evidence, were then to be directed to excise from their evaluation of the qualifying trigger the matters said to constitute sexual infidelity, and to put them into distinct compartments to be disregarded. In our judgment, where sexual infidelity is integral to and forms an essential part of the context in which to make a just evaluation whether a qualifying trigger properly falls within the ambit of subsections 55(3) and 55(4), the prohibition in section 55(6)(c) does not operate to exclude it."

Appeal allowed

The result of this case is that sexual infidelity may be taken into account as part of the background of a case (i.e. when assessing other triggers), but cannot itself constitute a trigger.[259] The irony of the case is, though, that having had his conviction for murder quashed and won a retrial at which loss of control should, according to the Court of Appeal, be put to the jury, the defendant went on to plead guilty to murder and discarded his opportunity to be found guilty of manslaughter instead.[260]

Why might that be? Could it be an appreciation that even if a jury were to be directed to take into account sexual infidelity in considering the defence of loss of control they were still likely to have convicted of murder in any case (which does raise the question of why launch an appeal in the first place)? If social mores have changed to the extent that sexual infidelity is no longer accepted as an excuse for loss of self-control, one assumes that the jury would not accept that the defendant had experienced a *justifiable* sense of feeling seriously wronged. Further, and again assuming this change in social mores, it would be unlikely that the "objective test", discussed below, would be satisfied in such cases.

There are those who do not accept that such a change in social mores has occurred to the extent that juries, when given the option, will deny operation of the defence of loss of control:

"In [*Clinton*], the Court of Appeal has likely ensured that the sexual infidelity provision within the loss of control partial defence will be largely ineffective in minimizing the use of the defence by men who kill a female intimate partner in the context of sexual infidelity. As described by one media commentator, the decision 'restores the defence in so-called crime of passion cases', and as such raises the fear that in practice this new partial defence will do little to overcome the problems associated with the now abolished—'jealous man's'—provocation defence. Importantly, if the new partial defence is to operate in essentially the same manner as the former provocation defence, it is essential that ongoing monitoring and analysis be undertaken to ensure that the law's operation

---

[259] Ashworth, Commentary to *Clinton* [2012] 539 at 544.
[260] "Jon-Jaques Clinton makes U-turn at retrial for wife's murder" *BBC News*, September 3, 2012: *http://www.bbc.co.uk/news/ uk-england-berkshire-19469372* [Accessed April 4, 2014].

does not continue to reproduce problematic narratives of victim blame and denigration in the law's response to male-perpetrated intimate homicide."[261]

Should the law be used to enforce a particular response to male-perpetrated intimate homicide? It was suggested at the time that the law was reformed that there might be other triggers which ought to be similarly excluded. If the statute were to go so far as to list one trigger that under no circumstances would provide a partial defence to murder, why not add others,[262] such as honour killings? The response was that:

"The Government fully agrees that anyone involved in a so-called 'honour killing' should not be able to reduce a charge of murder to manslaughter on the basis of the victim's behaviour. The Government believes that the high threshold for the words and conduct limb of the partial defence will have the effect of excluding situations which might be characterised as 'honour killings' because such cases will not satisfy the requirements that the circumstances were of an extremely grave character and caused a justifiable sense of being seriously wronged. In addition we intend to introduce an exemption for cases where there is a 'considered desire for revenge' which will also have a role to play in ensuring that so-called honour killings do not benefit from a partial defence."[263]

It is unclear why the Government did not have the same faith in its test's ability to exclude unmeritorious cases of sexual infidelity without the need to specify the exclusion of such cases from the defence's remit.

(c) The objective test

It is not sufficient to show that the defendant lost control. There is also, by virtue of s.54(1)(c), the question of whether "a person of D's sex and age, with a normal degree of tolerance and self-restraint and in the circumstances of D, might have reacted in the same or in a similar way to D". This test has been designed to accord with the Privy Council's most recent interpretation of the "reasonable man" test under s.3 of the Homicide Act 1957.[264]

Whether this amounts to a partial justification is, as already discussed, open to question. One issue is what is meant by "reacted in the same or in a similar way"? Does this mean that, a person with a normal degree of tolerance and self-restraint would have reacted by doing exactly as the defendant did in killing the deceased (with the same use of a weapon, degree of force, etc.), or does it simply mean that the provocation would have been such to make such a person lose their self-control? Under the common law, cases such as *van Dongen*[265] appeared to suggest that the former interpretation applied, whilst Ashworth argues that the latter proposition is correct since the former is too "particularistic".[266] It is a pity that neither the Law Commission nor the Ministry of Justice saw fit to clarify this in considering reform of the law.

---

[261]   K. Fitz-Gibbon, "Replacing Provocation in England and Wales: Examining the Partial Defence of Loss of Control" (2013) 40 J. of Law and Society 280–305 at 298.

[262]   Horder gives the example of disqualifying as provocation anything said or done by a child in order to explicitly overrule *Doughty*: J. Horder, *Homicide and the Politics of Law Reform* (Oxford: OUP, 2012), p.211.

[263]   Ministry of Justice, CP(R) 19/08, para.56.

[264]   *Attorney General for Jersey v Holley* [2005] 2 A.C. 580.

[265]   *R. v Van Dongen (Anthony Gerrard) (Appeal against Conviction)* [2005] Crim. L.R. 971.

[266]   A. Ashworth, *Principles of Criminal Law*, 6th edn (Oxford: OUP, 2009), p.259.

State v Hoyt, 128 N.W. 2d 645, 21 Wis. 2d 284 (1964) (Supreme Court of Wisconsin)

WILKIE J:

"The 'reasonable man' concept in the law generally has two distinct meanings. There is the statistical concept under which the reasonable man does what most people do in fact under the circumstances. Yet if this is the meaning of the test, it is clear that as a matter of fact a great majority of people will never commit murder no matter how violently provoked by another. A consistent application of this test, viewing the reasonable man as the statistical factual norm would, in effect read . . . [the defence] . . . out of existence.

However, in other contexts there is the ethical concept under which the reasonable man functions as the person the law *expects* everyone to be, regardless of whether a majority, in fact, fall short of the *moral* normal in actual conduct. To take this view of the reasonable man for the purposes of the provocation test would propel courts and juries into the strange task of deciding when a person, taken as the ethical ideal, would commit murder. This may well result in reading . . . [the partial defence] out of existence. The person we expect people to be like would not solve his problems by murder. If we conclude that an ethical ideal—that person whom all others aspire to emulate—would be driven to kill under the circumstances of a given case, logically the verdict should be not guilty, not morally blameworthy to any degree . . .

The basic question is whether [the defendant] . . . is as culpable as a person who kills solely for self-aggrandizement or out of sheer malevolence. To answer this question, we must place ourselves emphatically in the actual situation in which the defendant was placed, a situation which may be relatively unique. Therefore, an inquiry into what most people would do in such circumstances cannot be completely determinative of the issue. The test cannot be wholly objective or wholly subjective . . . The victim's conduct must be such that we conclude that the feeling and conduct of the defendant can be understood sympathetically, albeit not condoned. The trier-of-fact must be able to say: although I would have acted differently, and I believe most people would have acted differently, I can understand why this person gave way to the impulse to kill."

Prior to the Coroners and Justice Act 2009, the courts had managed to evade the real question (a moral question) of whether the defendant could be expected to control the impulse to kill, by constructing the reasonable man test, which has been used in provocation cases since the nineteenth century.[267] Prior to the Homicide Act 1957, judges were able to control the test in two ways. First, they could withdraw the issue from the jury on the basis that there was no evidence on which the jury could find that a reasonable man would have been provoked, and secondly, they were able to keep the test objective. In other words, the courts excluded from the reasonable man any of the characteristics of the defendant which might have had an impact on why, and the extent to which, they were provoked.

Thus, in *Bedder*[268] the House of Lords held that the fact that the defendant was impotent should be ignored in assessing whether his killing of the prostitute who had taunted him (as well as hitting and kicking him) was something a reasonable man might have done. The courts were loath to include any unusual physical characteristic for fear of "not knowing where to draw the line".[269] However, it became clear following the enactment of s.3 that the approach taken in *Bedder* was too strict. One of the major tasks for the Law Commission in recommending reform of the law on provocation was, however, to bring to an end the ambiguity and inconsistency in relation to the interpretation of the reasonable man test. Following a long line of judgments from the House of Lords and Privy Council

---

[267]   From the dicta of Keating J in *Welsh* (1869) 11 Cox C.C. 336 at 339 who stated that provocation would be sufficient if it was "something which might naturally cause an ordinary and reasonably minded man to lose his self-control and commit such an act".

[268]   *Bedder* [1954] 1 W.L.R. 1119.

[269]   G.P. Fletcher, *Rethinking Criminal Law* (Boston: Little, Brown, 1978), p.249.

starting with *DPP v Camplin*,[270] and including *Morhall*,[271] *Luc Thiet Thuan*,[272] and *Smith*,[273] the case of *Attorney General for Jersey v Holley*[274] supplied the final instalment, providing an interpretation of the reasonable man test from which the Law Commission took inspiration in drafting the test adopted by the Government in passing the new law. It is worth exploring the controversies surrounding this issue in order to understand the weakness that the reform is designed to strengthen.

The question with which the courts grappled was what, if any, characteristics of the accused ought to be attributed to the reasonable person in applying the objective test? Although *Holley* was the most recent authority on the question prior to the enactment of the Coroners and Justice Act, *Camplin* remained the source of the law's interpretation of the test within s.3 of the Homicide Act.

DPP v Camplin [1978] A.C. 705 (House of Lords)

[The facts appear from the judgment of Lord Diplock]

LORD DIPLOCK:

"The respondent, Camplin, who was 15 years of age, killed a middle-aged Pakistani, Mohammed Lal Khan, by splitting his skull with a chapati pan, a heavy kitchen utensil like a rimless frying pan. At the time the two of them were alone together in Khan's flat. At Camplin's trial for murder before Boreham J. his only defence was that of provocation so as to reduce the offence to manslaughter. According to the story that he told in the witness box but which differed materially from that which he had told to the police, Khan had buggered him in spite of his resistance and had then laughed at him. Whereupon Camplin had lost his self-control and attacked Khan fatally with the chapati pan . . .

The point of law of general public importance involved in the case has been certified as being:

'Whether, on the prosecution for murder of a boy of 15, where the issue of provocation arises, the jury should be directed to consider the question, under s. 3 of the Homicide Act 1957 whether the provocation was enough to make a reasonable man do as he did by reference to a "reasonable adult" or by reference to a "reasonable boy of 15." ' . . .

[F]or the purposes of the law of provocation the 'reasonable man' has never been confined to the adult male. It means an ordinary person of either sex, not exceptionally excitable or pugnacious, but possessed of such powers of self-control as everyone is entitled to expect that his fellow citizens will exercise in society as it is today. A crucial factor in the defence of provocation from earliest times has been the relationship between the gravity of provocation and the way in which the accused retaliated, both being judged by the social standards of the day. When Hale was writing in the seventeenth century, pulling a man's nose was thought to justify retaliation with a sword; when *Mancini v D.P.P.* . . . was decided by this House, a blow with a fist would not justify retaliation with a deadly weapon. But so long as words unaccompanied by violence could not in common law amount to provocation the relevant proportionality between provocation and retaliation was primarily one of degrees of violence. Words spoken to the accused before the violence started were not normally to be included in the proportion sum. But now that the law has been changed so as to permit of words being treated as provocation, even though unaccompanied by any other acts, the gravity of verbal provocation may well depend on the particular characteristics or circumstances of the person to whom a taunt or insult is addressed. To taunt a person because of his race, his physical infirmities or some shameful incident in his past may well be considered by the jury to be more offensive to the person addressed, however equable his temperament, if the facts on which the taunt is founded are true than it would be if they were not. It would stultify much of the mitigation of the previous harshness of the common law in ruling out verbal provocation as capable of reducing murder to manslaughter if the jury could not take into

270   *R. v Camplin (Paul)* [1978] A.C. 705.
271   *Morhall* [1996] 1 A.C. 90.
272   *Luc Thiet Thuan v The Queen* [1997] A.C. 131.
273   *Smith* [2001] 1 A.C. 146.
274   *Attorney General for Jersey v Holley* [2005] 2 A.C. 580.

consideration all those factors which in their opinion would effect the gravity of taunts and insults when applied to the person to whom they are addressed. So to this extent at any rate the unqualified proposition accepted by this House in *Bedder v D.P.P.* . . . that for the purposes of the 'reasonable man' test any unusual physical characteristics of the accused must be ignored requires revision as a result of the passing of the Act of 1957. . .

In my opinion a proper direction to a jury on the question left to their exclusive determination by s. 3 of the Act of 1957 would be on the following lines. The judge should state what the question is using the very terms of the section. He should then explain to them that the reasonable man referred to in the question is a person having the power of self-control to be expected of an ordinary person of the sex and age of the accused, but in other respects sharing such of the accused's characteristics as they think would affect the gravity of the provocation to him; and that the question is not merely whether such a person would in like circumstances be provoked to lose his self-control but also whether he would react to the provocation as the accused did."

Appeal dismissed

What Lord Diplock made clear in *Camplin* was that, first, not all characteristics of the defendant had to be taken into account by the court and, secondly, in determining which characteristics to include, a distinction needed to be drawn. Lord Diplock broadly adopted Ashworth's argument that:

"the proper distinction . . . is that individual peculiarities which bear on the gravity of the provocation should be taken into account, whereas individual peculiarities bearing on the accused's level of self-control should not."[275]

Thus, the fact that a defendant is impotent may be highly relevant if the defendant is claiming to have been taunted about his impotence, but is irrelevant in determining the level of self-control he should possess. However, Lord Diplock made an exception to this in the model direction which has survived the recent reform of the law. Two characteristics are deemed to be relevant to the standard of self-control which may be expected of a defendant: age and sex. Age is included because "to require old heads on young shoulders is inconsistent with law's compassion of human infirmity". The reason why this concession was also extended to sex has never been made clear.[276] In fact, the Law Commission's recommendation for the objective test contained reference to the defendant's age alone, and omitted any reference to gender.[277] "Sex" was added to the draft provision by the Government without comment, and although responses to the public consultation raised the question of whether it should be omitted, on the grounds that it might reinforce sexism,[278] the Government was not persuaded by these.[279] Whilst some commentators have welcomed the retention of sex as a relevant factor, as a way of addressing gender bias,[280] others have argued that the law would more effectively tackle gender stereotypes by leaving sex as something that should be taken account of as part of the wider circumstances of D.[281]

Beyond the need to include sex and age in applying the reasonable man test, Lord Diplock's speech was not free from ambiguity. While endorsing a distinction between characteristics which affect the

---

[275]   "The Doctrine of Provocation" [1976] C.L.J. 292 at 300.
[276]   The Australian decision of *Masciantonio v R* (1995) 69 A.L.J.R. 598 decided that age was the only factor relevant to the issue of self-control.
[277]   Law Commission Paper No.304, para.5.11.
[278]   Ministry of Justice, CP(R) 19/08, para.77.
[279]   Ministry of Justice, CP(R) 19/08, para.78.
[280]   See, for example, S. Edwards, "Anger and Fear as Justifiable Preludes for Loss of Self-Control" (2010) 74 J. of Criminal Law 223 and A. Carline, "Reforming Provocation: Perspectives from the Law Commission and the Government" [2009] 2 Web J. of Current Legal Issues.
[281]   N. Cobb and A. Gausden, "Feminism, 'Typical' Women, and Losing Control", in Reed and Bohlander, *Loss of Control and Diminished Responsibility: Domestic, Comparative and International Perspectives* (Aldershot: Ashgate, 2011).

gravity of the provocation and characteristics which affect the power of self-control, Lord Diplock, nevertheless, added that this was of "too great nicety" for the jury whose task it is to determine whether the defendant was provoked. Acceptance or rejection of the distinction lies at the core of subsequent decisions of the House of Lords and Privy Council. These cases alternated in their view taken of the distinction Lord Diplock made between the two categories of characteristics in provocation cases, which can be labelled as characteristics of "provocativeness" (those relevant to the gravity of the provocation) and "provocability" (those which affect the level of self-control exercised by the defendant).[282]

In *Smith* the House of Lords decided by a majority of 3/2 that aspects of the defendant which affected her ability to exercise control should be considered. The two dissenting judges were of the view that those in the majority were removing the objective element and in doing so were subverting the moral basis of the defence, and that mental abnormalities such as clinical depression are catered for by the alternative partial defence of diminished responsibility. *Smith* was, however, disapproved in the case of *Holley*.

Attorney General for Jersey v Holley [2005] 2 A.C. 580 (Privy Council)

The defendant, who was a chronic alcoholic, was charged with the murder of his girlfriend whom he had killed in a quarrel while under the influence of drink. At trial he raised the defence of provocation under art.4 of the Homicide (Jersey) Law 1986 (enacted in terms identical to s.3 of the Homicide Act 1957). He adduced expert medical evidence to the effect that his alcoholism was a disease, and in consequence a characteristic, of which the jury should take account when assessing his loss of self-control. The deputy bailiff referred the jury to the medical evidence and invited them to consider whether any particular characteristic reduced the defendant's power of self-control so as to excuse his action. He qualified this by adding that drunkenness at the time of the killing which rendered a defendant more susceptible to being provoked could not be taken into account in his favour. The defendant was convicted of murder. The Court of Appeal of Jersey concluded that the disease of chronic alcoholism, unlike drunkenness which afforded no defence, was the type of characteristic which the jury could have taken into account when determining whether his loss of self-control was excusable. The appeal was allowed on the ground that the deputy bailiff's qualification amounted to a misdirection. The Attorney-General appealed to the Privy Council.

LORD NICHOLLS OF BIRKENHEAD:

"[1] In July 2000 the House of Lords considered the ingredients of [the defence of provocation] in the Morgan Smith case (*R v Smith (Morgan)*). The decision of the House in that case is in direct conflict with the decision of their Lordships' board in *Luc Thiet Thuan v The Queen*. And the reasoning of the majority in the Morgan Smith case is not easy to reconcile with the reasoning of the House of Lords in *R v Camplin* or *R v Morhall*. This appeal, being heard by an enlarged board of nine members, is concerned to resolve this conflict and clarify definitively the present state of English law, and hence Jersey law, on this important subject . . .

[12] [Lord Nicholls explained the case of *Morhall* and the effect of the House of Lords' decision in that case.] Of course, assessing the conduct of a glue-sniffing defendant against the standard of a glue-sniffing man having ordinary powers of self-control may mean the defendant is assessed against a standard of self-control he cannot attain. He may be exceptionally excitable or pugnacious. But this is so with every defendant who seeks to rely upon provocation as a defence. The objective standard of self-control is the standard set by the common law and, since 1957, by the statutory reference to a 'reasonable man'. It is of general application. Inherent in the use of this prescribed standard as a uniform standard applicable to all defendants is the possibility that an individual defendant may be temperamentally unable to achieve this standard.

[13] Taking into account the age and sex of a defendant, as mentioned in *Camplin*, is not an exception to this

---

[282]   A. Norrie, "From Criminal Law to Legal Theory: The Mysterious Case of the Reasonable Glue Sniffer" [2002] 65 M.L.R. 538.

uniform approach. The powers of self-control possessed by *ordinary* people vary according to their age and, more doubtfully, their sex. These features are to be contrasted with abnormalities, that is, features not found in a person having ordinary powers of self-control. The former are relevant when identifying and applying the objective standard of self-control, the latter are not . . .

[22] Th[e] majority view [in *Smith*], if their Lordships may respectfully say so, is one model which could be adopted in framing a law relating to provocation. But their Lordships consider there is one compelling, overriding reason why this view cannot be regarded as an accurate statement of English law. It is this. The law of homicide is a highly sensitive and highly controversial area of the criminal law. In 1957 Parliament altered the common law relating to provocation and declared what the law on this subject should thenceforth be. In these circumstances it is not open to judges now to change ('develop') the common law and thereby depart from the law as declared by Parliament. However much the contrary is asserted, the majority view does represent a departure from the law as declared in section 3 of the Homicide Act 1957. It involves a significant relaxation of the uniform, objective standard adopted by Parliament. Under the statute the sufficiency of the provocation ('whether the provocation was enough to make a reasonable man do as [the defendant] did') is to be judged by one standard, not a standard which varies from defendant to defendant. Whether the provocative act or words and the defendant's response met the 'ordinary person' standard prescribed by the statute is the question the jury must consider, not the altogether looser question of whether, having regard to all the circumstances, the jury consider the loss of self-control was sufficiently excusable. The statute does not leave each jury free to set whatever standard they consider appropriate in the circumstances by which to judge whether the defendant's conduct is 'excusable'.

[23] On this short ground their Lordships, respectfully but firmly, consider the majority view expressed in the Morgan Smith case is erroneous . . .

[24] If the defendant was taunted on account of his intoxication, that may be a relevant matter for the jury to take into account when assessing the gravity of the taunt to the defendant. But the defendant's intoxicated state is not a matter to be taken into account by the jury when considering whether the defendant exercised ordinary self-control."

Appeal allowed[283]

The intention of the Privy Council was to provide a judgment that would take precedence over the House of Lords' decision in *Smith*, and this intention is made clear at the beginning of Lord Nicholl's speech where he states that they wished to resolve the conflict between previous cases and state definitively the position of English law.[284] At long last this area of law seemed to have been provided with the foundation for some degree of stability. The Coroners and Justice Act 2009 has now stepped in as an attempt to ensure that the objective test as confirmed in *Holley* remains objective in relation to the new defence of loss of control. The Law Commission, in deciding on the wording of the new provision, identified the mischief that it sought to avoid.

Law Commission No.304, Murder, Manslaughter and Infanticide (2006):

"5.35 Disagreement in the courts has focused on the extent to which D's own characteristics, or other factors, can, or must, be taken into account in judging how the reasonable person might have responded to the provocation.

5.36 One key question in making that judgement is 'how gravely provocative really was the provocation'? It is obvious that D's own characteristics must be relevant to this question. To give a simple example, D's own height would be relevant in assessing the gravity of the provocation constituted by an accusation that he or she was 'a midget'. The courts have not encountered significant difficulties in recent years in deciding how such characteristics or factors affecting the gravity of provocation should be dealt with in law. The jury is obliged to take such characteristics into account.

5.37 More controversial has been the question whether the jury should be required, or permitted, to take into account individual characteristics of D (or other factors) liable to affect the level of self-control that he or she can be expected to show in the face of *any* provocation. It may be, for example, that a drunken D, an immature D or a

---

[283] Although the appeal was allowed the manslaughter conviction was permitted to stand due to an undertaking given by the Attorney-General not to seek to restore the conviction for murder.

[284] In *R. v James (Leslie)* [2006] 1 Cr. App. R. 29 the Court of Appeal endorsed the decision in *Holley* over that of *Smith*.

mentally deficient D, is unable to exercise the same level of self control, in the face of provocation generally, as a sober adult with normal mental capacities. The courts have disagreed over whether the jury should be required or permitted to take such factors into account.

5.38 . . . In our view, the function of the reasonable person requirement is to test D's own reaction against the standards of someone of his or her age possessed of an ordinary temperament: someone who is neither intolerant nor lacking in a reasonable measure of self-restraint when facing provocation. Unless the jury concludes that D's reaction might have been that of such a person, the defence ought to fail, even if D only killed as a result of a provoked and momentary loss of temper.

5.39 We are reluctant to speculate on how the courts would interpret the provisions [proposed] above. Still less would we wish to insist that they interpret them in a given way. None the less, the following examples may provide some guidance on the kinds of distinctions we think that it would be helpful to draw.

5.40 Our provisions impose a duty on the judge to instruct the jury to ignore factors that affect D's general capacity to exercise self-control. Alcoholism, for example, or another mental deficiency or disorder that is liable to affect temper and tolerance are obvious examples. A person who has killed because his or her capacity for self-control was reduced by such a characteristic must look to the defence of diminished responsibility for a partial defence, because such characteristics constitute an abnormality of mental functioning, unlike, for example, D's age.

5.41 Abnormal states of mind, such as intoxication or irritability, should also be left out, as should other factors that affect a general capacity to exercise adequate self control, like a claim that D is 'more jealous or obsessive than most'. This approach to the general capacity to exercise adequate self-control will produce some hard cases. Examples might be ones in which, at the time of the provoked killing, D's general capacity for self-control was temporarily impaired by the effect of taking prescribed medicine, by having suffered a stroke, by involuntary intoxication, by an allergic reaction of some kind or by a bang on the head.

. . .

5.43 By way of contrast, a low IQ could be taken into account as part of the circumstances of D . . . if it meant, for example, that D misinterpreted a provocation, thinking it to be more grave than a person of higher intelligence might have done. To give a different example, the fact that D was dumb and thus unable to respond verbally, is a factor that might legitimately be taken into account when considering D's reaction to a particular provocation given on a particular occasion. In each example, the characteristic is not being used as evidence that the D lacked a general capacity to exercise adequate self control.

5.44 By way of contrast, some of the evidence given by a psychiatrist in *Roberts* [1990] Crim LR 122 would not be relevant to the provocation plea, under our recommendations. This was evidence that 'irrational violence was to be expected from some immature prelingually deaf persons when emotionally disturbed'. This is evidence relevant to a plea of diminished responsibility, rather than to a plea of provocation, because it is evidence of an impaired general capacity for self-control.

5.45 In many instances, the circumstances liable quite properly to influence the jury in D's favour will bear on how 'gross' the provocation was, or on how justifiable it was for D to feel seriously wronged . . . An example is the cumulative effect of repeated provocations given, quite possibly over many years, in circumstances where it may also have been impossible for D to escape the provocation's effects. There is usually no theoretical difficulty about taking such background factors into account because they do not necessarily suggest that D is someone with a reduced general capacity to exercise self control. A classic example would be the intimidated spouse who has been subject to abuse, the cumulative effect of which has become intolerable over the years.

5.46 This area of law will always remain difficult. As we indicated in the [consultation paper], however, a trial judge is under a duty to explain to the jury the full context in which a provoked killing has taken place, and the form of his or her direction ought to be discussed in advance with prosecution and defence advocates. These safeguards should go some way towards minimising the chance of misdirections, and hence appeals."

There are still those, however, who argue that the test in *Smith* which allowed the jury to take account of characteristics affecting the defendant's ability to control herself is preferable, in that it is unfair to measure an individual against a standard she is incapable of attaining.[285] Holton and Shute have argued that the difficulties with which the Law Commission has grappled in finding an acceptable

---

[285] R.D. Mackay, B. Mitchell and W.J. Brookbanks, "Pleading for Provoked Killers: In Defence of *Morgan Smith*" (2008) 124 L.Q.R. 675.

objective test for the loss of control defence are better dealt with by reassessing the meaning of the subjective element of "loss of self-control".[286] As noted above, they argue that the loss of control test ought to involve an examination of whether the defendant possessed such self-control to begin with. One of the benefits of such an approach, they argue, is that defendants who possess certain undesirable characteristics such as irascibility or alcoholism will fail in their defence, not because they fail in satisfying the objective test, but because those characteristics remove the power of self-control to begin with.

Section 54(1)(c) specifies that the issue is whether a person of D's sex and age, with a normal degree of tolerance and self-restraint *and in the circumstances of D*, might have reacted in the same or in a similar way to D. Section 54 (3) explains what "the circumstances of D means".

> "[T]the reference to 'the circumstances of D' is a reference to all of D's circumstances other than those whose only relevance to D's conduct is that they bear on D's general capacity for tolerance or self-restraint."

This would seem to confirm the pre-existing law under *Camplin* and *Holley* in that characteristics affecting the provocativeness are part of "all the circumstances". For example, if one is taunted about being a glue-sniffer (as in *Morhall*), this can be taken into account because it has a relevance beyond D's general capacity for tolerance or self-restraint. However, being intoxicated will not, of itself, be a relevant characteristic, as specified in para.5.41 of the Law Commission's Report above. This has been confirmed in the case of *Asmelash*.[287] Here the defendant had been drunk at the time that he stabbed the victim, and said that he had lost self-control and did not really know what had happened, but (somewhat inexplicably) was not so drunk that he did not know what he was doing. The judge directed the jury that they should consider whether a person unaffected by drink would have reacted in a similar way. On appeal against conviction for murder, arguing that this had been a misdirection, defence counsel attempted to rely on the Crown Court Bench Book, which had suggested that "in the circumstances" will "include the consumption of alcohol. The jury will no longer be directed that the reasonable man is a sober man".[288] The Court of Appeal, however, held that the judge was right to direct the jury as he had done, implying that the Crown Court Bench book will have to be rewritten.

It is only right that a defendant's intoxication should be ignored when applying s.54(1)(c) and s.54(3) of the 2009 Act, unless, perhaps, it caused the defendant to act out of a mistaken belief.[289] However, it would seem that this provision has (perhaps unintentionally) opened the door to a wide variety of characteristics being taken into account—as long as their *only* relevance is not that they bear on the defendant's general capacity for tolerance or self-restraint. So, while s.54(1)(c) only specifies the characteristics of sex and age, under s.54(3) there is no reason why the defendant's impotence, pregnancy, physical disability, sensitivity or even mental disability cannot be taken into account—unless the only relevance of these characteristics is that they affect the defendant's capacity for tolerance or self-restraint. As can be seen from the case of *Clinton*, above, sexual infidelity on the part of the deceased may be seen as a relevant factor in assessing the defendant's reaction to a qualifying trigger.

---

[286]   R. Holton and S. Shute, above fn.217.
[287]   *R. v Asmelash (Dawit)* [2014] Q.B. 103.
[288]   *Directing the Jury* (2011), quoted in *Asmelash* [2014] Q. B. 103 at [17].
[289]   D. Ormerod, *Smith and Hogan's Criminal Law*, 13th edn (Oxford: OUP, 2011), p.526.

Richard Taylor, "The Model of Tolerance and Self-Restraint", in Reed and Bohlander (eds), Loss of Control and Diminished Responsibility (2011), p.57

"The new test is not primarily about powers of self-control but about normal temperament which includes the concept of self-restraint, which may be similar to self-control, but the new test is wider in including also the notion of tolerance. It is the inclusion of tolerance which enables it, in effect, to exclude unpalatable characteristics such as jealousy and racial, religious, sexual and other forms of intolerance, prejudice and bigotry and other unacceptable attitudes such as those underpinning so-called 'honour killings'. The definition of 'the circumstances of D' was developed as a response to the unduly wide and imprecise standard which the decision in *Smith (Morgan)* had approved and was intended in general terms to return the law to the *Camplin* approach which the Privy Council in any event subsequently reintroduced for the law of provocation in *Holley*. However, the new test is subtly different from the *Campin/Holley* test, not only in the new (and potentially very significant) reference to tolerance as well as to self-restraint, but also in that all the circumstances of the accused are in principle brought in provided that they do not bear only on the capacity for tolerance or self-restrain but can be shown to have some other relevance to D's conduct, even if not necessarily to the gravity of the triggering conduct. There may not be many circumstances which neither bear on the gravity of the triggering conduct nor bear only on the capacity for tolerance and self-restraint, but defendants will no doubt seek to present their circumstances or highlight them in a manner which shows some relevance to D's conduct, other than to his/her capacity for tolerance and self-restraint, even if the circumstances do not directly affect the gravity of the triggering conduct."

2. Diminished responsibility

Where a defendant is suffering from "diminished responsibility" he will have a partial defence to murder and will instead be convicted of manslaughter—again giving the court the necessary flexibility as to sentence. The defence is important not only to allow such a defendant to avoid the mandatory penalty for murder, but it has also been recognised by some that it is necessary and desirable for labelling purposes, in avoiding the label of "murderer",[290] particularly given the narrowness of the M'Naghten rules in pleading insanity.

(i) Introduction

Royal Commission on Capital Punishment, Cmnd.8932 (1949–1953), para.411:

"It must be accepted that there is no sharp dividing line between sanity and insanity, but that the two extremes of 'sanity' and 'insanity' shade into one another by imperceptible gradations. The degree of individual responsibility varies equally widely; no clear boundary can be drawn between responsibility and irresponsibility. The existence of degrees of responsibility has been recognised in . . . [other] legal systems. . . . The acceptance of the doctrine of diminished responsibility would undoubtedly bring the law into closer harmony with the facts."

The doubts that have led many to argue for the abolition of the insanity defence[291] have here been used to justify a half-way house for those who kill while suffering from mental disorder; some device, it was felt, was needed to reflect the view that where there was less responsibility there ought to be less punishment. Such acceptance of partial responsibility would enable the courts to do what, after all discussion of responsibility was ended, they really desired: to avoid the fixed penalty for murder by convicting the killer of manslaughter instead. For all other crimes which do not carry a fixed penalty, a

---

[290] This was the view of several consultees to the Law Commission's review of partial defences to murder: Law Commission Paper No.290, para.5.18.

[291] Above, Ch.4.

partial defence was unnecessary. The lesser degree of responsibility could be reflected at the sentencing stage by "less punishment".

(ii) The law

Homicide Act 1957 s.2 (as amended by the Coroners and Justice Act 2009 s.52)

"(1) A person ('D') who kills or is a party to the killing of another is not to be convicted of murder if D was suffering from an abnormality of mental functioning which—
  (a)   arose from a recognised medical condition,
  (b)   substantially impaired D's ability to do one or more of the things mentioned in subsection (1A), and
  (c)   provides an explanation for D's acts and omissions in doing or being a party to the killing.
(1A) Those things are—
  (a)   to understand the nature of D's conduct;
  (b)   to form a rational judgment;
  (c)   to exercise self-control.
(1B) For the purposes of subsection (1)(c), an abnormality of mental functioning provides an explanation for D's conduct if it causes, or is a significant contributory factor in causing, D to carry out that conduct.
(3) . . . A person who but for this section would be liable, whether as principal or accessory, to be convicted of murder shall be liable instead to be convicted of manslaughter."[292]

The plea is raised by the defence on whom, as with insanity, the burden rests. Attempts to argue that this contravened art.6(2) of the ECHR which guarantees the presumption of innocence were rejected outright by the Court of Appeal in *Lambert*.[293] This was confirmed in *Foye*,[294] where it was stated that the fundamental reason why a reverse burden of proof applies is that because the defence depends on the inner workings of the defendant's mind, it would be a practical impossibility for the Crown to disprove an assertion that the defendant suffered from diminished responsibility, since the defendant might refuse to submit to or cooperate with a medical examination.

Before the amendments to s.2 were made by the Coroners and Justice Act 2009, the provision required that the defendant suffered an "abnormality of mind" arising from one of a number of "bracketed causes" (arrested or retarded development of mind or any inherent causes or induced by disease or injury). "Abnormality of mind" was extremely vague; the concept was only slightly clarified by the case of *Byrne*.[295] The appellant strangled and then mutilated a girl. It was alleged that he suffered from violent perverted sexual desires which he found difficult or impossible to control. He was, in fact, described as a sexual psychopath. In the course of his judgment (allowing the appeal) Lord Parker CJ defined "abnormality of mind" thus:

"[it is] a state of mind so different from that of ordinary human beings that the reasonable man . . . would term it abnormal. It appears to us wide enough to cover the mind's activities in all its aspects, not only the perception of physical acts and matters, and the ability to form a rational judgment as

[292] *R. v Antoine (Pierre Harrison)* [2001] 1 A.C. 340 decided that once a defendant has been found unfit to plead they cannot go on to plead diminished responsibility (to avoid indefinite mandatory commitment) because the trial terminates. Since the defendant is no longer liable to be convicted of murder the defence in s.2 cannot arise.
[293] *R. v Lambert (Steven)* [2001] 1 Cr. App. R. 14. The subsequent appeal to the House of Lords did not deal with diminished responsibility. The prosecution may raise the plea if the defendant is pleading insanity: *R. v Campbell (Colin Frederick)* (1987) 84 Cr. App. R. 255.
[294] *R. v Foye (Lee Robert)* [2013] EWCA Crim 475.
[295] *R. v Byrne (Patrick Joseph)* (1960) 44 Cr. App. R. 246.

to whether the act was right or wrong, but also the ability to exercise will-power to control physical acts in accordance with that rational judgment."

As the evidence to the Butler Committee suggested, this interpretation still left the meaning of "abnormality of mind" somewhat imprecise. It was a quasi-legal, quasi-medical formula that could satisfy no-one.

In recommending reform of the law, the Law Commission saw the need to bear in mind the needs and practices of medical practitioners, and drew inspiration from a definition of the defence adopted in New South Wales in 1997, to replace the requirement of an "abnormality of mind" with an abnormality of mental functioning arising either from a medically recognised condition or, in defendants under the age of 18, developmental immaturity.[296]

The developmental immaturity limb was always a controversial aspect of the Law Commission's proposal,[297] and was abandoned by the Government in drafting the new provision. It was dropped on the basis that it was not felt that the lack of such provision had caused any practical problems up until then, and because there was concern that every juvenile defendant accused of murder would attempt to rely on it to reduce their liability to manslaughter.[298] There was some opposition to this change to the proposals, one reason being that it is unfair to allow a 40-year-old defendant with the mental age of 10 to be able to rely on diminished responsibility due to them being recognised as suffering from a recognised mental condition, whilst excluding the defence in the case of a 10-year-old child because their development has not been arrested. This would suggest the law expects more of children than adults.[299] Such concerns were, however, rejected by the Government.

One might assume that the "abnormality of mental functioning" requirement will more or less fall by the wayside, and that a defence of diminished responsibility will succeed providing that the defendant was suffering from a recognised medical condition and that there is expert evidence that this substantially impaired their ability to do one of the things specified in s.2(1A). If "abnormality of mental functioning" is to mean anything, it may be that reference to the test in *Byrne* is made to help juries determine the meaning of "abnormality". The Law Commission's most recent report says no more on this point than that "mental functioning" was a term preferred by psychiatrists to that of "mind" under the old law. However, the Commission's earlier report of 2004 suggests that the impairment of the defendant's ability to do one of the things that now appear in s.2(1A) actually amounts to a definition of "abnormality of mental functioning".[300] What is clear is that the new law is intended to be a lot more user-friendly for psychiatrists who are asked to provide evidence for the prosecution and defence in such cases. The abnormality of mental functioning must have arisen from a "recognised medical condition", meaning that the law can now keep pace with developments in diagnostic practice. For a medical condition to be recognised, it would seem that it would have to be listed in one of the accepted classificatory systems such as The World Health Organisation's *International Classification of Diseases* or the American Psychiatric Association's *Diagnostic and Statistical Manual of Mental Disorders*.[301]

---

[296] Law Commission Paper No.304, para.5.112.

[297] As acknowledged by the Law Commission itself: Law Commission Paper No.304, para.5.129.

[298] Ministry of Justice, CP 19/08, para.53.

[299] Ministry of Justice, CP(R) 19/08, para.98.

[300] Law Commission Paper No.290, *Partial Defences to Murder*, para.5.95.

[301] Ministry of Justice, CP 19/08, para.49. See also R. Mackay, "The Coroners and Justice Act 2009—partial defences to murder (2) the new diminished responsibility plea" [2010] Crim. L.R. 290–302 at 294. However, the fact that a condition is listed in such a guide does not in itself, it appears, make it an abnormality of mental functioning for the purposes of s.2(1). See *Dowds* [2012] 1 Cr. App. R. 34.

The abnormality of mental functioning must substantially impair the defendant's ability to either understand the nature of his conduct; to form a rational judgment; or to exercise self-control. The question of "substantial" impairment remains one for the jury.[302]

Law Commission No.304, Murder, Manslaughter and Infanticide (2006):

"5.121 [T]he new provisions seek to make clear what impact on capacity the effects of an abnormality of mental functioning must have, if the abnormality is to be the basis for a successful plea of diminished responsibility. It might be helpful to illustrate this by example, although it is not our case that on the actual facts given below the defence should necessarily succeed.

(1) Substantially impaired capacity to 'understand the nature of his or her conduct':

(a) a boy aged 10 who has been left to play very violent video games for hours on end for much of his life, loses his temper and kills another child when the child attempts to take a game from him. When interviewed, he shows no real understanding that, when a person is killed they cannot simply be later revived, as happens in the games he has been continually playing.

(2) Substantially impaired capacity to 'form a rational judgement':

(a) a woman suffering from post-traumatic stress disorder, consequent upon violent abuse suffered at her husband's hands, comes to believe that only burning her husband to death will rid the world of his sins;

(b) a mentally sub-normal boy believes that he must follow his older brother's instructions, even when they involve taking take part in a killing. He says, 'I wouldn't dream of disobeying my brother and he would never tell me to do something if it was really wrong';

(c) a depressed man who has been caring for many years for a terminally ill spouse, kills her, at her request. He says that he had found it progressively more difficult to stop her repeated requests dominating his thoughts to the exclusion of all else, so that 'I felt I would never think straight again until I had given her what she wanted.'

(3) Substantially impaired capacity to 'control him or herself':

(a) a man says that sometimes the devil takes control of him and implants in him a desire to kill, a desire that must be acted on before the devil will go away."

Under the original drafting of s.2 of the Homicide Act, the final question of whether the defendant's responsibility was substantially impaired was a moral question for the jury on which expert psychiatrists should not have given their own views.[303] It has been found, however, that whilst a minority of psychiatrists tended to restrict themselves to the first part of the test in s.2 in giving evidence at trials, almost 70 per cent of them expressed an opinion in relation to whether the defendant's responsibility was substantially impaired.[304] Despite this statistic, it seems that psychiatrists were not comfortable with expressing an opinion on this matter, and the Royal College of Psychiatrists suggested that psychiatrists should resist requests from lawyers to do so.[305] The difficulty faced by psychiatrists is illustrative of the central problem with s.2 prior to the amendment to the law: the compromise it achieved

---

[302]   Law Commission Paper No.304, para.5.118.

[303]   Little was said on the meaning of "substantially" impaired under the previous law. It was stated in *R. v Ramchurn (Jayant)* [2010] 2 Cr. App. R. 3 that "substantially" is an ordinary English word, which imports neither uncertainty nor ambiguity into the statutory language. Lord Judge CJ said the use of "substantially" was "designed to ensure that the murderous activity of a defendant should not result in a conviction for manslaughter rather than murder on account of any impairment of mental responsibility, however trivial and insignificant; but equally that the defence should be available without the defendant having to show that his mental responsibility for his actions was so grossly impaired as to be extinguished" At [23].

[304]   Law Commission Paper No.290 (2004), para.5.51.

[305]   Law Commission Paper No.304 (2006), para.5.118.

between medical and legal issues left neither side on safe ground. Neither medical experts nor the jury could satisfactorily answer the questions demanded of them. Indeed, the process had been described by psychiatrists as "an expensive farce" and a "blot on psychiatric practice".[306] What happened was the familiar story of medical experts being made to determine the issue of responsibility.

Mackay predicts that it is likely that experts will continue to give their opinions on this issue as before.[307] However, under the new law the jury will no longer have to address the impossible issue of whether "responsibility" was substantially impaired and psychiatrists will no longer go through the charade of testifying about such a non-medical concept. Instead, juries will have to assess whether the defendant's recognised psychiatric condition substantially impaired her ability to do one of the specified things. In doing this, they will undoubtedly be guided by psychiatric evidence but, now, psychiatrists will be testifying about matters within their medical expertise (for example, whether a defendant could form a rational judgement) rather than matters beyond their competence (issues of responsibility).

The final (and new) requirement is that the recognised medical condition must have caused the defendant's involvement in the killing. The Law Commission noted that it was never clear under the pre-existing law whether the abnormality of mind had to in some sense "cause" the defendant to kill.[308] The new s.2(1)(c) requires that the abnormality of mental functioning provides an explanation for D's acts and omissions in doing or being a party to the killing, and s.2(1B) further provides that this means that D's conduct must cause or be a significant contributory factor in causing D to carry out that conduct. The inclusion of a strict causal requirement has been criticised by Mackay, who notes that there is no real support for such a requirement and other jurisdictions, such as New South Wales, have not seen the need to include one.[309] The law now makes it clear that there must be a connection between the abnormality of mental functioning and the killing. This means that where the jury think that the abnormality of mental functioning made no difference to the defendant's behaviour, he will not succeed in his plea of diminished responsibility.[310] But the test is more than one of "but for" causation. How is it envisaged that it will operate in practice?

"Let us consider a hypothetical case where the psychiatric evidence is as follows. D suffers from schizophrenia and killed V while experiencing delusions to the effect that God ordered him to kill. Schizophrenia is a recognised medical condition which led to D's experiencing delusions to the effect that God ordered him to kill. Schizophrenia is a recognised medical condition which led to D's experiencing an abnormality of mental functioning. This in turn is likely to have impaired D's ability to form a rational judgement and so clearly provides an explanation for the killing. The prosecution psychiatrist concurs with all this but unlike the psychiatrist for the defence expresses doubts as to whether the abnormality of mental functioning was the cause or a significant contributory factor in causing D to carry out the killing. One can only hope that this sort of dispute will be rare. But there is nothing to prevent it. A sensible way forward might be for the courts to interpret this provision so that . . . proof of all the other elements of the new plea would mean that in giving his opinion the psychiatrist is entitled, without more, to reach a conclusion that the causal requirement is satisfied."[311]

---

[306]   *Report of the Committee on the Penalty for Homicide* (1993), p.33.
[307]   Mackay, "The Coroners and Justice Act 2009—partial defences to murder (2) the new diminished responsibility plea" [2010] Crim. L.R. 290–302 at 295.
[308]   Law Commission Paper No.304, para.5.122.
[309]   Mackay, "The Coroners and Justice Act 2009—partial defences to murder (2) the new diminished responsibility plea" [2010] Crim. L.R. 290–302 at 300.
[310]   Ministry of Justice, 19/08(R), para.95.
[311]   R. Mackay, "The New Diminished Responsibility Plea", in Reed and Bohlander, *Loss of Control and Diminished Responsibility:*

There remain further concerns over the types of cases that the new law is likely to cover. Under the pre-existing s.2, the woolliness of the language enabled psychiatrists, as expert witnesses (with the collusion of judges and juries) to simply stretch the interpretation of the provision to cover cases where a conviction of murder was thought to be inappropriate. Persons suffering from reactive depressions and alcoholism, as well as mercy-killers, have been brought within the ambit of the defence. Indeed, the Law Commission has noted that long-term carers of terminally ill spouses who kill with their spouse's consent "are already quite commonly dealt with under s.2 of the Act as persons suffering from diminished responsibility. It is the prosecution that normally accepts the plea".[312] Women suffering from pre-menstrual syndrome[313] have also been included as have, most importantly, psychopaths and persons acting under "irresistible impulse".[314] Mackay has conducted research to shed light on the frequency with which different conditions are used to support a plea of diminished responsibility. His findings are that the most common condition used in connection with the defence was depression (28.7 per cent) followed by schizophrenia (23.6 per cent), and personality disorder and psychosis (both at 12.7 per cent).[315] The question is whether the new drafting of the provision will have narrowed the ambit of the defence to exclude any of these conditions. Only those that are "recognised medical conditions" will have the capacity to provide a basis for the defence, but the success or otherwise of the plea will depend on the requirements under s.2(1)(b) and s.2(1)(c). Depression giving rise to a mercy killing or stemming from domestic abuse could amount to a recognised medical condition, for example.[316]

More difficult is perhaps the case of the alcoholic.[317] It was held in *Tandy* that alcoholism may amount to an "injury",[318] one of the bracketed causes required of an abnormality of mind under the previous incarnation of the defence, if the first drink of the day was "involuntary". However, for policy reasons the courts have consistently upheld the distinction between alcoholism and mere intoxication. In *Dietschmann*,[319] the House of Lords held that where a defendant pleads diminished responsibility resulting from the combination of mental abnormality and intoxication the jury should be satisfied that, despite the drink, the defendant's mental abnormality substantially impaired his mental responsibility for his fatal acts. Shortly before the Coroners and Justice Act was passed, however, the case of *Wood*[320] dealt with this matter in relation to a defendant whose abnormality of mind arose from alcoholism (alcohol dependency syndrome), where he was also drunk at the time of the killing. In this case the Court of Appeal reassessed the way in which *Tandy* applied in cases of alcohol dependency syndrome and noted that the jury would have to focus its minds on two issues in a case of an alcoholic charged with murder who was attempting to rely on s.2. The first was whether the defendant's dependency amounted to an abnormality of mind. This question was more easily answered in cases

---

Domestic, Comparative and International Perspectives (Aldershot: Ashgate, 2011), pp.18–19. For arguments as to why the problem with the causation requirement is more apparent than real, see R. Fortson, "The Modern Partial Defence of Diminished Responsibility", in Reed and Bohlander, *Loss of Control and Diminished Responsibility: Domestic, Comparative and International Perspectives* (Aldershot: Ashgate, 2011), p.35.

[312]   Law Commission Consultation Paper No.177, *A New Homicide Act for England and Wales?* (2005), para.8.84.

[313]   *Reynolds*, April 23, 1988 (CA). For discussion of this and other cases of PMT (including that of *Smith (Sandie)* [1982] Crim. L.R. 531), see S. Edwards, "Mad, Bad or Pre-Menstrual?" (1988) 138 N.L.J. 456.

[314]   *Byrne*, above, fn.295.

[315]   R. Mackay, "The Diminished Responsibility Plea in Operation—An Empirical Study", Appendix B to Law Com. No.290 (2004), table 15b.

[316]   Classifications F30–F39 of the WHO's *International Classification of Diseases* list "mood [affective] disorders" which cover a range of depressive illnesses, including reactive depression and depressive reaction (F32).

[317]   For a discussion of intoxication and diminished responsibility, see M. Gibson "Intoxicants and Diminished Responsibility" [2011] Crim. L.R. 909–924.

[318]   *R. v Tandy (Linda Mary)* [1988] Crim. L.R. 308.

[319]   *R. v Dietschmann (Anthony)* [2003] 1 A.C. 1209.

[320]   *R. v Wood (Clive)* [2008] 2 Cr. App. R. 34.

where observable brain damage had occurred, but nevertheless, had to be addressed in all cases even if there had been no brain damage. Secondly, in cases where the jury decided that the alcohol dependency syndrome did amount to an abnormality of mind, they then had to address the question of whether the defendant's actions at the time of the killing were substantially impaired as a result of the syndrome. This approach was confirmed again by the Court of Appeal in *Stewart*.[321]

In *Dowds*,[322] decided in relation to the reformed version of s.2, a far more simple matter was dealt with than that in *Woods*. The defendant was drunk at the time that he stabbed his partner 60 times, killing her, but there was no suggestion that he was suffering from alcohol dependency syndrome. Instead he tried to argue diminished responsibility on the basis that "acute intoxication" is listed in the WHO ICD-10 and should therefore amount to a recognised medical condition for the purposes of pleading diminished responsibility. The Court of Appeal rejected this argument on the basis that the Law Commission explicitly did *not* include writing the terms of ICD-10 and/or DSM-IV[323] into the legislation, for which purpose those terms are "demonstrably unsuited". Pleading diminished responsibility successfully is not as simple as relying on the presence of a particular condition on any such diagnostic list. Being on the list is a necessary but not sufficient condition for diminished responsibility to apply.

Will battered women who kill their abusive partners fall within the ambit of the new defence? The Law Commission assumes that in the worst cases of domestic violence, the victim of that violence will be able to rely on diminished responsibility as a partial defence.[324] In the past, however, a battered woman's ability to do so, whilst recognised in law, has not necessarily been seen to be desirable. Such women have had to fall back on diminished responsibility when both self-defence and provocation have been unlikely to succeed. For example in *Ahluwalia*,[325] the defendant was beaten and threatened with death for over 10 years before she poured petrol over her husband whilst he was asleep and then set light to him. At her trial she pleaded provocation (or alternatively lack of mens rea) but was found guilty of murder. The Court of Appeal, however, very exceptionally, permitted medical evidence that was not brought before the court at the trial to be admitted at the appeal stage. On the basis of the evidence of her depressive condition her conviction was quashed; at the re-trial a plea of manslaughter on the basis of diminished responsibility was accepted and she was sentenced to 40 months' imprisonment (exactly the amount she had already served).[326] Forcing such defendants to resort to diminished responsibility has been severely criticised, however, on the basis that it labels them as "abnormal" or "crazy".[327]

What is the outcome of a successful plea of diminished responsibility if widely divergent cases are going to be brought within its protection? Simply because the conviction is for manslaughter rather than murder does not ensure lenient treatment. A finding of mental imbalance does not automatically entail a hospital order under s.37 of the Mental Health Act 1983 although this is imposed in approximately 50 per cent of diminished responsibility cases.[328] The use of imprisonment has increased to over

---

[321]   *R. v Stewart (James)* [2009] EWCA Crim 593.

[322]   *Dowds* [2012] 1 Cr. App. R. 34.

[323]   This has now been updated to the DSM-V. The fact that conditions listed in the DSM do not remain static from edition to edition might in itself prove problematic.

[324]   Law Commission Paper No.304, para.5.100.

[325]   *Ahluwalia* (1993) 96 Cr. App. R. 133.

[326]   See also *R. v Hobson (Kathleen)* [1998] 1 Cr. App. R. 31 where the Court of Appeal ordered a retrial on the basis that the issue of "Battered Women's Syndrome" (added to the British Classification of Mental Diseases after her trial but prior to the appeal) should have been put to the jury.

[327]   See, for example, K. O'Donovan, "Defences for Battered Women Who Kill" (1991) 18 J.L. and Soc. 219.

[328]   R. Mackay, "The Diminished Responsibility Plea in Operation—An Empirical Study", Appendix B to Law Com. No.290 (2004). This figure combines both hospital orders and restriction orders. A "restriction order" (Mental Health Act 1983 s.41) is an order that can be attached to the hospital order to prevent the offender being transferred to another hospital, given leave of absence or discharged without the Home Secretary's consent.

one-third of cases although life sentences are fairly rare.[329] In *Brown*[330] the Court of Appeal confirmed that the approach to sentencing in cases of manslaughter by reason of diminished responsibility has not been significantly changed by the introduction of the revised definition of diminished responsibility. In a case where a life sentence is appropriate the judge can have regard to Sch.21 to the Criminal Justice Act 2003 to determine what minimum term would be appropriate had the defendant been convicted of murder, and apply an appropriate discount to reflect that the defendant's responsibility was diminished.[331] In *Welsh*[332] the schizophrenic defendant's life sentence with a minimum term of 12 years was upheld on the basis that the defendant's propensity for violence, even before he suffered from schizophrenia, and the gravity of the offence, meant that public confidence would not be met by making a hospital order coupled with a restriction order, and there was a substantial risk that the defendant would remain a source of danger even if his condition substantially improved once he received treatment and medication. Determinate sentences of imprisonment can be imposed where there is no proper basis for a hospital order, but where the defendant's degree of responsibility is not minimal. The residual cases "which have been felt to merit sympathetic consideration have resulted in more lenient disposal".[333]A recent example of a case that can be classified as a "mercy killing" is that of *Webb*,[334] where the defendant, having been requested on many occasions by his wife to help end her life, smothered her after the overdose she had taken seemed not to have been effective and she had told him not to let her wake up. His sentence of two years' imprisonment was reduced to a suspended 12-month sentence of imprisonment.

This last case raises the question of whether those that kill out of compassion should have to rely on the defence of diminished responsibility to avoid the label of murder and a mandatory life sentence. It has been seen that where a killing is motivated by the emotion of fear or anger, the killer may be able to rely on the partial defence of loss of control to reduce a murder conviction to one of manslaughter. Keating and Bridgeman have noted that compassion, like fear and anger, is an emotion, but unlike those emotions it is an altruistic emotion and reflects well on the person who experiences it and acts upon it. Should we not, then, afford a defence of compassionate killing to those such as the defendant in *Webb* who act to end another's suffering?

Heather Keating and Jo Bridgeman, "Compassionate Killings: The Case for a Partial Defence" (2012) 75 M.L.R. 697–721 at 720

"In cases such as these, where there is objective evidence of extreme and unbearable suffering experienced by the deceased prior to death, together with requests for help to die, the argument for a partial defence of compassionate killing may be one which would garner support. However, our case studies prompt us to go further to argue that the partial defence should not be confined to those cases in which the deceased was, at the time of death, able to articulate her suffering. [In this respect differing from assisted suicide where there must of course be a request; see below.] The knowledge and understanding of a loved one which is gained from the intensive experiences of care which are characteristic of these cases means that the suffering of another can be understood even when it is not articulated. As our case studies reveal, the intimate relationship of love and care can bring an understanding of another not achievable by one more distant. This is both because their caring relationship ensures a focus upon the experiences and needs of the loved one who is suffering and also because it brings

---

329   In his study of 126 convictions for diminished responsibility manslaughter over the years 1997–2001, Mackay found that a discretionary life sentence was imposed in 10 cases.
330   [2012] 2 Cr. App. R. (S.) 27.
331   *R. v Brown (Robert)* [2012] 2 Cr. App. R. (S.) 27.
332   *R. v Welsh (Colin Christopher)* [2011] 2 Cr. App. R. (S.) 68.
333   Butler Committee on Mentally Abnormal Offenders, Cmnd.6244, para.19.7.
334   *R. v Webb (George Hugh)* [2011] 2 Cr. App. R. (S.) 61.

understanding of their values important to an assessment of suffering. We recognise that a proposal to extend the partial defence beyond instances where there is a competent, autonomous decision on the part of the sufferer is controversial. In order to address the risks involved and, heeding the warnings given by Penney Lewis . . . about the dangers of a compassion-based approach, we stress that there would need to be evidence that the deceased was experiencing extreme and unbearable suffering prior to death. It would not be enough for the accused to have an honest belief about the level of the suffering being experienced; it would need to one based on reasonable grounds and thus a reasoned and caring response to the suffering of their loved one. In sum, the partial defence of compassionate killing we propose would be available to a relative or family member who had been fulfilling intensive caring responsibilities for the deceased and who, in response to an honest and reasonable belief that he or she had been experiencing extreme and unbearable suffering, ended the deceased's life in order to end his or her suffering."

3. Killing in pursuance of a suicide pact

Homicide Act 1957 s.4

"(1) It shall be manslaughter, and shall not be murder, for a person acting in pursuance of a suicide pact between him and another to kill the other or be a party to the other being killed by a third person . . .

(3) For the purposes of this section 'suicide pact' means a common agreement between two or more persons having for its object the death of all of them, whether or not each is to take his own life, but nothing done by a person who enters into a suicide pact shall be treated as done by him in pursuance of the pact unless it is done while he has the settled intention of dying in pursuance of the pact."

The law acts with some clemency towards a defendant who survives a suicide pact when they had intended to die themselves. Such clemency does not, however, extend to other situations. If the agreement to "kill and then die" is merely a front for murder where the defendant has no intention of killing himself, then he will be convicted of murder. This will be the case even if the deceased consented to die and even if, furthermore, it can be described as a mercy-killing. It is, therefore, thought to be more blameworthy to kill in such situations than where a suicide pact exists. The basis of this distinction in blameworthiness must lie in the "settled intention" of the defendant to die himself. Perhaps it is felt that the person killed would not have consented had she not been aware of the intention of the other; more probably, however, the consent of the "victim" is still irrelevant and the partial defence represents "a concession to human frailty". It recognises with compassion the state of despair of one who would kill and then die themselves.[335] Or could it be that this is a remnant of the Biblical historical origins of the law of homicide—that one who kills intending to die themselves immediately thereafter does not "acquire the [same] control over the blood—the life force—of the victim"[336] —and therefore deserves less punishment?

Killing in pursuance of a suicide pact is distinguished from the separate crime of encouraging or assisting suicide.

V. ENCOURAGING OR ASSISTING SUICIDE

Suicide Act 1961 s.2 (as amended by the Coroners and Justice Act 2009 s.59)

"(1) A person ('D') commits an offence if—
(a) D does an act capable of encouraging or assisting the suicide or attempted suicide of another person, and
(b) D's act was intended to encourage or assist suicide or an attempt at suicide.

---

[335] In *Dunbar v Plant* [1997] 3 W.L.R. 1261 it was stated that the public interest does not generally call for the survivor of a suicide pact to be prosecuted.
[336] G.P. Fletcher, *Rethinking Criminal Law* (Boston: Little, Brown, 1978), p.236.

(1A) The person referred to in subsection (1)(a) need not be a specific person (or class of persons) known to, or identified by, D.

(1B) D may commit an offence under this section whether or not a suicide, or an attempt at suicide, occurs.

(1C) An offence under this section is triable on indictment and a person convicted of such an offence is liable to imprisonment for a term not exceeding 14 years."

The amendments made by the Coroners and Justice Act 2009 were intended solely to modernise the language used and bring it in line with the law under the Serious Crime Act 2007.[337] Previously, the provision was couched in the same terms as those used in the Accessories and Abettors Act 1861, requiring that the defendant aid, abet, counsel or procure the suicide or attempted suicide of another. The change is not intended to extend the law or alter the kinds of cases in which a prosecution will be brought.[338] Hirst notes, however, that the key change is the substitution of a conduct crime for a result crime.[339] Now that it is a purely inchoate offence the chances are that it could bring within its ambit more cases than it did previously, given that it can be charged in cases where the would-be "victim" has not got as far as attempting to commit suicide, as required under the old law.

It has been pointed out that

"[t]he distinction between . . . [complicity in suicide and manslaughter by suicide pact] . . . may be very fine. If D and V agree to gas themselves and D alone survives, it appears that he will be liable under the Homicide Act if he turned on the tap and under the Suicide Act if V did."[340]

The distinction is of importance in terms of punishment. Killing in pursuance of a suicide pact is punishable as manslaughter by a maximum of life imprisonment, while encouraging or assisting suicide is punishable by a maximum of 14 years' imprisonment. The Draft Criminal Code recognised the strength of this point and proposed to make both offences subject to a seven-year maximum sentence.[341] The Law Commission proposed repealing s.4 of the Homicide Act on the basis that its proposed reformulation of the definition of the partial defence of diminished responsibility would cater adequately for the deserving cases.[342] However, following consultation the Law Commission retracted this proposal and recommended that s.4 of the Homicide Act be retained pending the outcome of a further consultation on the question of whether a separate partial defence of mercy killing ought to be created.[343]

The consent of the DPP is required before a prosecution may be brought under the Suicide Act 1961.[344] In *Pretty*,[345] the first case on assisted suicide to reach the House of Lords, it was held that the DPP is unable to give an undertaking to people that they will not be prosecuted if they assist their spouse to commit suicide—even if that spouse, by virtue of their incurable condition, is unable to carry out her wishes herself.[346] The House of Lords in *Purdy*[347] has again had occasion to consider the issue

---

[337]   See Ch.5.

[338]   This was confirmed by the then DPP, Kier Starmer QC, in evidence to the House of Commons Public Bill Committee on the Coroners and Justice Bill at its fourth sitting on February 5, 2009: *http://www.parliament.the-stationery-office.co.uk/pa/cm200809/cmpublic/cmpbcor.htm* [Accessed April 2014].

[339]   M. Hirst, "Assisted Suicide after Purdy: The Unresolved Issue" [2009] Crim. L.R. 870 at 875.

[340]   D. Ormerod, *Smith and Hogan: Criminal Law*, 12th edn (Oxford: OUP, 2008), p. 558.

[341]   Law Commission Paper No.177 (1989), cl.63.

[342]   Law Commission Consultation Paper No.177 (2005), para.10.32.

[343]   Law Commission Paper No.304 (2006), para.7.50.

[344]   Section 2(4).

[345]   *R. (on the application of Pretty) v DPP* [2002] 1 A.C. 800.

[346]   Mrs Pretty brought her case under a number of the Articles of the ECHR: arts 2, 3, 8, 9, 14. It was decided that s.2 of the Suicide Act 1961 was not incompatible with the ECHR and thus did not breach the Human Rights Act 1998. See generally, M.D.A. Freeman, "Death, Dying and the Human Rights Act 1998" (1999) 52 C.L.P. 218.

[347]   *R. (Purdy) v DPP* [2010] 1 Cr. App. R. 1.

of how prosecutorial discretion should be controlled in such cases. The facts were similar to those of *Pretty*, with the claimant arguing that, if the DPP could not give an undertaking not to prosecute, he should at least be obliged to provide clear guidance as to what factors would be taken into account when deciding whether to prosecute. The House of Lords allowed the appeal, finding that the right to respect for private life under art.8 of the ECHR was engaged and that if the law was to interfere with that right, there should be accessible and precise guidance to enable an individual to foresee the consequences of his actions so that he could regulate his conduct without breaking the law. The Code for Crown Prosecutors did not provide sufficient or specific guidance on this issue and so the DPP would be required to issue offence-specific policy, similar to charging standards already in existence in relation to offences such as driving offences or non-fatal offences against the person.

In response, the DPP embarked on a consultation process in September 2009, following which he issued a policy in February 2010 providing a list of factors for and against prosecution in the public interest in cases of assisted suicide.[348] Such guidance should assure those suffering from a terminal illness, a severe and incurable physical disability or severe degenerative condition, such as the claimants in *Pretty* and *Purdy*, that if they seek to take their own lives, assisted by their loved ones, that said loved ones will not be prosecuted if they can be said to be truly motivated by compassion. However, where the suspect was acting in his or her capacity as a medical doctor, nurse, other healthcare professional, a professional carer, or as a person in authority, such as a prison officer, and the victim was in his or her care, this will act as a factor in favour of prosecution. The Supreme Court in Nicklinson,[349] in addition to finding that s.2 does not impose what would be regarded under the ECHR as a "blanket ban" on assisted suicide, meaning that the UK is acting within the margin of appreciation and not in breach of the Convention, also declined to order the D.P.P. to amend the prosecution policy in response to arguments that it was insufficiently clear. This raises general questions not only about the degree of discretion that should be afforded to the CPS in prosecuting cases, and how that discretion ought to be controlled but, more fundamentally, about whether the criminal law ought to criminalise conduct it does not seek to punish, and whether the law on assisted suicide, mercy killings and euthanasia needs amending. The Law Commission recommended that the Government ought to undertake a consultation process on the question of whether the law should allow for a partial defence to murder of mercy killing or create a new offence of mercy killing.[350] It would appear that the CPS's consultation on its prosecution policy overlapped considerably with the kinds of issues such a public consultation would seek to explore. Arguably "mercy killing" could involve cases where the victim was unable herself to choose to end her own life and to communicate that to the defendant, whereas the DPP's guidance makes it clear that a defendant would ordinarily only avoid prosecution for assisted suicide if the victim had been the one to instigate the suicide and had been able to communicate her wishes clearly to the defendant. Leaving such issues to the discretion of Crown prosecutors is, however, less desirable than legislating clearly on what is or is not a criminal offence.

The maximum penalty is 14 years' imprisonment. Prosecutions are rare, making the sentencing task for the judge quite difficult. In *Howe*,[351] the first case prosecuted since *Purdy* was decided and the guidance was issued by the DPP, a 12-year custodial sentence was reduced to one of 10 years. The defendant, who was 19, walked to a petrol station to fill a petrol can with petrol and buy a lighter which he returned to his 30-year-old friend. The friend, who was of a vulnerable character, had mental health problems and had on a number of occasions threatened to kill himself, poured petrol over

---

[348] See *http://www.cps.gov.uk/publications/prosecution/assisted_suicide_policy.html* [Accessed April 2014].
[349] *R (on the application of Nicklinson) v. Ministry of Justice* [2014] UKSC 38. For more on this case see Ch.4 above.
[350] Law Commission Paper No.304 (2006), para.7.49.
[351] *Howe* [2014] EWCA Crim 114.

himself and lit himself on fire. Miraculously he survived, albeit suffering 95 per cent burns. The Court of Appeal, in reducing the sentence, considered that it was wrong of the trial judge to make reference to the sentencing guidelines in relation to s.18 Offences against the Person Act and provided guidance as to relevant factors for a court to consider in dealing with the offence.

VI. INFANTICIDE

1. The current position

Infanticide Act 1938 s.1

"(1) Where a woman by any wilful act or omission causes the death of her child being a child under the age of twelve months, but at the time of the act or omission the balance of her mind was disturbed by reason of her not having fully recovered from the effect of giving birth to the child or by reason of the effect of lactation consequent upon the birth of the child, then, if[352] the circumstances were such that but for this Act the offence would have amounted to murder or manslaughter,[353] she shall be guilty of . . . infanticide, and may for such offence be dealt with and punished as if she had been guilty of the offence of manslaughter of the child.

(2) Where upon the trial of a woman for the murder of her child, being a child under the age of twelve months, the jury are of opinion that she by any wilful act or omission caused its death, but that at the time of the act or omission the balance of her mind was disturbed by reason of her not having fully recovered from the effect of giving birth to the child or by reason of the effect of lactation consequent upon the birth of the child, then the jury may, if the circumstances were such that but for the provisions of this Act they might have returned a verdict of murder or manslaughter, return in lieu thereof a verdict of infanticide."

Infanticide is similar to voluntary manslaughter in that in one respect it is effectively a partial defence to murder.[354] It has especially close links with the partial defence of diminished responsibility and, indeed, there is some question as to whether infanticide is redundant given the existence of this wider defence. The changes made by the Coroners and Justice Act 2009 may seem minor, but they will provide welcome clarification of the law for many. Prior to the changes there had been some question over whether the prosecution could only charge infanticide in cases where they could prove the necessary mens rea for murder, and whether infanticide was available as a defence to women charged with manslaughter as well as those charged with murder.[355] Although the Court of Appeal in *Gore*[356] had suggested that it should be clear that the prosecution need not be able to prove intention to kill or cause grievous bodily harm, given that the only mens rea term appearing in the statute was "wilful", that part of the court's decision was only obiter. The Government was, however, happy to accept the Court of Appeal's interpretation of the law and the amendment made by the Coroners and Justice Act 2009 to add the words "or manslaughter" to both s.1(1) and s.1(2) is a welcome clarification to the law. This amendment has the added benefit of making it clear that infanticide cannot be charged in cases that would not otherwise amount to unlawful homicide. The Government was concerned that

---

[352]   The word "if" was substituted for "notwithstanding that" by the Coroners and Justice Act 2009 s.57.

[353]   The words "or manslaughter" were added by the Coroners and Justice Act 2009 s.57.

[354]   In *Gore* [2007] EWCA Crim 2789 the Court of Appeal noted that infanticide is an offence under s.1(1) of the Infanticide Act 1938, but a partial defence to murder is provided under s.1(2) of the Infanticide Act 1938. Mackay has found that in practice infanticide is charged as an offence rather than being raised as a partial defence at a murder trial. However, of 49 cases prosecuted between 1990 and 2003, 37 were initially charged as murder, with the charge being altered to infanticide following pre-trial negotiations. There was no jury trial in all but two of these 49 cases: R. Mackay, "Infanticide and Related Diminished Responsibility Manslaughters: An Empirical Study", Appendix D to Law Commission Paper No.304, *Murder, Manslaughter and Infanticide* (2006), paras D17–D.18. It is therefore usually up to the defence to raise the issue, leading the prosecution to alter the charges.

[355]   Ashworth argued that it should be available as both: A. Ashworth, Commentary to *Gore* [2008] Crim. L.R. 388 at 390.

[356]   *Gore* [2007] EWCA Crim 2789.

one of the consequences of the reading of s.1 in *Gore* was that a woman who committed a "wilful act or omission" might be accused of infanticide even though her culpability in relation to an omission to act would fall below the standard of gross negligence required for manslaughter.[357]

When introduced in its modern form,[358] infanticide was seen by many as a welcome solution to juries' reluctance to convict distressed women of the murder of their babies—with the consequence that they would be sentenced to death. One of the reasons for the welcome that the introduction of the crime of infanticide received was that it avoided the hypocrisy of passing a death sentence that all in authority (at least) knew would not be carried out; the sentence of death would invariably be commuted to one of life imprisonment by the Royal Prerogative of Mercy. Since 1849, no mother had been executed for the murder of her own child under the age of one year.[359]

While the existence of the offence is useful in giving effect to both a judicial and societal desire to express understanding for and sympathy with the defendant's plight, the medical basis upon which infanticide has rested since the twentieth century[360] has never been beyond doubt. It is estimated that about half of new mothers experience "baby blues" in the first few days after giving birth and that in about 10 per cent of cases more severe depressions result. The most severe forms of psychiatric illnesses of postpartum psychosis and psychotic depression are thought to be much less common but do exist. Medically, therefore, it can be argued that there is a case for a special defence (although no one is suggesting that all these women are likely to kill their children).[361] However, the most serious cases would probably fall within the defence of diminished responsibility. Moreover, there are clear problems with both the terminology employed in the Infanticide Act and its use in practice.

The Report of the Committee on Mentally Abnormal Offenders (Butler Committee), Evidence of the Governor and Staff of Holloway Prison, Cmnd.6244 (1975), para.19.24:

"The disturbance of the 'balance of mind' that the Act requires can rarely be said to arise directly from incomplete recovery from the effects of childbirth and even less so from the effects of lactation.[362]

Infanticide due to puerperal psychotic illness is rare. The type of killing where the child is killed immediately after birth and which is usually associated with illegitimate concealed pregnancies is also very uncommon. Most cases of child murder dealt with by the courts as infanticide are examples of the battered child syndrome in which the assault has had fatal consequences and the child is aged under 12 months. A combination of environmental stress and personality disorder with low frustration tolerance are the usual aetiological factors in such cases and the relationship to 'incomplete recovery from the effects of childbirth or lactation' specified in the Infanticide Act is often somewhat remote. The Act is nevertheless nearly always invoked in cases of maternal filicide when the victim is aged under 12 months, in order to reduce the charge from murder to manslaughter. The illogical

---

[357] Ministry of Justice CP 19/08, para.122.

[358] The Infanticide Act 1922 s.5(1), first made a finding of manslaughter instead of murder possible if "at the time of the act or omission [in killing her *newly-born* child] she had not fully recovered from the effect of giving birth to such child".

[359] Royal Commission on Capital Punishment (1953), Cmnd.8932, p.11.

[360] It was not until 1922 that infanticide was framed with reference to the medical effects of childbirth; previously it had been more concerned with social conditions and moral values. Originally, for example, infanticide applied only to the killing of illegitimate children and was more concerned with the concealment of death (which acted as a presumption of guilt to murder) rather than the death itself (21 Jac. 1, c.27, 1623). See A. Loughnan, "The 'Strange' Case of the Infanticide Doctrine" (2012) 32 O.J.L.S. 685–711.

[361] D. Maier-Katkin and R. Ogle, "A Rationale for Infanticide Laws" [1993] Crim. L.R. 903 at 906–909.

[362] D.J. West in *Murder followed by Suicide* (Cambridge: Harvard University Press, 1955) found no significant connection between women who killed their children and this period of time. In a survey of cases of infanticide it was found that psychiatric experts made no reference in their reports to the effects of lactation and often had to be prompted to refer to the effects of childbirth: R. Mackay, "The Consequences of Killing Very Young Children" [1993] Crim. L.R. 21 at 29.

operation of the Act is illustrated by the fact that an exactly similar type of case where the victim happened to be over the age of 12 months can no longer be dealt with as infanticide."

This illogicality is reinforced by the lack of any mitigating provision to protect the woman who does not succeed in killing her child. She may be charged with attempted murder or wounding with intent. The Criminal Law Revision Committee has stated that the particular drafting of s.1 of the Infanticide Act 1938 makes the charging of *attempted infanticide* impossible.[363] Despite this, in the case of *Smith*,[364] the trial judge accepted a plea of guilty to attempted infanticide. Whilst the means by which this was done are suspect, the result is admirable. Such a woman in these circumstances is trying to commit infanticide and the law should recognise this. Further, if found guilty of attempted murder she may be sentenced to imprisonment.[365] The woman who is convicted of infanticide[366] (which, like attempted murder and wounding with intent, carries a maximum sentence of life imprisonment) is almost never sent to prison—and presumably this would also be true of attempted infanticide. The sentence is almost always one of probation.[367] In more serious cases of imbalance the woman may be made subject to a hospital order and committed to her local hospital.

The Draft Criminal Code recognised the present anomaly: attempted infanticide would become the appropriate charge where a woman in such circumstances fails to kill her child.[368]

If the current use of the defence rests much more on the effects of child-rearing than on childbirth, then is it not illogical that the defence is open to mothers only? Clearly, fathers may be subject to similar pressures. As the law stands such defendants will have to plead diminished responsibility.[369] Mackay's research leads him to conclude that "as far as females were concerned, these were viewed as tragic cases which the prosecution was prepared to deal with leniently, while the males, although avoiding murder convictions, were considered much more culpable".[370] Such defendants are very likely to be sentenced to prison.[371] However, Mackay's more recent research indicates that where women are successful in pleading infanticide, the basis of the conviction is one which is linked to her recent experience of childbirth rather than the effects of child-rearing. Of 49 women convicted of infanticide between 1990 and 2003, 15 killed their child within 24 hours of childbirth and 11 killed between one day and one month following childbirth.[372] In 14 of the cases the primary diagnosis was one of postnatal depression.[373] This information provides some support for retention of the defence as one available only to biological mothers of young babies.

---

[363] 14th Report, *Offences against the Person*, Cmnd.7844 (1980), para.113.

[364] *R. v Smith (KA)* [1983] Crim. L.R. 739.

[365] See N. Walker, *Crime and Insanity in England* (Edinburgh: Edinburgh University Press, 1968).

[366] In the past five years (to 2012/13) there have only been four convictions for infanticide: one each in 2008/09 and 2011/12; two in 2010/11 and none in 2009/10 or 2012/13: ONS, *Focus on: Violent Crime and Sexual Offences, 2012/13* (2014), table 11.

[367] Mackay found that of the 49 women convicted of infanticide between 1990 and 2003, 20 were sentenced to probation with treatment and 19 to a probation order alone. Only three were sentenced to imprisonment of terms ranging from three to five years: R. Mackay, Appendix D to Law Commission Paper No.304 (2006), table 9. See also A. Wilczynski and A. Morris, "Parents Who Kill Children" [1993] Crim. L.R. 31 at 35; Wilczynski, "Images of Women Who Kill Their Infants: The Mad and the Bad" (1991) 2 *Women and Criminal Justice* 71.

[368] Law Commission Paper No.177 (1989), cl.6(2).

[369] Although fathers might have been able to plead provocation as in the case of *Doughty* (1986) 83 Cr. App. R. 319, the new defence of loss of control will not be available to fathers in the same way.

[370] R. Mackay, *Mental Defence Conditions in the Criminal Law* (1995), p.211.

[371] Mackay, *Mental Defence Conditions in the Criminal Law* (1995), p.30. However, the position may be somewhat complicated by the fact that the male defendants in the survey tended to have previous convictions whilst female defendants did not.

[372] R. Mackay, Appendix D to Law Commission Paper No.304 (2006), table 3b.

[373] Mackay, Appendix D to Law Commission Paper No.304 (2006), table 12b.

2. Is infanticide redundant?

In the following case the defendant's conviction for murder of her three-month-old baby was upheld. The appellant had not sought to rely upon the defence of infanticide, as her defence had been that the baby had died of natural causes, but the Court of Appeal took the opportunity to express dissatisfaction with the current law.

R. v Kai-Whitewind [2005] 2 Cr. App. R. 31

JUDGE LJ

"133 . . . The appellant was a woman of good character with two children. She had apparently given them natural maternal love and affection before she gave birth to Bidziil. He was conceived in the course of an alleged rape. She resisted suggestions that her pregnancy should be terminated. Immediately after the birth she underwent some unspecified level of depression, but was anxious about the possible implications of taking anti-depressants on the baby's feeding. Within a very short period, for understandable reasons arising from an injury to Bidziil for which the appellant herself was not responsible, after a period in hospital, he was cared for by her mother, and not by her. All this inevitably weakened the natural bonding process. When the baby returned home, the appellant was unable to breast feed the baby successfully, something to which she attached great importance. She seems to have believed that as a result of the difficulties, they were not bonding properly. It was in those circumstances that the baby was killed, less than three months after the appellant had given birth to him. Following conviction, the inevitable mandatory sentence of life imprisonment was imposed on her . . .

139 The issues raised in these cases are delicate and sensitive. In October 2004 the Home Office announced a comprehensive review of the law of murder . . . We shall highlight two particular areas of concern. The first is whether, as a matter of substantive law, infanticide should extend to circumstances subsequent to the birth, but connected with it, such as the stresses imposed on a mother by the absence of natural bonding with her baby: in short, whether the current definition of infanticide reflects modern thinking. The second problem arises when the mother who has in fact killed her infant is unable to admit it. This may be because she is too unwell to do so, or too emotionally disturbed by what she has in fact done, or too deeply troubled by the consequences of an admission of guilt on her ability to care for any surviving children. When this happens, it is sometimes difficult to produce psychiatric evidence relating to the balance of the mother's mind. Yet, of itself, it does not automatically follow from denial that the balance of her mind was not disturbed: in some cases it may indeed help to confirm that it was.

140 The law relating to infanticide is unsatisfactory and outdated. The appeal in this sad case demonstrates the need for a thorough re-examination."

Law reform bodies have long been concerned about the ambit of infanticide. Given the disputed medical basis of the statute and the illogical limitations it imposes, the Butler Committee on Mentally Abnormal Offenders[374] decided that infanticide could be subsumed in the partial defence of diminished responsibility. Not only would the limitations to 12 months and to the mother be abolished, but it concluded that there would be little difficulty in establishing the necessary medical evidence for a finding of diminished responsibility. However, the Criminal Law Revision Committee was opposed to any such reform, on the basis that: (i) it was not satisfied that diminished responsibility could cover all cases of infanticide;[375] and (ii) infanticide should remain a separate offence with a maximum penalty of no more than five years' imprisonment.[376]

The first of these reasons is supported by Mackay's survey of infanticide cases. Whilst there were a few cases where either s.1 of the Infanticide Act or s.2 of the Homicide Act could have been employed,

---

374 Cmnd.6244, paras 19.22, 19.26.
375 Criminal Law Revision Committee, 14th Report, *Offences against the Person*, Cmnd.7844 (1980), para.102.
376 Criminal Law Revision Committee, 14th Report, *Offences against the Person*, Cmnd.7844 (1980), para.104.

there were many where the psychiatric evidence could not support a finding of diminished responsibility. Mackay continues:

> "the overall impression gained from an examination of the psychiatric reports which were used in support of infanticide leaves little room to doubt that the criteria within the 1938 Act were being used primarily as a legal device for avoiding the mandatory penalty and thus ensure that leniency could be shown in appropriate cases."[377]

It can be argued, of course, that if the 1938 Act provisions were not there experts would stretch the evidence to fit the test of diminished responsibility. This would still be a gamble, however, and might result in some cases which are currently dealt with as infanticide being dealt with as murder.[378]

In its Consultation Paper on homicide the Law Commission put forward three options for reform: minimal, moderate and radical. The minimal option involved discarding reference to "the effect of lactation" and extending the age limit of the victim to two years, a proposal supported by evidence heard by the Victorian Law Reform Commission that most infanticide cases occur within two years of birth.[379] The moderate option went further by also including disturbance of the mind arising from circumstances consequent upon birth, as well as the effects of birth, and by requiring a causal link between the disturbance of the mother's mind and the killing.[380] The radical option for reform involved abandoning the age limit of the child victim and extending the offence/defence to persons in a caring relationship with the child at the time of the killing other than the biological mother.[381] This last option begs the question: why could such killers not be dealt with satisfactorily using the defence of diminished responsibility?

The Law Commission's provisional proposal was the adoption of the minimal option for reform. However, following a full consultation exercise it came to the decision, informed by responses and research from specialists in the field, that infanticide should be retained without amendment, and would apply as a defence to both first and second degree murder.[382] This recommendation was based on medical evidence that the incidence of certain psychiatric disorders is higher following childbirth.[383] In addition, some evidence, albeit inconclusive, was submitted that there is a connection between lactation and psychosis.[384] It is notable, however, that not all experts were in favour of maintaining the separate offence/defence, and some, including the Royal College of Psychiatrists, thought that it ought to be merged with diminished responsibility.[385]

This recommendation that the substantive law remain unchanged was adopted by the Government, who agreed that the law works satisfactorily in practice.[386] What of the problems raised in the case of *Kai-Whitewind*? The Law Commission recommended, in attempting to address the Court of Appeal's

---

[377] Above, fn.362 at 29. See also, R. Mackay, above, fn.370, p.210.

[378] An alternative possibility is that abolition would bring about an increase in the number of cases in which it is decided not to bring prosecutions. This is already relatively common, for example, where the defendant is very young and the offence is an attempt to conceal the pregnancy and birth: R. Mackay, above, fn.362 at 30. See also A. Wilczynski and A. Morris, above, fn.367.

[379] Law Commission Consultation Paper No.177 (2005), para.9.17.

[380] Law Commission Consultation Paper No.177 (2005), para.9.18.

[381] Law Commission Consultation Paper No.177 (2005), para.9.19.

[382] Law Commission Paper No.304 (2006), para.8.23.

[383] Law Commission Paper No.304 (2006), para.8.25.

[384] Law Commission Paper No.304 (2006), para.8.26.

[385] Law Commission Paper No.304 (2006), para.8.35.

[386] Ministry of Justice CP 19/08, para.120.

concern in that case, that a new procedure should be introduced in potential infanticide cases. This would allow the trial judge in the case of a woman convicted of murder of her child of the relevant age to order a thorough medical examination of the defendant in order that an appeal might be granted if evidence supporting a charge of infanticide is found.[387] Wells concludes that rather than substantive or procedural reform being capable of meeting such concerns, "[o]ne . . . comes back to the notion of improving the quality and understanding of forensic evidence as the core, unfulfilled task for the legal system".[388] These calls have gone unheeded. Loughnan suggests the following explanation:

"In the current era, in the absence of an expert medical consensus, the 'strange' doctrine of infanticide is sustained by a lay or non-expert knowledge about the interrelation of gender, childbirth and 'madness', which underpins legal evaluation of infanticidal women and their acts."[389]

VII. Causing or Allowing the Death of a Child or Vulnerable Adult

In considering the options for reform available in relation to the law on infanticide, the Law Commission noted that "a comprehensive review of infanticide cannot be considered without looking at recent legislative changes on domestic violence".[390] It was referring to the new offence created by the Domestic Violence, Crime and Victims Act 2004.

Domestic Violence, Crime and Victims Act 2004 s.5

"(1) A person ('D') is guilty of an offence if—

(a) a child or vulnerable adult ('V') diess as a result of the unlawful act of a person who—

   (i) was a member of the same household as V, and

   (ii) had frequent contact with him,

(b) D was such a person at the time of that act,

(c) at that time there was a significant risk of serious physical harm being caused to V by the unlawful act of such a person, and

(d) either D was the person whose act caused V's death or—

   (i) D was, or ought to have been, aware of the risk mentioned in paragraph (c),

   (ii) D failed to take such steps as he could reasonably have been expected to take to protect V from the risk, and

   (iii) the act occurred in circumstances of the kind that D foresaw or ought to have foreseen . . .

(7) A person guilty of an offence under this section is liable on conviction on indictment to imprisonment for a term not exceeding 14 years or to a fine, or to both."

Why was such an offence deemed to be necessary and why would a charge of manslaughter not accommodate such behaviour?

---

[387] Law Commission Paper No.304 (2006), para.8.46. This provisional proposal is adopted by the Law Commission as a formal recommendation at para.8.58.

[388] Commentary to *Kai-Whitewind* [2006] Crim. L.R. 348 at 351.

[389] A. Loughnan, "The 'Strange' Case of the Infanticide Doctrine" (2012) 32 O.J.L.S. 685–711 at 689.

[390] Law Commission Consultation Paper No.177 (2005), para.9.68.

Law Commission No.282, Children: Their Non-Accidental Death or Serious Injury (Criminal Trials) (2003), paras 1.1–1.2:

"1.1 . . . The recommendations in this Report are intended to address a problem which has been recognised for many years . . . It can be exemplified at its most intractable in the following situation: A child is cared for by two people (both parents, or a parent and another person). The child dies and medical evidence suggests that the death occurred as a result of ill-treatment. It is not clear which of the two carers is directly responsible for the ill-treatment which caused death. It is clear that at least one of the carers is guilty of a very serious criminal offence but it is possible that the ill-treatment occurred while one carer was asleep, or out of the room.

1.2 As the law stands, as a result of the Court of Appeal's ruling in *Lane and Lane* it is likely that a trial in such a case would not proceed beyond a defence submission of 'no case to answer'. As a result, neither parent can be convicted, and one or other parent, or both, might well have literally 'got away with murder'. It should be remembered that even though one parent may not have struck the fatal blow or blows, he or she may be culpable, as an accessory, either through having participated in the killing actively or by failing to protect the child. In many cases of this type it is difficult, or impossible, to prove even this beyond reasonable doubt and therefore neither parent can be convicted."

The new offence provides that any parent or carer has a duty not only to refrain from abusing the child, but to prevent anyone else within the household from doing so. However, this duty is not new; the offence of child neglect or cruelty under s.1 of the Children and Young Persons Act 1933 would apply in such a case, with a maximum penalty of 10 years' imprisonment. The question is, should someone who has failed to prevent the abuse of their child which has ended in that child's death be liable for a more serious offence because of their failure to prevent that death?

It should be remembered that, in *Lowe*,[391] it was held that an offence of child neglect, as an omission, cannot amount to the unlawful act on which a conviction for constructive manslaughter can be based. It might be possible, however, that a parent or carer could be liable under the species of gross negligence manslaughter. Whilst there have been reported cases of neglect of vulnerable family members resulting in manslaughter convictions,[392] such cases are rare. It is not entirely clear, however, why such cases are not prosecuted in this way, and why the new statutory offence will succeed where gross negligence manslaughter would fail. Parents will satisfy the requirement of owing a duty of care to their child, in accordance with *Adomako*.[393] The question is whether they breached that duty either by abusing the child themselves or by allowing someone else to do so. If this is established, the issue then becomes whether the breach caused the death of the child. This is where the difficulty arises in relation to manslaughter. If one parent omitted to prevent another parent harming their child, can that first parent be said to have caused the child's death? The statutory offence makes provision for an alternative of *allowing* the child's death to avoid this problem. As an alternative to the defendant causing death themselves, he may be liable under subs.(1)(d) on the basis that he knew of, or should have known of, the significant risk of serious physical harm and failed to take reasonable steps to protect the victim.

Are parents who fail to prevent abuse directed at their children sufficiently culpable to warrant punishment for an offence of homicide (particularly given that they will probably be suffering tremendously from the loss of that child)? The mens rea requirement can be said to amount to mere negligence.[394] The Court of Appeal has, however, been unhelpful in its interpretation of the mens rea requirement. In *Khan* it stated that in relation to the requirement that D either was, or ought to have been, aware of the risk of serious physical harm:

---

391 *Lowe* [1973] Q.B. 702. See above, p.710.
392 For example: *Stone and Dobinson* [1977] 1 Q.B. 354; *Barrass* [2012] 1 Cr. App. R. (S.) 80.
393 [1995] 1 A.C. 171.
394 J. Herring, "Mum's Not the Word: An Analysis of Section 5", in C.M.V. Clarkson and S. Cunningham (eds), *Criminal Liability for Non-Aggressive Death* (Aldershot: Ashgate, 2008), p.135.

"The objective therefore is to bring within the ambit of the offence, not only those who are actually aware of the risk and foresaw the unlawful act, but those who chose to close their eyes to a risk of which they ought to have been aware, and which they ought to have foreseen".[395]

As noted by Ormerod, however, this confuses willful blindness, where D has some awareness of the risk, with negligence, where D need not have any awareness provided that the reasonable person would.[396] This is misleading, given that s.5(1)(d)(i) does not require any awareness of the risk.

Much of the terminology used in s.5 is rather woolly. Herring identifies as many as 11 ambiguities within the definition of the offence.[397] The question of what amounts to a "significant risk" of serious physical harm was addressed by the Court of Appeal in *Stephens; Mujuru*.[398] Whilst it was clear to the court that the trial judge had set the bar too low by interpreting "significant risk" to mean "more than minimal", the court went no further in giving its own interpretation other than stating that it should be given its ordinary meaning by the jury. In *Khan* the Court of Appeal addressed a number of other issues of definition within s.5 in the context of the death of a vulnerable adult, rather than a child. First, in relation to the requirement that D was a member of the same household as V, it noted that this was a question of fact and that any adult living in the household was a member of it, but that visitors to the house, including carers, were not members of the household for the purposes of the provision. The judgment appears to have narrowed the offence somewhat in stating that even if D lived in the same house as V, s.5 would not apply unless D came into frequent contact with V.[399] Only if the jury was sure that a particular D had frequent contact with V should they go on to consider the question of mens rea in s.5(1)(d). Secondly, in relation to the requirement that the deceased's death occur in circumstances of the kind that D foresaw or ought to have foreseen, it was noted that this does not mean that the circumstances of which D ought to have been aware need be *identical* to those that occurred, only that they are of the same kind.[400]

In some cases of child abuse the parent is arguably just as blameworthy in standing by and watching her partner abuse the child as if she had abused the child herself. But what of the abused woman who is too afraid to intervene when her husband is chastising their child for fear that he could turn on her and do worse? Some may argue that a mother should sacrifice herself for her child, but it is difficult to see that if she fails to do so she should be charged with having caused or allowed the child's death. In the first case resulting in conviction for the new offence, the facts were such that the case seems to fall outside the offence's concern. A young mother was convicted of the offence after she left her baby with her partner, who had previously injured the baby.[401] He was convicted of murder. This was not, then, a case in which it was impossible to prove which partner was the killer. The mother was convicted of allowing her baby's death, in addition to the offence of child cruelty. It is uncertain that she warranted the former conviction, particularly given the judge's description of her as "a decent young woman who was in a vulnerable position". She received a two-year community punishment order.

Whilst the new offence will catch within its remit some who are victims of abuse themselves it may well overcome the practical problems and evidential obstacles involved in prosecuting those who systematically abuse their children and refuse to give evidence against each other at trial. The main driving force behind the reform seems to have been the shocking statistics that three

---

[395]   *R. v Khan (Uzma)* [2009] 1 Cr. App. R. 28 at [32].
[396]   Commentary to *Khan* [2009] Crim. L.R. 348 at 352.
[397]   J. Herring, above fn.394, pp.129–137.
[398]   *R. v Stephens (Jerry)* [2007] 2 Cr. App. R. 26.
[399]   Above fn.395 at [28].
[400]   Above fn.395 at [39].
[401]   "Mother is First to be Found Guilty of Family Homicide", *The Times*, May 6, 2006, p.31.

children under the age of 10 suffer death or serious injury every week in England and Wales, and that only a small proportion of these result in a conviction for murder, manslaughter or one of the more serious non-fatal offences.[402] The kind of case for which the offence was designed is the now infamous case of Baby P, or Peter as his name was later revealed to be, in which a toddler died after 10 months of abuse and was the victim of broken ribs and a broken spinal cord.[403] Three adults were convicted of causing or allowing his death under s.5: his mother, her boyfriend and her boyfriend's brother, Jason Owen. In Jason Owen's appeal against sentence Hughes LJ noted that after the nine-week trial

> "It was impossible at the end for the jury to resolve the question of who had inflicted those injuries which had been maliciously done, as some of them clearly must have been. No defendant as a result was convicted of either murder or manslaughter."[404]

Jason Owen had had his charge of murder withdrawn from the jury by the judge when the evidence showed that it was either Peter's mother or her boyfriend who had inflicted the violence upon him.

Although there will no doubt continue to be cases where a mother is either complicit in violence towards her child, or even where she is herself guilty of inflicting violence on him, such cases are likely to be rare. Herring argues that the problem with s.5 is that it deflects attention away from the main problems faced by society in such cases and makes criminals out of mothers who are themselves victims of domestic violence.

Jonathon Herring, "Mum's Not the Word: An Analysis of Section 5", in C.M.V. Clarkson and S. Cunningham (eds), Criminal Liability for Non-Aggressive Death (2008), pp.152–153:

"The motivation behind this offence is undoubtedly good. It is designed to protect children's rights. However, the offence must be viewed in the context within which it operates. Evidence from other jurisdictions indicates that it is primarily used against women who fail to protect their children from their violent male partners. [I have] argued that its use in such cases is highly problematic. It tends to lead to prosecution of women who are themselves the victims of domestic violence. It assumes escape routes from the violence which are either not there or are not reasonable to expect the woman to take. Further, the offences are often based on a glamorised view of motherhood which regards the mother in an idealistic way as an all-knowing all-sacrificing protector. The prosecution of women who fail to live up to this image can lead to the focus of legal and public attention not being on the abuser but on the mother who 'left her children to die'. The offence also disguises the state's responsibility for abused and endangered children. The offence was promoted as the way of protecting children from abuse and violence. The way to do that is not section 5, but an effective and thorough raft of measures to protect women and children from violence. For the state to prosecute a mother who has been seeking to protect her children and herself from a violent man when the state has done so little to protect them cannot be justified. The time and effort in prosecuting abused women who fail to protect their children would be better spent on ensuring there was effective and adequate protection of women and children from violence."

Few cases have been prosecuted since the offence came into force, although there appears to have been a sudden upsurge in the most recent statistics. There were between three and eight cases

---

[402] Law Commission Paper No.282 *Children: Their Non-Accidental Death or Serious Injury (Criminal Trials)* (2003), para.2.29, citing Judge Isobel Plumstead, Papers for the NSPCC, "Which of you did it?" Conference in Cambridge, November 2, 2002.
[403] See S. Laville, "Baby P Case: The final chapter in a story of appalling cruelty and deprivation", *The Guardian*, May 22, 2009.
[404] *R. v Owen (Jason)* [2009] EWCA Crim 2259.

prosecuted per year from 2005/06 to 2011/12; but 16 cases were prosecuted in the 12-month period up to September 2013.[405] It should be noted that the offence also applies to the death of vulnerable adults, as well as children. The death of a vulnerable adult may involve an equal or even higher level of blameworthiness than in cases where a child has been killed, as indicated by the severe sentence passed in the first reported case of allowing the death of a vulnerable adult. In *Liu; Tan*[406] T was convicted of allowing his wife's death, whilst his mistress, L, was convicted of manslaughter and inflicting grievous bodily harm with intent. T's wife had the mental age of a 12-year-old and had been kept as a slave by T and L. She had frequently been beaten by L and died from hypothermia after being left outside in the back yard overnight. T's sentence of six years' imprisonment was upheld by the Court of Appeal, as was L's sentence of nine years' imprisonment for manslaughter. In the case of *Khan*[407] the question of what constitutes vulnerability in an adult for the purposes of s.5 was addressed. In that case the victim had no disability or illness, but was isolated in the family home, speaking no English and not having any local friends. The Court of Appeal applied a broad interpretation of "vulnerability", suggesting that it might include temporary vulnerability and stating that it could arise from the deceased's dependence on others. Ormerod notes that this raises problems relating to the mens rea of the offence, since D might be under a duty to protect V even though D does not know that V is in fact a vulnerable adult.[408] Arguably the offence, whilst being based on laudable aims, is just too broad.

Cases involving vulnerable adults might also risk criminalising those who are the victim of domestic violence in the same way that Herring fears cases involving children may do. Women such as the defendants in *Khan* who live within the same household as the deceased might themselves be victims of domestic violence and find themselves under threat if they try to intervene to protect the deceased. The Court of Appeal in *Khan* sought to allay such fears by noting that whether the defendant has taken reasonable steps to protect the deceased under s.5(1)(d)(ii) will depend on the defendant's own personal position. It was suggested that if one of the defendants themselves had been experiencing violence at the hands of her brother (the husband of the deceased), she would not be expected to protect the deceased.[409] It is not clear, however, whether this addresses Herring's concerns in relation to mothers who fail to intervene to protect their own children, and are faced with a criminal conviction in addition to the loss of their child. Ashworth is of the opinion that there was a good reason for creating some such offence as that under s.5, but that the offence as drafted is much wider than necessary to cover such cases, and raises questions about how many people at which it might be aimed are unaware of its existence.[410] The offence, however, does have its supporters, such as Morrison, who argues that "[t]he current framework is the fairest and most appropriate way of determining the liability of defendants who have been victims of domestic violence",[411] since she interprets *Khan* as applying a test of "qualified objective" reasonableness, meaning that D's abuse can be taken into account when judging whether she did what could have been reasonably expected of her.

---

[405] ONS, *Crime in England and Wales, year ending September 2013* (2014), Appendix table A4.
[406] *R. v Su Hua Liu* [2007] 2 Cr. App. R. (S.) 12.
[407] *Khan* [2009] 1 Cr. App. R. 28.
[408] Commentary to *Khan* [2009] Crim. L.R. 348 at 351.
[409] At [33].
[410] A. Ashworth, "Ignorance of the Criminal Law, and Duties to Avoid it" (2011) 74(1) M.L.R. 1 at 18.
[411] S. Morrison, "Should there be a Domestic Violence Defence to the Offence of Familial Homicide?" [2013] Crim. L.R. 826–838 at 838.

VIII. Vehicular Homicide

There are five statutory offences of vehicular homicide in English law: causing death by dangerous driving; causing death by careless driving; causing death by careless driving while under the influence of drink or drugs; causing death by unlicensed, disqualified or uninsured driving; and causing death by aggravated vehicle-taking. In *Government of USA v Jennings*,[412] it was held that that "motor manslaughter" had not been impliedly repealed by the Road Traffic Act 1956 and that causing death by reckless driving (the predecessor of causing death by dangerous driving) co-existed alongside the common law offence. In cases where persons are killed by motor vehicles the prosecution has a choice. It can either charge the defendant with one of these statutory offences, it can charge with manslaughter, or it can, in theory at least, charge both.[413] Following *Adomako*, although, strictly speaking, Lord Mackay's discussion of vehicular homicide was obiter, it is now clear that whatever the method of killing, the test of gross negligence is to be applied if a manslaughter charge is brought. The jury, having regard to the risk of death involved, should consider whether the conduct of the defendant was so bad in all the circumstances as to amount to a criminal act or omission. Lord Mackay acknowledged that, as a consequence of this, cases of involuntary motor manslaughter will become rare. There have been several reported sentencing cases since *Adomako* in which drivers have been convicted of gross negligence manslaughter,[414] although the official statistics would suggest that charges for motor manslaughter reached a peak in 2004/05 and have reduced again more recently.[415] It is, of course, also possible for a driver to be convicted of manslaughter on the basis of an unlawful and dangerous act if she uses her car as a weapon of assault (by driving directly at the victim in order to cause fear) and in doing so kills.[416] Guidance issued by the CPS makes it clear that manslaughter will be the appropriate charge in cases where a motor vehicle has been used as an instrument of attack, but also recognises that there may be some cases in which manslaughter ought to be charged based on gross negligence.

---

[412] *Government of USA v Jennings* [1983] 1 A.C. 624.

[413] The statutory causing death by driving offences are now lesser included offences of manslaughter in cases involving mechanically propelled vehicles, by virtue of the Road Traffic Offenders Act 1988 s.24, amended by the Road Safety Act 2006. In 1996, charging standards were introduced, agreed by the police and CPS, in an attempt to improve consistency in charging practices across the country and reduce the number of occasions in which charges are subsequently amended. This guidance has been reviewed following the enactment of the Road Safety Act 2006 and again in 2013: http://www.cps. gov.uk/legal/p_to_r/road_traffic_offences_guidance_on_prosecuting_cases_of_bad_driving/ [Accessed April 2014].

[414] See, for example, *AG's Reference (No.14 of 2001) (Michael John Emm)* [2002] 1 Cr. App. R.(S.) 25; *AG's Reference (No.134 of 2004) (Roberts)* [2005] Crim. L.R. 321; *Ballard* [2005] Crim. L.R. 323; *Attorney General's Reverence (No.111 of 2006)* [2007] 2 Cr. App. R. (S.) 26; *Bissell* [2008] 1 Cr. App. R.(S.) 79. The cases of *Rule* [2003] 1 Cr. App. R.(S.) 47, *Parfitt* [2005] 1 Cr. App. R.(S.) 50, *Dwyer* [2005] Crim. L.R. 320 and *Bennett* [2008] 1 Cr. App. R.(S.) 11. All involved defendant drivers who pleaded guilty to manslaughter but it is not clear from the reports whether the basis of the plea was gross negligence manslaughter or constructive manslaughter (see below). It is also possible that a defendant might be guilty of the rare species of reckless manslaughter when he kills with a car. See *Hussain* [2012] 2 Cr. App. R. (S.) 75 where D was convicted of manslaughter where the Crown's case was one of reckless manslaughter. A young child had run out into the road from between parked cars. D, having struck the child, stopped momentarily but then continued to drive so that V was trapped under his wheels and was killed. The Crown's case was that D knew that it was a child who was under the car rather than some other object, that he foresaw the risk of serious injury or death by continuing to drive and yet chose to take that risk and death resulted (at [25]).

[415] In 2004/05 there were 22 cases of homicide (murder or manslaughter) where the method of killing was with a motor vehicle. There was some fluctuation in the number of cases per year, with the most recent figures being 18 in 2009/10 and 8 in 2010/11: K. Smith et al., *Homicides, Firearms Offences and Intimate Violence 2010/11*, Home Office Statistical Bulletin 02/12, table 1.03. Unfortunately the Office of National Statistics no longer publishes separate statistics on homicides where the method of killing is a motor vehicle, with such homicides now recorded as "other" method (along with burning, drowning, explosion, poison etc.).

[416] See, for example: *Ripley* [1997] 1 Cr. App. R.(S.) 19; *AG's Reference (No.62 of 2001) (David Little)* [2002] 1 Cr. App. R.(S.) 94; *Wright* [2004] 1 Cr. App. R.(S.) 4; *Franks* [2004] EWCA Crim 1241; *Clarke* [2006] 1 Cr. App. R.(S.) 132; *Dudley* [2006] 2 Cr. App. R.(S.) 77; *Abu Kwaik* [2013] EWCA Crim 2397. Constructive manslaughter has also been successful in a case of driving causing death where the unlawful act on which the charge was based was burglary: *Bristow* [2013] EWCA Crim 1540.

Crown Prosecution Service, Policy for Prosecuting Cases of Bad Driving (2007):

"5.12 Some sections of the public consider that we should often charge gross negligence manslaughter instead of causing death by dangerous driving.

5.13 There are two arguments put forward to support this view:

- first, that the public is now increasingly less tolerant of bad driving and convictions for gross negligence manslaughter may be more likely;

- secondly, because manslaughter carries a higher maximum penalty, it better reflects the gravity of the offence.

5.14 However, the position is not straightforward. Prosecutors may have one or more statutory offences available to them (causing death by dangerous driving and causing death by careless driving whilst unfit through drink or drugs) in cases where there has been a fatal collision caused by bad driving. Before a charge of gross negligence manslaughter will be preferred, there must be something to set the case apart from one where one of the statutory offences can be proved.

5.15 As a matter of law, it is more difficult to prove an offence of gross negligence manslaughter than it is to prove an offence of causing death by dangerous driving. It is not necessary to have evidence of an obvious and serious risk of death to prove an offence of causing death by dangerous driving. All that is required is evidence that the driving was dangerous and that the driving caused the death of another person.

5.16 Whilst it is correct that the offence of manslaughter carries the possibility of a more severe sentence than an offence of causing death by dangerous driving, the courts have, over the years, generally passed sentences well within—sometimes significantly below—the maximum sentence available for causing death by dangerous driving.

5.17 We will, therefore, only charge gross negligence manslaughter in cases where there is evidence to show a very high risk of death, making the case one of the utmost gravity.

5.18 Under the provisions of Section 33 of the Road Safety Act 2006, juries are now able to return alternative verdicts for offences of causing death by dangerous driving, dangerous driving, causing death by careless driving when under the influence of drink or drugs and furious driving where they are not satisfied that the prosecution has made out its case for manslaughter. This has not previously been the case.

5.19 This alternative verdict provision provides something of a safety net for the prosecution, but there must still be sufficient evidence for a realistic prospect of conviction of manslaughter and it must still be the most appropriate charge, before a decision to charge manslaughter will be made.

5.20 In most cases where a death occurs as a result of dangerous driving, the statutory offence of causing death by dangerous driving will remain the correct charge."

This discussion of the appropriateness of charging manslaughter has been omitted from the latest version of the guidance, updated in 2013. Instead, that guidance notes merely that, in relation to gross negligence manslaughter:

"Gross negligence manslaughter should not be charged unless there is something to set the case apart from those cases where a statutory offence such as causing death by dangerous driving or causing death by careless driving could be proved. This will normally be evidence to show a very high risk of death, making the case one of the utmost gravity. This is in contrast to the statutory offences where all that is required is evidence that the driving was dangerous and that the manner of driving caused the death of another person."[417]

---

[417] http://www.cps.gov.uk/legal/p_to_r/road_traffic_offences_guidance_on_prosecuting_cases_of_bad_driving/ [Accessed April 2014].

A. Causing Death by Dangerous Driving

1. Introduction

Section 1 of the Road Traffic Act 1988, as amended by the Road Traffic Act 1991, provides as follows:

"A person who causes the death of another person by driving a mechanically propelled vehicle dangerously on a road or other public place is guilty of an offence."

The offence is triable only on indictment and is punishable by a maximum penalty of 14 years' imprisonment.[418]

Before 1977, the offence covered causing death by reckless or dangerous driving. In 1977, it was narrowed to causing death by reckless driving.[419] The *Lawrence* test of recklessness, as qualified in *Reid*, applied. In 1991 this was abolished and replaced by the new offence of causing death by dangerous driving. Why did this occur?

Department of Transport and Home Office, Road Traffic Law Review Report (The North Report) (1988), para.5.8:

"5.8 . . . There is a general . . . view that . . . the test in *Lawrence* is too subjective. It is said that the more subjective the test, and the further removed from an objective assessment of the standard of driving, the harder it is to provide cogent evidence of the commission of the offence and that this deters the bringing of prosecutions for reckless driving in serious instances of bad driving . . .

There is criticism that the test in *Lawrence* allows a defendant to exculpate himself by admitting that, in retrospect, his driving created an obvious risk but by showing also that he did at the time apply his mind to the question of the existence of the risk and (foolishly perhaps) concluded that there was none . . .

The *Lawrence* test can also be interpreted as being too wide in scope . . . [as including cases] when the behaviour involved was no more than mere thoughtless incompetence."

2. Rationale of law

Why is it necessary to have a special offence? Why are such persons not simply charged with manslaughter? Is it less blameworthy to kill another with a motor vehicle than with some other instrument?

Sir Brian MacKenna, "Causing Death by Reckless or Dangerous Driving: a Suggestion" [1970] Crim. L.R. 67:

"By 1955–56 it was clear to all that prosecutions for motor manslaughter were a failure: juries just would not convict. Different reasons were assigned for their perversity . . . 'The very word "manslaughter" is ugly and is associated in the minds of most people with brawls and sordid offences of various kinds. A jury is therefore reluctant to convict of this offence a person who is obviously very decent, and about whom the jury may think "there but for the grace of God, go I"' (Mr. Molson, *Hansard*, H.C. Vol. 534, Cols. 782–783). For those who favoured this diagnosis the remedy seemed obvious: a new offence of causing death by reckless driving . . . punishable by a maximum of five years' imprisonment."

---

[418]   The penalty was raised from 10 years' imprisonment by the Criminal Justice Act 2003 s.285(3). The Criminal Justice Act 1993 had already increased the maximum penalty from five to 10 years.

[419]   Criminal Law Act 1977 s.50(1).

Sally Lloyd-Bostock, "The Ordinary Man, and the Psychology of Attributing Causes and Responsibility" (1979) 42 M.L.R. 143 at 156–157:

"[It has been pointed out] that the more relevant a particular type of accident becomes to the perceiver, the more he is forced to find ways of avoiding acknowledging that he could be blamed for, as distinct from just injured in, such an accident. He may therefore be expected to attribute less blame in accidents which are situationally relevant to himself. For example, a motorist may be more lenient in his judgment about someone involved in a road accident. As well as situational relevance, a misfortune may be personally relevant, *i.e.* the actor or victim may be similar to the perceiver. Similarity to oneself has often been found to relate to empathy and liking and to a tendency to judge another's actions more leniently . . . [Another possibility is that where] the judger can identify with an actor and his act, he is more likely to perceive the situation as if he were himself the actor and hence assign less personal responsibility."

This attitude to drivers who kill appears to be changing. Road safety charities and victims' groups such as Brake and RoadPeace have been calling for drivers to be charged with manslaughter and have the support of some national newspapers. The argument is that whilst the number of road deaths has been declining in recent years,[420] it still remains unacceptable, and cases need to be treated more seriously, with penalties reflecting the fact that death has been caused. In 2004 there were 3,221 persons killed on the roads[421] yet in that year only 405 people were charged with causing death by dangerous driving.[422] This led some to argue that prosecutors were not proceeding with charges of causing death by dangerous driving in as many cases as they should, because they were undercharging or accepting a plea to careless driving in place of a charge of causing death by dangerous driving that should have been proceeded with.[423] Despite such claims, there is little evidence supporting the view that cases which should be charged as causing death by dangerous driving slip through the net.[424] Others have, in the past at least, argued that the special offence is in fact not needed: prosecutions should simply be brought under s.2 of the Road Traffic Act 1988 for dangerous driving, punishable by a maximum of two years' imprisonment. Manslaughter could be charged in the very worst cases.

Criminal Law Revision Committee, 14th Report, Offences against the Person, Cmnd.7844 (1980), para.142:

"We consider that the fact that death occurs in motoring cases should not enable a graver charge than reckless driving to be preferred unless the facts are that the full mental element appropriate to manslaughter can be proved. The real mischief where that mental element cannot be proved is the very bad driving, and the fact that it causes death should be treated as no more than an aggravating factor of that road traffic offence for sentencing purposes in appropriate cases."

This is the simple view that it is the bad driving that is reprehensible and the defendant should be blamed for that. The fact that death has been caused is "chance" and should be irrelevant in terms of

---

[420] 1,754 people were killed on the roads in 2012, a reduction of 38 % compared with the average over the years 2005–09: Department for Transport, *Reported Road Casualties Great Britain: 2012* (2013), table RAS30059.
[421] Department for Transport, *Transport Statistics Great Britain* (2009), table 8.1.
[422] *Offences relating to motor vehicles, England and Wales 2004* (Supplementary Tables) (2006), table 7.
[423] Home Office, *Review of Road Traffic Offences Involving Bad Driving: A Consultation Paper* (2005), para 2.1.
[424] S. Cunningham, "The Unique Nature of Prosecutions in Cases of Fatal Road Traffic Collisions" [2005] Crim. L.R. 834. Further research conducted since the new offence of causing death by careless driving was introduced again suggests that this is still the case and causing death by dangerous driving is generally charged where appropriate: S. Kyd Cunningham, "Has Law Reform Policy Been Driven in the Right Direction? How the New Causing Death By Driving Offences are Operating in Practice" [2013] Crim. L.R. 711–728.

substantive criminal liability.[425] This approach was not adopted by the North Report nor accepted by the Government.

Department of Transport and Home Office, Road Traffic Law Review Report (The North Report) (1988), paras 6.5–6.9, 6.23–6.27:

"6.5 . . . The detailed arguments for abolishing the offence [causing death by reckless driving] (excluding the argument that all such cases should be charged as manslaughter) included the following:

there is a danger that the existence of the offence would be seen as downgrading cases where there is *no* death or injury;

it is improper to create greater liability based on consequences which may to a degree be fortuitous, resulting for example from the non-availability at the time of medical help or the presence of a pedestrian who happens to be struck;

although the offence is not unique in the fact that its seriousness depends on the results of unintended conduct (the whole of involuntary manslaughter being so based), it is desirable to limit the number of such instances;

why should the road user continue to be singled out as the only kind of person whose act causing death constitutes a separate offence?

it is wrong, in England and Wales, to have a complete overlap with the offence of manslaughter;

the law takes no account of injury short of death as a constituent element of an offence;

the maximum sentence of two years' imprisonment for reckless driving is adequate in the vast majority of reckless driving cases involving death; and if the case is very bad, then manslaughter or culpable homicide should be charged.

6.6 The arguments in favour of retaining a causing death offence concentrated more on practicality and on public expectations of the law. They included the following:

it is generally accepted in the law that consequences can affect the nature of an offence, as may be illustrated by the different offences of murder and attempted murder, and murder where there is no intent to kill but where there is intent to cause grievous bodily harm which has resulted in death;

the public sense of justice requires that the very bad driver who has killed should be guilty of a more serious offence;

the seriousness of the offence (and penalty) is desirable in order to have a deterrent effect;

juries are reluctant to convict of manslaughter in most causing death cases. Death should be singled out for special treatment because it is the most serious consequence of a criminal act, and so doing would exemplify the concern of the law for the sanctity of life;

though logic might suggest that consequences should be irrelevant, public opinion is strongly in favour of the retention of such an offence;

the case for the retention of an offence of causing death by bad driving is strong if there is no longer a complete overlap with the offence of manslaughter or culpable homicide;

outside the motoring sphere, reckless acts may amount either to no offence at all or, if death happens to result, to manslaughter or culpable homicide; so consequences should be no less relevant in the road traffic context;

---

[425] Such an approach was adopted in *Krawec* [1985] 149 J.P. 709 but disapproved in *R. v Simmonds (Derek)* [1999] 2 Cr. App. R. (S.) 218. See further, C.M.V. Clarkson, *Understanding Criminal Law*, 4th edn (London: Sweet & Maxwell, 2005), pp.163–168.

> if someone drives so badly as to be reckless, the consequences are not 'fortuitous,' for the driver has created a real risk of death or injury;
>
> if there continues to be some overlap between causing death by reckless driving and manslaughter, it would be strange to be able to take consequences into account in the latter but not in the former . . .

6.9 Taking all these arguments into consideration, we have concluded that, on balance, an offence of causing death by very bad driving, however defined, should be retained. Two main factors have influenced our thinking. To abolish the offence in the absence of compelling reasons for doing so would mean that some cases of very bad driving were not dealt with with appropriate seriousness. Repeal of s.1 would be seen as a down-grading of bad driving as a criminal activity. This is not a message which we wish to convey. Secondly, though logic might pull us towards arguments in favour of abolition, neither English nor Scots law in fact relies entirely on intent as the basis for offences. There seems to be a strong public acceptance that, if the consequence of a culpable act is death, then this consequence should lead to a more serious charge being brought than if death had not been the result. We concur with this view. We recommend that a separate causing death offence be retained, but that it be reformulated in terms consistent with our recommended very bad driving offence.

6.27 We have considered carefully the merits of recommending the introduction of injury related offences, taking account of the disquiet expressed over conduct which maims but does not kill. We recognise that some very serious injuries are caused by bad drivers, and that these can in many respects be considered to be as bad as causing a death. We have, however, concluded that the arguments in favour of the injury offences . . . are not sufficiently compelling to outweigh the disadvantages of extending consequence linked offences to injuries as well as to death. The special emphasis which society places on the wrong created by causing a death justifies the retention of an offence from which death results, but we do not recommend the introduction of new offences based on the causing of injury."

As seen in Ch.7 above, a new offence of causing serious injury by dangerous driving was created by the Legal Aid, Sentencing and Punishment of Offenders Act 2012, carrying a maximum penalty of five years' imprisonment. It appears that society no longer places such a special emphasis on death, raising questions as to what further offences might be created to penalise the causing of injury through negligence.[426]

3. The law

Road Traffic Act 1988 (as amended by the Road Traffic Act 1991) s.2A

"2A. Meaning of dangerous driving.

(1) For the purposes of sections 1 and 2 above a person is to be regarded as driving dangerously if (and, subject to subsection (2) below, only if)—

(a)   the way he drives falls far below what would be expected of a competent and careful driver, and

(b)   it would be obvious to a competent and careful driver that driving in that way would be dangerous.

(2) A person is also to be regarded as driving dangerously for the purposes of sections 1 and 2 above if it would be obvious to a competent and careful driver that driving the vehicle in its current state would be dangerous.

(3) In subsections (1) and (2) above 'dangerous' refers to danger either of injury to any person or of serious damage to property; and in determining for the purposes of those subsections what would be expected of, or obvious to, a competent and careful driver in a particular case, regard shall be had not only to the circumstances of which he could be expected to be aware but also to any circumstances shown to have been within the knowledge of the accused.

(4) In determining for the purposes of subsection (2) above the state of a vehicle, regard may be had to anything attached to or carried on or in it and to the manner in which it is attached or carried."

---

[426]   S. Cunningham, "Taking 'Causing Serious Injury by Dangerous Driving' Seriously" [2012] Crim. L.R. 261–274.

The Road User and The Law (The Government's Proposals for Reform of Road Traffic Law) Cmnd.576 (1989), paras 2.6–2.9:

"2.6 There are already helpful precedents in Scottish case law which it is intended to follow in formulating the new section 2 offence. It will have two ingredients:

(a)   a standard of driving which falls far below that expected of a competent and careful driver; and

(b)   the driving must carry a potential or actual danger of physical injury or serious damage to property.

2.7 *The standard of driving* will be judged in absolute terms, taking no account of factors such as inexperience, age or disability (though such factors are relevant in sentencing). It is not intended that the driver who merely makes a careless mistake of a kind which any driver might make from time to time should be regarded as falling *far* below the standard expected of a competent and careful driver.

2.8 The *danger* must be one which a competent and careful driver would have appreciated or observed. It means any danger of injury (however minor) to a person, or of serious damage to property. It will not be necessary to establish that any person or property was actually endangered. It will be sufficient for the prosecution to establish that a competent and careful driver would have appreciated that some person or property might be endangered by the accused's manner of driving.

2.9 The requirements will be met if the state of the vehicle driven is such that a competent and careful driver would not drive at all. They will not be met simply by the physical condition of the driver, which will be dealt with by the proposed amendment to the offence of driving while unfit. However, if an unfit driver drives dangerously as defined above he will be guilty of the reformulated reckless driving offence, and his unfitness will not be an excuse."

The emphasis is thus on the objective nature of the driving rather than on the defendant's state of mind.[427] However, one element of subjectivity is imported. Under s.2A(3) if the defendant knows of circumstances rendering the driving dangerous (for example, a defect in the car)—even though the driving was not obviously dangerous—such knowledge can be imputed to the competent and careful driver.

What is the difference between this test of dangerous driving and that required for gross negligence manslaughter as laid down in *Adomako* (apart from the fact that causing death by dangerous driving can only be committed on a road or other public place whereas manslaughter can be committed anywhere)? The most important distinction is that for manslaughter the driving must have involved a *risk of death*: it must be "not only dangerous but inherently life-threatening".[428] However, given the potential danger of all motor vehicles, "measuring the risk to determine whether it was one of death or one of mere physical injury is surely a near impossible task, given that death did in fact occur".[429]

4. Sentencing

Following the enactment of the Road Safety Act 2006, the Sentencing Guidelines Council issued a new definitive guideline to replace the previous judicial guideline in the case of *Cooksley*.[430] The

---

[427] In *Milton v CPS* [2007] R.T.R. 43, the High Court used the rule in s.2A(3) to argue that it should be possible to take into account the fact that a driver has special skills when deciding the issue of dangerousness. A police officer's conviction for dangerous driving was quashed on the basis that the fact that he was a police-trained advanced driver should have been taken into account when deciding whether driving at speeds of up to 148 mph was dangerous. *Milton* was, however, overruled by the Court of Appeal in *Bannister* [2010] R.T.R. 4. In this case, involving another police driver, the Court of Appeal noted that to take account of the special skill of a police driver would be to substitute the test of the competent and careful driver in the statute and to re-write the test Parliament had laid down.

[428] I.D. Brownlee and M. Seneviratne, "Killing with Cars after Adomako: Time for Some Alternatives" [1995] Crim. L.R. 389.

[429] S. Cunningham, "The Reality of Vehicular Homicide: Convictions for Murder, Manslaughter and Causing Death by Dangerous Driving" [2001] Crim. L.R. 679.

[430] *R. v Cooksley (Robert Charles)* [2004] 1 Cr. App. R. (S.) 1. The guidelines had been reassessed in the case of *R. v Richardson*

maximum penalty for causing death by dangerous driving is 14 years' imprisonment. The new guidelines set out three levels of seriousness, each with their own starting point and sentencing range. Level 1 covers the most serious offences

"encompassing driving that involved a deliberate decision to ignore (or a flagrant disregard for) the rules of the road and an apparent disregard for the great danger being caused to others"

and has a starting point of eight years with a range of seven to 14 years. Level 2 covers driving that created a "substantial" risk of danger, with a starting point of five years and a range of four to seven years. Level 3 covers driving that created a "significant" risk of danger, with a starting point of three years and a range of two to five years.[431]

Such sentencing levels raise critical questions relating to "motor manslaughter". When is such a charge appropriate? When cases of killing with cars result in convictions for manslaughter, the sentence is unlikely to exceed the maximum available on conviction for causing death by dangerous driving.[432] In *Attorney General's Reference (No.111 of 2006)*[433] the Court of Appeal concluded that an analysis of authorities at first instance of cases of vehicular manslaughter suggested a range of between four and seven years' imprisonment. This corresponds with level 2 of the SGC's range for causing death by dangerous driving. That in itself suggests that there is a mismatch between charging practice and sentencing practice. If the most serious cases of driving causing death are prosecuted as gross negligence manslaughter, as the CPS policy suggests, such cases should not end up being sentenced to a lesser term of imprisonment than if they had been charged as causing death by dangerous driving.[434] A recent case of constructive manslaughter where a car was used as "a weapon of revenge" sought to apply the sentencing guidelines for causing death by dangerous driving, meaning that a ceiling of 14 years' imprisonment was imposed in sentencing for manslaughter. The sentence of eight-and-a-half years' imprisonment was upheld.[435] Whilst this suggests that there is little to be gained in terms of sentencing in the CPS charging manslaughter rather than the statutory offence, it can be argued that manslaughter ought to be charged in such cases in order that the defendant be labelled according to his wrongdoing.

B. Causing Death by Careless Driving

The arguments against the offence of causing death by dangerous driving are even more forceful when applied to this offence, created by the Road Safety Act 2006.

(Jack Virgil) [2007] 2 Cr. App. R. (S.) 36 following the increase of the maximum penalty to 14 years following the enactment of the Criminal Justice Act 2003.

[431]   Sentencing Guidelines Council, *Causing Death by Driving: Definitive Guideline* (2008), p.11.

[432]   See S. Cunningham, "The Reality of Vehicular Homicide: Convictions for Murder, Manslaughter and Causing Death by Dangerous Driving" [2001] Crim. L.R. 679. In recent years, the highest sentence for vehicular manslaughter has been 14 years, as in the case of *R. v Dudley (Leayon Davi)* [2006] 2 Cr. App. R. (S.) 77.

[433]   *Attorney General's Reference (No.111 of 2006)* [2007] 2 Cr. App. R. (S.) 26.

[434]   Further, Hirst has pointed out that the sentence a driver might receive for causing death on the basis of a "grave driving error" may well be greater than that which an individual would get for constructive manslaughter arising from an unprovoked road rage assault: M. Hirst, "Causing Death by Driving and Other Offences: A Question of Balance" [2008] Crim. L.R. 339 at 352.

[435]   *R. v Kwaik (Abid Abu)* [2013] EWCA Crim 2397.

Road Traffic Act 1988 s.2B (as amended by the Road Safety Act 2006)

"2B Causing death by careless, or inconsiderate, driving

A person who causes the death of another person by driving a mechanically propelled vehicle on a road or other public place without due care and attention, or without reasonable consideration for other persons using the road or place, is guilty of an offence."

This is a constructive crime that can be committed in one of two ways. Either the defendant must have driven carelessly (without due care and attention) or inconsiderately (without reasonable consideration for other persons) and in doing so caused death. The Road Safety Act 2006 introduces a statutory definition of careless and inconsiderate driving, which had previously been governed by case law.[436]

Road Traffic Act 1988 s.3ZA (as amended by the Road Safety Act 2006)

"3AZ Meaning of careless, or inconsiderate, driving

(1) This section has effect for the purposes of sections 2B[437] and 3[438] above and section 3A[439] below.

(2) A person is to be regarded as driving without due care and attention if (and only if) the way he drives falls below what would be expected of a competent and careful driver.

(3) In determining for the purposes of subsection (2) above what would be expected of a careful and competent driver in a particular case, regard shall be had not only to the circumstances of which he could be expected to be aware but also to any circumstances shown to have been within the knowledge of the accused.

(4) A person is to be regarded as driving without reasonable consideration for other persons only if those persons are inconvenienced by his driving."

It is unlikely that many, if any, cases will be prosecuted as causing death by inconsiderate, rather than careless.[440]

The offence of causing death by careless driving is triable either way, with a maximum penalty of five years' imprisonment following conviction at the Crown Court. The reason why this offence was created is that it was perceived that a gap existed in the legislation for careless drivers who kill. Before this offence was created, such drivers could only be punished for careless driving which was punishable by a fine and penalty points on the defendant's licence. Where a driver was prosecuted for causing death by dangerous driving, but that prosecution failed because the jury did not find the defendant had fallen *far* below the standard of the competent driver, or because the Crown accepted a plea of guilty to careless driving, the defendant would escape a custodial sentence. Victims' groups put pressure on the Government to change the law following cases in which it was thought that drivers had received a conviction for careless driving when they should have been convicted of causing death by dangerous driving and deserved a prison sentence.

The North Report of 1988 espoused the view that careless driving is not serious enough for it to be fair to give much weight to its consequences but in trying to head-off such claims when it proposed

---

[436] *Simpson v Peat* [1952] 2 Q.B. 24. Careless driving is an offence under s.3 of the Road Traffic Act 1988.

[437] Causing death by careless driving.

[438] Careless driving.

[439] Causing death by careless driving whilst under the influence of drink or drugs.

[440] None of the cases in a sample of 79 prosecutions under s.3 of the Road Traffic Act 1988 following a fatal road traffic collision were based on inconsiderate, rather than careless, driving: S. Cunningham, *Criminal Charges Brought in Cases of Road Death in the East Midlands: Implications for Law Reform*, PhD Thesis, University of Leicester, 2004. In a study of the new offence, none of the 22 cases prosecuted under s.2B were based on inconsiderate driving: S. Kyd Cunningham, "Has Law Reform Policy Been Driven in the Right Direction? How the New Causing Death by Driving Offences are Operating in Practice" [2013] Crim. L.R. 711–728.

the new offence, the Government stated that "in principle, consequences are as relevant to the culpability of careless drivers as they are to drivers guilty of dangerous driving".[441] Little consideration was given to the question of why it is justified to punish careless drivers who kill whilst other methods of killing usually require gross negligence on the part of the defendant before liability for homicide is incurred.[442]

This new offence extends the law too far. Careless driving is an offence of negligence, but the degree of negligence required is below that required for dangerous driving. In advance of the offence coming into force the Court of Appeal stated

"absent the consumption of alcohol, careless driving on its own almost always involves culpability at the lowest possible scale. In one sense, every driver is careless when he makes a mistake. Every driver, even the best, and most experienced, and normally careful, does so from time to time".[443]

Most acts of "momentary inattention" behind the wheel will luckily have no adverse effects and will likely not even be noticed by those involved. But where circumstances are such that the result of momentary inattention is catastrophic, a prosecution for causing death by careless driving is likely to ensue.[444] In cases of fatal collisions involving carelessness there may be a number of factors contributing to the collision and death, including the carelessness of the driver who dies.[445] Is it fair that any death be attributed to the driver who was lucky to survive? Arguably, in allowing this, luck plays too great a role in determining liability.

The Sentencing Guidelines Council's guidance on sentencing in cases of causing death by careless or inconsiderate driving dictate that those cases arising from momentary inattention where there are no aggravating factors should be sentenced to a community order. At the top end where a case falls just short of dangerous driving, the starting point is 15 months' custody, with a range of 36 weeks to three years' custody. All other cases would fall within the middle range with a starting point of 36 weeks' custody and a range of a community order at the low end up to two years' custody at the high end.[446] Although one of the motives behind the creation of the new offence was to allow careless drivers who kill to be sent to prison to satisfy victims' needs for justice to be done, it may be that victims remain disappointed under the new law.[447]

---

[441] Home Office, *Review of Road Traffic Offences Involving Bad Driving: A Consultation Paper* (2005), para.3.30.
[442] The one exception to this is possibly the offence of causing or allowing the death of a child or vulnerable adult, discussed above.
[443] *R. v Richardson (Jack Virgil)* [2007] 2 Cr. App. R. (S.) 36 at [29].
[444] S. Kyd Cunningham, above, fn.440.
[445] This is recognised by lawyers who prosecute and defend such cases. See S. Kyd Cunningham, above, fn.440 at 719.
[446] Sentencing Guidelines Council, *Causing Death by Driving: Definitive Guideline* (2008), p.15. The Court of Appeal has stated that it does not find it easy to apply the categories in the sentencing guidelines: *Campbell* [2009] EWCA Crim 2459 at [31].
[447] Although victims groups are often reported as being in favour of custodial sentences, this is not necessarily true of the public as a whole. Roberts et al. found that only 17% of the public would expect to see a prison sentence in a case of careless driving causing death. However, it was also found that the public's expectations did not correlate with their *preferred* sentence. 38% of respondents endorsed a custodial term for a hypothetical case of careless driving causing death: J.V. Roberts et al., "Public Attitudes to the Sentencing of Offences Involving Death by Driving" [2008] Crim. L.R. 525 at 530–532. For a discussion of when custody is likely to be imposed in cases of causing death by careless driving, see N. Padfield, "Time to Bury the Custody 'Threshold'?" [2011] Crim LR 593–612.

C. Causing Death by Careless Driving when Under the Influence of Drink or Drugs

Road Traffic Act 1988 s.3A (as amended by the Road Traffic Act 1991)

"3A. Causing death by careless driving when under influence of drink or drugs.

(1) If a person causes the death of another person by driving a mechanically propelled vehicle on a road or other public place without due care and attention, or without reasonable consideration for other persons using the road or place, and—

(a) he is, at the time when he is driving, unfit to drive through drink or drugs, or

(b) he has consumed so much alcohol that the proportion of it in his breath, blood or urine at that time exceeds the prescribed limit, or

(c) he is, within 18 hours after that time, required to provide a specimen in pursuance of section 7 of this Act, but without reasonable excuse fails to provide it, he is guilty of an offence.

(2) For the purposes of this section a person shall be taken to be unfit to drive at any time when his ability to drive properly is impaired.

(3) Subsection (1)(b) and (c) above shall not apply in relation to a person driving a mechanically propelled vehicle other than a motor vehicle."

This offence is punishable by a maximum of 14 years' imprisonment.[448] Why was it introduced?

Department of Transport and Home Office, Road Traffic Law Review Report (The North Report) (1988), paras 6.18–6.23:

"Our consultation identified a strongly held view . . . that bad drivers who have been drinking and who cause death are frequently dealt with too leniently. Under present legislation a driver who is over the prescribed alcohol limit . . . and whose driving causes an accident in which someone is killed may often be charged with only an alcohol or drugs offence, or with this offence coupled with one of careless driving . . . [P]rosecuting authorities will, we are told, often settle for a drink driving charge as being easier to prove . . . [There is a] growing concern among the public over drinking and driving and in particular over drinking drivers who kill. There is understandable revulsion that innocent lives can be lost in such a fashion. We share these anxieties . . . [T]he availability of such a specific offence would be of real value in further marking out the dangers to the community of drinking and driving . . .

[One] alternative might be to have an absolute offence of killing someone while driving with more than the legal limit of alcohol in the body or while unfit to drive through drink or drugs . . . Under such an offence it would be enough to prove involvement by a drinking driver in an accident where a person was killed . . . [T]here are problems with this type of approach. There is no doubt that drivers should not take so much alcohol as to put them over the legal limit; but it is easy to visualise circumstances where an accident leading to a death may have occurred and yet the drinking driver was not in any way to blame. Where, for example, a drunken pedestrian dashes out in front of a car in circumstances such that no driver could have avoided him, it would seem unduly harsh to charge the driver not only with the drink offence but also with a new causing death offence.

The final possibility which we have considered is that of an offence in which two elements would have to be proved. The first would be that the driver was over the legal alcohol limit or unfit to drive through drink or drugs; the second that there had been a level of bad driving amounting at least to driving without due care. By including a requirement to prove that some legally bad driving had occurred, such a formulation would protect from prosecution for this new offence drivers who had indeed been over the alcohol limit or who were otherwise unfit but the standard of whose driving had had no part in causing the death."

Like causing death by dangerous driving, this offence eschews the view that the focus ought to be solely on the quality of the driving. As in so many areas of criminal law, the degree of resulting harm

---

[448] Increased from 10 to 14 years by the Criminal Justice Act 2003 s.285(4). The penalty had already been increased from five to 10 years' imprisonment by the Criminal Justice Act 1993 s.67(1).

is critical in determining the extent of liability and punishment. The aggravating factor, in comparison with the new offence of causing death by careless driving, is that the defendant was under the influence of drink or drugs and, having chosen to drive in such a condition, can be said to be more blameworthy.

The Sentencing Guidelines Council's guidelines for sentencing the offence are rather complex, setting out nine levels of seriousness, dependent on a combination of the amount of alcohol in the defendant's breath and the level of carelessness displayed.[449] The current legal limit is 35 micrograms of alcohol in 100ml of breath or 80mg in 100ml of blood. Other European countries have a limit of 50mg in 100ml of blood or lower but, despite a recent report commissioned by the Labour Government recommending that England and Wales follow suit and lower the limit,[450] the coalition Government has decided to leave it unchanged.

D. Causing Death by Unlicensed, Disqualified or Uninsured Driving

Road Traffic Act 1988 s.3ZB (as amended by the Road Safety Act 2006)

"3ZB Causing death by driving: unlicensed, disqualified or uninsured drivers
    A person is guilty of an offence under this section if he causes the death of another person by driving a motor vehicle on a road and, at the time when he is driving, the circumstances are such that he is committing an offence under—

(a) section 87(1) of this Act (driving otherwise than in accordance with a licence),

(b) section 103(1)(b) of this Act (driving while disqualified), or

(c) section 143 of this Act (using motor vehicle while uninsured or unsecured against third party risks)."

This offence is triable either way and punishable by a maximum of two years' imprisonment following conviction at the Crown Court.[451] The offence is entirely constructive; the only requirement on the face of the provision is that the defendant's driving caused death and at the time he was driving whilst either uninsured, disqualified or without a licence. This offence construction was rejected by the North Report in relation to drink driving in the extract above, where the example of a blameless drunk driver colliding with a pedestrian who ran into the road was provided. However, the Government attempted to justify the allocation of blame in such cases on the basis that the "mere fact of taking a vehicle on a road when disqualified is, in the Government's view, as negligent of the safety of others as is any example of driving below the standard expected of a competent driver, even if the disqualified driver, at a particular time, is driving at an acceptable standard".[452] These arguments can be countered, however.

---

[449] Or, alternatively, in cases based on refusal to submit to a breath test, the deliberate nature or otherwise of such refusal.
[450] Sir Peter North CBE QC, *Report of the Review of Drink and Drug-driving Law* (2010) available at *http://northreview.independent.gov.uk/docs/NorthReview-Report.pdf* [Accessed April 2014]. For an analysis of the report, see S. Cunningham, "The North Review of Drink-Driving: Some Sobering Proposals" [2011] Crim. L.R. 296–310.
[451] The Sentencing Guidelines Council's guidelines are that a straightforward offence involving an uninsured or unlicensed driver with no aggravating factors should have a sentencing starting point of a community order. Where one aggravating factor is present, the starting point is 26 weeks' custody. Where the defendant was disqualified from driving or was unlicensed or uninsured and two aggravating factors are present the starting point is 12 months' custody. See Sentencing Guidelines Council, *Causing Death by Driving: Definitive Guideline* (2008), p.17.
[452] Home Office, *Review of Road Traffic Offences Involving Bad Driving: A Consultation Paper* (2005), para.4.2.

R.A. Duff, "Whose Luck Is It Anyway?" in C.M.V. Clarkson and S. Cunningham (eds), Criminal Liability for Non-Aggressive Death (2008), pp.76–77:

"What justifies increasing the endangerer's punishment if she causes death is that the causation of death actualises the risk that made her conduct wrongfully dangerous: what we say to her is 'Look what you have done by your carelessness'. Now it is true that if the unlicensed (or disqualified or uninsured) driver had not been driving, he would not have caused death (at least in that way); and given that he was unlicensed, disqualified or uninsured, it follows that if he had not been driving whilst unlicensed, disqualified or uninsured he would not have caused death. But it is still not true that he caused death by driving whilst unlicensed, disqualified or uninsured, unless it was his being unlicensed, disqualified or uninsured that made his driving especially dangerous. Now there is of course *some* connection between being unlicensed, or disqualified, and driving dangerously: under an appropriate system, being licensed gives both drivers and others some assurance that drivers are competent to drive safely, and being disqualified is often the result of driving dangerously or being incompetent to drive safely. However, there is no such connection between being uninsured and driving dangerously, because insurance has to do with paying for harm caused rather than with avoiding causing it; and even in the cases of driving when unlicensed or disqualified it is far from clear that the connection is close enough to treat the causation of death as the actualisation of a risk that made the driving wrongful in the first place."

The Government's position, as set out in its consultation paper, has been tempered somewhat by the statutory interpretation applied by the Supreme Court in the case of *Hughes*.[453] As discussed in Ch.2 above, the previous case of *Williams*[454] had applied a very broad interpretation of causation to the offence, which was in line with the Government's aspirations for the offence. The facts of *Hughes* involved a defendant whose driving could not be faulted, who was involved with a collision when the deceased, who was fatigued and under the influence of drugs, swerved across the carriageway. The Supreme Court held that while D's acts were a "but for" cause of death (in that if he had not been driving, the deceased would not have collided with his car and died), his actions could not be the legal cause of death. The offence required that there must be "something which he did or omitted to do by way of driving [the car] which contributed in a more than minimal way to the death[455]" and that there needs to be "something properly to be criticised in the driving of the defendant".[456]

Quite what is needed in terms of the quality of driving to prove the offence is yet to be seen. The court noted that the driving does not need to be as severe as careless or inconsiderate driving, but there has to be an action or omission that amounts to more than mere presence at the scene. If the driving were to be as bad as careless driving then clearly the defendant ought to be charged under s.2B of the Road Traffic Act 1988. Research conducted to examine how the new offence under s.3ZB was being utilised soon after it was introduced has found that the offence is often only used as a back-stop to other more serious charges in any case; in eight of 14 cases where the s.3ZB offence was charged it was charged alongside offences under either s.1, s.2B or s.3A of the RTA 1988 or s.12A Theft Act (see below), and the defendant pleaded guilty to those more serious offences.[457]

Whilst it is true that the offences of unlicensed, disqualified and uninsured driving are problematic, involving a high standard of reoffending, it does not follow that this problem will be tackled by the creation of a new homicide offence. Where an unlicensed, disqualified or uninsured driver causes the death of another by her bad driving then she may be punished according to the level of her driving, for either causing death by dangerous driving or causing death by careless driving. The effect of *Hughes* may be that prosecutions under s.3ZB become even more of a rarity.

---

[453] *R. v Hughes (Michael)* [2014] 1 Cr. App. R. 6.
[454] *R. v Williams (Jason John)* [2010] EWCA Crim 2552.
[455] *R. v Hughes (Michael)* [2014] 1 Cr. App. R. 6 at [28].
[456] *Hughes* [2014] 1 Cr. App. R. 6 at [32].
[457] S. Kyd Cunningham, above, fn.440.

E. Causing Death by Aggravated Vehicle-Taking

Section 12 of the Theft Act 1968 makes it an offence for any person to take any conveyance without the consent of the owner. The mens rea of the offence is that the defendant must know that the conveyance has been taken without authority. This offence was introduced to deal with the problem of "joy-riding" where an intention permanently to deprive the other of the car, as required for theft, cannot be established.

The Aggravated Vehicle-Taking Act 1992 s.1(1), inserting s.12A of the Theft Act 1968, created an offence of aggravated vehicle-taking covering situations where the taken vehicle is driven dangerously or causes injury to any person or damage to any property. This offence is punishable by a maximum of two years' imprisonment but under s.12A(4) if death is caused, the maximum punishment is increased to 14 years' imprisonment.[458]

The death that is caused must be "owing to the driving of the vehicle". This is a straightforward matter of factual causation. It is unnecessary to prove that the driving was bad or that the driver was in any way culpable.[459] This again is a clear example of constructive crime. If one commits crime A (taking a conveyance) one becomes automatically liable for crime B if the specified consequence (death) occurs. The object of the statute is simply to increase the penalty for joy-riders who cause death.

IX. CORPORATE MANSLAUGHTER

The Corporate Manslaughter and Corporate Homicide Act 2007 introduced a new separate homicide offence: corporate manslaughter. This offence is considered in Ch.3 where the criminal liability of corporations for all offences is discussed.

X. THE STRUCTURE OF HOMICIDE OFFENCES

In England and Wales, there are several categories of homicide. The main distinction is between murder and involuntary manslaughter, a distinction resting on the presence or absence of a mental element, malice aforethought. However, murder is also distinguished from voluntary manslaughter, this distinction being based either on the mental condition of the defendant (diminished responsibility), or on the circumstances of the killing (the "loss of control" defence and suicide pacts). As we have seen, there are three further species of homicide:[460] infanticide, which refers specifically to the death of a particular type of victim (child under one year of age); the offence under s.5 of the Domestic Violence, Crime and Victims Act 2004, which is also defined with reference to the victim (children or vulnerable adults); corporate manslaughter (which can only be committed by organisations); and the various offences of vehicular homicide, which refer to death being caused in a particular manner.

In this section we shall be concerned with four questions:

1. Why do we distinguish between different categories of homicide?

2. Do we distinguish between these categories with sufficient particularity?

3. On what basis ought such distinctions to be made?

4. Should we abolish these categories and replace them with a single offence of unlawful homicide?

---

[458] Increased from five years by the Criminal Justice Act 2003 s.285(1).
[459] *R. v Marsh (William)* [1997] 1 Cr. App. R. 67.
[460] It should be noted that "homicide" within the official statistics refers only to murder, manslaughter and infanticide.

A. Rationale of Distinction between Different Categories of Homicide

Homicides range from cold-blooded, malicious killings to killings not far removed from accidents or killings where there are severe mitigating circumstances, such as fear of serious violence triggering a loss of control. It is necessary to differentiate between these homicides in terms of their perceived seriousness. This differentiation is useful for two purposes:

(a) Different penalties can be attached for the different categories of homicide. Thus the fact that murder is perceived as being far more serious than manslaughter is clearly reflected in the sentence: capital punishment before 1965 and mandatory life imprisonment since then, as opposed to a *maximum* of life imprisonment for manslaughter. Similarly, the fact that the crime of causing death by dangerous driving is perceived as being less serious than manslaughter can be reflected by its sentence of a maximum of 14 years' imprisonment. That said, this grading of offences determined by sentence with murder at its pinnacle has been eroded in recent years, as noted by Norrie: "the 2003 Act[461] has in symbolic terms chipped away at the notion of one, uniquely serious, crime possessing one, uniquely serious, penalty".[462]

(b) Differentiating between homicide offences emphasises the different stigma attached to each and enables us to differentiate between different kinds of moral wrong. For example, the label "murder" emphasises the special stigma attached to that crime. One of the main purposes of the criminal law and punishment is its symbolic value in communicating messages to the public as to what is permissible or not. Different labels are used for different crimes to communicate the degree of rejection of the specific crime. The label "murder" is used to emphasise the "dreadfulness"[463] and the "uniquely horrible [nature of the] crime".[464] Also, it may have a significant deterrent value.[465] Abolishing the label "may appear to have the effect of lessening the seriousness of taking life".[466] Similar arguments may be put forward to explain why we retain the label "manslaughter" and treat separately the offences of infanticide and vehicular homicide.

T. Morris and L. Blom-Cooper, A Calendar of Murder (Criminal Homicide in England since 1957) (1964), pp.271–272:

"[W]anton murder is dramatically defined as the most dreadful of crimes, a view which has been upheld by the laws and customs of civilised societies down the ages. The act of murder occupies a unique place in the feelings of men in that it falls into a class of actions the results of which are irreversible . . . Around the notion of death a whole series of institutional beliefs and practices have arisen creating a sense of social balance in which the realisation of mortality is incorporated into the fabric of human experience; only thus is death made tolerable.

. . .

Murder produces a sense of profound social shock—heightened in our own society by dissemination of the details through modern mass media. It can normally be relieved only by some highly dramatic act on the part of the community towards the offender. In days gone by this act was the public imposition of capital punish-

---

[461] Referring to Criminal Justice Act 2003 s.269.
[462] A. Norrie, "Between Orthodox Subjectivism and Moral Contextualism: Intention and the Consultation Paper" [2006] Crim. L.R. 489–501 at 489.
[463] *La Fontaine* 11 A.L.R. 507 at 535, per Jacobs J.
[464] Cross, "Penal Reform in 1965 . . ." [1966] Crim. L.R. 184 at 189.
[465] C.L.R.C., Working Paper on Offences against the Person, 1976, para.7.
[466] C.L.R.C., Working Paper on Offences against the Person, 1976, para.7.

ment; latterly . . . the criminal trial and the dramatisation of its preliminaries may be gradually taking its place . . . Clearly, it is the special character of murder, the attendant sensationalism of the re-enactment of the killing with its actual risk of imitation, which wide advertisement brings in its trial, that gives murder its quintessential quality—a crime apart."

Horder identifies the labelling function of different homicide offences as one of a number of elements distinguishing two competing models of homicide offences. He compares the common law model (encompassing murder and manslaughter) with the regulatory model (including offences such as causing or allowing the death of a child or vulnerable adult and the causing death by driving offences).

Jeremy Horder, Homicide and the Politics of Law Reform (2012), pp.75; 86–87

"Common law/traditional-codificatory model

1. General applicability (not context specific).
2. Application to all citizens equally.
3. Fault element required.
4. Classical view of responsibility and causation.
5. Comprised of *mala in se.*
6. Legitimacy not tied to consequentialist evaluation.
7. Labels descriptively evaluative.

Regulatory or bureaucratic—administrative model

1. Context-specific application.
2. Targeted at particular groups.
3. Fault elements dispensable or watered down.
4. Responsibility and causation elements malleable.
5. Blurring of *mala in se/mala prohibita* distinction.
6. The outcomes that law produces are crucial to legitimacy.
7. Labels descriptively factual.

. . .

The conclusion I seek to draw . . . is that a wholesale shift from a common law to a regulatory approach in the law of homicide may have few clearly proven advantages, and many real disadvantages, most especially in relation to fault or to punishment, and hence in relation to legitimacy . . . [I]n these respects a regulatory approach may sometimes be too harsh on accused persons (causing death on the roads; causing the death of a child or vulnerable person), but sometimes also too general to them (Assisted Dying for the Terminally Ill Bill). The direction of my argument is towards a system of criminal law in which common law and regulatory approaches are regarded as mutually reinforcing, rather than as rival claimants to exclusive occupancy of the relevant legal space. How can such a system be developed?

The offence of corporate manslaughter provides one model . . . to give effect to a regulatory objective ensuring that a company can in appropriate circumstances be found liable for homicide, brought about at least in part by glaring deficiencies in the senior managers' management or organization of the company's activities. The common law and regulatory approaches are mutually reinforcing in this sense. The powers available to the court upon conviction are classically regulatory in form . . .

However, most importantly, these regulation-oriented powers available upon conviction—probably far less punitive than many groups advocating corporate liability would have liked—are themselves in part reinforced and supported by the way in which the offence takes a common law approach to labelling and fault. Liability is for 'manslaughter', and the fault element—'a gross breach of a relevant duty of care'—mirrors the common law requirement in manslaughter for gross negligence. In taking this approach, the new offence recognizes that the labelling element of conviction for common law homicide offences (murder; manslaughter) can *itself* be regarded as part of the punishment, so long its currency has not been debased by substantial diminution of fault requirements."

B. Greater Specificity

Given the above views, another question presents itself. Does English law distinguish with sufficient precision between different homicides? Many would assert that it does not. Murder and manslaughter, in particular, are far too broad, each encompassing too many different types of conduct, circumstances and offenders—in short, too many different degrees of "heinousness". Murders, for example, vary widely: they cover planned, cold-blooded killings, deliberate killings with torture all the way down to killings only marginally qualifying as intentional under *Woollin*. They cover people who coldly kill for no reason, down through all the different motivations and explanations to mercy killings, where an anguished defendant kills a loved one to end their suffering. Manslaughters, too, cover a vast field: they range from conduct just short of murder to just above the non-criminal category of justifiable or accidental death. Is not each crime, each label, covering too vast a field?

When the English common law was introduced into the United States, these points were taken. The English categories of murder and manslaughter were each seen to be too broad to serve any useful purpose. In particular, it was felt to be wrong for the death penalty to apply to all murders. The crime of murder should be divided into categories with the death penalty only applying to the "worst". In 1794, the pioneering Pennsylvania Code divided murder into two degrees, with the death penalty only applying to first degree murder. Similarly, manslaughters were divided into different degrees, each degree carrying a separate penalty. This approach has been widely adopted with the result that both murder and manslaughter are now divided into degrees or categories in most states. In addition, the majority of states have yet further homicide offences, apart from murder and manslaughter, such as reckless homicide, negligent homicide and vehicular homicide.

Arizona Revised Statutes 2013

"13–1102. Negligent homicide; classification
   A. A person commits negligent homicide if with criminal negligence the person causes the death of another person, including an unborn child.
   B. An offense under this section applies to an unborn child in the womb at any stage of its development . . .
   C. Negligent homicide is a class 4 felony [presumptive penalty for first offence is 2.5 years[467]].

13–1103. Manslaughter; classification
A. A person commits manslaughter by:

1. Recklessly causing the death of another person; or

2. Committing second degree murder as defined in section 13–1104, subsection A upon a sudden quarrel or heat of passion resulting from adequate provocation by the victim; or

3. Intentionally aiding another to commit suicide; or

4. Committing second degree murder as defined in section 13–1104, subsection A, paragraph 3, while being coerced to do so by the use or threatened immediate use of unlawful deadly physical force upon such person or a third person which a reasonable person in his situation would have been unable to resist; or

---

[467]   This and ensuing presumptive penalties are increased where the offender has two or more prior felony convictions or commits the offence with a deadly weapon or dangerous instrument.

5. Knowingly or recklessly causing the death of an unborn child by any physical injury to the mother.

B. An offense under subsection A, paragraph 5 of this section applies to an unborn child in the womb at any stage of its development . . .

C. Manslaughter is a class 2 felony [presumptive penalty for first offence is 5 years].

13–1104. Second degree murder; classification

A. A person commits second degree murder if without premeditation:

1. The person intentionally causes the death of another person, including an unborn child or, as a result of intentionally causing the death of another person, causes the death of an unborn child; or

2. Knowing that the person's conduct will cause death or serious physical injury, the person causes the death of another person, including an unborn child or, as a result of knowingly causing the death of another person, causes the death of an unborn child; or

3. Under circumstances manifesting extreme indifference to human life, the person recklessly engages in conduct that creates a grave risk of death and thereby causes the death of another person, including an unborn child or, as a result of recklessly causing the death of another person, causes the death of an unborn child.

B. An offense under this section applies to an unborn child in the womb at any stage of its development . . .

C. Second degree murder is a class 1 felony . . .[468]

13–1105. First degree murder; classification

A. A person commits first degree murder if:

1. Intending or knowing that the person's conduct will cause death, the person causes the death of another person, including an unborn child, with premeditation or, as a result of causing the death of another person with premeditation, causes the death of an unborn child.

2. Acting either alone or with one or more other persons the person commits or attempts to commit sexual conduct with a minor . . ., sexual assault . . ., molestation of a child . . ., terrorism . . ., marijuana offenses . . ., dangerous drug offenses . . ., narcotics offenses . . ., drive-by shooting . . . , kidnapping . . ., burglary . . ., arson . . ., robbery . . ., escape . . ., child abuse . . ., or unlawful flight from a pursuing law enforcement vehicle . . . and in the course of and in furtherance of the offense or immediate flight from the offense, the person or another person causes the death of any person.[469]

3. Intending or knowing that the person's conduct will cause death to a law enforcement officer, the person causes the death of a law enforcement officer who is in the line of duty.

B. Homicide, as prescribed in subsection A, paragraph 2 of this section, requires no specific mental state other than what is required for the commission of any of the enumerated felonies.

C. An offense under subsection A, paragraph 1 of this section applies to an unborn child in the womb at any stage of its development. . . .

D. First degree murder is a class 1 felony and is punishable by death or life imprisonment."

Vehicular homicide is a separate offence in about half of the states. In some states, for example Colorado, criminally negligent homicide and vehicular homicide co-exist as separate offences (in addition to manslaughter and two degrees of murder).[470]

There is a major problem with such precise gradations of homicide offences. It assumes that one can isolate those factors or criteria that *always* makes a homicide more or less reprehensible. Let us

---

[468] Under A.R.S. 13–710 a person who stands convicted of second degree murder shall be sentenced to a presumptive term of 16 calendar years, with a minimum of 10 calendar years and maximum of 25 calendar years. Where the victim was a child under the age of 15 the presumptive term is 20 years (A.R.S.: 13–705).

[469] Details of each of these felonies have been omitted.

[470] Colo. Rev. Stat. Ann. ss.18–3–101 to 18–3–106.

take the deliberation/premeditation formula as an example. In most states in the United States the "worst" murders, first degree murders, are reserved for deliberate and premeditated killings.[471] One can perhaps understand the rationale behind such provisions, namely that it

"reflect[s] a belief that one who meditates an intent to kill and then deliberately executes it is more dangerous, more culpable or less capable of reformation than one who kills on sudden impulse; or that the prospect of the death penalty is more likely to deter men from deliberate than from impulsive murder."[472]

There are, however, severe problems with such an approach:
(a) It is almost impossible to distinguish between a "premeditated" and a "merely intentional" killing. In the United States most statutes have defined "intention" in terms of "conscious objective". If something is your objective, that, of necessity, means you have made a decision to bring about that objective. The making of that decision must, by definition, involve premeditation and deliberation. As Cardozo J. put it:

"an intent to kill is always deliberate and premeditated . . . There can be no intent unless there is a choice, yet by the hypothesis, the choice without more is enough to justify the inference that the intent was deliberate and premeditated . . . [Such statutes are] framed along the lines of a defective and unreal psychology."[473]

(b) A "purely impulsive" murder may be just as, if not more, reprehensible than the cold-blooded, premeditated killing. As Stephen put it:

"As much cruelty, as much indifference to the life of others, a disposition at least as dangerous to society, probably even more dangerous, is shown by sudden as by premeditated murders. The following cases appear to me to set this in a clear light. A, passing along the road, sees a boy sitting on a bridge over a deep river and, out of mere wanton barbarity, pushes him into it and so drowns him. A man makes advances to a girl who repels him. He deliberately but instantly cuts her throat. A man civilly asked to pay a just debt pretends to get the money, loads a rifle and blows out his creditor's brains. In none of these cases is there premeditation unless the word is used in a sense as unnatural as 'aforethought', in 'malice aforethought'; but each represents even more diabolical cruelty and ferocity than that which is involved in murders premeditated in the natural sense of the word."[474]

(c) Many premeditated killings are clearly not the most reprehensible. Mercy killings, for example, are invariably premeditated killings, yet they are generally regarded as far less blameworthy than most other types of killings. A good example of this is to be found in the United States case of *Repouille v United States*.[475] In this case the defendant's son was aged 13, had been bedridden since infancy and was described as an "incurable imbecile" who could not walk or talk; he had been blind for five

---

[471] In France, murder committed with premeditation amounts to the separate offence of "assassination", punished by life imprisonment (French Penal Code art.221–3).
[472] *Bullock v US*, 122 F.2d 213 (D.C. Cir. 1941).
[473] B. Cardozo, "What Medicine Can Do for Law," in *Law and Literature and other Essays and Addresses* (New York: Harper & Bros, 1930), pp.99–100.
[474] J.F. Stephen, 3 *A History of the Criminal Law* (1883), p.94.
[475] 165 F. 2d 152 (2d Cir. 1947).

years. The defendant had spent all his savings on an operation for the child but his condition had not improved. The defendant began to talk of putting the boy out of his misery and one day soaked a rag with chloroform and applied it to the boy's face, while he lay in his bed, until he died. This was a clear case of a planned, premeditated killing which would be first degree murder. Yet the jury convicted the defendant of second degree manslaughter and requested sentencing leniency. The judge suspended execution of a five-year sentence and placed the defendant on probation. Commenting on this, Learned Hand J. stated:

"... the jury ... did not feel any moral repulsion at his crime. Although it was inescapably murder in the first degree, not only did they bring in a verdict that was flatly in the face of the facts and utterly absurd—for manslaughter in the second degree presupposes that the killing was not deliberate— but they coupled even that with a recommendation which showed that in substance they wished to exculpate the offender. Moreover, it is also plain, from the sentence which he imposed, that the judge could not have seriously disagreed with their recommendation."

A case such as this highlights the total inadequacy of the premeditation/deliberation formula in that it has not succeeded in isolating the worst killings. Categories of homicide become meaningless if they do not reflect common views of reprehensibility.

At the other end of the spectrum from murder, we have seen that more specificity is being added to the law of homicide. Whilst manslaughter exists as a common law "dustbin" crime, new homicide offences with a determinate sentence have been created in recent years in the form of causing or allowing the death of a child or vulnerable adult and various offences of causing death by driving (offences under Horder's regulatory model).. In addition, corporate manslaughter has been created to punish deaths caused by corporate gross negligence. What all of these new offences have in common is that they cater for killings that take place outside the context of a violent attack where the defendant has chosen to engage in violence against another person.[476] Further specific offences could be added to this category, however. Medical negligence leading to death might warrant a separate offence.[477] As noted above, drug supply causing death is an offence in some jurisdictions, and could form the basis of a new offence here.[478] However, Wilson's arguments against such a move are forceful.[479] A further suggestion for a separate homicide offence has been made by the Association of Chief Police Officers, which has called for a new offence of "liability for suicide".[480] This would be targeted at those who are guilty of domestic abuse, and whose partners, such as the deceased in the case of *Dhaliwal*,[481] are driven to suicide. Such offenders are not caught by the scope of the law on encouraging suicide, since they would not have the necessary mens rea for that offence. They might be guilty of constructive manslaughter, if it could be proved that they committed an unlawful and dangerous act which caused death. In *Dhaliwal* it was suggested that such a charge would be possible in cases where the victim was suffering from a recognised psychiatric illness which was caused by the abuse suffered

---

[476] See generally, C.M.V. Clarkson and S. Cunningham (eds), *Criminal Liability for Non-Aggressive Death* (Aldershot: Ashgate, 2008).

[477] O. Quick, "Medical Killing, Need for a Special Offence?", in C. M. V. Clarkson and S. Cunningham (eds), *Criminal Liability for Non-Aggressive Death* (Aldershot: Ashgate, 2008).

[478] For arguments in favour of such a move, see C. Elliott and C. de Than, "Prosecuting the Drug Dealer When a Drug User Dies: *R v Kennedy (No.2)*" (2006) M.L.R. 986; and C. Elliott and C. de Than, "Restructuring the Homicide Offences to Tackle Violence, Discrimination and Drugs in a Modern Society" (2009) 20 K.L.J. 69.

[479] Wilson, "Dealing with Drug-induced Homicide" in C.M.V. Clarkson and S. Cunningham (eds), *Criminal Liability for Non-Aggressive Death* (Aldershot: Ashgate, 2008).

[480] *The Independent*, November 17, 2009, p.12

[481] [2006] 2 Cr. App. R. 24, discussed in Ch.7 above.

at the hands of her partner, and which in turn caused her to commit suicide. However, in many cases it will be difficult to show that this was the case, and yet arguably the deceased's partner can be blamed for her death.[482] If we were to entertain the idea of creating such a specific offence, however, where would such specificity end?

Andrew Ashworth, "'Manslaughter': Generic or Nominate Offences?" in C.M.V. Clarkson and S. Cunningham (eds), Criminal Liabillity for Non-Aggressive Death (2008), pp.243; 246–247:

"[W]e must now confront the question whether the law should be structured around generic homicide offences or nominate offences. Three arguments in favour of nominalism stand out—that it is much more communicative, thereby emphasising the special duties of citizens in certain roles or positions; that the circumstances of some types of case are so unlike others that a separate category is a more accurate label; and that, if there were not a nominate offence for certain conduct, the law might be misapplied by juries. One argument against nominate offences is that their creation may convey the impression, however wrongly, that they are regarded as less serious than manslaughter because they are labelled separately and differently. Another counter-argument raises questions about the deliberate mis-labelling of certain homicides in order to avoid controversy . . .

One general argument against nominate offences is that they may amount to a down-grading of the offence. Classifying the offences as manslaughter or culpable homicide would be an appropriate signification of the degree of wrongdoing, but a nominate offence (perhaps using the less censuring term, 'causing death by . . .') may not be a proper valuation. In order to grapple with this we need to separate the label from the essence. Applying a separate label to an offence (causing death by dangerous driving, infanticide) may lead people to believe—and this would be an empirical question—that certain forms of wrongdoing are being taken less seriously. But then there is the further and arguably more important question of whether that amounts to a real under-valuation, i.e. whether the 'valuation' consists not merely of the label attached but also of the level of sentence imposed. That, too, would be an empirical question. As intimated above, this question is rendered complex by the increasing levels of sentencing for causing death by dangerous driving in recent years, sentences that are often higher than those for manslaughter by gross negligence and unlawful act manslaughter, and sometimes higher than for manslaughter upon provocation (where the considerations are, of course, very different).

A further argument against nominalism, though limited in its scope, draws our attention back to the political context in which proposals for homicide law have to be assessed. Any proposal explicitly to reduce the censuring of homicides resulting from assisted suicide, suicide pacts and mercy killing tends to stir up formidable political opposition. Fears about the effects of such opposition led the Law Commission to leave these cases out of its final report in 2006. Some will decry this as cowardice, but the pragmatic truth is that recommendations that were viewed as relaxations of the law in those areas might well undermine all the other proposals in a package of reforms, so strong is the feeling among some religious groups and others. The tendency is therefore to leave these difficult cases aside, consigning them to a twilight world in which other doctrines (notably diminished responsibility) are stretched to accommodate such cases but only if sympathetic medical witnesses can be found. This is an unusual face of nominalism: there seems to be less controversy and greater public acceptance to be gained through mislabelling these cases, often as manslaughter by reason of diminished responsibility, than through using a clear and representative label that draws attention to the circumstances."

C. Basis of Distinctions

Whether we have generic offences or specific offences of homicide, the question remains as to how we should distinguish between such offences. In the previous chapter on non-fatal offences against

---

[482] Elliott and de Than argue that liability could arise in such cases under either constructive manslaughter or gross negligence manslaughter but that, given the practical difficulties in proving such cases, a new statutory offence with a maximum term of 10 years' imprisonment ought to be introduced: C. Elliott and C. de Than, "Restructuring the Homicide Offences to Tackle Violence, Discrimination and Drugs in a Modern Society" (2009) 20 K.L.J. 69 at 84.

the person it was argued that appropriate levels of criminal liability and punishment ought to be fixed by reference to a combination of *blame* and harm, and that "blame" could involve a consideration of other factors in addition to cognitive mens rea. Thus, as we saw, we might blame someone more because of the method or circumstances of the crime—e.g. torturing the victim. In homicide the harm is, of course, constant: the victim is dead. There is, however, no particular reason why the blame element giving rise to different offence categories, *must* be limited to a consideration of the mental element of the defendant.

Indeed, a glance at other jurisdictions reveals that classifications of homicide offences could be made to depend on a variety of other factors. The identity of the victim, for instance, could be regarded as the key factor distinguishing two homicides with identical mental states.[483] In Louisiana it is first degree murder to kill intentionally a fireman or a peace officer engaged in the performance of their duties.[484] Or, it could be the identity of the killer that is regarded as decisive as in New York where it is first degree murder if the murderer was confined in prison.[485]

Alternatively, the categorisation could be made to depend on the method and circumstances of the killing. In Louisiana it is first degree murder to kill after being offered anything of value for the killing,[486] and in Idaho it is first degree murder to kill by poisoning or torturing a victim to death.[487]

Such an approach would not be totally alien to English law where the identity of the victim and the killer are highly relevant for the crimes of infanticide and causing or allowing the death of a child or vulnerable adult, and the method and circumstances of the killing are equally relevant for the crime of causing death by dangerous driving and the other vehicular homicide offences. An objection to such an approach might be that it would be impossible to achieve agreement as to what factors rendered a killing more or less reprehensible. The Law Commission has specifically rejected the suggestion that killing a police officer on duty be first degree murder if the killer did not have the requisite fault element, on the basis that such a rule would create the potential for too much arbitrariness and legalism.[488] However, the starting points for sentencing in murder cases already list the following factors as those justifying a particularly high minimum term: the murder of a police or prison officer in the course of his duty; a murder involving firearms or explosives; a murder done for gain; a murder involving sexual or sadistic conduct; and a murder that is racially or religiously aggravated.[489] Would the law not be more transparent if, rather than requiring that these factors not be considered until the sentencing stage, they were utilised to provide distinctions within the substantive law and define different degrees of murder? As noted above, however, these factors appearing within the statute do not provide an exhaustive list of factors which a sentencing judge can take into account, and judges retain discretion in sentencing. It is one thing to list factors which can be a helpful tool in sentencing and quite another to use them in order rigidly to define specific offences.

Elliott and de Than have argued that there is no need to have such rigidity in defining specific offences, but that an aggravated form of murder ought to be introduced to signify that an extra level of "harm" may be caused in cases of homicide which causes particular anxiety amongst the community.

---

[483] Such a proposal was considered and rejected by the Criminal Law Revision Committee in relation to assaults (14th Report, para.162).
[484] La. Rev. Stat. s.14.30(2).
[485] N.Y. Penal Law s.125.27(1)(a)(iv).
[486] La. Rev. Stat. s.14.30(4).
[487] Idaho Code s.18–4003(a).
[488] Law Commission Paper No.304, *Murder, Manslaughter and Infanticide* (2006), paras 2.67–2.169.
[489] Criminal Justice Act 2003 Sch.21.

Catherine Elliott and Claire de Than, "Restructuring the Homicide Offences to Tackle Violence, Discrimination and Drugs in a Modern Society" (2009) 20 K.L.J. 69–88 at pp.73, 75, 76:

"The proposed aggravated murder offence would recognise that certain forms of murder target members of a particular community within our society, such as a racist or homophobic murder, or target our society as a whole, such as a terrorist bombing. Such offences can create considerable public distress and insecurity. The impact of these crimes goes beyond the immediate victim, family and friends, and affects the community as a whole. The significance of this wider impact has been recognised in international criminal law, through offences such as crimes against humanity. It is this heightened impact on society that would justify a more serious response from the criminal law . . .

The proposed new offence of aggravated murder would . . . apply in two situations. The first is where the victim was chosen by the defendant because of a general characteristic, such as their race, gender, homosexuality or age; the defendant's conduct created an obvious risk of death; the defendant either intended the death or was subjectively reckless as to causing death; and the conduct was premeditated. In the case of a terrorist attack the victims could have been selected purely on the basis that they were members of British society, and this would amount to a relevant characteristic for these purposes, as the broader the characteristic the greater the potential impact on society, and therefore it would be illogical to restrict this offence to situations where there is reliance upon a very precise characteristic. A terrorist attack might target employees of a particular organisation, such as a scientific laboratory carrying out tests on animals or a foreign embassy. This offence would not deny that all human life is equally valuable, but it would recognise that the loss of certain human lives in certain circumstances will have a greater impact on society than others, and would end the undervaluing of multiple deaths—which is the case with the current homicide offences. Note that the definition of this offence would not seek to lay down a prescribed list of victim characteristics which would be relevant to its commission, because prejudices are irrational and cannot be ranked. Instead, what is important is that the victim has been identified because of that general characteristic, as it is this method of victim selection that generates the broader fear in those members of the public sharing that characteristic . . .

The second way in which the offence of aggravated murder would be committed would be where the offender was a mass or multiple murderer who killed with an intention to kill. As an indication of gravity, conviction of aggravated murder could give rise to a mandatory life sentence and a minimum period in custody of 30 years."

Elliott and de Than do not provide a draft provision to demonstrate how these ideas would be put into practice. Although their suggestion avoids the need to provide a definitive list of which characteristics will be sufficient to fall within it thus avoiding the complex issues of valuing human life, such a provision would be likely to be too loosely defined to provide clear guidance. There are, in addition, conceptual problems with this. An example relates to the treatment of child-murderers. Elliott and de Than recognise that children are most at risk from members of their own family, but argue that aggravated murder should only apply when the defendant targets a child to whom they are not related, on the basis that it is the latter type of child-murder which causes the most amount of disquiet. However, rather than provide a tool in educating the public as to the real dangers posed to their children as Elliott and de Than suggest,[490] surely the distinction would instead lend itself to perpetuating the moral panics often resulting from stranger murders whilst undermining the seriousness of child abuse that turns fatal.

Can homicide offences be graded exclusively in terms of different mental elements? The Law Commission in England and Wales has proposed a new hierarchy of homicide offences incorporating two distinct degrees of murder.

---

[490]   At p.74.

Law Commission No.304, Murder, Manslaughter and Infanticide (2006):

"1.64 In structuring the general homicide offences we have been guided by a key principle: the 'ladder' principle. Individual offences of homicide should exist within a graduated system or hierarchy of offences. This system or hierarchy should reflect the offence's degree of seriousness, without too much overlap between individual offences . . .

1.65 The 'ladder' principle also applies to sentencing. The mandatory life sentence should be confined to the most serious kinds of killing. A discretionary life sentence should be available for less serious (but still highly blameworthy) killings.

1.66 Partial defences currently only affect the verdict of murder. This is because a verdict of murder carries a mandatory sentence. That sentence is not appropriate where there are exceptional mitigating circumstances of the kind involved in the partial defences. These mitigating circumstances necessitate a greater degree of judicial discretion in sentencing. The law creates this discretion by means of the partial defences which reduce what would otherwise be a verdict of murder, which carries a mandatory sentence, to manslaughter, which does not. Therefore, our recommended scheme does not extend the application of the partial defences to second degree murder or manslaughter. These offences would permit the trial judge discretion in sentencing and they therefore lack the primary justification for having partial defences.

The structure of offences

1.67 We believe that the following structure would make the law of homicide more coherent and comprehensible, whilst respecting the principles just set out above:

(1) **First degree murder** (mandatory life penalty)

   (a) Killing intentionally.
   (b) Killing where there was an intention to do serious injury, coupled with an awareness of a serious risk of causing death.

(2) **Second degree murder** (discretionary life maximum penalty)

   (a) Killing where the offender intended to do serious injury.
   (b) Killing where the offender intended to cause some injury or a fear or risk of injury, and was aware of a serious risk of causing death.
   (c) Killing in which there is a partial defence to what would otherwise be first degree murder.

(3) **Manslaughter** (discretionary life maximum penalty)

   (a) Killing through gross negligence as to a risk of causing death.
   (b) Killing through a criminal act:
      (i) intended to cause injury; or
      (ii) where there was an awareness that the act involved a serious risk of causing injury.
   [(c) omitted]"

There is much to recommend these proposals.[491] The "ladder" principle attempts to facilitate a logical approach being taken to the question of distinguishing between different offences and appears to succeed. The proposals shed the areas of homicide law which are often seen as most objectionable at present, namely the GBH rule for murder and the offence of constructive manslaughter. Yet they do so without sacrificing the underlying principles which some might say justify the current position. Those who intend to cause GBH and kill are blameworthy, since whether their victim will die or not is beyond their control. The proposals place this level of blameworthiness on the same rung of the ladder as foresight of a risk of death whilst intending to cause injury. Similarly, those who would fall under the current law of constructive manslaughter through assault resulting in death remain liable for manslaughter, but only where they foresee that injury could result. One issue with the final

---

[491] For a critique of the recommendations, see A. Ashworth, "Principles, Pragmatism and the Law Commission's Recommendations on Homicide Law Reform" [2007] Crim. L.R. 333.

recommendations from the Law Commission is, however, that unlike its original proposals, it recommends that manslaughter would attract a discretionary life maximum penalty as it does under the current law. Rogers suggests that this "would seem to undermine the integrity of the whole new structure of homicide offences", given that there would be nothing in the sentence to differentiate manslaughter from second degree murder.[492]

We have already seen that deciding where to draw the line between murder and manslaughter through the use of mens rea is a much debated topic. The Law Commission has sought to blur the line between the offences by inserting between them the offence of second degree murder to incorporate what would, under the current law, fall within the lower ranks of murder and the upper reaches of manslaughter. Questions remain, however, over where on the ladder certain levels of blameworthiness should be placed. In its provisional proposals the Law Commission singled out killing with intention to kill as the most serious form of homicide and proposed that this be the only way of committing first degree murder.[493] Following consultation, the Law Commission has been persuaded that intention to kill is not always more blameworthy than other forms of mens rea. In the Report an alternative form of mens rea for first degree murder is added: killing with intention to cause serious injury whilst aware of a serious risk of death. Norrie, in commenting on the Law Commission's Consultation Paper which suggested that "reckless indifference" would provide one form of mens rea for second degree murder,[494] provides some arguments in favour of the view that an extreme form of recklessness might actually be sufficient for first degree murder, and that it would equate in terms of blameworthiness with an intention to kill. His view is that there is something, in addition to intentionality, that determines how serious a killing is.[495] This can be referred to as the defendant's "attitudinal state". Norrie's view is that if we take account of the attitude of killers who display "reckless indifference" we might find that they are just as blameworthy as those who intend to kill:

"[d]oing harm so serious as to endanger life can be regarded *substantively* as of the same order of culpability [as intention to kill]. It exhibits a practical indifference that is as bad as intending to kill."[496]

The Law Commission's provisional proposals received criticism in relation to the definition of the term "reckless indifference". It was thought that the term was "unacceptably vague and liable to create a very blurred line between second degree murder and manslaughter".[497] The Law Commission has therefore provided a clear formula for exactly what is needed in terms of recklessness for both first and second degree murder. The defendant must have adverted to a risk of death. But in addition to this, for first degree murder he must have intended to cause serious injury, and for second degree murder he must have intended to cause injury. This last requirement is designed to distinguish those liable for second degree murder from those who are guilty of gross negligence manslaughter,[498] where a risk of death may have been foreseen but it was not the defendant's purpose in acting to harm the victim (e.g. a surgeon operating on a patient). The distinction between first and second degree murder may now lie in the seriousness of harm intended whilst being aware of a risk of death.

---

[492]   J. Rogers, "The New Homicide Ladder" (2007) 157 N.L.J. 48.
[493]   Law Commission Consultation Paper No.177, *A New Homicide Act for England and Wales?* (2005).
[494]   See extract, above, p.695.
[495]   A. Norrie, "Between Orthodox Subjectivism and Moral Contextualism: Intention and the Consultation Paper" [2006] Crim. L.R. 486–513.
[496]   At p.494.
[497]   Law Commission Paper No.304 (2006), para.2.102.
[498]   Law Commission Paper No.304 (2006), para.2.110.

Given that the Law Commission has abandoned its plan to define "serious" injury,[499] this leaves a great deal of discretion to the jury with little guidance on how to distinguish between the offences. Further, it is arguable that an intention to kill should be singled out as the most serious form of blameworthiness and would be effective in singling out the worst forms of killings. Some, such as Norrie and Wilson,[500] may disagree, but it should be noted that the ladder structure within the original proposals provided at least the possibility for those who are aware of death to be labelled as murderers, albeit in the second degree.

The other area of concern surrounding the ladder of offences is how the partial defences would operate. A preliminary point is that mercy killing, except in cases in which the defendant can show diminished responsibility, would amount to first degree murder with no partial defence to accommodate the lesser blameworthiness that many would argue such killers demonstrate. The main reason for this, the Law Commission states, is that euthanasia was outside the terms of its reference.[501] However, in its Report the Law Commission recommends that a further consultation exercise take place to explore the possibility of creating a separate partial defence of mercy killing.[502]

The defences are, however, extended beyond the current law by the proposal to allow duress to act as a full defence to first degree murder, second degree murder and attempted murder.[503] This is in addition to the two partial defences of provocation (now replaced by loss of control) and diminished responsibility which would operate only in relation to first degree murder, reducing the offence to second degree murder rather than to manslaughter. The reasoning behind this is that the existing partial defences were created in order to avoid the mandatory life penalty for murder; with the mandatory sentence being confined to first degree murder and judges enjoying discretion in sentencing for second degree murder there would be no need to reduce the liability of such killers to that of manslaughter. Or would there?

Oliver Quick and Celia Wells, "Getting Tough with Defences" [2006] Crim. L.R. 514 at pp.515–516:

"(a) What's in a label?
A person entitled to a partial defence will nonetheless be convicted of second degree murder, whereas now they would be convicted of manslaughter. The unlawful homicide with which they currently share that label—involuntary manslaughters—will in the main still remain as manslaughters. Partial defence killings would therefore be elevated in seriousness to a tier above and carry the murder label. Since second degree murder could also under the proposals include some killings that would currently amount to murder (those where there is intention to cause serious harm), this is more than just a rebranding. The Commission seems relatively untroubled by this promotion of cases from manslaughter to second degree murder. This is 'not seen as a problem' yet the accompanying counter-argument addresses a rather different point. . . .

(b) Like with unlike?
Partial defence murders would be bedfellows with those who are recklessly indifferent to causing death. Some of the hidden premises can be deduced in the arguments about reckless indifference to death. First, the [Consultation Paper] argues that this should not be included in first degree murder. The following paragraph then states that

---

[499] Law Commission Paper No.304 (2006), para.2.93.
[500] Cited in Law Commission Paper No.304 (2006), para.2.60.
[501] Law Commission Consultation Paper No.177 (2005), para.8.3.
[502] Law Commission Paper No.304 (2006), para.7.49.
[503] Law Commission Paper No.304 (2006), para.6.212. At present duress is not a defence to murder or attempted murder. Some have in the past argued that there are compelling reasons for adding duress to the current group of partial defences: see, for example, Lacey, "Partial Defences to Homicide: Questions of Power and Principle in Imperfect and Less Imperfect Worlds", in A. Ashworth and B. Mitchell (eds), *Rethinking English Homicide Law* (Oxford: OUP, 2000), p.107.

a person should only be guilty of second degree murder if the reckless indifference was to death (and not merely to serious harm) because 'as the most serious homicide after first degree murder [it] should require a very high level of culpability.' The combined effect of restricting the partial defences to first degree murder and of then placing them in the same category as killings accompanied by either intention to cause serious harm or reckless indifference to causing death, is that they would in future represent a quite different level of culpability than they do now. Antony Duff has noted, and we agree, that grouping someone who deliberately killed but had a partial defence with someone who killed through reckless indifference is 'quite misleading' as a matter of fair or accurate labelling. In their response to [Partial Defences to Murder], Justice for Women pointed out that shaking off the shackles of a murder label is often as important a focus of the post-conviction struggle of abused women who kill, as is their quest for freedom."

Thus, Quick and Wells are of the view that the Law Commission "over-emphasises *relative culpability* at the expense of the significance of labelling".[504] The ladder of offences is neat and logical, but there remains the argument of whether those that suffer from diminished responsibility ought to be labelled as murderers, albeit in the second degree, rather than manslaughterers. Part of the reasoning behind the Law Commission's recommendations relates to the need for the partial defences to operate in the same manner. The law would become too complex if provocation (or loss of control) reduced liability from first degree murder to second degree murder but it was felt that for labelling purposes it was better that diminished responsibility were able to reduce liability to manslaughter. Given that defendants often plead these defences together, the jury's task would be overcomplicated if they were told that the effect of each of the partial defences was different and this would lead to the potential for "split juries" who agree that the case for first degree murder is not made out but cannot decide whether the verdict should be one of second degree murder or manslaughter.[505] Whilst many support the view that an offender suffering from diminished responsibility deserves a label of "manslaughterer" rather than "murderer", the same is not true of those who react to provocation.

D. Unlawful Homicide—A Single Offence

Should English law abandon any such thoughts of further categorisation, indeed abandon its existing categories of homicide offences, and replace them with a single offence of unlawful homicide?

In *Hyam v DPP* Lord Kilbrandon said:

"There does not appear to be any good reason why the crimes of murder and manslaughter should not both be abolished, and the single crime of unlawful homicide substituted; one case will differ from another in gravity, and that can be taken care of by variation of sentences downwards from life imprisonment."[506]

The main argument that can be adduced in favour of the introduction of a single offence of unlawful homicide is that murder varies so widely both in character and in culpability that the judge ought to have a discretion as to sentence. Writing before the abolition of the death penalty, Morris and Blom-Cooper espoused the view that murder is a unique crime set apart from other homicide offences.[507] Experience, it seems, has persuaded them that they were wrong.

---

[504]   At p.515.
[505]   Law Commission Paper No.304 (2006), paras 2.132–2.145.
[506]   *Hyam v DPP* [1975] A.C. 55 at 98. A similar proposal was made by the New Zealand Law Reform Committee but has not been implemented (*Report on Culpable Homicide*, 1976, pp.3–4).
[507]   See extract, above, p.784.

L. Blom-Cooper and T. Morris, With Malice Aforethought (2004), pp.56–57:

"[T]he distinction between murder and other unlawful homicides is essentially artificial. 'Murder' is a term used in common parlance, often without much discrimination, to describe incidents of violent and unnatural death to which social opprobrium is attached, notwithstanding that a court may conclude at trial (if any) that the proper verdict under the law is one of manslaughter. Murder is essentially a term of art; a construct having its origins in the intellectual patchwork of the common law that, responsive to the currents of opinion but without any over-arching logic—still less philosophy—that has evolved over the centuries. In no way can it be regarded as a phenomenon *sui generis*, since the boundary between murder and manslaughter shifts as readily as the precise limits of a sand bar under the influence of wind and tide.

The defences which may be employed to identify the crime as manslaughter, rather than murder, are as chimerical in character as the attempts to create categories of murder to which may be attached a range of differential penalties. The question must, therefore, be posed whether it is profitable to expend further intellectual energy and resources in pursuit of the *ignis fatuus* of their perfection.

Were the mandatory penalty of life imprisonment for murder to be abolished, the incentive for defendants to persuade the courts that, if they plead guilty it is to manslaughter and not to murder, would cease to exist, and with it the problems of interpretation of motives and states of mind that presently demand so much legal attention. That incentive removed, the existence of a common sentencing tariff to reflect the proportionality of penalty to the specific nature of the criminal event, would make plain the underlying imperative; the establishment of a single offence of criminal homicide."

Thus, other benefits of such reform are pragmatic. In many cases where a murder conviction could probably have been obtained, prosecutors are content to charge with manslaughter, or accept pleas of guilty to manslaughter. This saves much time and expense and indicates that prosecutors, at least, are often willing to rely on judges exercising their sentencing discretion reasonably.[508] For example, in the Iranian Embassy siege case[509] the prosecution accepted a plea of guilty to manslaughter in a fairly clear-cut case of murder; the defendant was promptly sentenced to life imprisonment, the same sentence he would have received after a long, expensive trial resulting in a murder conviction. Similar considerations, coupled with a desire to shield the relatives of victims from hitherto unrevealed details, prompted the prosecution in *Sutcliffe* (the so-called Yorkshire Ripper case)[510] to agree to a plea to manslaughter (the judge declined to accept such a plea). If there were a single offence of unlawful homicide, one would avoid the present anomalous situation of some prosecutors accepting lesser pleas, while other prosecutors insist on pursuing a murder charge.

Further, juries appear unwilling to convict of murder except in clear cases as this is tying the judge's hands as to sentence. By returning verdicts of manslaughter in many cases, they are allowing the judge to take all the circumstances into account before imposing an appropriate sentence.[511] Lord Denning has said that "in many cases which are in law plainly murder, juries return verdicts of manslaughter,

---

[508] A single homicide offence has also been supported by Victim Support who are concerned that in trying to reduce their crime from murder to manslaughter defendants often attack the character of the victim: Law Commission Consultation Paper No.177 (2005), para.2.33.

[509] *The Times*, May 8, 1981, p.1, col.2.

[510] *The Times*, April 30, 1981, p.1, col.1.

[511] An alternative method of avoiding the operation of "jury equity" in this way would be to abolish the mandatory life sentence for murder. During debates in the House of Lords, Lord Lloyd of Berwick tabled an amendment to the Coroners and Justice Bill, at the suggestion of Professor John Spencer, that would have given the jury in a murder trial the option to find "extenuating circumstances" whilst convicting of murder. This in turn would have permitted the judge to impose a sentence other than life imprisonment. This amendment was opposed by the Government on the basis that it would blur the boundary between murder and manslaughter and undermine the mandatory life sentence for murder: Ministry of Justice, *Homicide Reform Bulletin No.2*, August 2009. See also: I. Dennis, "Reforming Murder: the Coroners and Justice Bill" (Editorial) [2009] Crim. L.R. 687 and above, fn.54.

because they do not think the death sentence is appropriate".[512] Such a practice seems to have survived the abolition of the death penalty. In *Repouille v US*,[513] a case described as "inescapably first degree murder", the jury, quite perversely, returned a verdict of second degree murder enabling the judge to impose a suspended sentence. If the law is in a strait-jacket, judges, prosecutors and juries will start ignoring the law. If this starts happening too extensively, should not the law be changed?

A single offence of unlawful homicide would mean that life imprisonment would be restricted to the worst cases. Such persons would actually remain in prison for a substantial period of time. This would increase public confidence in the life sentence. At the moment, the judge has discretion in setting the minimum term to be served in prison, although that discretion should be exercised in accordance with the guidance provided by the Criminal Justice Act 2003 Sch.21. In some ways this guidance makes the exercise very similar to setting a determinate sentence in cases of manslaughter, although it ought to be borne in mind that the time actually spent in prison will depend upon the perceived dangerousness of the murderer and the whole of the term must be served, unlike determinate sentences. The different sentencing bands for minimum terms in murder cases demonstrate the variation in culpability that murderers display under the current system. It might be less opaque, however, to admit defeat in trying to single out the worst types of killing for the mandatory sentence and simply allow judges to impose sentences of life imprisonment when they come across those cases that deserve it.

The creation of a single offence would also mean that the somewhat artificial rules on loss of control, diminished responsibility, infanticide and suicide pacts could be abandoned.[514] These matters could then simply be treated as mitigating factors relevant to sentencing.

What are the arguments against the introduction of a single offence of unlawful homicide?

Criminal Law Revision Committee, Working Paper on Offences against the Person, 1976:

"5. To have a single offence of homicide, combining murder with a lesser offence of manslaughter, would mean that the jury's verdict would leave the judge with no guidance as to the gravity of the offence. In the absence of any new provision introducing a system of special verdicts, the judge would have to assess, in deciding what penalty to impose, whether intent to kill or a less serious degree of criminality amounting to what is now manslaughter had been proved. If the accused pleaded not guilty, the facts of the case would come out in the evidence, but the verdict of the jury would be confined to the issue of guilt or innocence of the offence of homicide. The judge would be left to decide, for example, whether the provocation alleged in mitigation (with the merger of murder and manslaughter, provocation would be a matter of mitigation only) existed in fact. If the accused pleaded guilty to homicide, the judge would have even less material on which to decide such questions since he would not have had the benefit of hearing detailed evidence. Thus the offence of homicide would apply to a very wide range of circumstances, varying in their degree of gravity, and the judge would be left to determine the true nature of the offence without the assistance of the jury. The majority of us think that the argument discussed in this paragraph is a very strong one; a minority of members, however, consider that it is overstated.

6. To have a single offence of homicide covering such a wide range of acts would make a conviction of the offence relatively uninformative in that it would be used to describe the most heinous case of murder and the least serious case of manslaughter. Although the Committee's proposals about the existing offence of manslaughter would reduce the scope of the single offence of homicide (combining murder and manslaughter), it would still be a wide-ranging offence classifying under the same head both a person who killed under provocation or while

---

[512]   Royal Commission on Capital Punishment, Cmnd.8932 (1953), para.27.

[513]   Above, fn.475.

[514]   Of course, it does not follow that these defences would *have* to be abolished. See R. Mackay, "Diminished Responsibility and Mentally Disordered Offenders", in A. Ashworth and B. Mitchell, *Rethinking English Homicide Law* (Oxford: OUP, 2000), pp.80–81.

suffering from diminished responsibility and a person who killed deliberately without any provocation and not suffering from any mental disorder.

7. To abolish the offence of murder as such, although retaining it as part of a wider offence of homicide, may appear to have the effect of lessening the seriousness of taking life. We think that, in the public's mind, there is a stigma attaching to a conviction of murder and that this rightly emphasises the seriousness of the offence and may have a significant deterrent value . . .

8 . . . [T]he majority of us see advantages in the mandatory sentence and think that there is a need for a special penalty for the most serious cases of homicide in order to reassure the public and also for the purposes of prevention and deterrence."[515]

There are two further objections to a suggested new offence of unlawful homicide. First, such a proposal would result in a substantial increase of judicial discretion in sentencing. In Ch.1, the dangers of such discretion were considered. Over the past three decades there has been a strong movement away from judicial discretion in sentencing which ought to lead to a more precise classification of offences. It can only be a retrograde step to propose reforms to the substantive law that would involve an *increase* in judicial discretion in sentencing.

Secondly, the Law Commission makes the following point:

"If, for Blom-Cooper and Morris, fault is merely a factor to reflect in sentence, then that could logically be said to be true of the outcome (the victim's death) as well. Why single out unlawful *killing* for separate treatment, when it may purely have been chance that the victim died, and the result could have been more or less serious bodily harm done?"[516]

If we were to abolish the distinction between murder and manslaughter would it not follow that we should abolish the distinction between such offences as malicious wounding and inflicting grievous bodily harm and wounding and causing grievous bodily harm with intent?

---

[515] Similar views were expressed by Lord Hailsham in *Cunningham* [1982] A.C. 566 at 580.
[516] Law Commission Consultation Paper No.177 (2005), para.2.34.

9

OFFENCES AGAINST PROPERTY

I. INTRODUCTION

There is a wide variety of offences against property in English law, for example, theft, fraud, robbery, burglary, taking a motor vehicle or other conveyance without authority, abstracting electricity, blackmail, handling stolen goods, forgery, criminal damage—and many more.

A. The Level of Offending

So widespread are these offences that people are more likely to be the victim of a property offence than of any other kind of crime. In the year ending September 2013, offences of theft, robbery and fraud accounted for approximately 58 per cent of total recorded crime.[1] Of this, theft offences (including burglary, vehicle related thefts and other thefts of property) amounted to 50 per cent.[2] Robbery, which was formerly categorised in the official statistics as an offence of violence rather than a property offence, but is now recorded in a stand-alone category, accounts for just under 2 per cent of all recorded crime.[3] However, police statistics only deal with those offences which are recorded and thus this source of information about the extent of many forms of property crime is not accurate. The Crime Survey for England and Wales (CSEW), formerly known as the British Crime Surveys (BCS) attempts to shed some light upon the dark figure of crime, by surveying householders in England and Wales asking them whether they have experienced crime in the past year, and inviting them to give details of offences against them.[4] The 2010/11 BCS illustrates that the public's likelihood of reporting crime varies considerably by the type of offence. For instance, in that year, 96 per cent of vehicle thefts were reported[5] (largely for insurance reasons). However, for theft from a person only 29 per cent were reported.[6]

The reasons for the differences between the police and the CSEW/BCS figures are not hard to identify. For example, the value of the property involved may be perceived by the victim (and the police) as being too trivial to proceed; the cost and inconvenience of taking action may make some victims

---

[1]   1,885,983 offences out of 3,725,281 total recorded offences. Office for National Statistics, Statistical Bulletin, *Crime in England and Wales Year Ending September 2013* (2014), pp.17–19. Crime statistics were transferred from the Home Office to the Office for National Statistics (ONS) in April 2012. The ONS quarterly release now presents the most recent crime statistics from both the police and the CSEW, as well as drawing upon data from other sources, including crime reports from the National Fraud Intelligence Bureau.

[2]   ONS, Statistical Bulletin, *Crime in England and Wales Year Ending September 2013* (2014), p.50 and table A4.

[3]   ONS, Statistical Bulletin, *Crime in England and Wales Year Ending September 2013* (2014), p.35 and table P1.

[4]   Available at *http://www.crimesurvey.co.uk/index.html* [Accessed March 2014].

[5]   R. Chaplin, J. Flatley and K. Smith, *Home Office Statistical Bulletin 2010/2011* (2011), p.37 and table 2.11.

[6]   Chaplin, Flatley and Smith, *Home Office Statistical Bulletin 2010/2011* (2011), p.37 and table 2.11.

reluctant to proceed; it may be viewed as a private matter to be dealt with themselves; it may be impossible to identify offenders (as will be the case with much shoplifting); the behaviour may not be seen by even the victim as truly criminal (as may be the case with the problem of bad cheques); and, in some cases, the victim may never even learn of their loss. When asked why they had not reported a crime to the police in the 2010/11 BCS, 72 per cent of victims gave the reason that they perceived it as too trivial, there was no loss or they believed that the police would or could not do much about it.[7]

The cost of property crime is vast. For instance, Levi and Burrows have estimated that fraud in the United Kingdom financial community resulted in direct losses of £12.98 billion in 2005, with the total known cost of fraud and dealing with fraud amounting to "at least" £13.9 billion.[8] The National Fraud Authority, part of the Attorney General's Office, as a result of collecting better quality data, found that the overall cost of fraud to both the private and public sector is more than double this conservative estimate, suggesting that it was as much as £41.8 billion in 2013.[9] Loss through fraud committed with the use of plastic payment cards reached £388 million in the United Kingdom in the year 2011–2012, of which £245.8 million involved "card-not-present" (CNP) fraud (where a card has been used on the internet, over the phone or by mail order).[10] This figure represented a rise of 11 per cent since 2011, with CNP fraud accounting for 63 per cent of all card fraud (up from 26 per cent in 2002), although this needs to be seen in the context of a huge rise in CNP spending over the past decade, particularly over the internet.[11] In the year 2011/12 4.7 per cent of plastic card owners (an estimated 2 million adults) reported that they had been a victim of card fraud.[12] This is the second consecutive year in which there has been a statistically significant fall in plastic card fraud, with levels returning to those seen in the 2007/08 survey.[13] The introduction of chip and pin technology has been heralded as a success in reducing losses in respect of face-to-face fraud, which in 2012 amounted to £54.5 million (an increase of 26 per cent from 2011, down 75 per cent from peak losses of £218.8 million in 2004),[14] but such technology cannot be used over the internet. Initiatives such as secure payment systems introduced by card providers are designed to go some way to reducing card fraud on the internet, and a special police unit operated by the Metropolitan Police and City of London Police entitled the Dedicated Cheque and Plastic Crime Unit (DCPCU) has been working alongside banking industry fraud investigators to try to reduce fraud since 2002.[15] In addition to measures being taken by the retail and banking industries to try to reduce this type of fraud, the government has also reacted by creating agencies and organisations to combat fraud. In 1988 the Serious Fraud Office was established as an independent government organisation to investigate and prosecute serious and complex fraud cases.[16] In 2006 the Serious Organised Crime Agency (SOCA), was established as a national

---

[7]   Chaplin, J. Flatley and K. Smith, *Home Office Statistical Bulletin 2010/2011* (2011), p.55 and table 2.12.

[8]   M. Levi and J. Burrows, "Measuring the Impact of Fraud in the UK" (2008) 48 Brit. J. Criminol. 293–318.

[9]   National Fraud Authority, *Annual Fraud Indicator* (2013), available at *https://www.gov.uk/government/uploads/system/uploads/attachment_data/file/206552/nfa-annual-fraud-indicator-2013.pdf* [Accessed March 2014], pp.13–21. The Authority was closed in 2014 and its functions transferred to other bodies, including the National Crime Authority and Action Fraud: *https://www.gov.uk/government/speeches/national-fraud-authority* [Accessed March 2014].

[10]   Financial Fraud Action UK, *Card Fraud: the Facts 2013* (2013) available at *http://www.financialfraudaction.org.uk/publications/files/assets/downloads/Fraud%20The%20Facts%202013.pdf* [Accessed March 2014], pp.10–14.

[11]   Financial Fraud Action UK, *Card Fraud: the Facts 2013* (2013), fn.10 above, pp.12–15.

[12]   ONS, *Chapter 3: Plastic Card* Fraud (2013), available *http://www.ons.gov.uk/ons/dcp171776_309774.pdf* [Accessed March 2014], pp.3–4

[13]   ONS, *Chapter 3: Plastic Card* Fraud (2013), fn.12 above.

[14]   ONS, *Chapter 3: Plastic Card* Fraud (2013), fn.12 above, p.26. It has been suggested that some of this recent increase is due to fraudsters finding ways of stealing both the card and the pin.

[15]   ONS, *Chapter 3: Plastic Card* Fraud (2013), fn.12 above, pp.44–45; also *http://www.financialfraudaction.org.uk/Police-The-dcpcu.asp* [Accessed March 2014].

[16]   See *http://www.sfo.gov.uk/* [Accessed March 2014]; Criminal Justice Act 1987 s.1.

law enforcement agency, working in close collaboration with UK intelligence and law enforcement partners (including the UK police forces and HM Revenue and Customs (HMRC), to prevent and detect serious organised crime).[17] SOCA has now been abolished,[18] and its operations merged into the National Crime Agency, an intelligence-led organisation, which will provide leadership and collaborate with law enforcement agencies and other agencies in relation to the fight against fraud and cyber crime through its Organised Crime Command (OCC), Economic Crime Command (ECC) and National Cyber Crime Unit.[19]

There is a wide diversity of offences thrown together under the umbrella of property offences. The harm done may vary from damage that endangers life, through robbery and "professional" theft to behaviour that lies at the very fringes of criminality. There is no typical offender (although the chances of it being a young male are even higher than for other types of offences). The public imagination may conjure up images of Fagin, Bill Sikes or Ronald Biggs and those large-scale professional crimes that capture the news headlines such as the robbery in Kent of a security company which was hailed as biggest robbery in UK history,[20] but, although professional criminals do exist, there also exist a vast army of occasional criminals: the opportunist burglar, the shoplifter, the juvenile joy-rider, the naïve passer of dud cheques, and the "respectable" employee who takes advantage of his employer's trust to embezzle funds. Property offences encompass crime that could be described as violent[21] to crime that could be labelled as white-collar crime.[22]

B. The Sociological Background

Given the diversity of property offenders and offences, it is not surprising that there exists a multiplicity of theories attempting to account for such criminality. Some attempts have tried to establish links between economic conditions and the rate of property offending.[23] Overall conclusions are difficult to draw and any causal relationship is unlikely to be straightforward. There are many varied explanations as to why people commit property offences, and discussion of these is beyond the scope of this book. However, an understanding of the law is assisted by an appreciation of the context in which such offences occur and the extent to which the law is utilised as a response to offending behaviour.

---

[17]   Serious Organised Crime and Police Act 2005 s.1; Serious Organised Crime Agency, *SOCA Annual Plan 2013/14*, available at *http://www.octf.gov.uk/getattachment/bc73bdfc-9688-43a4-a3b1-897164f3c04b/SOCA-Annual-Plan-2013-14.aspx* [Accessed March 2014].

[18]   Crime and Courts Act 2013 s.15 and Sch.8.

[19]   Crime and Courts Act 2013 Pt 1; National Crime Agency, *The NCA Commitment to Working in Partnership with UK Operational Partners* (2014), available at *http://www.nationalcrimeagency.gov.uk/publications/178-the-nca-commitment-to-working-in-partnership-with-uk-operational-partners/file* [Accessed March 2014].

[20]   S. Tendler and C. Merrell, "Armed raiders steal £40m in Britain's biggest cash robbery" *The Times*, February 23, 2006.

[21]   Robbery, although a violent offence, is described here as a property offence because the violence is incidental to the main aim, the acquisition of property.

[22]   This term was invented by E.H. Sutherland in *White-Collar Crime* (New York: Reinhart and Winston, 1949) to illuminate crime committed not by young working-class males but by persons of apparent respectability in the course of their employment. There now exists a wealth of literature on this subject. See, for example, D. Nelkin, "White Collar Crime", in M. Maguire, R. Morgan and R. Reiner, *The Oxford Handbook of Criminology*, 5th edn (Oxford: OUP, 2012), pp.623–659 and M. Levi, *Regulating Fraud* (London: Tavistock Press, 1987).

[23]   See, for example, A. Sidebottom et al., "Theft in Price Volatile Markets: On the Relationship Between Copper Price and Copper Theft" (2011) 48 J. of Research in Crime and Delinquency 396–418 and A. Sidebottom, M. Ashby and S.D. Johnson, "Copper Cable Theft: Revisiting the Price-Theft Hypothesis" (2014) 51 J. of Research in Crime and Delinquency 684-700, which support the hypothesis that there is a link between increases in the price of copper between 2006 and 2012 and a rise in the incidence of copper cable theft.

J. Hepburn, Occasional Property Crime, in R. Meier (ed.), Major Forms of Crime (1984), pp.88–89:

"Among the earliest criminal laws were those pertaining to property. In a highly stratified society, especially one with a capitalistic economy, power and status depend to a large degree on the economic resources a person accumulates. Consequently, there generally is a strong, negative public reaction to property offenses in the United States. The reaction is particularly strong against armed robbery, mugging, and arson, because these offenses combine loss of property with a potential for physical harm to the victim. Residential burglary, which violates the sanctity of the home, also generates a strong condemnation. In contrast, the public outcry against shoplifting, vandalism, and other 'petty' forms of property crime is least vocal.

The magnitude of the public's reaction to property offenses does not seem to be associated with the amount of financial loss involved. Compared to the multimillion-dollar losses which result from corporate crime and organized crime, the losses incurred by occasional property crimes are quite small . . .

Armed robbery netted a total of $339 million in property loss, for example, while the total loss due to burglary was $3 billion. According to the FBI, the total cost of all Part I property offenses was slightly over $10 billion. In comparison, the annual cost to the public of faulty goods, monopolistic practices, and other corporate crimes has been estimated at between $174 and $231 billion . . . Furthermore, the financial losses due to the criminal activities of organized crime are estimated to be upwards of $50 billion annually . . . Despite the greater loss due to corporate and organized crime, these crimes receive less public condemnation than the more traditional property crimes.

The public's reaction to property crimes is reflected in the legal reaction taken by law enforcement agencies. Police agencies are largely reactive; they respond to the crimes that are brought to their attention by citizens. Legislators also are responsive to their constituency's concern with property crimes. As a result, a significant amount of the time, money, and energy of law enforcement agencies is directed toward ordinary property crimes. Increased police patrols are justified on the (false) assumption that they reduce the opportunity for crime and increase the risk of arrest. Merchants and residents are advised by the police of various 'target-hardening' tactics, such as exterior lighting and barred windows, designed to reduce the opportunity for crime. Prosecutors and legislators champion the view that more severe legal penalties are needed to deter crime.

Although the public and legal reaction to property crimes in general is rather severe, the reaction to those who are occasional offenders tends to be more restrained. Compared to other offenders processed routinely by the courts, the occasional offender is (1) less likely to have a criminal record of prior arrests and convictions, (2) more likely to have been charged with a minor offense, (3) more respectable, as defined in terms of employment history, residential stability, and family relationships, and (4) more repentant. As a result of these characteristics of the offender and the offense, the occasional offender is treated less harshly by the criminal justice system. The prosecutor's office is less likely to file initial charges against the offender. If it does, there is a strong probability that the offender will be diverted from prosecution to some special restitution-oriented program or that the charges will be dismissed before trial. Should the offender be convicted, a prison sentence is most unlikely."

The Crime Survey for England and Wales (CSEW) results are a useful source of information about public attitudes towards property offences, in two main contexts. First, such surveys have a great deal to say about the sorts of crime that people are most anxious about and the steps they take to reduce their vulnerability. Fear of being "mugged" is a commonly expressed concern; for some people this may cause them to avoid going out at night at all if it can be avoided; for others it might (especially in the case of women) mean never going out alone. Fear of burglary might cause some to support neighbourhood watch schemes. Fear of having their computers used for fraud might cause executives to spend large amounts of money on security systems and security experts.

Secondly, such surveys are a valuable means of ascertaining what the public thinks about sentencing practices in relation to property offences. Generally, public opinion polls reveal a punitive approach to sentencing[24] but it appears that "people overestimate the leniency of the

---

[24]   P. Mayhew, D. Elliott and L. Dowds, *The 1988 British Crime Survey* (1989), p.43. See also N. Walker and W. Hough (eds), *Public Attitudes to Sentencing* (Aldershot: Gower, 1988), pp.203–217. The 2009/10 BCS reported that 11 % of people identified that "too lenient sentencing" was the main cause of crime (the third most popular perceived single cause after drugs

courts".[25] Results obtained from the 2010/11 CSEW show that, when asked the question; "Out of every 100 men aged 21 or over who are tried and found guilty of house burglary how many are sent to prison?", 86 per cent of respondents provided a large under-estimate of the actual custody rate.[26] Research in Victoria, Australia, found that judges are not more lenient than the local community and that the community does not "speak with one voice" on sentencing, meaning that there were huge ranges in opinion as to the appropriate sentences to impose in particular cases.[27] The community does not have firm views as to what is an appropriate sentence for a case and those who are more certain they are right are the harsher ones.[28]

Further, surveys indicate that while members of the public may have a generalised preference for tough sentences, when asked about a specific case study, their attitude is less punitive.[29] There is evidence that some victims of crime have similar attitudes, and that their views as to what should happen in their own case may appear lenient in comparison to their general opinion about sentencing.[30] Other research concludes that most victims have no idea at all about the sentence which should be imposed: "As far as the justice of their case is concerned, they have suffered a lobotomy".[31]

Even in abstract terms, the attitudes expressed in such surveys are not always in favour of stiffer penalties. Where the offence is perceived as less serious, there may be considerable support for non-custodial alternatives to imprisonment. One in 12 of the respondents in the second British Crime Survey favoured the use of informal police warnings for shoplifters over the age of 25 with previous convictions.[32] In the 2010/11 CSEW 37 per cent of respondents favoured the use of a caution/warning in the case of a 30-year-old man with no previous convictions who admitted a minor theft of clothing from a small independent shop.[33] This raises once again the issue whether some offences are properly the concern of the criminal law.

C. The Legal Background

Discussion so far makes it clear that the structure of property offences is very different from the offences against the person already covered. With the latter, the seriousness of the injury was critical in the structuring of offences and concomitant levels of punishment: for example, causing death is more serious than causing grievous harm, which in turn is worse than causing actual bodily harm—

---

and lack of discipline from parents), J. Flatley et al., Home Office Statistical Bulletin 12/10, *Crime in England and Wales 2009/10* (2009), table 5a.

25   P. Mayhew et al., fn.24 above, p.43. This finding has been confirmed by numerous studies, including N. Walker and W. Hough (eds), fn.24 above, pp.185–202, and M. Hough et al., *Attitudes to Sentencing and Trust in Justice: Explaining Trends from the Crime Survey for England and Wales* (2013), who found that attitudes had changed little over a 25-year period (pp.22–23). Studies of other jurisdictions have indicated similar findings: M. Hough and J.V. Roberts, "Public Opinion, Crime and Criminal Justice", in M. Maguire, R. Morgan and R. Reiner, *The Oxford Handbook of Criminology*, 5th edn (Oxford: OUP, 2012), p.286.

26   M. Hough et al., fn.25 above, pp.19–21.

27   A. Lovegrove, "Public Opinion, Sentencing and Lenience: An Empirical Study Involving Judges Consulting the Community" [2007] Crim. L.R. 769 at 777.

28   Lovegrove "Public Opinion, Sentencing and Lenience: An Empirical Study Involving Judges Consulting the Community" [2007] Crim. L.R. 769 at 778.

29   M. Hough et al., fn.25 above, p.25; J.V. Roberts and M. Hough, "Custody or Community? Exploring the Boundaries of Public Punitiveness in England and Wales" (2011) 11 Criminology & Criminal Justice 181–197; A. Lovegrove, "Sentencing and Public Opinion: An Empirical Study of Punitiveness and Lenience and its Implications for Penal Moderation" (2013) 46 Australian & New Zealand J. of Criminol. 200–220.

30   J. Shapland, J. Willmore and P. Duff, *Victims in the Criminal Justice System* (Aldershot: Gower, 1985).

31   A. Cretney and G. Davis, *Punishing Violence* (London: Routledge, 1995), pp.156–157. This research examined victims of assault but there is no reason to suppose victims of property crimes have a clearer view.

32   P. Mayhew et al., fn.24 above,, p.44.

33   M. Hough et al., fn.25 above, pp.25–26.

and so on. Offences against property, however, are not structured in such a clear manner. It is not possible to follow the same pattern in structuring liability because of the difficulty in measuring the "harm" done. One possible method here is by assessing the value of the property involved. English law, however, has eschewed such an approach at a substantive level (although this is an important factor at the sentencing stage) and instead has chosen to distinguish property offences by the method of taking or dealing with the property. According to this approach, deceiving someone into agreeing to part with their property (formerly, the offence of obtaining property by deception) is treated differently from coercing someone with threats into parting with property (blackmail). Whether each grouping is sufficiently precise and/or meaningful is a matter to be returned to after an examination of the offences themselves.

Another distinctive feature of the offences against property is that they are mainly statutory and largely found in modern statutes, in particular, the Theft Act 1968, the Theft Act 1978, the Fraud Act 2006, the Criminal Damage Act 1971, the Forgery and Counterfeiting Act 1981 and the Proceeds of Crime Act 2002. These statutes are somewhat distinctive in that they are similar to a code. Most English statutes consolidate, amend or add to the pre-existing law. The approach here is different. Take, for instance, the Theft Act 1968. This Act swept away all the previous law on the subject, creating entirely new law dealing with most forms of dishonest dealings with property. As English law enters an era possibly culminating in a codification of the whole of the criminal law,[34] it becomes particularly important and interesting to see how our courts have handled these areas of law.

Before examining the property offences themselves two important preliminary points must be made.

The Criminal Law Revision Committee, in putting forward its proposals[35] which largely became the Theft Act 1968, wished to avoid the technicality and complexity of the old law under the Larceny Acts and, accordingly, deliberately tried to frame as much of the legislation as possible in ordinary "simple" language capable of being easily understood by the layman. Accordingly, many key concepts (for example, "dishonesty") were inserted in the legislation without definition. The courts could, of course, have developed their own legal definitions of such concepts but have instead preferred to leave the meaning of such words to the jury, as questions of fact. The jury are ordinary people; they know what ordinary words mean—and do not need judges to explain their meaning to them. This approach, leading to a lack of fixed standards and inconsistency, has proved highly controversial, as will be seen in this chapter.

The second preliminary issue in some ways completely contradicts the above point. Offences against property deal with interference with other persons' rights or interests in property. One is free to do as one likes with one's own property. It is therefore always necessary to ascertain that there is some other person who has some right or interest in the property. For instance, in *Corcoran v Whent*[36] a defendant ate a meal in a hotel restaurant and left without paying. In order to determine his liability for theft it became necessary to determine whether at the time he decided not to pay (after he had eaten the food), the food (in his stomach) belonged to anyone else! If it belonged to him he could commit no crime as he would not be interfering with anyone else's rights or interests in property.[37]

---

[34] Law Commission Working Paper No.143, *Codification of the Criminal Law* (1985). At present, the codification project has been "removed" from the Law Commission's programme (Law Com. No.311, *Tenth Programme of Law Reform* (HC 605, 2008)). Although the Law Commission still supports codification as a longer-term aim, it is currently focusing upon the simplification of the criminal law: *http://lawcommission.justice.gov.uk/areas/codification-of-the-general-principles-of-the-criminal-law.htm* [Accessed March 2014].

[35] Criminal Law Revision Committee, Eighth Report, *Theft and Related Offences*, Cmnd.2977 (1966).

[36] *Corcoran v Whent* [1977] Crim. L.R. 52.

[37] The defendant's conviction for theft was quashed. Once he had eaten the food he could not "deal with it" and it was no

However, how is one to determine whether anyone else has such a proprietary right or interest in the property? There is a whole body of law—the law of property, contract and quasi-contract—devoted to answering such questions. The Theft Act 1968, for example, uses many technical legal terms such as "trespasser",[38] "proprietary right or interest",[39] "trust",[40] etc. As these terms are undefined it would appear reasonable that they be assigned their established civil law meaning. Such an approach would, however, fly in the face of the philosophy that words in such legislation be assigned their ordinary meaning by ordinary people, the jury. There is some force in such an approach. Civil law meanings of words need adaptation to the purposes of the criminal law, for instance, to accommodate the normal requirement of mens rea. Further, the criminal law ought to reflect everyday values and "the way we live". Who better to reflect such values than those "everyday folk", the jury? This appears to be the prevailing articulated view. In *Morris*,[41] one of the leading House of Lords' decisions on theft, Lord Roskill was highly critical of the approach that relied on the civil law meaning of concepts. For instance, whether a contract was void or voidable, was "so far as possible" not a relevant question in relation to the law of theft.

As will be seen, however, courts are not always prepared to jettison established legal meanings and replace them with "ordinary meanings". (What is the ordinary meaning of those ordinary words, "trust" or "equitable interest"?) Accordingly, one of the fascinations of this area of law is to observe the lurchings along the tightrope as the English courts try to achieve an impossible balance between these two competing and irreconcilable approaches.

A thorough consideration of all property offences is not possible, even in a book of this size. Accordingly, the enquiry will be limited to those offences that tell us most about the purposes and structures of this area of law. The main offences to be considered will be theft and fraud. Briefer consideration will also be given to the offences of obtaining services dishonestly, robbery, burglary, handling stolen goods and making off without payment.

II. Theft

A. Extent and Context

Theft offences accounted for approximately half of all recorded crime in England and Wales in 2012–2013 (1.9 million offences).[42] However, as already seen, such official figures do not reveal the dark figure of crime. Many thefts are simply not reported or recorded. Whereas a high proportion of thefts of motor vehicles are reported (because of the value of vehicles and for insurance purposes),[43] the picture of theft *from* vehicles and theft from the person is rather different. In relation to thefts from the person, the 2012/13 CSEW estimates that only just over a third of such offences (36 per cent) are

---

longer property "belonging to another". This would now be dealt with as making off without payment under s.3 of the Theft Act 1978.

[38] Section 9.

[39] Section 5(1).

[40] Section 5(2).

[41] [1984] A.C. 320.

[42] ONS, *Crime in England and Wales, year ending September 2013* (2014), available at *http://www.ons.gov.uk/ons/dcp171778_349849.pdf* [Accessed March 2014], p.50. This includes burglary, vehicle-related theft, theft from the person and bicycle theft. The statistics show an overall downwards trend in theft offences. The 2012/13 figures show a 4% decrease compared with the previous year and there has been a 45% decrease in volume since 2002/03.

[43] The 2012/13 CSEW showed that 91 % of incidents of theft of a vehicle were reported to the police: ONS, *Focus on Property Crime 2012/13* (2013), available at *http://www.ons.gov.uk/ons/rel/crime-stats/crime-statistics/focus-on-property-crime--2012-13/rpt-chapter-1.html* [Accessed March 2014], p.22

reported to the police.[44] In relation to shoplifting (a particularly difficult crime to observe) it has been estimated that only 3 per cent of such incidents come to police attention.[45] Astor's research concluded, for example, that one in 15 people stole goods from stores with store detectives noticing only about 1 per cent of those.[46] More recently, the 2013 Commercial Victimisation Survey found that 42 per cent of retailers reported the last incidence of theft by customers that they had experienced to the police.[47] Such research renders almost meaningless the official figure of recorded thefts from shops of 313,693 in 2012/13.[48] This, together with the variable value of goods being taken in shoplifting offences, with a recent average value of £177 per incident of customer theft being estimated,[49] means that only very rough estimates about overall losses can be given.

Under-reporting occurs, as we have seen, for a variety of reasons, but it does reflect to some extent the degree of seriousness with which the offence is regarded. Vehicle thefts, for instance, are viewed seriously and are almost always reported.[50] These surveys also enable assessments of seriousness to be made on the basis of the penalties chosen by respondents for a variety of offences. In the second BCS, 23 per cent of respondents thought that prison was the appropriate penalty for a 25-year-old car thief with previous convictions, in comparison with 12 per cent who felt it to be the appropriate penalty for shoplifting.[51] One might be tempted to conclude from this, and the lower rate of reporting of theft from shops, that this crime is regarded less seriously than other forms of theft. The development of the term "shoplifting" may even be seen as evidence of this, separating this form of activity from "theft". But any such conclusions would have to be highly qualified. The relationship between reporting and seriousness is by no means a perfect one. Sexual crimes, for example, are rated highly seriously, yet are grossly under-reported. In other words, there are other reasons for not reporting an offence other than an attitude as to its seriousness.[52] Despite this, it is probably the case that shoplifting is regarded as a comparatively minor offence: the amount involved will generally be small; the victim of the offence may be perceived as being a large, impersonal organisation able to absorb the loss; and there may even be at times a "there but for the grace of God . . ." sentiment. All this does not, of course, amount to an argument for the decriminalisation of "shoplifting"—but it may well be an argument for the creation of a separate lesser offence.[53]

A type of theft that is very likely to be reported is theft of a mobile phone, although statistics indicate that such thefts are more likely to be reported to a network service provider than to the police. The 2011/12 CSEW indicated that two-thirds of people who had a mobile phone stolen via robbery or theft from the person (e.g. by pick pocketing) reported the crime to the police, whilst 81

---

[44]   ONS, *Focus on Property Crime 2012/13* (2013), fn.43 above.

[45]   J. Shury et al., *Crime Against Retail and Manufacturing Premises*, Home Office Online Report 37/05 (2005).

[46]   S.D. Astor, "Shoplifting Survey", *Security World*, Vol.8, Part 3 (1971), pp.3–4; Sentencing Advisory Panel, Sentencing Guidelines for Theft from a Shop: Consultation Paper (2006), para.10.

[47]   Home Office, *Crime Against Businesses: Headline findings from the 2013 Commercial Victimisation Survey* (2014), p.9. The British Retail Consortium (BRC), *Retail Crime Survey 2013* (2014), available at *http://www.brc.org.uk/brc_show_document. asp?id=4428&moid=8064* [Accessed March 2014], found that only 9% of respondents reported customer theft offences to the police, p.17.

[48]   ONS, Statistical Bulletin, *Crime in England and Wales Year Ending September 2013* (2014), p.64.

[49]   BRC, fn.47 above, p.17. This was an increase of 62% on the BRC average value for the previous year and the highest average value for nine years, p.4. Anecdotal evidence suggests that a key factor in this upward trend has been the impact of criminal gangs targeting higher value goods, p.13.

[50]   See fn.5 and fn.43 above.

[51]   M. Hough and D. Moxon, "Dealing with Offenders: Popular Opinion and the Views of Victims. Findings from the British Crime Survey" (1985) 24 Howard J. of Crim. Justice 160–175.

[52]   C.M.V. Clarkson, A. Cretney and G. Davis, "Assaults: the Relationship between Seriousness, Criminalisation and Punishment" [1994] Crim. L.R. 4.

[53]   Below, pp.906–908.

per cent reported it to their network provider.[54] Around half (52 per cent) of households who experienced theft of a mobile phone in other circumstances in 2011/12 reported it to the police, whilst three-quarters (75 per cent) reported it to their network service provider.[55] This high reporting rate may reflect the relative value of mobile phones compared with other personal possessions typically carried on the person.[56] Overall, 2 per cent of mobile phone owners experienced theft of a mobile phone,[57] although it would seem that in a substantial number of cases victims could do much to prevent this. In 2011/12 39 per cent of such thefts (the largest single category) were reported to have occurred when the phone was stolen away from the victim's home but was not being carried on the person, for example, where unattended property was stolen in pubs, restaurants, entertainment venues or workplaces.[58]

B. The Legal Background

Prior to the Theft Act 1968, what is now the crime of theft was dealt with by three separate offences: larceny, embezzlement and fraudulent conversion. Each of these offences and the distinction between them was technical and highly complex. Further, the offences were felt to be defective in that certain conduct that would ordinarily be regarded as stealing did not come within the definitions of the offences.

Criminal Law Revision Committee, Eighth Report, Theft and Related Offences, Cmnd.2977 (1966), paras 33, 60:

"33. The committee generally are strongly of opinion that larceny, embezzlement and fraudulent conversion should be replaced by a single new offence of theft. The important element of them all is undoubtedly the dishonest appropriation of another's property—the treating of 'tuum' as 'meum'; and we think it not only logical, but right in principle, to make this the central element of the offence. In doing so the law would concentrate on what the accused dishonestly achieved or attempted to achieve and not on the means—taking or otherwise—which he used in order to do so. This would avoid multiplicity of offences . . .
      60. We recommend that the maximum penalty for stealing should be 10 years' imprisonment in all cases."

This proposal was accepted by the Theft Act 1968 but in 1991 the penalty was reduced to a maximum of seven years' imprisonment.[59] It is interesting to compare this with the actual practice. In the 12 months ending September 2013, 23,133 PNDs (Penalty Notice for Disorder) were issued for

---

54   ONS, *Crime Statistics, Focus on Property Crime 2011/12* (2013), Ch.2: Mobile Phone Theft, available at *http://www.ons.gov. uk/ons/dcp171776_309652.pdf* [Accessed March 2014], p.20, Appendix table 2.12. Of course, many such crimes will be reported both to the police and the network service provider. This reporting rate is considerably higher than that for theft from the person overall, where only a third (32%) of incidents were reported to the police.
55   ONS, *Crime Statistics, Focus on Property Crime 2011/12* (2013), fn.54 above.
56   ONS, *Crime Statistics, Focus on Property Crime 2011/12* (2013), fn.54 above, p.20. The network service provider would need to be contacted to put a 'stop' on the mobile, so that the victim would not be liable for further unauthorised use of the phone. Of those who did not report the theft to the network service provider, the main reason given for not reporting the theft was either that the phone was returned to the owner (43%), or that it was a pay as you go phone (42%).
57   ONS, *Crime Statistics, Focus on Property Crime 2011/12* (2013), fn.54 above, p.4.
58   ONS, *Crime Statistics, Focus on Property Crime 2011/12* (2013), fn.54 above, pp.14–15.
59   Theft Act 1968 s.7, as amended by the Criminal Justice Act 1991 s.26. The Sentencing Guidelines Council issued definitive sentencing guidelines for use when sentencing offences of theft in breach of trust, in a dwelling, from a person and from a shop: *Theft and Burglary in a Building other than a Dwelling*, December 2009, Part E. In April 2014 the Sentencing Council launched a consultation on proposed new sentencing guidelines for theft offences: *http://sentencingcouncil.judiciary.gov. uk/* [Accessed April 2014].

shoplifting.[60] This is a £90 fine issued by the police when the value of the goods stolen from a shop is less than £100.[61] In the same year, less than 20 per cent of those convicted of theft or handling stolen goods were given absolute or conditional discharges,[62] 21.2 per cent of those convicted of theft or handling stolen goods were given custodial sentences, and the average length of such sentences was just over four months.[63]

C. The Law

1. Definition

Theft Act 1968 s.1(1)

"A person is guilty of theft if he dishonestly appropriates property belonging to another with the intention of permanently depriving the other of it; and 'thief' and 'steal' shall be construed accordingly."

The maximum penalty for this offence is seven years' imprisonment.

In *Lawrence*,[64] it was stressed by the House of Lords that this definition involves several elements, all of which must be proved to coincide before liability can be imposed. Each of these elements is defined, wholly or partially, in the ensuing sections of the Theft Act 1968 as follows:

— s.2: dishonesty,

— s.3: appropriation,

— s.4: property,

— s.5: belonging to another, and

— s.6: intention of permanent deprivation.

We shall deal first with the actus reus elements, namely, appropriation of property belonging to another—before turning to the mens rea elements, dishonesty and intention of permanent deprivation.

2. Appropriation

Theft Act 1968 s.3

"(1) Any assumption by a person of the rights of an owner amounts to an appropriation, and this includes, where he has come by the property (innocently or not) without stealing it, any later assumption of a right to it by keeping or dealing with it as owner.

(2) Where property or a right or interest in property is or purports to be transferred for value to a person acting in good faith, no later assumption by him of rights which he believed himself to be acquiring shall, by reason of any defect in the transferor's title, amount to theft of the property."

---

60 Ministry of Justice Statistics Bulletin, *Criminal Justice Sentencing Statistics Quarterly Update to September 2013 England and Wales* (2014), table Q1.6(1).
61 Criminal Justice and Police Act 2001 ss.1–11, as amended by the Legal Aid, Sentencing and Punishment of Offenders Act 2012. Ministry of Justice Guidance, *Penalty Notices for Disorder (PNDs)* (2013): An offender may only receive one PND for shoplifting, para 3.12. Such a notice is not regarded as a conviction: *Hamer* [2010] EWCA Crim 2053.
62 22,007 out of 103,627 convictions: Ministry of Justice Statistics Bulletin, fn.60 above, table Q1.6(1).
63 Ministry of Justice Statistics Bulletin, fn.60 above, table Q1.6(1).
64 *Lawrence v Metropolitan Police Commissioner* [1972] A.C. 626.

Criminal Law Revision Committee, Eighth Report, Theft and Related Offences, 1966, Cmnd.2977, paras 34–35:

"34. We hope, and believe, that the concept of 'dishonest appropriation' will be easily understood even without the aid of further definition. But there is a partial definition of 'appropriates' in . . . (section) 3(1) . . . It seems to us natural to refer to the act of stealing in ordinary cases as 'appropriation'. We see no reason why the word should seem strange for more than a short time . . .

35. There is an argument for keeping the word 'converts' because it is well understood. But it is a lawyers' word, and those not used to legal language might naturally think that it meant changing something or exchanging property for other property. 'Appropriates' seems altogether a better word."

An appropriation is an *assumption of the rights of an owner*. But what are the rights of an owner?

F.H. Lawson and Bernard Rudden, The Law of Property (1982), pp.8–9:

"The main elements (of ownership) are (a) the right to make physical use of a thing; (b) the right to the income from it, in money, in kind, or in services; and (c) the power of management, including that of alienation. Thus the owner of a car may drive it, hire it out, or sell it. And of course within these areas he may do the same things more generously: take the children for a drive, lend it to a friend, give it away."

In short, as Roman law used to put it, an owner has the right to "use, enjoy and abuse" their property as they see fit.[65] An owner of property may keep it, sell it, give it away or destroy it. *Assuming* the rights of an owner is laying claim to be in such a position. The method of acquiring the property is not important. There does not have to be a taking or removal although this is, of course, what occurs in the paradigmatic theft. The second part of s.3(1) makes this clear. If the owner accidentally leaves a book in the defendant's room there can be an appropriation the moment the defendant decides to keep the book. At this point they will be assuming a right to the book by keeping or dealing with it as owner, despite the fact they originally came by the property quite innocently.

This last point leads directly to the central problem in the interpretation of an "appropriation". When the book has been accidentally left in the defendant's room they assume the right of an owner the moment they *decide* to keep it. At this point they are exercising one of the rights of ownership. However, if it were held that this amounted to an appropriation this would mean that there could be a theft by a defendant who has *done* nothing *wrong*—other than have a blameworthy state of mind. Following this logic, a defendant in a supermarket who places goods in a trolley but who has a secret intention of stealing them will be guilty of theft. They have decided not to pay for the goods and to make off with them as and when they see fit. The argument runs that this is treating the goods as one's own and is thus an appropriation.

Lawrence v M.P.C. [1972] A.C. 626 (House of Lords)

Occhi, an Italian visitor who spoke little English, arrived in England at Victoria station and asked the defendant, Lawrence, a taxi driver, to take him to an address in Ladbroke Grove. The defendant informed Occhi that it was a long way and would be expensive. (In reality the correct fare would have been about 10s. 6d. [52½p].) Occhi got into the taxi and offered a £1 note. Lawrence said that this was not enough and, with Occhi holding out his wallet for him, helped himself to a further £6 from the wallet. He then drove Occhi to his destination. The defendant was convicted of the theft of the approximate sum of £6 contrary to s.1(1) of the Theft Act 1968 and appealed against his conviction.

---

[65]   This is subject, of course, to numerous restrictions aimed at protecting the interests of others.

VISCOUNT DILHORNE:

"Mr Occhi, when asked whether he had consented to the money being taken, said that he had 'permitted' . . . It may well be that when he used the word 'permitted', he meant no more than that he had allowed the money to be taken. It certainly was not established at the trial that he had agreed to pay to the appellant a sum far in excess of the legal fare for the journey and so had consented to the acquisition by the appellant of the £6.

The main contention of the appellant in this House and in the Court of Appeal was that Mr Occhi had consented to the taking of the £6 and that, consequently, his conviction could not stand. In my opinion, the facts of this case to which I have referred fall far short of establishing that Mr Occhi had so consented.

Prior to the passage of the Theft Act 1968, which made radical changes in and greatly simplified the law relating to theft and some other offences, it was necessary to prove that the property alleged to have been stolen was taken 'without the consent of the owner' (Larceny Act 1916, section 1(1)).

These words are not included in section 1(1) of the Theft Act, . . .

I see no ground for concluding that the omission of the words 'without the consent of the owner' was inadvertent and not deliberate, and to read the subsection as if they were included is, in my opinion, wholly unwarranted. Parliament by the omission of these words has relieved the prosecution of the burden of establishing that the taking was without the owner's consent. That is no longer an ingredient of the offence . . .

That there was an appropriation in this case is clear. Section 3(1) states that any assumption by a person of the rights of an owner amounts to an appropriation. Here there was clearly such an assumption . . .

Belief or the absence of belief that the owner had with such knowledge consented to the appropriation is relevant to the issue of dishonesty, not to the question whether or not there has been an appropriation. That may occur even though the owner has permitted or consented to the property being taken. So proof that Mr Occhi had consented to the appropriation of £6 from his wallet without agreeing to paying a sum in excess of the legal fare does not suffice to show that there was not dishonesty in this case. There was ample evidence that there was."

Appeal dismissed

Following this decision there can be an appropriation even though the victim is consenting to hand over the property. Thus the shopper who places the goods in the supermarket trolley can be held to appropriate the goods at that stage. The only thing that distinguishes the legitimate shopper from the thief is the mental state of the latter.

In 1984, the House of Lords in *Morris* cast doubt on this proposition by holding that the defendant must have done something objectively wrong for there to be an appropriation. As we shall see, however, this case (and its progeny) is no longer good authority.

R. v Morris, Anderton v Burnside [1984] A.C. 320 (House of Lords)

Two defendants took goods from a shelf in a supermarket and removed the proper price labels, and replaced them with labels from cheaper goods. The goods, bearing their incorrect price labels were presented at the check-out counter. One defendant was arrested before, and the other after, paying for the goods. The appeals were heard together.

LORD ROSKILL:

"It is to be observed that the definition of 'appropriation' in section 3(1) is not exhaustive . . .

The starting point . . . must, I think, be the decision of this House in *R. v Lawrence* . . . [in which] Viscount Dilhorne also rejected the argument that even if [the] four elements were all present there could not be theft within the section if the owner of the property in question had consented to the acts which were done by the defendant. That there was in that case a dishonest appropriation was beyond question and the House did not have to consider the precise meaning of that word in section 3(1).

Mr Denison submitted that the phrase in section 3(1) 'any assumption by a person of *the rights*' (my emphasis) 'of an owner amounts to an appropriation' must mean any assumption of '*all* the rights of an owner.' Since neither respondent had at the time of the removal of the goods from the shelves and of the label switching assumed *all* the rights of the owner, there was no appropriation and therefore no theft. Mr Jeffreys for the prosecution, on the other hand, contended that *the* rights in this context only meant *any* of the rights. An owner of goods has many rights—they have been described as 'a bundle or package of rights'. Mr Jeffreys contended that on a fair reading of the subsection it cannot have been the intention that every one of an owner's rights had to be assumed by the alleged thief before an appropriation was proved and that essential ingredient of the offence of theft established.

My Lords, if one reads the words 'the rights' at the opening of section 3(1) literally and in isolation from the rest of the section, Mr Denison's submission undoubtedly has force. But the later words 'any later assumption of a right' in subsection (1) and the words in subsection (2) 'no later assumption by him of rights' seem to me to militate strongly against the correctness of the submission. Moreover the provisions of section 2(1)(a) also seem to point in the same direction. It follows therefore that it is enough for the prosecution if they have proved in these cases the assumption by the respondents of *any* of the rights of the owner of the goods in question, that is to say, the supermarket concerned, it being common ground in these cases that the other three of the four elements . . . [of theft] had been fully established.

My Lords, Mr Jeffreys sought to argue that any removal from the shelves of the supermarket, even if unaccompanied by label switching, was without more an appropriation. In one passage in his judgment in Morris's case, the learned Lord Chief Justice appears to have accepted the submission, for he said [1983] Q.B. 587, 596:

'it seems to us that in taking the article from the shelf the customer is indeed assuming one of the rights of the owner—the right to move the article from its position on the shelf to carry it to the check-out.'

With the utmost respect, I cannot accept this statement as correct. If one postulates an honest customer taking goods from a shelf to put in his or her trolley to take to the checkpoint there to pay the proper price, I am unable to see that any of these actions involves any assumption by the shopper of the rights of the supermarket. In the context of section 3(1), the concept of appropriation in my view involves not an act expressly or impliedly authorised by the owner but an act by way of adverse interference with or usurpation of those rights. When the honest shopper acts as I have just described, he or she is acting with the implied authority of the owner of the supermarket to take the goods from the shelf, put them in the trolley, take them to the checkpoint and there pay the correct price, at which moment the property in the goods will pass to the shopper for the first time . . .

If, as I understand all your Lordships to agree, the concept of appropriation in section 3(1) involves an element of adverse interference with or usurpation of some right of the owner, it is necessary next to consider whether that requirement is satisfied in either of these cases. As I have already said, in my view mere removal from the shelves without more is not an appropriation. Further, if a shopper with some perverted sense of humour, intending only to create confusion and nothing more both for the supermarket and for other shoppers, switches labels, I do not think that that act of label switching alone is without more an appropriation, though it is not difficult to envisage some cases of dishonest label-switching which could be. In cases such as the present, it is in truth a combination of these actions, the removal from the shelf and the switching of the labels, which evidences adverse interference with or usurpation of the right of the owner. Those acts, therefore, amount to an appropriation and if they are accompanied by proof of the other three elements to which I have referred, the offence of theft is established. Further, if they are accompanied by other acts such as putting the goods so removed and re-labelled into a receptacle, whether a trolley or the shopper's own bag or basket, proof of appropriation within section 3(1) becomes overwhelming . . .

I would answer the certified questions in this way:

'There is a dishonest appropriation for the purposes of the Theft Act 1968 where by the substitution of a price label showing a lesser price on goods for one showing a greater price, a defendant either by that act alone or by that act in conjunction with another act or other acts (whether done before or after the substitution of the labels) adversely interferes with or usurps the right of the owner to ensure that the goods concerned are sold and paid for at that greater price.'

I would dismiss these appeals."

Appeals dismissed

This requirement that the defendant must do acts objectively inconsistent with the rights of the owner is consistent with what Fletcher calls the "theory of manifest criminality". We saw when examining the law of attempts how this theory leads to an "objectivist orientation", with insistence that the acts must come close to the completed crime so as to be manifestly dangerous and a threat to security. This was the theory endorsed by the House of Lords in *Anderton v Ryan*[66] where a distinction was drawn between "objectively innocent" acts on the one hand and "criminal" or "guilty" acts on the other.

Fletcher states that "manifestly criminal" activities must exhibit at least the following essential features. First, the criminal act must manifest, on its face, the actor's criminal purpose. And secondly, the conduct should be "of a type that is unnerving and disturbing to the community as a whole".

George P. Fletcher, Rethinking Criminal Law (1978), pp.82–89:

"The principle of manifest criminality supported the expansion of the law to include all acts of taking that conformed to the shared paradigms of stealthful and forcible taking. A guest sneaking out with his host's dining utensils looked as much like a thief as any then punished. So, too, the customer that runs from the store with the shopkeeper chasing after him . . . The purpose of raising an issue of *animus* was to challenge the authenticity of appearances. Someone who looked like a thief in the act of taking might not have been one in fact . . . The primary inquiry was the act of larceny (theft), and only in extraordinary cases might there have been a dispute about whether someone who acted like a thief had the 'spirit' or *animus* of a thief. Thus the law was structured so as to render intent a subsidiary issue. It was a basis for defeating the implications of the primary element of acting manifestly like a thief . . . Routine business transactions, deliveries and takings by consent do not bear this imprint of larceny, and therefore . . . lack the features of manifest thievery . . . The value implicitly protected in the pattern of manifest criminality is the privacy of criminal suspects. Judges may not enquire about the accused's mental state, self-control and culpability unless they find preliminarily that the accused's conduct meets an objective standard of liability. The objective standard is the manifestly criminal act."

The approach adopted in *Morris* can be seen as consistent with the "harm principle": conduct should only be criminalised to prevent the causing of harm, albeit of a "second-order" nature,[67] to others. The defendant by doing something manifestly observable as wrong, for example, switching price labels, is doing something that is a threat to the security of the store; the interests of the store have been violated and they have sustained a "second-order harm". This approach stands in sharp contrast to "protectionalist criminology"[68] sustained by the utilitarian philosophies of punishment. Where the main interest is the protection of the property of others, then whatever measures are necessary to effect such protection become acceptable, even if this means imposing liability at an early stage when a defendant has done nothing observably wrong. If an individual has a blameworthy state of mind, then for deterrent, incapacitative and rehabilitative reasons they need punishment.

The operation of the *Morris* principle can best be seen by applying it to the facts of several cases on theft.

In *Eddy v Niman*[69] the defendant, intending to steal goods from a store, took them from a shelf and placed them in the provided receptacle. He was not liable for theft because he had done nothing manifestly wrong. He was doing precisely what the store expected all its customers to do, namely, place goods in a receptacle provided by the store.

---

[66]   *Anderton v Ryan* [1985] A.C. 567.
[67]   Above, pp.11–15.
[68]   G.P. Fletcher, *Rethinking Criminal Law* (Boston: Little, Brown, 1978), p.101.
[69]   *Eddy v Niman* (1981) 73 Cr. App. R. 237.

In *Skipp*[70] the defendant, posing as a genuine haulage contractor, obtained instructions and collected two loads of oranges and onions to be delivered from London to Leicester. He had the intention of stealing the goods from the outset but only after loading them did he actually make off with them. It was held that he did not appropriate the goods when he loaded them because at that stage he was not doing anything inconsistent with the owner's rights. The appropriation occurred when the goods were "diverted from their true destination". In *Fritschy*[71] the defendant, acting under the instructions of the owner, collected a quantity of krugerrands in London to deliver them to Switzerland. All along he had a secret intention to steal the coins, which he did in Switzerland. The Court of Appeal held that there was no appropriation in England because the defendant had acted with the owner's authority at that stage. The coins were only appropriated in Switzerland where the defendant committed the acts that amounted to an adverse interference with the owner's rights.

These cases were, of course, difficult to reconcile with *Lawrence*. The House of Lords in *Gomez* strongly confirmed *Lawrence*, disapproved much of *Morris* and overruled *Skipp* and *Fritschy*. In doing so, much reliance was placed on the following civil decision.

Dobson v General Accident Fire and Life Assurance Corp Plc [1989] 3 W.L.R. 1066 (Court of Appeal, Civil Division)

The claimant had a home insurance policy with the defendant which covered him against loss by "theft". He advertised a Rolex watch and diamond ring for sale for £5,950. The goods were purchased by a rogue using a stolen building society cheque which was worthless. The claimant claimed under his insurance policy and the question was whether there had been a "theft".

PARKER LJ:

"On the basis of *R. v Lawrence* . . . the facts of the present case appear to establish that the rogue assumed all the rights of an owner when he took or received the watch and ring from the plaintiff. That he did so dishonestly and with the intention of permanently depriving the plaintiff of it are matters beyond doubt . . .

After anxious consideration I have reached the conclusion that whatever *R. v Morris* did decide it cannot be regarded as having overruled the very plain decision in *R. v Lawrence* that appropriation can occur even if the owner consents and that *R. v Morris* itself makes it plain that it is no defence to say that the property passed under a voidable contract . . . I would therefore dismiss the appeal."

BINGHAM LJ:

"I do not find it easy to reconcile . . . [*Lawrence*] with the reasoning of the House in *R. v Morris*. Since, however, the House in *R. v Morris* considered that there had plainly been an appropriation in *Lawrence's* case, this must (I think) have been because the Italian student, although he had permitted or allowed his money to be taken, had not in truth consented to the taxi driver taking anything in excess of the correct fare. This is not a wholly satisfactory reconciliation, since it might be said that a supermarket consents to customers taking goods from its shelves only when they honestly intend to pay and not otherwise. On the facts of the present case, however, it can be said, by analogy with *Lawrence's* case, that although the plaintiff permitted and allowed his property to be taken by the rogue, he had not in truth consented to the rogue becoming owner without giving a valid draft drawn by the building society for the price. On this basis I conclude that the plaintiff is able to show an appropriation sufficient to satisfy s.1(1) of the 1968 Act when the rogue accepted delivery of the articles."

Appeal dismissed

---

[70]   *R. v Skipp* [1975] Crim. L.R. 114.
[71]   *R. v Fritschy* [1985] Crim. L.R. 745.

R. v Gomez [1993] A.C. 442 (House of Lords)

The appellant, an assistant manager of an electrical goods shop, lied to the manager of the store that two cheques were valid, with the result that £16,000 worth of goods were supplied to a rogue. The appellant and the rogue were convicted of theft. Their appeal was allowed by the Court of Appeal (Criminal Division). The Crown appealed to the House of Lords.

LORD KEITH OF KINKEL (with whom Lord Jauncey of Tullichettle and Lord Slynn of Hadley agreed):

"Lord Roskill was undoubtedly right [in *Morris*] . . . that the assumption by the defendant of any of the rights of an owner could amount to an appropriation . . . But there are observations [from his speech] . . . that I must regard as unnecessary . . . and as being incorrect. In the first place, it seems to me that the switching of price labels on the article is in itself an assumption of one of the rights of the owner, whether or not it is accompanied by some other act such as removing the article from the shelf and placing it in a basket or trolley. No one but the owner has the right to remove a price label from an article or to place a price label upon it. If anyone else does so, he does an act, as Lord Roskill puts it, by way of adverse interference with or usurpation of that right. This is no less so in the case of the practical joker figured by Lord Roskill than in the case of one who makes the switch with dishonest intent. The practical joker, of course, is not guilty of theft because he has not acted dishonestly and does not intend to deprive the owner permanently of the article. So the label switching in itself constitutes an appropriation and so to have held would have been sufficient for the dismissal of both appeals. On the facts of [*Morris*] . . . it was unnecessary to decide whether . . . the mere taking of the article from the shelf and putting it in a trolley or other receptacle amounted to the assumption of one of the rights of the owner, and hence an appropriation. There was much to be said in favour of the view that it did, in respect that doing so gave the shopper control of the article and the capacity to exclude any other shopper from taking it. However, Lord Roskill expressed the opinion that it did not, on the ground that the concept of appropriation in the context of section 3(1) 'involves not an act expressly or impliedly authorised by the owner but an act by way of adverse interference with or usurpation of those rights'.

While it is correct to say that appropriation for purposes of section 3(1) includes the latter sort of act, it does not necessarily follow that no other act can amount to an appropriation and in particular that no act expressly or impliedly authorised by the owner can in any circumstances do so. Indeed, *R. v Lawrence* is a clear decision to the contrary since it laid down unequivocally that an act may be an appropriation notwithstanding that it is done with the consent of the owner. It does not appear to me that any sensible distinction can be made in this context between consent and authorisation . . .

[His Lordship then cited extensively from *Dobson* agreeing with Parker LJ but finding Bingham's L.J.'s suggested reconciliation of *Morris* with *Lawrence* to be unsound.]

The actual decision in *Morris* was correct, but it was erroneous, in addition to being unnecessary for the decision, to indicate that an act expressly or impliedly authorised by the owner could never amount to an appropriation. There is no material distinction between the facts in *Dobson* and those in the present case. In each case the owner of the goods was induced by fraud to part with them to the rogue. *Lawrence* makes it clear that consent to or authorisation by the owner of the taking by the rogue is irrelevant. The taking amounted to an appropriation within the meaning of section 1(1) of the Act of 1968. *Lawrence* also makes it clear that it is no less irrelevant that what happened may also have constituted the offence of obtaining property by deception under section 15(1) of the Act . . .

The decision in *Lawrence* was a clear decision . . . which had stood for 12 years when doubt was thrown upon it by obiter dicta in *Morris*. *Lawrence* must be regarded as authoritative and correct, and there is no question of it now being right to depart from it . . .

In my opinion . . . [*Skipp* and *Fritschy*] were inconsistent with *Lawrence* and were wrongly decided."

LORD BROWNE-WILKINSON:

"The fact that Parliament used that composite phrase—'dishonest appropriation'—in my judgment casts light on what is meant by the word 'appropriation'. The views expressed (obiter) by this House in *Morris* that 'appropriation' involves an act by way of adverse interference with or usurpation of the rights of the owner treats the word appropriation as being tantamount to 'misappropriation'. The concept of adverse interference with or usurpation of rights introduces into the word appropriation the mental state of both the owner and the accused. So far as concerns the mental state of the owner (did he consent?), the Act of 1968 expressly refers to such consent when it is a material factor: see section 2(1)(b), 11(1), 12(1) and 13. So far as concerns the mental state of the accused, the composite phrase in section 1(1) itself indicates that the requirement is dishonesty.

For myself, therefore, I regard the word 'appropriation' in isolation as being an objective description of the act done irrespective of the mental state of either the owner or the accused. It is impossible to reconcile the decision in *Lawrence* (that the question of consent is irrelevant in considering whether there has been an appropriation) with the views expressed in *Morris*, which latter views in my judgment were incorrect."

LORD LOWRY (DISSENTING):

"The ordinary and natural meaning of 'appropriate' is to take for oneself, or to treat as one's own, property which belongs to someone else. The primary dictionary meaning is 'to take possession of, take to oneself, especially without authority', and that is in my opinion the meaning which the word bears in section 1(1). The act of appropriating property is a one-sided act, done without the consent or authority of the owner. And, if the owner consents to transfer property to the offender or to a third party, the offender does not appropriate the property, even if the owner's consent has been obtained by fraud . . .

Coming now to section 3, the *primary* meaning of 'assumption' is 'taking to oneself', again a unilateral act, and this meaning is consistent with subsections (1) and (2). To use the word in its secondary, neutral sense would neutralise the word 'appropriation', to which assumption is here equated, and would lead to a number of strange results. Incidentally, . . . 'the rights' may mean '*all* the rights', which would be the normal grammatical meaning, or (less probably, in my opinion) 'any rights' see *R. v Morris* . . .

I would respectfully agree with [Lord Roskill's description in *Morris*] . . . in relation to dishonest actions, of appropriation as involving an act by way of adverse interference with or usurpation of the owner's rights, but I believe that the less aggressive definition of appropriation which I have put forward fits the word as used in an honest sense in section 2(1) as well as elsewhere in the Act . . . [He then expressly declined to discuss whether *Morris* itself was really an example of theft.]

[T]here was no theft [in *Dobson*] because the property passed with the fraudulently obtained consent of the owner and the buyer was guilty of obtaining by deception in the false pretences sense . . .

It is true that *Morris* contains no disapproval or qualification of *Lawrence*, but, in my view, the main statements of principle in these cases cannot possibly be reconciled and the later case therefore must not be regarded as providing any support for the earlier . . .

[In the Court of Appeal in the present case] Lord Lane C.J. said:

'. . . We therefore conclude that there was a de facto, albeit voidable, contract between the owners and Ballay [one of Gomez's associates]; that it was by virtue of that contract that Ballay took possession of the goods; that accordingly the transfer of the goods to him was with the consent and express authority of the owner and that accordingly there was no lack of authorisation and no appropriation . . .'

I respectfully agree . . . [and] would dismiss the Crown's appeal."

Appeal allowed

R. v Hinks [2001] 2 A.C. 241 (House of Lords)

The defendant made friends with a man of limited intelligence. She regularly accompanied him to his building society where he made withdrawals from his account amounting to a total of about £60,000 which was deposited in the defendant's account. A consultant psychiatrist gave evidence that the man was naïve and trusting and had no idea of the value of his assets or the ability to calculate their value, and that, although he was capable of making the decision to divest himself of money, it was unlikely he could make that decision alone. The defendant was convicted of theft of the money withdrawn from his account. The Court of Appeal dismissed her appeal. She appealed to the House of Lords.

LORD STEYN:

"The certified question before the House is as follows: 'Whether the acquisition of an indefeasible title to property is capable of amounting to an appropriation of property belonging to another for the purposes of section 1(1) of the Theft Act 1968.' In other words, the question is whether a person can 'appropriate' property belonging to another where the other person makes him an indefeasible gift of property, retaining no proprietary interest or any right to resume or recover any proprietary interest in the property . . .

[I]t is immaterial whether the act was done with the owner's consent or authority. It is true of course that the certified question in *Gomez* referred to the situation where consent had been obtained by fraud. But the majority judgments do not differentiate between cases of consent induced by fraud and consent given in any other circumstances. The ratio involves a proposition of general application. *Gomez* therefore gives effect to section 3(1) of the Act by treating 'appropriation' as a neutral word comprehending 'any assumption by a person of the rights of an owner'. If the law is as held in *Gomez*, it destroys the argument advanced on the present appeal, namely that an indefeasible gift of property cannot amount to an appropriation.

Counsel for the appellant submitted in the first place that the law as expounded in *Gomez* and *Lawrence* must be qualified to say that there can be no appropriation unless the other party (the owner) retains some proprietary interest, or the right to resume or recover some proprietary interest, in the property. Alternatively, counsel argued that 'appropriates' should be interpreted as if the word 'unlawfully' preceded it. Counsel said that the effect of the decisions in *Lawrence* and *Gomez* is to reduce the *actus reus* of theft to 'vanishing point'. He argued that the result is to bring the criminal law 'into conflict' with the civil law. Moreover, he argued that the decisions in *Lawrence* and *Gomez* may produce absurd and grotesque results. He argued that the mental requirements of dishonesty and intention of permanently depriving the owner of property are insufficient to filter out some cases of conduct which should not sensibly be regarded as theft . . .

[I]n such cases a prosecution is hardly likely and if mounted, is likely to founder on the basis that the jury will not be persuaded that there was dishonesty in the required sense. And one must retain a sense of perspective . . . If the law is restated by adopting a narrower definition of appropriation, the outcome is likely to place beyond the reach of the criminal law dishonest persons who should be found guilty of theft . . .

Counsel for the appellant further pointed out that the law as stated in *Lawrence* and *Gomez* creates a tension between the civil and the criminal law. In other words, conduct which is not wrongful in a civil law sense may constitute the crime of theft. Undoubtedly, this is so. The question whether the civil claim to title by a convicted thief, who committed no civil wrong, may be defeated by the principle that nobody may benefit from his own civil *or* criminal wrong does not arise for decision. Nevertheless, there is a more general point, namely that the interaction between criminal law and civil law can cause problems . . . The purposes of the civil law and the criminal law are somewhat different. In theory the two systems should be in perfect harmony. In a practical world there will sometimes be some disharmony between the two systems. In any event, it would be wrong to assume on *a priori* grounds that the criminal law rather than the civil law is defective . . . The tension between the civil and the criminal law is therefore not in my view a factor which justifies a departure from the law as stated in *Lawrence* and *Gomez*. Moreover, these decisions of the House have a marked beneficial consequence. While in some contexts of the law of theft a judge cannot avoid explaining civil law concepts to a jury (*e.g.* in respect of section 2(1)(a)), the decisions of the House of Lords eliminate the need for such explanations in respect of appropriation. That is a great advantage in an overly complex corner of the law.

My Lords, if it had been demonstrated that in practice *Lawrence* and *Gomez* were calculated to produce injustice that would have been a compelling reason to revisit the merits of the holdings in those decisions. That is, however, not the case. In practice, the mental requirements of theft are an adequate protection against injustice. In these circumstances I would not be willing to depart from the clear decisions of the House in *Lawrence* and *Gomez*. This brings me back to counsel's principal submission, namely that a person does not appropriate property unless the other (the owner) retains, beyond the instant of the alleged theft, some proprietary interest or the right to resume or recover some proprietary interest. This submission is directly contrary to the holdings in *Lawrence* and *Gomez*. It must be rejected. The alternative submission is that the word 'appropriates' should be interpreted as if the word 'unlawfully' preceded it so that only an act which is unlawful under the general law can be an appropriation. This submission is an invitation to interpolate a word in the carefully crafted language of the 1968 Act. It runs counter to the decisions in *Lawrence* and *Gomez* and must also be rejected. It follows that the certified question must be answered in the affirmative . . . I would dismiss the appeal to the House"

LORD HOBHOUSE (DISSENTING):

"The reasoning of the Court of Appeal therefore depends upon the disturbing acceptance that a criminal conviction and the imposition of custodial sanctions may be based upon conduct which involves no inherent illegality and may only be capable of being criticised on grounds of lack of morality. This approach itself raises fundamental questions. An essential function of the criminal law is to define the boundary between what conduct is criminal and what merely immoral. Both are the subject of the disapprobation of ordinary right-thinking citizens and the distinction is liable to be arbitrary or at least strongly influenced by considerations subjective to the individual members of the tribunal. To treat otherwise lawful conduct as criminal merely because it is open to such disapprobation would be contrary to principle and open to the objection that it fails to achieve the objective and transparent certainty required of the criminal law by the principles basic to human rights . . .

If one treats the 'acceptance' of the gift as an appropriation, and this was the approach of the judge and is implicit in the judgment of the Court of Appeal (despite their choice of words), there are immediate difficulties with section 2(1)(a). The defendant did have the right to deprive the donor of the property. The donor did consent to the appropriation; indeed, he intended it. There are also difficulties with section 6 as she was not acting regardless of the donor's rights; the donor has already surrendered his rights. The only way that these conclusions can be displaced is by showing that the gift was not valid. There are even difficulties with section 3 itself. The donee is not 'assuming the rights of an owner': she has them already . . .

Section 3 does not use any qualitative expression such as '*mis*appropriates' nor does it repeat the Larceny Act expression 'without the consent of the owner'. It has thus been read by some as if 'appropriates' was a wholly colourless expression. This reading declines to draw any guidance from the context in which the word is used in the definition in section 1(1) and the scheme of sections 2 to 6. It also declines to attach any significance to the use of the word 'assumption'. This led some curious submissions being made to your Lordships.

It was for example suggested that the garage repair mechanic employed to change the oil of a car would have appropriated the car. The reasoning is that only the owner has the right to do this or tell someone to do it therefore to do it is to assume the rights of the owner. This is an absurdity even when one takes into account that some of the absurd results can be avoided by other parts of the definition of theft. The mechanic is not assuming any right; he is merely carrying out the instructions of the owner. The person who accepts a valid gift is simply conforming to the wishes of the owner. The words 'appropriate' (property belonging to another) and 'assume' (the rights of that other) have a useful breadth of meaning but each of them in its natural meaning includes an element of doing something which displaces the rights of that other person. The rights of that other (the owner) include the right to authorise another (the defendant) to do things which would otherwise be an infringement of the rights of the owner . . .

My Lords, the relevant law is contained in sections 1 to 6 of the Act. They should be construed as a whole and applied in a manner which presents a consistent scheme both internally and with the remainder of the Act. The phrase 'dishonestly appropriates' should be construed as a composite phrase. It does not include acts done in relation to the relevant property which are done in accordance with the actual wishes or actual authority of the person to whom the property belongs. This is because such acts do not involve any assumption of the rights of that person within section 3(1) or because, by necessary implication from section 2(1), they are not to be regarded as dishonest appropriations of property belonging to another.

Actual authority, wishes, consent (or similar words) mean, both as a matter of language and on the authority of the three House of Lords cases, authorisation not obtained by fraud or misrepresentation. The definition of theft therefore embraces cases where the property has come to the defendant by the mistake of the person to whom it belongs and there would be an obligation to restore it—section 5(4)—or property in which the other still has an equitable proprietary interest—section 5(1). This would also embrace property obtained by undue influence or other cases coming within the classes of invalid transfer . . .

In cases of alleged gift, the criteria to be applied are the same. But additional care may need to be taken to see that the transaction is properly explained to the jury. It is unlikely that a charge of theft will be brought where there is not clear evidence of at least some conduct of the defendant which includes an element of fraud or overt dishonesty or some undue influence or knowledge of the deficient capacity of the alleged donor. This was the basis upon which the prosecution of the appellant was originally brought in the present case. On this basis there is no difficulty in explaining to the jury the relevant parts of section 5 and section 2(1) and the effect of the phrase 'assumption of the rights of an owner'. . .

I would answer the certified question in the negative. But, in any event, I would allow the appeal and quash the conviction because the summing up failed to direct the jury adequately upon the other essential elements of theft, not just appropriation."

Appeal dismissed

Certain conclusions can be drawn from *Gomez* and *Hinks* as to the present meaning of "appropriation".

First, an appropriation involves the assumption of *any* of the rights of the owner. There need not be an assumption of *all* of the rights of the owner.

Secondly, where the defendant obtains property by deception there is an appropriation: it is irrelevant that the owner of the property "consents" to the transfer. For example, in *Atakpu*[72] the defendants, using false passports and licences, deceived a car-rental firm in Germany into parting with cars to them. They brought the cars to England with a view to selling them here. It was held that the theft had been committed in Germany and therefore there could be no theft in England. This meant that there was an almost[73] complete overlap between theft and the former offence of obtaining property by deception contrary to s.15 of the Theft Act 1968 (now abolished by the Fraud Act 2006). In any case where the defendant deceived the victim into parting with property the prosecution had the choice of charging either offence.[74]

Thirdly, because the victim's consent is irrelevant, it is unnecessary for the defendant to do anything involving "adverse interference with or usurpation of" the owner's rights. For example, in *Atakpu* the defendants who rented the cars in Germany did nothing beyond what they were permitted to do but were nevertheless held to have stolen the cars in Germany. The method of receiving the property is irrelevant: it can be pursuant to a valid contract or a gift.

Finally, it is irrelevant that the person receiving the property acquires an indefeasible title to the property. On the facts of *Hinks* itself the woman might only in fact have acquired a voidable title in civil law if there had been undue influence. It was emphasised, however, that the validity of the gift was irrelevant.

The approach adopted by the House of Lords in *Lawrence*, *Gomez* and, particularly, *Hinks* is most unfortunate. First, it is lamentable that leading House of Lords' decisions on the meaning of "appropriation" such as *Gomez* and *Hinks* do not even bother to specify the precise actions that constitute the appropriation. This leads to a failure to consider whether *at the time of the appropriation* the property still belongs to another. For instance, it is arguable that if the appropriation in *Gomez* occurred when the goods were physically collected by the rogue, ownership had already passed to him and so there was no appropriation of property belonging to another.[75]

Secondly, the concept of appropriation has become "wholly colourless" (Lord Hobhouse in *Hinks*); it has been emasculated of any practical meaning and has become no more than a minimal triggering condition for theft with the entire emphasis transferred to whether the conduct was dishonest or not. The absurdity of this approach is revealed in the following examples, considered obiter in *Gallasso*, a case decided prior to *Hinks*:

> "for example, the shopper carelessly knocks an article off the shelf; if he bends down and replaces it on the shelf nobody could regard that as an act of appropriation. Or suppose a lady drops her purse in the street. If a passer-by picks it up and hands it back there is no appropriation even though the passer-by is in temporary control."[76]

---

[72]   *R. v Atakpu (Austin)* [1993] 4 All E.R. 215.

[73]   Certain categories of land, wild flowers and wild animals cannot be stolen (s.4(2)–(4)) but could be obtained by deception as these subsections did not apply to s.15 (s.34(1)). Further, R. Heaton ("Deceiving without Thieving" [2001] Crim. L.R. 712) has argued that there could have been cases where, as a result of the defendant's deception, ownership passed to the defendant prior to any appropriation so while property had been obtained by deception, there was no theft because the defendant was not appropriating property belonging to another.

[74]   In *R. v Briggs (Linda Joan)* [2004] 1 Cr. App. R. 34 a narrow interpretation of appropriation was adopted in order to avoid too great an overlap between theft and obtaining by deception. This approach is not consistent with the leading House of Lords' decisions.

[75]   R. Heaton, "Deceiving without Thieving" [2001] Crim. L.R. 712.

[76]   *R. v Gallasso (Lesley Caroline)* (1994) 98 Cr. App. R. 284 at 289.

As a result of *Hinks*, these actions, along with those of Lord Hobhouse's motor mechanic, all now amount to an appropriation. An appropriation has become a neutral, value-free act with the mental element of the defendant being irrelevant. This purely objective description ignores the definition of appropriation in s.3(1) that it must involve an *"assumption* by a person of the rights of the an owner". As seen above, "assumption" is not a value-free word. It suggests that one is laying claim to rights one does not have over property. There must be an assertion of dominion over the property; it involves a positive decision to treat the property as one's own.[77] It has been argued that there should be an element of "proprietary subjectivity" by the defendant towards the property: "a mental connection of the person with the thing, the sense of dominion . . . he behaves as if the property were *his*".[78] It is absurd to assert that picking up a dropped purse to hand it back to the owner is assuming the rights of the owner.

For similar reasons it is objectionable that persons who have done nothing wrong yet, but have secret dishonest intentions, should be liable for theft. As seen above, the defendant in *Eddy v Niman* took goods from a shelf in a store and, intending not to pay for them, placed them in a trolley. Following *Hinks* this would now be an appropriation and, because of the mens rea, theft. Again, it is difficult to accept that this is *assuming* the rights of an owner. One can surely only lay claim to, or assert, the rights of an owner if there is an open representation that one is assuming such a right. In the supermarket situation, as long as the goods are in the trolley the defendant is recognising and respecting the rights of the owner by doing exactly what he is expected to do. It is quite different if the defendant slips the goods into their own pocket. They are thereby laying claim to the goods; they are treating them as owner without any recognition of the rights of another. Using Fletcher's test of "manifest criminality" discussed earlier, the reasonable observer would recognise the theftuous criminality of the defendant's actions.[79] However, following *Hinks*, such considerations are irrelevant. This marks an alarming return to "protectionist criminology" whereby liability is imposed primarily on the basis of the defendant's blameworthy state of mind—even if they have done nothing observably wrong.

A third objection to the ruling in *Hinks* is that persons can be liable for theft despite committing no civil wrong thus creating a conflict between the civil law and the criminal law: "It is surely intolerable that the performance of a perfectly valid contract should be a crime."[80] With regard to valid gifts, the recipient acquires an indefeasible title to property and can sue the donor if they take the property back. This amounts to the civil law "assisting [the defendant] to enjoy, or to recover, the fruits of his crime".[81] It has been argued, however, that congruence between these two areas of law is not possible: criminal courts are not well placed to determine whether a valid title has been acquired; civil courts are unable to determine liability for theft which depends on the establishment of dishonesty (a question of fact for a jury or magistrate). Nor is harmony necessary because the relevant rules of civil and criminal law are not aimed at the same thing: for example, the civil law has an interest, inter alia, in protecting the rights of third parties who subsequently acquire property.[82] The problem with these views is that criminal courts do

---

[77]   A.T.H. Smith, *Property Offences* (London: Sweet & Maxwell, 1994), p.163.

[78]   E. Melissaris, "The Concept of Appropriation and the Offence of Theft" [2007] 70 M.L.R. 581 at 590–591.

[79]   See also M. Giles and S. Uglow, "Appropriation and Manifest Criminality in Theft" (1992) 56 Jo. C.L. 179. E. Melissaris, fn.78 above, argues that "it is necessary the act [should] be manifested and sensibly identifiable" (p.596). Obviously one could not expressly employ a test of manifest criminality as this would involve asking the jury vague questions such as: does this conduct look like theft to you? What is suggested is that in developing a suitable test of appropriation the courts should have been, and hopefully Parliament will be, *guided* by this test.

[80]   J.C. Smith, [2001] Crim. L.R. 163 at 165.

[81]   D. Ormerod, *Smith and Hogan: Criminal Law*, 13th edn (Oxford: OUP, 2011), p.784.

[82]   S. Gardner, "Property and Theft" [1998] Crim. L.R. 35. See also A.L. Bogg and J. Stanton-Ife, "Protecting the Vulnerable: Legality, Harm and Theft" (2003) 23 *Legal Studies* 402.

have to decide questions of civil law[83] and civil courts do have to decide questions of dishonesty.[84] More significantly, this argument misses the central point that the law of theft is there to protect persons' interests in property. These interests can only exist at civil law: "remove dependence on the law of property, and property offences have no rationale".[85] A different argument in favour of the *Hinks* position is that it is legitimate to criminalise conduct that does not breach civil law proprietary rights because such conduct "may nonetheless have a *tendency* to undermine property rights, either directly by attacking the interests that they protect, or indirectly by weakening an established system of property rights and so threatening the public good that that system represents".[86] Of course, it is legitimate to criminalise conduct that threatens security interests—but that is the function of the law of attempt and the other inchoate and endangerment offences. Attepted theft, for example, involves criminalising conduct that threatens the interests protected by the law of theft. The substantive law of theft should, however, be aimed at protecting existing property rights which can only be established by reference to the civil law.

A final objection to the decisions of *Lawrence, Gomez* and *Hinks* is that it was quite wrong to have collapsed the distinction between theft and the former offence of obtaining property by deception (now abolished by the Fraud Act 2006).

P.R. Glazebrook, "Thief or Swindler: Who Cares?" [1991] C.L.J. 389:

"Should it matter tuppence whether a crook snitched his victim's property or tricked him out of it? Parliament evidently thought not [by originally enacting the same penalties for the two offences] . . .

In the ensuing 22 years the courts decided accordingly . . . [holding] that though property had been, or might have been, obtained by deception the crook could still be convicted of theft for there was nothing in the definition of stealing in section 1 of the 1968 Act that required the courts to make the trivial and morally irrelevant distinction between someone who dishonestly appropriated another's property by stealth, and one who did so by deceit. The crook is as dishonest in the one case as the other, and the gain to him, and the loss to his victim, is exactly the same . . . It would certainly be bizarre if a defendant who appropriated property he had received because the transferor had made a mistake to which the defendant had not contributed were guilty of theft (as he is: s.5(4)), but was not guilty if the property had come to him because of a mistake which he had deliberately induced.

What is more, it may be either difficult to decide, or the merest matter of chance, whether the crook had resorted to deception in order to get his sticky mitts on to the property he coveted. In *Lawrence* it would have been as difficult as it would have been pointless to set about deciding whether the travel-weary and English-less Signor Occhi had been deceived by taxi-driver Lawrence . . . or whether Signor Occhi was just too bemused to know what exactly was happening as Lawrence helped himself to the notes in his wallet . . . Can it really be that Her Majesty's judges think that they must indulge the sensitivities of a con-man who feels hurt at being called a common thief? Indeed, the decision (the Court of Appeal judgment in *Gomez*) looks even sillier now that Parliament has decided to reduce the maximum sentence for theft (but not that for obtaining) from 10 years to 7, for it will enable defendants to demand that they should be acquitted of one offence because they are guilty of a more serious one."

Stephen Shute and Jeremy Horder, "Thieving and Deceiving: What is the Difference?" (1993) 56 M.L.R. 548 at 549–553:

"It has long been recognised that there is some common sense distinction between theft and obtaining property by deception . . . The criminal law seeks to find appropriate labels for different kinds of wrongdoers, as part of its

---

[83]   For example, in relation to "belonging to another" under s.5.

[84]   See, for example, *Twinsectra Ltd v Yardley* [2002] 2 All E.R. 376; *Starglade Properties Ltd v Nash* [2010] EWCA Civ 1314; *Vivendi SA v Richards* [2013] EWHC 3006 (Ch).

[85]   J. Beatson and A.P. Simester, "Stealing One's Own Property" (1999) 115 L.Q.R. 372 at 374. Cf. A.P. Simester and G.R. Sullivan, "On the Nature and Rationale of Property Offences", in R.A. Duff and S.P. Green (eds), *Defining Crimes: Essays on the Criminal Law's Special Part* (Oxford: OUP, 2005) pp.170–181.

[86]   S. Shute, "Appropriation and the Law of Theft" [2002] Crim. L.R. 445 at 455.

'representative labelling' function. The label 'thief' does not carry the same moral import as the label 'conman'
. . .

   There is in our society a general social practice of uncoerced voluntary transfers ('givings'), even when they are the product of another's advice, influence or persuasion . . . [which] serve[s] to enhance the transferor's autonomy . . . [T]he nature of the wrongdoing in theft has a separate moral foundation from that of obtaining by deception. The wrongful conduct in obtaining by deception is internal to the practice of voluntary transfer. Its wrongfulness centres on the abuse of what should have been an autonomy enhancing transaction. The fraudster abuses the control that he or she has over the information on which victims make their decisions about an admittedly voluntary transfer: the victim's chances of making an authentic choice are deliberately or recklessly undermined by the fraudster. The wrongful act in theft, however, is external to the legitimate social practice of voluntary transfers of property. Its wrongfulness centres on the fact that the thief bypasses the entire social practice at the victim's expense. Putting it metaphorically, whereas the thief makes war on a social practice from the outside, the deceiver is the traitor within."

These latter views are surely preferable to those of Glazebrook. Offences should be structured, labelled and punished to reflect the extent of wrongdoing and harm involved. Crimes are generally described in terms of their paradigms. The paradigmatic theft involves a surreptitious or forcible taking while deception offences involved a confrontation and a participation by the victim in the loss of the property.[87] With theft, the owner is generally helpless against such a taking. If interrupted there is a risk of violence. With the typical obtaining by deception, the victim has a real opportunity to prevent the commission of the crime. With greater alertness they might not have been deceived. They have agreed to part with the property. In our society where mutual transactions based on trust are valued and encouraged, the wrong of *deceiving* another into parting with property is a distinctive wrong—quite different in quality from the paradigmatic theft. Parliament recognised this by providing different penalties for the two offences. It is unacceptable to brush over these important moral distinctions by the creation of broad morally uninformative offences.

   As shall be seen later, the Fraud Act 2006 has abolished all the deception offences and replaced them with two new offences: fraud (which can be committed in one of three ways) and obtaining services dishonestly. One of the three ways in which fraud can be committed is through the making of a false representation with a dishonest intention to make a gain or cause a loss. The new offence thus differs significantly from the previous offence of obtaining property by deception. First, there need be no deception. It does not have to be established that the victim believed the false representation and that that caused them to part with property. Secondly, no property need actually be obtained. The new offence adopts an inchoate model. What is criminal is making the false representation with the requisite intent. It can, however, be anticipated that prosecutions will mostly be brought in cases where property has actually been obtained and the victim has sustained a loss. In such cases there will still be an overlap between fraud and theft and the above criticisms of the over-broad interpretation of appropriation will still apply. However, the overlap is no longer nearly so complete. In cases where no property has been obtained there will very seldom be an appropriation and so fraud will be the only available charge. The next section, however, demonstrates that even in such cases there will sometimes be an appropriation.

(i) Appropriation and control

Another problem that has arisen is whether there can be an appropriation by a defendant who is not in a position to exercise power or control over the property. Can a defendant sitting in a pub in Leicester

---

[87]   C.M.V. Clarkson, "Theft and Fair Labelling" (1993) 56 M.L.R. 554.

appropriate the Crown Jewels (situated in the Tower of London) by "selling" them to the mythical, ever-gullible foreign tourist?

R. v Pitham and Hehl (1976) 65 Cr. App. R. 45 (Court of Appeal, Criminal Division)

A man called Millman, knowing that his friend McGregor was in prison, decided to take advantage of his friend's hapless plight and steal furniture from his house. He took the two appellants to the house and sold them some furniture. Millman was convicted of burglary on the basis that he had entered the building as a trespasser and committed theft therein, contrary to s.9(1)(b) of the Theft Act 1968. The two appellants were convicted of handling stolen goods. They argued that their handling was still "in the course of stealing"; the goods were not yet stolen and therefore they were not handling stolen goods.

LAWTON LJ:

"What was the appropriation in this case? The jury found that the two appellants had handled the property *after* Millman had stolen it . . . What had Millman done? He had assumed the rights of the owner. He had done that when he took the two appellants to 20 Parry Road, showed them the property and invited them to buy what they wanted. He was then acting as the owner. He was then, in the words of the statute, 'assuming the rights of the owner'. The moment he did that he appropriated McGregor's goods to himself. The appropriation was complete. After this appropriation had been completed there was no question of these two appellants taking part, in the words of the section 22, in dealing with the goods 'in the course of the stealing'."

Appeal dismissed

It has been argued that there can be no assumption of a right of an owner in such a case because an owner has no general right that others shall not contract to sell or purport to pass ownership in their property: "He does not need such a right, because other people, generally, can do him no harm by offering to sell his goods, and cannot pass ownership without his authority."[88] Such an argument seems to suggest that "everyone has the right to sell anyone else's property—which seems rather bizarre".[89] Further, the fact that the owner suffers no harm because ownership cannot be passed is irrelevant. It is only in rare cases that theft deprives the owner of their ownership (as opposed to possession) of the goods[90] and causing loss of ownership is simply not a prerequisite of the law of theft.

However, while an offer to sell another's property can probably amount to an appropriation,[91] this should only be so where the actor is in a position to threaten the owner's rights.[92] Sitting in a pub offering the sell the Crown Jewels poses no threat whatsoever and therefore does not amount to an assumption of a right of an owner. Indeed, viewed from another perspective, it would not even amount to an attempted theft as the acts would still be preparatory. On the other hand, the rogue Millman in *Pitham* was in a position to threaten his friend's rights. His was an act of adverse interference with the rights of owner and was an assumption of the rights of owner.

---

[88]   A.T.H. Smith (A.T.H.), *Property Offences* (1994), p.160.
[89]   D. Ormerod, *Smith and Hogan: Criminal Law*, 12th edn (Oxford: OUP, 2008), p.748.
[90]   Ormerod, *Smith and Hogan: Criminal Law*, 12th edn (2008), p.748.
[91]   On its particular facts, *Pitham* is probably wrong. As all the parties concerned knew that Millman had no authority to sell the property, Millman was not "assuming the rights of owner"; it was a proposal for a joint theft (D. Ormerod, *Smith and Hogan: Criminal Law*, 13th edn (Oxford: OUP, 2011), p.794).
[92]   E. Melissaris, fn.78 above, states that under present English law: "The greater the proximity, the greater the risk to the owner's rights" (p.588).

(ii) Timing of appropriation

One of the criticisms, mentioned above, of *Gomez* and the other leading House of Lords' decisions was their failure to consider the precise point in time when the appropriation occurs. This matter has been considered in other cases—mainly ones where an act is done in one place which affects property in another place. Often this property is a thing in action such as a debt owed by a bank to an account holder.[93] In *Chan Man-sin*, the Privy Council held that

> "one who draws, presents and negotiates a cheque on a particular bank account is assuming the rights of the owner of the credit in the account or (as the case may be) of the pre-negotiated right to draw on the account up to the agreed figure."[94]

In *Hilton*,[95] it was held that the appropriation occurred when the defendant instructed the bank to make a transfer of funds *and the transfer was made*. The decision in *Chan Man-sin* is to be preferred. Presenting a cheque is undoubtedly as clear an assumption of ownership as swapping price labels. Whether the transfer of money is ever made is as irrelevant as whether the shopkeeper is fooled by the switched price labels. In *Sui Soi Ngan*,[96] it was held that the drawing and signing of a cheque (in England) were merely preparatory acts and that the appropriation occurred when the cheque was presented to the bank (in Scotland).

In *Osman*[97] the defendant in Hong Kong sent a telex to a New York bank instructing payment from the victim's account into another account. It was held that one of an owner's rights is the right to draw on an account: "It is that right which the defendant assumes by presenting a cheque, or by sending a telex instruction without authority." Accordingly, the act of sending the telex in Hong Kong was the appropriation.[98] More usually today, it would be the act of sending an email in these circumstances that would constitute the appropriation.

A somewhat different approach was adopted in *Levin*.[99] Using a computer in Russia the defendant gained unauthorised access to an American bank and diverted funds into false accounts. Beldam LJ favoured the view that a crime could have a dual location: "It seems to us artificial to regard the act as having been done in one rather than the other place." Nevertheless he felt that if "having to choose" the appropriation occurred in America:

> "The fact that the applicant was physically in St Petersburg is of far less significance than the fact that he was looking at and operating on magnetic discs located in Parsipenny. The essence of what he was doing was done there. Until the instruction is recorded on the disc, there is in fact no appropriation."

---

[93]   When a customer places money in a bank account, the bank owns that money but owes the customer a debt. This debt is a thing in action which is regarded as property under s.4.
[94]   *Chan Man-sin v Att-Gen of Hong Kong* (1988) 86 Cr. App. R. 303 at 306.
[95]   *R. v Hilton (Peter Arnold)* [1997] 2 Cr. App. R. 445.
[96]   *R. v Ngan (Sui Soi)* [1998] 1 Cr. App. R. 331.
[97]   *R. v Governor of Pentonville Prison, Ex p. Osman* (1990) 90 Cr. App. R. 281.
[98]   In *Sui Soi Ngan* [1998] 1 Cr. App. R. 331 the court equated the presenting of a cheque with the sending of a telex.
[99]   *R. v Governor of Brixton Prison, Ex p. Levin* [1997] 1 Cr. App. R. 225.

(iii) Continuing appropriation

Is an appropriation complete as soon as there is an assumption of a right of an owner or does it continue for as long as the owner continues to assume that right? This can be important. For example, there can only be liability for handling stolen goods if the handling is "otherwise than in the course of stealing".

R. v Atakpu [1994] Q.B. 69 (Court of Appeal, Criminal Division)

The defendants hired cars in Germany and Belgium dishonestly intending to sell them in England.

WARD J:

"It would seem that (1) theft can occur in an instant by a single appropriation but it can also involve a course of dealing with property lasting longer and involving several appropriations before the transaction is complete; (2) theft is a finite act—it has a beginning and it has an end; (3) at what point the transaction is complete is a matter for the jury to decide upon the facts of each case; . . . In our judgment, if goods have once been stolen, even if stolen abroad, they cannot be stolen again by the same thief exercising the same or other rights of ownership over the property.

We find it more difficult to answer . . . whether or not theft is a continuous offence. On a strict reading of *Reg. v. Gomez* any dishonest assumption of the rights of the owner made with the necessary intention constitutes theft and that leaves little room for a continuous course of action.

We would not wish that to be the law. Such restriction and rigidity may lead to technical anomalies and injustice. We would prefer to leave it for the common sense of the jury to decide that the appropriation can continue for so long as the thief can sensibly be regarded as in the act of stealing or, in more understandable words, so long as he is "on the job". [However], since the matter is not strictly necessary for our decision we will leave it open for further argument. It is not necessary for us to decide because no jury properly directed could reasonably arrive at a conclusion that the theft of these motor cars was still continuing days after the appellants had first taken them. If the jury had been asked when and where these motor cars were stolen they could only have answered that they were stolen in Frankfurt or Brussels. The theft was complete abroad and the thieves could not steal again in England."

Inevitably, such a fluid test of whether the defendant is "on the job" raises problems. If a burglar steals valuables from a house and hands them to a "fence" in a car parked outside on the street, is he still "on the job"? The liability of the "fence" for theft or handling will depend upon such a determination.

(iv) No need for loss

As long as there is an appropriation, accompanied by an intention to permanently deprive someone of property, there is no need for that person actually to sustain any loss. In one of the two cases in *Morris* the defendant was arrested before reaching the check-out point; the supermarket suffered no loss. In *Wheatley*[100] the decision of *Re (A) Snaresbrook Crown Court*[101] was approved: in this case it had been accepted that the alleged theft had been carried out for a purpose which could have financially benefited the company. In *Chan Man-sin*[102] presenting a forged cheque was held to be an appropriation even though the defendant's actions were legally ineffective as the transaction was a nullity and the bank would have had to repay the money. These decisions reveal the almost inchoate nature of the crime of theft.

---

[100]   *Wheatley v Commissioner of Police of the British Virgin Islands* [2006] 2 Cr. App. R. 21.
[101]   *Re (A) v Snaresbrook Crown Court* [2001] All E.R. (D) 123.
[102]   *Chan Man-sin v Att-Gen. of Hong Kong* (1988) 86 Cr. App. R. 303 at 306.

(v) Bona fide purchasers

Section 3(2) provides a special exemption for the bona fide purchaser for value of stolen goods. If a person bought goods at a reasonable price not knowing they were stolen and then later discovered they were, but decided to keep them, this would (without s.3(2)) come within the latter half of s.3(1), namely, they would have come by the property innocently without stealing it but would be appropriating it when they decided to keep it. The Criminal Law Revision Committee specifically proposed this exception on the ground that while there was a case for the imposition of criminal liability in such cases, "on the whole it seems to us that, whatever view is taken of the buyer's moral duty, the law would be too strict if it made him guilty of theft".[103] Accordingly, in *Wheeler* the defendant innocently purchased some stolen military antiques. He was later informed by the police that the goods were stolen but, nevertheless, sold one of the items. It was held that he could not be guilty of theft if he kept the goods for himself or sold them to another.[104] It is, however, possible that in selling such goods the defendant could be liable for the offence of fraud (if they represented that they had good title) or of aiding and abetting the offence of handling stolen goods by the purchaser (if both knew the goods were stolen).[105]

3. Property

Theft Act 1968 s.4

"(1) 'Property' includes money and all other property, real or personal, including things in action and other intangible property.

(2) A person cannot steal land, or things forming part of land and severed from it by him or by his directions, except in the following cases, that is to say—

(a) when he is a trustee or personal representative, or is authorised by power of attorney, or as liquidator of a company, or otherwise, to sell or dispose of land belonging to another, and he appropriates the land or anything forming part of it by dealing with it in breach of the confidence reposed in him; or

(b) when he is not in possession of the land and appropriates anything forming part of the land by severing it or causing it to be severed or after it has been severed; or

(c) when, being in possession of the land under a tenancy, he appropriates the whole or part of any fixture or structure let to be used with the land.

For purposes of this subsection 'land' does not include incorporeal hereditaments; 'tenancy' means a tenancy for years or any less period and includes an agreement for such a tenancy, but a person who after the end of a tenancy remains in possession as statutory tenant or otherwise is to be treated as having possession under the tenancy, and 'let' shall be construed accordingly.

(3) A person who picks mushrooms growing wild on any land, or who picks flowers, fruit or foliage from a plant growing wild on any land does not (although not in possession of the land) steal what he picks, unless he does it for reward or for sale or other commercial purpose.

For purposes of this subsection 'mushroom' includes any fungus, and 'plant' includes any shrub or tree.

(4) Wild creatures, tamed or untamed, shall be regarded as property; but a person cannot steal a wild creature not tamed nor ordinarily kept in captivity, or the carcass of any such creature, unless either it has been reduced into possession by or on behalf of another person and possession of it has not since been lost or abandoned, or another person is in course of reducing it into possession."

---

[103]   CLRC, 8th Report, *Theft and Related Offences* (1966), Cmnd.2977, para.37.

[104]   *R. v Wheeler (Stephen Godfrey)* (1991) 92 Cr. App. R. 279 at 283.

[105]   *R. v Bloxham (Albert John)* [1983] 1 A.C. 109 at 114, approved in *Wheeler* (1991) 92 Cr. App. R. 279 at 284.

Theft is an offence against property and inevitably the question arises as to the meaning of "property". Section 4(1) provides an extremely wide definition that property includes:

1. Money: This refers to current coins and bank notes, including foreign ones. Obsolete coins and notes would constitute other personal property. It does not cover money placed in a bank account, which then constitutes a debt owed by the bank to the account holder and is a thing in action (see below).

2. All real property: i.e. land and things attached to the land such as houses. However, the breadth of this provision is greatly limited by ss.4(2), (3) and (4):

Section 4(2) isolates the only circumstances in which land and the things attached to the land may be stolen. Where a defendant dishonestly tries to dispose of an interest in another's land, a charge of fraud under s.1 of the Fraud Act 2006 is likely to be most appropriate charge. By virtue of s.4(2)(a), a trustee authorised to sell or dispose of trust land would commit theft if they dishonestly made an unauthorised disposal of the property. Section 4(2)(b) deals with the appropriation by persons not in possession of the land: for example, it is not theft where D moves the fence to his garden so as to annex part of his neighbour's lawn into his own garden. Nor do squatters steal the land that they 'squat' on.[106] However, a person not in possession of land can steal anything forming part of the land by severing it from the land or appropriating it after severance, so it would be theft if D were to remove trees or shrubs planted in his neighbour's garden.[107] Under s.4(2)(c), a tenant may be guilty of theft where he appropriates any fixture or structure let to be used with the land, e.g. removing a bath. This subsection does not require that the thing actually be severed from the land, merely that the fixture be wholly or partly appropriated. So "if the tenant contracted to sell the unsevered fireplace in the house leased by him, he would be guilty of theft".[108]

Section 4(3) deals with the circumstances in which things growing wild on land may be stolen. A person is not guilty of theft if they pick wild mushrooms, or "flowers, fruit or foliage from a plant growing wild on any land", unless the picking is done "for reward or sale or other commercial purpose". This exemption would not apply to cultivated flowers or crops, or if the whole plant were taken (except in the case of mushrooms), or if part of the plant was removed by an act which cannot be regarded as "picking" for example, taking cuttings with a knife, cutting grass with a lawnmower or strimmer, or sawing off branches.[109]

Section 4(4) deals with wild animals. All tame creatures may be stolen. Wild creatures cannot be stolen,[110] except where (i) the creature has been tamed or is ordinarily kept in captivity (so animals in a circus or the zoo could be stolen), or (ii) the creature either has been reduced into the possession of another person, or is in the course of being reduced into the possession of another person.

---

[106] Specific offences have been created to criminalise certain squatters: Criminal Law Act 1977 ss.6–7, Legal Aid; Sentencing and Punishment of Offenders Act 2012 s.144; N. Cobb, "Property's Outlaws: Squatting, Land Use and Criminal Trespass" [2012] Crim LR 114–127.

[107] Whether an item 'forms part of the land' is a question of land law, depending on the degree of annexation and the object of annexation. For guidance re this, see *Elitestone Ltd v Morris* [1997] 1 W.L.R. 687 (HL); C. Harpum, S. Bridge and M. Dixon, *Megarry and Wade, The Law of Real Property*, 8th edn (London: Sweet & Maxwell, 2012), paras 23-005–23-010.

[108] D. Ormerod and D.H. Williams, *Smith's Law of Theft*, 9th edn (Oxford: OUP, 2007), para.2.139.

[109] The Wildlife and Countryside Act 1981 makes it an offence intentionally to pick, uproot or destroy certain wild plants: s.13 and Sch.8. See M. Welstead, "Seasons of Mist and Mellow Fruitfulness" (1995) 145 N.L.J. 1499.

[110] Cf. *Cresswell v DPP* [2006] EWHC 3379 (Admin). There are, however, a number of statutory provisions which criminalise the poaching of various animals: see D. Ormerod, *Smith and Hogan: Criminal Law*, 13th edn (Oxford: OUP, 2011), pp.802–803.

If, for example, Lord G shoots a grouse on his country estate, and before his dog can retrieve the carcass, a dishonest beater bags the bird for himself, the beater will commit theft.

3. All personal property: i.e. all property that is not real property. Nothing in the Theft Act "suggests that what would otherwise constitute or be regarded as 'property' for the purposes of the Theft Act 1968 ceases to be so because its possession or control is, for whatever reason, unlawful or illegal or prohibited".[111] Personal property includes:

4. Things in action: a thing in action is non-physical property; one's rights in it can only be enforced by a legal action. The best example of such a "thing in action" is a debt. We saw above that a bank owns the money in an account but owes a debt to the account holder. This debt is a thing in action; it is property and can be stolen.[112] For example, in *Williams*[113] the defendant dishonestly overcharged elderly householders for building work; by cashing their cheques he was causing a diminution of their credit balances and so was appropriating their thing in action, namely part of the debt owed to them.

Problems have arisen with regard to whether cheques can be stolen in the situation where the defendant induces a victim to draw a cheque in her favour. Following dicta in *Preddy*[114] it has been held in *Graham*[115] and *Clark*[116] that cheques cannot be stolen in such cases. This is because the moment the cheque is written, the thing in action belongs to the defendant. It does not belong to the victim because he cannot sue himself. However, the better view is that the requisite property here is not the thing in action, but the cheque itself which is a valuable security ("any document . . . authorising the payment of money"[117]); it is a piece of paper with special qualities like a key to a safe[118] and is, therefore, capable of being stolen. Other examples of things in action are a copyright, a trademark and shares in a company.[119]

5. Other intangible property: this is also non-physical property in which one can have a legal interest: for example, statute has declared that a patent is intangible property but not a thing in action.[120] In *Nai Keung*[121] it was held that export quotas were "other intangible property" and capable of being stolen.

Three areas are of particular interest and deserve consideration.

---

[111]   *R. v Smith (Michael Andrew)* [2011] EWCA Crim 66, [2011] 1 Cr. App. R. 30 at [7] (defendants guilty of robbery when they attacked a drug dealer and stole his heroin). A.T.H. Smith, "Can proscribed drugs be the subject of theft?" (2011) 70(2) C.L.J. 289–291.

[112]   *R. v Kohn (David James)* (1979) 69 Cr. App. R. 395; *R. v Hilton (Peter Arnold)* [1997] 2 Cr. App. R. 445.

[113]   *Williams* [2001] 1 Cr. App. R. 362.

[114]   *R. v Preddy (John Crawford)* [1996] A.C. 815.

[115]   *R. v Graham (Hemamali Krishna)* [1997] 1 Cr. App. R. 302.

[116]   *Clark* [2002] 1 Cr. App. R. 14. This case concerned obtaining property by deception. The same principles, with regard to the meaning of property, apply to theft.

[117]   Theft Act 1968 s.20(3).

[118]   J.C. Smith, "Obtaining Cheques by Deception or Theft" [1997] Crim. L.R. 396 at 400.

[119]   If a defendant presents, or intends to present the cheque, problems also arise in relation to the issue of whether he intends to permanently deprive the owner of the cheque: see below at p.861–863.

[120]   Patents Act 1977 s.30.

[121]   *Attorney-General of Hong Kong v Nai Keung* [1987] 1 W.L.R. 1339.

(i) Electricity

In *Lowe v Blease*[122] it was held that electricity is not property for the purposes of theft. Section 13 of the Theft Act creates a special offence of abstracting electricity, carrying a maximum of five years' imprisonment. The s.13 offence has been used to prosecute those who dishonestly bypass the electricity meter to avoid paying for electricity.[123] Gas, however, is property that can be stolen.[124]

(ii) Confidential information

In *Oxford v Moss*[125] a university student acquired a proof of one of his examination papers. He read the questions but did not intend to deprive the university of the piece of paper on which the questions were printed. He was charged with theft of intangible property, namely, the confidential information contained in the examination questions. On appeal it was held that this was not intangible property within the meaning of s.4. Following this, in *Absolom*,[126] it was held that a person who obtained valuable trade secrets relating to oil exploration, worth between £50,000 and £100,000, and tried to sell them to a rival oil company could not be guilty of theft as such information did not amount to property. While there are other offences of infringing rights in intellectual property,[127] counterfeiting registered trade marks,[128] and gaining unauthorised access to data held on a computer,[129] it is nonetheless "absurd and disgraceful that we should still be making do without any legislation specifically designed to discourage this modern form of commercial piracy".[130] On the other hand, it has been argued that

> "misconduct such as exploiting confidential information can raise complex issues of fair competition, access to markets, free movement of employees, and freedom of speech. To the extent that such questions are significantly more complex in the realm of non-proprietary economic value, they may be better mediated by more fine-grained and specific legislation, and not simply overpainted by the broad brush of theft."[131]

The Law Commission has investigated this issue and provisionally concluded that confidential information is not "property" and that it "would be a mistake for the criminal law to pretend that it is".[132] However, because "there is no distinction in principle between the harm caused by such misuse and

---

[122] *Low v Blease* [1975] Crim. L.R. 513.
[123] *R. v Herber (Peter)* [2014] EWCA Crim 519. It is not, however, necessary to prove that the meter has been tampered with to prove the s.13 offence: *R. v McCreadie (Malcolm)* (1993) 96 Cr. App. R. 143.
[124] *Firth* (1865–1872) L.R.1 C.C.R. 172; *R. v Hughes (Colin David)* [2000] 2 Cr. App. R. (S.) 399.
[125] *Oxford v Moss* (1978) 68 Cr. App. R. 183.
[126] *Absolom, The Times,* September 14, 1983.
[127] Copyright, Designs and Patents Act 1988 ss.107, 198.
[128] Trade Marks Act 1994 s.92.
[129] Computer Misuse Act 1990 s.1.
[130] G. Williams, *Textbook of Criminal Law,* 2nd edn (London: Stevens & Sons, 1983), p.739. Cf. C.R. Davies, "Protection of Intellectual Property—A Myth?" (2004) J.C.L. 398
[131] A.P. Simester and G.R. Sullivan, "On the Nature and Rationale of Property Offences", in R.A. Duff and S. Green (eds), *Defining Crimes* (Oxford: OUP, 2005), pp.182–183. For further consideration of the issues in relation to the criminalisation of unauthorised access to data, see J. Clough, "Data Theft? Cybercrime and the Increasing Criminalization of Access to Data" (2011) 22 *Criminal Law Forum* 145–170.
[132] Law Commission Consultation Paper No.150, *Legislating the Criminal Code: Misuse of Trade Secrets* (1997), para.3.26. See J. Hull, "Stealing Secrets: A Review of the Law Commission's Consultation Paper on the Misuse of Trade Secrets" [1998] Crim. L.R. 246.

the harm caused by theft"[133] the Commission has proposed a new offence covering the use or disclosure of another's trade secret where the "owner does not consent to its use or disclosure".[134]

(iii) The human body and its parts

Can one steal a human body or any parts thereof? It is often stated that "nobody owns my body, not even me".[135] However, in relation to the criminal law the answer may not be that simple and to answer the question, some distinctions need to be drawn.

First, for most practical purposes it seems unlikely that parts of the human body, while still a part of a live person, can be property for purposes of theft. In *Bentham*,[136] the House of Lords held that one does not possess one's hand or any part of the body that is not separate and distinct from oneself:

"A person's hand or fingers are not a thing. If they were regarded as property . . . the court could, theoretically, make an order depriving the offender of his rights to them and they could be taken into the possession of the police".

However, once a limb, organ or sample has been removed from the body and stored in, say, a sperm or blood bank, it possesses all the attributes of personal property and should fall within s.4(1). In *Yearworth*[137] it was held that semen stored in a hospital's fertility storage unit was property owned by the men who had provided the samples. Indeed, it has been held that blood[138] and urine[139] are property capable of being stolen. In the United States it has been held that a university hospital owned a patient's spleen and other body substances after they had been removed.[140] Such organs and tissue can be extremely valuable and while, for policy reasons, it might be appropriate to ban the purchase or sale of, say, organs for transplantation,[141] that should not alter the basic proposition that such organs, once removed, can be property capable of being stolen.[142]

Secondly, in relation to corpses there was a commonly accepted view that a corpse was not prop-

---

[133]   Law Commission Consultation Paper No.150, fn.132 above, para.3.60.

[134]   Law Commission Consultation Paper No.150, fn.132 above, para.1.30.

[135]   J.W. Harris, "Who Owns My Body?" (1996) 16 O.J.L.S. 55. See, generally, A.T.H. Smith, "Stealing the Body and its Parts" [1976] Crim. L.R. 622; J. Herring and P.-L Chau, "My Body, Your Bodies, Our Bodies" (2007) 15 Med. L. Rev. 34.

[136]   *R. v Bentham (Peter)* [2005] 2 Cr. App. R. 11.

[137]   *Yearworth v North Bristol NHS Trust* [2010] Q.B. 1.

[138]   *R. v Rothery (Henry Michael)* [1976] R.T.R. 550. The defendant was charged with theft of the capsule containing the blood, not the actual blood itself. The appellant did not appeal the conviction for theft, but it may be argued that the Court of Appeal (albeit obiter) suggested that blood was property capable of being stolen: P. Matthews, "Whose Body? People as Property" (1983) C.L.P. 193 at 224.

[139]   *R. v Welsh* [1974] R.T.R. 478. In *Herbert* (1961) 25 Jo. C.L. 163, a defendant was convicted of larceny and common assault by magistrates for cutting a girl's hair without consent and "taking and carrying away" the hair once it had been cut. No point appears to have been taken as to whether "hair" could amount to "property", and the case was not appealed. Cf. *DPP v Smith* [2006] EWHC 94 (Admin), above pp.615–616.

[140]   *Moore v Regents of the University of California* [1990] 271 Cal. Rptr 146. In *Washington University v Catalona* (2006) 437 F. Supp. 2d 985 a US District Court held that the university owned samples provided by participants enrolled in cancer research conducted by one of their employees. This was subsequently affirmed on appeal: (2007) 490 F. 3d 667 (8th Circuit Court of Appeals).

[141]   Human Tissue Act 2004 s.32. The prohibition on commercial dealings does not apply to "material which is the subject of property because of an application of human skill": s.32(9)(c).

[142]   In 2005, Christopher Ibbotson, a laboratory manager, used his position to steal bones from a bone bank at Sheffield Hospital and to sell them to private clinics. He was charged with stealing the bones and with obtaining money by deception. The judge directed the jury to acquit him of the theft charges after Ibbotson pleaded guilty to 10 counts of obtaining money by deception and asked for 34 offences to be taken into consideration: *The Guardian*, January 20, 2005; *The Independent*, December 23, 2005.

erty and nobody could have a proprietary right or interest in it.[143] For the purposes of the criminal law this is clearly outmoded. Take, for instance, a cadaver "owned" by a University Medical Faculty. If the University does not "own" the cadaver under property law, it does have a bailment of the corpse,[144] or, at least, "possession or control" over it. However, although there might be a "proprietary right or interest" or "possession or control" over a corpse as required by s.5, that does not conclusively establish that the corpse is "property" under s.4. The traditional rule that a corpse, or part of a corpse, is not property was confirmed in *Kelly*,[145] but it was added that parts of a corpse can become property for the purpose of s.4 if they have "acquired different attributes by virtue of the application of skill, such as dissection or preservation techniques, for exhibition or teaching purposes". In this case the defendant was held liable for the theft of some 40 body parts (heads, a part of a brain and an assortment of arms, legs and feet) from the Royal College of Surgeons. These parts were used for the training of surgeons. Rose J did add that in future body parts might be held to be property "even without the acquisition of different attributes, if they have a use or significance beyond their mere existence . . . if, for example, they are intended for use in an organ transplant operation, for the extraction of DNA, or. . .as an exhibit in a trial". This was confirmed in *Yearworth* where it was stated that if an amputated finger was damaged, it should make no difference whether any work or skill had been applied to the finger to change its attributes.

4. Belonging to another

Theft is an interference with the proprietary rights of another. One of the central problems here has been identifying who has sufficient "rights" in property to be afforded protection by the criminal law. The owner clearly needs protection, but ownership is only one form of proprietary right and others, particularly those with possession of property, need similar protection. Accordingly, s.5 of the Theft Act 1968 identifies the situations in which property is regarded as "belonging to another". It must be stressed that in some of these situations the property does not *really* (under the civil law) belong to anyone else, but someone else has an interest thought to be worth protecting and, therefore, the property is artificially *deemed* to belong to that person. Section 5 lays down five situations where property "belongs to another". There is substantial overlap between some of these situations but they are "essentially intended to be cumulative in effect".[146] It is convenient to deal with each of them separately.

(i) Possession or control; proprietary right or interest

Theft Act 1968 s.5(1)

"Property shall be regarded as belonging to any person having possession or control of it, or having in it any proprietary right or interest (not being an equitable interest arising only from an agreement to transfer or grant an interest)."

(a) *Possession or control*

"Possession" is a complex legal concept which involves both physical control and an intention to possess. "Control," on the other hand, signifies no more than its literal meaning, namely, physical

---

[143]   *Dr Handyside's Case* (1749) 3 East P.C. 652; *Sharpe* [1857] Dears & B. 160; *Williams v Williams* (1852) 20 Ch.D. 657.
[144]   D. Brahams, "Bailment and Donation of Parts of the Human Body" (1989) 139 N.L.J. 803. Cf. *Yearworth v North Bristol NHS Trust* [2010] Q.B. 1.
[145]   *R. v Kelly (Anthony Noel)* [1999] Q.B. 621. In *In the Matter of X* [2003] J.C.A. 050, the Jersey Court of Appeal held that an aborted human foetus was incapable of forming the subject of a true property interest.
[146]   *R. v Arnold (Lydon Ewart)* [1997] 4 All E.R. 1 at 9.

control—and, therefore, covers many of the cases that could be described as possession, making it unnecessary to draw any distinction between the two concepts. Thus a customer in a shop examining a book has control of the book; a diner in a restaurant has control over the cutlery with which they are eating; a golf club has either possession or control (it does not matter which) over balls lost on its golf course;[147] and a person has possession or control over any articles in their house or on their land even if they have forgotten or do not know they are there.[148] Property that has been intentionally abandoned does not belong to anyone and cannot be stolen, but where this issue has arisen in criminal cases, the courts have been reluctant to decide that property has been abandoned. So, for example, it has been decided that a householder who puts rubbish in the dustbin does not abandon the rubbish,[149] and property is not abandoned merely because it has been lost by the owner.[150]

Theft by owner:

The law of theft is designed to protect a variety of interests in property. The result is that theft can be committed by a person with an interest in the property against another with an interest (even a lesser interest) in the same property. In particular, this means that the real owner may be guilty of stealing their own property from another who has possession or control of that property. For instance, if a defendant pawns his watch as security for a loan and then surreptitiously takes the watch back, he would be appropriating property (the watch) belonging to another (the pawnbroker who, at a minimum, has possession or control over the watch).

R. v Turner (No.2) [1971] 1 W.L.R. 901 (Court of Appeal, Criminal Division)

The defendant took his car to a garage to be repaired. The repairs were almost completed and the car parked outside in the road. The defendant, without telling the garage or offering to pay for the repairs, drove his car away. He was convicted of theft and appealed against his conviction.

LORD PARKER CJ:

"[T]he judge directed the jury that they were not concerned in any way with lien and the sole question was whether Mr Brown [the garage proprietor] had possession or control. This court is quite satisfied that there is no ground whatever for qualifying the words 'possession or control' in any way. It is sufficient if it is found that the person from whom the property is taken . . . was at the time in fact in possession or control. At the trial there was a long argument whether that possession or control must be lawful, it being said that by reason of the fact that this car was subject to a hire-purchase agreement, Mr Brown could never even as against the appellant obtain lawful possession or control . . . As I have said, this court is quite satisfied that the judge was quite correct in telling the jury that they need not bother about lien, and that they need not bother about hire-purchase agreements. The only question was: was Mr Brown in fact in possession or control?"

Appeal dismissed

---

147 *Hibbert v McKiernan* [1948] 2 K.B. 142; *R. v Rostron (Terry)* [2003] EWCA Crim 2206.
148 *R. v Woodman (George Eli)* [1974] Q.B. 754.
149 *Williams v Phillips* (1957) 121 J.P. 163. Under the Environmental Protection Act 1990 s.60 it is an offence to interfere with waste sites and receptacles for waste. For a discussion of the legal issues in relation to "freegans", who take and make use of discarded items, see S. Thomas, "Do Freegans Commit Theft?" [2010] 30 L.S. 98–125. Cf. *R. (on the application of Ricketts) v Basildon Magistrates' Court* [2010] EWHC 2358 (Admin): it was open to magistrates to find that bags of donated items left outside a charity shop had not been abandoned. The donors had not intended to abandon the property, but to gift it to the charity.
150 *Hibbert v McKiernan* [1948] 2 K.B. 142; *Rostron* [2003] EWCA Crim 2206.

Glanville Williams described this case as "one of the most extraordinary cases decided under the Theft Act" and stated that "it is hard to believe that the decision represents the law".[151] The gist of his argument is that, if one ignores the lien, which the jury were instructed to do, the defendant had a right to repossess his car whenever he liked and one should not be held guilty of theft for doing what one has a right to do. In similar vein, it has been argued that, if a defendant takes back their television set from a thief who has stolen it (but who now has possession), there should be no liability because the thief has "no property right in the television maintainable against D. Vis-à-vis D, the television set belongs to no-one else".[152]

It is submitted that this criticism is misplaced. The Theft Act has chosen to protect a wide range of proprietary interests, including possession and control—irrespective of the rights or interests of the defendant. In *Turner (No.2)*, there can be little doubt that the defendant appropriated property belonging to another (Mr Brown, by virtue of his possession or control). In most cases defendants with greater property rights than their victims, such as rights to repossession of their property, will not be acting dishonestly. Generally, the owner who takes back their own property would not be condemned by ordinary community standards as dishonest and would thus not be convicted of theft. The owner retrieving the stolen television set would argue that they believed that they had a legal right to take the property and so was not dishonest under s.2(1)(a) of the Theft Act 1968. But the defendant in *Turner (No.2)* surreptitiously removed his car without paying for the repairs and without the garage proprietor knowing his name or address so as to be able to send him his bill. In such a case a conviction for theft, based on the ordinary meaning of the words "possession or control", does seem more appropriate than an acquittal based on a technical analysis of the meaning of a "bailment at will", which is what Mr Brown had at civil law if he did not have a lien. The short point is that whatever else he might have had at civil law, Mr Brown clearly had possession or control of the car and the defendant acted dishonestly and satisfied the remaining elements of the offence of theft. A conviction was inevitable.[153]

(b) *Proprietary right or interest*

The most obvious instance of a proprietary right or interest is that of ownership. Ownership is a proprietary right and thus property belongs to an owner. With co-owners of property, each owner has a proprietary right and therefore one co-owner can steal from another.[154]

Particular problems have arisen here with regard to the "passing of property". This phrase is used to signify ownership passing from one person to another. When goods are bought and paid for in a shop "property passes" from the shop to the purchaser. The basic rule at civil law is that property passes when the parties intend it to pass. For example, in a supermarket parties are deemed normally to intend that property should pass only on payment for the goods.[155]

In some cases, however, the transaction might be defective because one of the parties has made a mistake. Such a mistake might prevent property passing. The basic rule here is that if one of the parties has made a *fundamental mistake*, the transaction is rendered *void* and property does not pass

---

[151] G. Williams, *Textbook of Criminal Law*, 2nd edn (London: Stevens & Sons, 1983), pp.749, 750.

[152] A.P. Simester et al., *Simester and Sullivan's Criminal Law: Theory and Doctrine*, 5th edn (Oxford: Hart Publishing, 2013), p.503.

[153] cf. *R. v Meredith* [1973] Crim. L.R. 253 where a defendant who had had his car towed away to a police yard took his car back without paying any fee. It was held that a charge of theft was improper as "The police had no right, as against the owner to retain it." This Crown Court decision cannot be accepted. The police had possession or control of the car; it therefore "belonged" to them for the purposes of theft. The only proper route to an acquittal on these facts should have been lack of dishonesty.

[154] *R. v Bonner (George Andrew)* [1970] 1 W.L.R. 838.

[155] For fuller discussion, see fn.152 above, pp.505–507.

pursuant to a void transaction. On the other hand, a lesser or *non-fundamental mistake* can render a contract merely *voidable* and property *does* pass pursuant to a voidable transaction.[156]

The requirement that at the time of the appropriation the property must "belong to another" used to mean that the imposition of criminal liability and punishment could depend entirely on whether property passed pursuant to a transaction. For example, in *Kaur v Chief Constable of Hampshire*[157] the defendant chose a pair of shoes from a rack of shoes marked £6.99 per pair. One shoe was marked at £6.99 and the other at £4.99. The cashier charged her £4.99. On appeal against a conviction for theft it was held that the appropriation occurred when, having paid, she put the shoes in her bag. The issue was whether property had passed to her when she paid for the goods. If the cashier had made a fundamental mistake, the contract would have been void. As ownership would not then have passed she would have been appropriating property belonging to another. It was held, however, that the cashier had made a mere mistake as to quality, rendering the contract, at most, voidable. Accordingly, the ownership had passed to the defendant and she was not liable as she had not appropriated property belonging to another.

Such cases would be decided differently after *Gomez* and *Hinks* because the appropriation would be held to have taken place at the earlier stage when she took the shoes from the rack. At that point they still belonged to the store. The same would be true of the infamous case of *Gilks*,[158] where a punter at the races was mistakenly paid out £106 even though his horse came nowhere. It was held that the bookmaker in paying out the money in the mistaken belief that a certain horse had won was making a fundamental mistake. Accordingly, property did not pass and so when the punter decided to keep the money he was appropriating property that did still belong to another. Again, after *Gomez* and *Hinks* the appropriation would be held to occur as the money was handed over and, at that moment (or, at any rate, the split second before) the money would still have belonged to the bookmaker.[159]

There are interests in property less than ownership that also qualify as "proprietary rights or interests". These interests may be either legal or equitable. An example of a legal right can be seen in *Turner (No.2)* where the garage proprietor had a lien on the car (although, as seen, the case was not decided on that basis). An example of an equitable interest is that the beneficiary of a trust has an equitable interest in the trust property.

With regard to equitable interests it is important to note that there have been significant changes in the civil law relating to constructive trusts since the coming into force of the Theft Act 1968. For example, it is now possible that even though property has passed, the person who made a mistake in delivering the goods retains an equitable interest in them[160] and so the property "belongs" to them by virtue of s.5(1).[161] Whether these developments in the civil law of constructive trusts should be reflected by a corresponding broadening of the law of theft is considered below.

However, s.5(1) specifically excludes "equitable interests arising only from an agreement to transfer or grant an interest". With some contracts, for example, contracts to buy land or shares, the person

---

[156] A.P. Simester et al., fn.152 above, pp.507–510.

[157] *Kaur v Chief Constable of Hampshire* [1981] 1 W.L.R. 578.

[158] *Gilks* [1972] 1 W.L.R. 1371.

[159] In *R. v Goodwin (Phillip)* [1996] Crim. L.R. 262, where a defendant inserted foreign money (of less value than the required coin) into a gaming machine, it was held that ownership in any coins paid out would not have passed. Such a ruling was unnecessary. The appropriation would occur as the defendant received each coin. At that moment the property still belonged to the owner of the machine.

[160] *Chase Manhattan Bank v Israel British Bank* [1981] Ch. 105.

[161] For fuller discussion, see fn.152 above, A.P. Simester et al., *Simester and Sullivan's Criminal Law: Theory and Doctrine*, 5th edn (Oxford: Hart Publishing, 2013), pp.512–519.

contracting to purchase acquires an equitable interest, while the other party retains legal ownership. If that legal owner then sells to a third party they do not commit theft as the original contracting party only has an "equitable interest arising from an agreement" which is not sufficient for the property to be regarded as belonging to them.

It is with regard to this ascertainment of whether a person has a "proprietary right or interest" that we see the sharpest tensions between the criminal law and the civil law because the criminal law, with its traditional emphasis on blame and harm, is having to define part of the harm component in terms of the civil law. We saw in the introduction to this chapter that there is a conflict between two views. On the one hand, there is the view that criminal liability should only be imposed on blameworthy actors who cause harm and that this determination should be divorced from technical analyses of the civil law. This view tends to maintain that words in the Theft Acts be given their "ordinary meanings" by ordinary people, the jury. This was the view adopted in *Turner (No.2)* where the judge refused to direct the jury in terms of liens. This approach has been supported by the House of Lords where dissatisfaction was expressed at allowing criminal liability to turn on fine points of civil law.

R. v Morris, Anderton v Burnside [1984] A.C. 320 (House of Lords)

LORD ROSKILL:

"I respectfully suggest that it is on any view wrong to introduce into this branch of the criminal law questions whether particular contracts are void or voidable on the ground of mistake or fraud or whether any mistake is sufficiently fundamental to vitiate a contract. These difficult questions should so far as possible be confined to those fields of law to which they are immediately relevant and I do not regard them as relevant questions under the Theft Act 1968."

Reliance on civil law concepts, particularly whether there is a constructive trust or not, can present extremely complicated questions of civil law and generate uncertainty. For example, in *Powell v MacRae*,[162] the defendant, a turnstile operator at Wembley Stadium, accepted a bribe and allowed a member of the public to enter the ground without a ticket. On a charge of theft the justices ruled that as the money had been received in the course of employment it belonged to the employer. On appeal, this view was rejected: there was no constructive trust and so the employer had no fiduciary interest in the property. The longstanding authority which supports this approach is the case of *Lister & Co v Stubbs*,[163] in which Stubbs, a foreman employed by the plaintiffs, took substantial sums by way of bribes from a firm which supplied large quantities of goods to the plaintiff company. The Court of Appeal held that the monies paid to Stubbs by way of bribes did not belong to the plaintiffs and were not held by Stubbs as a trustee for the company: the relationship between the foreman and the plaintiffs was one of debtor and creditor, not one of trustee and beneficial owner. However, *Lister & Co v Stubbs* has since been ruled to be wrongly decided on this point by, the Privy Council in *Attorney General for Hong King v Reid*,[164] a case in which Reid, a senior figure in the Hong Kong Government legal service, had, in breach of the fiduciary duty which he owed as a Crown servant,[165] accepted bribes

---

[162] *Powell v MacRae* [1977] Crim. L.R. 571, 141 J.P. Jo. 432.
[163] *Lister & Co v Stubbs* (1890) 45 Ch.D. 1.
[164] *Attorney-General for Hong Kong v Reid* [1994] 1 A.C. 324.
[165] Company directors, agents and partners are in a fiduciary position. Employees may be in a fiduciary position, depending on their position and role within their employer's organisation. For further discussion, see A. Arlidge, A. Milne and P. Springer, *Arlidge and Parry on Fraud*, 4th edn (London: Sweet & Maxwell, 2014), paras 6-016–6-029; A.P. Simester et al., fn.161 above. See A.T.H. Smith, "Constructive Trusts in the Law of Theft" [1977] Crim. L.R. 395 at 398, re the argument in favour of there being a fiduciary relationship between employers and employees.

in order to obstruct prosecutions. The Privy Council ruled that a person who receives a bribe holds it on a constructive trust for the person injured:

"The decision in *Lister & Co v Stubbs* is not consistent with the principles that a fiduciary must not be allowed to benefit from his own breach of duty, that the fiduciary should account for the bribe as soon as he receives it and that equity regards as done that which ought to be done."[166]

Following this, an employer on facts similar to those in *Lister & Co v Stubbs* would have a proprietary interest in the bribe, and the employee would fall within the terms of s.5(1). However, in *Sinclair Investments (UK) Ltd v Versailles Trade Finance Ltd* the Court of Appeal, Civil Decision, has recently declined to follow the Privy Council decision in *Reid*, preferring to follow the decision of the Court of Appeal in *Lister*, holding that where a bribe or secret commission was paid to an agent in breach of his fiduciary duty to his principal, the sum received was not held on trust by the agent for his principal since the bribe was not an asset which the fiduciary was under a duty to take for the beneficiary, and the principal therefore did not have a proprietary claim to it. This was a highly controversial and much criticised decision,[167] and in the Australian case of *Grimaldi v Chameleon Mining NL*,[168] the full Federal Court of Australia declined to follow it, preferring instead the decision in *Reid*.

The issue has recently been resolved by the Supreme Court in *FHR European Ventures v Cedar Capital Partners LLC*.[169] In that case, the Supreme Court in a unanimous decision overruled *Lister v Stubbs* and subsequent decisions relying on that case (including *Sinclair*) and followed the approach adopted in *Reid* in holding that a bribe or secret commission accepted by an agent is held on trust for the principal and the principal has a proprietary claim to it. The position is therefore now clear: where an employee in a fiduciary position enriches himself by taking a bribe, the amount of the bribe is treated as the property of the employer and it is caught by s.5(1). Following this, an employer on facts similar to those in *Powell v MacRae* would have a proprietary interest in the bribe.[170]

It must be questionable whether criminal liability for theft should depend on changes in the law relating to constructive trusts, particularly as the purposes of the law of constructive trusts are very different to those of the criminal law.[171]

Further, holding such persons liable for theft raises the risk of false labelling. The essence of the defendant's wrongdoing in *Powell v MacRae* was that he took a bribe. A defendant in such circumstances should be found liable for that[172] rather than for the subsequent theft of the proceeds.

---

[166]   *Reid* [1994] 1 A.C. 324 at 336.

[167]   See, for example, FHR European Ventures LLP v Mankarious [2013] EWCA Civ 17, [2014] Ch 30; P. Millett, "Bribes and Secret Commissions Again" (2012) 71 C.L.J. 583–614; R. Hedlund, "Secret Commissions and Constructive Trusts: Yet Again!" (2013) 7 J.B.L. 747–764, and S. Worthington, "Fiduciary Duties and Proprietary Remedies: Addressing the Failure of Equitable Formulae" (2013) 72 C.L.J. 720–752. Cf. G. Virgo, "Profits Obtained in Breach of Fiduciary Duty" (2011) 72 C.L.J. 502–504.

[168]   Grimaldi v Chameleon Mining NL (2012) 287 A.L.R. 22.

[169]   FHR European Ventures LLP and others v Cedar Capital Partners LLC [2014] UKSC 45.

[170]   See p.836, fn.162.

[171]   A.T.H. Smith, "Constructive Trusts in the Law of Theft" [1977] Crim. L.R. 395.

[172]   Bribery Act 2010 s.2. See A.P. Simester et al., fn.161 above, p.518. An employee receiving a secret commission or bribe might also be charged with fraud by abuse of position (Fraud Act 2006 ss.1, 4): *R. v Knowles (Ross)* [2013] EWCA Crim 646 at [14].

Responding to these concerns, the Court of Appeal in *Attorney-General's Reference (No.1 of 1985)*[173] doubted whether a secret profit made by an employee would give rise to a trust but indicated that, even if it did, it would not give rise to a proprietary interest for the purposes of s.5(1) because if conduct is "so far from the understanding of ordinary people as to what constitutes stealing, it should not amount to stealing".[174] This approach was not, however, adopted in *Shadrokh-Cigari*[175] where it was held that an equitable interest arising under a constructive trust was a proprietary interest for the purposes of s.5(1).

While one can sympathise with the approach adopted in *Attorney-General's Reference (No.1 of 1985)*, the fact remains that theft is an offence involving interference with the property rights of another and such property rights can only exist at civil law (whether the law of property, contract or quasi-contract). It is not justifiable to convict a defendant of theft if nobody else has any interest in the property because, as seen, an owner is generally free to use, enjoy and abuse their own property as they see fit. Equally, while other charges might be more appropriate, it is not justifiable to acquit a defendant of theft on the ground that the property does not belong to another when, by civil law, it plainly does. If the existence of property rights is not to be ascertained by reference to the civil law, then how are they to be ascertained?

Of course, it would be possible for the Theft Act 1968 to be amended so that certain property interests, particularly those arising under a constructive trust, are excluded for the purposes of the law of theft. But unless and until that occurs, it is inappropriate for criminal courts to depart from the civil law and proceed on an "if it doesn't look like theft, then it isn't theft" basis.

In *Dobson v General Accident, Fire and Life Insurance Corp Plc*[176] it was stressed that the issue of whether goods belong to another "is a question to which the criminal law offers no answer and which can only be answered by reference to civil law principles".

The CPS has advised that:

"The criminal law is not a suitable vehicle to regulate such disputes [over ownership of property]. Before a criminal charge can proceed the ownership of any property must be absolutely clear. If that ownership is in real dispute the criminal law should not be invoked until ownership has been established in the civil courts."[177]

(ii) Trusts

Theft Act 1968 s.5(2)

"Where property is subject to a trust, the persons to whom it belongs shall be regarded as including any person having a right to enforce the trust, and an intention to defeat the trust shall be regarded accordingly as an intention to deprive of the property any person having that right."

With most trusts the beneficiary already has a "proprietary right or interest", making s.5(2) unnecessary.[178] However, with charitable trusts there are no specified beneficiaries having beneficial interests

---

[173]   *Attorney-General's Reference (No.1 of 1985)* [1986] 1 Q.B. 491.
[174]   *Attorney-General's Reference (No.1 of 1985)* [1986] 1 Q.B. 491 at 507.
[175]   *R. v Shadrokh-Cigari (Hamid)* [1988] Crim. L.R. 465.
[176]   *Dobson v General Accident Fire and Life Insurance Corp Plc* [1989] 3 All E.R. 929 at 937.
[177]   CPS, *The Fraud Act 2006: Legal Guidance* (2008).
[178]   *Arnold* [1997] 4 All E.R. 1 at 9.

in the trust property. Such trusts are enforced by the Attorney-General[179] and under s.5(2) the trust property is deemed to belong to the Attorney-General.[180]

(iii) obligation to deal with property in particular way

Theft Act 1968 s.5(3)

"Where a person receives property from or on account of another, and is under an obligation to the other to retain and deal with that property or its proceeds in a particular way, the property or proceeds shall be regarded (as against him) as belonging to the other."

If a person receives property and ownership passes to him then he is generally free to do as he likes with the property. Sometimes, however, even if the recipient has become the "true owner" of the property,[181] he may be obliged to deal with it in a particular way. For instance, a person collecting for charity is obliged to hand over the money to the appropriate charity. When the donor places their coin in the tin can this is the clear understanding between donor and collector. Accordingly, s.5(3) deems that money still belongs to the donor and if the collector makes off with the money he is appropriating money "belonging to" the donor.

In many cases, where s.5(3) could apply, the person to whom the obligation is owed will have a legal or equitable interest in the property and so the property will still belong to that person under s.5(1). Under s.5(3), however, it is not necessary for courts to engage with the intricacies of establishing that a trust has been created and that the person supplying the property retains an equitable interest in it.[182] As said in *Klineberg*,[183] s.5(3)

"is essentially a deeming provision by which property or its proceeds 'shall be regarded' as belonging to another, even though, on a strict civil law analysis, it does not".

Nevertheless, for s.5(3) to apply, there are several conditions that need to be satisfied:

(a) *The property must have been received from or on account of another to whom the obligation is owed*

Two alternative situations are covered here. First, as with the charity-collector above, the property is received from the person to whom the obligation is owed. Secondly, it can be received from one person on account of another; in this situation the obligation must be owed to that other person. On this basis the charity-collector could also be said to have received the property on account of the charity. The operation of these two principles can be seen in *Floyd v DPP*[184] where the defendant collected money weekly from work colleagues who had ordered goods from a Home Farm but failed to pay the money to the farm. On these facts it would be possible to invoke either of the above bases. First, she received money from her colleagues; being under an obligation to pay the money to the Home Farm, the money would be regarded as belonging to her colleagues. Secondly, and this was the basis of the actual decision, she received money on account of the Home Farm and owed them an obligation to hand over the money,[185] and so the property was regarded as belonging to the Home Farm.

---

179   Charities Act 2011 s.115(7); *Halsbury's Law of England*, vol.8, *Charities*, 5th edn (2010), paras 508, 583.
180   This obvious point was overlooked in *R. v Dyke (Ian James)* [2002] 1 Cr. App. R. 30.
181   *Arnold* [1997] 4 All E.R. 1.
182   *R. v Klineberg (Jonathan Simon)* [1999] 1 Cr. App. R. 427; *Floyd v DPP* [2000] Crim. L.R. 411.
183   *Klineberg* [1999] 1 Cr. App. R. 427; *Floyd* [2000] Crim. L.R. 411.
184   *Floyd v DPP* [2000] Crim. L.R. 411.
185   As there was no evidence of any contract between the defendant and the Home Farm, it is far from clear that she did in fact owe them any obligation. See J. Smith, "Commentary to *Floyd v D.P.P.*" [2000] Crim. L.R. 412.

While establishing receipt of property from another is normally a simple matter,[186] the same is not always true where it is alleged that property has been received on account of another.

Attorney-General's Reference (No.1 of 1985) (1986) 83 Cr. App. R. 70. (Court of Appeal, Criminal Division)

The defendant, a salaried manager of a tied public house, was only allowed to sell his employer's beer and was under a duty to pay all his takings into his employer's account. However, he sold other beer and kept the profit for himself. He was charged with theft from his employers on the basis that the money he received from his customers belonged to his employers by virtue of s.5(3).

THE LORD CHIEF JUSTICE:

"We are told at the outset of this hearing that this sort of behaviour by managers of 'tied' houses is becoming more prevalent. They do not, it seems, appear to be deterred by the prospect of losing their job or of being compelled by civil action to disgorge their illicit profit. An additional deterrent, it is suggested, in the shape of a conviction for theft would not be inappropriate.

That is not a matter which concerns us. We have to decide whether Parliament intended to bring such behaviour within the ambit of the criminal law . . .

[Liability] depends on whether A can properly be said to have received property, (*i.e.* the payment over the counter for the beer he has sold to the customer) 'on account of the employers'. We do not think he can. He received the money on his own account as a result of his private venture. No doubt he is in breach of his contract with the employers; no doubt he is under an obligation to account to the employers at least for the profit he has made out of his venture, but that is a different matter."

Declaration accordingly

In similar circumstances an employee might now be charged with fraud by abuse of position.[187]

(b) *There has to be an obligation to deal with that property or its proceeds in a particular way*

Under s.5(3) there has to be an obligation to deal with *the property handed over* or *its proceeds* in a particular way. If I give my decorator £100 in order to buy paint, an obligation to use that money or its proceeds is imposed. If I give him £100 as a down-payment, no such obligation is imposed. This simple distinction (in theory) has caused problems in practice, particularly in cases where deposits have been paid.

R. v Hall [1973] Q.B. 496 (Court of Appeal, Criminal Division)

The defendant was a travel agent who accepted deposits for air trips to the United States. The flights never materialised and the money was not refunded. The appellant paid all the monies into the firm's general trading account. He was convicted of theft and appealed on the ground that the monies paid to him became his and therefore did not "belong to another".

EDMUND-DAVIES LJ:

"Counsel for the appellant . . . concedes that [by receiving the monies] the travel agent undertakes a contractual obligation in relation to arranging flights . . . But what counsel for the appellant resists is that in such circum-

---

[186]   However, where the alleged receipt of the property occurs by way of a bank transfer, then, following *Preddy* [1996] A.C. 815, it has not been "received from" anyone as it is a newly created property that never belonged to anyone else: see J.C. Smith, Commentary to *Klineberg and Marsden* [1997] Crim. L.R. 417. In this case the court failed to distinguish between money handed over by cash or cheque and that secured by bank transfer.

[187]   Fraud Act ss.1, 4. Below, pp.885–887.

stances the travel agent 'is under an obligation' to the client 'to retain and deal with . . . in a particular way' sums paid to him in such circumstances.

What cannot of itself be decisive of the matter is the fact that the appellant paid the money into the firm's general trading account . . .

Nevertheless, when a client goes to a firm carrying on the business of travel agents and pays them money, he expects that in return he will, in due course, receive the tickets and other documents necessary for him to accomplish the trip for which he is paying, and the firm are 'under an obligation' to perform their part to fulfil his expectation and are liable to pay him damages if they do not. But, in our judgment, what was not here established was that these clients expected them 'to retain and deal with that property or its proceeds in a particular way', and that an 'obligation' to do so was undertaken by the appellant. We must make clear, however, that each case turns on its own facts. Cases could, we suppose, conceivably arise where by some special arrangement (preferably evidenced by documents), the client could impose on the travel agent an 'obligation' falling within section 5(3). But no such special arrangement was made in any of the seven cases here being considered. It follows from this that, despite what on any view must be condemned as scandalous conduct by the appellant, in our judgment on this ground alone this appeal must be allowed and the convictions quashed."

Appeal allowed

R. v Klineberg and Marsden [1999] 1 Cr. App. R. 427 (Court of Appeal, Criminal Division)

The appellants sold timeshare apartments in Lanzarote. The purchasers paid money, to be held by a trust company until the apartments were ready to be occupied. Almost none of the money was in fact transmitted to the trust company. The appellants were convicted of theft and appealed.

KAY J:

"The intending purchasers in each case, and prior to the handing over of any money, were made aware by documents and in at least some cases by oral representations that, if they were to enter into an agreement, they would have the security of knowing that any money they handed over would be held in independent trusteeship until the apartment in question was ready for occupation . . . One of the pivotal features of the whole scheme was that their money would be safeguarded by trusteeship pending completion. In such circumstances there must have been, at the very least, an implied obligation in favour of each intending purchaser to transfer his money into the appropriate trusteeship without undue delay."

Appeal allowed in part on other grounds

Similarly, in *Re Kumar*,[188] a travel agent was held to be under an obligation to use money paid to secure flight tickets because there was an agreed trustee relationship for such money to be transferred into specific bank accounts. In *McHugh*,[189] it was stressed that both the defendant and the client must "clearly understand" that the client's money is to be kept separate from the defendant's business money. In other cases, whether one is under an obligation to keep a separate fund in existence depends entirely on the facts of each case.

Davidge v Bunnett [1984] Crim. L.R. 297 (Queen's Bench Divisional Court)

The defendant shared a flat with three other women. When the gas bill arrived the others all gave the defendant their shares in cheques made payable to the defendant's employer. They expected her to pay the bill, either by cashing the cheques with her employer and adding her own share, or,

---

188   *Germany v Kumar (No.1)* [2000] Crim. L.R. 504.
189   *R. v McHugh (Christopher John)* (1993) 97 Cr. App. R. 335.

alternatively, that her employer, on receipt of all the monies, would write out a cheque for the Gas Board. Instead, the defendant spent most of the money on her Christmas shopping; the gas bill went unpaid. She was convicted of theft and appealed.

HELD,

"D was under an obligation to use the cheques or their proceeds in whatever way she saw fit so long as they were applied *pro tanto* to the discharge of the gas bill. This could have been achieved by one cheque from her employer, or a banker's draft, or her own cheque . . . Hence the magistrates' finding that she was not obliged to use the actual banknotes. Using the proceeds of the cheque on presents amounted to a very negation of her obligation to discharge the bill. She was under an obligation to deal with the proceeds in a particular way. As against D, the proceeds of the cheques were properly belonging to another within section 5(3) of the Act."

Appeal dismissed

In *Lewis v Lethbridge*,[190] the defendant collected sponsorship money for a colleague who had entered the London Marathon. He never handed this money over to the charity. In the Divisional Court it was held that the defendant was not under an obligation to keep a separate fund in existence equivalent to the amount of money he had received. The money thus did not "belong to another" under s.5(3). The defendant was "a civil debtor and a naughty one without question, but not a thief".[191] This decision has now been disapproved.

R. v Wain [1995] 2 Cr. App. R. 660 (Court of Appeal, Criminal Division)

The appellant raised money for a "Telethon" held for charity by Yorkshire Television. He paid the money raised first into a separate bank account and then, with Yorkshire Television's permission, into his own bank account and then spent it. He was convicted of theft and appealed.

MCCOWAN LJ:

"[Referring to *Lewis v Lethbridge*] the learned judge was forgetting that section 5(3) of the Theft Act 1968 referred not merely to dealing with that property but also its proceeds . . .
Professor Smith . . . in his *Law of Theft* (6th ed.) at p. 39 [states]

'In *Lewis v Lethbridge* . . . no consideration was given to the question whether any obligation was imposed by the sponsors. Sponsors surely do not give the collector (whether he has a box or not) the money to do as he likes with. Is there not an overwhelming inference . . . that the sponsors intend to give the money to the charity, imposing an obligation in the nature of a trust on the collector?'

It seems to us that the approach of the court in the *Lethbridge* case was a very narrow one based, apparently, on the finding by the justices that there was no requirement of the charity that the appellant hand over the same notes and coins. Neither was there in the present case. But what the Divisional Court does not appear to have considered in that case was the trust aspect . . . In our judgment, the criticisms of that case by Professor Smith are fully justified . . . [His Lordship approved *Davidge v Bunnett*.]
[I]t seems to us that by virtue of section 5(3), the appellant was plainly under an obligation to retain, if not the actual notes and coins, at least their proceeds, that is to say the money credited in the bank account which he opened for the trust with the actual property. When he took the money credited to that account and moved it over to his own bank account, it was still the proceeds of the notes and coins donated which he proceeded to use for his own purposes, thereby appropriating them."

Appeal dismissed

---

190   *Lewis v Lethbridge* [1987] Crim. L.R. 59.
191   Cited in *R. v Wain (Peter)* [1995] 2 Cr. App. R. 660 at 664.

In *Huskinson*[192] the defendant fell into arrears with his rent. He applied for housing benefit and was sent a cheque for £479 to pay off some of the arrears which then amounted to £800. He gave his landlord £200 and spent the remainder on himself. He was acquitted of theft and on appeal the Divisional Court held that, as the relevant regulations did not require him to apply the cheque or proceeds directly in satisfaction of the rent, he was not under a legal obligation to the Housing Services Department to deal with the cheque in a particular way.

(c) The defendant must have direct knowledge of the obligation

In *Wills*[193] the appellant and two assistants operated a business as financial consultants advising clients on investments and loans. The assistants each received money from different clients with instructions to invest the money with an insurance company. Those monies were used for the general purposes of the business and not invested in accordance with the clients' instructions. The appellant was not present when either transaction took place and there was no evidence that he personally knew of the obligation. The appellant was convicted of theft (as were the assistants). On appeal, it was held that, for section 5(3) to apply, the prosecution must prove that the defendant has knowledge of the nature and extent of the obligation to deal with the property in a particular way. It is not enough merely to show that the property was not dealt with in a manner that conformed with the obligation.

In *Wain*, it was stated that whether the defendant "is a trustee is to be judged on an objective basis. It is an obligation on him by law. It is not essential that he should have realised that he was a trustee, but of course the question remains as to whether he was acting honestly or dishonestly".[194] Thus the defendant must have knowledge of the facts giving rise to the obligation but need not know that they are under a civil legal obligation.[195] However, if a defendant genuinely believes that they are legally justified in doing what they do with the money, it will be difficult to establish the requisite dishonesty.

(d) The obligation must be a legal one

It is not enough that the defendant is under a social or moral obligation to deal with the property in a particular way. They must be under a legal obligation. This means that the party imposing the obligation must be able to commence legal proceedings against the defendant at civil law for a failure to perform their obligation. One must be careful here to distinguish a legal obligation to do something (for example, pay one's rent as in *Huskinson*) from a legal obligation to use particular property or its proceeds in the performance of that obligation (for example, using the housing benefit to pay one's rent). It is only when there is a legal obligation of the latter kind that property is deemed to belong to another for the purposes of the law of theft.

Whether the obligation for the purposes of s.5(3) had to be a "legal" one or not used to be controversial. One school of thought was that "obligation" was an ordinary word—like many of the other "ordinary words" used in the Theft Act. Whether or not an obligation existed was simply a matter of fact to be left to the jury. As the jury know no law, this means that they can only decide on the basis of whether they think the defendant ought to be under an obligation, i.e. whether a moral obligation exists.[196]

However, it was the opposing school of thought that won the day here in the continuing see-saw battle between "ordinary meaning" and "civil law meaning". In *Mainwaring*,[197] it was held that there

---

[192]   *DPP v Huskinson* [1988] Crim. L.R. 620 (QBD).
[193]   *R. v Wills* (1991) 92 Cr. App. R. 297.
[194]   *Wain* [1995] 2 Cr. App. R. 660 at 666.
[195]   See also *R. v Dubar (David Nicholas)* [1995] 1 Cr. App. R. 280 at 287.
[196]   *R. v Hayes (John Allan)* (1977) 64 Cr. App. R. 82. There are also dicta in *Hall* [1973] 1 Q.B. 496 to this effect.
[197]   *R. v Mainwaring (Paul Rex)* (1982) 74 Cr. App. R. 99.

must be a legal obligation at civil law for the purposes of s.5(3). This was confirmed in *Dubar*, where it was stated that it is

> "the trial judge's function to direct the jury as to matters of law, including the existence of an obligation within s.5(3) if, but only if, he fully and fairly leaves it to the jury to decide the facts which give rise to such an obligation."[198]

While this means, yet again, that criminal liability can depend on highly complex points of civil law,[199] nevertheless such an approach can be supported on the basis that:

> "Parliament is not in the habit of legislating about moral obligations as such; and that Parliament should do so without making its meaning plain is inconceivable."[200]

1. Section 5(3) and fair labelling:

A large proportion of reported cases involving s.5(3) involve dishonest business operations by travel agents, estate agents, investment companies and so on. Assuming criminalisation is justified in such cases (as opposed to using civil remedies or administrative disabilities such as disqualification of directors), the question becomes: is s.5(3) so defined as to criminalise behaviour that ought to be subject to criminal sanctions and, if so, is theft the correct label to describe such wrongdoing?

In *Hall*, the defendant was dishonest (the jury at first instance convicted him) and Edmund-Davies LJ described his conduct as scandalous. Yet he escaped liability. Is it justifiable to draw a moral line between his conduct and that of the applicant in *Re Kumar* purely because there was an agreed trustee relationship in the latter case? Part of the problem is that s.5(3) is embracing conduct too far removed from the paradigm of theft. This explains the comments in some of the above cases such as *Lewis v Lethbridge* that the defendant was a "civil debtor and a naughty one without question, but not a thief" and *Attorney-General's Reference (No.1 of 1985)* that the defendant's conduct was "so far from the understanding of ordinary people as to what constitutes stealing, it should not amount to stealing". In *Klineberg and Marsden* the essence of the prosecution case was that the appellants "were involved in a timeshare fraud". Indeed, in many of the above cases the real wrongdoing constituted fraud and not theft. As shall be seen, the Fraud Act 2006 has introduced a new offence of fraud and many of the above defendants would fall within the provisions of this offence. It is thus doubtful whether s.5(3) any longer performs a useful role.

2. Criminalising breach of contract

In many of the above cases, the defendant was in breach of contract. In some of these cases (for example, *Re Kumar*) there was liability; in others (for example, *Attorney-General's Reference (No.1 of 1985)*) there was no liability. Whether a dishonest breach of contract should be criminalised has also arisen in cases not turning on s.5(3). For example, in *Clowes (No.2)*[201] a central point on appeal was whether signed agreements were contracts or trust documents. Criminal liability could only be imposed in the latter situation as only then would the property "belong to another".

---

[198] *R. v Dubar (David Nicholas)* [1995] 1 Cr. App. R. 280 at 287. Approved in *Arnold* [1997] 4 All E.R. 1 at 10 and *Breaks and Huggan* [1998] Crim. L.R. 349.

[199] See, for example, *Williams and Lamb* [1995] Crim. L.R. 77. In *Hallam and Blackburn* [1995] Crim. L.R. 323 the Court of Appeal was highly critical of the civil law technicalities that have been grafted on to s.5.

[200] G. Williams, *Textbook of Criminal Law*, 2nd edn (London: Stevens & Sons, 1983), p.752.

[201] *R. v Clowes (Peter) (No.2)* [1994] 2 All E.R. 316.

Quite apart from the above point concerning the appropriateness of "theft" as the offence label, this raises the broader question whether *all* dishonest breaches of contract should be criminalised. A breach of contract can have as disastrous an impact upon the innocent party as stealing from them. If accompanied by dishonesty, why should it not be criminalised?

It could be asserted that there is the entire structure of the civil law to provide remedies for breach of contract. Criminalisation is unnecessary. This argument, however, collapses when one recalls that there are similar civil remedies provided for those who "lose" their property wrongfully. The existence of civil remedies is no argument for the decriminalisation of theft. So the question remains: why is theft a crime but *dishonest* breach of contract not a crime?

Apart from historical explanations relating to the evolution of the law of larceny and its metamorphosis into theft, an explanation of principle is not easy. It is perhaps best to focus on the paradigmatic instances of theft and breach of contract. A typical theft involves a surreptitious or forceful taking. The victim is helpless against such a taking. If the thief is interrupted there is a risk of violence. Owing to their anonymity there is extra difficulty in identifying and apprehending the thief. With the typical breach of contract, however, one is dealing with two parties, both "free" and "equal" who have both chosen to enter into a contractual nexus. The risk of one party breaching their contract is always there and, in a free market economy, a factor to be assessed at the time of entering into the contract—taking account of the civil remedies available. Bearing in mind the basic proposition that conduct should not be made criminal merely because it is immoral, but that, additionally, criminalisation should be "necessary" and "profitable"[202] one should only expand the reaches of the criminal law with the utmost caution. Certain instances of dishonest breach of contract have already been made criminal, particularly where the contract is breached by a false representation, or the defendant is attempting unilaterally to avoid their liability in circumstances where it would be difficult to trace them.[203] Beyond such cases the criminal law should not go. Section 5(3) does extend the tentacles of the law of theft beyond the paradigmatic instances. Great caution must be exercised to keep some rein over the subsection so that it does not stray too far from ordinary understandings of criminality. In this regard, the CPS has advised that: "Prosecutors should guard against the criminal law being used as a debt collection agency or to protect the commercial interests of companies and organisations".[204]

(iv) Obligation to make restoration

Theft Act 1968 s.5(4)

"Where a person gets property by another's mistake, and is under an obligation to make restoration (in whole or in part) of the property or its proceeds or of the value thereof, then to the extent of that obligation the property or proceeds shall be regarded (as against him) as belonging to the person entitled to restoration, and an intention not to make restoration shall be regarded accordingly as an intention to deprive that person of the property or proceeds."

This subsection was specifically enacted to combat the mischief revealed in the case of *Moynes v Coopper*[205] where an employee was given a pay packet which, owing to a mistake, contained too much money. When he opened the packet and saw the excess he dishonestly kept the whole. He was acquitted of larceny. If these facts were to reoccur, the case could be brought within s.5(4) and, therefore,

---

202   Above, pp.18–23.
203   Making off without payment contrary to the Theft Act 1978 s.3.
204   CPS, *The Fraud Act 2006: Legal Guidance* (2008).
205   *Moynes v Coopper* [1956] 1 Q.B. 439.

even though property in the excess money might have passed to the employee when his wages were handed over, he could be liable: on discovering and keeping the excess money there is an appropriation of property (the money) which is deemed to belong to the employer by virtue of s.5(4) because he has got the money by mistake and is under an obligation to make restoration of the excess—or its proceeds or value.

Section 5(4) is in fact of limited use. Where a person receives property by another's mistake, the mistake may be fundamental, in which case property does not pass at all and the property will still belong to the other by virtue of s.5(1) (proprietary right or interest). Section 5(4) is not needed in such cases. On the other hand, where the mistake is not sufficiently fundamental as to prevent property passing, the receiver of the property will not necessarily be under an obligation to make restoration of the property. Whether there is an obligation to make restoration is a complex matter governed by the law of restitution.

Accordingly, the following points can be made about s.5(4):

1. The obligation must be a legal one—i.e. under the civil law of restitution.[206]

2. The obligation must be to return *the* property or *its* proceeds or the *value* thereof. (Under s.5(3) only the property or its proceeds is specified.)

3. The subsection says "is" under an obligation. The use of the present tense is significant here. If in a supermarket a cashier makes a mistake as a result of which the contract is *voidable*, property does pass, but the recipient of the property *is* not *there and then* under an obligation to make restitution. The obligation to make restitution only comes into existence when the person who made the mistake "avoids" the contract. At that point the recipient will become under an obligation to make restitution and only then does the present tense "is" become applicable. However, as Heaton[207] points out, upon rescission ownership in the property will revert to the person who made the mistake and any subsequent "keeping or dealing with it as owner" will be an appropriation of property that belongs to another by virtue of s.5(1).

It ought to be pointed out, however, that courts have not been rigorous in their application of these civil law principles and, while insisting with one breath that the obligation be a legal one, they have at the same time tended to adopt a more cavalier approach.

Attorney-General's Reference (No.1 of 1983) [1985] Q.B. 182 (Court of Appeal, Criminal Division)

The defendant, a policewoman, was overpaid her wages. The money was paid by direct debit straight into her bank account. When she realised the mistake she decided to keep the excess. The judge directed an acquittal and the Attorney-General referred a question on a point of law for the court's opinion under s.36 of the Criminal Justice Act 1972.

LORD LANE CJ:

"In order to determine the effect of that subsection upon this case one has to take it piece by piece to see what the result is read against the circumstances of this particular prosecution. First of all: 'Did the respondent get property?' The word 'get' is about as wide a word as could possibly have been adopted by the draftsman of the

---

[206]   *Gilks* [1972] 1 W.L.R. 1341.
[207]   "Deceiving without Thieving" [2001] Crim. L.R. 712 at 723.

Act. The answer is 'Yes', the respondent in this case did get her chose in action, that is, her right to sue the bank for the debt which they owed her—money which they held in their hands to which she was entitled by virtue of the contract between bank and customer.

Secondly: 'Did she get it by another's mistake?' The answer to that is plainly 'Yes'. The Receiver of the Metropolitan Police made the mistake of thinking she was entitled to £74.74 when she was not entitled to that at all.

'Was she under an obligation to make restoration of either the property or its proceeds or its value?' We take each of those in turn. 'Was she under an obligation to make restoration of the property?'—the chose in action. The answer to that is 'No'. It was something which could not be restored in the ordinary meaning of the word. 'Was she under an obligation to make restoration of its proceeds?' The answer to that is 'No'. There were no proceeds of the chose in action to restore. 'Was she under an obligation to make restoration of the value thereof?'—the value of the chose in action. The answer to that seems to us to be 'Yes'.

I should say here, in parenthesis, that a question was raised during the argument this morning as to whether 'restoration' is the same as 'making restitution'. We think that on the wording of section 5(4) as a whole, the answer to that question is 'Yes'. One therefore turns to see whether, under the general principles of restitution, this respondent was obliged to restore or pay for the benefit which she received. Generally speaking, the respondent, in these circumstances, is obliged to pay for a benefit received when the benefit has been given under a mistake on the part of the giver as to a material fact. The mistake must be as to a fundamental or essential fact and the payment must have been due to that fundamental or essential fact. The mistake here was that this police officer had been working on a day when she had been at home and not working at all . . .

As a result of the provisions of section 5(4) the debt of £74.74 due from the respondent's bank to the respondent notionally belonged to the Receiver of the Metropolitan Police; therefore the prosecution, up to this point, have succeeded in proving—remarkable though it may seem—that the 'property' in this case belonged to another within the meaning of section 1 in the Theft Act 1968 from the moment when the respondent became aware that this mistake had been made and that her account had been credited with the £74.74 and she consequently became obliged to restore the value . . .

Before parting with the case we would like to say that it should often be possible to resolve this type of situation without resorting to the criminal law. We do, however, accept that there may be occasions—of which this may have been one—where a prosecution is necessary."

Opinion accordingly

The defendant here owed a debt and dishonestly tried to avoid paying that debt. This is yet another instance of the grey area of criminality discussed above: when, if ever, should not paying one's debts or breaching one's contract be a crime? In one sense the defendant in this case was even more blameless than most debtors because she did not choose to incur the debt. It was thrust upon her by the mistake of another. And again, there were civil remedies available. The money could have been recovered. The court rightly stressed that such cases could usually be dealt with without resort to the criminal law. In *Attorney-General's Reference (No.1 of 1983)* the amount of the overpayment was some £74. In *Shadrokh-Cigari*[208] a bank account was credited $286,000 instead of $286. English law does not formally take account of the value of property in assessing criminality, or level thereof. Yet this is surely an instance where the sums involved are so huge that perhaps criminal liability is appropriate. Or is it that the value of the property affects our assessment as to dishonesty? We can conceive of perhaps "turning a blind eye" to an extra £74 credited to our bank account, but when the excess amount is some $286,000, an assessment of dishonesty becomes inevitable.

It was noted earlier that there have been considerable changes in the civil law since the coming into force of the Theft Act 1968. Some of these changes have rendered s.5(4) largely superfluous. In *Chase Manhattan Bank v Israel British Bank*[209] it was held that a person who pays money to another under a mistake of fact retains an equitable interest in the money. Accordingly, in such cases the money

---

[208] *R. v Shadrokh-Cigari (Hamid)* [1988] Crim. L.R. 465.
[209] *Chase Manhattan Bank v Israel British Bank* [1981] Ch. 105.

"belongs" to that person by virtue of s.5(1) and s.5(4) is unnecessary. This point was recognised in *Shadrokh-Cigari*, discussed above, although s.5(4) was used as an alternative basis to establish liability.

5. Dishonesty

The mens rea of theft is twofold: dishonesty and intention of permanent deprivation. Mens rea is normally taken to refer to a state of mind in relation to consequences or circumstances of a defendant's actions—for example, did they intend, foresee or know of something happening? But, apart from the requirement of intending permanent deprivation, this traditional concept of mens rea fits ill with property offences where, in essence, a judgment is being made about behaviour and the general state of mind of the defendant in relation to their actions. As was said in one of the leading cases, *Feely*,[210] the taking of property must be one to which "moral obloquy can reasonably" be attached.

The interference with property rights must be such that we can blame the defendant for disregarding the value system inherent in the law of theft. The requirement of "dishonesty" is introduced as a mechanism by which moral judgments can be made and blame attributed.

S.P. Green, 13 Ways to Steal a Bicycle: Theft Law in the Information Age (2012), pp.112–113

"Dishonesty connotes some additional moral content. It suggests that the offender lacked integrity or probity. It conveys a moral sense that is independent of the law. To say that a defendant acted honestly or dishonestly is to say something more generally about his character as a person, beyond merely his specific acts . . .

In short, the term *dishonesty* seems a useful one for distinguishing between those appropriations that should count as stealing and those that should not, particularly when the term is compared to the alternatives. Unlike *unlawfully*, the term *dishonesty* is not based exclusively on law; and unlike *fraudulently*, it does not connote any overly narrow sense of deceit or duplicity. *Dishonesty* connotes a lack of honesty, probity, or integrity; a thievishness. It exists as a free-standing concept of morality. As such, it offers an appropriate label for the wrongful element in stealing."

Dishonesty is only partially defined by the Theft Act 1968. Where defined, the meaning of dishonesty is a question of law. Where undefined, it is a question of fact.

(i) Question of Law

Theft Act 1968 s.2

"(1) A person's appropriation of property belonging to another is not to be regarded as dishonest—

  (a) if he appropriates the property in the belief that he has in law the right to deprive the other of it, on behalf of himself or of a third person; or

  (b) if he appropriates the property in the belief that he would have the other's consent if the other knew of the appropriation and the circumstances of it; or

  (c) (except where the property came to him as trustee or personal representative) if he appropriates the property in the belief that the person to whom the property belongs cannot be discovered by taking reasonable steps.

---

[210] *Feely* [1973] 1 Q.B. 530.

(2) A person's appropriation of property belonging to another may be dishonest notwithstanding that he is willing to pay for the property."

Theft Act 1968 s.1(2)

"It is immaterial whether the appropriation is made with a view to gain, or is made for the thief's own benefit."

(a) *Belief in legal right*

Section 2(1)(a) provides that a person who genuinely believes that they have a legal right to the property is not to be regarded as dishonest—irrespective of the reasonableness or otherwise of the belief.[211] There is a well-known maxim that "ignorance of the law is no defence". This, however, relates to ignorance of the criminal law, for instance, to a defendant who claims that they did not know theft was a crime. Section 2(1)(a) only applies to persons who have made a mistake as to the *civil law*—believing they have legal rights to property when, perhaps, they have no such rights.

(b) *Belief in consent*

It will be recalled that, under *Gomez*, a defendant can appropriate property even though the other has consented to such appropriation. However, if the defendant genuinely believes that they have the other's real consent to deal with the property they cannot be condemned as dishonest. Again, the reasonableness of their belief is irrelevant except in evidential terms.

(c) *Belief that property is lost*

Lost property continues to belong to the owner and so the finder of lost property is appropriating property belonging to another. However, if they genuinely (again, a subjective test) believe that the owner "*cannot* be discovered by taking reasonable steps", they are not to be condemned for deciding to keep the property. Obviously, factors such as the type and value of the property and the location where it was found will be important evidence in assessing the defendant's belief.

It should be noted that s.2(1)(c) relates to lost property which does still belong to someone else. It does not concern property which the defendant believes is abandoned. Of course, if property actually is abandoned, it does not belong to another and so the actus reus of theft will not be made out. However, what is the position if property is not abandoned but the defendant believes that it has been abandoned? As a matter of strict interpretation, because this situation is not covered by the exclusions in s.2, whether there is dishonesty should be determined as a matter of fact under the rules about to be examined.[212] However, in *Wood*[213] it was held as a *matter of law* that if the defendant genuinely believed that the property was abandoned there would be no dishonesty.

(d) *Willingness to pay*

Section 2(2) makes it clear that a willingness to pay will not necessarily exempt one from a finding of dishonesty. The owner might not wish to sell at whatever price, and it would be unthinkable to allow the unscrupulous to help themselves to other people's property and escape liability simply by being able to pay. In *Wheatley*,[214] it was held that the fact that no loss was suffered was not determinative of dishonesty.

---

[211]   *R. v Small (Adrian Anthony)* (1988) 86 Cr. App. R. 170; *R. v Holden* [1991] Crim. L.R. 478.
[212]   Also, there could hardly be an intention permanently to deprive another of the property if the defendant believes it has been abandoned.
[213]   *R. v Wood (Peter)* [2002] EWCA Crim 832.
[214]   *Wheatley v Commissioner of Police of the British Virgin Islands* [2006] 2 Cr. App. R. 21 (PC).

(e) *Not for the thief's benefit*

Despite dishonesty being a moral concept, s.1(2) makes it clear that, even though the theft is for the good of others, with the thief gaining nothing, they can still be found dishonest.[215]

(ii) Question of Fact

Apart from the above specific instances, the concept of dishonesty was left undefined in the Theft Act 1968 although judges soon began to give the concept a legal meaning.[216] However, in 1973 the Court of Appeal embarked on a new course.

R. v Feely [1973] 1 Q.B. 530 (Court of Appeal, Criminal Division)

The defendant was employed by a firm of bookmakers as manager of one of their branches. The employer sent round a circular to all managers stating that the practice of borrowing from tills was to stop. The defendant, knowing this, "borrowed" £30. When the deficiency was discovered (but not yet attributed to him) he immediately offered an IOU. He was owed more than twice that sum by his employers. The trial judge directed the jury that this was dishonest, and he was convicted of theft and appealed on the ground that this question should have been left to the jury.

LAWTON LJ:

"The design of the new Act is clear . . . Words in everyday use have replaced legal jargon in many parts of the Act . . .

In section 1(1) of the Theft Act 1968 the word 'dishonesty' can only relate to the state of mind of the person who does the act which amounts to appropriation. Whether an accused person has a particular state of mind is a question of fact which has to be decided by the jury . . . We do not agree that judges should define what 'dishonesty' means.

This word is in common use . . . Jurors, when deciding whether an appropriation was dishonest can be reasonably expected to, and should, apply the current standards of ordinary decent people. In their own lives they have to decide what is and what is not dishonest. We can see no reason why, when in a jury box, they should require the help of a judge to tell them what amounts to dishonesty."

Appeal allowed

It is for the jury (or magistrates) to determine whether the defendant has acted dishonestly by the standards of ordinary and decent people. To do this they must, of course, try to establish what was in the defendant's mind. For example, in *Price*[217] the defendant issued cheques, which were later dishonoured, claiming that he was the beneficiary of a £100,000 trust fund. The jury first has to decide whether they believe the defendant's story, that is, whether they genuinely believed that he was such a beneficiary. Having established the defendant's state of mind, they must decide, applying their own moral standards,[218] whether it is dishonest.[219] *In Price* the jury disbelieved the defend-

---

215   The Criminal Law Revision Committee gave two more limited instances that s.1(2) was designed to meet, *viz.*, taking property that is either useless to the taker or which they intend to destroy (8th Report, *Theft and Related Offences* (1966) Cmnd.2977, p.125).

216   *R. v Rao* [1972] Crim. L.R. 451.

217   *R. v Price (Ronald William)* [1990] Crim. L.R. 200.

218   It is a misdirection to use a witness reaction (for example, of shock) as the yardstick for measuring objective standards of dishonesty (*R. v Green (Barry Roland)* [1992] Crim. L.R. 292).

219   The courts sometimes fall into error here. For example, in *R. v Buzalek* [1991] Crim. L.R. 115 the defendant admitted he had lied about certain payments. The court concluded for itself that he "was confessing to being dishonest". This was, in fact,

ant's story and decided he was dishonest. Thus, using the facts of *Feely*, the jury might find that the defendant did believe he could, and did intend to, repay the money. The jury, now armed with this knowledge, must make a moral assessment as to whether such conduct, in the circumstances, was dishonest.

However, what of the defendant whose actions might be regarded as dishonest by the jury applying their standards but who insists (and is believed) that, according to *his* system of values, he was acting honestly? For example, in *Gilks*[220] the defendant claimed that he thought he was honest in keeping money mistakenly paid to him by a bookmaker because he thought bookmakers were "a race apart" and thus fair game.

R. v Ghosh [1982] Q.B. 1053 (Court of Appeal, Criminal Division)

The defendant was a consultant who acted as a locum at a hospital. He falsely claimed fees in respect of an operation that he had not carried out. He claimed that he thought he was not dishonest by his standards because the same amount of money was legitimately payable to him for consultation fees. The judge directed the jury that they must simply apply their own standards. He was convicted of an offence contrary to the now-repealed s.15 of the Theft Act 1968 (which used the same concept "dishonesty") and appealed against his conviction.

LORD LANE CJ:

"The sentence [in *Feely*] requiring the jury to apply current standards leads up to the prohibition on judges from applying *their* standards. That is the context in which the sentence appears. It seems to be reading too much into that sentence to treat it as authority for the view that 'dishonesty can be established independently of the knowledge or belief of the defendant'. If it could, then any reference to the state of mind of the defendant would be beside the point.

This brings us to the heart of the problem. Is 'dishonestly' in section 1 of the Theft Act 1968 intended to characterise a course of conduct? Or is it intended to describe a state of mind? If the former, then we can well understand that it could be established independently of the knowledge or belief of the accused. But if, as we think, it is the latter, then the knowledge and belief of the accused are at the root of the problem.

Take for example a man who comes from a country where public transport is free. On his first day here he travels on a bus. He gets off without paying. He never had any intention of paying. His mind is clearly honest; but his conduct, judged objectively by what he has done, is dishonest. It seems to us that in using the word 'dishonestly' in the Theft Act 1968, Parliament cannot have intended to catch dishonest conduct in that sense, that is to say conduct to which no moral obloquy could possibly attach. This is sufficiently established by the partial definition in section 2 of the Theft Act itself. All the matters covered by section 2(1) relate to the belief of the accused. Section 2(2) relates to his willingness to pay. A man's belief and his willingness to pay are things which can only be established subjectively. It is difficult to see how a partially subjective definition can be made to work in harness with the test which in all other respects is wholly objective.

If we are right that dishonesty is something in the mind of the accused (what Professor Glanville Williams calls 'a special mental state'), then if the mind of the accused is honest, it cannot be deemed dishonest merely because members of the jury would have regarded it as dishonest to embark on that course of conduct.

So we would reject the simple uncomplicated approach that the test is purely objective, however attractive from the practical point of view that solution may be.

There remains the objection that to adopt a subjective test is to abandon all standards but that of the accused himself, and to bring about a state of affairs in which 'Robin Hood would be no robber': *R. v Greenstein* [1975] 1 W.L.R. 1353. This objection misunderstands the nature of the subjective test. It is no defence for a man to say

---

a legal pronouncement and so inconsistent with *Feely*. Having ascertained he had lied, it should have been for the jury to establish whether he was dishonest. (The defendant claimed these were "white lies" which he believed were justified in the circumstances.)

[220] *Gilks* (1972) 56 Cr. App. R. 734.

'I knew that what I was doing is generally regarded as dishonest; but I do not regard it as dishonest myself. Therefore I am not guilty.' What he is however entitled to say is 'I did not know that anybody would regard what I was doing as dishonest.' He may not be believed; just as he may not be believed if he sets up 'a claim of right' under section 2(1) of the Theft Act 1968, or asserts that he believed in the truth of a misrepresentation under section 15 of the Act of 1968. But if he *is* believed, or raises a real doubt about the matter, the jury cannot be sure that he was dishonest.

In determining whether the prosecution has proved that the defendant was acting dishonestly, a jury must first of all decide whether according to the ordinary standards of reasonable and honest people what was done was dishonest. If it was not dishonest by those standards, that is the end of the matter and the prosecution fails.

If it was dishonest by those standards, then the jury must consider whether the defendant himself must have realised that what he was doing was by those standards dishonest. In most cases, where the actions are obviously dishonest by ordinary standards, there will be no doubt about it. It will be obvious that the defendant himself knew that he was acting dishonestly. It is dishonest for a defendant to act in a way which he knows ordinary people consider to be dishonest, even if he asserts or genuinely believes that he is morally justified in acting as he did. For example, Robin Hood or those ardent anti-vivisectionists who remove animals from vivisection laboratories are acting dishonestly, even though they may consider themselves to be morally justified in doing what they do, because they know that ordinary people would consider these actions to be dishonest."

Appeal dismissed

The enquiry is thus two-fold:

1. The jury, applying their own standards, must judge the defendant's actions and beliefs and decide whether he was honest or dishonest.

2. If the jury find that according to their standards he was dishonest, they must then establish whether the defendant knew that ordinary people would regard such conduct as dishonest.[221]

In *Roberts*,[222] it was held that this second limb of the *Ghosh* direction need only be put to the jury in those cases where the defendant raised the special plea that he did not think he was being dishonest by his own standards.[223] This was confirmed in *Wood*:

"the *Ghosh* direction . . . is best left only for that kind of case where there is a dispute about whether ordinary people would have different views from a defendant as to whether what he was doing was honest or not."[224]

Edward Griew, "Dishonesty: The Objections to Feely and Ghosh" [1985] Crim. L.R. 341:

"The question tends to increase the number of trials. Whereas a different approach to the dishonesty issue might make it clear that given conduct was dishonest as a matter of law and therefore constituted an offence, the *Feely* question leaves the issue open. It may be worth a defendant's while to take his chance with the jury . . . [B]efore *Feely* defendants might have felt constrained to plead guilty.

The question tends to complicate and lengthen contested cases . . . [I]t may be in the interests of some defendants to extend and complicate trials in order to obfuscate the issue . . .

---

[221] When utilising this two-fold test it must be put to the jury in this order (*Green* [1992] Crim. L.R. 292).

[222] *R. v Roberts (William)* (1987) 84 Cr. App. R. 117.

[223] It has been suggested (A. Halpin, "The Test for Dishonesty" [1996] Crim. L.R. 283) that *Roberts* allows the second limb of the *Ghosh* direction to be withheld from the jury in cases of "obvious dishonesty" even if the defendant raises the possibility that he believed others would not regard his conduct as dishonest. This view is not reflected in the practice of the courts. See, for example, *Price* [1990] Crim. L.R. 200; *Hyam* [1997] Crim. L.R. 439; *R. v Clarke (Victor Edward)* [1996] Crim. L.R. 824.

[224] *R. v Wood (Peter)* [2002] EWCA Crim 832, and in *R. v Jouman (Bibi Shameera)* [2012] EWCA Crim 1850 at [22].

The *Feely* question carries an unacceptable risk of inconsistency of decision . . .

[It] implies the existence of a relevant community norm. In doing so it glosses over differences of age, class and cultural background . . . It is simply naive to suppose . . . that there is, in respect of the dishonesty question, any such single thing as 'the standards of ordinary decent folk . . .'

[It is] unsuitable where the context of the case is a specialised one, involving intricate financial activities or dealings in a specialised market. It is neither reasonable nor rational to expect ordinary people to judge as 'dishonest' or 'not dishonest' conduct of which, for want of relevant experience, they cannot appreciate the contextual flavour . . . [O]rdinary people (might) have no standards in relation to the conduct in question . . .

A person may defend his attack on another's property by reference to a moral or political conviction so passionately held that he believed (so he claims) that 'ordinary decent' members of society would regard his conduct as proper, even laudable. If the asserted belief is treated as a claim to have been ignorant that the conduct was 'dishonest' by ordinary standards . . . and if the jury think (as exceptionally they might) that the belief may have been held, *Ghosh* produces an acquittal. The result is remarkable. Robin Hood must be a thief even if he thinks the whole of the right-thinking world is on his side.

A person reared or moving in an environment in which it is generally regarded as legitimate to take advantage of certain classes of people—perhaps bookmakers or employers—may plausibly claim that he did not realise that his conduct, of which a member of such a class was a victim, was generally regarded as dishonest. It is not acceptable that a claim of that sort should be capable even of being advanced."

These views are supported by research which revealed huge variations in ordinary people's ideas of what constitutes dishonesty. Women are more likely than men, and older people are more likely than younger people, to categorise certain behaviour as dishonest. But, interestingly, men are more likely to convict someone of a dishonesty offence in court.[225] The result is that it becomes a lottery—dependent, inter alia, on the sex and age profile of the jury (or, perhaps of the magistrate)—whether someone will be convicted of an offence of dishonesty. There may also be regional or cultural variations in attitudes towards the relative honesty/dishonesty of conduct. For example, in 2007 the ship *MSC Napoli* was grounded off the South Devon coast and 37 of its cargo containers were washed up on a nearby beach at Branscombe. Large crowds came to the beach to "salvage" property that that had come ashore (including BMW motorbikes). Yet no arrests were made and there were no prosecutions for theft. It has been suggested that at least part of the reason for this was that, because the local Westcountry culture appeared to be tolerant of the looting of wrecks, "the police were not satisfied that a court would regard the "salvors" as dishonest because of the uncertainty surrounding the concept of dishonest in the offence of theft".[226]

Glanville Williams, Textbook of Criminal Law, 2nd edn (1983), pp.726–730:

"The practice of leaving the whole matter to the jury might be workable if our society were culturally homogeneous, with known and shared values, as it once very largely was. But the object of the law of theft is to protect property rights; and disrespect for these rights is now widespread. Since the jury are chosen at random, we have no reason to suppose that they will be any more honest and 'decent' in their standards than the average person . . .

Evidence of the poor level of self-discipline now prevailing abounds—and this without taking any account of tax defaults. Observers agree upon a very large scale of theft: not merely shoplifting and fare bilking but stealing from employers by employees and an assortment of frauds perpetrated upon customers by employees. Great numbers of employed people of all classes believe, or affect to believe, that systematic dishonesty of various

---

[225]   The "Honesty Lab" study conducted by S. Fafinski and E. Finch: S. Connor, "Sexes Differ Over Dishonesty Says New Study", *The Independent*, September 7, 2009; M. Henderson, "Many Potential Jurors Find it Hard to Tell Right From Wrong", *The Times*, September 7, 2009.

[226]   R. Glover, "Can Dishonesty be Salvaged? Theft and the Grounding of the MCS Napoli" (2010) 74 J.C.L. 53–76 at 55.

kinds is a 'perk'. It is tolerated by many employers, provided that it does not exceed some ill-defined limit; and some employers even encourage fiddles when they are at the expense of customers, since this is a way of increasing employees' remuneration without cost to the employers. For the employee, illicit remuneration has the advantage of being untaxed. Fiddling also brings non-material rewards: it is a pleasant departure from routine, a game of chance against the risk of detection, all the better since the consequences of detection are now rarely serious. So highly do some workers value the practice that a change in the system of work threatening to interfere with it, or an attempt by employers to prosecute offenders, is met by strikes. Notable examples were the strike at Heathrow Airport when baggage loaders were arrested for pilferage in 1973 . . . If ordinary people in steady employment develop these lax notions about the right of property, it seems from the judgment in *Feely* that the law of theft is to be automatically adjusted to suit . . .

[Commenting on *Gilks* Professor Williams continues] Subjectivism of this degree gives subjectivism a bad name. The subjective approach to criminal liability, properly understood, looks to the defendant's intention and to the facts as he believed them to be, not to his system of values . . .

What must be found is a definition of dishonesty . . . I would suggest that the definition should be that dishonesty involves a disregard for rights of property. Professor Smith's suggestion, however, is that a judicial definition of dishonesty might be . . .: a person appropriates dishonestly 'where he knows that it will or may be detrimental to the interests of the other in a significant practical way' ([1982] Crim.L.R. 609). We can at least be certain that almost any definition making the position independent of current social attitudes would be better than the rule in *Ghosh*."[227]

Williams assumes that because large numbers of employees "fiddle" from their employers, for example, that such employees have lost all standards of knowing right from wrong and therefore, being in a moral vacuum, would be unable to assess "dishonesty" if sitting in a jury box. But surely a plausible explanation is that most such employees know perfectly well that their conduct is dishonest, but have chosen nevertheless to go ahead and do it. Such persons are perfectly capable of sitting on a jury and judging standards of dishonesty. Research has revealed that people are less likely to regard conduct as dishonest if they have done similar things themselves but are still capable of making a judgment of dishonesty. For example, nearly two-thirds of people have taken stationery home from work but 82 per cent thought it was dishonest.[228] Charges of hypocrisy will not do, otherwise any juror who had ever committed a (relevant) offence would have to be disqualified—an impossible task given the vast unknown figure of unrecorded property crime.

Law Commission, Report No.276, Fraud (2002), paras 5.9–5.10:

"5.9 There is some evidence that people's moral standards are surprisingly flexible. A MORI poll for the *Sunday Times* in October 1985 found that only 35% of those questioned thought it morally wrong to accept payment in cash in order to evade liability for tax. On the other hand, it does not follow that the other 65%, if sitting on a jury in a case of tax evasion where dishonesty was in issue, would necessarily have acquitted. Indeed, the proportion of those questioned who thought that such conduct was morally acceptable to most people was only 37%. This may suggest that people do not generally assume that their own moral standards are the norm. Indeed it indicates that a majority of respondents thought that their own moral standards fell below those of most others.

5.10 It seems, therefore, that the first stage of the *Ghosh* test may not necessarily result in the jury simply applying their own standards of honesty. It may, indeed, be quite natural for fact-finders to form a view of what reasonable, honest, people would consider dishonest, as distinct from their decision reflecting their own personal moral view."

The earlier Glanville Williams extract also challenges the view that the defendant's system of values are relevant in an assessment of culpability.

---

227   Further calls have been made for a comprehensive statutory definition of dishonesty: P.R. Glazebrook, "Revising the Theft Act" (1993) 52 C.L.J. 191; A. Halpin, "The Test for Dishonesty" [1996] Crim. L.R. 283.

228   S.Connor, above, fn.225.

C.M.V. Clarkson, Understanding Criminal Law, 4th edn. (2005), pp.236–238:

"The courts were faced with a quandary here. Acceptance of such pleas [*viz.*, that the defendant did not think he was dishonest by his own standards] would undercut the moral imperative laid down by the criminal law. The criminal law largely reflects (and attempts to uphold) community values. The *Feely* test allows these community values to be enunciated by a so-called representative section of the community, namely, the jury. If the values of the jury and the community are to be ignored and replaced by the values of the defendant (who, for example, might endorse the political ideology that 'property is theft'), the result would be a complete absence of any objective standard. The door would be open to the 'Robin Hood defence'. The defendant would effectively become his own judge and jury.

On the other hand, the courts were reluctant to dismiss such pleas totally. The criminal law is based largely on the premise of moral responsibility. We blame those who are morally at fault. If a defendant openly rejects the value system inherent in the law of theft, he can be blamed even if, according to his own values, he thinks his actions are honest. He has knowingly 'declared war' on the values of society and can be blamed for doing this. It can never be an excuse in the criminal law that one does not agree with any given law. But what of the defendant who genuinely thinks he is acting honestly according to his values—*and* who really believes that most other people would agree with him as to the morality of his conduct—and can convince a jury of these beliefs? Such a defendant is not openly defying the law; he believes he is upholding the value system inherent in the law of theft. The case for exempting such a defendant from blame becomes strong.

This latter thinking was endorsed in the leading decision of *Ghosh* . . . The quest throughout the criminal law is for the isolation of the blameworthy. If the jury, reflecting community standards, can attach 'moral obloquy' to the defendant's actions and are satisfied that the defendant knows he is acting contrary to the moral standards of ordinary people, a judgment of blameworthiness is truly appropriate. The test has tried to combine the need to preserve objective standards within the criminal law with the need to maintain the importance of moral fault."

Such thinking, allowing a context-dependent and individualised assessment of moral blameworthiness, was initially disapproved by the Law Commission.

Law Commission Consultation Paper No.155, Fraud and Deception (1999), para.7.52:

"7.52 [W]e are not aware of any other area of criminal law which recognises an open-ended defence that the conduct in question is morally blameless. The general approach in English law is for elements of the offence to spell out the conduct it is sought to criminalise, and similarly to provide defences by specifying excusable forms of conduct which would otherwise be caught. There is no specific requirement of morally blameworthy conduct in the law of (for example) assaults, sexual offences, corruption or criminal damage . . . [O]ffences are defined in such a way that conduct which satisfies their requirements (and does not fall within a recognised general defence) will *normally* be blameworthy; but the element of moral blame is incorporated in the definition of the conduct prohibited, not superimposed upon it. There is always the possibility that blameless conduct may occasionally be caught, but that possibility is dealt with via prosecutorial discretion and sentencing options. It is not clear why theft and deception should be thought unique in this respect."

However, in its subsequent Report, the Law Commission partially resiled from this position.

Law Commission, Report No.276, Fraud (2002), paras 5.5–5.8:

"5.5 It may be that moral elements such as dishonesty can only be defined with reference to the fact-finder's judgment. Richard Tur argues that 'what may constitute a just excuse is so context-dependent that exhaustive definition must necessarily limit the range of circumstances which might excuse' ("Dishonesty and the Jury" in Griffiths (ed.), *Philosophy and Practice* (1985), p. 75). Therefore, if an exhaustive definition of 'just excuse' or 'dishonesty' were incorporated into the law, there would inevitably be examples of behaviour which were legally dishonest, but which the fact-finders would characterise as morally blameless.

5.16 . . . We have also concluded that it would not be possible to define dishonesty exhaustively . . .

5.17 . . . We have come to agree with the argument put forward by Richard Tur . . .

5.18 The fact that *Ghosh* dishonesty leaves open a possibility of variance between cases with essentially similar facts is, in our judgment, a theoretical risk. Many years after its adoption, the *Ghosh* test remains, in practice, unproblematic. We also recognise the fact that the concept of dishonesty is now required in a very large number of criminal cases, so to reject it at this stage would have a far-reaching effect on the criminal justice system."

6. Intention of permanent deprivation

The defendant must intend to permanently deprive the other of the property. If they intend to return the goods, this is not theft. Dishonest borrowings are not theft.

What is required is an *intention* of permanent deprivation. Whether the victim is actually deprived of the property is irrelevant. This demonstrates again the inchoate nature of the offence of theft.

"Intention of permanently depriving the other of it" (s.1) is not defined by the Theft Act. However, s.6 *extends* the natural meaning of the phrase and provides that in certain circumstances even though the defendant did not "mean" the other to lose the thing permanently they are "to be regarded" as having an intention of permanent deprivation.

Theft Act 1968 s.6

"(1) A person appropriating property belonging to another without meaning the other permanently to lose the thing itself is nevertheless to be regarded as having the intention of permanently depriving the other of it if his intention is to treat the thing as his own to dispose of regardless of the other's rights; and a borrowing or lending of it may amount to so treating it if, but only if, the borrowing or lending is for a period and in circumstances making it equivalent to an outright taking or disposal.

(2) Without prejudice to the generality of subsection (1) above, where a person, having possession or control (lawfully or not) of property belonging to another, parts with the property under a condition as to its return which he may not be able to perform, this (if done for purposes of his own and without the other's authority) amounts to treating the property as his own to dispose of regardless of the other's rights."

In *Lloyd*,[229] it was made clear that s.6 should only be referred to in exceptional cases; for most purposes it would be unnecessary to go beyond s.1(1).[230]

Section 6(1) contains two limbs. The first refers to a defendant whose "intention is to treat the thing as his own to dispose of regardless of the other's rights". The second limb is a specific illustration of this in that certain borrowings "may amount to so treating it" as his own. Section 6(2) provides that the situation covered therein "amounts to treating the property as his own to dispose of regardless of the other's rights". This is thus just another specific illustration of the principle contained in the first limb of s.6(1).[231] Nevertheless, it is useful to look at the three situations separately.

---

[229] *R. v Lloyd (Sidney Douglas)* [1985] Q.B. 829.
[230] *Warner* (1970) 55 Cr. App. R. 93; *R. v Cocks (Eugene George)* (1976) 63 Cr. App. R. 79; *Mitchell* [2008] EWCA Crim 850.
[231] *R. v Fernandes (Roland Anthony)* [1996] 1 Cr. App. R. 175 at 188.

(i) Section 6(1)

(a) *If his intention is to treat the thing as his own to dispose of regardless of the other's rights*

R. v Raphael [2008] EWCA Crim 1014 (Court of Appeal, Criminal Division)

The defendant drove off in a car belonging to Adeosun and then demanded money for its return.

PRESIDENT OF THE QUEEN'S BENCH DIVISION:

"[T]he section itself demonstrates that the necessary intention may sometimes be established when the person appropriating property belonging to another does not in fact intend that its true owner should be deprived of it permanently. It is properly described as a deeming provision. As Lord Lane LJ . . . observed in *Lloyd*:

> 'It must mean, if nothing else, that there are circumstances in which a defendant may be deemed to have the intention permanently to deprive, even though he may intend the owner eventually to get back the object which has been taken. . . . The first part of section 6(1) seems to us to be aimed at the sort of case where a defendant takes things and then offers them back to the owner for the owner to buy if he wishes. If the taker intends to return them to the owner only upon such payment, then, on the wording of section 6(1) that is deemed to amount to the necessary intention permanently to deprive . . .'

He continued that there were other cases of 'similar intent': for instance, 'I have taken your valuable painting. You can have it back on payment to me of £X000. If you are not prepared to make that payment, then you are not going to get your painting back.'
   The express language of section 6 specifies that the subjective element necessary to establish the mens rea for theft includes an intention on the part of the taker 'to treat the thing as his own to dispose of regardless of the other's rights'. In our judgment it is hard to find a better example of such an intention than an offer, not to return Adeosun's car to him in exactly the same condition it was when it was removed from his possession and control, but to sell his own property back to him, and to make its return subject to a condition or conditions inconsistent with his right to possession of his own property."

Appeal dismissed

In *Lavender*[232] a defendant removed doors from one council property undergoing repairs and used them to replace damaged doors at another council property. It was held that this was a "disposal" under s.6(1) because the defendant "intended to treat the doors as his own, regardless of the council's rights". The problem with this interpretation is that it renders s.6 redundant in that an intention to treat property as one's own is already a necessary requirement for an appropriation.

   In *Marshall*,[233] ticket touts obtained unexpired London Underground tickets and sold them to other potential customers. It was argued that there was no intention of permanent deprivation because the tickets would, in due course, be returned to the possession of London Underground. It was held, however, that the ticket touts had, under s.6(1), an intention to treat the tickets as their own to dispose of regardless of London Underground's rights.

   The issue of intention of permanent deprivation needs to be approached with care by a trial judge in cases where goods are taken and abandoned shortly thereafter. Appropriation and intention of permanent deprivation are separate elements of the offence of theft, and it would be wrong for a trial judge in such a case to give the impression that a taking, even if violent, was sufficient in itself

---

[232] *DPP v Lavender (Melvyn)* [1994] Crim. L.R. 297.
[233] *R. v Marshall (Adrian John)* [1998] 2 Cr. App. R. 282. See J.C. Smith, "Stealing Tickets" [1998] Crim. L.R. 723. See also *DPP v SJ (A Juvenile)* [2002] EWHC 291 where it was held that an intention to render something useless demonstrated an intention of treating an article as one's own to dispose of.

to establish an intention permanently to deprive the owner of the property. In *Mitchell*[234] the defendant, being pursued by police officers and needing a getaway car, pulled a woman out of her car and drove off in it and abandoned it shortly afterwards. The trial judge ruled that this taking, using and abandoning of the vehicle was sufficient evidence capable of amounting to an intention to dispose of property regardless of the owner's rights. On appeal, this was declared to be wrong. Section 6 was not meant to widen greatly the basic s.1 requirement of an intention of permanent deprivation. It was simply dealing with "a small number of difficult cases". Such a brief use of the car before abandoning it did not come within s.1. The relevance of abandonment must also be properly explained to the jury. In *Vinall*[235] two cyclists riding along a cycling path were approached by the two defendants and another man. One of the cyclists was punched from his bicycle and chased off, and the three men walked off with his bicycle. The bicycle was found abandoned by a bus stop on a main road 50 yards from where the owner had left it. The trial judge invited the jury to consider whether the fact of the abandonment of the bicycle at the bus stop itself demonstrated: (1) an intention to assume the rights of an owner and, therefore, an appropriation of the bicycle; and (2) a deemed intention permanently to deprive the owner of it. The Court of Appeal held that the judge had allowed the "separate concepts of appropriation and intention permanently to deprive" to become "fatally confused".[236] The taking of the bicycle was a sufficient assumption of the rights of the owner to amount to an appropriation, and the abandonment of the bicycle was capable of being additional evidence that by taking the bicycle the appellants were assuming the rights of the owner over it. But the jury had also to be directed that they had to be sure that at the time of taking the bicycle either the appellants had an intention permanently to deprive (s.1) or they intended to treat the bicycle as their own to dispose of regardless of the other's rights (s.6).[237]

(b) *Borrowing or lending for a period and in circumstances making it equivalent to an outright taking or disposal*

This makes it clear that certain borrowings are to be treated the same as outright takings. The classic example here is borrowing another's football season ticket and then returning the piece of paper at the end of the season after watching all the matches. At that stage the ticket has no value and is useless; the "virtue" has gone out of the thing.

R. v Lloyd [1985] Q.B. 829 (Court of Appeal, Criminal Division)

Films were removed from a cinema for a few hours and "pirate" copies made of them; the originals were then returned. The defendant appealed against his conviction for conspiracy to steal.

LORD LANE CJ:

"[T]he intention of the appellants could more accurately be described as an intention temporarily to deprive the owner of the film and was indeed the opposite of an intention permanently to deprive . . .

Borrowing is *ex hypothesi* not something which is done with an intention permanently to deprive. This half of the subsection, we believe, is intended to make it clear that a mere borrowing is never enough to constitute the necessary guilty mind unless the intention is to return the 'thing' in such a changed state that it can truly be said

---

234   *Mitchell* [2008] EWCA Crim 850.
235   *R. v Vinall (George Alfred)* [2011] EWCA Crim 2652, [2012] 1 Cr. App. R. 29. L.H. Leigh, "Robbery, Contemporaneity and intent Permanently to Deprive" (2012) 176 J.P.N. 201–202.
236   *Vinall* [2011] EWCA Crim 2652 at [10].
237   This case is further discussed below, at p.899, in relation to the offence of robbery. See also *R. v Zerei (Samuel Michael)* [2012] EWCA Crim 1114.

that all its goodness or virtue has gone: for example *R. v Beecham* (1851) 5 Cox C.C. 181, where the defendant stole railway tickets intending that they should be returned to the railway company in the usual way only after the journeys had been completed. He was convicted of larceny . . .

That being the case, we turn to inquire whether the feature films in this case can fall within that category. Our view is that they cannot. The goodness, the virtue, the practical value of the films to the owners has not gone out of the article. The film could still be projected to paying audiences . . .

Our view is that those particular films which were the subject of this alleged conspiracy had not themselves diminished in value at all. What had happened was that the borrowed film had been used or was going to be used to perpetrate a copyright swindle on the owners whereby their commercial interests were grossly and adversely affected in the way that we have endeavoured to describe at the outset of this judgment. That borrowing, it seems to us, was not for a period, or in such circumstances, as made it equivalent to an outright taking or disposal. There was still virtue in the film."

Appeals allowed

Difficult questions of fact will, of course, remain. In *Lloyd* Lord Lane spoke of "all" the virtue or goodness being gone. This raises the problem of the football season ticket which is returned after it has been used for 19 matches, but is still valid for one final match. The ticket clearly has *some* value or virtue left. Presumably, questions such as these, were they to arise, would be left to the jury as questions of fact.

(ii) Section 6(2)

This deals with the situation of a person who takes unacceptable risks with the property of another. For example, they may pawn such property realising that they may be unable to redeem it. In *Fernandes* a solicitor dishonestly made an insecure investment of a client's money. It was held that

"section 6 may apply to a person in possession or control of another's property who, dishonestly and for his own purpose, deals with that property in such a manner that he knows he is risking its loss".[238]

It is uncertain whether the defendant must realise that they may be unable to redeem the property or whether it suffices that they "may" objectively be so unable. Griew says: "The former view is doctrinally the purer; the latter is more readily suggested by the terms of the poorly-drafted section."[239] However, in *Fernandez* it was stated that the defendant must *know* that they are risking the loss of the property.[240]

(a) *Dishonest borrowings*

Apart from these specific situations where s.6 has deemed dishonest borrowings to be the equivalent of an intention to permanently deprive, the Theft Act 1968 has generally chosen not to punish dishonest borrowings. Why?

---

[238] *R. v Fernandes (Roland Anthony)* [1996] 1 Cr. App. R. 175 at 188.
[239] E. Griew, *The Theft Acts*, 7th edn (London: Sweet & Maxwell, 1995), p.66.
[240] This view is supported by D. Ormerod and D. Williams, *Smith's The Law of Theft*, 9th edn (Oxford: OUP, 2007), pp.123–124.

Criminal Law Revision Committee, 8th Report, Theft and Related Offences (1966), Cmnd.2977, para.56:

"[A]n intention to return the property, even after a long time makes the conduct essentially different from steal-ing. Apart from this . . . [criminalising temporary deprivations] would be a considerable extension of the criminal law, which does not seem to be called for by any existing serious evil. It might moreover have undesirable social consequences. Quarrelling neighbours and families would be able to threaten one another with prosecution. Students and young people sharing accommodation who might be tempted to borrow one another's property in disregard of a prohibition by the owner would be in danger of acquiring a criminal record. Further, it would be difficult for the police to avoid being involved in wasteful and undesirable investigations into alleged offences which had no social importance."

Glanville Williams, "Temporary Appropriation should be Theft" [1981] Crim. L.R. 129, 131–132, 135:

"Suppose that a person removes a small piece of sculpture from a private exhibition, or a valuable book from a University library, and returns it after a year. During that time it has of course been lost to its owner; and both the owner and the police have been put to trouble . . . The taker of the article may use it in such a way as to put it at risk, or he may make a profit from it, or he may return it in an impaired condition; and if he is a person of no substance the owner's civil remedy against him will be insufficient penalty . . .

If a person has gone off with the property of another, and upon being apprehended and charged with theft swears that he meant to return it, is his statement to be accepted or not? To accept it too readily gives guilty defendants an easy line of escape; to reject it carries the risk of convicting people who are technically innocent, even though they are morally guilty because they have taken the article dishonestly . . . Why should not the dishonest taking be sufficient to constitute the offence of theft, thus relieving the prosecution of a very difficult burden of proof? . . .

When an article is unlawfully taken, even if only for a temporary purpose and without substantial risk of permanent loss of the article, the owner suffers an immediate loss, namely in respect of the use of it . . . Sometimes the economic loss resulting from the loss of use of an article that is essential to an undertaking can be considerable.

One of the principal arguments for changing the law is that the value of articles lies in their use. More and more things are used by way of hiring . . . Many articles of use have comparatively short useful 'lives'. In a few years they wear out or become unfashionable or technically obsolete . . . Besides, the owner is in a dilemma of either being without the article for that time or putting himself to the expense of buying another—an expense that may turn out to have been unnecessary if the article is returned."

This reasoning was largely accepted by the Law Commission whose provisional view was that tempo-rary deprivation of property is wrong in principle and so should be criminal.[241]

There are two well-known exceptions to the intention of permanent deprivation rule (apart from the exceptions within s.6 itself).[242] Section 11 creates the offence of removing articles from places open to the public, for example, removing works of art from museums or galleries albeit intending to return them at some time. Section 12 of the Theft Act 1968 creates the second exceptional offence of taking a motor vehicle or other conveyance without authority. This is designed to prevent "joyriding", where a car is taken and, after being driven around, abandoned. In such cases an intention of permanent deprivation would be difficult to establish.

---

[241] Law Commission Consultation Paper No.155, *Fraud and Deception* (1999), para.19. While this proposal was made in rela-tion to deception offences, the reasoning is equally applicable to theft.

[242] Section 12A provides for an offence of aggravated vehicle taking to cover instances where a vehicle is taken by D contrary to s.12 and, after it is taken but before it is recovered, damage is caused, or injury inflicted in the circumstances specified in s.12A(2). See D. Ormerod, *Smith and Hogan's Criminal Law*, 13th edn (Oxford: OUP, 2011), pp.861–863. For further excep-tions, see e.g. Postal Services Act 2000 s.84, and G. Williams, "Temporary Appropriation should be Theft" [1981] Crim. L.R. 129 at 130.

It is interesting to contrast this last activity of joyriding with the conduct of a person who walks into a bookshop and dishonestly removes a book which they take home and read before returning it to the shop. It appears that the only reasons for the criminalisation of the former but not the latter activity are, first, the prevalence of joyriding[243] and secondly, the difficulty of proving the necessary intent with taking cars (with the book example, a finding of intention of permanent deprivation would be almost irresistible and thus a conviction for theft would result in fact).

It is worth pausing at this point to reflect whether some insight can be gleaned into the real harm that is sought to be prevented by the crime of theft. When the book is dishonestly taken from the store, the store clearly suffers a harm. First, there is economic harm. The book is removed from their shelves, meaning it cannot be sold to another. The used book that is returned is not the same thing that was taken, which was a new book. The store sustains an economic loss of the difference in value between the new book and the secondhand book.[244] Secondly, there is all the non-economic harm associated with most thefts. The shop has had its rights of ownership assaulted. It has lost control of its property, lost the power to make choices and decisions about it. The identity of the borrower is probably unknown and, therefore, there can be no certainty as to when and if the property will be returned. For instance, the Criminal Law Revision Committee considered the striking example of someone who "borrowed" Goya's portrait of the Duke of Wellington from the National Gallery for four years.[245]

It should be repeated at this stage that it is not necessary for a victim to lose her property permanently. What matters is that the defendant, at the time of the appropriation, *intends* that she shall lose it permanently. Thus the result may be the same as with cases of borrowing. In our example, the book is ultimately returned. It is the intention of the taker that distinguishes the cases. Is this approach justifiable?

O.W. Holmes, The Common Law (1882), pp.70–72:

"[In theft] acts are punished which of themselves would not be sufficient to accomplish the evil which the law seeks to prevent, and which are treated as equally criminal, whether the evil has been accomplished or not . . .

In larceny the consequences immediately flowing from the act are generally exhausted with little or no harm to the owner. Goods are removed from his possession by trespass, and that is all, when the crime is complete. But they must be permanently kept from him before the harm is done which the law seeks to prevent. A momentary loss of possession is not what has been guarded against with such severe penalties. What the law means to prevent is the loss of it wholly and forever . . .

The reason is plain enough. The law cannot wait until the property has been used up or destroyed in other hands than the owner's, or until the owner has died, in order to make sure that the harm which it seeks to prevent has been done . . .

There must be an intent to deprive such owner of his ownership . . . But why? . . . The true answer is, that the intent is an index to the external event which probably would have happened, and that, if the law is to punish at all, it must, in this case, go on probabilities, not on accomplished facts. The analogy to the manner of dealing with attempts is plain. Theft may be called an attempt to permanently deprive a man of his property, which is punished with the same severity whether successful or not. If theft can rightly be considered in this way, intent must play the same part as in other attempts. An act which does not fully accomplish the prohibited result may be made wrongful by evidence that but for some interference it would have been followed by other acts co-ordinated with it to produce that result. This can only be shown by showing intent. In theft the intent to deprive

---

[243]   CLRC, fn.103 above, p.788. The offence was first created by s.28 of the Road Traffic Act 1930 "to deal with a mischief which had even then become common" (para.82).

[244]   G.P. Fletcher, *Rethinking Criminal Law* (Boston: Little, Brown, 1978), p.48.

[245]   CLRC, fn.103 above, p.788.

the owner of his property establishes that the thief would have retained, or would not have taken steps to restore, the stolen goods."

The real harm in theft is, thus, that when a defendant intends permanent deprivation there is a greater risk to the victim that they will lose their property permanently. (In most cases they will, in fact, have already lost the property.) As with the law of attempt, the threat to the property amounts to a "second order harm". This, however, only explains why the actual loss of property need not occur—but still does not explain why there must be an intention of permanent deprivation as opposed to an intention to borrow dishonestly.

What is being punished is disapproved-of behaviour which poses an unacceptable risk to the property of another. It is fairly obvious that where there is an intention of permanent deprivation there is a greater risk of actual permanent deprivation occurring (for much the same reason that there is greater danger when a defendant is intending a consequence than when they are being reckless as to it: they are trying to achieve the objective and must, in general, stand more chance of success than if not so trying). So the question reduces itself to whether permanent deprivation is sufficiently "worse" than temporary deprivation to justify criminalisation of the former but not the latter. Most people would surely agree that, in general, a permanent loss is qualitatively worse than a temporary loss. The owner has been deprived completely and irrevocably of their property. Insurance, if obtainable, will not compensate for such loss of power and control over the property. Whether it is *so much* worse as to justify the criminalisation line being drawn between the two is uncertain. Perhaps, it is best at this stage to conclude that while a temporary loss caused by dishonest conduct is unfortunate and deserves moral condemnation, one should refrain from expanding the role of the criminal law without clear and strong reasons.

(b) *Particular property*

There must be an intention permanently to deprive the other of the *particular* property alleged to be appropriated. It is no defence that similar property was to be returned. This rule is most often applied to coins and banknotes. It is clear law that if one "borrows" money, intending to repay it the next day, one is not intending to return the same notes or coins; one therefore does have an intention of permanently depriving the other of the particular property alleged to be stolen.[246] Of course, actual liability still depends on a finding of dishonesty which, in such cases, may be difficult to establish.

(c) *Cheques*

There is a particular problem with cheques in that if a defendant wrongfully obtains and cashes another's cheque, under former banking practices the cheque would often ultimately be returned to that other or be available for their collection and so the defendant could assert that they had no intention of permanently depriving the other of that piece of paper.[247] In *Duru*,[248] it was held that in such a case the defendant would have an intention of depriving the other permanently of the thing in action represented by the cheque. *Duru* was overruled by *Preddy*[249] on the ground that the thing in action (the defendant's right to sue the other on the cheque) was not property belonging to another.[250] In addition, although the defendant in such circumstances acquires the cheque form, in *Preddy*, Lord Goff

---

[246] *R. v Williams (Hywell Rhys)* [1953] 1 Q.B. 660; *R. v Velumyl* [1989] Crim. L.R. 299.
[247] A similar argument was advanced in relation to London Underground tickets in *Marshall* [1998] 2 Cr. App. R. 282.
[248] *Duru* (1973) 58 Cr. App. R. 151.
[249] *Preddy* [1996] A.C. 815.
[250] This was followed in *Clark* [2001] EWCA Crim 884. See the discussion above, p.829 regarding cheques as 'property'.

stated (*obiter*) that, if the defendant intends to present the cheque for payment, he will not be guilty of theft of the cheque form, because he has no intention to deprive the owner of the cheque, since he knows that on presentation to the bank the cheque will be returned to the drawer via the bank.[251] Lord Goff's comments in *Preddy* were followed in *Graham*[252] and treated as binding in *Clark*.[253] There are two ways of overcoming this problem. First, when the defendant presents the cheque to the bank they are appropriating the other's bank balance—a thing in action. In *Hilton*[254] it was held that the thing in action (the debt from the bank to the other person) in such cases has been wholly or partially destroyed. An intention to destroy the property of another amounts to an intention to permanently deprive the other of it. Secondly, with regard to the cheque itself, it has been argued that, when receiving the cheque, the defendant could be regarded as appropriating a piece of paper with special qualities in that it is effectively the key to the drawer's bank account.[255] When that piece of paper is returned to the other (or their bank) it will simply be a worthless piece of paper with all its virtue gone. The defendant therefore had an intention of permanently depriving the other of the piece of paper with special qualities. The problem with this analysis is that these "special qualities" are simply those that render the cheque a thing in action. As demonstrated by *Preddy*, this thing in action never belonged to another. However, Smith's analysis could be utilised in cases where the property is *deemed* to belong to another as in s.5(3). In such a case an intention that "the document should find its way back to the transferor only after all benefit to the transferor has been lost or removed as a result of its use in breach of such obligation"[256] can amount to an intention to deprive the other permanently of the cheque.

The problem does not arise if the defendant intends to keep the cheque, and not to present it. In these circumstances, it appears from the case of *Roach*[257] that the defendant can be convicted of theft of the cheque form because:

"In such circumstances there is no difference between these cheques and any other form of property. If they were taken dishonestly and there was an intention permanently to deprive the owner of them, they would have been stolen."

(iii) Conditional intention

R. v Easom [1971] 2 Q.B. 315

The defendant picked up a woman's handbag in a cinema, rummaged through it and, having taken nothing, put it back near to the owner, who repossessed it. On appeal, Easom's conviction for stealing the handbag and specified contents (tissues, cosmetics etc.) was quashed: the defendant never had intention of permanently depriving the owner of the handbag of any of those things.

EDMUND DAVIES LJ

"In every case of theft the appropriation must be accompanied by the intention of permanently depriving the owner of his property. What may be loosely described as a 'conditional' appropriation will not do. If the appro-

[251] *Preddy* [1996] A.C. 815 at 836–837. In fact, as the Court of Appeal in *Roach* acknowledged, "it is not now the practice of the banks in any event to return cheques which have been cashed to the original drawer of the cheque": *R. v Roach (Daniel)* [2011] EWCA Crim 918 at [7].
[252] *Graham* [1997] 1 Cr. App. R. 302.
[253] *Clark* [2001] EWCA Crim 884.
[254] *R. v Hilton (Peter Arnold)* [1997] 2 Cr. App. R. 445, approving *Kohn* (1979) 69 Cr. App. R. 395.
[255] J.C. Smith, "Obtaining Cheques by Deception or Theft" [1997] Crim. L.R. 396.
[256] *Arnold* [1997] 4 All E.R. 1 at 15.
[257] *Roach* [2011] EWCA Crim 918 at [8].

priator has it in mind merely to deprive the owner of such of his property as, on examination, proves worth taking and then, finding that the booty is valueless to the appropriator, leaves it ready to hand to be repossessed by the owner, the appropriator has not stolen. If a dishonest postal sorter picks up a pile of letters, intending to steal any which are registered, but, on finding that none of them are, replaces them, he has stolen nothing, and this is so notwithstanding the provisions of section 6 (1) of the Theft Act 1968."

Easom could not be convicted of the theft of the handbag, tissues etc., because he did not intend to keep any of these items. His intention was to steal anything that he found that was worth stealing, and "it cannot be said that one who has it in mind to steal only if what he finds is worth stealing has a present intention to steal".[258] Nor, since he replaced the bag near to the position from which it had been removed, could it be established that he had exercised such dominion over the property that it could be inferred that, at the time of the taking, he intended to treat the bag as his own to dispose of regardless of the owner's rights.[259] The defendant in such circumstances might be convicted of attempted theft if the charge were suitably worded as "attempting to steal from a handbag".[260]

III. Fraud

A. The Criminological Background

The terms "theft", "robbery", and "burglary" evoke immediate understanding in the hearer (even if that understanding is less than perfect); the same is less true of offences involving fraud. The behaviour encompassed by fraud may, however, be just as devastating to the victim, or just as close to the fringes of criminality. It may be the classic con-man who tricks an elderly lady into parting with her valuable antique for vastly less than it is worth; it may be the individual passing bad cheques or falsely claiming social security; it may be the employee who abuses their position of trust to defraud their employers; or it may be a company perpetrating a fraud against the public or the state. An increasing threat is perceived in the rise in the use of computers and the internet to commit crime. The use of the internet to shop, manage bank accounts, interact with friends and acquaintances, and even to find a new partner, has become a commonplace feature of modern life. Unfortunately, it has also provided fraudsters with many new opportunities to seek out and take advantage of victims.[261]

Jonathan Clough, Principles of Cybercrime (2010), pp.183–185:

"The Internet is a paradise for those who prey upon the gullible, the greedy or the vulnerable. First, it provides unprecedented access to victims . . . The advent of the Internet has allowed offenders to reach millions of potential victims at virtually no cost. The more people who can be contacted, the greater the chance someone will be taken in by the scam.

Secondly, the Internet is a large marketplace. In 2003, 17.6% of adults in the United States conducted banking online and 32.3% purchased a product or service online. In Canada, 44% of adults had purchased goods or services over the internet in 2003, whilst in the UK the figure in 2009 was 80%, with 55% banking online . . .

This increase in commercial and financial transactions conducted online provides an environment where people are less wary of responding to emails or providing information via websites. It also provides opportunities

---

[258] *Husseyn* (1979) 67 Cr. App. R. 131. But cf. the position in relation to s.9(1)(a) burglary: *Attorney-General's References (Nos 1 and 2 of 1979)* [1980] Q.B. 180. See below, p.903.
[259] *Vinall* [2011] EWCA Crim 2652, [2012] 1 Cr. App. R. 29 at [19].
[260] D. Ormerod, *Smith and Hogan's Criminal Law*, 13th edn (Oxford: OUP, 2011), p.840. Cf. A.P. Simester et al., fn.161, pp.539–541.
[261] G. Kirwan and A. Power, *Cybercrime: The Psychology of Online Offenders* (Cambridge: CUP, 2013), pp.102–118.

for fraudsters to mimic legitimate organisations . . . there is an immediacy about online transactions which is also conducive to fraud . . .

Thirdly, it provides anonymity. Offenders are not only able to conceal their real identities, they are able to assume realistic looking alternative identities. Finally, the multi-jurisdictional nature of online fraud makes investigation and prosecution more difficult, particularly if relatively small amounts are involved."

Computer and internet fraud comes in many forms. For example, "advance fee frauds" (also known as "Nigerian mail frauds" or "419 schemes" (after the provision of the Nigerian Criminal Code criminalising such schemes), frequently target victims via email, suggesting that they may be entitled to obtain a financial or other benefit, but that, in order to receive this benefit, a sum of money has to be paid upfront. The benefit never materialises.[262] In the case of online dating 'scams', fraudsters pretend to form romantic attachments and then use the opportunity to defraud their victims of substantial sums of money, causing their victims to suffer what might be seen as a "double hit": "the loss of money as well as the loss of a relationship".[263] Large amounts of money may be stolen through "salami" methods, where by rounding up, or down, small amounts are diverted from accounts into the offender's account or, for example, by "trojan horse" methods where secret codes are hidden in somebody else's computer program.[264] Such offending may go on for years without detection and then only come to light through accident. To try to prevent or detect computer crime, companies may be told by security specialists to watch for staff living beyond their means, staff having drug or alcohol problems, or staff being unwilling to take holidays, change jobs or be promoted.[265]

Certainly, such advice ties in with classic studies on embezzlement such as that by Cressey. He discovered that much embezzlement occurred in situations where a trusted person found themselves with a financial problem which was non-shareable, but was in an occupation where his difficulties could be secretly resolved by violating his position of trust. The offender then felt able to rationalise and justify his behaviour to himself.[266]

The examples given should indicate two other features of offences involving fraud: that the amount of money involved, as with theft, may vary from small to huge and it is inevitable that much of the offending will remain hidden and not appear in the official statistics. According to such statistics there is far less offending of this nature than there is of theft. In the year ending September 2013, there were 201,035 fraud offences recorded by the police in England and Wales,[267] compared with 1,8850,983 total theft offences.[268] This 2012/13 figure for fraud represented an increase of 34 per cent on the

---

[262] Kirwan and Power, *Cybercrime: The Psychology of Online Offenders* (Cambridge: CUP, 2013), pp.116–118; J. Clough, *Principles of Cybercrime* (Cambridge: CUP, 2010), pp.187–188; R.G. Smith, M.N. Holmes and P. Kaufman, "Nigerian Advance Fee Fraud", Trends and Issues in Criminal Justice No.121 (Australian Institute of Criminology, 1996).

[263] M.T. Whitty and T. Buchanan, "The Online Romance Scam: A Serious Cybercrime" (2012) 15 *Cyberpsychology, Behavior and Social Networking* 181–183 at 181.

[264] A. Bequcai, *Computer Crime* (Aeco Publishers Inc., 1978); M. Levi, *Regulating Fraud* (London: Tavistock Publications, 1987), pp.37–41; J. Clough, fn.262 above, pp.192–194.

[265] R. Doswell and G.L. Simons, *Fraud and Abuse of IT Systems* (Manchester: National Computing Center, 1986).

[266] D.R. Cressey, *Other People's Money* (Glencoe: Free Press, 1953). Cressy's explanatory framework for financial fraud is known as the "Fraud Triangle". For a more recent consideration of the significance of the Fraud Triangle in relation to white-collar crime, see A. Schucter and M. Levi, "The Fraud Triangle Revisited" (2013) *Security Journal*, 1–24.

[267] ONS, *Crime in England and Wales, Year Ending September 2013* (2014), p.86. It should be noted that, since the Fraud Act 2006 came into force in 2007, fraud is defined differently for the purposes of recorded crime compared to previously. One might have expected this to lead to a higher rate of recorded fraud, due to the broader definition of the offence (see below). Following the National Statistician's *Review of Crime Statistics for England and Wales* in 2011, in 2013 changes were made to the presentation of fraud statistics, which now include offences recorded by Action Fraud, police recorded crime, CSEW and the National Fraud Intelligence Bureau (NFIB) figures. A clearer picture is likely to emerge once these new arrangements have matured: pp.85–88.

[268] ONS, *Crime in England and Wales, Year Ending September 2013* (2014), Appendix table A4.

previous year, but this may not necessarily be due to an increase in the volume of fraud offences (although it may be a contributing factor). Other possible contributing factors may be changes in the recording of fraud offences and greater numbers of victims reporting fraud in the wake of publicity in relation to the launch of Action Fraud.[269]

Given the secretive nature of fraud (the victim may never learn of the loss), reliable estimates about the level of offending are impossible to come by, although it would seem reasonable to conclude that more is left hidden than is the case with other property offences.[270] However, work has been done to estimate the financial losses involved in fraud. Levi's major study on fraud gathers together statistics from a variety of sources to conclude that "those data that are available show that in purely financial terms losses from fraud dwarf all other types of property crime".[271] As noted above, fraud resulted in direct losses of £12.98 billion in 2005.[272] Benefits fraud amounted to £0.9 billion a year in 2004/05, having more than halved since 2001 when it stood at £2 million,[273] whilst Customs and Excise fraud totalled around £5 billion in 2004/05, showing a drop of around £2 billion from the year 2001/02.[274] More recent and reportedly reliable figures from 2013 show that of the estimated £52 billion lost to the UK economy from fraud, £20.6 billion was to the public sector, £15.9 billion was to the private sector, £9.1 billion was to individuals and £147.3 million to the charity sector.[275]

Research has attempted to discover the prevalence of fraud offences compared to mainstream offences. The 2003 *Offending, Crime and Justice Survey* asked around 10,000 people if they had committed different types of offences in the past year. The results suggest that fraud is in fact slightly more prevalent than the more "mainstream" property offence of theft, although the difference is only marginal. This shows a clear discrepancy from the amount of fraud recorded in the official statistics. The survey also sought to establish how fraud links with mainstream offending, and attempted to establish how many mainstream offenders commit fraud offences and vice versa. The results were that those who commit fraud offences are significantly more likely to commit mainstream offences than other adults, with 16.1 per cent of those admitting to having committed fraud in the past 12 months also admitting that they had committed a theft offence in the same period.[276] Whilst more research is necessary in this area, one thing is clear: it is fundamentally flawed to conceive of the "crime problem" in terms of traditional street activities; it does contain within it the stereotypical working-class villain and his species of fraud, but it also contains the sophisticated frauds by "respectable", powerful members of society.

From a starting point of not being regarded as warranting criminal status, cases involving fraud

---

[269] ONS, *Crime in England and Wales, Year Ending September 2013* (2014), pp.85–86. Since April 2013, Action Fraud has been the UK national fraud reporting centre. When a crime is reported to Action Fraud, the complainant is given a crime reference number and the crime is referred to the National Fraud Intelligence Bureau (NFIB), run by the City of London Police, who provide the national policing lead for economic crime: http://www.actionfraud.police.uk/home [Accessed March 2014].

[270] See, for example, Association of Certified Fraud Examiners, *2012 Report to the Nations* (2012), available at http://www.acfe.com/uploadedFiles/ACFE_Website/Content/rttn/2012-report-to-nations.pdf [Accessed March 2014]; National Fraud Authority, *Annual Fraud Indicator* (2013), available at : https://www.gov.uk/government/uploads/system/uploads/attachment_data/file/206552/nfa-annual-fraud-indicator-2013.pdf [Accessed March 2014], p.3; M. Tunley, "Uncovering the Iceberg: Mandating the Measurement of Fraud in the United Kingdom" (2011) 39 Int. J. of Law, Crime & Justice 190–203.

[271] M. Levi, *Regulating Fraud* (London: Tavistock Publications, 1987), p.23.

[272] M. Levi and J. Burrows, "Measuring the Impact of Fraud in the UK" (2008) 48 Brit. J. Criminol. 293–318.

[273] D. Wilson et al., Home Office Online Report 09/06, *Fraud and Technology Crimes: Findings from the 2003/04 British Crime Survey and 2004 Offending, Crime and Justice Survey and Administrative Sources* (2006), p.11.

[274] D. Wilson et al., fn.273, p.13.

[275] National Fraud Authority, *Annual Fraud Indicator* (2013), figures 1 and 2 and pp.15–24, available at https://www.gov.uk/government/uploads/system/uploads/attachment_data/file/206552/nfa-annual-fraud-indicator-2013.pdf [Accessed March 2014].

[276] J. Allen et al., Home Office Online Report 34/05, *Fraud and Technology Crimes: Findings from the 2002/03 British Crime Survey and 2003 Offending, Crime and Justice Survey* (2005), p.10.

may well be regarded more seriously by the courts than those involving theft (perhaps because of the element of rational execution or betrayal of trust), although not as seriously as robbery or burglary. Fraud, for example, bears a higher maximum penalty than theft, i.e. 10 years rather than seven years. The Sentencing Guidelines Council has considered the relative seriousness of different kinds of fraud in preparing its sentencing guideline.[277]

One form of fraud which has become prevalent in recent years is often referred to as "identity theft". This involves using the personal information of another person to conduct financial transactions in that person's name, enabling the fraudster to obtain goods and services at no cost to themselves.[278] Other jurisdictions have enacted specific offences to catch such fraudsters, whilst in the United Kingdom it remains under the umbrella of the general offence of fraud. In the United States, for example, the Identity Theft Assumption and Deterrence Act was passed in 1998 at federal level, criminalising the use of another's personal data, with sentences ranging from three to 15 years' imprisonment, depending on the financial extent of the fraud.[279] The harm resulting from such offences is obviously financial, but Marron argues that it extends beyond the mere loss of money:

> "What the fear or prospect of identity theft appears to strike at is the capacity of individuals to sustain an ability to consume, to create and recreate their lives as a 'reflexive project of the self' and so sustain that personal freedom through which they are integrated as subjects and objects of government."[280]

It is also seen as a separate phenomenon for the reasons that rather than focusing efforts on finding out who commits these offences, blame is often laid at the door of the victims, who are accused of failing to protect themselves against the threat.[281] Whilst many of the "card-not-present" frauds can be classed as instances of identity theft, the actual prevalence of this type of fraud, in the absence of a separate offence, is not measured.

B. The Law Prior to the Fraud Act 2006

Whilst the protection of property by means of a law of theft (or larceny) has very early origins in the common law, the emergence of laws protecting those who parted with their property because of fraud or deceit was rather slower. The ruling spirit of "caveat emptor" made it inappropriate to use the criminal law in such instances. "[W]e are not to indict one for making a fool of another",[282] and similarly, "[It is] needless to provide severe laws for such mischiefs, against which common prudence and caution may be a sufficient security."[283]

Just as elsewhere in the law, however, the principle of "caveat emptor" was gradually eroded, so that by the time of the Theft Act 1968 distinct offences existed dependent upon the type of title obtained. If *ownership* passed by means of deception the offence was obtaining by false pretences. If

---

[277] Sentencing Guidelines Council, *Sentencing for Fraud—Statutory Offences: Definitive Guideline* (2009). Guidelines have recently been issued in respect of corporate offenders: Sentencing Council, *Fraud, Bribery and Money Laundering: Corporate Offenders: Definitive Guideline* (2014), effective from October 1, 2014.

[278] E. Finch, "What a Tangled Web We Weave: Identity theft and the Internet", in Y. Jewkes (ed.), *Dot.cons: Crime, Deviance, and Identity on the Internet* (Cullompton: Willan, 2003), pp.86–104.

[279] D. Marron, "Alter Reality: Governing the Risk of Identity Theft" (2008) 48 Brit. J. Criminol. 20–38 at 21; J. Clough, fn.262 above, pp.207–209.

[280] D. Marron, fn.279 above, p.23.

[281] D. Marron, fn.279 above, p.34.

[282] Per Holt CJ in *Jones* (1703) 91 Eng. Rep. 330.

[283] W. Hawkins, *Pleas of the Crown* 344, 6th edn (1788).

the defendant gained *possession* only, the offence was larceny by a trick. Not only did this cause difficulties in distinguishing the two but there were other separate offences as well, such as larceny by a servant, fraudulent conversion and embezzlement.

All of these were swept away by the reforms of 1968.

Criminal Law Revision Committee, Theft and Related Offences, Eighth Report (1966) Cmnd.2977, para.38:

"The sub-committee for a considerable time proposed that the general offence of theft should be made to cover the present offence of obtaining by false pretences under [the Larceny Act] 1916, s.32(1). It might seem appropriate to extend theft in this way in order to make it cover as many ways as possible of getting property dishonestly. But in the end the sub-committee gave up the idea (to the regret of some members), and the full committee agreed. In spite of its attractions, it seemed to the majority of the committee that the scheme would be unsatisfactory. Obtaining by false pretences is ordinarily thought of as different from theft, because in the former the owner in fact consents to part with his ownership; a bogus beggar is regarded as a rogue but not as a thief, and so are his less petty counterparts. To create a new offence of theft to include conduct which ordinary people would find difficult to regard as theft would be a mistake. The unnaturalness of including obtaining by false pretences in theft is emphasised by the difficulty of drafting a satisfactory definition to cover both kinds of conduct."

Following this, the Theft Acts 1968 and 1978 created eight offences of dishonestly obtaining something by deception:

1. obtaining property,[284]

2. obtaining a money transfer,[285]

3. obtaining a pecuniary advantage,[286]

4. procuring the execution of a valuable security,[287]

5. obtaining services,[288]

6. securing the remission of liability,[289]

7. inducing a creditor to wait for or to forgo payment,[290] and

8. obtaining an exemption from, or an abatement of, a liability.[291]

Over time, major problems emerged in relation to these deception offences.

First, it was necessary to prove that the deception *caused* the obtaining of the specified commodity. This caused immense difficulties. For instance, in one of the leading House of Lords' decisions, *Lambie*,[292] a defendant, who had exceeded her credit limit and knew the bank was trying to recover

---

[284] Theft Act 1968 s.15.
[285] Theft Act 1968 s.15A, inserted by Theft (Amendment) Act 1996.
[286] Theft Act 1968 s.16.
[287] Theft Act 1968 s.20(2).
[288] Theft Act 1978 s.1.
[289] Theft Act 1978 s.2(1)(a).
[290] Theft Act 1978 s.2(1)(b).
[291] Theft Act 1978 s.2(1)(c).
[292] *R. v Lambie (Shiralee Ann)* [1982] A.C. 449.

the credit card, used the card to purchase goods. It was tolerably clear that the shop assistant who accepted the credit card had little interest in the defendant's relationship with her bank. She knew the transaction would be honoured by the bank. That is the point of credit cards. Accordingly, it was difficult to see that the deception (the representation that the defendant has actual authority to use the card) caused the shop assistant to hand over the property. To prevent such credit card frauds the House of Lords was forced to adopt the tortuous reasoning that the shop assistant was deceived and for that reason handed over the property:

> "if she had been asked whether, had she known the respondent was acting dishonestly and, in truth, had no authority whatever from the bank to use the credit card in this way, she would have completed the transaction, only one answer is possible—no."

It was subsequently stated in the Court of Appeal that the court had "the gravest possible doubt" whether the supplier of goods in a credit card transaction was interested in the authority of the card-user:

> "suppliers of goods were generally concerned to ensure that they would receive payment when a credit card was issued, but there was room to doubt whether they were interested in how the holder got the card, provided that the transaction would be honoured."[293]

The decisions in *Lambie* and other similar cases generated much debate. A.T.H. Smith argued that their combined effect was to extend

> "the concept of deception beyond what it meant when the Theft Act was framed in 1968, to mean something much more like fraud . . . [W]hereas elsewhere in the criminal law the conduct objected to must be an 'operating and substantial cause' the courts are now saying that a man has been deceived when he has been told an untruth (verbally or by conduct) and where it may be assumed that he would have done otherwise had he known the truth."[294]

In other words, causation was reduced to the sine qua non level.

Secondly, the requirement that the deception be operative, that is, deceive someone, meant that machines could not be "deceived".[295] While this might not have been a particular problem in 1968 (other than in cases relating to vending machines, etc.), technological advances in a commercial world now dominated by credit cards, electronic transfers of money and the provision of goods or services through the internet and call centres meant that there were significant gaps in the law in relation to deceiving machines. Accordingly, the Law Commission proposed replacing the concept of deception with the requirement of a misrepresentation.

Law Commission, Report No.276, Fraud (2002), para.7.16:

"We now believe that [the misuse of credit cards and other payment instruments] would be covered in a more convincing and less artificial way if the concept of deception were replaced by that of misrepresentation. Since the merchant who accepts the card in payment does not care whether the defendant has authority to use it, it is debatable whether the merchant can be said to be *deceived*. It is clear from . . . *Lambie*, however, that by

---

[293] *Nabina* [2000] Crim. L.R. 481.
[294] "The Idea of Criminal Deception" [1982] Crim. L.R. 721.
[295] *Re Holmes* [2004] EWHC 2020; *Poland v Ulatowski* [2010] EWHC 2673 (Admin) at [30]–[32].

tendering the card the defendant is impliedly and falsely *representing* that he or she has authority to use it for the transaction in question. In our view that should suffice, even if the defendant knows that the representee is indifferent whether the representation is true. We have therefore concluded that this form of the new offence should be defined in terms of misrepresentation rather then deception."

Under this approach the focus is on the wrongdoing of the defendant rather than on whether the other person was induced to act in reliance on the misrepresentation. This approach has the advantage that it makes no difference whether the misrepresentation was directed at a person or a machine.

Thirdly, the various deception offences were over-specific with the result that specific offences were often wrongly charged. There was an enormous overlap between the offences—quite apart from the overlap, already discussed, with theft. Such blurring of offences was morally confusing in fair labelling terms and made it difficult for prosecutors to know which charge to select.

Fourthly, some of the offences were unduly complex: a lawyer's dream or nightmare, depending on one's point of view.

Finally, the sentencing maxima for the deception offences were haphazard. For instance, while s.15 carried a 10-year maximum penalty, s.16 (obtaining a pecuniary advantage by deception—for example, obtaining an overdraft or employment by deception) carried a maximum penalty of five years' imprisonment. Obtaining services by deception and evasion of liability by deception, contrary to ss.1 and 2 of the Theft Act 1978 respectively, also carried a five-year maximum penalty. Fair labelling involves encapsulating the wrongdoing involved and reflecting its seriousness by an appropriate level of punishment. The essence of the wrongdoing in all these deception offences was the same: the defendant was acting dishonestly and fraudulently. The particular ways or means of committing each type of fraud should not be relevant.

Accordingly, the Law Commission proposed abolition of all the deception offences and their replacement by a general offence of fraud along with one separate offence of obtaining services dishonestly.

Law Commission, Report No.276, Fraud (2002), paras 1.6–1.9:

"1.6 [The issue is] whether the introduction of a general fraud offence would improve the criminal law. We have come to the conclusion that it would . . .

(1) It should make the law more comprehensible to juries, especially in serious fraud trials. The charges which are currently employed in such trials are numerous, and none of them adequately describe or encapsulate the meaning of 'fraud'. The statutory offences are too specific to offer a general description of fraud; while the common law offence of conspiracy to defraud is so wide that it offers little guidance on the difference between fraudulent and lawful conduct . . .

(2) A general offence of fraud would be a useful tool in effective prosecutions. Specific offences are sometimes wrongly charged, in circumstances when another offence would have been more suitable. This can result in unjustified acquittals and costly appeals . . .

(3) Introducing a single crime of fraud would dramatically simplify the law of fraud. Clear, simple law is fairer than complicated, inaccessible law. If a citizen is contemplating activities which could amount to a crime, a clear, simple law gives better guidance on whether the conduct is criminal . . .

(4) A general offence of fraud would be aimed at encompassing fraud in all its forms. It would not focus on particular ways or means of committing frauds. Thus it should be better able to keep pace with developing technology.

1.7 In line with these recommendations, we recommend that the eight offences of deception created by the Theft Acts 1968–96 should be repealed and that the common law offence of conspiracy to defraud should be abolished. In their place we recommend the creation of two new statutory offences—one of fraud, and one of obtaining services dishonestly."

Of course, more radical options were possible. The Law Commission's proposed offences (enacted in the Fraud Act 2006) pre-suppose the existence of the remaining property offences such as theft, handling stolen goods and so on. Reform could have gone further and have introduced an even broader offence, such as a general offence of dishonesty. Such ideas are considered later in this chapter.

C. The Fraud Act 2006

Following the above recommendations by the Law Commission, the various deception offences cited above were all abolished by the Fraud Act 2006. In their place there is a new offence of fraud, supported by ancillary offences. There is also an independent offence of obtaining services dishonestly.

1. Fraud

Section 1 creates a new broad offence of fraud, punishable on conviction on indictment by a maximum of 10 years' imprisonment.[296] Sentencing guidelines have been issued in respect of this offence.[297]

Fraud Act 2006 s.1

"(1) A person is guilty of fraud if he is in breach of any of the sections listed in subsection (2) (which provide for different ways of committing the offence).
  (2) The sections are—

(a) section 2 (fraud by false representation),

(b) section 3 (fraud by failing to disclose information), and

(c) section 4 (fraud by abuse of position)."

Each of these three ways of committing the offence of fraud will be discussed in turn. As fraud by false representation is the broadest of these forms of committing the offence and is the one likely to be most frequently charged, those elements that are common to all three (dishonesty and intent to make a gain or cause loss) will be discussed in relation to this form of the offence.

(i) Fraud by false representation

Fraud Act 2006 s.2

"(1) A person is in breach of this section if he—

(a) dishonestly makes a false representation, and

(b) intends, by making the representation—

  (i) to make a gain for himself or another, or

---

[296] Section 1(3).
[297] Sentencing Guidelines Council, *Sentencing for Fraud—Statutory offences: Definitive Guideline* (2009).

(ii) to cause loss to another or to expose another to a risk of loss.

(2) A representation is false if—

(a) it is untrue or misleading, and

(b) the person making it knows that it is, or might be, untrue or misleading.

(3) 'Representation' means any representation as to fact or law, including a representation as to the state of mind of—

(a) the person making the representation, or

(b) any other person.

(4) A representation may be express or implied.
(5) For the purposes of this section a representation may be regarded as made if it (or anything implying it) is submitted in any form to any system or device designed to receive, convey or respond to communications (with or without human intervention)."

Under s.5 (discussed later) "gain" and "loss" extend only to gain and loss in money or other property.

The essence of this offence is telling lies for economic purposes. With the abolition of the requirement that there be a deception, there is no need to establish that anyone believed the lies or was induced to act in a certain way because of the lies. There is no need for the defendant to obtain any advantage (economic or otherwise). All that is required is that there is a dishonest intention to secure a gain or cause a loss. The offence thus adopts an inchoate model of liability. The emphasis is on the wrongdoing of the defendant.

David Ormerod, "The Fraud Act 2006—Criminalising Lying?" [2007] Crim. L.R. 193 at 196–197:

"This wholly inchoate offence appears to criminalise lying.
  Should lying be a sufficient basis for criminal liability? What is the wrong which D performs which warrants the criminal sanction? It is not one derived from intentionally harming V's interests directly—there need be no such harm. Similarly, it is not one of potentially damaging V's interests. The wrong seems to be the act of lying or misleading with intent to gain or cause loss; the harm might be construed as one of destabilising society's processes of property and financial transfers. Even if this is sufficient to warrant criminalisation, is it properly called fraud?"

(a) *Actus reus*

The actus reus of this form of the offence requires that there be a representation which is false.

1. Express or implied representations

Section 2(4) provides that a representation may be express or implied. Express representations are an obvious way of lying: for example, telling a purchaser that one is selling a diamond when it is, in fact, glass. The representation may be written, spoken, posted on a phishing website or sent by email.[298] In *McDermott*[299] the defendant was convicted of fraud when, having stolen clothing from a department store, he then returned the clothes and, representing that he had bought them, sought to recover a refund. In *Wenman*[300] the defendant told a complainant that his roof was in a poor state of repair and

---

[298] CPS, *The Fraud Act 2006; Legal Guidance, http://www.cps.gov.uk* (2008), p.6.
[299] *R. v McDermott (Joseph Mark)* [2008] EWCA Crim 1713.
[300] *R. v Wenman (Joseph William)* [2013] EWCA Crim 340. Cf. *R. v Davies (Tudor)* [2008] EWCA Crim 980, where contracts for

quoted him a total of £25,600 for repair works, in circumstances in which there was nothing basically wrong with the roof. In both of these cases there was a clear false representation.

No definition of an implied representation is given. In *United Arab Emirates v Allen*[301] it was suggested that "Implied representations are legal constructs intended to give effect to that which honest parties involved in a transaction would reasonably read into the conduct of the other". Under the law before the Fraud Act 2006, proof of a deception involved, inter alia, establishing that there was an untrue representation. The courts, after the Fraud Act 2006, will presumably draw on this established body of law as to the meaning of an implied representation. There are many established instances where the conduct of the defendant will be regarded as amounting to an implied representation:[302]

(a) Hotels: If one books into a hotel one is taken to be representing that one intends to pay the bill at the end of one's stay.[303]

(b) Restaurants: Ordering and eating a meal in a restaurant is a representation that one intends to pay for that meal. If during or after the meal one decides not to pay, then remaining at the table thereafter is a false representation that one still intends to pay.[304]

(c) Quotations:

R. v Silverman (1988) 86 Cr. App. R. 213 (Court of Appeal, Criminal Division)

The appellant charged two elderly sisters grossly excessive prices for work done to the central heating and wiring of their flat. They had trusted him to charge a fair price because of previous work done by him for their family. The appellant placed no pressure on them to accept his quotation and there was nothing wrong with the work done. He was charged and convicted under s.15 (the now abolished offence of obtaining property by deception). He appealed on the grounds, inter alia, that an excessively high quotation did not amount to a false representation and that the trial judge had erred in not putting his defence (that the sisters seemed happy with his work) to the jury in express terms.

WATKINS LJ:

"Mr Hopmeier, who appears here for the appellant, has argued, first, that the appellant made no representations to the complainants. He has not shrunk from conceding that the appellant was dishonest. He has submitted that the appellant quoted the sisters for the work to be done but that it was open to them either to accept or reject the quotation upon such advice as they might seek and perhaps in the light of tenders by others, and that the appellant was in much the same position as anyone else who is asked to quote for work to be done. He has argued that it is a dangerous concept to introduce into the criminal law that an excessively high quotation amounts to a false representation under section 15(1) of the Theft Act 1968. In certain circumstances that submission may we think be well founded. But whether a quotation amounts to false representation must depend upon the circumstances.

It seems clear to us that the complainants, far from being worldly wise, were unquestionably gullible. Having left their former home, they relied implicitly upon the word of the appellant about their requirements in their maisonette. In such circumstances of mutual trust, one party depending upon the other for fair and reasonable conduct, the criminal law may apply if one party takes dishonest advantage of the other by representing as a fair charge that which he but not the other knows is dishonestly excessive . . .

There was material for a finding that there had been a false representation although it is true that the appellant had said nothing at the time he made his representations to encourage the sisters to accept the quotations.

---

building work were solicited and cash deposits obtained, but the work was not done.

[301] *United Arab Emirates v. Allen* [2012] EWHC 1712 (Admin); [2012] 1 W.L.R. 3419 at [56].

[302] See further, A.T.H. Smith, *Property Offences* (London: Sweet & Maxwell, 1994), pp.472–480.

[303] *Harris* (1975) 62 Cr. App. R. 28.

[304] *DPP v Ray* [1974] A.C. 370.

He applied no pressure upon them, and apart from mentioning the actual prices to be charged was silent as to other matters that may have arisen for question in their minds . . .

Here the situation has been built up over a long period of time. It was a situation of mutual trust and the appellant's silence on any matter other than the sums to be charged were, we think, as eloquent as if he had said: 'What is more, I can say to you that we are going to get no more than a modest profit out of this.'

There is, we think, no foundation for the criticism of the judge in the first ground of appeal nor any substance in this ground in law . . .' [However, it was decided that the judge should have included D's defence 'worthless though it might have been in the minds of the jury' in the summing up]."

Appeal allowed

The implications of this decision are immense. In a free-market economy it is regarded as acceptable to maximise one's profits—in short, to make as big a profit as possible. Those making grossly inflated quotations had, in the past, only to contend with the risk of their quotation being rejected. Since this case the risk of criminal prosecution is a possibility. Again, we are dealing with dubious business practice being criminalised. Rather than continually extending the reaches of the criminal law, it would surely be better here for the victim to resort to civil remedies. More recently, in *Greig*[305] the defendant did £300 worth of gardening work for a 77-year-old man with mental health problems. Two cheques for a total of £5,000 signed by the man were paid into the defendant's bank account. A further cheque for £1,850 made payable to a co-defendant was returned unpaid by the bank. The Court of Appeal upheld the defendant's conviction for an offence of fraud by false representation under s.2. The amounts charged by Greig were so far removed from a reasonable charge that the jury were entitled to infer that a dishonest false representation had been made

Of course, "there may be different prices for the same type of work", and the Fraud Act does not criminalize all bad bargains.[306] It is important to stress that it is necessary to prove dishonesty before an inflated quotation could give rise to liability. It is highly unlikely that any jury would convict in cases of excessive quotations unless there were some very special circumstances as in *Silverman* (the taking advantage of a relationship of mutual trust) or *Greig* (the taking advantage of a vulnerable client).

(d) Cheques: Generally, handing over a signed cheque is an implied representation that the existing state of facts is such that, in the ordinary course of events, when the cheque is presented to the bank it will be honoured.[307] However, in *United Arab Emirates v Allen*[308] the defendant had obtained a mortgage from a bank, which was repayable by monthly instalments over 20 years. As security for this loan, she had provided the bank with an undated cheque in a sum approximately equal to the loan amount, which was to be presented for payment by the bank if she defaulted on the mortgage repayments. When the loan repayments were not met, the bank presented the cheque for payment, but it was not honoured because there were insufficient funds in the defendant's account. The Administrative Court refused to accept that in this case the defendant, when she provided the cheque, was making an implied representation that her current financial circumstances were such as to be able to say with confidence that, if the cheque was presented at any stage during the lifetime of the mortgage, it would, "in the ordinary course" be met. In this case, the bank had required the

---

305 *R. v Greig (Thomas Andrew)* [2010] EWCA Crim 1183.

306 This was recognised by the trial judge in *Greig* [2010] EWCA Crim 1183 at [14].

307 *R. v Gilmartin (Anthony)* [1983] Q.B. 953 p.962. *MPC v Charles* [1977] A.C. 177 at 182. In *R. v Hamilton (Winston)* (1991) 92 Cr. App. R. 54 it was held that presenting a signed withdrawal slip at the bank is a representation that the bank is indebted to the person to that amount.

308 *Allen* [2012] EWHC 1712 (Admin); [2012] 1 W.L.R. 3419. The defendant's conduct took place in the United Arab Emirates (UAE), where it is a criminal offence to issue an uncovered cheque and the UAE were seeking her extradition. Under the Extradition Act 2003 she could only be extradited if the conduct amounted to an offence under UK law punishable by 12 months or more detention or imprisonment.

cheque to be provided as security for the loan, in case the mortgage payments were not met at any stage during the 20 year lifetime of the loan.

(e) Cheque cards: The nature of the representation changes when one uses a cheque card to support a cheque. This is because the cheque is bound to be honoured by the bank if certain conditions have been fulfilled and, therefore, the representation made with respect to the cheque is in fact true.

The representation thus is not about the cheque but about the cheque card itself. Issuing a cheque supported by a cheque card is an implied representation by conduct that one has actual authority from the bank to use the card and to contract on behalf of the bank that it will honour the cheque.

(f) Credit and debit cards: Acceptance of a credit card gives rise to a contract between the acceptor and the card-issuing company under which the latter must honour the relevant voucher on presentation. Use of a credit card is thus an implied representation that one has actual authority from the card-issuing company:

1. to use the card to make contracts on behalf of that company; and

2. to bind the card-issuing company to honour the relevant voucher on presentation.

So, if a defendant uses a credit or debit card to purchase goods knowing that they lack authority to do so—because, for example, they are exceeding their credit limit or because the card is not theirs—there is a false representation. It is irrelevant that the trader will in fact be paid.[309]

(g) Insurance: "It is elementary law that a person applying for insurance is obliged to disclose all facts material to be known by the insurer".[310] An omission to disclose material facts on an application for insurance cover may amount to a false representation. For example, in *Martin*[311] it was held that the defendant's failure to inform motor insurers that he was a disqualified driver, when he was applying for car insurance, amounted to a false representation.

(h) Change of circumstances: If a representation, which was true when made, becomes untrue, the failure to reveal the change of circumstances may amount to a false representation. In *DPP v Ray*[312] the defendant ordered a meal in a restaurant with the intention of paying for it. He subsequently decided not to pay. It was held that by remaining at the table, without notifying the waiter of his changed intention, he was practising a deception that he still intended to pay. This would now be a false representation. In *Rai*,[313] the defendant applied for a council grant for a bathroom for his elderly mother. Before the work was done, his mother died. It was held that his failure to inform the council of the change of circumstances amounted to a deception and would now be a false representation. In these cases involving a change of circumstances, it could well be that there is a legal duty to disclose the change of circumstances. The defendant in *Rai* would have been under such a duty. In such cases, the prosecution has a choice whether to charge fraud by false representation or fraud by failing to disclose information (s.3).

It is interesting to compare the behaviour in all these cases with that required for theft. We saw

---

309 In *R. v Awosika (Oluwabunmi)* [2009] EWCA Crim 625 the defendant was convicted of fraud when she tried to purchase a Rolex watch with an unauthorized Amex card. Cf. *R. v Augunas (Darius)* [2013] EWCA Crim 2046, considered below at pp.879–880.

310 *R. v Martin (Derek Paul)* [2013] EWCA Crim 1986 at [8].

311 *Martin* [2013] EWCA Crim 1986 at [8].

312 *DPP v Ray* [1974] A.C. 370.

313 *R. v Rai (Thomas)* [2000] 1 Cr. App. R. 242.

earlier that the paradigmatic case of theft involves actions which are objectively inconsistent with the rights of the owner and thus accords with Fletcher's theory of manifest criminality.[314] Fraud, on the other hand, is more indicative of a theory of subjective liability: the actions of the defendant will tend to look innocent, but their state of mind renders them criminal.[315] However, as a result of the case of *Gomez*, this distinction is all but lost in cases where the false representation leads to the obtaining of property. Such cases, that have all the hallmarks of fraud, may be charged as theft under s.1. One suggestion (prior to the Fraud Act 2006) was that we should regard obtaining by deception as an aggravated form of theft in much the same way as robbery, the aggravating feature being "a feeling of intellectual vulnerability".[316] If this translates into a fear of being made a fool of and distrusting one's own judgment, it is hard to see why this particular feature should be singled out. After all, the employer who employs somebody who subsequently steals from them might feel similarly threatened but may not be able to point to any relevant false representation.

The decisions in *Rai* and *Ray* may be contrasted with the decision in *Allen*.[317] Here the Administrative Court rejected an argument that, after the mortgage advance had been made to the defendant she was under a continuing obligation to provide information about any later change in her financial circumstances, or that, by remaining silent about such a change, there was an implied continuing representation that she would be able to meet the mortgage repayments when they fell due.[318] It has been suggested that the outcome of this case might have been different if the loan had been payable by instalments and the defendant had, "like the defendant in *Rai*", allowed the bank "to confer a benefit on her after she knew that the situation had changed".[319]

Of course, the new offence of fraud is much broader than the old offence of obtaining property by deception. There will now be instances where nothing is obtained—and nothing appropriated—but the fraud offence is committed by an *intention* to make a gain or cause a loss.[320]

2. Fact or law including state of mind

Section 2(3) provides that a representation means

"any representation as to fact or law, including a representation as to the state of mind of—(a) the person making the representation, or (b) any other person."

The inclusion of a representation as to a state of mind is appropriate: the implied representation of the restaurant customer that they intend to pay is just as much a representation as the fact that they have sufficient money to pay. Under the old law, a deception was defined to include "the present intentions" of the person making the representation. This gave rise to some controversy as to whether this included statements of opinion. This problem is solved by the broader formulation in s.2(3) that what is required is a representation as to "the state of mind" of the representor or another person. Whether an opinion is held is a "state of mind". As a matter of logic, "any representation by a person

---

[314] Above, p.814.
[315] G.P. Fletcher, *Rethinking Criminal Law* (Boston: Little, Brown, 1978), p.118.
[316] S. Gardiner, "Appropriation in Theft: The Last Word?" (1993) 109 L.Q.R. 194 at 198.
[317] *Allen* [2012] EWHC 1712 (Admin), [2012] 1 W.L.R. 3419. Cf. *R. v Forrest (Nathan)* [2014] EWCA Crim 308.
[318] *Allen* [2012] EWHC 1712 (Admin) at [56].
[319] A.P. Simester et al., fn.161 above, p.618.
[320] For example, in *Idrees v DPP* [2011] EWHC 624 (Admin) the defendant, who had failed his driving theory test 15 times, procured another person to impersonate him to take the test. That person presented himself at the driving test centre on the relevant day, but was not allowed to take the test because he was identified as an imposter. Mr Idrees was convicted of fraud by false representation and his conviction was upheld by the Administrative Court.

about their state of mind can only be about their present (or past) state of mind. Their state of mind as to the future can only be a current perception."[321]

What is the position with advertising "puffs"? Some of these will be representations as to fact, for example, "our make-up will last longer than any others". Others will be representations as to opinion, for example "as good as a Rolex". Under the old law of deception, it was widely accepted that advertising "puffs" would not count as deceptions because potential victims would not be fooled by them. However, under the present law, such exaggerated advertising amounts to a representation either as to fact or as to the state of mind of the advertiser. It must be doubted whether such an expansion of the law is warranted. The CPS has stated:

"Prosecutors should bear in mind that the principle of *caveat emptor* applies and should consider whether civil proceedings or the regulatory regime that applies to advertising and other commercial activities might be more appropriate. Not every advertising puff should lead to criminal conviction but it is also the case that fraudsters prey on the vulnerable."[322]

3. Representations to machines

As seen earlier, a major problem with the old law was that because a machine has no mind, it cannot be deceived.[323] Section 2(5) makes it clear that a representation is made if it is "submitted in any form to any system or device designed to receive, convey or respond to communications (with or without human intervention)". Thus representations can be made to cash machines, internet service providers, automated call centres and so on.[324]

This provision is not unproblematic. It is not entirely clear when a representation is "submitted". Ormerod argues that a document could be regarded as submitted when the defendant saves typing on to the hard drive of a computer.[325] The alternative view, however (as he concedes),[326] is that, drawing an analogy with business contracts in e-commerce where the communications only have operative effect when received, "the time of acceptance is when the electronic message was received by the ISP's network". However, as only "submission" (and not receipt) is required, it would most likely be regarded as submitted as soon as it is sent. The CPS state that it is uncertain when a submission to a machine takes place: it could be when the card is pushed into the card reader, when the PIN number is typed, or when "enter" is pressed. In cases where the last stage has not been reached, they advise charging attempted theft.[327]

In many of these cases, however, the false representation made to a machine will result in the provision of a service and the Law Commission envisaged that such cases would usually be prosecuted as obtaining services dishonestly.[328] This offence is discussed below.

---

[321] *Allen* [2012] EWHC 1712 (Admin), [2012] 1 W.L.R. 3419 at [49]. Cf. *Voros v Hungary* [2012] EWHC 518 (Admin): in concluding a hire-purchase agreement in respect of a car, the defendant was making a false (and dishonest) representation about his current intentions when he stated that he would pay the instalments as they fell due, when he knew that the car was shortly to be seized to satisfy a debt owed to a third party.

[322] CPS, *The Fraud Act 2006: Legal Guidance* (2008), p.11.

[323] Cf. above, p.869, *Holmes* [2004] EWHC 2020 (Admin).

[324] e.g. *R. v Saunders (Gabrielle Yinka)* [2012] EWCA Crim 1380, [2012] 2 Cr. App. R. (S) 26: use of a laptop to make fraudulent online applications for credit card accounts.

[325] "The Fraud Act 2006—Criminalising Lying?" [2007] Crim. L.R. 193 at 200.

[326] D. Ormerod, *Smith and Hogan: Criminal Law*, 13th edn (Oxford: OUP, 2011), p.886.

[327] CPS, *The Fraud Act 2006: Legal Guidance* (2008), p.7.

[328] Law Commission Paper No.276, *Fraud* (2002), para.8.2, n.5.

4. False

Section 2(2) provides that a representation is false if it is untrue or misleading.

Whether a representation is true or not is a matter of fact. In many situations, however, a person may make a representation that is largely, but not wholly, true. If I say that my car, which I have driven for five years, has "never given me any trouble" when, in fact, I once had to replace a rear brake light, my representation is literally untrue. There is no requirement that the untrue representation be material or significant. However, in some cases a court may need to consider complex issues of civil law in order to determine whether a representation is true or false. In *Cornelius*[329] a solicitor had acted in eight property sale transactions and had provided bridging loans to the purchasers, which had been repaid out of the mortgage advances. As security for the bridging loans, the defendant required each purchaser to execute a declaration of trust in his favour. The issue was whether the defendant had made a false representation when he had provided a Certificate of Title stating that the property was free from "onerous encumbrances" and that he had no interest in the property as mortgagor. The Court of Appeal held that both of these representations were true. First, the trust deeds executed by the purchasers were not expressed to be by way of security or registered with HM Land Registry, and the defendant was not in actual possession of the property. In these circumstances, the mortgages took priority over the interests created by the trust deeds[330] and the mortgagee therefore

> "acquired a good and marketable title free from the interest created by the trust. Even if it could be described as an encumbrance (which is itself doubtful) it could not be described as an 'onerous' encumbrance."[331]

Secondly, the statement that the defendant had no interest in the property as mortgagor was also true. The word mortgagor was a technical legal term, meaning "the person who grants the mortgage".[332] In this case the mortgage had been granted not by the defendant, but by the registered proprietor. The Court of Appeal took the view that it would be wrong to interpret this technical term more widely, given that it was included in a standard form of Certificate.[333] As there was no false representation, the defendant could not be convicted of the s.2 offences.

It is important to stress that there must be a causative link between the false representation and the defendant's intention: the defendant must intend "by making the representation" to make a gain or cause loss.[334] So, if the untrue part of the representation relates to a peripheral matter which the defendant thinks will be of no importance to the other, they will not be liable. Also, of course, in cases where the untruth is trivial, dishonesty is unlikely to be established.

Whether a misrepresentation is "misleading" is more difficult. The Government, in enacting this legislation, stated that "misleading" meant "less than wholly true and capable of an interpretation to the detriment of the victim".[335] If I have just had my unreliable car serviced so that, for the moment, it is performing well and, on trying to sell it, I say: "This car is a really good runner", this is not an untrue statement: at the moment the car is running well. Whether, however, this statement represents that

---

[329]   *R. v Cornelius (Benjamin Jason)* [2012] EWCA Crim 500.
[330]   *Cornelius* [2012] EWCA Crim 500 at [28]–[29]. This is by virtue of the Land Registration Act 2002 s.29 and Sch.3: *Halifax plc v Curry Popeck* [2008] EWHC 1692 (Ch).
[331]   *Cornelius* [2012] EWCA Crim 500 at [30].
[332]   *Cornelius* [2012] EWCA Crim 500 at [33].
[333]   *Cornelius* [2012] EWCA Crim 500 at [25], relying on *Barclays Bank plc v Weeks, Legg and Dean* [1999] Q.B. 309 and *Midland Bank v Cox McQueen* [1999] P.N.L.R. 593. The Court refused to substitute a conviction for attempted fraud on the basis that he had dishonestly made a representation which, contrary to his belief, was in fact true.
[334]   *R. v Gilbert (Stephanie Rae)* [2012] EWCA Crim 2392 at [29].
[335]   Home Office, *Fraud Law Reform: Government Response to Consultations* (2004), para.19.

it has always (or usually) performed well or whether my statement is misleading is more difficult. It is unclear whether the representation must be misleading to the person to whom it is made or misleading to reasonable people. With the emphasis in fraud having shifted away from deception and the effect of the representation on the mind of the victim, it seems that what is required is that the representation be objectively misleading.

The fact that misrepresentations need only be misleading, coupled with the fact that the intention need only be to make a gain for another, can potentially lead to extraordinary results. If I write a reference for a student to obtain a job (a gain for them) and I gloss over their weaknesses and exaggerate their strengths thus creating a misleading picture as to their overall abilities, this is (subject to dishonesty) fraud. It is questionable whether it is appropriate that misleading statements should suffice to make a representation false. Arguably there is a moral distinction between the actions of a person who tells a clear lie and one who is "merely economical with the truth, allowing the hearer to infer facts for which he must take some responsibility".[336]

Stuart P. Green, Lying, Cheating and Stealing: A Moral Theory of White-Collar Crime (2006), pp.78–80:

"Merely misleading is less wrongful than lying because what I call the principle of *caveat auditor*, or 'listener beware', applies to cases of merely misleading but does not apply to lying. Like the principle of *caveat emptor*, which says that a buyer is responsible for assessing the quality of a purchase before buying, the principle of *caveat auditor* says that, in certain circumstances, a listener is responsible, or partly responsible, for ascertaining that a statement is true before believing it.

When A lies to B, A tells B that she herself believes what she is saying. As a result B is justified in putting her faith in A; B need not be on her guard or question A's veracity. If A is mistaken about her assertion, then she is wholly responsible for B's false belief. And if A's untrue statement has been intentional, it is A who is wholly to blame.

Merely misleading involves a very different dynamic. When A misleads B without making an assertion, she has not told B that she believes what she is saying is true (since what she is saying is neither true nor false). There is thus no warranty of truth that B could rely on. . . .

Lying and merely misleading can also be distinguished on the grounds that each tends to elicit a different set of 'emotive reactions', and cause a different set of harms, it its victims. A victim who is deceived by a non-lie feels foolish and embarrassed, presumably because he believes he has contributed to his own harm by drawing unwarranted inferences from misleading premises. By contrast, a victim of lies is much more likely to feel 'brutalised' . . . by some external force."

(b) *Mens rea*

The mens rea required for this form of the offence is threefold:

1. Knowledge that the representation is, or might be, untrue or misleading

The offence is committed not only where the defendant knows that they are making a representation that is untrue but also where they know it might be untrue or misleading. Knowledge includes "wilful blindness".[337]

R. v Augunas [2013] EWCA Crim 2046 at [9]

McCOMBE LJ:

"What is required is that the accused person knows that the representation is, or might be, misleading. It is not enough that a reasonable person might have known this; what matters is the accused person's actual knowledge. In

---

[336] D. Ormerod, *Smith and Hogan: Criminal Law*, 13th edn (Oxford: OUP, 2011), p.897.

[337] Cf. *Taylor's Central Garages (Exeter) v Roper* [1951] 2 T.L.R. 284.

our judgment, it is not good enough for the prosecutor to satisfy the jury that the accused ought to have appreciated that the representation made by him was or might be untrue or misleading, nor is it enough that the circumstances must have given rise to a reasonable suspicion that the representation was, or might be, untrue or misleading. Of course, if an accused person wilfully shuts his eyes to the obvious doubts as to the genuineness of the misrepresentation that he is making, then he knows that it might be untrue or misleading and he would be guilty of the offence."

Given that "misleading" is a vague and imprecise term, the potential net of criminal liability is being cast wide by requiring only that a defendant know that a representation might be misleading.

2. Dishonesty

As with theft, where the concept of appropriation is broad and colourless, the requirement of dishonesty will play a crucial role in this offence. The slightest lie for economic purposes satisfies the actus reus of the offence. It is left to the concept of dishonesty to determine which lies are criminal.

The partial definition of dishonesty contained in s.2 of the Theft Act 1968 does not apply to the offence of fraud. It is assumed that the test of dishonesty established in *Ghosh* will be applicable.[338] The position was the same with the deception offences prior to the Fraud Act 2006. In *Woolven*,[339] the defendant claimed that whilst ordinary people might have found his behaviour dishonest he did not think it was because he was trying to get the money for his employer (to whom he thought the money belonged). The Court of Appeal concluded that it was unnecessary to direct the jury in terms similar to those in s.2(1)(a) relating to a claim of right: a direction based on *Ghosh* was likely to say everything that was needed. This does not mean, however, that a *Ghosh* direction has to be given in every case. Indeed, in *Price*, it was held that it was both unnecessary and potentially misleading in the majority of cases to do so.[340] The direction must be given where the defendant "might have believed that what he is alleged to have done was in accordance with the ordinary person's idea of honesty".[341]

The Law Commission in its Consultation Paper[342] suggested that there should be a defence along the lines of s.2(1)(a) of the Theft Act 1968 where the defendant has, or believes that they have, a legal right to do what they do. In its final Report this recommendation was abandoned.

The Law Commission No.276, Fraud (2002), paras 7.66, 7.67, 7.69:

"7.66 We do not therefore recommend that a 'claim of right' should be a complete defence to the offence of fraud, nor do we recommend that 'belief in a claim of right' should be a complete defence. However, we believe that in the vast majority of such cases the requirements of *Ghosh* dishonesty will suffice to ensure that justice is done, and that the civil and criminal law are kept closely in line with each other.

7.67 The first limb of the *Ghosh* test requires the jury to consider, on an objective basis, whether the defendant's actions were dishonest. If the defendant may have believed that she had a legal right to act as she did, it will usually follow that the jury will be unable to conclude that they are sure that she was dishonest, on an objective basis . . .

7.69 We think it likely that using the *Ghosh* approach as a means of analysing cases of 'belief in a claim of right' would ensure that defendants who genuinely believe that they have a claim of right will be acquitted. However, it would not operate as an automatic and complete defence as it does to theft by reason of section 2(1)(a) of the Theft Act 1968. We believe that this is right, as a matter of policy, not only because we are seeking to ensure that the criminal law is not tied to the civil law, but also because there may be cases where a belief in a claim of right should not lead to an acquittal. For example a 'Robin Hood' defendant could seek to exploit legal 'loopholes' in order to redistribute property in a way, not amounting to theft, which she believes to be morally right, but which

---

[338] Home Office, *Fraud Law Reform: Government Response to Consultations* (2004), para.10.
[339] *R. v Woolven (Johnathan Robert)* (1983) 77 Cr. App. R. 231.
[340] *Price* (1990) 90 Cr. App. R. 409 at 411. Cf. *R. v Razoq (Adil)* [2012] EWCA Crim 674 at [81].
[341] *Price* (1990) 90 Cr. App. R. 409 at 411.
[342] Law Commission Consultation Paper No.155, *Fraud and Deception* (1999).

she knows most reasonable, honest people would consider dishonest. She may then argue that she genuinely believed that she had a legal right to act as she did, despite knowing that most reasonable, honest people would categorise her actions as dishonest. If there were a complete 'belief in a claim of right' defence, such a defendant would have to be acquitted. Under the *Ghosh* test, however, it would be for the jury to decide whether her exploitation of legal loopholes was in fact dishonest, on the ordinary standards of reasonable, honest people."

It is likely, however, that the concept of dishonesty in fraud will have a more important role than it had in the deception offences. With the deception offences the defendant had to practice a deception and obtain something as a result. Where a lie led to the obtaining of, say, property, it was difficult for the concept of dishonesty to have any role in cases other than a claim of right. Fraud is, however, a much broader offence. Nothing need be obtained. All that is required is an intention to make a gain (or cause a loss) and, as we shall see, "gain" includes "keeping what one has". So, for example, if one tells a charity collector with a tin on the street, "Sorry, but I have no loose change" (when one does have loose change), this satisfies all the other elements of the offence. It is a false representation made with a view to gain. In such cases, all the real work will be left to the concept of dishonesty to distinguish between harmless lies and the serious offence of fraud. Similarly, an undercover journalist (falsely representing their identity) could act with a view to exposing another and causing them a loss. Commenting on such cases, and rejecting a possible defence of public interest, the Law Commission said: "If no moral obloquy can attach to the defendant's conduct, the fact-finders are unlikely to be satisfied that it was dishonest."[343]

With theft, dishonesty performs a *positive* role. As seen, particularly after *Gomez* and *Hinks*, it is an inculpatory requirement. It is what can render otherwise innocent conduct criminal. With the offence of fraud, however, it has a *negative* or exculpatory role. As there must be a false representation, it is in fewer cases that the conduct would not automatically be regarded as dishonest. Accordingly, the Law Commission in its Consultation Paper[344] recommended abolishing the dishonesty requirement and replacing it with specific defences, for example, that the defendant believed that they were legally entitled to the property. However, in its final Report[345] the Law Commission was persuaded by the view of Tur that "what may constitute a just excuse is so context-dependent that exhaustive definition must necessarily limit the range of circumstances which might exist".[346] Accordingly, the requirement of dishonesty as a negative requirement for fraud offences remains.

3. Intention to make gain or cause loss

For the repealed deception offences, causation had to be established. The deception had to cause the other to part with property, etc. One of the reasons for the enactment of the new offence of fraud was to dispense with this requirement and all its associated problems. Accordingly, it is not necessary that the victim believe the false representation. However, s.2(1)(b) requires that the defendant "intends, *by making the representation*" to make a gain for themselves or another, to cause a loss to another, or to expose another to a risk of loss.[347] So, if a street trader advertises a T-shirt "As worn by Michael Jackson" they would not expect anyone actually to believe such a claim which is probably being made simply to attract attention. They would not intend that *by making that representation* they would make a gain. This provision is the distinguishing feature of the offence of fraud and is what transforms a lie into a criminal offence.

---

343   Law Commission Paper No.276, *Fraud* (2002), para.7.77.
344   Law Commission Consultation Paper No.155, *Fraud and Deception* (1999), paras 7.39–7.53.
345   Law Commission Paper No.276, *Fraud* (2002).
346   "Dishonesty and the Jury", in J. Griffiths (ed.), *Philosophy and Practice* (1985), p.75.
347   *Gilbert* [2012] EWCA Crim 2392.

Fraud Act 2006 s.5

"(1) The references to gain and loss in sections 2 to 4 are to be read in accordance with this section.
(2) 'Gain' and 'loss'—

(a) extend only to gain or loss in money or other property;

(b) include any such gain or loss whether temporary or permanent;

and 'property' means any property whether real or personal (including things in action and other intangible property).
(3) 'Gain' includes a gain by keeping what one has, as well as a gain by getting what one does not have.
(4) 'Loss' includes a loss by not getting what one might get, as well as a loss by parting with what one has."

This is extremely broad.[348] If a defendant makes a false representation so that a rich person will take them to an expensive restaurant, they intend to make a gain for themselves of the food. It is clear mislabelling to describe such conduct as fraud—and highly dubious whether such actions should be criminalised at all.

In 2009 a defendant was prosecuted for fraud when she used a false address to apply for a place for her son at a popular primary school. The prosecution was abandoned because she had not intended to make a gain or cause a loss in money or other property. A school place is not "money or other property".[349]

It is not necessary that the defendant intend any gain for themselves. It is enough that they intend a gain for another, intend to cause a loss to another, or to expose another to a risk of loss. For example, if a defendant spreads malicious rumours that their enemy's company is in dire straits hoping that the value of its shares will fall, they have acted with intent to cause loss—even though they have no intention to buy the shares at the reduced price.

Unlike theft, it is not necessary that the defendant intend to make a permanent gain. So, if a student falsely tells me that this book is currently out-of-stock and not available in the library and asks to borrow the book from me for a few hours, the elements of the offence (subject to dishonesty) are made out. Again, it must be questioned whether such "white lies" deserve criminalisation.

Law Commission No.276, Fraud (2002), paras 7.54–7.55:

"7.54 Arguably the full offence should not be committed unless the defendant has succeeded in *actually* causing a loss or making a gain: where the defendant has acted with *intent* to cause loss or make a gain, but that intent has been frustrated, a conviction of attempt would adequately reflect the criminality of the defendant's conduct. It may sometimes be debatable, however, whether a loss has actually been caused or a gain made, whilst it is clear beyond doubt that the defendant *intended* to bring about one or both of these outcomes. We think it would be unfortunate if, in such a case, it had to be determined whether there had in fact been gain or loss within the meaning of the Act, when that question had little bearing on the gravity of the defendant's conduct or the appropriate sentence . . . [I]t should be sufficient if the defendant acts *with intent* to make a gain or to cause a loss.

7.55 In the light of this conclusion we have considered whether it should be possible to prosecute for an *attempt* to commit the new offence . . . Under our recommendations there would be no need to charge an attempt in these cases, because the defendant would be guilty of the full offence."

The approach shifts the focus away from the "victim" and effectively adopts an inchoate model of liability with the emphasis on the "anti-social" conduct of the defendant. One way of rationalising this

---

[348] See e.g. *Martin* [2013] EWCA Crim 1986 (granting of contract of insurance a gain for the purposes of s.5 because it conferred valuable rights which were of monetary value).

[349] *The Guardian*, July 4, 2009; C. Monaghan, "To Prosecute or Not to Prosecute? A Reconsideration of the Over-zealous Prosecution of Parents under the Fraud Act 2006" (2010) 74 J.C.L. 259–278.

approach is that liability should not depend on whether the so-called victims suffer harm to their "net wealth" but on whether their autonomy to direct their assets, without being influenced by another's fraud, has been infringed.[350] The interest the law is seeking to protect is commercial freedom and the defendant is seen as threatening this interest.

(ii) Fraud by failing to disclose information

Fraud Act 2006 s.3

"A person is in breach of this section if he—

  (a) dishonestly fails to disclose to another person information which he is under a legal duty to disclose, and

  (b) intends, by failing to disclose the information—

      (i) to make a gain for himself or another, or
      (ii) to cause loss to another or to expose another to a risk of loss."

There is a significant overlap between this method of committing fraud and that under s.2. In many cases where a defendant breaches a legal duty to disclose information, they can be regarded as making a false implied representation.

There must be a legal duty to disclose. The Law Commission Report and the Home Office Consultation both proposed that this form of the offence should also extend to cases where there is no legal duty to disclose but where three conditions were satisfied:

"The information is of a kind which the person trusts the defendant to disclose to him;
The defendant knows the other person is trusting him to disclose information or is 'aware that he might be'; and
Any reasonable person would expect the defendant to disclose the information to the other person."[351]

This additional proposal was eventually abandoned by the Government for the following reasons:

Home Office, Fraud Law Reform: Government Response to Consultations (2004), paras 22–25:

"22. The point of controversy was the proposal that this offence should extend to situations where a person dishonestly fails to disclose information which he is under no legal duty to disclose, but which the other person trusts him to disclose. There was substantial opposition to this proposal. One of the main arguments was that this would intrude on the caveat emptor principle, and create a conflict between civil and criminal law, in that it would become criminal not to provide information which you are entitled to withhold under civil law . . . [T]his result would be 'bizarre' . . .

23. The other main objection was the lack of certainty . . . [I]t will be necessary to make a judgement in each cases as to whether the 'victim' is trusting the defendant to disclose the information. The example of a person selling a car who does not reveal that he has successfully camouflaged some damage to the bodywork with filler is one example presented to us of a situation where it is arguable that the purchaser trusts a disclosure to be made, but consensus is lacking and it will be hard to say where the line should be drawn. It was pointed out that this is a problem not only for juries but for police in deciding what to investigate. It was argued that the conduct . . . may be dishonest and morally reprehensible, but that does not mean it should be criminal.

---

[350] cf. G.P. Fletcher, *Rethinking Criminal Law* (Boston: little, Brown, 1978), pp.51–57.
[351] Home Office, Fraud Law Reform: Consultation on Proposals for Legislation (2004), para.20.

24. Others argued against this that if the offence is restricted to situations where there is already a legal duty to provide information . . . criminal prosecutions may then hinge on civil arguments about whether the duty exists . . .

25. . . . [It] should not be fraud unless (inter alia) a legal duty is breached. In particular, we share concerns over extending the criminal law into areas where something may be morally dubious, but not clearly seen as criminal."

(a) *Actus reus*

The defendant must fail to disclose to another person information which they are under a legal duty to disclose.

The legal duty may arise from statute, from the express or implied terms of a contract,[352] from the custom of a particular trade or market,[353] or from the existence of a fiduciary relationship between the parties.[354]

For example, in *Rasoq*[355] a hospital doctor had been excluded and suspended from work pending disciplinary proceedings. He then signed up with a number of locum agencies to obtain work as a physician, but did not disclose his exclusion. The Court of Appeal held that the evidence was "over-whelming" that the defendant was legally bound to inform these agencies of his exclusion.[356] Section 3 could also have been charged in the case of *Twaite*,[357] where an RAF officer obtained service family accommodation by falsely stating on a form that he was married, and lived there for almost a year, in breach of service regulations and without saying anything to the RAF, before he finally did get married. Whether there is a legal duty to disclose is not always a clear-cut matter and it is likely that the criminal courts will have to grapple with intricate questions of civil law. For example, in certain areas of social security law there has been a dispute as to the nature of any obligation to disclose matters relating to entitlement to benefit, there being controversy over whether certain obligations to disclose are moral or legal obligations.[358]

As with theft, the relationship between the civil and criminal law can be problematic.

David Ormerod, "The Fraud Act 2006—Criminalising Lying?" [2007] Crim. L.R. 193 at 206:

"In practice, it is unclear whether s.3 will prove workable. Which will be worse: the criminal courts shunning the civil law, as they are wont to do, leaving these offences lacking in solid foundation or, becoming unduly burdened by the complexity of civil law questions, particularly as to some of the less explicit duties such as the

---

[352] For example: contracts of insurance are contracts of 'utmost good faith' and those taking out insurance must disclose material facts to the insurer (*Martin* [2013] EWCA Crim 1986); an employee may be contractually required to disclose criminal convictions, or to give an undertaking that they are not working elsewhere (*R. v Daley (Patricia Rose)* [2010] EWCA Crim 2193).

[353] cf. *Forrest* [2014] EWCA Crim 308, where the CA rejected an assertion that it was the usage or custom of the mortgage lending market that applicants for mortgages make full disclosure of matters relevant to the bargain beyond the information sought in the mortgage application form itself.

[354] Home Office, *Fraud Law Reform: Consultation on Proposals for Legislation* (2004), para.20. For examples of cases in which it was held that, on the facts, no legal duty to disclose information arose, see *Allen* [2012] EWHC 1712 (Admin), [2012] 1 W.L.R. 3419 at [58]; *Forrest* [2014] EWCA Crim 308,

[355] *R. v Razoq (Adil)* [2012] EWCA Crim 674.

[356] *Razoq* [2012] EWCA Crim 674 at [83]. The defendant was also convicted of s.2 offences in respect of lies made on application forms.

[357] *R. v Twaite (Timothy)* [2010] EWCA Crim 2973, [2011] 1 W.L.R. 1125. The defendant's conviction for fraud by false representation was quashed because he had been convicted on the wrong basis.

[358] M. Rowland and R. White, *Social Security Legislation 2013. Vol.III, Administration, Adjudication and the European Dimension*, 14th edn (London: Sweet & Maxwell, 2013), para.1.93. Cf. *B v Secretary of State for Work and Pensions* [2005] EWCA Civ 929.

expectations in a particular trade or custom? Added to the task of identifying the relevant duty, and determining its scope, is the complexity of deciding whether D has complied with the duty: a further civil law question. Unless the Crown can show that D has not fully complied, there may be difficulties. Where the dispute is whether D's partial disclosure of the relevant information is sufficient, is this a matter of law for the judge, or for the jury?"

(b) *Mens rea*

The defendant must act dishonestly and intend to make a gain for themselves or another, or to cause loss to another or to expose another to a risk of loss. These requirements are discussed above.[359]

The section is silent as to whether the defendant must know (or believe or suspect) that they are under a legal duty to disclose. Presumably, if the defendant has no idea that they are under a legal duty to disclose, dishonesty would be unlikely to be established.

(iii) Fraud by Abuse of Position

Fraud Act 2006 s.4

"(1) A person is in breach of this section if he—

(a) occupies a position in which he is expected to safeguard, or not to act against, the financial interests of another person,

(b) dishonestly abuses that position, and

(c) intends, by means of the abuse of that position—

(i) to make a gain for himself or another, or

(ii) to cause loss to another or to expose another to a risk of loss.

(2) A person may be regarded as having abused his position even though his conduct consisted of an omission rather than an act."

The Law Commission had proposed that secrecy be an element of this offence. This proposal was abandoned by the Government.

Home Office, Fraud Law Reform: Government Response to Consultations (2004), para.28:

"[S]ecrecy is a 'hallmark' of fraud, as one of our respondents put it. It was accepted that an open abuse is no less reprehensible than a secret abuse, but while an open abuse might be rightly subject to sanction, the argument was that it should not fall under the criminal law of fraud. A secrecy requirement helps separate fraud from other offences (eg blackmail) and matters better dealt with under civil law. However some were concerned that, while secrecy would almost invariably be part of the offending behaviour in practice, it was difficult to define and represented an unnecessary complication, which could lead to technical arguments in court. There could be arguments about whether there had been an intention to disclose in the future, and about whether the employer knew what was going on, if a surveillance operation was in place. It was argued that the mischief lay in the dishonest abuse and that the value-laden concepts of 'dishonesty' and 'abuse' were sufficient in themselves to set the parameters for the offence."

---

[359] Above, pp.880–883.

(a) *Actus reus*

There must be an abuse of a position of trust.

1. Abuse

No definition of "abuse" is provided other than that the conduct may consist of an omission rather than an act. So, for example, there could be an abuse where an employee omits to take up a chance of a crucial contract, intending to enable an associate to pick up the contract instead.[360] This section has been used to prosecute employees who steal from their employers by writing out company cheques in their own favour,[361] or divert money held in client accounts,[362] or which is due to their employer[363] into their own bank accounts. Obviously, the mens rea requirement that the abuse be dishonest and with the intention of making a gain or causing a loss will limit what can count as an abuse. So, the lazy or incompetent employee who abuses their position (in ordinary language terms) by not bothering to make required phone calls to secure customers will not fall within this provision unless the failure to make the calls is considered dishonest and there was the requisite intent to make a gain or cause a loss. It is likely that all the real work here will be done by the mens rea requirement and so, like appropriation, "abuse" will become a neutral or colourless concept always satisfied if the requisite mens rea is present.

2. Position

The statute does not use the phrase "position of trust". Instead, the requisite position is defined as existing when a person "occupies a position in which he is expected to safeguard, or not to act against, the financial interests of another person".

The Law Commission No.276, Fraud (2002), paras 7.37, 7.38:

"7.37 The essence of the kind of relationship which in our view should be a prerequisite of this form of the offence is that the victim has voluntarily put the defendant in a privileged position, by virtue of which the defendant is expected to safeguard the victim's financial interests or given power to damage those interests. Such an expectation to safeguard or power to damage may arise, for example, because the defendant is given authority to exercise a discretion on the victim's behalf, or is given access to the victim's assets, premises, equipment or customers. In these cases the defendant does not need to enlist the victim's *further* co-operation in order to secure the desired result, because the necessary co-operation has been given in advance.

7.38 The necessary relationship will be present between trustee and beneficiary, director and company, professional person and client, agent and principal, employee and employer, or between partners. It may arise otherwise, for example within a family, or in the context of voluntary work, or in any context where the parties are not at arm's length. In nearly all cases where it arises, it will be recognised by the civil law as importing fiduciary duties, and any relationship that is so recognised will suffice. We see no reason, however, why the existence of such duties should be essential. This does not of course mean that it would be entirely a matter for the fact-finders whether the necessary relationship exists. The question whether the particular facts alleged can properly be described as giving rise to that relationship will be an issue capable of being ruled upon by the judge and, if the case goes to the jury, of being the subject of directions."

Section 4 extends beyond fiduciary duties[364] and, as stated in the above extract, may arise in family

---

[360] Law Commission Paper No.276, *Fraud* (2002), para.7.39.
[361] *R. v Moss (Pamela Jane)* [2013] EWCA Crim 1554.
[362] *R. v Turner (Ruth Louise)* [2013] EWCA Crim 1206. Cf. *R. v Woods (Natalie Frances)* [2011] EWCA Crim 1305.
[363] Cf. *Knowles* [2013] EWCA Crim 646.
[364] For further discussion of the circumstances in which a fiduciary relationship arises, see A. Arlidge, A. Milne and P. Springer, *Arlidge and Parry on Fraud*, 4th edn (London: Sweet & Maxwell, 2014), paras 6-009–6-043.

and other voluntary arrangements. Such matters, extending beyond the ambit of the civil law, will create immense difficulties for judges and juries and "open up the possibility that all sorts of trivial civil law contractual disputes become the subject of prosecution".[365]

The Crown Prosecution Service, The Fraud Act 2006: Legal Guidance (2008), pp.16–17:

"Examples of the type of conduct that would give rise to a charge under Section 4 are:

- an employee of a software company who uses his position to clone software products with the intention of selling the products on his own behalf;

- where a person is employed to care for an elderly or disabled person and has access to that person's bank account but abuses that position by removing funds for his own personal use.[366] (This may also be theft . . .)

- an Attorney who removes money from the grantor's accounts for his own use. The Power of Attorney allows him to do so but when excessive this will be capable of being an offence under Section 4;

- an employee who fails to take up the chance of a crucial contract in order that an associate or rival company can take it up instead;

- an employee who abuses his position in order to grant contracts or discounts to friends, relatives and associates;[367]

- a waiter who sells his own bottles of wine passing them off as belonging to the restaurant; . . .

- a tradesman who helps an elderly person with odd jobs, gains influence over that person and removes money from their account. (This may also be theft . . .)

- the person entrusted to purchase lottery tickets on behalf of others . . . , this will probably be theft as well."

The position must be one in which the defendant is *expected* to safeguard, etc. the financial interests of another person. Expected by whom? The particular victim? The defendant? The reasonable person? The courts are most likely to adopt an objective interpretation and ask whether reasonable people would expect the defendant to act in a particular way.[368]

(b) *Mens rea*

The defendant must dishonestly abuse the position and must intend, through that abuse, to make a gain for herself or another or to cause a loss to another, or to expose another to a risk of loss. These matters were discussed earlier.[369]

There is no express requirement that the defendant must know that they occupy a position of trust whereby they are expected to safeguard, etc. the financial interests of another person. Liability on this

---

[365] Ormerod, *Smith and Hogan: Criminal Law*, 13th edn (2011), p.907. For discussion re the rationale of the s.4 offence, see J. Collins, "Fraud by Abuse of Position: Theorising Section 4 of the Fraud Act 2006" [2011] Crim. L.R. 513–523.

[366] *Marshall* [2009] EWCA Crim 2076.

[367] cf. *R. v Gale (Mark Diego)* [2008] EWCA Crim 1344 (defendant used his position as an office manager for DHL to send a large crate from Heathrow to New York, certifying it as "known cargo" so that it avoided airport screening. In fact, the crate contained Khat, an illegal drug in the United States).

[368] Ormerod, *Smith and Hogan: Criminal Law*, 13th edn (2011), p.908.

[369] Above, pp.880–883.

issue would appear to be strict. However, it will be very difficult to establish dishonesty without such knowledge.

2. Offences ancillary to fraud

The Fraud Act 2006 creates two ancillary offences to fraud. First, there is the offence of possession of articles for use in frauds[370] (punishable with a maximum of five years' imprisonment). Secondly, there is the offence of making or supplying articles for use in frauds[371] (punishable with a maximum of 10 years' imprisonment).

3. Obtaining services dishonestly

Under the Theft Act 1978 s.1, it was an offence to obtain services by deception. This covered situations where someone was deceived into providing a service rather than parting with property. For example, someone could be induced to mow a lawn or provide a ride in a taxi by being falsely told they would be paid. Owing to the problems involved with the concept of "deception", particularly in relation to machines, this offence is now replaced by a new offence of obtaining services dishonestly.

Fraud Act 2006 s.11

"(1) A person is guilty of an offence under this section if he obtains services for himself or another—

(a) by a dishonest act, and

(b) in breach of subsection (2).

(2) A person obtains services in breach of this subsection if—

(a) they are made available on the basis that payment has been, is being or will be made for or in respect of them,

(b) he obtains them without any payment having been made for or in respect of them or without payment having been made in full, and

(c) when he obtains them, he knows—

(i) that they are being made available on the basis described in paragraph (a), or

(ii) that they might be,

but intends that payment will not be made, or will not be made in full."

The offence is punishable by a maximum of 10 years' imprisonment.[372] The CPS has indicated that on average between 305 and 446 charges per year are brought for this offence.[373]

---

[370] Section 6.
[371] Section 7.
[372] Section 11(3).
[373] Ministry of Justice, *Post-legislative Assessment of the Fraud Act 2006*, cm.8372 (2012), para.25.

The Law Commission No.276, Fraud (2002), paras 8.1–8.2:

"8.1 Because it requires proof of deception, the offence under section 1 of the 1978 Act fails to catch a person who succeeds in obtaining a service dishonestly but without deceiving anyone. This may happen in various ways . . .

(2) The service may not be provided for the defendant *personally*, but for anyone who is there to receive it. For example, the defendant climbs over the fence of a football ground and watches the match without paying the admission charge.

(3) The service may not be provided directly by *people* at all, but through a machine. For example, the defendant downloads, via the internet, software or data for which a charge is made, or which is available only to those within a certain category of person who have paid to be included within that category, by giving false credit card or identification details; or receives satellite television transmissions by using an unauthorised validation card in a decoder.[374]

(4) Some cases are a hybrid of types (2) and (3). For example, the defendant gives false credit card details to an automated booking system, or tenders a forged or stolen credit card to an electronic vending machine, and thus obtains a ticket for a journey or entertainment. There is no deception of the booking system (because it is not a person), nor of the staff who check the tickets of the passengers or audience (because the staff are only interested in whether each person has a ticket, not how they got it)."

Many of the examples provided in this extract would fall under the new offence of fraud (by false representation). The defendant is making a false representation (for example, false credit card details) and is thereby obtaining a service. The Law Commission felt, however, that the new offence was necessary to cover all such cases of obtaining services whether false information was provided or not.

The Law Commission No.276, Fraud (2002), paras 8.4–8.5:

"8.4 . . . We are persuaded that we should tackle the problem head on . . . [W]here a person dishonestly obtains a service by giving false information to a machine, the gravamen of that person's conduct is not the provision of the false information but the taking of a valuable benefit without paying for it.

8.5 Suppose, for example, that an internet website offers valuable information to subscribers, who are supposed to gain access to the information by giving their password. If a non-subscriber dishonestly downloads the information, it hardly matters whether she does so by giving the password of a genuine subscriber (and thus impliedly representing herself to be that subscriber) or by somehow bypassing the password screen altogether. To distinguish between these two situations would be like distinguishing between the person who puts a foreign coin into a vending machine and the one who gets at the contents by opening up the machine with a screwdriver, on the basis that the former makes a 'misrepresentation' to the machine (that the coin is legal tender) whereas the latter does not. This would be absurd. Both are guilty of stealing the contents. Equally, in our view, a person who 'steals' a service should be guilty of an offence, whether it is obtained by providing false information or in any other way."

Recognising the overlap with fraud, the Law Commission stated it "would expect prosecutors to use [the offence of obtaining services dishonestly] against defendants who have obtained services from machines, even if such defendants have done so by providing false information and might arguably be guilty of the fraud offence as well."[375]

---

[374] cf. *Mikolajczak v Poland* [2013] EWHC 432 (Admin), where the defendant had used the telephone numbers of three other people to obtain credit on his SIM card and had then made calls, which were charged to these three people. The conduct pre-dated the Fraud Act 2006, but the Administrative Court appeared to accept that it would now amount to an offence under s.11 (at [9]).

[375] At para.8.2, n.5.

(i) Actus reus

(a) *Act*

The requirement that there be an "act" is designed to ensure that the offence cannot be committed by omission alone. So, if services were not requested there is no offence to refuse payment.[376] The Law Commission give the example of a person who innocently happened to be on a boat and, despite hearing an announcement that anyone who had not paid for the next trip should disembark, remained on the boat and received a free ride. Such a person would not come within the ambit of the offence.[377]

(b) *Obtains*

Unlike the general offence of fraud, this offence is not inchoate in character. An actual obtaining of the service is required. Causation must be established.

(c) *Services*

"Services" is undefined other than that it must be something that is made available on the basis that it has been, is being, or will be, paid for. Any act done on the understanding that it will be paid for amounts to a service. For example, in *Widdowson*,[378] it was held that obtaining a van on hire-purchase was obtaining services.

The Crown Prosecution Service, The Fraud Act 2006 Legal Guidance (2008), p.25:

"Section 11 will cover circumstances where the Defendant:

- obtains chargeable data or software over the internet without paying;
- orders a meal in a restaurant knowing he has no means to pay;
- attaches a decoder to his TV to enable him to access chargeable satellite services without paying;
- uses the services of a members' club without paying and without being a member."

It is irrelevant that the service is obtained pursuant to an illegal or otherwise unenforceable contract. So, for example, a man who, without intending to pay, induces a prostitute to provide sexual services is liable even though the contract is illegal and unenforceable.[379]

What is the position if the services amount to a criminal offence? Under the Theft Act 1978, "services" were defined as involving the conferring of a "benefit".[380] No such requirement is specified here. Accordingly, it could be argued that if a 17-year-old dishonestly induces another into tattooing them, there would be liability. Under the 1978 Act, it was likely that there would be no liability is such a scenario because the offence in question (under the Tattooing of Minors Act 1969) was designed to protect them and so there would be no benefit to them.[381] The better view, however, is that there

---

[376] CPS, *The Fraud Act 2006: Legal Guidance* (2008), p.24.
[377] At para.8.11. It could, however, be argued that deliberately remaining on someone else's boat after hearing the announcement and thus knowingly choosing to receive a free ride constitutes an "act".
[378] *R. v Widdowson (Stanley)* (1986) 82 Cr. App. R. 314.
[379] Law Commission Paper No.276, *Fraud* (2002), para.7.53.
[380] Section 1(2).
[381] J.C. Smith, *The Law of Theft*, 8th edn (London: Lexis Nexis, 1997), p.133.

should be no liability in such cases. For example, if a gangster induces a "hit-man" to kill another by falsely promising payment, it would be absurd to assert that the gangster obtained services dishonestly—quite apart from the obvious point that the gangster would be guilty of far more serious offences. The purpose of this offence is to protect persons from wasting their labour which, like property, has intrinsic economic value. It is not the purpose of the law to protect those, like the "hit-man", who devote their labour and time to the commission of criminal offences.

(d) *Without payment*

The section only applies to those services induced on the understanding that they will be paid for. Thus the more effective one's lies, the less the chance of liability here. If one's dishonesty is so convincing that a service is provided free, there is no liability.

What is meant by "paid for" here? One view is that it extends to recompense in forms other than money.[382] The better view is that the criminal law should not extend its reach into non-commercial, perhaps purely social, transactions, such as where a person induces another into fixing a broken tap by falsely stating that, in return, dinner will be cooked for the tap-mender.

One of the examples given in the Law Commission extract above of when this offence will apply is where false credit card details are given to an automated booking system. It would appear, however, that the offence will not actually cover such conduct. Provided the card details (PIN and security number, etc.) are correct, payment *will* be made by the bank or issuing company.[383] Such conduct will, however, be covered by the fraud offence under s.2.

(ii) Mens rea

The mens rea requirements of s.11 are:

(a) *Dishonesty*

The act leading to the obtaining of the services must be dishonest. Again, the partial definition of dishonesty in s.2 of the Theft Act 1978 does not apply and whether the act is dishonest will be governed by the *Ghosh* test.

(b) *Knowing payment required*

At the time when the services are obtained, the defendant must know that the services are made available on the basis that payment has been, is being or will be made for or in respect of them or that they might only be available on that basis.

(c) *Intention not to pay*

The defendant must intend that payment will not be made, or that it will not be made in full. So, if the defendant is uncertain whether the services have been paid for (say, because they think another person *might* have already paid for them), there will be no liability. Recklessness will not suffice.

---

[382] Ormerod, *Smith and Hogan, Criminal Law*, 11th edn (2005), p.776 (discussing the 1978 Act).
[383] Ormerod, *Smith and Hogan, Criminal Law*, 13th edn (2011), p.912.

4. Conspiracy to defraud

The Law Commission proposed abolition of this offence as did the Home Office Consultation Paper on Fraud. This proposal was not, however, implemented on the basis that changing the law could lead to unforeseen circumstances with the developing technologies enabling fraudsters to exploit gaps in the law. Accordingly, to provide a "safety net",[384] the rather broad and unsatisfactory offence of conspiracy to defraud still remains. The Government stated that it was committed to a review of the operation of the Fraud Act 2006 three years after its implementation and that it might at that point abolish the offence of conspiracy to defraud.[385] However, in its 2012 post-legislative assessment of the Fraud Act 2006, the Ministry of Justice concluded that the offence should be retained because it

> "continues to be an effective and essential tool in combating fraud. This is particularly pertinent where there are various levels of criminal activity involved and the court would not otherwise be aware of the full extent of criminality involved".[386]

This offence was discussed in Ch.5.

IV. Making Off Without Payment

A. Introduction

We have already examined the general rule that the criminal law does not punish non-payment of debt even when dishonest, unless there has been a fraud, usually by means of a false representation. It is the dishonest false representation in securing such non-payment that marks conduct out as deserving of criminal liability.

However, in certain situations where debts have been incurred, such as at restaurants, hotels and petrol stations, it has been felt necessary to criminalise dishonest avoidance of payment even in the absence of a false representation. This is because of problems of law enforcement. Normally in contractual situations the identity of the other person is known (or where it is not, as in contracts in shops, a charge of theft will often be possible) and, therefore, it is appropriate to leave remedies to the civil law. However, in restaurants or petrol stations, for example, debts are incurred by anonymous debtors in circumstances where a charge of theft is not possible because property might have passed prior to the appropriation. Accordingly, a special criminal offence has been created to deal with such situations.

B. The Law

Theft Act 1978 s.3

"(1) Subject to subsection (3) below, a person who, knowing that payment on the spot for any goods supplied or service done is required or expected from him, dishonestly makes off without having paid as required or expected and with intent to avoid payment of the amount due shall be guilty of an offence.

(2) For purposes of this section 'payment on the spot' includes payment at the time of collecting goods on which work has been done or in respect of which service has been provided.

(3) Subsection (1) above shall not apply where the supply of the goods or the doing of the service is contrary to law, or where the service done is such that payment is not legally enforceable."

---

[384] Home Office, *Regulatory Impact Assessment: Fraud Bill* (2006).
[385] Hansard (HC), March 13, 2006, col.1110.
[386] Ministry of Justice, *Post-legislative Assessment of the Fraud Act 2006*, Cm.8372 (2012), para.42.

Strange though it may seem to start with a list of what does not have to be proved under this section, it is, nevertheless, a useful way of proceeding. Thus, one does not need to determine whether or not property has passed; one does not need to establish a false representation at any stage of the conduct and, finally, one does not have to show dishonesty any earlier than at the time of making off.

1. Actus reus

(i) Makes off

In *Brooks*,[387] the court said that making off "may be an exercise accompanied by the sound of trumpets or a silent stealing away after the folding of tents". In more prosaic words, there is no need for the leaving to be done by stealth. All that making off requires is that the defendant leave the place where payment is required for another place. So, if a dissatisfied diner openly storms out of a restaurant without paying, they clearly "make off". (Criminal liability in such a case would turn on whether their actions were regarded as dishonest.) It would appear to be irrelevant that the defendant has the victim's consent to their leaving, whether it is obtained by false representation (for example, pretending that payment has already been made) or not (for example, leaving a name and address). In both cases, the defendant "makes off" but, again, criminal liability will depend on other elements of the crime such as dishonesty or, in the case of the name and address being left, whether payment was expected on the spot.

(ii) The spot

What constitutes the "spot" is a matter of some importance: it will determine whether the defendant can be charged with the full offence or only with an attempt. If the spot is deemed to be the premises, as is likely, for example, in the case of leaving a restaurant without paying, then the offence is only committed when the defendant has left the premises. So, in *McDavitt*,[388] where the spot was held to be the restaurant, the defendant, who was apprehended as he made for the door, could only be convicted of attempting to make off without payment.

(iii) Goods supplied or service done

In order to understand the phrase "goods supplied" four situations may be compared. In the first, the defendant drives into a petrol station and fills his tank with petrol. He then decides not to pay and makes off. The defendant had "goods supplied" to him and will be liable under s.3. In the second situation, the defendant takes goods from a shelf in a supermarket and then leaves without paying. The supermarket, by displaying the goods, can be regarded as having "supplied" them and, accordingly, the defendant can be liable under s.3.[389] In the third situation, the defendant walks into a non-self-service shop and asks for and receives a pack of cigarettes. He then walks off without paying and is again liable under s.3 because he has had "goods supplied" to him. In the fourth situation, the defendant leans over the counter and helps himself to the cigarettes. If the defendant makes off without paying he cannot be liable under s.3 because he has not had "goods supplied" to him.

Neither the term "goods" nor "service" is defined by s.3, but it seems unlikely that this omission will lead to practical difficulties. Just as the goods must be "supplied", so the service must be "done".

---

387 *R. v Brooks (Edward George)* (1983) 76 Cr. App. R. 66 at 69.
388 *R. v McDavitt* [1981] Crim. L.R. 843. See also *R. v Aziz* [1993] Crim. L.R. 708.
389 D. Ormerod and D. Williams, *Smith's Law of Theft*, 9th edn (Oxford: OUP, 2007), p.230.

Clearest examples of this will be the meal provided in a restaurant or the accommodation provided by a hotel, but it would also seem broad enough to cover the defendant who parks his car in someone's car park, thereby taking up the offer to do so.

(iv) Without having paid

In practice, the main area likely to cause difficulties here is in relation to payment by dud cheques. The issue is whether such cheques are to be regarded as payment or not. Various views have been expressed about this. On the one hand, it is argued that such payment is not "as required or expected"[390] and should not, therefore, be regarded as payment. The other view is that such cheques should be regarded as payment because they conditionally discharge the defendant's liability to pay (although this does not apply to forged cheques because they do not amount to such a conditional discharge of liability).[391]

With payment by improperly-used credit or debit cards, provided the required information (PIN, etc.) has been supplied, the bank or issuing-company is bound to pay the victim and so the defendant cannot be liable for this offence.

(v) As required or expected

The only situation likely to cause a problem here is where payment is normally required or expected at a certain time but the creditor, because of a deception, agrees to accept payment at a later time. In *Vincent*,[392] the proprietors of hotels agreed to accept postponed payment at a time later than normally required or expected. It was held to be irrelevant that they had only agreed to this because of the defendant's dishonest deception. Section 3 creates a "simple and straightforward offence". Payment was not required or expected at the usual time. The reasons were irrelevant. Where the consent of the supplier to postponement of payment is obtained by deception, then the debtor would be guilty of fraud by misrepresentation (Fraud Act 2006 s.2) if he was dishonest and intended by making the misrepresentation to gain or to cause loss.

(vi) Unenforceable debts

Making off without payment will not be an offence where the payment is legally unenforceable or the supply of goods or services is contrary to law. The defendant who leaves a prostitute without paying commits no offence under s.3. In *Troughton*[393] a taxi driver had agreed to take the defendant, who was very drunk, to his home in Highbury. The defendant had not told the driver his actual address, and the driver had to stop to obtain directions from him. There was then an argument, and the defendant accused the driver of making an unnecessary diversion. Eventually, as he was unable to obtain an address, the taxi driver drove to the police station. On appeal, it was held that *Troughton* was not guilty of the s.3 offence because he was never in a situation in which he was bound to pay the money for the taxi fare. By driving to the police station, the driver had breached his contract with the defendant to take him to his home. As a result of this breach of contract, the driver was not lawfully entitled to demand the fare.

---

[390]   Ormerod and Williams, *Smith's Law of Theft*, 9th edn (2007), p.233.
[391]   G. Syrota, "Are Cheque Frauds Covered by Section 3 of the Theft Act 1978?" [1981] Crim. L.R. 413 and *R. v Hammond* [1982] Crim. L.R. 611.
[392]   *Vincent* [2001] Cr. App. R. 150.
[393]   *Troughton v The Metropolitan Police* [1987] Crim. L.R. 138 (QBD).

2. Mens rea

The mens rea required under s.3 is: that the defendant must *know* that payment on the spot is required and must make off *dishonestly with intent to avoid payment*.

It is clear that there has to be an intention to make permanent default.[394]

3. Punishment

The maximum penalty for an offence under s.3 is two years' imprisonment.[395] A Penalty Notice for Disorder cannot be issued in respect of this offence.[396]

V. OTHER PROPERTY OFFENCES

There are a large number of other property offences, some serious like blackmail, robbery, burglary, criminal damage and handling stolen goods and some not so serious, like taking a conveyance. Whilst it is beyond the scope of this book to deal with all these offences in detail, the chief provisions of some of these offences will be sketched.

A. Sociological Background

The gravity of the conduct encompassed by these offences varies enormously. Robbery is regarded as the most serious because it is not only a property offence, but also an offence of violence. Robberies, which account for less than 2 per cent of recorded crime,[397] range from professional armed robberies on banks and the causing of serious injury to relatively minor street "muggings" where the victim is threatened with a punch if they do not hand over some money or a mobile phone.[398]

In 2012/13 there were 61,836 recorded robbery offences in England and Wales, a decrease of 10 per cent compared with the previous year. Apart from a rise in the number of robberies in 2005/06 and 2006/07 there has been a general downward trend in recorded robbery offences between 2002 and 2013.[399] Over half of the recorded offences in 2012/13 (31,986) took place in the Metropolitan Police force area.[400] One in five (20 per cent) of recorded robberies in England and Wales in 2012/13 involved a knife or sharp instrument.[401] The 2012/13 CSEW figures indicate that 29 per cent of "muggings" and 37 per cent of "robberies"[402] result in some form of physical injury, the most common injury being

---

[394] *Allen* [1985] A.C. 1029.

[395] The guideline sentence for magistrates where the goods or services are worth less than £200 and there is little or no evidence of pre-planning is a fine (Sentencing Guidelines Council, *Magistrates' Court Sentencing Guidelines: Definitive Guideline* (2009)), p.79.

[396] Ministry of Justice, *Penalty Notices for Disorder (PNDs)* (2013), para 3.18, this guidance, issued under s.6 of the Criminal Justice and Police Act 2001, may be accessed at *https://www.justice.gov.uk/downloads/oocd/pnd-guidance-oocd.pdf* [Accessed March 2014].

[397] ONS, Statistical Bulletin, *Crime in England and Wales Year Ending September 2013* (2014), p.35 and table P1.

[398] In the 2011/12 CSEW, approximately 2% of mobile phone owners reported that their mobile phone had been stolen in the last 12 months: ONS, *Crime Statistics, Focus on Property Crime 2011/12* (2013), Ch.2: Mobile Phone Theft, available at *http://www.ons.gov.uk/ons/dcp171776_309652.pdf* [Accessed March 2014], p.1.

[399] ONS, fn.397 above, p.36.

[400] ONS, fn.397 above, p.38.

[401] ONS, fn.397 above, p.37.

[402] The CSEW uses the term "mugging" to include robbery, attempted robbery and snatch theft (where supposedly no force was used or there is a minimal threat or force), whereas the term "robbery" maintains its legal meaning as defined below: ONS, *User Guide to Crime Statistics for England and Wales: January 2014* (2014), p.38.

cuts, scratches or severe bruising.[403] Around 12 per cent of muggings and 13 per cent of robberies require some form of medical attention.[404] The most serious kind of robbery is no doubt perceived to be armed robbery, which is fairly uncommon, since in 2010/11 just 3.9 per cent of robberies involved the use of a firearm.[405]

Less than 50 per cent of all robberies are reported[406] and, although robbery is seen as a serious offence, the detection rate for this crime is only approximately 20 per cent.[407]

The other major property offence that is the subject of much media attention is burglary which in 2012/13 accounted for 17 per cent of all recorded property crime[408] (about half of which is from a dwelling)[409] and 9 per cent of all property crime according to the CSEW.[410]

The threat of burglary has been a particular source of anxiety in the past, but the level of worry has reduced considerably over the past decade. In 1998, 19 per cent of adults indicated they had "high levels of worry" about burglary, and this had fallen to 12 per cent by 2012.[411] This drop in anxiety is most likely caused by the fact that people are much less likely to be victims of burglary than they were 10 years ago. Between 1995 and 2012/13, for example, burglaries dropped by 63 per cent.[412] The success in tackling this offence may be due to measures taken by householders against burglary. Indeed, a higher proportion of English and Welsh households have taken security measures (such as burglar alarms) to protect their property against the risk of burglary than in other countries.[413] Such measures appear to be effective, since it has been found that the level of home security is an important predictor of whether a household will experience burglary or not. In 2012/13 around half of all households that had been the victim of burglary in the past 12 months had no or "less than basic" security at the time of the incident, and households with no security had about twice the level of burglary of those with "at least basic" security.[414] Where security is ineffective and a burglar gains entry to a house, items are taken in 68 per cent of cases, with purses, wallets, money, computers and computer goods, jewellery, electrical goods and cameras, and mobile phones being the most commonly stolen items.[415] Offenders admit that they target homes in the hope of taking cash, jewellery, laptops and credit cards.[416]

Victims of burglary run a greatly increased risk of repeat victimisation. Offenders are likely to return to a property which they have successfully burgled in the past, with two-thirds of burglars claiming

---

[403] ONS, *Crime Survey for England and Wales 2012/13*, table 3.07.

[404] ONS, *Crime Survey for England and Wales 2012/13*, table 3.07.

[405] G. Berman, *Firearm Crime Statistics*, House of Commons Standard Note SN/SG/1940 (2012) available at *http//www.parliament.uk/briefing-papers/sn01940.pdf* [Accessed April 2014], p.6.

[406] ONS, *Crime Survey for England and Wales 2012/13*, table 2.11. In the year 2010/11 49% of robberies were reported to the police.

[407] K. Smith, P. Taylor and M. Elkin, Home Office Statistical Bulletin, *Crimes Detected in England and Wales 2012/13*, 2nd edn (2013), table 1.

[408] ONS, *Focus on Property Crime 2012/13, Chapter 1: Overview of Property Crime* (2013), figure 1.2.

[409] ONS, *Crime Survey for England and Wales 2012/13*, table 12a.

[410] ONS, *Crime Survey for England and Wales 2012/13*, figure 1.1

[411] CSEW, *Perception Measure Tables—Crime in England and Wales*, Year Ending December 2012 (2013), table PM1.

[412] ONS, *Focus on Property Crime 2012/13, Chapter 3: Burglary and Home Security* (2013), p.2.

[413] P. Mayhew and J.J.M. van Dijk, *Criminal Victimisation in Eleven Industrialised Countries: Key Findings from the International Crime Victims Survey* (1997).

[414] ONS, *Focus on Property Crime 2012/13, Chapter 3: Burglary and Home Security* (2013), pp.8–9. In 2012/13 the proportions of households burgled once was similar for various levels of house security (from "basic" to "enhanced"), but the proportion of households burgled more than once in the 12-month period was greater for households with no security (3%) than for households with higher levels of home security (0.5%): p.10.

[415] ONS, *Crime Survey for England and Wales 2012/13*, p.15 and table 3.06. In 2012/13 the average value of goods stolen was £3,068: table 3.07.

[416] I. Hearnden and G. Magill, *Decision-making by House Burglars: Offenders' Perspectives*, Home Office Research Findings 249 (2004).

that they had returned to a property they had burgled before and taken items from it on a second occasion.[417] The types of property most likely to be targeted are rented properties, particularly those inhabited by students.[418] It would seem that offenders are most likely to burgle those from a similar socio-economic background to themselves, which is supported by research which has found that offenders tend to know their victims, with over half of burglars saying that they knew who lived in the property they were burgling.[419]

The reporting and recording rates for burglary are higher than for robbery largely because insurance claims cannot be made without the crime being reported. In 2008/09, 61 per cent of burglaries where there was no loss were reported to the police, but where there had been property lost in the burglary, this rose to 85 per cent.[420] However, the detection rate for burglary of a dwelling is only 17 per cent.[421]

B. The Legal Background

Some of the offences incorporated in the Theft Act of 1968 were already statutory, such as burglary and handling stolen goods under the Larceny Act of 1916; others were common law offences, such as robbery. There can be no doubt, however, that the reforms introduced were timely. Burglary had become a particularly complex offence, with distinctions having to be drawn between "breaking in the night" and "breaking in the day". Fletcher makes the point that the insistence upon the requirement of "breaking" in the development of this offence marks an adherence to a theory of manifest liability, where the actions of the defendant had to be manifestly criminal for an offence to be committed.[422] What has happened since has been a retreat from that position; the new law not only does away with the archaic distinction between breaking by day and night but does away with the requirement of breaking altogether. The replacement, trespass, however, "retains at least a trace of the traditional rule that the entry must be manifestly suspicious".[423]

The severity with which most of these offences are regarded is indicated not only by the maximum sentences available: robbery and aggravated burglary are punishable by up to life imprisonment and domestic burglary and handling stolen goods by up to 14 years' imprisonment,[424] but also by the sentences actually handed down by the courts. Of those adults convicted of robbery in the 12 months ending September 2013, 59.8 per cent received immediate custodial sentences (average length: 35.5 months).[425] The sentencing range for street robbery or "muggings" and robberies of small commercial businesses by adult offenders (which involve the use of minimal force) is 12 months to three years custody;[426] for violent personal robberies in the home it is 13 to 16 years;[427] and for the most serious professional planned commercial armed robberies it is in the region of 25 years.[428] Robbery is a

---

[417] I. Hearnden and G. Magill, fn.416 above..

[418] ONS, *Crime Statistics—Focus on Property Crime, Chapter 1: Property Crime Overview* (2013), Appendix table 1.01. In the 2012/13 CSEW it was found that only half (49%) of student households had "at least basic" security, compared with 80% of rented households: ONS, *Focus on Property Crime 2012/13, Chapter 3: Burglary and Home Security* (2013), p.6.

[419] I. Hearnden and G. Magill, fn.416 above.

[420] ONS, *Crime Survey for England and Wales 2012/13*, figure 1.9.

[421] K. Smith, P. Taylor and M. Elkin, fn.407 above.

[422] G.P. Fletcher, *Rethinking Criminal Law* (Boston: Little, Brown, 1978), pp.124–128.

[423] Fletcher, *Rethinking Criminal Law* (1978), p.128.

[424] Theft Act 1968 ss.8(2), 9(4), 10(2) and 22(2).

[425] Ministry of Justice Statistics Bulletin, *Criminal Justice Statistics, Quarterly Update to September 2013, England and Wales* (2014), table Q1.6(i).

[426] Sentencing Guidelines Council, *Robbery: Definitive Guideline* (2006), p.11.

[427] Sentencing Guidelines Council, *Robbery: Definitive Guideline* (2006), p.13; O'Driscoll (1986) 8 Cr. App. R. (S.) 121.

[428] *R. v Jenkins (David)* [2009] 1 Cr.App. R. (S.) 20; *R. v Thomas (Thomas)* [2012] 1 Cr. App. R. (S.) 43.

specified violent offence and a serious offence for the purposes of the measures dealing with dangerous offenders under the Criminal Justice 2003.[429]

Of those sentenced for burglary in the 12 months ending September 2012 in all courts, 53.7 per cent
were given immediate custodial sentences (average length: 20.3 months).[430] The Sentencing Council
has issued a definitive sentencing guideline for burglary offences which indicates that, for a "Category
3" domestic burglary, where there is limited damage or disturbance to property and property of low
value is stolen, and where the offence is committed on impulse, the sentencing range is from a low level
community order to 26 weeks' custody.[431] A court sentencing a defendant for a third qualifying domestic
burglary must impose a custodial term of at least three years, unless it is satisfied that there are particular circumstances in relation to the offences or the offender which would make it unjust to do so.[432]

C. The Law

Only the main features of these offences will be highlighted.

1. Robbery

Theft Act 1968 s.8

"(1) A person is guilty of robbery if he steals, and immediately before or at the time of doing so, and in order to
do so, he uses force on any person or puts or seeks to put any person in fear of being then and there subjected
to force.
  (2) A person guilty of robbery, or of an assault with intent to rob, shall on conviction on indictment be liable to
imprisonment for life."

Robbery is theft aggravated by the threat or use of force. The elements of theft must be established
if a conviction for robbery is to be obtained. If the defendant believes that they have a legal right to
the property they take (even if not to the way they take it) then there can be no theft and, therefore,
no robbery.[433]

The element additional to theft is that of force and a number of points need to be made about
this. First, "force" is a question of fact to be determined by a jury, although it would seem that very
little force is actually required.[434] Wrenching a shopping basket[435] or handbag[436] from the owner
can suffice, although the mere snatching of a cigarette from between the victim's fingers will not.[437]
Secondly, the force or threat of force must take place immediately before or at the time of the theft.[438]
Thirdly, the fact that the victim was not put in fear is irrelevant; the issue is whether the defendant
sought to put the victim in fear of force.[439] Lastly, the threat of force must be used in order to steal and

---

[429] See e.g. *R. v Knight (Neville Wayne)* [2010] 2 Cr. App. R. (S.) 84.
[430] Ministry of Justice Statistics Bulletin, fn.425 above, table Q1.6(i)..
[431] Sentencing Council, *Burglary Offences: Definitive Guidelines* (2011), pp.9–10.
[432] Sentencing Council, *Burglary Offences: Definitive Guidelines* (2011), pp.9–10; Powers of the Criminal Courts (Sentencing) Act
      2000, s.111.
[433] *R. v Robinson* [1977] Crim. L.R. 173.
[434] *Dawson and James* (1976) 64 Cr. App. R. 170; *R. v Clouden* [1987] Crim. L.R. 56.
[435] *Clouden* [1987] Crim. L.R. 56.
[436] *Corcoran v Anderton* (1980) 71 Cr. App. R. 104.
[437] *P v DPP* [2012] EWHC 1657 (Admin), [2013] 1 W.L.R. 2335, discussed by D. Ormerod in the case commentary at [2013] Crim.
      L.R. 151–152.
[438] In *R. v Atakpu (Austin)* [1994] Q.B. 69 the court was of the view that it should be left to the common sense of the jury to
      decide at what point the theft finished. This will determine whether the force was used at the time of the theft. See p.826.
[439] *R. v DPP* [2007] EWHC 739 (Admin).

not for any other purpose such as rape.[440] While the mens rea of theft is not spelt out in s.8, it is clear that there must be the mens rea of theft,[441] and the force or threatened force must be *in order to steal*; an accidental, negligent or even reckless use of force will not suffice.

Robbery is an extremely broad offence and while some robberies can be extremely serious, others can be relatively minor as where there is no more than a threat of a punch in order to steal a mobile phone. As the threat by itself would amount to no more than an assault (carrying a maximum penalty of six months' imprisonment) and the theft, although carrying a maximum penalty of seven years' imprisonment, would not be severely punished, one is forced to question whether the combination of the two elements justifies such a serious offence carrying a maximum penalty of life imprisonment.

Andrew Ashworth, "Robbery Re-assessed" [2002] Crim. L.R. 851 at 871:

"Violence can be a serious matter, and the law distinguishes serious from less serious degrees. Robbery can also be serious, but the law fails to distinguish very serious from less serious degrees. The result is that the label 'robbery' carries connotations that sometimes grossly misrepresent the seriousness of an offence. A radical approach would be to abolish the offence of robbery, leaving its ingredients to be charged separately. Another approach would be to divide the offence into at least two degrees, using the law of offences against the person as the basis. That would have the procedural benefit of ensuring that lesser offences become triable either way, rather than sending all offenders aged 18 and over to the Crown Court.

One desirable consequence of such a re-assessment would be that sentencing guidance is focused on the amount of the theft and the degree of force used or threatened."

Recognising the breadth of this offence, sentencing guidelines have been developed for different types of robbery: street robbery or "mugging"; robberies of small businesses; less sophisticated commercial robberies; violent personal robberies in the home; and professionally planned commercial robberies.[442]

2. Burglary and aggravated burglary

Theft Act 1968 ss.9 and 10

"9.—(1) A person is guilty of burglary if—

(a) he enters any building or part of a building as a trespasser and with intent to commit any such offence as is mentioned in subsection (2) below; or

(b) having entered any building or part of a building as a trespasser he steals or attempts to steal anything in the building or that part of it or inflicts or attempts to inflict on any person therein any grievous bodily harm.

(2) The offences referred to in subsection (1)(a) above are offences of stealing anything in the building or part of a building in question, of inflicting on any person therein any grievous bodily harm therein, and of doing unlawful damage to the building or anything therein . . .

(3) A person guilty of burglary shall on conviction on indictment be liable to imprisonment for a term not exceeding—

(a) where the offence was committed in respect of a building or part of a building which is a dwelling, fourteen years;

(b) in any other case, ten years.

---

[440] In a situation such as this the defendant may be convicted of theft or possibly attempted rape.
[441] Including intention permanently to deprive the owner at the moment of taking the property: *Vinall* [2011] EWCA Crim 6252, [2012] 1 Cr. App. R. 29 at [12]; *R. v Zerei (Samuel Michael)* [2012] EWCA Crim 1114. See above p.858.
[442] Sentencing Guidelines Council, *Robbery: Definitive Guideline* (2006).

(4) References in subsections (1) and (2) above to a building, and the reference in subsection (3) above to a building which is a dwelling, shall apply also to an inhabited vehicle or vessel, and shall apply to any such vehicle or vessel at times when the person having a habitation in it is not there as well as at times when he is.

10.—(1) A person is guilty of aggravated burglary if he commits any burglary and at the time has with him any firearm or imitation firearm, any weapon of offence, or any explosive; and for this purpose—

(a) 'firearm' includes an airgun or air pistol, and 'imitation firearm' means anything which has the appearance of being a firearm, whether capable of being discharged or not; and

(b) 'weapon of offence' means any article made or adapted for use for causing injury to or incapacitating a person, or intended by the person having it with him for such use; and

(c) 'explosive' means any article manufactured for the purpose of producing a practical effect by explosion, or intended by the person having it with him for that purpose.

(2) A person guilty of aggravated burglary shall on conviction on indictment be liable to imprisonment for life."

The original s.9(2) also included the ulterior offence of rape. As can be seen in the case of *Collins* below it would be burglary under the old law if a person entered a building as a trespasser with the intention of raping anyone therein. The Sexual Offences Act 2003 removed rape as an ulterior offence in s.9(2)[443] and created a new offence of trespass with intention to commit a sexual offence.[444] This new offence is much wider than the old provision on burglary in that the person must be a trespasser "on any premises" (which is wider than "building or part of a building") and there must be an intention to commit "a relevant sexual offence" on the premises (which covers many sexual offences in addition to rape).

There are now four offences of burglary within s.9. Under s.9(1)(a), there are two offences of entering a building as a trespasser with the intention of stealing, inflicting grievous bodily harm, or doing unlawful damage—one committed where the building is a "dwelling" and one where it is not. The former offence is known as "domestic burglary".[445] Similarly, under s.9(1)(b) having entered a "dwelling" as a trespasser and then stealing, etc. is distinguished from other buildings or parts thereof. Section 10 creates a more serious offence: burglary aggravated by the presence of weapons.

R. v Collins [1973] Q.B. 100 (Court of Appeal, Criminal Division)

[The facts appear in the judgment]

EDMUND-DAVIES LJ:

"Let me relate the facts. Were they put into a novel or portrayed on the stage, they would be regarded as being so improbable as to be unworthy of serious consideration and as verging at times on farce. At about 2 o'clock in the early morning of Saturday, July 24, 1971, a young lady of 18 went to bed at her mother's home in Colchester. She had spent the evening with her boyfriend. She had taken a certain amount of drink, and it may be that this fact affords some explanation of her inability to answer satisfactorily certain crucial questions put to her at the trial.

She has the habit of sleeping without wearing night apparel in a bed which is very near the lattice-type window of her room . . .

At about 3.30 or 4 o'clock she awoke and she then saw in the moonlight a vague form crouched in the open window. She was unable to remember, and this is important, whether the form was on the outside of the window sill or on that part of the sill which was inside the room, and for reasons which will later become clear, that seemingly narrow point is of crucial importance.

---

[443] Schedule 6 para.17.
[444] Section 63.
[445] This is the terminology employed by the Powers of Criminal Courts (Sentencing) Act 2000 s.111.

The young lady then realised several things: first of all that the form in the window was that of a male; secondly, that he was a naked male; and thirdly, that he was a naked male with an erect penis. She also saw in the moonlight that his hair was blond. She thereupon leapt to the conclusion that her boyfriend, with whom for some time she had been on terms of regular and frequent sexual intimacy, was paying her an ardent nocturnal visit. She promptly sat up in bed, and the man descended from the sill and joined her in bed and they had full sexual intercourse. But there was something about him which made her think that things were not at as they usually were between her and her boyfriend. The length of his hair, his voice as they had exchanged what what was described as 'love talk', and other features led her to the conclusion that somehow there was something different. So she turned on the bed-side light, saw that her companion was not her boyfriend and slapped the face of the intruder, who was none other than the defendant. He said to her, 'Give me a good time tonight', and got hold of her arm, but she bit him and told him to go. She then went into the bathroom and he promptly vanished.

The complainant said that she would not have agreed to intercourse if she had known that the person entering her room was not her boyfriend. But there was no suggestion of any force having been used upon her, and the intercourse which took place was undoubtedly effected with no resistance on her part.

The defendant was seen by the police at about 10.30 later that same morning. According to the police, the conversation which took place then elicited these points: He was very lustful the previous night. He had taken a lot of drink . . . He went on to say that he knew the complainant because he had worked around her house. On this occasion, desiring sexual intercourse—and according to the police evidence he added that he was determined to have a girl, by force if necessary, although that part of the police evidence he challenged—he went on to say that he walked around the house, saw a light in an upstairs bedroom, and he knew that this was the girl's bedroom. He found a step ladder, leaned it against the wall and climbed up and looked into the bedroom. He could see through the wide-open window a girl who was naked and asleep. So he descended the ladder and stripped off all his clothes, with the exception of his socks, because apparently he took the view that if the girl's mother entered the bedroom is would be easier to effect a rapid escape if he had his socks on than if he was in his bare feet. That is a matter about which we are not called upon to express any view, and would in any event find ourselves unable to express one.

Having undressed, he then climbed the ladder and pulled himself up on to the window sill. His version of the matter is that he was pulling himself in when she awoke. She then got up and knelt on the bed, she put her arms around his neck and body, and she seemed to pull him into the bed. He went on: 'I was rather dazed because I didn't think she would want to know me. We kissed and cuddled for about 10 or 15 minutes and then I had it away with her but found it hard because I had had so much to drink.' . . .

Now, one feature of the case which remained at the conclusion of the evidence in great obscurity is where exactly Collins was at the moment when, according to him, the girl manifested that she was welcoming him. Was he kneeling on the sill outside the window or was he already inside the room, having climbed through the window frame, and kneeling upon the inner sill? It was a crucial matter, for there were certainly three ingredients that it was incumbent upon the Crown to establish. Under section 9 of the Theft Act, 1968, which renders a person guilty of burglary if he enters any building or part of a building as a trespasser and with the intention of committing rape, the entry of the accused into the building must first be proved. Well, there is no doubt about that, for it is common ground that he did enter this girl's bedroom. Secondly, it must be proved that he entered as a trespasser. We will develop that point a little later. Thirdly, it must be proven that he entered as a trespasser with intent at the time of entry to commit rape therein.

The second ingredient of the offence—the entry must be as a trespasser—is one which has not, to the best of our knowledge, been previously canvassed in the courts . . .

What does that involve? . . .

. . . In the judgment of this court there cannot be a conviction for entering premises 'as a trespasser' within the meaning of section 9 of the Theft Act unless the person entering does so knowing that he is a trespasser and nevertheless deliberately enters, or, at the very least, is reckless as to whether or not he is entering the premises of another without the other party's consent.

Having so held, the pivotal point of this appeal is whether the Crown established that this defendant at the moment that he entered the bedroom knew perfectly well that he was not welcome there or, being reckless as to whether he was welcome or not, was nevertheless determined to enter. That in turn involves consideration as to where he was at the time that the complainant indicated that she was welcoming him into her bedroom. If, to take an example that was put in the course of argument, her bed had not been near the window but was on the other side of the bedroom, and he (being determined to have her sexually even against her will) climbed through the window and crossed the bedroom to reach her bed, then the offence charged would have been established. But in this case, as we have related, the layout of the room was different, and it became a point of nicety which had to be conclusively established by the Crown as to where he was when the girl made welcoming signs, as she unquestionably at some stage did . . .

Unless the jury were entirely satisfied that the defendant made an effective and substantial entry into the bedroom without the complainant doing or saying anything to cause him to believe that she was consenting to his entering it, he ought not to be convicted of the offence charged. The point is a narrow one, as narrow maybe as the window sill which is crucial to this case . . .

We have to say that his appeal must be allowed on the basis that the jury were never invited to consider the vital question whether this young man did enter the premises as a trespasser, that is to say knowing perfectly well that he had no invitation to enter or reckless of whether or not his entry was with permission."

Appeal allowed

(i) Actus reus

From this case it can be seen that the offence of burglary contrary to s.9(1)(a) involves the following elements.[446]

(a) *Enters*

Whether there has been an entry is a question of fact for the jury. In giving them guidance, the court in *Collins* held that there had been to be an "effective and substantial" entry. In *Brown*[447] the court qualified this approach requiring only an "effective" entry. Thus it is unnecessary for the entire body of the defendant to be inside the building but minimal intrusions such as a few fingers would be generally insufficient. In *Ryan*,[448] it was held that the jury was entitled to consider whether there was an entry in a case where the defendant's head and arm were inside a window when he became trapped. It is difficult to see how this could amount to an "effective" entry.

(b) *As a trespasser*

Reference must be made to the civil law in order to understand the term "trespass". Under civil law, trespass is entry without the consent of the lawful possessor. No conviction for burglary can be obtained without a finding of civil trespass but, as *Collins* makes clear, more than this is required: the defendant must enter "knowing that he is a trespasser . . . or, at the very least, is reckless whether or not he is entering the premises of another without the other party's consent". This was the point at issue in *Collins*. Had he entered the building prior to being invited in? If so, he was a trespasser.

Even if there is consent, if the defendant acts in a way that goes beyond what the possessor would have consented to, they may be deemed to enter as a trespasser. Thus in *Jones*[449] the defendant had left his parents' home but was a frequent, welcome visitor. One night he entered their home and stole two television sets. Despite the father's loyal statement that his son was welcome at any time, the court held that an inference could be drawn that he would not have consented to entry for the purposes of theft. The son was thus held to have entered as a trespasser.

(c) *Any building or part of a building*

Two issues are raised here. First, what constitutes a "building"? Section 9(4) gives an extended meaning to the term by including within it inhabited vehicles and vessels such as caravans and house-

---

[446] The same elements are required under s.9(1)(b) subject to the necessary modifications.
[447] *R. v Brown (Vincent)* [1985] Crim. L.R. 212.
[448] *R. v Ryan (Lee Bernard)* [1996] Crim. L.R. 320.
[449] *R. v Jones (John)* [1976] 1 W.L.R. 672.

boats.[450] The occupant does not have to be present at the time in order to render it "inhabited" but it would seem that it would have to be lived in.

Little other statutory guidance is given as to the ambit of "building"; generally it would seem appropriate to take a commonsense view of it. It would be too restrictive to think in terms of just houses, flats, offices and the like. Outbuildings such as garages and sheds must also be included. The courts have tended to regard both a degree of permanence and considerable size as appropriate criteria to determine whether something constitutes a "building".[451] So, tents and telephone kiosks are, therefore, probably not buildings for the purposes of burglary.[452]

The second issue relates to "part of a building". This does not necessarily mean a separate room. It includes areas such as those behind counters in shops from which the defendant is excluded.[453]

(ii) Dwelling

The Criminal Justice Act 1991 created the new offences of domestic burglary in respect of s.9(1)(a) and (b) where the building is a "dwelling".[454] Dwelling is not defined but presumably means a building (or vessel or vehicle[455]) in which someone lives as their home.[456]

(iii) Mens rea

The mens rea requirement for burglary under s.9(1)(a) is:

  (i)   intention or recklessness as to trespass,

  (ii) intention to commit one of the offences in s.9(2),[457] and

  (iii) with regard to domestic burglary, it has been argued that because this is an aggravating element it should import a requirement of mens rea; the defendant should only be guilty if they know or thinks somebody might be living there.[458]

---

[450] *R. v Coleman (Kenneth)* [2013] EWCA Crim 544, [2013] 2 Cr. App. R. (S.) 79: an inhabited narrow boat was held to be a building for the purposes of s.9(4).

[451] *Stevens v Gorley* (1859) 7 C.B.(N.S.) 99.

[452] Ormerod and Williams, *Smith's The Law of Theft*, 9th edn (2007), pp.257–258.

[453] Either expressly or impliedly: *R. v Walkington (Terence John)* [1979] 1 W.L.R. 1169.

[454] The indictment must specify that the property is a dwelling, and where this is disputed there should be alternative counts on the indictment, one specifying that the property is a dwelling and one charging non-domestic burglary, and the jury should determine the issue: *R. v Flack (Perry)* [2013] EWCA Crim 115, [2013] 2 Cr. App. R. (S.) 56.

[455] An inhabited houseboat or caravan is a 'dwelling': *Coleman* [2013] EWCA Crim 544, [2013] 2 Cr. App. R. (S.) 79. See the case commentary by D. Thomas at [2013] Crim. L.R. 694–696.

[456] Ormerod and Williams, *Smith's The Law of Theft*, 9th edn (2007), p.266; K. Laird, "Conceptualising the Interpretation of 'Dwelling' in Section 9 of the Theft Act 1968" [2013] Crim. L.R. 656–673.

[457] A defendant who enters a building as a trespasser intending to steal only if he finds items worth stealing has sufficient mens rea for the purposes of s.9(1)(a) burglary: *Attorney-General's References (Nos 1 and 2 of 1979)* [1980] Q.B. 180; Ormerod and Williams, *Smith's The Law of Theft*, 9th edn (2007), p.263. Cf. The position in relation to conditional intention and theft, above pp.863–864.

[458] Ormerod and Williams, *Smith's The Law of Theft*, 9th edn (2007), p.266.

(iv) Aggravated burglary

If a person "commits any burglary and at the time has with him any firearm or imitation firearm, any weapon of offence, or any explosive", the offence becomes aggravated burglary.[459] For the purposes of this offence it does not matter whether the burglary is of a dwelling or not.

For the purposes of s.9(1)(a) (entry with intent), the defendant must have the article of aggravation with him at the time of entry. For the purposes of s.9(1)(b) (having entered), the relevant time is when the specified offence is committed. So, if a defendant, having entered as a trespasser, picks up a kitchen knife and uses it to force the householder to hand over the property, aggravated burglary is committed. In *Klass*,[460] it was held that the weapon must be carried by the person at the time of entering the building. Although s.10 refers to the person having with him a weapon of offence, "there can be no doubt that the offence of aggravated burglary may be committed by a person who does not have the weapon if he is aiding and abetting the person with him".[461] However, the offence is not committed if another party outside the building (e.g. a getaway driver in a car) is in sole possession of a weapon.[462] In *Chevannes*, a case invloving a s.9(1)(b) burglary, the alleged weapon of offence (a bottle containing ammonia and water) had been left downstairs whilst two of the burglars stole items upstairs. The Court of Appeal stated that what mattered in such cases was

> "not whether the accused, or one of those with whom he was engaged in a joint enterprise, was actually holding the weapon at the time the theft took place, but whether the weapon was within his control so that it could be taken up and used if necessary."[463]

(v) Punishment

A person found guilty of burglary of a dwelling is liable to imprisonment for up to 14 years. In other circumstances the maximum is now 10 years.[464] If the burglary is aggravated the maximum sentence is life imprisonment.[465]

3. Handling stolen goods

(i) Introduction

The offence of handling stolen goods is closely related to that of theft and there is a considerable overlap between the two offences. Many thieves literally handle the property they have stolen and so, to prevent such persons being liable for both offences, careful demarcation of the two crimes is necessary. Also, many handlers satisfy the test of appropriation and the other elements in the definition of theft. The Criminal Law Revision Committee was fully aware of this overlap, but saw "no reason in principle or convenience" against it, although circumstances and evidentiary requirements may dictate the more natural charge.[466] Handling is a very broad offence covering a wide range of

---

[459]   Theft Act 1968 s.10.
[460]   *R. v Klass (Kennedy Francis)* [1998] 1 Cr. App. R. 453. Followed in *R. v Wiggins (Zaro Pierre)* [2012] EWCA Crim 885.
[461]   *Klass* [1998] 1 Cr. App. R. 453 at 456.
[462]   *Klass* [1998] 1 Cr. App. R. 453 at 456.
[463]   *R. v Chevannes (Justin Lee)* [2009] EWCA Crim 2725, per Moore-Bick J at [20]. This is a matter of fact for the jury.
[464]   For sentencing guidelines, see above, p.898.
[465]   Section 10(2) of the Theft Act 1968.
[466]   Criminal Law Revision Committee, Eighth Report (1966), Cmnd.2977, para.132.

circumstances. The handler could be a professional "fence" or an otherwise law-abiding person buying a stolen DVD player at a car-boot sale. It is thought that without professional handlers of stolen goods, so-called "fences" and "placers", there would be a lot less theft. Handling thus has a higher maximum sentence (of 14 years' imprisonment) than theft to deal with large-scale handling operations. However, the majority of handlers are not such professional criminals.[467] In 2012, 6,329 handlers were sentenced, 70 per cent of them being dealt with in the magistrates' courts.[468] Of these, 35 per cent received a community order, 15 per cent a fine, and 11 per cent a conditional or absolute discharge. The second most common form of disposal was a sentence of immediate imprisonment (24 per cent), but the sentences imposed appear generally to be short: in 2012 the average sentence was 6 months and 3 weeks imprisonment, and the median term was 4 months.[469]

(ii) The law

Theft Act 1968 s.22

"(1) A person handles stolen goods if (otherwise than in the course of the stealing) knowing or believing them to be stolen goods he dishonestly receives the goods, or dishonestly undertakes or assists in their retention, removal, disposal or realisation by or for the benefit of another person, or if he arranges to do so.

(2) A person guilty of handling stolen goods shall on conviction on indictment be liable to imprisonment for a term not exceeding 14 years."

It should be noted that s.22 creates only *one* offence, although there are a large number of ways in which this offence can be committed. In fact, it renders culpable almost any way of dealing with stolen goods as long as there is mens rea. So, for example, the person who arranges to handle stolen goods commits the offence under s.22 despite the fact that, but for the provision, they would not even have done enough to be liable for an attempt.

(a) *Actus reus*

The elements of the actus reus are:

1. The goods must be stolen at the time of handling:

Section 34(2)(b) defines "goods" as including money and every other description of property, except land. In addition, s.24 defines stolen goods as goods obtained by theft under s.1, by fraud under the Fraud Act 2006, by blackmail under s.21 and money dishonestly withdrawn from a wrongful credit under s.24A(8). Importantly, the goods must remain stolen at the time the handling occurs; so, for example, where the goods have been reduced to police custody and used to bait a trap to catch handlers there can be no conviction under s.22.[470]

The handling must be "otherwise than in the course of the stealing". This provision is necessary to prevent thieves being simultaneously guilty of both theft and handling. This raises the problem

---

[467]   Mode of trial guidelines state that handling cases should be tried summarily unless the handler commissioned the theft, the offence has professional hallmarks or the property is of high value (the Consolidated Practice Direction—Criminal Procedure Rules (2013), para.V51.8, available at *http://www.justice.gov.uk/courts/procedure-rules/criminal/practice-direction/part5* [Accessed April 2014]).

[468]   Sentencing Council, *Theft Offences: Sentencing Data* (2014), pp.14–17, available at *http://sentencingcouncil.judiciary.gov.uk/docs/Theft_offences_bulletin_-_FINAL.pdf* [Accessed April 2014], p.51

[469]   Sentencing Council, *Theft Offences: Sentencing Data* (2014), fn.468 above.

[470]   See s.24(2) and (3) and *Attorney-General's Reference (No.1 of 1974)* [1974] 2 All E.R. 899. The exception will be where it is possible to establish arranging to handle at some earlier time. Alternatively, a charge of attempting to handle stolen goods may be possible.

of when theft ends which depends upon whether an appropriation can be regarded as a continuing act.[471] This matter was discussed earlier in relation to the meaning of an appropriation.[472]

2. There must be a handling of the goods:

Although the preferred view, as indicated above, is that there is only one offence, there are 18 ways in which the property may be handled.[473] The stereotypical case of handling will involve receiving the goods but it will also encompass disposal (even by way of destruction) and assisting another to deal with the stolen goods. A brief look at the interpretation of this latter form of handling reinforces how very wide this offence is. In *Kanwar*,[474] the Court of Appeal held that "assistance" requires that something be done to aid the retention, removal, disposal or realisation of the goods but that this was not limited to physical acts. On the facts of the case, lying to protect one's husband who had brought stolen goods into the house was held to be sufficient.

(b) *Mens rea*

The mens rea requirement for handling under s.22 is:

1. The defendant must know or believe the goods to be stolen. There seems to be hardly any difference in the meaning of these words in this context. Belief, if anything, falls only just short of knowledge: where no other reasonable conclusion can be drawn by the defendant but that the goods were stolen.[475] Mere suspicion that the goods could be stolen is, however, not sufficient.

2. There must be dishonesty. Dishonesty here bears the same meaning as for theft. Accordingly, a person could receive stolen goods knowing that they are stolen but intending to return them to the owner. In such a case a finding of dishonesty would be unlikely under the *Ghosh* test.

(c) *Punishment*

The maximum penalty for handling stolen goods is 14 years' imprisonment.[476]

VI. Conclusion

An evaluation of these property offences cannot be undertaken until the underlying elements and rationale of such offences have been exposed. Only then can comment about structure and sentencing levels be made.

---

[471] See *R. v Hale (Robert Angus)* (1979) 68 Cr. App. R. 415; *Lockley* [1995] Crim. L.R. 656.

[472] At p.824.

[473] *R. v Nicklin (David John)* [1977] 1 W.L.R. 403 at 407.

[474] *R. v Kanwar (Rena Louise)* [1982] 1 W.L.R. 845.

[475] In directing the jury, the judge should avoid trying to distinguish the two terms: *R. v Forsyth (Elizabeth)* [1997] 2 Cr. App. R. 299 at 321.

[476] Sentencing guidelines were laid down in *R. v Webbe (Bernard)* [2001] EWCA Crim 1217. Based on these there are now definitive guidelines for sentencing in the Magistrates' Courts (Sentencing Guidelines Council, *Magistrates' Court Sentencing Guidelines: Definitive Guideline* (2009)). In April 2014 the Sentencing Council issued draft guidelines for theft offences, including handling: Sentencing Council, *Theft Offences: Guideline Consultation, April 2014* (2014), available at *http://sentencingcouncil.judiciary.gov.uk/docs/Final_Sentencing_Council_Theft_Consultation_web.pdf* [Accessed April 2014].

A. Underlying Rationale

What do all the different property offences have in common? Clearly, the common denominator in such offences is that they all involve an interference with the property interests of the victim. But what degree of interference is necessary?

We have already seen that the emphasis is *not* on actual loss of property. Indeed, there need not be any loss of property. In theft, for example, there need only be an *intention* of permanent deprivation; there need be no actual deprivation. In burglary, there need only be an entry to a building with one of the specified intents. No property need be taken. It was noted earlier in this chapter when dealing with the non-criminalisation of breach of contract that losses from such a breach can be significant while losses from theft can be minimal, or non-existent and many losses from theft and other property offences can be made good—either by actions for recovery of the goods or by insurance.

It is thus clear that the emphasis is not on the loss of the property (which could be described as the direct or "first order" harm), but on the quality of the defendant's actions. The focus is on *wrongdoing*. The requirement of dishonesty for most property offences underlines this. The defendant's actions must be such that the community as a whole can reject them as "wrong". The defendant's actions pose a threat to the value system inherent in our whole concept of property; it involves an "indirect undermining of the proprietary regime".[477] This threat, which raises the risk that there will be actual loss to property, can be seen as the real harm in the property offences. It is not the only harm. Many of the offences have their own special and distinctive harms, but this threat is the harm common to all of them and can be seen as a "second-order" harm analogous to the "second-order" harms encountered in the law of attempt.

B. Structure of Property Offences

Many of the property offences are so similar that perhaps one ought to consider abolishing most of them and introducing a single broad offence of dishonesty or wrongful interference with property rights. The Law Commission[478] considered this option and rejected it on the grounds that it could extend the reach of the criminal law too far, would place too much reliance on the elusive concept of "dishonesty" and would probably be incompatible with arts 5 and 7 of the European Convention on Human Rights which have been interpreted to require that offences be formulated with sufficient precision to enable people to regulate their conduct. Such a broad offence would clearly breach the principle of fair labelling whereby different offences should encapsulate different wrongs in a morally informative manner. It would be unthinkable to conflate all the existing property offences into a single new crime. For example, burglary and robbery involve wrongs quite separate from mere interference with property rights. The same is equally true of other offences such as handling and blackmail. Green argues that the

"reactive emotions [that the different crimes are] likely to evoke . . . will differ depending on which wrong has been committed. That is, such wrongs generally feel different from each other—a significant psychological phenomenon since differences in reactive emotions, though not conclusive, are usually a reliable indicator of differences in moral content."[479]

---

[477] A.P. Simester and G.R. Sullivan, "On the Nature and Rationale of Property Offences", in R.A. Duff and S. Green (eds), *Defining Crimes* (Oxford: OUP, 2005). See also, S.P. Green, *13 Ways to Steal a Bicycle: Theft Law in the Information Age* (Massachusetts: Harvard University Press, 2012), p.141.

[478] Law Commission Consultation Paper No.155, *Fraud and Deception* (1999).

[479] S.P. Green, *Lying, Cheating and Stealing: A Moral Theory of White-Collar Crime* (Oxford: OUP, 2006), p.128.

An alternative solution could be the introduction of a smaller (than at present) number of more broadly drawn offences. A step in this direction has been taken by the abolition of all the deception offences and their replacement by a single offence of fraud and the new offence of obtaining services dishonestly. Other possibilities remain. For example, the offence of theft could be expanded to encompass the present offence of handling stolen goods. In most cases a person who handles stolen goods is "assuming the rights of owner" over property and is thereby appropriating it, becoming guilty of theft.[480] The official Criminal Statistics do not even distinguish between these two offences.

It is submitted, however, that such an approach would be misguided. While there is much to be said for the introduction of the new broad offence of fraud, most of the core central property offences should be retained in something like their present form. Criminal offences should describe as accurately as possible the conduct which is prohibited. The moral messages sought to be communicated by the criminal law and by the punishment of offenders become confused if offence categorisations are not clearly understood by the public. There are important moral distinctions between these offences which the public, albeit only intuitively, recognise and which need protecting.

Let us take, for example, the proposal to merge the present offences of theft and handling stolen goods. Apart from the fact that the overlap between these two crimes is not complete, with not all cases of handling amounting to theft, there are important differences between these offences in terms of fair labelling. Handling is a very different offence in terms of public perception (see below) and in terms of the need to be able to impose high deterrent sentences (hence the 14 years maximum). Handlers of stolen goods provide (and arguably create) much of the market for theft; their activities are a significant source of the economic motivation behind much theft.[481] If the law could stamp out professional handlers much of the incentive to commit theft would be reduced.

Alternatively, we should consider whether the present offences are too broadly drawn. Should there be some further subdivision? This has already been achieved with burglary. Burglary involves a special harm, namely the violation of the security and sanctity of the home. This can cause psychological harm: distress, alarm, and the fear of knowing one is not safe even in one's own home.[482] Accordingly, the Criminal Justice Act 1991 drew a distinction between burglaries of dwellings where these harms would be most acutely felt (maximum 14 years' imprisonment) and burglaries of non-dwellings (maximum 10 years' imprisonment). Further, s.10 of the Theft Act 1968 creates the separate offence of aggravated burglary where there is the extra harm of possession of a weapon of offence at the scene of the burglary. This is not only more frightening but increases the risk of violence actually being used, in that the burglar might be "tempted to use it if challenged".[483]

C.M.V. Clarkson, Understanding Criminal Law, 4th edn (2005), p.248:

"Most people today regard handling as a lesser offence in terms of moral stigma; defendants will often plead guilty to handling on condition that all charges of theft are dropped. This attitude has come about because of a growing view that handlers and purchasers of stolen goods are 'only slightly dishonest people' (Spencer, 1985) who are not as blameworthy as those who actually steal or burgle. Buying and selling stolen goods are the most common offences amongst young offenders (Graham and Bowling, 1995). Theft and burglary create an immediate sense of danger in the community; there must often be a risk of violence with such activities; the thief or burglar is the primary cause of harm, directly invading the rights of the owner of property. In contrast, the criminal

---

[480]   Cf. S.P. Green, fn.479 above, pp.187–189.
[481]   S.P. Green, fn.479 above, p.188.
[482]   The lives of a large majority of victims of burglary are affected for some weeks after a burglary, and over a quarter of such victims suffer serious shock (M. Maguire, "The Impact of Burglary upon Victims" (1980) 20 Brit. J. Criminol. 261).
[483]   *R. v Stones (James)* [1989] 1 W.L.R. 156.

receiver, the 'fence', is regarded only as a shady, somewhat disreputable character—and the secondary purchaser as simply someone who has succumbed to the 'natural temptation' of buying something very cheap.

   The law is accordingly faced with a dilemma. On the one hand, it recognises that the punishment of handlers is crucial if theft and burglary is to be reduced but, on the other hand, it is faced by an apathetic public almost prepared to 'turn a blind eye' to handling. A possible way out of this dilemma could be to divide the offence of handling stolen goods into degrees. The more serious offence could be reserved for the professional 'fence', the lesser offence covering secondary purchasers. Such a division might be a fairer reflection of the moral stigma felt by most to attach to the two categories of handlers and could have the advantage of underwriting the necessity of enforcement against, and harm caused by, the professional handler. The danger with such an approach, however, could be that even less moral stigma would be attached to secondary purchasers than at present and, after all, it is these purchasers who buy stolen goods from fences who are the 'key element in the incentive structure that supports property crime.'"

Another suggestion is that property offences should be subdivided into separate offences based on the value of the property interfered with. In the United States the Model Penal Code states that theft of property worth less than $50 constitutes a petty misdemeanour, theft of property valued at between $50 and $500 constitutes a misdemeanour, and theft of property with a value exceeding $500 constitutes a felony of the third degree.[484] Each offence category carries its own range of penalties. In England, on the other hand, the same crime of theft is committed whether it is a magazine or a million pounds that is stolen.

Criminal Law Revision Committee, Eighth Report, Theft and Related Offences, Cmnd.2977 (1966), para.62:

"We considered whether instead of a general maximum of 10 years there should be different maximum penalties depending on the value of the property stolen. But although there is a case for specially high penalties for stealing large sums, we are not in favour of such a provision. Apart from the difficulty of laying down a satisfactory scale, the value of the property is only one of the possible aggravating features of theft, and it seems to us wrong to single this out. Besides, the property may be far more or far less valuable than the thief imagined."

The value of property is at present taken into account procedurally. For example, criminal damage is only triable summarily if the value of the property does not exceed £5,000.[485] Mode of Trial Guidelines state that theft, fraud and handling offences should be tried summarily unless the property is of high value. "High value" is defined for this purpose as £10,000 or more.[486] Further, as we shall see, in cases of shoplifting where the value of the property stolen is less than £100 the police can issue a PND (Penalty Notice for Disorder). The value of property is also an important factor in sentencing. Sentencing guidelines for fraud and theft provide that high value (including sentimental value) of the property to the victim or substantial consequential loss is an aggravating factor. So, for example, the sentencing guideline for confidence fraud (contrary to s.1 of the Fraud Act 2006) has four starting points based on the value of the property or consequential loss (less than £20,000; £20,000–£100,000; £100,000–£500,000; more than £500,000).[487] The current sentencing penalty for making off without payment depends on whether the goods or services are worth less than £200 and for handling stolen goods whether the property is worth less than £1,000.[488] The sentencing

---

[484] Model Penal Code s.223.1(2). For further discussion in relation to the MPC consolidation of theft and the effects of this in practice, see S.P. Green, fn.479 above, pp.20–23.

[485] Magistrates' Courts Act 1980 s.22.

[486] The Consolidated Practice Direction—Criminal Procedure Rules (2013), paras V.51.4–V.51.8.

[487] Sentencing Guidelines Council, *Sentencing for Fraud—Statutory offences: Definitive Guideline* (2009).

[488] Sentencing Guidelines Council, *Magistrates' Court Sentencing Guidelines: Definitive Guideline* (2009).

guideline for burglary offences, on the other hand, merely indicates that in domestic burglaries, theft of/damage to property causing a significant degree of economic, sentimental or personal value to the victim is a factor indicating greater harm.[489] Other particularised guidelines, for example, making off without payment, have been drafted on the assumption that they generally do not involve property of high monetary value.[490] Accordingly, the real debate is not as to *whether* the value of the property should be taken into consideration, but *how* this should be achieved: whether at the decision to prosecute stage, the mode of trial stage, the substantive level, or the sentencing stage.

The present approach of substantive English law, however, is consistent with the underlying rationale of the property offences that the focus is on the wrongdoing of the defendant and not on the direct harm caused. If it is not necessary that *any* direct harm be caused, it follows that the *extent* of that harm is not important and thus the value of the property interfered with should not be taken into account. This accords with the widely held view that the causing of resulting harm (and the extent thereof) is irrelevant as it can be "chance" whether a large or small sum is stolen. It is also argued that the value of property in abstract terms is irrelevant. What matters is the impact on the particular victim. Stealing £20 from an impoverished person is worse than stealing £20 worth of goods from a large supermarket. Further, it is argued that the value of the property is only one way of assessing the extent of the harm and should not be made decisive. Other factors are equally important: the characteristics of the offender (e.g. theft by persons in positions of trust); the characteristics of the victim (e.g. theft from the vulnerable); and the circumstances of the offence (e.g. pick-pocketing, thefts committed jointly with others).

On the other hand, it is interesting to contrast these property offences with offences against the person where the level of harm (physical and psychiatric injury) is crucial in distinguishing offences of different gravity (e.g. actual bodily harm as opposed to grievous bodily harm), whereas the other factors, such as characteristics of the victim, are taken into account at the sentencing stage. There is logic to this. At the substantive stage the law can only deal with *standard* harms.

Andrew von Hirsch and Nils Jareborg, "Gauging Criminal Harm: A Living-Standard Analysis" (1991) 11 Oxford J. of Legal Studies 1 at 4–5:

"Why this emphasis on standard harm? Particular criminal acts are too diverse to be rated on an individualised basis. The analysis is aided when one (1) rates the standard case of an offence, and then (2) addresses unusual cases through principles of aggravation and mitigation . . . The standard harm in any given type of criminal conduct is, ordinarily, foreseeable. However, when one is talking about atypical harms, foreseeability diminishes. The burglar may be expected to understand the typical consequences of a burglary, but not, ordinarily, Mary Smith's particular situation—*e.g.* the extraordinary value the vase had for her as a gift from a deceased friend. The rules on aggravation/mitigation will thus have to be more complex, because they need to consider not only the special harm involved in unusual cases, but also . . . the foreseeability of such special harm . .

The criminal law is a system of rules, not an arena for personalized judgments. If the law can assess crimeseriousness in the standard case, and then make deviations from that assessment for certain types of special circumstances, this is all one can reasonably hope to accomplish."

Following this, it is possible to argue that the most appropriate measure of the standard harm (or threat thereof) in property offences is the value of the property which, like the level of personal injury or success or failure in the law of attempt, is critical in our moral assessments of the defendant's

---

[489]   Sentencing Council, *Burglary Offences: Definitive Guideline* (2011), p.8. Or "economic, commercial or personal value" in the case of non-domestic burglaries, p.12.

[490]   Sentencing Guidelines Council, *Magistrates' Court Sentencing Guidelines: Definitive Guideline* (2009), p.79; Sentencing Council, *Theft Offences: Guideline Consultation, April 2014* (2014), pp.95–95.

actions. Such an approach might well help to counteract the commonly held view that there is one law for wealthy, white-collar criminals and another for the rest of those who steal. Other factors such as the circumstances of the offence which are simply too diverse to be reduced to substantive rules are best left to the "rules on aggravation/mitigation", i.e. to the sentencing stage.

The logic of the argument to this point has been that there could be different levels of property offences based purely on the economic value of the goods interfered with. However, an alternative solution could be to subject to separate treatment certain property offences where the economic value of the goods is *generally* small. Shoplifting might be regarded as a prime candidate for this and, as we shall see, this is to a certain extent already being done. A case can also be made for the decriminalisation of some of the activities presently covered by the Theft Acts—particularly in those areas where civil remedies such as breach of contract seem more appropriate. However, it is highly questionable whether such thinking can or should be applied to shoplifting.

Daniel J.I. Murphy, Customers and Thieves—an Ethnography of Shoplifting (1986), p.240:

"[T]here are essentially two methods for controlling shoplifters on the shopfloor: 'law-enforcement' and 'peace-keeping'. It is obvious that the numbers of suspects who are handed to the police differ dramatically according to which model is being pursued. The peace-keeping model is the preferred one of a few retailers who acknowledge the temptation to steal which modern marketing techniques create and they accept the responsibility to convert ordinary shoppers who have succumbed to this temptation. Retailers who pursue the law-enforcement model would criticise the peace-keeping model for being an insufficient deterrent to shoplifters, and the Home Office Standing Committee supports their position: 'A reminder to pay without fear of penalty is no deterrent, and in effect would mean that the thief could not lose.' However, the research clearly demonstrates that all stores on occasions use this method to control shoplifting . . . The point made here is that there are methods of controlling shoplifting which do not involve the criminal justice system and these should be given more public discussion."

Since 2004, the police have been able to issue a penalty notice for disorder (PND) for an offence of retail theft (shoplifting). Originally these could be issued to those 16 or over, where the value of the goods stolen was under £200,[491] but the age limit for a PND has since been raised to 18, and financial limit decreased to £100. This is an on-the-spot £90 penalty rather like a speeding ticket. In the 12 months ending September 2013, 23,133 PNDs were issued for shoplifting.[492]

This demonstrates that there are alternative ways of dealing with offenders without having to resort to prosecution. This is particularly appropriate for shoplifting which is in most cases

"a nuisance, particularly to shopkeepers, [but] is not dangerous or frightening, nor does it, particularly when compared to other offences, damage the confidence of the public. Its victims are not usually particularly vulnerable by reason or age or youth."[493]

It must be stressed that such PNDs are issued within the criminal justice system. The offence has not been decriminalised. However, a case could be made for treating shoplifting as a separate and lesser offence.

---

[491]   Criminal Justice and Police Act 2001 ss.1–11 (as amended by the Legal Aid, Sentencing and Punishment of Offenders Act 2012); Ministry of Justice Guidance, *Penalty Notices for Disorder (PNDs)* (2013).

[492]   Ministry of Justice Statistics Bulletin, *Criminal Justice Sentencing Statistics Quarterly Update to September 2013 England and Wales* (2014), table Q1.6(1).

[493]   *R. v Page (Cyril Edward)* [2005] 2 Cr. App. R. (S.) 37 at [3].

Andrew Ashworth, Sentencing and Penal Policy (1983), pp.186–187:

"[T]here are three major reasons for regarding offences against larger companies, such as Woolworth and Marks and Spencer, as less serious than an offence involving the same amount of property but committed against an individual victim. First, an individual's possessions are more likely to have a personal ('sentimental') value to him which is additional to, and may indeed be more important to him than, the economic value . . . Secondly, thefts from individuals are more likely to cause fear and alarm than thefts from companies . . . Thirdly, companies would generally be better able than individuals to afford and to off-set any loss through theft."

The case for a separate lesser offence is strengthened when one considers that the value of the property stolen in shops is generally small,[494] such thefts are regarded by the public as the least serious of the various types of theft that can be committed,[495] and even when shoplifters are detected prosecutions are often not brought[496]

"in order to avoid 'image' problems, because of the claimed risk of false arrest tort actions by innocent customers, and because of the claimed cost of time away from work when security personnel have to testify".[497]

In an attempt to minimise the economic costs of shoplifting, businesses focus upon investing in security measures such as CCTV, security tagging for valuable items, security guards and store detectives,[498] and a number of the larger high-street retailers now employ civil recovery agents to recover from shoplifters the alleged costs arising from their actions.[499]

On the other hand, there is the clear view expressed by Lawton LJ, in *Wood*, that "Shoplifting is stealing and stealing is a serious offence."[500] A Home Office Working Party Report on internal shop security was to similar effect:

"We also noted the suggestion . . . that shoplifting should be made an administrative offence. This would do nothing to reduce the number of shoplifting offences. Indeed, it might increase it. We see no reason why shoplifting should be treated differently from any other type of crime."[501]

A central problem with this approach, as with all attempts to divide offences into narrower subcategories, is that the subdivision has to be rational and must not miss any important moral distinctions. This raises the question: What is so special about shoplifting? Why not make pick-pocketing or employee theft a separate offence?

---

[494] In 2006, the median value of goods stolen from shops was £40 (Sentencing Advisory Panel, Sentencing Guidelines for Theft from a Shop: Consultation Paper (2006), para.49). However, in 2013 the British Retail Consortium (BRC) estimated that the average value of shoplifting offences was £177 per theft: BRC, fn.47 and fn.49, above, p.808.

[495] R.F. Sparks, H.G. Genn and D.J. Dodd, *Surveying Victims* (Chichester: John Wiley, 1977).

[496] Only 3% of shoplifting incidents come to police attention and only 1% result in a conviction (Sentencing Advisory Panel, *Sentencing Guidelines for Theft from a Shop: Consultation Paper* (2006), para.10; and see above, p.808).

[497] C. Foote and R.J. Levy, *Criminal Law: Cases and Materials* (Kingston: Wolters Kluwer, 1981), p.757.

[498] S.P. Green, fn.477 above, pp.167–168.

[499] Citizens Advice, *CAB Evidence Briefing: Uncivil Recovery* (2010).

[500] *R. v Wood (Maurice)* (1979) 1 Cr. App. R. (S.) 34.

[501] Home Office, *Shoplifting, and Theft by Shop Staff* (1973), para.6.16.

L.R. Zeitlin, "A Little Larceny Can Do a Lot for Employee Morale," Psychology Today (June 1974), 22–26, 64:

"Thefts of merchandise alone amount to approximately five per cent of the yearly sales of American retail establishments, and internal losses outweigh external losses by about three to one. That is, the stores' own employees steal three times as much as do shoplifters . . . [W]ell over 75 per cent of all employees participate to some extent in merchandise shrinkage . . . [I]n retail establishments internal theft averages out to an unevenly distributed five per cent to eight per cent of the typical employee's salary . . .

When the average retail employee becomes dissatisfied with his job, if he doesn't quit, he starts stealing from his employer. He gets back at the system. In a sense, the intellectual and physical challenges provided by opportunities to steal represent a significant enrichment of the individual's job. He can take matters into his own hands, assume responsibility, make decisions and face challenges . . . He is in business for himself . . .

The dishonest worker is enriching his own job in a manner that is very satisfactory (for him) . . . [and] management gets a bargain. By permitting a controlled amount of theft, management can avoid reorganising jobs and raising wages . . .

[M]anagement may decide that the monetary cost of enforcing honesty is too great . . . [M]anagement would have to maintain a figurehead security system. After all, the major benefit of employee theft is the job enrichment provided by the individual's attempt to beat the system. If all need for precaution is eliminated, then the employee gets no satisfaction from theft. All he gets is a slight addition to his income in merchandise instead of cash . . .

Uncontrolled theft can be disastrous for any business concern but *controlled* theft can be useful. Employee theft, used as a motivational tool, can be an economic benefit to an organisation, if management finds it too costly to meet its traditional responsibilities to make jobs rewarding and to pay a living wage."

In the United States, an examination was made into several substantive offences to ascertain whether sub-categorisation was feasible.[502] The bulk of the examination was devoted to the crime of armed robbery with the conclusion that armed robbery be divided into six degrees. Yet these six divisions only take account of two variables: the type of weapon used and the extent of physical violence threatened. No account is taken of the numerous other variables that would normally affect the type and length of sentence imposed. Accordingly, it has been pointed out that:

> "if the legislature actually *tried* to anticipate every conceivable offence and offender variation, the result would be a penal law of enormous length and complexity, replete with hair-splitting distinctions. We doubt whether any legislature would be willing or able to spend all its time hammering out a definition of robbery in the 68th degree (and deciding upon the appropriate penalty); but even if it were, it is doubtful whether all offence variations could really be anticipated."[503]

Further,

> "excessively specific offences risk clogging the trial process with unmeritorious technical argument, and obfuscating the moral clarity of the law's communications . . . [P]eople . . . need to know the law's requirements *in gist* and not precisely."[504]

The over-particularisation of offences may lead to a defendant facing "the wrong charge, or too many charges".[505] It thus seems clear that little can be gained from subdividing the property offences into

---

[502] Report of the Twentieth Century Fund Task Force on Criminal Sentencing, *Fair and Certain Punishment* (1976), p.18.

[503] Executive Advisory Committee on Sentencing in New York, *Crime and Punishment in New York* (1979), p.220.

[504] A.P. Simester and G.R. Sullivan, fn.477 above, p. 187. Cf. J. Chalmers and F. Leverick, "Fair Labelling in Criminal Law" (2008) 71 M.L.R. 217 at 239.

[505] Law Commission Paper No.276, *Fraud*, Cm.5560 (2002), para.3.20.

smaller separate offences such as shoplifting. No area of law can be adequately, and with sufficient specificity, subcategorised to reflect the nuances of situation, blameworthiness and harm that condition the seriousness of particular criminal acts.

Accordingly, perhaps the best way forward is to build on the approach already being adopted by English law. Some reform of the substantive offence definitions and categories clearly needs to be undertaken. Movement in this direction has already occurred with the abolition of all deception offences and their replacement by a broad offence of fraud. At the procedural mode of trial level, more thought should be given to making other offences only triable summarily where the value of the property is low.

The one area where significant steps have already been taken is in relation to the development of sentencing guidelines. In 2008, recognising that some of the property offences such as theft and fraud are too broad for a "one size fits all" sentencing guideline, the Sentencing Guidelines Council issued definitive guidelines for different types of theft: theft in breach of trust; theft in a dwelling; theft from the person; and theft from a shop.[506] Unfortunately, in its 2014 *Theft Offences Sentencing Consultation*, the Sentencing Council appears to have had second thoughts about such an approach in relation to theft, and has instead proposed separate guidelines for theft from a shop, and "general theft" (to include theft from the person, theft in breach of trust, theft of and from a motor vehicle and theft of a bicycle), on the basis that the harm and culpability factors in relation to these offences were very similar and that to issue separate guidelines in respect of each would make the overall guideline very lengthy.[507] Whilst theft offences inevitably vary enormously in their seriousness, a strong argument may be made for maintaining the approach of the current guidelines, on the basis that these different types of theft are not generally regarded as having equivalent levels of culpability. In particular, thefts from the person and in a dwelling are regarded as being significantly more intrusive and serious than the theft of a bicycle.

Guidelines have also been developed for different types of fraud: confidence fraud; possessing, making or supplying articles for use in fraud; banking and insurance fraud, obtaining credit through fraud; benefit fraud; and revenue fraud (against HM Revenue and Customs),[508] and for domestic and non-domestic burglary.[509] However, while these developments are to be welcomed, they do not foreclose further consideration of the structure of property offences at the substantive level—for example, whether there should be two categories of robbery and handling stolen goods. But, of course, this whole question of the structure of property offences raises similar issues to those already canvassed with regard to the structure of offences against the person. As suggested there, answers to all such questions depend on the basic philosophy underlying the construction of criminal liability and the criminal justice system.

---

[506] Sentencing Guidelines Council, *Theft and Burglary in a Building Other than a Dwelling: Definitive Guideline* (2008). This also contains a definitive guideline for burglary in a building other than a dwelling.

[507] Sentencing Council, *Theft Offences: Guideline Consultation* (2014).

[508] Sentencing Guidelines Council, *Sentencing for Fraud—Statutory Offences: Definitive Guideline* (2009).

[509] Sentencing Council, *Burglary Offences: Definitive Guideline* (2011).

INDEX